HOLT

Lifetime HEALTH

HOLT, RINEHART AND WINSTON

A Harcourt Education Company

Orlando • **Austin** • New York • San Diego • Toronto • London

AUTHORS

David P. Friedman, Ph.D.
Professor, Department of Physiology & Pharmacology
Deputy Associate Dean for Research
Wake Forest University School of Medicine
Winston-Salem, North Carolina

Curtis C. Stine, M.D.
Professor
Department of Family Medicine
  and Rural Health
College of Medicine
Florida State University
Tallahassee, Florida

Shannon Whalen, Ph.D.
Associate Professor
Department of Health Studies, Physical
  Education and Human Performance
Adelphi University
Garden City, New York

Acknowledgments

CONTRIBUTING AUTHORS

Mary B. Grosvenor, M.S., R.D.
Science and Health Writer
Delta, Colorado

Shahla Khan, Ph.D.
Adjunct Professor
Department of Health Science
University of North Florida
Jacksonville, Florida

Anjum Khurshid, M.D.
The Medical Institute for Sexual
   Health
Austin, Texas

Mitchell Leslie
Science and Health Writer
Portland, Oregon

Josh R. Mann, M.D., M.P.H.
Clinical Assistant Professor
Department of Family and
   Preventive Medicine
University of South Carolina
Columbia, South Carolina

Joe S. McIlhaney, Jr., M.D.
President
The Medical Institute for Sexual
   Health
Austin, Texas

Margaret J. Meeker, M.D., F.A.A.P.
Pediatrician
Traverse City, Michigan

Jane A. Petrillo, Ed.D.
Assistant Professor
Department of Health, Physical
   Education, and Sport Science
Kennesaw State University
Kennesaw, Georgia

Lori A. Smolin, Ph.D.
Department of Nutritional
   Sciences
University of Connecticut
Storrs, Connecticut

Robert Wilson III
Chairman
Department of Health and
   Physical Education
Morehouse College
Atlanta, Georgia

Kathleen J. Young, Ph.D.
Assistant Professor
Department of Health Sciences
California State University,
   Northridge
Northridge, California

CONTRIBUTING WRITERS

Sandra Alters, Ph.D.
Science and Health Writer
Montreal, Canada

Daniel H. Franck, Ph.D.
Science and Health Writer
Spencertown, New York

Linda K. Gaul, Ph.D.
Epidemiologist
Texas Department of State Health
   Services
Austin, Texas

Rosemary E. Previte
Science and Health Writer
Lexington, Massachusetts

Inclusion Specialist

Ellen McPeek Glisan
Special Needs Consultant
San Antonio, Texas

Teacher Edition Development

Sandra Alters, Ph.D.
Science and Health Writer
Montreal, Canada

Linda K. Gaul, Ph.D.
Epidemiologist
Texas Department of State Health
   Services
Austin, Texas

Marilyn Massey-Stokes, Ed.D., C.H.E.S.
Associate Professor
Health, Exercise, and Sport
   Sciences
Texas Tech University
Lubbock, Texas

Su Nottingham
*Health and Life Management
   Teacher*
Central Michigan University
Mt. Pleasant, Michigan

Jane A. Petrillo, Ed.D.
Assistant Professor
Department of Health, Physical
   Education, and Sport Science
Kennesaw State University
Kennesaw, Georgia

Debbie Rummel
Health Teacher
Antioch Community High School
Antioch, Illinois

Wendy Schiff, M.S.
Adjunct Lecturer
St. Louis Community College—
   Meramec
St. Louis, Missouri

Joan A. Solorio
Special Education Director
Austin Independent School
   District
Austin, Texas

Kathleen J. Young, Ph.D.
Assistant Professor
Department of Health Sciences
California State University,
   Northridge
Northridge, California

(continued on p. 684)

CONTENTS In Brief

UNIT 1 Health and Your Wellness

UNIT 2 Health and Your Body

UNIT 3 Drugs

UNIT 4 Diseases and Disorders

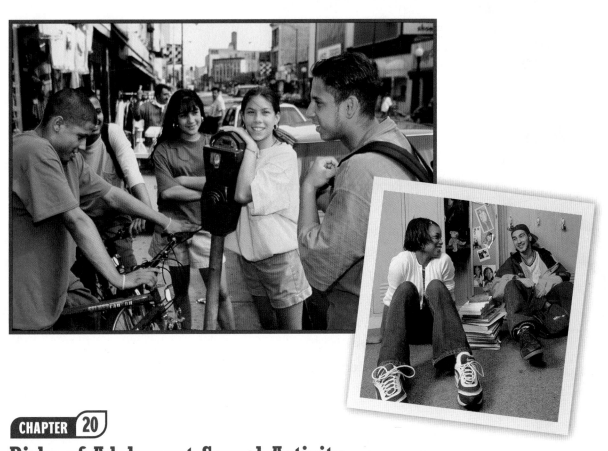

HEALTH Handbook
EXPRESS Lessons

How Your Body Works

What You Need to Know About...

First Aid and Safety

LIFE SKILLS QUICK REVIEW

REFERENCE Guide

FEATURES

Building Character

Explore the relationship between strong character and your health.

LIFE SKILL Activity

You'll use these skills every day to enhance your health.

MAKING GREAT DECISIONS

Five easy steps show you how to make the right decisions!

Analyzing DATA

Interpret health data, and draw accurate conclusions.

real life Activity

Use these hands-on activities to practice what you've learned.

YOUR Health YOUR World

Analyze the influence of media, technology, and culture on your health.

HOW TO USE YOUR TEXTBOOK

Your Road Map for Success with *Lifetime Health*

Read the Objectives

Objectives tell you what you'll need to know.

STUDY TIP Reread the objectives when studying for a test to be sure you know the material.

Study the Key Terms

Key Terms are listed for each section. Learn the definitions of these terms because you will most likely be tested on them. Use the glossary to locate any definition quickly.

STUDY TIP If you don't understand a definition, reread the page where the term is introduced. The surrounding text should help make the definition easier to understand.

Take Notes and Get Organized

Keep a health notebook so that you are ready to take notes when your teacher reviews the material in class. Keep your assignments in this notebook so that you can review them when studying for the chapter test.

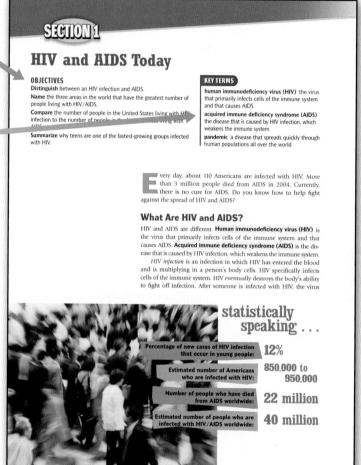

SECTION 1

HIV and AIDS Today

OBJECTIVES

Distinguish between an HIV infection and AIDS.

Name the three areas in the world that have the greatest number of people living with HIV/AIDS.

Compare the number of people in the United States living with HIV infection to the number of people in the United States living with AIDS.

Summarize why teens are one of the fastest-growing groups infected with HIV.

KEY TERMS

human immunodeficiency virus (HIV) the virus that primarily infects cells of the immune system and that causes AIDS

acquired immune deficiency syndrome (AIDS) the disease that is caused by HIV infection, which weakens the immune system

pandemic a disease that spreads quickly through human populations all over the world

Every day, about 110 Americans are infected with HIV. More than 3 million people died from AIDS in 2004. Currently, there is no cure for AIDS. Do you know how to help fight against the spread of HIV and AIDS?

What Are HIV and AIDS?

HIV and AIDS are different. **Human immunodeficiency virus (HIV)** is the virus that primarily infects cells of the immune system and that causes AIDS. **Acquired immune deficiency syndrome (AIDS)** is the disease that is caused by HIV infection, which weakens the immune system.

HIV infection is an infection in which HIV has entered the blood and is multiplying in a person's body cells. HIV specifically infects cells of the immune system. HIV eventually destroys the body's ability to fight off infection. After someone is infected with HIV, the virus

statistically speaking . . .

Percentage of new cases of HIV infection that occur in young people:	12%
Estimated number of Americans who are infected with HIV:	850,000 to 950,000
Number of people who have died from AIDS worldwide:	22 million
Estimated number of people who are infected with HIV/AIDS worldwide:	40 million

↗ Be Resourceful, Use the Web

Internet Connect boxes in your textbook take you to resources that you can use for health projects, reports, and research papers. Go to **scilinks.org/health**, and type in the HealthLinks code to get information on a topic.

Visit go.hrw.com
Find worksheets, articles from *Current Health*, and other materials that go with your textbook at **go.hrw.com**. Click on the textbook icon and the table of contents to see all of the resources for each chapter.

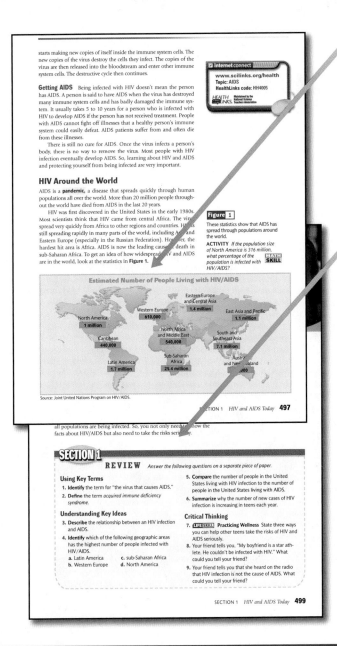

Use the Illustrations and Photos

Art shows complex ideas and processes. Learn to analyze the art so that you better understand the material you read in the text.

Tables and graphs display important information in an organized way to help you see relationships.

A picture is worth a thousand words. Look at the photographs to see relevant examples of health concepts you are reading about.

Answer the Section Reviews

Section Reviews test your knowledge of the main points of the section. Critical Thinking items challenge you to think about the material in greater depth and to find connections that you infer from the text.

STUDY TIP When you can't answer a question, reread the section. The answer is usually there.

Do Your Homework

Your teacher will assign Study Guide worksheets to help you understand and remember the material in the chapter.

STUDY TIP Answering the items in the Chapter Review will prepare you for the chapter test. Don't try to answer the questions without reading the text and reviewing your class notes. A little preparation up front will make your homework assignments a lot easier.

Visit Holt Online Learning

If your teacher gives you a special password to log onto the Holt Online Learning site, you'll find your complete textbook on the Web. In addition, you'll find some great learning tools and practice quizzes. You'll be able to see how well you know the material from your textbook.

UNIT 1

Health and Your Wellness

CHAPTER 1

Leading a Healthy Life

What's Your Health IQ?
KNOWLEDGE

Which of the statements below are true, and which are false? Check your answers on p. 638.

1. Most deaths are caused by our behaviors.

2. If you have a history of heart disease in your family, there is nothing you can do about your risk for heart disease.

3. The leading cause of death in teens is motor vehicle accidents.

4. Smoking is the single leading preventable cause of death in the United States.

5. Eating at least five servings of fruits and vegetables a day can lower your chances of suffering from cancer or heart disease.

6. If you are not physically sick, then you are healthy.

SECTION 1

Health and Teens

SECTION 2

Health and Wellness

SECTION 3

Health in Your Community

Visit these Web sites for the latest health information:

HEALTH LINKS
THE WORLD'S A CLICK AWAY

Find more information whenever you see a HealthLinks box. Go to **scilinks.org/health**, and type in the HealthLinks code.

go.hrw.com

Find worksheets and other materials that go with your textbook at **go.hrw.com**.

Current Health

Check out *Current Health*® articles related to this chapter by visiting **go.hrw.com**. Just type in the keyword **HH4 CH01**.

Health and Teens

OBJECTIVES

Compare the major causes of death in the past with the major causes of death today.

Distinguish between controllable risk factors and uncontrollable risk factors.

Compare the major causes of death for teens with those for other age groups in the United States.

List the six health risk behaviors that lead to health problems in teens.

Name three behaviors you can adopt now to improve your health. **LIFE SKILL**

You have the power to protect yourself from the dangers that threaten your health. The first step to protecting yourself is learning what these dangers are and what you can do to prevent them.

Health Today

What does being healthy mean to you? Focus on the first thing you think of when you read the word *healthy*. Did you think of not having diseases? being physically fit? eating right? Many people think that being healthy simply means not being sick. In the past, this was true.

Health in the Past: Infectious Diseases In the 1800s and early 1900s, the leading causes of death in the United States were *infectious diseases*—diseases caused by pathogens, such as bacteria. Infectious diseases can be passed from one person to another. Examples of infectious diseases include polio, tuberculosis, pneumonia, and influenza (the flu). Infectious diseases were a constant threat. That is why people thought of being healthy as being free from disease!

Health Today: Lifestyle Diseases Over the years, medical advances, better living conditions, and a focus on preventative medicine have helped bring infectious diseases of the past under control. As a result, most of the diseases that were common 50 to 100 years ago can now be prevented or cured. Today, most health problems in the United States are related to the way we live, or our lifestyle. **Lifestyle diseases** are diseases caused partly by unhealthy behaviors and partly by other factors. They are diseases influenced by the choices you make that affect your health. Examples of diseases that can be influenced by lifestyle are some types of diabetes, some types of heart disease, and some types of cancer.

"Our generation **will live longer than** people did a hundred years ago **because we are learning to live healthier lives.**"

Table 1   Controllable Risk Factors for Heart Disease

Controllable factor	Behavior		
	Bad	**Better**	**Best**
Physical activity	▶ watching TV very often	▶ walking the stairs instead of taking elevator	▶ playing a team sport three times a week
Smoking	▶ smoking a pack a day	▶ smoking a pack a week	▶ not smoking
Weight	▶ weighing 20 percent or more above recommended body weight	▶ weighing 10 percent to 19 percent more than recommended body weight	▶ weighing a maximum of 9 percent more than recommended body weight
Diet	▶ eating fast food every day	▶ eating junk food several times a week	▶ eating healthful, nutritious meals

Health Risk Factors

All health problems have risk factors. A **risk factor** is anything that increases the likelihood of injury, disease, or other health problems. For example, the risk factors for heart disease include a history of heart disease in your family, a high-fat diet, stress, being overweight, smoking, and lack of exercise. All of these factors increase a person's chance of developing heart disease. Notice that some of the risk factors can be controlled by your behavior, while others cannot.

Controllable Risk Factors   *Controllable risk factors* are risk factors that you can do something about. They can be controlled by your behavior. For example, what can you do to decrease your risk of developing heart disease? As shown in **Table 1,** you can exercise regularly, avoid smoking, manage a healthy weight, and eat healthful, nutritious meals.

Uncontrollable Risk Factors   Unfortunately, not all health risk factors are controllable. The ones that can't be changed are called *uncontrollable risk factors.* Examples of uncontrollable risk factors for heart disease are age, race, gender, and heredity. For example, the older a person is, the more likely he or she is to develop heart disease. African Americans are more likely to have high blood pressure, which can lead to heart disease, than European Americans are. Men are more likely to develop heart disease than women are.

You can't make yourself younger or change your race or gender. However, by focusing on controllable risk factors, which you can change through your behavior, you can protect your health.

Uncontrollable Risk Factors

▶ **Age**
▶ **Race**
▶ **Gender**
▶ **Heredity**

Everyone, no matter what age, can do things to take control of his or her health.

Risk Factors and Your Health

You can't control the uncontrollable risk factors. However, you can protect your health by focusing on controllable risk factors, which you can change through your behavior. What behaviors can you focus on at this point in your life? First, you should know the leading causes of death for people your age in the United States:

▶ motor vehicle accidents
▶ homicide
▶ suicide
▶ other accidents

These four causes of death make up almost three-fourths of all teen deaths. For children and infants, motor vehicle accidents are also the No. 1 cause of death.

Your health behaviors affect not only your health today but also your future health. Thus, you should be aware of the leading causes of death for other age groups. For example, the leading cause of death for adults between 19 and 65 years of age is cancer. The leading cause of death for adults over 65 years of age is heart disease.

The next section describes the health behaviors that most affect you and other teens. By learning these risk behaviors, you can take control in improving your health today and in the future.

internet connect

www.scilinks.org/health
Topic: Motor Vehicle Safety
HealthLinks code: HH4101

HEALTH *LINKS* Maintained by the
National Science
Teachers Association

Analyzing DATA ⟶

Health Today

1. Each slice of the pie represents the percentage of deaths among *teens* that are a result of the cause indicated.

2. Each slice of the pie represents the percentage of deaths for *all ages* that are a result of the cause indicated.

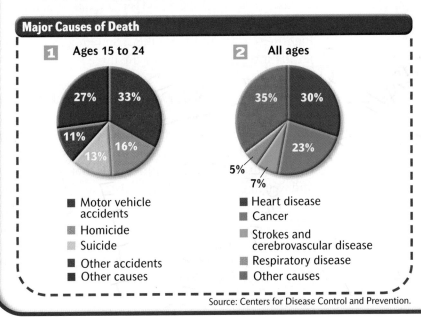

Major Causes of Death

1 Ages 15 to 24

- 33%
- 27%
- 11%
- 13%
- 16%

■ Motor vehicle accidents
■ Homicide
■ Suicide
■ Other accidents
■ Other causes

2 All ages

- 30%
- 35%
- 23%
- 5%
- 7%

■ Heart disease
■ Cancer
■ Strokes and cerebrovascular disease
■ Respiratory disease
■ Other causes

Source: Centers for Disease Control and Prevention.

Your Turn

1. What is the No. 1 cause of death for your age group?

2. What percentage of deaths for all ages are caused by heart disease and cancer? **MATH SKILL**

3. Using one or both pie charts, list at least four causes of death that are affected by health risk behaviors.

4. **CRITICAL THINKING** Describe what you can do to protect yourself from each of the causes of death that you listed in item 3.

Six Health Risk Behaviors

There are six types of risk behaviors that cause the most serious health problems.

1. **Sedentary lifestyle** Not taking part in physical activity on a regular basis is referred to as being **sedentary.** Those who have sedentary lifestyles, even if they are not overweight, raise their risk of certain diseases such as heart disease and diabetes.

2. **Alcohol and other drug use** Alcohol abuse can cause liver disease, certain types of cancer, heart disease, and brain damage. Alcohol and drug use are also major factors in car accidents, physical fights, depression, suicide, and mental disorders. Alcohol and drug use are also factors in the spread of *sexually transmitted diseases* (STDs). These are diseases that are spread through sexual activity. An example of a sexually transmitted disease is acquired immune deficiency syndrome (AIDS), caused by the human immunodeficiency virus (HIV).

3. **Sexual activity** Sexual activity outside of a committed relationship, such as marriage, puts people at risk for health problems. These health problems include HIV infection, other sexually transmitted diseases, and unplanned pregnancy.

Figure 1

You have the power to protect yourself from the six types of risk behaviors.

ACTIVITY *What risk behaviors do you think are the most common at your school?*

4. **Behaviors that cause injuries** As mentioned, the four major causes of death for teenagers are motor vehicle accidents, other accidents, homicide, and suicide. For example, a risk behavior that can lead to homicide is carrying a weapon. Not using a seat belt is a risk behavior that can lead to death in a motor vehicle accident.

5. **Tobacco use** Smoking is the single leading preventable cause of death in the United States. Smoking is a controllable risk factor for heart disease, cancer, and respiratory disease. These are three of the leading causes of death for all age groups. The choice to smoke often takes place in high school, if not before then. Smoking as a teenager greatly increases your risk for the three leading causes of death.

6. **Poor eating habits** Your eating habits can either increase or lower your chances of developing many diseases. Eating at least five servings of fruits and vegetables a day can lower your chances of suffering from cancer or heart disease. On the other hand, eating foods that are high in fat and weighing more than your recommended weight puts you at risk for heart disease, cancer, and stroke.

The choices you make can either raise your risk for certain health concerns or lower your risk. Learning about the risk behaviors summarized in **Figure 1** will help you make better choices to protect yourself.

SECTION 1

REVIEW   *Answer the following questions on a separate piece of paper.*

Using Key Terms

1. **Identify** the term for "a disease caused partly by unhealthy behaviors and partly by other factors."

2. **Identify** the term for "not taking part in physical activity on a regular basis."

Understanding Key Ideas

3. **State** the type of disease that causes most deaths in the United States today.

4. **List** three examples of uncontrollable risk factors.

5. **Identify** which of the following is *not* a controllable risk factor.
   a. exercise   c. age
   b. diet   d. weight

6. **Compare** the leading causes of death for teens with those of all ages.

7. **State** the six risk behaviors that lead to health problems in teens.

8. **Identify** the risk behavior that leads to the most deaths in teens.

9. **Identify** the risk behavior that is the leading preventable cause of death in the United States.

Critical Thinking

10. **LIFE SKILL** **Practicing Wellness** List three of your behaviors that you can change to improve your health.

11. **LIFE SKILL** **Practicing Wellness** Use Table 1 to give another example of a "best" behavior you can do for the controllable factor physical activity.

Health and Wellness

OBJECTIVES

Describe each of the six components of health.

State the importance of striving for optimal health.

Describe four influences on wellness.

Describe three ways to take charge of your wellness.

Name two ways you can improve two components of your health. **LIFE SKILL**

KEY TERMS

health the state of well-being in which all of the components of health—physical, emotional, social, mental, spiritual, and environmental—are in balance

value a strong belief or ideal

wellness the achievement of a person's best in all six components of health

health literacy knowledge of health information needed to make good choices about your health

ris was in good physical shape. Abel couldn't remember the last time he had to stay home because he had a cold. Do you think Iris and Abel are healthy?

Six Components of Health

Being healthy is much more than being physically fit and free from disease. **Health** is the state of well-being in which all of the components of health—physical, emotional, social, mental, spiritual, and environmental—are in balance. To be truly healthy, you must take care of all six components. The six components are described in more detail below.

Physical Health Abel used to think that being physically healthy meant being strong and muscular like an Olympic athlete. Being in good physical shape is part of physical health. However, you don't have to be an athlete or even good at sports to be physically healthy. *Physical health* refers to the way your body functions. Physical health includes eating right, getting regular exercise, and being at your recommended body weight. Physical health is also about avoiding drugs and alcohol. Finally, physical health means being free of disease and sickness.

Emotional Health *Emotional health* is expressing your emotions in a positive, nondestructive way. Everyone experiences unpleasant feelings at one time or another. Emotionally healthy people can cope with unpleasant emotions and not get overwhelmed by them. For example, when Abel feels down, he knows he can go to his best friend or his family for support. Are you aware of how you feel and to whom you can go for support?

Myth

"As long as I work out, I'm healthy."

Fact

Being healthy is more than being physically fit.

Six Components of Health

Physical Health

▸ eats a well-balanced, diet

▸ exercises regularly

▸ avoids tobacco, alcohol, and drugs

▸ is free of disease

Emotional Health

▸ expresses emotions constructively

▸ asks for help when sad

Social Health

▸ respects others

▸ has supportive relationships

▸ expresses needs to others

Mental Health

▸ has high self-esteem

▸ enjoys trying new things

▸ is free of mental illness

Spiritual Health

▸ has a sense of purpose in life

▸ follows morals and values

▸ feels a unity with other human beings

Environmental Health

▸ has access to clean air and water

▸ has a clean and uncrowded living space

▸ recycles used paper, glass products, and aluminum

Figure 2

To be healthy, a person must attend to all six components of health.

ACTIVITY *Which component of your health do you think needs the most improvement?*

Social Health Social health does not mean being the most popular kid in school. A person who is popular can be socially unhealthy! *Social health* is the quality of your relationships with friends, family, teachers, and others you are in contact with. As listed in **Figure 2,** a person who is socially healthy respects others. A socially healthy person also stays clear of those who do not treat him or her with respect and tolerance. For example, Abel gets together with his friends each week. However, he avoids his neighbor who bullies him. He is also learning to better work out disagreements with his parents.

Mental Health   Your mental health can be strongly influenced by your emotional health. *Mental health* is the ability to recognize reality and cope with the demands of daily life. Sometimes people who have gone through intensely troubling times develop mental illnesses. An example of a mental illness is a phobia. A phobia is an irrational and excessive fear of something, such as a fear of heights. But mental health is about more than not having mental illness. Mental health is also having high self-esteem. Having high self-esteem is feeling comfortable and happy about yourself. For example, Iris is now trying out for the drama club. She had been hesitant to try out because none of her friends liked acting, but she decided to try out anyway.

Spiritual Health   *Spiritual health* is maintaining harmonious relationships with other living things and having spiritual direction and purpose. Spiritual health means different things to different people. For some people, spiritual health is defined by the practice of religion. For others, it is understanding their purpose in life.

Spiritual health also includes living according to one's ethics, morals, and values. A **value** is a strong belief or ideal. Being spiritually healthy may mean you live in harmony with your environment. It may also mean that you are at peace with yourself and those around you. For example, Iris says she feels most valuable and united with others when she helps out at her city's homeless shelter.

Environmental Health   The environment is made up of the living and nonliving things in your world. The environment includes air, water, and land. Your environment is your surroundings—where you live, work, or play. *Environmental health* is keeping your air and water clean, your food safe, and the land around you enjoyable and safe. Iris started a recycling program for her family when she realized the importance of her environmental health to her well-being.

Wellness: Striving for Optimal Health

As you may have noticed, many of the components of health can be affected by the other components. If one component of health is weak, it can affect a person's overall health. This is why being healthy is defined as the balance of all the components of health. **Wellness** is the achievement of a person's best in all six components of health.

It would be unrealistic to think that a person could achieve complete wellness all of the time. Think of striving for wellness in the same way you think of always striving to have a good day. Do you always have a really good day or a really bad day? Most of your days are most likely somewhere in between. That is how the wellness continuum works, too.

The wellness continuum represents the idea that a person is neither completely healthy nor completely unhealthy. Think of the wellness continuum as resembling the scale on a bellringer, commonly seen at amusement parks. As shown in **Figure 3,** at the top of the scale is optimal health, and at the bottom of the scale is illness and death. The harder you strive to hit the hammer on the pedal, the higher the ball goes on the scale. For most of us, the ball reaches somewhere in the middle of the scale.

People who can cope with their emotions, have healthy relationships, and make smart decisions probably fall near the optimal wellness side of the continuum. On the other hand, people who eat poorly, engage in health risk behaviors, never exercise, and are unhappy probably fall closer to the illness side. Where you fall on the continuum can change on a yearly, monthly, and even daily basis. Fortunately, you have the power to change your behaviors to move closer to optimal health.

Figure 3

The wellness continuum shows that wellness is about always striving for optimal health, even though most people are never completely healthy.

Influences on Your Wellness

As you strive for optimal health, it's important to recognize that there are many factors that influence your health.

Hereditary Influences   Your health can be influenced by your *heredity*—the traits you inherit from your parents. For example, if several members of your family have developed diabetes, you may be at risk for diabetes. However, if you have a hereditary disease in your family, it doesn't mean you will definitely develop that disease. By focusing on controllable risk factors, you can decrease your risk for hereditary diseases.

Social Influences   Your health is also influenced by the relationships you have with other people. For example, if your friends convince you to go to a party where alcohol is available, your friends are influencing your health in a negative way. If your parents or grandparents deal with anger by talking out their problems instead of yelling and fighting, you will be more likely to talk out your problems. Your parents are influencing your health in a positive way.

Cultural Influences   *Culture* is the values, beliefs, and practices shared by people that have a common background. Your culture can strongly influence your health. For example, some Asian cultures eat a lot of vegetables and seafood in their diet. This cultural influence is thought to be one of the reasons people from some Asian cultures have a lower risk of heart disease. What cultural influences do you think influence your health?

Many factors influence your health, including hereditary, social, cultural, and environmental influences.

Social
"My friends and I would rather play **video games** together than play sports."

Cultural
"My father makes the best shrimp with lemongrass."

Environmental
"The air is so fresh in the country. I'm glad we moved here."

Hereditary
"My grandfather had Alzheimer's disease."

Environmental Influences Your surroundings, the area where you live, and all the things you have contact with are part of your environment. Pollutants, safety regulations, and the availability and use of medical care are aspects of your environment that affect your health. The government enforces air- and water-quality regulations to keep your environment free from pollutants. The government also maintains safety regulations, such as traffic laws, to keep you safe.

Taking Charge of Your Wellness

Three ways you can take charge of your health are through your knowledge, through your lifestyle, and through your attitude.

Knowledge An important way to improve your health is through your knowledge. **Health literacy** is the knowledge of health information needed to make good choices about your health. Studying health in school will certainly increase your health literacy. However, it's important to keep up with current health issues. Your parents, teachers, healthcare providers, and library are great resources for health information. They can also lead you to other resources for health information.

Lifestyle One of the most important ways to improve your health is to make behavioral changes in your lifestyle. Putting your knowledge into action is a sure way to take charge of your wellness.

Unfortunately, most people don't always behave in a way that shows they know what is healthy. For example, most smokers know that smoking cigarettes can lead to lung cancer, but they still smoke. **Table 2** shows some examples of consequences that can happen when health behavior doesn't follow health knowledge. Some ways you can put your health knowledge into action are to exercise regularly, always wear a seat belt, and eat healthy and nutritious foods.

Table 2 Health Knowledge Versus Health Behavior		
Health knowledge *knowing the consequences of your behavior on your health*	**Health behavior** *taking action that affects your health, either negatively or positively*	**Consequences** *facing the effect of your behavior on your health*
Example 1 ▸ Steven knows that eating junk food can make him overweight and may lead to heart disease later in life.	▸ Steven eats candy bars and chips and drinks soda almost every day.	▸ Steven starts putting on weight which increases his risk for diabetes and heart disease.
Example 2 ▸ Karen knows she needs enough sleep to stay healthy.	▸ Karen doesn't plan her studying well and stays up late all week cramming for final exams.	▸ Karen does poorly on her exams, gets sick, and misses the junior prom.

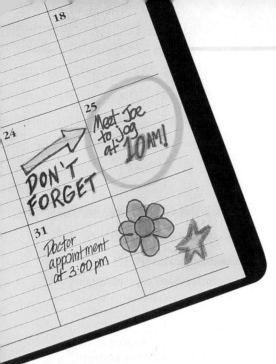

Attitude A person's way of thinking, or attitude, greatly affects that person's health. By changing your attitude, you can act in ways that work to make you a healthier person. For example, you could try to change your attitude toward stress. You can try to relax and stop letting the "little things" bother you. If you can keep stress from affecting you, you will find that you feel better mentally and physically. You can also try to change your attitude about anger. Don't get so worked up about things you can't control!

Your attitude can also help you make the best of a bad situation. People who have suffered through a long-term illness have benefited by having a positive attitude. People with positive attitudes are more hopeful and will strive harder to overcome illness. Having a positive attitude can be critical when overcoming an illness.

Perhaps the most important attitude you can change is the way you feel about yourself. To achieve wellness, you have to feel good about yourself, or have positive self-esteem. *Self-esteem* is a person's confidence, pride, and self-respect. You can be free from disease, be physically active, have a healthy diet, and have many supportive relationships. However, if you don't feel good about yourself, you will never be truly healthy. Eventually, low self-esteem can affect your health and actually make you physically ill. As a result, it is important to build a healthy self-esteem.

Taking charge of your wellness will help you lead a healthy life. Leading a healthy life is about balancing the six components of health. Getting the best out of each component of health has a lot to do with the choices you make and the actions you take. The good news is that you have the power to make the right choices and live life to its fullest!

> **"Health knowledge is useless without positive health behavior. You must put what you know into action for it to work!"**

SECTION 2

REVIEW *Answer the following questions on a separate piece of paper.*

Using Key Terms

1. **Define** the term *health*.
2. **Identify** the term for "a strong belief or ideal."
3. **Define** the term *wellness*.
4. **Identify** the term for "knowledge of health information needed to make good choices about your health."

Understanding Key Ideas

5. **Describe** each of the six components of health.
6. **Identify** the health component that involves working on the quality of your relationships with others.
   - **a.** mental health
   - **b.** social health
   - **c.** emotional health
   - **d.** environmental health

7. **Describe** the importance of striving for wellness.
8. **Discuss** each of the four influences on your wellness.
9. **Describe** how your attitude can help you take charge of your health.

Critical Thinking

10. **LIFE SKILL Practicing Wellness** State two ways you can improve two components of your health.
11. **Describe** how your family members influence and promote health in your family.

Health in Your Community

OBJECTIVES

Describe four ways society addresses health problems.

List three ways you can promote an issue to improve the health of others. **LIFE SKILL**

KEY TERMS

public health the practice of protecting and improving the health of people in a community

advocate to speak or argue in favor of something

public service announcement (PSA) a message created to educate people about an issue

Three years ago, Maureen's mother was so sick from diabetes that she had to be hospitalized. Thanks to new developments in medicine, she's feeling better than she has in years. Maureen's mother is now more free to do the things she loves.

Four Ways Society Addresses Health Problems

Everyone has the responsibility of taking care of his or her health. However, many health problems need to be tackled by the cooperation and experience of many people. **Public health** is the practice of protecting and improving the health of people in a community.

Our community is able to promote and protect the health of people in many ways. Four ways in which our community addresses health problems are through medical advances, technology, public policy, and education.

1. **Medical advances** Conducting medical research is one way our society addresses health concerns. One medical advancement that came about through medical research was the development of the insulin pump.

   The implanted insulin pump is being developed for people with a certain type of diabetes. *Diabetes* is a serious disease in which the body is not able to obtain glucose (better known as *sugar*) from the blood. Diabetes kills tens of thousands of people every year in the United States. People who live with diabetes must constantly manage the levels of glucose in their bloodstream. To do so, diabetics must monitor their diet, exercise regularly, and, in many cases, receive daily insulin shots.

   The surgically implanted insulin pump is being developed to replace the need for daily insulin shots. A microchip embedded in the pump makes monitoring and controling blood-sugar levels possible. If a diabetic's blood-sugar level is high, the pump will release insulin. With the insulin pump, the diabetic will no longer need daily insulin shots and can easily manage blood-sugar levels.

Medical advances and technology have saved lives and helped people recover from many diseases.

HEALTH Handbook For more information about public health, see the Express Lesson on p. 552 of this text.

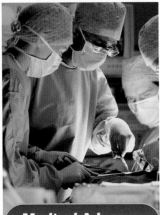
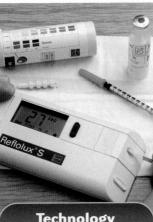

Medical Advances
Doctors are developing insulin pumps that can be surgically implanted to make managing blood-sugar levels easier.

Technology
Glucose meters indicate blood-sugar levels for diabetics.

Public Policy
Congress passes laws that provide funds for research on diseases such as diabetes.

Education
School health classes teach students how to decrease their risk of developing diabetes.

Figure 4

Society has worked in many ways to address health problems such as diabetes.

ACTIVITY *Can you think of how another health problem has been addressed for one of these four ways?*

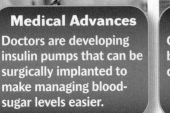

internet connect

www.scilinks.org/health
Topic: Diabetes
HealthLinks code: HH4041

HEALTH LINKS. Maintained by the National Science Teachers Association

2. **Technology** Another way in which our society works to solve health problems is through technology. Through the use of computers, lasers, and other revolutionary technologies, new and better products have been made to help people lead healthier lives.

   One example of a product made through the use of technology is the glucose meter, such as the one shown in **Figure 4.** The glucose meter was designed to let diabetics know their blood-sugar level by requiring only a very small amount of blood. The glucose meter makes monitoring blood-sugar levels easier.

3. **Public policy** Governmental policies and regulations can also help to address health problems. Tobacco regulation is one way that laws can help prevent disease. Examples of these laws are placing taxes on cigarettes, enforcing an age limit to buy tobacco products, and limiting how tobacco companies can advertise. These laws are aimed at trying to keep people from smoking. Smoking can cause diseases such as lung cancer.

   Congress can also pass laws that provide tax dollars for research on diseases. This money helps fund the development of products such as the glucose meter. The money also helps advance medical research, such as surgically implanting insulin pumps.

4. **Education** Health education has been a key factor in the prevention of disease and illness in this country. For example, most states require that students take some form of health class. Health teachers teach students about the benefits of exercising and eating nutritious foods. Health teachers also discuss the risks of smoking, drinking, and behaving violently.

   In addition, many community agencies provide health education. For example, the American Diabetes Association teaches the public about diabetes and ways to prevent it.

What You Can Do

Many people have improved the health of others by speaking out and promoting health issues. To speak out or argue in favor of something is to **advocate.** You may know of people in your community who work tirelessly to promote health issues. Maybe they help take hot meals to elderly people in their homes or serve food at a homeless shelter. Or perhaps they organize rallies to promote certain health issues. Others may work in a health field.

You Can Be an Advocate! Although few people devote their lives to being advocates, we all have the potential to better our own wellness as well as the wellness of others. For example, you could volunteer at a local health clinic or public agency. You could become involved at school in addressing health issues important to teens. You could serve as an example to others by practicing your best health behaviors. You can even be an advocate by training for a career in a health field!

HEALTH Handbook For more information about health careers, see the Reference Guide on p. 628 of this text.

real life Activity

SPEAK OUT!

LIFE SKILL
Communicating Effectively

Materials

✔ magazines
✔ scissors
✔ colored paper
✔ poster board
✔ glue
✔ markers

Procedure

1. **Choose** a health issue in your school or community that you would like to address by supporting others in making positive health choices.

2. **Think** about the message you want to communicate and the audience you want to receive your message.

3. **Cut** out magazine pictures that can help you express your health message.

4. **Use** magazine pictures, colored paper, poster board, glue and markers to create a poster that expresses your message.

Conclusions

1. **Summarizing Results** What was the main health message of your poster?

2. **Evaluating Information** What technique or style did you use to make your health message stand out?

3. **Predicting Outcomes** How do you think the audience you want to send your message to will respond to your poster?

4. **CRITICAL THINKING** Using other methods, such as the Internet or a video camera, how would you communicate your health message differently?

"My mother survived cancer. Now, I'm helping others with cancer and having fun!"

Getting Your Point Across One way to reach many people about health issues is through a public service announcement. A **public service announcement (PSA)** is a message created to educate people about an issue. Most PSAs are in the form of a commercial that you hear on the radio or on television. You can also create a PSA in other forms. For example, you can publish an essay in the school newspaper. You could also create posters and post them around your school.

There are several things you should think about when choosing the way to communicate your message:

▶ **Make sure you have the most current and accurate information.** Be sure to research your topic. Ask a family member or teacher about an organization that specializes in your topic. Your parents can also help you find information on the Internet.

▶ **Know your audience.** To whom are you trying to send your message? How do you think your audience will respond to your message? Some issues bring up strong feelings and opinions in people. The success of your message can depend on how sensitive you are to these feelings and opinions.

For example, imagine that after waiting for many years, your uncle recieves a kidney transplant. He is now much healthier and feels great. You can see the positive difference a person's decision to be an organ donor has made on the life of your uncle. You would therefore like to spread the message that people who are willing to donate their organs need to talk to family members about their decision. A national organ donation or transplant organization could give you current and accurate information to help you create a PSA for you school or community.

Advocating for your health and others' health is one of the most important things you can do in your life. Being well informed about your health, knowing how you feel about yourself, and making an effort to maintain a healthy lifestyle are the foundations for your and others' wellness.

SECTION 3

REVIEW   *Answer the following questions on a separate piece of paper.*

Using Key Terms

1. **Define** the term *public health*.

2. **Identify** the term for "a message created to educate people about an issue."

Understanding Key Ideas

3. **List** four ways society addresses health issues.

4. **Identify** the way in which society teaches others to live healthy lives.
   a. medical advances   c. technology
   b. education   d. public policy

5. **Identify** which of the following areas addresses community health through governmental decisions.
   a. public policy   c. technology
   b. medical advances   d. education

Critical Thinking

6. **LIFE SKILL** **Communicating Effectively** Describe why good communication skills are important for advocating a health issue.

7. **LIFE SKILL** **Practicing Wellness** List three ways you can communicate a health issue to your community.

Highlights

Key Terms

SECTION 1

lifestyle disease (6)
risk factor (7)
sedentary (9)

SECTION 2

health (11)
value (13)
wellness (13)
health literacy (15)

SECTION 3

public health (17)
advocate (19)
**public service
announcement (PSA)** (20)

The Big Picture

✔ In the past, deaths were caused mainly by infectious diseases. Today, most health problems are related to the way we live, or our lifestyle.

✔ All health problems have risk factors. You have the power to change controllable risk factors.

✔ The major cause of death for adults over the age of 65 is heart disease. The major cause of death for adults between 19 and 65 years of age is cancer. The major causes of death for teens are motor vehicle accidents, homicide, suicide, and other accidents. The major cause of death for children and infants is motor vehicle accidents.

✔ The six types of behavior that lead to health problems for teens are sedentary lifestyle, alcohol and drug use, sexual activity, behaviors that result in unintentional and intentional injuries, tobacco use, and poor eating habits.

✔ Health is the state of well-being in which all of the components of health—physical, emotional, social, mental, spiritual, and environmental—are in balance.

✔ Wellness is the achievement of your best in all of the components of health.

✔ The four influences on your wellness are hereditary, social, cultural, and environmental influences.

✔ You can take charge of your wellness through your lifestyle, through your attitude, and through your knowledge.

✔ Society addresses health problems in four ways: medical advances, technology, public policy, and education.

✔ Everyone has the power to try to improve the wellness of others.

✔ Public service announcements are an effective way to advocate for a health issue.

✔ Communication skills are very important when you advocate for a health issue.

Review

Using Key Terms

advocate (19)
health (11)
health literacy (15)
lifestyle disease (6)
public health (17)
public service announcement (PSA) (20)

risk factor (7)
sedentary (9)
value (13)
wellness (13)

1. For each definition below, choose the key term that best matches the definition.
   a. the practice of protecting and improving the health of people in a community
   b. a message created to educate people about an issue
   c. the achievement of a person's best in all six components of health
   d. a strong belief or ideal
   e. not taking part in physical activity on a regular basis
   f. anything that increases the likelihood of injury, disease, or other health problems
   g. knowledge of health information needed to make good choices about your health

2. Explain the relationship between the key terms in each of the following pairs.
   a. *health* and *lifestlyle disease*
   b. *advocate* and *public service announcement*

Understanding Key Ideas
Section 1

3. How have the causes of health problems changed from the past to today?

4. Heart disease is an example of which type of disease: infectious or lifestyle?

5. Which of the following is a controllable risk factor?
   a. race
   b. age
   c. gender
   d. exercise

6. Which of the following is *not* a common cause of death for your age group?
   a. heart disease
   b. motor vehicle accidents
   c. suicide
   d. homicide

7. Describe how a sedentary lifestyle can lead to health problems.

8. Driving without a seat belt is an example of which of the six health risk behaviors?

9. Describe how the risk behavior tobacco use can lead to health problems.

10. **CRITICAL THINKING** What are some behaviors you can practice now that will improve your chances of living a long, healthy life?

Section 2

11. Which component of health involves avoiding drugs and alcohol?

12. The ability to cope with the demands of daily life is part of which component of health?

13. Describe how you can reach higher levels on the wellness continuum.

14. Give an example for how each of the following factors influences your wellness.
    a. heredity
    b. culture
    c. society
    d. the environment

15. Describe how you can take charge of your wellness through your attitude. **LIFE SKILL**

16. **CRITICAL THINKING** Describe how you can use health knowledge to improve the physical component of your health.

Section 3

17. Which of the following is *not* an example of how society addresses health problems?
    a. education
    b. public policy
    c. smoking
    d. medical advances

18. Explain why it's important to know your audience when you advocate for better health.

19. Why is it important to have the most current and accurate information when you advocate for a health issue?

20. **CRITICAL THINKING** Describe how technology has improved your health and the health of others in the world.

Understanding Graphics

Study the figure below to answer the questions that follow.

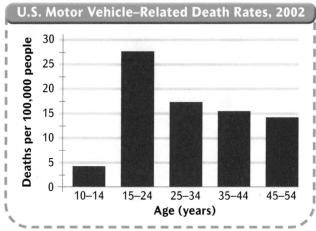

U.S. Motor Vehicle–Related Death Rates, 2002

Deaths per 100,000 people / Age (years)

Source: Centers for Disease Control and Prevention

21. What is the motor vehicle death rate for your age group?

22. Which age group has the highest motor vehicle death rate?

23. CRITICAL THINKING Why do you think the age group that you answered in item 22 has the highest motor vehicle death rate?

Activities

24. Health and Your Community Interview a person over the age of 70 to find out what health problems were most common d his or her teenage years. Prepare a one-page comparing what you learned in the interview what you learned in this chapter about health problems facing teens today.

25. Health and You For 1 week, keep a diary of everything that influences your well-ness. Separate the influences into four catego hereditary, social, cultural, and environment

26. Health and Your Community Collect newspa or magazine pictures that show healthful beh iors and harmful behaviors. Glue these pictu on a poster board. Show your poster to the c and discuss how advertisements can influenc your health choices.

Action Plan

27. LIFE SKILL Practicing Wellness Create a pers health plan that improves or promotes each the six components of health.

Standardized Test Prep

Read the passage below, and then answer the questions that follow. **READING SKILL** **WRITING SKILL**

Kent knows that there are many benefits to exercising regularly. He knows that regular exercise makes him feel as if he has more energy. He also knows that it will help him maintain his weight. However, Kent can't remember the last time he exercised. Kent prefers to play video games after school. After he gets bored playing video games, he usually watches some TV. When Kent put his jeans on this morning, he noticed they were tight. Today, he was feeling too lethargic to pay attention in math class. Kent couldn't understand why he was so tired if he slept 9 hours last night. He felt that he was getting sick.

28. In this passage, the word *lethargic* means
A hungry.
B excited.
C lacking in energy.
D bored.

29. What can you infer from reading this passage
E Kent's health behavior does not reflect his health knowledge.
F Kent has an infectious disease that is maki him sick.
G Kent needs more sleep each night.
H none of the above

30. Explain what may happen to Kent's energy lev Kent starts exercising at least three times a we

31. Write a paragraph describing how Kent can change his daily routine to find more time to exercise.

CHAPTER 2

Skills for a Healthy Life

What's Your Health IQ?
BEHAVIOR

Indicate how frequently you engage in each of the following behaviors (1 = never; 2 = occasionally; 3 = most of the time; 4 = all of the time). Total your points, and then turn to p. 638.

1. I review all of my choices before I make a decision.

2. I think about the outcome for each possible choice.

3. I make decisions that support my beliefs.

4. I think about the decisions I make afterward so that I can learn from them.

5. I stop to think about who might be affected by the decisions I make.

6. I usually ask for advice when I have a tough decision to make.

7. If I make a bad decision, I try to correct any problem my decision caused.

Visit these Web sites for the latest health information:

  Current Health

Find more information whenever you see a HealthLinks box. Go to **scilinks.org/health**, and type in the HealthLinks code.

Find worksheets and other materials that go with your textbook at **go.hrw.com**.

Check out **Current Health®** articles related to this chapter by visiting **go.hrw.com**. Just type in the keyword **HH4 CH02**.

Building Life Skills

OBJECTIVES

State the importance of practicing life skills for lifelong wellness.

List 10 life skills that you need for a healthy life.

Predict how you can use each of the 10 life skills in your daily life.
LIFE SKILL

KEY TERMS

life skill a tool for building a healthy life

coping dealing with problems and troubles in an effective way

consumer a person who buys products or services

media all public forms of communication, such as TV, radio, newspaper, the Internet, and advertisements

resource something that you can use to help achieve a goal

Just like you need skills to build a house, you also need skills to build a happy, healthy life.

Amin has been so frustrated. He argues with his dad every day. His allergies are driving him crazy, and he doesn't know which medicine to buy. What's worse is that the class bully has been following him around school. Amin knows things need to get better, but he isn't sure where to begin.

What Are Life Skills?

Like Amin, everybody wants to enjoy the benefits of a healthy life. We all want to be free from sickness. We want to feel good about who we are. However, having a healthy life doesn't come without effort.

Just like you need skills to build a house, you need skills to build a happy, healthy life. Building a house is not an easy task. A lot of hard work is required, and you need the right tools, such as a hammer, nails, and wood. You need tools for building a healthy life, too. These tools for building a healthy life are called **life skills.**

Life skills will help you improve the six components of health: physical, emotional, social, mental, spiritual, and environmental. For example, one life skill can improve your social component of health by teaching you how to communicate more effectively. Another life skill can help your emotional health by suggesting ways to deal with difficult times, such as the death of a family member.

Some life skills can affect all components of your health. For example, one life skill provides suggestions for making good decisions. From the foods you choose to the friends you choose, the decisions you make can affect every component of your health.

Learning to use life skills will boost your wellness throughout your lifetime. However, using life skills takes practice. Just as an experienced builder makes a better house, you can practice life skills to build a healthier life!

Ten Life Skills

Figure 1 lists 10 life skills that can help you lead a healthy life. You will find these life skills throughout this textbook. The life skills are identified by this icon: **LIFE SKILL**

1. **LIFE SKILL** **Assessing Your Health** How healthy are you? How do you know if you are doing the right thing for your health? This life skill will help you evaluate your health. It will also help you to evaluate how your actions and behaviors affect your health. This will enable you to find out what you need to do to improve your health!

2. **LIFE SKILL** **Communicating Effectively** Have you ever had trouble dealing with a classmate or your parents? Have you ever struggled for the right word to say how you feel? This life skill will teach you good communication skills, which include knowing how to listen and speak effectively. These skills will help improve your relationships with your family, friends, classmates, teachers, and other adults.

3. **LIFE SKILL** **Practicing Wellness** This life skill will show you how to practice healthy behaviors daily so that you can have good life-long health. Examples of healthy behaviors you may practice are getting enough sleep, choosing nutritious foods, and avoiding risky behaviors.

4. **LIFE SKILL** **Coping** Dealing with troubles or problems in an effective way is referred to as **coping.** This life skill will help you deal with difficult times and situations and with emotions such as anger, depression, and loss of a loved one.

5. **LIFE SKILL** **Being a Wise Consumer** A **consumer** is a person who buys products (such as food, CDs, or clothing) or services (such as

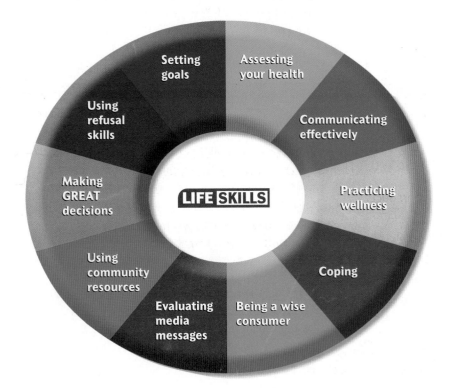

Figure 1
Practicing these 10 life skills will help you lead a healthy life.

medical care or auto repair). Therefore, you are a consumer! This life skill will help you make good decisions when buying health products and services. It will show you how to decide what is appropriate for your health.

6. **LIFE SKILL** **Evaluating Media Messages** Public forms of communication, such as TV, radio, movies, newspaper, the Internet, and advertisements are referred to as the **media.** The media have a significant influence on what you learn about the world. This life skill will give you the tools to analyze media messages. Knowing how to analyze media messages will help you make better decisions about your health.

7. **LIFE SKILL** **Using Community Resources** A **resource** is something that you can use to help achieve a goal. For example, health clinics, libraries, and government agencies are all community resources. Every community has a wealth of services that provide help for all six components of health. This life skill will help you find these services and will describe how they can assist you.

The following three life skills will be described in more detail in the next three sections of this chapter.

8. **LIFE SKILL** **Making GREAT Decisions** Everyone wants to make the right decisions for themselves. This life skill will provide you with steps to help you do just that. Section 2 of this chapter will discuss these steps in more detail.

9. **LIFE SKILL** **Using Refusal Skills** This life skill will provide you with different ways you can say "no" to something you do not want to do. Section 3 of this chapter will describe refusal skills in more detail.

10. **LIFE SKILL** **Setting Goals** This life skill will provide you with tips to help you reach your goals. Section 4 of this chapter will discuss these tips on setting goals in more detail.

> **The average number of advertisements a person sees in 1 day is 3,000.**

SECTION 1

REVIEW
Answer the following questions on a separate piece of paper.

Using Key Terms

1. **Define** the term *coping*.

2. **Identify** the term for "a person who buys products and services."

3. **Identify** the term for "something that you can use to help achieve a goal."

Understanding Key Ideas

4. **Summarize** the importance of practicing life skills for lifelong wellness.

5. **Name** the life skill that teaches you good listening skills.

6. **Identify** the life skill that helps you make good decisions when buying health products or services.
   a. Coping
   b. Practicing Wellness
   c. Assessing Your Health
   d. Being a Wise Consumer

7. **Name** the life skill that will help you say no to something you don't want to do.

Critical Thinking

8. **LIFE SKILL** **Practicing Wellness** Choose three life skills. Then, describe how you can apply each of these life skills in your life.

Making GREAT Decisions

OBJECTIVES

Describe the importance of making decisions.

Summarize what you should do if you make a wrong decision.

Apply the Making GREAT Decisions model to make a decision. **LIFE SKILL**

Describe a time when you worked with someone else to make a decision. **LIFE SKILL**

On her way to school, Sina was daydreaming about Marty, the cute senior she met yesterday. To her surprise, he pulled up in his car with his friends. Marty and his friends were planning to skip school and wanted her to come along. Sina froze as she quickly tried to decide what she should do.

Importance of Making Decisions

How many decisions have you made today? You've probably made more decisions than you even realize. Every day, people make decisions about what clothes to wear, what to eat, what channel to watch on TV, and whether to press the snooze button on the alarm clock again. These decisions often happen on the spur of the moment. You may even make these decisions without even thinking about them.

Making snap decisions without really thinking about them is all right for the easy things. But if you make impulsive decisions all of the time, you may run into some negative consequences. **Consequences** are the results of your actions and decisions. Sexually transmitted diseases, pregnancy, tobacco and alcohol addiction, overdoses, and car accidents are examples of negative consequences that many teens have faced because they made fast decisions.

Making decisions is important because you are responsible for the consequences of your decisions. The decisions you make not only affect your health but also can affect the health of others. For example, choosing to drink and drive not only puts the driver in danger but also puts everyone on the road in danger.

Your decisions can also promote the health of your family and the health of your community. For example, you can start a recycling project with your family. You can also start a neighborhood watch program in your community.

Deciding not to take part in risky behavior will protect you from negative consequences.

MAKING GREAT DECISIONS

Give thought to the problem.

Review your choices.

Evaluate the consequences of each choice.

Assess and choose the best choice.

Think it over afterward.

Figure 2

The Making GREAT Decisions model will help you make great decisions.

ACTIVITY *Use the steps of the Making GREAT Decisions model for a decision you need to make today.*

Using the Making GREAT Decisions Model

How many times have you made a decision that you regretted later? This is where the life skill for making GREAT decisions can help you by providing a decision-making model. The Making GREAT Decisions model is useful because it requires you to think about the choices and the consequences before making a decision. If you learn how to use the decision-making model, you are more likely to make decisions that have positive consequences.

The steps of the Making GREAT Decisions model are listed in **Figure 2**. Notice that each step uses the first letter of the word *great*. Let's use the model for the decision Sina was facing at the beginning of this section. Recall that Sina has just been asked to skip school with Marty.

GIVE Thought to the Problem If Sina doesn't stop to think about the decision, she might do something she regrets. Therefore, Sina pauses before giving Marty an impulsive answer.

REVIEW Your Choices At first glance, you might say that Sina has two choices. One choice is skip school and get into the car with Marty. Another choice is to tell Marty, "No, thanks," and keep walking to school. Are those two choices the only ones that Sina has? Can you think of any others? Why is Sina tempted to skip school with Marty in the first place? She probably likes him. Maybe she can suggest that they get together at another time.

EVALUATE the Consequences of Each Choice In this step, Sina weighs the pros and cons of each possible choice. If Sina skips school, she could get caught and could be suspended from school. If her parents found out, she would be grounded. These consequences would be the short-term consequences.

Sina could also face long-term consequences. These consequences would affect her years from now. Sina thinks that she spotted a six-pack of beer in the back seat. What would happen if she were in the car and they were arrested? She could have an arrest on her record. Or they could get into an accident!

What if Sina follows her second choice—not to get into the car with Marty but to keep walking to school? If she makes this decision, she will not face any serious consequences. But she will miss a chance to be with Marty.

What if she follows her third choice—to turn down Marty's offer but to suggest that they get together another time? Sina won't get into trouble for skipping school. Also, she won't risk getting into a car with people who drink and drive. Wait a minute. If Marty drinks and drives and skips school now, is he likely to do so again? If Sina gets together with Marty, might she find herself in this situation in the future?

ASSESS and Choose the Best Choice During this step, Sina makes her choice. She decides which choice best reflects her values. You may recall that a value is a strong belief or ideal. For example, honesty is one of Sina's values. Values have a big effect on your decision making. If you make a decision that goes against your values, you will feel bad about the decision later. Respecting your values is respecting yourself.

Sina chose not to skip school with Marty. She also did not offer to get together with him later. Lying to her teachers and parents about her whereabouts went against her values. She would face too many negative consequences for skipping school. Going straight to school was a lot less stressful. Sina politely told Marty, "No, thanks."

THINK It Over Afterward Sina thought about her decision. She was glad she didn't have to lie to her parents. She was also glad that she didn't have to worry about getting in trouble.

Making GREAT Decisions Together

You will likely face situations in which you are not sure what the right decision is. These decisions generally affect your life and health significantly. For this reason, you may feel more pressured to make the right decision. When you have to make difficult decisions, seeking advice from your friends, teachers, and parents can be very helpful. They might see a positive or negative consequence that you didn't. They can also support you when you need to make an unpopular decision.

Sometimes, we don't realize how our decisions affect others. For example, if you decide to baby-sit when you feel sick, you might pass the sickness on to the baby. These are the decisions about which you probably would want to ask for advice.

For some decisions, you may need more than just advice. Many decisions require you to collaborate with others. To **collaborate** is to work together with one or more people. For example, working on a science project with your classmate requires you to collaborate. Some collaborations are more serious. For example, you discover your friend has been talking about suicide. You need to collaborate with your parents to find out how to help your friend. No matter how serious the situation is, learning to work with others helps you find the right solution.

As you get older you will find that skills in collaborative decision making will be very useful. You will use these skills to make decisions with co-workers at your current or future jobs. You will also use collaborative decision making skills with the family you will form. Learning these skills now will help you make better decisions in the future.

Collaborating with parents can help you make GREAT decisions.

Everyone Makes Mistakes

What happens if you find you made a poor decision? It is possible, even likely—even after practicing your decision-making skills! Sometimes, the consequences of wrong decisions are embarrassing or humiliating. Everybody has had that kind of experience. Sometimes, however, wrong decisions can be dangerous to you and to the people around you. These kinds of decisions need to be dealt with as soon as possible.

Stop, Think, and Go If you made a poor decision, you can use the Stop, Think, and Go process to correct the problem. The Stop, Think, and Go process uses the following steps:

- ▶ **STOP** First, stop and admit that you made a poor decision. When you admit that you made a wrong decision, you take responsibility for what you've done.
- ▶ **THINK** Then, think about to whom you can talk about the problem. Usually, a parent, teacher, school counselor, or close friend can help you. Tell whomever you choose about your decision and its consequences. Discuss ways to correct the situation.
- ▶ **GO** Finally, go and do your best to correct the situation. Maybe you simply need to leave the situation you are in. You may have to tell someone about an unsafe situation. You may have to apologize to someone you hurt. In any case, you have had the opportunity to learn from your mistake.

Admitting that you have made the wrong decision is not always easy. You might risk getting in trouble with your parents or teachers. You might make your friends angry. In the long run, though, you'll feel better. You will know that you adhered to your values and tried to do the right thing.

SECTION 2

REVIEW   *Answer the following questions on a separate piece of paper.*

Using Key Terms

1. **Identify** the term for "a result of your actions and decisions."
2. **Define** the term *collaborate*.

Understanding Key Ideas

3. **Describe** the importance of making decisions.
4. **Identify** the step that is *not* a part of the Making GREAT Decisions model.
   a. Review your choices.
   b. Assess and choose the best choice.
   c. Think it over afterward.
   d. Think quickly.

5. **Summarize** why it is important to think about decisions you make afterward.
6. **Describe** what you can do if you make a wrong decision.

Critical Thinking

7. **LIFE SKILL** **Making GREAT Decisions** Apply the Making GREAT Decisions model to a situation in which you need to make a decision.
8. **LIFE SKILL** **Making GREAT Decisions** Describe a time when you worked effectively with someone else to make a decision.

Resisting Pressure from Others

OBJECTIVES

State the people and groups that influence our behavior.

Identify three types of direct pressure.

Identify three types of indirect pressure.

State an example of each of the 12 types of refusal skills.

Apply one of the refusal skills to a pressure in your life. **LIFE SKILL**

KEY TERMS

peer pressure a feeling that you should do something because that is what your friends want

direct pressure the pressure that results from someone who tries to convince you to do something you normally wouldn't do

indirect pressure the pressure that results from being swayed to do something because people you look up to are doing it

refusal skill a strategy to avoid doing something you don't want to do

"Here, take this! Don't say anything or I'll say it was your idea!" Maiyen's friend Jeff stuffed candy that he was planning to steal into Maiyen's pocket. At that moment, Maiyen's uncle came out from behind the store counter. "Maiyen! How's your dad?"

Who Influences You?

What style of clothes do you wear? What kind of hairstyle do you have? Your behaviors and decisions are often influenced by many people. For example, your friends can influence you through peer pressure. **Peer pressure** is a feeling that you should do something because that is what your friends want. Your family can also influence your behaviors and decisions. Even the media (movies, TV, books, magazines, newspapers, the Internet, and radio) influence the decisions you make every day. These influences can be positive or negative.

Positive Influences Having positive role models and being influenced to improve yourself can be good. For example, let's say that your closest friends are joining the track team. You decide to join the team, too, to spend more time with your friends. Running around the track improves your physical health, doesn't it?

Negative Influences On the other hand, being pressured to do something that you don't want to do is not healthy. For example, Maiyen is being pressured to steal from her uncle's store. The consequences of negative pressure can be serious. Some pressures can be life threatening. Examples of pressures that can threaten your life include smoking, drinking alcohol, and using drugs. These pressures often come from your own friends.

Everybody has felt some type of pressure from his or her friends at one time or another.

Table 1 Types of Pressure

Direct pressure		Indirect pressure	
Pressure	**Example**	**Pressure**	**Example**
Teasing	Your friends tease you about your clothes being out of style.	TV	You start using phrases or slogans from your favorite TV show.
Persuasion	You're too tired to go to the party, but your friend says that a lot of cool people will be there.	Radio	A song's lyrics encourage violent acts or criminal behavior.
Explanations	The doctor says that your risk of heart disease increases if you do not exercise.	Advertising	You buy a product because the ad says the product will solve a particular problem for you.
Put-downs	Some kids call you a wimp because you won't try out for the soccer team.	Role models	Your coach volunteers at a fund raiser. You donate money to the fund.
Threats	Your sister threatens to tell on you for failing your math test if you tell on her for getting a detention.	Popular people	You like the way a certain jacket looks on a popular person, and you want to get one for yourself.
Bribery	Your parents tell you that they will give you $10 for every A you get on your report card.	Famous people	Your hairstyle matches the hair style of a famous actress.

Types of Pressure

The people and groups that influence you can pressure you either directly or indirectly. These two types of pressure—direct and indirect—are described below. Examples of each type of pressure are given in **Table 1.**

Direct Pressure The pressure that results from someone who tries to convince you to do something you normally wouldn't do is referred to as a **direct pressure.** Refer to Table 1 to determine which kind of direct pressure Maiyen faced. If you answered "threat," you are correct.

Indirect Pressure The pressure that results from being swayed to do something because people you look up to are doing it is referred to as **indirect pressure.** Indirect pressure is much more subtle than direct pressure. When you are pressured indirectly, you are not directly told or asked to do something. However, you may still feel pushed to do it.

When making a decision, make a conscious effort to determine why you are making that decision. Are you being pressured to behave in a certain way? Does this decision support your values? If your choice harms you or someone else in any way, you might want to rethink the decision.

Refusal Skills

What happens if someone is directly pressuring you to do something that you do not want to do? There are many different ways to refuse to do something. A **refusal skill** is a strategy to avoid doing something you don't want to do.

Table 2 lists and gives examples of twelve different refusal skills. You can use one or more of these refusal skills in any situation where you are feeling pressured. For example, Asaf promised his dad he would help clean out the garage on Saturday afternoon. However, his friend Joey wants him to ride bikes instead. Asaf has already told Joey about his promise to his dad, but Joey keeps pressuring him.

How do you think Asaf can use the twelve refusal skills in this situation? Which ones do you think Asaf should try? Can you think of any other possible responses Asaf could use?

Some of the refusal skills might be familiar to you. You might have even used a couple of them. Some refusal skills are better than others for certain situations. Sometimes, you have to refuse in several different ways before people will accept your answer. The more options you know, the more successful you will be at refusing pressure. Practicing each of the refusal skills will help even more.

Table 2 Twelve Refusal Skills	
Refusal skill	**Sample response**
1. Blame someone else.	"My dad would kill me if I didn't help him."
2. Give a reason.	"No, my dad said he'd pay me $20 if I helped out."
3. Ignore the request or the pressure.	Pretend that you don't hear them asking you. Refuse to talk about it.
4. Leave the situation.	"I've got to get going. I'm running late."
5. Say, "no, thanks."	"No, thanks. I'm not interested."
6. Say no, and mean it.	"NO, I don't want to!"
7. Keep saying no.	"How many times do I have to say no? Stop bugging me!"
8. Make a joke out of it.	"You probably couldn't keep up with me on a bike ride anyway."
9. Make an excuse.	"No, I'm not feeling well."
10. Suggest something else to do.	"Let's go on a bike ride on Sunday instead."
11. Change the subject.	"I heard Nick and Mary are dating."
12. Team up with someone.	"Hey David, didn't dad say we had to do the garage or we'd be grounded?" Ask one or more people who share your values to help you in the refusal. Many voices are better than one!

Practicing Refusal Skills

When you do something again and again, you get good at it. That isn't a surprise. You know that if you practice playing the guitar, you'll get better and better at it. If you practice working on those math problems, you'll get a better grade on the exam. It's the same thing with refusal skills. The more you practice them, the more natural they will sound when you actually have to use them.

Practicing refusal skills can help you know what to do when you are in a "real-life" situation. If you are experienced in using refusal skills, you will probably make better decisions. The reason is that the decisions you make will be your own, and you will not be pressured by others.

Refusal skills will be helpful for you during your entire life, not just now. Usually, when you hear about peer pressure, people are talking about the teenage years. The truth is that throughout your life you will be in situations in which you feel pressured to do things that you don't want to do. For example, your boss invites you to the game on Saturday, which happens to be the day your friends planned your birthday celebration. Refusal skills can help you gracefully say "no, thanks." They will also increase your self-confidence. People will notice your confidence and will be less likely to pressure you.

LIFE SKILL Activity

Using Refusal Skills

Role-Playing Refusal Skills

Drinking alcohol when under the legal drinking age is one of the most common pressures many teens face. Underage drinking has been related to car accidents, suicide, and other accidents that lead to death.

Imagine that you have a couple of friends over to play video games. Your parents went out to dinner so you have the house to yourselves. One friend finds beer in the refrigerator. She suggests that you and your friends drink it. You know your parents will notice if the beer is gone.

1 Reread the list of refusal skills in **Table 2.**

2 Apply each one of the refusal skills to the situation described above, and role-play each skill with a classmate.

LIFE SKILL **Using Refusal Skills** Describe which refusal skill was the most effective.

Saying No with Respect When you practice refusal skills, two basic points are important to remember—always respect others, and don't put anyone down. One reason that people feel pressured to do things they don't want to do is that they don't want to seem disrespectful. However, you can deliver a firm no without being disrespectful. You do not have to insult someone when you are refusing to give in to their pressure. For example, don't call someone a loser to get the person off your back. That isn't a positive way to deal with the situation and it won't get a positive reaction either.

Disagreeing with others or saying no does not mean that people will stop liking you, although it may seem so at the time. If someone gets angry with you for saying no, you should not feel as if you should have said yes.

Persistent Pressure Some people might not stop bothering you. You might have said no in 10 different ways, and they are still pushing you. In this case, you have to leave the situation. (If you can't leave, find a teacher, a parent, or another trusted adult to help you.) Remember, that even if someone doesn't respect your no, you don't have to do what he or she is pressuring you to do. Your values and rights are important.

What do you do if the person who won't stop pushing you is your friend? You may have to ask yourself if this person is a good person for you to be around. Does he or she respect you and the things that are important to you? If you stopped hanging around with the person, would you have less pressure and stress in your life?

Practicing refusal skills now will help you cope with difficult situations that you might face. The more you practice, the more confident you will be. Before you know it, you'll be an expert!

> **Even if someone doesn't respect your NO, you don't have to do it.**

SECTION 3

REVIEW *Answer the following questions on a separate piece of paper.*

Using Key Terms

1. **Define** the term *peer pressure*.

2. **Identify** the term for "a strategy to avoid doing something that you do not want to do."

Understanding Key Ideas

3. **State** five things that influence our behavior.

4. **Compare** three types of direct pressure.

5. **Compare** three types of indirect pressure.

6. **Identify** the example of a direct pressure.
   a. teasing
   b. advertising
   c. radio
   d. popular people

7. **Identify** the example of an indirect pressure.
   a. persuasion
   b. TV
   c. bribery
   d. threats

8. **Apply** five refusal skills you can use if a friend suggests that you skip school.

9. **Describe** why people feel pressured to do things that they don't want to do.

Critical Thinking

10. **LIFE SKILL** **Practicing Wellness** Use one of the 12 refusal skills to deal with a pressure you currently have in your life.

Setting Healthy Goals

OBJECTIVES

Differentiate between short-term goals and long-term goals.

Describe six suggestions for setting goals.

Develop an action plan to achieve a personal goal. **LIFE SKILL**

KEY TERMS

goal something that you work toward and hope to achieve

action plan a set of directions that will help you reach your goal

Beth's New Year's resolutions are to apply to colleges, get a part in the school play, and save money to buy the latest CD of her favorite band. Like most people, Beth has a long list of things she plans to do.

Kinds of Goals

You've probably been asked many times about your goals by parents, relatives, teachers, and guidance counselors. A **goal** is something that you work toward and hope to achieve. If you haven't been asked about your goals yet, just wait until you interview for a job or fill out a college application! Questions about goals usually come up at interviews and on applications. Knowing what your goals are will help you answer these questions.

Goals are directions for helping you achieve your dreams.

Goals are directions for your life. Setting goals can help you stay focused so that you can reach your goals. If you set your goals for the future, you will have a map of where to go. Instead of driving aimlessly around, you know where you are going and what you have to do to get there. There are two types of goals: short-term goals and long-term goals.

Short-Term Goals Goals that can be achieved quickly—in days and weeks—are called short-term goals. What is Beth's short-term goal? She wants to save money to buy a CD. Other examples of short-term goals that you might have are doing well on an exam or getting up the nerve to ask someone on a date.

Long-Term Goals Some goals may take months or years to achieve. Those goals are called long-term goals. If you know what you want to be "when you grow up," you have a long-term goal. For example, you may have goals of being a mechanic, traveling around the world, or getting into college.

Achieving long-term goals takes a lot of hard work and determination. You cannot reach them overnight. In fact, some long-term goals consist of a series of smaller, short-term goals. Setting short-term goals makes achieving the ultimate long-term goal easier.

For example, Beth's long-term goal is to be an actress. Because she knows there are many steps to reach this goal, she broke the goal into smaller goals. This year, she will apply to several colleges to study acting. Also, she will try out for the school play.

Six Suggestions for Setting Goals

Long-term goals, such as becoming an actress, may seem too hard to accomplish. Don't be discouraged. Remember what we said about goal setting being like making a map? You are much more likely to reach your goal if you map out how to get there. Below are six suggestions for setting goals. To help you remember them, think of them as the six S's.

1. **Safe** The first thing to ask yourself is if this goal can harm you. For example, let's say that you are overweight and your goal is to lose weight. Losing weight to get in shape and become healthier is a good thing, right? The question is *how* do you plan to lose weight? If your goal is to starve yourself until you feel sick and weak, your goal is not safe. A safe goal would be to stop eating junk food and start exercising regularly. Do you see the difference?

2. **Satisfying** Goals should be satisfying. You should feel good about yourself when you reach your goals. You might think, Why wouldn't I feel good about reaching any goal that I have set? Let's say your goal was to do well on an exam. You did well on the exam, but you cheated. You have no satisfaction because you didn't reach your goal using your own effort. But if you had earned the grade by studying, you would have felt fantastic!

3. **Sensible** It's also important that your goals, especially your short-term goals, be sensible, or realistic. For example, setting a goal to become fluent in a second language in a one-month period is not realistic. This is a good long-term goal, but not a good short-term goal. However, like Beth, you can break your long-term goals into short-term goals. For example, each day make a short-term goal to learn five new words in the second language.

   Another part of making a sensible goal is to make sure it is a goal that you can achieve. Don't set a goal that would be impossible for you to achieve. For example, let's say you have soccer practice and band practice and you are also on the yearbook committee. It probably wouldn't be a sensible goal for you to run for student council on top of all of your other responsibilities.

4. **Similar** The goal you set for yourself should be similar to goals you have set in the past. This means that your new goals should not contradict your earlier ones. Let's go back to the goal of losing weight. But now you have another goal. You want to learn how to bake fancy desserts. Something should tell you that these goals might not work well together. When you have a goal to kick a bad habit, don't create another goal that will make reaching the first goal difficult.

Beth got the part! When setting a goal, remember the six S's: safe, satisfying, sensible, similar, specific, and supported.

Building Character

SELF-DISCIPLINE

Self-Discipline is the ability to set a realistic goal or to make a plan and then stay focused on that goal or plan. If you have self-discipline, you can follow through on your commitments and resist doing things that might get in the way of your goal. Having self-discipline means tht you have the willpower necessary to make good decisions.

Think about a goal that you have achieved in the past year. In what ways did you show self-discipline in reaching your goal? Did you have difficulty maintaining self-discipline while trying to reach your goal? Explain your answer.

internet connect

www.scilinks.org/health
Topic: Setting Goals
HealthLinks code: HH4121

HEALTH
LINKS® Maintained by the
National Science
Teachers Association

Staying focused on all of the benefits of achieving your goal will be your strongest motivation to reach your goal.

5. **Specific** Good goals are specific. That is, the steps to achieve those goals are very clear. When people say they want to "be happy," their goal is not specific. Being happy is a good thing to want to be, but is it a good goal? How do you achieve happiness? Do you plan to be happy by the time you're 85 or by this weekend? The goal of being happy is too vague.

A more specific way to approach the goal of happiness is to identify what makes you happy. Then you can spend more time doing it. For example, let's say that you are happiest when you are listening to music. Your goal could be to work in a music store. Then you could listen to music at work and get discounts on CDs!

6. **Supported** The last thing to ask yourself when setting a goal is whether your parents or other responsible adults would support this goal. Most of the time, your goals are positive and would be supported by others. However, some goals might not be supported. For example, let's say you set a goal to be more successful on your athletic team by using steroids. Most parents would not agree with the way you chose to achieve this goal.

Having your family's support will help you reach your goal. Share with your family how you plan to reach the goal. They may have suggestions that can help. They also might find problems that you didn't notice.

Make an Action Plan

Now that you know six suggestions for setting goals, you can use these suggestions to check your goal. The next step is to create an action plan. An **action plan** is a set of directions that will help you reach your goal. An action plan describes the step-by-step process you will take as you work towards your goal. An action plan also states the date you plan to meet the goal. You may want to record your action plan in a notebook.

Rewards   Your action plan should contain suggestions that will make reaching your goal easier. One idea that helps is to make a list of rewards you will reap for reaching your goal. This list will remind you why you are working so hard. For example, let's return to Beth's long-term goal of becoming an actress. What would some of Beth's rewards be? She is doing what she enjoys. She feels good about her accomplishment. Her talent is admired and respected by other people and by other actors and actresses. If she becomes a really successful actress, she might even become rich and famous!

> "If we did all the things we are capable of, we would literally astound ourselves."
>
> — *Thomas Edison*

real life Activity

REACHING YOUR GOALS

LIFE SKILL
Setting Goals

Materials

✔ pencil
✔ notebook

Procedure

1. **Choose** a *short*-term health goal for yourself. Record it in your notebook.

2. **Write** how your goal satisfies each of the six suggestions for setting goals. **WRITING SKILL**

3. **Create** a step-by-step action plan in your notebook. Record each action you will need to take. Don't forget to record a goal date!

4. **State** why you want to reach this goal.

5. **Write** the positive and negative influences related to reaching your goal. **WRITING SKILL**

6. **Track** your progress daily. Write down each accomplishment and each setback.

Conclusions

1. **Analyzing Methods** How can you take advantage of the positive influences that you listed?

2. **Analyzing Methods** What can you do to control or minimize the negative influences that you listed?

3. **Predicting Outcomes** List the benefits and rewards you will gain by achieving this goal.

4. **CRITICAL THINKING** Do you think this goal is realistic? Why or why not?

Achieving long-term goals requires work and determination. Making an action plan will help you reach your goals.

Influences   It is important to know what influences can hurt you and what influences can help you when working on your goal. For example, the six risk behaviors that are common among teens are drug and alcohol use, sexual activity, behaviors that cause injury, poor dietary patterns, tobacco use, and sedentary lifestyle. In Beth's case, these behaviors not only would harm Beth's physical health but also could keep her from reaching her goal. What would happen if Beth used drugs? What would happen if she became pregnant before graduating from high school? How would her plans change?

On the other hand, Beth notes the positive influences related to meeting her goal. Your family can be a significant positive influence on your goals. For example, her parents are a big help when she practices her lines. They also drive her to rehearsals and support her in the audience on opening night.

Tracking Your Progress   Another important part of the action plan is to track your progress. Every week, Beth writes down what she has accomplished and what has set her back on her road to becoming an actress. This record encourages her when she sees progress. Beth remembers how satisfying it was to write in her notebook the day she got a part in the school play.

Writing down how rehearsals have gone also helps Beth see certain problems. For example, Beth has noticed that forgetting her lines during rehearsal distracts her. Beth has solved this problem by spending a few minutes reviewing her lines on the way to school each day!

Beth also uses her notebook to see which steps she needs to prepare for next. Because Beth's goal is a long-term goal, she broke it down into smaller, short-term goals. Her next short-term goal is to apply to colleges. She looks forward to the day when she can write down that her favorite college accepted her!

SECTION 4

REVIEW   *Answer the following questions on a separate piece of paper.*

Using Key Terms

1. **Identify** the term for "something that you work toward and hope to achieve."

2. **Define** *action plan.*

Understanding Key Ideas

3. **Compare** short-term goals and long-term goals.

4. **Summarize** the six suggestions for setting goals.

5. **Name** the suggestion for setting goals that recommends that you avoid a goal that hurts your health.

6. **Identify** the suggestion for setting goals that recommends that you choose a goal that is realistic.
   a. sensible
   b. smart
   c. safe
   d. simple

7. **List** three things you should do when making an action plan.

8. **State** the six risk factors that can keep you from reaching any goal.

Critical Thinking

9. **LIFE SKILL** **Setting Goals** Create an action plan to achieve one of your personal goals.

CHAPTER 2

Highlights

Key Terms

The Big Picture

SECTION 1

life skill (26)
coping (27)
consumer (27)
media (28)
resource (28)

✔ Practicing life skills will help you improve your wellness throughout your life. The ten life skills are Assessing Your Health, Communicating Effectively, Practicing Wellness, Coping, Being a Wise Consumer, Evaluating Media Messages, Using Community Resources, Making GREAT Decisions, Practicing Refusal Skills, and Setting Goals.

✔ You can use life skills when you buy health products, make decisions, deal with loss, build relationships, and improve many aspects of your health.

SECTION 2

consequence (29)
collaborate (31)

✔ The decisions you make affect not only your health but also other people.

✔ The five steps of the Making GREAT Decisions model are as follows: (1) **G**ive thought to the problem. (2) **R**eview your choices. (3) **E**valuate the consequences of each option. (4) **A**ssess and choose the best choice. (5) **T**hink it over afterward.

✔ Learning to collaborate with others will help you make better decisions.

✔ If you make a wrong decision, STOP and take responsibility for it. THINK about talking to a trusted adult to help you correct the situation. GO and do your best to correct the problem.

SECTION 3

peer pressure (33)
direct pressure (34)
indirect pressure (34)
refusal skill (35)

✔ You can be positively or negatively influenced by friends, family, or the media

✔ Different types of direct pressures include teasing, persuasion, explanations, put-downs, threats, and bribery.

✔ Different sources of indirect pressures include TV, radio, advertising, role models, popular people, and famous people.

✔ A refusal skill is a strategy to avoid doing something you don't want to do.

✔ Practicing refusal skills can help you say no to peer pressure with confidence and respect.

SECTION 4

goal (38)
action plan (41)

✔ Short-term goals can be achieved in days or weeks. Long-term goals may take months or years to achieve.

✔ The six S's for setting goals are safe, satisfying, sensible, similar, specific, and supported.

✔ An action plan is a set of directions that can help you reach your goal.

Review

Using Key Terms

action plan (41)

collaborate (31)

consequence (29)

consumer (27)

coping (27)

direct pressure (34)

goal (38)

indirect pressure (34)

life skill (26)

media (28)

peer pressure (33)

refusal skills (35)

resource (28)

1. For each definition below, choose the key term that best matches the definition.
   a. all public forms of communication, such as TV, radio, newspaper, the Internet, and advertisements
   b. something that you can use to help achieve a goal
   c. to work together with one or more people
   d. a strategy to avoid doing something you don't want to do
   e. a person who buys products or services
   f. a feeling that you should do something because your friends want you to
   g. dealing with problems and troubles in an effective way
   h. a result of your actions and decisions
   i. a tool for building a healthy life

2. Explain the relationship between the key terms in each of the following pairs.
   a. *direct pressure* and *indirect pressure*
   b. *goal* and *action plan*

Understanding Key Ideas

Section 1

3. Choose a life skill, and describe how you could use it effectively for long-term wellness.

4. Identify the life skill you would use to evaluate how your actions affect your health.

5. Identify the life skill you would use to help you say no to peer pressure.
   a. practicing wellness
   b. setting goals
   c. using refusal skills
   d. coping

6. **CRITICAL THINKING** Explain how you could use the Communicating Effectively life skill.

Section 2

7. Why is it important to evaluate the consequences of each option before you make a decision?

8. Identify the step in the Making GREAT Decisions model in which you determine whether you made the right decision.

9. Which of the following is *not* a step to take if you have made a wrong decision?
   a. think
   b. forget
   c. stop
   d. go

10. **CRITICAL THINKING** Write a paragraph about a decision that you made that affected other people. **WRITING SKILL**

11. **CRITICAL THINKING** Name a situation in which you would use collaborative decision-making skills? **LIFE SKILL**

Section 3

12. Describe how each of the following influences affects your behavior.
    a. friends
    b. family
    c. the Internet
    d. TV

13. Which three kinds of direct pressure do you experience most often? **LIFE SKILL**

14. Which three kinds of indirect pressure do you experience most often? **LIFE SKILL**

15. Describe a refusal skill you have used before.

16. Identify the refusal skill that requires support from others.

Section 4

17. What is the difference between a short-term goal and a long-term goal?

18. State an example of a short-term goal that you would like to reach this week. **LIFE SKILL**

19. Which of the following suggestions for setting goals recommends you choose a goal that will make you feel good about yourself?
    a. similar
    b. specific
    c. satisfying
    d. safe

20. State how each of the six risk behaviors could affect one of your goals. **LIFE SKILL**

Interpreting Graphics

Study the table below to answer the questions that follow.

Refusal Skills	
Pressure	**Response**
1. "Everyone else is doing it."	1. "Do you have to do what everyone else does?"
2. "Don't you want to know what it's like?"	2. "Okay, just this once."
3. "Please, do it for me."	3. _____

21. Which response above is a good example of a refusal skill?

22. **CRITICAL THINKING** Change the bad example of a refusal skill into a good example of a refusal skill.

23. **CRITICAL THINKING** Use a refusal skill to fill in a response for item 3.

Activities

24. **Health and You** Draw a map for a long-term goal you have set for yourself. Draw and label a road to show the path you will take. Use symbols such as rivers for challenges you expect to face. Draw and label bridges to symbolize ways to overcome these challenges. Draw a triumphant image to show the accomplishment of your goal.

25. **Health and Your Family** Write about a time when your family made a group decision on something you were going to do, such as where to go for dinner or how to spend a vacation. **WRITING SKILL**

26. **Health and You** Write about a real or imaginary situation in which you used or could use three or more of the life skills discussed in this chapter to improve your life. **WRITING SKILL**

Action Plan

27. **LIFE SKILL** **Setting Goals** Write an action plan for a *long*-term goal of yours. Apply the six suggestions for setting goals. Break up the goal into short-term goals. Set a date to accomplish the long-term goal. Determine the positive and negative influences that may affect your goal.

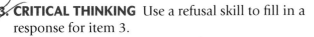

Standardized Test Prep

Read the passage below, and then answer the questions that follow. **READING SKILL** **WRITING SKILL**

As Marty pulled away from the curb, he thought about Sina's answer. He didn't understand it. Her response was <u>ambiguous</u>. Marty thought that maybe she wouldn't skip school with him and his friends because she was afraid to get caught. As Marty reached for a beer, he thought it was silly to fear getting caught. He skips school all the time. Suddenly, Marty heard sirens. He looked up in his rearview mirror and saw a police car behind him.

28. In this passage, the word *ambiguous* means
   A negative.
   B not clear.
   C complicated.
   D hopeful.

29. What can you infer from reading this passage?
   E Sina skipped school with Marty.
   F Marty was pulled over by the police.
   G Marty had a great day with his friends.
   H all of the above

30. Write a paragraph describing all of the reasons why Sina shouldn't skip school with Marty.

Self-Diagnosis and the Internet

More and more people are using the Internet to diagnose their medical conditions. This Internet research has some benefits but has a lot of serious drawbacks, too.

Self-diagnosis is our personal evaluation of our own health issues. We usually use self-diagnosis, for example, when we are coming down with a cold, when we have the flu, or when we have a rash from poison ivy. In the past, if a condition were more complex or more dangerous, people went to a doctor for a professional diagnosis. Most people still do, but today many people are turning to the Internet to find the answers to their medical questions.

Web Sites Often Have Inaccurate Information

One health issue that many people go to the Internet to understand is skin cancer. Doctors at the University of Michigan wanted to find out if Internet sites that provide information on skin cancer were accurate. What they found was quite alarming. Their study revealed that most sites contained incomplete information and that one in eight contained wrong information. It is important to remember that many Web sites lack accurate information about prevention, diagnosis, and treatment.

Some Sites Are Not What They Claim To Be

Unfortunately, some sites contain areas of self-diagnosis simply to sell you a worthless product. Many unscrupulous Internet merchants are simply seeking to make a lot of money in a hurry. If someone sells you a bracelet to cure a rash, it does more harm than only costing you money. If you buy the bracelet, you may be using a useless trinket to ignore a serious condition. Such bogus sites often spring up on the Internet and then disappear just as quickly. Other sites mean well but offer cures that have not been fully tested. The people behind these sites may have your best interest at heart, but their sites may not have the objectivity of a carefully trained doctor.

How Can the Internet Help?

The Internet has many sites that offer self-diagnosis charts, tests, and evaluations. For example, if you have a skin problem, you can go to a site, answer a few questions, and arrive at a medical conclusion. In many cases, such Internet sites can help you understand your problem. By comparing your symptoms with those listed on a site, you may figure out what is wrong.

As good as Web self-diagnosis may be, it is also filled with dangers. Self-diagnosis on the Web

▶ is not a substitute for a doctor's professional evaluation

▶ may be based on information that is inaccurate or false

▶ is often conducted on sites that want to sell you something or that contain highly questionable health practices

Your Doctor Knows

A doctor has been trained to look carefully for all of the evidence of a disease or disorder. In addition, your doctor is less likely to make a mistake than you are while you are sitting and worrying in front of a computer. For example, suppose that moving the left side of your face became difficult and you couldn't blink your left eye. If you looked up the symptoms on a computer, you might think you had Bell's Palsy, an annoying disruption of your facial nerves. According to the Internet, your problem will go away on its own. Your doctor, however, may ask you if you had a recent rash, had joint pain, or had been hiking. Your doctor knows that nerve problems in the face can be a symptom of something else. He or she will evaluate all of your symptoms and might diagnose Lyme disease and take appropriate steps. Your self-diagnosis would have prevented you from getting the antibiotics needed to combat Lyme disease.

Wise Use of the Web

The Internet can help you see the seriousness of a symptom or can provide additional information. For example, if you have already seen a doctor, you can

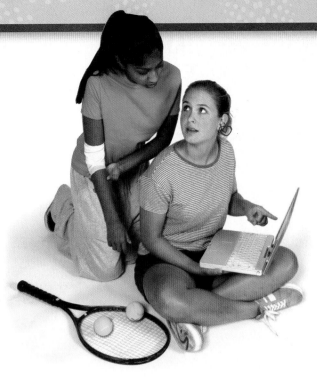

read more about your diagnosis and can educate yourself. In addition, you can use the Internet to gather information in private. But the Internet is only one tool to support your health. Use it wisely in addition to consulting health professionals.

YOUR TURN

1. **Summarizing Information** What are three dangers of using Internet sites for self-diagnosis of health issues?

2. **Applying Information** How has Internet technology changed self-diagnosis from the way people diagnosed themselves in the past?

3. **CRITICAL THINKING** How can you determine if a Web site contains medically accepted information?

internet connect

www.scilinks.org/health
Topic: Internet
HealthLinks code: HH4047

HEALTH LINKS® Maintained by the National Science Teachers Association

CHAPTER 3

Self-Esteem and Mental Health

What's Your Health IQ?
BEHAVIOR

Indicate how frequently you engage in each of the following behaviors (1 = never; 2 = occasionally; 3 = most of the time; 4 = all of the time). Total your points, and then turn to p. 638.

1. I praise myself when I do a good job.

2. I do what I know is right, even if others use pressure to try to stop me from doing the right thing.

3. I am confident enough to try new things, even if I might fail at them.

4. I ask people for help if I need it.

5. I like to volunteer to help others when I can.

6. I concentrate on my strengths and work to improve my weaknesses.

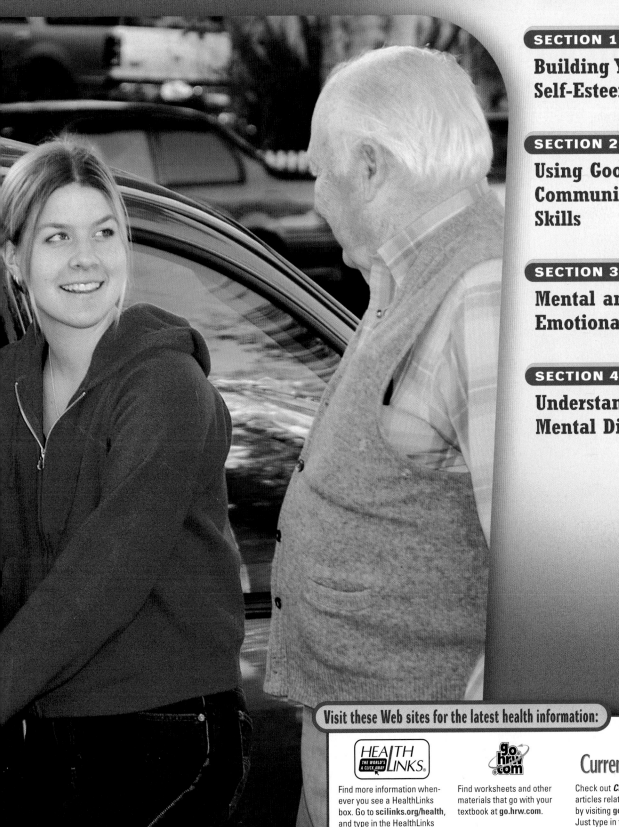

Visit these Web sites for the latest health information:

HEALTH LINKS®
THE WORLD'S A CLICK AWAY

Find more information whenever you see a HealthLinks box. Go to **scilinks.org/health**, and type in the HealthLinks code.

go.hrw.com

Find worksheets and other materials that go with your textbook at **go.hrw.com**.

Current Health®

Check out *Current Health®* articles related to this chapter by visiting **go.hrw.com**. Just type in the keyword **HH4 CH03**.

SECTION 1

Building Your Self-Esteem

OBJECTIVES

Define self-esteem.

List the benefits of high self-esteem.

Identify factors that influence the development of self-esteem.

Describe ways you can improve your self-esteem. **LIFE SKILL**

KEY TERMS

self-esteem a measure of how much you value, respect, and feel confident about yourself

self-concept a measure of how you view yourself

integrity the characteristic of doing what you know is right

One characteristic of high self-esteem is not being afraid to try new things.

Leyla started taking ballet 3 months ago. She doesn't dance as well as the rest of the class. The other dancers have been practicing ballet much longer than Leyla has. However, Leyla loves every minute of rehearsal. She can't wait to perform on stage.

What Is Self-Esteem?

Self-esteem is a measure of how much you value, respect, and feel confident about yourself. How you feel about yourself affects everything you do. It affects how you communicate with people and what decisions you make about your health. For example, if you feel good about yourself, you can more easily talk with people and share your feelings. However, if you don't feel good about yourself, you might not have the confidence to use your refusal skills or to avoid disrespectful people.

Benefits of High Self-Esteem   Below is a list of the benefits people who have high self-esteem experience.

▶ **Increased respect** People with high self-esteem respect themselves by taking care of themselves. They will not do anything to harm themselves, such as smoking or abusing drugs and alcohol. They don't criticize or put themselves down. Furthermore, they exercise, eat right, and get plenty of rest.

People with high self-esteem respect their values and beliefs. They are less likely to let others pressure them to take part in risky behavior. Nor will they pressure others to take part in harmful behavior.

▶ **Increased ability to reach goals** If you have confidence in yourself, you are more likely to set realistic goals and stick with the goals you set for yourself until you reach those goals. The longer you stick with a goal and the harder you try, the better the chance you have at reaching it. Because people with high self-esteem are more likely to reach their goals, they are more likely to challenge themselves to set higher goals and accomplish more.

▶ **Increased willingness to try** People with high self-esteem have the will to try new things and don't get discouraged easily. For example, Leyla had the courage to try something new—ballet dancing. More important, when she found out she wasn't as good as the others, she didn't give up. Instead, she kept trying her best. She did it for herself, not for competition.

▶ **Increased feelings of value** People with high self-esteem feel like they are a valuable part of their family, school, and community. They are more likely to ask for help when they need it. They are also more likely to volunteer in their communities because they know they have the power to help others.

Risks of Low Self-Esteem People with low self-esteem share many characteristics as listed in **Figure 1.** For example, people with low self-esteem are more vulnerable to peer pressure. As a result, they are more likely to make unhealthy decisions, such as smoking.

People with low self-esteem may not be respectful to themselves or others. Those who do not feel good about themselves will often put themselves down. They are also more critical of others.

Low self-esteem is also harmful to one's mental health. People with low self-esteem are at risk for depression and suicide. Low self-esteem is also linked to eating disorders, running away, and violence.

People with low self-esteem do not have to experience the risks of low self-esteem. Everyone has the power to choose healthy behaviors that show respect for others and themselves.

Figure 1

You can't tell if someone has high self-esteem or low self-esteem just by looking at him or her.

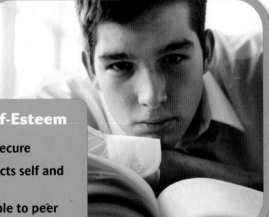

High Self-Esteem

▶ **Speaks up for self**
▶ **Respects self and others**
▶ **Has confidence**
▶ **Tries new things**
▶ **Feels valuable to society**
▶ **Adjusts to change**
▶ **Feels optimistic**
▶ **Makes decisions based on values**

Low Self-Esteem

▶ **Feels insecure**
▶ **Disrespects self and others**
▶ **Vulnerable to peer pressure**
▶ **Doesn't feel valuable**
▶ **Feels depressed**
▶ **Fears failure**
▶ **Uses drugs and alcohol**
▶ **Feels pessimistic**
▶ **Behaves destructively**

Ten Tips for Building Self-Esteem

▶ Volunteer at a soup kitchen or other community service.

▶ Make a list of your strengths.

▶ Speak positively about yourself and others.

▶ Take care of your physical health.

▶ Reward yourself when you do well.

▶ Try something new.

▶ Choose friends who support you and your positive choices.

▶ Set a goal to improve a weakness.

▶ Cheer yourself through hard times.

▶ Have fun.

The Development of Self-Esteem

Self-esteem begins to develop the day you are born. Across your entire life, your level of self-esteem can vary. At one time, it may be high, and at a different time or in a different situation, it may be low.

Self-Concept   A measure of how one views oneself is **self-concept.** For example, if you think of yourself as a valuable and likeable person, you have a positive self-concept. If you have a positive self-concept, you have high self-esteem. However, if you don't think of yourself as very likeable or valuable, you probably have a negative self-concept and therefore, have low self-esteem.

Interpreting Messages From Others   How you interpret messages about yourself has a lot to do with how you view yourself. These messages come from family, friends, teachers, neighbors, and even strangers. The messages can be positive, such as "You are fun to be around." Messages can also be negative, such as "You always complain about everything." These messages shape what you think about yourself. How you think about yourself shapes your self-esteem.

Some negative messages can serve as good advice. Good advice on how to improve yourself is called *constructive criticism*. For example, if you have not been getting along well with your parents, your brother might recommend that you try being more cooperative with your parents.

Other negative messages can be hurtful. But your self-esteem doesn't have to suffer. Remember that self-esteem is how you feel about yourself, not how others feel about you or what others say about you. Only you have the power to control your self-esteem.

Improving Your Self-Esteem

Everyone can work at improving his or her self-esteem. You can improve your self-esteem by using positive self-talk, acting with integrity, choosing supportive friends, and accepting yourself.

Use Positive Self-Talk   You learned that the messages you receive from others influence your self-esteem. The same is true for the messages *you* send to yourself. The things you say to yourself strongly influence your self-esteem.

We are constantly talking to ourselves, whether we realize it or not. You may say or think things like, "My painting really looks neat!" or "I'm too stupid for this class." The things you say about yourself can make you feel good, or they can make you feel not so good.

To practice treating yourself well, you can use a technique called *self-talk*. Self-talk is a way of coaching yourself about your own self-worth. Go ahead and talk to yourself. Tell yourself you can do what you set out to do when you set realistic goals and ask for help. Tell yourself that you are a valuable person.

internet connect

www.scilinks.org/health
Topic: Building a Healthy
Self-Esteem
HealthLinks code: HH4024

HEALTH LINKS.   Maintained by the National Science Teachers Association

---

real life Activity

SELL YOURSELF

LIFE SKILL
Practicing Wellness

Materials

- ✔ poster board
- ✔ magazines
- ✔ markers
- ✔ scissors
- ✔ paste

Procedure

1. **Think** about why you are a wonderful person.

2. **List** five reasons why you are wonderful on your poster board.

3. **Think** of different techniques advertisers use to sell their products. Use these techniques in your own advertisement to express why you are fabulous.

4. **Cut** out magazine clippings to help express the five reasons you are great.

Conclusions

1. **Summarizing Results** What are the five reasons you are great?

2. **Evaluating Information** What technique or style did you use to make yourself stand out?

3. **Analyzing Methods** Describe why this activity may have been hard for you or easy for you.

4. **CRITICAL THINKING** List at least five additional reasons that you are special.

Act with Integrity The characteristic of doing what one knows is right is **integrity.** For example, your integrity prompts you to be honest and return the extra $10 the cashier mistakenly gave you, even if your friends want you to spend it on a movie with them.

When you have integrity, you respect others, yourself, and your values. You don't let people pressure you to go against what is right and important to you. People who have low self-esteem may be unsure of themselves and can be swayed to do something they don't feel right about. On the other hand, people who have high self-esteem recognize when they need to stand up for their beliefs to continue to respect themselves.

Choose Supportive Friends It is easier for you to treat yourself well if the people you know also speak well of you. Avoid critical or disrespectful people. Maintain friendships with people who acknowledge your strengths and support you in your goals and values.

Accept Yourself People who have high self-esteem do not think they are perfect. They know they are not perfect. People who have high self-esteem accept who they are. They see all their imperfections and still think of themselves as valuable.

People who accept themselves celebrate their strengths and concentrate on what they do well. They also strive to improve weaknesses by setting short-term goals. However, if they can't change a weakness, they let it go. For example, if you're not as tall as you would like to be, wishing and hoping won't make you taller. However, dwelling on your height may lower your self-esteem.

Once you accept yourself, you'll find that others will accept you, too. If you project a confident attitude, others will sense—and respect you for—your confidence. You will then feel better about yourself!

> **Until you accept who you are, you will never be happy with what you have.**

SECTION 1

REVIEW
Answer the following questions on a separate piece of paper.

Using Key Terms

1. **Define** the term *self-esteem*.

2. **Identify** the term for "the characteristic of doing what one knows is right."

Understanding Key Ideas

3. **State** the positive benefits of high self-esteem.

4. **Identify** which of the following is *not* a characteristic of high self-esteem.
   a. feels valuable   **c.** confidence
   b. pessimistic   **d.** self-respect

5. **Summarize** the effects of low self-esteem.

6. **Identify** factors that influence the development of self-esteem.

7. **Identify** which of the following is *not* a way to improve your self-esteem.
   a. using positive self-talk **c.** acting with integrity
   b. accepting yourself   **d.** denying your faults

Critical Thinking

8. **Describe** how respecting yourself and respecting your values can improve your self-esteem.

9. **LIFE SKILL** **Practicing Wellness** Describe three ways you can improve your self-esteem.

SECTION 2

Using Good Communication Skills

OBJECTIVES

Summarize why good communication is important.

Differentiate between passive, assertive, and aggressive communication styles.

Name five characteristics of good listening skills.

List three examples of body language.

List five ways to improve your speaking skills. **LIFE SKILL**

Rina was planning to have some friends over for her birthday. But her friends have been acting strange. They whisper when they think she isn't looking. They pretend not to see her when she walks down the hall. No one will even return her phone calls.

Good Communication Is Important

Communication is a process through which two or more people exchange information. One person sends the message, and one or more people receive it. However, if the message is not properly sent or is unclear, misunderstandings can arise.

Miscommunication can result in hurt feelings.

Preventing Misunderstandings Rina's situation shows how easy it is to miscommunicate. Rina was receiving messages that made her feel unwanted. What she found out later was almost the opposite. Rina's friends were being secretive because they were planning a surprise for her birthday. Fortunately, her situation had a positive outcome; she was pleasantly surprised. However, miscommunication can have some negative effects such as arguments and hurt feelings.

Building Healthy Relationships Communication is important for building caring and satisfying relationships with your family, friends, co-workers, and society. How you communicate with others affects how people relate to you. For example, if you are mean or insult others, they probably won't want to be around you. However, if you let people know how important they are to you, they will be more likely to treat you the way you want to be treated.

Expressing Yourself Good communication skills are also important for letting others know what you need and want. These skills also help you to express how you feel. Just think how difficult life would be if you couldn't tell someone that you needed help.

Communication Styles

There are three communication styles: passive, aggressive, and assertive. The following descriptions compare these three communication styles.

Passive   A person who has a communication style that is **passive** does not offer opposition when challenged or pressured. Such a person tends to go along with what other people want and does not protest or resist when challenged. For example, let's say your brother borrowed your shirt and tore it. If you had a passive response, you would give your brother the silent treatment and then just throw your shirt away.

Aggressive   To be hostile and unfriendly in the way one expresses oneself is to be **aggressive.** For example, an aggressive response in the same situation with your brother would be to tell him, "You are such a jerk! Let's see how you feel when I ruin your things!" Aggressive communication is not effective and usually leads to a bigger conflict.

Assertive   The third and most healthy communication style is the assertive style. To be **assertive** is to express oneself in a direct, respectful way. For example, you could say to your brother, "My favorite shirt is ruined. I spent a lot of money on this shirt. I would like you to replace it." With this response, you calmly expressed to your brother how his action affected you. This response was also respectful to your brother, which is an important part of being assertive.

Using the assertive communication style might not be easy when someone has done something that really upsets you. However, practicing can help you improve. **Table 1** lists more examples of passive, aggressive, and assertive communication responses. See if you can think of some examples of your own.

Use assertive communication if someone is disrespectful to you, such as cutting in front of you in line.

Table 1 Communication Styles

Situation	Passive response	Aggressive response	Assertive response
Someone cuts in front of you in line.	You don't say anything.	"Well, you must think you're special!"	"Excuse me, but I believe I'm next in line."
Your best friend tells someone else one of your secrets.	You don't say anything, but you vow never to tell her another secret.	"I hate you! I'm never going to trust you again!"	"It hurt me to find out you told my secret to someone else. Please don't repeat my secrets again."
Your boss asks you to work late for the third night in a row.	You agree but feel worried about finishing your homework tonight.	"You are so inconsiderate! I quit!"	"Sorry, I can't work tonight. I have a lot of homework to do."

Speaking Skills

Think about the way you communicate. Are there any areas that you would like to improve? Have you ever been at a loss for words? Have you ever been frustrated because you can't get someone to understand you? Everyone has felt that way before. There are many skills you can learn to help you communicate better.

One of the main ways we communicate is verbally. *Verbal* communication refers to the specific words and tones that we use when we speak. Because most of us can speak, we frequently use speech to communicate.

You may ask yourself, what could I possibly need to learn about talking, something I've been doing almost my whole life? It is true that you have a lot of practice with this type of communication. However, learning effective speaking skills can be helpful when you need to give a speech in class. Effective speaking skills also can give you the confidence to discuss sensitive issues with your parents, such as sexual activity or marriage.

Voice Volume   How loud or soft you are speaking is called *voice volume*. If someone increases how loud he or she says something, what does that increase in voice volume generally mean? You don't even have to know what the person is saying to know that he or she may be mad. What does it mean if someone lowers the volume of communication to a whisper? That person may be either trying to tell you a secret or trying not to get caught talking to you in class! Be aware of the voice volume you use when speaking with others.

Tone and Pitch   Tone of voice and pitch refer to the *inflections* or emphasis in your voice when you speak. Tone and pitch convey the attitude you are trying to express.

For example, if your older sister says, "What are you doing?" the tone and pitch of her voice tell you that she is asking you a question. But if she says, "WHAT are you doing!" you know she is angry. If she says, "What ARE you doing?" she sounds arrogant. She could also say, "What are you DOING?" and sound very upset. See if you can say, "What are you doing?" and sound questioning, angry, arrogant, and upset. Can you think of any other tones and pitches that you could use with the same phrase?

"I" Messages and "You" Messages   A good technique for communicating assertively is to use "I" messages. An "I" message is a way of talking that explains how you feel while remaining firm, calm, and polite. Sometimes, when people are mad or upset, they say things that seem like they are blaming another person. This type of statement is called a "you" message. "You" messages sound like the following: "You did this" or "You are so selfish." It is very easy to get in a fight when "you" messages are being sent. An "I" message, on the other hand, is a tool that allows you to express your feelings without blaming another person.

WHAT are you doing?

What **ARE** you doing?

What are you **DOING?**

When using "I" messages, say how you feel and why you feel that way. For example, suppose you put your bag on the front seat of the bus to save it while you run to get something. When you come back, someone has moved your bag and taken your seat. To use an "I" message, you could say, "I'm upset that you moved my bag and took my seat. I want to sit there because my stop is the first stop."

Let's say your sister is playing music so loud that you can't study for your history test. You could use "I" messages to tell her, "I can't study for my test because the music is so loud. Please turn it down."

Empathy The ability to understand another person's feelings, behaviors, and attitudes is called **empathy.** Showing empathy can be an effective way to communicate. For example, let's say you ask your neighbor if you can borrow his bike. He tells you he needs it for his job delivering newspapers. If you respond by telling him he can deliver newspapers later, that would not show empathy. Your neighbor would probably respond, "Go take a hike." However, if you responded by asking to borrow the bike when he's done, he might be more likely to lend it to you.

LIFE SKILL Activity

Communicating Effectively

Say What?

Practicing "I" messages will help you communicate more effectively. Try role-playing a situation in which "I" messages would be helpful.

1. Decide who will be the "parent" and who will be the "teen."

2. Decide on a situation in which you need to talk to your parent about something that upset you, such as chores or going out with friends.

3. First, use "you" messages to talk to the "parent."

4. Now, try "I" messages to tell the "parent" how you feel.

5. Switch roles with your partner, and repeat steps 4 and 5.

LIFE SKILL **Communicating Effectively**

1. When you were the "parent," describe how you felt when the "teen" was using "you" messages.

2. Now, describe how you felt when the "teen" used "I" messages. Which form of communication do you think would be most effective? Explain your answer.

Listening Skills

Have you ever spent a lot of energy explaining how you felt to someone but found out that the person wasn't paying attention? How did the situation make you feel? What did it do to your self-esteem?

Communication includes not only sending messages but also receiving messages, or listening. It makes people feel good when they know you are listening and that you really care about what they are saying. Two important ways to show you are listening are to use active listening and to paraphrase. **Figure 2** lists more suggestions for being a good listener.

Active Listening *Active listening* means letting the speaker know you are listening and clarifying anything that is confusing. You can do so by asking the speaker questions and by using expressions such as

▶ "I guess you must have felt . . . "
▶ "Tell me about . . . "
▶ "Hmmm."
▶ "Really?"
▶ "Uh-huh."

To practice active listening, give the speaker your full attention. Giving your full attention means you should not think about what you are going to say next. Try to identify the main concepts and ideas that are being communicated. Provide feedback to the speaker, but wait until the speaker is finished before you start talking.

Paraphrasing *Paraphrasing* is using your own words to restate what someone else said. You may have heard teachers use this term when telling you how to write a research paper. When writing a paper, you paraphrase other authors to show the teacher that you understood what you read. In a conversation, you paraphrase to show the other person that you understand what he or she is saying.

Here is an example of paraphrasing. Your friend spends 10 minutes telling you how unhappy he is because his parents are divorced, and you say, "The divorce really is making you unhappy, isn't it?" Paraphrasing allows you to show the person that you care about what he or she is saying. Paraphrasing may seem like restating the obvious, but you would be amazed how sometimes you hear something differently from what the speaker means. Paraphrasing helps you to accurately understand the speaker.

Paraphrasing can also be used if you don't understand what someone is saying. For example, imagine your health teacher is talking about the fat content in food. If you were paraphrasing, you might say, "So, what you are saying is that white-meat chicken has less fat than dark-meat chicken does?" Then, the teacher could either agree or try to explain the topic in a different way.

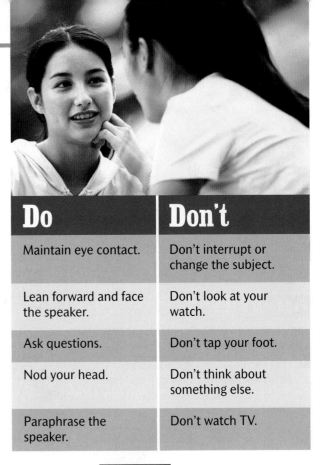

Do	**Don't**
Maintain eye contact.	Don't interrupt or change the subject.
Lean forward and face the speaker.	Don't look at your watch.
Ask questions.	Don't tap your foot.
Nod your head.	Don't think about something else.
Paraphrase the speaker.	Don't watch TV.

Figure 2

Maintaining eye contact is a good way to show that you are listening. Here are some more tips to show that you are listening.

Body Language

Earlier, you learned that one way to communicate is to speak. However, you can communicate without saying a word. You reveal a lot about how you feel through facial expressions, gestures, and posture. This nonverbal communication is called *body language.* Below are some examples of body language. See if you can guess what each one may be communicating.

- ▶ opening your eyes wide
- ▶ scratching your head
- ▶ opening your mouth wide
- ▶ snarling
- ▶ scrunching your eyebrows in a V shape
- ▶ standing up straight and tall
- ▶ winking

Can you think of any other examples of body language? Try some body language of your own. Act excited. Go on—do it. What did you do? You probably smiled, looked alert, and clapped your hands. Now, act bored. You probably slumped your shoulders and drooped your face. If someone was watching you, he or she would have been able to tell how you were feeling even though you didn't say a word. What do you think the people in **Figure 3** are feeling?

Misunderstandings often occur when our body language says one thing but our mouths say another. Think back to the example of Rina and her friends. What made her suspicious of her friends? What type of body language was she receiving from them? Usually, when body language is giving a message that is different from what you are saying, people tend to believe the body language message. Therefore, paying attention to the messages you are sending nonverbally is important. Also, you can learn a lot about what others are feeling by watching their body language.

Figure 3

Body language can tell a lot about how a person is feeling.

ACTIVITY *What are the first three people in line feeling? How can you tell?*

SECTION 2

REVIEW *Answer the following questions on a separate piece of paper.*

Using Key Terms

1. **Identify** the term for "direct and respectful in the way one expresses oneself."

2. **Define** the term *empathy*.

Understanding Key Ideas

3. **Describe** why good communication is important.

4. **Identify** the communication style that is most likely to lead to conflict.

5. **List** five characteristics of good listening skills.

6. **Identify** which of the following behaviors is *not* an example of a good listening skill.
   a. watching TV   **c.** paraphrasing
   b. facing the speaker   **d.** leaning forward

7. **Identify** which of the following behaviors is *not* an example of body language.
   a. winking   **c.** snarling
   b. raising your voice   **d.** clapping hands

Critical Thinking

8. **LIFE SKILL** **Communicating Effectively** List five ways you can improve your speaking skills.

SECTION 3

Mental and Emotional Health

OBJECTIVES

Describe characteristics of positive mental health.

Compare the stages of Maslow's hierarchy of needs.

Describe how you can learn to express emotions in positive ways.

Identify the limitations of defense mechanisms.

Describe three positive strategies for managing your emotions. **LIFE SKILL**

KEY TERMS

mental health the state of mental well-being in which one can cope with the demands of daily life

self-actualization the achievement of the best that a person can be

emotion the feeling that is produced in response to life experiences

defense mechanism an unconscious behavior used to avoid experiencing unpleasant emotions

L ast night, John's girlfriend broke up with him. He lay in bed feeling sad for hours before he fell asleep. The next morning, he still felt sad. He wanted to try to make himself feel better, so he decided to talk to a friend about his sadness.

Mental Health

Mental health is the state of mental well-being in which one can cope with the demands of daily life. Good mental health means having high self-esteem and being able to develop healthy, intimate relationships. Having high self-esteem, handling daily frustrations, and building relationships depend on your ability to express and manage your emotions in positive ways. Therefore, to be mentally healthy, you also must be emotionally healthy.

People who are mentally and emotionally healthy have the following characteristics:

▶ **A sense of control** Mentally healthy people have a sense of control and take charge of their lives. Because they feel in control, they also take responsibility for their behavior. They are less likely to blame others for situations they may face.

▶ **Ability to endure failures and frustrations** Mentally healthy people are more likely to persist through setbacks because they understand that frustrations are part of learning.

▶ **Ability to see events positively** Mentally healthy people are optimistic and see the challenges of life as opportunities.

▶ **Ability to express emotions in a healthy way** Mentally healthy people do not hold in emotions or deny how they feel. They express their emotions in healthy ways and talk with friends when they need support.

For example, when John was feeling sad he decided to talk with a friend. He did not deny his emotions or express them destructively. John has characteristics of someone who has good mental health.

Myth

Crying is a sign of weakness.

Fact

Holding your emotions in can be destructive to your health.

Maslow's Hierarchy of Needs

Having good mental health has benefits. For example, mentally and emotionally healthy people are more likely to reach self-actualization. **Self-actualization** is the achievement of the best that a person can be. People who have achieved self-actualization have reached their potential and feel that they have received the most out of life.

Abraham Maslow, a *psychologist*, a person who studies emotions and behaviors, believed that everyone has a basic drive to reach self-actualization. Maslow stated that to reach self-actualization, a person has to first achieve some very basic needs. He listed these needs and called the list the *hierarchy of needs*, which is shown in **Figure 4.**

According to Maslow, the first needs a person must meet are the basic physical needs of the body, such as the need for food, water, sleep, and exercise. Once these needs are met, the next need is safety. This need includes the needs for shelter and protection from danger. After the need for safety is achieved, the person is free to strive for social needs, such as love, acceptance, and friendship. Once social needs are met, the person can focus on achieving esteem. Esteem is met through self-respect and the achievement of goals. Finally, after all of the other needs are met, the person could reach self-actualization.

Figure 4

Everyone has basic needs he or she strives to meet in order to get the most out of life.

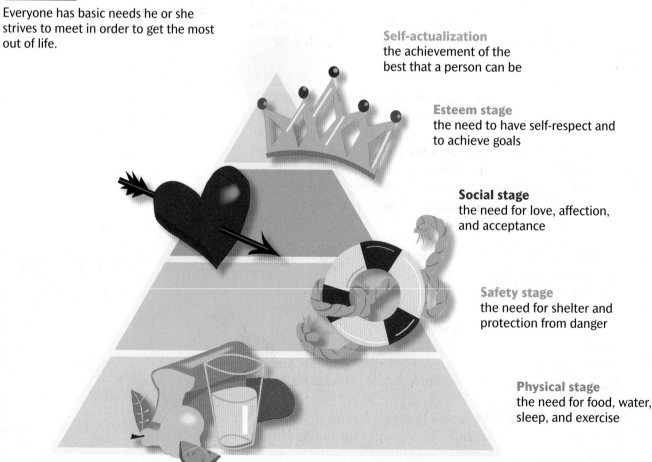

Self-actualization
the achievement of the best that a person can be

Esteem stage
the need to have self-respect and to achieve goals

Social stage
the need for love, affection, and acceptance

Safety stage
the need for shelter and protection from danger

Physical stage
the need for food, water, sleep, and exercise

Most people work on more than one stage at a time. Even people who have reached self-actualization may have to struggle with hardships that threaten their basic needs throughout their lives. Basic needs such as love and safety may not be met all of the time. However, you can still strive for the higher stages. Some ways you can work toward self-actualization in your teen years are by building healthy relationships, setting goals, and working toward achieving those goals.

Expressing Emotions

An **emotion** is the feeling that is produced in response to life experiences. Emotions aren't categorized as good or bad. However, the expression of emotions can have positive or negative effects. For example, pretend you can't study for your test because your family is making a lot of noise. Feeling frustrated is normal. But if you run around the house tearing at your hair and screaming, you probably won't get a positive response from your family.

Whether the emotion is anger, sadness, or joy, expressing it in a positive way is important. Denying an emotion will not make it go away. Instead, the emotion can build up inside of you and be expressed in a negative way. Learning to express and manage emotions in healthy ways is key to mental and emotional health and to self-actualization.

Learning to Express Emotions
How you decide to express your emotions is based in large part on how others around you express their emotions. For example, your family might deal with anger by yelling and throwing things. It is likely you would learn to deal with your anger in the same way.

You can learn to express your emotions more constructively regardless of how others around you express their emotions. To relearn how to express an emotion, practice expressing the emotion in a positive way. For example, role-play with a friend a situation in which you lost your temper with someone. This time, use the speaking skills you learned earlier to calmly tell that person what made you upset. Practicing will help you positively express your emotions naturally.

ZITS reprinted with special permission of King Features Syndicate, Inc.

Managing Emotions

Emotions can be overwhelming, especially during your teenage years. Understanding and recognizing the emotions you feel can be challenging.

It is especially difficult if you are feeling more than one emotion at a time. For example, should you go up and talk to that cute, new student? Or should you run and hide in the bathroom? Trying to deal with so many emotions can be frustrating. The following are suggestions to help you manage your emotions.

1. **Talk it out.** One way you can make sense of what you are feeling is by talking with someone you trust. For example, John made plans to talk with his friend after his girlfriend broke up with him. Just talking about a problem can help you manage your emotions.

2. **Blow off steam.** When emotions become bottled up inside of you, releasing that energy in some positive way often helps. Activities such as exercising, building something, or playing a sport are positive ways to let off steam.

3. **Be creative.** You can also release emotions in creative ways. Some people write or draw when they are troubled. Some people enjoy singing, playing a musical instrument, or painting. All of these activities help release tension.

Some emotions are more difficult to manage than other emotions. These emotions deserve special attention and are discussed in more detail below.

Anger   Often, anger results from frustration or helplessness. For example, the computer crashes and causes you to lose the report that is due next class. You may want to grab the computer and smash it on the floor. That response will definitely not get your report back. In fact, that response may get you into a lot of trouble. Understanding that there was nothing you could do and letting things like this go will release a lot of tension.

Anger can *always* be dealt with in an appropriate manner. A person may make you angry, but that person doesn't make you hit him or her. You and only *you* are responsible for how you express your emotions.

The first step in keeping your anger from getting out of your control is learning to recognize when you feel angry. If you can recognize quickly when you start to become angry, you can more easily control your anger. When you get angry, do you clench your fists? Does your heart beat faster? When you feel the anger coming on, stop. Count to 10, take a deep breath, and calm down before you react. You may want to walk away and think about how best to deal with the situation. You may want to talk with someone or jog a few blocks while you think.

Once you feel in control of your anger, you may want to talk with the person who made you upset. This can help resolve your feelings. Be sure to use the "I" messages you learned earlier.

Yelling at others when you are angry may make you feel better but it may cause more problems later.

Fear Fear may not be a pleasant emotion, but it can be a helpful one. For example, our sense of fear is what helps protect us from danger. You jump out of the way of a speeding car because you fear getting run over.

Speeding cars are good things to fear. However, many people fear things that are not harmful. The fear may even get in the way of your normal life. For example, the fear of speaking in front of class can prevent you from giving a good speech.

To get over a fear, you can use self-talk. Instead of thinking about being scared, tell yourself that you have nothing to be afraid of. Another way to manage your fear is through controlled exposure to the fearful situation. For example, if you are afraid of speaking in front of a large group of people, you can start by speaking in front of one person. You can then work your way up to speaking in front of a large group.

Guilt Guilt is another emotion that may not be pleasant but can serve a purpose. It alerts you that you are behaving in a way that goes against your values. Guilt can keep you true to yourself.

The best way to deal with guilty feelings is to do your best to right the wrong. If someone was hurt, apologize. If you stole something from a store, return it. Making amends lifts the weight of guilt off your shoulders because you are taking responsibility for your behavior. You'll feel much better in the long run.

Jealousy Jealousy is often caused by a fear that something you own or love will be lost. For example, if John's ex-girlfriend starts to date another person, John may feel jealous. A twinge of jealousy now and then is natural. However, if jealousy is not controlled, it can make you bitter and ruin your relationships.

If your girlfriend's or boyfriend's flirting has been bothering you, try talking about it with your boyfriend or girlfriend. However, remember that dating someone doesn't mean you own the person. If you don't trust your partner, you should examine your relationship and why you feel distrustful.

Loneliness Loneliness is an emotion that makes you feel isolated from others—not physically isolated, but emotionally isolated. You can be in a room of people, but if you don't feel close to any of them or feel rejected, you can still feel lonely. On the other hand, you can be by yourself and not feel lonely at all. In fact, being able to enjoy time by yourself is a sign of positive mental health.

A good way to manage loneliness is to join a group or club. You could also do volunteer work or start a job. Don't wait for people to approach you. You'll never be able to make close friends unless you go out and meet people.

Tips for Managing Emotions

▶ Sing, or play a musical instrument.

▶ Write down how you feel.

▶ Talk to a friend.

▶ Exercise, or play a sport.

▶ Let go of what you can't control.

▶ Draw or paint a picture.

Defense Mechanisms

Sometimes, painful emotions such as fear and guilt can be difficult to cope with. Even if you deal with a difficult emotion in a healthy way, you may still feel upset. If an emotion gets too overwhelming, you may use a technique called a *defense mechanism*. A **defense mechanism** is an unconscious thought or behavior used to avoid experiencing unpleasant emotions. **Table 2** shows a list of these defense mechanisms and some examples.

Because defense mechanisms are unconscious behaviors, you don't plan or decide to use them. However, you can observe yourself and become aware of how you react and treat others.

Table 2 Defense Mechanisms		
Mechanism	**What is it?**	**Example**
Compensation	making up for weakness in one area by achieving in another	trying to get an A in your other classes because you are doing poorly in math
Daydreaming	imagining pleasant things that take your mind off the unpleasant reality	daydreaming in detention about what it will be like when you graduate and when teachers can't tell you what to do anymore
Denial	refusing to accept reality	telling everyone that you are still going out with your boyfriend or girlfriend even though he or she broke up with you
Displacement	shifting feelings about one person or situation to another person or situation	yelling at your family when you are angry at your teacher
Idealization	copying someone you think highly of because you don't feel good about who you are	copying the clothing and appearance of a famous musician
Projection	seeing your own faults or feelings in someone else	accusing your boyfriend or girlfriend of flirting with others because you flirt
Rationalization	making excuses for or justifying behavior	not studying for a test because you need the time to practice for the school play
Regression	reacting to emotions in a childlike or immature fashion	kicking the lockers because you were sent to the principal's office
Repression	blocking out painful thoughts or feelings	ignoring your memories about all the times your divorced parents had fights
Sublimation	redirecting negative impulses into positive behavior	painting a mural when you are mad instead of creating graffiti

Limitations of Defense Mechanisms Some defense mechanisms, such as compensation and sublimation, can be helpful. They can even have a positive outcome. However, most of the defense mechanisms have few if any long-term benefits. In the short-term, defense mechanisms may make a person feel better and allow one to get through a tough time. However, they do not make the upsetting emotions disappear. Instead, they tend to mask the unwanted feelings.

Often, the longer a feeling is ignored, the more problematic it becomes. For example, you could use displacement to deal with the frustration of a classmate picking on you. When you come home from school, you yell at your younger sister. If you do not realize what you are doing, you will never solve the problem between you and your classmate. Displacing your frustration on your sister has also put a strain on your relationship with her.

Some defense mechanisms, such as sublimation, can channel unpleasant emotions into positive behaviors.

Finding the Right Balance Each person needs to find the right balance between managing emotions and using defense mechanisms. All people use defense mechanisms at one time or another. These mechanisms can be a healthy way to temporarily cope with one's feelings. But if the defense mechanisms become the only way a person can cope, that person is not managing emotions effectively.

Your best bet is to take a close look at the way you cope with your own feelings. Are you using the positive methods that were discussed earlier? Practice the tips for managing your emotions on some of your small frustrations. Once you have mastered some of the techniques, you may find that you don't need to use defense mechanisms.

SECTION 3

REVIEW *Answer the following questions on a separate piece of paper.*

Using Key Terms

1. **Define** the term *self-actualization*.
2. **Identify** the term for "the feeling that is produced in response to life experiences."

Understanding Key Ideas

3. **Identify** which of the following characteristics is *not* a characteristic of positive mental health.
   a. enduring failures
   b. seeing life events positively
   c. having a sense of control
   d. denying feelings

4. **Compare** the stages of Maslow's hierarchy of needs.
5. **Describe** how you can learn to express emotions in a positive way.
6. **Summarize** the limitations of defense mechanisms.
7. **Identify** the defense mechanism in which a person makes excuses for a behavior.

Critical Thinking

8. **LIFE SKILL** **Practicing Wellness** Describe three strategies you can use to manage your emotions in a positive way.

Understanding Mental Disorders

OBJECTIVES

Describe what mental disorders are.

List seven signs of a mental disorder.

Summarize causes of mental disorders.

Identify community resources available for mental health problems.

KEY TERMS

mental disorder an illness that affects a person's thoughts, emotions, and behaviors

symptom a change that a person notices in his or her body or mind and that is caused by a disease or disorder.

depression a sadness and hopelessness that keeps a person from carrying out everyday activities

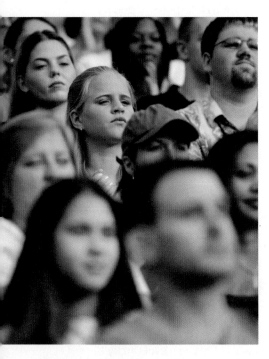

Anyone can be affected by a mental disorder.

t is just after noon, and Lisa is still in bed. She doesn't see any point in getting up. She doesn't want to do anything. She has felt this way for days. She doesn't even want to be around her friends. She feels that anything she does is useless.

What Are Mental Disorders?

In the last section, you learned that mental health is being able to meet the daily challenges of life, having high self-esteem, and developing healthy relationships. Sometimes, however, people are not mentally healthy. They may suffer from a mental disorder. A **mental disorder** is an illness that affects a person's thoughts, emotions, and behaviors. Those who suffer from a mental disorder may not be able to have fun. They may not feel good about themselves or may have a difficult time developing intimate relationships. They may have difficulty dealing with everyday routines. Many homeless people suffer from a mental disorder.

Lisa is an example of someone experiencing a mental disorder. She feels hopeless and doesn't have the energy to do regular activities or build relationships.

Mental Disorders Are Often Misunderstood Unfortunately, many people who have a mental disorder don't get help because they don't understand mental disorders. Some people are afraid of mental disorders or the people who have the disorders. Identifying and understanding different kinds of mental disorders can help prevent the fear associated with the disorder. Most of these mental disorders are treatable.

To understand mental disorders, you need to learn about their symptoms. A **symptom** is a change that a person notices in his or her body or mind and that is caused by a disease or disorder. For example, Lisa's symptoms were hopelessness and low energy.

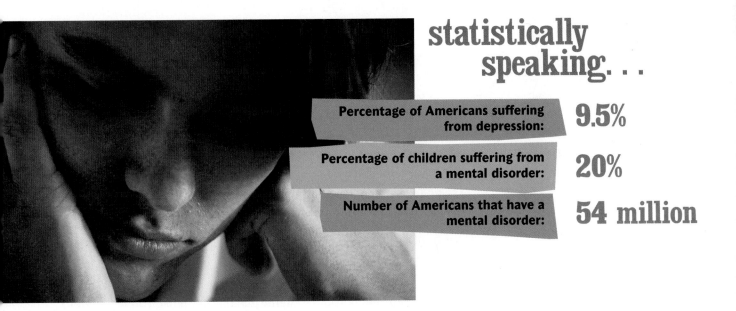

statistically speaking. . .

Percentage of Americans suffering from depression: **9.5%**

Percentage of children suffering from a mental disorder: **20%**

Number of Americans that have a mental disorder: **54 million**

Types of Mental Disorders

There are many types of mental disorders, and they have a variety of symptoms. If you experience any of the symptoms listed below, talk to a trusted adult. However, only licensed professionals can diagnose a mental disorder.

- ▶ too much or too little sleep
- ▶ feeling of extreme sadness
- ▶ unexplained mood changes
- ▶ drug or alcohol abuse
- ▶ inability to concentrate
- ▶ extreme anxiety or irrational fear
- ▶ personality changes
- ▶ false perceptions of reality

Several disorders are common and require some additional description. These disorders are depression, attention-deficit/hyperactivity disorder, and anxiety disorders.

Depression   Everyone feels sad or down at times. However, sadness and hopelessness that keep a person from carrying out everyday activities is called **depression.** Depression, also known as major depressive disorder, is a serious disorder that if left untreated can lead a person to consider suicide. Some of the symptoms of depression are listed below.

- ▶ lack of energy
- ▶ withdrawal from people
- ▶ loss of appetite or overeating
- ▶ too much or too little sleep
- ▶ feelings of helplessness and hopelessness

Experiencing one or more of these symptoms from time to time is not uncommon. However, if you experience several of these symptoms for several days, you should seek professional help.

internet connect

www.scilinks.org/health
Topic: Depression
HealthLinks code: HH4040

HEALTH LINKS. Maintained by the National Science Teachers Association

Below are suggestions a person can follow if he or she is experiencing depression.

1. **Face the problem.** Don't wait for depression to go away. Seek professional help immediately. Also, don't use drugs or alcohol to solve your problems. They will only create more problems.

2. **Identify the problem.** What is causing the depression? Could it be the result of a loss or loneliness? A licensed professional may determine that it's caused by biological factors, such as a chemical imbalance.

3. **Take action.** Responding actively to depression can make one feel more in control and can help release unpleasant feelings. The following are some examples of actions one can take.
   ▶ Change negative thinking, and use positive self-talk.
   ▶ Seek out support from others.
   ▶ Be active. Physical activity, such as playing a sport, can make your body produce chemicals that can make you feel better.

Attention-Deficit/Hyperactivity Disorder Attention-deficit/hyperactivity disorder (ADHD) is the most commonly diagnosed disorder of childhood. However, ADHD is a lifelong condition. A person who has ADHD is frequently inattentive or impulsively hyperactive to the point that he or she has problems accomplishing daily activities. For example, a teen who has ADHD may have problems doing school work. He or she may become easily distracted, have difficulty following instructions, or have difficulty completing tasks.

The causes of ADHD are unknown. However, treatment is available for those who have ADHD. Some medications have proven to be helpful by increasing one's ability to concentrate.

Phobias, such as the fear of heights, may be learned behaviors that result from an event that was very frightening.

Anxiety Disorders It is normal to feel nervous or worried in some situations. For example, you may feel anxiety every time you take a test. However, if the anxiety gets in the way of taking part in daily activities, if it occurs frequently, or if it causes terror, then it may be an anxiety disorder.

Panic disorder is one type of anxiety disorder. In a panic attack, the person may feel extreme fear for his or her life even though he or she is not really in danger.

Phobias are anxiety disorders characterized by excessive or persistent fear of something that may or may not cause real danger. For example, acrophobia is fear of being in high places.

Obsessive-compulsive disorder is an anxiety disorder triggered by uncomfortable thoughts called *obsessions* and by repetitive behaviors called *compulsions*. Post-traumatic stress disorder is anxiety over a past traumatic event. To learn more details about these and other mental disorders, see **Table 3.**

Causes of Mental Disorders

Many mental health specialists believe that some mental disorders, such as phobias, develop from traumatic or stressful experiences in a person's life. Some examples of stressful or traumatic experiences are a death, an accident, or an abusive event.

Other disorders can be inherited. For example, researchers are trying to determine if schizophrenia is an inherited disorder. Some disorders can be caused by an injury or a physical disorder that affects the brain. For example, brain tumors, alcoholism, and some infections can cause mental disorders. Whatever the cause, many disorders are treatable. Some disorders can be cured. A person who has a mental disorder must get help to treat the disorder.

Table 3 Mental Disorders

Disorder	Description
Major depression	▶ feelings of hopeless and sadness that last for more than a few days ▶ inability to take part in daily activities
Attention-deficit/hyperactivity disorder (ADHD)	▶ difficulty concentrating ▶ difficulty completing tasks ▶ difficulty following instructions ▶ impulsive and hyperactive
Panic disorder	▶ sudden feelings of terror that strike without warning ▶ putting oneself in danger by desperately trying to escape the situation
Phobias	▶ excessive or persistent fear of something that may or may not cause real danger, such as spiders, elevators, or giving a speech ▶ possible panic attacks
Obsessive-compulsive disorder	▶ repeated, disturbing, and unwanted thoughts ▶ ritual behaviors that are perceived as impossible to control such as repeatedly washing one's hands
Post-traumatic stress disorder	▶ avoidance of experiences that could trigger memories of a traumatic experience such as wartime experiences or abuse
Eating disorders	▶ obsessive behavior and thoughts about weight control ▶ starvation of oneself such as anorexia nervosa ▶ consumption of large amounts of food followed by vomiting
Hypochondria	▶ belief of illness when none is present
Bipolar disorder	▶ uncontrollable cycles of extreme happiness and then depression
Schizophrenia	▶ false perceptions of reality ▶ hallucinations and/or delusions

Help for Mental Disorders

If you think that you or a friend may have a mental disorder, the first step is to talk to a parent, school nurse, religious leader, or other trusted adult. He or she can then help you find the resources to treat the disorder. Many resources in your community are available to help those who have a mental disorders. Hospitals, clinics, private agencies, and school-linked services can provide a variety of treatments.

Talking about problems to other people who are experiencing the same problems can be comforting.

Psychotherapy   If a disorder is caused by a traumatic experience, psychotherapy can be useful. Psychotherapy is a form of counseling received from a licensed therapist. Psychotherapy can help the person resolve issues from the past trauma. If the mental disorder is a phobia, a licensed therapist can help the patient discover the source of the fear.

Group Therapy   Group therapy is led by a licensed therapist. The therapist leads a group of people who have a similar disorder. Those in the group find it comforting to talk about their problems with others who are experiencing the same problem.

Medication   Some people who have a disorder benefit from certain medications. Antidepressants can help treat people who have depression. People who have schizophrenia or ADHD also can benefit from medication that eases symptoms and makes the disorder more manageable.

However, prescription drugs are not the answer to all mental health problems. Psychiatrists are trained to prescribe the right drug and the right amount only to those who will benefit. Frequently, a psychiatrist will recommend group therapy or psychotherapy as well as prescribed medication.

SECTION 4

REVIEW *Answer the following questions on a separate piece of paper.*

Using Key Terms

1. **Define** the term *symptom*.
2. **Define** the term *depression*.

Understanding Key Ideas

3. **Describe** what is meant by the term mental disorder.
4. **Identify** which of the following descriptions is *not* a symptom of a mental disorder.
   a. personality change   c. too much sleep
   b. crying when sad   d. alcohol abuse
5. **LIFE SKILL** **Describe** three things you can do if you are experiencing depression.

6. **List** six mental disorders.
7. **Describe** three possible causes of mental disorders.
8. **Identify** which of the following is *not* a treatment for a mental disorder.
   a. denial   c. group therapy
   b. medication   d. psychotherapy

Critical Thinking

9. **LIFE SKILL** **Practicing Wellness** If you think that you are suffering from a phobia, what type of treatment should you seek?

Highlights

Key Terms

The Big Picture

✔ People who have high self-esteem respect themselves and others, reach their goals, recover from disappointment, and feel valuable to family, friends, and community.

✔ Our self-esteem is influenced by the messages we receive about ourselves.

✔ You can improve your self-esteem by using self-talk, acting with integrity, choosing supportive friends, and accepting yourself.

✔ Communication is important for avoiding misunderstandings, building our relationships,and expressing our feelings.

✔ Assertive communication is the most effective way to communicate because it is direct and respectful to others.

✔ When using good speaking skills be aware of your voice volume, tone, and pitch. Also, use "I" messages and show empathy.

✔ Some examples of good listening skills are maintaining eye contact, nodding your head, and paraphrasing.

✔ Misunderstandings can happen if your body language communicates a different message than what you say.

✔ People who have positive mental health have high self-esteem, meet the daily challenges, and develop healthy relationships.

✔ The five stages of Maslow's hierarchy of needs are the physical stage, the safety stage, the social stage, the esteem stage, and self-actualization.

✔ You can learn to express your emotions in a positive way by practicing a positive example of expressing that emotion.

✔ You can manage your emotions by talking about your feelings with others, by blowing off steam, and by expressing your emotions creatively.

✔ Defense mechanisms are often ineffective ways of dealing with unpleasant emotions.

✔ A mental disorder is an illness of the mind that affects thinking, behavior, and mood. A mental disorder makes dealing with everyday routines difficult.

✔ Learning about the symptoms of mental disorders is important for identifying the disorder and getting help.

✔ Many mental disorders can be caused by heredity, by injury, by physical illness, or by traumatic experiences.

✔ Three forms of treatment for mental disorders are psychotherapy, group therapy, and medication.

Review

Using Key Terms

aggressive (56)
assertive (56)
defense mechanism (66)
emotion (63)
empathy (58)
integrity (54)
depression (69)

mental health (61)
mental disorder (68)
passive (56)
self-actualization (62)
self-concept (52)
self-esteem (50)
symptom (68)

1. For each definition below, choose the key term that best matches the definition.
   a. the ability to understand another person's feelings, behaviors, and attitudes
   b. the achievement of the best that a person can be
   c. a change that a person notices in his or her body or mind and that is caused by a disease or disorder
   d. the characteristic of doing what one knows is right
   e. not offering opposition when challenged or acted upon
   f. an illness that affects a person's thoughts, emotions, and behaviors
   g. a sadness and hopelessness that keeps a person from carrying out everyday activities
   h. an unconscious behavior used to avoid experiencing unpleasant emotions

2. Explain the relationship between the key terms in each of the following pairs.
   a. *aggressive* and *assertive*
   b. *self-concept* and *self-esteem*
   c. *emotion* and *mental health*

Understanding Key Ideas

Section 1

3. Describe how you can show respect for yourself.

4. List the benefits of high self-esteem.

5. Describe how self-esteem develops.

6. Explain how accepting yourself can improve your self-esteem.

Section 2

7. Which of the following is *not* a reason why communication is important?
   a. builds healthy relationships
   b. leads to unclear messages
   c. lets you express yourself
   d. prevents misunderstandings

8. Which of the following statements is *not* an example of assertive communication?
   a. I don't want to talk to you ever again!
   b. I have to go because I'm running late.
   c. Don't yell at me.
   d. I don't want to see that movie.

9. Describe how to be an active listener.

10. List three examples of body language.

11. **CRITICAL THINKING** Describe a situation in which you can use "I" messages. **LIFE SKILL**

Section 3

12. Describe characteristics of positive mental and emotional health.

13. State the stage of Maslow's hierarchy of needs that requires food.

14. How can you learn to express your emotions in a positive way?

15. Which defense mechanism is being used when someone refuses to accept reality?

16. **CRITICAL THINKING** Describe a positive strategy for managing your anger. **LIFE SKILL**

Section 4

17. List three characteristics of mental disorders.

18. Which of the following symptoms is *not* a sign of depression?
   a. lack of energy   c. high self-esteem
   b. loss of appetite   d. too much sleep

19. Give two examples of disorders that can be treated with medication.

20. **CRITICAL THINKING** List two mental disorders that could be caused by a traumatic experience.

Interpreting Graphics

Study the figure below to answer the questions that follow.

Assertive Communication

Situation	Response
1. Your boyfriend/girl-friend tells you to stop wearing a certain shirt	1. _____ _____ _____
2. Your mother throws out your favorite torn jeans.	2. You respectfully ask your mother not to throw out your things.
3. Your little sister borrows your tennis racket without asking.	3. You yell at your sister and then take her stuff so she can see what it feels like.

21. Which response in the table is an assertive response?

22. Which response in the table is an aggressive response?

23. **CRITICAL THINKING** Fill in an assertive response for the first situation.

Activities

24. **Health and You** Optimism helps a person reach his or her goals or overcome hard times. Think of a situation that you will face this week and that you have been worried about. Now, write a detailed description of how you want that situation to turn out. **WRITING SKILL**

25. **Health and Your Community** Ask each classmate to write down one nice thing about each other student in the class. Have your classmates give their anonymous lists to you. Organize the comments according to student names. Hand back the nice comments to the students so that they can read the nice things written about them!

26. **Health and You** Identify a person you admire for their community involvement. Compare this person's characteristics with characteristics you already possess or hope to acquire. **WRITING SKILL**

Action Plan

27. **LIFE SKILL** **Communicating Effectively** Use the communication skills you learned in this chapter to create a step-by-step action plan to improve communication in one of your relationships.

Standardized Test Prep

Read the passage below, and then answer the questions that follow. **READING SKILL** **WRITING SKILL**

Rina's birthday party on Saturday night was a big hit. Everyone had fun except Jessica and Tessa, who had an argument. Jessica became <u>agitated</u> when Tessa broke Jessica's necklace. Tessa was trying it on when it caught on her watch and the clasp snapped. Jessica called Tessa an idiot and yelled, "Don't ever touch my things again!" Tessa was so offended that she told Jessica she didn't want to be friends with her anymore. Jessica left the party early. Tessa stayed, but she was very quiet and withdrawn.

28. In this passage, the word *agitated* means
    A worried.
    B angry.
    C jealous.
    D curious.

29. What can you infer from reading this passage?
    E Tessa knows how to manage her anger.
    F Rina will never have another party again.
    G Both Jessica and Tessa were hurt by the argument.
    H none of the above

30. Write a paragraph describing how the situation would have turned out more positively if Jessica and Tessa used the communication skills listed in this chapter.

CHAPTER 4

Managing Stress and Coping with Loss

What's Your Health IQ?
BEHAVIOR

Indicate how frequently you engage in each of the following behaviors (1 = never; 2 = occasionally; 3 = most of the time; 4 = all of the time). Total your points, and then turn to p. 638.

1. I exercise and eat well.

2. I make time in my schedule to do the things that I really enjoy.

3. I ask for support from family and friends when I feel too much stress.

4. I have an optimistic view of changes in my life.

5. I do the most important projects I want to accomplish first.

6. I say no if my boss repeatedly asks me to work late on a school night.

Visit these Web sites for the latest health information:

HEALTH LINKS.
THE WORLD'S A CLICK AWAY®

Find more information whenever you see a HealthLinks box. Go to scilinks.org/health, and type in the HealthLinks code.

go.hrw.com

Find worksheets and other materials that go with your textbook at **go.hrw.com**.

Current Health®

Check out *Current Health®* articles related to this chapter by visiting go.hrw.com. Just type in the keyword **HH4 CH04**.

Stress and Your Health

OBJECTIVES

Describe five different causes of stress.

Describe the body's physical response to stress.

Differentiate between positive and negative stress.

Describe how stress can make you sick. **LIFE SKILL**

Many people experience stress because they take on too many responsibilities or don't manage time well.

I t's 1:05 P.M. Paula is running down the hall and is late for algebra class. Halfway to class, she realizes that she forgot her algebra homework in her locker. She'll get a detention if she goes back to get it and is late to class again. When she gets to class, she is marked late. Paula's head begins to pound with an intense headache.

What Causes Stress?

Do you ever feel stressed? **Stress** is the body's and mind's response to a demand. You may not even be aware that you are under stress until you get a headache, as Paula did.

Stress can be caused by many different situations or events. For example, going out on a date can cause stress and so can taking a test or watching a football game. Stress is caused by stressors. A **stressor** is any situation that puts a demand on the body or mind. There are several different types of stressors.

Environmental Stressors Environmental stressors are conditions or events in your physical environment that cause you stress. For example, pollution, poverty, crowding, noise, and natural disasters are things in your environment that can cause you stress.

Biological Stressors Some stressors are biological. These are conditions that make it difficult for your body to take part in daily activities. For example, having an illness, a disability, or an injury are biological stressors.

Thinking Stressors Any type of mental challenge can cause stress. A good example of this is taking a test. Paula's algebra homework is probably a stressor for her.

Behavioral Stressors Unhealthy behavior, such as not getting enough sleep or exercise, can lead to stress. Using tobacco, alcohol, or drugs also puts stress on your body. Paula was experiencing behavioral stress because she didn't manage her time well.

Life Change Stressors Any major life change, whether positive or negative, can be a cause of stress. For example, death of a loved one, getting married, and other personal events can cause stress. The teen years are a time when you experience many changes and, thus, stress. **Table 1** lists some common life changes that can lead to stress.

ACTIVITY *To measure how much your life has changed, add up the life change units below for the changes that you experienced in the past year. Compare your score with the scale below.*

Table 1 Life Changes That Can Lead to Stress

Life event	Life change units	Life event	Life change units
Experiencing the death of a parent	▶ 119	Having more arguments with parents	▶ 51
Experiencing the death of a brother or sister	▶ 102	Getting married	▶ 50
Going through your parents' divorce	▶ 98	Failing a grade in school	▶ 42
Having a serious illness	▶ 77	Seeing an increase in arguments between parents	▶ 40
Having a parent go to jail	▶ 75	Beginning or ending school	▶ 38
Experiencing the death of a close friend	▶ 70	Breaking up with a boyfriend or girlfriend	▶ 37
Being pregnant	▶ 66	Making an outstanding achievment	▶ 36
Getting a new job	▶ 62	Moving to a new school district	▶ 35
Gaining a new family member	▶ 57	Being suspended from school	▶ 29
Experiencing a significant change in family's financial status	▶ 56	Having trouble with a teacher	▶ 28
Experiencing the serious illness of a parent	▶ 56	Change in sleeping habits	▶ 26
Being excluded from a social circle	▶ 53	Going on vacation	▶ 25
		Getting a traffic ticket	▶ 22

Your Life Change Score: If your score is less than 100, your life has changed little. If your score is between 100 and 200, you have experienced moderate change. If your score is more than 200, your life has changed significantly.

Adapted from Mark A. Miller and Richard H. Rahe, "Life Changes Scaling for the 1990s," *Journal of Psychosomatic Research* 43 (1997).

Physical Response to Stress

Imagine that you are riding your bike and you suddenly find yourself in the path of a fast-moving car. You feel a sudden burst of energy that allows you to get out of the way of the car. Now imagine that you are a goalie in a soccer game. The ball has been kicked by an opposing team player and it's headed straight to the goal. Your heart starts to beat faster as you jump for the ball and make the block.

In both of these situations, your body responded to a stressful situation, but in a different way. When the car was in the path of your bike, the response was to move away, or "take flight." When the soccer ball was coming to the goal, the response was to confront the situation, or "fight." The physical changes that prepare your body to respond quickly and appropriately to stressors is called the *fight-or-flight response.*

The Fight-or-Flight Response During the fight-or-flight response, your body provides you with the energy, reflexes, and strength you may need to respond to the stressor. As part of the fight-or-flight response, your body releases epinephrine. **Epinephrine** (EP uh NEF rin), formerly called *adrenaline*, is one of the hormones that are released by the body in times of stress. Epinephrine prepares the body for quick action by triggering the changes listed below.

▶ Your breathing speeds up, which helps get more oxygen throughout your body.

▶ Your heart beats faster, which increases the flow of blood to carry more oxygen to your muscles.

▶ Your muscles tense up, which prepares you to move quickly.

▶ The pupils of your eyes get wider, which allows extra light for more sensitive vision.

▶ Your digestion slows down, because digestion is an unnecessary activity during an emergency.

▶ Blood sugar increases to provide more fuel for fighting or running.

Emotional and Behavioral Response to Stress

The way you respond to a stress emotionally and behaviorally depends on whether you consider the stress to be positive or negative, as shown in **Figure 1.**

Positive Stress Let's say you have to give a speech in front of your class. If you choose to consider this in a positive way, this type of stress can motivate you to do your best. Positive stress can help you respond well in a stressful situation. A positive stress that energizes one and helps one reach a goal is called **eustress.** Eustress will make you feel alert and lively. You will appear confident and in control.

A person who presents speeches when experiencing eustress often attracts and holds the attention of the audience. The words roll off the speaker's tongue. One point flows into the others, and the speaker rarely forgets what to say next.

The physical changes in response to stress prepare the body to run away or stay and fight.

HEALTH Handbook For more information about the endocrine system, see the Express Lesson on p. 545.

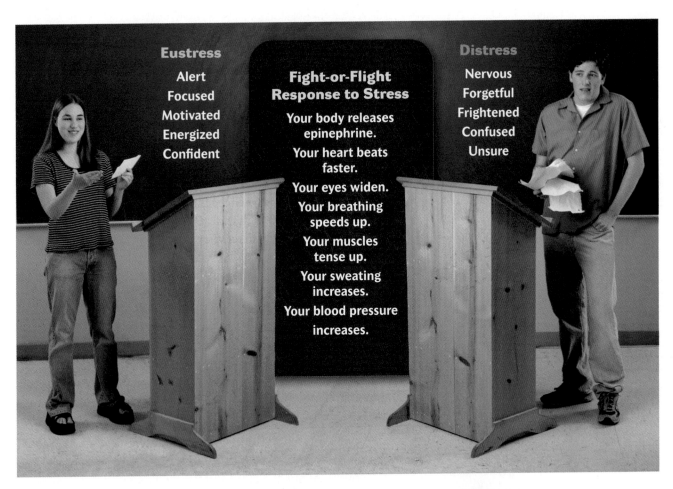

Eustress	Fight-or-Flight Response to Stress	Distress
Alert	Your body releases epinephrine.	Nervous
Focused	Your heart beats faster.	Forgetful
Motivated	Your eyes widen.	Frightened
Energized	Your breathing speeds up.	Confused
Confident	Your muscles tense up.	Unsure
	Your sweating increases.	
	Your blood pressure increases.	

Negative Stress   If you choose to consider giving a speech to be a negative stress, you may experience distress. **Distress** is negative stress that can make a person sick or keep a person from reaching a goal. Distress can keep you from doing your best, no matter how capable you are.

People who attempt to give a speech while experiencing distress may forget the points they want to make. They may have practiced the speech for days, but when they stand up in front of a room full of people, they lose their concentration. Their words don't flow well. Their voice may sound too soft and shaky, revealing a lack of confidence. The audience may become bored or confused.

Try to Make Stress Positive   Obviously, it is better to approach stressful situations as positive and not negative. However, it is not always easy to control your response to a stressor. One way you can help yourself experience eustress is to be optimistic about dealing with a stressor. Instead of thinking, I can't do this, think, What can I do to accomplish this? Concentrate only on what you can control in the situation. Let go of what you cannot control. Do what you can to build confidence that you can succeed in the situation. If you set your mind to it and prepare to meet the challenge, you will find yourself approaching situations in a positive way!

Figure 1

Everybody experiences the same physical responses to stress—the fight-or-flight response. But each person's emotional and behavioral response differs depending on whether he or she views the stress as positive (eustress) or negative (distress).

ACTIVITY *Which student do you think has a better chance at winning the debate? Explain your answer.*

Stress-Related Diseases and Disorders

▶ **Tension headache**

▶ **Cold and flu**

▶ **Asthma**

▶ **Migraine headache**

▶ **Backache**

▶ **Temporomandibular joint dysfunction (TMJ)**

▶ **Heart disease**

▶ **Stroke**

▶ **High blood pressure**

▶ **Chronic fatigue**

▶ **Ulcer**

▶ **Anxiety disorder**

▶ **Insomnia**

▶ **Depression**

Long-Term Stress Can Make You Sick

If your body experiences stress continuously over a long period of time, you increase your risk for a wide range of stress-related diseases. For example, stress causes the muscles in your neck and head to tense, which can cause headaches. Long-term stress can cause changes in your body that can lead to a heart attack. Long-term stress can also weaken your immune system, the system of your body that defends against infections. As a result, you are more likely to suffer from infections, such as colds.

The *general adaptation syndrome* is a model that describes the relationship between stress and disease. Learning the stages will help you understand how stress can affect your health. There are three stages in the model:

1. **Alarm stage** In the alarm stage, the body and mind become alert. This stage includes the events brought on by the fight-or-flight response. All of your body's efforts go into responding to the demand. A person in this stage may experience headaches, stomachaches, difficulty sleeping, and anxiety.

2. **Resistance stage** If the stress continues, your body becomes more resistant to disease and injury than normal. You can cope with added stress, but only for a limited time.

3. **Exhaustion stage** In this stage, your body cannot take the resistance to the stressor any longer, especially if several stressors occur in a row. You become exhausted, not in the normal sense like after a long, busy day, but in a more serious way. Organs such as your heart may suffer, and your immune system can no longer fight illness.

By learning to manage stress, you can protect yourself from many illnesses and can enjoy a healthier life.

SECTION 1

REVIEW *Answer the following questions on a separate piece of paper.*

Using Key Terms

1. **Compare** the terms *stress* and *stressor*.

2. **Identify** the term for "a positive stress that energizes a person and helps a person reach a goal."

Understanding Key Ideas

3. **List** five different causes of stress.

4. **Identify** which of the following is *not* a part of the fight-or-flight response.
   a. heart rate speeds up   c. muscles tense
   b. increased sweating   d. digestion speeds up

5. **Identify** a hormone that is released during the fight-or-flight response.

6. **Compare** positive and negative stress.

7. **LIFE SKILL** **Assessing Your Health** Using the stages of the general adaptation syndrome, describe how stress can make you sick.

Critical Thinking

8. **LIFE SKILL** **Practicing Wellness** Describe how two stressors led you to experience eustress.

9. What do you think would be the consequences of not having a fight-or-flight response?

Dealing with Stress

OBJECTIVES

Describe how you can take care of yourself to avoid stress-related illnesses.

Describe two relaxation techniques.

List eight skills or resources for building resiliency.

Evaluate the effect of a positive attitude on stress reduction.

List three ways that you can manage your time more efficiently. **LIFE SKILL**

KEY TERMS

resiliency the ability to recover from illness, hardship, and other stressors

asset a skill or resource that can help a person reach a goal

prioritize to arrange items in order of importance

Anthony has a final exam tomorrow. He told his friend Ricardo that he couldn't help him fix his bike because he needed to study for a couple of hours. It's now 10 P.M. Anthony has studied for 3 hours and is now listening to music to relax. He plans to go to bed when the CD finishes so that he can get a good night's sleep.

Take Care of Yourself

Stressful events will occur throughout your life. At this time, you may be experiencing stressors such as tests and peer pressure. When you get older, your stressors may be managing money or raising children. Whatever stressors you experience, learning to manage them will help you remain healthy throughout your life.

In the last section, you learned how your body responds to stress. If stress continues over time, stress-related illnesses can develop. People who are in better physical health are more likely than others to resist developing an illness. An important way to defend yourself from stress-related illness is to take care of yourself! Exercising regularly, getting enough rest, and eating right will help you prevent some of the negative consequences of stress.

Exercise Regularly Exercise will not only keep you physically fit, but it will also relieve tension. *Tension* is a physical effect of stress marked by straining of muscles. During the fight-or-flight response, the body is tensed and ready for a great amount of physical activity. However, many stressors, such as taking a test, don't require much physical activity. Keeping the body in a heightened state of alertness when you don't need to run or fight stresses your heart, muscles, and immune system. Health problems such as tension headaches and heart disease can result from such long-term stress. Exercise can relieve this tension in a healthy way.

Taking care of yourself is one of the best ways to fight off the negative effects of stress.

Get Enough Rest You should get at least 9 hours of sleep every night. Not getting enough sleep can lead to exhaustion, which can cause illness. Also, if you haven't slept enough, you are less alert and less capable of dealing with a stressor. For example, Anthony knows that if he has a good night's sleep, his mind will be prepared and alert for the exam.

Eat Right Eating nutritious foods gives you the vitamins, minerals, and energy you need to deal with everyday demands. You need vitamins and minerals for your immune system to function properly. The better shape your immune system is in, the better it can defend you from stress related illnesses.

Learn to Relax

During the response to stress, you build up a lot of tension. At the same time, energy is pulled away from body systems that need the energy to fight sickness. Using relaxation techniques can help you relieve tension and reserve energy for fighting illness. The following are a couple of relaxation techniques you can try.

Breathing Exercises One relaxation technique is deep breathing. It requires completely filling the lungs with air instead of taking shallow breaths. Deep breathing brings more oxygen to all parts of your body. More oxygen helps muscles and organs function more effectively. More oxygen also helps keep your brain alert and focused. Deep breathing also produces a calming effect that helps relax you. When you practice deep breathing, your heart rate slows down and your blood pressure drops.

To practice deep breathing, find a comfortable place to sit. Close your eyes, and concentrate only on your breathing. Inhale slowly until your lungs cannot hold any more air. Then, exhale slowly. Repeat this process for at least 15 minutes.

Tension-Releasing Exercises When you are under stress, it's common to hold the tension in your muscles. You may not even notice the tension in your muscles until they start to ache.

To release tension, start by tensing the muscles in one part of your body, such as your shoulders. Notice how it feels to have those muscles tensed. Now, relax those muscles. Notice how those muscles feel relaxed. You can then move to another muscle group and repeat the tensing and relaxing until your entire body is relaxed.

Deep breathing and tension-releasing exercises are only two ways for you to relax. You can put your body at ease in many other ways. For example, Anthony relaxes by listening to music. Someone else may relax by reading a book. You may already have your own special technique. Keep in mind that although relaxation techniques can help you manage the symptoms of stress, this should not stop you from dealing with the stressor directly.

"Playing guitar is my way to relax."

Table 2 Eight Assets for Building Resiliency

Asset	Description	Example
Support	▶ having family, friends, and others to help you	▶ You talk to the school counselor about a problem.
Empowerment	▶ feeling as if you are a valuable member of your community and family	▶ You volunteer to start a drug-free campaign at school.
Boundaries	▶ having a clear set of rules and consequences for school, family, and relationships	▶ You know that if another teen bullies you at school, a teacher will speak with that teen.
Productive use of time	▶ choosing creative and productive activities	▶ You join a school club instead of playing video games after school.
Commitment to learning	▶ understanding the value of schoolwork	▶ You spend time every day working on homework assignments.
Positive values	▶ having values that include caring, integrity, honesty, self-responsibility, equality, and justice	▶ You support a friend who tells the truth even though doing so may get him or her in trouble.
Social skills	▶ communicating effectively, respecting others, and avoiding peer pressure	▶ You talk out a disagreement instead of yelling.
Positive identity	▶ having high self-esteem, having a sense of control, and feeling as if you have a purpose	▶ You use positive self-talk to prepare yourself for a speech.

Source: Adapted from Benson, Peter L., Ph.D., Espeland, Pamela, and Galbraith, Judy, M. A., *What Teens Need to Succeed.*

ACTIVITY *Provide an additional example of how you can strengthen each asset.*

Build Resiliency

The ability to recover from illness, hardship, and other stressors is called **resiliency.** Resilient people continue to be optimistic when life gets tough. They seem to struggle less and succeed more. They accomplish difficult tasks and make other people ask, "How did they do that?"

Many resilient people get their strength from their assets. An **asset** is a skill or resource that can help you reach a goal. For example, support is an asset. Having people to support you can get you through some hard times. You don't have to have a big family or be popular to have a strong support system. Resilient people build strong support systems by asking for help. They ask for support from their family, friends, teachers, school counselors, neighbors, community leaders, and religious leaders.

You have the power to strengthen these assets. **Table 2** lists eight assets and provides examples of how each asset can work for you. For example, if you want to strengthen the asset entitled "positive identity," you can use the skills such as positive self-talk to improve your self-esteem. The stronger you make your assets, the stronger you will feel, and the healthier you will be.

internet connect

www.scilinks.org/health
Topic: Stress
HealthLinks code: HH4129

HEALTH LINKS. Maintained by the National Science Teachers Association

Change Your Attitude

You have control over the number of stressors in your life. Because stress is caused by how you perceive a new or potentially threatening situation, you can choose to see the situation as a challenge instead of as a problem. Having a positive attitude about the outcome of potentially stressful events can eliminate a lot of stress. If you approach the situation with a positive attitude, you won't feel as nervous. If you don't feel so nervous, a positive consequence is more likely to happen.

Use Positive Self-Talk   Say or think positive things to yourself. For example, let's say you are invited to go on a date to go see a movie. You are nervous about the date because you really like the person that invited you on the date. You can think to yourself, I must be fun and desirable if this person wants to go out with me. You can also predict a realistic, positive outcome. You can imagine that you and your date have a great time and make plans to meet again.

LIFE SKILL Activity

Coping

Positive Attitude

Approaching the stressors in your life with a positive attitude will not only help you produce additional positive effects, but it will also relieve a lot of tension. How can you have a positive attitude about the stressors in your life?

1. List five stressors. If you would like to, you can list your own stressors.

2. Describe how you could have a positive emotional response to each stressor.

3. Describe how you could have a positive physical response to each stressor.

4. Describe a positive outcome to each stressor.

LIFE SKILL   Practicing Wellness

1. Predict how this activity will affect your actual responses to these stressors.

2. Describe how you felt when you finished step 4. Did you see the stressors more optimistically?

Be Confident About Yourself The better you feel about yourself, the more positive your perception of a situation will be. The more positive your perception is, the more positive your response and the consequences will be! To build your self-confidence, you can remember similar challenges you have met successfully.

Don't Worry About Things Out of Your Control Accept the things you can't change, and then make the best out of the situation. Put your energy only into things you can control.

Manage Your Time

One of the most common stressors that people experience is the feeling of not having enough time. Many people feel overwhelmed by the pace of their lives. However, by organizing your time, you can feel in control of your life. Having a sense of control will minimize the effects of stress.

Topic: Stress Management
HealthLinks code: HH4130

Many of us get into trouble when we take on more things to do than we have time for. Helene is overwhelmed because today she has to go to swim practice, study for a French test, do her history homework, go to dance rehearsal, cover the late shift at work, and help prepare dinner.

List and Prioritize Your Projects The first step in managing your time is to make a list of your projects and to prioritize your goals. To **prioritize** is to arrange items in order of importance. You may not be able to do everything on your list. However, if you put the most important items first, you can be sure to get them done. Prioritizing also helps you decide which activities can be eliminated.

Helene organized her priorities as follows: (1) French test, (2) swim practice, and (3) history homework. Helene was able to eliminate three activities. She didn't have to prepare dinner because she traded nights with her sister. She arranged to have a co-worker cover her shift at work. Finally, she went to dance practice as a way to relieve stress through exercise and having fun.

Know and Set Your Limits One major reason that some people have hectic schedules is that they don't know their limits when they commit to projects. For example, Helene has taken on much more than she can handle. Signing up for dance, swimming, and a part-time job is too much for anybody. If Helene does not drop some of her responsibilities, her health will begin to suffer.

Helene can also manage her time by learning to say no. Helene shouldn't have promised her boss that she would work. Some people have a hard time saying no. They are afraid people will think that they don't care. However, saying no sometimes is a healthy way of taking care of yourself.

"I don't have time to be stressed out!"

Make a Schedule Once you have prioritized your projects and have decided what you can accomplish, you can make a schedule. Some people use calendars or planners to keep track of their schedule. But all you really need is a pen and a notebook. The following points will help you make your schedule.

▶ **Enter your priorities first.** When setting aside time for projects, start with the projects at the top of your list to make sure that you give them the time needed. Schedule your most difficult tasks for the hours when you are most productive. Consider scheduling your least favorite tasks first.

▶ **Be realistic.** Set realistic goals. Don't cram your day with more activities than you can possibly do. Make sure you plan enough time for each activity. Break up long-term goals into short-term goals. For example, if you have a big research paper to turn in, break the paper down into manageable parts. Schedule one day to gather your references, a second day to write the outline of your paper, and so on. Your steady progress will motivate you to continue.

▶ **Prepare for problems.** Life is never perfect. Therefore, it helps to think about possible problems ahead of time. You may want to give yourself a little more time in your schedule, just in case.

▶ **Make time to relax.** Don't forget to fit in time to have fun or to do the things you really enjoy. Remember that relaxing is important to your health.

▶ **Do it.** Stop thinking about what you have to do and just do it. Sometimes you can get overwhelmed by just thinking of all of the things you have to do. Tackle each task one at a time.

If you practice the stress management techniques you learned in this chapter, you can begin to control the stress in your life. Not only will you protect your health, you will have more time to enjoy your life!

Five Tips for Managing Your Time

1 Prioritize your goals.

2 Learn to say no.

3 Keep a schedule.

4 Don't overload yourself.

5 Plan for fun activities.

SECTION 2

REVIEW
Answer the following questions on a separate piece of paper.

Using Key Terms

1. **Define** the term *resiliency*.

2. **Identify** the term for "a skill or resource that can help a person reach a goal."

3. **Identify** the term for "to arrange items in order of importance."

Understanding Key Ideas

4. **Describe** how taking care of yourself can help you avoid stress-related illness.

5. **Describe** two techniques you can use to relax.

6. **Name** eight assets for building resiliency.

7. **Describe** how a positive attitude can change your response to stress.

8. **LIFE SKILL** **Practicing Wellness** Describe three ways to manage your time more efficiently.

Critical Thinking

9. Why do you think the phrase "burned out" is used to describe a person who has been under a lot of stress?

Coping with Loss

OBJECTIVES

Describe the effects of loss.

Name the stages of the grieving process.

Describe how funerals, wakes, and memorial services help people cope with the loss of a loved one.

Propose three ways you can cope with the loss of a loved one. **LIFE SKILL**

KEY TERMS

grieve to express deep sadness because of a loss

wake a ceremony to view or watch over the deceased person before the funeral

funeral a ceremony in which a deceased person is buried or cremated

memorial service a ceremony to remember the deceased person

Fidencia cannot imagine life without Ben. She can't believe her parents are making her move away from him. She was so angry with them that she wanted to scream. Today is the day that they move. She feels as if she is losing a part of herself.

Effects of Loss

There are many forms of loss. Some examples of loss are the death of a family member, the divorce of one's parents, the death of a pet, a breakup with a boyfriend or girlfriend, and a move away from your home.

All forms of loss can cause you to experience a range of emotions, from sadness to anger to numbness. These feelings are normal and common reactions to loss. You may not be prepared for how intense your emotions may be or how suddenly your moods may change. You may even begin to doubt your mental stability. It is important to know that these feelings are healthy and normal and will help you cope with your loss. However, if the feelings don't pass over time, you should seek the help of a parent or trusted adult.

Loss Can Cause Stress When you experience loss, you can feel the physical and emotional effects of stress. For example, after a loss, you may develop tension headaches or an increase in blood pressure. You may also feel irritable and confused. Just like other stressors, the stress caused by a loss needs to be managed or it can lead to a stress-related illness. The tension-relieving skills that you learned in the last section can keep you healthy. The last thing you need through a trying time is to have a sickness weigh you down.

Moving away from someone you care deeply for is an example of a loss that can cause stress.

The Grieving Process

To express deep sadness because of a loss is to **grieve.** Allowing yourself to grieve is important because grieving helps you heal from the pain of a loss.

When grieving, you may feel agitated or angry. You may find concentrating, eating, or sleeping difficult. You might even feel guilty. For example, you may wish you had told a loved one that died how you felt about him or her. This period of unpredictable emotions may turn to short periods of sadness, silence, and withdrawal from family and friends. During this time, you may be prone to sudden outbursts of tears that are triggered by reminders and memories of this person. Over time, the pain, sadness, and depression will start to lessen. You will begin to see your life in a more positive light again.

This journey to recovery is called the *grieving process.* There are five stages of the grieving process. Not everyone goes through all of the stages or goes through the stages in the same order. However, understanding these stages and the importance of expressing feelings of grief will help you recover from a loss.

Stages of Grief

▶ **DENIAL**
  "This can't be happening to me!"

▶ **ANGER**
  "Why me? It's not fair."

▶ **BARGAINING**
  "I'd do anything to have him back."

▶ **DEPRESSION**
  "There is no hope. I'm so sad. I just want to be alone."

▶ **ACCEPTANCE**
  "It's going to be OK."

The Five Stages of the Grieving Process Although you may never completely overcome the feelings of loss, the grieving process can help you accept the loss. Try to move forward through the stages. If you feel stuck in a stage, ask your parents or a trusted adult for help.

1. **Denial** The first reaction you may face when dealing with a loss is denial. In denial, the person refuses to believe the loss occurred. Denial can act as a buffer to give you a chance to think about the news. However, you must eventually reach the other stages in order to heal.

2. **Anger** Experiencing anger or even rage is normal when you face a loss. You may even try to blame yourself or others for the loss. Be careful about accusing others, and use anger management skills.

3. **Bargaining** Bargaining is the final attempt at avoiding what is true. For example, some people make promises to change if the person or thing they lost is returned to them.

4. **Depression** Sadness is a natural and important emotion to express when you experience loss. However, if feeling very sad keeps you from daily activities for more than a few days, ask a parent or a trusted adult for help.

5. **Acceptance** During this stage, you begin to learn how to live with a loss. The loss continues to be painful, yet you know you will get through it and that life will go on.

Funerals, Wakes, and Memorial Services

Different types of ceremonies may take place after the death of a loved one. These ceremonies honor the person who has passed away. They also help the family and friends of the loved one to get through the grieving process. Different cultures and religions have different ceremonies for handling grief. However, most people use some form of service to help them grieve.

A **wake** is a ceremony that is held to allow family and friends to view or watch over the deceased person before the funeral. Viewing the body of the deceased can help family and friends accept the death. A wake also gives family members and friends an opportunity to come together and to support each other emotionally. For example, in Ireland, the wake is commonly held in the home of the deceased's family.

A **funeral** is a ceremony in which a deceased person is buried or cremated. To *cremate* means to burn the body by intense heat. During a funeral, the death is formally acknowledged. The funeral honors the deceased and offers family and friends the opportunity to pay tribute to the loved one.

A **memorial service** is a ceremony to remember the deceased person. A memorial service provides the same opportunity to mourn the loss of a loved one that funerals and wakes do. However, memorial services can take place long after the death of the loved one. These services may also present a memorial or structure, such as the Vietnam War Memorial, to remember and honor the deceased.

The Vietnam Veterans Memorial Wall is dedicated to honoring those who died in the Vietnam War. Visiting the memorial has helped many people cope with the loss of a loved one who died in the war.

You have mixed feelings about seeing Nate at school this morning. He has just lost his brother, and you want to show your support. However, you and your friends feel awkward. You are not sure how to relate to Nate after his tragic loss.

Write on a separate piece of paper how you might give your friend Nate support. Remember to use the decision-making steps.

Give thought to the problem.

Review your choices.

Evaluate the consequences of each choice.

Assess and choose the best choice.

Think it over afterward.

Help for Dealing with a Loss

There are several things you can do to help yourself as you cope with a loss.

▶ Get plenty of rest and relaxation, but try to stick to any routines you kept before the loss.

▶ Share memories and thoughts about the deceased.

▶ Express your feelings by crying or by writing in a journal.

▶ If the loss was unintentional, do not blame yourself or others. Blaming only creates a way of avoiding the truth about the loss.

Helping Others Sometimes people feel uncomfortable in the presence of a person who has experienced a loss. Small, kind actions such as the touch of a hand on a shoulder is a powerful way to show your support. There are other ways you can help a friend cope with a loss.

▶ Show your support through simple actions, such as offering to run errands or cook a meal.

▶ Let the person know that you are there for him or her, and allow the person to talk about his or her thoughts and feelings.

▶ Tell the person that you have faith that he or she is strong and will learn to live with this loss.

▶ If the person seems depressed, avoids family and friends, or doesn't seem to be making any progress, tell a trusted adult.

Your support can help your friend accept his or her loss. He or she will appreciate your help.

SECTION 3

REVIEW *Answer the following questions on a separate piece of paper.*

Using Key Terms

1. **Define** the term *grieve*.

2. **Identify** the term for "a ceremony to view or watch over the deceased person before the funeral."

3. **Identify** the term for "a ceremony to remember the deceased person."

Understanding Key Ideas

4. **Describe** the effects of loss.

5. **Identify** which of the following is *not* a stage of the grieving process.
   a. death
   b. acceptance
   c. bargaining
   d. anger

6. **Identify** in which of the following stages you might say, "Why me?"
   a. acceptance
   b. bargaining
   c. anger
   d. depression

7. **Compare** how funerals, wakes, and memorial services help people grieve.

8. **LIFE SKILL** **Coping** Describe three ways that you can help someone cope with a loss.

Critical Thinking

9. Why should a person not be afraid to show emotion, such as crying, when faced with a loss?

SECTION 4

Preventing Suicide

OBJECTIVES

List four facts about suicide.

Describe why teens should be concerned about suicide.

State seven warning signs of suicidal behavior.

Describe steps that you can take to help a friend who has talked about suicide. **LIFE SKILL**

KEY TERMS

suicide the act of intentionally taking one's own life

Talking to someone is one of the best things you can do when you feel hopeless or sad.

Kim had six types of pills in a variety of colors in front of her. She didn't know what half of them were for. It didn't matter. Nothing mattered. Or did it? Kim decided to make one last phone call.

Facts About Suicide

Suicide is the act of intentionally taking one's own life. It is shocking to think that someone would want to die. The truth is that most people who attempt suicide don't really want to die. They feel helpless about how to end their emotional pain. However, suicide is never the solution. There are other ways to deal with emotional suffering. Asking someone for help is the first step in making yourself feel better.

Suicide is an uncomfortable topic for many people. Because so many people avoid the subject, many myths about it have arisen. Knowing the following truths about suicide can put an end to the myths and can help prevent suicide.

▶ Many people who have considered suicide considered it only for a brief period in their life.

▶ Most people who have attempted suicide and failed are usually grateful to be alive.

▶ Suicide does not happen without warning. People who have attempted suicide often asked for help in an indirect way. All talk of suicide should be taken seriously.

▶ The use of drugs or alcohol can put people at risk of acting on suicidal thoughts because their judgment is impaired.

Suicide is a serious issue for all teens. Any talk or mention of suicide by a friend should not be taken lightly. If you think a friend is in trouble, talk with your friend. More important, tell a parent or trusted adult about your friend's intentions right away.

Teens and Suicide

Suicide is the fifth leading cause of death for ages 25 to 64. However, it is the third leading cause of death for people between the ages of 15 and 24. Thus, suicide is a serious problem for your age group. Fortunately, suicide is preventable, and you are the best person to protect yourself from it. Being aware of the challenges of the teen years will help.

Changes During the Teen Years   Sometimes the physical and emotional changes during the teen years may make teens feel more emotional, impulsive, and focused on today. Some teens may feel confused and helpless at times, especially if they are having troubles at home or at school. Don't be tempted to find quick solutions that may make the situation worse. Ask a parent or trusted adult for help if you are not sure about what to do.

It is important to realize that feeling impulsive, emotional, or focused on today are part of growing up. As you get older, you will gain more experience, connect with more people, and become more independent. You will have a greater awareness of who you are, what you value, and what you need. You will then feel better prepared for the challenges that face you.

Teens often feel . . .

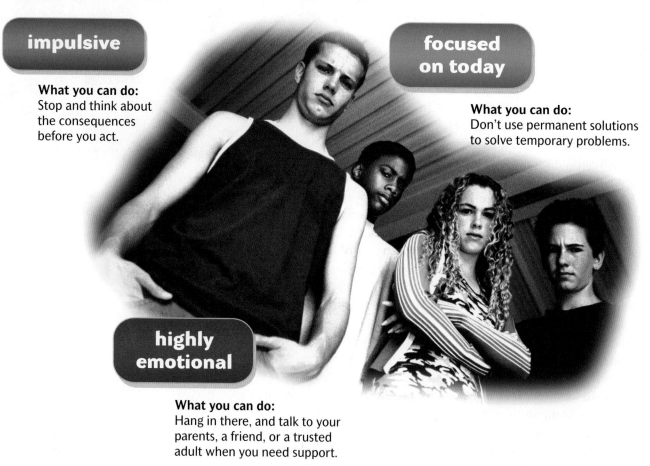

impulsive

What you can do:
Stop and think about the consequences before you act.

focused on today

What you can do:
Don't use permanent solutions to solve temporary problems.

highly emotional

What you can do:
Hang in there, and talk to your parents, a friend, or a trusted adult when you need support.

Warning Signs for Suicide

Recognizing the warning signs of suicide in yourself or in others could help save your life or someone else's life. If you notice any of the following signs in yourself or in another person, talk to a parent or trusted adult.

▶ **Feeling hopeless** If feelings of sadness interfere with a person's daily activities, he or she might be depressed. If feelings of hopelessness have lasted for more than a few days, the person may be headed in a dangerous direction. The person needs help right away.

▶ **Withdrawing from family and friends** Withdrawing from family and friends is a strong sign that someone is considering suicide. However, if you or someone you know is thinking of suicide, this is the most important time to look for support from the people closest to you. If you notice a friend becoming withdrawn, talk with him or her to find out if he or she needs help.

▶ **Neglecting basic needs** People who no longer take care of their appearance, start to lose weight, or have trouble sleeping could be depressed and suicidal. Some examples of neglecting appearance are not brushing hair, not showering regularly, or not changing clothes.

▶ **Experiencing loss of energy** People who feel hopeless and depressed don't feel like making an effort at anything. They no longer take part in things that interest them and may sleep more than usual.

▶ **Taking more risks** Rebellious, self-destructive, or reckless behavior can be a sign of someone who is struggling about wanting to hurt himself or herself. He or she may also become violent toward others or himself or herself.

▶ **Using alcohol and drugs** In attempts to escape the pain, depressed people will often use drugs and alcohol. However, this behavior not only is self-destructive, but it also leads to more anxiety and depression.

▶ **Giving away personal things** When someone feels that he or she is coming to the end of his or her life, the person may feel a need to take care of things. Giving away personal belongings is a way to say goodbye without words. If someone gives you something that is very precious to him or her, you might want to ask why.

These signs indicate that the person is feeling unheard, confused, depressed, and frightened. They are signs that the person needs help.

Understand that suicide is not the solution to temporary problems. Suicide is permanent. A person who commits suicide cannot go back and change his or her mind later. Also, find comfort knowing that if you are depressed, you are not alone. Everyone goes through hard times. Everyone has experienced loneliness. Learning to cope and manage pain and sadness is an important part of human development. Usually, the first step is to ask someone for help. Remaining silent can only cause isolation and further withdrawal from daily life.

Words That Warn

▶ "I wish I were dead."

▶ "I just want to go to sleep and never wake up."

▶ "I won't be a problem for you much longer."

▶ "I won't have to put up with this much longer."

▶ "I can't take it anymore."

▶ "This pain will be over soon."

▶ "Nothing matters."

 TOPIC link For more information about depression, see Chapter 3.

Giving and Getting Help

When you or someone you know is thinking of suicide, do not ignore the problem. Thoughts of suicide are a cry for help. You should act immediately by talking with a friend, parent, or trusted adult. The following are things that you can do if a friend has talked about suicide.

▶ **Take all talk of suicide seriously.** If your friend mentions suicide, tell a trusted adult even if you think your friend is joking.

▶ **Tell your friend that suicide is not the answer.** Emphasize to your friend that suicide is not the answer to temporary problems. Remind your friend of all the things that would be missed if he or she were no longer alive. Suggest that your friend talk to a trusted adult.

▶ **Change negative thoughts into positive thoughts.** Help your friend use positive self-talk to look at things with a different perspective.

▶ **Don't keep a secret.** Do not agree to keep a secret if your friend asks you not to tell anyone that he or she is thinking of suicide. This is a serious situation that requires the help of a trusted adult.

Anyone who is suicidal needs professional help and cannot fix the problem by himself or herself. It is very important that you get help for a friend who is suicidal. Likewise, if you are feeling depressed, don't delay asking a trusted adult for help.

Most cities have a variety of health organizations that offer services to people in need. Some of these services are free. A parent or guardian can help you find the right organization. The important thing is to tell someone and to get the help that you or your friend needs.

"I know what it feels like to be really down.

I'm glad I talked with someone."

SECTION 4

REVIEW
Answer the following questions on a separate piece of paper.

Using Key Terms

1. **Define** the term *suicide.*

Understanding Key Ideas

2. **Name** four facts about suicide.

3. **Describe** why suicide is an especially serious problem for teens.

4. **Identify** the number that suicide ranks as the cause of death in teens.
   a. first   c. fifth
   b. third   d. ninth

5. **State** seven warning signs that someone may be thinking about committing suicide.

6. **Describe** how positive self-talk can help a person who is thinking of suicide.

7. **LIFE SKILL** **Practicing Wellness** Describe four things that you can do if your friend is thinking about suicide.

Critical Thinking

8. **LIFE SKILL** **Practicing Wellness** Describe how you can protect yourself from the risks of suicide during the teen years.

CHAPTER 4

Highlights

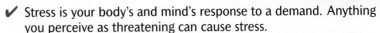

Key Terms

SECTION 1

stress (78)
stressor (78)
epinephrine (80)
eustress (80)
distress (81)

SECTION 2

resiliency (85)
asset (85)
prioritize (87)

SECTION 3

grieve (90)
wake (91)
funeral (91)
memorial
service (91)

SECTION 4

suicide (93)

The Big Picture

✔ Stress is your body's and mind's response to a demand. Anything you perceive as threatening can cause stress.

✔ The fight-or-flight response is your body's physical response to help you deal with a stressor.

✔ Eustress is positive stress and can motivate and energize a person to reach a goal. Distress is negative stress and can make a person sick or keep a person from reaching a goal.

✔ If your body is under stress for a long period of time, you may become exhausted and may develop a stress-related illness.

✔ Eating right, exercising regularly, and getting enough rest will keep you healthy so that your body can avoid stress-related illnesses.

✔ You can learn to relax by practicing deep breathing exercises and tension-releasing exercises.

✔ Assets are skills or resources that can help a person build resiliency against stressors.

✔ Having a positive attitude about a potentially threatening situation can help relieve stress.

✔ You can manage your time more effectively by listing your projects in order of priority, knowing your limits, and making a schedule.

✔ Loss may cause the same emotional and physical effects that characterize stress.

✔ The stages of the grieving process are denial, anger, bargaining, depression, and acceptance.

✔ Funerals, wakes, and memorial services can help you accept the loss of a loved one and receive emotional support from family and friends.

✔ Sharing memories of the deceased and listening to your friend are a couple of ways you can help a friend cope with a loss.

✔ Learning the facts about suicide can prevent the development of myths about suicide and can help prevent suicide.

✔ Teens should be concerned about suicide because it is the third leading cause of death in people between the ages of 15 and 24.

✔ Giving away personal things, feeling hopeless, and sleeping too much are a few of the warning signs for suicide.

✔ Taking all talk of suicide seriously, suggesting that your friend talk to a trusted adult, and not keeping any talk of suicide secret are a few ways you can help a friend who may be considering suicide.

Review

Using Key Terms

asset (85)
distress (81)
epinephrine (80)
eustress (80)
funeral (91)
grieve (90)
memorial service (91)

prioritize (87)
resiliency (85)
stress (78)
stressor (78)
suicide (93)
wake (91)

1. For each definition below, choose the key term that best matches the definition.
   a. any situation that puts a demand on the body or mind
   b. the ability to recover from illness, hardship, and other stressors
   c. to arrange items in order of importance
   d. a ceremony in which a deceased person is buried or cremated
   e. a skill or resource that helps a person reach a goal
   f. the act of intentionally taking one's own life
   g. to express deep sadness because of a loss
   h. the body's and mind's response to a demand made upon it
   i. one of the hormones that are released by the body in times of stress

2. Explain the relationship between the key terms in each of the following pairs.
   a. *wake* and *memorial service*
   b. *distress* and *eustress*

Understanding Key Ideas

Section 1

3. What is the difference between a biological stressor and an environmental stressor?

4. Describe how the fight-or-flight response can help you respond to a threatening situation.

5. Which of the following does *not* describe someone in distress?
   a. confused
   b. unsure
   c. nervous
   d. motivated

6. In which stage of the general adaptation syndrome are you most likely to get sick from response to stress?

Section 2

7. Explain how exercise can help you deal with stress.

8. Explain how breathing deeply can help you deal with stress.

9. Which of the following is *not* an asset for building resiliency?
   a. occasional exercise
   c. positive values
   b. support
   d. empowerment

10. Explain how self-talk can help you deal with a stressor.

11. Which of the following is *not* a helpful suggestion for making a schedule? **LIFE SKILL**
    a. Be realistic.
    b. Make time to relax.
    c. Order your activities randomly.
    d. Prepare for problems.

12. **CRITICAL THINKING** Use the tips you learned in the chapter to make a schedule for yourself for today.

Section 3

13. Describe how loss can cause stress.

14. List the stages of the grieving process.

15. Describe three ceremonies that honor a loved one who has passed away.

16. Describe why you should not blame others for a loss if the loss was an accident. **LIFE SKILL**

Section 4

17. Explain why it is important to know the facts about suicide.

18. Which of the following does *not* describe a behavior that can lead teens to react quickly on thoughts of suicide?
    a. impulsive
    c. silent
    b. highly emotional
    d. focused on today

19. Explain why giving away personal things might be a sign of someone considering suicide.

20. Explain why it is important not to ignore a friend's talk about suicide. **LIFE SKILL**

Interpreting Graphics

Study the figure below to answer the questions that follow.

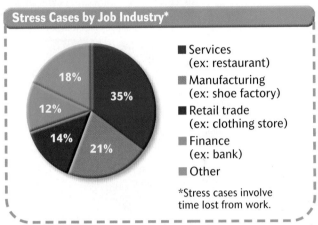

Stress Cases by Job Industry*

- 18%
- 35%
- 12%
- 14%
- 21%

■ Services
  (ex: restaurant)
■ Manufacturing
  (ex: shoe factory)
■ Retail trade
  (ex: clothing store)
■ Finance
  (ex: bank)
■ Other

*Stress cases involve time lost from work.

Source: U.S. Department of Labor Bureau of Statistics.

21. Which job industry accounts for the highest percent of stress cases?

22. What is the total percent of stress cases for the services and manufacturing job industries?

23. CRITICAL THINKING What types of stress cases do you think workers experience in the job industries listed?

Activities

24. Health and You Using the time management skills you learned in this chapter, develop a schedule for the next 7 days.

25. Health and Your Community Research and write a two-page report on the ways that people in the United States cope with loss. **WRITING SKILL**

26. Health and You Describe the grieving process as it relates to a loss you have experienced or a loss you could have experienced.

27. Health and Your Community Create a list of family members and friends you can turn to for help if you or a person you know is considering suicide.

Action Plan

28. LIFE SKILL Practicing Wellness Use the stress management techniques—taking care of yourself, building resiliency, changing your attitude, and managing your time—to create a stress management program. Follow the program for 1 week. Keep track of your stress management activities and how these activities affect your stress level.

Standardized Test Prep

Read the passage below, and then answer the questions that follow. **READING SKILL WRITING SKILL**

> As Cindy hung up the phone, she thought about Hallie's comments. Cindy didn't understand why Hallie was so <u>adamant</u> about not going to her sister's funeral. Cindy tried to talk Hallie into going to the funeral. She told Hallie that the funeral might be uncomfortable but that she would be happy later if she went. However, Hallie's last words to Cindy were "I love my sister, but I hate funerals. My parents will be so angry with me, but I just can't imagine sitting through a funeral." Cindy sat in silence, thinking. She wanted to help and comfort her friend, but didn't know how.

29. In this passage, the word *adamant* means
  A negative.
  B not clear.
  C not giving in.
  D hopeful.

30. What can you infer from reading this passage?
  E Hallie is sad and confused.
  F Cindy will be going to the funeral.
  G Cindy's sister died.
  H all of the above

31. Write a paragraph that describes ways that Cindy could help Hallie with her loss.

32. Write a paragraph that describes why it may help Hallie through the grieving process if she goes to her sister's funeral.

Preventing Violence and Abuse

What's Your Health IQ?
BEHAVIOR

Indicate how frequently you engage in each of the following behaviors (1 = never; 2 = occasionally; 3 = most of the time; 4 = all of the time). Total your points, and then turn to p. 638.

1. I calm down before telling someone that what he or she said or did upset me.

2. I respect others even if they are different from me.

3. I don't pick on or tease others.

4. I don't carry weapons.

5. I don't solve arguments with fights.

6. I am assertive and communicate directly and respectfully, not aggressively.

SECTION 1
Conflict Resolution and Violence Prevention

SECTION 2
Recognizing and Preventing Abuse

SECTION 3
Sexual Abuse and Violence

Visit these Web sites for the latest health information:

 HEALTH LINKS THE WORLD'S A CLICK AWAY

Find more information whenever you see a HealthLinks box. Go to **scilinks.org/health**, and type in the HealthLinks code.

 go. hrw .com

Find worksheets and other materials that go with your textbook at **go.hrw.com**.

Current Health

Check out *Current Health* articles related to this chapter by visiting **go.hrw.com**. Just type in the keyword **HH4 CH05**.

101

Conflict Resolution and Violence Prevention

OBJECTIVES

Describe how people are affected by the violence around us.

Identify five factors that lead to conflict between teens.

Describe three ways to resolve a conflict without violence.

State four ways you can avoid dangerous situations. **LIFE SKILL**

Develop a personal plan of how to handle a situation in which you or a friend is bullied. **LIFE SKILL**

<table>
<tr><td>KEY TERMS</td></tr>
</table>

violence physical force that is used to harm people or damage property

tolerance the ability to overlook differences and accept people for who they are

bullying scaring or controlling another person by using threats or physical force

negotiation a bargain or compromise for a peaceful solution to a conflict

peer mediation a technique in which a trained outsider who is your age helps people in a conflict come to a peaceful resolution

From the games we play to the music we listen to and the movies we see, violence is all around us.

When Milos first moved to his new town, older kids made fun of the way he dressed and how he talked. He was beaten up three times in the first month. He eventually joined a gang for protection. Now, he's pushing others around.

Violence Around Us

Violence is any physical force that is used to harm people or damage property. Unfortunately, violence has started to become a way of life in our society. We see it on TV, in the movies, in the newspaper, in video games, in our schools, and even in our own homes. We are literally surrounded by violence. Many have come to think about violence as no big deal. We see violence not only as a quick solution to a problem, but also as entertainment such as in many action movies.

Some people think that if they don't actually get injured, violence doesn't affect them. This is not true. Seeing and experiencing violence can often make a person insensitive to others who might be in trouble. For example, kids who frequently observe teasing might consider the behavior as normal. When teasing becomes common, it is easier to be *apathetic*, or unconcerned, of others who have been hurt.

Observing and experiencing violence can also make a person more violent towards others. For example, Milos was beaten up when he moved to his town. Now he beats other kids.

Being hardened and becoming violent are responses to experiencing and seeing violence. These responses to violence don't make anyone safer. On the contrary, the responses escalate violence and make society unsafe and helpless to stop the violence.

Factors That Lead to Conflicts Between Teens

A *conflict* is another name for a fight or a disagreement. A conflict can be small, like a disagreement over how to play a game. A conflict can also be large, like the tensions between two countries.

Some people wrongly choose violence to resolve a conflict. Violence does not solve a problem, it makes the problem worse. Violence can lead to injury and even death. Often, violence provokes further violence in the form of revenge. Understanding the factors that can lead to conflict can help prevent conflicts from getting out of control.

Feeling Threatened The stress from being threatened can often lead to violence. Milos's situation is a good example. He reacted to threats and violence against him with more violence. Violence is never a good solution to a problem. Violence only makes the problem bigger. Bringing a gun or a weapon to school will not protect you. It will put you and others in greater danger.

Unmanaged Anger Unmanaged anger can also contribute to conflict. Being *fatigued*, or very tired, or living in an over-crowded area can cause a person to be more irritable and act out with anger. However, it is important to deal with anger effectively. If you feel you have problems managing your anger, ask your parents or a trusted adult where you can get help. Remember that only you are responsible for how you express your anger.

Lack of Respect Being disrespectful to others can lead to conflict. For example, picking on someone, or destroying one of his or her belongings is one form of disrespect. Having negative opinions about people because of their race, their ethnicity, their gender, their religion, or the way they dress are other ways of being disrespectful.

 TOPIC link For more information about managing anger, see Chapter 3.

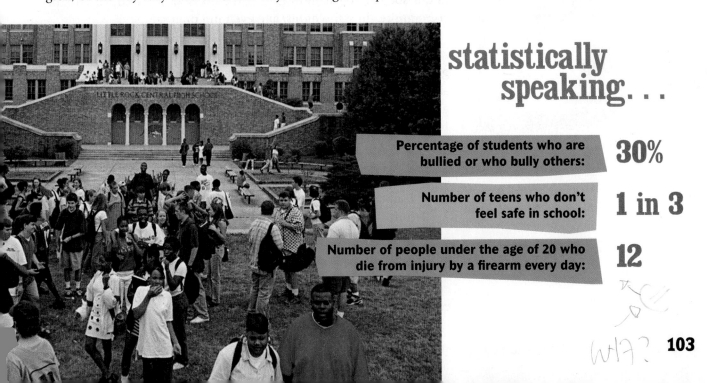

statistically speaking...

Percentage of students who are bullied or who bully others:	**30%**
Number of teens who don't feel safe in school:	**1 in 3**
Number of people under the age of 20 who die from injury by a firearm every day:	**12**

Bullies threaten, hassle, or intimidate smaller or weaker people.

A violent act against someone just because he or she is different in race, religion, culture, or ethnic group, is called a *hate crime*. Many forms of violence could be stopped if people were more tolerant. **Tolerance** is the ability to overlook differences and accept people for who they are.

Bullying   Scaring or controlling another person by using threats or physical force is called **bullying.** Bullies can use physical force, such as hitting, kicking, or damaging one's property. Bullies can also use words to hurt or humiliate another person by name-calling, insulting, making racist comments, taunting, or teasing.

Bullies can be manipulative in less obvious ways, such as by spreading nasty rumors. Bullies often form *cliques*. A clique is a close peer group that includes certain people and excludes others.

The following list provides suggestions on how to prevent bullying or being bullied.

▶ Be tolerant of others. Encourage your friends to respect others.
▶ If you see someone being bullied, tell a trusted adult.
▶ Don't be embarrassed to ask for help from friends, teachers, or parents. Bullies won't pick on you if they can't get away with it.
▶ Be assertive, not aggressive. Bullies like to pick on those they think are weak, but responding aggressively to a bully may make the situation worse.
▶ Avoid bullies or any people who are disrespectful or threatening.
▶ Respect yourself. No matter what bullies may say to you, stand by what you believe and be proud of who you are.

Gangs   Gangs often cause conflict and violence. A *gang* is a group of peers who claim a territory. Most gangs have a leader and use recognizable symbols or tattoos. Often gangs commit acts of vandalism and carry weapons. They often use drugs, and alcohol, which can play a role in many dangerous situations. Gangs are destructive to the community, the people who live in it, and themselves.

People join gangs for many reasons. Gangs may make people feel as if they fit in or make them feel safe, or powerful. Some people join gangs for excitement, recognition, or what they think is respect. TV shows and movies often make gangs seem glamorous and may make a person want to join a gang. A gang can provide a lonely person with friendship. Teens may join gangs because their family members are in the gang. Regardless of the reason, joining a gang is a bad idea.

There are many other choices besides joining a gang. You do not have to support or take part in violence. The following are other ways to find support and your own place in your community.

▶ join a sports team or school club
▶ volunteer with your neighborhood watch group
▶ coach a sports team for younger kids

There is no excuse for joining a gang. If you feel unsafe in your community, work with community leaders to fight for improvements.

Avoiding Dangerous Situations

To avoid dangerous situations, you should not only stay clear of potentially violent people, but also avoid situations where you might cause conflict or violence. For example, don't join gangs and don't carry weapons. **Figure 1** shows some other ways to avoid conflicts.

Some dangerous situations happen unexpectedly. You may find yourself in a conflict that starts to get out of control and could lead to violence. Follow these steps to avoid dangerous situations.

1. **Recognize the signs.** Part of avoiding dangerous situations is being able to recognize when a situation is getting out of control. People who are beginning to lose control of their anger will show it in the tone and volume of their voice. Nonverbal signs of anger can also appear in body language. For example, clenching one's fists or teeth, getting red in the face, or narrowing one's eyes are signs that anger is getting out of control. Also, look for these signs in yourself.

2. **Calm things down.** If you see signs that a situation might end in conflict, there are things you can do to calm down the situation and avoid a conflict. Always be respectful to the other person. If someone says something that makes you upset, take a deep breath and count to 10 before responding. Use the tips for managing anger and using "I" messages you learned in Building Self-Esteem and Mental Health.

3. **Leave the situation.** If things look like they might get out of control, you can arrange to discuss the matter later when you both cool down. If you no longer feel as if you have control of the situation or of your own anger, you should leave immediately.

4. **Offer alternatives.** Even if someone insists that you fight, you don't have to. Firmly say that you will not fight. You can offer alternatives to a physical battle, such as a basketball contest. You can make an excuse for why you need to leave. Act like the other person is making a big deal over something small. The important thing is to get yourself and others out of danger.

Everyone deserves to feel safe. People should not be so worried about their safety that they are afraid to go to school or take part in their favorite activities. Every teen should feel confident that there are adults and authorities that are committed to protecting him or her. If you feel unsafe and don't know what to do about a situation, these adults and authorities can be your best defense. If someone tells you that he or she is planning a violent act, tell a responsible adult. Even if you believe the person is joking, it is important for your safety and the safety of others that you tell a responsible adult.

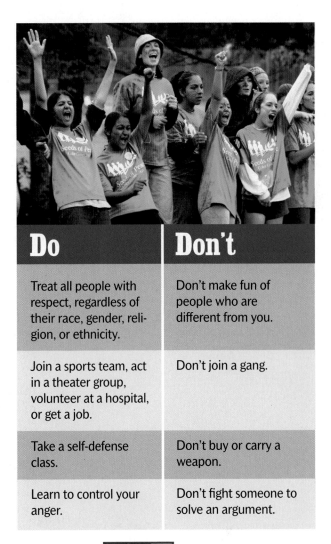

Do	Don't
Treat all people with respect, regardless of their race, gender, religion, or ethnicity.	Don't make fun of people who are different from you.
Join a sports team, act in a theater group, volunteer at a hospital, or get a job.	Don't join a gang.
Take a self-defense class.	Don't buy or carry a weapon.
Learn to control your anger.	Don't fight someone to solve an argument.

Figure 1

These teens from Pakistan, India, the Middle East, and the Balkans respect and support each other as teammates in a soccer game. As indicated in the figure above, showing respect to others who are different from you is one important way to avoid conflict.

Resolving Conflict Without Violence

Let's say you have followed all the steps to avoid dangerous situations yet find yourself in a serious conflict. There are ways to resolve conflicts effectively without using violence, but they require work. It's not easy to work out a problem with someone who has made your blood boil. It's hard to be respectful to someone who hasn't been respectful to you. That's why resolving a conflict nonviolently takes more courage and strength than using violence does.

TOPIC link For more information about communicating effectively, see Chapter 3.

Conflict Resolution Skills   *Conflict resolution* is a nonviolent way to deal with arguments. All people involved in the conflict sit down together and express their points of view. Everyone works together to find a solution acceptable to all parties involved. A common and successful approach is through negotiation. A **negotiation** is a bargain or compromise for a peaceful solution to a conflict.

Being able to successfully negotiate a conflict depends on your communication skills. Here are some tips for communicating effectively to resolve conflicts.

- ▶ Be respectful, yet be assertive.
- ▶ Use the steps of the Making GREAT Decisions model.
- ▶ Don't call each other names or raise your voice.
- ▶ Allow the other person time to speak.
- ▶ Don't make assumptions.
- ▶ Focus on the real issue.
- ▶ Be open to change and look for shared interests.
- ▶ Use "I" messages, not "you" messages.
- ▶ Use listening skills and try to understand what the other person wants.

If negotiating a conflict on your own isn't working, don't give up. You can also try *peer mediation*. **Peer mediation** is a technique in which a trained outsider who is your age helps people in a conflict come to a peaceful resolution.

Peer mediators help people involved in a conflict work out the problem in a nonviolent way.

Peer Mediation Having nonbiased outsiders organize a negotiation for you can be a big help in resolving conflicts. Peer mediators are trained to keep discussions fair. They make sure each person has a chance to speak, and they make sure the discussion focuses on the real issue.

Many schools provide peer mediation services. If students in the school want help solving a conflict, they usually fill out a form describing the problem and submit the form to the mediation program. Sometimes, mediation referrals come from third parties, such as students or teachers who know trouble is brewing between two people.

In peer mediation, each student tells his or her side of the conflict. Students get a chance to vent their feelings and talk to each other if they want to. They can ask questions and clarify facts. The parties brainstorm solutions. Usually, at least two mediators keep track of the solutions that are discussed. However, the mediators don't make suggestions unless they are asked. Their job is to ensure that everyone has a voice to guide the group toward a solution and to make sure things are worked out "fair and square."

Eventually, the arguing students agree to one of the suggestions on their brainstorming list that they created. Both parties sign a contract agreeing to the solution. The peer mediators follow up by checking to see if both sides are following the agreement.

With peer mediation, both parties in a conflict are guaranteed to work out the problem in a safe, nonviolent way. A lot of students like peer mediation because it is run by students. Adults only supervise. Is there a peer mediation program in your school? If not, you may want to talk to a teacher or principal about starting one.

MAKING GREAT DECISIONS

Max and Ryan have been friends since kindergarten. Now they are in high school together. One day, Max and Ryan are talking in the cafeteria. Ryan starts telling Max about some kids who have been bullying him after school. Ryan swears Max to secrecy, unzips his bag, and shows Max a gun. Max asks Ryan why he needs a gun. Ryan says, "Just in case."

Write on a separate piece of paper what you would do if you were in Max's situation. Remember to use the decision-making steps.

G ive thought to the problem.
R eview your choices.
E valuate the consequences of each choice.
A ssess and choose the best choice.
T hink it over afterward.

SECTION 1

REVIEW
Answer the following questions on a separate piece of paper.

Using Key Terms

1. **Identify** the term for "the ability to overlook differences and accept people for who they are."
2. **Define** the term *bullying*.
3. **Identify** the term for "a bargain or compromise for a peaceful solution to a conflict."

Understanding Key Ideas

4. **Describe** how violence affects us.
5. **State** five factors that can lead to conflict.

6. **Identify** which of the following is *not* a skill for successfully resolving conflict.
   a. negotiation   **c.** bullying
   b. peer mediation   **d.** compromise
7. **Describe** why peer mediation has been successful in high schools.
8. **LIFE SKILL** **Practicing Wellness** List four ways you can avoid dangerous situations.

Critical Thinking

9. **LIFE SKILL** **Coping** Develop a plan on how to handle a situation in which you are being bullied.

Recognizing and Preventing Abuse

OBJECTIVES

Identify abusive behavior.

Describe four types of abuse.

Summarize the effects of abuse.

Identify help that is available for those in abusive relationships.

List actions you can take to protect yourself from abuse.

LIFE SKILL

KEY TERMS

abuse physical or emotional harm to someone

neglect the failure of a caretaker to provide for basic needs, such as food, clothing, or love

domestic violence the use of force to control and maintain power over a spouse in the home

hazing harassing newcomers to a group in an abusive and humiliating way

Often, people who are abused are abused by someone they should be able to trust.

T ad was watching TV when he heard screaming from the apartment next door. His neighbors were fighting again, but this time the fight sounded really bad. He could hear furniture being thrown and something breaking. One of the voices sounded very frightened.

What Is Abuse?

Abuse is physical or emotional harm to someone. Abuse can take place anywhere, including at school, on the street, or at home. Unfortunately, the most common forms of abuse come from people one should be able to trust, such as family members, friends, boyfriends, or girlfriends. For this reason, people who are being abused don't feel as if they can leave the abuser or demand to be treated respectfully. However, it is necessary for them to do so. Many forms of abuse are illegal. No one should have to tolerate abuse.

It is difficult to imagine what would make someone inflict harm on a loved one, such as a child, a spouse, a girlfriend, a boyfriend, a peer, or an elderly parent. You may be surprised to find out that the abuser is often someone who was once abused himself or herself. If people grow up in a family in which they were abused, they learn that abusive behavior is the normal response to tension or conflict.

Abusive Behavior Learning to recognize inconsiderate and disrespectful behavior will help you avoid abusive people. For example, an abusive relationship may exist if a person is controlling, obsessive, manipulative, selfish, aggressive, or needy. An abusive person may get jealous easily, have difficulty controlling anger, or demand that the other person not see certain people or wear certain clothes. An abuser will often insult, humiliate, or put down others. Abusers often use *coercion*, which is force or threats. If you know of someone who has been abusive to others, chances are that he or she could be abusive to you, too.

Types of Abuse

There are many types of abuse. The following is a description of the most common types of abuse.

Child Abuse As many as 3 million cases of child abuse are reported every year in the United States. Many more cases never get reported. Children are frequent targets of abuse because they are young and can't or don't know how to respond appropriately. Sometimes one sibling will abuse another. Child abuse is usually categorized in four different ways: physical abuse, emotional abuse, sexual abuse, and neglect. **Neglect** occurs when a caretaker fails to provide basic needs, such as food, clothing, or love.

Domestic Violence The use of force to control and maintain power over a spouse in the home is called **domestic violence.** A former spouse, a fiancé, a boyfriend, or a girlfriend can also commit domestic violence. Women can abuse their male partners, but women are much more likely to be the victims of domestic violence. It is estimated that an act of domestic violence occurs somewhere in the United States every 15 seconds.

Often an abusive relationship goes through a cycle of three stages, as shown in **Figure 2.**

1. **Tension-building phase** A time of emotional abuse such as insults or threats.
2. **Violent episode phase** An act of physical abuse occurs such as choking or hitting.
3. **Honeymoon phase** The time when the couple makes up. This phase is often the reason people stay in abusive relationships.

internet connect

www.scilinks.org/health
Topic: Abuse and Violence
HealthLinks code: HH4003

HEALTH LINKS. Maintained by the National Science Teachers Association

Figure 2

Violence in domestic relationships often cycles through three stages. The cycle will often repeat itself continuously, sometimes for years, until the partners get help or the relationship ends.

insults

arguments   accusations

Tension-Building Phase   threats

apologies

Honeymoon Phase

reconciliation

promises

pushing   hitting

Violent Episode Phase

choking

use of weapons

Elder Abuse   The elderly are often viewed as the wisest people in the community. Unfortunately, elderly people are not always treated with respect by all people. Because elderly people are often frail, they can be easily taken advantage of. For example, people will sometimes steal from them. They may be neglected in nursing homes or in their own homes. Elder abuse can also take the form of physical abuse and emotional abuse.

Hazing   Harassing newcomers to a group in an abusive and humiliating way is called **hazing.** Hazing may happen when people join sports teams, gangs, fraternities, or sororities. The idea behind hazing is that it proves you are truly committed to joining the group. However, hazing is unacceptable. When people are beaten up, sexually taken advantage of, or humiliated, hazing becomes abusive and illegal.

It's important to be able to recognize abusive behavior. Abusive behavior can then be reported to stop the immediate violence and to prevent future violent acts.

Effects of Abuse

After reading about some of the types of abuse, you can imagine that abuse may have an impact on a person's life in more ways than one. If a person is physically harmed, he or she might have obvious physical injuries that need to be tended to. However, the effects of abuse are not merely physical. Abuse affects all parts of a person's health.

Take Rosa, for example. Rosa was hazed during her tryouts for the swim team. She really wanted to make the team, so she went through the process. In addition to the bruises from the paddling, she feels so humiliated and depressed at what the team members made her do. She doesn't think she can ever tell anyone. Now it's all she thinks about—night and day. She feels isolated. How can she turn around and be friends with people who abused her?

The effects of hazing are similar to the effects of other forms of abuse. Some examples of the effects of abuse are as follows:

▶ depression

▶ low self-esteem

▶ poor appetite or overeating

▶ low energy or fatigue

▶ poor concentration and difficulty making decisions

▶ difficulty sleeping

▶ feelings of worthlessness

▶ feelings of guilt, shame, and anxiety

An abused person might lose his or her ability to trust or might develop relationship difficulties. Victims of abuse may turn to alcohol or drugs. Some victims may develop an eating disorder. Others may contemplate suicide or may start to suffer from post-traumatic stress disorder, anxiety disorder, or panic attacks.

Protecting Yourself from Abuse

If anyone abuses you, tell your parents, the police, or other trusted adult. Tell the abuser you will let an authority know about his or her behavior. Many forms of abuse, such as physical and sexual abuse, are illegal. Often, the abuser will stop if you threaten to tell because he or she will be afraid of getting into trouble.

Create a Supportive Network of Friends and Family   Make sure there are people you can trust and talk to openly. If abuse does occur, you want people to whom you can turn for help. The more positive relationships you have in your life, the more options you will have in case of abuse.

Avoid Disrespectful People   If you know of someone who has been abusive to you or to others, you should stay away from that person. Whenever possible, don't go somewhere if you know that person will be there. Leave where you are if that person arrives. Choose friends who treat you and others with respect. Choose friends who make you feel good about yourself. If you let people know that you respect yourself and expect respect from others, chances are that they will treat you with respect.

Be Assertive   Abusers frequently prey on people who appear vulnerable or who have low self-esteem. Assertive people set down boundaries that let others know they will not accept hurtful behavior. Being assertive toward an abuser will make it difficult for him or her to abuse you. However, if you act passively toward an abuser, that person will think he or she can abuse you again and again. If you act aggressively, depending on who the abuser is, that person may become angrier and make the abuse worse. Using assertiveness skills can help you protect yourself from abuse. **Figure 3** has examples of assertive statements.

Figure 3

Assertive statements respectfully tell the other person how you feel.

ACTIVITY   *If a boyfriend or girlfriend is wrongfully accusing you of cheating on him or her, how would you respond assertively?*

Assertive Statements

"I don't like it when you tell me to whom I can and cannot talk.**"**

"You scare me when you yell like that.**"**

"It hurts when you criticize me and put me down, especially in front of other people.**"**

"I don't want to be around you when you drink or get angry.**"**

HEALTH Handbook For more information about practicing refusal skills, see the Express Lesson on p. 618 of this text.

Show Disapproval If a person does not treat you in an acceptable way, show your disapproval. Showing disapproval lets the abuser know that his or her behavior is not acceptable, that you won't tolerate it, and that you want it to stop.

There are many ways you can show disapproval. One subtle way is to refuse to laugh at an offensive joke. One active way is to yell for help. Earlier you learned about body language, tone of voice, and other means of communication. Use this knowledge to stand up for yourself and to let others know that their behavior is unacceptable. Because you know it is important to behave and speak politely, it can be hard to show disapproval. However, showing disapproval is a necessary part of stopping abuse.

It's important to know that the abuser probably won't stop abusing on his or her own. You may have to tell an abuser more than once that you will not tolerate the hurtful behavior. The refusal skills you learned earlier can be a big help in saying no to abuse. However, it is also important to tell your parents or other trusted adult about the abuse.

LIFE SKILL Activity

Communicating Effectively

Stopping Abuse Before It Starts

Can you think of any situations in which you might need to be assertive or show disapproval? Practicing skills such as showing disapproval and being assertive will help you use these skills confidently.

1. Choose a partner to practice your assertiveness and disapproval skills with.

2. Think of a potentially abusive situation in which you and your partner would like to use assertiveness and disapproval skills.

3. Write down possible things a disrespectful person might say.

4. Write down ways to show disapproval or to be assertive toward the disrespectful person.

5. Now role-play your responses. Decide which partner will be the disrespectful person and which partner will be the victim.

6. After you have gone through all the possible responses, switch roles. If you come up with more responses while role-playing, go ahead and try them. Remember to be assertive, not aggressive.

LIFE SKILL Practicing Wellness Did you find your responses effective as you role-played them? Compare how it felt to take the role of the abusive person to how it felt to take the role of the assertive person.

Help for The Abused

Not only is abuse a crime, but *no one* should allow abuse to occur. Something can be done to stop the abuse.

Tell Someone If you are currently being abused in any way, tell your parents, coach, school administrators, school counselor, or any other trusted adult. The police also have information about shelters and other agencies that help victims of abuse.

Go Somewhere Safe If you are in immediate danger, leave the situation and go somewhere safe—a friend's or relative's house, the police station, a religious institution, a hospital, a school, or any supervised place where you will be out of harm. Do not think about running away. Running away is not a safe way to escape abuse at home. Runaways almost always find themselves in situations that are worse than the one they left.

Consider Counseling Abuse leaves mental and emotional scars that last long after the victim is safe. Counselors and other mental health professionals can help victims of abuse deal with low self-esteem, depression, shame, and guilt. Many times, the family of the victim takes part in the therapy, too.

Victims are not the only ones who need help—abusers also need to get help. Abusers need help to realize that their behavior is hurtful, illegal, and unacceptable. There are programs available to help abusers change their behavior.

Family counseling can help family members deal with the long-term effects of abuse and can also stop future acts of abuse.

SECTION 2

REVIEW *Answer the following questions on a separate piece of paper.*

Using Key Terms

1. **Define** the term *neglect*.

2. **Identify** the term for "harassing newcomers to a group in an abusive and humiliating way."

Understanding Key Ideas

3. **List** five examples of inconsiderate and disrespectful behavior abusive people do.

4. **Identify** the form of abuse that occurs between a husband and wife or between a boyfriend and girlfriend.
    - **a.** child abuse
    - **b.** elder abuse
    - **c.** domestic violence
    - **d.** hazing

5. **List** the three phases of the cycle of violence.

6. **Describe** why children and the elderly are especially vulnerable to abuse.

7. **Describe** the effects of abuse.

8. **LIFE SKILL** **Coping** List people you can go to for help if you or someone you know has been abused.

9. **LIFE SKILL** **Practicing Wellness** Describe actions you can take to prevent and avoid abuse.

Critical Thinking

10. Why do you think abused children often have trouble making friends?

Sexual Abuse and Violence

OBJECTIVES

Define sexual abuse.

Describe sexual harassment.

Describe facts about sexual assault and rape.

Name five things a person should do if he or she has been sexually assaulted.

List three ways you can protect yourself from sexual abuse and violence. **LIFE SKILL**

KEY TERMS

sexual abuse any sexual act without consent

incest sexual activity between family members who are not husband and wife

sexual harassment any unwanted remark, behavior, or touch that has sexual content

sexual assault any sexual activity in which force or the threat of force is used

date rape sexual intercourse that is forced on a victim by someone the victim knows

Boys as well as girls are victims of sexual abuse.

Alex was excited when he got his first job at the ice-cream stand. But, now he hates to go to work. His boss sometimes touches him in places he doesn't want to be touched. Tonight, he is really worried. He has to close up the stand alone with the boss.

Sexual Abuse

Sexual abuse is any sexual act without consent. Any act in which a person touches you in a sexual way that makes you feel uncomfortable is an act of sexual abuse. The acts can range from kissing and fondling to forced intercourse. For example, it is considered sexual abuse if the abuser touches the victim in a sexual way or if the victim is forced to touch the abuser in a sexual way. It is also considered sexual abuse if either the victim or abuser is indecently exposed or if the victim is shown pornography.

Children and Sexual Abuse Sexual activity between family members who are not husband and wife is known as **incest.** Incest traumatizes a child not only physically but also emotionally. Because the child is being abused by someone he or she knows and trusts, the child may find it difficult to tell when he or she is being abused.

Another reason children find it hard to admit that they are being sexually abused is that the abuse tends to begin "innocently" with affectionate hugs and kisses. The abuser may manipulate the child into feeling special. The behavior progresses to caresses and sexual teasing and then to sexual activity. Because the behavior started in an innocent fashion, children feel as if they did something to encourage the abuse. They then feel too ashamed to tell someone. However, if no one finds out, the abuse can continue.

Anyone being sexually abused should tell a trusted adult. All forms of sexual abuse are illegal and should be reported to the police.

Sexual Harassment

Every time James sees Tiffany, he has something to say about how she looks. The way he looks up and down her body makes her feel so uncomfortable. She has started wearing baggy clothes. She has even started walking to school the long way just so she doesn't bump into him.

Matt went out with Lydia. The date turned into a bad evening. She kept pressuring him to have sex. He said no many times. Then, she accused him of not liking girls. She became angry and left early. At school today, she avoided him. He saw her whispering to her friends and looking at him from across the room. Matt felt so embarrassed. He couldn't wait for the bell to ring so that he could leave.

The two situations above are examples of sexual harassment. **Sexual harassment** is any unwanted remark, behavior, or touch that has sexual content. Can you identify the harassing behaviors? If the behavior makes your school, home, or work environment intimidating, hostile, or offensive, the behavior is sexual harassment. In the cases of Tiffany and Matt, the harassers were making the school environment uncomfortable.

When people are confronted about sexual harassment, they will often say they were only flirting. How do you feel when someone flirts with you? You might feel flattered, respected, and attractive. But, Tiffany and Matt felt uncomfortable, cornered, and ashamed. Do you see the difference? Whatever intention you may have, if someone tells you that he or she doesn't like your behavior, you are not flirting. If you are unsure how someone feels about your flirting, you can always ask.

Power and Sexual Harassment Sexual harassment is most dangerous when the harasser holds a position of power, such as a doctor, teacher, boss, or older friend of the family. In such a case, the victim is often afraid to complain about the behavior. He or she doesn't want to risk his or her health, get a bad grade, lose a job, or embarass the family. Victims may even get direct messages, such as "If you have sex with me, I'll give you a raise."

Responding to Sexual Harassment If you are being sexually harassed, there are things you can do to stop the harassment.

1. **Tell the harasser to stop.** The harasser might not know that he or she is making you feel uncomfortable. If you never say anything, he or she will never know that you disapprove of the behavior.

2. **Report the harassment.** If the harassing continues after you told the person to stop, avoid the person and complain about the harassment to a higher authority. The higher authority might be a parent, guidance counselor, principal, or owner of a business. Sexual harassment is illegal. Most schools and businesses have rules prohibiting sexual harassment. Use those rules and government laws to stop the behavior.

Examples of Sexual Harassment

▶ **Telling unwanted sexual stories or jokes**

▶ **Making sexual remarks about a person's clothing and the way it fits on the person's body**

▶ **Staring at a person's body or body parts**

▶ **Continuously asking a person out or sending gifts, e-mails, or love notes after he or she asked you to stop**

▶ **Touching, patting, or pinching a person in a sexual way**

▶ **Standing too close to or brushing up against a person's body**

▶ **Making sexual gestures**

▶ **Offering the person something he or she needs in return for sex**

Sexual Assault and Rape

Sexual assault is any sexual activity in which force or the threat of force is used. Sexual assault can range from forced kissing to pulling off clothes and grabbing body parts. Forced sexual intercourse, or *rape*, is an extreme form of sexual assault.

Some people think that sexual assault and rape are committed by strangers. The truth is that about 80 percent of victims of sexual assault and rape know their attacker. **Date rape**, also referred to as acquaintance rape, is sexual intercourse that is forced on a victim by someone the victim knows. The rapist uses the trust that he or she has developed with the victim to take advantage of the victim. Rape can also happen between married couples. This is a form of domestic violence. Some people believe that rape occurs because the attacker wants sexual intercourse. However, the real reason that people rape is to gain power and control.

Using alcohol and drugs as well as being around people who use alcohol and drugs can put you in a dangerous situation. About 45 percent of rapists were under the influence of alcohol when they raped somebody. Also, rapists sometimes give alcohol and drugs to victims so that they will be more vulnerable. Rapists have also been known to slip drugs into the victim's drink. These drugs are commonly known as *date-rape drugs*. The drugs cause the victim to lose consciousness. In some cases, date-rape drugs can be fatal.

Effects of Sexual Assault and Rape   Like victims of other types of violence, victims of rape and sexual assault suffer both physical and emotional trauma. Survivors may experience injuries such as bruises, cuts, and broken bones. They may also be exposed to pregnancy and sexually transmitted diseases (STDs). Victims may feel guilt and shame about the assault. They may have trouble sleeping or eating. They may even suffer from post-traumatic stress disorder.

Rape and sexual assault are not only morally wrong, they are illegal. Depending on the state, the sentences for a conviction of sexual assault or rape range from fines and community service to years in prison.

Beliefs Vs. Reality

"Only young, beautiful people are raped."	People of all ages are victims of rape.
"Men and boys are never raped."	One out of 10 victims of rape is male.
"People who wear sexy clothes are asking to be raped."	It doesn't matter what a victim wears. No one asks to be raped.
"Rape is an act of sexual frustration."	Rape is an act of power and control.
"Most rapes are committed by someone unknown to the victim."	Most rapes are committed by a person known to the victim.

Protecting Yourself from Sexual Abuse and Violence

There are many things you can do to decrease your risk of sexual abuse and violence. The following are some suggestions.

At Home   You can keep your house safe by making sure all the windows and doors are locked. Don't open the door to strangers. Don't hide a spare key in an obvious place.

Know your neighbors, and make sure your neighbors know you. If everyone knows each other, then people can be on the lookout for strangers in the community.

If you are home alone, make sure you have the phone number where your parents or guardians will be if you need to call them. Do not tell callers that you are home alone. Keep other emergency numbers readily available.

On the Street   The first rule of preventing abuse on the street is don't go out alone, especially at night. Be alert. Walk purposefully, and act as if you know where you are going. If you look lost, you will appear vulnerable. Always make sure you have enough money to make a phone call if you feel threatened. If you do feel threatened, yell and run into a store or other public place.

By People You Know   Most of the sexual violence that occurs comes from someone the victim knows. Preventing sexual abuse and violence from people we know is a little different from preventing it from people we don't know. The people we know don't have to sneak up next to us on the street. Chances are that we let them into our house or are walking with them on the street.

Know signs of abusive people, and don't get involved with those people. Be careful about people you meet on the internet, especially if they discuss or show pornography. Do not agree to meet them in person. Avoid people who are hostile or disrespectful. Rapists are often motivated to make the person feel powerless, degraded, dirty, and ashamed. If someone you know makes you nervous or makes offensive jokes or comments, tell him or her you don't like the behavior and also tell a parent or other trusted adult.

No one, not your friends, your family members, or your boyfriend or girlfriend, has a right to sexually abuse you. Use the communication skills, refusal skills, and decision-making skills you have learned to protect yourself. Use body language and voice tone, volume, and pitch to discourage a sexual offender. Say no clearly and loudly over and over again. Make it clear that you think that the person's behavior is inappropriate.

If you are being attacked, call out for help. Call as much attention to the situation as you can. Break things. Do whatever you can to protect yourself.

Protecting Yourself from Date Rape

▶ **When going on a date, know who the person is, where you are going, and what you will be doing. Make sure friends and family know this information too.**

▶ **Don't be alone with your date. Go on dates in public places.**

▶ **Go on double dates or group dates.**

▶ **Do not accept drugs or alcohol.**

▶ **Do not allow anyone to have an opportunity to put drugs in your beverage.**

▶ **Be wary of meeting anyone on the Internet.**

▶ **Know where a phone is at all times.**

▶ **Set limits, and communicate these limits clearly and firmly ahead of time.**

Help After a Sexual Assault

If you have been raped or assaulted, there are several things you should do.

1. Make sure you are away from further harm.

2. Call for help. You can call your family, the police, a neighbor, a friend, or any other trusted adult.

3. Don't change anything about your body or your environment. Don't shower or go to the bathroom. Don't change your clothes or wash or comb your hair. Don't clean up the place where you are. There might be evidence that can be collected by the police or at a hospital. You can cover yourself with a blanket to feel more comfortable.

4. Ask someone to take you to the hospital.

5. Seek therapy or counseling. Remember, abusers want to make the victim feel ashamed and humiliated. Counselors can help reassure victims that they are not to blame for the assault.

Sometimes, people who are sexually assaulted just want to forget the whole incident and put it behind them. There are two problems with forgetting the assault. First, if you are in denial about the incident and don't seek medical care, then you can't get physical or emotional treatment from trained personnel.

The second problem is that if you don't report it, the abuser cannot be stopped. If you report the attack, you may be preventing another person from going through what you did. Many victims do not report crimes because they don't want to go through a trial. However, you can report an assault without prosecuting. This way, the incident is on record, so you can prosecute later. If you do not report the assault immediately and if you destroy any evidence, prosecuting later will be very difficult.

One of the first steps after a sexual assault is calling for help.

SECTION 3

REVIEW
Answer the following questions on a separate piece of paper.

Using Key Terms

1. **Define** the term *sexual harassment*.

2. **Identify** the term for "any sexual activity in which force or the threat of force is used."

Understanding Key Ideas

3. **Describe** sexual abuse.

4. **Describe** why victims of sexual abuse find it difficult to admit they are being abused.

5. **State** five examples of sexual harassment.

6. **Describe** three facts about sexual assault and rape.

7. **Identify** which of the following is *not* a way to protect yourself from date rape.
   a. double dating
   b. going out with people who drink
   c. going on dates in public places
   d. being assertive

8. **List** five things a person should do if he or she has been sexually assaulted.

Critical Thinking

9. **LIFE SKILL** **Practicing Wellness** Describe three ways you can protect yourself from sexual abuse and violence.

Highlights

Key Terms

The Big Picture

✔ Being exposed to violence can make people fearful, unsympathetic to others, and more likely to use violence themselves.

✔ Factors that lead to violence include feeling threatened, not managing anger, not showing respect for others, bullying, and gangs.

✔ You can avoid dangerous situations by recognizing signs, calming things down, leaving the situation, offering alternatives, avoiding gangs, and avoiding weapons.

✔ Conflict resolution skills, such as negotiation and peer mediation, are effective, nonviolent ways to deal with arguments.

✔ Being assertive and asking for help are two ways you can protect yourself from bullying.

✔ Being able to identify disrespectful and inconsiderate behavior such as selfishness, aggression, and excessive jealousy, will help you avoid abusive people.

✔ Four types of abuse are child abuse, domestic violence, elder abuse, and hazing.

✔ Besides causing physical injury, some effects of abuse are depression, low self-esteem, guilt, shame, anxiety, distrust, and difficulty developing relationships. Many who are abused turn to alcohol or drugs.

✔ Creating a supportive network, avoiding disrespectful people, being assertive, and showing disapproval will help you protect yourself from abuse.

✔ Victims of abuse should tell a trusted adult, go somewhere safe, and get counseling.

✔ Sexual abuse is any physical sexual act that happens without one's consent. It can cause physical and emotional trauma.

✔ Sexual harassment is unwanted sexual attention, such as telling offensive jokes, staring at someone's body, or touching people in sexual ways.

✔ Most rapes are committed by someone the victim knows.

✔ A few ways you can protect yourself from sexual abuse and violence are keeping your house locked up, not going out alone, and avoiding disrespectful people.

✔ If someone has been sexually assaulted, he or she should find safety, call for help, not clean up, report the incident to the police, and seek counseling.

Review

Using Key Terms

abuse (108)
bullying (104)
date rape (116)
domestic violence (109)
hazing (110)
incest (114)
neglect (109)

negotiation (106)
peer mediation (106)
sexual abuse (114)
sexual assault (116)
sexual harassment (115)
tolerance (104)
violence (102)

1. For each definition below, choose the key term that best matches the definition.
   a. a technique in which a trained outsider who is your age helps people in a conflict come to a peaceful resolution
   b. the ability to overlook differences and accept people for who they are
   c. the use of force to control and maintain power over a spouse in the home
   d. sexual activity between family members who are not husband and wife
   e. harassing newcomers to a group in an abusive and humiliating way
   f. sexual intercourse that is forced on a victim by someone the victim knows
   g. any unwanted remarks, behavior, or touch that has sexual content
   h. a bargain or compromise for a peaceful solution to a conflict
   i. any sexual activity that involves the use of force or the threat of force
   j. any sexual act without consent

2. Explain the relationship between the key terms in each of the following pairs.
   a. *bullying* and *violence*
   b. *neglect* and *abuse*

Understanding Key Ideas

Section 1

3. Explain how observing and experiencing violence can cause a person to become apathetic.

4. Which of the following does *not* contribute to conflict?
   a. gangs
   b. feeling threatened
   c. negotiating
   d. bullying

5. Explain how using tolerance can help prevent a conflict.

6. Why might someone join a gang?

7. List the 4 steps for avoiding a dangerous situation in a conflict that is getting out of control.

8. Describe three ways to communicate effectively to resolve conflict. **LIFE SKILL**

9. **CRITICAL THINKING** Create an action plan to help someone who is being bullied.

Section 2

10. Which is *not* a sign of inconsiderate or disrespectful behavior common in abusive people?
    a. manipulation
    b. aggression
    c. obsession
    d. empathy

11. Neglecting an older person is an example of _____ abuse.

12. Why are children frequently targets for abuse?

13. Which of the following is *not* an effect of abuse?
    a. eating disorder
    b. high self-esteem
    c. drug and alcohol abuse
    d. depression

14. Describe how you can show disapproval for inconsiderate and disrespectful behavior. **LIFE SKILL**

15. **CRITICAL THINKING** Create a list of trusted adults you could go to for help if you were being abused.

Section 3

16. Give an example of sexual abuse.

17 Explain effective ways of dealing with sexual harassment.

18. Explain how being around people who drink alcohol and use drugs can put you at risk for sexual assault.

19. Which of the following should you *not* do immediately after you have been sexually assaulted?
    a. call the police
    b. call a trusted adult
    c. get to safety
    d. take a shower

20. What are three ways you can protect yourself from sexual abuse and violence? **LIFE SKILL**

Interpreting Graphics

Study the figure below to answer the questions that follow.

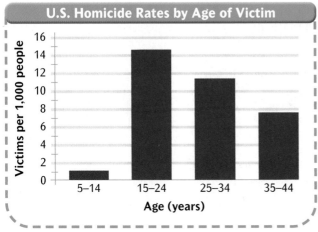

U.S. Homicide Rates by Age of Victim

Victims per 1,000 people / Age (years): 5–14, 15–24, 25–34, 35–44

Source: Centers for Disease Control and Prevention.

21. What is the difference between homicide rates for your age group and homicide rates for 25- to 34-year-olds? **MATH SKILL**

22. CRITICAL THINKING Why do you think 15- to 24-year-olds have the highest homicide rate?

Activities

23. Health and Your Community Start a neighborhood watch program, or join one that already exists in your community. Work with neighbors to write a plan for contacting authorities if a disturbance occurs.

24. Health and You Describe an example of a conflict that you have recently had. Evaluate your style of resolving the conflict. Now, use the conflict management skills you learned to explain all the possible ways you could improve your style of resolving conflicts.

25. Health and Your Community Meet with a local law enforcement officer to discuss potentially dangerous situations in your community. Write a paper on these potentially dangerous situations and ways you can avoid them.

Action Plan

26. LIFE SKILL Practicing Wellness Develop an action plan to deal with a conflict you might have with a family member or friend.

Standardized Test Prep

Read the passage below, and then answer the questions that follow. **READING SKILL** **WRITING SKILL**

A man moved into the apartment next door to Tasi last week. He makes her nervous. Whenever she passes him in the hall, he looks over her whole body. Yesterday, when Tasi came home from school, the man asked her to come over to his apartment to watch a movie. When she said she didn't want to, he became <u>irate</u>. His voice started getting louder and he moved closer to her. She ran into her apartment. She locked the door and called her father at work.

27. In this passage, the word *irate* means
 A angry.
 B sensitive and caring.
 C silent.
 D playful.

28. What can you infer from reading this passage?
 E The man is happy.
 F Tasi doesn't know how to say no.
 G The man might abuse or assault Tasi.
 H Tasi's father needs a new job.

29. Write a paragraph that describes how Tasi protected herself. Describe what further action Tasi and her father can take in the future to protect Tasi from the man.

UNIT 2
Health and Your Body

CHAPTER 6

Physical Fitness for Life

What's Your Health IQ?
KNOWLEDGE

Which of the following statements are true, and which are false? Check your answers on p. 638.

1. To gain the benefits of exercise, you must exercise every day.

2. Exercise can help improve depression.

3. Girls will develop large, manly muscles if they lift weights.

4. Lifting weights develops cardiorespiratory endurance.

5. The longer and harder you train, the better your health will be.

6. Anabolic steroids are illegal drugs.

7. Teens need more sleep than their younger siblings or their parents need.

Visit these Web sites for the latest health information:

HEALTH LINKS®
THE WORLD'S A CLICK AWAY

Find more information whenever you see a HealthLinks box. Go to **scilinks.org/health**, and type in the HealthLinks code.

go.hrw.com

Find worksheets and other materials that go with your textbook at **go.hrw.com**.

Current Health

Check out *Current Health*® articles related to this chapter by visiting **go.hrw.com**. Just type in the keyword **HH4 CH06**.

125

SECTION 1

Physical Fitness and Your Health

OBJECTIVES

State the benefits of being fit.

Describe the five health-related components of physical fitness.

Summarize the role of skill-related fitness.

Describe the importance of physical fitness for all ages and abilities.

Name three things you can do to be a good sport. **LIFE SKILL**

KEY TERMS

physical fitness the ability of the body to perform daily physical activities without getting out of breath, sore, or overly tired

chronic disease a disease that develops gradually and continues over a long period of time

health-related fitness fitness qualities that are necessary to maintain and promote a healthy body

resting heart rate (RHR) the number of times the heart beats per minute while at rest

Figure 1

Adding physical activity to your daily life can be easy.

ACTIVITY *How could these people add more physical activity to their daily lives?*

"**M**iracle Life anti-aging pills will keep you feeling young and give you more energy, guaranteed!" You've probably seen or heard ads just like this. The makers of such products claim to have the secret to a long healthy life. Well, the secret is out, and as you'll discover, it's not really much of a secret.

The Benefits of Being Physically Active

An important part of living a long, healthy life is to stay physically active. **Physical fitness** is the ability of the body to carry out daily physical activities without getting out of breath, sore, or overly tired. Regular physical activity leads to a physically fit body.

A certain amount of physical activity every day has been shown to keep you healthy and lowers your risk of certain diseases. As shown in **Figure 1,** many modern conveniences, such as escalators, cars, computers, and even TV remote controls, have reduced the need for us to be physically active in our daily lives. An overall reduction in the daily activity levels of children, teens, and adults has led to an increasingly unfit population.

Exercise is an excellent way of keeping a high level of activity in your daily life. *Exercise* is any physical activity that improves or maintains physical fitness. Exercise can be a formal set of activities or can be informal play. However, other everyday activities, such as raking leaves and walking to school, can also help keep you fit and healthy.

Stay Active, Stay Alive   Having a sedentary lifestyle has been linked to an increased risk of developing many illnesses, such as chronic diseases. A **chronic disease** is a disease that develops gradually and persists over a long period of time. A chronic disease can take a long time to treat. Examples of chronic diseases related to lifestyle include cardiovascular (heart) disease, stroke, high blood pressure, type 2 diabetes, and certain forms of cancer. Staying fit through regular exercise has been shown to be a significant factor in preventing the development of some of these chronic diseases.

Physical Benefits Leading an active lifestyle also has many physical benefits. Most people feel that exercising improves their appearance and makes them feel good about themselves. Exercise also leads to many improvements within your body.

▶ The heart and lungs get stronger, allowing more blood and oxygen to circulate around the body.

▶ Blood cholesterol levels are kept within a healthy range, and blood vessels are kept strong and healthy.

▶ Building muscular strength and endurance and also flexibility of our joints makes our muscles more efficient at controlling our movements and protects against injuries.

▶ A good ratio of muscle mass to fat mass is maintained.

▶ Metabolic rate is increased. Your metabolic rate is the rate at which your body converts food energy into the energy that keeps you alive.

▶ More Calories are burned because of an increase in muscle mass.

Being fit can increase your enjoyment of life!

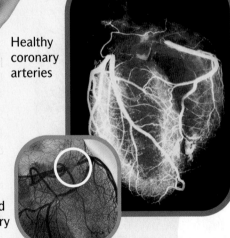

Healthy coronary arteries

Blocked coronary artery

Social Benefits
Regular exercise can be a great way to meet people.

Mental Benefits
Exercise can help
▶ reduce anxiety
▶ reduce depression
▶ increase self-confidence
▶ improve self-image

Physical Benefits
Being fit helps prevent the high blood cholesterol levels and coronary plaque buildup that can lead to a heart attack.

Mental Benefits Many people use regular exercise as a way to feel good mentally. Regular exercise has positive effects on feelings of depression and anxiety. Exercise can help reduce your stress levels and help you sleep better. How? Exercise takes your mind off of your worries and causes the release of certain body chemicals called *endorphins* (en DAWR finz). Endorphins can give you a feeling of wellness and happiness after a good workout. Increased oxygen to the brain during exercise can help you feel more alert. This in turn helps you feel more energized and better able to deal with day-to-day tasks.

Social Benefits Many people feel increased self-esteem as they exercise to stay fit. Part of this feeling is a result of the positive body changes that occur because of exercise. As a result of the increased self-esteem, such people are more likely to socialize with others.

Engaging in physical activity is also an opportunity to socialize with others who have the same interests. Working together on a team can help you develop your communication skills. It also gives you a chance to interact with many different people of differing abilities.

Five Components of Health-Related Fitness

Physical fitness can be classified into five components. These are commonly called the *health-related components of fitness*. **Health-related fitness** describes qualities that are needed to maintain and promote a healthy body. The five components of health-related fitness are muscular strength, muscular endurance, cardiorespiratory endurance, flexibility, and body composition.

Good muscular strength and endurance are important, even for small, everyday activities.

Muscular Strength Muscles move and apply force to objects and to each other by contracting. *Muscular strength* is the amount of force that a muscle can apply in a given contraction. Lifting a weight, climbing the stairs, and pushing a large piece of furniture are acts of muscular strength. During weight (or resistance) training, muscles are challenged to contract more than they are used to doing. The muscle cells themselves become larger in response to this extra work. This growth increases the overall strength of the muscle.

Muscular Endurance *Muscular endurance* is the ability of the muscles to keep working (contract) over a period of time. Muscular endurance allows you to carry out tasks that require muscles to remain contracted for a period of time. Examples of sports that require good muscular endurance include cross-country skiing and gymnastics. Muscular strength and endurance are closely related; as one improves, the other improves. Both muscular strength and muscular endurance can be developed by regular weight training.

Weight training is considered to be an anaerobic activity. During *anaerobic activity*, muscle cells produce energy without using oxygen. Anaerobic activity is intense and short in duration.

Cardiorespiratory Endurance   Cardiorespiratory endurance (KAHR dee oh RES puhr uh TAWR ee en DOOR uhns) is the ability of your heart, blood vessels, lungs, and blood to deliver oxygen and nutrients to all of your body's cells while you are being physically active. It is the single most important component of health-related fitness. As your cardiorespiratory endurance increases, your heart beats more efficiently. An indicator of poor cardiorespiratory endurance is running out of breath while doing strenuous activity.

Resting heart rate and recovery time are indicators of your level of cardiorespiratory endurance. **Resting heart rate (RHR)** is the number of times the heart beats per minute while at rest, such as just before you get up from a good night's sleep. *Recovery time* is the amount of time it takes for the heart to return to RHR after strenuous activity. Good cardiorespiratory endurance reduces recovery time and RHR.

Aerobic activity tends to improve your cardiorespiratory endurance. During *aerobic activity,* muscle cells use oxygen to produce energy for movement. The intensity of aerobic exercise is low enough so that the heart, lungs, blood vessels, and blood are all able to bring enough oxygen to your muscles. This allows your heart and muscles to continue with the activity for a long period of time (at least 20 to 60 minutes). Aerobic activity is continuous, uses large muscle groups, and tends to be rhythmic in nature. Examples include walking, jogging, dancing, swimming, cycling, and jumping rope.

Flexibility   *Flexibility* is the ability of the joints to move through their full range of motion. Good flexibility keeps joint movements smooth and efficient. Strong and healthy ligaments and tendons allow greater flexibility of a joint. Ligaments are the tissues that hold bones together at a joint. Tendons are the tissues that join muscles to bones. Any activity that involves a joint moving through a full range of motion will help maintain flexibility. As shown in **Figure 2,** stretching exercises, when done correctly, improve flexibility.

Having good flexibility alone is not the most important component of physical fitness. However, keeping a good level of flexibility is important because lack of use can cause joints to become stiffer as you become older.

Together with muscular strength and muscular endurance, flexibility is very important for overall fitness. These three components promote the health of bones and muscles.

Body Composition   *Body composition* refers to the ratio of lean body tissue (muscle and bone) to body-fat tissue. A healthy body has a high proportion of lean body tissue compared to body-fat tissue. Women naturally have more body fat than men do. Also, body fat increases with age as muscle mass decreases.

Figure 2

Maintaining good flexibility through regular stretching as a part of warm-ups and cool-downs may help reduce the risk of muscle tears, strains, and stress injuries.

internet connect

www.scilinks.org/health
Topic: Physical Fitness
HealthLinks code: HH4113

HEALTH LINKS
THE WORLD'S A CLICK AWAY
Maintained by the National Science Teachers Association

Having a certain amount of fat is necessary for good health. However, too much body fat increases the risk of getting certain lifestyle-related diseases, such as diabetes and cardiovascular disease. Excess body fat is almost always due to being inactive as well as having poor eating habits. Also, because of the stress of excess weight on the joints, people who have excess body fat are more likely than people who do not have excess body fat to have joint problems and back pain. Regular exercise and good eating habits are the best ways to develop a favorable body composition.

Skills Developed by Fitness

Skill-related fitness describes components of fitness that are important for good athletic performance. The six components of skill-related fitness are coordination, balance, agility, power, speed, and reaction time. The components of skill-related fitness are not as important for developing health as the health-related fitness components are. However, skill-related components are important for good athletic performance. For example, agility, coordination, and power are important in sports such as basketball, karate, football, and soccer. Athletic training concentrates on developing components of skill-related fitness.

Sport and Fitness

A great way to achieve total physical fitness is to get involved in an organized sport. Organized sports allow you to improve your social and communication skills and to interact with people of different abilities. Taking part in sports such as hiking, fishing, or camping will also enable you to explore the natural environment.

What Sport Can You Do? Sports are not limited to athletes. What sport you enjoy or choose to participate in is up to you. You should consider several things when deciding what sport to take part in.

▶Do you want to improve your abilities in a sport you have tried in the past or try something completely new?

▶Do you want to participate in an individual sport or a team sport? Individual sports are suited to people who enjoy one-on-one competition. Team sports allow you to interact with many people at one time. Working as a team helps develop problem-solving and conflict-resolution skills.

▶What activities are available in your area? Go to your local community center or youth club, and find out what activities are offered. Also, your school may have after-school activity programs that you can join.

▶What facilities do you need? If facilities such as a pool are needed, make sure they are easy for you to get to.

A person can achieve total fitness by taking part in an activity, such as football, to improve both health-related and skill-related fitness.

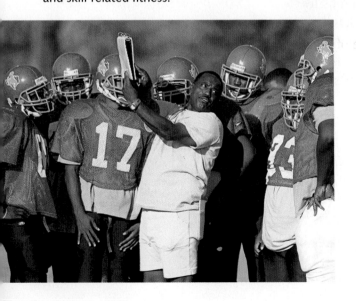

Sport and Competition Competition takes different forms—from the informal games between friends to formal competition with official rules and referees or umpires. Whether you compete in informal or formal play, competition will help develop your motivation, leadership, and cooperation skills. These are life skills that will help you in many areas of your daily life. Competition can also be valuable for the enjoyment you can get from just taking part in a sport.

Be a Good Sport To have winners, there must be losers. Losing competitors will naturally be disappointed at the loss. Likewise, winning teams have the right to be excited and proud. However, winning is never an excuse to be inconsiderate or hurtful to the losing team or individual.

Rules and regulations are meant to encourage fair play between competitors. Obeying and respecting game officials' decisions in any sport is necessary for fair play. Few coaches will tolerate disrespect on the field. Being removed from the game will hurt only yourself and your team's chances in competition.

Physical Activity Is for Everyone

It is never too early for you to develop a healthy lifestyle of lifelong physical activity. However, the benefits of maintaining fitness can be obtained only through a lifetime commitment to regular exercise.

A Lifetime of Physical Activity Even though a person may begin suffering from cardiovascular disease late in life, he or she likely began to develop the disease much earlier. By beginning good habits in your early years and making a commitment to lifelong activity, you can delay or even prevent some of the chronic diseases associated with growing older. Frequent strength training and eating a healthful diet may help prevent the bone-thinning disease osteoporosis (AHS tee oh puh ROH sis) in later life. Strength training even at an older age will help maintain bone density, muscle tone, muscle strength and endurance, and flexibility. The lifestyle choices you make now will affect your health for the rest of your life.

Activity and Asthma and Diabetes People who suffer from exercise-induced asthma often do not want to take part in physical activity or sport. Asthma causes a feeling of tightness in the chest and can cause coughing during and after exercise. And yet, physical activity is part of the treatment plan for people who have asthma. Gaining fitness helps decrease the severity of asthma symptoms. Exercise is also a very important part of the treatment plan for people who have diabetes because exercise helps control blood sugar levels. Exercise can also help with weight problems that are often associated with diabetes.

Fitness and Disability Have you ever thought about how you could dribble a basketball while steering yourself around in a wheelchair? How could you sprint 100 meters with an artificial leg? Many individuals have taken on the challenges of physical and mental disabilities and have become great athletes.

The Special Olympics and Paralympics show us that mental and physical disabilities do not stop people from becoming world-class athletes. The *Special Olympics* is an organization that enables and encourages people who are learning disabled to become physically fit. The organization also encourages such people to become more involved in society through sports training and competition. The *Paralympics* are Olympic-style games for athletes with physical disabilities.

No matter what your age or abilities are, being physically active—whether it is done through an exercise program, an organized sport, or just your everyday activity—is of great value to everyone. So, in short, part of the answer to a longer, healthier life is to be active!

People of all ages and abilities should take part in regular physical activity to reduce their risks of chronic diseases and to help them feel their best.

SECTION 1

REVIEW *Answer the following questions on a separate piece of paper.*

Using Key Terms

1. **Name** the term that means "the ability of the body to carry out daily activities without getting out of breath, sore, or overly tired."

2. **Identify** which condition is *not* a chronic disease.
   a. diabetes
   b. cancer
   c. heart disease
   d. cold

3. **Identify** the single most important component of health-related fitness.
   a. muscular strength
   b. body composition
   c. cardiorespiratory endurance
   d. muscular endurance

4. **Define** *resting heart rate.*

Understanding Key Ideas

5. **List** six benefits of being fit.

6. **Name** a health-related component of fitness and a sport that develops that component.

7. **Contrast** the functions of health-related components and skill-related components of fitness.

8. **Name** one common disease for which physical activity can be part of the treatment.

9. **LIFE SKILL** **Communicating Effectively** Identify four ways you can show you are a good sport.

Critical Thinking

10. **LIFE SKILL** **Practicing Wellness** Discuss the statement "Physical activity can actually prevent you from having a heart attack."

Planning Your Fitness Program

OBJECTIVES

Describe the important factors to think about before starting a fitness program.

Describe the steps involved in designing a fitness program.

Calculate your resting heart rate, target heart rate zone, and maximum heart rate.

Evaluate the use of the FITT formula in fitness training.

Design and implement a personal fitness program and set your fitness goals. **LIFE SKILL**

KEY TERMS

target heart rate zone a heart rate range within which the most gains in cardiorespiratory health will occur

FITT a formula made up of four important parts involved in fitness training: **f**requency, **i**ntensity, **t**ime, and **t**ype of exercise

repetitions the number of times an exercise is performed

set a fixed number of repetitions followed by a rest period

Maria's mom has heart disease. Maria has done some research and believes she could develop heart disease, too. Maria also read that regular exercise can help lower her chance of developing heart disease. Now she's determined to become more fit, but she's not sure where to start.

Getting Started with Your Fitness Program

You don't have to be an athlete to be physically fit, and you do not have to be fit to start a fitness program. Before you start any fitness program, however, there are many factors you should consider.

" Bob and I have started swimming **three times a week** at the school pool. "

▶ **Do you have any health concerns, such as diabetes or asthma?** Be sure to consult your doctor about your program if you do have health concerns.

▶ **Are you healthy enough to start a program?** You should schedule a physical examination with your doctor. Your doctor will be able to assess your level of health. He or she will check your heart rate, blood pressure, height, weight, and reflexes and may also check any health concerns you have.

▶ **What types of activities do you enjoy?** Be sure to choose activities that fit into your schedule and that won't bore you easily. Ask a friend to join you.

▶ **How much will your planned activities cost?** Cost is something to think about before choosing an activity. Many fitness activities such as walking or jogging do not require expensive clothing or shoes. However, for activities that require special equipment, you should rent or borrow the equipment from a reliable source. This will allow you to decide if you like the activity before you buy your own equipment. A little research may save you money and time in the long run.

Designing a Fitness Program

The steps to designing a fitness program are very straightforward. Remember that developing your cardiorespiratory endurance should be part of the foundation of your fitness program.

Determine Your Resting Heart Rate (RHR) Ideally, your RHR should be taken three mornings in a row to get your average RHR. Your RHR should be calculated when you are very relaxed, such as before getting up from a good night's sleep. Use step 1 of **Figure 3** to find your pulse. Count your pulse for 60 seconds. The average adult RHR is 50 to 80 beats per minute (bpm); teens' RHR is a little higher. Some of the world's best endurance athletes have resting heart rates below 40 bpm. Your RHR will decrease as a result of regularly exercising within your target heart rate zone.

Calculate Your Target Heart Rate Zone For you to maximize cardiorespiratory health benefits from exercise, your heart rate range should reach your **target heart rate zone.** Your target heart rate zone is normally between 60 and 85 percent of your maximum heart rate. Maximum heart rate (MHR) is the maximum number of times your heart should beat per minute while doing any physical activity.

Calculate your MHR and then your target heart rate zone to find how hard you should be exercising. Here's a quick way of estimating your MHR and target heart rate zone:

1. Determine your MHR by subtracting your age from 220.
2. Multiply your MHR by 60 percent (0.6) and 85 percent (0.85) to calculate your target heart rate zone.

Using this method, a 16-year-old would calculate his or her target heart rate zone to be 122 to 173 beats per minute. If you are an athlete, your doctor or a sports physician can calculate your MHR more accurately by using a special formula.

Figure 3

Monitoring your heart rate, before, during, and after exercising is an important part of a personal fitness program. Pushing your heart rate above the upper range of your target heart rate zone is not needed for cardiorespiratory benefits.

ACTIVITY *Estimate your MHR and your target heart rate zone.*

How to Calculate Your Heart Rate

1. Using the tips of your index and middle fingers, locate your carotid artery. Your carotid artery is located just below your jaw in the groove where your head and neck meet. Search around until you can feel a steady beat under the skin.

2. Use a clock or stopwatch to count your pulse for 10 seconds. Multiply the number of beats in 10 seconds by six to get your heart rate.

Table 1 Health Fitness Standards for Teens

Muscular Endurance

Curl-ups (number completed)

Age (years)	Boys	Girls
14	24 to 45	18 to 32
15–17	24 to 47	18 to 35

Cardiorespiratory Endurance

One-mile run (minutes:seconds)

Age (years)	Boys	Girls
14	9:30 to 7:00	11:00 to 8:30
15	9:00 to 7:00	10:30 to 8:00
16–17	8:30 to 7:00	10:00 to 8:00

Muscular Strength

Push-ups (number completed)

Age (years)	Boys	Girls
14	14 to 30	7 to 15
15	16 to 35	7 to 15
16–17	18 to 35	7 to 15

Flexibility

Back saver sit and reach (inches)

Age (years)	Boys	Girls
14	8	10
15–17	8	12

Source: Cooper Institute of Aerobic Research, *FITNESSGRAM Test Administration Manual.*

Assess Your Fitness Assessing your fitness levels will measure your level of fitness against commonly used standards. **Table 1** presents fitness standards for components of health-related fitness. The ranges of numbers found in each table represent *healthy fitness zones* (HFZ). There is an HFZ for boys and girls of each age in each component of health-related fitness. Achieving scores that place you within an HFZ indicates that you have a healthy level of physical fitness.

Set Your Fitness Goals Setting goals will help make your fitness program more effective. Writing down your fitness goals will help you define them.

▶ Make sure your goals are based on your physical abilities and are well planned. For example, if you are at the lower portion of the HFZ for your age, setting a goal of exceeding the HFZ for your age within 2 weeks would be dangerous.

▶ Choose goals that you want to achieve. Doing so will ensure that you have the motivation to stick with your fitness program.

▶ Break your goals into short-term and long-term goals. Short-term goals should help divide a fitness program into more manageable "pieces."

▶ Write down specific objectives that will help you reach each short-term goal. Make sure one of your objectives is to eat healthfully.

Keep Track of Your Progress Keep an activity log in which you record the date, how long you trained, what exercises you did and how you felt. You'll be able to review the log, check your progress, and make changes to your program when needed. Keeping a log will also help you stick with your objectives and reach your goals.

Building Character

GOOD JUDGMENT

People with *good judgment* consider all of the consequences of a decision and then act to achieve the best outcome. Healthy people use good judgment when making decisions that affect their wellness. By using good judgment, you can honestly assess your strengths and weaknesses to create a realistic fitness plan that you will stick with and that will not lead to injuries.

Imagine that you have set a goal of joining your school's track team in two months. You do not currently have an exercise routine and have never competed in any track events. Describe how using good judgment could help you achieve your goal.

Getting FITT

After you choose an activity you may still have many questions, such as, How many times per week should I do the activity? How hard should the activity be? How long should each workout take? The FITT formula can be used as a helpful guide to answer these questions.

The **FITT** formula is made up of four important parts of fitness training: *frequency, intensity, time,* and *type*. For exercise to be effective, it must be done enough times per week (*frequency*), hard enough (*intensity*), and for long enough (*time*). Finally, the kind (*type*) of exercise is important. The FITT formula recommendations differ slightly for each health-related component of fitness. **Figure 4** presents many types of activities that develop the health-related components and identifies the frequency with which each activity needs to be done.

Developing Your Cardiorespiratory Endurance   Recommendations for cardiorespiratory fitness are as follows:

▶ **Frequency** Exercise must be performed three to five times a week.

▶ **Intensity** If you are training at 85 percent of your MHR, 20 minutes per session is enough. If you are training at 50 to 60 percent of your MHR, 60 minutes of training per session may be needed to gain health benefits.

Figure 4

The Activity Pyramid can help you develop your fitness program. If you are currently sedentary, begin at the bottom of the pyramid (everyday activities) and gradually increase your level of activity. If you are already fairly active, you can increase the amount of time you spend doing physical activities.

The Activity Pyramid

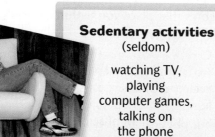

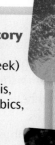

Sedentary activities
(seldom)

watching TV, playing computer games, talking on the phone

Muscular strength and endurance, and flexibility
(2 to 5 times a week)

push-ups, curl-ups, ballet, stretching, martial arts, yoga

Cardiorespiratory endurance
(3 to 5 times a week)

swimming, tennis, running, gym aerobics, jumping rope, aerobic dance

Household and recreational activities
(every day)

walking the dog, gardening, cleaning your room, soccer, sweeping the floor, hiking, dancing, golf, walking or cycling to the store

▶ **Time** Twenty to sixty minutes per session is recommended, depending on the intensity of the exercise. Intensity means how hard your heart is working and how difficult the activity is to do. The higher the intensity of the exercise, the less time you need to do it.

▶ **Type** Any aerobic activity that keeps heart rate within your target heart rate zone is good.

Developing Your Muscles Muscular strength and muscular endurance are closely related. As one improves, so does the other. Training programs are designed to address each of these health related components. FITT recommendations that address muscular development are as follows:

▶ **Frequency** Weight train 2 to 3 times a week.

▶ **Intensity** Select a weight that you can safely lift at least 8 times but no more than 12 times. The weight being lifted is called the *resistance*. Each lift is called a repetition. **Repetitions** are the number of times an exercise is repeated. A fixed number of repetitions

There is no difference between the same amount of male muscle and female muscle in terms of strength.

real life Activity

DEVELOP YOUR FITNESS PLAN

LIFE SKILL
Setting Goals

Materials

✔ paper
✔ pencil
✔ ruler

Procedure

1. **Draw** a table that has seven columns. Title the table "Activity Plan for the Week." Label the columns with the days of the week.

2. **Write** your fitness goal below the table. For example, you might write, "I want to run a 5 kilometer race in under 30 minutes."

3. **Create** a week of activities that are based on developing the five components of physical fitness. Remember to include at least 60 minutes of activity daily.

Conclusions

1. **Summarizing Results** What resources in your community can you use to carry out your fitness plan?

2. **Applying Information** Describe how your fitness plan will help you reach your goal.

3. **CRITICAL THINKING** Develop ways to address possible barriers to your training program, such as bad weather, expensive equipment, or lack of time.

4. **CRITICAL THINKING** Identify ways you can assess your progress.

5. **CRITICAL THINKING** How can you reward yourself for following your plan?

Activity Plan for the		
Mon.	Tue.	Wed.

Tips to Keep You Motivated

▶ **Look at it as down time. Training can be the perfect "time out" from a busy day.**

▶ **Train with a friend. A training partner will keep you company and may introduce some healthy competition.**

▶ **Set realistic goals. Make a contract for yourself, and reward yourself often for sticking with your program.**

▶ **Understand that you'll have bad days. When you don't reach a day's workout goals do not be discouraged—just start up again the next day.**

▶ **Keep the appointment. Consider your workout an important appointment that you cannot miss, and you'll be more likely to keep to it.**

followed by a rest period is called a **set.** Rest periods between sets are between 1 and 3 minutes long. Do one to three sets of 8 to 12 repetitions for all the major muscle groups.

▶ **Time** A total workout can be about 30 minutes long but should not be longer than 60 minutes.

▶ **Type** Anaerobic activities such as weight lifting and sit-ups tend to develop muscular strength and endurance. To build muscular endurance, you lift lighter weights (less resistance) with more (8 to 15) repetitions. To build strength, you should lift heavier weights (more resistance) with fewer (3 to 8) repetitions.

Increasing Your Flexibility
The following are FITT recommendations for flexibility:

▶ **Frequency** Perform stretching 3 to 5 days a week. For the best results, stretch daily.

▶ **Intensity** Stretch muscles, and hold at a comfortable stretch for about 15 to 30 seconds. Relax into the stretch, and as you breath out, you will stretch a little further. Never bounce as you stretch. Repeat each stretch three to five times.

▶ **Time** Stretch for 15 to 30 minutes.

▶ **Type** Stretching can be done on its own or as part of a warm-up and cool-down. Yoga is also a popular form of flexibility exercise.

When Will I See Changes?
The length of time it takes to see a difference varies from person to person. On average, it takes about 6 weeks to really notice the difference in the health-related components. So, don't get discouraged!

SECTION 2

REVIEW
Answer the following questions on a separate piece of paper.

Using Key Terms

1. **Define** the term *target heart rate zone.*

2. **List** the four parts of fitness training that FITT stands for.

3. **Name** the term that refers to the number of times an exercise is performed.

4. **Identify** the term that means "a fixed number of repetitions followed by a rest period."
   a. frequency   c. repetition
   b. intensity   d. set

Understanding Key Ideas

5. **List** the important things to consider before beginning a fitness program.

6. **Summarize** the steps to designing a fitness program.

7. **List** the steps of how to calculate your target heart rate zone.

8. **Identify** what each letter of the acronym FITT means in relation to a fitness plan.

Critical Thinking

9. **LIFE SKILL** **Practicing Wellness** Is it a good idea to do both aerobic exercises and anaerobic exercises as parts of a fitness program? Explain.

10. Why is it important to monitor your heart rate before, during, and after exercising or training?

SECTION 3

Exercising the Safe Way

OBJECTIVES

Describe six ways to avoid sports injuries.

Identify four signs of overtraining.

Describe the RICE method of treating minor sports injuries.

State the dangers posed by the use of performance enhancing drugs.

Summarize the importance of wearing safety equipment to prevent sports injuries. **LIFE SKILL**

KEY TERMS

dehydration a state in which the body has lost more water than has been taken in

overtraining a condition that occurs as a result of exceeding the recommendations of the FITT formula

dietary supplement any product that is taken by mouth that can contain a dietary ingredient and is also labeled as a dietary supplement

anabolic steroid a synthetic version of the male hormone testosterone used for promoting muscle development

"**A**n ounce of prevention is worth a pound of cure." These words are cold comfort to someone who has pulled a muscle or strained a tendon. However, most sports injuries are easy to prevent.

Avoiding Sports Injuries

The most common sports injuries are injuries to muscles, tendons, ligaments, and bones. These injuries are classified as either acute—having a sudden onset and short duration—or chronic—having a gradual onset and long-term effects.

Most acute injuries are minor bumps and scrapes that heal quickly and don't require much treatment. However, some acute injuries are more serious. Prompt medical attention is always required for a serious injury such as a fracture or concussion. Chronic injuries can take months or even years to treat.

Beliefs VS. Reality

"No pain, no gain."	Exercise can sometimes be uncomfortable but should never be painful. Pain means injury.
"Doing two or three 30-minute cardiovascular workouts a day will help me lose those extra pounds."	Not allowing your body to rest between training sessions will cause injury. Also, it is wise to review your eating habits as part of any fitness program.
"Working out in heavy sweats will help burn fat quicker."	Wearing excess clothing during a workout increases water loss and the chance of heat exhaustion or even heatstroke.

Many sports injuries can be prevented by having a properly conditioned body, by warming up and cooling down, by stretching correctly after a workout, by avoiding dehydration, and by avoiding overtraining. In addition, wearing the correct safety equipment and clothing can prevent many other injuries.

Get Conditioned Properly preparing your body for the activity you want to do is a very important step in preventing injury. Suddenly starting into an intense training program or being a "weekend warrior" puts strain on unprepared muscles and joints. Lack of conditioning is often the reason for injury in the early weeks of schools' sport seasons.

Conditioning is an exercise program that promotes cardiorespiratory and muscular endurance. Conditioning is developed through the progressive overload principle. The *progressive overload principle* states that the physical demands or overload placed on the body will cause the body to develop in response to the overload. The overload must be increased or progress over time for continued physical improvement to occur.

Placing enough overload on muscles will cause them to become fatigued and sore or achy after a workout. This short-term muscle soreness (less than 24 hours) is normal. Resting helps develop muscular strength and endurance as sore muscles need time to recover. During *recovery*, the body heals the fatigued muscle cells. To prepare the body for similar physical demands in the future, the body increases muscle mass and blood flow to the muscles. The body responds best to a gradual progression in overload. Excess overload or too fast a progression will lead to injury.

> "Records are meant
> to be broken,
> not athletes."
>
> —Cal Ripken, Jr.

To reduce the risk of injuries, wear the correct clothing and equipment, consider the weather conditions, and obey posted warning signs.

Warm Up and Cool Down   Starting a workout without warming up can cause injury. Warming up increases blood flow to muscles, stretches your muscles and ligaments, and increases your heart rate. About 10 minutes of activities such as slow jogging will increase your heart rate enough for you to begin a workout safely. An all-over sweat is a good sign that you have warmed up enough.

After a workout do not just stop moving. Instead, spend 5 to 10 minutes moving the muscles that were used at a pace that is slower than the workout pace. Cooling down will help prevent next-day stiffness and may prevent injuries. Skipping a cool-down may result in dizziness or feeling faint.

Stretch   Stretching is an important part of any warm-up and cool-down. Stretching regularly and properly will help you avoid tight muscles and may prevent injuries. Always stretch slowly; don't bounce. Stretch only as far as is comfortable. Concentrate on the major muscle groups you will use in your workout. Hold stretches for about 7 to 10 seconds. Hold the stretches for up to 30 seconds to increase flexibility.

Avoid Dehydration   **Dehydration** is a state in which the body has lost more water than has been taken in. Dehydration is a major health threat in any kind of weather. Drinking water during a workout ensures that your blood volume is maintained so that circulation and sweating can continue at a normal level. Good blood circulation helps maintain correct body temperature and minimizes stress on your heart. Dehydration can negatively affect your athletic performance.

Stop your activity immediately if you begin to feel lightheaded or weak, if your muscles begin to spasm, if you get a headache, or if you have a rapid, weak pulse. Immediately tell your coach or workout partner how you feel—don't go off alone until you feel better. Be sure to drink plenty of cool fluids, such as water or diluted fruit juice.

Avoid Overtraining   Some people may think that pushing themselves very hard will help them meet their fitness goals more quickly or give them the competitive edge. But your body needs rest between workouts so that it can recover from the exertion. **Overtraining** is caused by exceeding the recommendations of the FITT formula—training too much, too intensely, or too quickly for your abilities.

Overtraining has many negative effects, many of which are long-term effects. To avoid overtraining, always include periods of rest in your training program. To rest does not necessarily mean to stop activity. *Active rest* involves lowering the intensity of a workout or taking part in other activities. Knowing the warning signs of overtraining can help prevent you from developing a serious injury. Recovery from overtraining can take weeks to months.

Avoid Overuse Injuries   Repetitive activity causes stress to bones, ligaments, tendons, or muscles. Small, repetitive injuries to the tissue cause swelling and the release of substances that damage the tissue.

Warning Signs of Overtraining

▶ **Feelings of chronic fatigue**

▶ **Getting injured easily**

▶ **Feelings of irritability and depression**

▶ **Dehydration**

▶ **Loss of interest in working out**

▶ **Loss of appetite and loss of weight**

▶ **Increased resting heart rate (RHR)**

▶ **Poor athletic performance and possibly poor school performance**

▶ **Loss of menstrual period in females**

internet connect

www.scilinks.org/health
Topic: Overuse Injuries
HealthLinks code: HH4111

HEALTH LINKS. Maintained by the
National Science
Teachers Association

This damage results in chronic injury. Continued stress on the tissue can lead to weakness, loss of flexibility, and chronic pain.

Overuse injuries are becoming more common in adolescents, particularly in adolescents who are gymnasts, runners, or swimmers. Children and adolescents are very prone to overuse injuries because their bones are still growing. Damage to growing bones and other tissues can cause lifelong weakness and loss of flexibility. Treatment of overuse injuries should include resting the injured site, applying ice or heat as required, and undergoing physical therapy and rehabilitation to rebuild strength and flexibility at the site of injury.

Choose the Correct Equipment and Clothing

▶ **Wear comfortable clothing.** Your clothing should allow free movement of your body. Choose fabrics that draw moisture away from the skin.

▶ **Dress suitably for the weather and exercise intensity.** Many thin layers together insulate better than one or two thick layers. In cold weather, wear thin layers that can be removed if you get too warm. Wearing a brimmed hat, sunscreen, and sunglasses are musts when exercising outdoors, even in winter!

▶ **Always wear safety equipment, and wear it correctly.** Get training or advice from a reliable person on the correct use and fit of safety equipment.

▶ **Choose shoes that are made for your activity.** Good shoes play a very important role in preventing injury. However, you do not need an expensive pair of shoes unless you are training a lot or have a diagnosed foot problem. Ask for advice from a person who works in a specialty shoe store.

▶ **Make sure you can be seen.** Wear bright, reflective clothing if training at night.

▶ **Obey laws, regulations, and warning signs.** Ignoring these could lead to injury or even death.

Rest

Ice

Compression

Elevation

The RICE technique is used for the early treatment of sports-related injuries. RICE plays a critical role in limiting swelling.

Treating Minor Sports Injuries

Most injuries, regardless of type, have one thing in common: swelling. Swelling causes pressure in the injured area, and this increase in pressure causes pain. You must quickly control swelling because swelling slows down the healing process.

Apply the RICE principle to control swelling: rest, ice, compression, and elevation. As shown in **Table 2,** the RICE principle can be applied to both acute and chronic injuries.

▶ **Rest** It is important to protect the injured muscle, ligament, tendon, or other tissue from further injury.

▶ **Ice** Apply ice bags or cold packs to the injured site, and leave the ice on the injured site for no longer than 15 to 20 minutes. Leaving ice on any longer or placing ice directly on the skin can damage the skin.

▶ **Compression** Compression reduces swelling. Wrap a cloth bandage around the affected area. If you feel a throbbing or the bandage is too tight, remove the bandage and reapply it.

▶ **Elevation** Raising the injured site above heart level when possible can help reduce swelling.

Medical advice must be sought immediately if there is unconsciousness, excessive swelling, or persistent pain or bleeding. It would be a wise decision to get certified in first aid so that you can confidently and correctly treat an injury until you get to a doctor or hospital.

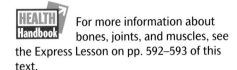
For more information about bones, joints, and muscles, see the Express Lesson on pp. 592–593 of this text.

Recovery from Injury The RICE principle is applied as first aid when an injury occurs, but it is also useful during recovery. Muscles in an injured limb lose strength and flexibility when they are not used. Rehabilitation is the process of regaining strength and coordination during recovery from an injury. Returning to activity before an injury is fully healed and rehabilitated puts you at risk of reinjury. Therefore you should always let an injury completely heal before attempting any activity that may stress the injured site. However, to keep doing activities that do not stress the injury is also important.

Table 2 Common Injuries and Treatments

Injury	Cause	Treatment
Sunburn (acute)	overexposure of the skin to ultraviolet (UV) rays in sunlight	drinking plenty of fluids; applying light moisturizer; consulting a doctor if blistering occurs
Tendon and muscle strain (acute)	overstretching or over contraction of muscles causes muscle fibers or tendons to tear	rest and immobilization (a mildly pulled muscle can recover in as little as a week; tendons can take longer)
Ligament sprain (acute)	forcing a joint to move beyond its normal limits can cause ligament fibers to tear	RICE and strengthening of the muscles and tendons around the joint through rehabilitation
Fracture (acute)	extreme stress and strain causes cracks in bone	immediate medical attention; rest and immobilization for 6 to 8 weeks
Heat exhaustion (acute)	training in hot or humid weather; extreme dehydration	immediate medical attention; moving to a shady spot, drinking plenty of cool water, and applying cool water to body
Concussion (acute)	a blow to the head, face, or jaw that causes the brain to be shaken in the skull	rest under observation; immediate medical attention if there is unconsciousness, vomiting, a seizure, or a change in the size of the pupils
Tendinitis (chronic)	inflammation of a tendon due to trauma or overuse	RICE (healing can take from 6 to 8 weeks); apply heat after 36 to 48 hours if swelling is gone
Stress fracture (chronic)	repeated stress or overuse causes tiny fractures in the bone	RICE and sometimes immobilization; female athletes with a stress fracture may need a bone scan
Shin splint (chronic)	straining of muscles that are attached to the shin bone	RICE; applying ice several times a day; strengthening of the lower leg muscles

Supplements, Drugs, and Athletic Performance

Some athletes feel that taking dietary supplements or drugs gives them a competitive edge. A **dietary supplement** is any product taken by mouth that can contain a dietary ingredient and that is labeled as a dietary supplement. Makers of these supplements can claim that their dietary supplement may help improve athletic performance. For example, some protein supplements are advertised as helping to increase muscle mass. **Table 3** summarizes some common ingredients of dietary supplements and drugs used by some athletes.

Dietary Supplements Supplements are not regulated by the Food and Drug Administration (FDA). Makers of these products can make certain claims for their product without any scientific proof. The strength of a supplement can vary widely. Claims that dietary supplements improve performance are often based on improvements that result from training, not from taking supplements. Some supplements that contain non-nutrient ingredients, such as caffeine, ephedrine, andro, or GBL, may have dangerous side effects or are banned by certain athletic associations. Athletes and healthy nonathletes who have a wholesome, well-balanced diet do not need supplements.

Table 3 Common Supplement Ingredients and Drugs

Name	How does it affect the body?	Dangers
Caffeine	a central nervous system stimulant that makes you feel awake and alert	raises blood pressure and heart rate if used in excess; affects sleep, mood, and behavior; can lead to dehydration by increasing urination
Amphetamines	mask fatigue, increase sense of well-being and mental alertness	raise blood pressure, increase aggressiveness, increase risk of injury, and circulatory collapse (shock)
Ephedrine (ephedra, ma huang)	stimulates the brain and nervous system, increases alertness, and may mask signs of fatigue	may lead to abnormal heartbeat, dizziness, psychiatric episodes, and seizures
Adrenal androgens (includes DHEA and Andro)	claimed to increase muscle strength and improve athletic performance when taken as a supplement	can cause behavioral, sexual, and reproductive problems; causes liver damage, muscle disorders, and increased risk of heart disease; can stunt growth in teens
Gamma-butyrolactone (GBL)	claimed to induce sleep, release growth hormone, increase athletic performance, and relieve stress	can cause vomiting, an increase in aggression, tremors, slow heartbeat, seizures, breathing difficulties, and coma
Anabolic steroids	increase muscle size and strength	increase aggressive behavior, cholesterol levels, and risk of kidney tumors; can cause severe acne, testicular shrinkage, liver cysts, and fatal damage to heart muscle; can stunt growth in teens

Anabolic Steroids **Anabolic steroids** are synthetic versions of the male hormone *testosterone* that are used to promote muscle development. Doctors use small amounts of anabolic steroids to treat some conditions, such as muscle disease, kidney disease, and breast cancer. However, anabolic steroids are often abused because of their muscle building properties.

Anabolic steroid abuse can cause serious health problems for both male and female abusers. Reported effects for females include excessive growth of facial and body hair, baldness, increased risk of cancer, and menstrual problems. Other effects are the side effects listed in **Table 3**, that affect both males and females.

Despite the harmful effects of anabolic steroids and the fact that abusing them is illegal, many men, women, and teens use them. It is estimated that more than a million male and female athletes are taking or have taken anabolic steroids. The incidence of steroid use among high school athletes is estimated to be 6 to 11 percent. Many athletes who abuse anabolic steroids start using the drugs as early as age 15.

Playing It Safe!

Exercising is a great way to stay physically fit. If you follow the basic rules to avoid sport injuries and avoid supplements and drugs, you will find out how much fun it can be to exercise and be fit.

In addition, remember to exercise or train in open areas that have good lighting, bring a friend, and always let someone know where you'll be and what time you'll return.

MAKING GREAT DECISIONS

A close friend of yours has always been into bodybuilding and weight lifting. Over the last few months, he has not been doing well in his competitions. He has a few friends who have suggested that taking a steroid will give him a competitive edge and will put him back on top.

Write on a separate piece of paper the advice that you would give your friend. Remember to use the decision-making steps.

Give thought to the problem.
Review your choices.
Evaluate the consequences of each choice.
Assess and choose the best choice.
Think it over afterward.

SECTION 3

REVIEW *Answer the following questions on a separate piece of paper.*

Using Key Terms

1. **Identify** the term for "a state in which the body has lost more water than has been taken in."
   a. chronic injury
   b. dehydration
   c. overtraining
   d. testosterone

2. **Define** *overtraining*.

3. **Define** what an anabolic steroid is.

Understanding Key Ideas

4. **Identify** three ways to prevent sports injuries.

5. **Describe** how overtraining can lead to chronic injury.

6. **State** why it is important to follow the RICE steps right after an injury.

7. **Evaluate** the statement "All athletes need to take some kind of supplement."

Critical Thinking

8. **LIFE SKILL** **Practicing Wellness** How could wearing the wrong type or size of safety equipment lead to an injury?

9. What advice would you give a friend who started exercising hard every day and whose body now hurts too much to move?

Sleep

OBJECTIVES

Describe why sleep is an important part of your health.

List the effects of sleep deprivation.

Compare how the amount of sleep needed by teens differs from the amount needed by adults or children.

Identify the two different types of sleep.

List three ways that you can improve your sleeping habits. **LIFE SKILL**

"I should have stopped playing video games earlier last night."

Can you remember a time when you were so tired that you couldn't concentrate in class? When you are tired, your concentration declines, it's hard to finish your tasks, and you are less able to handle stressful situations.

Sleep: Too Little, Too Often

A recent poll conducted by the National Sleep Foundation, "Sleep in America," found that over 60 percent of adults in the United States experience sleep problems. Sleep is not just a "time out"; it is essential for your health and safety. You need sleep for good health, and you need to get enough of it.

What is sleep, and why do we need it? The answer is not completely clear, but we do know that sleep is needed by the brain. Even mild sleepiness has been shown to hurt all types of performance—in school, sports, and even when playing video games!

Sleep deprivation is a lack of sleep. People who are sleep deprived over a long period of time suffer many problems. For example, they may have the following problems:

▶ **Stress-related problems** Even occasional periods of sleep deprivation can make everyday life seem more stressful and can cause you to be less productive.

▶ **Increased risk for getting sick** Long-term sleep deprivation decreases the body's ability to fight infections.

▶ **Increased risk for dangerous accidents** Sleepiness can cause a lack of concentration and a slow reaction time which can lead to dangerous and even fatal accidents. For example, drowsy driving is a major problem for drivers aged 25 or under.

Getting enough good quality sleep is as important as being physically fit and having good nutrition. The amount of sleep a person needs varies. Most adults need an average of 8 hours of sleep per night. But some adults need as little as 6 hours; others need 10 hours.

Teens and Sleep

Teens need more sleep than their parents and younger siblings do. Teens need about 9 hours and 15 minutes of sleep a night.

Why do teens need more sleep? When puberty takes place, the timing of a teen's circadian rhythm is delayed. The **circadian rhythm** (also known as a circadian clock or body clock) is the body's internal system for regulating sleeping and waking patterns. In general, our circadian rhythm is timed so that we sleep at night and wake during the day. When the rhythm is delayed at puberty, the body naturally wants to go to sleep later at night and wake up later in the morning. So, teens usually have more difficulty falling asleep until late at night and have a little more difficulty waking up early in the morning. Many teenagers are not alert until after the typical high school day has already begun.

The good news is that you can adjust your circadian clocks for the school year. This process may take several weeks but it is worth the time. Adjusting your circadian rhythm to fit your schedule can reduce morning crankiness, make you feel happier, and help you face the day ahead.

Myth

I need only 6 hours of sleep a night.

Fact

Teens need between 8.5 and 9.25 hours of sleep every night.

LIFE SKILL Activity **Practicing Wellness**

Getting Enough Sleep

Does the following passage sound familiar?

Greg rolled out of bed after hitting the snooze button for the 10th time. As he shuffled out of the room, he turned off the TV—he had left it on all night. His shower woke him up long enough to grab a muffin and get to school. Greg's first class period was a blur. All he could think of was sleeping. After class, he couldn't remember a thing the teacher said. He grabbed a soda from the vending machine to help himself wake up. He had a busy day, but when bedtime arrived, he just couldn't sleep!

You can develop better sleeping habits. Begin by keeping a week-long sleep log that records the following information:

1 The times you go to sleep and wake up

2 The things that affect your sleeping patterns

3 The reasons you cannot fall asleep or do not sleep well

4 The ways in which lack of sleep affects your activities or behaviors during the day

LIFE SKILL Assessing Your Health

1. What patterns did you find from your sleep log?

2. What types of things affect your sleep patterns?

3. Write down three things you can do to improve your sleeping habits.

Six Tips for Getting a Good Night's Sleep

1 Develop a routine. Go to bed and get up at the same time, even on weekends!

2 Exercise every day. The best time is in the late afternoon or early evening, but not too close to bedtime.

3 Limit caffeine. After about lunch time, stay away from coffee, colas, or foods with caffeine.

4 Relax. Avoid heavy reading, studying, and computer games within 1 hour of bedtime.

5 Say no to all-nighters. Staying up all night, even to study for an exam, will disturb your sleep pattern and your ability to function the next day.

6 Your bed is for sleep. Do not eat, watch TV, or study in bed.

The Stages of Sleep

While you sleep, your brain and body go through cycles of deep and light sleep. These two types of sleep are called NREM and REM. NREM stands for "nonrapid eye movement," and REM stands for "rapid eye movement."

In the beginning of a sleep cycle, we go into NREM sleep. The body recovers from the stress of the day's activities during this part of the sleep cycle. Brain activity is at its lowest during NREM sleep. The REM portion of the sleep cycle is called *dream sleep*. It first happens about 1.5 hours into sleep. REM sleep got its name from the rapid movement of the eyes during this phase of sleep. During a normal sleep cycle, periods of NREM sleep alternate with periods of REM sleep. Both types of sleep are essential in helping us lead healthy, active lives.

Insomnia and Other Sleep Disorders Sleep deprivation can result from insomnia. **Insomnia** is an inability to sleep, even if one is physically exhausted. Caffeine, alcohol, smoking, stress, and lack of exercise are all common causes of insomnia. Insomnia seems to become more of a problem as we age. Insomnia can often be treated by a simple change in daily habits, such as limiting caffeine late in the day.

Sleep apnea is a serious sleeping disorder in which there are interruptions in normal breathing patterns during sleep. These pauses in breathing can put great stress on the heart. People with sleep apnea can be constantly tired because of nights of disturbed sleep. Sleep apnea is most common in older people and people who are obese. See your doctor if you have sleeping problems for 3 weeks or longer or if you fall asleep during the day.

SECTION 4

REVIEW
Answer the following questions on a separate piece of paper.

Using Key Terms

1. **Name** the term that means "lack of sleep."

2. **Define** *circadian rhythm*.

3. **Identify** the term that means "the inability to fall asleep even if one is physically exhausted."
   a. sleep deprivation   c. circadian rhythm
   b. insomnia   d. sleep apnea

4. **Name** the condition in which a person has an interrupted breathing pattern during sleep.

Understanding Key Ideas

5. **List** the effects of sleep deprivation on your health.

6. **Describe** how sleep deprivation can affect daily life.

7. **Describe** what happens during NREM and REM sleep.

8. **LIFE SKILL** **Assessing Your Health** Which common causes of insomnia can you control? What changes would make the most improvement to your sleep?

Critical Thinking

9. Do you think insomnia can affect teens? Explain.

10. Give reasons why teens need more sleep than adults do.

CHAPTER 6

Highlights

Key Terms

SECTION 1

physical fitness (126)
chronic disease (126)
health-related fitness (128)
resting heart rate (RHR) (129)

SECTION 2

target heart
rate zone
(134)
FITT (136)
repetitions
(137)
set (138)

SECTION 3

dehydration (141)
overtraining (141)
dietary supplement (144)
anabolic steroid (145)

SECTION 4

sleep deprivation (146)
circadian rhythm (147)
insomnia (148)
sleep apnea (148)

The Big Picture

✔ Staying physically fit reduces the risk for certain chronic diseases.

✔ There are five components to health-related fitness; muscular endurance, muscular strength, cardiorespiratory endurance, flexibility, and body composition.

✔ Developing skill-related fitness is important for good athletic performance.

✔ People of all ages can benefit from regular physical activity.

✔ A fitness program must be suited to your abilities, your level of fitness, and your access to facilities and equipment.

✔ Calculating your resting heart rate (RHR) and your target heart rate zone are some of the first steps to designing a fitness program.

✔ Monitoring your heart rate during cardiorespiratory exercise is one of the best ways to monitor the intensity of the activity.

✔ Following the FITT formula can help you develop a safe and effective fitness program.

✔ Setting realistic fitness goals is the foundation of any fitness program.

✔ Most sports injuries can be avoided by proper conditioning, warming up and cooling down, stretching, avoiding dehydration, wearing safety equipment, and wearing the correct clothing and shoes.

✔ The damaging effects of overtraining and overuse can be long term.

✔ Most acute injuries should be treated immediately before swelling sets in. Rest, ice, compression, and elevation (RICE) is the most effective treatment.

✔ The usefulness of dietary supplements in improving athletic performance is not scientifically proven. The use of anabolic steroids for enhancing athletic performance is illegal.

✔ Sleep deprivation can increase stress, reduce productivity, lead to illness, and cause accidents.

✔ Teens need more sleep that children and adults.

✔ People with normal sleep patterns have a predictable alternating pattern of REM (dream sleep) and NREM (nondreaming) sleep.

✔ Sleeping habits can be improved by making simple dietary changes and by having a quiet, restful place to sleep.

Review

Using Key Terms

anabolic steroid (145)
chronic disease (126)
circadian rhythm (147)
dehydration (141)
dietary supplement (144)
FITT (136)
health-related fitness (128)
insomnia (148)
overtraining (141)
physical fitness (126)
repetitions (137)
resting heart rate (RHR) (129)
set (138)
sleep apnea (148)
sleep deprivation (146)
target heart rate zone (134)

1. For each definition below, choose the key term that best matches the definition.
   a. a fixed number of repetitions followed by a rest period
   b. synthetic form of the male hormone testosterone
   c. a disease that develops over a long period of time and, if treatable, takes a long time to treat
   d. the body's internal "clock"
   e. a formula used to assess how long, how often, and how hard you should exercise
   f. the number of times an exercise is performed

2. Explain the relationship between the key terms in each of the following pairs.
   a. *physical fitness* and *chronic disease*
   b. *overtraining* and *RICE*
   c. *sleep apnea* and *sleep deprivation*
   d. *RHR* and *target heart rate zone*

Understanding Key Ideas

Section 1

3. Describe five benefits of being physically fit.

4. List the five health-related components of fitness and an activity that develops each component.

5. What is the importance of skill-related fitness?

6. Explain how being a good sport can help you develop healthy life skills. **LIFE SKILL**

7. **CRITICAL THINKING** A friend says, "I don't have to bother to exercise. There'll be a cure for all of those diseases by the time I'm old!" Reply to these comments.

Section 2

8. What are the important factors to consider before starting a fitness program?

9. Describe each step in designing a fitness program.

10. Calculate the target heart rate zone of a 15-year-old.

11. Explain how the FITT formula can act as a guide when you are developing a fitness program.

12. In which of the following is the term *repetitions* used?
    a. running
    b. cycling
    c. weight lifting
    d. swimming

13. **CRITICAL THINKING** Explain the role of health fitness standards in designing a fitness program.

Section 3

14. What can you do to help prevent a sports injury?

15. List three signs of overtraining.

16. Describe the first steps in treating a minor sports injury.

17. Identify the effects of abusing anabolic steroids.

18. How can the FITT formula help you in avoiding a sports injury.

19. **CRITICAL THINKING** Your little sister who has just learned how to ride her bicycle says she no longer wants to wear her bicycle helmet because she "looks like a baby" while wearing it. What can you say to your sister to highlight the importance of wearing her bicycle helmet? **LIFE SKILL**

Section 4

20. Why is sleep so important?

21. Describe four consequences of not getting enough sleep.

22. How many hours of sleep a night do teens need?

23. In what phase of sleep does dreaming occur?

24. Identify four things you can do to get a good night's sleep. **LIFE SKILL**

Interpreting Graphics

Study the figure below to answer the questions that follow.

Six Leading Causes of Death

Cause of death	Percentage of total deaths	Lifestyle factors*
Heart disease	30	I, D, S
Cancer	23	I, D, S, A
Stroke	7	I, D, S
Respiratory disease	5	S
Accidents	4	
Diabetes	3	I, D

*I = inactivity, D = diet, S = smoking, A = alcohol

Source: Centers for Disease Control and Prevention.

25. Equal numbers of people die from heart disease as die from cancer, accidents, and diabetes combined. How can you determine this information from the graph? **MATH SKILL**

26. CRITICAL THINKING Based on the information in this chart, what is one of the most important lifestyle changes you can make to prevent heart disease?

Activities

27. Health and You Identify your target heart rate zone. Identify the purpose of knowing your target heart rate zone.

28. Health and You Keep an activity log for 1 day. Write down everything you do in a day and the length of time you do each activity. Identify wasted time, and see if you can fit in exercise time and more sleep time.

29. Health and Your Community Prepare a brochure that identifies locations in your community in which people of all ages can exercise regularly and safely. Include facility information, available classes, and fees.

Action Plan

30. LIFE SKILL Setting Goals Write a list of reasons you want to get more fit. Identify your short- and long-term goals. Write out an exercise contract that shows when, where, and what your program will be. Write down the day you will start.

Standardized Test Prep

Read the passage below, and then answer the questions that follow. **READING SKILL** **WRITING SKILL**

Jorge was always tired. He felt that he was always studying for an exam or writing reports for school. He was also depressed because his dad had some kind of heart disease and was in and out of the hospital. Jorge was often so tired after school that all he wanted to do was to flop down in front of the TV. Although he was exhausted, he found it difficult to fall asleep before midnight. However, he would often fall asleep much later in front of the flickering TV. He was on the school track team but had not been making training recently. The quality of his school work was also <u>deteriorating</u> and he was really fed up.

31. In this passage, the word *deteriorating* means
  A staying the same.
  B getting better.
  C getting worse.
  D often on time.

32. What can you infer from reading this passage?
  E Jorge is depressed.
  F Jorge is sleep deprived.
  G Jorge is probably going to lose his place on the track team.
  H all of the above

33. Write a paragraph describing how Jorge could change his life for the better. Suggest healthful changes Jorge can make in his lifestyle to feel better both physically and emotionally.

34. If Jorge sleeps an average of four and a half hours a night, how much sleep is he missing out on to get the recommended amount of sleep for teens? **MATH SKILL**

CHAPTER 7

Nutrition for Life

What's Your Health IQ?
KNOWLEDGE

Which of the statements below are true, and which are false? Check your answers on p. 638.

1. Consuming too many Calories, whether from protein, carbohydrate, or fat, will make you gain weight.

2. Peanut butter and potato chips are high in cholesterol.

3. Fiber isn't important because it cannot be absorbed.

4. You don't need to worry about getting enough vitamins and minerals because they are needed in such small amounts.

5. Water is a nutrient.

6. The Recommended Dietary Allowances are guidelines for the amounts of nutrients we need.

7. Snacking is bad for you.

Visit these Web sites for the latest health information:

HEALTH LINKS.
THE WORLD'S A CLICK AWAY

Find more information whenever you see a HealthLinks box. Go to **scilinks.org/health**, and type in the HealthLinks code.

go.hrw.com

Find worksheets and other materials that go with your textbook at **go.hrw.com**.

Current Health

Check out *Current Health* articles related to this chapter by visiting **go.hrw.com**. Just type in the keyword **HH4 CH07**.

SECTION 1

Carbohydrates, Fats, and Proteins

OBJECTIVES

Name the six classes of nutrients.

Identify the functions and food sources of carbohydrates, proteins, and fats.

Describe the need for enough fiber in your diet.

Identify one health disorder linked to high levels of saturated fats in the diet.

Describe how diet can influence health. **LIFE SKILL**

The saying "You are what you eat" reflects the idea that the food you eat affects how healthy you are.

Would you rather eat fruit salad, a hamburger, or yogurt? Each choice contains different amounts and combinations of the nutrients you need to stay healthy. But no one food provides them all.

What Is Nutrition?

How do you know if you are eating a balanced, healthy diet? **Nutrition** is the science or study of food and the ways in which the body uses food. It is also the study of how and why we make food choices. Nutrition is also the study of the nutrients foods contain. **Nutrients** are substances in food that provide energy or help form body tissues and are necessary for life and growth.

Six Classes of Nutrients There are six classes of nutrients in food—carbohydrates, fats, proteins, vitamins, minerals, and water. **Carbohydrates** are a class of energy-giving nutrients that includes sugars, starches, and fiber. **Fats** are a class of energy-giving nutrients and are the main form in which energy is stored in the body. **Proteins** (PROH teens) are a class of energy-giving nutrients made up of amino acids, which are needed to build and repair body structures and to regulate processes in the body.

A Balanced Diet Keeps You Healthy To stay alive, healthy, and growing, a person must eat and drink the right amounts of nutrients. Eating too little food causes weight loss, poor growth, and, in severe cases, death. But eating too much food can also cause poor health.

When you take in too much fat, too many carbohydrates, or too much protein, the extra energy is stored as body fat. Having excess body fat (also known as being *overweight)* increases the risks of *obesity* (weighing more than 20 percent above one's recommended weight). Excess body fat also increases the risk of developing heart disease, high blood pressure, and many other chronic diseases and disorders. Thus, if you have a healthy diet, you are more likely to be healthy and to stay healthy.

What you eat today not only affects how you look and feel right now but also can affect your health in the long term. The diet you follow during your teens can affect your risk of becoming overweight and developing obesity, heart disease, diabetes, osteoporosis, and cancer when you are in your 30s, 40s, or 50s. These diseases, which are common causes of death in the United States, are affected by diet.

Food Has Fuel for Your Body   Food provides the fuel that runs your body. The sum of the chemical processes that take place in your body to keep you alive and active is called *metabolism.* Metabolism requires energy and nutrients. The nutrients in food that provide energy are carbohydrates, fats, and proteins. In this section, we will look at carbohydrates, proteins, and fats. Vitamins, minerals, and water are also nutrients needed for metabolism, but they do not provide energy. These nutrients are discussed in the next section.

The energy in food is measured in Calories. **Figure 1** shows the amount of energy, in Calories, that certain foods offer. Carbohydrate and protein each provide 4 Calories per gram. Each gram of fat provides 9 Calories. So, 100 grams of bread, which is mostly carbohydrate, provides about 250 Calories. But 100 grams of chocolate cake, which contains more fat, provides about 100 additional Calories.

> **Healthy eating in adolescence is important for proper growth and development and can help prevent health problems such as obesity and diabetes.**

Figure 1

The number of Calories in a food depends on the amount of carbohydrate, fat, and protein that the food contains.

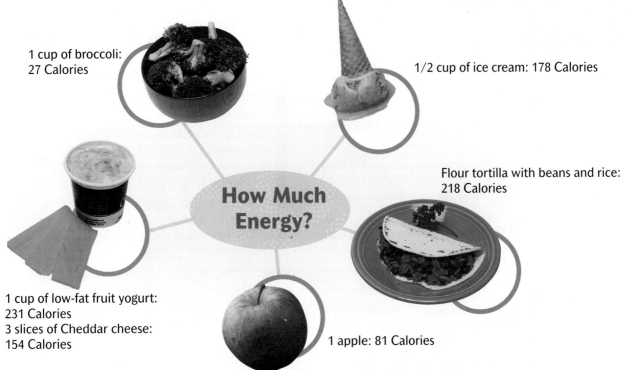

1 cup of broccoli: 27 Calories

1/2 cup of ice cream: 178 Calories

Flour tortilla with beans and rice: 218 Calories

How Much Energy?

1 cup of low-fat fruit yogurt: 231 Calories
3 slices of Cheddar cheese: 154 Calories

1 apple: 81 Calories

Carbohydrates

Carbohydrates, which are found in foods such as fruit, milk, cookies, and potatoes, are all made up of the same thing—sugars. There are two basic types of carbohydrates: simple and complex. Simple carbohydrates are made up of single or double sugar molecules. Complex carbohydrates are made of many sugar molecules that are linked together. The different types of carbohydrates are listed in **Figure 2**.

Sugars: Sweet and Simple Sugars are the simplest form of carbohydrate. The sugar that circulates in your blood and provides energy for your cells is a single-unit sugar called *glucose*. That is, glucose is a single molecule sugar. Other sugars are made of two single sugar molecules that are linked together. These are called *double sugars*. For example, table sugar is a double sugar called *sucrose* that is made of the single sugars glucose and fructose, which are linked together.

Sugars are found naturally in some foods and are added to others. The sweet taste of fresh fruit comes from the single sugar fructose. And about half the Calories in low-fat milk come from the milk sugar lactose. These unrefined foods are also sources of many other nutrients.

Foods such as candy, soda, and cakes are sweetened with added sugars. The sugar added to these foods is called *refined* because it has been separated from the plant that produced it. Refined sugar provides energy but hardly any nutrients. When you eat a lot of these foods you may be missing out on foods rich in nutrients.

Starches: Not So Simple Starches are a type of complex carbohydrate. Complex carbohydrates are made of many sugars that are connected together. Starch eaten in food is broken down by the body into sugars that can be used by the body.

Figure 2

Below are listed some simple and complex carbohydrates. Some foods, such as fruit, are healthier sources of simple carbohydrates than cookies are.

ACTIVITY *Give reasons why fruit is considered to be a healthier source of simple carbohydrates than cookies are.*

Simple

Glucose a single sugar that circulates in the blood (*blood sugar*); the most important sugar in the body because it provides energy to the body's cells; usually found as a part of the double sugar sucrose or in starch

Fructose a single sugar that is called *fruit sugar;* is sweeter than table sugar; found naturally in fruit and honey; added to many sweetened drinks

Lactose a double sugar made by animals that is also called *milk sugar;* found in dairy products

Sucrose a double sugar refined from sugar beets or sugar cane that we call *table sugar;* found in candies and baked goods and used as a table sweetener

Complex

Starch made of many glucose units linked together; found in foods like potatoes, beans, and grains

Glycogen made in the body; made of many glucose units linked together; stored in the muscle and liver of humans and animals; can be broken down to provide a quick source of glucose

Fiber made of many glucose units linked together; found in fruits and vegetables; cannot be digested by humans; needed for a healthy digestive system

The starches in our diet come from plant foods. Starchy vegetables (such as potatoes), legumes (beans and peas), and grains (rice, corn, and wheat) are all good sources of complex carbohydrates. It is recommended that 45 to 65 percent of the Calories in your diet come from carbohydrates. Most of these Calories should come from unrefined simple and complex carbohydrates.

Glycogen: Storage Carbohydrate If you consume more carbohydrates than your body needs, some will be stored as glycogen (GLIE kuh juhn). Glycogen is your body's quick energy reserve. It is made of highly branched chains of glucose, which can quickly be broken down into individual glucose units to be used by body cells. If glycogen stores become full, the body is able to convert carbohydrates from the diet into body fat.

Fiber Fiber is a type of complex carbohydrate that provides little energy and cannot be digested by humans. However, fiber is very important for your health. Fiber keeps your intestines healthy, prevents constipation, and may help prevent colon cancer and heart disease.

Fiber increases the amount of fluid and bulk in your digestive tract. Some kinds of fiber, called *soluble fiber*, dissolve in water. These soluble fibers hold water in your intestines, which increases the volume of material in your digestive tract. Soluble fibers are found in the soft pulp of oatmeal, apples, beans, and some vegetables. They help protect you against heart disease by "trapping" cholesterol from eaten food, therefore lowering blood cholesterol.

Other fibers do not dissolve in water. These *insoluble fibers* add bulk to your body's waste and are found in the hard or stringy part of fruits, vegetables, and grains. Wheat bran, corn, brown rice, and the skins of fruits and vegetables are good sources of insoluble fiber. Refined-grain products, such as white flour, are made by removing the germ and bran from each grain. Refining of grains results in a food that is lower in fiber and nutrients.

Fats

Fat is unhealthy, isn't it? Well, it depends on how you think about it. Fat is an essential nutrient. You need fat in your diet for your body to function properly. Fats also add to the texture, flavor, and aroma of our food. But eating too much fat and eating the wrong kinds of fat can increase your risk of weight gain, heart disease, and cancer.

What Is Fat? Fats belong to a class of chemical compounds called lipids (LIP idz), which are fatty or oily substances that do not dissolve in water. Fats are large molecules that are made up of two kinds of smaller molecules—*fatty acids* and *glycerol*. Three fatty acids are linked to one glycerol, which is why fats are also called *triglycerides.*

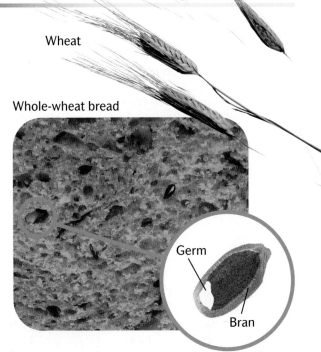

Wheat

Whole-wheat bread

Germ

Bran

Whole-grain products, such as whole-wheat bread, are made from the entire grain, including the bran and germ, which are rich in vitamins, minerals, and fiber.

Figure 3

The fat in foods is a mixture of saturated and unsaturated fat. Choosing foods that contain lower amounts of saturated fat can help protect you from heart disease.

ACTIVITY *Which foods contain the lowest percentage of saturated fats?*

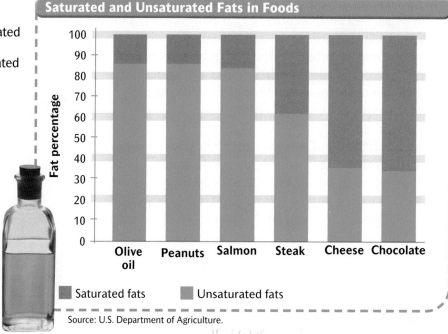

Saturated and Unsaturated Fats in Foods

Fat percentage: Olive oil, Peanuts, Salmon, Steak, Cheese, Chocolate

■ Saturated fats   ■ Unsaturated fats

Source: U.S. Department of Agriculture.

Four Fat Facts

1 Too little dietary fat can lead to a fatty-acid deficiency, but eating too much of the wrong types of fats can raise blood cholesterol levels.

2 Fat in your adipose tissue cushions your body's organs and helps keep your body temperature stable.

3 Fat is needed to make regulatory molecules in the body such as certain types of hormones. Fat is also needed to form the coating on nerves and the membranes that surround body cells.

4 Fats add to the taste and texture of food and help you feel full for several hours after you have eaten.

Fatty acids are long chains of carbon atoms that are chemically bonded to each other and are attached to hydrogen atoms. The length of the carbon chains and the number of hydrogen atoms attached affect how the fatty acid functions in the body. Likewise, the type of fatty acids in each type of fat affects how "good" or "bad" the fat is for you.

Saturated Fats   Some fatty acids are made up of a chain of carbon atoms with single bonds between each other. Each carbon atom is said to be *saturated* because it is bonded to as many hydrogen atoms as is chemically possible. *Saturated fats* are fats that are made up of saturated fatty acids.

Most saturated fats in our diets are solid at room temperature and come from animal foods such as meat and milk. A few vegetable oils such as coconut and palm oil also contain saturated fat. If you eat a lot of meat, whole milk, butter, and ice cream, your diet will be high in saturated fat. This type of diet can cause weight gain and can increase your blood cholesterol levels and your risk of heart disease.

Unsaturated Fats   Some fatty acids are made up of a chain of carbon atoms with one or more double bonds between the carbon atoms. These fatty acids are said to be *unsaturated* because the carbon atoms do not hold the maximum number of hydrogen atoms that is chemically possible. *Unsaturated fats* are fats that are made up of unsaturated fatty acids. They are more common in plants and tend to be liquid at room temperature. **Figure 3** shows the proportions of unsaturated and saturated fats that are found in some common foods.

Unsaturated fats that contain fatty acids that have only one set of double bonded carbons are called *monounsaturated fats*. Monounsaturated fats are found in olive oil, canola oil, and peanut oil. Diets in which the fats are mostly from monounsaturated fats are believed to lower the risk of heart disease. Fats that contain fatty acids with more than one double bond are called *polyunsaturated fats*. Corn oil, sunflower oil, and soybean oil are good sources of polyunsaturated fat. A polyunsaturated fatty acid called *omega-3* is found in seafood and some vegetable oils and may provide extra protection against heart disease. *Trans fats* are unsaturated fatty acids that are formed when vegetable oils are processed into margarine and shortening. They may increase the risk of heart disease. Total fat intake for teens should be 25 to 35 percent of total Calorie intake with limited amounts of saturated fat, cholesterol, and *trans* fat.

Cholesterol Cholesterol is another type of lipid. It is found in all human and animal tissues. Cholesterol is needed to make vitamin D, cell membranes, certain hormones, and bile (a substance that aids in fat digestion). Your body makes cholesterol, but you also get cholesterol from your diet.

Cholesterol combines with other molecules to circulate in the blood. One kind of cholesterol-containing molecule called *low-density lipoprotein* (LDL) brings cholesterol to the body cells. When levels of LDL cholesterol in the blood get too high, deposits called *plaque* (PLAK) form on the walls of blood vessels. Plaque can block blood flow to the heart muscle. Lack of blood flow starves the heart muscle of oxygen, causing a heart attack. Therefore, LDL cholesterol is known as "bad cholesterol."

Another molecule, called *high-density lipoprotein* (HDL), carries cholesterol back to the liver, where it is removed from the blood. High levels of HDL cholesterol called "good cholesterol" are linked to a reduced risk of developing heart disease.

Cholesterol is found only in animal tissue, so dietary cholesterol is found only in foods such as meat, fish, poultry, eggs, and dairy products. Cholesterol is not found in plants, so foods that come from plants are cholesterol free. The amount of cholesterol in the foods you eat is of concern because dietary cholesterol, like saturated fat, can increase blood cholesterol levels. When blood cholesterol levels rise, the risk of heart and blood vessel disease also increases.

Proteins

Your muscles, skin, hair, and nails are made up of mostly protein. Proteins in the body help build new cells and repair existing ones. Protein is also needed to form hormones, enzymes, antibodies, and other important molecules. If you eat more protein than is needed for these essential functions, it can be stored as fat.

Proteins are made up of chains of molecules called *animo acids*. The amino acids are linked together like beads on a necklace to make each type of protein. Twenty different amino acids make up body proteins. Nine of the amino acids needed to make body protein cannot be made in our bodies. These amino acids are called *essential*

Myth

Eating extra protein is important if you want to build bigger muscles.

Fact

Muscles grow in response to strength training, not to an increase in protein intake.

Legumes . . .

Grains . . .

Complete protein

Plants are sources of incomplete proteins. Eating a variety of plant proteins will supply you with all the essential amino acids.

amino acids and must be eaten in your diet to meet your body's needs. The other 11 amino acids can be made by the body and are called *nonessential amino acids*.

If one amino acid is missing when making a body protein, the protein cannot be made. If the missing amino acid is one of the nonessential amino acids, the body can make that amino acid and the protein can continue to be made. If the missing amino acid is an essential amino acid, it must be supplied by the diet or taken from other body proteins before the protein can be made again.

Complete and Incomplete Proteins   Protein in our diet comes from both animal and plant foods. For the body to maintain itself and grow, these proteins must provide all of the essential amino acids. Animal proteins such as meat, eggs, and dairy products contain all the essential amino acids. These proteins are therefore called *complete proteins*. Most plant proteins, found in foods such as legumes, grains, and vegetables, have smaller amounts of some essential amino acids than your body needs. These proteins are called *incomplete proteins*.

A healthy diet must include all the essential amino acids. A diet that contains both plant and animal foods can easily meet all of your amino acid needs. You can do this by eating a wide variety of foods, such as red and white meats, fish, dairy foods, legumes, nuts, and grains. People who don't eat meat can eat a variety of plant proteins to get enough of all of the amino acids to meet their needs. The combination of grains and legumes (as in a peanut butter sandwich) provides two different plant proteins that together supply all of the amino acids to meet the body's needs. Ten to thirty-five percent of your total Calorie intake should be from protein.

SECTION 1

REVIEW   *Answer the following questions on a separate piece of paper.*

Using Key Terms

1. **Define** the term *nutrition*.

2. **State** two functions of nutrients in your body.

3. **Name** the class of nutrients to which sugars and starches belong.

4. **Name** the class of nutrients that is made up of chains of amino acids.

5. **State** two functions of fats.

Understanding Key Ideas

6. **List** the six classes of nutrients.

7. **State** two functions of complex carbohydrates.

8. **Describe** how refining grains affects their fiber and nutrient content.

9. **Identify** the food that is *not* a source of cholesterol.
   a. beef   c. chicken
   b. beans   d. cheese

Critical Thinking

10. Which of these high-fat foods contains the healthiest type of fat? (Hint: See Figure 3.)
    a. olives   c. steak
    b. ice cream   d. coconut oil

11. **LIFE SKILL**   **Practicing Wellness** How can a person's diet affect his or her quality of life?

Vitamins, Minerals, and Water

OBJECTIVES

Describe the function and food sources of seven vitamins.

Describe the function and food sources of seven minerals.

Identify the importance of drinking enough water every day.

Name two ways to increase your calcium intake. **LIFE SKILL**

Carbohydrate, protein, and fat alone can't keep you alive and healthy. You also need the right proportions of vitamins, minerals, and water. Vitamins, minerals, and water do not provide energy but are needed for the body to function normally.

Vitamins

Vitamins are a class of nutrients that contain carbon and are needed in small amounts to maintain health and allow growth. Vitamins are sometimes added to foods that are low in certain vitamins. Vitamins are classified by whether they dissolve in fat or water. This affects how they are taken into the body, used, stored, and eliminated.

Fat-Soluble Vitamins As shown in **Table 1,** fat-soluble vitamins include vitamins A, D, E, and K. Because they dissolve in fat, most can be stored in fat tissue and remain in the body for a long time.

Table 1 Fat-Soluble Vitamins		
Vitamin	**Foods that have it**	**What it does**
A	▶ milk; yellow and orange fruits and vegetables; dark-green, leafy vegetables; eggs; cheese; butter	▶ keeps eyes and skin healthy; needed for growth and for strong bones and teeth
D	▶ fish oils, fortified milk, liver, egg yolk, salmon, butter, tuna; produced in the body by exposure of skin to ultraviolet light (UV) in sunlight	▶ promotes absorption of calcium and phosphorus in the intestine; needed for strong bones and teeth
E	▶ vegetable oils, beans, peas, nuts, dark-green vegetables, whole grains	▶ protects cell membranes from damage by reactive oxygen (free radicals)
K	▶ leafy vegetables such as spinach, kale, and broccoli; also produced in the intestine by bacteria	▶ aids in blood clotting

Water-Soluble Vitamins The eight B vitamins and vitamin C shown in **Table 2** are water soluble. Unlike fat-soluble vitamins, most water-soluble vitamins are not stored in the body very well. Although the B vitamins do not provide energy, most of them are needed to release energy from carbohydrates, fats, and proteins. Some also have other important functions. For example, folate helps prevent birth defects. Vitamin C is an antioxidant that probably helps protect us from heart disease and cancer. An *antioxidant* is a substance that is able to protect body structures from a highly chemically reactive form of oxygen called a *free radical*. Free radicals are normal byproducts of metabolism.

Table 2 Water-Soluble Vitamins

Vitamin	Foods that have it	What it does
B₁ (*Thiamin*)	▶ pork, liver, peas, beans, enriched and whole grains and cereals, nuts, seeds	▶ needed to produce energy from carbohydrates; helps the nervous system to function properly
B₂ (*Riboflavin*)	▶ milk; meat; eggs; whole grains; green, leafy vegetables; dried beans; enriched breads and cereals; pasta	▶ needed to produce energy from carbohydrates and fats; important for growth and healthy skin
B₃ (*Niacin*)	▶ meat, liver, fish, enriched and whole-grain breads and cereals, peas and beans, seeds	▶ needed to produce energy from carbohydrate, fat, and protein; needed for the nervous system and healthy skin
B₅ (*Pantothenic acid*)	▶ whole grains, meat, liver, broccoli, eggs, nuts, peas, beans	▶ needed to produce energy from carbohydrate, fat, and protein
B₆ (*Pyridoxine*)	▶ whole grains; liver; meat; fish; bananas; green, leafy vegetables; peas; beans	▶ needed for protein metabolism, the production of hemoglobin in red blood cells, and for the nervous system
B₁₂ (*Cobalamin*)	▶ meat, liver, dairy products, eggs	▶ necessary for forming cells (including red blood cells) and for a healthy nervous system
Folate (*Folic acid or folacin*)	▶ green vegetables, liver, whole and fortified grains, peas, beans, orange juice	▶ needed for forming cells (including red blood cells); helps prevent birth defects
Biotin	▶ liver, yogurt, egg yolk, peas, beans, nuts	▶ necessary for metabolism
C (*Ascorbic acid*)	▶ citrus fruits, melons, strawberries, green vegetables, peppers	▶ promotes healthy gums and teeth, the healing of wounds, and the absorption of iron; acts as an antioxidant to protect cells from damage

Minerals

More than 20 minerals are essential in small amounts to maintain good health. **Minerals** are a class of nutrients that are chemical elements that are needed for certain processes, such as enzyme activity and bone formation. Many of the common minerals are presented in **Table 3.**

Table 3	Some Important Minerals	
Mineral	**Foods that have it**	**What it does**
Calcium	▶ milk; dairy products; dark-green, leafy vegetables; tofu; legumes; shellfish; bony fish	▶ needed for development and maintenance of bones and teeth, transmission of nerve impulses, muscle contraction, blood clotting
Chromium	▶ meat, dairy products, whole grains, herbs, nuts, seeds	▶ helps regulate blood sugar
Copper	▶ liver, shellfish, peas, beans, nuts, seeds	▶ needed for the production of bone and red blood cells and the absorption of iron
Fluoride	▶ tea, fish, fluoridated toothpaste and water	▶ helps the strengthening of tooth enamel; helps in the prevention of cavities
Iodine	▶ iodized salt, seafood	▶ needed for production of thyroid hormones and normal cell function
Iron	▶ red meat, whole and enriched grains, dark-green vegetables, peas, beans, eggs	▶ necessary for production of hemoglobin
Magnesium	▶ milk; dairy products; green, leafy vegetables; peas; beans	▶ needed for bone growth, metabolism, and muscle contraction
Potassium	▶ meat; poultry; fish; bananas; oranges; dried fruits; potatoes; green, leafy vegetables; peas; beans	▶ needed for maintenance of fluid balance, transmission of nerve impulses, and muscle contraction
Phosphorus	▶ cereals, meats, milk, poultry	▶ needed for bone formation and cell reproduction
Selenium	▶ tuna, other seafood, whole grains, liver, meat, eggs	▶ needed for healthy heart function, antioxidant action, and healthy thyroid function
Sodium	▶ table salt, high-salt meats (ham), processed foods, dairy products, soy sauce	▶ needed for the regulation of water balance in cells and tissues and for transmission of nerve impulses
Sulfur	▶ meat, milk, eggs, nuts, grains	▶ needed for protein metabolism
Zinc	▶ seafood, meat, milk, poultry, eggs	▶ needed for growth and healing and for production of digestive enzymes

Vitamin and Mineral Supplements **Nutrient deficiency** is the state of not having enough of a nutrient to maintain good health. For most of us, a balanced diet can meet all of our vitamin and mineral needs. Supplements are available for those who cannot meet their vitamin or mineral needs with foods. However, supplements are not normally recommended for healthy people who can meet their nutrient needs through their normal diet.

If you need to take a supplement, take one that meets but does not exceed your needs. Too much or too little of a nutrient can result in malnutrition (improper nutrition, caused by poor diet or inability to absorb nutrients from foods). Most nutrient toxicities result from misuse of vitamin and mineral supplements.

Sodium Unfortunately, most of us eat far more salt than we need or than is healthy. Salt is made up of the minerals sodium and chloride. Sodium is needed by your body in very small amounts—about 500 milligrams, or 1/4 teaspoon of salt per day. It is recommended that your sodium intake should be no more than 2,400 milligrams per day, or about 1 1/4 teaspoon of salt. For some people, eating too much sodium causes an increase in blood pressure. High blood pressure can lead to heart disease, stroke, and kidney failure.

In the body, sodium and chloride, along with potassium, magnesium, and calcium act as *electrolytes*. Electrolytes are vital for processes such as muscle movement, nerve signals, and the transport of nutrients into and out of body cells. Electrolytes also help control fluid levels in your body.

Table salt is not the biggest source of sodium in our diets. Most of the sodium we eat comes from processed foods such as baked goods, snack foods, canned goods, and lunchmeats. Unprocessed foods, such as fresh fruits and vegetables, are low in sodium.

Calcium How much calcium do you need each day? The recommended daily intake for teens is 1,300 milligrams. One cup of milk (8 fluid ounces) has about 300 milligrams of calcium. Milk and other dairy products are the best sources of calcium in the American diet. Nondairy sources of calcium include

▶ green, leafy vegetables, such as spinach and broccoli
▶ calcium-fortified foods, such as bread and orange juice

Most of the calcium in your body is found in bone. About 45 percent of your skeleton forms between the ages of 9 and 17. People who don't eat or drink enough calcium when they are young have lighter, weaker bones than people who get a lot of calcium do. These people are more likely to develop a condition called *osteoporosis* as they grow older. Osteoporosis is a disorder in which the bones become brittle and break easily. One-half of all women over 50 will break a bone because of osteoporosis. Building strong bones now through eating or drinking foods high in calcium (as well as vitamin D and other minerals) can prevent such problems in the future. However, as **Figure 4** shows, many teens today are not getting enough calcium.

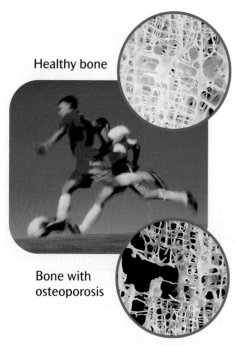

Healthy bone

Bone with osteoporosis

Too little calcium in the diet during childhood and the teen years can cause a person to have low bone density even before he or she reaches adulthood. Low bone density can lead to osteoporosis later in life. Osteoporosis is a condition in which bones are thin and porous and can break easily.

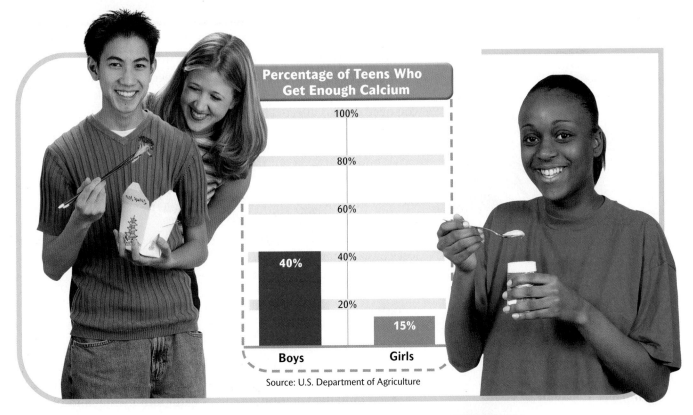

Percentage of Teens Who Get Enough Calcium

Boys: 40%
Girls: 15%

Source: U.S. Department of Agriculture

Iron Iron-deficiency anemia (uh NEE mee uh) is one of the most common nutritional deficiencies in the world. Anemia is a condition in which there are not enough red blood cells or hemoglobin to carry oxygen around the body. Iron is needed to make hemoglobin, the molecule in red blood cells that carries oxygen. When there is not enough iron in the diet, the blood cannot deliver enough oxygen to the cells. Anemia causes you to feel tired and weak.

The best sources of iron in the diet are red meats because they contain a form of iron that is easily absorbed. The iron in plant foods such as green vegetables is not absorbed as well as iron from meat but is still an important source of dietary iron. Teen girls need 18 milligrams of iron and teen boys need 12 milligrams of iron daily. People who have anemia are often given iron supplements. Too much iron can be poisonous. Iron toxicity from iron supplements is one of the most common forms of poisoning among young children.

Water

You can live for many weeks without food but only for a few days without water. How can a substance that has no taste, no color, and no Calories be so important? One reason is that about 60 percent of your body is water. Water is essential because it is necessary for almost every function that keeps you alive.

Eight Glasses a Day Every day, your body loses a large amount of water by excretion of urine and solid wastes, by evaporation through breathing, through your skin, and as you sweat. Extra water cannot be stored in the body; therefore, water intake must balance what your body loses.

Figure 4

Getting enough calcium during childhood and teenage years helps build bone density. However, most teens don't get enough calcium in their diets.

Myth

Sports drinks are always the best choice during a workout or exercise.

Fact

Plain water is often the best choice during activity that is less than 60 minutes long.

Some of your water intake can come from food. About 80 to 90 percent of the weight of most fruits and vegetables is water. The rest of your water needs must be met from fluids you drink. The amount you need daily is affected by your diet, your activity level, and by how hot and humid the weather is. You can usually get enough water by drinking eight glasses of fluid each day. Water, juice, and low-fat milk are healthy sources of fluid. Drinks containing caffeine are poor water sources. The reason is that caffeine increases the amount of water excreted in urine.

Dehydration Is Dangerous   Dehydration occurs when the body loses more water than has been taken in. It can occur when you don't drink enough fluid or when you lose more water than normal. You can lose even more water when you are ill. For example, a fever, vomiting, and diarrhea all increase water loss. Exercise also makes you lose water through sweating. When your body becomes too hot, your sweat glands in the skin make sweat. As the water in sweat evaporates, heat is lost and your body temperature drops. Exercising in hot weather can cause you to lose up to a quart of water in an hour!

Even mild dehydration interferes with both mental and physical performance. Symptoms of dehydration include thirst, headache, fatigue, loss of appetite, dry eyes and mouth, and dark-colored urine. As dehydration becomes more severe, nausea, difficulty concentrating, confusion, and disorientation result. If the dehydration is severe enough, death may occur. As you lose water from your body, you lose weight. Weight lost through dehydration is not fat loss, and the weight is quickly put back on when you replace the lost water.

Three Reasons Why Water Is Important

1 It transports nutrients and oxygen through the body and helps to get rid of wastes from the body.

2 It provides the proper environment for the body's chemical reactions to occur.

3 It helps regulate body temperature.

SECTION 2

REVIEW   *Answer the following questions on a separate piece of paper.*

Using Key Terms

1. **Name** the term for "a class of nutrients that contain carbon and are needed in small amounts to maintain health and allow growth."

2. **Identify** the term for "chemical elements that are needed for enzyme activity and bone formation."
   - **a.** vitamin
   - **b.** protein
   - **c.** mineral
   - **d.** water

3. **Name** the term that means "not having enough of a nutrient to maintain good health."

Understanding Key Ideas

4. **List** the functions of vitamin A, vitamin C, and vitamin D.

5. **Name** the nutrient that is related to osteoporosis.

6. **Identify** why the following people are at risk of dehydration: Sara, who just ran a marathon, and Jeff, who has been vomiting

7. **LIFE SKILL** **Practicing Wellness** Identify some nondairy sources of calcium.

Critical Thinking

8. **LIFE SKILL** **Assessing Your Health** Give possible reasons for the decrease in calcium intake by teens.

9. **LIFE SKILL** **Practicing Wellness** How can food processing affect the sodium content of foods?

Meeting Your Nutritional Needs

OBJECTIVES

Describe what the Recommended Dietary Allowances (RDAs) are.

Analyze the nutritional value of a food by using the information on the food label.

Identify the purpose of the MyPyramid food guidance system and identify foods from each of its food groups.

Summarize the Dietary Guidelines for Americans.

Determine whether your daily diet meets the MyPyramid recommendations. **LIFE SKILL**

KEY TERMS

Recommended Dietary Allowances (RDAs) recommended nutrient intakes that will meet the needs of almost all healthy people

Daily Value (DV) recommended daily amount of a nutrient; used on food labels to help people see how a food fits into their diet

MyPyramid a food guidance system that encourages healthy food choices and daily activity

Dietary Guidelines for Americans a set of diet and lifestyle recommendations developed to improve health and reduce nutrition-related disease risk in the U.S. population

K nowing which nutrients your body needs and what foods contain them is a good first step towards a healthy diet. The government has developed several types of recommendations to help you choose how much of each nutrient you need to eat to have a healthy, balanced diet.

The aim of the RDAs is to guide you in meeting your nutrition needs with food.

How Much of Each Nutrient?

Nutrition scientists and public health agencies have developed guidelines for how much of each nutrient we need. The current guidelines are the *Dietary Reference Intakes* (DRIs). The DRIs provide recommendations for the number of Calories and amounts of nutrients and other food components needed to prevent deficiencies, avoid toxicities, and promote best health.

The DRIs have separate recommendations for males and females, different age groups, and special conditions, such as pregnancy. Two types of reference values—Recommended Dietary Allowances and Tolerable Upper Intake Levels—are discussed in more detail below.

What Are RDAs? **Recommended Dietary Allowances (RDAs)** are the recommended nutrient intakes that will meet the needs of almost all healthy people. The RDAs are not exact requirements but are meant to serve as general guidelines for correct nutrient intake. The *Tolerable Upper Intake Levels* (ULs) are the largest amount of a nutrient you can take without risking toxicity. The ULs are helpful for checking that the amount of a nutrient in a supplement is safe.

Food Labels: The Nutrition Facts

Food labels provide a convenient source of nutritional information about foods and the way foods fit into your diet. The Nutrition Facts panel on the labels of packaged foods can help you make healthy choices easily and quickly.

Serving Size The size of a single serving is shown at the top of the Nutrition Facts panel. The amounts of nutrients given below the serving size are the amounts found in one serving. Often, the portion in which certain foods (such as snacks) are sold contains more than one serving.

Calories The label must list total Calories and the Calories from fat in a serving of the food. Any food that has more than 400 Calories per serving is considered to be high in Calories.

Daily Values Nutrients are listed on food labels by amounts and as percentages of Daily Values. The **Daily Value (DV)** of a nutrient is the recommended amount that a person should consume in a day. Knowing the DVs of nutrients can help you ensure that you are not getting too much or too little of any nutrient.

The percentage of the DV of a nutrient (shown under the heading "% Daily Value") tells you what percentage of the recommended amount of the nutrient is provided by one serving of the food if your diet contains 2,000 Calories. For example, a food that provides 10 percent of the DV for fiber provides 10 percent of the amount of fiber recommended per day for a 2,000-Calorie diet. If a food provides 5 percent or less of the DV of a nutrient, the food is considered low in that nutrient. If a food provides 20 percent or more of the DV of a nutrient, the food is considered high in that nutrient.

▶ **Total fat** The Nutrition Facts panel lists total fat and the subsets of saturated fat and *trans* fat. To keep your fat intake at a healthy level, look for foods that provide low percentages of the DVs for total fat and saturated fat. There is no DV for *trans* fat.

▶ **Cholesterol** To help keep your blood cholesterol within a healthy range, look for foods that provide a low percentage of the DV for cholesterol.

▶ **Sodium** Most of the sodium in a typical American diet comes from processed foods. Keep your sodium intake at a healthy level by choosing foods that provide a low percentage of the DV for sodium. Look for foods labeled "low sodium" (140 milligrams of sodium or less) or "reduced sodium" (25 percent less sodium than the regular food).

▶ **Total carbohydrates** The Nutrition Facts panel lists total carbohydrate and the subsets of fiber and sugar. Choosing foods labeled "high fiber" (20 percent or more of the DV of fiber) or a "good source of fiber" (10 percent or more of the DV of fiber) can help increase your fiber intake. The sugars subset includes natural sugars, such as the sugar in milk, and added sugar, such as the refined sugar in cookies.

▶ **Protein** Because most Americans eat more than enough protein, the percentage of the DV of protein is usually not listed.

Food labels can help you see how a food fits into your daily diet. Foods that appear to be similar to each other, such as breakfast cereals, may in fact contain different amounts of nutrients.

How to Use Food Labels

1 "Serving Size" shows the amount of food that counts as one serving.

2 "Calories" lists the number of Calories in one serving and the number of Calories that come from fat.

3 Total fat, saturated fat, *trans* fat, cholesterol, sodium, total carbohydrates, dietary fiber, sugars, and protein are listed.

4 "% Daily Value" shows the percentage of the recommended amount of the nutrient that is met by one serving of food.

5 Calcium, iron, vitamin C, vitamin A, and some B vitamins are listed.

6 Recommended daily intakes for 2,000- and 2,500-Calorie diets are listed.

Your Turn

1. Calculate the percentage of Calories from total fat in the food. **MATH SKILL**

2. CRITICAL THINKING If you needed 2,500 Calories a day, what percentage of the DV for fiber does a serving of this food provide? **MATH SKILL**

Nutrition Facts

Serving Size 1 bar (37g)
Servings Per Container 8

Amount Per Serving

Calories 140	Calories from Fat 25

	% Daily Value*
Total Fat 2.5g	**4%**
Saturated Fat 0.5g	**3%**
Trans Fat 0g	
Cholesterol 0mg	**0%**
Sodium 60mg	**2%**
Total Carbohydrate 27g	**9%**
Dietary Fiber 1g	**4%**
Sugars 14g	
Protein 1g	

Vitamin A 15%	Vitamin C 0%
Calcium 20%	Iron 20%
Thiamin 35%	Riboflavin 35%
Niacin 35%	Vitamin B6 40%

*Percent Daily Values are based on a 2,000 calorie diet. Your daily values may be higher or lower depending on your calorie needs:

	Calories:	2,000	2,500
Total Fat	Less than	65g	80g
Sat Fat	Less than	20g	25g
Cholesterol	Less than	300mg	300mg
Sodium	Less than	2,400mg	2,400mg
Total Carbohydrate		300g	375g
Dietary Fiber		25g	30g
Protein		50g	60g

Vitamins and Minerals Some of the vitamins and minerals that you need are also listed. Calcium, iron, vitamin C, vitamin A, and some B vitamins are given on labels only as a percentage of the DV.

Other Terms on Food Labels

You may sometimes be confused by the terms used in the ingredients list or on the food packaging. **Figure 5** on the next page lists and explains what some of these terms are.

Ingredient List The ingredients in a product are listed on the label in order of weight—those present in the largest amounts are listed first. Knowing the ingredients in a food is helpful to people who choose to avoid certain foods or who have food allergies. For example, to identify foods containing whole grains, look for terms such as *whole wheat* or *rolled oats* in the ingredient list.

Additives are also included in the ingredient list. Additives are substances added to foods to keep the foods from spoiling or to improve the taste, smell, texture, appearance, or nutrient content of a food.

Figure 5

Certain ingredient names and terms used on food packaging may be confusing.

ACTIVITY *List three terms not shown in the table that are commonly found on food labels.*

Calories Some foods are *calorie free* (less than 5 Calories), *light* or *lite* (one-third fewer Calories than the regular food has), *low calorie* (no more than 40 Calories), or *reduced calorie* (25 percent fewer Calories than the regular food has) to help a person reduce his or her Calorie intake.

Cholesterol Foods can be called *low cholesterol* (20 milligrams or less) or *cholesterol free* (less than 2 milligrams).

Sugars Sugars added to foods are included in the ingredient list, but sugars are not always called *sugar*. Look for *sucrose, fructose, dextrose, maltose, lactose, honey, syrup, corn syrup, high-fructose corn syrup, molasses, invert sugar,* and *fruit juice concentrate.* If any of these ingredients are listed first or second on the list or if several of them appear, the food is probably high in added sugar. Foods that have little or no added sugars can carry the words *sugar free* (less than 0.5 grams of sugar), *no sugar added, without added sugar,* or *reduced sugar* (25 percent less sugar than the regular food has).

Fats Food can be described as *fat free* (less than 0.5 grams fat), *low fat* (3 grams of fat or less), or *extra lean* (less than 5 grams of fat). Foods may also claim to be *low in saturated fat* (1 gram or less). It is important to remember that even though a food may be labeled *low fat*, it can still be high in Calories.

Other Ingredients and Terms on Food Labels

Aspartame, sucralose, and saccharine
artificial sweeteners

Monosodium glutamate (MSG)
flavor enhancer

Artificial colors
(*such as FD&C colors*) food colors added to make the food look more appealing

Sulfites, BHA, and BHT
food preservatives

Enriched
a food to which nutrients have been added to restore some of those lost in the processing of the food

Fortified
a food to which nutrients have been added

Treated by irradiation
food that has been exposed to radiation to kill microorganisms and slow ripening and spoilage

Pasteurized
food that has been heated to kill disease-causing organisms (seen on the labels of products such as milk, apple juice, and eggs)

Genetically modified
a food whose genes have been modified to produce desirable characteristics

Organic
a food produced under certain standards without the use of synthetic pesticides or fertilizers

Freshness date
the last day a food should be used to ensure best quality

Sell by date
the last date a perishable food should be sold

Expiration date
the last date a food should be used before the chance of spoilage increases

Health and disease claims
(*such as "May help reduce blood cholesterol"*) government approved claims made about the relationship between a nutrient or food and a disease or health

MyPyramid: Steps to a Healthier You

To build a healthy diet, you should choose foods that give you the right amounts of the nutrients that your body needs. The **MyPyramid** food guidance system is a tool that can help you choose what to eat and how much to eat every day. The MyPyramid symbol, shown below, includes six colored stripes. Five of the stripes represent food groups. The sixth (yellow) stripe represents oils, which are also part of a healthy diet.

Each food group is made up of foods that contain similar nutrients. The width of each stripe shows you the relative proportion of your diet that should be made up of foods from that group. The groups that have the widest stripes are grains, vegetables, fruits, and milk. The amount of food from each group that a person needs each day depends on the person's age, sex, and level of physical activity.

The person shown climbing the steps of the MyPyramid symbol serves as a reminder that being physically active every day is important for good health. For teens, about an hour of activity every day is recommended.

The U.S. Department of Agriculture named this food guidance system *MyPyramid* in order to emphasize that "one size doesn't fit all" when it comes to health. To find out MyPyramid's recommendations for you, visit **go.hrw.com** and type in the keyword **HOLT PYRAMID.**

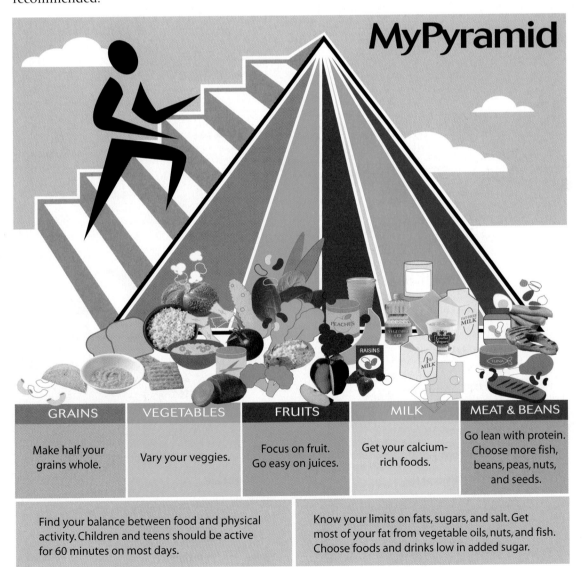

GRAINS	VEGETABLES	FRUITS	MILK	MEAT & BEANS
Make half your grains whole.	Vary your veggies.	Focus on fruit. Go easy on juices.	Get your calcium-rich foods.	Go lean with protein. Choose more fish, beans, peas, nuts, and seeds.

Find your balance between food and physical activity. Children and teens should be active for 60 minutes on most days.

Know your limits on fats, sugars, and salt. Get most of your fat from vegetable oils, nuts, and fish. Choose foods and drinks low in added sugar.

A Closer Look at MyPyramid

The MyPyramid food guidance system emphasizes five food groups that everyone should include in his or her diet. Recommended amounts from each food group are provided below for a 2,000-Calorie diet, which is an average amount of Calories needed per day. Your daily Calorie needs may be higher or lower depending on your age, sex, and activity level.

Grains

The orange band of the MyPyramid symbol represents grains. Foods in this group are high in complex carbohydrates, fiber, B vitamins, and minerals. These foods are also low in cholesterol. At least half of your grain choices should be whole-grain foods, such as whole-wheat bread, oatmeal, brown rice, and barley.

For a 2,000-Calorie diet, you should eat 6 ounces of grains every day.

Each of the following counts as 1 ounce from the grains group:
- 1 slice of bread
- 1 packet of instant oatmeal
- 1 cup of breakfast cereal
- ½ cup of cooked rice or pasta
- 3 cups of popcorn

Vegetables

Fruits

The green stripe represents vegetables, and the red stripe represents fruits. Both groups are good sources of vitamins, minerals, and fiber. Fruits and vegetables are low in Calories and fat and do not have cholesterol. Try to eat plenty of dark green vegetables (such as broccoli and spinach) and orange vegetables (such as carrots and sweet potatoes). Eat a variety of fruit, but limit fruit juices.

For a 2,000-Calorie diet, you should eat 2½ cups of vegetables and 2 cups of fruit every day.

Each of the following counts as 1 cup from the vegetable group:
- 2 cups of leafy salad greens
- 2 medium carrots or 12 baby carrots
- 1 large ear of corn
- 1 large tomato

Each of the following counts as 1 cup from the fruit group:
- 1 small or ½ large apple
- 1 large banana
- 8 large strawberries
- ½ cup of dried fruit

Milk

The blue stripe represents the milk group. The milk group includes dairy foods, such as milk, yogurt, and cheese. These foods are high in calcium, protein, and vitamins A and D. Choose low-fat and fat-free products to keep the amount of saturated fat in your diet low. You can also choose other calcium sources such as fortified foods and beverages.

For a 2,000-Calorie diet, you should eat 3 cups from the milk group every day.

Each of the following counts as 1 cup from the milk group:
- 1 half-pint container of milk
- an 8-ounce container of yogurt
- 3 slices of processed cheese
- $1\frac{1}{2}$ cups of ice cream

Meat and Beans

The purple stripe represents meats, such as beef, poultry, and fish, as well as dried beans, nuts, seeds, and eggs. Foods in this group are high in protein, B vitamins, and minerals. However, because many of these foods are from animals, they can be high in fat and cholesterol. Choose lean meats and poultry. Vary your protein choices by eating more fish, nuts, and seeds. These choices are low in saturated fat and do not have cholesterol.

For a 2,000-Calorie diet, you should eat $5\frac{1}{2}$ ounces from the meat and beans group every day.

Each of the following counts as 1 ounce from the meat and beans group:
- 1 egg
- 1 tablespoon of peanut butter
- $\frac{1}{4}$ cup of tofu
- $\frac{1}{4}$ can of tuna
- 1 slice of lunch meat

Oils

The thin yellow stripe in the MyPyramid symbol represents liquid oils, which are unsaturated fats. Liquid oils are not considered a food group in the MyPyramid food guidance system, but they are represented in the symbol because they are an important part of a healthy diet. Liquid oils include olive oil, canola oil, and other oils that come from nuts, seeds, and fish. Some of these oils are part of the foods you eat, and some are added to foods during cooking. You should limit solid fats, such as butter, margarine, and beef fat, in your diet.

Dietary Guidelines for Americans

The **Dietary Guidelines for Americans** are a set of recommendations designed to improve the diets and health of Americans. These guidelines focus on helping Americans get more nutrients in fewer Calories, improve the balance between the amount of food that they eat and the amount of exercise that they get, and limit dietary items that may contribute to disease.

More Nutrients, Fewer Calories Americans are eating more food but getting fewer nutrients. Thus, the Dietary Guidelines for Americans encourage the consumption of foods that are rich in nutrients (such as vitamins, minerals, and fiber) but low in Calories. Such foods include fruits, vegetables, whole grains, and low-fat milk products.

Balancing Food and Physical Activity Regular exercise can help you stay in a healthy weight range by balancing the energy that you take in from food with the energy that your body uses each day. The guidelines recommend that teens get 60 minutes of exercise every day.

Limiting Certain Types of Nutrients Although you need fat and carbohydrates, some types are healthier than others. The guidelines recommend low intakes of saturated fat, *trans* fat, cholesterol, and added sugars. Salt should be limited, too.

The Dietary Guidelines for Americans also indicate that adults who drink alcohol should do so in moderation. The guidelines also provide recommendations on how to prepare, handle, and store food safely.

SECTION 3

REVIEW   *Answer the following questions on a separate piece of paper.*

Using Key Terms

1. **Name** the standard that is used on food labels to help you find out how a food fits into your daily diet.

2. **Identify** the food guidance system that helps you choose amounts and types of food.

3. **Name** the set of recommendations designed to improve the diets and health of Americans.

Understanding Key Ideas

4. **State** the purpose of RDAs.

5. **State** the function of food labels.

6. **Identify** the purpose of the MyPyramid system.

7. **Name** the food group to which each of the foods below belongs in MyPyramid.
   a. rice   **c.** bean sprouts
   b. peanut butter   **d.** salmon

8. **Describe** how the Dietary Guidelines for Americans can fit into your daily life.

Critical Thinking

9. **LIFE SKILL** **Evaluating Information** Anne's diet contains foods from each of the food groups. The only vegetable that Anne eats is French fries, her dairy intake is ice cream, and many of her grain servings are from baked goods. Does Anne have a healthy diet? Explain.

SECTION 4

Choosing a Healthful Diet

OBJECTIVES

Identify why certain foods are called junk foods.

Describe examples of healthful snacks.

Compare the dietary needs of infants, children, teenagers, and adults.

Describe the special dietary needs of athletes, pregnant women, and people who are ill.

Identify reasons why vegetarians need to carefully plan their diet.

Identify ways to reduce saturated fat, sugar, and salt in your diet.

LIFE SKILL

Potato chips or popcorn? Chicken fried steak or stir fried vegetables? The foods you choose can make the difference between a diet that provides all of your nutrient needs and protects you from disease and one that does not.

Simple Steps to a More Healthful Diet

Does a healthy diet sound boring and unappetizing? It doesn't have to be! Many simple steps can improve your diet without cutting out your favorite foods. For example, just skipping one can of soda will cut 10 teaspoons of added sugar from your diet.

Is Junk Food a Problem?   Depending on whom you talk to, candy bars, potato chips, cookies, tacos, or pizza may be called *junk food*. But none of these foods are really junk, and they don't have to be cut from your diet.

The key to whether a food is a healthy food or a junk food is how many nutrients it provides relative to how many Calories it contains. The foods we think of as junk food are usually high in Calories and have large amounts of fat, sugar, or salt but contain few other nutrients. These foods have a low nutrient density. **Nutrient density** is a measure of the nutrients in a food compared with the energy the food provides. For example, a chocolate candy bar may taste good and fill you up, but it provides few nutrients in its 200 or more Calories. Therefore, the candy bar is not a nutrient-dense food and is said to have "empty" Calories.

If you really want a candy bar, having one is OK, but try to make up for the nutrients missing from the candy bar by eating healthier foods at other times during the day. The key words to remember are *variety, moderation,* and *balance.* Junk food is only a problem if it makes up a large part of your diet.

Choosing healthy snacks throughout the day can keep you from eating too much junk food.

Instead of this: Try this:

To lower your sugar intake:

Instead of this:	Try this:
Soda with your meals	Water, real fruit juice, or skim milk
Cake for dessert	Fresh fruit
Candy for snacks	Grapes, raisins, or trail mix

To lower your intake of unhealthy fats:

Instead of this:	Try this:
A hamburger and fries for lunch	A broiled chicken sandwich and a shared order of fries with a friend
Sausage and pepperoni pizza	Olive and mushroom pizza
Creamy chip dip	Salsa
Blue cheese salad dressing	Low-fat or fat-free dressing
Fried cheese sticks	Vegetables and ranch dressing

To increase your intake of fiber:

Instead of this:	Try this:
White rice	Brown rice or baked potatoes with the skin
A white bread sandwich	A whole-wheat bread sandwich
Apple juice	A fresh apple
Frosted cornflakes	Oatmeal or granola

Some of the foods you think of as junk foods may actually be healthy foods depending on how they are prepared and what choices you make. For example, a slice of pizza includes a vegetable in the tomato sauce, a grain in the crust, and a dairy product in the cheese. If you add some pineapple or bell peppers, you are adding to your fruit and vegetable servings. A taco includes meat or beans, vegetables, cheese and bread—all of which are part of the MyPyramid recommendations. Be careful when having these foods at fast-food restaurants because they may be prepared with more added fat and salt than you would use at home.

Learning to make these foods at home can save you money, reduce your fat and sodium intakes, and increase your vegetable servings. Preparing foods correctly will also reduce vitamin losses.

Choose the Right Snacks   Snacking isn't a "bad habit." When done right, it increases your nutrient intake and helps you maintain a healthy weight. A piece of fruit and a yogurt on the way to school is much better than not having any breakfast.

The problem with snacking is that we don't always choose healthy foods. Sometimes, chips and a candy bar from the vending machine may seem like your only choice. But planning ahead can improve your options. For example, if you know you will be staying late at school, bring an extra sandwich, a carton of yogurt, or an apple from home. If you do get chips or candy from the vending machine, make sure to balance these choices, which have low nutrient density, with meals that include a variety of healthy foods.

Nutrition Throughout Life

Would you feed an apple to a newborn baby? Of course not—the baby wouldn't be able to eat it and it certainly wouldn't meet his or her nutrient needs. Nutrient needs change with each stage of life—infancy, childhood, adolescence, and adulthood.

A Healthy Start in Infancy
In the first months of your life, your diet was fairly simple: milk from either your mother's breast or a bottle. A baby who is breast-fed gets the best nutrition possible for a human infant—the right mix of nutrients, Calories, and substances that help protect the baby from infections. Formula-fed infants get a diet designed to provide the same nutrients as breast milk does. This liquid diet provides all the energy and nutrients an infant needs until about 6 months of age. It is higher in fat than diets recommended for older children and adults are because infants need fat to provide energy and to allow their rapid growth and brain development.

After 4 to 6 months of life, the infant's diet can begin to include soft foods such as cereals and puréed fruits or vegetables. And soon the infant can eat foods such as crackers and soft meats. On this diet, a healthy 1-year-old will have tripled his or her weight since birth.

Continuing Good Nutrition in Childhood
From 2 years of age onward, children can generally meet their nutrient needs by following the recommendations of the MyPyramid food guidance system. The amount of food a child eats depends on his or her size, growth rate, and activity level. A larger, more active child will need more Calories and other nutrients than a smaller, less active child needs. Like adolescents and adults, children should eat plenty of whole grains, fruits, and vegetables.

A person's nutritional needs change at each stage of life—infancy, childhood, adolescence, and adulthood. For example, infants and children need more food energy per pound of body weight than adults do.

Teens Need to Eat Right to Grow When was the last time you had a fast-food meal? If it was within the past 2 days, you're not alone. Many teens have busy schedules, so they frequently eat meals away from home or skip meals altogether. Teenagers also tend to drink too little milk and too many sodas. As a result, teen diets are often low in important nutrients, such as calcium for strong bones and iron for blood and muscle growth. Teens' diets also tend to be low in folate for tissue growth and riboflavin for energy production.

During your teen years, your body experiences a major growth spurt. As growth and development speed up, your body needs more energy, protein, vitamins, and minerals. As a general rule, the more active you are, the more Calories and nutrients your body needs to grow and be healthy.

Most U.S. teens eat enough to meet their energy needs. In fact, many teens are consuming too many Calories and gaining more weight than is healthy. Teens should choose foods to meet nutrient needs and not exceed energy needs. They can do so by eating plenty of nutrient-dense foods and minimizing the amount of high-fat and high-sugar foods.

real life Activity

HOW HEALTHFUL IS YOUR DIET?

LIFE SKILL
Assessing Your Health

Materials

✔ paper
✔ pencil
✔ colored pencils

Procedure

1. **Record** everything you ate yesterday.

2. **Compare** what you ate to the recommendations of the MyPyramid food guidance system.

3. **Draw** a pyramid to represent the foods that you ate yesterday. Using the same colors used in the MyPyramid symbol, draw six stripes on your pyramid to represent the food groups. The width of each stripe should correspond to the amount of food eaten from each food group.

Conclusions

1. **Evaluating Information** Did you eat something from each food group? If not, which food group(s) did you miss?

2. **Predicting Outcomes** Write down three ideas that will help you eat from each food group every day.

3. **Summarizing Results** How does your one-day pyramid compare with the MyPyramid recommendations?

4. **CRITICAL THINKING** Explain why you would need to do this activity several days in a row to get an accurate idea of how well your diet follows the MyPyramid recommendations.

Adults Aren't Growing As you enter adulthood, growth in height slows and then stops. As a result, the number of Calories a person needs to maintain a healthy weight decreases. Recommended fat intake for adults is 20 to 35 percent of total Calorie intake. With this lower Calorie requirement, one must carefully plan the diet to include nutrient-dense foods that provide for nutrient needs without exceeding Calorie needs. As adults become less active, their Calorie needs continue to decrease. This often leads to weight gain that is commonly known as "middle-age spread." In addition, in older adults the absorption of some nutrients decreases, which makes a nutrient dense diet even more important.

Special Dietary Needs

Athletes, pregnant women, and people who are ill have special dietary needs. Food is fuel and your body is like a machine that cannot run without it. Putting the optimum "mix" of foods into your body will ensure good nutrition, whatever your nutrient needs.

Special Requirements of Athletes Whether training, competing, or just wanting to stay fit, athletes need extra energy and water to maintain their performance and endurance. The best strategy for athletes is to follow a diet based on the MyPyramid recommendations and to drink plenty of fluids.

Athletes need a diet high in carbohydrates to provide the quick energy required for exercise. Following the MyPyramid recommendations will provide a diet that is high in complex carbohydrates and rich in the B vitamins.

Even athletes who have increased protein needs, such as weight lifters and endurance athletes, get more than enough protein in their daily diet. A common misconception is that athletes need to eat large amounts of protein to build larger muscles. In fact, it is weight training combined with a well-balanced diet that is needed to develop muscles. Protein, especially protein from meat, is also a good source of iron. Iron is needed to carry oxygen to tissues and prevent muscle fatigue. Female athletes should be extra careful to get enough iron in their diets as iron is lost each month during menstruation.

Athletes Must Eat and Drink to Compete Competitive athletes may find that eating specific foods before, during, and after competition can affect their performance. Whatever your sport, exercising is never wise when you have not eaten recently. About 2 hours before exercising, you should eat a high-carbohydrate snack, such as a half a bagel, a handful of low-salt pretzels, or yogurt and fruit. However, eating too much just before exercising may cause nausea and cramping.

For an activity lasting longer than 60 minutes, drinking a sports drink containing 6 to 8 percent sugar or a 100- to 300-Calorie snack during the event will help maintain blood glucose levels.

The right foods and beverages in the right amounts are important for optimum performance. Following the MyPyramid serving recommendations is the best option for athletes.

Recommended Fluid Intake for Athletes

Timing	Amount of fluid
in the 2 hours before activity	2 cups (16 fluid ounces)
immediately before activity	2 cups (16 fluid ounces)
every 15 minutes during activity	1 cup (8 fluid ounces)
after activity	2 to 3 cups for every pound of body weight lost

Even mild dehydration can hurt athletic performance. Dehydration causes the blood to lose water and thicken, which makes the job of pumping the blood to the muscles more difficult. The risk of overheating increases as a person becomes more dehydrated.

Despite the effects of dehydration, athletes who need to fit into specific weight classes, such as wrestlers and rowers, often use dehydration to lose weight a day or so before a competition. They reduce their fluid intake and increase their water losses in sweat or by spitting. This strategy may allow them to fit into a weight class, but it can hurt their performance and severely threaten their health.

Nutrient Supplements   Despite the advertisements, dietary supplements are not necessary for optimal athletic performance. Such supplements can be dangerous and should be used with caution. Unlike prescription drugs, nutrient supplements are not regulated by the Food and Drug Administration (FDA). Some supplements may even contain ingredients that are banned by athletic associations.

Most athletes can meet all of their nutrient needs with a carefully chosen, well balanced diet. If you do choose a nutrient supplement, choose one that does not exceed the Tolerable Upper Intake Level (UL) for any nutrients. Non-nutrient supplements are not needed; the benefits of some are outweighed by the health risks.

Eating Well During Pregnancy   Food choices during pregnancy must meet the nutrient needs of the mother and the growing baby. To meet energy needs, pregnant women need up to 450 additional Calories each day. They also need to add protein, vitamin B_6 and B_{12}, folate (folic acid), iron, and zinc to their daily diet. Additional folate is important before pregnancy and very early in pregnancy to prevent certain birth defects. To meet these needs, the diet must be carefully planned. Meals must be regular, and fasting should be avoided.

In addition to needing extra energy, expectant mothers may need to take supplements to meet their nutrient needs. Supplements of folic acid and iron are often recommended. Before a woman takes supplements during pregnancy, she should consult her doctor.

Eating Well During Poor Health "Starve a cold, feed a fever," or is it "feed a cold, starve a fever"? Meeting your nutrient needs is important to keep you healthy. However, what you eat for a few days while you have a cold or flu really doesn't affect your overall health much— as long as you drink plenty of fluids. When you have a cold and are breathing through your mouth, you lose extra fluids. And if you have the flu, fever, vomiting, or diarrhea, your fluid losses will increase. Drinking plenty of fluids will prevent dehydration and speed recovery.

If you have a long-term illness, then your energy and nutrient intake become extremely important for maintaining your ability to fight the disease. Diet is also important in managing chronic disease. For example, people who have diabetes must balance their carbohydrate intake with their insulin doses to keep their blood sugar at a healthy level.

Choosing a Vegetarian Diet

A **vegetarian** diet is one in which few or no animal products are eaten. Vegetarians limit their intake of animal foods, such as meat, poultry, fish, dairy foods, and eggs, but don't necessarily leave them out completely. A semivegetarian may choose not to eat red meat but to eat poultry, fish, or both. A lacto-ovo vegetarian will not eat any meat but will eat eggs and dairy products. Only the strictest vegetarians, called *vegans*, do not eat any animal products.

More than 12 million Americans are vegetarians, and the number appears to be increasing. People choose to be vegetarian for many reasons, ranging from religious, ethical, and dietary to personal taste. A vegetarian diet can be very healthy and is not difficult to prepare food for, as **Figure 6** shows. A plant-based diet usually provides more fiber, vitamin A, and vitamin C than meat-based diets do. Also, because vegetarian diets contain less animal fat, they are lower in saturated fat and cholesterol than a meat-based diet is. This can reduce the risk of heart disease. Vegetarians appear to have lower risks for obesity, heart disease, diabetes, high blood pressure, and certain types of cancer.

Protein in a Meat-Free Diet The protein in animal foods provides enough of all the amino acids that are essential for humans, so we need less animal protein than plant protein to meet our dietary needs. Vegetarians who eat some animal foods, such as fish, eggs, or dairy products, should have no trouble meeting their protein needs. Vegans, however, must choose more carefully to meet their needs. Plant foods contain protein, but not enough of all the essential amino acids. By eating proteins from different plant sources, vegans can get all the amino acids to meet their needs.

VEGGIE TACOS
2 corn taco shells
1/2 cup vegetarian refried beans
4 tablespoons chopped lettuce
2 tablespoons chopped tomatoes
1 tablespoon chopped onions
2 tablespoons salsa
1/4 cup shredded cheese (optional)

Fill the taco shells with refried beans, and top with salsa, chopped lettuce, tomatoes, onions, and shredded cheese.

Serves one to two people

Figure 6

A vegetarian diet can be a healthy choice, but it takes careful planning to get all the needed nutrients. Many of our favorite meals are already vegetarian.

ACTIVITY *Suggest how this recipe could be adapted to make a healthy meat lover's meal.*

A well-planned vegetarian diet can be very healthy, and vegetarian meals can be easy to prepare.

A carefully planned vegetarian diet that provides plenty of nutrient dense plant foods, such as legumes, nuts, seeds, and whole grains, can easily meet the protein needs of vegetarian and vegan athletes.

A common misconception about vegetarian diets is that they are always healthier than diets in which meats are eaten. In general, vegetarian diets offer many health benefits, but it is possible for vegetarians to make poor food choices. For example, potato chips, fries, cookies, and sugar candies are all foods vegetarians can eat. A diet made up of a lot of these foods will be high in fat and sugar and low in other nutrients.

Meeting Other Nutrient Needs Despite their health benefits some vegetarian diets may be lacking in certain vitamins and minerals. Vegan diets, especially, may be low in iron, zinc, calcium, vitamin D, and vitamin B_{12}. Iron and zinc may be deficient because meats are the best sources of these minerals. Vegans must eat a lot of plant foods that are high in these minerals. Good vegan sources of iron include beans; dried fruits; green, leafy vegetables; tofu; and enriched cereals and grains. Whole grains, dried beans, and nuts are good sources of zinc. Because the form of iron in plants is not absorbed as well by the body as the form of iron from meat is, the RDA for iron for vegetarians is higher than the RDA for meat eaters.

Most of the calcium in the American diet comes from dairy products, so vegans need other sources of calcium. Calcium is found in spinach and other green leafy vegetables; dried beans; and in fortified foods such as breakfast cereals. Most vitamin D in the American diet comes from fortified dairy products, so vegans must get their vitamin D by getting enough exposure to sunshine or eating other vitamin D-fortified foods. Vitamin B_{12} is found only in animal foods, so vegans must eat foods fortified with vitamin B_{12} such as breakfast cereals or take a vitamin B_{12} supplement to meet their needs.

SECTION 4

REVIEW   Answer the following questions on a separate piece of paper.

Using Key Terms
1. **Identify** the correct term for the measure of the amount of nutrients in a food compared to the energy the food provides.

Understanding Key Ideas
2. **Explain** what is meant by "junk food."
3. **LIFE SKILL** **Practicing Wellness** Give reasons why a pizza can be a healthier fast food than a burger and fries are.
4. **Compare** the energy needs of adults with those of teens.

5. **Identify** a nutrient that is at risk of deficiency for each of the following groups:
   a. teens   c. athletes
   b. pregnant women   d. vegans
6. **LIFE SKILL** **Practicing Wellness** Identify foods that are lower in fat or sugar than the choices below.
   a. French fries   c. creamy chip dip
   b. soda   d. fried chicken

Critical Thinking
7. Your friend on the wrestling team uses water-loss pills to help him "make weight." He says they're not harmful. What would be your reply?

Highlights

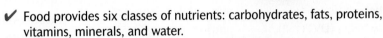

Key Terms

SECTION 1

nutrition (154)
nutrient (154)
carbohydrate (154)
fat (154)
protein (154)

SECTION 2

vitamin (161)
mineral (163)
nutrient deficiency (164)

SECTION 3

Recommended Dietary Allowances (RDAs) (167)
Daily Value (DV) (168)
MyPyramid (171)
Dietary Guidelines for Americans (174)

SECTION 4

nutrient density (175)
vegetarian (181)

The Big Picture

✔ Food provides six classes of nutrients: carbohydrates, fats, proteins, vitamins, minerals, and water.
✔ Carbohydrates, including sugars and starches, are the body's main energy source.
✔ Essential amino acids are needed by the body to make proteins that provide structure, regulation, and, in some cases, energy.
✔ Fat is a concentrated source of energy that is needed in the diet.
✔ Fiber is important for healthy digestion.
✔ Diets high in saturated fat and cholesterol increase the risk of excessive weight gain and heart disease.

✔ Vitamins and minerals are found in all foods in varying amounts. A well-planned diet can meet all your vitamin and mineral needs.
✔ Too little calcium in the diet early in life increases the risk of osteoporosis later in life.
✔ The body is about 60 percent water. To maintain health and to prevent the dangerous effects of dehydration, one must replace lost water.
✔ Increasing your intake of low-fat dairy products and calcium-fortified foods can help meet calcium needs.

✔ The RDAs are nutrient intakes that are sufficient to meet the needs of almost all healthy people.
✔ The Nutrition Facts section of a food label provides information about how much energy the food gives and how much of each nutrient the food contains.
✔ The Dietary Guidelines for Americans are a set of recommendations designed to improve the diets and health of Americans.

✔ Healthy snacks, such as fresh fruit, low-fat yogurt, or low-salt pretzels, provide a good source of essential nutrients without excessive Calories and fat.
✔ As children grow, their total nutrient and energy requirements increase, with total needs being greatest in the teenage years.
✔ Athletes need a well balanced diet that is higher in energy and fluids than the diet of a less active person.
✔ Simple dietary changes, such as switching to low-fat dairy products and eating fresh fruits and vegetables in place of sweet or salty snacks, can reduce the amount of fat, sugar, and salt in your diet.

Review

Using Key Terms

carbohydrate (154)
Daily Value (DV) (168)
Dietary Guidelines for
Americans (174)
fat (154)
MyPyramid (171)
mineral (163)
nutrient (154)

nutrient deficiency (164)
nutrient density (175)
nutrition (154)
protein (154)
Recommended Dietary
Allowances (RDAs) (167)
vegetarian (181)
vitamin (161)

1. For each definition below, choose the key term that best matches the definition.
   a a diet containing few or no animal foods
   b. recommendations for improving diet and health

2. Explain the relationship between the key terms in each of the following pairs.
   a. *nutrition* and *nutrient*
   b. *vitamin* and *mineral*

3. For each set of key terms, choose the term that does not fit and explain why it does not fit.
   a. *vitamin, mineral,* and *carbohydrate*
   b. *carbohydrate, protein,* and *water*

Understanding Key Ideas

Section 1

4. Name the six classes of nutrients.

5. Carbohydrates
   a. provide energy.   b. prevent obesity.
   c. are not needed.   d. cause weight loss.

6. Whole-grain products are high in what indigestible carbohydrate?

7. Why are saturated fats considered "bad"?

8. Name the "building blocks" that make up protein.

9. Can your current diet affect your future health? Explain.

Section 2

10. Name three fat-soluble vitamins and three water-soluble vitamins and the foods in which they are found.

11. Name two mineral deficiencies and identify the minerals involved.

12. If you usually eat less than the recommended amount of calcium, what symptoms do you expect to experience immediately? in 5 years? in 45 years? **LIFE SKILL**

13. Which of the following statements about dehydration is false?
    a. Dehydration is not common.
    b. Dehydration can be life threatening.
    c. Dehydration is a deficiency of water.

Section 3

14. Are the RDAs exact requirements? Explain.

15. For breakfast, you eat a cup of cooked oatmeal and 1/4 cup of raisins. For lunch, you have turkey on 2 ounces of whole-wheat bread and 3/4 cup of orange juice. How much food have you had from the fruit group? from the grain group? **MATH SKILL** **LIFE SKILL**

16. List five foods from each of the MyPyramid food groups.

17. Summarize what the Dietary Guidelines for Americans recommend.

18. **CRITICAL THINKING** Why aren't the colored bands of the MyPyramid symbol the same width?

Section 4

19. Can junk food be part of a healthful diet?

20. Give an example of a healthful snack, and explain why it is healthful.

21. Explain how the MyPyramid food guidance system can be used to plan a diet for an athlete.

22. Why do pregnant women need more energy and protein than nonpregnant women do?

23. Vegetarian diets
    a. can contain beef.   c. are always healthy.
    b. are boring.   d. can be low in iron.

24. **CRITICAL THINKING** The typical U.S. teen diet is low in fruits and vegetables, fiber, and dairy products. Suggest how teens could increase their intake of each of these foods. **LIFE SKILL**

Interpreting Graphics

Study the figure below to answer the questions that follow.

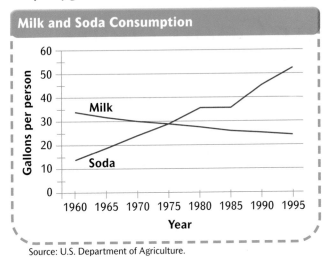

Milk and Soda Consumption

Source: U.S. Department of Agriculture.

25. How many gallons of soda did the average person drink per year in 1960? in 1995?

26. How did the consumption of milk and soda change over time?

27. CRITICAL THINKING Infer how the change in the consumption of milk and soda has affected the health of Americans. **WRITING SKILL**

Activities

28. Health and Your Community Do a snack survey at your school. Make a list of what kinds of snacks are available. Write up a plan for how you could improve the choices that are available. **MATH SKILL**

29. Health and Your Family Select a recipe for a meal that you or your family enjoys. Create a poster in which you show how you could reduce the fat, sugar, or salt content of the recipe, and increase its fiber, vitamin, and mineral content.

30. Health and You Make a list of seven foods that you snack on. Write the MyPyramid group that each food belongs to. Are all of the MyPyramid groups represented? If not, describe how you could substitute snack foods to ensure that you eat foods from all of the MyPyramid groups each day. **LIFE SKILL WRITING SKILL**

Action Plan

31. LIFE SKILL Practicing Wellness List five changes you could make in your diet to reduce your risk of heart disease and osteoporosis.

Standardized Test Prep

Read the passage below, and then answer the questions that follow. **READING SKILL WRITING SKILL**

Mark's father recently found out he has high blood <u>cholesterol</u> and is worried that he might have a heart attack. Mark's mother is planning a new heart-healthy diet for the whole family. Mark is only 14 years old, but his mother believes that the foods he eats now could affect his health later. She plans to start serving more vegetarian meals and buying more fruit, vegetables, and other low-fat snacks. After a week of the new diet, Mark can't wait to go out with his friends for burgers and ice cream. Mark tells his mother that he likes the foods he eats at home but seems to get hungry more often.

32. In this passage, the word *cholesterol* means
A a type of lipid that, when present in high levels in the blood, increases the risk of heart disease.
B the fat found in plant foods.
C a nutrient made up of amino acids.
D that Mark's father has high blood pressure.

33. What can you infer from reading this passage?
E Mark is not getting enough food energy from foods at home.
F Mark eats too much fat.
G Fat is bad for you.
H Mark doesn't like his father.

34. For what reasons did Mark's mother decide to plan a new diet for the family?

Healthy Meal— or Good Deal?

Restaurant and fast-food serving sizes are increasing dramatically. We are told that we can eat more food for less money. But is all of this food making us less healthy?

The last time you went into a restaurant and ordered a hamburger or a fish sandwich, did someone ask you if you wanted a bigger size for just a few pennies more? Did you order the "Super Portion" or the "Gigantic Burger?" Did the waitperson bring you a plate that had enough food to feed a football team? Many of us would answer yes to these questions.

Big—and Bigger

Study after study has shown that the average size of a serving in a restaurant, fast-food establishment, or convenience store has skyrocketed over the past 10 years. The message is *More is better*. In the past, the average soda serving was about 8 ounces. Today, a 20-ounce soda is not unusual. It's almost impossible to find an 8-ounce soda. One convenience store now sells a soda portion that is 64 ounces—a half gallon—and that contains more than 600 Calories. Most fast-food restaurants offer super or extra-large portions that were unheard of even 5 years ago.

Think Before You Buy

The excessiveness of our food culture is also reflected in advertising. The food industry spends more than $7 billion a year on food advertisements. The majority of this money goes to promote processed foods. For example, hardly anyone advertises potatoes, yet millions of dollars are spent to advertise potato chips. For food companies, processed foods bring in much more profit than nonprocessed foods do.

When you see food advertisements, pay attention to what they are trying to tell you. Most people know a chicken sandwich tastes good, so the ads often sell you something else. "Triple-burger for just 99 cents; extra-large fries for only 29 cents more." How many ads are actually telling you that what you're buying is not a good meal but a good deal?

Portion Sizes Affect People

Doctors, nutritionists, and health experts agree that people are at greater risk of obesity and other disorders when they are constantly bombarded with messages to eat more food. In fact, many people are eating more because they don't know when to stop. For example, people who are served large food portions often eat all that they are served. This tendency may reflect our cultural training to "clean one's plate." Many doctors and nutritionists suggest that the food portions served greatly exceed the amounts that a person needs for good health.

Eating Smart in a Huge Food Culture

Healthful living is about making smart choices. Having some good strategies for eating helps you stay healthy in a world of giant-sized portions. Nutritionists have some good advice that you may consider as you make your choices about how much food to eat.

▶ **Serve yourself.** If possible, be the one to put your food on your plate. You can ask your parents to place all of the food on the table "family style." This way, each member of the family can put food on his or her own plate. This approach greatly reduces overeating.

▶ **Be aware of portion sizes.** Recognize that the modern world is telling you to eat, eat, eat. Ads often direct you to spend less to eat more. What you have to do is see through all of this advertising and make smart eating choices. Take control of your health by making your own decisions on how much you eat. If you have doubts about how much you eat, talk about your eating with someone you trust.

▶ **Be aware of messages to eat more.** Messages to eat more food are all around you. To make yourself more aware, keep a list of all of the ads and cultural messages that you see in a week. Awareness of how our culture affects us is a great tool that you can use to stay healthy.

YOUR TURN

1. **Summarizing Information** In what three ways may modern food ads take your attention away from healthful eating choices?

2. **Inferring Relationships** Name three things in our culture other than food ads that encourage overeating.

3. **CRITICAL THINKING** Find one food ad that stresses large portions. Discuss how the ad goes about influencing the amount that people eat.

▶ internet connect

www.scilinks.org/health
Topic: Portion Size
HealthLinks code: HH4187

HEALTH LINKS. Maintained by the National Science Teachers Association

Weight Management and Eating Behaviors

What's Your Health IQ?
KNOWLEDGE

Which of the statements below are true, and which are false? Check your answers on p. 638.

1. Your friends, family, and environment can influence what foods you eat.

2. Eating breakfast can help your performance in school.

3. It is possible for a person with a high body weight to have a healthy level of body fat.

4. Weight loss is the focus of any weight management plan.

5. Eating disorders are serious problems that require medical help.

6. Diarrhea can be life threatening.

7. Most food-borne illnesses are caused by food eaten at restaurants.

Visit these Web sites for the latest health information:

HEALTH LINKS
THE WORLD'S A CLICK AWAY

Find more information whenever you see a HealthLinks box. Go to **scilinks.org/health**, and type in the HealthLinks code.

Find worksheets and other materials that go with your textbook at **go.hrw.com**.

Current Health

Check out *Current Health* articles related to this chapter by visiting **go.hrw.com**. Just type in the keyword **HH4 CH08**.

Food and Your Body Weight

OBJECTIVES

Discuss the difference between hunger and appetite.

Summarize why eating a healthy breakfast is important.

Describe how the balance between food intake and exercise affects body weight.

Identify how excess body fat can affect health.

Describe how obesity is linked to poor health.

Name three factors that influence the foods you choose to eat. **LIFE SKILL**

Both hunger and appetite play important roles in our eating habits. If you stop eating when you are no longer hungry, you are less likely to gain excess weight.

H ave you ever found yourself feeling full after a meal and then digging into a piece of pie for dessert? You've probably never thought of how you seem to make room for more food, even when you feel full. Many things influence why and when you eat.

Why Do You Eat?

Why do people eat even when they aren't hungry? **Hunger** is the body's physical response to the need for food. It is triggered by signals in your body that tell you to eat. The food you eat provides you with energy and nutrients that you need to remain healthy.

Are You Really Hungry?   But most people don't eat just to stay healthy. Most people also eat because of their appetite. **Appetite** is a desire, rather than a need, to eat certain types of foods. For example, the decision to eat an ice-cream cone with your friends, even though you just ate a meal, was triggered by appetite rather than hunger. Appetite may be triggered by many factors, including the sight or smell of food, the time of day, or the time of year. What your friends are eating—and even what mood you are in—can trigger your appetite.

You skipped breakfast because you got up late. You're in class, and your stomach is growling. It is almost lunchtime, and you are feeling a little lightheaded and are unable to concentrate. These feelings are your body's way of telling you that you are hungry and your body needs fuel. They are caused by a number of different signals in your body.

Some of these signals come from your digestive tract, and some come from other parts of your body. For example, your empty

stomach tells you to eat by sending messages to your brain. The levels of nutrients and other substances in your bloodstream also signal the brain that you need to eat. When you have eaten enough, other signals from the brain and digestive system make you feel full and satisfied. This full feeling is called *satiety* (suh TIE uh tee). Food in your stomach causes the stomach to stretch. This stretching is sensed by nerves, which send a "stop eating" message to the brain. The sensations of hunger and satiety help you eat the right amount to feed your body and to stay at a healthy weight.

What Foods Do You Choose?   The amount and type of food you choose to eat are affected by many factors as shown in **Figure 1.** These factors include

▶ the smell and taste of the food
▶ mood
▶ family traditions and ethnic background
▶ social occasions
▶ religious traditions
▶ health concerns
▶ advertising
▶ cost and availability

For example, you may eat sandwiches for lunch because they are easy to carry to school. Americans often eat turkey on Thanksgiving day because of tradition. Where you grew up also plays a role in what you generally eat. If you grew up in the southwestern United States, you may eat Mexican food regularly, even if it isn't part of your ethnic background. And someone who is growing up on the East Coast may eat more seafood than someone in the Midwest does. Some of us eat when we are bored or upset. We also avoid certain foods because we think they are unhealthy.

Figure 1

There are many reasons for choosing the foods we eat. Some of these reasons can lead you to choose healthy or unhealthy foods.

ACTIVITY *List the reasons why these teens are eating. Did they make healthy choices?*

Food Provides Energy

Carbohydrates, fats, and proteins are the energy-giving nutrients. This energy is measured in units called *Calories*. The amount of energy in a certain food depends on how much carbohydrate, fat, and protein the food contains. Carbohydrates and proteins each provide 4 Calories per gram. Fats provide 9 Calories per gram. Foods high in fat are high in Calories because fat provides the most Calories per gram.

After you have eaten a meal, your digestive system breaks down the food. Some of the energy released from food is used almost immediately to fuel the thousands of reactions in your body that keep you alive. Extra food energy that is not needed immediately is stored by the body in two forms—glycogen and fat. **Figure 2** shows how excess food energy is stored by the body. Most of the energy stored in the body is stored as fat. Fat can provide most of the body's energy, but small amounts of glucose are also needed. Glycogen can be broken down quickly to glucose. When the limited glycogen stores are used up, body proteins are needed to form glucose.

The Right Breakfast Keeps You Going
When you wake up in the morning, you usually haven't eaten for 10 to 12 hours. If you go to school without breakfast, you must depend on stored energy to fuel your body and brain. By lunchtime, you may not have eaten for more than 16 hours! The food you eat at breakfast gives you a quick source of energy for your body and glucose for your brain.

How long your breakfast or any other meal keeps you going depends on how much you have eaten and what foods you eat. Meals with fat and protein keep you feeling full longer than meals made of mostly carbohydrates. So a slice of dry toast and orange juice for breakfast will likely cause you to feel hungry long before lunchtime. However, a meal with a mixture of carbohydrate, protein, and some fat, such as yogurt, cereal, and fruit, will keep you feeling full and energized longer.

How Much Energy Do You Need?
How much food energy, or Calories, you need depends on how much energy your body is using. Everyone knows you need energy for running, swimming, and playing basketball. But did you know that your body needs energy even when you aren't moving?

Most of the food energy the body needs is used for basic functions, such as breathing, circulating blood, and growing. The amount of energy needed for these basic functions is called the basal metabolic rate. **Basal metabolic rate (BMR)** is the rate at which your body uses energy to stay alive when you are in a rested, fasting state, such as just after you wake up in the morning. The amount of energy that is used for BMR is different for each person.

Also, the Calorie requirements of boys and girls differ. On average, boys require more Calories per day than girls do. For example, active 15-year-old boys need about 3,000 Calories per day, and active 15-year -old girls need about 2,300 Calories per day.

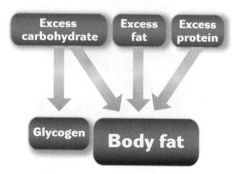

How Excess Food Energy Is Stored

Excess carbohydrate · Excess fat · Excess protein

Glycogen · Body fat

Figure 2

Excess dietary fat is easily stored as body fat. Excess dietary protein is also stored as body fat. When glycogen stores are full, excess dietary carbohydrates are stored as fat.

TOPIC link For more information about exercising and keeping fit, see Chapter 6.

The more active you are, the more energy your body uses. **Figure 3** provides several examples of the amount of energy burned during different activities. For example, it takes more energy for a person to run for 15 minutes than to walk for the same amount of time. But if you walk for an hour, you may use more energy than you would during a 15-minute run. The amount of energy needed for an activity also increases as body weight increases. For example, it takes more energy for a 130-pound person to walk a mile than for a 110-pound person to walk the same distance.

Balancing Energy Intake with Energy Used

When the amount of food energy you take in is equal to the amount of energy you use, you are in *energy balance*. Eating more or less food than you need will cause you to be out of energy balance. Eating extra food energy increases the body's fat stores and causes weight gain. Eating less food than you need decreases the body's fat stores and causes weight loss.

Some body fat is essential for health. It is needed for normal body structures and functions, as an energy store, for insulation, and for protection of the body's internal organs. A healthy amount of body fat for young women is 21 to 33 percent of body weight. For young men, the amount is 8 to 20 percent of body weight. We build up storage fat when we put on weight. Most people who are overweight have excess stored fat.

Overweight is the term used to describe a person who is heavy for his or her height. Generally, people who are overweight have excess body fat.

Research has shown that students who eat breakfast perform better in school than those who skip breakfast.

Figure 3

Different activities have different energy demands. The more intense the activity level, the greater the number of Calories that are burned per hour.

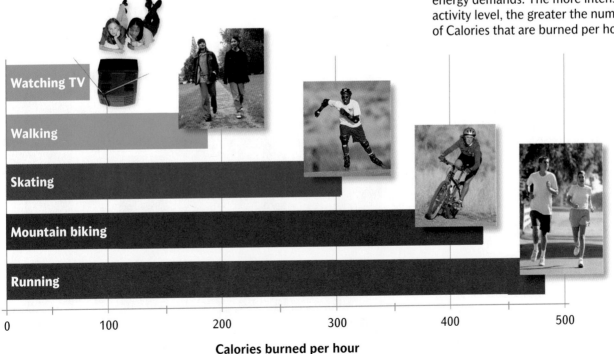

Watching TV

Walking

Skating

Mountain biking

Running

0   100   200   300   400   500

Calories burned per hour

Figure 4

Over the years, the increase in the size of portions served at restaurants has contributed to the increase in the number of Calories consumed by Americans.

ACTIVITY *Use the Calorie table on pp. 622–627 to compare the Calories in a plain, single-patty hamburger, a small order of fries, and a small soda with the Calories in an extra large meal.* **MATH SKILL**

Being Overweight May Lead to Health Problems Having excess body fat increases the risk of suffering from many chronic diseases. Some of these health problems include

▶ type 2 diabetes, heart disease, and high blood pressure
▶ certain forms of cancer, including prostate, colon, and breast cancer
▶ sleeping problems, such as sleep apnea

If you are overweight, it is not too late to begin a weight management plan. It's best to check with your healthcare provider before undertaking such a plan.

Overweight and Obesity: A Growing Problem

Obesity (oh BEE suh tee) is a condition in which a person has a significant amount of excess body fat. A person is considered obese if he or she weighs more than 20 percent above his or her recommended weight range. Being obese or being overweight is most common in developed countries, such as the United States.

More people are overweight or obese than ever before. As **Figure 5** shows, more than 60 percent of all adult Americans are currently overweight, and about 30 percent are classified as obese. Adults are not the only ones getting heavier. About 16 percent of children and teenagers in the United States are overweight. This trend is worrisome because being overweight when young increases the risk of being overweight as an adult. Overall, physical inactivity and poor diet pose the greatest risk to health. However, an overweight person who is active regularly may be at lower risk than a person of correct weight who is not active.

Figure 5

Lack of physical activity and poor dietary habits have lead to an increase in the percentage of people who are overweight or obese.

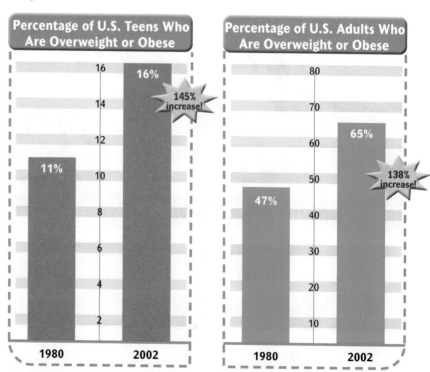

Source: Centers for Disease Control and Prevention and National Center for Health Statistics.

Why Are So Many People Overweight?   There are two main reasons why increasing numbers of Americans are overweight. The first reason is our lack of physical activity. Many modern conveniences have helped decrease our daily levels of activity. We drive more often than we walk, and we play video games and watch TV more often than we ride our bikes.

The second reason people are gaining so much body fat is our changing diet. Many Americans eat more food than they need, and they choose large portions of food that are high in fat and sugar. In these busy days, grabbing a snack from the vending machine or buying lunch at a fast-food restaurant is far more convenient for many people than preparing a healthy meal is. Supermarkets, fast-food restaurants, and all-night shopping marts provide easy access to high-Calorie snack foods, drinks, baked goods, and candy.

What Can You Do?   With a little preplanning and goal setting, maintaining a healthy weight is something everyone can do. It is important to avoid becoming overweight in the first place. Exercise and a healthy diet can help you stay in a healthy weight range.

Every year, about half of American women and one-third of American men try to lose weight. Many never lose any weight, and most who do lose weight eventually regain it. When trying to lose weight, people often have unrealistic goals (such as losing 7 pounds per week) and try very strict diets. Failure to achieve these unrealistic goals often causes a cycle of dieting and disappointment throughout life. A successful weight management plan should include foods that you like and physical activities that you enjoy.

Regardless of age or level of fitness, everyone can benefit from regular exercise.

SECTION 1

REVIEW   *Answer the following questions on a separate piece of paper.*

Using Key Terms

1. **Identify** the term that means "the body's physical response to the need for food."
   a. appetite
   b. obesity
   c. basal metabolic rate
   d. hunger

2. **Name** the term used to describe the rate at which your body uses energy to stay alive while in a rested and fasting state.

3. **Compare** the terms *overweight* and *obese*.

Understanding Key Ideas

4. **Summarize** why appetite is more likely to lead to overeating than hunger is.

5. **State** the advantages of eating breakfast.

6. **Describe** how your energy balance and body weight would be affected if you walked home from school every day instead of taking the bus.

7. **Describe** what happens when energy intake exceeds the body's energy needs.

8. **Describe** how excess body fat affects health.

9. **Name** two reasons for the increase in the number of overweight or obese people.

Critical Thinking

10. **LIFE SKILL** **Being a Wise Consumer** You are cooking dinner for your family. You go to the grocery store to buy the ingredients. List four factors that may influence your food choices.

Maintaining a Healthy Weight

OBJECTIVES

Describe how heredity and lifestyle affect body weight.

Summarize the components of a healthy weight management plan.

Evaluate the dangers of fad diets and weight-loss practices.

Calculate your body mass index. **LIFE SKILL**

Determine if your weight is in a healthy weight range. **LIFE SKILL**

KEY TERMS

heredity the passing down of traits from parents to their biological child

body composition the proportion of body weight that is made up of fat tissue compared to lean tissue

body mass index (BMI) an index of weight in relation to height that is used to assess healthy body weight

weight management a program of sensible eating and exercise habits that keep weight at a healthy level

fad diet a diet that requires a major change in eating habits and promises quick weight loss

The genes you inherit from your parents influence your body size and shape.

D o you know someone who appears to eat and eat and never gain an ounce? Do you know someone who is overweight yet seems to eat nothing at all? You are not imagining these differences. Some people gain weight more easily than others.

Why Do You Weigh What You Weigh?

Whether you gain or lose weight easily is in large part due to heredity. **Heredity** is the passing down of traits from parent to child. Having a body shape that is similar to the body shape of one of your parents is due to heredity. In fact, all of your genes, including the ones that control your energy balance, body size, and body shape, are inherited from your parents.

Genes are pieces of the hereditary material called *DNA*. Genes carry information on how your body is built and how your body works. Many genes play a role in controlling body weight. Some of these genes control the amount of body fat that you have, some control the signals of hunger and satiety, and some regulate activity. If one of these genes is defective, information about body fat, hunger, satiety, and activity levels may not be sent and received correctly.

If one or both of your parents are obese, your chances of becoming obese are high. However, the genes you inherit are not completely responsible for determining your body weight. Some of the differences in our body shapes and sizes are caused by lifestyle. For example, the choices you make about what you eat and how much you exercise affect your energy balance and body weight. Someone who has obese parents but who makes healthy food choices and exercises regularly may never be overweight.

What Is a Healthy Weight for *Me*?

There is more to a healthy body weight than just what the scales read. Healthy weights are different for different people, so weight recommendations are given as a range. When your weight is within a healthy weight range, your risk of getting diseases from having too much or too little body fat is low.

Body Composition **Body composition** is a measure of the proportion of body weight that is made up of fat tissue compared to bone and muscle (lean tissue). The percentage of body weight that is body fat is affected by sex and age. Women have a higher percentage of body fat than men do, and body fat percentage increases with age.

The term *overweight* makes no allowances for body composition. Therefore, using body weight alone to decide the need for fat loss is unreliable. A person can have excess body weight (be overweight) but not be obese. Obese individuals carry a large proportion of their body weight as fat tissue rather than as lean tissue. Because health risks are linked to amount of excess body fat, not body weight, it is important to be able to measure body composition.

Many methods of measuring body composition require large, expensive equipment. A simpler method is the measurement of *skinfold thickness*. An instrument called a caliper is used to pinch a portion of skin and the underlying fat at one or more locations on the body. The caliper measures the thickness of the pinched skin and fat. Body fat percentage can then be worked out using a mathematical equation. Another common method measures the flow of a low-level electric current through the body.

Body Mass Index (BMI) A popular way to find out if you are in a healthy weight range is to calculate your body mass index. **Body mass index (BMI)** is an index of weight in relation to height that is used to assess healthy body weight. The BMI is commonly used because it correlates well with body composition measurements.

Adults are said to have a healthy body weight if their BMI is between 18.5 and 25. Generally, adults who are overweight (BMI of 25.1 to 29.9) or obese (BMI of 30 or more) have too much body fat and are at a higher risk for diseases, but there are some exceptions. For example, athletes who have a lot of muscle and little fat, such as a weight lifter, may have a BMI in the unhealthy range. But if their body composition is measured, one can see that their level of body fat is within a healthy range. Therefore, their risk for disease is low.

People who have a lot of muscle may appear to have an unhealthy BMI. But an athlete who is 5 feet 11 inches tall and weighs 240 pounds is more likely to have extra muscle, not extra body fat.

Children, Teens, and BMI Adult BMI guidelines are not suitable for people younger than 20 years old. The definitions of *overweight* and *underweight* for children and adolescents are less clear because young people grow and develop at such different rates. A chart that compares BMI to age has been developed specifically for children and teens to account for changing body shapes and sizes. One chart is used for boys, and another chart is used for girls.

A Healthy Weight Management Plan

Once you have determined whether you are within a healthy weight range, you can develop your weight management plan. **Weight management** is a program of sensible eating and exercise habits that will help keep weight at a healthy level. For most overweight children and teens, the focus of weight management programs should be to slow or stop weight gain, not to cause weight loss. This approach allows the child or teen to continue to grow in height so they "grow into" their weight. Weight loss in children and teens is recommended only for those whose excess weight has caused health problems such as high blood pressure or difficulty breathing. Regular exercise in a weight management plan is just as important as a healthful diet.

Analyzing DATA ➡

Understanding Body Mass Index

1 Malik is 15. He is 5 feet 8 inches tall and weighs 158 pounds. He wants to find out if he is at a healthy weight. To do this, he needs to find his BMI by using the following equation:

$$BMI = weight \text{ (lb)} \div height \text{ (in.)} \div height \text{ (in.)} \times 703$$

Malik's BMI calculations would be

$$158 \div 68 \div 68 \times 703 = 24.0$$

Malik has a BMI of 24.

2 Malik now needs to find the healthy BMI range for 15-year-old boys.

3 His BMI of 24 is higher than the healthy range for his age. If he has a lot of muscle mass, the BMI chart may not be right for him. If he does not have a lot of muscle mass, he should then change factors such as his activity level and his snacking habits. Doing so will help him grow in height without growing in weight.

Healthy BMI Range

Age	Boys	Girls
12	14.9–21	14.8–21.6
13	15.4–21.8	15.3–22.5
14	15.9–22.6	15.8–23.3
15	16.5–23.4	16.2–24
16	17.1–24.2	16.7–24.6
17	17.6–25	17.3–25.2
18	17.8–25.6	17.5–25.7

Source: National Center for Health Statistics and National Center for Chronic Disease Prevention and Health Promotion.

Your Turn

1. Calculate your BMI. **MATH SKILL**

2. Is your BMI in the healthy range?

3. Why is the healthy BMI range different for each age group?

4. **CRITICAL THINKING** Let's say your BMI is slightly above the healthy range for your age. Predict what will happen to your BMI over the next year if your weight remains the same, but you grow an inch taller.

Eat Smart, Exercise More   The simplest and healthiest way to decrease the number of Calories you eat is to reduce portion sizes and to keep high-Calorie choices as a treat. This decision can be difficult to make if your friends are going out for ice cream. Sometimes the best way to avoid excess Calories is to skip the outing. But another way is to learn some lower-Calorie options. For example, instead of a double scoop ice cream, choose an ice pop, low-fat frozen yogurt, or sherbet. These options have fewer Calories than ice cream does.

Exercise increases your energy needs and makes managing your weight easier. Even small changes in activity levels, as shown in **Figure 6,** can result in weight loss. Exercise will also increase your muscle strength, improve fitness, and relieve boredom and stress. The recommended exercise goal for teens is at least 60 minutes of moderate activity daily.

Changing either eating habits or exercise involves changing your behavior. Keeping a log of your food intake and exercise may help you to make such changes. You can then review the log to see when you are likely to eat more than you intend or to see what prevents you from getting the exercise you planned.

Lose Fat, Not Muscle!   For those who need to lose weight, the goal for weight loss is to lose fat without losing muscle. A weight-loss rate of a half pound to one pound per week is recommended to prevent the loss of muscle. Faster weight loss is usually due to the loss of water and muscle, not fat. To lose a pound a week, an average person would need to eat 500 fewer Calories each day or burn 500 more Calories each day. Weight loss while dieting often stops and starts. Weight can drop one week and stay the same the next. This process can be frustrating to the dieter and can sometimes cause the dieter to try dangerous weight-loss practices.

> **"Your choice of diet can influence your long-term health prospects more than any other action you can take."**
>
> —*Former Surgeon General C. Everett Koop*

Figure 6

Even small changes in your daily activity levels can help you maintain a healthy weight.

ACTIVITY *Record and analyze your food intake and level of activity for a week. Do you need to make changes to improve your activity levels and eating habits?*

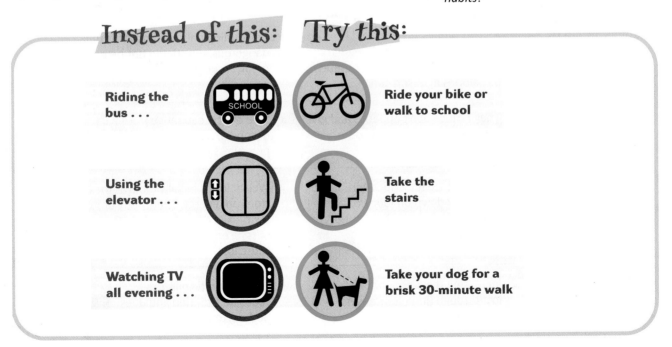

Instead of this: Try this:

Riding the bus . . .   Ride your bike or walk to school

Using the elevator . . .   Take the stairs

Watching TV all evening . . .   Take your dog for a brisk 30-minute walk

If You Are Underweight Consult with your doctor to help determine if your low weight is due to an illness. If you are otherwise healthy, a low weight may result from eating too little or exercising too much or may be due to heredity. To gain weight, gradually increase your food intake by having meals and snacks more frequently. Instead of junk food, choose nutritious foods that are high in Calories. Exercise, especially strength training, can also help an underweight person gain lean mass. Increasing muscle mass increases body weight.

Dangerous Weight-Loss Practices

People spend millions of dollars each year on weight-loss programs, low-Calorie foods, and diet aids. Many of these products and programs promise quick and easy weight loss. Programs that promise quick fixes generally do not promote long-term weight management. Some of these diets are presented in **Table 1.** Such diets do nothing to encourage exercise or promote permanent changes in eating habits that will maintain a healthy body weight for the long term. Many of these programs can even be dangerous.

Fad Diets A **fad diet** is a diet that requires major changes in your eating habits and promises quick results. Some fad diets suggest that specific foods, such as grapefruit, have weight-reducing properties. Others are based on incorrect ideas that the wrong combination of

Table 1	Types of Diets and Diet Products	
Diet or product	**How it works**	**Is it dangerous?**
Low-carbohydrate diets	▶ Restricting carbohydrate intake causes fat to be broken down to provide energy.	▶ They are not healthy in the long term because they are low in grains, fruits, and vegetables.
Liquid formulas	▶ A low-Calorie liquid "meal" is taken in combination with one regular meal per day to lower the number of Calories a person eats.	▶ Consuming only the liquid formula can be dangerous and should not be done without medical supervision.
Stimulants *bitter orange, caffeine*	▶ They reduce one's appetite and give a feeling of extra energy.	▶ Side effects can range from nervousness, dizziness, and headache to increased blood pressure, heart attacks, and seizures.
Fasting	▶ Energy intake is drastically reduced by cutting down on food consumption and, therefore, the number of Calories.	▶ Weight loss is initially rapid as the body uses fat stores for energy. Then, body proteins are broken down to provide the missing energy which will cause loss of muscle mass.
Diuretics *water pills*	▶ Increasing the amount of water lost through urination causes weight loss.	▶ Taking diuretic pills can cause dehydration and does nothing to reduce body fat.

foods or the times at which you eat promote weight gain. Some fad diets do result in some weight loss, but the weight loss is usually due to the decrease in energy intake that occurs while trying to eat the odd mix of foods. However, these diets often do not meet nutrient needs and are difficult and boring to follow.

Diet Pills Many attempts have been made to develop the perfect pill to cause weight loss without the need for low Calorie diets and exercise. However, no such safe drug exists. Drugs that do help with weight loss are available, but the lost weight is usually regained when the drug is no longer taken.

Surgery Surgery is a drastic method of reducing body weight. One such procedure changes the structure of the digestive tract by bypassing part of the stomach and sometimes the intestine. This procedure is called a *gastric bypass*. It reduces the amount of food you can eat, the nutrients absorbed, or both. This surgery is very risky and is recommended only for individuals whose weight-related health risks are so great that the health risks are more serious than the risk of surgery.

What Should You Do? Remember that the only safe and reliable way to manage your weight is to balance your food intake with your exercise. Also, work to change the habits that lead to weight gain. Although there is no single quick way to lose weight, many good diet programs promote healthy weight reduction and management.

The only safe and reliable way to lose weight is to reduce portion sizes, increase exercise, and work to change the habits that led to weight gain.

HEALTH Handbook For more information about health product claims, see the Express Lesson on p. 562.

SECTION 2

REVIEW   *Answer the following questions on a separate piece of paper.*

Using Key Terms

1. **Name** the term that means "the passing down of traits from parents to their biological child."
2. **Identify** the term that describes the proportion of body weight that is lean tissue compared to fat tissue.
   a. BMI
   b. weight management
   c. body composition
   d. heredity
3. **Write** the term that means "an index of weight in relation to height that is used to assess healthy body weight."
4. **Name** the term for "a diet that requires a major change in eating habits and promises quick weight loss."
5. **Define** the term *weight management*.

Understanding Key Ideas

6. **Compare** the roles of heredity and lifestyle in determining your body shape and body weight.
7. **Identify** which of the following is *not* an important part of a healthy weight management program.
   a. well-balanced diet
   b. exercise program
   c. diet supplements
   d. changes in behavior
8. **LIFE SKILL** **Assessing Your Health** Calculate what your BMI will be next year if you grow 1 inch and gain 5 pounds.   **MATH SKILL**

Critical Thinking

9. Should you expect your BMI to change in the next year? Explain.

SECTION 3

Eating Disorders

OBJECTIVES

Discuss the relationship between body image and eating disorders.

Describe the type of individual who is most at risk for an eating disorder.

List the symptoms and health dangers of the most common eating disorders.

Identify ways to help a friend who you think is developing an eating disorder. **LIFE SKILL**

Identify health organizations in your community that help people with eating disorders. **LIFE SKILL**

KEY TERMS

body image how you see and feel about your appearance and how comfortable you are with your body

anorexia nervosa an eating disorder that involves self-starvation, a distorted body image, and low body weight

bulimia nervosa an eating disorder in which the individual repeatedly eats large amounts of food and then uses behaviors such as vomiting or using laxatives to rid the body of the food

binge eating/bingeing eating a large amount of food in one sitting; usually accompanied by a feeling of being out of control

purging engaging in behaviors such as vomiting or misusing laxatives to rid the body of food

Eating disorders are complex illnesses that can involve having a distorted body image.

TOPIC link For more information about self-concept, see Chapter 2.

J enny had carried her dieting too far. She barely ate a thing and exercised all the time. When she was rushed to the hospital after fainting, she weighed only 85 pounds. Jenny didn't listen when her friends said that she was too thin. She hated how "fat" she looked.

What Are Eating Disorders?

Normally we eat when we are hungry and stop eating when we are full. However, eating patterns that are inflexible and highly structured are not normal. Abnormal eating patterns may include never eating enough, dieting excessively, eating only certain types of foods, eating too much, and not responding to natural feelings of fullness or hunger. These patterns may be warning signs of an eating disorder.

Eating disorders are conditions that involve an unhealthy degree of concern about body weight and shape and that may lead to efforts to control weight by unhealthy means. Examples of eating disorders include starving oneself, overeating, and forcefully ridding the body of food by vomiting or using laxatives. Eating disorders greatly affect all aspects of the sufferer's life and the lives of his or her loved ones.

Body Image and Eating Disorders Your **body image** is how you see and feel about your appearance and how comfortable you are with your body. Your body image can change with your mood, your environment, and your experiences. Your body image can also affect your eating habits and health. People who believe they are too fat may limit the food they eat even if they are not overweight. People with eating disorders often do not see themselves as they really are. In other words, they have a distorted body image.

Culture and society often define what we think of as a perfect body. In the 1950s, many women wanted to look like Marilyn Monroe—curvy and full figured. In the United States today, clothing styles and fashion models on television and in magazines suggest that thin is in and a perfectly toned, muscular body is best. The models we see in magazines and on television act as a standard for attractiveness and acceptability. But in fact, the women and men on magazine covers represent less than 1 percent of the population!

A Healthy Body Image   Having a healthy body image means you accept your body's appearance and abilities. It also means that you listen to what your body tells you. Developing a healthier body image requires paying attention to, appreciating, and caring for your body. You should have realistic expectations about your size that are based on your heredity and should realize that weight and body shape can change frequently and rapidly in teens.

The men and women on magazine covers represent less than 1 percent of the population.

real life Activity

SOCIETY AND BODY IMAGE

LIFE SKILL
Evaluating Media Messages

Materials

✔ colored paper
✔ teen, fashion, and fitness magazines
✔ scissors
✔ paste

Procedure

1. **Cut** out images of teenage girls and boys from the magazines.

2. **Paste** the images onto the colored paper to create a collage.

Conclusions

1. **Summarizing Results** Describe the body sizes and shapes in the images that you have collected.

2. **Comparing Information** How are these images like those of your friends and classmates? How are they different?

3. **Analyzing Results** Are these images used to sell a product? If so, what product is each image selling?

4. **CRITICAL THINKING** How can behaviors such as drug use and dieting develop from having an unrealistic body image?

5. **CRITICAL THINKING** From what other sources do you get messages about body image?

A Closer Look at Eating Disorders

Thousands of people die each year from complications related to eating disorders. Eating disorders often develop during adolescence, when children's bodies and responsibilities change from those of children to those of adults.

Many factors contribute to the development of eating disorders. Genetics, culture, personality, emotions, and family are all believed to play a role. Eating disorders are on the rise among athletes in sports that require athletes to be thin, such as gymnastics and figure skating. Eating disorders are also found in athletes who must fit into a particular weight class, such as wrestlers. Eating disorders are most common in young women who are overachievers and perfectionists and in adolescents who have a difficult family life. Eating disorders are also most common in people from cultures in which being thin is equated with being attractive, successful, and intelligent and in people whose jobs depend on their body shape and weight, such as dancers, actors, TV presenters, and models.

Common Eating Disorders   Three of the most common eating disorders—anorexia nervosa, bulimia nervosa, and binge eating disorder—are summarized in **Table 2.**

Anorexia nervosa is an eating disorder that involves self-starvation, a distorted body image, and low body weight. **Bulimia nervosa** is an eating disorder in which an individual repeatedly eats large amounts of food and then uses behaviors such as vomiting or using laxatives to rid the body of the food. **Bingeing** or **binge eating** is the eating of a large amount of food in one sitting. In some eating disorders, bingeing may be followed by purging. **Purging** is behavior that involves vomiting or misusing laxatives to rid the body of food.

Dangers of Eating Disorders

▶ Hair loss
▶ Dental problems
▶ Broken blood vessels in the face and eyes
▶ Dry, scaly skin
▶ Severe dehydration
▶ Loss of menstrual period in females
▶ Low bone density
▶ Heart irregularities
▶ Organ failure
▶ Death

Table 2 Common Eating Disorders

What is it?	Signs and symptoms	Treatment
Anorexia nervosa is an obsession with being thin that leads to extreme weight loss. Some people with anorexia binge and then purge as a means of weight control. Sufferers often have very low self-esteem and feel controlled by others. The average teen consumes about 2,500 Calories per day. But someone with anorexia may consume only a few hundred Calories.	▶ intense fear of weight gain ▶ overexercising ▶ preferring to eat alone ▶ preoccupation with Calories ▶ extreme weight loss ▶ loss of menstrual periods for at least 3 months ▶ hair loss on head ▶ depression and anxiety ▶ weakness and exhaustion	▶ medical, psychological, and nutritional therapy to help the person regain health and develop healthy eating behaviors ▶ family counseling  Extreme weight loss
Bulimia nervosa is a disorder that involves frequent episodes of binge eating that are almost always followed by behaviors such as vomiting, using laxatives, fasting or overexercising. During a typical binge, about 3,400 Calories are consumed in less than two hours.	▶ preoccupation with body weight ▶ bingeing and purging ▶ bloodshot eyes and sore throat ▶ dental problems ▶ irregular menstrual periods ▶ depression and mood swings ▶ feeling out of control ▶ at least two bulimic episodes per week for at least 3 months	▶ therapy to separate eating from emotions and to promote eating in response to hunger and satiety ▶ nutritional counseling to review nutrient needs and ways to meet them
Binge eating disorder is a disorder that involves frequent binge eating but no purging. It is frequently undiagnosed. About one-quarter to one-third of people who go to weight-loss clinics may have binge eating disorder.	▶ above-normal body weight ▶ bingeing episodes accompanied by feelings of guilt, shame, and loss of control	▶ psychological and nutritional counseling
Disordered eating patterns are disordered eating behaviors that are not severe enough to be classified as a specific eating disorder. They are often referred to as "disordered eating behaviors." Many teens are believed to have disordered eating behaviors that could lead to serious health problems.	▶ weight loss (less than anorexia) ▶ bingeing and purging less frequently than in bulimia ▶ purging after eating small amounts of food ▶ deliberate dehydration for weight loss ▶ hiding food ▶ overexercising ▶ constant dissatisfaction with physical appearance	▶ psychological and nutritional counseling

MAKING GREAT DECISIONS

You're worried about your best friend, Samantha. When she goes out to eat with you and your other friends, she talks about food a lot, but all she ever orders is a diet soda. She has lost weight and seems tired and cold all the time. You tell her that she looks too thin, but she complains that she is fat. You suspect Samantha may have an eating disorder.

Write on a separate sheet of paper the steps that you would take to help your friend. Remember to use the decision-making steps.

Give thought to the problem.

Review your choices.

Evaluate the consequences of each choice.

Assess and choose the best choice.

Think it over afterward.

Could You Be at Risk? People at risk of developing an eating disorder may find they have traits such as preferring to eat alone, being overly critical about their body size and shape, thinking about food often, weighing themselves every day, and/or eating a lot of "diet" foods. If your concerns about food or your appearance have led to trouble in school, at home, or with your friends, you should discuss your situation with a parent, a school nurse, a counselor, a doctor, or another trusted adult.

Getting Help Professional help from physicians, psychologists, and nutritionists is essential to manage and recover from an eating disorder. Unfortunately, people with eating disorders often deny that they have a problem and believe that their behavior is normal and a chosen lifestyle. As a result, they may not seek help early on when treatment can help prevent severe physical problems.

If you believe a friend has an eating disorder, it is important to encourage your friend to seek help. In private, let your friend know of your concern for his or her health. Listen to your friend. If you are unsuccessful, tell a trusted adult, or contact an agency that provides eating disorder counseling in your area. Remember, even if you are sworn to secrecy by your friend, it is important that a responsible adult knows about your fears. When a life is in danger, there is no confidentiality to keep.

SECTION 3

REVIEW

Answer the following questions on a separate piece of paper.

Using Key Terms

1. **Define** the term *body image*.

2. **Identify** the eating disorder that involves extreme weight loss.
   a. anorexia nervosa
   b. bulimia nervosa
   c. purging
   d. binge eating disorder

3. **List** the symptoms of bulimia nervosa.

4. **Name** the term that means "a rapid consumption of a large amount of food."

Understanding Key Ideas

5. **Describe** how a negative body image can affect eating behavior.

6. **Describe** how you could tell if a friend or family member was at risk of an eating disorder.

7. **Compare** the symptoms of anorexia with those of bulimia, and describe how the disorders affect health.

8. **LIFE SKILL** **Communicating Effectively** Describe how you could help a friend you think is developing an eating disorder.

9. **LIFE SKILL** **Using Community Resources** Identify resources in your local community that help people with eating disorders or their families.

Critical Thinking

10. Should someone who binges and purges about once a month be worried about the consequences of bulimia? Explain.

SECTION 4

Preventing Food-Related Illnesses

OBJECTIVES

Describe three of the most common digestive disorders.

Describe how diarrhea can be life threatening.

Discuss how food allergies can affect health.

Identify a common cause of food intolerances.

List things you can do to reduce your chances of getting a food-borne illness. **LIFE SKILL**

While in the library, Aaron started to feel bad. His stomach hurt, and he felt a little sick. It couldn't have been the burger he'd had for lunch—it was so good! He had barely packed up his bag before he had to run for the bathroom.

Food and Digestive Problems

To provide the body with nutrients, food must be digested and then the nutrients must be absorbed. Problems in any part of the digestive system can affect your health. Most digestive problems like Aaron's are not serious. But if you have severe or persistent symptoms, you should see a doctor.

Digestive problems can sometimes develop quickly.

Heartburn Have you ever had a burning feeling in your chest after a large meal? This burning feeling is called *heartburn* and is caused by stomach acid leaking into the esophagus. The esophagus is the tube that connects your throat with your stomach. The main cause of heartburn is overeating foods that are high in fat. Stress and anxiety can also cause heartburn by increasing the amount of acid made by the stomach. Heartburn is usually a minor problem that can be prevented by eating small, low-fat meals frequently and by not lying down soon after eating.

Ulcers Pain after eating can also be a symptom of a more serious ailment, such as an ulcer. Ulcers are open sores in the lining of the stomach or intestine. Recent studies have shown that most ulcers are caused by an infection of the stomach lining by the bacterium *Helicobacter pylori*. Such infections are treatable with antibiotics. Stress and an unhealthy diet can make ulcers worse.

Embarrassing Digestive Problems Some intestinal problems are as embarrassing as they are uncomfortable. Gas, diarrhea, and constipation can be difficult to discuss. However, they can often be avoided by changes in the diet.

Gas is produced when bacteria living in the large intestine break down undigested food. Normally, you don't notice the daily activities of these bacteria. Some foods, such as beans, contain a large amount of indigestible material. Although you cannot digest this material, it acts as a huge meal for the millions of bacteria that live in your large intestine. The bacteria produce a lot of gas while feasting on the beans. The end result for you is gas, or flatus. The buildup of this gas can make you feel bloated and can give you *flatulence*.

Diarrhea refers to frequent watery stools. Diarrhea can be caused by infections, medications, or reactions to foods. Occasional diarrhea is common and mostly harmless. But because diarrhea increases water loss from the body, prolonged diarrhea can lead to dehydration. Dehydration occurs when the amount of water in the body decreases enough to cause a drop in blood volume. Dehydration can make it difficult for the blood to carry nutrients and oxygen around the body and can become life threatening. Every year dehydration from diarrhea kills millions of children in the developing world. If you experience diarrhea, drink a lot of fluid, such as water or sports drinks, to replace lost water.

Constipation is difficulty in having bowel movements or is having dry, hard stools. Constipation can be caused by weak intestinal muscles or by a diet that is low in fiber or fluid. It can be prevented by getting plenty of exercise, drinking a lot of water (at least eight glasses a day), and eating a diet high in whole grains, fruits, and vegetables.

Common Causes of Food Allergies

- ▶ Peanuts
- ▶ Eggs
- ▶ Wheat
- ▶ Strawberries
- ▶ Soy foods
- ▶ Seafood
- ▶ Milk

Food Allergies

A **food allergy** is an abnormal response to a food that is triggered by the body's immune system. The immune system reacts to the food as if it were a harmful microorganism. The allergic reaction can cause symptoms throughout the body. Sometimes reactions are mild, but they can be life threatening. An upset stomach, hives, a runny nose, body aches, difficulty breathing, and a drop in blood pressure can all be food allergy symptoms. In some cases, these symptoms appear immediately. In others, they take up to 24 hours to appear.

Is It a Food Allergy? True food allergies are relatively rare. To find out if symptoms are due to a specific food, you must cut from your diet for 2 to 4 weeks all foods suspected of causing an allergic reaction. Then, a "food challenge" can be done by eating a small amount of one suspected food. You should do a food challenge in a doctor's office in case you have a serious reaction. If a reaction occurs, a diagnosis of a food allergy can be made. If no reaction occurs, a larger amount of the food can be eaten. If you still have no reaction, then an allergy to that food may be ruled out.

A food challenge should not be done with a suspected allergy to peanuts because reactions to peanuts can be deadly. Individuals who are allergic to peanuts can be so sensitive that exposure to tiny amounts, such as contamination from peanut-containing foods nearby, can cause serious reactions. Once this allergy is suspected, peanuts must be avoided.

Managing Food Allergies The best way to prevent an allergic reaction to food is to avoid eating the food to which you are allergic. Don't be afraid to ask about ingredients in food served in restaurants or at a friend's house. Food labels can help you find out if a food contains the ingredient. Individuals who have serious food allergies need to carry *epinephrine* with them. Injecting themselves with this hormone after exposure to the food can prevent a fatal reaction.

Food Intolerances

Although the symptoms of a food intolerance can be similar to those of a food allergy, food intolerances do not cause a specific reaction of the immune system. Food intolerances can be caused by eating foods or ingredients in a meal that irritate the intestine (such as onions).

An example of a food intolerance is lactose intolerance. **Lactose intolerance** is a reduced ability to digest the milk sugar lactose. It is not an allergy to milk. Lactose is found in dairy products, such as milk and cheese. Lactose intolerance causes gas, cramps, and diarrhea. These symptoms occur because undigested lactose passes into the large intestine, where it is digested by bacteria that produce acids and gas from the lactose. Most people who are lactose intolerant can eat some dairy foods if they eat only small amounts at a time. Lactose intolerance is rare in children but affects about a quarter of the American adult population. The incidence of lactose intolerance varies worldwide. Lactose intolerance affects less than 5 percent of people in northwestern Europe but nearly 100 percent of people in some parts of Asia and Africa.

Food-Borne Illness

A **food-borne illness** is an illness caused by eating or drinking a food that contains a toxin or disease-causing microorganism. Each year, about 76 million people in the United States suffer from food-borne illness. Food-borne illness can be caused by any kind of contamination in food. However, most food-borne illnesses in the United States are caused by eating food contaminated with pathogens, such as bacteria, viruses, fungi, or parasites. Many cases of food-borne illness are so mild that they are not reported to a doctor. So, in most cases, the cause of the illness is never discovered. However, sometimes food-borne illnesses can be life threatening, especially for young children, pregnant women, the elderly, and people who are ill.

"**Many** cases of food poisoning could be prevented if people **washed their hands** before handling food."

The Partnership for Food Safety Education has a campaign that aims to reduce the risk of food-borne illness. The partnership's FightBAC! message emphasizes Cook, Clean, Separate, and Chill.

Preventing Food-Borne Illness Most cases of food-borne illness can be prevented if everyone who handles or prepares food practices good food hygiene. Many cases of food-borne illness are due to unsanitary preparation of food at home. **Cross-contamination** is the transfer of contaminants, such as microorganisms or toxins, from one food to another. Cross-contamination can occur at home, for example, if the same cutting board is used to cut up raw chicken and to prepare vegetables for a salad or if raw and cooked foods are stored together. Cross-contamination can also happen in food-processing plants and restaurants. Contamination of foods in these locations could potentially affect hundreds of people. Therefore, there are many strict federal hygiene regulations that apply to food-processing plants and restaurants and that aim to minimize health risks to the public.

To reduce the risk of food-borne illness at home,

▶ wash your hands, utensils, and surfaces with hot, soapy water before and after each food preparation step

▶ clean surfaces with paper towels, and wash cloth towels frequently in hot, soapy water

▶ clean your refrigerator with hot, soapy water

▶ separate foods such as raw meat, eggs, or fish from other foods in your refrigerator

▶ place raw foods in containers to prevent juices from dripping onto other foods in the refrigerator

▶ use a refrigerator thermometer to ensure that your refrigerator is set at 40°F or below

▶ use a meat thermometer to ensure that food has been cooked at the correct temperature to kill microorganisms

SECTION 4

REVIEW
Answer the following questions on a separate piece of paper.

Using Key Terms

1. **Identify** the term used to describe an abnormal response to a food that is triggered by the immune system.
   a. food allergy
   b. lactose intolerance
   c. constipation
   d. food intolerance

2. **Write** the term that means "an inability to digest lactose."

3. **Name** the term for "an illness caused by eating a food that contains a contaminant such as a microorganism."

4. **Define** *cross-contamination.*

Understanding Key Ideas

5. **Describe** how excess gas can form in the intestines.

6. **Describe** how diarrhea can cause dehydration.

7. **Compare** the symptoms of a food allergy to the symptoms of a food intolerance.

8. **LIFE SKILL** **Practicing Wellness** Identify steps to reduce your chances of getting a food borne illness.

Critical Thinking

9. Can the bacteria on raw chicken that you buy from the store end up in your fresh fruit salad? Explain your answer.

CHAPTER 8

Highlights

Key Terms

SECTION 1

hunger (190)
appetite (190)
basal metabolic rate (BMR) (192)
overweight (193)
obesity (194)

SECTION 2

heredity (196)
body composition (197)
body mass index (BMI) (197)
weight management (198)
fad diet (200)

SECTION 3

body image (202)
anorexia nervosa (204)
bulimia nervosa (204)
binge eating (bingeing) (204)
purging (204)

SECTION 4

food allergy (208)
lactose intolerance (209)
food-borne illness (209)
cross-contamination (210)

The Big Picture

✔ What you eat and how much you eat are affected by both hunger and appetite.

✔ Personal choices as well as friends, tradition, ethnic background, availability of food, and emotions affect food choices.

✔ If you take in more Calories from food than you use to stay alive, grow, and move, you will gain excess weight.

✔ Eating breakfast every day is important for good health.

✔ Being overweight or obese increases the risk of heart disease, diabetes, cancer, and other chronic diseases.

✔ The genes you inherit from your parents and your lifestyle choices determine your body size and shape.

✔ Body mass index is an index of weight in relation to height that is used to assess healthy body weight.

✔ Keeping body weight in the healthy range requires a plan that encourages healthy food choices and good exercise habits.

✔ Fad diets may cause initial weight loss but can be dangerous and do not promote behaviors for long-term weight management.

✔ Individuals with eating disorders often have a distorted body image.

✔ Eating disorders are more common in teenage girls, especially overachievers who have a poor self-image, and in athletes who must restrict their weight.

✔ Anorexia nervosa is an overwhelming fear of gaining weight and can result in self-starvation. Bulimia nervosa involves frequent bingeing and purging, which can cause many health problems.

✔ Eating disorders should be identified and treated early to avoid long-term health problems.

✔ Common digestive disorders include heartburn, ulcers, constipation, diarrhea, and flatulence.

✔ Diarrhea causes water loss and can result in dehydration, which is very dangerous, especially to children and the elderly.

✔ A food allergy involves a reaction by the body's immune system to particular foods. A food intolerance may cause symptoms similar to those of an allergic reaction, but it is not a specific immune reaction.

✔ Proper handling and storage of food can prevent a food-borne illness.

Review

Using Key Terms

anorexia nervosa (204)
appetite (190)
basal metabolic rate (BMR) (192)
binge eating/bingeing (204)
body composition (197)
body image (202)
body mass index (197)
bulimia nervosa (204)
cross-contamination (210)
fad diet (200)

food allergy (208)
food-borne illness (209)
heredity (196)
hunger (190)
lactose intolerance (209)
obesity (194)
overweight (193)
purging (204)
weight management (198)

1. For each definition below, choose the key term that best matches the definition.
   a. eating a large amount of food at one time
   b. forcefully ridding the body of Calories
   c. heavy for one's height
   d. how you see and feel about your appearance
   e. sensible eating and exercise habits that keep weight at a healthy level
   f. a diet that promises quick weight loss

2. Explain the relationship between the key terms in each of the following pairs.
   a. *anorexia nervosa* and *bulimia nervosa*
   b. *hunger* and *appetite*
   c. *obesity* and *body mass index*
   d. *food allergy* and *lactose intolerance*
   e. *cross-contamination* and *food-borne illness*
   f. *body composition* and *heredity*

Understanding Key Ideas

Section 1

3. Is eating a piece of chocolate cake for dessert after a big dinner more likely to be motivated by hunger or by appetite? Explain your answer.

4. Why does eating breakfast each morning help you perform better in school?

5. Explain what happens to the extra energy if you eat more food than your body needs.

6. For what health conditions are people with excess body fat at increased risk?

7. What is the best plan for avoiding obesity?

Section 2

8. Explain why a person whose parents are obese may not necessarily become obese.

9. What is the BMI of an individual who is 5 feet 1 inch tall and weighs 127 pounds?

10. Explain why following a weight management plan that has a menu for only one week of meals is unlikely to promote long-term weight loss.

11. **CRITICAL THINKING** A magazine features the "tomato and lemon juice" diet. The diet promises a weight loss of 5 pounds a week. Why is this diet not a good way to manage weight?

Section 3

12. Explain why someone who has a poor body image is more likely to develop an eating disorder.

13. What types of individuals are most at risk for eating disorders?

14. Which of the following is *not* a symptom of an eating disorder?
    a. healthy body image
    b. fear of gaining weight
    c. extreme weight loss
    d. bingeing and purging

15. Identify people or health organizations you could look to for help with a friend who has an eating disorder. **LIFE SKILL**

Section 4

16. Identify actions you can take to help prevent heartburn and constipation. **LIFE SKILL**

17. Identify the main reason why diarrhea can be life threatening.

18. Identify ways you can avoid the symptoms of lactose intolerance. **LIFE SKILL**

19. Describe how washing your hands can protect you from food-borne illness.

20. **CRITICAL THINKING** You are at camp with a friend who is allergic to peanuts. How can you help determine which foods are safe for him to eat?

Interpreting Graphics

Study the figure below to answer the questions that follow.

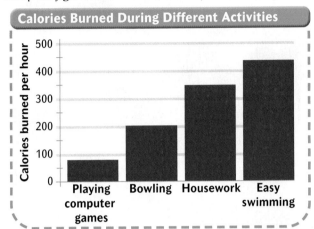

Calories Burned During Different Activities

(Calories burned per hour vs. Playing computer games, Bowling, Housework, Easy swimming)

21. Which of these activities requires the least bodily movement?

22. Estimate how many Calories in total are burned during 30 minutes of housework and 30 minutes of swimming. **MATH SKILL**

23. **CRITICAL THINKING** If you added 30 minutes of swimming every day and did not change your daily intake of food, how would your body weight likely be affected?

Activities

24. Health and You Find an advertisement for a diet plan in a magazine or in another source. Does the diet contain all of the components of a healthy weight management plan? Would it be safe to follow this plan for an extended period of time?

25. Health and Your Community Prepare a poster display that explores how body images have changed over the past 30 years.

26. Health and Your Family Write a short report that describes ways to avoid a food-borne illness in a home kitchen. **WRITING SKILL**

27. Health and You Think about how the availability of food can affect what you eat and when you eat. Write a healthy meal plan from what is on your school's lunch menu today. **WRITING SKILL**

Action Plan

28. **LIFE SKILL** **Assessing Your Health** List five things that you can do to improve your body image and to keep your weight in the healthy range.

Standardized Test Prep

Read the passage below, and then answer the questions that follow. **READING SKILL** **WRITING SKILL** **MATH SKILL**

Ann is studying for a history test. She had to cancel tennis after school because she needed the time to study. But now she is bored. To help <u>apply</u> herself to her studies she makes a bowl of buttery popcorn. When that is gone, she gets a bag of chips from the kitchen. When she discovers she has finished off the bag of chips too, she is angry with herself. She has been putting on weight lately. Skipping tennis and eating all this junk food is going to add to her weight gain. She decides that she needs a plan to help her focus on studying without gaining weight.

29. In the passage, the word *apply* means
A to put into action or use.
B to concentrate one's efforts.
C to ask for something.
D to select something.

30. What can you infer from reading this passage?
E Ann has an eating disorder.
F Ann is obese.
G Ann eats junk food when she is bored.
H Ann is not a good cook.

31. By skipping tennis, Ann uses 150 fewer Calories than usual that day. By eating popcorn and a bag of chips, she eats about 500 extra Calories. What has that done to her energy balance that day?

32. Write a paragraph describing some of the things Ann can do to help her study without gaining weight.

UNIT 3
Drugs

215

Understanding Drugs and Medicines

What's Your Health IQ?

KNOWLEDGE

Which of the statements below are true, and which are false? Check your answers on p. 638.

1. Side effects of over-the-counter medicines are rare.

2. Cold medicines can cause drowsiness when they are taken with antihistamines.

3. Not following doctor's orders while taking a prescription medicine can be dangerous.

4. Generic drugs work equally as well as brand-name drugs.

5. Nutritional supplements are not approved by the Food and Drug Administration in the same way medicines are.

6. Drugs that come from natural products are safer than drugs made from chemicals.

7. People cannot become addicted to prescription drugs.

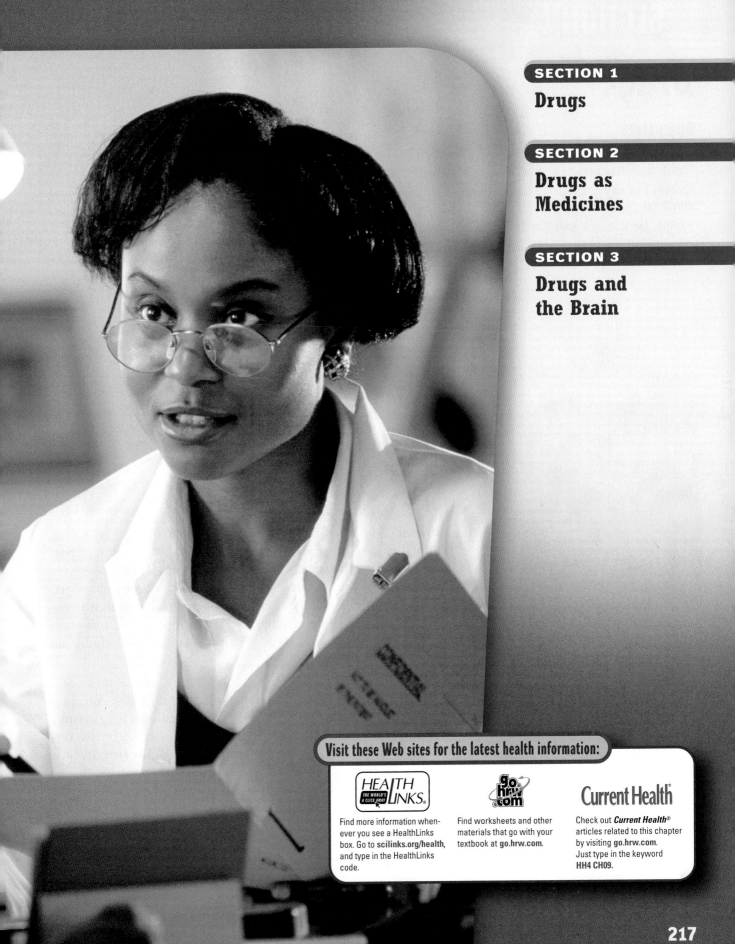

Visit these Web sites for the latest health information:

HEALTH LINKS.
THE WORLD'S A CLICK AWAY

Find more information whenever you see a HealthLinks box. Go to **scilinks.org/health**, and type in the HealthLinks code.

go.hrw.com

Find worksheets and other materials that go with your textbook at **go.hrw.com**.

Current Health

Check out *Current Health* articles related to this chapter by visiting **go.hrw.com**. Just type in the keyword **HH4 CH09**.

SECTION 1

Drugs

OBJECTIVES

List three qualities that make a drug useful as a medicine.

Name the two sources of all drugs.

Identify four different types of medicines and their effects on the body.

Identify five different ways that drugs can enter the body.

Describe why some drugs are considered drugs of abuse.

Taking medicine is serious business. Always make sure you are well informed about the medicines you are taking or need to take.

What do aspirin, caffeine, cortisone, and cocaine all have in common? They are all drugs. You encounter some drugs every day. Some drugs help sick people feel better. Some of these drugs you can get only from a doctor. Still, other drugs are taken for their effect on the brain.

What Are Drugs?

How can one class of substances be so many different things? A **drug** is any substance that causes a change in a person's physical or psychological state. Thousands of different drugs exist and they can have many different kinds of effects. Some drugs have one specific effect, while other drugs have many effects. Some drugs kill invading organisms. Other drugs, like the ones used for treating cancer, may even make someone who has cancer feel sick while they are helping the person to get better.

Some Drugs Are Medicines Any drug that is used to cure, prevent, or treat illness or discomfort is called a **medicine.** For example, the antibiotic penicillin is considered a medicine because it kills certain types of bacteria that can infect us and make us sick. To be a medicine, a drug must have the following qualities:

▶ **Effectiveness** When a medicine is good at carrying out its task, doctors say it is *effective*. For example, penicillin is effective at killing certain types of bacteria.

▶ **Safety** Medicines have to be safe when used as directed. For example, penicillin wouldn't be very useful if it damaged the heart while it killed bacteria. But penicillin does not damage the heart. So for most people, penicillin is safe to use.

Figure 1

Some medicines, such as aspirin, were originally developed from substances produced by plants. Today many medicines, including aspirin, are created by scientists in laboratories and are made by drug companies.

▶ **Minor side effects** No medicine is perfectly safe for everyone. Any effect that is caused by a drug and that is different from the drug's intended effect is called a **side effect.** Common side effects of medicines include headache, sleepiness, or diarrhea. Most drugs have very minor side effects. If a medicine has many side effects or if the side effects are severe, the medicine may be difficult to tolerate. However, some very important drugs are useful even though they have serious side effects. For example, the benefits of using anti-cancer medicines outweigh such side effects as fatigue and anemia.

Some Drugs Are "Drugs of Abuse" Drugs such as cocaine, alcohol, and marijuana change the way the brain works in ways that are not healthy. A person takes drugs like these to change how he or she feels or how he or she senses the world. The person may want to feel happier, or less sad or less anxious. Drugs that people take for mind-altering effects that have no medical purpose are called *drugs of abuse.*

Drugs that dramatically change your mood can be very dangerous. Over time, any drug that affects the brain can lead to changes in its structure and function. This can lead to permanent changes in behavior and serious long-term health problems.

Where Do Drugs Come From? Despite their differences, all drugs have one thing in common—they all contain chemicals. In the past, all drugs came from natural sources such as plants, animals, and fungi. For example, opium, which has been used for thousands of years to treat pain and diarrhea, comes from the unripe seed capsules of the opium poppy. **Figure 1** shows a willow tree, the bark of which is the source of salicin, the chemical from which aspirin was developed.

Many drugs are now created by scientists working in laboratories. Scientists can work on the structure of chemicals to change existing drugs or develop new drugs. Every year, drug companies test thousands of new chemicals to see if the chemicals might be effective as medicines.

internet connect

www.scilinks.org/health
Topic: Drugs and Drug Abuse
HealthLinks code: HH4050

HEALTH LINKS. Maintained by the National Science Teachers Association

Types of Medicines

Medicines can be classified in many ways. One useful way is to classify them by what they do. This is how you will find medicines organized in the drugstore or pharmacy. **Table 1** lists some common kinds of medicines. Among the most common medicines are analgesics, antihistamines, and antacids. Some of these medicines require a prescription (pree SKRIP shuhn), while over-the-counter medicines do

Table 1 Types of Medicines			
Classification	**Example**	**Effect**	**Availability**
Analgesic	▶ acetaminophen	▶ relieves pain	▶ OTC
Antihistamine	▶ diphenhydramine	▶ helps relieve minor allergy symptoms	▶ OTC
Antacid	▶ aluminum hydroxide	▶ neutralizes stomach acid for relief from heartburn	▶ OTC
Antibiotic	▶ amoxicillin	▶ kills bacteria to help cure infections	▶ prescription
Bronchodilator	▶ salmeterol	▶ opens airways to make breathing easier for people with asthma	▶ prescription
Steroid anti-inflammatory	▶ cortisone cream	▶ reduces inflammation and itching of skin	▶ OTC
Hormone	▶ insulin	▶ different hormones work differently; insulin lowers blood glucose levels to help treat diabetes	▶ prescription
Stimulant	▶ methylphenidate	▶ increases alertness; methylphenidate helps people with attention deficit hyperactivity disorder (ADHD) to focus their attention	▶ prescription
Antianxiety	▶ alprazolam	▶ helps people who are excessively nervous or panicked to calm down	▶ prescription
Vaccine	▶ meningitis vaccine	▶ prevents infections in people exposed to the infectious agent	▶ prescription
Sedative	▶ temazepam	▶ causes sleepiness	▶ prescription

not require a prescription. A **prescription** is a written order from a doctor for a specific medicine. **Over-the-counter (OTC) medicines** are medicines that can be bought without a prescription.

Analgesics are medicines that relieve pain. Three common types of OTC analgesics are aspirin, acetaminophen, and ibuprofen. However, some very powerful analgesics may be bought only with a prescription. Examples of such analgesics are the opiates codeine and morphine. *Antihistamines* are medicines that block the action of the body chemical histamine, which can cause allergy symptoms. *Antacids* are medicines that work against stomach acids which can cause heartburn.

How Drugs Enter Your Body   Most drugs are taken orally as capsules, liquids, or tablets. But **Figure 2** shows many other ways that drugs can be taken into the body. These methods include

- ▶ **Implanted pumps** Surgically implanted specialized pumps inject drugs directly into a specific part of the body.
- ▶ **Inhalation** The drug enters the body through blood vessels in the lungs when it is inhaled.
- ▶ **Injection** The drug is injected by using a hypodermic needle.
- ▶ **Transdermal patches** The drug is packaged into patches that are placed on the skin.
- ▶ **Ingestion** The drug is swallowed and absorbed through blood vessels in the intestines.
- ▶ **Topical application** The drug is applied directly to certain areas of the body and absorbed into the skin.

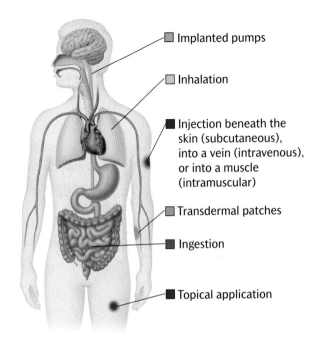

- ▪ Implanted pumps
- ▪ Inhalation
- ▪ Injection beneath the skin (subcutaneous), into a vein (intravenous), or into a muscle (intramuscular)
- ▪ Transdermal patches
- ▪ Ingestion
- ▪ Topical application

Figure 2

Drugs can enter the body in many different ways. The need to keep the correct concentration of a drug at the right place for the right amount of time is the reason behind the many delivery methods.

SECTION 1

REVIEW   *Answer the following questions on a separate piece of paper.*

Using Key Terms

1. **Compare** the term *drug* with the term *medicine*.
2. **State** the term used to describe an effect that is caused by a drug and that is different from the drug's intended effect.
3. **Compare** prescription medicines to OTC medicines.

Understanding Key Ideas

4. **List** three characteristics that make a drug useful as a medicine.
5. **Name** the two sources of all medicines and drugs.

6. **Name** four medicines and their effects on the human body.
7. **Identify** the delivery method of a drug that enters the body through the intestine.
8. **State** the reason why some drugs are considered drugs of abuse.

Critical Thinking

9. **Identify** the best method for a doctor to give a medicine to a patient if the medicine is required to act very quickly on the patient's heart. Explain your answer.

Drugs as Medicines

OBJECTIVES

Describe the process by which drugs are approved for medical use.

State two reasons why prescriptions are required for some medicines.

State two factors to consider when choosing over-the-counter (OTC) medicines.

Describe three problems that can occur when taking some medicines.

List six things you should do to be able to use medicines wisely. **LIFE SKILL**

KEY TERMS

psychoactive describes a drug or medicine that affects the brain and changes how a person perceives, thinks, or feels

generic medicine a medicine made by a company other than the company that developed the original medicine

active ingredient the chemical component that gives a medicine its action

drug interaction when a drug reacts with another drug, food, or dietary supplement such that the effect of one of the substances is greater or smaller

Myth

If stores are allowed to sell dietary supplements, they must really work.

Fact

Claims made by the makers of dietary supplements are not regulated by the FDA. Dietary supplement makers can sell their products without proving they are effective.

A century ago, anyone could put some chemicals in a bottle and call it a medicine. Men traveled across the country selling cures they had created themselves. Most of the time these cures did nothing but cost people money. On occasion the cures hurt or killed people.

Approving Drugs for Medical Use

Fake and dangerous drugs became such a problem that in the early part of the 20th century, the U.S. government started to make laws to help ensure that drugs were safe to use. In 1906, a government agency called the Food and Drug Administration (FDA) was created to control the safety of food, drugs, and cosmetics.

Testing a Drug The FDA has developed an approval process for companies that want to sell a drug in the United States. This process is needed to prove the drug is safe and effective. After scientists develop or discover a new drug, they test it. Initial testing takes place in laboratories and may include chemical tests or tests on cell cultures (cells grown in a lab). After the initial tests are completed, all drugs are tested again on animals to be sure that they work and are safe.

If the animal testing shows that the drug is safe, then testing for safety may begin on human volunteers. If the drug passes these first tests on humans, the drug is then tested on humans who have the illness that the drug is meant to treat. These larger tests are called *clinical trials.* During clinical trials, the new drug is compared to existing drugs to see if it is safe and effective.

If the clinical trials show that the drug is effective and safe, then the drug company can apply to the FDA for approval of the drug. The FDA then approves or rejects the drug for sale to the public.

Prescription Medicines

Even though the FDA has approved a drug or medicine as safe, some medicines can be bought only with a prescription. Such medicines often treat serious health conditions or are very powerful medicines. Prescription medicines should only be taken on recommendation by a doctor.

Why Do I Need to Follow a Prescription?
Prescriptions are always for a limited amount of a medicine, and they contain instructions on when and how often the medicine should be taken. If you don't follow the instructions for prescription medicines, the medicine may not work or the medicine may be harmful.

Antibiotics are examples of prescription medicines. You must continue taking antibiotics for a bacterial infection for as long as your doctor instructs. Even though you may start to feel better after a few days, the bacteria that caused the infection may not be completely eliminated. If you stop taking the antibiotic too soon, the remaining bacteria can cause the infection to return. Because not all antibiotics work against all bacteria, your doctor will prescribe a specific antibiotic for a specific illness.

What Information Does a Prescription Have?
When the doctor writes a prescription, the following information is included:
- ▶ the dose (how much of the medicine you should take)
- ▶ when you should take the medicine
- ▶ how often you should take the medicine
- ▶ the length of time you should take the medicine

When the prescription is filled at the pharmacy, the pharmacist should make sure you receive the correct medicine. Specific instructions are printed on the container. The pharmacist should also tell you the information you need in order to take your medicine safely.

Many pharmacies will also give you a *drug information sheet*. This sheet has all the information about the medicine, such as possible side effects and known interactions with other medicines. You should ask for this drug information sheet if you do not get it with your medicine.

Misuse of Prescription Medicines
The only person who should take a prescription medicine is the person whose name appears on the label. For example, even if you and your friend think you have the same illness, never take your friend's prescription medicine. You may not have the same illness, or the strength of your friend's medicine may be more or less than you need, or you could be allergic to the medicine.

Many prescription drugs are abused. This abuse can involve taking medicine when it is not needed, taking too much medicine, or mixing more than one kind of medicine. Drugs and medicines that affect the brain and change how we perceive, think, or feel, are called **psychoactive.** Psychoactive medicines and drugs are especially likely to be abused. You should take a psychoactive medicine only if it has been prescribed for you by a doctor.

Questions to Ask When Your Doctor Prescribes a Medicine

- ▶ **Why do I need to take this medicine?**
- ▶ **When should I take the medicine?**
- ▶ **For how long should I take the medicine?**
- ▶ **Are there any side effects?**
- ▶ **What should I do if a side effect occurs?**
- ▶ **Should I avoid any other medications, dietary supplements, foods, drinks, or activities while I take the medicine?**
- ▶ **What do I do if I miss a dose?**
- ▶ **What are the brand names and generic names of this medicine?**
- ▶ **Can I take the generic medicine?**

Sometimes, choosing an OTC medicine can be overwhelming.

Over-the-Counter (OTC) Medicines

Most grocery stores and drugstores have at least one aisle of OTC medicines. You can buy OTC medicines without a prescription. Over-the-counter medicines include analgesics, cold remedies, antacids, and medicines to treat rashes and other skin problems.

Benefits of OTC Medicines   Most OTC medicines are used for common illnesses, injuries, and disorders. For example, you can treat a headache with acetaminophen (AS i tuh MIN uh fuhn), a seasonal allergy with diphenhydramine (DIE fen HIE druh meen), an itchy skin rash with a cortisone cream, and a stuffy nose with pseudoephedrine (SOO doh e FE drin). If you use OTC medicines carefully, they can help relieve your minor illnesses.

Choosing an OTC Medicine   A wide variety of OTC medicines are available. But there are often many different brands of medicines that have different prices and that are used to treat the same problem. How should you choose one medicine over another?

1. **Decide what kind of OTC will work for you.** Read the list of uses to find out if the medicine can relieve your illness. Some OTC drugs may *sound* like they do the same thing but they have very different effects on the body. Take cough suppressants and cough expectorants for example. Both are called cough medicines, but a cough suppressant stops a dry, tickly cough whereas a cough expectorant loosens up chest congestion in a person with a chest infection.

2. **Decide whether you want generic or a brand-name medicine.** There are both brand-name and generic formulations of many OTC medicines. A **generic medicine** is a medicine that is made by a company other than the company that developed the original medicine. Generic drugs are chemically identical to the original drug. Both generic medicines and brand-name medicines contain the same active ingredient. The **active ingredient** is the chemical

Beliefs Vs. Reality

❝OTC medicines are sold without a prescription, so they must be completely safe.❞	OTC medicines can be dangerous when used improperly or if you are allergic to them.
❝OTC medicines can cure diseases so that you don't have to go to the doctor.❞	OTC medicines treat symptoms but cannot cure a disease.
❝Herbal medicines are safe because they're natural.❞	Herbal medicines are not regulated by the FDA, so they're not proven safe or effective.
❝I should take more of an OTC medicine if my symptoms get worse.❞	You should never take more than your recommended dosage level without first checking with your doctor.

How to Read an OTC Label

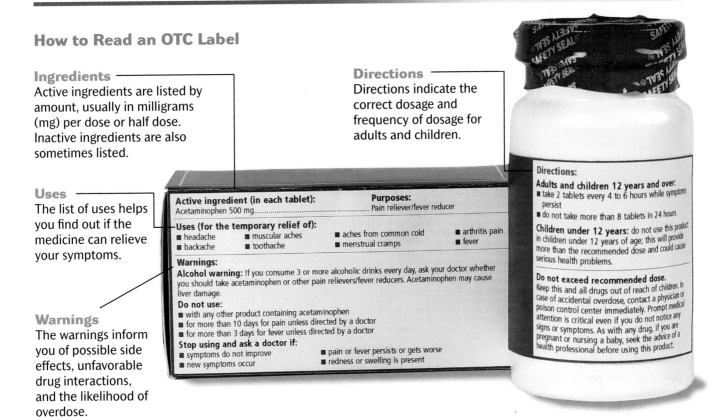

Ingredients
Active ingredients are listed by amount, usually in milligrams (mg) per dose or half dose. Inactive ingredients are also sometimes listed.

Uses
The list of uses helps you find out if the medicine can relieve your symptoms.

Warnings
The warnings inform you of possible side effects, unfavorable drug interactions, and the likelihood of overdose.

Directions
Directions indicate the correct dosage and frequency of dosage for adults and children.

Active ingredient (in each tablet):   **Purposes:**
Acetaminophen 500 mg................................ Pain reliever/fever reducer

Uses (for the temporary relief of):
- headache
- muscular aches
- backache
- toothache
- aches from common cold
- menstrual cramps
- arthritis pain
- fever

Warnings:
Alcohol warning: If you consume 3 or more alcoholic drinks every day, ask your doctor whether you should take acetaminophen or other pain relievers/fever reducers. Acetaminophen may cause liver damage.
Do not use:
- with any other product containing acetaminophen
- for more than 10 days for pain unless directed by a doctor
- for more than 3 days for fever unless directed by a doctor

Stop using and ask a doctor if:
- symptoms do not improve
- new symptoms occur
- pain or fever persists or gets worse
- redness or swelling is present

Directions:
Adults and children 12 years and over:
- take 2 tablets every 4 to 6 hours while symptoms persist
- do not take more than 8 tablets in 24 hours

Children under 12 years: do not use this product in children under 12 years of age; this will provide more than the recommended dose and could cause serious health problems.

Do not exceed recommended dose.
Keep this and all drugs out of reach of children. In case of accidental overdose, contact a physician or poison control center immediately. Prompt medical attention is critical even if you do not notice any signs or symptoms. As with any drug, if you are pregnant or nursing a baby, seek the advice of a health professional before using this product.

Figure 3

The labels on OTC medicines provide the information you need to take the medicine safely.

ACTIVITY *Compare the recommended dose for an adult with the dose for a 10-year-old child.*

component that gives a medicine its action. For example, ibuprofen is made by many companies and is the active ingredient in many products that relieve pain. The difference between generic and brand-name medicines is mainly in the inactive ingredients. These ingredients include fillers that give pills their size, shape, color, and coating and that add to the color and flavor of liquid medicines.

3. **Read the label.** All medicines can be dangerous if they are not taken properly. Because of this, all OTC medicines have very specific warnings on their labels. These warnings, as shown in **Figure 3,** alert you to potential dangers. The label also tells you what dose of medicine you should take.

Misuse of OTC Medicines In general, OTC medicines treat symptoms, not the disease that causes the symptoms. For example, you may use ibuprofen for a headache that lasts an evening. Or you may use a decongestant, such as pseudoephedrine, to help you breathe easier for a few days while you have a cold.

However, long-term use of OTC medicines can cover up pain or discomfort that is your body's way of telling you something is wrong. Treating a chronic headache or any other pain with regular use of painkillers may delay the diagnosis of a more serious condition. If symptoms last longer than a few days you should consult a doctor. Examining your daily habits may help you find the reasons for some of your symptoms. Chronic stress, for example, can lead to headaches and stomachaches. A change in lifestyle could solve those problems.

HEALTH Handbook For more information about evaluating health products, see the Express Lesson on pp. 562–563 of this text.

Herbal Remedies and Dietary Supplements Most pharmacies now sell herbal remedies and dietary supplements. The makers of these products may claim their product prevents or treats certain diseases and conditions. However, dietary supplements and herbal remedies do not have to be approved by the FDA before they are sold. Therefore, they do not have to be proven to be effective in the same way as OTC and prescription medicines do.

The health claims made about prescription and OTC medicines are supported by scientific research that has been evaluated by the FDA. The only way claims about a dietary supplement can be similar to health claims about OTC medicines is if supplement makers put on the label a disclaimer that says, "This statement has not been evaluated by the FDA. This product is not intended to diagnose, treat, cure, or prevent any disease." Evidence from scientific research, especially well-designed clinical trials, is the best way to know if a drug works and if it is safe.

Many people think that products derived from plants and animals—natural products—are purer and safer than products that are made in a laboratory. However, anything, including a plant, that is put into a bottle to be sold as a supplement has been purified in a laboratory. Also, even though something is a natural product, it does not mean it is safer. Some of the most toxic compounds known to science are completely natural!

Possible Problems with Medicines

When taken as directed, most medicines are safe. However, problems can occur when using medicines. These problems include allergic reactions, side effects, and drug interactions.

Allergic Reactions Allergic reactions are the most serious risks to taking medicines. Medicines such as penicillin and some related antibiotics are known to cause allergic reactions in some people. Insulin derived from animals, medicines used to treat epilepsy, and some sleeping pills are also known to cause allergic reactions.

Allergic reactions can range from mild itchiness to severe skin rashes, as shown in **Figure 4.** A life-threatening condition called *anaphylactic shock* (AN uh fuh LAK tik SHAHK) is the most serious kind of allergic reaction. Anaphylactic shock is a severe allergic response of almost the entire body that includes the following conditions:

- itching all over the body
- swelling, especially in the mouth or throat
- wheezing or difficulty in breathing
- a pounding heart
- fainting and unconsciousness

These symptoms signal a life-threatening medical emergency that needs immediate medical attention. If you or anyone you know develop these symptoms shortly after taking a medicine, emergency medical help should be sought right away.

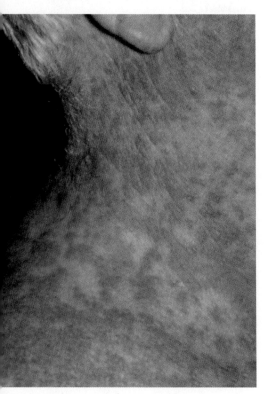

Figure 4

This is an example of someone who had an allergic skin reaction to a medicine.

ACTIVITY *Identify what this person should do.*

The first place to spot most allergic reactions is on your skin. So if you start to itch or if you get a rash after taking a medicine, stop taking it immediately and call your doctor. Be sure to tell your doctor about your allergic reaction before the doctor prescribes any kind of medicine for you again or before you decide to take an OTC medication.

Side Effects Another potential problem with medicines is that they may produce side effects. While medicine allergies are rare, side effects are common. Antibiotics, for example, not only kill invading bacteria, but they also kill bacteria that normally live in your intestines and help keep you healthy. When these helpful bacteria are killed, you can get diarrhea. Drowsiness is a common side effect of many antihistamines and cough medicines.

Aspirin is another example of a frequently used medicine that can have side effects. One of its side effects is to cause damage to the lining of the stomach. This side effect can lead to bleeding or ulcers. So if you get pains in your stomach while taking aspirin, you should stop taking the drug right away. Drugs that contain ibuprofen and related pain relievers can also cause stomach ulcers.

In addition, any child or teen who has symptoms of a cold, the flu, chickenpox, or a viral disease that causes a fever should never take aspirin. The combination of aspirin and these diseases can cause or increase the risk for a dangerous condition called Reye's (RIEZ) syndrome. Reye's syndrome is a relatively rare disease that primarily affects children and teens under the age of 16. Reye's syndrome can cause liver failure and brain damage, and the syndrome can sometimes be fatal.

Drug Interactions Drug interactions are another potential problem with medicines. **Drug interactions** occur when a drug reacts with another drug, food, or dietary supplement to increase or decrease the effect of one of the substances. Drug interactions are described on the label on any OTC package or the drug information sheet that comes with a prescription medicine.

For example, sedatives, tranquilizers, alcohol, and some antihistamines cause drowsiness. Taking any combination of these drugs at the same time could make you very drowsy and decrease your coordination. At that point, driving a car or doing anything else that requires concentration and coordination could be dangerous.

You must know about drug interactions before you start mixing medicines. Always check the label or drug information sheet before you take any medicine. You should tell your doctor and pharmacist if you are taking any other medicines or herbal remedies or dietary supplements before you start to take a new prescription or OTC medicine. By volunteering information about yourself and asking questions about new medicines, you can reduce your risk of drug allergies, side effects, and drug interactions.

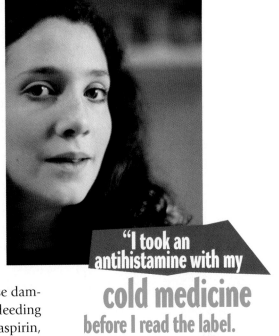

"I took an antihistamine with my **cold medicine** before I read the label. The cold medicine had an **antihistamine** too. I couldn't **stay awake** for the rest of the day."

Using Medicines Wisely

Taking the correct amounts of the correct medicine is very important. There are several important things you can do to make your medicines as safe and as effective as possible.

1. **Make yourself a part of your own healthcare team.** This team includes you, at least one parent or guardian, and any healthcare providers. Once you realize that you are part of the team, and not just a passive recipient of care, you have taken a big step towards ensuring your own health and safety. You must speak up. Your healthcare team can only do its best job caring for you if it knows all about you. Tell members of the team your complete medical history and be especially careful to mention any previous drug reactions or known allergies. Also, be sure to note any medicines and dietary supplements you already take. Your parents can help with your childhood medical history.

2. **Be prepared to ask questions.** Make sure you know and understand what is going on with your health. You may want to write down important questions ahead of time. You can also take notes or have a parent or other adult with you to hear what the doctor or healthcare professional is saying.

Analyzing DATA

Reading a Prescription Label

1 Patient's name and address

2 Prescription number and dates prescription was written and filled

3 Instructions for taking medicine

4 Quantity of medicine provided, name and strength of medicine, and doctor's name

5 Side-effect warnings

6 Refill information and expiration date

PHARM STORE   Ph. (555) 520-1302

12611 Sahara Ave., Las Vegas, NV 89109

1 **Zola Cobb**
9515 Decatur Blvd., Las Vegas, NV 89110

3 **Take 1 tablet 3 times a day**

4 Qty: **90 TABS**
BACLOFEN 10 MG TABS
DR. F. RANDALL

5 MAY CAUSE **DROWSINESS.** ALCOHOL MAY INTENSIFY THIS EFFECT. USE CARE WHEN OPERATING A CAR OR DANGEROUS MACHINERY.

2 Rx# 6842571
Orig Rx
date 10/03/07
Date
filled 11/13/07

6 Two refills remain.
Refill authorization expires on 02/22/08.

Your Turn

1. How often should this patient take her medicine?

2. When the patient finishes the medicine, will she be able to get a refill?

3. What is a possible side effect of this medicine?

4. How many days will it take for the person to finish the medicine provided? **MATH SKILL**

5. **CRITICAL THINKING** Do you think it's safe for this person to stop taking this medicine once she begins to feel better?

3. **Learn the facts about any medicine you are going to take.** If you are considering an OTC medicine, talk to the pharmacist about drug interactions and side effects.

4. **Listen to your body.** Once you have the medication, make sure that you read the label and drug information sheet carefully. Be sure to follow the instructions completely. You must pay attention to your own body. If you notice anything strange (like itching or headaches) or anything your doctor didn't warn you about, tell your parents and talk to your doctor right away.

5. **It's not always safe to suddenly stop taking a drug.** Try to get your doctor's advice before changing your dosage or intervals between doses, unless you have symptoms of an allergic reaction.

6. **Speak up and enlist your parents' help.** If you feel uneasy about your medicine, speak up. Even though a medicine is effective, it may be the wrong medicine for you. It's your job to protect yourself by being careful about how you use medicines and by becoming an active member of your healthcare team.

Remember, when you take medicines, knowledge is power. You can get the best results from your medicine and take your medicine in the safest way by knowing about the medicine you have to take and by following the tips in **Figure 5.** If you're not sure about something, ask your doctor or pharmacist.

Do	Don't
Tell your doctor your health history and any drug reactions you have.	Don't hide health information from your doctor—even the embarrassing stuff.
Pay attention to warning labels.	Don't mix medicines that cause drowsiness.
Ask your doctor or pharmacist before combining medicines.	Don't take medicines that are prescribed for someone else.
Call your doctor immediately if you notice signs of an allergic reaction.	Don't continue to take medicines that make you feel worse.
Complete the whole prescription of antibiotics.	Don't stop taking your antibiotics when you feel better.

Figure 5

Failing to use prescription medicines correctly can have very serious consequences.

SECTION 2

REVIEW
Answer the following questions on a separate piece of paper.

Using Key Terms

1. **Name** the term that describes a drug that changes how a person perceives, thinks, or feels.

2. **Define** the term *generic medicine.*

3. **Distinguish** the active ingredient from other ingredients in medicines.

4. **Name** the term for what can happen if you take an antihistamine and cold medicine together.

Understanding Key Ideas

5. **Summarize** the role of the FDA in the drug approval process.

6. **List** three reasons you need a prescription to get certain medicines.

7. **List** the important things to consider when choosing an OTC medicine.

8. **Describe** three problems that can occur when taking a medicine.

9. **LIFE SKILL** **Communicating Effectively** List five questions you should ask your doctor if you are given a prescription for a medicine.

Critical Thinking

10. **LIFE SKILL** **Practicing Wellness** Your friend regularly takes an antacid after meals. She says they are harmless and "help settle her stomach." Is your friend using her medicine wisely? Explain.

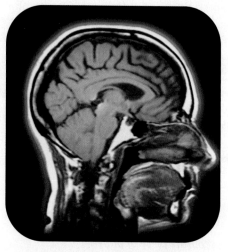

Drugs and the Brain

OBJECTIVES

Describe how drugs that affect the brain work.

State how drugs can affect a person's emotions.

Describe how addiction can develop from drug use.

Summarize the role of withdrawal in maintaining a drug addiction.

Describe why addiction is considered a treatable and avoidable disease. **LIFE SKILL**

KEY TERMS

addiction a condition in which a person can no longer control his or her drug use

drug tolerance a condition in which a user needs more of a drug to feel the same effect felt when first using the drug

physical dependence a state in which the body relies on a given drug in order to function

psychological dependence a state of emotionally or mentally needing a drug in order to function

withdrawal uncomfortable physical and psychological symptoms produced when a physically dependent drug user stops using drugs

People abuse drugs because of their effects on the brain. No one abuses a drug because of what it does to his or her stomach, lungs, or liver.

Your brain creates all of your thoughts, perceptions of the world, feelings, personality, and physical responses. Drugs that affect your brain can change all of these things.

How Drugs That Affect the Brain Work

Your brain is made up of billions of nerve cells called *neurons*. Each neuron makes many connections with other neurons. The brain uses all these neurons and their billions of connections to process information.

How Messages Are Sent in the Brain The information processing in the brain takes place at the connections between neurons. These connections are called *synapses*. What happens at the synapse is very important. As shown in **Figure 6,** for the brain to send a message, one neuron releases a special chemical messenger, called a *neurotransmitter,* at the synapse. The neurotransmitter moves across the synapse and attaches to the neuron that is to receive the message. This attachment, called *binding,* is the actual receiving of the chemical message. There are many different types of neurotransmitters including serotonin (SIR uh TOH nin), dopamine (DOH puh MEEN), and epinephrine (EP uh NEF rin).

Drugs Can Change How Messages Are Sent Some drugs can change the way neurons communicate with each other. These drugs act like neurotransmitters, block neurotransmitters, or change the amount of a neurotransmitter in synapses. Changing the communication between neurons by interfering with neurotransmitters changes the way we sense, feel, and respond to the world around us. Changing chemical messages between neurons by use of drugs can in some cases benefit health but in other cases is harmful.

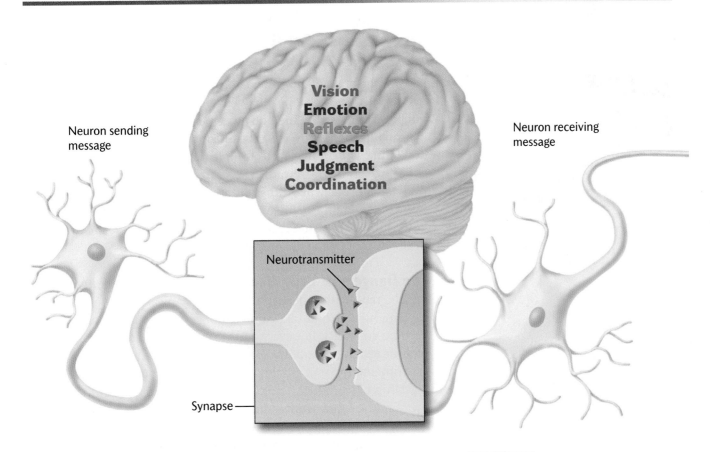

Vision
Emotion
Reflexes
Speech
Judgment
Coordination

Neuron sending message

Neuron receiving message

Neurotransmitter

Synapse

Messages in the Brain Determine Our Moods   When you are feeling relaxed, having your dog nuzzle you and lick your face is fun. When you are feeling rushed and stressed, her playfulness is annoying, so you push her away. The action of certain neurotransmitters is the basis for our different moods and emotions. How you view your dog's behavior on those two different days depends on which neurotransmitters are released in your brain. Serotonin, for example, is a neurotransmitter that greatly affects our actions and reactions to the outside world. People who are depressed may have a reduced amount of the neurotransmitter serotonin to activate neurons.

Drugs Can Affect Emotions   Antidepressants are examples of drugs that change the way the brain works in a beneficial way. By correcting the levels of serotonin in synapses, certain antidepressant medicines can help reduce depression. Other mood-altering medicines work by changing the levels or effectiveness of other neurotransmitters.

Drugs of abuse, such as marijuana, cocaine, and nicotine, interrupt the balance between the many neurotransmitters needed for normal brain functioning. These drugs alter our judgment in ways that affect our ability to understand and deal with reality. If drugs like these are taken over a long period of time, they can create the powerful changes in feelings and behavior that lead to addiction. **Addiction** is a condition in which a person can no longer control his or her drug use. When a person becomes addicted to a drug, he or she has developed a physical need for the drug, and can't function without it.

Figure 6

Neurons communicate with each other by neurotransmitters. Drugs that affect the brain change how the neurotransmitters are sent or received. Thus, such drugs can change one's feelings, perceptions, and actions.

 HEALTH Handbook   For more information about your brain, see the Express Lesson on pp. 516–519 of this text.

www.scilinks.org/health
Topic: Drug and Alcohol Abuse
HealthLinks: HH4048

HEALTH **LINKS.** Maintained by the
National Science
Teachers Association

The Path to Addiction

Almost all drugs of abuse activate one set of brain structures. These parts of the brain are together called the *brain reward system*. This system serves to reinforce healthy behavior, such as eating when you are hungry. To encourage the body to repeat such healthy behaviors, the neurons of the brain reward system release the neurotransmitter dopamine. Dopamine lets us feel pleasure.

The pleasure or "reward" we get from activities like eating is relatively small. But when drugs of abuse, such as cocaine or alcohol, turn on the brain reward system, the reward or pleasure can be very powerful. The pleasure that these drugs produce tricks the brain into believing that taking the drug is good for the body.

The Dangers of Drug Use Getting pleasure is one reason why people repeatedly abuse drugs. But the pleasure alone does not explain how people get addicted. No one starts using drugs to become an addict. But every addict starts as someone experimenting with drugs. At some point, people who become addicts move from experimentation to a more regular pattern of abuse.

Drug use produces biological changes in the brain that change the way the brain works—possibly permanently. Adolescent brains are more vulnerable to the effects of drugs than adult brains are. This is because the adolescent brain, along with the adolescent personality and body, is still growing and developing. Taking drugs interferes with the normal changes that occur at this important time of life.

Tolerance One of the first developments in the addiction process is a condition called *drug tolerance*. **Drug tolerance** develops after repeated drug use when the user finds that it takes more of a drug to feel the same effect felt when first using the drug. Because drug tolerance requires a person to take more drug to get the same effect, it sets the stage for another biological response to continue drug use—dependence.

Behavioral Warning Signs of Addiction

▶ **Loss of interest in schoolwork**

▶ **Dramatic change of appearance**

▶ **Change of friends**

▶ **Unexplained mood swings**

▶ **Absences from school**

▶ **Dramatic change in eating habits**

▶ **Excessive secretiveness or lying**

▶ **Unexplained need for money**

Drug Addiction

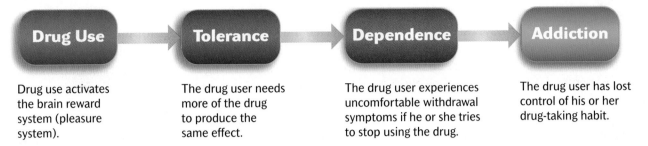

Drug Use — Drug use activates the brain reward system (pleasure system).

Tolerance — The drug user needs more of the drug to produce the same effect.

Dependence — The drug user experiences uncomfortable withdrawal symptoms if he or she tries to stop using the drug.

Addiction — The drug user has lost control of his or her drug-taking habit.

Dependence After repeated drug use, a person finds that he or she cannot function properly without taking the drug. The state in which the body relies on a given drug in order to function normally is known as **physical dependence.** The state of emotionally or mentally needing a drug in order to function normally is called **psychological dependence.** When people become physically dependent, the brain neurons and body cells respond to the presence of the drug by changing how they work. Because drugs of abuse interfere with the production of certain neurotransmitters, the neurons then try to "cancel" the effects of the drugs by becoming more responsive or less responsive to those neurotransmitters.

Addiction While drugs are changing the abuser's brain, he or she is also learning drug abuse behaviors and attitudes. When people become addicted to drugs, they lose control of their behavior. Addicts even use drugs when drug use leads to severe consequences such as dropping out of school or being arrested.

An addict learns how to get drugs, how to take them, and, sometimes, how to lie and steal to get drugs. Also, an addict learns to be distrustful and paranoid. But most of all, addicts learn to use drugs to deal with their emotional problems. This way of dealing with problems prevents the development of normal coping skills that are a part of growing up. An addict's brain is not like a normal brain. This is why drug addiction is now known as a brain disorder. **Figure 7** outlines how this complex disorder develops.

Withdrawal Neurons can keep the working balance that has been established during physical dependence as long as the person keeps taking the drug. But if the drug is suddenly removed, the neurons work abnormally. The uncomfortable physical and psychological symptoms produced when a physically dependent drug user stops using drugs is called **withdrawal.**

Withdrawal is characterized mostly by symptoms that are opposite of the drug's effect. Withdrawal keeps addiction going because the distressing symptoms drive the addict to take more drug to alleviate the symptoms. Craving the drug is the brain's way of telling the body it needs more of the drug. By now, the addict feels normal only when he or she has the drug in his or her body.

Figure 7

No one starts using drugs to become an addict.

You and Dave used to spend a lot of time together shooting hoops and surfing the Internet. But for the last few months, Dave has been hanging out with a new group. He used to really care about how he looks, but now he looks terrible. Today he asked you for the third time if he could borrow $10. When you told him he hadn't paid you back from the last time, he stormed off and warned you to stay away from him. You suspect that Dave is using drugs.

Write on a separate piece of paper how you would ask your friend if he has a drug problem. Remember to use the decision-making steps.

Give thought to the problem.

Review your choices.

Evaluate the consequences of each choice.

Assess and choose the best choice.

Think it over afterward.

Addiction Is a Treatable Disease

Many people believe that when a person becomes addicted, he or she will use drugs for the rest of his or her life. This belief is not true. Many drug abusers and addicts free themselves from drug dependency every day. However, fighting an addiction to any drug is not easy because all people who are addicted to drugs are both physically and psychologically dependent on drugs.

Most communities offer a variety of treatment programs. In treatment, patients receive help in getting off the drug to which they are addicted, as well as counseling to understand why they have become addicted. Counseling also helps the addict cope with life without the drug. The sooner treatment is started, the easier it is to do. So the sooner an addict, or a drug abuser who is on his way to becoming an addict, starts treatment, the better. And despite all the brain changes that happen and behaviors that addicts learn, they can recover.

There is one foolproof way to avoid addiction—don't use drugs of abuse. Nicotine and alcohol, both of which are highly addictive, are illegal for teens to use. So you don't need an excuse not to use them. And despite the way it may seem, everybody is not doing drugs. Two-thirds of 16-year-olds don't drink alcohol. More than 80 percent of 16-year-olds don't smoke cigarettes or use marijuana, and 99 percent don't use cocaine or Ecstasy. You can find friends who don't do drugs because you know it's the smart thing to do.

SECTION 3

REVIEW

Answer the following questions on a separate piece of paper.

Using Key Terms

1. **Define** the term *addiction*.

2. **Differentiate** drug tolerance from physical dependence.

3. **Name** the term that means "the uncomfortable physical and psychological symptoms produced when a physically dependent drug user stops using drugs."

Understanding Key Ideas

4. **Describe** how drugs can change the way the brain works.

5. **Describe** how drugs can affect your emotions.

6. **Identify** the term that is *not* a stage in the path to addiction.
   a. tolerance   c. drug use
   b. dependence   d. side effect

7. **State** reasons why addiction can be difficult to overcome.

8. **Describe** the relationship between physical dependence and withdrawal.

9. **LIFE SKILL** **Using Community Resources** What resources are available to a drug addict to help him or her begin recovery from a drug addiction?

Critical Thinking

10. **LIFE SKILL** **Practicing Wellness** Why is it important to avoid starting to take drugs?

Highlights

Key Terms

drug (218)
medicine (218)
side effect (219)
prescription (221)
over-the-counter (OTC) medicine (221)

psychoactive (223)
generic medicine (224)
active ingredient (224)
drug interaction (227)

addiction (231)
drug tolerance (232)
physical dependence (233)
psychological dependence (233)
withdrawal (233)

The Big Picture

✔ A drug is any substance that causes a change in a person's physical or emotional condition.

✔ The term *drug* can refer either to a medicine or to a drug of abuse.

✔ Drugs come from nature and are also created in laboratories.

✔ Medicines are considered safe and effective when they have tolerable side effects.

✔ Drugs are classified by what they do.

✔ Drugs can enter the body in many ways, including by inhalation, ingestion, transdermal application, injection, as well as topically and through implanted pumps.

✔ The Food and Drug Administration (FDA) is the government agency that regulates the safety and effectiveness of medicines.

✔ A doctor's prescription is needed to get medicines that treat serious health conditions or that are very powerful drugs.

✔ Over-the-counter medicines usually treat symptoms rather than cure diseases. When choosing an OTC medicine, you should consider whether the OTC medicine is best suited to treating your illness.

✔ Some medicines can cause allergic reactions or side effects or can react negatively with other medicines.

✔ To use a medicine properly, safely, and effectively, be sure you are informed about the medicine before you take it.

✔ Health claims made about herbal remedies and dietary supplements do not have to be not backed by scientific research.

✔ Areas of the brain called the *brain reward system* are involved in feelings of pleasure. These areas are stimulated by almost all drugs of abuse.

✔ Drugs that affect your emotions do so by changing the way neurons send and receive neurotransmitters.

✔ Addiction can develop from drug use because drugs change the way the brain works.

✔ The unpleasant physical and mental effects of withdrawal can keep an addiction going.

✔ Addiction is a brain disorder. Treating an addict involves helping the addict get over his or her physical dependence, learning new behaviors to stay drug free, and understanding the reasons that the drug use started.

✔ The majority of teens do not use illegal drugs.

Review

Using Key Terms

active ingredient (224)
addiction (231)
drug (218)
drug interaction (227)
drug tolerance (232)
generic medicine (224)
medicine (218)
over-the-counter (OTC) medicine (221)
physical dependence (233)
prescription (221)
psychoactive (223)
psychological dependence (233)
side effect (219)
withdrawal (233)

1. For each definition below, choose the key term that best matches the definition.
   a. a medicine that can be obtained only with a written order from a doctor
   b. a term used for a drug or medicine that changes how a person perceives, thinks, or feels
   c. a medicine that is made by a company other than the company that developed the medicine
   d. an unintended and sometimes harmful effect of a drug

2. Explain the relationship between the key terms in each of the following pairs.
   a. *physical dependence* and *withdrawal*
   b. *drug* and *medicine*
   c. *drug tolerance* and *addiction*
   d. *over-the-counter medicine* and *prescription*
   e. *active ingredient* and *drug interaction*

Understanding Key Ideas

Section 1

3. Why are all drugs not medicines?

4. What are three key characteristics of a good medicine?

5. From what two sources do all drugs and medicines come from?

6. Analgesics
   a. relieve allergy symptoms.
   b. kill harmful bacteria.
   c. relieve pain.
   d. soothe itchy skin.

7. List the ways that drugs can enter the body.

8. Explain why some drugs are called drugs of abuse. **LIFE SKILL**

9. **CRITICAL THINKING** How do you think medicines have affected how long you will live?

Section 2

10. What is the role of clinical trials in the drug approval process?

11. Why are some medicines available only by prescription?

12. Which of the following is the least important to consider when choosing an OTC medicine?
    a. active ingredient
    b. possible side effects
    c. brand name
    d. drug interactions

13. List four side effects of some medicines.

14. List the things you should ask your doctor about any medicine she or he prescribes to you. **LIFE SKILL**

15. **CRITICAL THINKING** Explain the advantages of being an active member of your healthcare team.

Section 3

16. Describe how messages are sent in the brain.

17. How do some drugs affect emotions?

18. Identify four behaviors that could be warning signs of drug abuse and addiction.

19. Describe the role of withdrawal in maintaining a drug addiction.

20. **CRITICAL THINKING** Evaluate the following statement: "Drug addiction is preventable." **LIFE SKILL**

Interpreting Graphics

Study the figure below to answer the questions that follow.

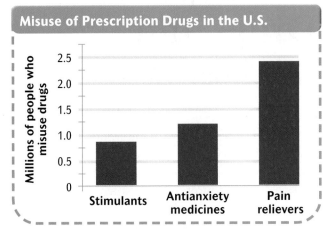

Misuse of Prescription Drugs in the U.S.

Millions of people who misuse drugs

Stimulants | Antianxiety medicines | Pain relievers

Source: National Household Survey on Drug Abuse.

21. What are the most commonly abused prescription drugs?

22. Using the data in the graph, estimate the total number of people who abuse prescription drugs. **MATH SKILL**

23. CRITICAL THINKING Why do you think these particular drugs are the most commonly abused?

Activities

24. Health and You Select an advertisement for an OTC drug. Analyze the claims and benefits given in the advertisement. How does the advertisement try to sell the drug? Rewrite the advertisement, and give suggestions for relieving the problem without use of the drug.

25. Health and Your Community Long-term self-medication with OTC medicines is becoming more common. Write a one-page report that presents possible reasons for this trend. Explain possible health problems the overuse of OTC medicines can lead to.

26. Health and You Write a reply to the following statement: "Just try it once; one try won't harm you. It's not like you'll become an addict overnight!"

Action Plan

27. LIFE SKILL Setting Goals You have a choice about how much you rely on drugs to relieve symptoms brought on by stress. Create a plan to restrict your reliance on drugs.

Standardized Test Prep

Read the passage below, and then answer the questions that follow. **READING SKILL** **WRITING SKILL**

We have created a product to blast your body with pure energy. Star Energy is an all-natural substance made from the flowers of *Grameninis energicium*. We have now <u>harnessed</u> the natural goodness of *Grameninis* for you to enjoy its health benefits. Star Energy is the most complete and dynamic natural energy formula ever developed. You'll instantly feel the difference in your energy levels. Many nutrition experts use Star Energy as a part of their weight-training program to boost muscle development. Just one tablet a day!

28. In this passage, the word *harnessed* means
A made.
B promoted.
C captured.
D distributed.

29. What can you infer from reading this passage?
E Star Energy will work for you.
F This is an advertisement.
G Star Energy is an OTC medicine.
H Star Energy has been approved by the FDA.

30. Write a paragraph on the methods that are used in this advertisement to make the product sound effective.

31. Because it is natural, is Star Energy any safer or more effective than a drug made in a laboratory? Explain.

32. Do you think this product could be abused?

There was a time when drug companies did not advertise prescription drugs on TV or in magazines. Now, we see such ads often. But are these advertisements good for your health?

Prescription Drugs and the Media

In 1555, the Royal College of Physicians in London declared that no doctor could tell a patient anything about a medicine, including its name. Doctors in those days were concerned that patients would hurt themselves by using medicines unwisely. This cautious attitude persisted in the medical community for more than 450 years, but things have changed in modern times.

Direct-to-Consumer Advertising

Prescription drugs are now so widely advertised in magazines, on the Internet, on the radio, and especially on TV that they affect every person living in this country. This kind of advertising is called *direct-to-consumer (DTC) advertising.* In 2001, the pharmaceutical industry spent $2.5 billion on DTC advertising in the United States. Pharmaceutical companies spent $1.5 billion on TV advertising alone.

Drug Advertising Affects People's Actions

In 1999, one national newsmagazine contained more than 18 pages of advertisements for prescription drugs. Does all of this advertising affect people's choices about medicine? The answer appears to be yes. Thirty percent of all people who see these ads and then go to a doctor ask for an advertised product. More astoundingly, almost half of the doctors give the patient a prescription for the specific drug requested. Only one in four doctors recommends another drug. In short, people are motivated by the ads, and their doctors are likely to give them requested drugs.

Advertising Prescription Drugs Has Benefits

Many people in the drug and medical field suggest that these ads provide great benefits to you, the consumer. They argue that a consumer has a right to learn about the drugs that are available to treat a symptom. Advertising, they say, is a form of education. If you have asthma, for example, shouldn't you have a right to know which asthma drugs you can use? Why should only a doctor have access to such information?

Another argument in favor of DTC advertising is that it makes money for the pharmaceutical industry. This money, supporters of DTC argue, helps pay for the costly development of current drugs and for the development of new drugs.

Drug Advertising Has Drawbacks

Along with the growth in drug advertising has come a steady growth of criticism. Consumer groups and physicians have complained that advertising sometimes causes people to make bad choices. One argument is that drug ads blur the distinction between providing information and promoting good healthcare. When doctors tell patients that the specific drug they asked for may not be good for them, the patients often react with anger and frustration. They may demand a specific drug even when another is as good, better, or even cheaper. Many doctors say that they feel pressured by patients who have read ads.

Being Aware of the Media's Influence

The media—TV, radio, Internet, newspapers, and magazines—affects everybody's life. The sudden growth in DTC advertising of prescription drugs means that all of us must become wise consumers. Advertising should not be accepted without question.

Your best course of action is to use your physician as a partner in your healthcare. Ask your doctor questions, and listen responsibly to the answers and suggestions. Likewise, all of us must bring skepticism to what we see and hear, especially when someone is trying to sell us something. Drug advertisements may indeed help us make better choices, but if used unwisely, they may compromise our health.

YOUR TURN

1. **Summarizing Information** Give one argument for and one argument against advertising prescription drugs.

2. **Analyzing Methods** Check some current magazines in terms of numbers and types of drug advertisements. How does each ad attempt to sell the drug? Discuss your findings.

3. **CRITICAL THINKING** How can you determine if a drug advertisement is telling you all of the facts about treating a specific illness or using a specific drug?

internet connect

www.scilinks.org/health
Topic: Prescription Drugs
HealthLinks code: HH4239

HEALTH LINKS. Maintained by the National Science Teachers Association

CHAPTER 10

Alcohol

What's Your Health IQ?
KNOWLEDGE

Which of the statements below are true, and which are false? Check your answers on p. 638.

1. A shot of vodka has the same amount of alcohol that a can of beer has.

2. Many of the problems caused by alcohol are due to loss of judgment.

3. One drink can affect a person's ability to drive.

4. Alcohol overdose can be fatal.

5. Children of alcoholics have an increased risk of becoming alcoholics.

6. Alcoholism affects only the alcoholic.

7. Drunk driving is the No. 1 cause of death among teens in the United States.

Visit these Web sites for the latest health information:

HEALTH LINKS
THE WORLD'S A CLICK AWAY®

Find more information whenever you see a HealthLinks
box. Go to **scilinks.org/health**,
and type in the HealthLinks
code.

go.
hrw.
com

Find worksheets and other
materials that go with your
textbook at **go.hrw.com**.

Current Health®

Check out **Current Health®**
articles related to this chapter
by visiting **go.hrw.com**.
Just type in the keyword
HH4 CH10.

Alcohol Affects the Body

OBJECTIVES

State why alcohol is considered a drug.

List the short-term effects of alcohol use.

Describe the long-term damage that alcohol does to the organs of the body.

Identify three reasons you should not drink alcohol. **LIFE SKILL**

KEY TERMS

alcohol the drug in wine, beer, and liquor that causes intoxication

intoxication the physical and mental changes produced by drinking alcohol

blood alcohol concentration (BAC) the amount of alcohol in a person's blood, expressed as a percentage

binge drinking the act of drinking five or more drinks in one sitting

cirrhosis a deadly disease that replaces healthy liver tissue with scar tissue; most often caused by long-term alcohol abuse

Alicia was throwing a party. David thought the party would be fun, but he was nervous. There was going to be beer at the party, but he didn't want to drink. Would others think he wasn't cool if they found out he wouldn't drink?

Alcohol Is a Drug

Alcohol is the drug found in beer, wine, and liquor that causes intoxication. Alcohol is considered a drug because it causes a change in a person's physical and emotional state. The physical and mental changes produced by drinking alcohol are called **intoxication.**

All forms of alcohol are dangerous. Many people think that beer is safer than liquor because beer is not as strong. This is not true. One beer contains the same amount of alcohol as a glass of wine or a shot of vodka. No alcoholic beverage is safe. And for people in the United States under the age of 21, no alcoholic beverage is legal to consume.

Beliefs Vs. Reality

"Drinking a beer will make me look more mature."	Stumbling around and acting silly will not make you look mature.
"If alcohol were that dangerous, it wouldn't be legal for adults."	Alcohol is dangerous for adults as well as teens.
"If I've had a few beers, I can drink some coffee before I drive and still be safe."	Coffee can make you feel more awake, but it can't make you sober. Only time can do that.
"Parties make me nervous, so I need a beer to loosen up."	When people "loosen up" with alcohol, they often say and do things they will regret later.

Short-Term Effects of Alcohol

Many people are not aware of alcohol's dangerous and unhealthy effects. The short-term effects of alcohol depend on several factors, including the amount of alcohol consumed, the presence of food in the person's stomach, genetic factors, any medicine or drug the person has taken, and the person's gender and size.

Effects on the Body When alcohol enters the stomach, it is quickly absorbed into the bloodstream and carried throughout the body. The short-term effects of alcohol on the body include the following:

1. **Alcohol irritates the mouth, throat, esophagus, and stomach.** Alcohol can cause a person to feel nauseated and to vomit.

2. **Alcohol makes the heart work harder.** Alcohol dilates, or widens, the blood vessels. The heart has to work harder to pump blood through the wide vessels.

3. **Alcohol makes the body lose heat.** When the blood vessels in the skin widen, they make the person feel warm and look flushed. But, the person may actually be getting too cold. Drinking alcohol in cold weather or while in the water can drain too much heat from the body, which leads to hypothermia.

4. **Alcohol causes the liver to work harder.** The liver breaks down toxic substances, such as alcohol, to neutralize any poisonous effects. But the liver can break down only about one alcoholic drink per hour. Drinking more than that amount causes alcohol to build up and to stress the liver.

5. **Alcohol causes dehydration.** Dehydration occurs because breaking down alcohol requires water. As a result, the kidneys produce more urine. The water used to break down alcohol is taken from the rest of the body, including the brain. The cells of the brain shrink and may even begin to die. Many of the symptoms of a hangover, such as headache, nausea, and dizziness, are a result of severe dehydration. A *hangover* is a set of uncomfortable physical effects that are caused by excessive alcohol use.

Effects on the Mind Alcohol has dramatic effects on the brain. As a depressant, alcohol slows down the nervous system. About 15 minutes after finishing one or two drinks, most people begin to feel more relaxed and more talkative, and they laugh more easily.

But after only two drinks, the drinker loses the ability to make good decisions, pay attention, follow complex thoughts, or cope with difficult situations. The drinker loses his or her inhibitions. *Inhibitions* are the natural limits that people put on their behavior.

After a few more drinks, a person loses the ability to focus his or her eyes. The person slurs his or her speech, loses coordination, and may experience drastic mood swings. The person loses judgment and may do things he or she would never do sober. For example, an intoxicated person may become sexually aggressive or engage in unplanned or unprotected sexual activity.

Short-Term Effects of Alcohol

▶ **Nausea**
▶ **Vomiting**
▶ **Dehydration**
▶ **Loss of judgment and self-control**
▶ **Reduced reaction time**
▶ **Poor vision**
▶ **Memory loss**
▶ **Blackout**
▶ **Coma**
▶ **Death**

Table 1 Blood Alcohol Concentration (BAC)

Weight	Drinks per hour*	BAC	
90 to 110 pounds	1	Male	0.04
		Female	0.05
	3	Male	0.11
		Female	0.14
	5	Male	0.19
		Female	0.23
110 to 130 pounds	1	Male	0.03
		Female	0.04
	3	Male	0.09
		Female	0.11
	5	Male	0.16
		Female	0.19
150 to 170 pounds	1	Male	0.02
		Female	0.03
	3	Male	0.07
		Female	0.09
	5	Male	0.12
		Female	0.14

*A 12-ounce beer, a 6-ounce glass of wine, and a 1.25-ounce glass of whiskey each qualify as one drink and have the same alcohol content.

Effects of alcohol at different blood alcohol concentrations

0.02 slowed reaction time; feeling of relaxation, warmth, and well-being

0.05 feeling of euphoria; loss of inhibitions; decreased judgment

0.10 impaired vision, judgment, reflexes, and coordination; mood swings

0.15 seriously affected coordination; blurred vision; severely impaired speech; difficulty walking and standing; memory problems, mood swings; violent behavior

0.2 blackouts; memory loss; stomach irritation; vomiting

0.25 loss of consciousness; numbness; dangerously slowed breathing

0.3 coma

0.4–0.5 death from alcohol poisoning

ACTIVITY *If a female weighs 120 pounds and has three drinks in 1 hour, what will her BAC be? How will she be affected?*

Source: National Clearinghouse for Alcohol and Drug Information.

Myth

If I weigh 160 lbs, I can drink three beers without affecting my driving because I'll still be under the legal limit of 0.08.

Fact

The ability to drive is affected even at a BAC of 0.02. Just one drink can affect a person's ability to drive safely.

Effects at Different Blood Alcohol Concentrations **Blood alcohol concentration (BAC)** is the amount of alcohol in a person's blood, expressed as a percentage. **Table 1** shows the BACs for men and women depending on the person's weight and the number of drinks consumed per hour. The list next to the table summarizes the effects of alcohol depending on the person's BAC. A BAC of 0.08 is the legal limit for driving under the influence of alcohol (DUI). However, even a BAC of 0.02, which is much lower than the legal limit, can affect a person's ability to drive.

The Dangers of Binge Drinking The act of drinking five or more drinks in one sitting is called **binge drinking.** A person can drink a fatal amount of alcohol before the effects of severe intoxication set in.

For most people, eight drinks or more in an hour cause the areas of the brain that control breathing and heart rate to become dangerously depressed. The brain and heart may stop working. This is called *alcohol poisoning,* or alcohol overdose, and it can be fatal.

Three symptoms of alcohol poisoning are extreme vomiting, loss of consciousness, and dangerously slowed breathing. If a person has passed out from drinking alcohol, get medical help immediately. Then turn the victim onto his or her side. Alcohol overdose causes vomiting, even when a person is unconscious. If the person is lying face up, he or she may choke and die. If the person is not breathing and has no pulse, someone certified in cardiopulmonary resuscitation (CPR) should administer CPR.

HEALTH Handbook For more information about CPR, see the Express Lesson on pp. 582–585 of this text.

Long-Term Effects of Alcohol

The long-term effects of alcohol use are serious. You do not have to be an alcoholic to suffer the effects in **Figure 1.** Repeatedly stressing your body with a toxic chemical eventually takes a toll on your health.

Permanent Damage to the Body Alcohol can damage the heart. Alcohol can cause an irregular heartbeat, high blood pressure (hypertension), and enlargement of the heart. Alcohol can also cause *anemia*, a decrease in red blood cells or hemoglobin. Red blood cells carry oxygen to the body.

Figure 1

Long-term alcohol use damages the body in many ways.

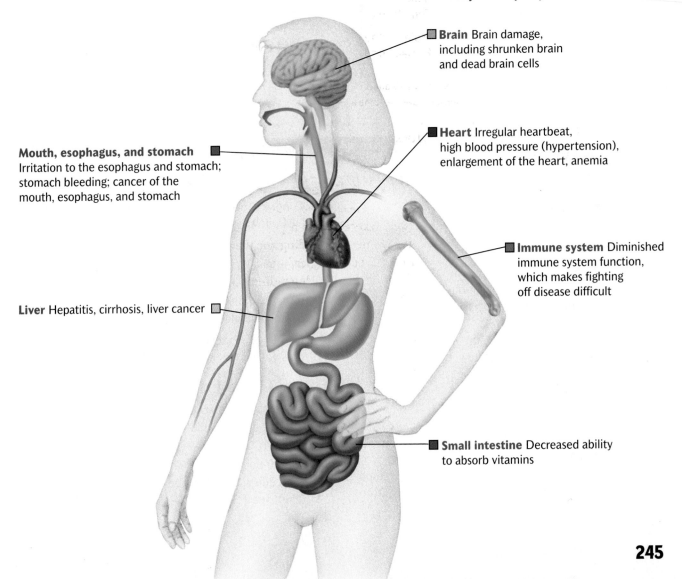

Brain Brain damage, including shrunken brain and dead brain cells

Heart Irregular heartbeat, high blood pressure (hypertension), enlargement of the heart, anemia

Mouth, esophagus, and stomach Irritation to the esophagus and stomach; stomach bleeding; cancer of the mouth, esophagus, and stomach

Immune system Diminished immune system function, which makes fighting off disease difficult

Liver Hepatitis, cirrhosis, liver cancer

Small intestine Decreased ability to absorb vitamins

Alcohol can have devastating effects on the liver. Long-term drinking can lead to *hepatitis* (inflammation of the liver), liver cancer, and cirrhosis. **Cirrhosis** (suh ROH sis) is a disease that replaces healthy liver tissue with scar tissue and is usually caused by long-term alcohol use. Cirrhosis is the 12th leading cause of death in the United States. Half of these deaths are due to chronic alcohol abuse.

Alcohol can also damage the esophagus and stomach. For example, alcohol causes irritation and bleeding of the stomach lining. Long-term alcohol abuse has been linked to cancer of the mouth, esophagus, and stomach.

Alcohol also damages the small intestine and makes absorbing vitamins and minerals difficult. It irritates the pancreas and may increase the risk of pancreatic cancer. It also affects the body's immune system—it reduces the body's ability to fight disease.

Over time, heavy drinking can put too much strain on the kidneys. Excessive drinking can also result in loss of bladder control.

> Alcoholism is a leading cause of dementia in the United States.

Permanent Damage to the Brain Alcohol causes permanent changes in the brain due to cell death from repeated dehydration and lack of oxygen. Alcoholism is a leading cause of dementia in the United States. *Dementia* is a decrease in brain function that includes personality changes and memory loss. While alcohol-related dementia is seen only in people who have been alcoholic for a very long time, some evidence suggests loss of brain function occurs in virtually all heavy drinkers.

SECTION 1

REVIEW
Answer the following questions on a separate piece of paper.

Using Key Terms

1. **Identify** the term for "the drug in wine, beer, and liquor that causes intoxication."

2. **Define** *intoxication*.

3. **Identify** the term for "the amount of alcohol in a person's blood, expressed as a percentage."

4. **Define** *cirrhosis*.

Understanding Key Ideas

5. **Identify** why alcohol is considered a drug.

6. **Summarize** the short-term effects of alcohol on the body.

7. **Identify** which of the following is *not* a short-term effect of alcohol.
   a. poor vision
   b. poor judgment
   c. reduced reaction time
   d. increased self-control

8. **Compare** the BAC that represents the legal limit for DUI with the BAC at which driving is first impaired.

9. **Describe** the dangers of binge drinking.

10. **Identify** which of the following is a long-term effect of alcohol use.
    a. dead brain cells
    b. stomach bleeding
    c. irregular heart beat
    d. all of the above

11. **LIFE SKILL** **Practicing Wellness** Name three reasons you should not drink alcohol.

Critical Thinking

12. What type of behavior would you expect to find at a party where people are drinking? Why do you think teens drink?

13. If a 160-pound male drank five beers in 2 hours, what effects might the boy experience? **MATH SKILL** (Hint: See Table 1.)

Alcoholism Affects the Family and Society

OBJECTIVES

State the difference between alcohol abuse and alcoholism.

Describe the stages in which alcoholism develops.

Identify the warning signs of alcoholism.

List three ways that alcohol use can have a negative effect on family life.

Describe how alcoholism affects society.

Summarize two treatment options for overcoming alcoholism.

KEY TERMS

alcohol abuse drinking too much alcohol, drinking it too often, or drinking it at inappropriate times

alcoholism a disease that causes a person to lose control of his or her drinking behavior; a physical and emotional addiction to alcohol

enabling helping an addict avoid the negative consequences of his or her behavior

codependency a condition in which a family member or friend sacrifices his or her own needs to meet the needs of an addict

fetal alcohol syndrome (FAS) a set of physical and mental defects that affect a fetus that has been exposed to alcohol because of the mother's consumption of alcohol during pregnancy

Eva was in her room when she heard the arguing begin. "Where have you been?" her mother asked. "Don't start with me again," said her father, "I can have a beer if I want to." Eva knew the yelling would start, and then the crying would begin. When was this ever going to end?

What Is Alcoholism?

Alcohol is the most widely used and abused drug in our society. **Alcohol abuse** is drinking too much alcohol, drinking it too often, or drinking it at inappropriate times. **Alcoholism** is a disease that causes a person to lose control of his or her drinking behavior. The drinker is both physically and emotionally addicted to alcohol. Alcoholics don't just crave alcohol. They suffer painful physical symptoms when they do not have alcohol.

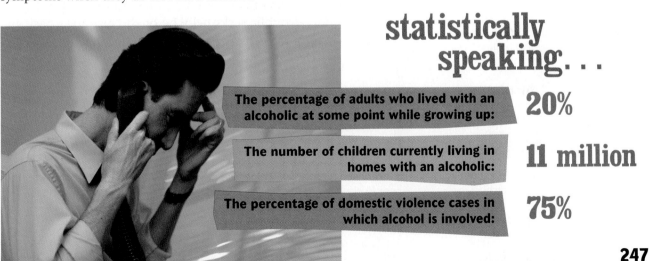

statistically speaking...

The percentage of adults who lived with an alcoholic at some point while growing up:	**20%**
The number of children currently living in homes with an alcoholic:	**11 million**
The percentage of domestic violence cases in which alcohol is involved:	**75%**

Alcoholism Develops in Stages

When Eva's dad lost his job, he started drinking more frequently. He had a new job now, but he couldn't seem to quit drinking.

Like all types of drug addiction, alcoholism develops over time. **Figure 2** shows how the stages of alcoholism are the same as those of any type of drug addiction.

1. **Problem drinking** Alcoholism begins with experimentation. No one who experiments with alcohol believes that he or she will become an alcoholic. Most alcoholics say that they first began drinking to have fun. At some point, people who become alcoholics move from experimental use to a regular pattern of abuse.

    In many cases, initial experimentation gradually becomes social drinking. *Social drinking* is drinking alcohol as part of a social situation, such as on a date or at a party. Social drinking has rules: Do not drink alone, and do not drink just to get drunk. The alcohol abuser starts drinking to avoid boredom, to escape anxiety, to relieve stress, or to cope with depression.

2. **Tolerance** As alcohol abuse continues, the person becomes tolerant to alcohol. *Tolerance* develops after repeated drinking when the user finds that it takes more alcohol to feel the same effect felt when first drinking alcohol. If alcohol abuse increases, the drinking or recovering from being drunk take up most of the individual's time. Family life, friends, work, schoolwork, and other activities are neglected. Drinkers become secretive, paranoid, and defensive as they try to hide their drinking behavior.

3. **Dependence** Over time the drinker's body begins to need alcohol to function normally. This condition is called *physical dependence.* Without alcohol, the drinker experiences withdrawal such as anxiety, sweating, shaking, and nausea.

4. **Alcoholism** Eventually, the drinker is addicted to alcohol. The person craves alcohol and cannot control his or her drinking. The alcoholic drinks and gets drunk with increasing frequency. Being addicted to alcohol means putting the drug before everything else. Some alcoholics will substitute alcohol for food, which can lead to serious health problems such as malnutrition.

Each stage leading to alcoholism may last a long time. However, by the time the alcoholic seeks help, he or she may look back and wonder how his or her drinking got so out of control.

Figure 2

Like any type of drug addiction, alcoholism happens gradually.

Alcoholism

Problem drinking	Tolerance	Dependence	Alcoholism
Drinker cannot drink alcohol in moderation or at appropriate times.	Drinker needs more alcohol to produce the same effect.	Drinker's body needs alcohol to function normally.	Drinker has lost control of his or her drinking behavior.

Risk Factors for Alcoholism It's not clear why some people can drink alcohol without becoming addicted, while others become alcoholics. Alcoholism probably results from a combination of psychological, environmental, behavioral, and physical factors. Examples of these factors are discussed below.

▶ **Age** For teens, the most important risk factor for alcoholism is age. Teens who start drinking before age 15 are four times more likely to become alcoholics than people who wait until they're 21 to drink. The brains of adolescents are undergoing tremendous growth and development, so they are particularly vulnerable to the effects of alcohol.

▶ **Social environment** Hanging out with friends who drink alcohol increases the chance that a person will drink. Peer pressure, persuasive advertising, and the desire to fit in can influence a person to drink.

▶ **Genetics** Research has shown that genetics may play a part in whether a person becomes an alcoholic. Alcoholism tends to run in families. The male children of alcoholic fathers have a 25 percent risk of becoming alcoholics. Children of nonalcoholics have a 7 to 9 percent risk.

▶ **Risk-taking personality** People who are impulsive, like novelty, and enjoy taking risks have a greater chance of becoming alcoholics than people who do not engage in risky behavior.

It is important to remember that a risk factor may increase the *chance* that something will happen, but risk factors can't determine your future. Regardless of how many risk factors you have, you still have a choice about whether or not to drink.

Warning Signs of Alcoholism

▶ **Drinking to deal with anger, frustration, and disappointment**

▶ **Changing friends, personal habits, and interests**

▶ **Being defensive about drinking**

▶ **Feeling depressed**

▶ **Drinking more for the same high**

▶ **Drinking alone**

▶ **Drinking to get drunk**

▶ **Experiencing memory lapses as a result of drinking alcohol**

Warning Signs of Alcoholism There are some warning signs that a person may be suffering from alcohol addiction. For example, as alcoholism develops, alcohol becomes an increasingly important part of a drinker's life. Alcohol may be used to deal with anger, disappointment, and frustration. The drinker begins to have a difficult time putting limits on drinking. The person finds it almost impossible to resist having another drink.

Alcoholics may be uncomfortable around friends who don't drink. Personal and professional relationships suffer, which causes additional stress for the alcoholic. Alcoholics usually battle feelings of depression or hopelessness. They might even talk about or try to commit suicide.

Most drinkers can't recognize these symptoms in themselves. The inability to see these symptoms is called *denial.* Denial is an important component of all addictions. Because addicts deny having a problem, friends or family members, employers, and sometimes the courts usually have to step in to stop the addictive process.

Alcoholism Affects the Family

Getting up in the morning is hard on Eva. She knows that she'll see her mom's red, swollen eyes. Eva always thinks that if she had helped out more when her dad lost his job, he might not drink so much now. She knows it isn't her fault, but she still feels guilty. Alcoholism affects everyone who interacts with the alcoholic. Families of alcoholics suffer in many ways, including

▶ **Guilty feelings** Family members often feel guilty, as if their loved one's alcoholism is somehow their fault. It is not.

▶ **Unpredictable behavior** The families of alcoholics never know what to expect. An alcoholic may be depressed in the morning, happy in the afternoon, and violently angry by nighttime.

▶ **Violence** Families of alcoholics are more likely to become victims of violence than families of nonalcoholics are.

▶ **Neglect and isolation** Alcoholics usually spend their time preoccupied with drinking. Children of alcoholics often feel as if the alcoholic parent does not have time to care for them.

▶ **Protecting the alcoholic** Family, friends, or employers sometimes enable an alcoholic. **Enabling** means helping an addict avoid the negative consequences of his or her behavior. For example, when Eva's dad has a hangover and can't go to work, her mom often calls his boss to say that he is sick.

▶ **Ignoring one's own needs** **Codependency** is the condition in which a family member or friend sacrifices his or her own needs to meet the needs of an addict. Family members are so wrapped up in taking care of the drinker that their own lives suffer.

In the end, alcoholism affects both the drinker and the people the drinker loves the most.

Families of Teen Alcoholics When teens drink they hurt not only themselves but also their families. Teens must acquire alcohol illegally. Teen alcoholics lie to their families to avoid getting caught. They often become angry or abusive when confronted about their drinking problem. Just as a parent's alcoholism puts stress on children, a teen's alcohol problem puts stress on his or her parents.

Alcohol and Pregnancy Alcoholism is so difficult to overcome that alcoholics who become pregnant find it difficult to stop drinking. In 2003, about 15 percent of pregnant women continued to use alcohol. Heavy drinking during pregnancy can lead to fetal alcohol syndrome. **Fetal alcohol syndrome (FAS)** is a set of physical and mental defects that affect a fetus that has been exposed to alcohol because of the mother's consumption of alcohol during her pregnancy. Children with FAS have various physical deformities and mental retardation. Some babies have to be cared for the rest of their lives. FAS is the leading preventable cause of mental retardation in our country.

"When my dad drinks everybody suffers."

Alcoholism Affects Society

If someone tells you that his or her drinking does not affect others, don't believe him or her. The truth is that alcoholism touches everyone. Society pays huge emotional, physical, and financial costs for the misuse of alcohol and for alcoholism. For example, alcohol abuse often leads to car wrecks, drowning, and other accidents that kill or injure both drinkers and nondrinkers. Do you know anyone in your community who has been injured or has died because of an alcohol-related accident?

Many cases of murder, family violence, child abuse, rape, and assault are attributed to alcohol-related voilence. Alcohol plays a major role in violence and crime. Alcoholism leads to the destruction of the family.

Alcoholism takes away money and resources from society. For example, drinkers get sick far more often than nondrinkers do. Alcoholism leads to missing days of school or work. Money is spent on treating alcohol-related illnesses, including alcohol abuse. Money is spent to cover losses due to alcohol-related crime. As a result of alcohol-related crime, more public services, such as ambulances, law enforcement, and legal services are needed.

Analyzing DATA

Costs of Alcohol to Society

1 Each slice of the pie indicates a percentage of the total cost of alcohol to society.

2 The asterisk indicates the total cost of alcohol to society.

Costs of Alcohol to Society*

- 9%
- 9%
- 14%
- 48%
- 20%

1
- ■ Lost productivity due to alcohol-related illness
- ■ Lost productivity due to premature death
- ■ Medical bills
- ■ Auto crashes
- ■ Crime

2 *Costs equaled $185 billion in 1998.

Source: National Institute on Alcohol Abuse and Alcoholism.

Your Turn

1. What percentage of the total costs of alcohol to society are due to health problems? **MATH SKILL**

2. What was the cost of alcohol due to crime, expressed in dollars? (Hint: Use the information next to the asterisk.) **MATH SKILL**

3. What fraction of the costs of alcohol to society are due to medical bills?

4. **CRITICAL THINKING** Why do you think the majority of the costs of alcohol to society are related to health problems?

Alcoholism Can Be Treated

Overcoming alcohol addiction is not easy, but it can be done. Because addiction changes the brain, freeing oneself from alcoholism takes a lot of support and, above all, help.

Treatment Programs To get help learning to live without drinking, alcoholics should participate in some form of treatment. The treatment helps the alcoholic endure the difficult stages of withdrawal (the process of discontinuing use of a drug to which the body is addicted). During withdrawal, a person may suffer extreme nervousness, headaches, chills, nausea, seizures, and uncontrollable shaking. Treatment programs also try to help the alcoholic understand why he or she became addicted to alcohol.

There are a variety of treatment options for alcoholics. Treatment programs include both inpatient and outpatient care. Inpatient centers provide a sheltered place to go through withdrawal while getting counseling. Alcoholics Anonymous (AA) is the most widely used program for treating alcoholism. The AA method for recovery involves 12 steps. Through regular meetings and shared experiences, AA members bring themselves and each other closer to a life that is free of alcohol and full of emotional, physical, social, and spiritual well-being.

Al-Anon and Alateen Al-Anon and Alateen are programs that provide treatment and support to the families of alcoholics. *Al-Anon* is designed to help family members talk about and share advice on the problem of living with an alcoholic. *Alateen* is specifically designed to help teenagers cope with this situation. There are local chapters of AA, Al-Anon, and Alateen in just about every community in the United States. Check the phone book for local chapters.

Coping with alcoholism can be difficult, confusing, and lonely. But many organizations offer teens support.

SECTION 2

REVIEW *Answer the following questions on a separate piece of paper.*

Using Key Terms

1. **Define** *alcohol abuse*.

2. **Compare** the terms *enabling* and *codependency*.

3. **Identify** the term for "the physical and mental defects that affect a fetus that has been exposed to alcohol because of the mother's consumption of alcohol during pregnancy."

Understanding Key Ideas

4. **Distinguish** between alcohol abuse and alcoholism.

5. **Describe** the stages leading to alcoholism.

6. **Name** six warning signs of alcoholism.

7. **Summarize** the effects of alcoholism on the family.

8. **Identify** which of the following is a way in which alcoholism affects society.
   a. destruction of the family
   b. increased medical costs
   c. increased crime
   d. all of the above

9. **Compare** two programs for treating alcoholism.

Critical Thinking

10. **LIFE SKILL** **Making GREAT Decisions** What would you do if you noticed a friend displaying several of the warning signs of alcohol abuse?

Teens and Alcohol

OBJECTIVES

Identify the role alcohol plays in teen driving accidents.

List the legal consequences of underage drinking.

Summarize how underage drinking can harm a teen's future.

List three ways you could refuse alcohol if it were offered to you. **LIFE SKILL**

Identify student groups and organizations that are involved in educating people about the dangers of alcohol. **LIFE SKILL**

KEY TERMS

designated driver a person who chooses not to drink alcohol in a social setting so that he or she can safely drive himself or herself and others

David heard the news on Sunday. Four people from his English class were in a car accident coming home from Alicia's party. The driver and one of the girls were seriously injured. The other two students were killed. David couldn't believe it. If he had asked the driver for a ride home after the party, he might have been killed or injured, too.

Drinking and Driving, a Deadly Combination

The No. 1 cause of death among teens is motor vehicle accidents. The majority of these accidents are alcohol related. All of the skills you need to drive are impaired by alcohol. For example, alcohol

- ▶ slows your reaction time
- ▶ affects your vision
- ▶ makes you drowsy
- ▶ reduces your coordination
- ▶ affects your judgment

As you learned earlier, even a small amount of alcohol can impair your ability to drive. A single drink can make you unsafe behind the wheel!

An estimated 513,000 people in the United States are injured in alcohol-related car crashes every year. About 3 in every 10 people in the United States will be involved in an alcohol-related crash at some point in their lives. When drunk driving results in an accident, the outcome is often deadly. While only 7 percent of motor vehicle crashes involve alcohol, about 39 percent of fatal crashes involve alcohol. Drunk driving is the nation's most frequently committed violent crime.

When alcohol and driving mix, the result is often tragic.

Oh, no! It was already 1:00 A.M., and Beto had promised his parents that he'd be home by 12:30 A.M. Beto wanted to ask Sarah for a ride home, but she had been drinking. On the other hand, he would have the chance to ask her out. Beto remembered that his parents had always said that they would pick him up if he needed a safe ride home. But Beto had wanted to go out with Sarah all year. He didn't want her to think he wasn't cool.

Write on a separate piece of paper the advice you would give Beto. Remember to use the decision-making steps.

G ive thought to the problem.

R eview your choices.

E valuate the consequences of each choice.

A ssess and choose the best choice.

T hink it over afterward.

. . . .
Every day, seven teens die in alcohol-related car crashes in the United States.
. . . .

Drinking, Driving, and the Law   Alcohol use is illegal for people under 21 years of age. To prevent drunk driving from claiming lives, the law has set heavy penalties for people caught driving drunk. Anyone caught driving with a blood alcohol concentration (BAC) of 0.08 percent or greater will be arrested for *driving under the influence* (*DUI*). In some states, a higher limit, about 0.10 percent, puts you into a more serious category, *driving while intoxicated* (*DWI*).

Zero Tolerance   All 50 states have enacted *zero tolerance* laws for people under the age of 21. This means that it is illegal for people under the age of 21 to drive with any amount of alcohol in their systems. Educational campaigns have been spreading the word to teens that zero tolerance means zero chances. Violating zero tolerance laws can result in loss of driver's license, expensive fines, and community service.

Among adults, penalties for drunk driving have been increasing to discourage people from driving drunk. Currently, penalties include arrest, heavy fines, suspension of one's driver's license, and possible jail time.

Getting Home Safe and Sober   Although you cannot control other people's drinking and driving behavior, there are ways you can protect yourself from dangerous situations caused by intoxicated drivers. So what can you do to protect yourself from the dangers of alcohol on the road?

1. **Don't drink.** Use the methods discussed later in this section to resist the pressures to drink.

2. **Plan ahead.** Before you go anywhere that alcohol may be served, plan a safe way home. You or someone else may need to volunteer to be the designated driver. A **designated driver** is a person who chooses not to drink in a social setting so that he or she can safely drive himself or herself and others.

3. **Have an arrangement with your parents or guardian to pick you up if you need a safe ride home.** Discuss this arrangement with your parents in advance. You may want to design a contract in which you promise never to drink and drive and your parents or guardian promises to provide you with a safe ride at any hour, no questions asked.

4. **Call a cab.** Many cities have programs that provide safe rides for free or at reduced rates to people who have been drinking. It's worth a cab fare to live to see tomorrow. Whatever you do, don't get into a car with someone who has been drinking.

What can you do if a friend is going to drink and drive? If all else fails, take their keys. They will probably be angry with you, but at least they'll be alive to thank you later. Once they sober up, they'll be glad to know that someone cares enough about them to save their lives.

Drinking Puts Your Future at Risk

Alcohol use is a high-risk behavior for many reasons. Drinking and driving claims the lives of thousands of teenagers every year. However, drinking and driving is not the only risk of alcohol use.

Drinking and Jail Because the legal age for drinking alcohol is 21, buying, trying to buy, or possessing alcohol is illegal for teens. Teens are automatically charged with *minor in possession* (*MIP*). And if teens are drinking in a public place, the charge of *public intoxication* (*PI*) is usually added on. Having a fake identification can cause a teen to get arrested, too.

If you get caught doing any of these things, you can end up in jail, on probation, and with a police record. You also risk losing the trust and respect of your family. A criminal record can also affect your chances of getting a job or getting into college.

Drinking and Sexual Activity Alcohol makes it hard to think clearly. For example, drinking can lead a person to participate in unplanned sexual activity. Sexual activity can result in an unplanned pregnancy, a sexually transmitted disease (STD), and the emotional pain of an unhealthy sexual relationship. Alcohol is also the most common drug associated with date rape. By choosing not to drink, you'll stay in control of your mind and your body.

Drinking and Diving Alcohol use plays a role in more than 38 percent of all drowning accidents in the United States. Diving under the influence of alcohol can lead to head and neck injury, brain damage, spinal cord injury, and paralysis.

Drinking and Teen Brains Alcohol use also affects the development of the brain. The effects of alcohol are much more potent in brains that are still rapidly developing, such as the brains of teens. The changes that alcohol causes in young brains greatly increases the risk of alcoholism.

Drunk driving is a serious crime that has very serious consequences.

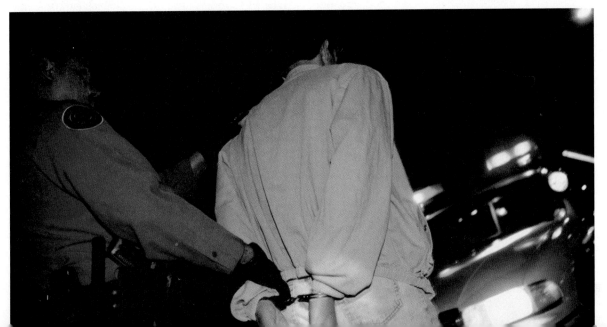

Saying No to Alcohol

Being a teenager is challenging. Teens face many kinds of pressures. Peer pressure is the most common reason teens start drinking. Teens also face pressure to drink from advertising, TV, and movies. Most of the time, teens aren't pressured directly. But just because no one says "drink this beer or I won't be your friend any more" doesn't mean that the pressure isn't there. It can be hard to say no to your friends if they want you to drink with them. To stick to your decision not to drink, you have to know how to say no.

Don't Set Yourself Up　The most effective way to avoid alcohol is to stay away from people who drink and places where others are drinking. If you're not there when the beer is passed around, you won't be tempted to take one or feel forced to join in. Surround yourself with friends who share your views about avoiding alcohol.

Practice Saying No　Even if you try, staying away from alcohol is not always possible. If you find yourself in a situation in which someone offers you a drink, you can use some of the ideas below.

1. **Buy yourself time.** Find a place where you can be alone to think about what you can do to get out of the situation. For example, you can go to another room, to the bathroom, or outside. Once you have time to collect your thoughts, saying no will be easier.

2. **Give good reasons why you choose not to drink.** For example, Hannah went to a party with her friend Angela. Angela said, "Come on Hannah, one wine cooler isn't going to hurt you." Hannah responded, "I promised I would get us both home safely. Do you want me driving you home if I'm drunk?"

3. **State the consequences that could result if you do drink.** For example, Angela said, "Hannah, give me a break. When did you become such a goody-two-shoes? It's just like drinking a fruit punch." Hannah then replied, "Angela, you know my parents would ground me forever if I came home drunk."

If You Hear This... / You Can Say This...

If You Hear This...	You Can Say This...
"Come on, just one."	"One is more than I want."
"Everyone is doing it."	"Then, at least one of us will be sober enough to drive home."
"It'll be fun."	"I'm already having a great time without it."
"What are you worried about?"	"I'm worried about how I'll look with my head in the toilet."
"Don't you want to party?"	"That's what I'm doing. Come on; let's go dance."

4. **Say no firmly.** *No* is a simple and powerful word. It sends a clear message about your intentions. If you say it clearly and look the other person in the eye while you're talking, the meaning is unmistakable. When Angela grabbed a wine cooler and stuck it right into Hannah's hand, Hannah said, "Angela, listen to me. I said *no!*"

5. **If necessary, say no again and include an alternate activity.** Angela pressured Hannah again. "Just have one. You'll be sober by the time we're ready to leave." Hannah responded, "No thanks, Angela. I really don't want to. Why don't we go dance instead?"

6. **Walk away.** What do you do if saying no isn't enough? You've stated your position. You've defended your decision. The person still insists. You have the option to walk away. Friends who don't respect your values and opinions aren't true friends anyway. Offer your friends the opportunity to join you. You may find that your friends will want to follow your example. For example, at this point, Hannah can say, "Angela, I'm going to go dance with John. Do you want to come, or should I meet you later?"

real life Activity

ALCOHOL AND ADVERTISING

LIFE SKILL
Evaluating Media Messages

Materials

✔ 5 popular magazines
✔ scissors
✔ poster board
✔ glue
✔ markers

Procedure

1. **Look** through several magazines for alcohol advertisements.

2. **Cut** out two ads to include in a poster.

3. **Glue** the ads to the top third of the poster board.

4. **Describe** below each ad ways you think companies try to get people to buy alcohol.

5. **Design** new advertisements on the bottom third of the poster that show the true consequences of alcohol use.

Conclusions

1. **Evaluating Information** Do alcohol ads represent the true results of alcohol use? Explain.

2. **Summarizing Results** What are some of the most common ways companies try to convince people to buy alcohol?

3. **Predicting Outcomes** How do you think ads for alcohol influence teens?

4. **CRITICAL THINKING** What can you do to help keep alcohol use from negatively affecting the lives of your friends and family?

5. **CRITICAL THINKING** What alternative activities can you suggest to a friend who wants to drink alcohol?

Figure 3

Life's healthiest and happiest activities never include drinking alcohol.

ACTIVITY *Plan a fun activity the whole class could participate in that does not include alcohol. Be sure to keep the cost per person very low.*

Joining the Fight Against Drunk Driving

People and organizations are aware of the great damage caused by alcohol and are doing something about it. For example, Mothers Against Drunk Driving (MADD) and Students Against Destructive Decisions (SADD), formerly Students Against Drunk Driving, are involved in this fight. MADD is an organization that promotes stricter penalties for people who drive drunk. SADD is a school-based organization dedicated to addressing underage drinking, impaired driving, drug use, and other destructive decisions and killers of young people.

You can join a SADD chapter at your high school. If your school doesn't have a chapter you can start one yourself. Planning and participating in alcohol-free activities, such as those shown in **Figure 3,** can help people see that no one needs alcohol to have a good time.

SECTION 3

REVIEW *Answer the following questions on a separate piece of paper.*

Using Key Terms

1. **Identify** the term that means "a person who chooses not to drink alcohol in a social setting so that he or she can safely drive himself or herself and others."

Understanding Key Ideas

2. **Identify** the No.1 cause of death among teens.
   - **a.** heart disease
   - **b.** suicide
   - **c.** motor vehicle accidents
   - **d.** AIDS

3. **List** the legal charges that a teen can face if he or she is caught drinking and driving.

4. **Identify** three ways that alcohol use can harm a teen's future.

5. **Evaluate** how alcohol use can affect a person's behavior.

6. **LIFE SKILL** **Practicing Wellness** Identify three ways that you can help prevent alcohol from harming your friends and loved ones.

7. **LIFE SKILL** **Refusal Skills** State five ways to refuse if a friend offers alcohol to you.

8. **Identify** two organizations that are involved in educating people about the dangers of alcohol.

Critical Thinking

9. **LIFE SKILL** **Evaluating Media Messages** Movies, TV, and advertisements often encourage audiences to drink by making alcohol consumption seem appealing and sophisticated. What is the media not telling viewers about alcohol?

CHAPTER 10

Highlights

Key Terms

The Big Picture

✔ Alcohol is a dangerous drug that has serious short- and long-term effects on the body and brain.

✔ The short-term effects of alcohol on the body include nausea, loss of body heat, dehydration, loss of judgment, reduced reaction time, memory loss, coma, and even death.

✔ The long-term effects of alcohol use include heart damage, several kinds of cancer, liver damage, kidney damage, and brain damage.

✔ Alcohol changes the brain in ways that lead to and maintain addiction.

✔ Alcoholism is a disease that causes a person to lose control of his or her drinking behavior. Alcoholism develops in four stages: problem drinking, tolerance, dependence, and alcoholism.

✔ The warning signs of alcoholism include drinking more in order to feel the same effect, drinking alone, drinking to get drunk, and changing one's friends, personal habits, and interests.

✔ Alcoholism is a disease that affects the entire family.

✔ If a pregnant woman drinks, she can cause her unborn child to suffer from fetal alcohol syndrome (FAS).

✔ Alcoholism affects society in many ways, including increased violence and crime, lower academic performance and productivity, and increased medical problems.

✔ Alcoholism can be treated. People who recover from alcoholism can lead happy and healthy lives.

✔ Motor vehicle accidents are the No. 1 cause of death among teens. The majority of these deaths are alcohol related.

✔ It is illegal for anyone under the age of 21 to possess alcohol.

✔ Teens caught with alcohol can be charged with minor in possession, driving under the influence, or public intoxication.

✔ Alcohol use has many negative effects on a teen's future, including a police record, unwanted sexual activity, unplanned pregnancy, sexually transmitted disease, rape, violence, injury, and death.

✔ The best way to protect yourself and your future from the dangers of alcohol is not to drink.

✔ There are many effective ways to refuse alcohol. Don't set yourself up, and practice saying "No."

✔ Teens can become involved in Students Against Destructive Decisions (SADD) to help educate other teens about the dangers of drinking alcohol.

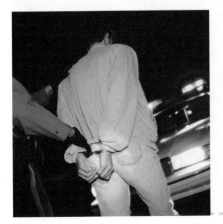

Review

Using Key Terms

alcohol (242)

alcohol abuse (247)

alcoholism (247)

binge drinking (244)

blood alcohol concentration (BAC) (244)

cirrhosis (246)

codependency (250)

designated driver (254)

enabling (250)

fetal alcohol sydrome (FAS) (250)

intoxication (242)

1. For each definition below, choose the key term that best matches the definition.
   a. the act of drinking five or more drinks in one sitting
   b. a disease that replaces healthy liver tissue with scar tissue
   c. helping an addict avoid the negative consequences of his or her behavior
   d. the set of physical and mental defects that affect a fetus that has been exposed to alcohol because of the mother's consumption of alcohol during pregnancy
   e. the drug in wine, beer, and liquor that causes intoxication
   f. a person who agrees not to drink in order to drive themselves and others safely

2. Explain the relationship between the following key terms.
   a. *alcohol abuse* and *alcoholism*
   b. *intoxication* and *blood alcohol concentration*
   c. *codependency* and *enabling*

Understanding Key Ideas

Section 1

3. State why alcohol is considered a drug.

4. List five short-term effects of alcohol use on the body.

5. List five long-term effects of alcohol on the body.

6. Describe the physical and mental effects of alcohol for each of the following blood alcohol concentrations:
   a. 0.05   c. 0.2
   b. 0.1   d. 0.4

7. **CRITICAL THINKING** Give three reasons why the following statement is not true: "If alcohol were dangerous, it wouldn't be legal for adults."

Section 2

8. What is the difference between alcohol abuse and alcoholism?

9. Describe each of the following stages that lead to alcoholism.
   a. dependence   c. problem drinking
   b. addiction   d. tolerance

10. List five warning signs of alcoholism.

11. Describe three ways alcoholism affects the family.

12. What condition is caused by using alcohol during pregnancy?

13. Describe some of the ways that alcohol reaches every member of a community.

14. **CRITICAL THINKING** Explain how you would address the following statement: "I'm too embarrassed to go to meetings to talk about my dad's alcoholism."

Section 3

15. What role does alcohol play in motor vehicle accidents involving teens?

16. Identify the laws that protect society from drunk driving.

17. How can alcohol use affect a teen's future?

18. List three things you would say to refuse alcohol. **LIFE SKILL**

19. What organizations are involved in educating people about the dangers of alcohol?

20. **CRITICAL THINKING** Write three things you might do to help reduce the number of teens at your school who drink alcohol.

Understanding Graphics

Study the figure below to answer the questions that follow.

Refusal Skills

Pressure	Response
1. "Come on, one beer won't hurt you."	1. "OK. But just one."
2. "Here, this beer will give you the courage to talk to Steve."	2. "No way. I'll just end up doing something stupid."
3. "If you aren't going to drink with me, I'm leaving without you."	3. _____

21. Which of the responses above is a good example of a refusal to drink alcohol?

22. Write a response that shows the use of a refusal skill to pressure item number three.

23. CRITICAL THINKING Why do you think people who drink try to pressure others to drink?

Activities

24. Health and Your Community Imagine that you notice a friend displaying many of the signs of alcoholism. How could you approach that friend and encourage him or her to seek help? **WRITING SKILL** Write a short report summarizing your suggestions.

25. Health and You Think about the goals you have for your future. Write a list of your goals. Evaluate how alcohol use could prevent you from reaching those goals.

26. LIFE SKILL Health and Your Community Work with a partner to organize a social group that would agree not to drink. Write a contract that lists the reasons that members do not drink and explains the promise that members make **WRITING SKILL** when they agree to live free of alcohol.

Action Plan

27. LIFE SKILL Practicing Wellness Make a plan to protect yourself from the dangers **WRITING SKILL** of drunk driving.

Standardized Test Prep

Read the passage below, and then answer the questions that follow. **READING SKILL** **WRITING SKILL**

Students, faculty, and staff of Davis High School are still in shock after the deaths of Mary Jones and Sammy Gray. Mary and Sammy were <u>pronounced</u> dead at the scene of a car accident last night. They were riding home from a party in a car driven by a friend who had been drinking. Although others at the party knew that the driver was impaired by alcohol, nobody thought to take his keys. Memorial services will be held tomorrow at Jackson Funeral Home. Contributions in memory of Mary and Sammy can be made to the Davis High School chapter of Students Against Destructive Decisions (SADD).

28. In this newspaper article, the word *pronounced* means
 A said to be.
 B spoken.
 C severely injured.
 D noticed to be.

29. What can you infer from reading this newspaper article?
 E Mary and Sammy didn't know the driver.
 F The driver probably didn't think it was unsafe to be driving.
 G Mary and Sammy were also very drunk.
 H Nobody at the party had noticed that the driver had been drinking.

30. Write a paragraph that describes the options that Mary and Sammy had to avoid riding with someone who had been drinking.

CHAPTER 11

Tobacco

What's Your Health IQ?
KNOWLEDGE

Which of the following statements are true, and which are false? Check your answers on p. 638.

1. At high doses, nicotine is a nerve poison.

2. Chewing tobacco is safer than smoking tobacco because no smoke gets into the lungs.

3. Herbal cigarettes are safer than tobacco cigarettes because they don't contain tobacco.

4. You can smoke for many years before you start to harm your lungs.

5. The smoke that escapes from a burning cigarette is dangerous to others.

6. The placenta protects a fetus from smoke in women that smoke during pregnancy.

7. Nonsmokers get fewer colds than smokers.

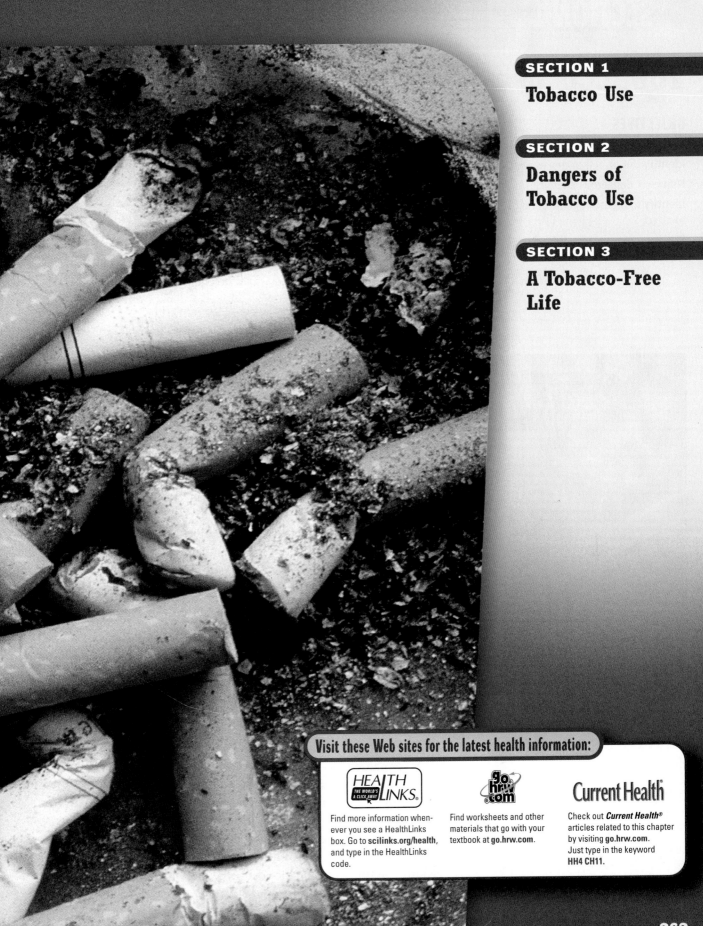

Visit these Web sites for the latest health information:

HEALTH LINKS.
THE WORLD'S A CLICK AWAY

Find more information whenever you see a HealthLinks box. Go to **scilinks.org/health**, and type in the HealthLinks code.

go.hrw.com

Find worksheets and other materials that go with your textbook at **go.hrw.com**.

Current Health

Check out *Current Health®* articles related to this chapter by visiting **go.hrw.com**. Just type in the keyword **HH4 CH11**.

Tobacco Use

OBJECTIVES

List six types of tobacco products.

Identify the drug that makes all forms of tobacco addictive.

Name six dangerous chemicals found in tobacco smoke.

Identify four carcinogens found in smokeless and other forms of tobacco.

State the reasons why herbal cigarettes are not a healthy choice for teens.

You'd never guess what's hiding in cigarette smoke.

Marcus pulled out a box of bidis. "Hey, you want one?" he asked Blanca. "I didn't know you smoked," replied Blanca. "Just herbal cigarettes," said Marcus. "They aren't bad for you like regular cigarettes are."

All Tobacco Products Are Dangerous

There are many types of tobacco products, including cigarettes, chewing tobacco, snuff (dip), pipe tobacco, cigars, and herbal cigarettes. Despite what many people think, all tobacco products have dangerous chemicals. **Nicotine** is the addictive drug that is found in all tobacco products. At low doses, it is a mild stimulant and muscle relaxant. At higher doses, it is a powerful nerve poison. Sixty milligrams of nicotine are enough to kill most people. One or two milligrams are inhaled when a cigarette is smoked.

Cigarette Smoke Has Poisonous Chemicals There are more than 4,000 chemicals in cigarette smoke. At least 40 of the chemicals in cigarette smoke are **carcinogens** (kahr SIN uh juhnz), chemicals or agents that cause cancer. **Tar** is a sticky, black substance in tobacco smoke that coats the inside of the airways and that contains many carcinogens, including the following:

▶ cyanide—a poisonous gas used to develop photographs
▶ formaldehyde—a substance used to preserve laboratory animals and as embalming fluid
▶ lead—a dangerous metal
▶ vinyl chloride—a flammable gas used to make plastic products

Other dangerous chemicals in cigarette smoke include carbon monoxide and ammonia. **Carbon monoxide** is a gas that blocks oxygen from getting into the bloodstream. It can be deadly. Ammonia is a chemical found in bathroom cleaners.

Other Forms of Tobacco Have Poisonous Chemicals Tobacco products that don't produce smoke are also harmful. Snuff contains two to three times more nicotine than cigarette smoke does. Eight dips per day have the same amount of nicotine that about 30 cigarettes do.

In addition to containing nicotine and tar, smokeless forms of tobacco, such as snuff (dip) and chewing tobacco, contain many different carcinogens. These carcinogens include arsenic, nickel, benzopyrene, and polonium (which gives off radiation). Snuff and chewing tobacco lead to mouth sores and oral cancer. Oral cancer can be severely disfiguring when large amounts of tissue and bone must be removed to treat it. Gruen Von Behrens, shown here, started using smokeless tobacco at age 13 to "fit in." By age 17 he was diagnosed with cancer.

Many teens think herbal cigarettes, such as *cloves, bidis,* and *kreteks,* are safe because they don't contain tobacco. This belief is not true. Herbal cigarettes do contain tobacco and a spice that makes them taste better, so their flavor is more attractive to teens.

Pipe tobacco and cigars may seem safer because they are usually not inhaled deeply. However, pipe tobacco and cigars have been linked with oral cancer. There is NO safe form of tobacco.

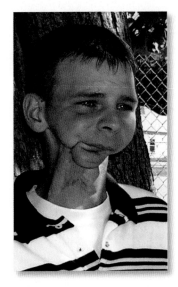

Gruen Von Behrens has had almost 30 surgeries to remove cancerous tumors resulting from smokeless tobacco use. Now he travels and shares his experience with young people so that others can learn about the dangers of tobacco.

Analyzing DATA

Cigarette Smoking Is Deadly

1 Each slice of the pie indicates a percentage of the total number of deaths due to cigarette smoking.

2 The asterisk indicates the average number of deaths per year from 1995 to 1999 in the United States.

Causes of Deaths Due to Cigarette Smoking*

1

- 4%
- 7%
- 17%
- 31%
- 20%
- 21%

- ■ Lung cancer
- ■ Heart disease
- ■ Chronic lung disease
- ■ Other diagnoses (ex: sudden infant death syndrome)
- ■ Other cancers
- ■ Stroke

2 * Shown as percentages of the average number of deaths per year (406,290) for the years 1995–1999 in the U.S.

Source: Centers for Disease Control and Prevention.

Your Turn

1. What is the total percentage of deaths due to smoking-related cancers?

2. Calculate the total **MATH SKILL** number of smoking-related deaths due to chronic lung diseases. (Hint: Use the information indicated by the asterisk.)

3. What percentage **MATH SKILL** of smoking-related deaths result from damage to the circulatory system?

4. **CRITICAL THINKING** What might be some of the smoking-related causes of death included in the group labeled "Other cancers"?

Debbie Austin warns teens about the dangers of cigarettes. After years of smoking, she had to have her larynx removed. She can speak only if she covers a hole in her throat that helps her breathe and cough. In the background, the poster shows Debbie still smoking through the hole.

Nicotine Is Addictive

Cigarette smoking kills more than 400,000 people in the United States each year. Almost all smokers start as teenagers. No one ever thinks he or she will become addicted. However, like all other addictive drugs, nicotine has effects on the brain and other parts of the body. The effects of nicotine on the brain and body lead to physical dependence and addiction. Tobacco companies once claimed that nicotine was not addictive. This claim has been proven to be false.

Nicotine addiction leads people to smoke over long periods of time despite the many health problems that smoking has been proven to cause. Even after losing her larynx to throat cancer, Debbie Austin, pictured above, still continued to smoke. She struggled to overcome addiction and is now working to educate young people about the dangers of cigarette smoking. Quitting smoking is difficult, and withdrawal is unpleasant. But the dangerous effects of tobacco use are far worse than withdrawal.

SECTION 1

REVIEW *Answer the following questions on a separate piece of paper.*

Using Key Terms

1. **Define** *carcinogen*.

2. **Identify** the term that means "a sticky, black substance in tobacco smoke that coats the inside of the airways and that contains many carcinogens."

Understanding Key Ideas

3. **Identify** three kinds of tobacco products.

4. **Identify** the addictive substance found in all tobacco products.
   - **a.** tar
   - **b.** nicotine
   - **c.** cyanide
   - **d.** carbon monoxide

5. **List** four dangerous chemicals in cigarette smoke.

6. **List** three carcinogens found in smokeless tobacco products.

7. **State** the reason clove cigarettes, bidis, and kreteks are dangerous for teens.

Critical Thinking

8. What would you tell a friend who thinks smoking herbal cigarettes is safe?

9. **LIFE SKILL** **Practicing Wellness** List four chemicals that are found in tobacco products and that also have other uses in society. Would you expect any of these chemicals to be healthy for you based on their other uses? Why or why not?

Dangers of Tobacco Use

OBJECTIVES

State the short-term effects of tobacco use.

Summarize the long-term health risks associated with tobacco use.

State the effects of secondhand smoke on a nonsmoker.

Describe how smoking affects unborn children whose mothers smoke during pregnancy.

List three reasons you would give a friend to encourage him or her not to smoke. **LIFE SKILL**

KEY TERMS

emphysema a respiratory disease in which air cannot move in and out of alveoli because they break down and lose their elasticity

sidestream smoke smoke that escapes from the tip of a cigarette, cigar, or pipe

mainstream smoke smoke that is inhaled through a cigarette and then exhaled by a cigarette smoker

environmental tobacco smoke (secondhand smoke) a combination of exhaled mainstream smoke and sidestream smoke

"Geoff, are you OK?" Asked Julian. Geoff had been coughing for about 5 minutes. "Sure, I'm fine," Geoff replied, still coughing. "Maybe you should cut back on the smoking," Julian suggested. "No way. I'm too young for smoking to cause me problems," said Geoff.

Short-Term Effects of Tobacco Use

Tobacco has many effects on the body. Some of these effects can be seen very soon after a person starts smoking. Because it takes only seconds for the nicotine inhaled from a cigarette to get into the bloodstream, the nicotine starts to act almost immediately. Nicotine has the following effects:

▶ stimulates the brain reward system
▶ increases heart rate and blood pressure
▶ increases breathing rate
▶ increases blood-sugar levels
▶ stimulates the vomit reflex

The other harmful substances in tobacco smoke cause other short-term effects. For example, carbon monoxide blocks oxygen from getting into the bloodstream. Tar irritates the insides of the lungs, which leads to coughing and to many of the long-term dangers of tobacco smoke.

The chemicals in dip damage the inside of the mouth. The gums become irritated and raw, which leads to open sores and cancer of the mouth.

In addition to the effects on your health, tobacco makes your breath and clothes stink and leaves black specks between your teeth. Snuff and chewing tobacco also cause you to spit often. None of these effects are very attractive.

Myth

Smoking causes diseases only when you are old.

Fact

If you start smoking at 15, you can start to develop bronchitis, sinus infections, and a chronic cough almost immediately.

Ronald Bowell testified in a lawsuit against the tobacco industry. Tobacco companies once claimed that tobacco use was safe and not addictive. Mr. Bowell smoked cigarettes for over 30 years. Now he suffers from emphysema and must use an oxygen tank at all times.

HEALTH Handbook For more information about the respiratory system, see the Express Lesson on pp. 536–537 of this text.

Long-Term Effects of Tobacco Use

As summarized in **Figure 1,** the long-term effects of tobacco use aren't just unpleasant—some of them can be deadly. Tobacco use is the leading cause of preventable death in the United States.

Addiction   Nicotine, the drug in tobacco products, stimulates the brain reward system (the area of the brain that registers pleasure) and changes the way the brain functions. In a process similar to that of any other addictive drug, these changes lead to addiction.

Bronchitis and Emphysema   The damage from tobacco smoke is most devastating in the respiratory system. The lungs are made up of large tubes called *bronchi* and smaller tubes called *bronchioles.* The tubes deliver oxygen to *alveoli,* tiny air sacks in the lungs. Oxygen passes from the alveoli into the bloodstream. Healthy people secrete a thin layer of mucus in their bronchi to trap harmful particles that they may inhale. This mucus is constantly removed from the lungs by tiny hairs, called *cilia.*

Cigarette smoke paralyzes and then kills cilia. As a result, mucus and inhaled particles (along with tar and other chemicals from tobacco products) build up deep within the lungs, which gives smokers a chronic cough. In addition, constant irritation of the bronchi causes them to swell, which makes breathing more difficult. This inflammation, combined with the built-up particles, tar, and mucus in the lungs, can lead to chronic bronchitis and infection.

Emphysema is a respiratory disease in which air cannot move in and out of the lungs because the walls of the alveoli break down and lose their elasticity. A person who has emphysema cannot breathe normally and is unable to get enough oxygen to the body. Emphysema worsens over time.

Chronic obstructive pulmonary disorder (COPD) is a disorder that is a combination of chronic bronchitis and emphysema. COPD causes chronic coughing, difficulty breathing, frequent infections, and eventually death due to respiratory failure. COPD is almost always linked with smoking.

Heart and Artery Diseases   Nearly 170,000 people die each year from heart and artery disease caused by cigarettes. Nicotine increases heart rate, narrows blood vessels, and eventually causes arteries to become hardened and clogged. All of these effects combine to increase the risk of heart attack, blood clots, and stroke.

Cancer   Cigarettes promote several kinds of cancers, including lung, pancreas, bladder, cervix, and kidney cancer. Tobacco products are the major causes of cancers of the mouth and throat. Lung cancer often spreads to other parts of the body, which is one of the factors that makes lung cancer so deadly. Lung cancer currently kills more people than any other form of cancer does.

Figure 1

Long-Term Effects of Tobacco on the Body

Long-term tobacco use damages the body in many ways.

Mouth

Smoking changes the natural chemical balance inside the mouth, leading to increased plaque, gum disease, and tooth decay. Tar in tobacco smoke stains teeth yellow.

Brain

Smoking reduces oxygen to the brain, narrows blood vessels, and can lead to strokes. Nicotine also changes the brain in ways that lead to addiction.

Healthy artery   Blocked artery

Heart

Nicotine increases heart rate and blood pressure and narrows the blood vessels. It also increases the risk of hardened and clogged arteries, which can lead to a heart attack.

Lungs

Cigarette smoke puts carcinogens directly into the lungs. It kills the tiny hairs that remove harmful substances from the lungs. The loss of these hairs increases the risk of bronchitis, emphysema, and lung cancer.

Healthy lung   Lung with cancer

Skin

Smoking breaks down the proteins that give skin elasticity. This leads to wrinkles and premature aging of the skin. Smoking also increases a person's chances of developing skin cancer.

Immune system

Chemicals in smoke reduce the activity of immune system cells. Damaging the immune system increases the chances of suffering from diseases such as cancer.

Immune System Suppression Chemicals in smoke reduce the activity of immune system cells. This makes the body more vulnerable to disease. The immune system is less able to fight lung diseases and remove cancer cells that are caused by smoking.

Other Long-Term Effects of Tobacco Use Smoking damages the stomach's ability to neutralize acid after a meal. This causes excess acid to build up and damage the stomach and small intestine, which leads to ulcers and to cancer.

Tobacco also makes you unattractive. Smokers have stains on their fingers. Both smokers and users of snuff develop discolored teeth and bad breath. People who dip also develop receding gums and sores in their mouths. Smoking leaves an odor of smoke and a film of tar on your clothes. Smoking also dulls the senses of smell and taste—you can no longer appreciate the good taste of foods.

Effects of Smoke on Nonsmokers

Unfortunately, even if you don't smoke, you can still be exposed to the harmful chemicals in cigarettes. When a smoker lights a cigarette, he or she creates two sources of smoke. The first source is called sidestream smoke. **Sidestream smoke** is the smoke that escapes from the tip of a cigarette, cigar, or pipe. Sidestream smoke can be as much as half of the smoke from a cigarette. The second source of smoke is mainstream smoke. **Mainstream smoke** is smoke that is inhaled through a tobacco product and exhaled by a tobacco smoker. **Environmental tobacco smoke (secondhand smoke)** is a combination of exhaled mainstream smoke and sidestream smoke. Environmental tobacco smoke is inhaled by anyone near the smoker.

The deadly contents of cigarette smoke affect everyone exposed to the smoke. For every eight people killed by their own smoke, a nonsmoker is killed by exposure to secondhand smoke.

Dangers of Secondhand Smoke Lung cancer caused by environmental tobacco smoke kills 3,000 nonsmokers in the United States each year. In addition, environmental tobacco smoke is linked with nasal sinus cancer and possibly cancers of the cervix, breast, and bladder.

Secondhand smoke also causes noncancerous illness. The children of smokers suffer from more lower respiratory infections, more asthma, and more ear infections than children who live in smoke-free homes do. Furthermore, heart function in healthy young men has been shown to be reduced by secondhand smoke. Secondhand smoke also causes headaches, nausea, and dizziness.

Dangers of Tobacco Use During Pregnancy Women who smoke while pregnant risk the health of their unborn child. Chemicals from cigarette smoke pass through the placenta to the developing infant and affect the baby the same way they affect the mother.

Smoking while pregnant can lead to miscarriage, premature birth, and low birth weight. Infants in homes where someone smokes are at a higher risk for *sudden infant death syndrome* (SIDS), a condition in which infants die in their sleep for unknown reasons.

Smoking can also affect a fetus's brain, causing developmental difficulties. Infants whose mothers smoke while pregnant can be physically dependent on nicotine when they are born.

If the pregnant mother does not smoke but lives with a smoker during her pregnancy, her baby faces many of the same risks faced by a baby born to a mother who smokes. Each year, passive smoking contributes to more than 150,000 cases of bronchitis and pneumonia in babies.

Effects of Tobacco on the Fetus and Baby

▶ Risk of miscarriage

▶ Risk of premature birth

▶ Low birth weight

▶ Slow growth rate

▶ Risk of sudden infant death syndrome (SIDS)

▶ Risk of developing respiratory illness

▶ Risk of developing learning difficulties

SECTION 2

REVIEW *Answer the following questions on a separate piece of paper.*

Using Key Terms

1. **Name** the disease in which air cannot move in and out of alveoli because they break down and lose their elasticity.

2. **Compare** mainstream smoke to sidestream smoke.

3. **Define** *environmental tobacco smoke.*

Understanding Key Ideas

4. **Identify** the short-term effect of smoking.
   a. emphysema
   b. cancer
   c. heart disease
   d. increased blood sugar

5. **Describe** the damage caused by long-term use of tobacco products.

6. **List** the effects that secondhand smoke has on nonsmokers.

7. **List** five problems that infants can have if they are born to mothers who smoke.

8. **LIFE SKILL** **Practicing Wellness** What would you tell a friend to discourage him or her from beginning to smoke?

Critical Thinking

9. **LIFE SKILL** **Practicing Refusal Skills** Imagine a friend responds to your efforts to discourage him or her from smoking by saying, "Just one cigarette won't hurt." What would your reply to this statement be?

A Tobacco-Free Life

OBJECTIVES

Discuss the factors that contribute to tobacco use.

Summarize three ways that tobacco use affects families and society.

List four things a person can do to make quitting smoking easier.

Name five benefits of being tobacco free.

List five ways to refuse tobacco products if they're offered to you. **LIFE SKILL**

> ### KEY TERMS
>
> **nicotine replacement therapy (NRT)** a form of medicine that delivers small amounts of nicotine to the body to help a person quit using tobacco

Smoking affects smokers and everyone around them.

Delaine was walking with her friend, Miguel, after school. Miguel pulled a pack of cigarettes out of his pocket and started to light one. "Hey, you want one?" he asked Delaine. "No thanks, you know I don't smoke," she answered.

Why Do People Use Tobacco?

Most tobacco users can name reasons they like tobacco. Some people say they use cigarettes to deal with stress. Some say smoking makes them look older; others say tobacco energizes them. But what makes people want to try tobacco in the first place?

- ▶ **Family and friends** If your parents smoke, smoking may seem normal to you. If your friends smoke, they'll almost certainly urge you to smoke, too. Being around smokers increases the possibility that you will try cigarettes.
- ▶ **Misconceptions** Messages about the dangers of tobacco to health are often not believed. People see others who have used tobacco for many years and who seem to be fine. Unfortunately, the effects of tobacco use may not be visible. Tobacco-related cancer is often not detected until it is large and may have spread.
- ▶ **Advertising** Tobacco advertising has been very effective in the past. Tobacco products have been marketed by the tobacco industry using rugged-looking cowboys, attractive models, and even cartoon animals. The idea they are selling is obvious—smoking makes men handsome and women attractive, and smoking is fun and makes people look cool.
- ▶ **Curiosity** Some people try tobacco because they're curious. They may see other people smoking and wonder what it's like.
- ▶ **Rebellion** Almost all adults tell you that you shouldn't try tobacco. Sometimes, teens get tired of being told what they can and can't do. Using tobacco can be one way to rebel against authority. But you can't prove your independence by becoming addicted to tobacco.

Tobacco Use Affects the Family and Society

Tobacco use causes health and financial problems for the family and costs society a lot of money.

Costs to Families Many of the costs of tobacco use to the family are related to health problems. For example, tobacco use costs the family

▶ over $1,500 per year for buying tobacco products
▶ lost wages due to illness
▶ medical bills
▶ funeral costs

Despite the best doctors and the most caring families, tobacco kills. Twenty percent of premature deaths in the United States are caused by tobacco use. Think of the devastation that loss causes families. After having cared for a sick smoker, family members have to watch him or her die. Then, they have to live without their loved one, who could be a father, mother, sister, or brother.

Costs to Society In addition to the cost of tobacco use to families, tobacco use creates a high cost to society. In fact, society is estimated to pay about $157 billion per year in financial costs due to smoking. These costs are related to medical care that cannot be paid by smokers. Businesses often pay part of a person's insurance costs, which can be very high when treating tobacco-related diseases. Another cost of smoking is the high number of accidental fires that are started by careless smokers.

Tobacco and the Law Selling tobacco to anyone under 18 years of age is illegal. Companies can pay very high fines if they are caught selling tobacco to a minor. In many states, teens are also fined or assigned community service if they are caught using tobacco.

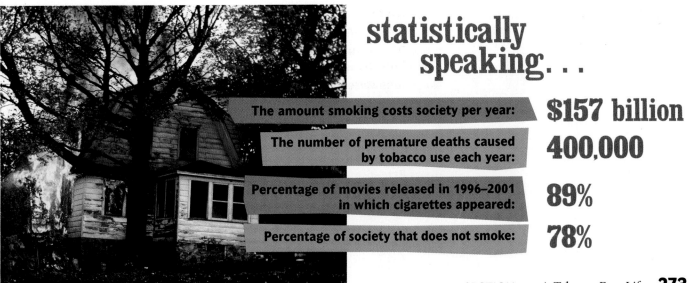

statistically speaking. . .

The amount smoking costs society per year:	**$157 billion**
The number of premature deaths caused by tobacco use each year:	**400,000**
Percentage of movies released in 1996–2001 in which cigarettes appeared:	**89%**
Percentage of society that does not smoke:	**78%**

"Smoking makes me look more mature."	Smoking can't make you look mature, but it can make you look older because smoking damages your skin.
"Smoking makes me look sexy."	Smokers get stained teeth, receding gum lines, bad breath, wrinkled skin, and stained fingers—traits not usually considered sexy.
"I can stop whenever I want."	Cigarettes are addictive. Three thousand teens start smoking every day; most will not be able to stop.
"All the cool kids smoke."	Does being hooked on tobacco really seem that cool?

Tips for Quitting

If you are a smoker, you may be wondering why you should quit. There are plenty of reasons to quit.

▸ **Smoking is unhealthy.** Obviously, the most important reason to quit smoking is for your health. The damage smoking does to your lungs and cardiovascular system makes smoking too dangerous to be worth the risk.

▸ **Smoking is expensive.** Twenty-five to fifty dollars a week is a lot to pay for a bad habit.

▸ **Smoking stinks.** Most people don't enjoy being around the smoke or the smell of cigarettes. Cigarettes also give you bad breath.

▸ **Smoking looks unattractive.** Many people start smoking thinking it will make them look attractive, but yellow fingers and teeth aren't attractive.

▸ **Smoking damages your skin.** Smoking can cause your skin to age prematurely, which causes you to look old before you actually are.

HEALTH Handbook For more information about making decisions, such as to quit smoking, see How to Make GREAT Decisions on pp. 616–617 of this text.

Decide That You Can Do It Quitting on your own requires dedication and determination. Withdrawal symptoms from stopping tobacco use can include nervousness, irritability, or difficulty sleeping. There are medical products available to help ease withdrawal. **Nicotine replacement therapy (NRT)** is a form of medicine that delivers a small amount of nicotine to the body to help a person quit smoking. Nicotine patches and nicotine gum are NRTs. Consult a doctor before using any medicine.

Many people find that withdrawal is actually easier to deal with than overcoming the psychological addiction that developed as cigarette smoking became part of their daily activities. People trying to quit will have many cues that trigger an urge to smoke as they go through their day. Doing the things a person usually did with a cigarette in hand will likely make the peron crave a cigarette.

Get Started   There are things you can do to make quitting easier. First, set a quitting date. Decide in advance when you want to quit using tobacco, and keep that date. Collect all your cigarettes, ashtrays, and lighters, and get rid of them all so you aren't tempted to start again.

Change Your Habits   Start healthy habits before you try to quit smoking. People who exercise are more likely to quit, so this is a good time to start exercising. Engaging in other activities will also help take your mind off quitting. The less time you spend sitting around thinking about how hard quitting is, the easier it will be.

This is also a good time to look at your diet and make sure it's healthy. Most people do gain some weight when they quit, but eating well and exercising will minimize any weight gain.

Set Goals   After you've quit, staying free of tobacco can be difficult. To help you stay tobacco free, set goals for yourself. Keep a calendar, and celebrate each week you don't use tobacco. You can reward yourself with the money you save by not buying tobacco. If you smoked a pack a day, you will have saved at least $25 in the first week. Twenty-five dollars a week really adds up. You will probably have a lot of money to celebrate quitting smoking. Celebrating your success can make quitting easier.

Get Support   Quitting can be hard, but you don't have to quit alone. There are many kinds of support groups that can help you. Your parents, teacher, school nurse, doctor, local health department, and local American Cancer Society or American Lung Association branches can help you find those groups.

Another approach is to join an after-school club that will keep you busy and take your mind off smoking. The new friends you make in these groups can encourage you when you're feeling like you just can't do it.

Reasons to Quit Smoking

▶ **You'll live longer.**
▶ **You'll smell better.**
▶ **You won't have bad breath.**
▶ **You'll have whiter teeth.**
▶ **You'll be able to taste food.**
▶ **You'll have extra money.**
▶ **You won't cough all the time.**
▶ **You'll be able to sit through a whole movie without shaking.**
▶ **You won't need a chemical to make you feel good.**

Skills for Refusing Tobacco

Have you ever been offered something you don't want? Sometimes, convincing people that you're not interested is difficult. Practicing effective refusal skills can help you know what you want to say before you're in a high-pressure situation. The following scenario is an example of using effective refusal skills to resist peer pressure to smoke.

"Hilary, come on. It's so boring in here. Let's go have a smoke."

"You know I don't smoke, Tiffany."

"Oh don't be such a goody-two-shoes. Just relax."

"Tiff, I spent all afternoon getting ready for this party. I'm wearing my favorite perfume. I really don't want to smell like a cigarette."

"Oh, Hilary. Don't you want to look cool?"

"Tiffany, you know I don't want to smoke. Why do you try to force me? Hey, look. There's Ian. You've wanted to go out with him all year, right? He won't even know you're here if you're out back smoking. Why don't we go dance? Maybe you can get his attention."

Refusing Effectively   Hilary did a good job of saying no without hurting her friendship. You can learn to do this by following the steps below.

1. **Be honest.** Hilary was direct with her friend. She stayed calm and didn't attack Tiffany or put her down.

2. **Give a reason.** Hilary gave her friend a reason she didn't want to smoke. It was a simple reason but one that made sense to her friend at that moment.

3. **Suggest an alternative.** Hilary suggested another activity that would appeal to both of them.

Of course, using effective refusal skills is not always easy. Telling your friends no can be very difficult. Many people find it impossible to keep resisting under pressure. But you know you don't want to smoke. And you don't want to lose your friends over a cigarette. Practicing refusal skills can help you turn down tobacco, or anything else you don't want, without losing your confidence or your friends.

"Thanks, but I don't smoke."

If You Hear This...   You Can Say This...

If You Hear This...	You Can Say This...
"Come on; just try one."	"Isn't that how *you* got addicted?"
"Smoking is sexy."	"There's nothing sexy about smelling like an ashtray."
"Don't be so paranoid. These are made from cloves, so they're healthy."	"They have tobacco, so they're still bad for you."
"Dipping makes you look as cool as a sports star."	"I don't think I'll look cool with brown spit."
"Everyone else is smoking."	"So, not smoking makes me unique? I like being unique."

Benefits of Being Tobacco Free

What are the benefits of **not** using tobacco? All the studies agree that people who don't use tobacco are healthier. They tend to live longer and are at a lower risk of lung cancer, oral cancer, heart disease, emphysema, and bronchitis. People who don't use tobacco also have other benefits, such as

- ▶ getting fewer colds, sore throats, and asthma attacks
- ▶ not coughing if they're not sick
- ▶ being less likely to have stained teeth, bad breath, or chronic gum disease
- ▶ being able to taste their food and smell flowers
- ▶ not smelling like smoke all the time
- ▶ not exposing loved ones to the harmful chemicals in smoke
- ▶ not having black bits of tobacco in their teeth
- ▶ not having to carry around a cup of brown spit

Finally, people who stay tobacco free never have to break an addiction to tobacco. Almost everyone who uses tobacco regularly for more than a few months becomes addicted. Staying tobacco free protects your brain from the changes caused by an addictive drug.

⊿ internet connect

www.scilinks.org/health
Topic: Anti-Smoking Campaigns
HealthLinks code: HH4012

HEALTH *LINKS.* Maintained by the National Science Teachers Association

---

LIFE SKILL
Activity
Setting Goals

Kicking the Habit

Imagine that you had decided to help a friend quit smoking. Design a plan of goals and rewards to encourage your friend to quit using tobacco and stay tobacco free.

1 Set a time limit. Decide with your friend that on a certain day your friend will quit smoking. Have everything organized so that your friend will have no temptations once he or she quits.

2 Set milestones. Mark dates on the calendar to divide up the one big goal into several smaller ones.

3 Reward your friend. List things you can do to celebrate your friend's achievement. As he or she reaches each milestone, mark the occasion with a reward for your friend's self-discipline and determination.

LIFE SKILL **Setting Goals**

1. Describe ways that you can provide support and encouragement to someone who is trying to quit smoking.

2. List some of the situations that may make it difficult for a person to stay tobacco free. List situations to avoid.

3. In what other situations might these goal-setting skills help?

World Cup Mountain Bike Champion Alison Dunlap and New Orleans Saints wide receiver Willie Jackson sign copies of a book that promotes a healthy lifestyle as an alternative to tobacco use for young people.

Life Without Tobacco   What does it mean if you've used tobacco? Is it too late to protect your health? Studies show that the sooner you quit using tobacco, the sooner your body can get back to normal.

Within half an hour after quitting smoking, your blood pressure and heart rate will fall back to normal. Eight hours later, you will have rid the carbon monoxide from your bloodstream, and you will have normal blood-oxygen levels. Within a few days, your sense of smell and taste will improve, and breathing will be easier.

During the following months, your lung health will improve, and you won't be short of breath anymore. You'll be reducing your risk of lung cancer by about 10 times, the threat of emphysema will almost disappear, and your risk of heart disease will decrease as well. Even in such a short time, living without tobacco makes a big difference.

Live Healthy and Tobacco Free   Life is better without tobacco. The 80 percent of teens who *don't* smoke agree. Tobacco is a dangerous and addictive drug. All forms of tobacco have been proven to cause major health problems that can be deadly. As a result of lawsuits, tobacco companies have paid billions of dollars to the states for exactly that reason.

People may have many reasons for trying tobacco. Friends, family, media influence, rebellion, boredom, and curiosity are all reasons people may smoke or dip for the first time. Most tobacco users generally have only one reason for continuing to use tobacco—addiction. And the best reason for staying tobacco free is life. Your life, your friends' lives, and the lives of all your loved ones will be better without tobacco.

SECTION 3

REVIEW   *Answer the following questions on a separate piece of paper.*

Using Key Terms

1. **Define** *nicotine replacement therapy (NRT).*

Understanding Key Ideas

2. **List** three reasons people may begin using tobacco.

3. **State** two ways that tobacco use affects families and society.

4. **Identify** which of the following is *not* a cost of tobacco use to society.
   a. tobacco products
   b. funeral costs
   c. fetal alcohol syndrome
   d. medical costs

5. **Describe** a strategy a person could use to make quitting smoking easier.

6. **Identify** five benefits of living tobacco free.

Critical Thinking

7. **LIFE SKILL** **Using Refusal Skills** List five reasons you can give for refusing to use tobacco. Which of these reasons is most important to you?

8. **LIFE SKILL** **Communicating Effectively** Imagine that you have a family member who smokes heavily. What do you think would be the best way to try to convince them to quit smoking?

Highlights

Key Terms

SECTION 1

nicotine (264)

carcinogen (264)

tar (264)

carbon monoxide (264)

SECTION 2

emphysema (268)

sidestream smoke (270)

mainstream smoke (270)

environmental tobacco smoke
(secondhand smoke) (270)

SECTION 3

nicotine replacement therapy (NRT)
(274)

The Big Picture

✔ There are many kinds of tobacco products, such as cigarettes, dip, snuff, chew, bidis, kreteks, and pipe tobacco.

✔ All forms of tobacco are dangerous because they contain many harmful chemicals and carcinogens, including nicotine, tar, carbon monoxide, cyanide, and formaldehyde.

✔ Nicotine can enter the body through the lungs, the gums, and the skin.

✔ Herbal cigarettes are thought to be more healthy but are actually just as dangerous as conventional cigarettes.

✔ People who use tobacco products find it very hard to quit because nicotine is a highly addictive drug.

✔ The short-term effects of tobacco use include increases in heart rate, blood pressure, and breathing rate, as well as a reduction in the amount of oxygen that reaches the brain.

✔ Long-term tobacco use leads to oral and lung cancer, bronchitis, emphysema, heart disease, artery disease, and other health problems.

✔ People who breathe environmental tobacco smoke are exposed to the same dangerous chemicals as smokers.

✔ Smoking while pregnant can lead to several kinds of problems for the infant, including miscarriage, developmental difficulties, and SIDS.

✔ There are many reasons not to smoke, including protecting your family, friends, and loved ones from the harmful effects of environmental tobacco smoke.

✔ People begin smoking for many reasons. Some want to fit in with friends who smoke, some find it normal after growing up around family members who smoke, and others want to look cool.

✔ Using tobacco is expensive. It costs families and society billions of dollars each year in healthcare and lost productivity.

✔ Quitting smoking can be difficult, but setting a quitting date, marking your progress, getting involved in other activities, and rewarding yourself can help make quitting easier.

✔ Refusing tobacco may be difficult, but practicing effective refusal skills makes it easier to resist pressure.

✔ There are many benefits to being tobacco free, including looking younger, feeling healthier, and living longer than you would if you used tobacco.

✔ Whether a person has used tobacco or not, choosing to live without tobacco dramatically improves a person's quality of life.

Review

Using Key Terms

carbon monoxide (264)
carcinogen (264)
emphysema (268)
environmental tobacco smoke (secondhand smoke) (270)
mainstream smoke (270)
nicotine (264)
nicotine replacement therapy (NRT) (274)
sidestream smoke (270)
tar (264)

1. For each definition below, choose the key term that best matches the definition.
   a. the smoke inhaled and exhaled by the smoker
   b. a gas that blocks oxygen from entering the bloodstream
   c. a lung disease in which the walls of the alveoli break down and lose their elasticity
   d. any chemical or agent that causes cancer
   e. a sticky substance in tobacco smoke that coats the inside of the airway and contains many carcinogens
   f. the addictive drug found in tobacco

2. Explain the relationship between the key terms in each of the following pairs.
   a. *nicotine* and *carbon monoxide*
   b. *tar* and *emphysema*
   c. *environmental tobacco smoke* and *carcinogen*
   d. *mainstream smoke* and *sidestream smoke*

Understanding Key Ideas
Section 1

3. Name four types of tobacco products.

4. State the reason it is difficult for people to quit using tobacco products.

5. Identify the carcinogens found in tobacco.
   a. benzene
   c. vinyl chloride
   b. formaldehyde
   d. all of the above

6. Compare the amount of nicotine in snuff with the amount in cigarette smoke.

7. Are herbal cigarettes safer than regular cigarettes?

8. **CRITICAL THINKING** Would you consider nicotine a dangerous drug? Explain.

Section 2

9. List three short-term effects of tobacco use.

10. Which of the following is a long-term effect of tobacco use?
    a. heart and artery disease
    b. cancer
    c. receding gums and mouth sores
    d. all of the above

11. Why is smoking dangerous to nonsmokers?

12. Infants of women who smoke while pregnant have a higher risk of
    a. low birth weight.
    c. SIDS.
    b. respiratory illnesses.
    d. All of the above

13. List four reasons not to smoke that you could give to a friend. **LIFE SKILL**

14. **CRITICAL THINKING** One of the negative aspects of smoking is that the clothes of smokers usually smell like tobacco smoke. Explain why smokers generally cannot smell tobacco smoke on their clothes.

Section 3

15. What factors do you think contribute to people using tobacco in your school? **LIFE SKILL**

16. Describe the financial and health costs of smoking on both the family and the community.

17. Which technique does *not* help a person quit smoking?
    a. setting a goal
    b. punishing yourself for failing
    c. changing your habits
    d. getting support

18. List five benefits both smokers and smokeless tobacco users can expect after quitting.

19. Describe an effective refusal method you could use if someone were to tell you, "Here, try these new cigarettes, almost everyone in our school smokes these." **LIFE SKILL**

20. **CRITICAL THINKING** Why might it be harder for a person to quit smoking if his or her friends and parents smoke?

Interpreting Graphics

Study the figure below to answer the questions that follow.

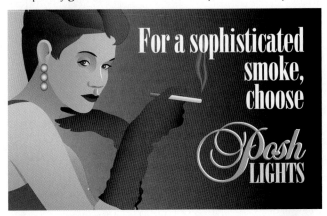

For a sophisticated smoke, choose *Posh* LIGHTS

21. What do you think the word *sophisticated,* as used in the ad above, means? **READING SKILL**

22. What message is this ad trying to convey about tobacco use?

23. CRITICAL THINKING Do you think this ad might encourage a young person to smoke? Explain.

Activities

24. Health and You Imagine you are riding in a car with someone who smokes. **WRITING SKILL** Write a paragraph explaining how you might politely and effectively ask the person not to smoke in the car.

25. Health and Your Community Environmental tobacco smoke is just as dangerous as mainstream smoke. Write a one-page **WRITING SKILL** report advocating for smoke-free environments for nonsmokers.

26. Health and You Write a reply to the following statement: "Just try this cigarette once; one try won't harm you. It's not like you'll become an addict."

Action Plan

27. Take Charge of Your Health Use of clove cigarettes, bidis, and kreteks has become more popular among teens. Research these products, and write a one-page report explaining why teens use these tobacco products.

Standardized Test Prep

Read the passage below, and then answer the questions that follow. **READING SKILL** **WRITING SKILL**

Cameron and Tony walked up to the counter at the convenient store. "What are you getting?" asked Tony. "Nothing. I'm out of cash," replied Cameron. "Didn't you have a bunch of money last week?" asked Tony. "Yeah, but I spent it on cigarettes." "Man, that just doesn't seem worth it. If you have a <u>finite</u> income, you should save it for the stereo system you want." "I know. Cigarettes keep getting more and more expensive, but I've been smoking for years. I can't stop," said Cameron. "It's not like quitting is impossible," replied Tony.

28. In this paragraph, the word *finite* means
  A limited.
  B endless.
  C spendable.
  D free.

29. What can you infer from reading this paragraph?
  E Tobacco products are cheap.
  F Tony makes more money than Cameron does.
  G Tony thinks tobacco is worth the expense.
  H Cameron is probably addicted to nicotine.

30. Write a paragraph discussing things that Cameron could do to make quitting easier. What could Tony do to help his friend quit smoking?

31. CRITICAL THINKING One reason that tobacco products are so expensive is that the U.S. government charges taxes that consumers must pay when they buy tobacco. Why do you think the government keeps raising these taxes?

CHAPTER 12

Illegal Drugs

What's Your Health IQ?
KNOWLEDGE

Which of the statements below are true, and which are false? Check your answers on p. 638.

1. If illegal drugs were really dangerous, people wouldn't use them.

2. People can't get addicted to marijuana.

3. Stimulants can help you study more effectively.

4. Anabolic steroids are male hormones, so they should make guys appear more masculine.

5. Barbiturates are safe because they're used as medicine.

6. Most prison inmates committed their crime while high on drugs.

7. Because I'm young, any damage drugs do to my brain will heal by the time I'm an adult.

Visit these Web sites for the latest health information:

Find more information whenever you see a HealthLinks box. Go to **scilinks.org/health**, and type in the HealthLinks code.

Find worksheets and other materials that go with your textbook at **go.hrw.com**.

Current Health

Check out **Current Health®** articles related to this chapter by visiting **go.hrw.com**. Just type in the keyword **HH4 CH12**.

SECTION 1

Drugs of Abuse

OBJECTIVES

List six ways illegal drug use can be dangerous.

State five reasons a person might try illegal drugs.

Identify the reason drug abuse is especially dangerous to teens.

Describe two ways illegal drug use conflicts with your values and goals. **LIFE SKILL**

KEY TERMS

drug abuse the intentional improper or unsafe use of a drug

overdose the taking of too much of a drug, which causes sickness, loss of consciousness, permanent damage, or even death

Drug abusers can be any age and be from any background. Each has a different reason for using drugs.

Tonya was the best point guard on the team until she tried cocaine. She liked how it made her feel, so she tried it again. Soon she was spending up to $100 a day on crack. When the team went to the state championship, Tonya couldn't go. She had been arrested for stealing. She had stolen to support her drug habit.

Illegal Drug Use Is Dangerous

Drug abuse is the intentional improper or unsafe use of a drug. Drugs that are used for recreational purposes are called *drugs of abuse.* Many drugs of abuse are *illegal drugs.* This means that possessing, using, buying, or selling these drugs is against the law for people of any age.

It may sometimes seem that our society is full of messages that tell us illegal drug use is normal and not dangerous. For example, characters in the movies and on television can make it seem as though illegal drug use is "cool." Many popular rock bands sing about illegal drugs. You can buy clothes and posters showing illegal drugs. But using illegal drugs is very dangerous for several reasons:

▶ Illegal drugs can have dangerous and permanent effects on the brain and the body.

▶ You can become addicted to almost all illegal drugs.

▶ Illegal drugs are a major factor in many suicides, motor vehicle accidents, and crimes.

▶ With illegal drug use that involves sharing needles, there is also the risk of catching infectious diseases such as hepatitis B and human immunodeficiency virus (HIV).

▶ Illegal drug use can result in overdose. **Overdose** is the taking of too much of a drug, which causes sickness, loss of consciousness, permanent health damage, or even death.

▶ While using illegal drugs, a person loses the ability to make responsible decisions. Having poor judgement while on drugs can result in risky sexual behavior, sexually transmitted diseases, car accidents, and other unsafe situations.

284 **CHAPTER 12** *Illegal Drugs*

Being caught in possession of illegal drugs is a crime that has serious penalties.

Why Do People Begin Using Drugs?

If illegal drug use is so dangerous, why does anyone even try illegal drugs? People try illegal drugs for many reasons, including the following:

▶ desire to experiment
▶ desire to escape from depression or boredom
▶ enjoyment of risk-taking behaviors
▶ belief that drugs solve personal, social, or medical problems
▶ peer pressure
▶ glamorization of drug use by the media

Often, people begin taking a drug because they like the way it makes them feel. Soon, however, they may find that they must keep taking the drug just to feel normal. Repeated use of drugs that change how the brain works can lead to addiction. Addiction to an illegal drug can be very difficult to overcome.

Regardless of a person's reason for trying an illegal drug, one thing remains the same—the physical, mental, social, and legal consequences for illegal drug use make it not worth the risk.

Teens and Illegal Drug Use Teens face many challenges during adolescence. These challenges include expectations on the part of parents and teachers and the desire for more freedom and responsibility. These challenges can make adolescence a very stressful time of life and can put teens at a greater risk for abusing illegal drugs.

Other challenges that teens face are intense peer pressure and a strong desire to fit in. There are many other reasons that teens might be tempted to try illegal drugs. The most common reasons that teens give for trying illegal drugs are listed below.

▶ Sometimes, just being around a group of people using drugs creates pressure to join in. This is a common type of peer pressure that doesn't involve direct pressure. Teens may give in and try a drug when they feel everyone else is trying drugs.

Some people start using drugs to get away from their problems and then can't get away from their drug problem.

▶ When faced with direct pressure to use drugs, teens who lack refusal skills or who feel intimidated may give in to pressure and use drugs.

▶ Many teens think that using illegal drugs is a way to escape from feelings of stress, anger, depression, or frustration. However, after a teen takes drugs, the problem that caused the negative feeling is still there, but now the teen may also have to deal with the consequences of drug use.

▶ Many teens try drugs out of curiosity. This seems natural when the media gives so much attention to drug abuse. Teens may see or hear of another person's experiences with drug use and wonder what it's like.

▶ Other teens may try drugs because they are risk takers or thrill seekers searching for a way to satisfy their desire for new experiences.

Unfortunately, teens have a higher risk of addiction to drugs than adults do. The risk of addiction is higher because young brains are still developing. Drug use or abuse can have irreversible effects on the function of the brain. Altering brain development with drug use can result in a lifetime of struggle to overcome addiction and to remain drug free.

SECTION 1

REVIEW   *Answer the following questions on a separate piece of paper.*

Using Key Terms

1. **Define** the term *drug abuse*.

2. **Identify** the term for "the taking of too much of a drug, which causes sickness, loss of consciousness, permanent damage, or even death."

Understanding Key Ideas

3. **Identify** which of the following is a type of media that seems to advocate drug use.
   a. music
   b. movies
   c. television
   d. all of the above

4. **Identify** the reasons illegal drugs are dangerous.

5. **Name** five factors that influence a person's choice to use illegal drugs.

6. **State** the reasons why teens might try illegal drugs.

7. **Defend** the statement that teens should never use illegal drugs.

8. **Predict** the outcome of using an illegal drug to escape from personal problems.

9. **LIFE SKILL** **Setting Goals** Describe two ways illegal drug use would affect your personal values and goals.

Critical Thinking

10. **LIFE SKILL** **Practicing Wellness** Why is it important to have healthy alternatives to drug use?

Commonly Abused Drugs

OBJECTIVES

List three things all types of illegal drugs have in common.

Summarize the effects of four commonly abused illegal drugs on the body.

Describe the effects of marijuana on a person's behavior.

Identify the reason abusing inhalants can be deadly after only one use.

Compare the dangerous effects of five types of club drugs.

Summarize the dangerous effects of anabolic steroids.

"Hey, you want a hit of this joint?" offered Randall. "No way. Do you know what that stuff can do to you?" Jen replied. Randall looked surprised. "Pot isn't dangerous, is it?" "It's dangerous" said Jen, "and it's addictive. Why would I want that?"

Types of Illegal Drugs

There are many types of illegal drugs. As shown in **Table 1,** each type of illegal drug has different effects on the body and the brain. Despite the differences in their effects, all illegal drugs have three things in common.

1. They affect the function of the brain.
2. They are dangerous to your health.
3. They can result in drug dependence and addiction.

Four commonly abused illegal drugs—marijuana, inhalants, club drugs, and anabolic steroids—will be described in this section.

Beliefs Vs. Reality

"Marijuana is a safe drug." Driving high on marijuana can be just as dangerous as driving drunk.

"It's okay to try a drug just once." Some drugs, such as crack cocaine or inhalants, can be fatal the first time they are used.

"I can stop any time I want." The more often you use drugs, the more difficult it can be to stop.

"If I want to use drugs, I only affect myself." Drug use affects you, your family, your friends, and society.

Table 1   Common Illegal Drugs and Their Effects

Drug and common or street names	How it is taken	Possible intoxication effects	Possible health consequences*
Marijuana *pot, weed, dope, blunt, grass, reefer, Mary Jane* **Hashish** *boom, chronic, hash, hemp*	smoked or mixed in food and eaten	▶ relaxation ▶ feelings of well being ▶ distortion of time and distance ▶ loss of short-term memory ▶ loss of balance and coordination ▶ increased appetite	▶ frequent respiratory infection ▶ impaired learning and memory ▶ panic attack
Inhalants *glue, paint thinner, propane, nitrous oxide, NO, poppers, snappers, whippets*	inhaled	▶ stimulation ▶ loss of inhibitions ▶ dizziness ▶ loss of coordination ▶ nausea and vomiting ▶ headache	▶ heart attack ▶ liver damage ▶ kidney damage ▶ brain damage ▶ coma ▶ death
Club (designer) drugs			
Ecstasy *MDMA, Ecstasy, X, XTC, Adam*	swallowed or snorted	▶ increased awareness of senses ▶ mild hallucinations ▶ increased energy ▶ loss of judgment	▶ impaired learning and memory ▶ hyperthermia (overheating) ▶ rapid or irregular heartbeat ▶ high blood pressure ▶ heart attack ▶ death
GHB *G, liquid X, grievous bodily harm*	swallowed or snorted	▶ relaxation ▶ nausea ▶ loss of inhibitions ▶ euphoria	▶ dangerously slowed breathing ▶ seizures ▶ coma
Ketamine and PCP *Special K, K, Vitamin K, angel dust (PCP)*	injected, snorted, or smoked	▶ confusion ▶ distortions of reality ▶ numbness	▶ loss of memory ▶ loss of muscle control ▶ dangerously slowed breathing
Anabolic steroids *roids, juice*	swallowed or injected	▶ no intoxication effects	▶ increased aggression ▶ shrinking of testes ▶ infertility ▶ growth of breasts in men ▶ growth of facial hair in women ▶ deepening of voice in women ▶ liver rupture/liver cancer ▶ heart damage/heart attack

*All of the drugs listed in this table can result in physical dependence, and some can result in addiction.

Marijuana

Marijuana (MAR uh WAH nuh), also called *pot*, *weed*, *reefer*, or *dope*, is the dried flowers and leaves from the plant *Cannabis sativa*. The active chemical in marijuana is *tetrahydrocannabinol* (THC). THC can be detected in the urine for up to several weeks after use. Different marijuana plants may contain very different levels of THC. Marijuana is usually smoked, but it can also be mixed with food and eaten.

Effects of Marijuana   The effects of smoked marijuana are felt within minutes and may last for 2 or 3 hours. The effects of swallowed marijuana are felt within 30 to 60 minutes. Although the short-term effects of marijuana differ depending on the person and the strength of the drug, they can include the following:

- ▶ slowed thinking ability
- ▶ difficulty paying attention
- ▶ distorted sense of time and distance
- ▶ giddiness
- ▶ loss of short-term memory
- ▶ loss of balance and coordination
- ▶ increased appetite
- ▶ anxiety
- ▶ panic attack

Smoking marijuana over a long period of time can cause some of the same health effects as smoking cigarettes. Marijuana smoke has been found to contain many of the same carcinogens as cigarette smoke. Long-term marijuana use may lead to chronic bronchitis, damaged lung tissue, and increased risk of lung cancer.

Marijuana use has a negative effect on learning and social behavior. THC changes the way sensory information gets into the brain. Long-term marijuana use can cause difficulty in remembering, processing, and using information. Marijuana users can have difficulty maintaining attention and shifting attention to meet changing demands in the environment.

Stopping marijuana growers is a major part of the war on drugs. Law enforcement officials frequently destroy large fields of marijuana.

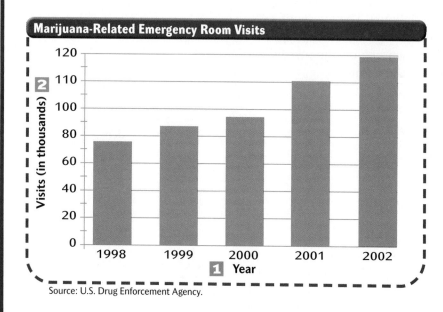

Analyzing DATA

Dangers of Marijuana Abuse

1 The horizontal axis (*x*-axis) shows the year.

2 The vertical axis (*y*-axis) shows the number of marijuana-related emergency room visits.

Marijuana-Related Emergency Room Visits

Visits (in thousands)

2

120
110
100
80
60
40
20
0

1998   1999   2000   2001   2002

1 Year

Source: U.S. Drug Enforcement Agency.

Your Turn

1. Approximately how many people visited the emergency room because of marijuana use in the year 1998?

2. How many more people were admitted to the emergency room with marijuana-related injuries in 2002 than in 1998? **MATH SKILL**

3. Using the trend shown in the graph, predict how many people visited the emergency room in 2004. How many persons might visit it in 2008? **MATH SKILL**

4. **CRITICAL THINKING** What do you think is the main cause of marijuana-related injury?

Dependence on Marijuana   People who use marijuana regularly build up a tolerance to the drug, so they need more and more to get high. This can lead to dependence on marijuana. After the effects of marijuana wear off, some users feel tired, unmotivated, and depressed. Once a marijuana user becomes dependent, he or she will experience the effects of withdrawal each time the drug wears off.

Marijuana and Driving   Because marijuana makes it difficult to pay attention and makes it harder to judge time and distance, marijuana use is dangerous when driving. People high on marijuana can show the same lack of coordination on standard drunk-driver tests as people who are drunk. The danger of driving under the influence of marijuana is increased when marijuana is combined with alcohol.

Hashish   Hashish (HASH EESH), also known as *hash*, is the darkbrown resin collected from the tops of the cannabis plant. The resin is compressed into various forms, such as balls or flat sheets. Pieces are then broken off, placed in pipes, and smoked. The effects of hashish are the same as those of marijuana, but stronger.

Inhalants

Drugs that are inhaled as vapors are called **inhalants** (in HAYL uhnts). Some inhalants have medical uses. For example, nitrous oxide (NIE truhs AHKS IED), also called *laughing gas,* is used by physicians and dentists as an anesthetic. Medicines to treat asthma also come in the form of inhalants.

But many inhalants are not used for medical reasons. For example, some people inhale common household chemicals, such as glue, paint thinner, gasoline, and felt-tip marker fluid. Other commonly abused inhalants include propane, butane, and nitrous oxide.

Inhalants can be sniffed (or *huffed*) directly from an open container or from a rag soaked in the substance. Sometimes, the container or the soaked rag is placed in a plastic bag where the vapors can become concentrated before they are inhaled.

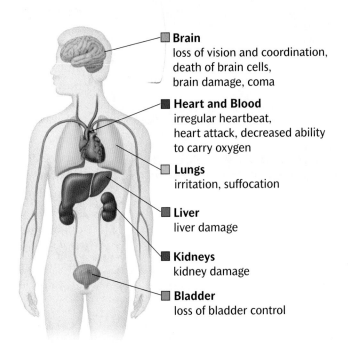

Brain
loss of vision and coordination, death of brain cells, brain damage, coma

Heart and Blood
irregular heartbeat, heart attack, decreased ability to carry oxygen

Lungs
irritation, suffocation

Liver
liver damage

Kidneys
kidney damage

Bladder
loss of bladder control

Figure 1

Simple household substances can be incredibly dangerous to the body when they're inhaled. Some of these effects are summarized above.

Effects of Inhalants The effects of inhalants range from mild to severe. The effects include hyperactivity, loss of inhibition, and dizziness. Stronger effects include loss of coordination, difficulty speaking or thinking, fear, anxiety, depression, nausea, vomiting, headache, and loss of consciousness.

Dangers of Inhalants As summarized in **Figure 1,** inhalants are very dangerous. Although different kinds of inhalants have different effects, almost all of them are damaging to the body.

▶ **Inhalants damage many organs.** Chemicals, such as solvents, in inhalants can cause permanent hearing loss, bone marrow damage, liver damage, kidney damage, and loss of bladder control.

▶ **Inhalants kill brain cells.** Inhalant vapors replace the oxygen found in the blood and can cause brain cells to die from lack of oxygen. Breathing high concentrations of inhalants can cause brain damage, coma, and death from suffocation.

▶ **Inhalants can cause sudden death.** Some people's bodies are sensitive to the solvents in some inhalants. The heart may suddenly stop beating, and the person may die. This is called *sudden sniffing death syndrome.* Unfortunately, people only discover that they are sensitive to organic solvents after it's too late.

Teens and Inhalants Because the substances used by people who huff drugs are easy to get, inexpensive to buy, and legal, huffing is often seen among younger teens. Huffing can be a first step on the path to trying other illegal drugs. Drugs that often lead to abuse of other drugs are called *gateway drugs.* Inhalants are a common gateway drug among teens, along with tobacco and alcohol.

Club (Designer) Drugs

Club (designer) drugs are drugs designed to closely resemble common illegal drugs in chemical structure and effect. These drugs used to be called *designer drugs*, but they are now more often called *club drugs*. Club drugs became very popular at parties and clubs but can now be found other places as well.

At one time, only drugs specifically listed under the law were illegal. A new drug with effects similar to those of an illegal drug but whose chemical structure differed slightly from that of the illegal drug was legal. Manufacturers became skilled at mixing legal versions of illegal drugs. The laws have now been changed to include all related forms of an illegal drug.

Club drugs are made in secret, illegal labs, so their strength and quality are unpredictable and unknown. Thus, the drugs can have unexpected effects. Overdose from club drugs may be hard to treat because no one can know for sure what drugs the user took. Club drugs include Ecstasy, GHB, ketamine, PCP, and look-alike drugs.

Ecstasy   The most commonly abused club drug is Ecstasy, or MDMA (methylenedioxymethamphetamine). Ecstasy is also called *X*, *Adam*, or *XTC*. Ecstasy has both stimulant and hallucinogenic properties. Ecstasy is normally taken as a pill, although it can also be crushed and snorted. The intoxication effects of Ecstasy include increased awareness of the senses, hallucinations, increased energy, and loss of judgment. The side effects of Ecstasy can include muscle tension, teeth clenching, impaired learning and memory, nausea, chills, rapid or irregular heartbeat, high blood pressure, heart attack, brain damage, and even death.

Ecstasy decreases the body's ability to control its temperature. As a result, it is easy to become overheated. People dancing in a night club, such as those shown in **Figure 2**, can pass out and even die from heatstroke while high on Ecstasy.

GHB   Gamma hydroxybutyrate (GHB) is a clear liquid or a white powder that causes euphoria, relaxation, dizziness, and loss of inhibitions. Higher doses cause vomiting, memory loss, respiratory problems, loss of consciousness, seizures, coma, and death. Some people who lose consciousness from GHB stop breathing and die. When it is combined with other depressant drugs, such as alcohol, death is even more likely. GHB can be highly addictive.

Some people incorrectly believe that taking GHB with Ecstasy can cancel out the effects of each of the drugs. Some also mistakenly believe that GHB makes Ecstasy last longer. However, GHB mixed with Ecstasy puts the user at a much higher risk of seizure.

GHB has been used in many sexual assaults because it makes the victim incapable of resisting and can cause memory problems. For this reason, GHB is part of a group of drugs known as *date-rape drugs*.

Figure 2

People are often pressured to use club drugs at parties and dance clubs.

ACTIVITY *State two ways you can refuse designer drugs if you are ever pressured. (Hint: Refer to the Life Skills Quick Review on p. 618 for ideas.)*

internet connect

www.scilinks.org/health
Topic: Drugs and Drug Abuse
HealthLinks code: HH4050

HEALTH LINKS. Maintained by the
THE WORLD'S A CLICK AWAY National Science
Teachers Association

Ketamine   Ketamine (KEET uh MEEN) is another type of club drug. Ketamine is also known as *Special K, Kit Kat,* or *Vitamin K.* The effects of ketamine include hallucination, numbness, inability to move, loss of memory, and dissociation (separation from reality). Some users of ketamine hurt themselves because they are unable to feel pain. Ketamine has also been known to cause memory loss and coma.

PCP   PCP (phencyclidine), also called *angel dust,* can produce effects that range from mild euphoria to distortions of reality, out-of-body experiences, and psychotic behavior. People on PCP often act violently toward others or toward themselves. Suicide, accidental suicide, seizures, and coma are risks when one is under the influence of PCP. Mental disturbances caused by PCP can last from a few hours to a few weeks.

Look-Alike Drugs   *Look-alike drugs* are abused substances that are only slightly different from other, better-known drugs. As with any street drug, users can never know exactly what drug they are getting, how strong it is, and what other drugs might be in it. For example, look-alike drugs such as PMA and DXM are often sold as Ecstasy.

Look-alike drugs are often cheaper than well-known drugs but are just as dangerous. Depending on what is in them, look-alikes can cause similar effects to any other club drug. If look-alike drugs are taken with other drugs such as alcohol, dangerous reactions can occur.

Anabolic Steroids

Hormones are substances that are made and released in one part of the body and that cause a change in another part of the body. **Anabolic steroids** are synthetic versions of the male hormone testosterone that are used to promote muscle development. *Anabolic* means "building."

When prescribed, anabolic steroids are used to treat muscle wasting in AIDS patients, to assist with wound healing in the elderly, and to treat abnormally low levels of testosterone in males. Most people who use steroids to build muscles use them illegally and without the guidance of a doctor.

Steroids are unique among abused drugs because they don't have immediate psychoactive effects. People take anabolic steroids for their effect on the body, not the brain. Unfortunately, steroids have severe side effects, as shown in **Figure 3.** Abusing anabolic steroids can lead to serious health problems.

Male	Female
▶ stunted growth	▶ severe acne
▶ aggression	▶ increased cholesterol
▶ paranoia	▶ increased facial hair
▶ liver cancer	▶ baldness
▶ increased cholesterol	▶ deeper voice
▶ heart disease	▶ disrupted menstrual cycle
▶ severe acne	▶ infertility
▶ baldness	▶ bloating
▶ shrinking of testes	▶ rapid weight gain
▶ reduced sperm count	▶ liver cancer
▶ infertility	

Effects of Steroids on the Body If adolescents take steroids, their bones will mature too early and their growth will be stunted. Steroids can also cause severe acne, increased cholesterol, rapid weight gain, liver damage, kidney tumors, heart disease, and heart attack in both men and women.

In males, steroids shut down normal testosterone production and can shrink the testes and reduce sperm production. Steroids can cause breasts to grow because the body breaks anabolic steroids down into compounds that act like the female hormone estrogen.

In females, steroids can cause facial hair to grow, toughen the skin, and deepen the voice, making a woman seem more like a man. Steroids can also disrupt the menstrual cycle, leading to infertility.

Effects of Steroids on the Mind Large doses of steroids tend to make abusers more irritable and aggressive. Aggression caused by steroid abuse is called *roid rage*. Roid rage can lead to violent crime, assault, and rape. People who abuse steroids may also experience hyperactivity, bizarre sounds, feelings of paranoia, panic attacks, depression, anxiety, and even suicidal urges. Many abusers also find that they have withdrawal symptoms, including depression, if they stop taking steroids.

Being the Best Drug Free Teens who want to win on the field should be aware that the only real way to win is naturally. Almost all sports now ban steroid use. If an athlete tests positive for steroids, he or she can be banned from the sport. Along with sparing your body the damaging side effects of steroids, you can have the satisfaction of knowing that any victory you achieve is a result of your own hard work. You don't need help from an illegal drug to succeed.

"I don't need steroids to be a good baseball player."

SECTION 2

REVIEW *Answer the following questions on a separate piece of paper.*

Using Key Terms

1. **Identify** the term for "drugs that are inhaled as vapors."
2. **Define** the term *club drugs*.

Understanding Key Ideas

3. **Summarize** three effects common to all illegal drugs.
4. **Compare** the effects of the following four commonly abused illegal drugs.
   a. marijuana
   b. inhalants
   c. club (designer) drugs
   d. anabolic steroids

5. **Identify** which of these are *not* effects of marijuana on the brain.
   a. impaired memory   c. increased alertness
   b. loss of coordination   d. increased appetite
6. **Identify** three dangers of inhalant abuse.
7. **List** the effects of five types of club drugs on the body.
8. **Compare** the effects of anabolic steroids on men with the effects of anabolic steroids on women.

Critical Thinking

9. **LIFE SKILL** **Communicating Effectively** If a friend told you he bought some pills at a party, what advice would you give him about trying the pills?

Other Drugs of Abuse

OBJECTIVES

Describe the dangerous risks of using stimulants, depressants, opiates, and hallucinogens for nonmedical uses.

Compare the dangers of two different types of stimulants.

Summarize the dangerous effects of the depressants Rohypnol and dextromethorphan (DXM).

Describe the dangerous physical and social effects of addiction to opiates such as heroin.

Summarize the dangerous emotional effects that can result from hallucinogen abuse.

"I have a huge test tomorrow, and I'll be up all night studying," Gilberto told Eric. "I've got some stuff that can help keep you awake," said Eric. "No, thanks. I heard it's easy to get hooked on those types of drugs," Gilberto replied.

Other Types of Abused Drugs

Besides the drugs listed in the previous section, there are many other drugs of abuse that teens may encounter, including stimulants, depressants, opiates, and hallucinogens.

- ▶ **Stimulants** are drugs that temporarily increase a person's energy and alertness.
- ▶ **Depressants** are drugs that cause relaxation and sleepiness.
- ▶ **Opiates** (OH pee its) are a group of highly addictive drugs derived from the poppy plant that are used as pain relievers, anesthetics, and sedatives.
- ▶ **Hallucinogens** (huh LOO si nuh juhnz) are drugs that distort perceptions and cause a person to see or hear things that are not real.

Many of these drugs have medical purposes. For example, the stimulant Ritalin® is used to treat attention deficit hyperactivity disorder (ADHD). Depressants can be used to help people who have difficulty sleeping. Some opiates are used as anesthetics during surgery. But despite their medical uses, all of these drugs can be highly addictive and very dangerous when abused. Most of these drugs have a very high risk of overdose and should never be used without a doctor's supervision. The effects of these drugs are summarized in **Table 2.**

Some drugs, such as the stimulant methamphetamine, can have many appearances. All forms of methamphetamines are dangerous.

Table 2 Other Drugs of Abuse

Drug and common or street names	How it is taken	Possible intoxication effects	Possible health consequences*
Stimulants *cocaine, coke, crack, snow, methamphetamines, uppers, candy, ice, meth, crystal, speed, crank, cross-tops*	snorted, injected, smoked, or swallowed	▶ increased alertness and energy ▶ loss of appetite ▶ euphoria ▶ hyperactivity ▶ restlessness ▶ anxiety ▶ increased heart rate ▶ increased breathing rate ▶ elevated blood pressure	▶ nervousness ▶ irritability ▶ panic ▶ aggressive behavior ▶ confusion ▶ loss of awareness of reality ▶ kidney damage ▶ liver damage ▶ heart failure ▶ death
Depressants *Rohypnol™, roofies, downers, barbs, tranqs*	swallowed	▶ euphoria ▶ reduced anxiety ▶ loss of inhibitions ▶ drowsiness	▶ loss of coordination ▶ slurred speech ▶ confusion ▶ slowed heart rate ▶ dangerously slowed breathing ▶ loss of consciousness ▶ loss of memory ▶ coma ▶ death
Opiates *heroin, H, horse, smack, junk*	smoked, injected, swallowed, or snorted	▶ euphoria ▶ feelings of well-being ▶ relaxation ▶ drowsiness ▶ pain relief	▶ nausea/vomiting ▶ constipation ▶ confusion ▶ loss of consciousness ▶ dangerously slowed breathing ▶ coma ▶ death
Hallucinogens *acid, dots, snowmen, mesc, buttons, magic mushrooms, tops*	swallowed or smoked	▶ sensory illusions ▶ distortions of reality ▶ dizziness ▶ weakness ▶ enhanced emotions ▶ feelings of being outside of the body	▶ panic ▶ self-injury ▶ chronic mental disorders ▶ recurring distortion of perception (flashbacks)

*All of the drugs listed here can result in tolerance. All, except for some hallucinogens, can result in physical dependence and addiction.

Stimulants

Stimulants are drugs that temporarily increase a person's energy and alertness. Stimulants include caffeine, nicotine, methylphenidate (Ritalin®), amphetamines (am FET uh meenz), cocaine, and crack cocaine. Caffeine and nicotine are relatively mild, legal stimulants. Methylphenidate is a prescribed stimulant that helps people with attention deficit hyperactivity disorder (ADHD) control their behavior. Cocaine and amphetamines are very potent illegal drugs. Regardless, all stimulants can be addictive and dangerous drugs.

Amphetamines Amphetamines are a group of stimulants produced in laboratories. Some types of amphetamines are prescribed to treat neurological disorders and life-threatening obesity. However, one type of amphetamine, methamphetamine (METH am FET uh MEEN), is highly abused.

Methamphetamine Illegal methamphetamine, commonly called *meth, crystal,* or *ice,* usually appears as white or yellowish crystals called "rocks" that are crushed and then either smoked, injected, or inhaled through the nose (snorted). Methamphetamine's intense effects, which can last for hours, include

- euphoria
- loss of appetite
- increased alertness
- hyperactivity

Repeated use of methamphetamine causes severe damage to the body, including permanent brain, kidney, or liver damage. Overdose can cause brain damage or death. Methamphetamine is extremely addictive, and tolerance develops very rapidly.

Methamphetamine is produced in illegal laboratories called *meth labs.* The byproducts of methamphetamine production include poisonous gas, toxic chemicals, and highly explosive substances. These hazardous wastes are an added danger of methamphetamine abuse.

Cocaine and Crack Cocaine Cocaine comes from the coca plant, which grows in South America. The leaves are processed into a fine, white powder that is snorted through the nose or liquefied and injected. Powdered cocaine can be converted into *crack cocaine,* a crystallized form that is smoked. The effects of cocaine are very similar to those of methamphetamine. The effects of crack cocaine are more intense than those of powdered cocaine, but they do not last as long.

Large doses or repeated use of cocaine cause agitation, paranoia, and aggression. Users can't eat or sleep and at times may lose touch with reality. When the drug wears off, the aftereffects, called a *crash,* include agitation, extreme sleepiness, depression, and intense craving for more of the drug. Addiction to these stimulants is very difficult to escape. Overdose can cause heart attack, stroke, seizures, or death.

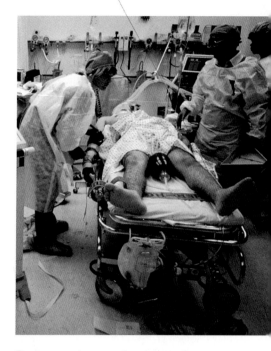

Doctors and nurses treat a crack cocaine user in the emergency room of Highland Hospital in Oakland, California. An overdose of crack cocaine can cause a heart attack, stroke, seizures, or death.

Depressants

Depressants are drugs that cause relaxation and sleepiness. Depressants slow down a person's breathing and reduce brain activity. Depressants include tranquilizers (mild depressants used to treat anxiety) and hypnotics (powerful depressants that are used to treat sleep disorders and seizures). When abused, depressants are highly addictive.

Most depressants have similar effects on the body. These effects include relaxation, loss of inhibition, drowsiness, loss of coordination, slurred speech, disorientation, loss of consciousness, and possible memory loss.

An overdose may cause a person to stop breathing altogether and may result in brain damage, coma, or death. Using depressants in combination with alcohol increases the effects. Most deaths due to depressants occur when they are used in combination with alcohol.

Rohypnol Rohypnol™ (roh HIP nahl) is a powerful hypnotic. Rohypnol, also called *roofies* or the *forget pill*, has developed a reputation as the most frequently used date-rape drug. It is easy to mix with alcohol, in which its bitter taste may not be noticed.

A person on Rohypnol will lose his or her inhibitions, become disoriented, and may not be able to remember what happened while on the drug.

DXM Dextromethorphan (DXM) is a legal ingredient in cough syrups that helps stop coughing. In high doses, its effects are similar to PCP's. The user feels spacey and may lose muscular control. DXM can also produce hallucinations and bizarre sensations.

3 Tips for Protecting Yourself from Date-Rape Drugs

1 Never leave your drink unattended.

2 Never accept an open drink or glass from a stranger.

3 Never drink a beverage that has an abnormal taste or appearance.

Opiates

Opiates are a classic example of a drug that can be both a highly valued medicine and a deadly drug of abuse. Opiates come from the flowering opium poppy plant (*Papaver somniferum*). Used as medicine, opiates reduce pain, relieve diarrhea, suppress coughing, and induce relaxation. Examples of opiates include heroin (HER oh in), opium, codeine (KOH DEEN), and morphine (MAWR FEEN).

When opiates are abused, they can result in addiction very quickly. People addicted to opiates experience very unpleasant withdrawal symptoms if they try to quit. These symptoms include cramps, vomiting, muscle pain, shaking, chills, and panic attacks.

Heroin Heroin is the most commonly abused opiate. It is a chemically altered form of morphine that can be swallowed, snorted, smoked, or injected. It creates an initial "rush" that quickly subsides into a dreamlike state, feelings of well-being, and drowsiness.

Tolerance to heroin develops rapidly. Smoking or snorting heroin loses its effectiveness, and users often begin to inject heroin to achieve the same high. Heroin is a very addictive drug. Heroin abuse and addiction are associated with a host of problems. Each year, thousands of people die under the influence of heroin. It is not uncommon for heroin users to

- lose their jobs because they can't stay sober long enough to work
- have poor living conditions
- suffer from many health problems
- engage in crime to finance their addiction
- choke on their own vomit when passed out

Along with cocaine, heroin is the drug most closely linked with violent crime. Because withdrawal symptoms are extremely unpleasant, heroin addicts will do almost anything to get another dose when the drug wears off. This is one reason heroin is such an addictive and destructive illegal drug.

Repeatedly injecting heroin can cause skin infections, open wounds, and scarring. Injected heroin use has also become an important factor in the spread of some diseases. Heroin addicts who share needles run a high risk of infecting themselves with hepatitis or HIV/AIDS.

Opium Opium, also called *black* or *dream stick*, is a bitter, brownish drug that is made of the dried juice of the opium poppy. It is a mild painkiller, but it also causes slowed heart beat, slowed breathing, loss of appetite, and loss of inhibitions.

Morphine and Codeine Morphine, also called *mister blue* or *morpho*, is very similar to heroin. It is used legally for patients in severe pain, such as terminal cancer patients. Codeine is used for the relief of milder pain and sometimes to stop coughing.

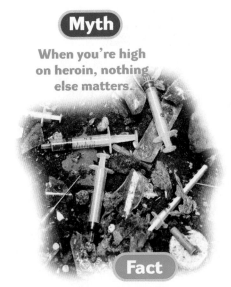

Myth

When you're high on heroin, nothing else matters.

Fact

It may seem like nothing matters until you're living on the street, infected with HIV/AIDS, or dying from an overdose.

Hallucinogens

Hallucinogens are drugs that distort perception and cause the user to experience things that are not real. Hallucinogens include LSD (lysergic acid diethylamide), peyote, and mushrooms. While a person is on hallucinogens, his or her emotional experiences seem deeper and more important. Hallucinogens can also produce extreme anxiety, fear, and paranoia.

LSD LSD is usually taken in the form of tablets or absorbed through the tongue on small paper squares. The effects of LSD are not easy to predict. Sometimes, LSD can increase energy, alter mood, and create strange thoughts and sensations. LSD can cause nausea and vomiting, dizziness, and bizarre body sensations. People on LSD may experience huge emotional swings.

Some LSD experiences are extremely frightening. Users may become panicked and confused when they find they can't control their thoughts and feelings. In addition, a person may feel the effects of a hallucinogen long after the drug has worn off. This is called a *flashback*. Flashbacks can be frightening even if the initial LSD experience wasn't.

Mushrooms Mushrooms (psilocybin) are hallucinogenic drugs with effects similar to LSD. Mushrooms are either eaten raw or mixed with food. Commonly called *magic mushrooms*, psilocybin produces altered perceptions of sight, sound, taste, smell, or touch. Other effects can include confusion, anxiety, and panic. Occasionally, flashbacks may be experienced days, weeks, or even months after use. It is difficult to distinguish psilocybin from more-toxic varieties of mushrooms. If an abuser takes the wrong kind, the mushroom can result in stomach pains, vomiting, diarrhea, and even death.

People who are high on some types of drugs may accidentally hurt or kill themselves.

SECTION 3

REVIEW *Answer the following questions on a separate piece of paper.*

Using Key Terms

1. **Define** *stimulant*.

2. **Identify** the term that means "a drug that causes relaxation and sleepiness."

3. **Identify** the term that means "a drug that distorts perception, causing users to see or hear things that are not real."

Understanding Key Ideas

4. **List** medical uses for three drugs of abuse.

5. **Summarize** why stimulants, depressants, opiates, and hallucinogens are dangerous when used for nonmedical uses.

6. **Compare** the effects of stimulants, depressants, opiates, and hallucinogens on the body and behavior.

7. **Evaluate** the reason Rohypnol and other depressants are especially dangerous for women.

8. **State** five reasons why heroin is a physically and socially destructive drug.

Critical Thinking

9. **LIFE SKILL** **Practicing Wellness** Why should police be cautious when confronting someone on LSD?

A Drug-Free Life

OBJECTIVES

Summarize how drug abuse can negatively affect a person's life.

Identify the ways that drug abuse can affect a family.

List four ways that drug abuse impacts society.

Describe the principles that describe effective drug abuse treatment.

List five ways that you could refuse illegal drugs. **LIFE SKILL**

Tina's newborn baby had not quit crying for hours. Because Tina had frequently abused heroin while she was pregnant, Kayla was born dependent. Now Kayla was going through withdrawal. "My poor baby. I'm so sorry," Tina whispered as she rocked her baby.

Drug Abuse Affects the Individual

When people abuse drugs, they risk losing the things that are good in life. Think for a moment about your goals. Do you want to do well in college, get a good job, or travel all over the world? Now think about how drug use would affect your goals. Drug use, abuse, or addiction can destroy your dreams. For a few moments of feeling "high," you risk everything else that is important to you.

Risks of Drug Use Illegal drugs cause damage to your body. Most illegal drugs can be deadly. Despite this, many people would like to believe that the consequences of drug use won't affect them. However, no matter how you try to manipulate the facts to make drugs seem safer, thousands of people are hospitalized because of drug use each year.

The dangerous intoxication and side effects are not the only risks of illegal drug abuse. Drug use can lead to

- ▶ car accidents
- ▶ accidental injury or death
- ▶ violence and other criminal activity
- ▶ unplanned pregnancy
- ▶ sexually transmitted diseases (STDs)

Most of the time, the activities that get people into trouble are things a person would never do if he or she were not high on drugs. It takes getting high only one time to engage in a behavior that will change the rest of your life.

Hal Carter has turned his life around. With treatment, hard work, and support, he was able to overcome an addiction to painkillers.

Drug Abuse and Crime   Many abused drugs are illegal, so simply having them is a crime. People get arrested every day for possession of illegal drugs or the supplies for making them. Addiction to an illegal drug is expensive. Many illegal drug users will steal or sell drugs to get money to buy their drugs. Making and selling illegal drugs is a crime that can result in many years of prison time.

In both small and large cities, between two-thirds and three-quarters of people arrested for violent crimes were on drugs when their crimes were committed. Some do not even remember committing their crime.

Drug Abuse Affects the Family

Drug abuse isn't just a problem for drug abusers. Drug abuse also affects a family in many ways.

Drug Abuse and Trust   Among the first things a family loses when a teen starts using drugs is trust. Parents don't want their children using drugs, so teens have to hide their drug use and lie about what they're doing. Eventually, parents find out. Once drug abuse becomes regular, finding money to buy drugs becomes more difficult. This can lead addicts to steal from their parents and siblings. Good relationships need trust to thrive.

There are warning signs you can look for if you suspect that someone you care about is using drugs. A person might be using drugs if he or she

- ▶ has unusual emotional reactions to situations
- ▶ withdraws from family intimacy and activities
- ▶ repeatedly breaks household or school rules
- ▶ hangs out with different friends
- ▶ starts to dress differently

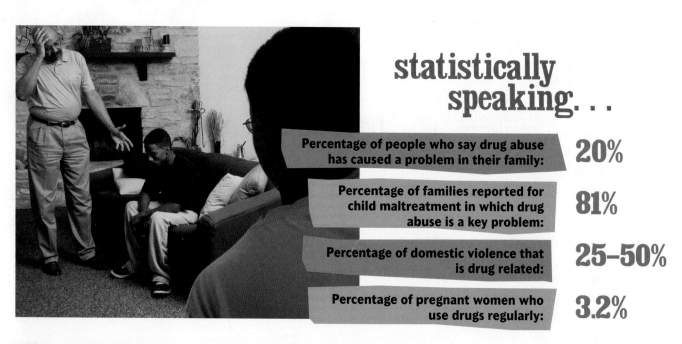

statistically speaking. . .

Percentage of people who say drug abuse has caused a problem in their family:	**20%**
Percentage of families reported for child maltreatment in which drug abuse is a key problem:	**81%**
Percentage of domestic violence that is drug related:	**25–50%**
Percentage of pregnant women who use drugs regularly:	**3.2%**

Drug Abuse and Violence Drug addicts are also at risk of physically hurting their family members or of being hurt themselves. Twenty-five to fifty percent of all family violence is drug related. Seventy-five percent of female victims of domestic violence were attacked by someone who was high or drunk. You or someone in your class may have been a witness to or even a victim of drug-related family violence. It's a terrible thing, but it's not uncommon.

Drug Abuse Affects Pregnancy Drug use can be dangerous to pregnant women and to the fetus developing inside the womb. In general, babies exposed to drugs in the womb are at risk of premature birth, low birth weight, and a variety of developmental problems.

Mothers who are addicted to certain drugs are at risk of delivering a baby who is physically dependent on that drug. This means the baby undergoes withdrawal after being born. Drug withdrawal occurring in newborn infants whose mothers were frequent drug users during pregnancy is called **neonatal abstinence syndrome.**

The withdrawal process can be uncomfortable and distressing. These infants may be more difficult to care for than normal babies. Caring for a drug-dependent baby is a challenge that many drug-addicted mothers may not be able to handle. If the child is kept by someone who is a frequent drug user, the infant may be neglected, abused, or abandoned. Children who are raised by drug abusers also have a higher risk of becoming drug abusers than children raised by drug-free parents do.

A healthcare worker checks the pulse of an infant whose mother went into labor while smoking crack cocaine.

Drug Abuse Affects Society

In 1962, only 4 million Americans had tried an illegal drug. Today, almost 90 million Americans have tried an illegal drug. This rise in drug use has had a profound effect on society.

Drug Abuse and Economics Drug abuse has become a very costly problem for society. The economic costs of drug abuse to the United States were estimated to be $181 billion in 2002. The healthcare costs resulting from drug abuse alone were $16 billion in 2002. AIDS accounted for $3.4 billion of these costs. Intravenous drug use is a major factor in the spread of AIDS and hepatitis. Although many programs have been initiated to help combat the spread of AIDS among IV drug users, AIDS still remains a serious problem.

Drug abuse costs society money in other ways as well. Drug-related costs resulting from lost productivity at work, accidental injuries, car crashes, suicide, and overdose all take a toll on society.

Drug Abuse and Crime The link between drugs and crime is undeniable. In 2002, the cost of drug-related crime was $108 billion. That is how much all of the 50 states together spent on their state-supported colleges in 2002. In 1983, only 1 prisoner in 11 was jailed for a drug-related crime. Now, that ratio is 1 in 4. There are so many arrests for drug possession that many states have been forced to establish special drug courts just to deal with the huge number of nonviolent drug offenders.

There is no way to estimate the costs of violent crime to the victims. Assault, rape, and murder take a toll on society that is more costly than can be assigned a financial value. Many people in prison for violent crimes were high on drugs when the crime was committed. Innocent victims of drug-related violence suffer physically, mentally, and emotionally.

Odds are that in our lifetime, each of us will know someone who has been a victim of a drug-related theft or violent crime. Therefore, how can anyone say that drug use is only dangerous to the abuser? The costs of drug use make it worthwhile for all of us to be involved in the effort to stop drug abuse.

real life Activity

DRUG ABUSE AFFECTS EVERYONE

LIFE SKILL
Setting Goals

Materials

✔ local newspaper
✔ scissors
✔ glue
✔ poster board
✔ markers

Procedure

1. **Use** a copy of your local newspaper to look for some articles that indicate the effects that drug use has on your community.

2. **Cut** out several articles or photos and glue them to your poster board.

3. **Write** below each photo how the articles or photos you chose illustrate a cost of drug use in your community.

4. **Write** one thing that can be done in your community to help combat each of the drug-related costs to society.

5. **Draw** a circle around any of the articles or photos that have affected you or your family in some way.

Conclusions

1. **Summarizing Results** Write a short paragraph summarizing the ways you think illegal drug use has had an effect on your community.

2. **Predicting Outcomes** How can your community work together to decrease drug abuse and its effects?

3. **Predicting Outcomes** If drug use increased in your community, how might it affect your life?

4. **CRITICAL THINKING** What are some ways that you and your friends might help combat drug use in your school?

POLICE LINE DO NOT CROS

"We didn't think we were hurting anyone else until we heard the cars crash. Now four people are dead."

Drug Abuse Affects Everyone   It is easy to see how drug abuse can hurt the abuser. However, many other people are affected as well. The costs of illegal drug use on people other than the drug abuser include the following:

▶ physical, mental, and emotional injuries from drug-related domestic violence

▶ health problems in babies born to mothers who abused drugs

▶ injury resulting from drug-related car accidents

▶ loss of job productivity resulting from drug use

▶ diseases caused by drug abuse

When you add up all of the ways that illegal drug abuse affects families and society, the users of illegal drugs are costing all of us.

Treatment for Drug Addiction

Because drugs affect the brain, addiction is a difficult and long-lasting problem. For people who are addicted to drugs, there are ways to escape the cycle of addiction. **Recovering** is the process of learning to live without drugs.

Most addictions cannot be overcome without support. No one should try to overcome a drug dependency on his or her own. Because recovering from a drug addiction is difficult, to be successful, treatment should be managed by a professional. There are a variety of treatment approaches, including 12-step programs, outpatient counseling, and residential communities. The goal of all drug treatment programs is to help the person battle both the drug dependency and the reasons why the drug abuse started in the first place.

Research on drug addiction and recovery has produced a set of principles that describe effective drug abuse treatment.

1. No single treatment works for everyone.

2. Treatment should be available and easy to access.

3. The best treatment addresses other problems that the abuser has, not just the drug addiction.

4. Treatment should offer multiple services, including medical services, family counseling, job training, and legal services.

5. The longer an abuser stays in treatment, the more effective it is.

6. Group therapy is useful for building skills for resisting drug use and developing interpersonal relationships that do not involve drugs.

7. Medications can be an important part of treatment. *Methadone* is a long-lasting synthetic opiate used to treat heroin addiction.

8. Mental illness should be treated at the same time as addiction.

9. Treatment does not need to be voluntary to be effective. **Intervention** involves confronting a drug user about his or her problem to stop him or her from using drugs. Family and friends often have to intervene to get someone to seek treatment for drug addiction.

10. Patients should be monitored for continued drug use.

11. Treatment programs should test for HIV/AIDS, hepatitis B and C, and other infectious diseases.

12. Recovery from addiction may require several periods of treatment to combat relapse. **Relapse** is a return to using drugs while trying to recover from drug addiction.

Group therapy plays an important role in most drug treatment programs. Group therapy helps build skills for resisting drug use and developing healthy relationships.

Saying No to Drugs

One of the best ways to protect yourself from drugs is to be involved in activities with others who want to stay drug free. You could get involved in a school activity. Or you could try volunteering for an organization in your community.

You should also stay away from people who do drugs or from situations where there may be pressure to use drugs. At some point, however, someone you know may pressure you to use drugs. If so, you are not alone—even adults have this problem. Often the people who pressure you are your friends, which can make the situation even more difficult. When this type of situation arises, it is important to remember that only you can protect your dreams and your future. If someone stops being your friend just because you refuse to take drugs, that person was not a true friend to begin with. Friendships are based on respect. Anyone who forces you to do something that could hurt your body, mind, relationships, and future does not respect you.

Practice Saying No Despite your efforts, you may someday be offered drugs. To protect yourself from being pressured into taking drugs, prepare ways in which you can turn down drugs using activities like the one in **Figure 4** or techniques such as the following:

1. **Say no firmly.** You can always say, "No, thanks." Make your refusal calmly, firmly, and confidently. If you seem unsure of yourself, others will think they can argue with you.

2. **Buy yourself time.** Find a place where you can be alone to think about what you can do to get out of the situation. For example, go to the bathroom or go to another room.

3. **Give good reasons why you choose not to do drugs.** For example, you might say, "No, thanks. I don't want to risk getting kicked off of the football team."

Figure 4

Practicing refusal skills can ensure that you can say no to drugs when you need to.

ACTIVITY *In pairs, practice resisting pressure to use drugs. Make a list of different ways you can say no to somebody pressuring you to use drugs.*

If You Hear This... / You Can Say This...

If You Hear This...	You Can Say This...
"Try this—only losers don't do drugs."	"What loser told you that?"
"Come on; everyone's doing it."	"I don't care that much about fitting in."
"Here, try this. It's so cool."	"I'm cool enough already."
"So what do you do for fun?"	"I definitely don't sit around and kill my brain cells."
"When are you gonna wise up and try some of this?"	"I'll try it when I see smart people using it."
"Just try one. It'll make you feel good."	"I feel fine already."
"Are you scared or something?"	"Yeah, I'm scared of ending up addicted."

"Some of us **have tried drugs** and some of us haven't.

None of us need drugs to have fun."

4. **State the consequences that could result if you do use drugs.** "I don't want to get arrested like Mary. Besides, I have a track meet tomorrow, and I don't want to be strung out."

5. **If necessary, say no again and include an alternate activity.** Come up with an idea for something that you could do that doesn't involved taking drugs. For example, you might say, "No thanks. Let's go get something to eat. I'm starving!"

6. **Walk away.** Sometimes the person offering you drugs will keep persisting. Or sometimes you may find yourself weakening even though doing drugs is not something you want to do. In these situations, just walk away. Nobody can pressure you to do drugs if you aren't there.

Live Drug Free Refusing drugs may be difficult, but choosing to be drug free will make your life a lot easier. Organizations such as Mothers Against Drunk Driving (MADD) and Students Against Destructive Decisions (SADD) work to reduce drug use among teens. Student organizations help promote activities that do not involve drug use. They provide a safe place for young people to have fun without having to face the pressure to use illegal drugs.

Teens these days are facing new challenges and many changes. Life can be stressful in many ways. Facing these challenges with courage and maturity are part of making the transition to adulthood. Living a healthy life without getting caught in a web of drug abuse and addiction can help you accomplish your goals for the future.

SECTION 4

REVIEW   *Answer the following questions on a separate piece of paper.*

Using Key Terms

1. **Identify** the term that means "drug withdrawal that occurs in newborn infants whose mothers were frequent drug users during pregnancy."

2. **Define** *intervention.*

3. **Identify** the term that means "a return to using drugs while trying to recover from drug addiction."

Understanding Key Ideas

4. **List** three ways that drug abuse can negatively affect a person's life.

5. **Summarize** the ways in which families may suffer as a result of illegal drug abuse.

6. **Describe** the ways that illegal drug abuse can have a negative effect on society.

7. **Summarize** the principles involved in successful drug treatment and recovery.

8. **Evaluate** three techniques for avoiding pressure to use illegal drugs.

9. **Sequence** how you would react to a situation in which you are pressured to use drugs.

Critical Thinking

10. Why do you think it is so difficult for people to stay off drugs once they have become addicted?

11. **LIFE SKILL** **Using Community Resources** Why do you think drug treatment doesn't have to be voluntary to be effective?

Highlights

Key Terms

drug abuse (284)
overdose (284)

marijuana (289)
inhalant (291)
club (designer) drug (292)
anabolic steroid (293)

stimulant (295)
depressant (295)
opiates (295)
hallucinogen (295)

neonatal abstinence syndrome (303)
recovering (305)
intervention (306)
relapse (306)

The Big Picture

- ✔ Illegal drug use results in many risks, including addiction, damage to the brain and the body, the contraction of diseases, suicide, violent crime, and overdose.
- ✔ People who try drugs often end up abusing drugs because most drugs are highly addictive.
- ✔ People begin using drugs for many reasons, including peer pressure.
- ✔ Teens can be under a lot of pressure to use drugs. Teens have a higher risk for addiction because their brains are still changing rapidly.

- ✔ All illegal drugs affect the brain, are dangerous to a person's health, and can result in abuse and addiction.
- ✔ Marijuana causes loss of concentration, disorientation, loss of sense of time and distance, paranoia, drowsiness, and several other effects.
- ✔ Huffing inhalants damages many organs of the body, including the brain, liver, kidneys, bone marrow, and bladder.
- ✔ Club drugs are addictive and can cause brain damage and death.
- ✔ Look-alike drugs are especially dangerous because there is no way to know what is in them.
- ✔ Anabolic steroids are used to increase muscle mass, but they have very harmful side effects.

- ✔ Many types of illegal drugs have medical uses but are unsafe if they are used without a doctor's supervision.
- ✔ Stimulants such as methamphetamines and cocaine are highly addictive and dangerous.
- ✔ Depressants are highly addictive and dangerous drugs.
- ✔ Hallucinogens such as LSD and PCP are dangerous drugs because their effects on the brain are unpredictable.
- ✔ Intravenous heroin use is a major factor in the spread of HIV/AIDS and hepatitis.

- ✔ Drug abuse hurts the individual addict and damages relationships with family and friends.
- ✔ Drug abuse damages a fetus exposed to illegal drugs in the womb.
- ✔ Drug abuse costs society billions of dollars every year in medical costs, injuries, accidents, lost productivity, and crime.
- ✔ There are many programs available to help drug addicts recover.
- ✔ Practicing refusal skills can help you avoid the dangers of drug abuse and addiction.

Review

Using Key Terms

anabolic steroid (293)
depressant (295)
club (designer) drug (292)
drug abuse (284)
hallucinogen (295)
inhalant (291)
intervention (306)
marijuana (289)

neonatal abstinence
syndrome (303)
opiates (295)
overdose (284)
recovering (305)
relapse (306)
stimulant (295)

1. For each phrase below, choose the most appropriate key term from the list above.
   a. the improper or unsafe use of a drug
   b. a drug that is inhaled as vapors
   c. a drug that temporarily increases energy and alertness
   d. drug withdrawal occurring in newborn infants
   e. laboratory-made drugs that closely resemble common illegal drugs in chemical structure and effect
   f. a drug that slows the body and the brain

2. Explain the relationship between the key terms in each of the following pairs.
   a. *drug abuse* and *overdose*
   b. *recovering* and *relapse*

Understanding Key Ideas
Section 1

3. Which of the following is a danger of illegal drug use?
   a. overdose   c. poor judgment
   b. car crash   d. all of the above

4. Evaluate the reasons people often give for trying illegal drugs.

5. List two reasons teens may be under pressure to use illegal drugs.

6. State the reason teens are at a higher risk of addiction from drug use than adults are.

7. **CRITICAL THINKING** Do you think using an illegal drug only once is safe?

8 List two goals you have after you graduate from high school. How would illegal drug use affect those goals? **LIFE SKILL**

Section 2

9. What are three effects that are common to all types of illegal drugs?

10. Which of the following is *not* an effect of marijuana use?
    a. poor concentration   c. drowsiness
    b. giddiness   d. increased alertness

11. List three long-term effects of inhalants on the body.

12. Compare the dangerous effects of Ecstasy and ketamine.

13. Women who take steroids are likely to
    a. have deeper voices.
    b. have increased body hair.
    c. develop severe acne.
    d. All of the above

14. List four reasons you would give your friend to discourage him or her from using steroids to enhance athletic performance. **LIFE SKILL**

Section 3

15. List three medical uses for drugs of abuse.

16. What dangerous effects do stimulants have?

17. List three effects of depressants on the body.

18. Why do you think heroin addiction is so difficult to overcome?

19. Describe how hallucinogens affect the mind.

Section 4

20. How can drug abuse make a person's life more difficult?

21. In what ways does family life suffer when a family member abuses illegal drugs?

22. What aspects of society are affected by drug abuse?

23. Name three types of treatment for drug addiction.

24. List five ways you could refuse illegal drugs if they were offered to you. **LIFE SKILL**

25. **CRITICAL THINKING** What healthy activities can teens participate in on weekends to help avoid the pressure to use drugs?

Interpreting Graphics

Study the figure below to answer the questions that follow.

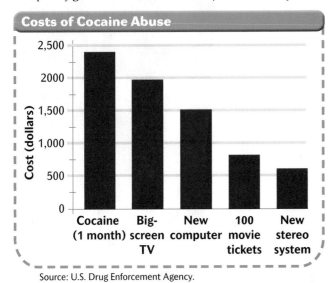

Costs of Cocaine Abuse

Source: U.S. Drug Enforcement Agency.

26. Which of the items above costs the most? 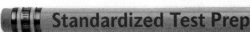 **MATH SKILL**

27. Do the costs of a stereo and a computer combined equal the cost of cocaine?

28. CRITICAL THINKING Explain why people may be driven to steal in order to support a cocaine habit.

Activities

29. Health and You Write down three things you may have heard about illegal drug use. Research each statement, and explain whether or not it is a myth.

30. Health and Your Community Find a newspaper or magazine article about a **READING SKILL** planned drug prevention event in your community. Analyze how much you think this event will affect your community. For example, do you think teens from your school will attend? How well is the event advertised? Suggest ways to make the event more successful.

31. Health and You Write a reply to the following statement: "Just try it; one time won't harm you. It's not like you'll become an addict overnight!"

Action Plan

32. LIFE SKILL Setting Goals List three goals you have for your future. Write down how these goals could be affected by illegal drug use. Write a plan for how you can avoid illegal drugs and accomplish your goals.

Standardized Test Prep

Read the passage below, and then answer the questions that follow. **READING SKILL** **WRITING SKILL**

Wayne grew up in a middle-class family in Wisconsin. When he was 17, he tried smoking marijuana. After marijuana, he tried Ecstasy and then crack cocaine. Soon he was spending over $100 a day on his cocaine habit. He started stealing small amounts of money from his family. When they noticed things missing from the house, they made him move out. He lived with some friends until they got kicked out. He started breaking into homes and was arrested. Wayne is currently <u>serving</u> 2 years. But he is off cocaine and plans to stay that way when he gets out.

33. In this passage, the word *serving* means
   A helping other people.
   B passing out food to the homeless.
   C spending time in jail.
   D volunteering at a prison.

34. What can you infer from reading this passage?
   E Drug addictions are easy to recover from.
   F People can easily control their addictions.
   G Drug addictions can make people do things they wouldn't otherwise do.
   H Drugs are a cheap and harmless habit.

35. Write a paragraph discussing how a drug abuse can develop from experimentation into addiction.

36. Do you think it will be easy for Wayne to stay off cocaine when he gets out of jail? If you were Wayne, what steps would you take to make sure you stay clean and drug free?

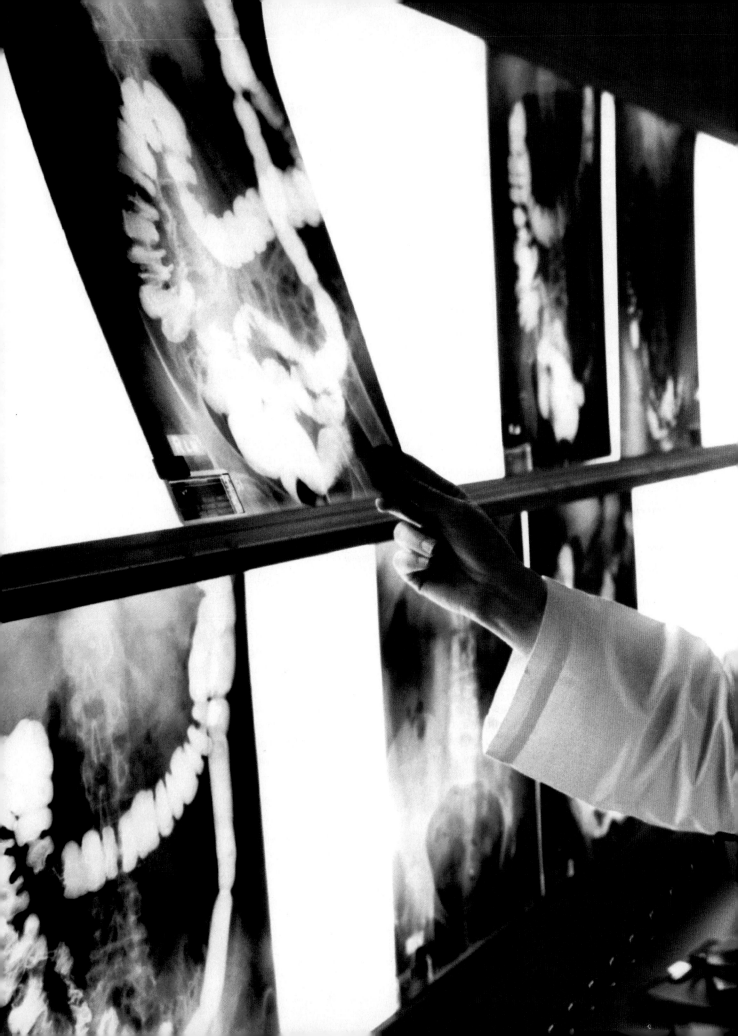

UNIT 4

Diseases and Disorders

313

Preventing Infectious Diseases

What's Your Health IQ?

BEHAVIOR

Indicate how frequently you engage in each of the following behaviors (1=never; 2=occasionally; 3=most of the time; 4=all of the time). Total your points, and then turn to p. 638.

1. I cover my mouth while sneezing or coughing.

2. I wash fruits and vegetables before eating them.

3. I do not go to public places when I am sick.

4. I have regular check-ups with my dentist and doctor.

5. I wash my hands before eating a meal.

6. When my doctor prescribes antibiotics, I follow and complete the prescription.

7. I make sure meat is thoroughly cooked before I eat it.

8. I get extra sleep when I am sick.

Visit these Web sites for the latest health information:

HEALTH LINKS.
THE WORLD'S A CLICK AWAY

Find more information whenever you see a HealthLinks box. Go to **scilinks.org/health**, and type in the HealthLinks code.

go.hrw.com

Find worksheets and other materials that go with your textbook at **go.hrw.com**.

Current Health®

Check out *Current Health®* articles related to this chapter by visiting **go.hrw.com**. Just type in the keyword **HH4 CH13**.

What Are Infectious Diseases?

OBJECTIVES

Identify five different agents that can cause infectious diseases.

List four ways that infectious diseases spread.

Describe two different treatments for infectious diseases.

Name two ways you can help prevent the development of antibiotic resistant bacteria. **LIFE SKILL**

While walking to his friend's house, Paul stepped on a rock and cut his foot. Because the cut was small, Paul just kept on walking. Paul didn't know, however, that a hidden army of organisms was starting an attack on his cut.

What Causes Infectious Diseases?

An **infectious disease** (in FEK shuhs di ZEEZ) is any disease that is caused by an agent that has invaded the body. Infectious diseases may be passed to a person from another person, from food or water, from animals, or from something in the environment. Colds, the flu, head lice, and tuberculosis (TB) are examples of infectious diseases.

Figure 1

Infectious diseases are caused by many different pathogens, such as viruses, bacteria, fungi, protozoa, and animal parasites.

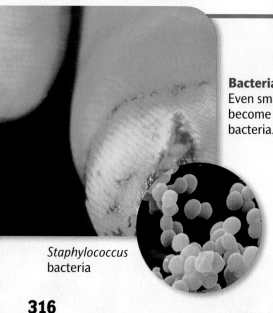

Bacteria
Even small cuts can become infected by bacteria.

Staphylococcus bacteria

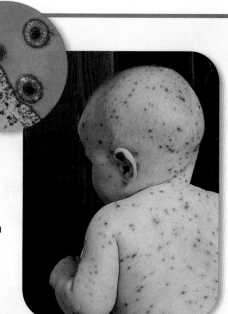

Varicella virus

Virus
Chickenpox, a common childhood illness, is caused by a virus.

All infectious diseases are caused by pathogens. A **pathogen** is any agent that causes disease. **Figure 1** shows some of the different kinds of pathogens that cause infectious diseases.

Bacteria Individually, bacteria are too small to be seen without a microscope. **Bacteria** are tiny, single-celled organisms, some of which can cause disease. Bacteria live almost everywhere on Earth. Some bacteria are even found in the frozen Arctic and in the boiling waters of hot springs.

You have more than 300 kinds of bacteria living in your mouth right now! There's no need to reach for the mouthwash, though, because most bacteria are harmless. Many are actually helpful. For example, bacteria living in your intestines make vitamins that you need to live. However, some kinds of bacteria make you sick when they grow on or inside your body. Some bacteria give off poisons, while other bacteria enter and damage cells. Tuberculosis, tetanus, and sinus infections are examples of diseases caused by bacteria.

Viruses Viruses are even smaller than bacteria. **Viruses** are tiny disease-causing particles made up of genetic material and a protein coat. The genetic material in the virus contains the instructions for making more viruses. Viruses replicate only inside living cells. They reproduce by taking control of body cells and forcing them to make many new viruses. After escaping from the cell, these new viruses seek out other cells to attack. Viral diseases include colds, the flu, measles, AIDS, and severe acute respiratory syndrome (SARS).

Fungi Organisms that absorb and use the nutrients of living or dead organisms are called **fungi** (singular fungus). The mushrooms in your salad are fungi. They don't cause disease, but other fungi do. Maybe you've had athlete's foot, which is caused by a fungus that lives and feeds on your feet and makes them burn and itch. A fungus, not a worm, is also responsible for the scaly, circular rash known as ringworm.

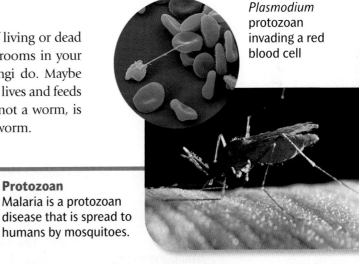

Plasmodium protozoan invading a red blood cell

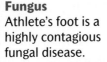

Fungus
Athlete's foot is a highly contagious fungal disease.

Protozoan
Malaria is a protozoan disease that is spread to humans by mosquitoes.

Parasite
Lice are parasites that attach to the hair on a person's head and cause itching.

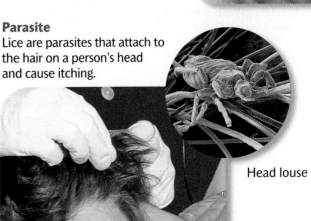

Tinea fungus

Head louse

Protozoans   Single-celled, microscopic organisms called protozoans are larger and more complex internally than bacteria. Protozoans account for diseases that are leading causes of death throughout some parts of the world. For example, malaria is a disease caused by protozoans. Malaria kills approximately 1 million people every year in tropical countries.

Parasites   Bacteria, viruses, fungi, and protozoans account for almost all of the infectious diseases in the United States. However, animal parasites cause a large number of diseases throughout the world. Animal parasites get their energy and nutrients by feeding on other living things. Examples of harmful animal parasites include lice, tapeworms, and certain roundworms.

internet connect

www.scilinks.org/health
Topic: Infectious Diseases
HealthLinks code: HH4087

HEALTH LINKS Maintained by the
National Science
Teachers Association

How Are Infectious Diseases Spread?

Before you can have the symptoms of a cold, the virus that causes the cold has to enter your body. This means that the virus has to travel from someone who has a cold to your body. Knowing how pathogens are spread will help you protect yourself against infectious diseases. Infectious diseases are spread in four main ways, as shown in **Figure 2.**

Person to Person   One way that pathogens can be spread is from person to person. For example, when you sneeze or cough, you send thousands of tiny drops of saliva and mucus into the air. The drops can remain in the air for quite a while and carry many pathogens with them. Anyone who breathes in one of these infected drops can become sick from the pathogens. Also, anyone who touches anything the drops fall on, such as a book, can become infected by the pathogens. Diseases such as the flu, colds, and measles are spread from person to person through the air.

Other ways pathogens can be spread from one person to another are by kissing, drinking from the same glass, and having sexual contact. Mononucleosis, commonly known as the "kissing disease," is spread through person-to-person contact. Although the disease can be passed through kissing, it may also be spread by drinking from the same glass or eating the food of someone who is infected.

Food and Water   The food you eat and the water you drink can also bring pathogens into your body. Foodborne diseases are often spread when pathogens from an infected person or animal contaminate food. This is why people who work with food are required to wash their hands thoroughly. Foodborne disease can also be spread when the food itself is contaminated. For example, meat from infected animals may contain the eggs of parasitic worms. Foodborne diseases include hepatitis A and botulism.

In the United States, it is relatively safe to drink tap water. Water from streams and lakes, however, must be purified before the water can be used for drinking. Water can become contaminated if it is

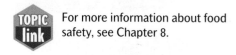

TOPIC link   For more information about food safety, see Chapter 8.

exposed to sewage or animal wastes that have not been treated. Water can be purified by boiling, by using water purification tablets, or by using a filtering system. Diseases caused by contaminated water include typhoid, cholera, giardiasis, and dysentery.

Environment Pathogens are present on most of the objects around you. Although many pathogens cannot live long outside of the human body, some are tougher and can survive on objects in the environment. These pathogens are on the phone you used this morning and even the money in your pocket. Many pathogens live in soil and can enter your body through cuts in your skin. The tetanus bacterium is an example of a pathogen that may be present in soil.

Animals Many pathogens live in or on animals' bodies and can carry diseases from one person to another. For example, you can get diseases from your pets. Children often contract ringworm by petting a dog or cat that has the fungus.

The pathogens that cause malaria, yellow fever, and encephalitis are carried by mosquitoes. When a mosquito carrying one of these pathogens bites you, it pierces your skin and can inject the pathogens into your blood. Certain ticks, such as the one shown in **Figure 2,** carry Lyme disease and Rocky Mountain spotted fever, which are bacterial diseases.

Figure 2

Infectious diseases are spread in many ways.

ACTIVITY *List two ways that diseases can be spread in your home.*

Person to Person People's body fluids may contain pathogens. Sneezing, coughing, sharing drink containers, and having sexual contact can spread diseases from person to person.

Environment Look around you—almost everything you see is covered with micro-organisms, a few of which can cause disease.

Western black-legged tick

How Infectious Diseases Are Spread

Food and Water Many types of food can contain pathogens. Without proper cooking or treatment of foods these pathogens can be passed on to the humans that eat the food. Unpurified water also carries pathogens.

Animals Like humans, animals can carry disease. When humans come into contact with infected animals, diseases can be spread.

Proper Uses of Antibiotics

1 Antibiotics should not be taken for a viral infection, such as a cold or the flu.

2 Antibiotics should not be saved for the next time you get sick. Finish the prescription.

3 Antibiotics should not be taken by anyone other than the person for whom they were prescribed.

Figure 3

Antibiotic-resistant bacteria can grow and multiply if a person does not finish his or her antibiotic prescription. These more resistant bacteria can then be spread to other people.

How Are Infectious Diseases Treated?

When you are sick from an infectious disease, your doctor will treat you based on what pathogen made you sick. For example, your doctor will treat a strep throat differently from athlete's foot. This is because each type of pathogen has its own characteristics.

Treating Bacterial Diseases   Medicines used to kill or slow the growth of bacteria are called *antibiotics*. The discovery of these bacteria-killing compounds completely changed medicine. Before the discovery of antibiotics, even a small cut on your finger could lead to a deadly bacterial infection!

Antibiotics work by preventing the growth and division of bacterial cells. Eventually, antibiotics cause antibiotic sensitive bacteria to die. Some of the antibiotics in use today include penicillin, tetracycline, and streptomycin. Because antibiotics have no effect on viruses, they can't be used to treat colds or other viral diseases.

Doctors and the public are worried about a growing problem called antibiotic resistance. **Antibiotic resistance** is a condition in which bacteria can no longer be killed by a particular antibiotic. As shown in **Figure 3,** improper use of an antibiotic promotes the growth of antibiotic-resistant bacteria. The antibiotic-resistant bacteria can spread to other people. Antibiotic resistance is a threat to everyone's health. Today, people are dying from infections that would have been easy to treat 10 to 15 years ago.

You can help prevent antibiotic resistance. First, you should not ask your doctor for antibiotics if you have a viral disease. Second, if your doctor does give you a prescription to treat a bacterial infection, be sure to follow the prescription and finish your medication.

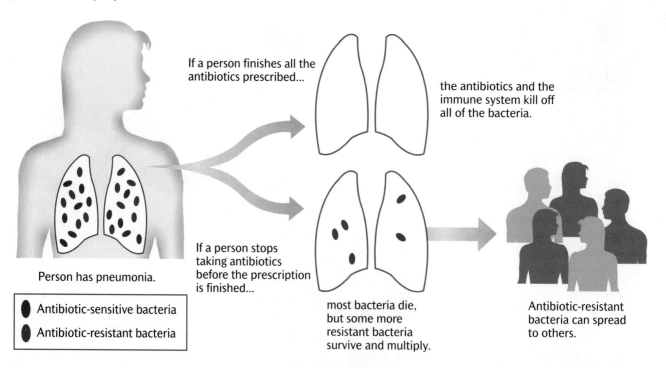

Person has pneumonia.

● Antibiotic-sensitive bacteria

● Antibiotic-resistant bacteria

If a person finishes all the antibiotics prescribed...

the antibiotics and the immune system kill off all of the bacteria.

If a person stops taking antibiotics before the prescription is finished...

most bacteria die, but some more resistant bacteria survive and multiply.

Antibiotic-resistant bacteria can spread to others.

Treating Viral Diseases Currently, there is less known about how to destroy viruses than bacteria. Unlike bacteria, viruses do not grow as living cells. Thus, viral infections cannot be treated with the same medications as bacterial infections can. Most antiviral medications concentrate on relieving symptoms and stopping the production of viruses inside the human cells. These medications must be taken early in the illness to have an effect.

Treating Fungal Infections Fungal infections are usually not as common as bacterial or viral infections, but they can sometimes be serious. Fungal infections of the skin, such as athlete's foot, can usually be treated with an over-the-counter antifungal medicine. Other fungal infections such as candidiasis (yeast infection), however, are more serious and often require stronger prescription medicines.

Treating Protozoan Infections Prevention is the best way to protect yourself from protozoan infections. Simple precautions such as maintaining good hygiene and sanitation keep many protozoans from being able to survive, reproduce, and spread. It is important for a person who has a protozoan infection to see a doctor to receive treatment with prescription medicines.

 For more information about the proper use of medicines, see Chapter 9.

Treating Parasitic Infections Although parasites such as roundworms and tapeworms are found throughout the world, head lice are more common in the United States. To prevent infection from head lice, people should not share combs and brushes with others or wear other people's clothes. Fortunately, head lice can usually be treated with medicated shampoos.

SECTION 1

REVIEW
Answer the following questions on a separate piece of paper.

Using Key Terms

1. **Define** the term *infectious disease.*
2. **Identify** the term for "an agent that causes disease."
3. **Define** the term *antibiotic resistance.*

Understanding Key Ideas

4. **Identify** the five types of pathogens that cause infectious diseases.
5. **Differentiate** between environmentally spread diseases and diseases that are spread from person to person.

6. **Identify** which disease can be spread by water.
   - **a.** ringworm
   - **c.** Lyme disease
   - **b.** cholera
   - **d.** head lice
7. **Identify** three ways to purify water before using it.
8. **State** how antibiotics work to treat bacterial diseases.
9. **Describe** how bacteria develop antibiotic resistance.
10. **Describe** two types of fungal infections, and explain how they are treated.

Critical Thinking

11. **LIFE SKILL** **Practicing Wellness** How can the failure to take antibiotics properly pose a risk to other peoples' health?

SECTION 2

Protecting Yourself from Infectious Diseases

OBJECTIVES

Describe how the body fights infectious diseases.

Summarize five things a person can do to stay well.

Describe how immunity to a disease develops.

State three things you should do when you are sick.

List three things you can do to prevent the spread of infectious diseases. **LIFE SKILL**

KEY TERMS

inflammation a reaction to injury or infection that is characterized by pain, redness, and swelling

lymphatic system a network of vessels that carry a clear fluid called *lymph* through the body

white blood cell a blood cell whose primary job is to defend the body against disease

vaccine a substance usually prepared from killed or weakened pathogens or from genetic material and that is introduced into a body to produce immunity

symptom a change that a person notices in his or her body or mind and that is caused by a disease of disorder

The best way to protect yourself from disease is to practice a healthy lifestyle.

Your head aches, your throat burns, and your muscles feel like you've just been tackled by a football team. When you've got the flu, you feel as if you'll never get better. But in a couple of weeks, your symptoms are usually gone. What happened? Although you were not aware of it, during those 2 weeks, your body was able to get rid of the flu virus and allowed you to recover.

How Your Body Fights Disease

Your body has many ways of fighting disease-causing bacteria, viruses, and other pathogens. Your body uses your skin and chemicals to fight pathogens. Your body also has more specialized defenses, such as the inflammatory response and the immune system. Because of these defenses, your body is able to protect itself from the pathogens that are continually attacking it.

Physical Barriers To make you sick, most pathogens have to enter your body, start growing, and cause damage. Luckily for most of us, this infection process is not easy! As shown in **Figure 4,** your body's first line of defense helps to keep many pathogens from entering your body. Your body's first line of defense includes

▶ **Skin** Your skin keeps pathogens from entering your body. Your skin also uses chemicals, such as sweat and oil, to kill pathogens that have settled on your skin. Your skin is always repairing and rebuilding itself by quickly closing any gaps (cuts) that pathogens could get through.

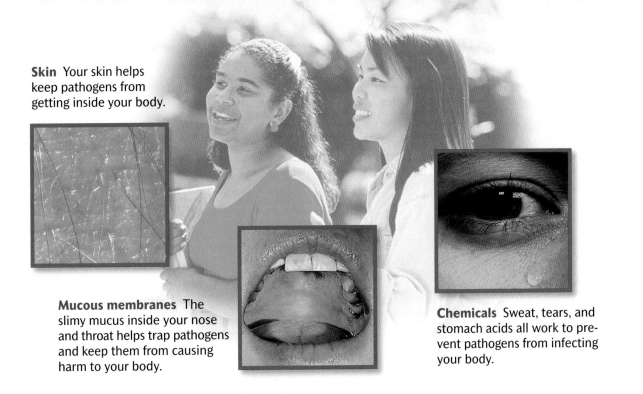

Skin Your skin helps keep pathogens from getting inside your body.

Mucous membranes The slimy mucus inside your nose and throat helps trap pathogens and keep them from causing harm to your body.

Chemicals Sweat, tears, and stomach acids all work to prevent pathogens from infecting your body.

▶ **Mucous membranes** The soft tissues that line the nose, mouth, throat, digestive tract, urethra, and vagina are all mucous membranes. Like the skin, mucous membranes form a barrier to pathogens. Mucous membranes make a slimy material known as *mucus.* One function of mucus is to trap pathogens. Bacteria you breathe in may get caught in mucus lining the tubes that carry air to the lungs. Tiny, hairlike structures called cilia grow from the lining of these tubes. Like an escalator, the waving cilia move the mucus and its bacterial passengers to the back of your throat. Then, by swallowing, you send these bacteria into your stomach where they are destroyed.

▶ **Chemicals** Many of the chemicals your body makes destroy pathogens. For example, sweat is acidic, and inhibits the growth of bacteria. Your stomach secretes acids that not only help you digest your food but also kill bacteria. Tears contain a protein that kills bacteria.

Inflammatory Response Sometimes pathogens are able to cross the protective barriers that are your skin and mucous membranes. This can happen, for example, when you cut or burn yourself. Inflammation is a second way your body protects itself from pathogens. **Inflammation** is a reaction to injury or infection that is characterized by pain, redness, and swelling.

When the protective barriers are broken and a part of your body becomes infected, the area around the injury becomes inflamed, and gets hot. This is caused by the small blood vessels that expand to bring more blood to the injured area. Sometimes, a yellowish substance called *pus* builds up around the injury. Pus includes dead and injured body cells that were fighting the bacteria and dead and injured bacteria. The inflammatory response shows that your body is attacking pathogens.

Figure 4

The body has many defenses to protect itself from pathogens. The first line of defense includes the skin, mucous membranes, and chemicals.

HEALTH Handbook For more information about the immune system, see the Express Lesson on p. 542 of this text.

Immune System Even though the skin and mucous membrane barriers and the inflammatory response are very effective, they can't protect against all pathogens. So your immune system gets ready for action. The immune system is made up of certain types of blood cells and certain proteins called *antibodies*. The blood cells and antibodies move through the blood vessels and are within your organs.

These infection-fighting cells also move through the **lymphatic system,** a network of vessels that carry a clear fluid called *lymph* throughout the body. The lymphatic system picks up fluid from all over the body. This system often sweeps up bacteria or viruses and carries them to your *lymph nodes*. You can feel one set of lymph nodes in your neck just below your ears and jaw. Lymph nodes are filled with white blood cells that scan the lymph for pathogens. **White blood cells** are cells in the blood whose primary job is to defend the body against disease. Certain white blood cells produce antibodies that then bind to specific pathogens and warn other white blood cells to destroy the pathogens. When you are sick, your lymph nodes often swell because of the growing number of white blood cells fighting the infection.

The immune system's defenses take time to defeat pathogens. The cells of the immune system typically attack a specific pathogen. In contrast, the body's other defenses—skin, mucous membranes, and inflammation—work to react to and fight any pathogen.

What You Can Do to Stay Well

Your immune system is always working to keep you well. But there are several things you can do to stay well. Here are a few tips.

- ▶ **Protect yourself.** Keeping your body healthy helps your immune system to fight infectious diseases.
- ▶ **Eat a healthy, balanced diet.** A lack of certain nutrients in your diet can weaken your immune system. Extreme dieting or fasting can reduce your defenses.
- ▶ **Drink water.** Drink 8 to 10 glasses of water a day to keep your immune system working effectively.
- ▶ **Reduce your stress levels.** While everyone feels stress at some time, stress that lasts weeks or months can weaken your immune system and may leave you more vulnerable to illnesses such as colds.
- ▶ **Exercise regularly.** Get at least 60 minutes of activity daily such as walking, running, cycling, or even doing housework.
- ▶ **Get regular medical checkups.** Seeing your doctor and dentist regularly can help prevent you from getting sick.
- ▶ **Try to avoid close contact with sick people.** When you must be exposed to people who are sick, wash your hands often. Do not share personal items, such as hairbrushes, or share drinks from the same container.
- ▶ **Get enough sleep.** Sleep is important to keep your body functioning properly.

Myth

If I spend all day outside on a chilly day, I'll get a cold.

Fact

Being cold does not make you more likely to get a cold.

TOPIC link For more information about stress management skills, see Chapter 4.

Get Vaccinated One of the most important ways to stay healthy is to stay up to date on all your vaccinations. **Vaccines** are substances usually prepared from killed or weakened pathogens or from genetic material and that is introduced into a body to produce immunity. When a vaccine is injected or swallowed, the immune system responds to the vaccine material by making white blood cells called memory cells. In the future, if the pathogen against which the vaccine was made enters the body, the memory cells and their antibodies fight the pathogen before it can cause disease.

Having a disease or being immunized for it may give many years of protection, but periodic boosters may be needed. *Boosters* are extra doses of a vaccine that help the body maintain the production of memory cells for a particular disease.

It is also possible to be immunized for diseases that develop new strains, such as the flu. However, every time a new strain of the flu virus appears, a new vaccine must be developed to protect against it. Thus, people must get a flu vaccine every year for maximum protection against the illness.

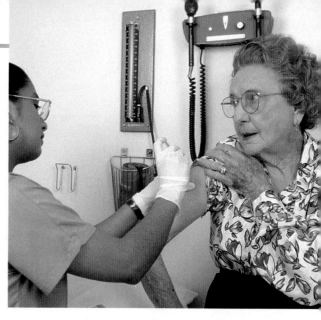

Keeping vaccinations up to date throughout life can help a person avoid many infectious diseases.

Analyzing DATA

Vaccinations

1 In the "Vaccine" column are listed the diseases that each vaccination protects against.

2 The age ranges indicate the age when each vaccination should be received. The blue boxes indicate that the vaccine can be received anytime during that period.

Your Turn

1. At what ages must a person receive the MMR vaccination?

2. What three diseases does the DTaP vaccination protect against?

3. At what age should a person receive his or her first varicella vaccination?

4. **CRITICAL THINKING** Why do you think people must be vaccinated for polio more than once?

Sample Vaccination Schedule for Several Diseases					
Vaccine 1	**Age** 2				
	Birth–6 mos	6 mos–2 yrs	2–6 yrs	11–12 yrs	14–18 yrs
Diphtheria, tetanus, pertussis (DTaP)	DTaP (3 doses)	DTaP	DTaP	Td (tetanus and diphtheria booster)	
Measles, mumps, rubella (MMR)		MMR	MMR		
Varicella (chicken-pox) (Var)		Var			
Inactivated polio (IPV)	IPV (3 doses)		IPV		

What to Do When You Are Sick

Think back to the last time you had a cold. Do you remember how you felt? You probably had a runny nose and a sore throat and were weak and tired. These are the typical symptoms of a cold.

Symptoms of Infection   **Symptoms** are the changes that you notice in your body or mind that are caused by a disease or disorder. Common symptoms of infection include fever, rash, sore throat, headache or muscle aches, fatigue, tired eyes, nausea, vomiting, and diarrhea.

Some symptoms are caused by the pathogens themselves as they multiply within your body. For example, the *Salmonella* bacteria that may be in raw eggs or in raw or undercooked chicken and meats cause diarrhea when they invade cells lining the intestine.

Some other symptoms are part of your body's response to infection. Fever, for instance, is an increase in body temperature. Sometimes fever is caused by the invading microorganisms, but sometimes it is a defense against pathogens. For example, some bacteria can't function or survive at higher temperatures, so your body temperature rises in an attempt to stunt their growth.

Taking Care of Yourself   Following a few simple rules can make your illness less unpleasant.
- Unless you have no other choice, stay home when you're sick. You'll get more rest, and you won't pass your illness to others.
- Drink plenty of fluids such as water and juice.
- Be sure to follow all the directions the doctor gives. Take all the medicine prescribed to you.
- Throw away any tissues you use right away. Wash your hands frequently.

Five Signs That You Need to Seek Medical Care

1 You have difficulty in breathing.

2 You have severe pain somewhere.

3 Your temperature is 101°F or more and lasts for more than 2 days.

4 You have a cut that does not heal properly.

5 Mucus from your nose, throat, or lungs is thick and yellowish green.

How to Prevent the Spread of Disease

Infectious diseases in the United States are common and can spread quickly. As a result, it is important that everyone works to prevent the spread of disease. There are several things you can do to prevent the spread of disease.

Get Vaccinated Public vaccination programs have been largely responsible for preventing the spread of infectious diseases. Vaccines can help protect people against certain diseases for long periods of time. Vaccines are particularly important for fighting viral diseases because few drugs can stop a virus once it has begun to reproduce inside the body. Scientists are currently developing vaccines for more infectious diseases.

Keep Clean Even with medical advancements, maintaining good hygiene is still one of the best ways you can help prevent the spread of disease. For example, bathing and washing with soap daily helps protect against infection by washing away many bacteria.

HEALTH Handbook For more information about public health, see the Express Lesson on p. 552 of this text.

OBSERVING UNHEALTHY BEHAVIORS

LIFE SKILL
Practicing Wellness

Materials

✔ pen or pencil
✔ paper

Procedure

1. **Choose** two students in your class to observe.

2. **Write** the following behaviors down the left side of the paper: "moving an object with hands," "chewing on fingernails," "touching pencil or pen to mouth," and "touching any part of the face with the hands."

3. **Note** the time, and then begin observing your subjects.

4. **Use** tick marks to record the number of times that each subject performs the activities on your list. Continue observing for 10 minutes. Add up the number of tick marks for each behavior.

5. **Record** your results on the board.

Conclusions

1. **Summarizing Results** Calculate the average number of times subjects engaged in each of the observed behaviors. **MATH SKILL**

2. **Analyzing Results** Which behavior did the subjects engage in the most? Which behavior did they engage in the least?

3. **CRITICAL THINKING** What are some consequences of the behaviors you observed on the spread of infectious diseases? Why might these behaviors be unhealthy?

4. **CRITICAL THINKING** Based on your results and analyses, what recommendations would you make that could improve individual health and help reduce the spread of diseases from person to person?

The most effective way to wash your hands is to count to ten while rubbing your hands in the soap and then rinse well. When should you wash your hands?

▶ before eating or preparing a meal
▶ after handling uncooked meats or raw vegetables
▶ after going to the bathroom or changing a baby's diaper
▶ after touching or playing with animals or working outdoors
▶ after you sneeze or cough into your hand
▶ after coming into contact with a sick person

Don't Share Personal Items You should also avoid sharing personal items, such as toothbrushes. Avoid sharing the same food or drink with others. Sharing these things increases the chance that you might pass an illness to another person or contract a disease from someone who is infected.

Cover Your Mouth! You should cover your mouth when you sneeze or cough. After sneezing, you should wipe your nose with disposable tissues and throw them away immediately. This practice helps reduce the chance that others will become infected.

Be On Guard Outdoors Following a few simple rules while outdoors can greatly reduce your chances of contracting a disease from animals or insects.

▶ When in long grass, wear long-sleeved shirts and pants.
▶ Use a safe and effective insect repellant when necessary.
▶ Avoid contact with animals that behave strangely.
▶ Avoid drinking and swimming in remote streams, rivers, or lake waters.

Count to 10, and then rinse well.

SECTION 2

REVIEW   *Answer the following questions on a separate piece of paper.*

Using Key Terms

1. **Define** the term *inflammation*.
2. **Define** the term *vaccine*.
3. **Name** the term for a "cell in the blood whose primary job is to defend the body against disease."

Understanding Key Ideas

4. **Name** two physical barriers that your body has to guard against pathogens.
5. **Identify** which of the following is *not* a part of the body's immune system.
   - **a.** antibodies
   - **b.** white blood cells
   - **c.** lymph nodes
   - **d.** heart

6. **Identify** which of the following activities can help you stay well.
   - **a.** avoiding exercise
   - **b.** getting enough sleep
   - **c.** sharing a toothbrush
   - **d.** sharing a drink
7. **Describe** how vaccinations work to protect the body from illness.
8. **LIFE SKILL** **Setting Goals** State three things you can do to help yourself when you are sick.
9. **LIFE SKILL** **Practicing Wellness** List four times when you should wash your hands.

Critical Thinking

10. **Explain** why it is important that your body has several different defenses to protect you from pathogens.

Common Infectious Diseases

OBJECTIVES

State why diseases affect everybody.

Identify two bacterial diseases, and describe their symptoms and ways that they are spread.

Identify two viral diseases, and describe their symptoms and ways that they are spread.

List examples of fungal, protozoan, and parasitic infections, and describe their symptoms.

Name two organizations in your community that help treat and prevent the spread of infectious diseases. **LIFE SKILL**

KEY TERMS

meningitis an inflammation of the membranes covering the brain and spinal cord

salmonellosis a bacterial infection of the digestive system, usually spread by eating contaminated food

hepatitis an inflammation of the liver

amebic dysentery an inflammation of the intestine caused by an ameba

Camelia could not believe that she was home in bed and sick with pneumonia. She did not understand how she could have become sick. After all, she ate a healthy diet, exercised regularly, and always had her yearly checkups at the doctor. Why was she sick?

Diseases Affect Everybody

No matter how healthy we are, we all become ill from infectious diseases sometime during our lives. There are so many different pathogens in so many places that it is impossible to avoid them. Sometimes, the illness may be minor. At other times, however, serious complications may arise. Although the young and the elderly are most susceptible to infectious diseases, we are all capable of being infected.

Our best defense against pathogens is to avoid behaviors that increase our chances of becoming infected. In general, the more you know about preventing a disease and identifying its symptoms, the better your chances are of avoiding it.

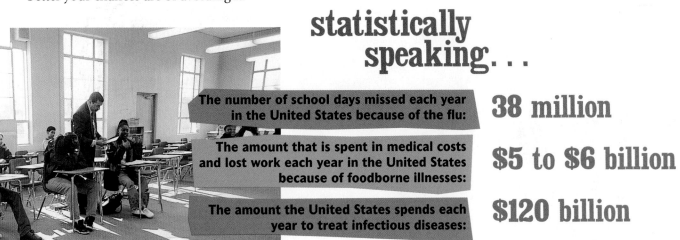

statistically speaking...

The number of school days missed each year in the United States because of the flu:	**38 million**
The amount that is spent in medical costs and lost work each year in the United States because of foodborne illnesses:	**$5 to $6 billion**
The amount the United States spends each year to treat infectious diseases:	**$120 billion**

Common Bacterial Diseases

Bacteria are found on almost everything around us, from our books and clothes to our food. Many bacteria, however, prefer to live in dark, warm, and moist places such as inside our bodies. In the human body, bacteria can grow and multiply quickly. As a result, it is not surprising that diseases caused by bacteria are very common.

Tetanus

Symptoms
severe muscle spasms

Transmission
tetanus causing bacteria are commonly found in soil; can enter body through cuts or wounds

Prevention
series of vaccinations during childhood; boosters every 5 to 10 years as an adult

Treatment
antibiotics

Tetanus immune globulin

Strep throat

Symptoms
sore throat, fever, and yellow or white specks on tonsils

Transmission
spread by contact with mucus from an infected person

Prevention
avoiding contact with infected person

Treatment
antibiotics

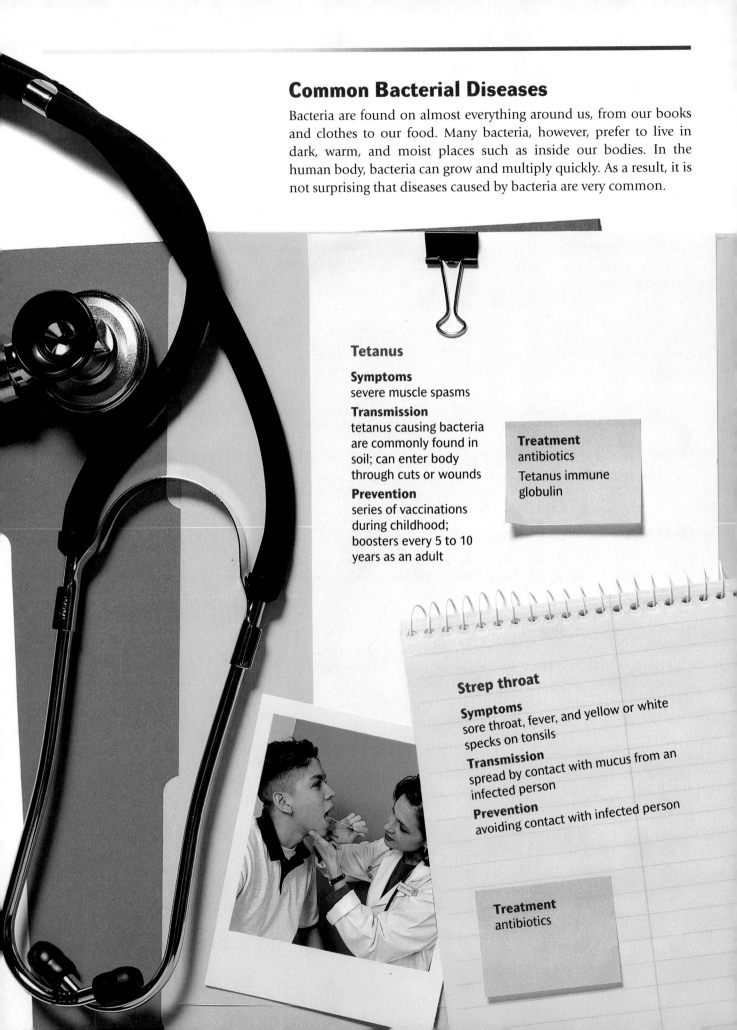

Maybe you've had strep throat or a sinus infection, or maybe you have gotten food poisoning after eating chicken that wasn't thoroughly cooked. Bacteria are responsible for causing these illnesses, in addition to **meningitis, salmonellosis,** and many others.

Meningitis
an inflammation of the membranes covering the brain and spinal cord; can also be caused by viruses or sometimes by fungi or parasites

Symptoms
severe headache, fever, stiff neck, sensitivity to light, and nausea

Transmission
pathogen is spread by contact with saliva or mucus from an infected person

Treatment
antibiotics, if bacterial disease is caught early

Prevention
vaccination for some bacterial forms of meningitis, avoiding contact with infected persons

Sinus infections

Symptoms
headache; tenderness of the sinuses; thick, greenish mucus; and feeling of pressure in your head

Transmission
bacteria are spread by contact with mucus from the nose or throat of an infected person

Prevention
avoiding infected person and allergens, such as cigarette smoke and other air pollutants

Treatment
antibiotics

Salmonellosis
a bacterial infection of the digestive system, usually spread by eating contaminated foods

Symptoms
headache, cramps, diarrhea, nausea, vomiting

Transmission
eating food from an infected animal or food contaminated by an infected person

Prevention
thorough cooking of animal food products, hand washing, refrigeration

Treatment
over the counter medicines to treat symptoms, sometimes requires antibiotics

Common Viral Diseases

You have probably contracted one or more viral diseases before. Maybe you have suffered through a few colds and the flu. Some viral diseases, such as the flu, can often be handled by your body, while others, such as **hepatitis,** are more serious. In **Table 1,** you'll learn about the symptoms, transmission, prevention, and treatment of several viral diseases.

Table 1	Common Viral Diseases			
Type	**Symptoms**	**Transmission**	**Prevention**	**Treatment**
Flu	headache, sore muscles, sore throat, fever, vomiting, fatigue, and cough	spread by contact with saliva or mucus of an infected person and by personal contact	vaccination and avoiding contact with infected person	rest and plenty of fluids; see doctor for flu medications and if symptoms become severe
Cold	scratchy, sore throat; sneezing and runny nose; and mild cough	spread by contact with saliva or mucus of an infected person	washing hands regularly and avoiding contact with infected person	rest and plenty of fluids; no specific treatments; see doctor if symptoms become severe
Mumps	pain and swelling of glands in the throat, fever, and headache	spread by contact with infected airborne droplets and personal contact	vaccination	see doctor; rest and plenty of fluids; no specific treatments
Measles	fatigue, runny nose, cough, slight fever, small white dots in mouth, and rash covering body	spread by contact with saliva or mucus of infected person	vaccination	see doctor; rest and plenty of fluids; no specific treatments
Mononucleosis	fever, swollen lymph nodes, sore throat, and weakness	spread by contact with saliva or mucus of an infected person	avoiding drinking from the same glass and eating from the same food as other people	see doctor; rest and plenty of fluids; no specific treatments
Hepatitis	inflammation of the liver, jaundice (yellowing of the skin), fever, and darkening of the urine	spread by contact with bodily fluids of infected person and by ingesting contaminated food or water	vaccination for hepatitis A and B, washing hands regularly, and avoiding contact with infected person	see doctor; rest and medications; no cure for hepatitis B and C

Other Common Infections

When we think of infections, we often think of infections caused by bacteria or viruses. We may forget that there are several other kinds of pathogens in our environment, such as fungi, protozoa, and parasites.

www.scilinks.org/health
Topic: Head Lice
HealthLinks code: HH4072

HEALTH LINKS.
THE WORLD'S A CLICK AWAY
Maintained by the National Science Teachers Association

Fungal Infections Fungi are an important source of food and drugs, but some kinds of fungi can actually be harmful. Athlete's foot, jock itch, and ringworm are examples of infections caused by fungi. These infections occur most often when the specific type of fungus comes into contact with skin that is warm and moist. With fungal infections, the skin can become itchy and red and lesions may appear.

The best way to prevent fungal infections is to keep clothing, such as socks and underwear, dry and to maintain good personal hygiene. If a fungal infection does arise, over-the-counter medications will usually kill the fungus. If the symptoms continue or become severe, it is important to see a doctor immediately.

Protozoan Infections Protozoa are most often found in water and soil. About 20,000 kinds of protozoa exist, but only a small number of them cause disease. Some infections caused by protozoa include amebic dysentery, malaria, and African sleeping sickness. **Amebic dysentery** (uh MEE bik DIS uhn TER ee) is an inflammation of the intestine caused by an ameba. Symptoms of amebic dysentery include nausea, diarrhea, and sometimes fever.

The most widespread and serious of the protozoan infections worldwide is malaria. Worldwide, several million people are infected with malaria each year. Approximately one million people die from malaria each year. Malaria is caused by a protozoan that is passed from one person to another by mosquitoes. Symptoms include fever, chills, headache, fatigue, and nausea. Malaria can be prevented and treated with antimalarial drugs prescribed by a doctor.

Tapeworms attach to the intestinal wall using suckers and hooks on their heads. Among the tapeworms that can infect humans are beef, pork, dog, rat, and fish tapeworms.

Parasitic Infections Diseases can also be caused by animal parasites. Animals such as hookworms, flukes, pinworms, and tapeworms can live inside the body and cause disease. Examples of animal parasites that live on the body are lice, leeches, ticks, and fleas. Animal parasites can be spread to and infect the body in several ways. Eating infected food, drinking infected water, having contact with infected soil, and being bitten by infected insects are some of the ways that a person can contract a parasitic infection.

Head lice are one of the most common parasitic infections in the United States. Head lice can often be seen with the naked eye and often cause itchiness and sores on the head. The best way to treat head lice is through a combination of using over-the-counter medications, washing linens, soaking brushes and combs in hot water and soap, and vacuuming carpet and furniture.

Working Toward a Healthy Future

Today you can travel almost anywhere in the world in just a few hours. International air travel not only has made it easier for people to see the world but also has made it easier for diseases to spread from country to country. Because diseases can be spread so easily, it is important for everyone throughout the world to work together to fight disease.

Because diseases can be spread so quickly and easily, doctors have had difficulty controlling infectious diseases. Government scientists at the Centers for Disease Control and Prevention (CDC) and the National Institutes of Health (NIH) are now watching for new diseases that may enter the country.

It is important to have an efficient and effective public health system to prevent or manage an infectious disease outbreak. Even though great progress has been made in the ability to protect the public's health, the methods and financial resources needed for such progress are not available in many parts of the world. As a result, public health problems and priorities vary throughout the world.

Public health organizations also work to control or eliminate diseases. Health organizations are working hard to control or eliminate diseases such as measles, mumps, rubella, and polio. Smallpox is an example of a disease that has been declared eradicated in nature. However, even with advances in medicine and great effort, eliminating a disease is very difficult.

Even if we are able to control or eliminate many diseases, new diseases may be discovered and diseases that we have under control may become resistant to our medicines. Thus, we must maintain healthy habits and lifestyles to ensure global health for the future.

Because it is so easy for diseases to travel from one country to another, it is important that the effort to improve public health be a global one.

SECTION 3

REVIEW

Answer the following questions on a separate piece of paper.

Using Key Terms

1. **Describe** the symptoms of salmonellosis.
2. **Identify** the term for "inflammation of the liver."
3. **Define** the term *amebic dysentery*.

Understanding Key Ideas

4. **Identify** why anyone can become affected by an infectious disease.
5. **Identify** one method used to prevent tetanus.
   a. antibiotics
   b. skin test
   c. series of vaccinations
   d. muscle spasms
6. **Identify** three symptoms of bacterial meningitis.

7. **Classify** the following as bacterial diseases or viral diseases.
   a. strep throat
   b. tuberculosis
   c. measles
   d. mononucleosis
8. **Describe** the symptoms of hepatitis.
9. **Identify** the most widespread disease caused by protozoa.
10. **Name** three ways to treat head lice.

Critical Thinking

11. **LIFE SKILL** **Using Community Resources** Explain why every community should have organizations that help treat and prevent the spread of disease.

Highlights

Key Terms

SECTION 1

infectious disease (316)
pathogen (317)
bacteria (317)
virus (317)
fungus (317)
antibiotic resistance (320)

SECTION 2

inflammation (323)
lymphatic system (324)
white blood cells (324)
vaccine (325)
symptom (326)

SECTION 3

meningitis (331)
salmonellosis (331)
hepatitis (332)
amebic dysentery (333)

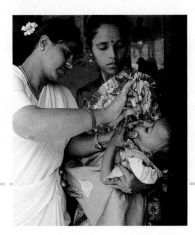

The Big Picture

✔ An infectious disease is any disease that is caused by an agent that has invaded the body.

✔ Infectious diseases can be caused by several kinds of pathogens, such as bacteria, viruses, fungi, protozoa, or parasites.

✔ Infectious diseases can be spread from one person to another or through food, water, the environment, or animals.

✔ Specific types of pathogens have specific treatments. Antibiotics are used to treat bacterial infections. Viral diseases cannot be treated with antibiotics.

✔ Antibiotic resistance is a growing problem that is a threat to everyone's health.

✔ The body's first line of defense against pathogens includes the skin, mucous membranes, and body chemicals.

✔ Inflammation protects your body from pathogens that cross the body's first line of defense. The injured area swells and turns red.

✔ The immune system uses immune cells to target and kill specific pathogens.

✔ Eating a balanced diet, reducing stress, exercising regularly, and keeping up to date on all your vaccinations are things a person can do to help maintain his or her health.

✔ When you are sick, it is important to stay home, rest, and follow the directions of your doctor.

✔ Being vaccinated, washing hands frequently, and not sharing personal items help prevent the spread of disease.

✔ Infectious diseases can affect everyone, especially the young and the elderly.

✔ Bacteria are found everywhere and are a common cause of disease. Strep throat, salmonellosis, and sinus infections are common bacterial diseases.

✔ Although there are no cures for many viral diseases, rest and fluids can help speed recovery. The common cold, flu, hepatitis, mononucleosis, and chickenpox are diseases caused by viruses.

✔ Diseases caused by fungi, protozoa, and animal parasites are treated differently than diseases caused by bacteria and viruses are. Worldwide, protozoa are the cause of several serious infections, such as malaria.

✔ Increases in world travel and poverty in many parts of the world have made it more difficult for doctors to fight infectious diseases.

✔ Public health organizations work to control or eliminate diseases.

CHAPTER 13

Review

Using Key Terms

amebic dysentery (333)
antibiotic resistance (320)
bacteria (317)
fungus (317)
hepatitis (332)
infectious disease (316)
inflammation (323)
lymphatic system (324)

meningitis (331)
pathogen (317)
salmonellosis (331)
symptom (326)
vaccine (325)
virus (317)
white blood cell (324)

1. For each definition below, choose the key term that best matches the definition.
   a. a bacterial infection of the digestive system, usually spread by eating infected food.
   b. a network of vessels that carries a clear fluid called lymph throughout the body
   c. any agent that causes disease
   d. a reaction to injury or infection, characterized by pain, redness, and swelling
   e. a change that a person notices in his or her body or mind that is caused by a disease or disorder
   f. blood cells whose primary job is to defend the body against disease

2. Explain the relationship between the key terms in each of the following pairs.
   a. *hepatitis* and *virus*
   b. *bacteria* and *antibiotic resistance*
   c. *amebic dysentery* and *meningitis*

Understanding Key Ideas

Section 1

3. Which of the following do not cause infectious diseases?
   a. bacteria
   b. white blood cells
   c. fungi
   d. viruses

4. Describe the differences between bacteria and viruses.

5. List four ways that infectious diseases can be spread.

6. What kinds of diseases can antibiotics cure?

7. What are three ways that you can help prevent the spread of antibiotic resistant bacteria?

Section 2

8. Which of the following is part of the body's first line of defense?
   a. the skin
   b. red blood cells
   c. white blood cells
   d. immune system

9. Which of the following is part of the body's inflammatory response?
   a. sleeping
   b. swelling
   c. sweating
   d. tears

10. What are three activities we can do to stay well?

11. Name three signs that indicate you need to seek medical care.

12. Describe the role of white blood cells in developing immunity from pathogens.

13. What are three things you should do when you are sick?

14. What are three things you can do to prevent the spread of infectious diseases?

Section 3

15. Which of the following statements describes why all people can become infected by an infectious disease?
    a. Pathogens are in so many places.
    b. Bacteria live inside our bodies.
    c. The elderly are more susceptible to infectious diseases than the young are.
    d. none of the above

16. What is the best way to keep from being infected with strep throat?

17. Tetanus is a _____ disease.
    a. viral
    b. fungal
    c. parasitic
    d. bacterial

18. Which of the following are symptoms of measles?
    a. inflamed liver
    b. swollen glands
    c. muscle spasms
    d. rash covering body

19. Worldwide, what is the most common protozoan disease?

20. **CRITICAL THINKING** Explain why it is important to have an efficient public health system if an outbreak of a disease occurs.

Interpreting Graphics

Study the figure below to answer the questions that follow.

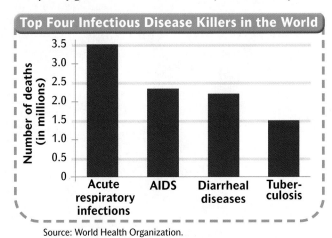

Top Four Infectious Disease Killers in the World

Source: World Health Organization.

21. What is the number of deaths due to acute respiratory infections?

22. What is the total number of deaths due to AIDS and tuberculosis? **MATH SKILL**

23. **CRITICAL THINKING** Why do you think acute respiratory infections are the cause of such a large number of deaths?

Activities

24. **Health and You** Contact your doctor, and ask for a copy of your immunization record. Make a list of diseases you have been vaccinated for, and research when you need your next booster shots.

25. **Health and Your Community** Choose a disease listed on pp. 326 and 327 and research that disease. Explore what measures are being taken by public health organizations to prevent the disease. Write a one-page report to explain your findings. **WRITING SKILL**

26. **Health and You** Work with a partner to create a list of all of the objects that come into contact with your eyes, nose, and mouth each day that could contain pathogens. **WRITING SKILL**

Action Plan

27. **LIFE SKILL** **Assessing Your Health** Establishing healthy patterns of living can help reduce the chance of spreading disease. Explain five habits that you can begin now to help keep you from spreading infectious diseases.

Standardized Test Prep

Read the passage below, and then answer the questions that follow. **READING SKILL** **WRITING SKILL**

Tanita went to the doctor 2 weeks ago for a sore throat. Her doctor told her that she had strep throat and that she needed to take antibiotics for 2 weeks and rest. After a few days of rest and taking her medicine, Tanita felt much better. She decided that she had taken an <u>adequate</u> amount of antibiotics to cure her strep throat. So she decided to stop taking the pills and went back to school. Yesterday, however, after band practice, she began to have a fever and sore throat again. Tanita couldn't understand why she felt bad again. After all, she had taken medicine and rested, as her doctor ordered.

28. In this passage, the word *adequate* means
    A wrong.
    B unfortunate.
    C enough.
    D expensive.

29. What can you infer from reading this passage?
    E Tanita does not like band practice.
    F Tanita did not take enough medicine to completely cure her infection.
    G Tanita works at a bank.
    H none of the above

30. Write a paragraph describing why Tanita might have become sick again. Explain what might happen if she takes the same antibiotic again.

31. Write a paragraph describing how Tanita could have prevented herself from getting strep throat in the beginning.

CHAPTER 14

Lifestyle Diseases

What's Your Health IQ?

BEHAVIOR

Indicate how frequently you engage in each of the following behaviors (1 = never; 2 = occasionally; 3 = most of the time; 4 = all of the time). Total your points, and then turn to p. 638.

1. I eat foods that are low in saturated fats and high in fiber.

2. I eat and drink foods that are low in added salt and sugar.

3. I exercise at least 60 minutes every day.

4. I avoid tobacco products and being in smoky environments.

5. I have yearly medical exams.

6. When outside, I wear sunscreen.

7. I eat at least 2 servings of fruit a day.

Visit these Web sites for the latest health information:

HEALTH LINKS
THE WORLD'S A CLICK AWAY

Find more information whenever you see a HealthLinks box. Go to **scilinks.org/health**, and type in the HealthLinks code.

Find worksheets and other materials that go with your textbook at **go.hrw.com**.

 Current Health

Check out *Current Health®* articles related to this chapter by visiting **go.hrw.com**. Just type in the keyword **HH4 CH14.**

Lifestyle and Lifestyle Diseases

OBJECTIVES

Describe how lifestyle can lead to diseases.

List four controllable and four uncontrollable risk factors for lifestyle diseases.

State two actions you can take now to lower your risk for developing a lifestyle disease later in life. **LIFE SKILL**

KEY TERMS

lifestyle disease a disease that is caused partly by unhealthy behaviors and partly by other factors

Myth

Because diabetes runs in my family, I will get it, too.

Fact

Many factors, some of which you can control, contribute to diabetes.

Even though Devon is only 16 years old, he is worried about his health. Both his father and one of his grandfathers have diabetes. Devon worries that he will also develop diabetes, but he doesn't know what to do. He decides to talk to his doctor about ways to reduce his risk.

What Are Lifestyle Diseases?

A hundred years ago, the main causes of death in the United States were infectious diseases, such as tuberculosis (TB) and the flu. Today, however, we are better protected from infections because of good hygiene practices, better living conditions, and medical advances. So, although infectious diseases are still a serious health problem, the top causes of death in the United States today are lifestyle diseases. **Lifestyle diseases** are diseases that are caused partly by unhealthy behaviors and partly by other factors.

What Causes Lifestyle Diseases? Lifestyle diseases are so called because a person's lifestyle (habits, behaviors, and practices) largely determine whether the person develops a lifestyle disease. Lifestyle diseases include cardiovascular disease, many forms of cancer, and two types of diabetes.

Personal habits, behaviors, and practices, however, are not the only factors that determine whether a person develops a lifestyle disease. Other factors that we cannot control, such as age, gender, and genes, also contribute to a person's chances of developing a lifestyle disease.

It is important to know the factors that contribute to lifestyle diseases, because behaviors that lead to lifestyle diseases later in life can start when you are very young. In Devon's case, diabetes runs in his family. The chance that Devon will develop diabetes is greater than it would be if there was not a history of diabetes in his family. However, by practicing a healthy lifestyle now, Devon can reduce his risk of developing diabetes.

Risk Factors for Lifestyle Diseases

When determining if a person might develop a disease, a doctor looks at the person's risk factors. A *risk factor* is anything that increases the likelihood of injury, disease, or other health problems.

Controllable Risk Factors   Taking charge of the risk factors that you can control may greatly decrease your chances of developing a lifestyle disease. Controllable risk factors include habits, behaviors, and practices that you can change, as shown in **Figure 1.** For example, controllable risk factors include

- ▶ your diet and body weight
- ▶ your daily levels of physical activity
- ▶ your level of sun exposure
- ▶ smoking and alcohol abuse

Thus, exercising regularly, eating a healthy diet, and not smoking will help you reduce your risk of lifestyle diseases later in life. Because there are many risk factors that you have little or no control over, it is important to start healthy habits that you can control early.

Uncontrollable Risk Factors   Some risk factors that contribute to your chances of developing a lifestyle disease are out of your control. However, it is important to understand what these factors are and how they affect your health. Uncontrollable risk factors include

- ▶ **Age** As you age, your body begins to change. As a result of aging, the body has a harder time protecting itself. Therefore, the chances of developing a lifestyle disease increase as you age.

Figure 1

Some of the risk factors for lifestyle diseases are beyond your control. But you can control many risk factors, such as smoking, physical activity, sun exposure, and diet.

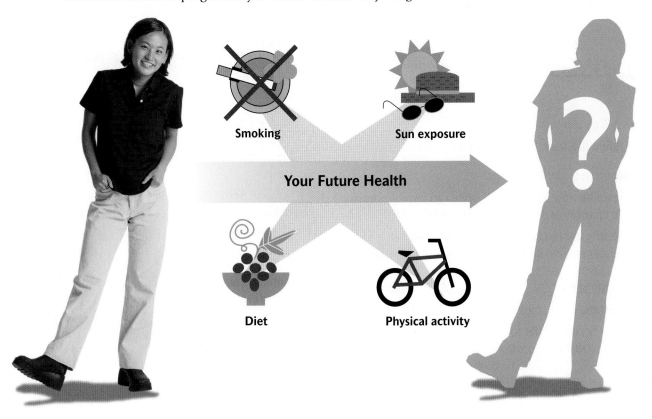

Smoking

Sun exposure

Your Future Health

Diet

Physical activity

Although we all have uncontrollable risk factors such as age, gender, ethnicity, and heredity, there are still many behaviors you can practice to help lower your risk of developing a lifestyle disease.

▶ **Gender** Certain diseases are more common among members of one gender. For example, men have a greater risk of heart disease than women do, especially earlier in life. Women have a greater risk of breast cancer than men do.

▶ **Ethnicity** Your ethnicity can also influence your chances of developing a lifestyle disease. For example, African Americans are more likely to develop high blood pressure than individuals of European descent are. Mexican Americans have a higher risk of developing diabetes than individuals of European descent do. Asian Americans historically have had a lower incidence of heart disease than people of European descent have had. However, Asian Americans have recently begun to develop heart disease in greater numbers. It is believed that a change to eating a high-fat, low-fiber diet is the main reason for the increase.

▶ **Heredity** In the same way that genes determine your natural hair color, genes can also determine your chances of developing certain lifestyle diseases. For example, in some families heredity may increase the chances that a family member will develop cancer.

However, it is important to remember that just because you have an uncontrollable risk factor for a lifestyle disease, you will not necessarily develop that disease. For example, if you have a hereditary tendency to develop heart disease, you can make healthy food choices and exercise regularly and you may never develop heart disease. You may, however, need to work harder to prevent heart problems than other people do.

SECTION 1

REVIEW   *Answer the following questions on a separate piece of paper.*

Using Key Terms

1. **Define** the term *lifestyle disease.*

Understanding Key Ideas

2. **Describe** how a person's lifestyle can increase his or her chances of developing a lifestyle disease.

3. **Identify** the term for "anything that increases the likelihood of injury, disease or other health problems."
   a. unavoidable chance c. hereditary tendency
   b. risk factor   d. none of the above

4. **List** three controllable risk factors for lifestyle diseases.

5. **Classify** each of the following risk factors as *controllable* or *uncontrollable.*
   a. age   c. diet
   b. smoking d. genes

6. **Summarize** how each of the following can increase your risk of developing a lifestyle disease.
   a. age   c. ethnicity
   b. gender   d. heredity

7. **LIFE SKILL** **Setting Goals** Describe two actions you can take today to help reduce your chances of developing a lifestyle disease.

Critical Thinking

8. Why might a person who has lead a healthy lifestyle develop a lifestyle disease?

9. Do people have an obligation to take the best care of themselves that they can? Explain.

Cardiovascular Diseases

OBJECTIVES

Summarize how one's lifestyle can contribute to cardiovascular diseases.

Describe four types of cardiovascular diseases.

Identify two ways to detect and two ways to treat cardiovascular diseases.

List four things you can do to lower your risk for cardiovascular diseases. **LIFE SKILL**

KEY TERMS

cardiovascular disease (CVD) a disease or disorder that results from progressive damage to the heart and blood vessels

stroke a sudden attack of weakness or paralysis that occurs when a blood vessel in the brain bursts or becomes blocked

blood pressure the force that blood exerts against the inside walls of a blood vessel

heart attack a sudden loss of blood flow to the heart muscle

atherosclerosis a disease characterized by the buildup of fatty materials on the inside walls of the arteries

X avier just got back from a physical exam. The doctor told Xavier that he had high blood pressure. Xavier knew that high blood pressure was common in his family. He felt that he had already taken some steps to lower his risk.

What Are Cardiovascular Diseases?

Together, the heart and blood vessels make up the cardiovascular system. The diseases and disorders that result from progressive damage to the heart and blood vessels are called **cardiovascular diseases (CVDs).** You may not have heard that term before, but you've probably heard of some kinds of cardiovascular disease: heart attack, stroke, atherosclerosis, and high blood pressure.

Cardiovascular disease is the leading cause of death in the United States. Nearly all of the people who die from CVD are over the age of 40. So why should you worry about CVD now? The damage that leads to CVD builds up over many years and may begin as early as childhood. So, the sooner you start taking care of your heart and blood vessels, the more likely you are to avoid developing a CVD.

Lifestyle and Cardiovascular Disease Why do some people die from cardiovascular disease while others never have any problems? Genetic differences between people are one reason. But whether you develop a cardiovascular disease and how serious it becomes also depend on how you live. For example, smoking, being overweight, having high blood pressure, having high blood cholesterol, or having diabetes greatly increase your risk of developing a cardiovascular disease.

"**High blood pressure runs in my family.** So, my dad and I are **cutting down** on the amount of **salt** we eat."

Types of Cardiovascular Diseases

About 70 million Americans have some form of cardiovascular disease. Heart attacks, strokes, and other kinds of cardiovascular disease kill about 1 million Americans every year. This number is almost twice the number of people who die from cancer.

Stroke

Each year about 163,000 people die from strokes. **Strokes** are sudden attacks of weakness or paralysis that occur when a blood vessel in the brain bursts or becomes blocked. In some cases, a blood clot (shown in yellow) lodges in one of the arteries in the brain. The clot cuts off circulation to nearby brain cells. If the clot isn't removed, the cells begin to die. Strokes can also occur when a hole forms in one of the vessels inside the skull and blood leaks into the brain. Internal bleeding can severely damage the brain.

Get medical help immediately if you or anyone around you has the following symptoms:

- ▶ sudden numbness or weakness of the face, an arm, or a leg
- ▶ trouble seeing in one or both eyes
- ▶ sudden dizziness or loss of coordination
- ▶ sudden, severe headache with no known cause

High Blood Pressure

Doctors call *high blood pressure*, or *hypertension*, the silent killer, because many people don't know that their blood pressure is high until they have a heart attack or stroke. **Blood pressure** is the force that blood exerts against the inside walls of a blood vessel. When blood pressure is too high, it puts extra strain on the walls of the vessels and on the heart.

High blood pressure can injure the walls of the blood vessels, which can lead to other cardiovascular diseases. It also makes the heart work harder, which can cause the heart to weaken or fail. High blood pressure can eventually damage the kidneys and eyes, too.

Heart Attack

The narrow *coronary arteries* that cover the heart deliver the nutrients and oxygen that the cells of the hard-working heart require. If a blood clot gets stuck in one of the coronary arteries, it can sharply reduce or shut off blood flow to the heart. As the heart cells stop functioning from lack of oxygen, the victim often has a crushing pain in the chest. The result of the reduced blood flow is a heart attack. A **heart attack** is a sudden loss of blood flow to the heart muscle. About one-third of heart attacks injure the heart so badly that they are fatal. Heart attacks can happen at any time, and sometimes they happen without any previous symptoms. Therefore, it is important to know the warning signs of a heart attack.

Warning Signs of a Heart Attack

▶ **Uncomfortable pressure, squeezing, or pain in the center of the chest that lasts for more than a few minutes**

▶ **Pain spreading to shoulders, neck, and arms**

▶ **Chest discomfort combined with lightheadedness, fainting, sweating, nausea, or shortness of breath**

Atherosclerosis

If you looked inside an old water pipe, you might find it clogged with buildup. Much less water can flow through such a pipe than through a new, clean one. Something similar can happen inside blood vessels. Fatty deposits known as *plaques* build up on the inside walls of arteries and interfere with blood flow. The disease characterized by the buildup of fatty materials on the inside walls of the arteries is called **atherosclerosis** (ATH uhr OH skluh ROH sis).

Atherosclerosis is dangerous for two reasons. First, it can reduce or stop blood flow to certain parts of the body. Second, these deposits can break free and release clots into the bloodstream. If one of these clots gets stuck in one of the coronary arteries, the result is a heart attack. If the clot lodges in the brain, a stroke results.

Normal artery

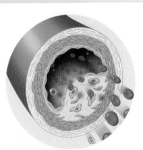

Artery with fatty buildup (Atherosclerosis)

Detecting and Treating Cardiovascular Diseases

The earlier you detect and treat a cardiovascular disease, the greater your chance of reducing the damage or danger of the disease.

Detecting Cardiovascular Diseases Doctors today can diagnose CVD earlier and more accurately than they could before. Methods to detect CVD include

▶ **Blood Pressure** To check your blood pressure, a healthcare provider wraps a cuff around your upper arm. The cuff is inflated until it is tight enough to stop bloodflow through the main artery in the arm. As air is slowly released from the cuff, the healthcare provider uses a stethoscope to listen for the heartbeat sound as blood begins to flow through the artery. He or she records the number that appears on the instrument recording the pressure. This number indicates the *systolic pressure*, the maximum blood pressure when the heart contracts.

As the cuff deflates further, the healthcare provider listens until the sound of the heartbeat disappears and the blood flows steadily through the artery. He or she records this second number. The second number, the *diastolic pressure*, indicates the blood pressure between heart contractions.

HEALTH Handbook For more information about the circulatory system, see the Express Lesson on pp. 532–535 of this text.

Analyzing DATA

Checking Blood Pressure

Blood pressure is measured in millimeters of mercury (mm Hg). Blood pressure is expressed as two numbers. In the diagram, the number read at the end of the yellow bar indicates the pressure.

1 The first number measured indicates the systolic pressure. Systolic pressure is the maximum pressure when the heart contracts.

2 The second number measured indicates the diastolic pressure. Diastolic pressure is the pressure between heart contractions.

Your Turn

1. What is this person's systolic pressure?

2. What is this person's diastolic pressure?

3. **CRITICAL THINKING** Does this person have high blood pressure? If so, what can he or she do to reduce it?

4. **CRITICAL THINKING** If a woman has a blood pressure of 100/70, what is the systolic pressure? What is the diastolic pressure? Is her blood pressure low, normal, or high?

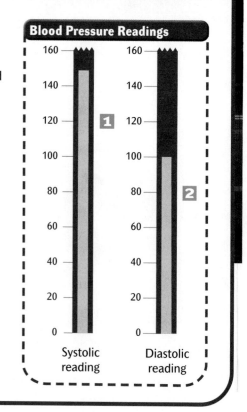

Blood Pressure Readings

Systolic reading Diastolic reading

Normal blood pressure generally falls between 80/50 and 130/85 mm Hg (a unit for measuring pressure). Blood pressure over 140/90 is considered high.

▶ **Electrocardiogram** One of the most common cardiovascular tests is the *electrocardiogram,* sometimes called an *ECG* or *EKG.* An EKG measures the electrical activity of the heart. EKGs can detect damage to the heart and an irregular beat.

▶ **Ultrasound** To look at the heart in action, doctors sometimes use ultrasound, which is also used to take pictures of babies in the womb. Doctors can see the pumping of the heart and the action of the heart valves.

▶ **Angiography** Angiography (AN jee AHG ruh fee) is a test in which dye is injected into the coronary arteries. An instrument called a fluoroscope is used to see where the dye travels and to look for blockages in the coronary arteries.

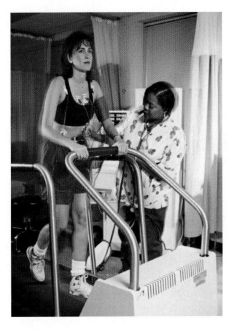

Using an EKG machine, doctors can detect damage to the heart and an irregular beat by monitoring the electrical impulses of the heart.

Treating Cardiovascular Diseases Today, we have many choices for treating cardiovascular disease (CVD).

▶ **Diet and Exercise** Changing the diet and exercise habits of a patient is an important step in treating CVD. A low-fat, low-salt, and a low-cholesterol diet, along with light physical activity, is often prescribed to people with signs of CVD. Exercise is normally carried out under a doctor's supervision.

▶ **Medicines** Many medicines are available to treat CVDs. For example, some medicines keep the blood vessels from constricting. This helps keep blood pressure down.

▶ **Surgery** If the coronary arteries are badly clogged, doctors often perform a *coronary artery bypass operation.* Surgeons remove a length of vein from the patient and transplant it to the heart. They attach one end of the vein to the aorta and the other end to the coronary artery just below the blockage. Thus, blood can detour around the blockage and reach the heart muscle.

▶ **Angioplasty** A technique called *angioplasty* requires a doctor to insert a tube with a balloon at the tip into a blood vessel in the patient's leg. The tube and balloon are guided through vessels into the blocked artery. Once the balloon is in place, it is inflated to flatten the plaque and open the artery. Sometimes, a metal cage called a *stent* is left in the artery to prop open the artery walls.

▶ **Pacemakers** Sometimes, the heart needs help to keep beating. If the heart cannot keep a steady rhythm, surgeons may implant an artificial pacemaker in the chest. *Artificial pacemakers* are small, battery-powered electronic devices that stimulate the heart to contract.

▶ **Transplants** If the heart becomes so weak or diseased that it can't do its job, surgeons may replace it. Depending on the emergency, doctors may use artificial hearts or hearts taken from people who gave permission for their organs to be removed after their death. An operation to replace a heart is called a *heart transplant.*

▣ **internet** connect

www.scilinks.org/health
Topic: Cardiovascular Problems
HealthLinks code: HH4030

HEALTH
LINKS. *THE WORLD'S A CLICK AWAY*

Maintained by the
National Science
Teachers Association

Preventing Cardiovascular Diseases

The doctors and surgeons who treat CVD would prefer that you protect your heart and blood vessels before you get sick. Because CVD can begin as early as childhood, it is important to take steps now, such as doing the healthy activity shown in **Figure 2,** to ensure a healthy future. The following advice can help you lower your risk of CVD.

▶ **Trim the fat, and hold the salt.** Limit your consumption of saturated fats, cholesterol, and salt. Instead, eat more fruits and vegetables, lean meats, and plenty of products made from whole grains.

▶ **Keep your weight near recommended levels.** Being overweight increases your risk of CVDs. Try to keep your weight near that recommended for your height and build.

▶ **Don't smoke.** Smoking speeds up atherosclerosis and increases your risk of having a stroke or heart attack. If you don't smoke, don't start. If you do smoke, the sooner you quit, the better.

▶ **Get moving.** Regular exercise benefits your cardiovascular system in many ways. It helps you feel less stressed by daily life and is also a good way to keep your weight under control.

▶ **Watch those numbers.** Have your blood pressure and cholesterol checked regularly. If you have a family history of CVD, you should get checked now. It may be wise to start a program to control your cholesterol, even this early.

▶ **Relax.** Stress, feelings of aggression, hostility, and anger have been shown to increase the risk of CVD. The increase in risk may be due to the physical effects of stress, such as raised blood pressure, or due to smoking, drinking, or poor eating—behaviors people sometimes use to deal with stress.

Figure 2

Exercising can help to lower your chance of developing a cardiovascular disease.

ACTIVITY *List two exercise activities that you enjoy or might enjoy doing to keep your heart healthy.*

SECTION 2

REVIEW   *Answer the following questions on a separate piece of paper.*

Using Key Terms

1. **Identify** the term for "a disease or disorder that results from progressive damage to the heart and blood vessels."

2. **Define** the term *stroke.*

3. **Name** the term for "the force that blood exerts against the inside walls of a blood vessel."

Understanding Key Ideas

4. **Describe** how lifestyle contributes to cardiovascular disease.

5. **Name** four types of cardiovascular diseases.

6. **Compare** the meaning of systolic pressure and diastolic pressure readings.

7. **Classify** each of the following as either a detection method or a treatment for cardiovascular diseases.
   a. EKG   c. angiography
   b. angioplasty   d. heart transplant

8. **LIFE SKILL** **Practicing Wellness** Identify the action that would help protect you from cardiovascular diseases.
   a. increasing salt intake c. exercising regularly
   b. smoking   d. eating a high-fat diet

Critical Thinking

9. Why do you think cardiovascular diseases are so common in the United States?

SECTION 3

Cancer

OBJECTIVES

Describe what cancer is.

Identify three causes of cancer.

Describe four types of cancer.

Identify three ways to detect and three ways to treat cancer.

List five things you can do to lower your risk for cancer. **LIFE SKILL**

KEY TERMS

cancer a disease caused by uncontrolled cell growth

malignant tumor a mass of cells that invades and destroys healthy tissue

benign tumor an abnormal, but usually harmless cell mass

chemotherapy the use of drugs to destroy cancer cells

Every day, millions of your body's cells die. At the same time, millions of cells divide to take the place of the dying cells. Healthy cells divide at a regulated rate. Sometimes, the cells keep dividing uncontrollably. The result is a common but dangerous disease called *cancer*.

What Is Cancer?

Cancer is a disease caused by uncontrolled cell growth. More than 1 million people in the United States are diagnosed with cancer every year. Cancer is the second leading cause of death, after CVD.

Cancer begins when the way that the body normally repairs and maintains itself breaks down. To replace cells that have died or are worn out, your body makes new ones. This process is usually carefully controlled to produce only a limited number of replacement cells. Sometimes, however, these controls break down, and some cells continue to divide again and again. These out-of-control cells quickly grow in number.

Tumors As the body produces more and more of these faulty cells, they form a clump known as a *tumor*. A **malignant tumor** (muh LIG nuhnt TOO muhr) is a mass of cells that invades and destroys healthy tissue. When a tumor spreads to the surrounding tissues, it eventually damages vital organs.

Sometimes, masses of cells that aren't cancerous develop in the body. A **benign tumor** (bi NIEN TOO muhr) is an abnormal, but usually harmless cell mass. Benign tumors typically do not invade and destroy tissue and do not spread. But these tumors can grow large enough that they negatively affect the nearby tissues and must be removed.

Teens who have successfully battled cancer, as Nicole Childs has, can continue to take part in normal activities and be successful in life.

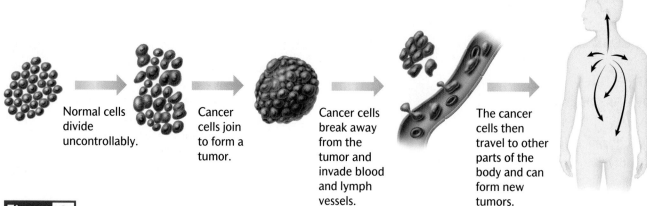

Normal cells divide uncontrollably.

Cancer cells join to form a tumor.

Cancer cells break away from the tumor and invade blood and lymph vessels.

The cancer cells then travel to other parts of the body and can form new tumors.

Figure 3

Occasionally, cells grow uncontrollably and become cancerous. Once this happens, the cancerous cells can then travel to other parts of the body.

Cancer Cells Are Destructive Cancer cells are very destructive to the body. They tear through and crush neighboring tissues, strangle blood vessels, and take nutrients that are needed by healthy cells. But what makes cancer especially dangerous is that the cells travel, as shown in **Figure 3.** This process is called *metastasis* (muh TAS tuh sis). The cancer cells get into the blood or lymph and move to other parts of the body. They then settle down and grow into new tumors. For example, lung cancer cells typically travel to the brain. Breast and prostate cancer cells often travel to the bones. Sometimes, the cancer cells that spread, not the original tumor, are what kill a person.

What Causes Cancer? Uncontrolled cell growth comes from damage to the genes that regulate the making of new cells. Genes that regulate cell division can become damaged in a variety of ways. A person can inherit "damaged," or mutated, genes from his or her parents. These genes make the person more likely to develop cancer than someone without those genes is. Cancer-causing agents or substances known as *carcinogens* can also be responsible for damaging genes. Some examples of carcinogens include

▶ certain viruses, such as human papilloma virus (HPV)
▶ radioactivity and ultraviolet (UV) radiation, an invisible type of energy from the sun (people are exposed to ultraviolet radiation while outside or in a tanning bed)
▶ chemicals found in tobacco smoke (for example, arsenic, benzene, and formaldehyde)
▶ asbestos (a material once widely used to make fireproof materials, electrical insulation, and other building supplies)

All of us are exposed to some carcinogens in our daily lives. They may be in our food, water, air, or environment. However, as you'll learn later, many cancers are caused by carcinogens that you can avoid. You can control how close you come to many of these carcinogens. Choosing to work, study, and live somewhere free from these carcinogens can reduce your chance of developing cancer.

internet connect

www.scilinks.org/health
Topic: Cancer Cells
HealthLinks code: HH4028

HEALTH LINKS. Maintained by the National Science Teachers Association

Types of Cancer

Although all kinds of cancer are the result of uncontrolled cell growth, each kind of cancer has its own characteristics. For example, cancer of the pancreas is very difficult to treat, while certain forms of skin cancer can be removed easily. **Table 1** describes several types of cancer.

Colon cancer

Table 1 Types of Cancer			
Name of cancer	What is it?	Estimated new cases each year	Estimated deaths each year
Breast	▶ cancer of the tissue of the breast; more common in women but can also be found in men	121,930	40,870
Prostate	▶ cancer of the prostate, a part of the male reproductive system	232,090	30,350
Respiratory	▶ cancer of the respiratory organs, such as the lungs, larynx, and bronchus; most forms linked to the use of tobacco	184,800	168,140
Colon	▶ cancer of the colon, an organ in the digestive system	104,950	56,290
Urinary	▶ cancer of the urinary organs, such as the bladder and kidneys	101,880	26,590
Lymphoma	▶ cancer of the lymph nodes or lymph tissue	63,740	20,610
Skin	▶ cancers that affect the skin, such as basal cell carcinoma and melanoma	66,000	10,590
Leukemia (loo KEE mee uh)	▶ cancer of the tissues that produce blood; more common in males than in females	34,810	22,570
Ovarian	▶ cancer of the ovaries, a part of the female reproductive system	22,220	16,210
Nervous system	▶ cancer of the brain, spinal cord, and other parts of the nervous system	18,500	12,760
Cervical (SUHR vi kuhl)	▶ cancer of the cervix, a part of the female reproductive system	10,370	3,710

Basal cell carcinoma

Source: American Cancer Society.

Detecting and Treating Cancer

Although all cancers have similar characteristics, they differ in how they are detected, how they are treated, and how they affect the person with the cancer.

Detecting Cancer   In addition to annual medical exams, there are many ways that cancer is detected.

> **Self-exams** Regular self-examinations of the skin, breasts, or testicles are important. Because skin cancer is so common, watch for any new growths; a sore that doesn't heal; and for shape, size, texture, or color changes to a mole or wart.

> **Biopsy** A *biopsy* is a sample of tissue taken from the body that is then examined. Biopsies are commonly used to determine what type of cancer a person has and whether a tumor is malignant or benign.

> **X rays** An X ray of the breasts to detect tumors is called a *mammogram*. Doctors recommend regular mammograms for women over the age of 40. Computerized axial tomography (CAT scan or CT) takes multiple X rays of some part of the body, which a computer then assembles into one image.

> **MRI** Magnetic resonance imaging, or MRI, uses a massive magnet and a computer to gather images of the body.

> **Blood and DNA tests** Blood tests can detect some cancers. For example, older men are often given a prostate specific antigen (PSA) test. This test looks for high levels of a protein produced by the prostate, a small gland near the bladder. DNA tests are used to detect the likelihood of developing cancer. More tests will become available as we learn more about human genes and the ways in which cancer develops and spreads.

You and your parents should talk to your doctor about getting regular cancer-screening tests. Use the CAUTION acronym in the margin to help you remember the warning signs of cancer.

Treating Cancer   Cancer is most treatable when it is caught early. Doctors battle the disease with several weapons. Techniques used to treat cancer include the following.

> **Surgery** An operation can remove some tumors. Surgery is most effective when the tumor is small, has not spread, and is located where removing it will not damage surrounding tissue.

> **Chemotherapy** Chemotherapy (KEE moh THER uh pee) is the use of drugs to destroy cancer cells. Unfortunately, chemotherapy also kills some of the body's healthy cells. It can cause side effects such as nausea, fatigue, vomiting, and hair loss.

> **Radiation therapy** As you learned earlier, radiation can cause cancer. But doctors also use radiation to destroy cancer cells, an approach called *radiation therapy*. Usually, a beam of radiation is fired at the tumor from outside the body.

Warning Signs of Cancer

Change in bowel or bladder habits

A sore that doesn't heal

Unusual bleeding or discharge

Thickening or a lump anywhere in the body

Indigestion or difficulty swallowing

Obvious change in a wart or mole

Nagging cough or hoarseness

Often, doctors recommend a combination of surgery, chemotherapy, and radiation. The success of any treatment depends on the type of cancer, how long the tumor has been growing, and whether the cancer has spread to other parts of the body. One promising treatment that scientists are trying to develop is to "starve" tumors by cutting off their blood supply. Another possibility is to create a cancer "vaccine" that would stimulate the immune system to destroy cancer cells.

Living with Cancer Cancer is difficult for the person who has cancer, as well as for loved ones. A person with cancer may often be tired or weak. They may also feel down. Children with cancer are often scared, confused, and upset by medical procedures and strange surroundings.

How can you help a person who has cancer? Be patient. Offer to spend time doing quiet things, such as talking, reading, or watching TV. Many people recover from cancer and go on to lead healthy lives. So, a positive outlook during the treatment process greatly helps.

LIFE SKILL Activity

Using Community Resources

Cancer Resources in Your Community

The first step toward learning more about cancer is to use the resources in your community. Taking advantage of these resources will help you protect yourself from having cancer in the future.

1. Your doctor can help you find reliable information on cancer.

2. Find out about nonprofit organizations in your city that are devoted to cancer awareness, such as the American Cancer Society.

3. The Internet can also provide valuable resources related to cancer. But be careful when using the Internet. Although many Web sites have reliable information, some have misleading and false information.

LIFE SKILL Using Community Resources

1. Identify programs offered by cancer resource centers in your community.

2. What are two ways that you can promote cancer awareness in your community?

 HEALTH Handbook For more information about evaluating health Web sites, see the Express Lesson on pp. 564–565 of this text.

Kick Butts Day is a national campaign that encourages students to speak out against tobacco use. Tobacco use increases your risk of certain cancers.

Preventing Cancer

Taking charge of these five controllable risk factors can greatly reduce your risk of getting cancer.

1. **No butts about it: don't smoke.** Tobacco use is responsible for about 30 percent of the deaths due to cancer in the United States. People who use tobacco are prone to cancers of the mouth, throat, esophagus, pancreas, and colon. Despite what you might hear, there is no safe form of tobacco.

2. **Safeguard your skin.** Limit your exposure to the damaging UV radiation that causes skin cancer. You can do so by protecting exposed areas of skin with sunscreen, even on cloudy days. Do not sunbathe, use tanning beds, or use sunlamps.

3. **Eat your veggies, and cut the fat.** No diet can guarantee that you won't get cancer. However, people who eat large amounts of saturated fat are more likely to get cancer of the colon and rectum. Studies suggest that people who eat fruits, vegetables, and foods high in fiber have a lower risk of some cancers.

4. **Stay active, and maintain a healthy weight.** Studies have shown that regular physical activity helps protect against some types of cancers. Exercising also helps prevent obesity, another risk factor for developing cancer. Teens should get at least 60 minutes of activity daily.

5. **Get regular medical checkups.** Your doctor can answer questions you may have about cancer risk factors, preventions, and treatments. He or she will also be able to advise you on self-examinations and when to begin regular cancer screening tests.

When we make positive choices with regard to these controllable risk factors, we can work toward a healthy future for ourselves.

SECTION 3

REVIEW   *Answer the following questions on a separate piece of paper.*

Using Key Terms

1. **Define** the term *cancer.*

2. **Compare** a benign tumor to a malignant tumor.

3. **Define** the term *chemotherapy.*

Understanding Key Ideas

4. **Describe** how cancer cells differ from normal body cells.

5. **State** three common carcinogens.

6. **Identify** the form of cancer that has the highest death rate. (Hint: See Table 1 on p. 351.)
   a. pancreas   c. lung
   b. liver   d. colon

7. **Describe** three methods that doctors use to detect cancer.

8. **Describe** how chemotherapy works to treat cancer.

9. **Identify** which of the following actions would help reduce your chances of developing cancer.
   a. not smoking   c. eating fruits
   b. wearing sunscreen   d. all of the above

10. **[LIFE SKILL] Practicing Wellness** Identify one part of your lifestyle that you can change to decrease your chance of developing cancer.

Critical Thinking

11. Why do you think cancer is more common in some families than in others?

SECTION 4

Living with Diabetes

OBJECTIVES

Describe the role of insulin in diabetes.

Compare type 1 and type 2 diabetes.

Identify two ways to detect and two ways to treat type 1 and type 2 diabetes.

Name two ways that you can prevent type 2 diabetes. **LIFE SKILL**

Estimates indicate that about 18 million people in the United States have diabetes. Unfortunately, about 5 million people who have diabetes do not know that they have it and are not being treated for it.

What Is Diabetes?

When you eat, the nutrients in foods are broken down to provide your cells with energy. Complex carbohydrates are broken down into glucose, which enters your bloodstream and circulates to the rest of your body. Once glucose reaches the cells, it moves from the bloodstream into the cells. The cells then use the glucose for energy.

Insulin The body can't use glucose without insulin. **Insulin** is a hormone that causes cells to remove glucose from the bloodstream. Thus, insulin lowers the amount of glucose traveling free in the bloodstream. Insulin is produced by special cells in the the pancreas. When blood glucose levels are high, more insulin is released into the bloodstream. When glucose levels are lower, less insulin is released into the bloodstream.

Insulin and Diabetes Sometimes, the pancreas doesn't produce enough insulin, or the body's cells don't respond to insulin. The result is diabetes. **Diabetes** is a disorder in which cells are unable to obtain glucose from the blood such that high blood-glucose levels result. The kidneys excrete water, resulting in increased urination and thirst. Cells then use the body's fat and protein for energy, which causes a buildup of toxic substances in the bloodstream. If this continues, a diabetic coma can result. A **diabetic coma** is a loss of consciousness that happens when there is too much blood sugar and a build up of toxic substances in the blood. Without treatment, diabetic comas can result in death.

Testing blood glucose is one way that people with diabetes can deal with their illness. Blood glucose is the amount of glucose in the blood.

Types of Diabetes

The three most common forms of diabetes are type 1 diabetes, type 2 diabetes, and gestational diabetes. As shown in **Table 2,** each kind of diabetes has its own characteristics.

Type 1 Diabetes Type 1 diabetes accounts for only 5 to 10 percent of diabetes cases in the United States. Type 1 diabetes develops when the immune system attacks the insulin-producing cells of the pancreas. Once these cells are destroyed, the body is unable to make insulin. Scientists believe that type 1 diabetes is caused by both genetic factors and viruses.

Type 1 diabetes is sometimes called *insulin-dependent* or *juvenile diabetes.* This type of diabetes is treated with daily injections of insulin and is usually diagnosed before the age of 18. Symptoms are usually severe and develop over a short period of time. Common symptoms include increased thirst, frequent urination, fatigue, and weight loss.

Type 2 Diabetes The most common form of diabetes in the United States is type 2, sometimes called *noninsulin-dependent diabetes.* Unlike type 1 diabetes, type 2 diabetes is most common among adults who are over 40 years of age and among people who are overweight.

In type 2 diabetes, the pancreas makes insulin, but the body's cells fail to respond to it. The result is the buildup of glucose in the blood and the inability of the body to use the glucose as a source of fuel. Common symptoms of type 2 diabetes include frequent urination, unusual thirst, blurred vision, frequent infections, and slow-healing sores. These symptoms usually appear gradually.

Medical alert bracelets alert medical personnel that a person, such as a diabetic, needs special care. Some warning signs of a diabetic emergency include feelings of weakness or faintness, irritability, rapid heartbeat, nausea, and drowsiness.

Table 2	Types of Diabetes		
Type of Diabetes	**What is it?**	**Symptoms**	**Treatment**
Type 1	▶ diabetes resulting from the body's inability to produce insulin	▶ increased thirst, frequent urination, fatigue, weight loss, nausea, abdominal pain, and absence of menstruation in females	▶ diet and insulin
Type 2	▶ diabetes resulting from the inability of the body's cells to respond to insulin	▶ frequent urination, increased thirst, fatigue, weight loss, blurred vision, frequent infections, and slow-healing sores	▶ diet, exercise, and occasionally insulin
Gestational	▶ diabetes that develops during pregnancy	▶ frequent urination, increased thirst, fatigue, weight loss, blurred vision, frequent infections, and slow-healing sores	▶ diet and occasionally insulin

A diet that includes lots of fruit and vegetables can help reduce the risk of developing type 2 diabetes.

Gestational Diabetes Occasionally, a pregnant woman can develop diabetes near the end of her pregnancy. Usually, the diabetes goes away after the baby is born. Gestational diabetes can increase the chances of complications during the pregnancy. The symptoms are the same as those of type 2 diabetes but milder. The risk of developing gestational diabetes increases if the mother has a family history of diabetes, is obese, is over 25 years of age, or has previously given birth to a child who weighed more than 9 pounds at birth.

Detecting and Treating Diabetes

Detecting and getting medical care for diabetes as early as possible can decrease your chances of developing serious side effects.

Detecting Diabetes Early detection is important in cases of diabetes. Diabetes patients risk complications such as blindness, kidney disease, strokes, and amputations of the lower limbs. The first step in detecting diabetes is to see your doctor if you have symptoms. Your doctor will use a variety of lab tests, such as urinalysis, a glucose-tolerance test, or an insulin test to determine if you have diabetes. Once diagnosed, a person can work with his or her doctor to keep the diabetes under control. Unfortunately, there is no cure for diabetes yet.

Treating Type 1 Diabetes The goal of treatment is to keep blood-glucose levels as close to normal as possible. People who have type 1 diabetes usually must test their blood glucose several times a day. Many people who have type 1 diabetes also need several doses of insulin each day to keep their blood-glucose levels within a normal range. Most diabetics must learn to give themselves insulin injections.

Treating Type 2 Diabetes Although insulin is sometimes used to treat type 2 diabetes, more common control measures focus on diet and exercise. A healthy diet can help people with type 2 diabetes control the amount of glucose they eat and can help them control

internet connect

www.scilinks.org/health
Topic: Diabetes
HealthLinks code: HH4041

HEALTH LINKS. Maintained by the National Science Teachers Association

Staying active through regular exercise can help reduce your risk of developing type 2 diabetes.

their weight. Foods with sugar do not need to be avoided completely, but must be eaten in moderation. Physical activity is also important because it helps the body use more of the glucose in the blood and keeps the person's weight at a healthy level.

New Treatments Researchers are working on new treatments for diabetes. The researchers are hoping that these new treatments will help diabetics monitor their blood-glucose better, will provide new methods of delivering insulin, and will help reduce the severity of symptoms. Scientists are also working on ways to transplant insulin-producing cells into people with type 1 diabetes.

Preventing Diabetes

As in so many diseases, genes play a role in diabetes. For example, people who have diabetes in their family are at a greater risk of developing diabetes. People in certain ethnic groups, particularly African Americans, Hispanics, and Native Americans, are also at a greater risk for developing type 2 diabetes.

There is currently no way to prevent type 1 diabetes. But exercise, a healthy diet, and insulin injections as needed can allow a person to lead a healthy life.

There are several things a person can do to reduce his or her risk of developing type 2 diabetes including:

▶ Maintain a healthy weight. Exercise regularly and eat a healthy diet. Physical activity and a healthy diet can greatly reduce the risk of developing type 2 diabetes in people who are overweight.

▶ Avoid tobacco products.

▶ Reduce the amount of stress in your life.

SECTION 4

REVIEW   *Answer the following questions on a separate piece of paper.*

Using Key Terms

1. **Name** the term for "a hormone that causes cells to remove glucose from the bloodstream."

2. **Define** the term *diabetes*.

3. **Define** the term *diabetic coma*.

Understanding Key Ideas

4. **Describe** the role of insulin in the body.

5. **Compare** type 1 and type 2 diabetes.

6. **Identify** when a person may develop gestational diabetes.
   a. as a child   c. after age 65
   b. as a teen   d. during pregnancy

7. **Name** three risk factors for developing type 2 diabetes.

8. **List** three symptoms that help a person detect type 1 and type 2 diabetes.

9. **Identify** which of the following is *not* a treatment for diabetes.
   a. urinalysis   c. healthy diet
   b. insulin injections d. regular exercise

10. **Describe** why it is important for a person who has diabetes to eat a healthy diet.

Critical Thinking

11. Why do you think type 2 diabetes is more common in the United States than in other countries?

Highlights

Key Terms

SECTION 1

lifestyle disease (340)

SECTION 2

cardiovascular
disease (CVD) (343)

stroke (344)

blood pressure
(344)

heart attack
(345)

atherosclerosis
(345)

SECTION 3

cancer (349)

malignant tumor (349)

benign tumor (349)

chemotherapy (352)

SECTION 4

insulin (355)

diabetes (355)

diabetic coma (355)

The Big Picture

✔ Lifestyle diseases are caused partly by a person's lifestyle, which includes habits and behaviors.

✔ Many risk factors, some controllable and some uncontrollable, contribute to a person's chances of developing a lifestyle disease.

✔ Diet, physical activity, smoking, sun exposure, and body weight are controllable risk factors. Age, gender, ethnicity, and genes are uncontrollable factors.

✔ People who inherit a tendency for a lifestyle disease can still do a lot to reduce their chances of developing such a disease.

✔ A person's lifestyle influences their chances of developing cardio-vascular diseases such as strokes, high blood pressure, heart attacks, and atherosclerosis.

✔ Doctors use many different methods, such as EKG, ultrasound, and angiography, to diagnose cardiovascular diseases.

✔ There are many treatment options for cardiovascular diseases including a healthy diet, exercise, medicine, and surgery.

✔ Eating sensibly, avoiding cigarettes, exercising, and having your blood pressure and cholesterol checked regularly can help prevent cardiovascular diseases.

✔ Cancer occurs when cells divide uncontrollably. Certain "damaged" genes can make a person more likely to develop cancer. Exposure to viruses, radioactivity, ultraviolet radiation, and tobacco can damage genes.

✔ There are many types of cancer. Each type has its own characteristics.

✔ Early detection and treatment of cancer can increase a person's chances of survival.

✔ Not smoking, protecting your skin from the sun, following a bal-anced diet, staying active, and getting regular medical checkups help reduce your chances of developing cancer.

✔ Diabetes occurs when cells are unable to obtain glucose from the blood such that high blood-glucose levels result.

✔ Type 1 diabetes is believed to be caused by an autoimmune response. Type 2 diabetes is usually the result of lifestyle choices.

✔ Although there is no cure for diabetes, lifestyle changes and medicines can often keep the disorder under control.

✔ The best way to prevent diabetes is to take control of the risk factors that you can change, such as diet, exercise, and weight.

Review

Using Key Terms

atherosclerosis (345)
benign tumor (349)
blood pressure (344)
cancer (349)
cardiovascular disease (CVD) (343)
chemotherapy (352)

diabetes (355)
diabetic coma (355)
heart attack (345)
insulin (355)
lifestyle disease (340)
malignant tumor (349)
stroke (344)

1. For each definition below, choose the key term that best matches the definition.
   a. a disease caused by uncontrolled cell growth
   b. the force that blood exerts against the inside walls of a blood vessel
   c. an abnormal, but usually harmless cell mass
   d. a hormone that causes cells to remove glucose from the bloodstream
   e. the damage and loss of function of an area of the heart muscle

2. Explain the relationship between the key terms in each of the following pairs.
   a. *malignant tumor* and *benign tumor*
   b. *insulin* and *diabetic coma*

Understanding Key Ideas

Section 1

3. Explain why infectious diseases have become less common and why lifestyle diseases are the most common causes of death.

4. _____ are uncontrollable risk factors for lifestyle diseases.
   a. Tobacco use, gender, and age
   b. Genes, age, and gender
   c. Age, exercise level, and family history of disease
   d. Gender, exercise level, and tobacco use

5. To help prevent the development of a lifestyle disease, a person should
   a. not smoke.
   b. exercise.
   c. have a low-fat diet.
   d. All of the above

6. What two steps could you take during school to lower your risk of developing a lifestyle disease. **LIFE SKILL**

Section 2

7. How can lifestyle contribute to cardiovascular disease?

8. Which of the following is *not* a type of cardiovascular disease?
   a. stroke
   b. atherosclerosis
   c. cancer
   d. high blood pressure

9. Which of the following is *not* a treatment for cardiovascular disease?
   a. angioplasty
   b. bypass surgery
   c. heart transplant
   d. echocardiography

10. How can regular exercise reduce your chances of developing cardiovascular disease? **LIFE SKILL**

11. CRITICAL THINKING Smoking decreases the amount of oxygen that the blood can carry. How can this effect increase the chances that a smoker will develop cardiovascular disease?

Section 3

12. Describe what cancer is and why it is so dangerous.

13. Refer to **Table 1** on p. 351. What is the main cause of the type of cancer that results in the most deaths each year? **READING SKILL**

14. _____ is *not* a method of detecting cancer.
   a. Prostate specific antigen testing
   b. MRI
   c. Regular self-examination
   d. Chemotherapy

15. Identify three cancer treatments used today.

16. What are two ways that a person can safeguard their skin from ultraviolet radiation?

Section 4

17. What is the relationship between insulin and glucose in diabetes?

18. What are the major differences between type 1 and type 2 diabetes?

19. What are two ways to detect and two ways to treat type 1 and type 2 diabetes?

20. List two steps you can take to lower your risk of developing type 2 diabetes. **LIFE SKILL**

Interpreting Graphics

Study the figure below to answer the questions that follow.

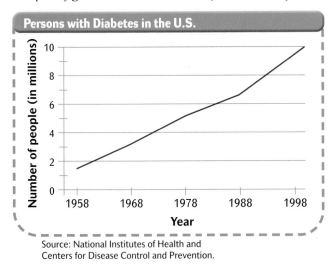

Persons with Diabetes in the U.S.

Source: National Institutes of Health and Centers for Disease Control and Prevention.

21. How many people were diagnosed with diabetes in 1978?

22. What is the difference in the number of people diagnosed with diabetes in 1988 and the number diagnosed in 1998? **MATH SKILL**

23. CRITICAL THINKING Why do you think diabetes has become more common since 1958?

Activities

24. Health and You Make a list of the uncontrollable risk factors for lifestyle diseases. Create a poster that explains how a person can reduce the risk of lifestyle diseases despite uncontrollable risk factors.

25. Health and Your Community Research one of the cancers listed in **Table 1.** Prepare an informational handout that describes how to detect, treat, and prevent the cancer. **WRITING SKILL**

26. Health and You Research a new approach to treating cancer. Write a one page paper that describes what the approach is, how it works, and when it is expected to be available to cancer patients. **WRITING SKILL**

Action Plan

27. LIFE SKILL Assessing Your Health Establishing healthy patterns of living during adolescence reduces the risks of developing a lifestyle disease. Discuss two risk factors over which you have control. How can you reduce or eliminate these risk factors?

Standardized Test Prep

Read the passage below, and then answer the questions that follow. **READING SKILL** **WRITING SKILL**

Heart disease is the leading cause of death in the United States. Heart disease causes over 900,000 deaths per year. These deaths <u>constitute</u> 40 percent of all deaths in the United States. Twenty-five percent of deaths due to heart disease occur in people under the age of 65. Death rates for the 10-year period ending in 1985 were 30 percent less than they were for the previous 10-year period. This decline in mortality is related to improvements in heart disease risk factor levels, as well as in diagnosis and treatment.

28. In this passage, the word *constitute* means
   A propose.
   B make up.
   C follow.
   D concern.

29. What can you infer from reading this passage?
   E There are more deaths due to heart disease in the United States than there are anywhere else in the world.
   F The number of deaths due to heart disease has not changed since 1985.
   G Changes in lifestyle risk factors have decreased the number of deaths due to heart disease.
   H Nothing can be done to prevent deaths from heart disease.

30. Write a paragraph describing how changes in lifestyle could reduce the number of deaths due to heart disease in the United States.

Every day, the newspapers are full of new discoveries in genetics, the science of heredity. How could the latest developments in genetics affect your health or the health of a family member?

Making Sense of Genetic Technology

In 2003, scientists published a complete list of all human genes. Genes are the set of instructions found in every person's body that describe how that person's body will look, grow, and function. Many scientists have now turned their attention to figuring out what each gene does. The application of our knowledge about genes to help meet human needs is known as *genetic technology*.

Our Growing Knowledge of Human Genetics

Scientists are asking how our genes determine the kind of blood that we have, the way that our skin cells work, or the color of our eyes. In addition, other researchers are working hard to apply this new knowledge to detect and cure genetic disorders. There are many kinds of genetic disorders. Down syndrome, sickle cell disease, hemophilia, cystic fibrosis, and muscular dystrophy are only a few well-known ones. In fact, more than 4,000 different human disorders are caused by errors in our genes. Someone you know might have cancer that has a genetic basis. In your lifetime, cures for cancers are likely to arise from today's research in genetic technology.

In addition to studying genetic disorders, scientists are using techniques in genetic technology in other ways. For example, scientists in pharmaceutical companies use genetic technology with bacteria to produce medicines that help humans. Doctors treat dwarfism by using human growth hormones made with new genetic technology. Using modern techniques, drug companies are manufacturing new vaccines. In fact, so much genetic work is being done that understanding these new developments can seem overwhelming.

Genetics and Technology

Let's look at some specific examples of the new genetic technology and see how it is affecting the world around us.

▶ **Transplanted Genes** It is possible to take a certain gene from one kind of organism, such as a human, and place it into another organism, such as a bacterium. This idea may seem strange, but the results can be remarkable. For example, a scientist can take the human gene that makes the hormone insulin out of a human cell and place it in a bacterial cell. Millions of these bacterial cells can then make pure human insulin.

Many very pure substances can be made in this way. The transfer of genes from one organism to another for medical or industrial use is called *genetic engineering*. Today genetic engineering is used to change the nature of many of our domestic plants and animals.

▶ **Genetic fingerprinting** Scientists are now able to take a sample of genetic material from a person and develop a "fingerprint" of that person's genetic makeup. The genetic material is first broken up into smaller fragments. These fragments are then placed into a gelatinous substance. Under the influence of an electric current, the pieces of genetic material are separated from one another. The way in which they separate is unique to each person. The result is a "fingerprint." Genetic fingerprinting can be used to research family trees or to identify an adult who carries a gene that causes a genetic disorder. It can also be used as legal evidence in criminal trials.

Understanding a New Technology

As you get older, scientists will make more and more discoveries in genetics. These discoveries are likely to change the way you live. Genetic disorders, such as Tay-Sachs, sickle cell disease, and thousands of other diseases, may be a thing of the past. The possibility of real change is awesome. For example, will you be

able to ensure that your children have certain traits? Will you or your children be able to eliminate genetic diseases? Genetics is the most powerful and exciting science to affect our lives, and its effects will be more profound as the years go by. How do you make sense of so many important discoveries? Here are some suggestions:

▶ **Read the latest news about science in newspapers, in magazines, and on the Internet.** The most important discoveries will be presented here for everyone to read and understand. However, be skeptical of what you read. So many exciting discoveries are being made that it is only natural that writers and reporters will sometimes exaggerate. Use your common sense. Get information from more than one source.

▶ **Use your research skills to look up information that you don't understand.** Books and reputable Internet sites are sources you can rely on to learn more about genetic technology.

YOUR TURN

1. **Summarizing Information** Why should all citizens become informed about genetic technology and modern genetic research?

2. **Inferring Conclusions** In what ways has modern medical and genetic technology improved our lives since the days of your grandmother and grandfather?

3. **CRITICAL THINKING** Do you think that people should be allowed to choose the traits of their children by changing their children's genes? How would you go about finding the information to make your point in a discussion?

☑ **internet** connect
www.scilinks.org/health
Topic: Genome
HealthLinks code: HH4363
HEALTH LINKS® Maintained by the National Science Teachers Association

Other Diseases and Disabilities

What's Your Health IQ?
KNOWLEDGE

Which of the statements below are true, and which are false? Check your answers on p. 638.

1. A person's chances of developing a hereditary disease are determined only by his or her genes.

2. The Human Genome Project may allow scientists to develop new treatments for hereditary diseases.

3. Autoimmune diseases are caused by viruses that attack the immune system.

4. Allergies, asthma, and arthritis are all examples of autoimmune disorders.

5. The most common cause of disabilities involving movement is injury to the nervous system.

Visit these Web sites for the latest health information:

HEALTH LINKS
THE WORLD'S A CLICK AWAY®

Find more information whenever you see a HealthLinks box. Go to **scilinks.org/health**, and type in the HealthLinks code.

go.hrw.com

Find worksheets and other materials that go with your textbook at **go.hrw.com**.

Current Health

Check out *Current Health*® articles related to this chapter by visiting **go.hrw.com**. Just type in the keyword **HH4 CH15**.

Understanding Hereditary Diseases

OBJECTIVES

Identify how genes are involved in hereditary diseases.

Compare the three different types of hereditary diseases.

Summarize three ways that a person with a genetic disease can cope with the disease.

Describe a future medical treatment for hereditary diseases.

KEY TERMS

hereditary disease a disease caused by abnormal chromosomes or by defective genes inherited by a child from one or both parents

gene a segment of DNA located on a chromosome that codes for a specific hereditary trait and that is passed from parent to offspring

genetic counseling the process of informing a person or couple about their genetic makeup

Human Genome Project a research effort to determine the locations of all human genes on the chromosomes and to read the coded instructions in the genes

gene therapy a technique that places a healthy copy of a gene into the cells of a person whose copy of the gene is defective

Just as hair color and height are determined by the genes that a person receives from his or her parents, so are certain diseases.

Julia has been lucky—she has had only a few colds, the flu, and chickenpox during her 16 years of life. Others in her family have had more serious diseases, such as diabetes and cancer. Julia is curious about whether she has inherited some of these diseases.

What Are Hereditary Diseases?

Unlike infectious diseases, hereditary diseases aren't caused by pathogens. Instead, **hereditary diseases** are diseases caused by abnormal chromosomes or by defective genes inherited from one or both parents.

Genes Genes are segments of DNA, located on chromosomes, that code for a specific hereditary trait. Genes are passed from parent to offspring. The genes that you inherited from your parents determine many of your characteristics. For example, whether you have blue or brown eyes is determined by your genes. The color of your hair is determined by your genes. Together, your genes tell your body how to grow, develop, and function throughout life. Your genes also determine your chances of developing certain diseases—hereditary diseases.

Genes and Hereditary Diseases How are genes involved in hereditary diseases? Occasionally, the instructions that a gene is carrying contain an error. When a gene carries incorrect instructions, this is called a *mutation*. Sometimes, a mutation can have a harmful effect on the person. In hereditary diseases, a mutation can cause a disease or increase a person's chances of getting a disease.

Types of Hereditary Diseases

Hereditary diseases can result from a mutation on one gene, on several genes, or from changes to an entire chromosome where the genes are found. Thus, hereditary diseases are sometimes classified as single-gene, complex, or chromosomal diseases.

Single-Gene Diseases Single-gene diseases occur when 1 gene out of the 20,000 to 25,000 genes in the body has a harmful mutation. The severity of the illness depends on what instructions the gene normally carries. **Table 1** summarizes the symptoms and treatments for several single-gene diseases.

Huntington's disease is an example of a disease caused by one defective gene. When people with Huntington's disease reach the age of 35 to 40, cells in their brain begin to die. Over time, their movements become jerky and uncontrollable, their personality changes, and their mental abilities deteriorate. Huntington's disease is always fatal.

Another example of a single-gene disease is *sickle cell anemia*. Sickle cell anemia occurs when the body makes a faulty version of *hemoglobin*, the protein that carries oxygen to your cells. Hemoglobin is found in red blood cells. As shown in **Figure 1**, the red blood cells of someone with sickle cell anemia have an abnormal shape. These cells tend to clog up small blood vessels, cutting off blood flow to some tissues.

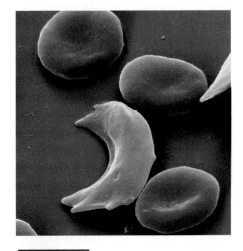

Figure 1

Normal red blood cells have a circular, biconcave shape. In sickle cell anemia, the red blood cells have an abnormal, sickle shape, making it difficult for the cells to carry oxygen to the body.

Table 1 Single-Gene Diseases			
Disease	**Description**	**Symptoms**	**Treatment**
Huntington's disease	▶ inherited disease that leads to the degeneration of brain cells	▶ involuntary movements, mood swings, depression, irritability, and inability to remember facts	▶ no cure; medicines to help control symptoms, such as emotional and movement problems
Sickle cell anemia	▶ inherited blood disease in which the body produces defective hemoglobin	▶ fatigue, paleness, shortness of breath, pain, infections, and stroke	▶ no cure; medicine to treat pain; blood transfusions
Hemophilia	▶ inherited blood disease in which the body produces little of or none of the blood proteins necessary for clotting	▶ severe bruising, excessive bleeding after a simple cut, hemorrhaging (internal bleeding), chronic joint disease, and joint pain	▶ no cure; blood transfusions; blood-clotting proteins
Cystic fibrosis	▶ inherited disease of the body's mucous glands; primarily affects the respiratory and digestive systems of children and young adults	▶ difficulty breathing, cough, accumulation of mucus in the intestines and lungs, infections, and weight loss	▶ no cure; medicines to treat symptoms, such as difficulty breathing and infections

Sickle cell anemia is the most common genetic disease among African Americans. This disease affects about 1 in 500 African Americans. Although sickle cell anemia isn't curable, with medical care people who have the disease usually live into their 50s.

Cystic fibrosis is another single-gene disease. It affects nearly 30,000 people in the United States. Cystic fibrosis causes large amounts of thick mucus to clog the lungs, the pancreas, and the liver. This buildup of mucus leads to malnutrition, breathing difficulties, and infections that can damage the lungs. Although there is currently no cure for cystic fibrosis, scientists are developing new treatments, such as gene therapy to help reduce the effects of this disease.

Complex Diseases In complex diseases, more than one gene influences the onset of the disease. Lifestyle behaviors also contribute to a person's chance of developing a complex disease. Cardiovascular diseases (strokes, heart attacks, high blood pressure, and atherosclerosis), type 2 diabetes, and cancer are examples of complex diseases. Many genes influence whether you get these diseases.

Is there anything you can do about complex diseases? Yes! Because you have control over your lifestyle, you can help lower your risk of developing a complex disease by making healthy lifestyle choices. Eating healthy foods and exercising regularly are two good ways to reduce your chances of developing a complex disease.

Chromosomal Diseases Genes are located on chromosomes. Humans normally have 23 pairs of chromosomes inside each of their cells (except for sperm and egg cells). Sometimes, a disease can occur when a person inherits the wrong number of chromosomes or when one of the chromosomes is incomplete. Because each chromosome carries a large number of genes, chromosomal diseases are usually fatal.

The most common chromosomal disease in the United States is *Down syndrome*. Down syndrome, also called Trisomy 21, occurs when a person inherits an extra copy of the 21st chromosome. People who suffer from Down syndrome often have varying degrees of mental retardation and difficulties with physical development. Down syndrome is typically not fatal.

Coping with Hereditary Diseases

Coping with a hereditary disease can be difficult. There are several things you can do if you or someone in your family has a hereditary disease.

1. **Genetic counseling** A genetic counselor is a specialist in human genetics. **Genetic counseling** is the process of informing a person or couple about their genetic makeup. As shown in **Figure 2,** the genetic counselor can study a family's chromosomes and medical history and explain the risks of passing on a hereditary disease to a child. Genetic counselors also provide information to help people accept a diagnosis and cope with a genetic disease.

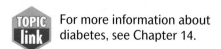

TOPIC link For more information about diabetes, see Chapter 14.

Figure 2

A genetic counselor can help potential parents understand the chances of passing on a hereditary disease to their child. Genetic counselors often examine each parent's chromosomes.

2. **Personal health records** Most of us can't remember all the details of our medical history, but this information is important for our doctors. You should keep your records up to date. Get copies of your health records if you change doctors.

It's also important to know what illnesses your relatives have experienced. Try to collect information on what hereditary diseases your relatives had, when these diseases appeared, and what your deceased relatives died from.

3. **Health information** Read the latest information about the hereditary disease. This will help you know what to expect and how to help a person with a specific hereditary disease. Knowing about the hereditary disease is a good first step in helping yourself or another person cope.

Future Medical Treatment for Hereditary Diseases

We know a lot more about human genes than we did in the past. This information is currently being used in treating hereditary diseases and developing treatments for the future.

Human Genome Project Scientists are trying to learn what all of our genes do and how they affect the development of diseases like cancer, heart disease, and diabetes. One major advancement in this research was the completion of the Human Genome Project. The **Human Genome Project** was a research effort to determine the locations of all human genes on the chromosomes and to read the coded instructions in the genes. The collection of all of our genes make up our *genome*. You can think of the genome as an instruction manual for human beings. The project was completed in 2003.

With the genetic information gathered from the Human Genome Project, scientists hope to treat hereditary diseases in different ways, including

▶ designing powerful drugs that target a particular hereditary disease
▶ making drugs to prevent diseases
▶ improving **gene therapy,** a technique that places a healthy copy of a gene into the cells of a person whose copy of the gene is defective
▶ creating genetic tests that can tell you which hereditary diseases you might develop in your lifetime

With the information from genetic tests, you can take steps early in life to head off the disease. For example, for heart diseases, these steps may include eating a diet low in saturated fats, exercising regularly, or controlling your weight.

MAKING GREAT DECISIONS

Imagine that your friend's father has just been diagnosed with Huntington's disease. There's a 50 percent chance that your friend has the defective gene too. She can know for sure by getting a genetic test that requires only a sample of blood. The problem is that there is no treatment or cure for Huntington's disease. However, even if she does have the faulty gene, she may not start to get sick for 10 years or even longer. Should she get tested?

Write on a separate piece of paper the advice you would give your friend. Remember to use the decision-making steps.

G ive thought to the problem.
R eview your choices.
E valuate the consequences of each choice.
A ssess and choose the best choice.
T hink it over afterward.

☑ **internet** connect

www.scilinks.org/health
Topic: Human Genome Project
HealthLinks code: HH4084

HEALTH LINKS Maintained by the National Science Teachers Association

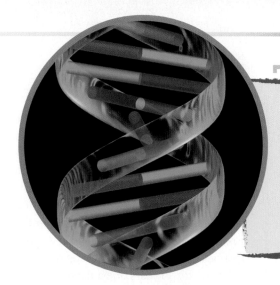

Positive Uses of Genetic Information

▶ **improved diagnosis of disease**
▶ **gene therapies**
▶ **vaccines incorporated into foods**
▶ **customized drugs for specific diseases**
▶ **improved ability to predict genetic diseases**
▶ **help in studying our past**

DNA molecules like this one are what make up our genes, the coded instructions for building our bodies.

Gene Therapy   Scientists are improving their ability to treat hereditary diseases by gene therapy. They are inserting working genes to cancel the effects of defective genes. Getting a gene into the body and making it work has been very difficult, but some diseases have been treated in this way. In the future, scientists hope to use gene therapy to insert missing genes or to replace the faulty genes that cause cystic fibrosis, sickle cell anemia, and other hereditary diseases.

Concerns About Genetic Information   Our growing knowledge of human genes raises concerns about how the information will be used. Some people worry that insurance companies might discriminate against people based on results of genetic tests. This is called *genetic discrimination*. Another worry is that genetic techniques might be abused to change characteristics such as eye color, height, or intelligence. In the next few years, society will be trying to decide what kinds of genetic changes are acceptable. The issue of genetic information may raise some troubling questions, but this new information is expected to help save many lives.

SECTION 1

REVIEW   *Answer the following questions on a separate piece of paper.*

Using Key Terms

1. **Define** the term *hereditary disease*.
2. **Compare** the terms *gene* and *gene therapy*.
3. **Define** the term *Human Genome Project*.

Understanding Key Ideas

4. **Summarize** how genes are involved in hereditary diseases.
5. **Classify** each of the following as a single-gene disease or a complex disease.
   a. hemophilia   **c.** cystic fibrosis
   b. diabetes   **d.** cancer

6. **Compare** three types of hereditary diseases.
7. **State** three ways that people can cope with a genetic disease.
8. **Identify** two ways information from the Human Genome Project may help treat hereditary diseases in the future.

Critical Thinking

9. What are two ways that society could deal with future concerns about genetic information?
10. Imagine you are a scientist working on the Human Genome Project. What would you say to news reporters about your research? **LIFE SKILL**

Understanding Immune Disorders and Autoimmune Diseases

OBJECTIVES

Compare immune disorders and autoimmune diseases.

Describe two types of immune disorders.

Describe two types of autoimmune diseases.

Summarize how people can cope with immune disorders and autoimmune diseases.

Imagine that your body begins to destroy its own cells. Even though this idea sounds far fetched, many common diseases occur when the immune system does just this.

What Are Immune Disorders and Autoimmune Diseases?

Your immune system is made up of special cells that protect your body from disease. These cells are constantly patrolling your blood and tissues. When an immune system cell does not recognize an object as part of the body, it attacks the foreign particle. Your immune system guards you from viruses, bacteria, foreign substances, and cancer cells.

Immune Disorders If the immune system does not function properly, the result is an immune disorder. Some immune disorders are relatively mild; others can be life threatening. Examples of immune disorders include allergies, asthma, acquired immune deficiency syndrome (AIDS), and severe combined immunodeficiency disease (SCID).

Autoimmune Diseases In people with **autoimmune diseases,** the immune system attacks the cells of the body that the immune system normally protects. Depending on the cells that are destroyed, these attacks can result in many conditions. For example, rheumatoid arthritis is caused when the immune system attacks the joints. In multiple sclerosis, the immune system attacks myelin, the fatty insulation of nerves in the brain and spinal cord.

Preventive medications are one way that many people are able to control immune disorders such as asthma.

Types of Immune Disorders

When immune system cells encounter a foreign particle, they send out chemical signals that cause the body to react. Usually, this reaction helps the immune system fight disease. Sometimes, however, the reaction causes more problems than the foreign particle would.

Allergies   An **allergy** is a reaction by the body's immune system to a harmless substance. A long list of things, including foods, dust, plant pollen, and animals, can cause allergic reactions. Do you sneeze when a cat comes around? Do your eyes itch and water when you go outside on a spring day? If so, you may have an allergy.

When inhaled substances, such as the pollen grains shown in **Figure 3,** cause an allergic attack, a person may experience a runny nose, sneezing, and itchy, watery eyes. Allergies to foods or certain drugs can sometimes cause *hives,* itchy swellings on the skin. Most allergies are a nuisance. But some people have extreme and life-threatening reactions to allergies. Their blood pressure falls, and the tubes carrying air into the lungs constrict, making it difficult to breathe.

One way to prevent allergic symptoms is to avoid things that cause a reaction. Some ways you can help reduce allergic symptoms include
▶ avoiding substances that you are allergic to
▶ washing sheets and blankets weekly
▶ cleaning bathrooms and kitchens to avoid molds

Avoiding allergenic substances is not always possible. Some people use over-the-counter drugs called *antihistamines.* Antihistamines work to suppress the symptoms of an allergy. A doctor can also prescribe a series of injections containing gradually larger doses of the substance to which the person is allergic. Over the course of 2 or 3 years, the person's sensitivity to the substance declines.

Asthma   **Asthma** is a disorder that causes the airways that carry air into the lungs to become narrow and to become clogged with mucus. This causes shortness of breath, wheezing, and coughing. The airways, called *bronchioles,* are shown in **Figure 4.** The bronchioles are covered with rings of muscle that adjust the width of the tubes. This allows your lungs to take in more or less air. For example, the width of the airways increase when you excercise.

Occasionally, the muscles covering the airways overreact to substances in the air, causing the airways to narrow. These airways can be too sensitive and tighten in response to things like dust, cigarette smoke, stress, exercise, foods, and pollution. The result is an asthma attack. During an asthma attack, the lining of these air passages may also swell and become inflamed, making breathing difficult.

When the tubes narrow, drawing a breath is very hard. Asthmatics often explain that breathing during an asthma attack is like trying to breathe through a straw. Other symptoms of asthma are coughing, wheezing, and chest tightness. Asthma attacks are very serious. Some attacks can even be life threatening. More than 5,000 people die from asthma each year.

Figure 3

Sinuses are hollow areas in the skull that open into the nasal cavity. When allergens, such as pollen grains, enter the sinuses, they can trigger an allergic reaction.

Sinuses

Pollen grains

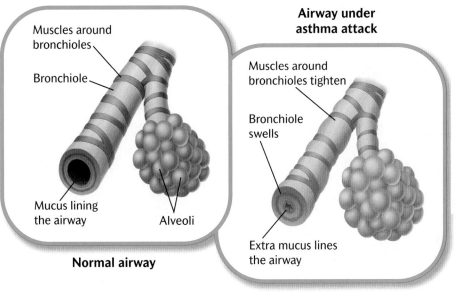

Airway under asthma attack

Muscles around bronchioles

Bronchiole

Mucus lining the airway

Alveoli

Normal airway

Muscles around bronchioles tighten

Bronchiole swells

Extra mucus lines the airway

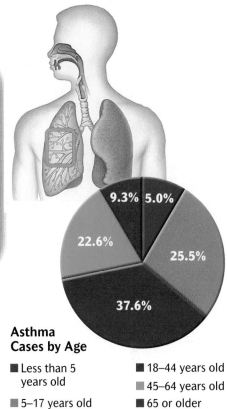

9.3% 5.0%

22.6%

25.5%

37.6%

Asthma Cases by Age

■ Less than 5 years old
■ 5–17 years old
■ 18–44 years old
■ 45–64 years old
■ 65 or older

Source: American Lung Association.

People can often prevent asthma attacks by avoiding the substances that irritate their lungs. Two kinds of drugs are also available to relieve asthma symptoms. Long-term control drugs are taken every day to soothe the airways. It is important that people with asthma take these drugs every day. For emergencies, asthmatics also have quick-relief drugs that, when inhaled, open the airways. These treatments have made it easier for people with asthma to lead normal, active lives. Moderate exercise can also strengthen the lungs of people who suffer from asthma.

Types of Autoimmune Diseases

When a person's immune system attacks the cells of the body it is meant to protect, the person has an autoimmune disease. There may be several factors that start the immune attack. An infection caused by pathogens with molecules similar to the body's own cells may cause the immune system to attack the cells in the body. If an infection enters a body tissue that is usually not patrolled by immune cells, the tissue may be attacked as well.

Arthritis Your joints move smoothly because the ends of the bones are covered with a smooth layer of cartilage that allows the bones to glide across one another. When this layer of cartilage is damaged, moving the bones and joints becomes difficult and painful. The result is **arthritis,** or inflammation of the joints. Arthritis is one of the most common joint diseases in the United States. There are two main kinds of arthritis: rheumatoid arthritis and osteoarthritis.

The disease known as *rheumatoid arthritis* is an autoimmune disease. For unknown reasons, the immune system begins to destroy the lining of the joints. The joints swell, become painful, and may become stiff or unable to move. This stiffness may be worse in the morning, just after waking, or after being inactive. Eventually, the bones of the joints may begin to deteriorate.

Figure 4

An asthma attack occurs when the muscles that encircle the airways of the lung (bronchioles) constrict, which makes breathing difficult.

ACTIVITY *Why do you think there are so many cases of asthma in 5- to 17-year-olds?*

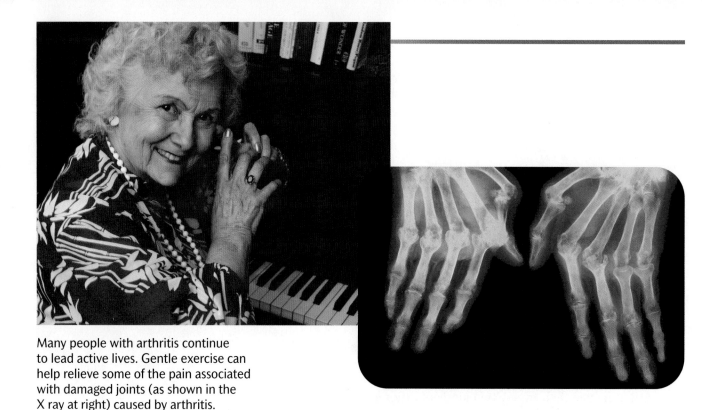

Many people with arthritis continue to lead active lives. Gentle exercise can help relieve some of the pain associated with damaged joints (as shown in the X ray at right) caused by arthritis.

Osteoarthritis is different from rheumatoid arthritis in that osteoarthritis is not an autoimmune disease. Instead, with osteoarthritis, the joints of the skeleton begin to wear out as a person grows older. The cartilage inside the joints begins to deteriorate and is not repaired as it would be in healthy joints. Movement, and even changes in the weather, can cause intense pain. The joints can swell, distort, or even develop bony knobs.

A plan that mixes medications, rest, and gentle exercise can help treat moderate forms of rheumatoid arthritis and osteoarthritis. Severe damage to a vital joint, such as the hip or knee, however, may require surgery to install a replacement joint made from plastic, metal, or porcelain. Drugs are also being developed to help reduce inflammation of the joints and to slow or stop joint damage.

Multiple Sclerosis Just like the power lines that carry electricity to your home, the nerves that carry impulses through the body are covered by a layer of insulation that speeds up nerve signals. The autoimmune disease known as **multiple sclerosis (MS)** occurs when the body attacks myelin, the fatty insulation on nerves in the brain and spinal cord. This damage causes the transmission of nerve impulses to slow down or stop.

Multiple sclerosis is twice as common in women as in men and usually strikes young adults. It can be hard to diagnose. Symptoms include blurred vision, tingling or burning sensations, weakness, numbness, mental problems, unsteadiness, slurred speech, or loss of bladder control. The symptoms of multiple sclerosis usually come and go. Months and sometimes years may pass between episodes. However, the disease usually gets worse over time and may eventually interfere with vision, balance, and walking. Patients may eventually become paralyzed. In some cases, the disease can be fatal.

internet connect

www.scilinks.org/health
Topic: Multiple Sclerosis
HealthLinks code: HH4102

HEA/TH LINKS. Maintained by the National Science Teachers Association

Although there is currently no cure for multiple sclerosis, many drugs and treatments can ease the symptoms and slow the deterioration of the nerves. Drugs such as steroids can reduce the length and severity of attacks. New drugs are currently being developed.

Coping with Immune Disorders and Autoimmune Diseases

Understanding immune disorders and autoimmune diseases can help you treat people with these types of diseases with compassion and respect. If you are diagnosed with an immune or autoimmune disease, be sure to do the following:

▶ **Understand your disorder and your doctor's treatment plan.** Ask questions, especially about the changes and symptoms you can expect to encounter. Learn about the side effects of medications and medical tests. Be aware of all aspects of your condition.

▶ **Follow the treatment plan designed by your physician.** Play an active role in determining your treatment plan. Do not be afraid to get a second or third opinion. Once you and your family are satisfied that the treatment is right for you, follow it.

▶ **Let your doctor know if a new symptom is occurring.** New symptoms can signal important changes in your disorder. It is very important to discuss any changes in your condition with your doctor. This is the only way to find out what the change might mean and how it might be treated.

▶ **Be honest with your doctor.** You hurt only yourself if you are not honest with your physician. A doctor cannot give you good advice without accurate information. Your health is too important to leave anything out.

People with multiple sclerosis, such as Sharon Jodoin, can enjoy physical activities. Being active helps maintain their health.

SECTION 2

REVIEW   *Answer the following questions on a separate piece of paper.*

Using Key Terms

1. **Define** the term *autoimmune disease*.

2. **Compare** *allergy* and *asthma*.

3. **Identify** the term for "inflammation of the joints."

Understanding Key Ideas

4. **Differentiate** between immune disorders and autoimmune diseases.

5. **Describe** two different types of immune disorders.

6. **Summarize** how common substances can trigger allergic reactions.

7. **Compare** the causes of rheumatoid arthritis and multiple sclerosis.

8. **Identify** the disease in which the body mistakenly attacks the fatty insulation on nerves in the brain and spinal cord.
   a. allergies
   b. asthma
   c. arthritis
   d. multiple sclerosis

9. **State** three ways that a person can better manage his or her autoimmune disease.

Critical Thinking

10. **Identify** how people with allergies or asthma can reduce the allergens in their homes.

Understanding Disabilities

OBJECTIVES

List three myths about disabilities.

Describe three different types of disabilities.

Identify two ways people cope with disabilities.

Identify one way that you can help create a positive environment for people with disabilities. **LIFE SKILL**

KEY TERMS

disability a physical or mental impairment or deficiency that interferes with a person's normal activity

tinnitus a buzzing, ringing, or whistling sound in one or both ears that occurs even when no sound is present

Americans with Disabilities Act (ADA) wide-ranging legislation intended to make American society more accessible to people who have disabilities

I n the past, people with disabilities were often discriminated against. They were believed to be unable to hold jobs or participate in other activities. Today, however, attitudes in society are changing as many people with disabilities are succeeding in all areas of life, despite their disabilities.

People in many different careers, such as artist Chuck Close, have been able to excel despite their disabilities. Chuck Close was partially paralyzed by a blood clot in his spinal cord.

What Are Disabilities?

Disabilities are physical or mental impairments or deficiencies that interfere with a person's normal activity. Disabilities can take many forms, including forms that involve vision, hearing, and movement.

Myths About Disabilities Over the years, there have been many myths about people who have disabilities. For example, one myth is that people with disabilities prefer to be around only other people with disabilities. Another common myth is that people with disabilities always need help. In reality, many people with disabilities live independantly and are part of mainstream society.

Actors with disabilities, such as Christopher Reeve and Michael J. Fox, have helped obtain funding for research to treat disabilities and bring special concerns to the attention of lawmakers and the public. People with disabilities also work as politicians, artists, lawyers, and doctors and in many other careers. Limits caused by disabilities do not limit the ability of a person to achieve his or her goals.

Educating others about the different types of disabilities is an effective way to help eliminate such myths and to build a positive atmosphere for all members of society.

Types of Disabilities

Disabilities are typically classified according to the body function that is affected by the disability. For example, disabilities involving vision include all disabilities that affect a person's ability to see. Although there are a variety of disabilities, the severity of the disabilities in each category can range from moderate to severe. Moderate disabilities may only slightly affect a person's ability to do everyday activities. Severe disabilities can sometimes require that a person have constant medical attention.

Disabilities Involving Vision   When people think of disabilities involving vision, they usually think of people who are completely blind. Although there are about 1.3 million Americans who are legally blind, there are nearly 10 million Americans with impaired vision. Thus, there are many people in the United States with disabilities involving vision who are not completely blind.

Accidents, diabetes, glaucoma, and macular degeneration account for most blindness in the United States. For example, in a condition

real life Activity

UNDERSTANDING DISABILITIES

LIFE SKILL
Coping

Materials

✔ bandana

Procedure

1. **Choose** two paths through the classroom. Make sure that the paths do not cross.

2. **Form** teams, with two people in each team.

3. **Choose** one team member to be blindfolded and one team member to be his or her guide.

4. **Tie** the bandana so that it completely covers the eyes of the "blind" team member so that he or she cannot see.

5. **Line up,** two teams at a time, at the beginning of each path.

6. **Guide** the blindfolded person through the path.

7. **Switch** roles, and repeat the activity.

Conclusions

1. **Summarizing Results** What did it feel like to walk through the classroom without any sense of sight?

2. **Summarizing Results** What challenges did you face when leading the person who was blindfolded?

3. **Predicting Outcomes** What changes could you make in your classroom to make it easier for a person with a vision disability to move around?

4. **CRITICAL THINKING** Other than moving around, what other daily activities might pose a problem for people who are blind?

HEALTH Handbook For more information about how to protect your vision and hearing, see the Express Lesson on pp. 574–575 of this text.

called *glaucoma*, increased pressure inside the eye causes vision impairment and eye damage. Damage to an area on the retina of the eye called the *macula* also leads to vision impairment. Worldwide, however, vitamin A deficiency is the leading cause of blindness. Luckily, many of the causes of visual impairment are controllable. Regular medical and vision checkups can help your doctor find problems early.

Currently, there are many treatment options for people with all levels of visual impairment. Traditionally, people with moderate vision problems have turned to eyeglasses or contact lenses for help. New treatments such as laser eye surgery are giving people more options in vision correction.

If you have vision problems that cannot be corrected, here are a few suggestions to help you cope with your disability:

▶ Communicate with your doctor about your condition and what to expect in the future.
▶ Educate yourself on your condition and the treatments that are being researched for the future.
▶ Find others with a similar disability for support.

Disabilities Involving Hearing Nearly 28 million Americans are hard of hearing or deaf. The majority of this group are over 65. The reason for this is that over time, noise contributes to hearing loss by damaging parts of the inner ear. A lifetime of excessive noise begins to destroy the cells of the inner ear that are involved in hearing. Many musicians suffer from severe hearing loss as a result of years of exposure to loud music. Exposure to loud noises can also lead to a condition called tinnitus. **Tinnitus** (ti NIET es) is a buzzing, ringing, or whistling sound in one or both ears that occurs even when no sound is present.

statistically speaking. . .

Approximate number of adults in the United States that have tinnitus to some degree: **50 million**

Number of children who are born deaf each year: **4,000**

Percentage of people in industrialized countries who experience tinnitus at some time in their lives: **20%**

Hearing loss can also be caused by age, environmental factors, medicines, infections, and inherited genes. For example, the most common cause of hearing loss in children is otitis (oh TIET is) media, an infection of the ear.

To find out the extent of a person's hearing impairment, a doctor may complete a general screening test or a more thorough test using a device called an *audiometer* (AW dee AHM uht uhr). Once the problem has been diagnosed, treatment options include the following:

▶ **Hearing aids** Although hearing aids cannot help with all forms of hearing loss, they can help improve hearing for many people. Hearing aids work by amplifying sounds through a speaker.

▶ **Cochlear implants** Cochlear (KAHK lee uhr) implants are small electronic devices that are surgically implanted under the skin behind the ear. Unlike hearing aids, cochlear implants do not restore normal hearing. Instead, they bypass damaged parts of the inner ear and provide direct electrical stimulation to the nerve that sends signals to the brain. The result is a better understanding of the surrounding voices and noises.

Disabilities Involving Movement Normally, we have control over the movements of our bodies. We decide when to walk, run, or lie down. Unfortunately, for millions of people these simple acts are difficult or impossible. Most disabilities involving movement (motor disabilities) are the result of a disorder of or an injury to the nervous system.

Movement disorders include multiple sclerosis, Parkinson's disease, Rett syndrome, and Tourette's syndrome. Although the symptoms of a movement disorder are usually apparent, diagnosing the cause of the problem can sometimes be difficult. A doctor may use laboratory tests, imaging techniques, or even surgical procedures to determine the cause of a movement disorder.

People with disabilities involving movements, such as Tom Mosca, enjoy many different hobbies and pastimes.

One of the most common causes of movement disabilities is spinal cord injury (SCI). About 80 percent of people in the United States who suffer SCIs are young men, and most are in their late 20s to early 30s. SCI can result in partial or complete loss of body movement. Paralysis affecting only the lower half of the body, not including arms, is called *paraplegia*. Paralysis affecting the upper and lower body is called *quadriplegia*. In the past, most people did not recover from paralysis due to SCI. New treatments make it more likely that a person will regain some movement after injury. Regular, intense therapy is the key to maximizing potential recovery. Recent research indicates that a cure for paralysis could be developed in the near future.

Learning how to sign is one way to gain a better understanding of deafness.

Coping with Disabilities

Learning to deal with disabilities in a positive way can help make disabilities more manageable. Becoming educated about a disability, maintaining a positive outlook, and taking an active role in treatment are a few ways to make living with a disability more tolerable.

No matter how moderate or severe, all disabilities challenge the person affected and those around him or her. In the United States, the Americans with Disabilities Act has resulted in many positive changes for people with disabilities. The **Americans with Disabilities Act (ADA)** is wide-ranging legislation intended to make American society more accessible to people with disabilities. The ADA has led to an increase in the number of handicapped parking spaces and wheelchair-accessible ramps to buildings.

With new research and changing attitudes, the outlook for people with disabilities has become increasingly positive. To continue this trend in the future, people with disabilities and those around them will have to continue to educate each other and work to create a positive environment.

SECTION 3

REVIEW   *Answer the following questions on a separate piece of paper.*

Using Key Terms

1. **Define** the term *disability*.

2. **Identify** the term for "a buzzing, ringing, or whistling sound in one or both ears that occurs even when no sound is present."

3. **Define** the term *Americans with Disabilities Act*.

Understanding Key Ideas

4. **Identify** three myths about disabilities.

5. **List** three different types of disabilities.

6. **Describe** two treatments for people with disabilities involving vision.

7. **Identify** which of the following treatments is used for disabilities involving hearing.
   a. contact lenses   c. cochlear implants
   b. spinal cord surgery   d. none of the above

8. **State** two examples of disorders that affect movement.

9. **Describe** two ways that the Americans with Disabilities Act helps people cope with disabilities.

Critical Thinking

10. **LIFE SKILL** **Practicing Wellness** How can you work to create a positive environment for people with disabilities?

CHAPTER 15

Highlights

Key Terms

The Big Picture

✔ Hereditary diseases are caused by defective genes inherited by a child from one or both parents.

✔ Hereditary diseases can be the result of a single-gene mutation, the mutation of several genes, or chromosome abnormalities.

✔ Examples of single-gene diseases include Huntington's disease, sickle cell anemia, hemophilia, and cystic fibrosis.

✔ Diseases that have both genetic and lifestyle risk factors are called complex diseases. Cardiovascular disease, cancer, and Type II diabetes are examples of complex diseases.

✔ Down syndrome is an example of a chromosomal disease.

✔ Receiving genetic counseling and keeping personal health records can make coping with hereditary diseases easier.

✔ In the future, the Human Genome Project will provide many new treatments for hereditary diseases.

✔ Immune disorders can occur when the immune system does not function normally.

✔ Autoimmune diseases occur when the immune system attacks the body's cells that it normally protects.

✔ Allergies and asthma are immune disorders. Allergies are caused by an immune response to a harmless substance. When a person's airways narrow and become swollen, the result is an asthma attack.

✔ Rheumatoid arthritis and multiple sclerosis are autoimmune diseases. Rheumatoid arthritis is caused when the immune system attacks the joints. Multiple sclerosis is caused by the body attacking myelin, the fatty insulation on nerves in the brain and spinal cord.

✔ Understanding the illness and following a treatment plan are two ways to cope with immune disorders and autoimmune diseases.

✔ Disabilities are physical or mental impairments or deficiencies that interfere with a person's normal activities.

✔ Accidents, diabetes, glaucoma, and macular degeneration account for most blindness in the United States.

✔ A lifetime of excessive noise can destroy the sound receptor cells in the ear, which leads to deafness.

✔ New medicines and surgical procedures are helping people with disabilities involving movement to have more-productive lives.

✔ The Americans with Disabilities Act has made American society more accessible to people with disabilities.

✔ Educating people is one way to help create a positive environment for people with disabilities.

Review

Understanding Key Terms

allergy (372)
Americans with Disabilities Act (ADA) (380)
arthritis (373)
asthma (372)
autoimmune disease (371)
disability (376)
gene (366)
gene therapy (369)
genetic counseling (368)
hereditary disease (366)
Human Genome Project (369)
multiple sclerosis (MS) (374)
tinnitus (378)

1. For each definition below, choose the key term that best matches the definition.
   a. a buzzing, ringing, or whistling sound in one or both ears that occurs even when no sound is present
   b. inflammation of the joints
   c. a technique that places a healthy copy of a gene into the cells of a person whose copy of the gene is defective
   d. a reaction by the body's immune system to a harmless substance
   e. the process of informing a person or couple about their genetic makeup
   f. a research effort to determine the locations of all human genes on the chromosomes and read the coded instructions in the genes

2. Explain the relationship between the key terms in each of the following pairs.
   a. *genes* and *hereditary disease*
   b. *disability* and *Americans with Disabilities Act*
   c. *autoimmune disease* and *multiple sclerosis*

Understanding Key Ideas

Section 1

3. Describe how genes are involved in hereditary diseases.

4. A person's eye color is determined by his or her
   a. age.
   b. genes.
   c. gender.
   d. All of the above

5. Describe one example of each of the three types of hereditary diseases.

6. Identify how keeping personal health records can help a person cope with hereditary diseases.

7. Describe how gene therapy might help people who have cystic fibrosis.

8. **CRITICAL THINKING** Explain why couples who are even distantly related might have a greater chance of having a child with a hereditary disease.

Section 2

9. What is the difference between immune disorders and autoimmune diseases?

10. Which of the following is an immune system disorder?
    a. multiple sclerosis
    b. rheumatoid arthritis
    c. allergies
    d. all of the above

11. Describe two treatments for asthma.

12. Which of the following is an autoimmune disease?
    a. multiple sclerosis
    b. flu
    c. osteoarthritis
    d. cardiovascular disease

13. What are three symptoms of multiple sclerosis?

14. How can asking questions of their doctors help people cope with their autoimmune diseases?

Section 3

15. State the reason it is important to know the difference between myths and truth about disabilities.

16. Describe three ways that people with uncorrectable vision problems can cope with their disability.

17. State the most common cause of hearing loss in children.

18. Compare the two different levels of paralysis.

19. Identify ways that you can help create a positive environment for people living with disabilities.

20. **CRITICAL THINKING** Why might a misconception that recovery cannot occur after a spinal cord injury prevent a person from maximizing his or her potential for recovery?

Interpreting Graphics

Study the figure below to answer the questions that follow.

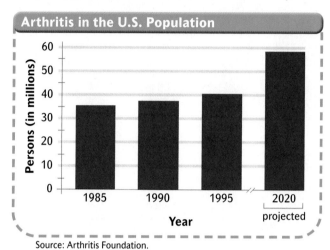

Arthritis in the U.S. Population

Persons (in millions) vs. Year

Source: Arthritis Foundation.

21. How many people in the United States had arthritis in 1985?

22. How many more people are expected to have arthritis in 2020 as compared to 1985?

MATH SKILL

23. CRITICAL THINKING Why do you think the number of people diagnosed with arthritis is expected to rise so dramatically from 1995 to 2020?

Activities

24. Health and Your Family Research the diseases that are common in your family. What hereditary diseases have been the cause of death for members of your family?

25. Health and Your Community Research several facilities in your community that are designed to help people who have disabilities. Create a poster detailing the different ways one of these facilities helps these people.

26. Health and You Research a new approach to treating hereditary diseases that has come from the Human Genome Project. Write a one-page paper describing the treatment and the way it works.

WRITING SKILL
READING SKILL

Action Plan

27. LIFE SKILL Communicating Effectively In the past, myths have led to many misconceptions about people with disabilities. Write one page summarizing how you could help eliminate these myths and help people better understand disabilities.

WRITING SKILL

Standardized Test Prep

Read the passage below, and then answer the questions that follow. **READING SKILL WRITING SKILL**

Sickle cell anemia affects millions of people throughout the world. The majority of these people have ancestors who came from Africa. In order for people to receive proper treatment for this disease, early diagnosis is critical. Approximately 40 U.S. states now perform a blood test to detect <u>faulty</u> versions of hemoglobin on all newborn infants. Hemoglobin is the protein in red blood cells that carries oxygen. If a child is found to have the disease, treatments begin immediately. Although there is currently no cure for sickle cell anemia, treatments can help control the side effects.

28. In this passage, the word *faulty* means
- **A** important.
- **C** unnecessary.
- **B** defective.
- **D** preferred.

29. What can you infer from reading this passage?
- **E** There are more deaths due to sickle cell anemia in the United States than anywhere else in the world.
- **F** Having ancestors from Africa increases a person's chances of developing sickle cell anemia.
- **G** Researchers expect a cure for sickle cell anemia very soon.
- **H** Blood tests for sickle cell anemia are inaccurate.

30. Write a paragraph describing how early diagnosis of sickle cell anemia could affect a person's life.

WRITING SKILL

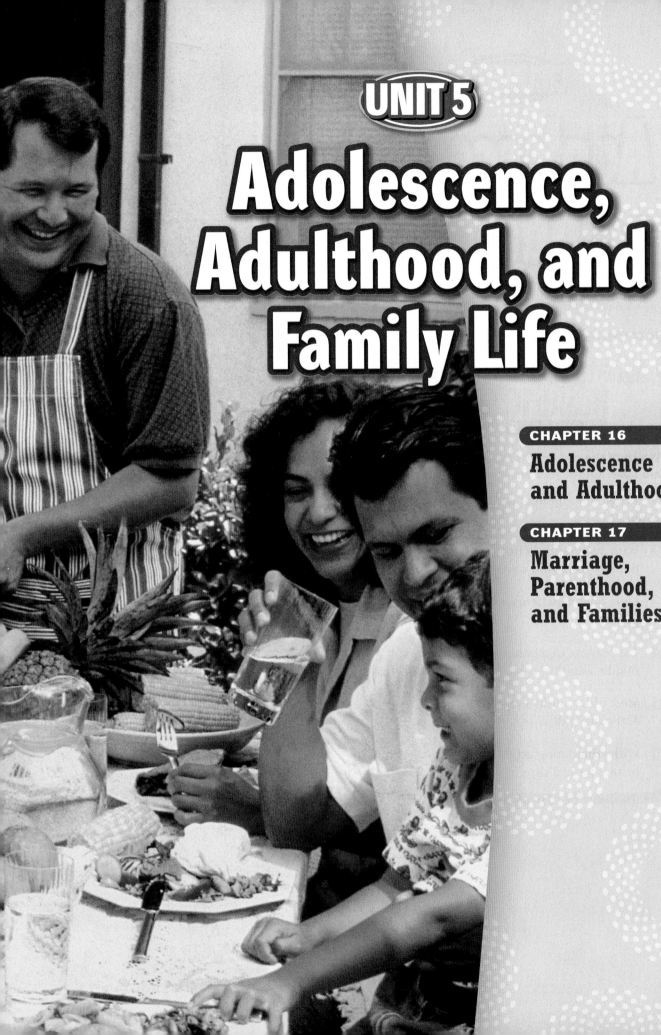

UNIT 5
Adolescence, Adulthood, and Family Life

CHAPTER 16
Adolescence and Adulthood

What's Your Health IQ?
KNOWLEDGE

Which of the statements below are true, and which are false? Check your answers on p. 638.

1. Breast development is the first sign of puberty in girls.

2. With successful dieting, a girl going through puberty can avoid developing extra body fat.

3. Only boys experience voice changes during puberty.

4. The leading causes of death in young and middle adulthood are cancer and heart disease.

5. Most older adults eventually develop Alzheimer's disease.

6. With stimulating activities, mental capacity can be maintained throughout adulthood.

Visit these Web sites for the latest health information:

HEALTH LINKS
THE WORLD'S A CLICK AWAY®

Find more information whenever you see a HealthLinks box. Go to **scilinks.org/health**, and type in the HealthLinks code.

go.hrw.com

Find worksheets and other materials that go with your textbook at **go.hrw.com**.

Current Health

Check out *Current Health®* articles related to this chapter by visiting **go.hrw.com**. Just type in the keyword **HH4 CH16**.

Changes During Adolescence

OBJECTIVES

Compare the physical changes that occur in boys and girls during adolescence.

Describe the mental and emotional changes that occur during adolescence.

Describe the social changes that occur during adolescence.

Identify added responsibilities teens have during adolescence.

Name three ways that changes during adolescence have affected your life. **LIFE SKILL**

Adolescence brings many changes and responsibilities.

Franco was both excited and nervous about his driving test. He had always looked forward to the day when he would get his driver's license. Now, though, he was beginning to realize all of the responsibilities that come with driving a car. He thought to himself, Am I ready for this?

Physical Changes

Franco's worries about the changes in his life are common to many teens during adolescence. **Adolescence** is the period of time between puberty and full maturation. It is a time of change—changing body, changing emotions, changing mental abilities, and changing social life. All these changes can cause teens to feel awkward and unsure of themselves. Knowing as much as possible about the changes that are taking place helps adolescents realize that these changes are normal.

The beginning of adolescence is typically marked by the onset of puberty. **Puberty** is the period of human development during which people become able to produce children. Puberty begins when specific hormones are released. **Hormones** are chemical substances made and released in one part of the body that cause a change in another part of the body. The changes typical of puberty start when the female and male reproductive organs begin to release hormones. The main male hormone is called *testosterone*. The main female hormones are called *estrogen* and *progesterone*.

Physical Changes in Both Girls and Boys Most girls start puberty between 8 and 14 years of age. Boys usually begin puberty later, between 10 and 16 years of age. While some changes are common to both girls and boys, many of the changes are unique to each sex, as shown in **Figure 1**. Some of the changes that both girls and boys can expect to experience include facial acne, growth spurts, an increase in muscle strength and deepening of the voice. However, girls' voices deepen much less than boys' voices deepen.

Physical Changes in Girls Girls experience many changes during puberty, all of which occur at different times for different girls. As girls reach puberty, they naturally develop more body fat than boys do. The fat is needed for normal development during puberty. Hormones cause the hip bones to widen and fat to be deposited around the hips. Fat is also used for development of the breasts. Shortly after development of the breasts, hair begins to appear under the arms and in the pubic area. These changes are typically followed by a growth spurt.

Menarche, or the start of menstruation, begins when estrogen and progesterone levels begin to rise. The average age for menarche is 12 years old, although the age range for menarche varies widely. Girls should remember that these physical changes are a natural and healthy part of puberty.

Physical Changes in Boys As testosterone levels rise in boys, the first physical change seen is an increase in the size of the testes. The **testes** are the male reproductive structures that make sperm and produce the male hormone testosterone. Afterwards, hair begins to appear under the arms and in the pubic and facial areas. At this time, many people notice that the voice deepens. A growth spurt usually occurs toward the end of puberty. Because growth spurts occur earlier

HEALTH Handbook For more information about skin care, see the Express Lesson on pp. 566–569 of this text.

Figure 1

As boys and girls go through puberty, they experience many changes. The most obvious are the physical changes.

Physical Changes of Puberty

Girls

Appearance of hair on underarms and around genitals

Development of the breasts

Widening of hips and pelvis

Start of menstruation and ovulation

Both

Growth spurts

Facial acne

Change in muscle strength

Rise in sex hormones

Boys

Appearance of hair on face, on underarms, and around genitals

Deepening of voice

Broadening of shoulders

Enlargement of testes and penis

in puberty for girls than for boys, girls are usually taller than boys during these first years of puberty. Boys develop larger, stronger muscles throughout puberty.

Because puberty is a time of dramatic change, the body needs special attention during this period. Increases in height and weight mean that the body has greater nutritional needs. Adolescence is a good time to set healthy diet and exercise habits that can be continued throughout adulthood.

Mental and Emotional Changes

While physical changes during puberty are easily seen, mental and emotional changes may not be as noticeable. Coping with mental and emotional changes can be difficult because they are felt by the person but are not visible to others. Mental changes are changes that occur in the thinking process. These changes happen because the brain is still developing. Emotional changes occur as teens learn to cope with all of the changes that occur during adolescence.

A New Way of Thinking Intellectually, teens undergo enormous changes. During early adolescence, boys and girls process information in a simple way. Situations are usually seen from only one side without considering the other person's point of view.

During the middle adolescent period, teens often believe that nothing bad will ever happen to them. For example, teens believe that others may get into accidents but that they themselves will not. They may think this way because the brain is still maturing.

As adolescence progresses, teens can learn to think in a more sophisticated and complex manner. They are able to understand that actions taken today can have consequences the following day or in 10 years. They are able to reason more effectively, compare options, and make logical, mature decisions. They are also able to view situations from another person's perspective. This development helps teens become more compassionate toward others and greatly improves their relationships.

A New Way of Feeling Emotional changes may be the toughest part of adolescence. Many new feelings arise, particularly during adolescence. These new feelings come not only from changes in thinking but also from differences in the way teens see themselves. The new feelings also come when adolescents are treated

Figure 2

Most adolescents feel that their parents don't understand them. Hang on, because these feelings will pass.

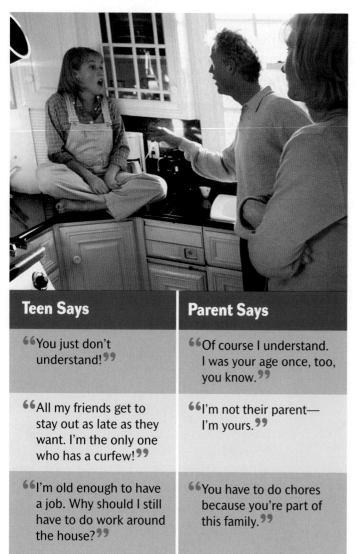

Teen Says	Parent Says
"You just don't understand!"	"Of course I understand. I was your age once, too, you know."
"All my friends get to stay out as late as they want. I'm the only one who has a curfew!"	"I'm not their parent—I'm yours."
"I'm old enough to have a job. Why should I still have to do work around the house?"	"You have to do chores because you're part of this family."

differently by friends and parents. Both boys and girls may find that their feelings get hurt more easily than they did before. Sometimes, these new feelings can cause teens to feel alone, insecure, and confused. These feelings are common during adolescence.

A New Desire for Independence Anger, loneliness, and even depression can be common during adolescence. Many of these feelings come from the teen's desire to become more independent. Frustration and confusion about how to become independent can sometimes seem overwhelming, as seen in **Figure 2.** These feelings arise mostly because up to this point teens have been dependent on other people.

The process of leaving dependence behind and forming a new identity is complex and sometimes scary. Teens may desire independence but feel dependent. These conflicting emotions exist together because the processes of leaving some emotions behind and getting new ones occur at the same time. Having conflicting emotions is healthy and normal. If prolonged periods of sadness or anxiety become too overwhelming, seeking help from a parent, school counselor, or doctor is important.

For more information about dealing with conflict, see Chapter 3.

LIFE SKILL Activity

Communicating Effectively

Communicating Effectively with Your Parents

Conflict with parents can be frustrating, but you can learn to resolve it. Consider the following situation.

John was tired when he came home from school. He put off cleaning his room until later. When John's mom came home, his room was a mess and he was watching TV. She started to yell at him. John ran to his room and yelled back, "You never give me a chance to get things done." John's mom called him disrespectful and lazy. John felt that his mom just did not understand.

Follow these guidelines to help you communicate more effectively with your parents and others.

1 Vent frustration and anger in a healthy way. Call a friend, or write about how you feel. Even when you are angry, hurting others, their stuff, or yourself is not an appropriate response.

2 Assess what happened. How were you right or wrong? How were your parents right or wrong?

3 Take action to resolve the conflict. Go to your parents, and apologize. Express how you felt during the argument.

4 Listen to your parents' side, and try to understand their point of view. Chances are that they are right in some way and are frustrated, too.

5 Plan with your parents to avoid conflict in the future. Ask for ways that you can show them that they can trust you.

LIFE SKILL **Communicating Effectively**

Write down two ways that John could have resolved the conflict with his mother. Then, write down two ways that John could build trust with his mother.

WRITING SKILL

"All my friends are allowed to..."
"YOU NEVER..."
"You just don't understand..."
"Things were different when you were young..."

Dealing with New Feelings   Learning how to deal with new, strong feelings is an important part of becoming a mature teenager. Along with these new feelings comes a greater desire to act on them. Controlling these desires is a serious challenge during adolescence. For example, when we are mad, we may want to express our anger by yelling. Feeling anger can be healthy, but yelling because one is angry is immature. Emotional maturity means learning to handle those strong feelings in an emotionally healthy way.

Controlling Your Emotions   Sometimes mental, emotional, or sexual emotions during adolescence can feel so strong that some teens believe that they do not have control over what they do. This belief is not true. Teens are very capable of learning to feel intense emotions and not act on them. Successfully separating feelings from behaviors makes a teen truly more mature and independent.

Social Changes

How teens communicate and interact with family, friends, and others is an important part of the teen years. Social changes refer to those changes that occur within the relationships in a teen's life. These relationships may be intimate ones with family or they may be more formal ones, such as with a boss at work. During adolescence, relationships change because mental, emotional, and physical changes are happening all at once. Parents, teachers, and siblings begin to respond differently to an adolescent because, in a sense, a new person is evolving in their presence.

Increased Expectations   As you mature, you may find that your parents expect more from you. And hopefully, you will find that your expectations of yourself increase as well. Evaluating these expectations and discussing which are negotiable and which are not are important for teens. It is normal for curfew, chores, and dating rules to change. It is also important to talk to parents about these expectations and to be willing to negotiate with your parents about them.

ZITS reprinted with special permission of King Features Syndicate, Inc.

Teens must also expect that some rules will be nonnegotiable, because everyone lives with some fixed rules. For example, no matter how old a person is, stopping at red traffic lights and abiding by other community rules are required. Social maturity means understanding, accepting, and living by each negotiable and nonnegotiable rule.

Changing Relationships Your relationships with your friends also change and become increasingly important during adolescence. As a teen, you may find yourself wanting to spend more time with friends than with family. Your changing relationships with your friends can be stressful for parents, too. Parents may feel hurt that their teen prefers spending more time with their friends than with them. Or parents may worry that their teenager is engaging in friendships that are unhealthy.

Evaluating Your Relationships Friendships can be difficult to assess during the teen years because emotions run high and can change quickly. Teens must take a hard look at their friendships and decide whether the friendships are good for them. You can evaluate your friendships by asking the following questions:
> Does this friendship bring out the best in me, or does it discourage me?
> Does the friendship make me a stronger or a weaker person?
> Does this person respect me and allow me to share my opinions and beliefs, or does this person insist that I conform to his or her ways?

A healthy friendship is one in which each person encourages the other. If the answers to the questions above indicate that a relationship is unhealthy, then the problems in the relationship must be addressed to resolve them. If they can't be resolved, then you must have the strength to end the relationship.

A teen's desire to be accepted can be very strong. Teens usually look to friends to find acceptance. But sometimes this strategy doesn't work. Take teen cliques, for example. *Cliques* are small, exclusive groups of friends that are judgmental of both their friends and others. Cliques can be painful to those on the outside, who may feel rejected. Gangs are another example of groups that can cause more harm than good.

Increased Responsibilities Independence is really about taking responsibility for one's feelings, thoughts, and behaviors. If a teen is to mature into an independent adult, taking responsibility in the teen's relationships at home is the best place to begin. As a teen's feelings and thoughts about his or her parents and siblings change, the teen's responsibilities toward them also change. Teens must start to communicate in a more mature manner, which entails listening well, allowing others to talk, and respectfully considering others' feelings and ideas. Good communication skills can also help to strengthen relationships with others. Some examples of

Evaluating Changing Relationships

1 **Ask questions.** Is this a healthy friendship? Is this friendship allowing me to grow?

2 **Take charge.** You can now think more like an adult, so decide on positive changes you can make to improve your relationships.

3 **Get tough.** Some of your friendships may become unhealthy. If you have difficulty breaking those relationships off, ask a good friend or teacher to help you.

4 **Commit yourself to improving.** You'll make some mistakes in your relationships, but you will learn from your mistakes.

Your best friend is 16 years old, and she is at a sleepover with eight other girls. At midnight, a good friend of hers sneaks over to the house, taps on the bedroom window, and asks her to a party at his friend's house. No parents are at the party. She tells her friend that she doesn't want to go because she doesn't feel right sneaking out. The others at the slumber party ask her to drive them to the party. What should she do?

Write on a separate piece of paper the advice you would give your best friend. Remember to use the decision-making steps.

Give thought to the problem.

Review your choices.

Evaluate the consequences of each choice.

Assess and choose the best choice.

Think it over afterward.

how you can take more responsibility in relationships at home include

- ▶ showing concern for how people are feeling by asking how they are doing
- ▶ listening to another's tone of voice, ideas, and opinions. If the person sounds tired or sad, ask what you can do to help
- ▶ looking for ways to encourage other people and support them with kind words

As teens begin to take on more responsibility, they will find that those around them will trust them more. Teens often complain that parents don't trust them, but trust is something that has to be demonstrated and earned. Teens must look for opportunities to show their trustworthiness.

Working Outside the Home The teen years often bring the first opportunity for a paid job outside of the home. This experience is exciting but requires maturity and responsibility. Employers expect workers to perform to the best of their ability. The consequences of a job poorly done can range from receiving a pay cut to being fired. A teen who hasn't been responsible around the house will likely have many problems at work. Teens must realize that in families and in the world at large, many rules exist. Some rules are negotiable, but many are not. Thus, the demand for teens to act mature, to dress appropriately and to have good hygiene habits is greater than ever on the job. Teens can behave maturely by understanding the expectations of their boss and following through with commitments.

SECTION 1

REVIEW

Answer the following questions on a separate piece of paper.

Using Key Terms

1. **Compare** the terms *adolescence* and *puberty*.

2. **Identify** three hormones that contribute to the start of puberty.

3. **Describe** the role of the testes in physical development.

Understanding Key Ideas

4. **Identify** a change that is common to boys and girls during puberty.
   a. broadening of the shoulders
   b. widening of hips and pelvis
   c. facial acne
   d. facial hair

5. **Describe** how teens' ways of thinking change during puberty.

6. **Describe** three ways that teens can take on more responsibility at home.

7. **State** three ways that teens can be more mature while working outside the home.

Critical Thinking

8. **LIFE SKILL** **Practicing Wellness** Identify ways that you can tell if a relationship is healthy. Discuss what you can do if the relationship isn't healthy.

9. **LIFE SKILL** **Coping** State three changes that you have experienced during adolescence. Then, identify two ways to cope with these changes.

Adulthood

OBJECTIVES

Describe the changes that occur during young adulthood.

Identify the opportunities middle adulthood offers.

Name three concerns that an older adult might have.

List behaviors that promote healthy aging.

State three ways in which you can help an older adult you know lead a healthy life. **LIFE SKILL**

KEY TERMS

menopause the time of life when a woman stops ovulating and menstruating

midlife crisis the sense of uncertainty about one's identity and values that some people experience in midlife

Alzheimer's disease a disease in which one gradually loses mental capacities and the ability to carry out daily activities

life expectancy the average length of time an individual is expected to live

Do you ever dream of the day when you will be completely independent? When you'll own your own car? Independence comes with many responsibilities. Knowing what is expected of adults will allow you to start now to prepare yourself for adulthood.

Young Adulthood

Even though Americans are considered legal adults at the age of 18, a person who is 18 is still technically a teenager. Young adulthood is considered to be the period of adulthood between the ages of 21 and 35. This period is full of changes, challenges, and decisions.

Physical Changes   During young adulthood, the growth rate of adults begins to slow down. As young adults' bodies begin to mature, they also enter a time of peak physical health. Many young adults take advantage of their health by playing sports or taking part in outdoor activities.

Mental and Emotional Changes   With the changing emotions of the teen years behind, many young adults experience a sense of settling. Many of the conflicting feelings that occur during adolescence disappear and allow young adults to feel better about life. They enjoy the independence from their family but continue developing close relationships. Young adults begin to relate to their parents on an adult level. Keeping in touch with family is one way to adjust to the separation young adults may feel.

Intellectually, young adults think more abstractly. They can more consistently make mature, responsible choices. All of these changes give young adults a clearer sense of their identity: who they are, what they want from friendships, and what job they want to have.

Along with the increased responsibilities of young adulthood come many rewards.

Social Changes Many young adults choose to marry and start a family during this time in their life. Before entering into such strong commitments, one must know oneself well—one's skills, values, strengths, weaknesses, and beliefs.

Commitment in relationships is very important. Some young adults choose to remain single. Others are afraid to marry. One reason may be that they have never seen a positive relationship. As a result, they may wonder if their marriage will fall apart. It is important that they know that they *can* make their marriage work. Seeking advice from older adults who have successful marriages is helpful.

Financial Concerns One exciting aspect of young adulthood is that you can start working toward your dream job. You might get a job or continue your education. You make decisions about the things you thought, planned, and prepared for as an adolescent. Young adults enjoy financial independence and freedom, perhaps for the first time in their lives. They are responsible for earning and spending their own money. While such independence can be scary, it can also be exciting. With this financial freedom comes the ability to choose where to work, where to live, and what car to buy.

real life Activity

CALCULATING A BUDGET

LIFE SKILL
Setting Goals

Materials

✔ paper
✔ calculator
✔ list of salaries and monthly expenses

Week	1	2	3
Housing	$300		
Food	$100		
Transportation	$100		
Entertainment	$50		
Total	$550		

Procedure

1. **Divide** into groups of three students. Each group should be assigned a salary and given a list of monthly expenses.

2. **Divide** your salary by 12 to calculate your monthly allowance.

3. **Calculate** how much money you need per month for each expense category.

4. **Analyze** with your partners how much money you need in total. Divide the monthly salary accordingly. Some categories will need more money than others.

5. **Decide** as a group which categories are more important than others.

Conclusions

1. **Calculating Data** **MATH SKILL** What is your group's monthly salary?

2. **Calculating Data** **MATH SKILL** How much money do you need per month for each expense category?

3. **Summarizing Results** Does your salary meet the needs of your budget? Discuss ways to help your budget meet your salary.

4. **CRITICAL THINKING** For most jobs, the higher the education level, the higher the salary. Discuss the decisions that you can make now to affect your future job. How will you carry out those decisions?

Maintaining Wellness Young adults face many of the same health risks as adolescents. The No. 1 cause of death in people between the ages of 15 and 24 is unintentional injuries. Auto accidents, many of which involve alcohol, account for most of these accidents. The second and third leading causes of death are homicide and suicide, respectively.

Young adults who smoke, drink, and fail to exercise may feel healthy for a number of years and believe that these habits aren't harmful. But later in life, the ill effects of these bad habits appear. Suddenly, it may be too late to reverse the effects of bad habits. Because patterns developed during young adulthood affect your life later on, it is important to develop healthy habits during this time.

Middle Adulthood

We often hear the teen years described as being the best years of life. In fact, for many adults, this is not true. Middle adulthood, the period between 35 and 65 years of age, can prove to be "the best years" for many reasons.

Physical Changes The body goes through many changes during middle adulthood. Middle age used to be seen as a time when your body would start to slow down. Fortunately, with changes in attitude, diet, and physical exercise, adults have enjoyed greater physical stamina. Muscle tone and strength naturally begin to diminish, but with regular, moderate exercise, they can be maintained.

Women typically begin menopause between the ages of 50 and 55. **Menopause** is the period of time in a woman's life when the woman stops ovulating and menstruating. As a woman's estrogen and progesterone levels fall, the body's reproductive capacity begins to slow down. After menopause, women no longer menstruate or ovulate (produce mature eggs). Changes that accompany menopause may include hot flashes, a decrease in breast size, anxiety, and sometimes depression. Lower levels of estrogen put women at risk for osteoporosis, or weakening of the bones. Taking supplemental calcium and exercising can decrease the risk of developing osteoporosis.

Men also experience many physical changes during middle adulthood. Just as women experience a decline in their ability to reproduce, so do males. As men age, their sex hormone and sperm production gradually decrease.

Mental and Emotional Changes Many middle-aged adults begin to accept their mortality as they see friends and loved ones die. They reflect on these changes and begin to evaluate their lives. A healthy mind will see mistakes made, accept them,

Many rewards accompany the added responsibilities of middle adulthood, such as a rewarding career and friendships with co-workers.

Midlife years are the best years of life for many people. Many are able to enjoy and focus on their families and job.

and move forward by trying to learn and change. Accepting the passage of time brings maturity. Satisfaction is gained from reflecting on the birth and growth of children, job accomplishments, and healthy relationships. A healthy, mature mind can accept changes and look forward to the later parts of life with hopeful anticipation.

Occasionally, an adult may experience a midlife crisis. A **midlife crisis** is the sense of uncertainty about one's identity and values that some people experience in midlife. If someone experiences a midlife crisis, it usually begins in the person's forties. Adults may feel that their life is slipping away and that they are losing their youth. Thus, they try to hold onto that youth rather than accept their maturation. They may make dramatic changes in their life, such as taking a new job, in an effort to feel better about themselves. However, such changes do not solve their problem because they do not deal with the root of the problem, which is fear of accepting the loss of their youth. Many middle-aged adults experience psychological changes. These changes are healthy and normal.

Social Changes   Adults in this stage often enjoy clearer identity formation—they know who they are. By the time adults reach the middle years, they are able to positively focus on their family and their job. They understand their role in each area and make choices accordingly. They guide their family through changes in life and take on leadership roles in child-rearing and in their job. Stresses do arise. When handled in a healthy manner, though, these stresses can mature a person and deepen one emotionally and intellectually.

Financial Concerns   Most adults learn to accept more responsibility during middle adulthood because other people depend on them for financial and emotional support. As with any responsibility, there are pleasures in addition to the strains. Some adults experience immense satisfaction from providing for others. These greater financial needs can also bring on greater stress.

The effects of stress can be serious, and adults must learn to cope. But for some people, the stress may get overwhelming. Health problems from stress can erupt. Such problems may include depression, ulcers, high blood pressure, or heart disease. Mental health deeply affects physical health during these years, and caring for both aspects of health is very important.

Maintaining Wellness   The leading cause of death during middle adulthood is cancer. Cancer is followed closely by heart disease as a cause of death. Adults can reduce their risks of cancer and heart disease by exercising, not smoking, and eating a low-fat diet to prevent high blood cholesterol. Many young adults do not feel the effects of eating a poor diet, smoking or chewing tobacco, not exercising, and being overweight. As these young adults grow older, however, they may begin to experience the ill effects of these habits.

Receiving yearly medical care from a physician is very important for preventing and treating problems. For example, one may have high blood pressure or cancer and not know it. To ensure good health, both women and men need regular medical exams from a physician.

Older Adulthood

The population of older adults (those 65 years of age and older) in the United States has grown rapidly during the past decade. This trend is predicted to continue well into the new century. Some reasons for this trend are improved understanding of nutrition, exercise, and disease prevention as well as advances in medical care. Sadly, our cultural attitudes have encouraged young people to view older adults as uninformed, unproductive, and unable to enjoy life. In reality, older adults may enjoy experiences that are not possible in the early or middle adult years. Descriptions of this and other stages of adulthood can be seen in **Table 1.**

Physical Changes As adults move into older adulthood, they continue the aging process. As they age, they may find that their ability to recover from illnesses or injuries is not as quick as before. In addition, the effects of years of unhealthy habits started during adolescence may become evident during this time of life. For example, smoking-related lung cancer and obesity-related diabetes are two common concerns for older adults.

Mental and Emotional Changes Most older adults are more emotionally stable than they were earlier in life. This stability is a natural consequence of maturity. They have endured hardships such as the death of a close friend, spouse, or family member. Many come to terms with the meaning of life—what is important and what is not. Young adults can learn much from older adults.

Table 1 Stages of Adulthood		
Age	**Stage**	**Description**
21–35	young adulthood	This period of life is marked by a first career job, marriage, children, and financial independence.
35–65	middle adulthood	Greater financial security, satisfaction with a growing family, and emotional maturity mark this time of life.
65 and older	older adulthood	Wisdom accumulated from a variety of life experiences marks this stage. Loneliness and isolation can be serious problems.

Ways to Interact with Older Adults

1 Visit them. Sit and listen to them. Ask them what they would do in certain situations. Ask for their opinion.

2 Offer to do simple household chores. They'll love having you around while you get work done that perhaps they can't do.

3 Bring them food. Bake cookies, and deliver them personally. Ask if they need groceries, and then get them.

internet connect

www.scilinks.org/health
Topic: Alzheimer's Disease
HealthLinks code: HH4009

HEALTH LINKS. Maintained by the National Science Teachers Association

Despite the extensive life experiences they have had, older adults are not immune from many of the same mental problems that are possible in the earlier years. Depression, anxiety, or loneliness may also plague the elderly. Younger family members must be alert for signs of such problems in older family members. The younger family members too can benefit from helping older loved ones. Such help could be as simple as an occasional visit or phone call. If we take time to listen to older adults, we find that many of their feelings are similar to ours—whether we are a teen or a middle-aged adult.

Many younger adults believe that older adults lose their intelligence and wisdom to age and disease. This belief is not true for most older adults. For example, Alzheimer's disease occurs in only a small percentage of the population of adults between the ages of 65 and 80. **Alzheimer's disease** is a disease in which one gradually loses mental capacities and the ability to carry out daily activities.

Alzheimer's disease affects the brain and usually progresses slowly. A person with this disease first begins losing short-term memory and then long-term memory. Sometimes the patient forgets where he or she is. Sometimes the patient does not recognize loved ones. Alzheimer's is an emotionally painful disease to both the patient and the family.

Social Changes   Many adults look forward to retirement after age 65. Leaving a career of many years can be enjoyable but also stressful. Any major lifestyle change is hard. Adapting to retirement usually requires time. Adapting may take a few weeks or even months. Believe it or not, when an adult has focused for many years on a career, shifting that focus onto an enjoyable hobby or recreation can be difficult. Most people eventually come to appreciate the freedoms and free time retirement offers.

Financial Concerns   Older adults who do decide to work less or retire may find that their financial situation has changed. Although taking advantage of this time period by enjoying such activities as traveling and visiting family members is important, planning ahead is also important. Some adults may require expensive healthcare. In some cases, they may even have to face moving into a retirement home and losing their independence.

Maintaining Wellness   Health problems that the elderly face are similar to those of middle-aged adults. Cancer and heart disease are the leading causes of illness in older adults. So, maintaining healthy habits is very important for older adults. There is no reason that age alone should make a person less productive in society or prohibit him or her from fully enjoying life.

"All old people get Alzheimer's, so I don't want to get old."	Less than 4 percent of people aged 65 to 74 get Alzheimer's disease.
"The teen years are always the best years of life."	The teen years can be difficult. Often, people feel more settled and satisfied with relationships and life later in adulthood.
"Most older people are sickly and are unable to take care of themselves."	The majority of older people are fairly healthy and self-sufficient.
"Older people should stop exercising and get a lot of rest."	Exercise at any age strengthens heart and lung function. Older people can benefit from exercising as much as anyone else.

Healthy Aging

When we look at the big picture of life from adolescence to older adulthood, we see the health risks shift from accidents and injuries to illnesses such as heart disease and various forms of cancer. We can see the importance of establishing healthy patterns of behavior early in adolescence to reduce serious health risks during the teen years as well as later in life. As a teen, you may rarely think of how eating, exercising, and risk-taking affect your health later in life. The truth is that healthy changes in your behavior during these critical years are extremely important to your health in older adulthood.

Common Concerns During Aging Building a positive attitude about each stage of life can ensure that a person will care for his or her health. Having a positive outlook is important because mental health and physical health affect each other. For example, physical exercise can reduce psychological depression by increasing the circulation of certain brain chemicals.

One of the tragic myths of aging is that as we age, we lose our intellectual sharpness and our ability to enjoy life and be productive. The truth is that advancing age brings greater wisdom and, in many ways, an ability to enjoy life more than we did during early adulthood. As adults mature, however, they must keep their minds stimulated. This can be accomplished through active work, such as reading, listening to music, and talking to others, rather than passively watching television and movies.

Many emotional challenges arise throughout adulthood. Loneliness, depression, or various stages of grief occur as we move through difficult life experiences, such as the death of friends, the death of a spouse, or perhaps divorce. It is very important for adults to pay attention to their feelings and moods and to seek help from loved ones.

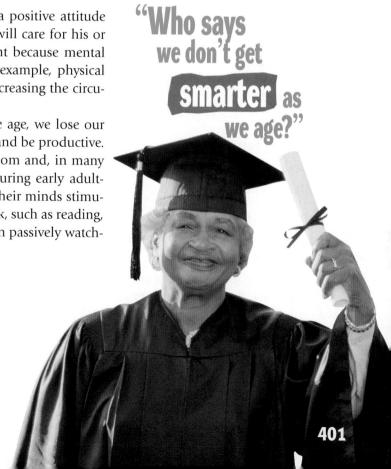
"Who says we don't get **smarter** as we age?"

Figure 3

Regular exercise is one way to maintain your health now and in the future.

ACTIVITY *What is one form of exercise you can start now?*

Tips for Healthy Aging The average length of time an individual is expected to live, or **life expectancy,** has risen dramatically since 1960. Most men and women who live to be 65 can also expect to live until age 80. Scientists predict that the greatest increase in population over the next few decades will occur in people over the age of 85. Thus, making certain that older adults are independent, healthy, mentally keen, and productive is important.

The most important habits to form during adolescence and early adulthood are those that keep us physically healthier, as seen in **Figure 3.**

▶ Establishing regular exercise can actually help us live longer. Regular exercise improves quality of life and may prevent premature death and disease.

▶ Even the simple measure of not smoking can dramatically reduce the risks of developing heart disease, cancer, and other diseases.

▶ Not drinking alcohol also decreases the risk of death by car accidents, alcoholism, and liver disease.

▶ Maintaining a healthy weight helps to prevent diabetes later in life.

▶ Lowering salt intake and keeping total Calories at a level at which normal weight for height is maintained are important to a person's health as they age.

The development from adolescence to adulthood is a miraculous journey, and life can get better with each passing year. Growing older is a privilege and process worthy of our respect and care. We should not reject the process but should look forward to and enjoy every part of this journey.

SECTION 2

REVIEW   *Answer the following questions on a separate piece of paper.*

Using Key Terms

1. **Describe** the symptoms of Alzheimer's disease.

2. **Define** *life expectancy.*

Understanding Key Ideas

3. **Describe** how emotions change during young adulthood.

4. **Identify** the leading cause of death in young adults, and describe actions they can take to reduce the risk of dying during this period.

5. **Describe** three changes that you might face during middle adulthood.

6. **State** the leading causes of illness in older adults.

7. **State** whether our culture portrays older adults as having less intelligence. Explain why this portrayal is true or why it isn't true.

8. **LIFE SKILL** **Practicing Wellness** State three ways that you can help an older adult to lead a healthier life.

9. **LIFE SKILL** **Practicing Wellness** Identify four habits that you can begin today to improve the quality of your life in 10 years.

Critical Thinking

10. Some people describe the teen years and young adulthood as the "best years of life." Do you agree or disagree? Why?

Highlights

Key Terms

SECTION 1

adolescence (388)
puberty (388)
hormone (388)
testes (389)

The Big Picture

✔ Changes in hormone levels mark the beginning of puberty.

✔ Puberty involves many physical changes, some of which are unique to boys and girls.

✔ As teens mature, they begin to think in a more complex and sophisticated manner.

✔ Adolescence is a process of gradually accepting more responsibility for one's behaviors, thoughts, and feelings.

✔ Mental maturity allows adolescents to see life from another person's viewpoint, not simply from their own. This maturity helps them respect others.

✔ During adolescence, teens' relationships change as more is expected from them.

✔ Working outside the home requires a high level of maturity and commitment on the part of the teen.

SECTION 2

menopause (397)
midlife crisis (398)
Alzheimer's disease (400)
life expectancy (402)

✔ Moving from young adulthood into older adulthood involves many mental, physical, and emotional changes.

✔ Young adulthood is a time marked by increased independence.

✔ Young adults can exert great influence over all areas of their health and can reduce their risk of developing diseases by making healthy lifestyle choices.

✔ During middle adulthood, the different aspects of adults' lives become more stable. This stability allows for greater focus on their job and family.

✔ With the increased financial responsibilities of middle adulthood also comes satisfaction from providing for others.

✔ Keeping physically, mentally, and socially active can ensure that older adulthood is an enjoyable time marked by good health.

✔ The older adult years can be a time of great satisfaction, productivity, and wisdom. Aging is a natural process that should be viewed positively.

Review

Understanding Key Terms

adolescence (388)

Alzheimer's disease (400)

hormone (388)

life expectancy (402)

menopause (397)

midlife crisis (398)

puberty (388)

testes (389)

1. For each definition below, choose the key term that best matches the definition.
   a. the sense of uncertainty about one's identity and values that some people experience in midlife
   b. a chemical present in the bloodstream that brings about changes during puberty
   c. the male reproductive structures that make sperm and produce the male hormone testosterone
   d. the average length of time that an adult is expected to live
   e. the years during which a woman makes the transition from menstruating to having her last period
   f. the period of human development during which people become able to bear children

2. Explain the relationship between the key terms in each of the following pairs.
   a. *adolescence* and *puberty*
   b. *hormone* and *testes*

Understanding Key Ideas

Section 1

3. Name one hormone responsible for changes in males during puberty.

4. Name one hormone responsible for changes in females during puberty.

5. Describe the changes in thinking that adolescents undergo as they mature.

6. Describe why it is important for teens to separate feelings and behaviors.

7. Important actions that an adolescent can take to protect their health during the teen years include
   a. refusing to smoke.   c. avoiding alcohol.
   b. exercising moderately. d. All of the above

8. Adolescence is a time for taking greater responsibility in what areas of life?

9. Communicating more maturely involves which of the following actions?
   a. listening actively   c. focusing on your feelings
   b. venting frustration   d. getting your way

10. **CRITICAL THINKING** List two ways that relationships change during adolescence. How can you cope with these changes? **LIFE SKILL**

Section 2

11. Which social change is one that young adults often face?
    a. Alzheimer's disease   c. midlife crisis
    b. menopause   d. marriage

12. In general, do young adults enjoy greater financial independence than adolescents do or less financial independence?

13. The No. 1 health risk that a young adult faces is
    a. cancer from smoking.
    b. heart attacks.
    c. unintentional injuries.
    d. diabetes.

14. At what age do women typically begin menopause?

15. Why is it important for middle-aged adults to visit the doctor annually?

16. The chance of developing osteoporosis, or thinning of the bones, can be reduced by
    a. getting extra rest.   c. exercising regularly.
    b. reading.   d. avoiding calcium.

17. Describe the types of financial concerns many older adults experience.

18. Since 1960, the life expectancy of Americans has
    a. stayed the same.   c. decreased slightly.
    b. increased.   d. decreased greatly.

19. **CRITICAL THINKING** Explain how someone might appropriately deal with a midlife crisis.

20. **CRITICAL THINKING** Why do you think that having a positive attitude about growing older is important? **LIFE SKILL**

Interpreting Graphics

Study the figure below to answer the questions that follow.

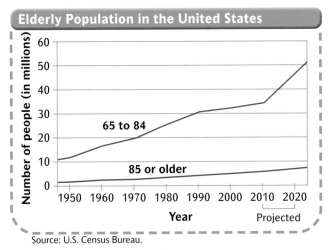

Elderly Population in the United States

Source: U.S. Census Bureau.

21. How many more people were age 65 to 84 in the year 2000 than in 1970? **MATH SKILL**

22. How has the number of people who are 85 or older changed over time? **MATH SKILL**

23. **CRITICAL THINKING** Why do you think the number of people who are 65 or older has risen so dramatically?

Activities

24. **Health and You** Interview one person from each stage of adulthood. Ask them about the concerns and advantages of their stage. Create a chart to summarize your results.

25. **Health and You** List each of the following problems on one side of a piece of paper: high blood pressure, heart attack, stroke, car accidents, and cancer. Now, beside each health hazard, write one thing that you can do to reduce the risk of the problem.

26. **Health and Your Community** Create a brochure explaining the changes that adolescents experience during puberty. Explain ways that the adolescents can positively cope with these changes.

Action Plan

27. **LIFE SKILL** **Assessing Your Health** Establishing healthy patterns of living during adolescence reduces the risks of dying early and makes life more enjoyable. Explain five habits that you can begin now that will make your life healthier and more enjoyable. How will you make these changes?

Standardized Test Prep

Read the passage below, and then answer the questions that follow. **READING SKILL** **WRITING SKILL**

Juan was a successful architectural engineer in San Francisco, California. He had two children and a wife. At age 42, he finally quit his smoking habit, which he started when he was 18. He began to jog every day and completed a marathon on his 45th birthday. After being <u>badgered</u> by his family, he finally went to see his doctor when he was 46. His physician told him that he had early lung cancer and high blood pressure. Juan was shocked because he felt that he was in the best shape of his life.

28. In this passage, the word *badgered* means
   A saddened.
   B asked to do something.
   C comforted.
   D laughed at.

29. What can you infer from reading this passage?
   E Juan does not like to jog.
   F Smoking may have contributed to Juan's cancer and high blood pressure.
   G Juan has lived in San Francisco for 10 years.
   H None of the above

30. Write a paragraph describing Juan and his family's life after finding out that Juan has lung cancer and high blood pressure.

31. Write a paragraph describing the factors that may have contributed to Juan's cancer and high blood pressure. Explain how Juan could have made healthier lifestyle choices to reduce his chances of developing these diseases.

Coming of Age

Almost every society has a ritual to mark the transition from childhood to adulthood. Some coming-of-age rituals are quite informal, while others are ceremonial.

What does it mean to be an adult? In answering this question, scientists and social scientists look at cultures all over the world to find what we have in common. One thing most cultures share is some sort of ritual marking the transition from childhood or adolescence to adulthood. The rituals associated with this transition are called *rites-of-passage* or *coming-of-age ceremonies.*

Rites of Passage

Think about your own life. What incidents do we use to mark your maturity? When does our society say to you, "Now you are an adult with its rights and responsibilities"? Some of our rituals are informal. For example, obtaining a driver's license has great significance to many teenagers. Voting at 18 gives you the rights and responsibilities of a political voice. Turning 21 gives you new rights and responsibilities. More-formal rites of passage may include your school's most formal dance.

Many religions have a very formal coming-of-age rite called *confirmation.* In the Catholic Church, for example, a bishop places his hands on a young person's head to signify that this person has received the wisdom to make his or her own decisions about faith.

Coming of Age Around the World

All over the world, people just like you engage in rites of passage. Although some of these rites may seem unusual, each has the same kind of significance that the various ways our society marks the transition to adulthood do.

▶ **Maasai** As part of elaborate coming-of-age ceremonies, Maasai boys from the African nation of Kenya go to live in *manyattas,* camps built by adult women of the society. Adult women also chaperone the girls who live in the camp. Boys practice ancient rituals, including using spears and wielding shields, to become *morans* (warriors).

DRIVER'S HANDBOOK

- **Mexico** When a girl reaches 15 years of age, many people mark that milestone with a rite of passage called a *quinceañera*. A girl of 15 arrives at a thanksgiving mass in a traditional white or pastel Mexican dress full of frills. Her friends, who act as attendants, may accompany the girl. After mass, there may be a birthday party, at which a dance with the girl's favorite boy highlights the festivities.

- **Navajo Nation** When a Navajo girl comes of age, she participates in a traditional ceremony called *Kinaalda*. This ceremony lasts for 4 days. It is based on a cycle of songs called the *Blessing Way*. The ritual ends on the fourth day with a traditional campfire in which the girl bakes a special corn cake to symbolize her acceptance of the hard work that comes with adulthood.

- **Judaism** Many coming-of-age rituals are religious in nature. When a young boy of the Jewish faith makes a transition into manhood, he is part of a ceremony called a *bar mitzvah*. This ceremony takes place around his 13th birthday. The ceremony takes place in a day, but learning about the Jewish faith may take months or years of preparation. Girls participate in a *bat mitzvah*. Both terms mean "commandment age" and signify that one has become an adult of the faith.

- **Japan** Coming of age in Japan takes on a national significance. *Seijin-no-hi*—"Coming of Age Day"—takes place every year on January 15 in Japan. This day is set aside to honor anyone who has turned 20 during the past year. Twenty is a significant legal age in Japan, too. People can vote, and other options become open to them. The day often begins with athletic events or town celebrations. People who are 20 dress up and go out with their friends for a night on the town.

One thing that characterizes all of these rituals is the society's enthusiasm for children. Although the message that one is becoming an adult is serious, the rites and rituals themselves can be exciting and show that the adults accept the youth as one of their own.

The quinceañera celebrates this teen's entry into young adulthood.

YOUR TURN

1. **Summarizing Information** Why does almost every society have coming-of-age rituals and rites?

2. **Interpreting Information** Research one culture, and write a paragraph about how that culture marks the transition from childhood to adulthood.

3. **CRITICAL THINKING** How do you think that coming-of-age rituals in your society help you focus on your rights and responsibilities?

CHAPTER 17

Marriage, Parenthood, and Families

What's Your Health IQ?
KNOWLEDGE

Which of the statements below are true, and which are false? Check your answers on p. 638.

1. In healthy marriages, the spouses try to meet all of each other's needs.

2. The serious emotional consequences of divorce are felt only by the couple divorcing.

3. A spouse should depend on his or her partner to solve all conflict in the marriage.

4. A parent's behavior affects how his or her children feel about themselves.

5. An increasing number of single fathers are raising their children.

SECTION 1
Marriage

SECTION 2
Parenthood

SECTION 3
Families

Visit these Web sites for the latest health information:

HEALTH LINKS.
THE WORLD'S A CLICK AWAY

Find more information whenever you see a HealthLinks box. Go to **scilinks.org/health**, and type in the HealthLinks code.

go.hrw.com

Find worksheets and other materials that go with your textbook at **go.hrw.com**.

Current Health

Check out *Current Health* articles related to this chapter by visiting **go.hrw.com**. Just type in the keyword **HH4 CH17**.

SECTION 1

Marriage

OBJECTIVES

Describe the responsibilities of married partners.

List five things couples should discuss if they are considering marriage.

Name three difficulties that teenagers who are married may face.

Identify four ways in which a teen can cope with a divorce or remarriage in the family.

KEY TERMS

marriage a lifelong union between a husband and a wife, who develop an intimate relationship

emotional intimacy the state of being emotionally connected to another person

emotional maturity the ability to assess a relationship or situation and to act according to what is best for oneself and for the other person in the relationship

divorce the legal end to a marriage

Two halves of one whole. The resting place for deep friendship. The blending of souls. All of these phrases have been used to describe marriage. But marriages do not form easily. Marriages are created by the strength of loving actions, commitment, compromise, and emotional intimacy.

Healthy Marriages: Working Together

You have probably observed many married couples. Have you noticed how the interactions of each couple differ? A **marriage** is a lifelong union between a husband and a wife, who develop an intimate relationship. Deciding whether to marry is one of the most serious decisions a person can make. Marriage can provide great rewards for both partners, such as deep friendship, emotional intimacy, and children. Knowing the responsibilities of a healthy marriage can help you prepare for this decision.

Mature love takes time to develop. To develop a serious relationship, the partners must be willing to learn about each other.

Responsibilities of Marriage A healthy marriage requires that both partners work together to meet each other's needs. Other responsibilities for each partner include the following:

▶ **Love** In a healthy marriage, spouses show their love for each other through actions and do not depend solely on feelings of love. Feelings of love change over time. Sometimes, couples may not feel the same intensity of love they felt when they were first married. However, if the spouses are patient and work together, they can regain feelings of love and support. Often, a couple's love grows deeper and stronger after the couple has worked through a hard time.

▶ **Commitment** A *commitment* is an agreement or pledge to do something. In a healthy marriage, spouses make a commitment to work through their differences, remain faithful to one another, and to make their relationship work. Commitment in marriage requires that both partners be willing to change themselves for the good of the couple. A person cannot change his or her spouse's habits; the person can change only his or her own.

▶ **Compromise** Compromise is essential in a healthy marriage. Compromise in marriage means not always getting your way and sometimes giving up what you want. Each partner must prioritize needs and desires and then discuss these priorities with his or her spouse. Although compromise requires sacrifice, both partners benefit from the stronger relationship that compromise brings.

▶ **Emotional intimacy** Intimacy, or familiarity with each other, is important in a healthy marriage. **Emotional intimacy** is the state of being emotionally connected to another person. The most common way for a couple to develop emotional intimacy is through good communication. Each partner is responsible for expressing feelings in a truthful, loving way if the relationship is to grow.

A person can have a healthy marriage even if he or she has not seen an example of one. Those who have not seen a healthy marriage need to know that a healthy marriage is possible for them through loving actions, commitment, compromise, and emotional intimacy.

Benefits of Marriage

▶ **Emotional and physical intimacy**

▶ **Companionship and deep friendship**

▶ **Financial support system**

▶ **Greater emotional stability**

Engagement: Developing Your Relationships

Developing emotional maturity is an important part of the engagement period. **Emotional maturity** is the ability to assess a relationship or situation and to act according to what is best for oneself and for the other person in the relationship. It is important for the couple to make sure that the relationship is built on mature love, not on *infatuation*, or exaggerated feelings of passion. In mature love, each partner tolerates and accepts the other person's flaws. With emotional maturity you can better determine what is needed to improve a relationship and to allow it to grow.

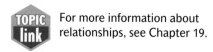 For more information about relationships, see Chapter 19.

Discussing Important Issues   Using the engagement period to talk about the commitment ahead is essential to building a strong relationship. Talking seriously can be difficult because each person feels intense love and is eager to marry. Each partner must ask some important questions and gain advice from others to make the best decisions possible. During the engagement period, couples should discuss issues such as the following:

> ▶ What are our values and beliefs?
> ▶ Should we have children?
> ▶ How will we handle conflict between family members?
> ▶ Should both of us work outside of the home?
> ▶ Where should we live?
> ▶ What are our economic expectations?

Couples should come to agreement on these issues to clearly understand each person's desires and goals.

Premarital Education Classes   Premarital education classes can help couples openly discuss their goals and expectations of marriage. Major differences may surface, and a counselor can help the couple decide if those differences can or cannot be resolved. If they cannot be resolved, couples may decide to break the engagement. Other good reasons to break an engagement include physical or emotional abuse or alcohol and drug abuse.

Teen Marriages

The teen years are a time of dramatic changes. As a teen, you leave behind old ways of thinking and behaving and emerge as a more grown up person. Your interests and concerns will be different from those you had when you were younger.

When teens marry, changes in thinking and behavior are not yet complete. Thus, the spouse a teenager chooses may be different from the spouse the teen would choose later in life.

When teens marry, they must cope with many stresses in addition to their physical and emotional changes. The stresses of teen marriages include

> ▶ independence from parents and family
> ▶ financial worries
> ▶ changes in relationships with close friends
> ▶ interaction with in-laws
> ▶ concern for a spouse's emotional and physical well-being
> ▶ possible parenthood

Many married teens also put education plans on hold. They are financially unable to meet the expenses of marriage and tuition. Delaying education can cause resentment and can keep a person from reaching his or her potential.

Some teenagers are unable to mentally, physically, and intellectually mature into adulthood while married. Those who can successfully mature into adulthood while married have a lot of help from parents or other adults.

"We never thought being married could be so hard."

Divorce and Remarriage

Unfortunately, not all marriages are successful. When a marriage has trouble, sometimes the couple tries *separating*, or living apart for awhile. If one or both partners decide that the marriage is over, they may seek a *divorce*. A **divorce** is a legal end to a marriage. Going through a divorce is often difficult not only for the adults, but also for the other family members. Everyone in the family must adjust to the new situation.

Reasons for Divorce   Many times, divorce seems like the best solution to an unhappy marriage. Problems such as abuse and addiction are often grounds for divorce. But marriages end in divorce for many other reasons including emotional immaturity, marital unfaithfulness, conflicts with family, and selfishness. Additional reasons for divorce include the following:

▶ **Communication problems** Breakdown in good communication is a common cause of divorce. If a couple fails to communicate well, anger may accumulate over the years. The spouses may then turn away from each other emotionally and refuse to openly communicate.

▶ **Unfulfilled expectations** Lack of fulfilled expectations accounts for other divorces. One partner may enter marriage hoping that life will become different or that his or her spouse can be changed as time passes. These expectations are unrealistic. Partners should enter marriage with the understanding that marriage will not solve life's problems and that one person cannot change the habits of another.

▶ **Different financial habits and goals** Differences in financial habits can also lead spouses to divorce. Before and during marriage, it is important to discuss finances, to make a budget, and to figure out how each partner will stay within the budget.

Impact of Divorce on Teens   Numerous losses occur in a teen's life after divorce. Some teens experience a change in the relationship with their parents. Others feel the financial stress of a divorce. Many teens face other emotional stresses. For example, some teens may experience feelings of abandonment. Others may feel angry at themselves for not having been able to change the situation.

Many of these feelings are hard to identify when experiencing them. Counseling can help a teen understand these feelings better. The tips listed in **Figure 1** can help teens cope with divorce.

Figure 1

A divorce or remarriage in the family can be difficult. A few tips for coping with these situations appear below.

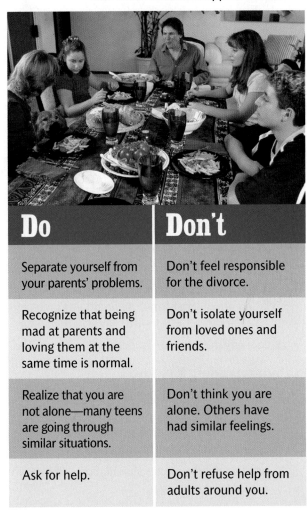

Do	**Don't**
Separate yourself from your parents' problems.	Don't feel responsible for the divorce.
Recognize that being mad at parents and loving them at the same time is normal.	Don't isolate yourself from loved ones and friends.
Realize that you are not alone—many teens are going through similar situations.	Don't think you are alone. Others have had similar feelings.
Ask for help.	Don't refuse help from adults around you.

When Carlos was 8, his mom and dad divorced. Carlos and his brother, Enrique, were devasted. They remember how sad and hard it was to cope after that. Enrique is 26 now and is considering getting married, but he is afraid. He doesn't want to go through a divorce. How will he know if he is making the right decision about marriage?

Write on a separate piece of paper the advice you could give Enrique. Remember to use the decision-making steps.

Give thought to the problem.
Review your choices.
Evaluate the consequences of each choice.
Assess and choose the best choice.
Think it over afterward.

Impact of Parents' Remarriage on Teens If a parent chooses to remarry, new problems may confront a teen. The teen may not have begun healing from his or her parent's divorce. Teens often feel resentment toward the remarrying parent, the step-parent, and any step-siblings. Teens may want their mother and father to remarry each other and see this new family as a threat to that happening. They may blame the remarrying parent for the distress of the other parent.

Coping with Divorce or Remarriage Teens will find the transitions involved in a divorce or remarriage easier if they keep a few things in mind.

- Your parents are doing their best to make their way through a difficult time. Even though you may be angry with them, it's normal to also love them.
- Although you may be angry with one or both of your parents, don't take your anger out on others.
- Find a way to constructively deal with your feelings. For example, write or talk out your feelings with friends or a close relative.
- Don't blame yourself for your parents' divorce. It is not your fault.

Accept the fact that you can't change your parents' decisions. Make the best of your situation. Patience and a positive attitude can help teens get through the difficult times of divorce and remarriage.

SECTION 1

REVIEW   *Answer the following questions on a separate piece of paper.*

Using Key Terms

1. **Define** the term *marriage*.

2. **Identify** the term for "the state of being emotionally connected to another person."
   a. emotional maturity   c. emotional intimacy
   b. custody   d. None of the above

3. **Identify** the term for "a legal end to a marriage."

Understanding Key Ideas

4. **Name** four responsibilities of married partners.

5. **Describe** characteristics that you would expect to see in an emotionally mature person.

6. **List** five things couples should discuss if they are considering marriage.

7. **Name** three difficulties that two teens who are married might face.

8. **Identify** which of the following are healthy ways teens can cope with a divorce.
   a. Don't blame yourself. c. Be patient.
   b. Express your feelings. d. all of the above

9. **Describe** three things that teens should avoid doing or feeling if their parents divorce. (Hint: See Figure 1.)

Critical Thinking

10. List three difficulties a teen may face if his or her parents divorce. Then, discuss how you could help the teen. Support your answers.

Parenthood

OBJECTIVES

Name three responsibilities of parenthood.

Identify how a parent's behaviors can affect his or her children.

Describe three traits you would like to develop before becoming a parent. **LIFE SKILL**

KEY TERMS

parental responsibility the duty of a parent to provide for the physical, financial, mental, and emotional needs of a child

discipline the act of teaching a child through correction, direction, rules, and reinforcement

Leon could not remember feeling such joy. He looked down and saw his baby smiling for the first time. As he saw his baby's beautiful smile and tiny hands, he realized how special having a child is.

Responsibilities of Parents

Nothing in life is as joyful, meaningful, or exhausting as being a parent. Raising children can be one of the richest experiences an adult can have. The decision to have a child is not to be taken lightly, however. Children require a lifetime of commitment, love, and support.

Parenting can seem like a frightening task—the moment a child is born, the child is completely dependent on the parents. The mother and father become the most important influences on their child's well-being and must take on many parental responsibilities. **Parental responsibility** is the duty of a parent to provide for the physical, financial, mental and emotional needs of a child. Being a parent means caring and providing completely for another human being.

Parenting requires time, patience, love, responsibility, and a great deal of emotional maturity.

Responsibilities Before Birth Parental responsibilities do not begin at their child's birth, though. Parenting begins at pregnancy. A mother's and father's habits before and during pregnancy directly affect the health of the baby. Smoking, drinking alcohol, and taking drugs can have serious effects on a developing baby. For example, alcohol consumed by a mother during pregnancy can cause fetal alcohol syndrome. *Fetal alcohol syndrome* is a set of physical and mental problems that affect a fetus because of the mother's consumption of alcohol during her pregnancy.

Emotional Responsibilities The early years of a child's life are very demanding on parents. Children look to parents to have their emotional needs met. Children need to be assured that they are loved. Children also need time with parents. Nothing can replace spending time alone with parents. Secure and healthy parents make certain that they meet the emotional needs of their children.

Safety Responsibilities Parents must always make sure that their child is safe. The number one cause of death in toddlers and young children is accidents. Most of these accidents happen in the home while a parent is present. Keeping watch over a child can be a great strain on the parents. If you have ever been a babysitter, you probably know how stressful ensuring a child's safety can be.

Financial Responsibilities Children also need basic items such as food, clothes, and medicines, all of which cost money. So, parents have to make sure that they have enough income to take care of their child's needs.

Disciplinary Responsibilities Healthy parenting requires discipline as well as love. **Discipline** is the act of teaching a child through correction, direction, rules, and reinforcement. Beginning discipline in a child's toddler years is necessary for the child to mature into a happy and secure person. Proper discipline can be difficult for parents because children naturally resist discipline. But when discipline is given with realistic expectations and support, the child will feel more secure, loved, and safe.

As children enter the early elementary years, parents must teach their children to show respect for themselves and for other people. Children learn from their parents' actions, so parents need to be good role models for their children.

Parents and Teens Parenting can be especially challenging as children move into the teen years. As children grow, parents' care-taking responsibilities—such as expenses and safety concerns—change to match the children's changing needs. As teens mature, their relationship with their parents may change. This change can be hard on both the teens and the parents. It is important both for parents to be supportive of their teens and for teens to try to understand their parents' point of view. Effective communication, trust, and understanding allow a relationship to grow.

ZITS reprinted with special permission of King Features Syndicate, Inc.

Effects of Parental Behavior

Before people become parents, they need to know that their behavior affects the children they raise. Children develop understanding about their worth from their relationship with their parents. Parents who communicate their love for their children from the moment the children are born give the children a secure emotional base from which to grow into confident adults.

Children learn to read their parents' behavior and speech. When parents are happy, children can feel secure about themselves. If a parent is unhappy, children can feel anxious and uncertain. The children may wonder if they are loved. When parents are emotionally or physically unavailable to children for extended periods, children may feel flawed and abandoned.

Parents must realize that children are highly attentive to parents' behavior. The security of their children's world depends on the parents' behavior. Parental behavior affects how children feel about themselves, life, and the future. Common parental behaviors that build healthy self-esteem in children include

▶ giving children time, attention, and physical intimacy
▶ establishing clear rules and limits
▶ taking the time to listen and communicate with children
▶ praising positive behaviors and good choices

Sometimes parents have trouble emotionally connecting with their children. This lack of connection is not related to anything the child did. Instead, the parents lack the skills to connect emotionally. Regardless of how parents behave, it is possible for their children to later develop positive parental behaviors. Parenting classes, mentors, support groups, and books can help people learn to be good parents.

It is important for parents to model positive behaviors for their children, such as showing affection, communicating, and listening.

SECTION 2

REVIEW   *Answer the following questions on a separate piece of paper.*

Using Key Terms

1. **Define** the term *parental responsibility*.

2. **Identify** the term for "teaching a child through correction, direction, rules, and reinforcement."

Understanding Key Ideas

3. **Name** the major influences in a child's life.

4. **Describe** one way that a parent's behaviors before birth can affect his or her child.

5. **Identify** which of the following is the responsibility of a parent to a child.
   a. safety
   b. discipline
   c. finances
   d. all of the above

6. **Summarize** why disciplining a child is important.

7. **Describe** the effects that a parent's behavior can have on a child.

8. **Identify** four ways that a parent can help to increase a child's self-esteem.

Critical Thinking

9. Why do you think that a parent modeling good behavior is more effective for teaching children about good behavior than telling them what to do is?

10. **LIFE SKILL** **Setting Goals** What are three character traits you would like to build before you become a parent?

Families

OBJECTIVES

Discuss why family relationships are important.

Describe different types of families

Name the characteristics of healthy families.

State four ways to cope with family problems.

List three ways that you could help make your family healthier. **LIFE SKILL**

KEY TERMS

sibling a brother or sister related to another brother or sister by blood, the marriage of the individuals' parents, or adoption

nuclear family a family in which a mother, a father, and one or more biological or adopted children live together

extended family the people who are outside the nuclear family but are related to the nuclear family, such as aunts, uncles, grandparents, and cousins

family counseling counseling discussions that are led by a third party to resolve conflict among family members

Have you ever noticed how many different types of families there are? Although families may have different structures, the relationships between family members are the most important part of all families.

Family Relationships Are Important

For most people, the relationships they have with their mother, father, sister, brother, aunts, grandparents, or other family members are sources of much joy and love. Family relationships teach us how to love and what being loved is like. They teach us who we are, who we want to be, and what feeling accepted or rejected is like.

Family relationships are powerful because they influence our emotions and help shape our character, either positively or negatively. Think about your own experiences with your family. Families provide for the emotional and physical needs of their members. Families help family members develop their individual identities. Families also instill moral values.

Families Need Time Because our families are so important, it makes sense for us to put energy into our family relationships. Unfortunately, not all of us do so. We sometimes spend more time concentrating on friendships, schoolwork, or athletic pursuits because doing these things is easier. As you mature, it is important to refocus on family relationships and take responsibility for working harder on them. This is particularly true if your family relationships are troubled or strained.

Regardless of the makeup of a family, the relationships between family members are the most important part of the family.

Types of Families

The members that make up a family of today may be different from those of families in years past. Children in a family are referred to as **siblings,** or brothers or sisters related to another brother or sister by blood, the marriage of the individual's parents, or adoption. Today, there are many different types of families.

Nuclear Families The traditional family structure is the nuclear family. A **nuclear family** consists of a family in which a mother, a father, and one or more biological or adopted children live together. Traditionally, the parents in a nuclear family have clearly-defined roles, such as providing for the family's needs and raising the children.

Blended Families Over the past few decades, family structures have changed for many reasons, including an increase in the number of divorces. A blended family may result if a divorced or widowed parent chooses to remarry. *Blended families* are made up of the biological mother or father, a step-parent, and the children of one or both parents. The parents may decide to have children together. The parent who is not a child's biological parent is known as a *step-parent*.

Single-Parent Families Some families consist of a single mother and her children or a single father and his children. This type of family is a *single-parent family*. Single-parent families can occur if the parent was divorced, never married, or widowed. Most single-parent families are headed by a mother. But, in recent years, an increasing number of single fathers are raising their children.

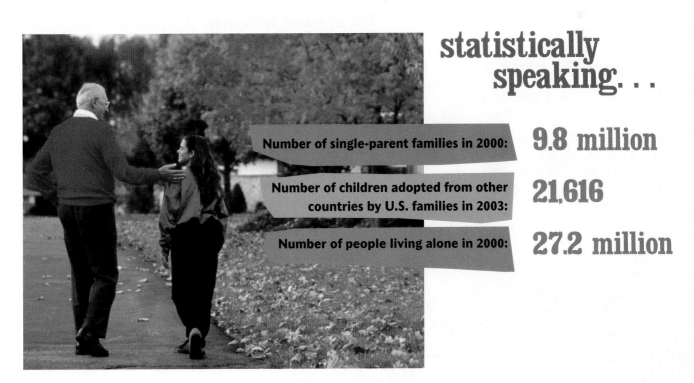

statistically speaking. . .

Number of single-parent families in 2000: **9.8 million**

Number of children adopted from other countries by U.S. families in 2003: **21,616**

Number of people living alone in 2000: **27.2 million**

Extended Families Occasionally, nuclear families are joined by other relatives to form extended families. **Extended families** are the people who are outside the nuclear family but are related to the nuclear family, such as aunts, uncles, grandparents, and cousins. Extended families can offer great emotional support to all members because the responsibilities of the family can be shared among the members.

Adoptive Families In some instances, parents are unable to continue parenting for a variety of reasons. They may decide that in the interest of providing the best for their child, the child should be offered up for adoption. *Adoption* is a legal process through which adults are given permanent guardianship of children who are not their biological children. When a child is adopted, he or she is placed with adoptive parents and a new nuclear family is formed.

Foster Families Children sometimes live in foster families when their own parents are unable to care for them. In *foster families,* a person or a married couple who is not related to the children agrees to house and raise the children for a period of time. Foster families are arranged through government agencies.

Characteristics of Healthy Families

Parents usually set the tone for the family; therefore, much of a family's health depends on the parents. Healthy families are ones in which the family members learn to cope with difficulties and grow stronger because of them. Regardless of the type of family, all healthy families share some basic characteristics: effective communication, respect, commitment, and love.

Effective communication The purpose of effective communication is to prevent misunderstanding, build healthy relationships, and to express yourself. When families communicate in a positive manner, the family strengthens as a unit.

Effective communication should be taught by parents. Unfortunately, many parents were not taught good communication skills when they were young. As a result, parents may have problems communicating with their children or with each other. Thus, the children become frustrated and occasionally discouraged. Mature communication means expressing feelings in a positive, truthful manner.

Respect As healthy families grow, the members learn to show respect for each other. Respect means refraining from verbally or physically hurting another person. Respect also means honoring each other's privacy and treating each other's possessions with care. Showing respect to a sibling or parent is particularly difficult when you are angry. Respect demands self-control and discipline.

Figure 2

Healthy families depend on good communication, respect, commitment, and love.

ACTIVITY *What is one activity that you could do to improve communication in your family?*

Commitment Commitment in healthy family relationships means being dedicated to recognizing and achieving what is best for family members. Part of our commitment to siblings and parents comes naturally, but much of it comes from hard work. Members of healthy families learn to accept one another in spite of each other's differences.

Love Love is the feeling we receive when others in the family express affection and unconditional support to us. Love is also the effort we expend to build better relationships with our siblings and parents. Healthy family members encourage, strengthen, and show compassion toward each other and are accountable to each other.

Unfortunately, many families do not express love in a healthy manner. For instance, a father may believe that he is expressing love to his children by buying them many gifts. He may not realize that the children would rather spend time with him than receive gifts from him. Family members should set their priorities together. Expressing love may require great effort and sacrifice, but love within a family is one of the greatest experiences in life.

Building Healthy Family Relationships Although everyone would love to have positive, rewarding family relationships, such relationships require much work from all members of the family. How can you improve how you behave in your family? How can you show your family love, compassion, and respect? When you behave in a mature and healthy manner toward parents and siblings, they often behave that way in return.

Growing up under the authority of parents commonly makes children feel that they are helpless to change anything. In particular, sometimes being told what to do causes teens to feel that their parents are too controlling. If you feel frustrated in your relationship with your family members, you can be sure that they hurt too. So, it benefits all of you when you all begin working on the relationship.

Coping with Family Problems

Your family has probably had problems. All families experience problems from time to time. Since family relationships are important, though, each member will benefit if the problems are resolved as soon as possible.

Problems in family relationships can occur because of many stresses. Financial problems, difficulty controlling anger, depression, and grief cause many family conflicts. When a family experiences one of these stresses, everyone can be affected. Thus, it is important for each member in a family to participate in solving the problem.

More serious family problems include cases of abuse. For example, one parent may abuse the other parent or the children. Family members should never find acts of verbal, sexual, or physical violence acceptable. Family members should seek help from a trusted adult.

Building Character

RESPONSIBILITY
People who show *responsibility* are dependable, use good judgment in making decisions, and accept the consequences of the decisions they make. A responsible person honors his or her commitments and acts in ways that earn the trust of those around them. Every member of a family shares responsibilities for keeping the family healthy. Describe three ways in which you can take responsibility for keeping your family relationships healthy and strong.

Tips for Coping with Family Problems

▶ **Confront the problem.** Ignoring the problem may make it worse.

▶ **Evaluate the problem as best you can.** Figure out what needs to change for the problem to be solved.

▶ **Take action.** Determine what can and cannot be changed, and work to change what you can.

▶ **Don't give up.** Decide that you will keep working toward resolving the problem despite the difficulty of doing so.

If your family is experiencing problems, help can be found. Find someone you trust who is willing and available to listen.

While the strategy for coping with each family problem may differ according to the problem, some methods are better than others. One good way to deal with your emotions is to communicate them to people you trust. In a situation like divorce, you might want to spend time talking with your friends, especially those who have also had a divorce in their family. Also, trusted adults, such as a grandparent, aunt, uncle, school guidance counselor, teacher, or religious leader, can sometimes give you some of the emotional support that you may be missing.

Another thing you could do is get involved in a new hobby or sport. Find something that absorbs your interest and takes your mind off problems that you cannot solve.

Family Counseling   Family counseling is sometimes necessary to help a family improve its relationships. **Family counseling** involves counseling discussions that are led by a third party to resolve conflict among family members.

Family counselors can give another perspective, help family members see each other's point of view in a positive way, and help to evaluate the family's problems. But the real work comes from the family members themselves. If a family needs counseling, it is more helpful if the entire family receives counseling. But if that is not possible, one family member should not hesitate to go by himself or herself.

Good family relationships are important to your emotional and physical well-being. Although it is often difficult to confront family problems and take action, by staying encouraged and not giving up you can be a part of the solution to the problem. The rewards are worth the effort!

SECTION 3

REVIEW   *Answer the following questions on a separate piece of paper.*

Using Key Terms

1. **Define** the term *nuclear family* .

2. **Identify** the term for "the people who are outside the nuclear family but related to the nuclear family, such as aunts, uncles, grandparents and, cousins."

3. **Define** the term *family counseling.*

Understanding Key Ideas

4. **Identify** two reasons that family relationships are important.

5. **Compare** three types of families.

6. **Identify** which one of the following is *not* a characteristic of a healthy family.
   a. commitment   c. love
   b. selfishness   d. good communication

7. **LIFE SKILL** **Coping** List four ways you can cope with problems in your family.

Critical Thinking

8. How would you help your family if a parent was recently diagnosed with cancer?

9. **LIFE SKILL** **Coping** Identify a problem a family might face and outline how a teen might work to resolve the problem.

Highlights

Key Terms

SECTION 1

marriage (410)
emotional intimacy (411)
emotional maturity (411)
divorce (413)

The Big Picture

✔ Love, commitment, compromise, and communication are essential to developing a healthy marriage.

✔ Couples should use the engagement period to ask questions and make decisions about the commitment of marriage.

✔ Teen marriages are often extremely difficult because the teen years involve many dramatic changes.

✔ Lack of communication, unfulfilled expectations, and different financial goals are common causes of divorce.

✔ Although parental divorce and remarriage affect many teens, it is important for teens to accept the situation, avoid blaming themselves, and to use healthy strategies to cope with their feelings.

SECTION 2

parental responsibility (415)
discipline (416)

✔ Parenting requires commitment, love, discipline, and support.

✔ Parents are responsible for the physical and emotional needs of their children from before birth through the teen years.

✔ Discipline provides guidance for children.

✔ It is important for parents to be supportive of their children, especially during the teen years.

✔ Because children learn from their parents, parents' behavior greatly affects children.

SECTION 3

sibling (419)
nuclear family (419)
extended family (420)
family counseling (422)

✔ Families provide guidance and support, help develop family members' identities, and instill moral values.

✔ As family structures have changed over the past few decades, many more children now live in different types of families including blended, single-parent, extended, adoptive, and foster families.

✔ Healthy family relationships are developed through effective communication, respect, commitment, and love.

✔ It is important that all family members try to work together to solve family problems.

Review

Understanding Key Terms

discipline (416)
divorce (413)
emotional intimacy (411)
emotional maturity (411)
extended family (420)
family counseling (422)
marriage (410)
nuclear family (419)
parental responsibility (415)
sibling (419)

1. For each definition below, choose the key term that best matches the definition.
   a. the people who are outside the nuclear family but are related to the nuclear family, such as aunts, uncles, grandparents, and cousins
   b. counseling discussions that are led by a third party to resolve conflict among family members
   c. a brother or sister related to another brother or sister by biology, marriage, or adoption
   d. teaching a child through correction, direction, rules, and reinforcement
   e. the duty of a parent to provide for the physical, financial, mental, and emotional needs of a child

2. Explain the relationship between the key terms in each of the following pairs.
   a. *divorce* and *marriage*
   b. *emotional maturity* and *emotional intimacy*

Understanding Key Ideas

Section 1

3. Name two responsibilities of partners in a healthy marriage.

4. The benefits of marriage include
   a. deep friendship.
   b. financial stability.
   c. emotional intimacy.
   d. All of the above

5. What is the purpose of premarital education classes?

6. Why is it important for individuals in a relationship to have realistic expectations of each other?

7. Explain why it is difficult for teen marriages to succeed.

8. Many marriages fail because of
   a. poor communication.
   b. lack of commitment.
   c. emotional immaturity.
   d. All of the above

9. Name four ways in which a teen can cope with a divorce or remarriage in the family.

10. **CRITICAL THINKING** Write one paragraph explaining why you think compromise plays such an important role in the success of a marriage. **WRITING SKILL**

Section 2

11. Describe what is meant by the term *parental responsibility*.

12. The responsibilities of parents begin
    a. before their child's birth.
    b. when their child can walk.
    c. after their child is born.
    d. during their child's teen years.

13. Describe the responsibilities of a parent.

14. **CRITICAL THINKING** Describe traits a person should work on before becoming a parent.

15. **CRITICAL THINKING** Write two paragraphs on why you think parents' behaviors have such a great effect on their children throughout the children's lives. **WRITING SKILL**

Section 3

16. What are two important things that family relationships teach us?

17. Compare two different family structures.

18. List qualities that are necessary for a healthy family.

19. Explain how family counseling might help families experiencing conflict.

20. **CRITICAL THINKING** List three ways you could help make your family relationships healthier. **LIFE SKILL**

Interpreting Graphics

Study the figure below to answer the questions that follow.

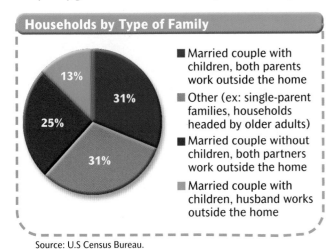

Households by Type of Family

- 13% ■ Married couple with children, both parents work outside the home
- 31% ■ Other (ex: single-parent families, households headed by older adults)
- 25% ■ Married couple without children, both partners work outside the home
- 31% ■ Married couple with children, husband works outside the home

Source: U.S Census Bureau.

21. What percentage of households are made up of married couples who have children and in which both parents work outside the home?

22. CRITICAL THINKING Why do you think the households made up of married couples who have children and in which only the husband works outside the home is the smallest category?

Activities

23. Health and Your Community Imagine you are a counselor advising a man and a woman who are engaged to be married in 3 months. Write three questions that you feel will help them decide if their marriage will be healthy. State why these questions are important. **WRITING SKILL**

24. Health and Your Community Choose a television program that portrays a marriage, and watch the program. Answer the following questions about the program: How is marriage portrayed? Do you agree or disagree with the show's portrayal of marriage? Support your answers.

25. Health and You Write five positive character traits that you possess and that you believe will make you a good parent. Then, explain why each trait is important to good parenting. **WRITING SKILL**

Action Plan

26. LIFE SKILL Coping It is important for families to develop problem-solving skills. Devise a plan for a family to work out its problems.

Standardized Test Prep

Read the passage below, and then answer the questions that follow. **READING SKILL** **WRITING SKILL**

Since Anne and Collin were married, Anne has wanted to move back to her home state. When they had a son, Anne went back to work to help pay bills. She loved her job, but Collin wanted her to stay home with the baby. One day, Collin told Anne that he had received a promotion. Anne knew the promotion meant they wouldn't move and that Collin might want her to quit her job. Both Anne and Collin told each other what they wanted. Then, each decided to <u>relent</u>. Collin took his promotion. They did not move back to Anne's home state. However, Anne requested a flexible work schedule and was able to keep her job.

27. In this passage, the word *relent* means to
- **A** resist.
- **B** state your desires clearly.
- **C** give way under pressure.
- **D** insist on something.

28. What can you infer from reading this passage?
- **E** Marriage requires that spouses consider each other's needs.
- **F** Marriage always interferes with your career plans.
- **G** Parenthood reduces one's chances of promotion.
- **H** The reason that most couples stay married is that they live close to their families.

29. Write a paragraph that compares the benefits of working through difficulties in marriage.

UNIT 6

Reproductive Health

CHAPTER 18

Reproduction, Pregnancy, and Development

What's Your Health IQ?
KNOWLEDGE

Which of the statements below are true, and which are false? Check your answers on p. 638.

1. Sperm are made in the vas deferens. F

2. Both sperm and urine travel through a man's urethra, although not at the same time. T

3. Testicular cancer is most common among men who are over the age of 50. F

4. Estrogen is the primary hormone in males. F

5. Eggs are made in the ovaries. T

6. The uterus is the organ in which a fetus develops. T

7. A woman produces several eggs every month. F

8. Fertilization of the egg usually occurs in the fallopian tubes. T

9. By the end of the sixth month of pregnancy, all the baby's major body structures are formed. T

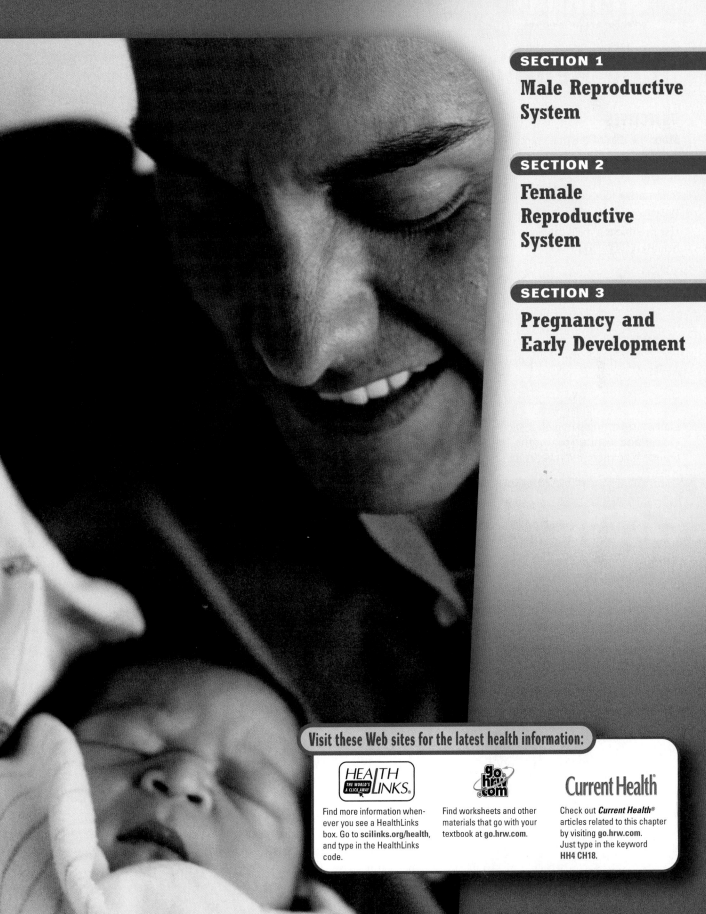

Visit these Web sites for the latest health information:

HEALTH LINKS
THE WORLD'S A CLICK AWAY

Find more information whenever you see a HealthLinks box. Go to **scilinks.org/health**, and type in the HealthLinks code.

go.hrw.com

Find worksheets and other materials that go with your textbook at **go.hrw.com**.

Current Health

Check out *Current Health* articles related to this chapter by visiting **go.hrw.com**. Just type in the keyword **HH4 CH18**.

Male Reproductive System

OBJECTIVES

State the role of the male reproductive system.

Describe the function of each of the organs of the male reproductive system.

Summarize four problems that can occur with the male reproductive system.

List five things a male can do to keep his reproductive system healthy. **LIFE SKILL**

Lance Armstrong survived testicular cancer and went on to win the Tour de France bike race seven years in a row.

Lance Armstrong raced through the Tour de France on the streets of Paris. He was minutes from winning his seventh victory. Winning the race 7 years in a row was special enough. Winning the race after recovering from testicular cancer was even more incredible!

What the Male Reproductive System Does

Maintaining good reproductive health is important to your total health. Lance Armstrong first noticed something was wrong with his reproductive health when he found a lump on his testicle. When he started to cough up blood, he went to the doctor. His cancer had spread, but luckily, it was treatable. Armstrong learned how important it is to be aware of health problems that can occur and to know how to keep the reproductive system healthy. He went on to create the Lance Armstrong Foundation for cancer research and awareness.

The male reproductive system works to produce sperm and deliver it to the female reproductive system. **Sperm** are sex cells that are produced by the male reproductive organs called the testes and that are needed to fertilize an egg. **Eggs,** or **ova** (singular, *ovum*), are the sex cells that are produced by the female reproductive organs called ovaries. The process by which a sperm and an egg and their genetic material join to create a new human life is called **fertilization.**

When a human sperm and egg combine, a new human being begins to grow. In most cases, about 9 months later, a mother gives birth to her baby. The process of producing a new human is called *reproduction.*

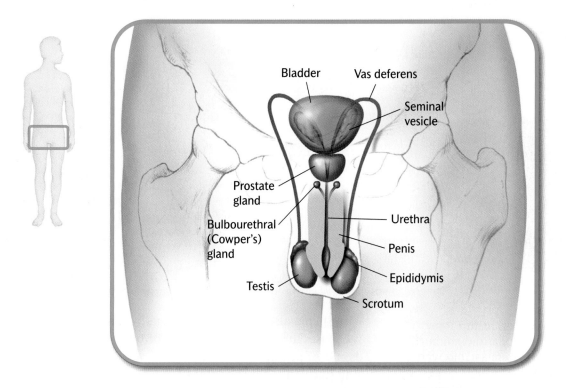

Bladder

Vas deferens

Seminal vesicle

Prostate gland

Bulbourethral (Cowper's) gland

Urethra

Penis

Epididymis

Testis

Scrotum

How the Male Reproductive System Works

The male reproductive system is made up of internal and external organs. **Figure 1** shows the organs of the male reproductive system.

Testes The **testes (testicles)** (singular, *testis*) are the male reproductive organs that make sperm and testosterone. At puberty and continuing throughout a male's life, the testes produce several hundred million sperm each day. The sperm are made inside the testes in tightly coiled tubules called *seminiferous tubules.*

Testosterone is the major sex hormone of males. During puberty, testosterone causes facial and body hair to grow, the shoulders to broaden, and the voice to deepen. Testosterone also influences sperm production.

The two testes rest in the *scrotum*, a skin-covered sac that hangs from the body. The small muscles in the scrotum move the testes closer or farther from the body. This movement keeps the sperm a little cooler than normal body temperature. Sperm cannot develop properly at the higher temperatures of the inner body.

Penis The **penis** is the male reproductive organ that removes urine from the male's body and that can deliver sperm to the female reproductive system. The penis is made of soft tissue and blood vessels. During sexual activity, the penis becomes erect, or firm. The erection occurs as the blood vessels in the penis fill with blood. The penis must be erect during ejaculation (ee JAK yoo LAY shuhn). *Ejaculation* occurs when sperm are released from the penis after sexual excitement. It is also normal for males to ejaculate while they are sleeping. These ejaculations are called *nocturnal emissions* or "wet dreams."

Figure 1

The male reproductive system produces and delivers sperm.

HEALTH Handbook For more information about the excretory system, see the Express Lesson on pp. 540–541 of this text.

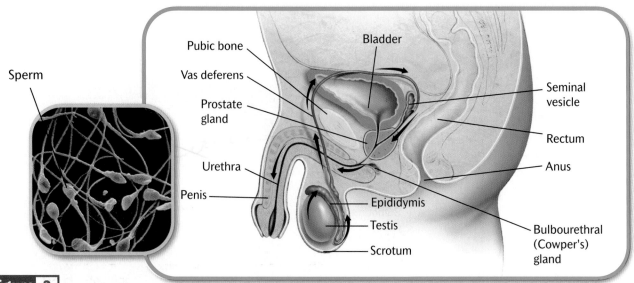

Figure 2

As sperm (photo inset) mature, they move (shown by black arrows) through the reproductive system and mix with fluids from several accessory organs.

ACTIVITY *Summarize the path that sperm take from the testes to the outside of the body.*

The penis also provides a passage for urine to leave the body. Urine passes through the *urethra*, a tube that starts at the bladder and ends at the opening of the penis. Sperm also pass through the urethra during ejaculation, but not at the same time as urine is carried.

The tip of the penis is covered by a sheath of skin called the *foreskin*. The foreskin is sometimes surgically removed shortly after birth in a procedure called *circumcision*. The health advantage of circumcision is under debate. Some parents circumcise their infant for religious or cultural reasons. Many males are never circumcised.

Epididymis and Vas Deferens From the testes, the sperm travel, as shown by the arrows in **Figure 2.** Sperm first travel into a tightly coiled tube called an *epididymis* (EP uh DID i mis), which is where sperm mature and are stored. The mature sperm in each epididymis then move into a long tube called the *vas deferens*. As sperm travel through the vas deferens, they mix with fluids made by three accessory reproductive organs—the seminal vesicles, the prostate gland, and the bulbourethral glands. The mixture of sperm and other secretions from the male reproductive organs is a fluid known as **semen.** Semen leaves the male body by passing through the urethra.

Seminal Vesicles The *seminal vesicles* are found near the base of the urinary bladder. They produce thick secretions that nourish the sperm and help sperm move easier.

Prostate Gland The *prostate gland* encircles the urethra near the bladder. The prostate gland secretes a thin, milky fluid that protects the sperm from acid in the female reproductive system.

Bulbourethral (Cowper's) Glands The *bulbourethral* (buhl boh yoo REE thruhl), or *Cowper's, glands* are found near the urethra below the prostate. Prior to ejaculation, this gland secretes a clear fluid that protects the sperm from acid in the male urethra.

Problems of the Male Reproductive System

Good hygiene and preventive healthcare are important for maintaining reproductive health. However, even with good care, problems with the male reproductive system can occur. Some of these problems are described in **Table 1.**

Table 1 Problems of the Male Reproductive System

Problem	What is it?	Symptoms	Treatment
Jock itch	▶ fungal infection of groin area; exposure to moisture and heat increases the risk of jock itch	▶ itchy rash in groin	▶ keeping area cool and dry; over-the-counter antifungal creams
Cystitis (bladder infection)	▶ inflammation of the urinary bladder; usually due to a bacterial infection	▶ inflammation of the bladder, burning during urination, blood in urine, strong-smelling urine, and fever	▶ antibiotics prescribed by a doctor
Prostatitis	▶ bacterial infection of the prostate; may be related to a sexually transmitted disease	▶ inflammation of the prostate, fever, pain in the pelvis, abdomen, testes, or lower back, and discomfort with urination	▶ antibiotics prescribed by a doctor
Inguinal hernia	▶ bulging of portion of the intestines or other structure through a weakness in the abdominal wall	▶ abnormal bulge in the abdomen, groin, or scrotum; can cause a sense of heaviness, fullness, or pain	▶ immediate medical care; surgery
Testicular torsion	▶ twisting of a testis on the nerves and blood vessels attached to it; can happen during athletic or other physical activities	▶ elevation of a testis, swelling and tenderness of the scrotum, or abdominal pain accompanied by nausea or vomiting	▶ immediate medical care; surgical removal of the affected testis may be necessary if not treated immediately
Undescended testes	▶ failure of one or both testes to move from the abdomen to the scrotum during fetal development	▶ one or no testes in the scrotum	▶ surgery or hormone therapy
Prostate cancer	▶ abnormal division of cells in the prostate; may be hereditary	▶ difficulty urinating or defecating, burning during urination, blood in urine, or no symptoms	▶ surgery, radiation, and/or chemotherapy
Testicular cancer	▶ abnormal division of cells in the testes; may be hereditary	▶ lump on testes, enlargement of testes, sense of heaviness in the scrotum, or no symptoms	▶ surgery, radiation, and/or chemotherapy

Testicular cancer cells

Keeping the Male Reproductive System Healthy

Protecting your reproductive health is important because your reproductive health is an essential part of your total health. Decisions you make and actions you take now can affect your health in the years ahead.

Preventing Problems   Males should watch for any changes or symptoms that might indicate a problem. If symptoms of any problem are present, see a doctor right away. In many cases, prompt care is the key to avoiding future problems. Here are specific ways to prevent some problems.

▶ **Preventing sexually transmitted diseases** Some male reproductive infections are transmitted by sexual activity. Chapters 19 and 20 discuss the prevention and treatment of STDs.

▶ **Preventing jock itch** *Jock itch* is a fungal infection that occurs in a male's groin area. Males who are physically active in hot and humid locations may be more likely to get jock itch. Males can usually prevent jock itch by wearing cotton clothing and by drying themselves thoroughly after a shower. It is also important to avoid wearing damp clothes for too long and to avoid sharing towels or clothes with others.

▶ **Preventing trauma** *Trauma* refers to injuries that are due to an external force, such as being hit in the genitals. Such injuries can happen while playing sports, from car or bicycle accidents, or during "horseplay" with friends. One way to reduce the risk of traumatic injuries to the testes is to wear protective gear (a "cup") when playing sports.

▶ **Preventing hernias** A *hernia* happens when a piece of the intestine bulges into a weak place in the wall of the abdomen or groin. Hernias often appear when abdominal pressure is increased by straining to lift or push something heavy. It can also appear when coughing or sneezing. Doctors check for signs of a hernia by feeling for bulges in the groin while a male coughs. One way for males to prevent hernias is to avoid strenuous lifting. For example, use your knees, and not your back, when lifting heavy objects.

▶ **Preventing infertility** Male *infertility* is the inability to fertilize an egg. Infertility can be genetic, but can also be caused by environmental conditions such as heat and trauma to the testes area. A young male can protect his fertility by avoiding injury to the genitals. Males should also avoid hot temperatures in the testes, which can lead to low sperm counts.

Early Detection of Testicular Cancer   Testicular cancer is a disease that can occur in young men. In fact, testicular cancer is the most common cancer in males between the ages of 15 and 35. A man is particularly at risk for testicular cancer if he had undescended testes as a child, or if testicular cancer runs in his family. However, if detected early, testicular cancer can be treated very effectively.

Six Ways to Keep Healthy

1 Wear appropriate protective gear (a "cup") when playing contact sports.

2 Avoid wearing tight clothing.

3 Wash the penis and scrotum every day, and dry yourself carefully after showering.

4 If you are not circumcised, wash underneath the foreskin.

5 Perform a monthly testicular self-exam.

6 Have an annual checkup with a doctor.

All males who have reached puberty should do routine testicular self-examinations about once per month. Males should also have an annual checkup by a doctor. Talk with a doctor or other healthcare provider to find out how to perform the exam correctly. Here is a brief summary of how to perform a testicular self-exam:

1. Perform the self-exam during or after a warm bath or shower, when the skin of the scrotum is relaxed.

2. Stand in front of a mirror, and hold the penis out of the way.

3. Examine each testicle separately. Hold each testicle between the thumbs and fingers with both hands, and roll each testicle gently between the fingers.

4. Look and feel for any lumps or any change in the size, shape, or consistency of the testicle.

5. Contact your doctor if you detect any troublesome signs.

Males should be aware of the signs for testicular cancer even if it does not run in their family. However, do not confuse lumps with blood vessels, supporting tissues, and tubes that carry sperm. Look for unusual lumps, swelling, or a feeling of heaviness, pain, and discomfort in your scrotum or abdomen. If you notice any of these signs or have any doubts, tell your parents and see a doctor right away.

Early Detection of Prostate Cancer Prostate cancer occurs primarily in older males. When men become older, testosterone can cause the prostate gland to enlarge. The gland can enlarge in either a cancerous or a noncancerous fashion. Prostate cancer can be found early during a physical examination or blood test given by a doctor. Treatment is more effective when prostate cancer is detected early. Males shouldn't wait until it's too late. Delaying treatment can be deadly.

"**My dad survived** prostate cancer because his dad taught him the symptoms of the disease. **I am going to make sure I stay healthy,** too."

SECTION 1

REVIEW   *Answer the following questions on a separate piece of paper.*

Using Key Terms

1. **Identify** the term for "the sex cell that is produced by the testes and that is needed to fertilize an egg."

2. **Define** the term *testis*.

Understanding Key Ideas

3. **State** the functions of the male reproductive system.

4. **Identify** one of the functions of the penis.
   a. delivers sperm to the female
   b. makes sperm more mobile
   c. carries sperm to the epididymis
   d. produces and stores sperm

5. **Order** the path of the sperm through the following male reproductive organs: penis, urethra, vas deferens, testes, and epididymis.

6. **Compare** the symptoms of testicular cancer with those of inguinal hernia.

7. **LIFE SKILL** **Practicing Wellness** List five things a male can do to keep his reproductive system healthy.

Critical Thinking

8. Why do you think the male reproductive system produces so many sperm cells?

9. How might the male reproductive system be affected if the seminal vesicles did not function?

Female Reproductive System

OBJECTIVES

State the role of the female reproductive system.

Describe the function of each of the organs of the female reproductive system.

Describe the changes in the body during the menstrual cycle.

Summarize four problems that can occur with the female reproductive system.

List five things a female can do to keep her reproductive system healthy. **LIFE SKILL**

Ann Curry, a news anchor and breast cancer awareness activist, carries the Olympic torch in Rockefeller Center, New York.

Ann Curry was scared when she found out her sister had breast cancer. This was the first case of cancer in her family. Ms. Curry, a TV news anchor, helped her sister fight the cancer. Then she became dedicated to the fight against breast cancer. A sister's love is saving thousands of lives!

What the Female Reproductive System Does

Keeping your reproductive system healthy is important for your total health. Ann Curry began spreading the message about the importance of maintaining good reproductive health after her sister's battle with and recovery from breast cancer. She often reports about breast cancer. Ms. Curry is involved with the Susan G. Komen Breast Cancer Foundation to support the fight against breast cancer. Ms. Curry has also appeared in public service announcements about the importance of early detection of breast cancer. She continues to empower women and their families with the knowledge that they need to protect their reproductive health.

So, how can you maintain good reproductive health? You should learn about how the reproductive system works. Another important part of maintaining good reproductive health is being aware of possible problems that can occur. You should also know important skills for keeping your reproductive system healthy.

Like the male reproductive system, the female reproductive system is well suited for reproduction. The function of the female reproductive system is to make eggs and to provide a place to support and nourish a developing human.

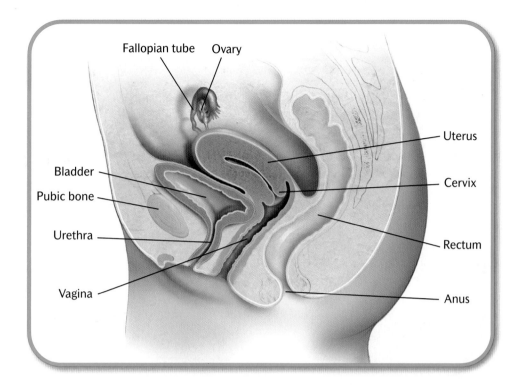

Fallopian tube   Ovary

Bladder

Pubic bone

Urethra

Vagina

Uterus

Cervix

Rectum

Anus

How the Female Reproductive System Works

The female reproductive system is made up of several internal and external organs. **Figure 3** shows the primary organs of the female reproductive system. Although breasts are not directly involved in producing a human life, they are considered secondary reproductive organs because they produce milk for the child.

Ovaries The two ovaries are found deep in the pelvic area. The **ovaries** (singular, *ovary*) are the female reproductive organs that produce eggs and the hormones estrogen and progesterone. Recall that eggs (ova) are the sex cells that are produced by the ovaries and that can be fertilized by sperm. A female is born with approximately 1 million to 2 million eggs.

The ovaries make the hormones estrogen and progesterone. During puberty, estrogen causes the reproductive organs to mature into their adult shape and size. Estrogen also causes the growth of pubic and underarm hair and helps strengthen the bones. Both estrogen and progesterone regulate the monthly release of an egg and prepare the body for a pregnancy.

Vagina The **vagina** is the female reproductive organ that connects the outside of the body to the uterus and receives sperm during sexual intercourse. This tubular organ runs from the lower end of the uterus to the outside of the body. In addition to functioning in reproduction, the vagina allows menstrual flow to exit the body. The vagina is also part of the birth canal through which a baby is delivered. Above and separate from the vagina is a tube called the *urethra*, which carries urine from the bladder to the outside of the body.

Figure 3

The female reproductive system produces eggs and supports a developing human.

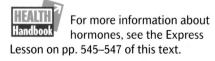 For more information about hormones, see the Express Lesson on pp. 545–547 of this text.

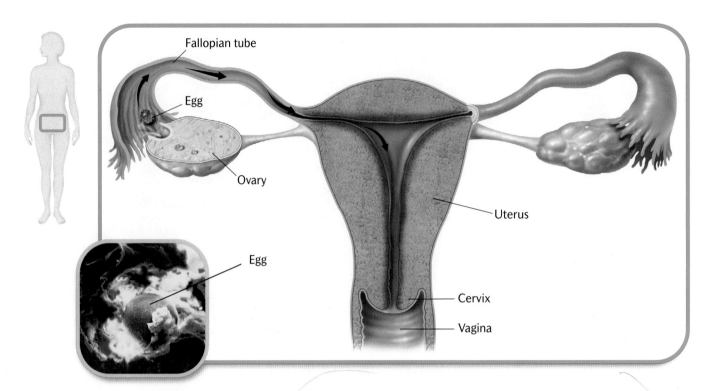

Fallopian tube

Egg

Ovary

Egg

Uterus

Cervix

Vagina

Figure 4

During ovulation, the egg (photo inset) is released from the ovary and travels through the female reproductive system, as shown by the black arrows.

ACTIVITY *Summarize the path that an egg takes from the ovary to the uterus.*

Fallopian Tubes and Uterus From the ovaries, the egg travels into the fallopian tube, as shown by the black arrows in **Figure 4.** The **fallopian tubes** are the female reproductive organs that transport an egg from the ovary to the uterus. The **uterus** is the female reproductive organ that provides a place to support a developing human. It is a muscular cavity (the size of a fist) found at the top of the vagina and between the bladder and rectum. The uterus meets the vagina at its lower end, called the *cervix*.

How the Menstrual Cycle Works

The menstrual cycle occurs in most females from puberty to menopause. The **menstrual cycle** is a monthly series of hormone-controlled changes that prepare the uterine lining for a pregnancy.

The menstrual cycle, shown in **Figure 5,** is a complex combination of hormonal and physical changes in the body. Increasing levels of two hormones (follicle stimulating hormone [FSH] and luteinizing hormone [LH]) cause the maturation and release of an egg. The release of an egg from a follicle in the ovary is called *ovulation*. Prior to ovulation, increasing levels of estrogen cause the uterine lining to thicken. This lining nourishes and supports the growing human during a pregnancy. Following ovulation, high levels of estrogen and progesterone further thicken and maintain the uterine lining.

If pregnancy does not occur (the egg is not fertilized), estrogen and progesterone levels quickly fall. *Menstruation*, or the breakdown and discharge of the uterine lining out of the vagina, then occurs. During this time, females use sanitary napkins or tampons to absorb the blood and tissue released during menstruation. Menstruation usually lasts between 3 and 7 days.

internet connect

www.scilinks.org/health
Topic: Female Reproductive System
HealthLinks code: HH4060

HEALTH LINKS. Maintained by the National Science Teachers Association

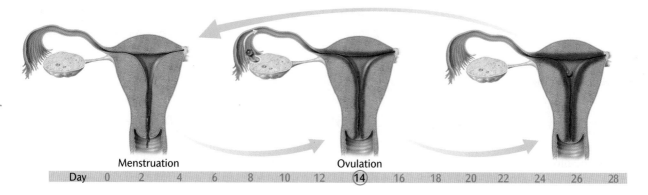

Menstruation   Ovulation

Day 0   2   4   6   8   10   12   (14)   16   18   20   22   24   26   28

Figure 5

Menstruation, ovulation, and thickening of the uterine lining, are the events that make up the menstrual cycle.

The Menstrual Cycle Can Vary The average menstrual cycle lasts 28 days. However, this length can vary from one individual to another and from month to month. Ovulation usually occurs on the 14th day of the cycle. Environmental factors, such as stress, diet, travel, exercise, weight gain or loss, and illness, can influence the timing of a female's cycle. It is important for a female to check with her healthcare professional if she has any questions about irregularity in her menstrual cycle.

Analyzing DATA

Menstrual Cycle Hormones

1 The horizontal (x) axis shows the independent variable, *Day of cycle*.

2 The vertical (y) axis shows the dependent variable, *Hormone level*.

3 Each line shows the level of a hormone at each day in the cycle.

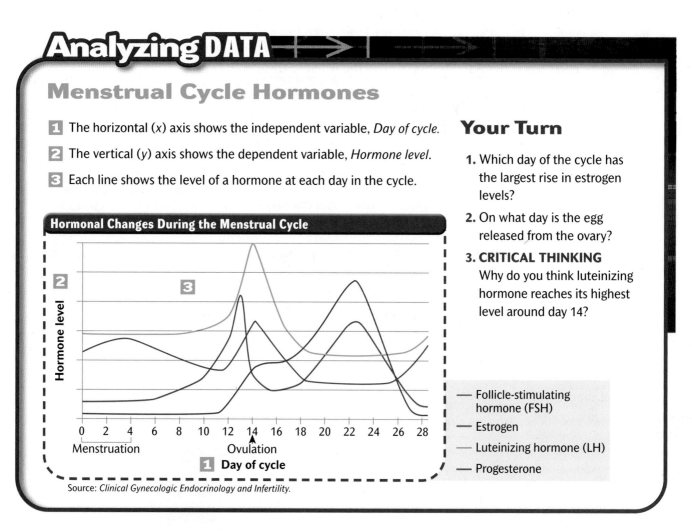

Hormonal Changes During the Menstrual Cycle

Hormone level

0   2   4   6   8   10   12   14   16   18   20   22   24   26   28

Menstruation   Ovulation

1 **Day of cycle**

— Follicle-stimulating hormone (FSH)
— Estrogen
— Luteinizing hormone (LH)
— Progesterone

Source: *Clinical Gynecologic Endocrinology and Infertility.*

Your Turn

1. Which day of the cycle has the largest rise in estrogen levels?

2. On what day is the egg released from the ovary?

3. **CRITICAL THINKING**
   Why do you think luteinizing hormone reaches its highest level around day 14?

Problems of the Female Reproductive System

Table 2 describes some problems and conditions of the female reproductive system.

Table 2	Problems of the Female Reproductive System		
Problem	**What is it?**	**Symptoms**	**Treatment**
Cystitis (bladder infection)	▶ inflammation of the urinary bladder; usually due to a bacterial infection	▶ burning during urination, strong-smelling urine, fever, or blood in urine	▶ antibiotics prescribed by a doctor
Vaginitis	▶ vaginal infection by fungus, bacteria, or protozoa; may be from an STD	▶ irritation or itching around the vagina, vaginal secretions of unusual color and/or unpleasant odor	▶ over-the-counter vaginal cream or medication prescribed by a doctor
Delayed puberty (amenorrhea)	▶ late puberty due to anorexia, endocrine problems, excessive weight loss, and/or overexercise	▶ no breast development and/or no menstrual periods	▶ determined by a doctor
Menstrual cramps	▶ cramps due to prostaglandin (hormone-like substance) production during menstruation	▶ contractions of uterine muscles, lower abdominal pain, and occasional nausea and vomiting	▶ over-the-counter medications and a warm bath; further treatment provided by a doctor
Premenstrual syndrome (PMS)	▶ mental and physical changes related to menstrual cycle, but not completely understood	▶ irritability, mood swings, depression, abdominal bloating, and breast tenderness	▶ determined by a doctor
Toxic shock syndrome (TSS)	▶ poisoning of body from bacterial toxins; often related to tampon use	▶ fever, chills, weakness, and rash on palms of hands	▶ antibiotics and immediate medical treatment
Endometriosis	▶ growth of tissue from uterine lining outside the uterus	▶ severe cramping and pain in lower abdominal area or pelvis	▶ determined by a doctor; hormone therapy or surgery may be required
Ovarian cyst	▶ failure of follicle in ovary to rupture and release an egg; may also be from growths or cancer	▶ pain in lower abdomen or pelvis for a month	▶ determined by a doctor; cysts often go away on their own but sometimes require surgery
Cervical cancer	▶ abnormal division of cells in the cervix; may also be from an STD	▶ vaginal bleeding, discharge, or pelvic pain; may not be any symptoms	▶ surgery, radiation, and/or chemotherapy

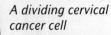

A dividing cervical cancer cell

Keeping the Female Reproductive System Healthy

Most healthy teenage females do not have any major problems with their reproductive system. But it is important to be on the lookout for any problems that may arise.

Preventing Problems Females can protect their reproductive health with good hygiene, self-examinations, and regular visits to the doctor. Here are some other specific ways to prevent problems:

▶ **Preventing sexually transmitted diseases** Some female reproductive infections are transmitted by sexual activity. Chapters 19 and 20 discuss the prevention and treatment of STDs.

▶ **Preventing vaginal irritation** One common problem that is confused with vaginitis is vaginal irritation. *Vaginal irritation* is redness, itching, or mild pain around the opening of the vagina. However, unlike vaginitis, no vaginal discharge is present. A female can reduce the chance of irritation by regular bathing and wearing loose cotton underclothes. Washing underclothes in mild, unscented soap, and avoiding soaps, toilet paper, and feminine products that are scented also help reduce the chance of irritation. Finally, avoid wearing pantyhose, tight jeans, or wet clothes for long periods of time.

▶ **Relieving menstrual cramps** Some females have cramps before or during a menstrual period. *Menstrual cramps* are cramps caused by contractions of the uterine muscles. Many over-the-counter, anti-inflammatory medicines are available for the temporary relief of menstrual cramps. Taking a warm bath, eating a balanced diet, exercising regularly, and reducing caffeine and sugar intake may also help reduce cramps. Females should see a doctor if cramps become very painful.

▶ **Preventing infertility** *Infertility*, the inability to get pregnant, is a problem that occurs in some females. Infertility may be genetic. However, endometriosis and STDs can also lead to infertility. Women can protect their future ability to have children by preventing STDs.

Annual Pelvic Exam Females should have an annual pelvic exam with a doctor. A doctor can find problems that females may not be able to detect. The annual exam includes a breast and genital exam, and a Pap smear. A *Pap smear* examines the cells of the cervix. A Pap smear is important for detecting and preventing cervical cancer. Cervical cancer rates are higher among older women. However, this cancer is on the rise in younger women due to certain STDs and the lack of regular screening with a Pap test.

Ovarian cancer can be detected during an annual exam, but it is difficult to find in early stages of the disease. Ovarian cancer is usually discovered late in its development during a physical exam. Tests are being developed to find the cancer earlier. Ovarian cancer occurs primarily in older women and may be hereditary.

Seven Ways to Keep Healthy

1 Exercise regularly, and maintain a balanced diet.

2 Gently wash the genital area every day with warm water and mild soap. Do not use feminine hygiene sprays and powders.

3 Wipe the vaginal opening from front to back after urination.

4 Change sanitary napkins or tampons every 4 to 6 hours when menstruating.

5 Avoid wearing tight clothing that can cause discomfort.

6 Have an annual pelvic exam with a doctor.

7 Do a breast self-exam each month.

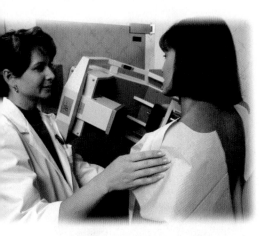

A mammogram is a procedure for detecting breast cancer that is very important for women over the age of 40 or anyone who has symptoms.

Early Detection of Breast Cancer Breast cancer is a disease that occurs primarily in older women. In fact, over 77 percent of the cases occur in women who are over the age of 50. However, females of any age (and some males too) can get breast cancer. Females are at risk for breast cancer if the disease runs in their family. Yet many women who do not have a family history of the disease get breast cancer.

The good news is breast cancer can often be treated effectively if it is detected early. A mammogram test usually detects breast cancer. Women should also have their breasts checked annually by a doctor. Another way to check for breast cancer is to do a breast self-examination (BSE) each month. To find out how to perform a BSE correctly, talk with a doctor. Here is a brief summary of how to perform a BSE:

1. Perform the BSE during or after a warm bath or shower, and at least 1 week after a menstrual period.
2. Stand in front of a mirror. Place one hand over your head and use the other hand to examine each breast separately.
3. Use your thumb and index finger to gently squeeze each nipple and look for any unusual discharge.
4. Check each breast for swelling, dimpling, or scaliness.
5. Use three or four fingers to feel each breast for unusual lumps or thickening under the skin. Check under the armpits and between the armpits and breasts, too.

Lumps, called cysts, may occur in breast tissue. Most cysts are noncancerous and do not need to be removed. Also, most breasts contain normal lumps. Be aware of any changes in your breasts from month to month. If you detect any signs or have any doubts, tell your parents and contact your doctor. Recognizing breast cancer early is important. It could save your life!

SECTION 2

REVIEW
Answer the following questions on a separate piece of paper.

Using Key Terms
1. **Define** the term *ovaries*.
2. **Identify** the term for "the female reproductive organ that provides a place to support a developing human."

Understanding Key Ideas
3. **Describe** the role of the female reproductive system.
4. **Identify** the female reproductive organ that transport eggs from the ovary to the uterus.
   - **a.** ovary
   - **b.** uterus
   - **c.** fallopian tube
   - **d.** urethra
5. **Summarize** the path of the egg through the female reproductive system.
6. **Describe** the changes that occur in the female reproductive organs during the menstrual cycle.
7. **Compare** the symptoms of the female reproductive problems, menstrual cramps and vaginitis.
8. **LIFE SKILL** **Practicing Wellness** List five things a female can do to keep her reproductive system healthy.

Critical Thinking
9. What should a girl do if she has severe menstrual cramps?
10. What do you think happens to the ovulated egg if it is not fertilized by a sperm?

Pregnancy and Early Development

OBJECTIVES

Describe how a human life begins.

Summarize how a baby develops during the three trimesters of pregnancy.

Identify five things a couple can do to stay healthy before and during pregnancy.

Summarize four problems that can occur during pregnancy.

Describe the stages of childbirth.

List three changes that occur during early child development.

KEY TERMS

sexual intercourse the reproductive process in which the penis is inserted into the vagina and through which a new human life may begin

embryo a developing human, from fertilization through the first 8 weeks of development

placenta a blood vessel–rich organ that forms in a mother's uterus and that provides nutrients and oxygen to and removes wastes from a developing human

fetus a developing human, from the start of the ninth week of pregnancy until delivery

prenatal care the healthcare provided for a woman during her pregnancy

H ow extraordinary it is that the female body can support the growth of a new human life. Isn't it amazing that one of the most complex and important events of your life took place inside your mother's body?

How Life Begins

Life begins with the union of an egg from a female and a sperm from a male. *Fertilization (conception),* or joining of the sperm and egg, can occur because of sexual intercourse. **Sexual intercourse** is the reproductive process in which the penis is inserted into the vagina and through which a new human life may begin. During sexual intercourse, the penis can deliver millions of sperm to the female.

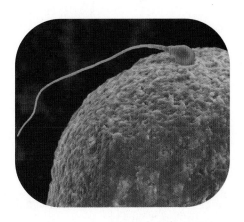

A sperm is about to penetrate the egg during fertilization. Notice the difference in size between the sperm and egg.

Fertilization From the vagina sperm travel through the uterus and into the fallopian tubes, where fertilization normally occurs. Only a small fraction of the sperm complete the journey to the egg. However, it takes only one sperm to fertilize an egg.

Once a sperm penetrates the egg, a chemical change prevents other sperm from entering the egg. The genetic material of the egg and sperm combine to form one cell, called a *zygote*. Genes play an important role in the development of a human. In fact, all of the genetic information needed to create a human is found in the zygote.

The Fertilized Egg Divides The zygote travels down the woman's fallopian tube toward her uterus. The journey takes about 3 to 5 days. As the zygote moves down the fallopian tube, it divides into two cells, then into four cells, and then into a ball of many cells.

4 Early Signs of Pregnancy

1 A missed menstrual period; often feels like a period is about to start

2 Positive urine or blood test for human chorionic gonadotropin hormone (HCG)

3 Tenderness and enlargement of the breasts and darkening of the nipples

4 Nausea ("morning sickness") and fatigue

The Embryo Implants in the Uterus A developing human from fertilization through the first 8 weeks of development is called an **embryo.** The embryo travels from the fallopian tube into the uterus. Within 3 to 5 days, this ball of hundreds of cells becomes embedded in the uterine wall. This event is called *implantation*. Once implantation of the embryo happens, the female is considered to be pregnant. The uterus will be the embryo's home until the baby is born.

A Placenta Supports the Baby The baby's growth in the uterus is dependent on a *placenta*. The **placenta** is a blood vessel–rich organ that forms in a mother's uterus and that provides nutrients and oxygen to and removes wastes from a developing human. Most substances, including drugs and alcohol, can pass through the placenta into the baby. If a mother eats, injects, or inhales anything harmful, her baby can be affected.

How a Baby Develops

The growth of a baby is a fascinating process. What begins as one cell develops into a baby made of trillions of cells over a 38 to 40 week period. **Figure 6** summarizes some of the developmental changes in the growing baby.

First Trimester The *first trimester*, or first 3 months, is a major time of growth and change. After implantation, the embryo starts growing rapidly. By the fourth week of development, the heart starts beating, arm and leg buds appear, and the eyes and brain begin to develop. The embryo is less than a fourth of an inch long, or about the size of a BB pellet.

Surrounding the embryo is a thin, fluid-filled membrane called the *amnion*. The amnion protects the growing embryo. The *umbilical cord* is another new development. It connects the embryo to the placenta.

The term for a developing human from the start of the ninth

Beliefs Vs. Reality

"A missed menstrual period is a sure sign of pregnancy."	It is common for women to have irregular periods. A woman is not necessarily pregnant if she misses a period.
"It takes the entire 38 to 40 weeks for the major structures in a growing baby to develop."	By the end of the first 3 months, all of the baby's major body structures have formed.
"Drugs cannot cross the placenta into the baby during pregnancy."	Most drugs can cross the placenta into the baby's body.
"Pregnant women do not have to visit the doctor until the last 3 months of pregnancy."	Regular doctor visits from the first sign of pregnancy are necessary to ensure the mother's and baby's health.

Development of the Fetus

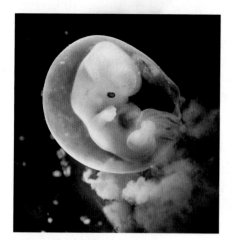

First trimester
At 6 weeks the embryo is almost an inch long. Eyelids and ears are forming. Even the tip of the nose can be seen.

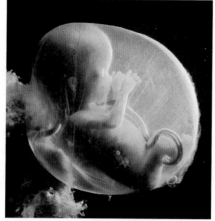

Second trimester
At 16 weeks the fetus is 5 to 6 inches long and weighs about 5 ounces. The fetus can yawn, stretch, and even make facial expressions.

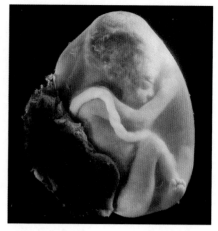

Third trimester
At 32 weeks the fetus is about 20 inches long and weighs almost 5 pounds. A layer of fat has formed underneath the skin.

week of pregnancy until delivery is **fetus.** Brain waves can be detected and muscle movement begins in the fetus. The bones and muscles are developing. By the end of the first trimester, all of the major body parts, such as the heart, brain, lungs, eyes, arms, and legs, have formed. The most critical development is complete. However, not all parts can function fully.

Second Trimester   The *second trimester*, or months 4 through 6, is a time when the organ systems continue to develop. By 4 months, the mother can feel the fetus move or "kick." The reproductive organs can be recognized as distinctly male or female. By the end of this trimester, the fetus can hear and recognize voices. Hair forms on the body. Head and facial features become apparent, and fingers and toes grow nails. Although development is not complete, a fetus born prematurely at the end of this trimester may be able to survive with medical assistance and support.

Third Trimester   The *third trimester*, or months 7 through 9, is a time when the fetus gains most of its weight. A fetus requires a lot of nutrients from the mother. A large percent of the iron and calcium in the mother's food will be delivered to the growing fetus. By 8 months, most fetuses are about 20 inches long. The brain develops further, and all other organs are almost complete. The fetus can even grasp with his or her hands. Fat deposited underneath the skin makes the fetus's skin become very smooth. By the end of 36 weeks, the fetus is almost ready to live outside the mother's body. However, the fetus' nervous system will continue to develop after birth.

Figure 6

The fetus steadily grows and develops throughout the 38 to 40 weeks of pregnancy.

📶 **internet** connect

www.scilinks.org/health
Topic: Growth and Development
HealthLinks code: HH4070

HEALTH LINKS. *THE WORLD'S A CLICK AWAY*   Maintained by the National Science Teachers Association

Keeping Healthy Before and During Pregnancy

Preparing for a pregnancy can help reduce the chance of problems during pregnancy. Both parents should support each other in leading a healthy life. The baby's health is affected by the parents' health before and during pregnancy. For example, sperm and eggs are susceptible to damage by environmental toxins, such as lead. Here are some tips pregnant women can follow:

1. **Avoid alcohol and other drugs (including caffeine and tobacco), and exposure to cigarette smoke.** Alcohol can interrupt the fetus' brain development. Smoking while pregnant can lead to miscarriage, sudden infant death syndrome (SIDS), premature birth, and low birth weight.

2. **Maintain a nutritious diet that follows the Food Guide Pyramid and eat regular meals.** A pregnant woman needs up to 450 extra Calories a day, but she should not eat for two people. Consult a healthcare provider about how to make those Calories count.

3. **Take prenatal vitamins, prescribed by a healthcare provider, before and throughout a pregnancy.** A very important element in a prenatal vitamin is folic acid (folate). Taking folate has been found to reduce the chance of birth defects in the baby.

4. **Get regular, moderate levels of exercise, if approved by a doctor.** Exercise improves circulation, prevents excessive weight gain during pregnancy, and prepares a mother for labor. However, do not overexercise during pregnancy, and avoid injury.

5. **Have all medical conditions evaluated by a doctor early in the pregnancy.** Pregnant women are routinely tested for diseases such as STDs, HIV, diabetes, and rubella (German measles). If a woman is not immune to rubella, she should be vaccinated before pregnancy. Rubella can lead to heart defects and mental retardation in a child. Also, illnesses such as STDs, HIV, or hereditary diseases in either parent, can hurt a fetus.

Prenatal Care During Pregnancy A pregnant woman should visit a doctor on a regular basis throughout pregnancy. The healthcare provided for a woman during her pregnancy is called **prenatal care.** The visits help make sure that the mother and baby are healthy, and provide education about fetal growth. The father can play an active role in a pregnancy by going to all doctor visits.

During the first visit, the doctor will do a complete physical examination. This includes blood tests and a discussion of childbirth options. Thereafter, prenatal visits should take place at least every 3 to 4 weeks.

Moderate exercise, if approved by a doctor, is good for pregnant women. Here are some other ways a woman can stay healthy before and during her pregnancy.

Take 0.4 to 0.8 milligrams of folate per day.

Eat regular meals, and do not fast.

Avoid tobacco, alcohol, and other drugs.

Have regular checkups with a healthcare provider.

Some of the routine procedures that are done during prenatal visits are blood pressure, weight, urine, and fetal heartbeat checks. The doctor will be on the lookout for any problems. Several tests also help provide information on the health of the baby. An *ultrasound* uses sound waves to draw pictures of a baby on a monitoring screen. This test can be used to determine if the baby is a boy or girl, how many babies there are, and whether the baby is growing in a healthy way. *Amniocentesis* tests the amniotic fluid to detect certain genetic problems and to determine the gender of the fetus.

Problems During Pregnancy

Even with the best of prenatal care, problems such as those listed in **Table 3** can occur during pregnancy.

A young boy with fetal alcohol syndrome

Table 3 Problems During Pregnancy			
Problem	**What is it?**	**Symptoms**	**Treatment or prevention**
Fetal alcohol syndrome (FAS)	▶ a set of birth defects that affect a fetus that has been exposed to alcohol during pregnancy	▶ physical and mental problems, such as mental retardation, growth deficiency, and hyperactivity in newborn baby	▶ none; prevented by a woman completely avoiding alcohol during her pregnancy
Miscarriage (spontaneous abortion)	▶ death of fetus from natural complications before the 20th week of pregnancy	▶ vaginal bleeding or pregnancy tissue expelled from uterus	▶ treatment determined by a doctor
Ectopic (tubal) pregnancy	▶ implantation of the fertilized egg in the fallopian tube	▶ abdominal pain early in the pregnancy, weakness, and faintness	▶ surgery or medical treatment is required immediately
Toxemia (preeclampsia)	▶ medical problem with unknown cause, but common in pregnant teens; may be related to the placenta or hormones	▶ swelling of face and ankles, high blood pressure, and protein in urine of mother; convulsions if severe	▶ medications, frequent checkups, and, in some cases, early delivery of baby; may be prevented with good prenatal care
Gestational diabetes	▶ diabetes during pregnancy	▶ high blood sugar levels in mother	▶ change in diet, medication, and, in some cases, early delivery of baby
Rh incompatibility	▶ a condition in which mother's immune system reacts against the fetus's blood due to an incompatibility in blood cell type	▶ anemia (low red blood cell count) in fetus or fetal death	▶ immunization of mother before and after pregnancy prevents this condition; monitoring of health of fetus
Premature birth	▶ early birth due to abnormal uterus, bleeding behind placenta, STD, multiple pregnancy, or other causes	▶ delivery of baby before 38th week	▶ good postnatal care in hospital's premature baby nursery

Stages of Childbirth

Childbirth begins with the onset of labor and goes through three stages, as shown in **Figure 7.** Contractions, or tightening of the uterine muscles, are the major sign of the onset of *labor.* The contractions feel like a bad cramp, which is why mothers call them "labor pains." The contractions help push the baby out of the uterus and through the vagina for delivery of the baby.

Dilation In the first stage of birth, called *dilation,* the uterus contracts, which causes the cervix to dilate or open up. The membranes surrounding the baby rupture. At this point, the mother's "water breaks"—the amniotic fluid surrounding the baby is released out of the vagina. The baby's head begins to push into the birth canal. The cervix and vagina have to dilate enough for the head and body of the baby to pass through it. The first stage ends when the cervix is fully dilated to 10 centimeters.

Expulsion During the second stage, called *expulsion,* the baby's head emerges fully and the shoulders rotate. An episiotomy may be done at this stage. An *episiotomy* is a surgical incision of the outer end of the vagina to allow more room for delivery of the baby. The second stage ends with delivery of the baby.

Placental The third, or *placental,* stage begins after the delivery of the baby and ends when the uterus expels the placenta (or "afterbirth") and umbilical cord out of the mother's body. After the baby is

Figure 7

Childbirth begins with the onset of labor and goes through three stages.

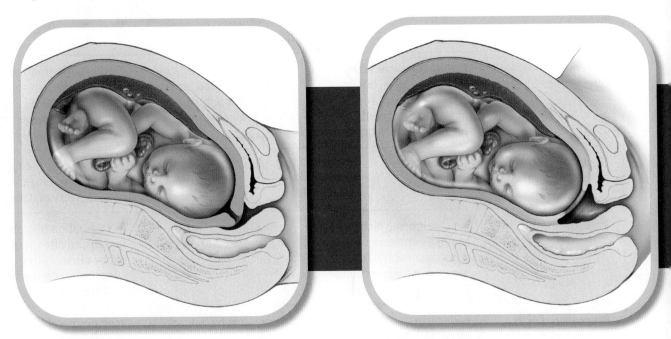

Before childbirth The fetus usually drops to a lower position in the mother's uterus about 1 month before childbirth.

First stage: Dilation During the dilation stage, the mother's cervix dilates and the membranes surrounding the baby rupture.

born, the doctor suctions mucus from the baby's mouth so the baby can breathe. The umbilical cord is tied and cut. Then, both the baby and mother are checked for signs of problems.

After birth, the mother may breast-feed her baby immediately if the baby is not ill. Most doctors recommend breast-feeding because breast milk provides all of the nutrients an infant needs and helps protect the baby from infections and stomach problems. Breast-feeding also helps establish the bond between a mother and her baby. However, some mothers prefer to bottle-feed their baby.

Types of Childbirth   The doctor and parents decide at the time of birth what type of birth is best for keeping the mother and her baby healthy. Most mothers can deliver a baby naturally through the vagina. This type of delivery is called *natural childbirth*.

Sometimes, for health reasons, a woman cannot safely have a vaginal delivery. The baby is then delivered by *Cesarean section*, or *C-section*. A C-section is a type of childbirth in which the baby and placenta are carefully lifted out of the mother's body by surgery. In this procedure, an incision is made in the mother's lower abdomen and then into the uterus. The baby is then lifted out. There are many reasons that a baby would be born by C-section. A C-section is often performed if a baby is under stress inside the uterus. For example, babies may not be in the correct position, with the baby coming "rear end" first (*breech birth*). Another reason for a C-section is if a baby is too large to fit through the birth canal.

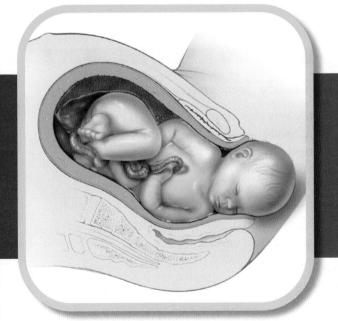

Second stage: Expulsion During the expulsion stage, the baby's head emerges from the birth canal (vagina) and the shoulders rotate.

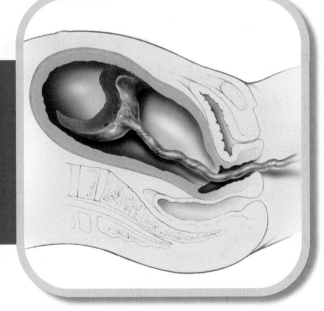

Third stage: Placental During the placental stage, the placenta and the umbilical cord are expelled after the baby is born.

Early Child Development

The fastest period of growth after birth takes place from birth to the age of one. By 2 months, a baby will spend several hours a day awake but mostly sleeps. Babies can raise their head at this age because of good neck control. Babies also begin smiling at faces they recognize.

At 4 months, babies are rolling from front to back, making "cooing" sounds, smiling, and spending more time awake. Their feeding schedules become more regular, and many babies can sleep through the night.

By 6 months, babies can sit up and have excellent head control. Most babies will crawl at 9 months and begin walking and talking by 1 year. The nervous system undergoes extraordinary development during the first year of life.

The "twos" are marked by social independence. "Temper tantrums" may occur as children desire healthy independence. Toilet training often begins this year. Encouraging a healthy diet at this age can help establish future healthy eating habits.

Between 5 and 6 years, most children are ready to begin school. By this age, they are toilet trained, have well-developed speech, and are ready for more social interactions with other children.

The late childhood years from age 6 to 12 are marked by dramatic intellectual and psychological changes. Children experience an important part of their social development in school. Children learn to read, do math, and interact with others. Parents should encourage their children to eat nutritious food, communicate their feelings, and respect all people. It is important for parents to be positive role models for their children. Childhood ends with the beginning of adolescence, which brings changes and responsibilities.

SECTION 3

REVIEW *Answer the following questions on a separate piece of paper.*

Using Key Terms

1. **Define** the term *embryo*.

2. **Identify** the term for "the healthcare provided for a woman during her pregnancy."

Understanding Key Ideas

3. **Describe** how a life begins.

4. **Identify** the development that occurs during the first trimester of pregnancy.
   a. baby moves
   b. arms and legs form
   c. lungs mature
   d. body hair grows

5. **Describe** the importance of prenatal care for keeping healthy before and during pregnancy.

6. **Identify** how fetal alcohol syndrome is prevented during pregnancy. (Hint: See Table 3.)

7. **Distinguish** the event that occurs during stage three of childbrith.
   a. "water breaks"
   b. cervix dilates
   c. baby's head emerges
   d. uterus expels placenta

8. **Summarize** the changes that occur in a baby during early child development.

Critical Thinking

9. Why do you think genes are so important in the development of a fetus?

10. What factors should a couple consider before they decide to have children?

CHAPTER 18

Highlights

Key Terms

sperm (430)
egg (ovum) (430)
fertilization (430)
testis
  (testicle) (431)
penis (431)
semen (432)

ovary (437)
vagina (437)
fallopian tube (438)
uterus (438)
menstrual cycle (438)

sexual intercourse (443)
embryo (444)
placenta (444)
fetus (445)
prenatal care (446)

The Big Picture

✔ The role of the male reproductive system is to produce sperm and deliver it to the female reproductive system.

✔ The penis deposits semen into the reproductive tract of a female to bring about fertilization of an egg. The penis also provides a passage for urine to leave the body.

✔ The testes are the primary organs of the male reproductive system. They produce both sperm and testosterone.

✔ Some problems of the male reproductive system include infections, trauma injuries, and cancer.

✔ Keeping the male reproductive system healthy requires practicing good hygiene, being able to detect problems, and getting checkups each year.

✔ The role of the female reproductive system is to make eggs and to provide a place to support and nourish a developing baby.

✔ The ovaries are the primary organs of the female reproductive system. They produce eggs and the female hormones estrogen and progesterone.

✔ The menstrual cycle functions to produce and release a mature egg each month and to prepare a female's body for pregnancy.

✔ Some problems of the female reproductive system include infections, menstrual cycle problems, and cancer.

✔ Keeping the female reproductive system healthy involves practicing good hygiene, being able to detect problems, and getting checkups each year.

✔ The joining of an egg from a female and a sperm from a male begins the process of a pregnancy and the development of a new human life.

✔ Development of a baby occurs over 3 trimesters, or 9 months. All of the major body structures are formed by the end of the first trimester.

✔ Maintaining a healthy diet, avoiding alcohol and drugs, doing moderate exercise, taking prenatal vitamins, and seeing a doctor on a regular basis are very important to have a healthy pregnancy and baby.

✔ Childbirth begins with the onset of labor and goes through 3 stages.

✔ Early development includes gaining head control, learning to walk, getting toilet trained, learning to speak, and learning to socialize.

Review

Using Key Terms

egg (ovum) (430)
embryo (444)
fallopian tube (438)
fertilization (430)
fetus (445)
menstrual cycle (438)
ovary (437)
penis (431)

placenta (444)
prenatal care (446)
semen (432)
sexual intercourse (443)
sperm (430)
testis (testicle) (431)
uterus (438)
vagina (437)

1. For each definition below, choose the key term that best matches the definition.
   a. the organ that produces sperm and testosterone
   b. healthcare for a woman during her pregnancy
   c. the female organ in which a human develops
   d. the organ through which sperm and urine exit a man's body
   e. the process by which a sperm and an egg join
   f. the female reproductive organ that receives sperm during sexual intercourse

2. Explain the relationship between the key terms in each of the following pairs.
   a. *semen* and *sperm*
   b. *egg* and *menstrual cycle*
   c. *fetus* and *placenta*

Understanding Key Ideas

Section 1

3. What is the role of the male reproductive system?

4. Where is sperm produced in the male body?
   a. testes
   b. seminal vesicles
   c. vas deferens
   d. prostate

5. Summarize the journey of the sperm within the male reproductive system.

6. What causes jock itch?

7. Which of the following is most likely to occur in older males?
   a. prostate cancer
   b. testicular cancer
   c. undescended testes
   d. inguinal hernia

8. Wearing a protective cup when playing sports can help prevent
   a. jock itch.
   b. testicular cancer.
   c. cystitis.
   d. testicular injury.

Section 2

9. What is the function of the female reproductive system?

10. What organ transports an egg from the ovary to the uterus after ovulation?

11. During the menstrual period, blood and tissue that exit the body are derived from the
    a. follicle.
    b. vaginal lining.
    c. uterine lining.
    d. fallopian tubes.

12. Which of the following problems may be due to the entry of bacteria into the urinary bladder?
    a. cystitis
    b. breast cancer
    c. menstrual cramps
    d. endometriosis

13. Which of the following will be least likely to help a woman stay healthy?
    a. good hygiene
    b. scented soaps
    c. annual checkups
    d. breast self-exams

14. **CRITICAL THINKING** What might happen if 2 eggs were released from the ovaries during 1 menstrual cycle?

Section 3

15. What events lead to the beginning of a new life?

16. Summarize what happens to the fetus during the second trimester of pregnancy.

17. Which of the following is *not* part of prenatal care?
    a. regular visits to a doctor
    b. ultrasound tests
    c. blood tests
    d. fertility testing

18. Summarize what happens during the second stage of childbirth.

19. During what time period of child development does the fastest period of growth occur?

20. **CRITICAL THINKING** How do you think both parents' lifestyle and responsibilities change after the birth of their baby?

Interpreting Graphics

Study the figure below to answer the questions that follow.

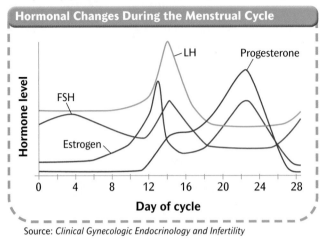

Hormonal Changes During the Menstrual Cycle

LH
Progesterone
FSH
Estrogen

Hormone level

Day of cycle
0 4 8 12 16 20 24 28

Source: *Clinical Gynecologic Endocrinology and Infertility*

21. On what day of the menstrual cycle is the progesterone level the highest?

22. Which hormones peak prior to ovulation?

23. CRITICAL THINKING Why do you think estrogen and progesterone levels decrease toward the end of the menstrual cycle?

Activities

24. Health and You Choose one type of cancer of the reproductive system (for example, testicular, prostate, or breast). Write a one-page report that describes the cancer. Include information on the symptoms of the cancer, ways the cancer can be prevented, and treatments. **WRITING SKILL**

25. Health and You Choose an environmental toxin that is harmful to the fetus, such as lead, alcohol, or tobacco. Write a one-page report that describes the effects of the hazard on the growing fetus. **WRITING SKILL**

26. Health and Your Family Write an essay about two hypothetical pregnant females who have different backgrounds, such as age, culture, financial status, or family support. Compare their experiences through pregnancy and delivery of the baby. **WRITING SKILL**

Action Plan

27. LIFE SKILL Practicing Wellness Discuss five things you can do as a teen to improve and protect your current and future reproductive health. **WRITING SKILL**

Standardized Test Prep

Read the passage below, and then answer the questions that follow. **READING SKILL** **WRITING SKILL**

Being pregnant is <u>laborious</u>. This is something Roberta and her husband, Ben, know firsthand. "A lot of changes started to happen soon after I got pregnant," Roberta says. "I couldn't lift grocery bags anymore. I got nauseated a lot at first and couldn't keep any of my food down." Roberta also suffered from swelling in her feet and face. She explains, "I had too much salt in my body." Excessive salt intake, even from eating potato chips, can cause swelling of the feet and other changes in the body. It is not easy being pregnant.

28. In this passage, the word *laborious* means
A simple
B nice
C difficult
D easy

29. What can you infer from reading this passage?
E Pregnancy does not change the body.
F Eating fatty foods is healthy for pregnant woman.
G Avoiding excess salt is healthy for pregnant women.
H Cramps can occur during pregnancy.

30. Write a paragraph describing some of the things that Roberta could do to feel better and to protect her health during her pregnancy.

31. Write a paragraph describing Roberta and her husband's life after the birth of their child.

CHAPTER 19
Building Responsible Relationships

What's Your Health IQ?
KNOWLEDGE

Which of the statements below are true, and which are false? Check your answers on p. 638.

1. Differences in values and personality don't really matter when choosing a dating partner.

2. There's really nothing a teen can do to avoid the pressures to become sexually active.

3. The majority of high school students have never had sexual intercourse.

4. Many teens who have had sex wish they'd waited.

5. Taking drugs or drinking alcohol can lead to unwanted sexual activity.

Visit these Web sites for the latest health information:

Find more information when- ever you see a HealthLinks box. Go to **scilinks.org/health**, and type in the HealthLinks code.

Find worksheets and other materials that go with your textbook at **go.hrw.com**.

Current Health

Check out *Current Health®* articles related to this chapter by visiting **go.hrw.com**. Just type in the keyword **HH4 CH19**.

SECTION 1

Responsible Relationships

OBJECTIVES

State why teen relationships are important.

List positive characteristics to look for in a dating partner.

Describe appropriate dating behavior.

State two things you can do to maintain a healthy relationship with your partner. **LIFE SKILL**

Good relationships are likely to develop when you make an effort to get to know the people around you.

onight, Carlos and Anne were going on their first date. Carlos had been on several dates before, but this date was different. He thought Anne was very special. And he wanted to make sure their first date was special. So, he felt nervous.

Teen Relationships Are Important

During the teen years, young people begin to form their own identity. Developing relationships with others of the same age is part of forming your own identity. Interest in dating and in serious relationships usually increases during the teen years.

Reasons for Dating Dating is one way for teens to get to know each other. Some teens decide to date because they want to develop friendships. Some teens date to find companionship and support. Others date to explore the characteristics they would like in a future spouse. Some teens, however, may have to wait to date until they reach an age set by their parents. Some are shy and may decide to delay dating. Others may choose not to date but to focus on building friendships with many people of both sexes.

Benefits of Dating Dating during your teen years has many benefits. Dating allows you to find out what different types of people are like. Dating also helps you find out to whom you relate most easily. You learn how to resolve disagreements and communicate more effectively. Finally, dating can enrich your life by providing emotional support during a challenging period of your life.

Possible Problems of Dating When dating relationships become more serious, difficulties may result. Spending increased time with your dating partner may interfere with your schoolwork, your home responsibilities, and your relationships with your friends and family. And engaging in sexual activity poses risks to your emotional and physical health. Refraining from sexual activity is one of the most important ways to create and sustain healthy relationships.

The two people get to know each other's values and feelings and enjoy doing things together. This is considered "dating".

Two people feel they can commit to each other for life. This relationship may lead to marriage.

The two people confide in, trust, and support each other. This is considered "going steady".

As the two people get to know each other better, they find they have some things in common.

Two people are attracted to each other and want to get to know each other better.

Developing Healthy Relationships Fortunately, *you* have the ability to make your relationships develop into a positive aspect of your life. The first step in a healthy relationship is to treat the people you date with respect and require that they treat you with respect. And remember, healthy relationships develop gradually. **Figure 1** shows the path that healthy relationships usually follow. A relationship can stop anywhere on this path and still be satisfying.

Finding the Right Person

Feeling both excitement and fear about dating is normal. It's also normal to be unsure about who to date. One of the best ways to make relationships and dating "work" is to make good decisions about the people you date. Unfortunately, the characteristics that make a person a good date are not always obvious at first glance.

Looking for the Right Person One of the most important things to know about a potential date is the quality of the person's character. It doesn't matter how attractive or popular a person is if he or she is selfish, inconsiderate, or abusive. Any one of these characteristics can make someone difficult to be around. Look for a friend or dating partner who
- ▶ is unselfish
- ▶ treats others well
- ▶ is tolerant and respectful
- ▶ has similar morals and values
- ▶ is fun to be with
- ▶ respects himself or herself

Figure 1

Healthy relationships develop gradually and can exist on many levels of closeness.

ACTIVITY *Think of a personal relationship that is current or past. What path did the relationship follow?*

A person with these characteristics is likely to make you feel better about yourself and to be a great friend, even if a lasting relationship never develops. Dating should be fun, so date someone you enjoy being around. If you decide not to continue dating each other, you can still remain good friends.

Avoiding the Wrong Person If someone hurts you physically or emotionally, *do not date that person.* If someone doesn't respect your morals and values or makes you feel badly about yourself, *do not date them.* You are too special to be treated in such unhealthy ways. A relationship cannot grow and survive without mutual respect.

Jealousy can also cause problems in teen relationships. This happens when your dating partner feels like another person is receiving too much of your attention. People who are jealous tend to be very possessive. Therefore, dating jealous individuals should be avoided as well.

Being the Right Person Becoming a good friend or dating partner is important. A good friend or dating partner is a person of integrity and character. Be the kind of person that you and others respect. Such a person is honest, trustworthy, generous, and not possessive. These characteristics will make you a great date and a great friend. They will also help you feel good about yourself because you will respect the kind of person you are becoming.

Appropriate Dating Behavior

Sometimes people do not have trouble finding the right person to date, but they are not sure how to act on their date. They may be nervous about dating because they are afraid that they won't know how to act or where to go on their date. **Figure 2** gives suggestions for how to act on a date.

Dating in Groups When young people are ready to date, they often begin dating in groups. Teens may attend movies, dances, or sporting events as a group. Dating in groups is a good idea because it allows you to get to know the other person without the pressure of being alone. Dating in groups also reduces the pressure to participate in sexual activity or other risky behaviors. Choose to go out with groups of people who will not pressure you into high-risk behaviors, such as using alcohol or drugs or engaging in sexual activity.

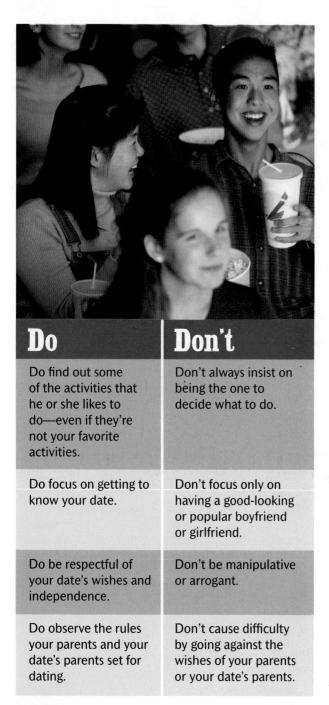

Do	Don't
Do find out some of the activities that he or she likes to do—even if they're not your favorite activities.	Don't always insist on being the one to decide what to do.
Do focus on getting to know your date.	Don't focus only on having a good-looking or popular boyfriend or girlfriend.
Do be respectful of your date's wishes and independence.	Don't be manipulative or arrogant.
Do observe the rules your parents and your date's parents set for dating.	Don't cause difficulty by going against the wishes of your parents or your date's parents.

Figure 2

The suggestions above will help make dating easier and more enjoyable.

Acting Appropriately When you are on a date, remember to treat the other person the way you want to be treated. Be prompt. Being late makes you appear to be either unreliable or uninterested in the date. Be courteous and polite. Think of activities you will both enjoy doing. Ask your date what he or she would like to do.

Don't break a date unless absolutely necessary. Breaking a date just because something better came along is not acceptable. Finally, let your date know if you had a good time. Saying "Thanks, you're fun to be with" is all you need to do.

Following the Rules Find out and follow the rules your parents and your date's parents have for your dating. Don't make your parents think you are untrustworthy or they may hesitate to offer you other privileges. If your date's parents think you are untrustworthy, they may not want you to go out with their son or daughter.

Ending Relationships When two people are dating each other, they usually don't think about the relationship ending. However, most dating relationships that begin during adolescence eventually end.

A person who has been rejected may find it difficult to believe the other person really wants to break up. Once the reality of the breakup is accepted, the rejected person may be hurt and angry. That emotional energy should be used instead to think of ways to become happy again.

When you are recovering from a breakup, remember that you will feel better eventually. Healing may take longer than you would like, but be patient. Stay in touch with your friends, and do the things that you enjoy doing most. If you feel seriously depressed for more than a few days, speak with an adult who you feel you can confide in.

Building Character

RESPECT

Having *respect* for others means that you value them and treat them fairly. To keep a relationship healthy, people who are dating must always remember to show respect for each other. Even when a dating relationship ends, the two people should treat each other respectfully. Doing so can be difficult, especially if one or both of the people are sad or angry. Having self-respect makes treating others with respect easier in such difficult circumstances. Self-respect helps you treat others as you want to be treated.

Imagine that a person you have been dating decides to end the relationship because he or she is transferring to another school. How can you show respect to this person even if you are hurt? How can you show self-respect?

SECTION 1

REVIEW *Answer the following questions on a separate piece of paper.*

Understanding Key Ideas

1. **Summarize** the reasons that relationships are important during the teen years.

2. **List** the reasons a teen might want to date.

3. **Name** one reason a teen might delay dating.

4. **Distinguish** between a casual friendship and a deep friendship. (Hint: See Figure 1.)

5. **State** the most important thing to know about a person you plan to date.

6. **Summarize** why dating in groups is a good idea for teens.

7. **Describe** how to maintain a healthy relationship with your date.

8. **Identify** which of the following actions is a "do" of dating.
   a. being prompt
   b. talking as much as possible
   c. being nervous
   d. making all decisions

Critical Thinking

9. **LIFE SKILL** Setting Goals Describe the type of person you would like to have as a friend and the type of person you would like to have as a dating partner. Are the two types similar?

Benefits of Abstinence

OBJECTIVES

Define the term *abstinence*.

Describe the health benefits of teen sexual abstinence.

Describe the emotional and social benefits of teen sexual abstinence.

Name two ways abstinence can help teens achieve their goals. **LIFE SKILL**

KEY TERMS

abstinence the conscious decision not to participate in sexual activity and the skills to support that decision

sexually transmitted disease (STD) an infectious disease that is spread by sexual contact

"**I'm not ready to be a dad.**"

internet connect

www.scilinks.org/health
Topic: Abstinence
HealthLinks code: HH4002

HEALTH THE WORLD'S CLICK AWAY *LINKS®* Maintained by the National Science Teachers Association

Carlos was finally feeling comfortable around Anne each time they went out on a date. But now his friends were pressuring him to go further in his relationship with her. He knew that he didn't want to be sexually active, but he wasn't sure how to tell Anne.

What Is Abstinence?

As teens begin to date, they have to make important decisions. During the teen years, a person's interest in sexual activity often increases. This increased interest is a normal part of becoming an adult. The ability to make good decisions about sexual activity is very important, not only to your current and future romantic relationships, but also to your health.

Sexual and emotional intimacy is a positive, pleasurable part of a married adult relationship. *Sexual intimacy* means sharing sexual feelings and sexual contact. Teen relationships, however, should focus on emotional intimacy, not sexual intimacy. *Emotional intimacy* means sharing thoughts and feelings, caring for and respecting others, and learning to trust one another.

Avoiding All Sexual Contact In broad terms, *abstinence* means the conscious decision not to participate in a behavior, and the skills to support that decision. For example, a person can choose to be abstinent from alcohol or tobacco. In this textbook, we will use the word *abstinence* to refer to sexual abstinence. **Abstinence** is the conscious decision not to partcipate in sexual activity and the skills to support that decision.

When some people talk about abstinence, they are referring only to the avoidance of sexual intercourse. They believe that one can participate in other forms of sexual activity and still be considered abstinent. This mistaken idea can put teens in very dangerous situations. There are forms of sexual activity that don't cause pregnancy but can cause a sexually transmitted disease.

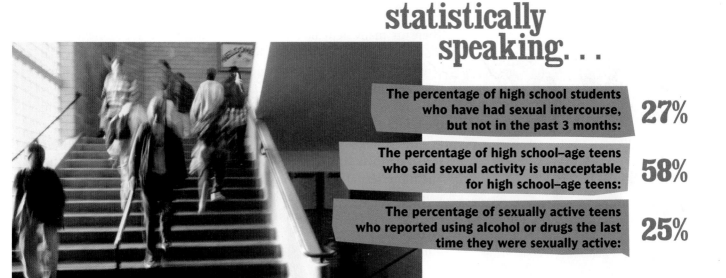

statistically speaking...

The percentage of high school students who have had sexual intercourse, but not in the past 3 months: **27%**

The percentage of high school–age teens who said sexual activity is unacceptable for high school–age teens: **58%**

The percentage of sexually active teens who reported using alcohol or drugs the last time they were sexually active: **25%**

A **sexually transmitted disease (STD)** is an infectious disease that is spread by sexual contact. Frequently, these types of activities lead to sexual intercourse, which can result in pregnancy or infection with an STD. (STDs are also referred to as *sexually transmitted infections,* or *STIs.*)

Remaining Abstinent Until Marriage For teens who have never been sexually active, abstinence means waiting until marriage to begin sexual activity. For teens who have already been sexually active, abstinence means making a decision to refrain from further sexual activity until marriage. The benefits of remaining abstinent are just as important to teens who have been sexually active as they are for teens who have never been sexually active.

Remaining abstinent until you are in a stable, committed relationship, such as marriage, will help you avoid feeling regretful later. Married individuals who were not sexually active before their marriage don't have to worry about STDs. Remaining abstinent until you are married will also help you avoid becoming a single parent.

Remember that a responsible relationship is much more than just physical contact. A responsible relationship should include the elements of emotional intimacy, such as trust, mutual respect, and love. These elements are most likely to be present when a couple has made a long-term commitment to each other through marriage. The lack of emotional intimacy in a sexually active relationship can create negative feelings between the two people in the relationship.

The teen years are often busy, and teens have a lot to think about. There are so many things that you want or need to do as a teen. It is difficult for teens to devote the amount of time and emotional energy needed to handle all of the demands created by a sexually active relationship. Handling the demands of a sexual relationship may be difficult for many adults also.

Three Rs for Remaining Abstinent

▶ **Respect for self**

▶ **Respect for others**

▶ **Responsibility for your own actions**

Teens have enough to juggle in their lives without having to deal with the stress of being sexually active.

Health Benefits

There are many benefits for teens who practice sexual abstinence. The most obvious benefits are the health benefits. By avoiding all sexual activities, an adolescent does not risk becoming pregnant or being infected with a sexually transmitted disease. Some STDs can cause serious consequences, such as cancer and the inability to have children in the future. In some cases, sexually transmitted diseases can be fatal.

The younger you are when you become sexually active, the more sexual partners you are likely to have over the course of your lifetime. The more sexual partners you have in your lifetime, the more likely you are to contract a sexually transmitted disease. Waiting until marriage will decrease the number of sexual partners you have in your lifetime and therefore will reduce your risk of contracting a sexually transmitted disease.

Emotional and Social Benefits

In addition to the health benefits, there are also significant social and emotional benefits for those who avoid sexual activity during their teen years. The social benefits of abstinence include

- ▶ the freedom to pursue a variety of friendships
- ▶ less complicated relationships
- ▶ the ability to focus on interpersonal aspects of relationships
- ▶ better relationships with parents and other trusted adults
- ▶ the chance to learn to build strong, lasting relationships based on mutual trust and respect
- ▶ better reputation among peers

The emotional benefits of abstinence include

- ▶ being free from worry and stress about sexually transmitted diseases and pregnancy
- ▶ allowing time to develop the maturity needed to make important decisions
- ▶ avoiding being manipulated or used by others
- ▶ having an increased sense of self-control and self-respect
- ▶ staying true to your personal values, such as respect, honesty, and morality

Beliefs Vs. Reality

"Sexual activity shows that a couple is in love."	Love can be expressed in many nonsexual ways.
"Sexual activity will make our relationship better."	Sexual activity creates stress in a teen relationship.
"Sexual activity is a healthy part of being a teen."	Many teens are physically and emotionally hurt by sexual activity.
"If a person has been sexually active in the past, there is no reason to avoid sexual activity in the future."	Teen pregnancy and STDs are always good reasons to avoid sexual activity.

Other Benefits of Abstinence

Being sexually active can prevent a young person from achieving his or her goals. Teens who are not sexually active can more easily focus on school and on accomplishing long-term personal, family, and career goals.

Being sexually active may simply distract you from other things that are more important, such as pursuing your education so that you can get a college degree and a good job. Adolescent girls who become mothers typically face difficulties finishing high school and supporting themselves financially. Adolescent boys who become fathers may need to find work to help support their child.

Sexual abstinence can also create a feeling of trust between teens. If a teen couple becomes sexually active, either partner may begin to have doubts about the other partner's values and ability to make good decisions. And when these relationships fail, they can be much more difficult to end than a failed friendship that did not include sexual activity.

The best way to avoid the health, emotional, and social risks of adolescent sexual activity is for both members of a couple to wait until marriage before becoming sexually active. Abstinence will allow you to enter into a long-term relationship without any worry of exposing your family to an STD. It will also allow you to achieve the goals you have set for yourself. But remaining abstinent may present challenges. It will require some planning and thought on your part ahead of time to be prepared for the possible challenges.

Agreeing as a couple to remain sexually abstinent can help form a respectful relationship.

SECTION 2

REVIEW   *Answer the following questions on a separate piece of paper.*

Using Key Terms

1. **Define** *abstinence.*

Understanding Key Ideas

2. **Explain** why it is important to abstain from all types of sexual activity.

3. **List** the health benefits of remaining sexually abstinent.

4. **Determine** which of the following is a social benefit of abstinence.
   a. less complicated relationships
   b. increase in self-esteem
   c. not getting pregnant
   d. not getting an STD

5. **List** the emotional benefits of remaining sexually abstinent.

6. **Determine** which of the following is an emotional benefit of sexual abstinence.
   a. better relationship with parents
   b. not getting an STD
   c. increased sense of self-control
   d. all of the above

7. **Discuss** how remaining sexually abstinent can help you achieve your future goals.

Critical Thinking

8. Why do you think some teens believe that they can't get pregnant the first time they are sexually active?

Coping with Pressures

OBJECTIVES

Describe the two types of pressures to become sexually active.

Discuss how to verbally and nonverbally refuse sexual advances.

Describe protective factors that help teens remain abstinent.

List risk factors that can cause teens to become sexually active.

Discuss nonsexual ways to show someone that you care. **LIFE SKILL**

"**I know there** are **pressures** but I've got **plans** for my **future** and I'm sticking with them."

" wish I had waited." This was the general response of the majority of sexually active teens in a survey about sexual activity. It is not unusual for teens to feel pressure to be sexually active. When teens are unprepared to deal with the pressures to become sexually active, however, the pressures become serious sources of stress.

Pressures to Be Sexually Active

If you plan ahead, you can learn how to successfully resist the pressures to be sexually active. Most teens experience two general types of pressure to be sexually active. The two types of pressure are internal pressure and external pressure. **Internal pressure** is an impulse a person feels to engage in a behavior. **External pressure** is pressure a person feels from another person or from a group to engage in a behavior.

Internal Pressures The internal pressure one feels to become sexually active comes from within oneself. All of us have an instinctive interest in sexual activity because sex is necessary for reproduction and the survival of humanity. Although teens experience an increase in hormone levels, it is important to remember that we all have self-control.

Internal pressure can also come from a desire for emotional intimacy. Emotional intimacy and sexual feelings are two different things. It may seem that sexual activity will help you become closer to another person. However, being sexually active as a teen can actually complicate your life and create distance in your relationship with a person.

External Pressures External sources of pressure to be sexually active include boyfriends or girlfriends, the media, and your peers. Remember, people who want you to go against your morals are usually not concerned with your well-being.

Setting Personal Limits

Given all of the pressures around you, you might think it is difficult to remain sexually abstinent. But in reality, you can learn ways to remain sexually abstinent and to resist the pressures to be sexually active.

Earlier in this chapter, you learned the importance of being sexually abstinent to avoid negative consequences. Sometimes a person understands the importance of abstinence but he or she has never set firm *personal limits* regarding sexual activity. When setting personal limits, you should commit not only to being abstinent but also to avoiding situations that could lead to sexual activity. Tell your dating partner *when you begin dating* that you have made a commitment to remain sexually abstinent.

Avoiding Pressure Situations

Even when you intend to be abstinent, you should avoid situations in which resisting sexual activity is difficult. Here are some suggestions for avoiding pressure situations.

▶ **Identify situations that could lead to sexual activity.** One such situation is being alone with your date. If you are alone with your date, avoid places or situations in which you may feel tempted. Avoid being home alone together and parking in cars in remote areas.

▶ **Avoid drinking alcohol or taking illegal drugs.** These substances impair your judgment and self-control. Avoid going out with others who drink alcohol or use drugs.

▶ **Look for dating partners who share your values about abstinence.** You are more likely to stick to your commitment to abstinence if you date someone who has made a similar commitment. Having other friends that share your values will also help you achieve your goals.

Dating in groups is a great way to avoid the pressures to be sexually active.

Refusing Verbally and Nonverbally

Even if you follow the suggestions for avoiding pressure situations, you may still find yourself being pressured to be sexually active. There are verbal and nonverbal ways to resist the pressures.

Verbal Refusals Use these steps to get out of a pressure situation.

1. **Clearly identify the problem.** In this case, the problem is that your dating partner is trying to convince you to be sexually active.

2. **State your thoughts and feelings about the problem.** For example, say "I've decided to remain abstinent until marriage, and I'm sticking with my decision."

3. **State what you would like to have happen instead.** For example, "Instead of staying here, let's go to a movie."

4. **Explain the results if the change in plans is made.** For example, say "If we go to the movies, we'll have a great time."

5. **Explain the results if the requested change in plans is not made.** For example, say "If you don't stop pressuring me, I'm going home."

Use a firm tone of voice, and be clear that you mean what you say. If you practice refusal lines ahead of time, figuring out what to say when you hear pressure lines is easy. People rarely come up with new lines. **Figure 3** gives examples of responses to such lines.

Nonverbal Refusal Your body language should match what you are saying. Stand up straight, and look the other person in the eyes while talking. Avoid laughter or other nervous behaviors, such as fidgeting. Good nonverbal skills are important because sending a mixed message may confuse the other person and weaken your refusal.

www.scilinks.org/health
Topic: Dating Responsibly
HealthLinks code: HH4039

HEALTH LINKS. Maintained by the National Science Teachers Association

---

Figure 3

Practicing refusal responses ahead of time will help you deal with the pressures to be sexually active.

If You Hear This...	You Can Say This...
"Everybody's doing it."	**I guess you don't know everybody, because more than half of high school students aren't sexually active.**
"If you loved me, you'd let me."	**If you loved me, you wouldn't ask.**
"No one has to know."	**I'll know, and that's one person too many.**
"Don't you want to know what it's like?"	**I do NOT want to know what it's like to get an STD, get pregnant, or live with memories I'd rather forget.**
"What are you afraid of?"	**AIDS, HPV, gonorrhea, syphilis, chlamydia, herpes, and about a dozen other STDs.**
"Come on, just this once."	**That's exactly what I'm afraid of. I'd rather save myself for someone who will love me for life.**

466 CHAPTER 19 *Building Responsible Relationships*

Standing Firm Sometimes, your date may keep pressuring you after the first time you say no. In that case, keep restating your position or remove yourself from the situation. If someone you are dating continues pressuring you to do something you do not want to do, *stop dating that person*. The continued pressure shows they don't have your best interests at heart.

Protective Factors and Risk Factors

Being sexually active is a risky behavior. There are many things in your environment that can either decrease or increase your likelihood of engaging in risky behaviors.

Protective Factors A **protective factor** is anything that decreases the likelihood of someone engaging in a risky behavior. Protective factors include a good relationship with parents and being involved in school and in the community. Teens who have protective factors are more likely to avoid sexual activity. Having made a personal commitment to remain abstinent may be the most important protective factor.

Top 5 Protective Factors

1 A close relationship with parents or guardians

2 Being involved in school activities

3 Good performance in school

4 Practicing religious beliefs

5 Being committed to being sexually abstinent

LIFE SKILL Activity   Refusal Skills

Know What to Say

You may find yourself wanting to get out of a situation where you are being pressured. Knowing what to say ahead of time can help you out of these situations. Below are some scenarios where teens may feel pressures to be sexually active.

1 You are at the movies when your date says "Let's leave now and go to my brother's apartment. Your parents will never know."

2 You are spending the night at the house of a friend whose parents are out for the evening. Your friend wants to invite over the two people you double-dated with a week ago.

3 Your date has a big surprise when picking you up—a bottle of wine his or her older sister bought.

4 Your date has driven to a secluded area and has stopped the car. You're uncomfortable and would like to leave.

LIFE SKILL Communicating Effectively

1. What would you say to get out of each of these situations?

2. What other pressure situations do teens often find themselves in?

There are many nonsexual ways to show someone that you care.

ACTIVITY *Think of three ways you have shown someone that you care for them.*

Risk Factors A risk factor is anything that increases the likelihood of injury, disease, or other negative health problems. Some of the more common risk factors for sexual activity include:

▶ **Alcohol and drugs** Drugs and alcohol reduce your inhibitions and make you more likely to engage in sexual activity.

▶ **Dating older people** Sometimes, resisting sexual pressure is harder when it comes from someone who is significantly older. Most states have laws prohibiting adults and older teens from having sex with teens that are significantly younger.

▶ **Sexually active friends** Hanging out with people who are sexually active may result in increased peer pressure to be sexually active. Spending your time with people who share your commitment to abstinence will make remaining abstinent much easier. Teens are more likely to avoid sexual activity if their friends are also abstinent.

▶ **Previous sexual activity** Previous sexual activity increases the likelihood of current sexual activity. However, teens who have been sexually active can choose to be sexually abstinent. This decision is the healthiest one.

Showing Someone You Care

There are many ways to show someone affection other than by being sexually active. Examples include making each other inexpensive gifts, spending time in conversation, or just being together.

Sometimes, the best way to show someone you care is simply to support the person during good times *and* bad times. Sharing common interests and supporting each other's individual interests are both good ways to show someone you care.

SECTION 3

REVIEW *Answer the following questions on a separate piece of paper.*

Using Key Terms

1. **Define** the term *internal pressure*.

2. **Define** the term *external pressure*.

3. **Identify** the term for "anything that helps someone from becoming involved in harmful behavior."

Understanding Key Ideas

4. **Compare** the two types of pressure to become sexually active.

5. **Identify** pressure situations that could lead to sexual activity and that should be avoided.

6. **Name** the two types of resistance that you can use against external pressure.

7. **Identify** which of the following is *not* a risk factor for sexual activity.
   a. using alcohol and drugs
   b. having sexually active friends
   c. dating someone significantly older
   d. dating in groups

8. **LIFE SKILL** **Communicating Effectively** List three ways other than sexual activity to show someone that you care.

Critical Thinking

9. **LIFE SKILL** **Using Refusal Skills** What would you do if someone was trying to pressure you to do something that you didn't want to do?

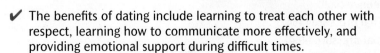

Highlights

Key Terms

The Big Picture

✔ The benefits of dating include learning to treat each other with respect, learning how to communicate more effectively, and providing emotional support during difficult times.

✔ Characteristics of a good dating partner include unselfishness, respectfulness, tolerance, and good moral values.

✔ Being prompt, courteous, polite, and observing parents' dating rules are all examples of good dating behavior.

✔ Having good character and treating others well are two things that you can do to maintain a healthy relationship with your partner.

SECTION 2

abstinence (460)

sexually transmitted disease (STD) (461)

✔ Abstinence is defined as the conscious decision not to participate in sexual activity and the skills to support that decision.

✔ By avoiding all sexual activities, an adolescent does not risk becoming pregnant or being infected with a sexually transmitted disease.

✔ Some of the benefits that practicing abstinence can offer to teens are less complicated relationships and having an increased sense of self-control and self-respect.

✔ Abstinence can help teens achieve their goals by freeing them to pursue their education and their relationships with their friends.

SECTION 3

internal pressure (464)
external pressure (464)
protective factor (467)

✔ Internal and external pressures can cause teens to become sexually active.

✔ Situations that create pressure to become sexually active should be avoided. Those situations include using drugs or alcohol, and dating someone that does not share your commitment to abstinence.

✔ You can refuse someone's sexual advances both verbally and nonverbally.

✔ Risk factors for sexual activity include using alcohol or drugs, dating someone considerably older than you are, and having sexually active friends.

✔ A good relationship with your parents, involvement in school activities, and your own morals are protective factors that help you remain abstinent.

✔ Making someone dinner or giving someone support during difficult times are good ways to show someone that you care.

Review

Using Key Terms

abstinence (460)
external pressure (464)
internal pressure (464)
protective factor (467)
sexually transmitted disease (STD) (461)

1. For each definition below, choose the key term that best matches the definition.
   a. anything that keeps a person from becoming involved in a harmful behavior such as adolescent sexual activity
   b. an impulse a person feels to become involved in a behavior
   c. the decision not to participate in sexual activity and the skills to support that decision
   d. pressure a person feels from another person to become involved in a behavior

Understanding Key Ideas

Section 1

2. What are two possible reasons for a teen to start dating?

3. Describe each step in the path of relationships. (Hint: See Figure 1.)
   a. initial attraction   b. close friendship
   c. deep friendship   d. lifelong love

4. What are positive characteristics to look for in a potential date?

5. Why is it best to avoid dating jealous people?

6. What are the benefits of dating in groups?

7. List three examples of behaviors that you should follow on a date.

8. **CRITICAL THINKING** What types of behavior would a date have to exhibit before you decided not to go on a second date with someone?

Section 2

9. Why should all types of sexual activity be included when talking about abstinence?

10. What is the percentage of high school-age teens who said sexual activity is unacceptable for high school-age teens?
    a. 10%   c. 58%
    b. 32%   d. 44%

11. Explain why people are more likely to contract a sexually transmitted disease during their lifetime if they become sexually active at a younger age.

12. What are some of the more serious consequences of contracting a sexually transmitted disease?

13. For each of the following choices, determine whether it is a health benefit, emotional benefit, or social benefit of remaining abstinent.
    a. avoiding infection with an STD
    b. avoiding a bad reputation
    c. avoiding being sexually manipulated by others
    d. having less complicated relationships

14. What goals can remaining sexually abstinent help teens achieve?

15. **CRITICAL THINKING** Teens often overestimate the percentage of their peers who are sexually active. Why do you think they do this?

Section 3

16. Define *internal pressure* and *external pressure*, and list sources for both types of pressure.

17. How does drinking alcohol or using drugs affect your decision making about being sexually active?

18. List and explain the steps to follow when verbally refusing another person's pressure to be sexually active.

19. Which of the following is *not* a protective factor for teens wishing to remain sexually abstinent?
    a. having a good relationship with one's parents
    b. being involved in school activities
    c. having a job
    d. practicing religious beliefs

20. **CRITICAL THINKING** Discuss three risk factors for teen sexual activity. What can teens do to avoid these factors?

Interpreting Graphics

Study the figure below to answer the questions that follow.

Primary Factors Encouraging Teen Abstinence	
Factors	**% of teens surveyed**
Morals, values, and beliefs	39%
Concerns about STDs	17%
Concerns about pregnancy	15%
Information about sex	10%
Other	19%

Source: National Campaign to Prevent Teen Pregnancy

21. Which factor influenced the most teens to practice abstinence?

22. What percentage of the teens surveyed were encouraged to remain sexually abstinent by one of the top four factors? **MATH SKILL**

23. CRITICAL THINKING What other factors might influence teens to remain sexually abstinent?

Activities

24. Health and You Watch two different television programs that portray teens. **WRITING SKILL** Write a paragraph for each program explaining whether the teens in these programs are making responsible decisions regarding relationships and possible sexual activity.

25. Health and Your Community Write one page describing what you think an ideal date would be like. Discuss details such as where you **WRITING SKILL** would go and what you would do in your community.

26. Health and Your Community Ask classmates for examples of adults who the classmates feel comfortable talking to about dating. Summarize the behaviors that make these adults easy to talk with.

Action Plan

27. LIFE SKILL Practicing Wellness Make a list of steps you can take to maintain healthy dating relationships.

Standardized Test Prep

Read the passage below, and then answer the questions that follow. **READING SKILL** **WRITING SKILL**

Kim and Rich are both seniors in high school and have been dating since they were freshmen. They only have one more week of school until graduation. Three other couples in their class are planning to skip school the last day of class to go have fun in a nearby large city. Kim and Rich know that it would be a fun day, but they are worried that if they are caught skipping, they may not be allowed to participate in their class's graduation <u>commencement.</u> They also know that their parents would be angry with them, and this would make their summer before leaving for college a difficult one at home.

28. In this passage, the word *commencement* means
- **A** meeting.
- **B** ritual.
- **C** trip.
- **D** test.

29. What can you infer from reading the passage?
- **E** Rich is only concerned for himself.
- **F** Kim and Rich have little in common.
- **G** Kim and Rich are concerned about the possible consequences of their actions.
- **H** Kim's and Rich's parents do not approve of their dating.

30. In this passage, Kim and Rich are
- **I** a couple just starting to date.
- **J** a high school couple in a dating relationship.
- **K** just friends who enjoy each other's company.
- **L** about to break up.

31. Describe three benefits for Kim and Rich if they don't skip class.

The Great American Date

Dating has been an issue for American teenagers throughout the ages. As society and culture change, so do their effects on dating.

Going on a date can be fun, awful, wonderful, and nerve wracking all at the same time. Whom do you ask out? How do you ask? Where do you go? If you think these questions are new ones, think again.

Dating in Early America

When America was new, people often lived far apart. Most teenagers didn't go to high school, and travel was difficult. So, boys and girls had few opportunities to meet. Young people often met at church on Sunday or perhaps at a dance on Saturday night. In addition, teenagers usually worked. They had to help on the farm or with the family business. Life was harder, and people expected teenagers to take life as seriously as adults did.

Because life was more demanding, early Americans were less tolerant about lighthearted teenage relationships. Early marriage not only was accepted but also was demanded by society. Young people were expected to go on a date only when they had the intention of getting engaged or marrying. A date meant that things were getting really serious—and everyone in town knew it.

Dating in the 1800s

As American society loosened up, more freedom and greater opportunities for teenagers to be alone frightened some adults. Dating became more formal. The teenage boy was expected to arrive on time, be well dressed, and bring a gift, such as flowers. The date consisted of sitting down and talking. Perhaps the boy and girl would sing at the piano. If the date was going well, the girl's parents might leave the room for a while. If the girl liked the boy, she would ask him to come again.

The Twentieth-Century Date

By the turn of the 20th century, America had changed again, and so had dating. Many adults felt that teenage girls no longer needed to be protected by a formal dating system. By the 1920s, teenage boys asked girls to go on dates, and teenagers had greater freedom to meet and socialize. A typical date might be picking up a girl in a car with a rumble seat and taking her to a dance. By the 1950s, after-school dates were also popular. A boy and girl might get a hamburger together at the local drugstore or meet at a friend's house to listen to records.

Greater freedom brought new challenges, however. The boy was expected to pay for things, which meant he had to have money. Although the 20th century brought greater freedom, this freedom placed more stress on girls and boys to control their behavior.

Dating Today

We live in a society that gives teenagers a lot more freedom than they had in the past. These days, it is not unusual for a girl to ask a boy out on a date, something that was unthinkable in past. This freedom can be wonderful, but unlike their counterparts from the 1800s, today's teenagers can face enormous emotional stresses because of these freedoms. Both boys and girls feel pressure to be cool, to have

money, to look good, and to keep the date entertaining. Despite the stress and awkwardness, dating is still a great way to get to know someone, test the waters of a relationship, and have a lot of fun.

YOUR TURN

1. **Summarizing Information** How has dating changed in American life from early days to the present?

2. **Inferring Conclusions** How does parents' influence today differ from their influence in the past?

3. **CRITICAL THINKING** Do you think that dating is easier and more fun today than it was in the past? Explain your answer.

CHAPTER 20

Risks of Adolescent Sexual Activity

What's Your Health IQ?
KNOWLEDGE

Which of the statements below are true, and which are false? Check your answers on p. 638.

1. Only about one-third of pregnant teenagers ever complete high school. *T*

2. Most teen mothers eventually marry the father of their child. *F*

3. Teen parents usually must interrupt their education to work. *T*

4. Babies born to teen mothers are more likely to suffer health problems. *T*

5. There is no effective way to prevent all of the risks of teen sexual activity. *F*

Visit these Web sites for the latest health information:

HEALTH LINKS.
THE WORLD'S A CLICK AWAY

Find more information whenever you see a HealthLinks box. Go to **scilinks.org/health**, and type in the HealthLinks code.

go. hrw. com

Find worksheets and other materials that go with your textbook at **go.hrw.com**.

Current Health

Check out *Current Health* articles related to this chapter by visiting **go.hrw.com**. Just type in the keyword **HH4 CH20**.

What Are the Risks?

OBJECTIVES

Identify the possible consequences, especially for teens, of sexual activity before marriage.

Describe how pregnancy can affect the lives of teen parents and babies of teens.

Identify how abstinence eliminates the risks of teen sexual activity.

Predict how a pregnancy now (yours or your partner's) would affect your life goals. **LIFE SKILL**

KEY TERMS

sexually transmitted disease (STD) an infectious disease that is spread by sexual contact, also referred to as a sexually transmitted infection (STI)

Sex is not a game, and neither is having a baby or a sexually transmitted disease. Yet many teens ignore the risks of teenage sexual activity. Ignoring the risks won't make the consequences go away.

Risks of Teen Sexual Activity

Although many teens don't want to admit it, a sexually active teen faces many risks. These risks include emotional and social consequences, such as feeling troubled about lying to one's parents. Many teens lose self-esteem and self-respect when they go against their own values and religious beliefs. Other serious consequences can include

▸ unplanned pregnancy

▸ **sexually transmitted diseases (STDs),** infectious diseases that are spread by sexual contact, such as HIV/AIDS

In spite of the risks, many teens have not thought about the realities of teenage sexual activity. Knowing the realities helps teens to be prepared when situations arise. Shown below are just some of the beliefs—and the realities—about teen sexual activity and its consequences.

Beliefs VS. Reality

"If I have a baby, I'll be the center of attention." Few teenagers want to constantly be around a baby.

"He won't leave me if I'm pregnant with his baby." Teen pregnancy adds stress to a teen relationship.

"I can't get pregnant the first time I have sex." You CAN get pregnant the first time you have sex.

"Jan is a really nice girl. She'd never have a sexually transmitted disease (STD)." All sexually active individuals are at risk of catching an STD regardless of their background.

Teen Pregnancy

Many teenage pregnancies occur because teens think, "It won't happen to me." But in fact it does happen to between 800,000 and 900,000 female teenagers each year. This means that 1 in 10 female teenagers gets pregnant each year. One in 5 sexually active female teenagers gets pregnant each year. One out of three girls becomes pregnant at least once before reaching the age of 20. With so many teen girls getting pregnant, it is not surprising to find out that the teen birth rate in the United States is very high. In fact, both the teen pregnancy rate and the teen birth rate are among the highest of any industrialized nation in the western world. The majority of these pregnant young women are not married.

Teen pregnancies are hard on the mother's health. The bones and muscles of teenagers are not ready for the physical stresses of pregnancy. Teenagers are still developing physically. Pregnant teens must eat well and get adequate medical care in order to stay healthy and to increase their chances of delivering a healthy baby. Otherwise, both the mother and the baby can have health problems.

> **One in five sexually active female teenagers gets pregnant each year.**

real life Activity

CHARTING YOUR COURSE

LIFE SKILL
Setting Goals

Materials

✔ 8 1/2 in. x 11 in. sheet of paper
✔ pencil
✔ ruler

Procedure

1. **Draw** a line lengthwise across the paper to represent your life.
2. **Draw** marks every inch along the line.
3. **Write** "0" at the left end of the line to show your birth. Label the first mark "10 years." Label each mark after that in 10-year increments (20 years, 30 years, etc.).
4. **Use** an X to mark the point that shows your current age.
5. **Draw** marks at four points that represent important events in your life. Label each mark with a descriptive phrase, such as "Moved to California."
6. **Draw** marks at four points that represent events that you hope will take place in the future. Label each mark with a descriptive phrase, such as "Buy a car."

Conclusions

1. **Summarizing Results** What future events did you mark?
2. **Predicting Outcomes** What things could change the expected events of your future?
3. **Predicting Outcomes** How might becoming a single teen parent change the expected events of your future?
4. **CRITICAL THINKING** What short-term goals do you need in order to reach each of the expected events of your future?

Teen Parents Caring for a baby is hard work. Teen parents must take on adult responsibilities at an early age. As shown in **Figure 1,** teen parents must make personal, social, and financial sacrifices. Many times they must interrupt their education. Often they have limited job options. Parents are legally responsible for the care and well-being of their children. Many teen parents are not prepared to make these sacrifices or to take on adult responsibilities.

Babies of Teen Parents Expectant teens often delay getting medical care. Thus, babies born to teen mothers are more likely to suffer from health problems. Babies born to teen mothers are also more likely to be born premature and to have a low birth weight (less than 5.5 lb). Babies with low birth weights are more likely to have physical and mental problems than babies with normal birth weights are.

Figure 1

The responsibilities of teen parenthood require personal, social, educational, and financial sacrifices.

Teen fathers earn, on average, less money per year than male teens who delay fatherhood until age 20 or 21.

Being a teen parent means having less free time for yourself.

Only about 20 percent of single teen mothers eventually marry the father of their child.

Only about 30 percent of pregnant teenagers ever finish high school.

Parents are legally responsible for their child's well-being.

If someone you know thinks she may be pregnant, encourage her to see a doctor right away. She and her partner should also talk to a parent or trusted adult. Many communities offer counseling, prenatal care, and classes on childbirth and parenting to pregnant teens.

Abstinence Eliminates the Risks of Teen Sexual Activity

Your dreams and goals for the future often begin during your high school years. One way you can protect your future is to remain abstinent from sexual activity. Only abstinence eliminates the risks of teen sexual activity.

Remember that there are many ways to show love and affection nonsexually. Make your partner feel special. Find hobbies to do together. When you go out on a date, get to know the person you're interested in. What builds a good relationship is the time two people spend together and the respect they show each other. Closeness and caring are as important as sexual attractiveness.

Many communities offer programs to help teenagers think more carefully about the decision to become sexually active. These programs often contain activities that help teenagers improve the skills they need to help them say no to sexual activity. Other programs connect teenagers with adult or peer mentors.

Some high school students say that it seems as if everyone around them has become sexually active. The reality is that a majority of teens in high school choose abstinence. Abstinence allows you to be in charge of your future and makes many options possible. Abstinence allows you to protect your health. By practicing abstinence, you can make sure that you will be able to finish your education and prepare for your career.

 TOPIC link For more information about the benefits of abstinence, see Chapter 19.

SECTION 1

REVIEW   *Answer the following questions on a separate piece of paper.*

Using Key Terms

1. **Identify** the term for "an infectious disease that is spread by sexual contact."

Understanding Key Ideas

2. **Identify** the risks of teen sexual activity before marriage and how abstinence eliminates those risks.

3. **Identify** the ratio of sexually active female teenagers who get pregnant each year.
   - **a.** 1 in 2
   - **b.** 1 in 10
   - **c.** 1 in 5
   - **d.** 1 in 20

4. **Describe** why teen pregnancies are hard on the mother's health.

5. **Classify** the following as risks to *teen mothers*, to *teen fathers*, or to *teen parents*.
   - **a.** interrupted education
   - **b.** limited job options
   - **c.** physical stress to bones
   - **d.** lower income

6. **State** the health risks that a baby born to a teen mother could face.

7. **Describe** the activities that many community programs offer to help teenagers remain abstinent.

Critical Thinking

8. **LIFE SKILL** **Assessing Your Health** How would your life change if you became a parent today?

What Are Sexually Transmitted Diseases?

OBJECTIVES

Describe why sexually transmitted diseases (STDs) are said to be a "silent epidemic."

Identify why teenagers are particularly at risk for being infected with STDs.

List steps you can take to prevent the spread of STDs. **LIFE SKILL**

KEY TERMS

epidemic the occurrence of more cases of a disease than expected

asymptomatic showing no signs of a disease or disorder even though an infection or disease is present

N ot me! That's what many sexually active teens think when they find out they have a sexually transmitted disease (STD). Each year about 19 million Americans are infected with an STD. Teenagers make up only 8 percent of the U.S. population. But about 25 percent of all new cases of STDs occur in teenagers between the ages of 15 and 19.

STDs: The Silent Epidemic

The occurrence of more cases of a disease than expected is called an **epidemic.** STDs are considered an epidemic among teens and young adults.

Mike was surprised to learn that he had a sexually transmitted disease (STD). The doctor wasn't. Mike's doctor told Mike that the STD epidemic is a "silent epidemic." The doctor explained that many STDs are asymptomatic. **Asymptomatic** means "showing no signs of a disease or disorder even though an infection or disease is present." Symptoms warn a person that he or she may be ill. Without symptoms, many people infected with an STD don't recognize that they are infected. So they don't get treatment, but they can spread the infection. Sexually transmitted diseases that are asymptomatic can be detected only by laboratory tests. Also, the symptoms of some STDs may not appear until many years after the person is infected.

The epidemic is also said to be silent because people don't often talk about sexually transmitted diseases. Many people feel too embarassed to see a doctor. People that are too embarassed to see a doctor may go untreated. This can increase the chance that the person will spread the disease to others.

STDs Are Serious STDs can cause serious problems, even years after one is infected. If not treated, some STDs can cause infertility, the inability to have children. Other STDs can cause serious illness or even death. Doctors recommend that people who are sexually active undergo regular testing, or screening, for STDs.

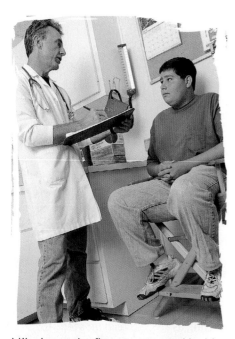

Mike is not the first teen treated by his doctor for an STD. About 25 percent of all new cases of STDs occur in teenagers between the ages of 15 and 19.

STDs and Teens

Teen behavior often places teens at higher risk for catching sexually transmitted diseases. One in 10 teenagers is infected with an STD. Among teens who are sexually active, 1 in 5 has an STD. Each of the following high-risk behaviors puts a teen at risk for STDs:

▶ **Being sexually active** Only abstinence eliminates the risk of catching an STD.

▶ **Having more than one sexual partner** The more sexual partners a person has, the higher the risk of getting an STD. Promiscuity, or engaging in sexual activity with many different people, puts one at an especially high risk for an STD.

▶ **Having a sexual partner who has had multiple sexual partners** A person can be exposed to any STDs that his or her partner was exposed to by other partners.

▶ **Using alcohol or drugs** People who use drugs or alcohol may make poor choices that they might not have made if they had been sober.

Communication between partners about STDs is difficult but important.

Analyzing DATA

STD Cases in Teens

1 The horizontal (*x*) axis shows the independent variable, *age*.

2 The vertical (*y*) axis shows the dependent variable, *number of cases per 100,000 females*.

3 The bars show the number of cases of chlamydia, a common STD, for each age group.

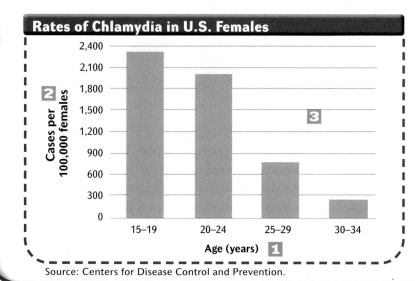

Rates of Chlamydia in U.S. Females

Source: Centers for Disease Control and Prevention.

Your Turn

1. What age group has the highest rate of infection?

2. Estimate the difference between the rate of chlamydial infection in females who are 15 to 19 years old and the rate in females who are 25 to 29 years old. **MATH SKILL**

3. **CRITICAL THINKING** Why do you think the rate of chlamydial infection in females who are 15 to 19 years old is higher than the rate in females who are 30 to 34 years old?

The most effective way to protect yourself from STDs is to remain abstinent before marriage and marry someone who has also been abstinent and is uninfected.

Teens Are at Higher Risk Teenagers are also at higher risk of getting STDs because their bodies may not fight infections as well as the bodies of healthy adults can. In addition, females have a higher risk of catching STDs than males do. First, females have large areas of mucous membranes that can be exposed to infectious particles during sexual intercourse. (Mucous membranes are the moist, pink tissues that line the openings into the body.) Second, during sexual intercourse, females receive a larger volume of potentially infected body fluid than males do. Finally, teenage females are especially at risk because the cells on the cervix of teenage females are more susceptible to infection than the cells of the adult cervix.

Preventing STDs

Mike suffered in many ways as a result of his STD. Besides dealing with the pain and discomfort of the disease, he risked causing permanent damage to his health. He also had to go through the embarrassment and emotional pain of telling his girlfriend and parents. Looking back, Mike realized that he had not made good decisions.

What can you do to make good decisions? First, remember that you are special. Your friends and family care about you. Next, remember that no one can protect you from STDs but YOU! Make the decision to stand up for yourself and take control. Follow these steps to protect yourself from STDs.

1. **Practice abstinence.** The best way to prevent STDs is to remain abstinent. Even if you have been sexually active, you can choose abstinence now. However, if you have been sexually active, you should be tested for STDs.

2. **Stay away from alcohol and drugs.** Alcohol and drugs will dull your ability to think clearly and make good decisions.

3. **Respect yourself.** Individuals with high self-esteem are less likely to let anyone pressure them into something they don't feel comfortable doing.

4. **Learn the facts about STDs, and use those facts to make good decisions.** You can do your part to fight the "silent epidemic" by learning about STDs. Knowledge helps you know the risks. Knowledge helps you make good decisions.

5. **Choose friends who influence you in a positive way.** The people you hang out with have a big influence on you. Choose friends who share your values and beliefs. You'll be more comfortable with people that won't ask you to do things that go against your better judgment.

Figure 2

Going out with a group of friends reduces the pressures you may feel when dating.

ACTIVITY *Create a list of healthy activities that you can do with a group of friends.*

6. **Get plenty of rest.** When you're tired, it's hard to think clearly. Don't put yourself in a situation in which you have to make a tough choice when you are tired.

7. **Go out as a group.** As shown in **Figure 2,** besides being lots of fun, you're a lot less likely to make poor decisions when you are around others. You can also take the pressure off by double-dating.

8. **Be aware of your emotions.** Don't try to ease the hurt of a painful emotional experience in your past by engaging in sexual behavior that does not agree with your beliefs and values.

SECTION 2

REVIEW *Answer the following questions on a separate piece of paper.*

Using Key Terms

1. **Define** the term *epidemic.*

2. **Identify** the term that means "showing no signs of illness or disease, even though an infection is present."

Understanding Key Ideas

3. **Describe** why STDs are called a "silent epidemic."

4. **State** two serious problems that sexually transmitted diseases can cause.

5. **Identify** the ratio of sexually active teens that have an STD.
   - **a.** 1 in 2
   - **b.** 1 in 5
   - **c.** 1 in 10
   - **d.** 1 in 20

6. **Identify** why each of the following behaviors puts a teen at high risk for catching STDs.
   - **a.** having more than one sexual partner
   - **b.** using alcohol or drugs

7. **Name** three reasons why teens are particularly at risk for being infected with STDs.

8. **LIFE SKILL** **Practicing Wellness** Describe steps you can take to prevent the spread of STDs.

Critical Thinking

9. Can someone transmit a sexually transmitted disease to another person without realizing it? Explain your answer.

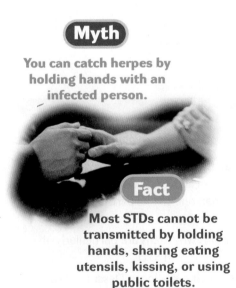

SECTION 3

Common STDs

OBJECTIVES

Describe how STDs can be spread from one person to another.

List example of ways in which STDs can damage a person's health.

Identify the symptoms and treatments of common bacterial STDs.

Describe the symptoms and treatments of common STDs caused by viruses and parasites.

State the responsibilities of people who think they may be infected with an STD.

Myth

You can catch herpes by holding hands with an infected person.

Fact

Most STDs cannot be transmitted by holding hands, sharing eating utensils, kissing, or using public toilets.

Some STDs can be fatal. Others have symptoms that are mild or unnoticeable. If untreated, all STDs eventually harm a person's health.

How Are STDs Spread?

Some sexually transmitted diseases are caused by bacteria. Other STDs are caused by viruses or parasites. Many of the bacteria, viruses, or parasites that cause STDs can be found in body fluids. These body fluids include semen, vaginal secretions, blood, and breast milk. Sexually transmitted diseases can be spread by

▶ any type of sexual activity that brings an uninfected person in contact with body fluids from an infected person

▶ any sexual activity that results in contact between one person's genitals and another person's skin or mucous membranes, in which one of the persons is already infected with an STD

▶ direct contact with open sores

▶ a mother to her baby before birth, during birth, or during breast-feeding

Mistaken Ideas   In most cases, the bacteria and viruses that cause sexually transmitted diseases cannot survive outside of the human body. For example, most of the bacteria and viruses that cause STDs cannot be spread through kissing, sharing eating utensils, holding hands, or using public toilets. And not all STDs can be cured. Some STDs, such as herpes, are permanent.

"It is best to see if an STD goes away on its own before going to a doctor."	Most STDs do not go away on their own. Even if the symptoms go away, the STD is not necessarily cured.
"Washing the genitals after sex prevents STDs."	Washing is not an effective way to prevent STDs.
"Birth-control pills prevent STDs."	Birth-control pills do not provide protection against STDs.
"The medicine prescribed for one kind of STD will cure any STD."	Each STD requires different treatment. A doctor must be consulted for proper treatment.
"If one sex partner is treated for an STD, the other partner does not need to be treated."	Both sex partners must be treated so that they will not reinfect each other.

STDs Can Cause Permanent Damage

All sexually transmitted diseases can harm a person's health. However, many people are not aware that sexually transmitted diseases can cause permanent damage. For example, there are some sexually transmitted diseases that can result in painful sores that can recur throughout one's life. Some STDs can lead to brain damage or cancer. Other sexually transmitted diseases can leave a person unable to have children. Some sexually transmitted diseases can even be fatal.

Babies and STDs Many people do not know that a sexually transmitted disease in a pregnant woman can threaten the health of her unborn baby, or fetus. Some STDs can cause a pregnant woman to have a miscarriage. Some STD infections in a newborn can result in blindness for the infant. The blindness is caused by certain bacterial STDs. These bacteria infect the baby's eyes as the baby passes through the birth canal. Most newborn babies in the United States are treated with medicated eyedrops soon after birth to eliminate the risk of transmission of bacterial eye infections during birth. The eyedrops contain an antibiotic or other substance that kills the bacteria. The drops are given to all babies, even if the mother is not believed to be infected.

The Facts About STDs Being informed about the facts of sexually transmitted diseases can help you avoid behaviors that lead to STDs. Being informed about sexually transmitted diseases also makes people aware of the symptoms of STDs. It is important to see a doctor or other health care professional as soon as you may have been exposed to a sexually transmitted disease. Early diagnosis and treatment of sexually transmitted diseases are essential to preventing long-term health effects. Common sexually transmitted diseases and their treatments are described on pp. 486–489.

"I took a risk as a teen and didn't see a doctor when I should have. As a result, my wife and I are unable to have children."

HEALTH Handbook For more information about male and female reproductive systems, see the Express Lessons on pp. 522–525 of this text.

STDs Caused by Bacteria

Table . 1 describes the four most common bacterial STDs— **chlamydia, pelvic inflammatory disease (PID), gonorrhea,** and **syphilis.** Although most bacterial STDs can be cured by antibiotics, early detection and treatment of STDs are very important. If left untreated for too long, each of these STDs can cause serious damage to the body. For example, some untreated bacterial STDs can scar the fallopian tubes. This scarring can later result in an ectopic pregnancy—the fertilized egg implants in the fallopian tube instead of the uterus.

Table 1 Bacterial STDs			
What is it?	**Symptoms**	**Treatment**	**If untreated**
Chlamydia (kluh MID ee uh) is an STD caused by a bacterium that infects the reproductive organs and may cause a mucous discharge. Chlamydia can be passed from pregnant women to infants during childbirth. The highest rates of chlamydial infections in the United States are found in 15- to 19-year-olds. There are more new cases of chlamydia than new cases of any other bacterial STD reported each year in the United States.	Often no symptoms **Females:** ▶ pain during urination ▶ vaginal discharge or bleeding ▶ pelvic pain **Males:** ▶ pain during urination ▶ discharge from the penis	Both partners take antibiotics at the same time.	**Females:** ▶ infertility ▶ pelvic pain ▶ ectopic pregnancies ▶ pelvic inflammatory disease (PID) **Males:** ▶ can injure reproductive organs ▶ swollen and tender testicles **Infants of infected mothers:** ▶ illness ▶ blindness
Pelvic inflammatory disease (PID) is an inflammation of the upper female reproductive tract caused by the migration of a bacterial infection from the vagina. PID is a common and serious complication of some STDs.	▶ pain in the pelvic area or abdomen ▶ vaginal discharge ▶ unusually long and painful menstrual periods ▶ spotting between periods ▶ fever ▶ painful urination ▶ nausea	Antibiotics are used to treat PID. Antibiotic treatment does not repair all of the damage that has already occurred. Surgery may be needed if infection is left untreated for too long.	▶ scars in the fallopian tubes or uterus that can lead to infertility or ectopic pregnancies ▶ chronic pelvic pain

Ectopic pregnancy

Table 1 Bacterial STDs, continued

What is it?	Symptoms	Treatment	If untreated
Gonorrhea (gahn uh REE uh) is an STD caused by a bacterium that infects mucous membranes, including the genital mucous membranes. Gonorrhea can be passed to infants during childbirth.	**Females:** Often no obvious symptoms ▶ pain during urination ▶ vaginal discharge or bleeding ▶ pain in the abdomen or pelvic area **Males:** ▶ pain during urination ▶ discharge from the penis	Both partners take antibiotics at the same time. Gonorrhea is becoming more difficult to treat because the bacteria that cause it have become more resistant to antibiotics.	**Females:** ▶ pelvic inflammatory disease (PID), which can result in ectopic pregnancies or infertility **Males:** ▶ scarring of the urethra, which makes urination difficult ▶ painful swelling of the testicles, which may lead to infertility **Newborns of infected mothers:** ▶ blindness ▶ joint infection ▶ life-threatening blood infections

Eyedrops are given at birth to prevent blindness caused by STDs passed from mother to newborn.

Syphilis (SIF uh lis) is an STD caused by a bacterium that can cause ulcers or chancres (SHANG kuhrz). Syphilis can spread through the blood, damaging the nervous system and other body organs. Syphilis can be passed to infants during childbirth.	**Males and Females:** **Phase 1** (10 to 90 days after infection): ▶ painless ulcer, called a chancre at the place where the bacteria entered the body **Phase 2** (2 to 8 weeks after infection): ▶ fever ▶ rash ▶ swollen lymph nodes ▶ joint pain ▶ muscle aches **Phase 3** (2 or more years after infection): ▶ heart and nervous system damage, including blindness and loss of mental abilities ▶ possible death	Both partners take antibiotics at the same time. If treated in the early stages, syphilis can be cured.	**Males and Females:** ▶ mental and physical disabilities ▶ premature death **Infants of infected mothers:** ▶ premature birth ▶ severe mental disabilities ▶ deafness ▶ death

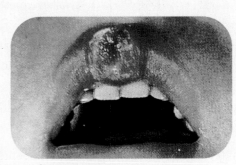

Syphilis chancre

STDs Caused by Viruses or Parasites

Table 2 describes the most common STDs caused by viruses. The symptoms of many viral STDs can be treated with drugs, but viral STDs, such as **human papilloma virus (HPV),** cannot be cured. **Table 3** describes some STDs caused by parasites.

Table 2 Viral STDs

What is it?	Symptoms	Treatment	If untreated
Human papilloma virus (HPV) is an STD caused by a group of viruses that can cause genital warts in males and females and cervical cancer in females. HPV is responsible for more new STD cases than any other STD in the United States.	Often no symptoms **Females:** ▶ genital and anal warts (pink or reddish warts that appear on the genitals) ▶ abnormal Pap smear (a screening test for cervical cancer) **Males:** ▶ genital and anal warts	There is no cure. Warts can be treated by surgical removal, freezing, or medication but will often return.	**Females:** Women have a higher risk of developing cervical cancer with certain types of HPV. **Males:** Men have an increased risk of developing genital cancers.
Genital herpes is an STD caused by a viral infection in the genital area. Genital herpes is caused by the herpes simplex virus (HSV). There are two types of herpes simplex viruses: HSV-1 and HSV-2. Both types can be passed to newborn infants if the mother has genital sores at the time of delivery.	**Males and Females:** **HSV-1:** ▶ cold sores, blisters around mouth and genitals **HSV-2:** ▶ mild or no symptoms ▶ red bumps, blisters, and recurrent sores usually on or around genitals ▶ fever with first infection ▶ swollen lymph nodes	There is no cure. Antiviral medications can shorten outbreaks and reduce their frequency.	An infected person remains infected for life. **Newborns of infected mothers:** ▶ Infections of liver, brain, skin, eyes, and mouth ▶ Death
Hepatitis is an inflammation of the liver. Two different viruses cause hepatitis B and hepatitis C, which are life-threatening forms of hepatitis. Both hepatitis B and hepatitis C can be sexually transmitted. There are other hepatitis viruses that are not sexually transmitted.	**Males and Females:** ▶ jaundice (yellowing of the skin) ▶ tiredness and muscle aches ▶ fever ▶ loss of appetite ▶ darkening of the urine	There is no cure for hepatitis B or hepatitis C. Medications may help stop the spread of the virus. Individuals with severe liver damage may need a liver transplant. A vaccine is available to prevent hepatitis B.	**Males and Females:** ▶ liver damage ▶ liver failure ▶ liver cancer ▶ premature death

A jaundiced eye caused by hepatitis.

Table 2 — Viral STDs, continued

What is it?	Symptoms	Treatment	If untreated
Human immuno-deficiency virus (HIV) is a virus that primarily infects cells of the immune system and causes AIDS. HIV is passed by exchange of infected body fluids—usually blood, semen, vaginal fluid, or breast milk. Exchange usually takes place during sexual activity or by sharing drug injection equipment.	**Males and Females:** **Phase 1** (initial exposure to ten years or more) ▶ fatigue ▶ weight loss ▶ fever ▶ diarrhea ▶ swollen lymph nodes **Phase 2** ▶ Phase 1 symptoms ▶ forgetfulness ▶ difficulty thinking **Phase 3** ▶ weakened immune system ▶ infections ▶ weight loss	There is no cure for AIDS. A combination of drugs can delay the start of serious symptoms.	**Males and Females:** ▶ weight loss ▶ malnutrition ▶ loss of mobility ▶ opportunistic infections (such as pneumonia and tuberculosis) ▶ cancer ▶ premature death

Table 3 — STDs Caused by Parasites

What is it?	Symptoms	Treatment	If untreated
Pubic lice are a strain of lice found in pubic hair of those infected. The lice crawl on the skin and lay eggs on the hairs. The lice are spread by skin-to-skin contact.	**Males and Females:** Pubic lice can cause intense itching in the pubic area.	Medication can kill the lice. Infected individuals must wash clothes and bed linens in hot water to kill any remaining lice and their eggs.	Skin damage can occur.
Scabies (SKAY beez) are tiny mites that burrow into the skin of an infected person. Scabies are spread by skin-to-skin contact.	**Males and Females:** Scabies can cause intense itching in the infected area.	Medication can kill the mites. Infected individuals must wash clothes and bed linens in hot water to kill any remaining mites and their eggs.	Skin damage can occur.
Trichomoniasis (TRIK oh moh NIE uh sis) is an STD caused by a protozoan, a single-celled animal that is just a little larger than a bacterium. Males may not have symptoms but can give the disease to others.	**Females:** ▶ itching in genital area ▶ discharge from the vagina ▶ painful urination **Males:** ▶ usually no symptoms	It can be cured with a prescribed medicine.	**Females:** ▶ bladder and urethral infections ▶ premature birth in pregnant women **Males:** ▶ inflamed urethra

Being Responsible About STDs

Sometimes people are too embarrassed or frightened to ask for help or information about sexually transmitted diseases. But sexually transmitted diseases are serious diseases. People who are sexually active must get screened regularly. People who think they might have a sexually transmitted disease should do the following:

1. **Seek medical help right away.** The earlier a person seeks treatment, the less likely the disease will do physical damage and spread to others.

2. **Complete the full course of medications.** The patient being treated should finish all prescribed medication, even if the symptoms disappear.

3. **Have follow-up testing done.** The patient should also undergo a follow-up test to ensure that the infection has been cured.

4. **Avoid all sexual activity while being treated.** Most sexually transmitted diseases can be spread while a person is being treated.

5. **Notify all sexual partners.** All previous and current sexual partners should be urged to get a check-up. One partner in a current relationship may be free of the sexually transmitted disease, but the other partner may not. Receiving treatment at the same time helps the couple avoid reinfecting each other.

Sexually transmitted diseases can affect anyone. Your behavior now will affect you the rest of your life. It is important to understand and avoid behavior that places you at risk for contracting a sexually transmitted disease. The most effective way to prevent a sexually transmitted disease is to avoid sexual contact of any kind. Practicing abstinence is the only sure way to prevent sexually transmitted diseases.

Seeking medical treatment right away is the responsibility of any couple that suspects one partner may have an STD.

SECTION 3

REVIEW *Answer the following questions on a separate piece of paper.*

Using Key Terms

1. **Identify** the bacterial STD that causes ulcers or chancres.

2. **Classify** each of the the following STDs as *bacterial* or *viral*.
   - **a.** gonorrhea
   - **b.** HPV
   - **c.** chlamydia
   - **d.** syphilis

3. **Identify** the possible symptom caused by HPV.
   - **a.** fever
   - **b.** genital warts
   - **c.** jaundice
   - **d.** blisters

Understanding Key Ideas

4. **List** three ways in which sexually transmitted diseases can be spread.

5. **Describe** the health damage that STDs can cause.

6. **State** the symptoms of each of the following STDs:
   - **a.** chlamydia
   - **b.** gonorrhea
   - **c.** HPV
   - **d.** scabies

7. **State** the treatment of each of the following STDs:
   - **a.** HIV
   - **b.** genital herpes
   - **c.** trichomoniasis
   - **d.** syphilis

8. **LIFE SKILL** **Practicing Wellness** List four things you should do if you suspect you have been exposed to an STD.

Critical Thinking

9. Can a person have more than one STD at one time? Explain your answer.

CHAPTER 20

Highlights

Key Terms

SECTION 1

sexually transmitted disease (STD) (476)

SECTION 2

epidemic (480)
asymptomatic (480)

SECTION 3

chlamydia (486)
pelvic inflammatory disease (PID) (486)
gonorrhea (486)
syphilis (486)
human papilloma virus (HPV) (488)

The Big Picture

✔ The risks of being sexually active include social and emotional consequences, unplanned pregnancy, and sexually transmitted diseases (STDs).

✔ Teen parents must make social, personal, educational, and financial sacrifices.

✔ Babies born to teen mothers are more likely to suffer from health problems.

✔ The risks of teen sexual activity can be avoided by practicing abstinence.

✔ Sexually transmitted diseases are spreading at an epidemic rate among teens and young adults.

✔ High-risk behaviors for getting STDs include being sexually active, having more than one sexual partner, and using alcohol or drugs.

✔ Teenagers are at a greater risk for contracting an STD than are adults because of their behavior. Also, teen bodies may not fight infections as well as the bodies of healthy adults can.

✔ Teens can protect themselves from STDs in several ways, including practicing abstinence, staying away from alcohol and drugs, and learning the facts about STDs.

✔ STDs can be spread by any type of sexual activity. Some STDs are also spread by direct contact with open sores and from a mother to her baby.

✔ Early detection and treatment of STDs can help prevent serious damage to one's health.

✔ Bacterial STDs include chlamydia, gonorrhea, pelvic inflammatory disease (PID), and syphilis. Most bacterial STDs can be cured with antibiotics.

✔ Viral STDs include human papilloma virus (HPV), genital herpes, hepatitis B, hepatitis C, and HIV/AIDS. Although the symptoms of many viral STDs can be treated with drugs, viral STDs cannot be cured.

✔ Pubic lice, scabies, and trichomoniasis infections cause intense itching in the pubic area and can be cured with medication.

✔ Anyone who suspects they may have an STD should seek testing and treatment immediately.

CHAPTER 20 *Highlights* **491**

Review

Using Key Terms

asymptomatic (480)

chlamydia (486)

epidemic (480)

gonorrhea (486)

human papilloma virus (HPV) (488)

pelvic inflammatory disease (PID) (486)

sexually transmitted disease (STD) (476)

syphilis (486)

1. For each definition below, choose the key term that best matches the definition.
   a. bacterial STD that causes ulcers
   b. showing no signs of illness or disease
   c. most common bacterial STD in the United States
   d. inflammation of the upper female reproductive tract
   e. virus that causes genital warts

2. Explain the relationship between the key terms in each pair below.
   a. *epidemic* and *sexually transmitted disease*
   b. *chlamydia* and *pelvic inflammatory disease*

Understanding Key Ideas

Section 1

3. Name one emotional consequence teens risk if they become sexually active.

4. One in _____ female teenagers gets pregnant each year.
   a. 5
   b. 10
   c. 20
   d. 100

5. Describe how the life of a teen parent differs from the life of a teen without a child.

6. Describe why babies born to teen mothers are more likely to have health problems than babies born to adult mothers are.

7. Name three ways that teenagers can show affection nonsexually.

8. **LIFE SKILL** **Setting Goals** How would becoming a parent now affect your goals for the future?

9. **CRITICAL THINKING** Look at the Beliefs Vs. Reality feature on p. 476. Suppose your friend says she is not worried about STDs because her boyfriend doesn't seem like the type of guy who would have an STD. What would you say to your friend?

Section 2

10. List two reasons STDs in teens are considered a "silent epidemic".

11. What percentage of all new STD cases occur in people between the ages of 15 and 19?
    a. 1 percent
    b. 10 percent
    c. 25 percent
    d. 50 percent

12. What are three reasons that teens are at high risk for being infected with STDs?

13. Describe how each of the following steps can protect you against STDs.
    a. practicing abstinence
    b. avoiding alcohol and drugs

Section 3

14. Describe four ways in which sexually transmitted diseases can be spread.

15. Why are most babies born in the United States treated with eyedrops at birth?

16. What symptom may occur in both males and females who have gonorrhea?
    a. fever
    b. painful urination
    c. bleeding
    d. blisters

17. Describe the health effects that can result if each of the following STDs is untreated.
    a. chlamydia
    b. syphilis
    c. genital herpes
    d. HPV

18. Which viral STD increases a woman's risk of developing cervical cancer?
    a. HPV
    b. HIV
    c. gonorrhea
    d. genital herpes

19. Describe the treatment of common STDs caused by parasites.

20. List four responsibilities of a person who suspects he or she is infected with an STD.

Interpreting Graphics

Study the figure below to answer the questions that follow.

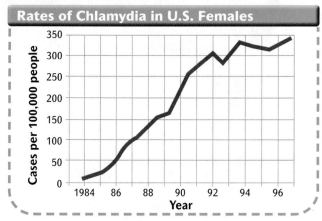

Rates of Chlamydia in U.S. Females

Source: Centers for Disease Control and Prevention.

21. What was the rate of chlamydial infections in 1996?

22. How has the number of cases of chlamydia changed over time?

23. CRITICAL THINKING Why do you think the number of cases of chlamydia changed so much between 1984 and 1996?

Activities

24. Health and Your Community What suggestions as to how to reduce the number of cases of STDs would you give your local health agency? Write a short report summarizing your suggestions. **WRITING SKILL**

25. Health and You Write a short report describing the benefits of waiting until you are a married adult before becoming a parent. **WRITING SKILL**

26. Health and Your Community Work with two classmates. Choose two of the STDs discussed on pp. 486–489. Then collect the Centers for Disease Control and Prevention (CDC) statistics on these two STDs. For each STD, draw a graph that shows the number of new cases each year since 1985.

Action Plan

27. LIFE SKILL Setting Goals Make a plan to protect yourself from becoming a teen parent or becoming infected with an STD.

Standardized Test Prep

Read the passage below, and then answer the questions that follow. **READING SKILL** **WRITING SKILL**

Gloria was <u>brooding</u> because she couldn't go with her friends to see a movie. She couldn't afford a babysitter, and she had to study. She had to pass all of her classes so that she could graduate from high school. Otherwise, she wouldn't be able to get a job that paid well. When her friend Juan called her, she talked about her feelings. "I wish I could go to the movie. I never realized that I would have to make so many sacrifices."

28. Write a paragraph describing the sacrifices Gloria is referring to in the last sentence of the reading passage. Explain why she has to make these sacrifices.

29. In this passage, the word *brooding* means
  A celebrating.
  B worrying about in a troubled way.
  C feeling sick.
  D feeling angry.

30. What can you infer from reading this passage?
  E Gloria does not like to dance.
  F Gloria is a teen parent.
  G Juan is Gloria's boyfriend.
  H none of the above

31. Write a paragraph describing Gloria's life after graduation.

CHAPTER 21

HIV and AIDS

What's Your Health IQ?
KNOWLEDGE

Which of the statements below are true, and which are false? Check your answers on p. 638.

1. Even young and healthy people are at risk of becoming infected with HIV. T

2. You cannot tell if a person is infected with HIV just by looking at him or her. T

3. You can get HIV after shaking hands with a person infected with HIV. F

4. If you drink from a water fountain after a person infected with HIV has, you are at risk of becoming infected with HIV. F

5. You cannot become infected with HIV by using a toilet after a person infected with HIV has used it. T

6. You are not at risk of becoming infected with HIV by kissing the cheek of a person infected with HIV. T

7. If you donate blood at the blood bank, you are at risk of becoming infected with HIV. F

8. Most people who are infected with HIV know they are infected and will warn others that they are infected. F

Visit these Web sites for the latest health information:

HEALTH LINKS.
THE WORLD'S A CLICK AWAY

Find more information whenever you see a HealthLinks box. Go to **scilinks.org/health**, and type in the HealthLinks code.

Find worksheets and other materials that go with your textbook at **go.hrw.com**.

Current Health

Check out *Current Health* articles related to this chapter by visiting **go.hrw.com**. Just type in the keyword **HH4 CH21**.

HIV and AIDS Today

OBJECTIVES

Distinguish between an HIV infection and AIDS.

Name the three areas in the world that have the greatest number of people living with HIV/AIDS.

Compare the number of people in the United States living with HIV infection to the number of people in the United States living with AIDS.

Summarize why teens are one of the fastest-growing groups infected with HIV.

KEY TERMS

human immunodeficiency virus (HIV) the virus that primarily infects cells of the immune system and that causes AIDS

acquired immune deficiency syndrome (AIDS) the disease that is caused by HIV infection, which weakens the immune system

pandemic a disease that spreads quickly through human populations all over the world

Every day, about 110 Americans are infected with HIV. More than 3 million people died from AIDS in 2004. Currently, there is no cure for AIDS. Do you know how to help fight against the spread of HIV and AIDS?

What Are HIV and AIDS?

HIV and AIDS are different. **Human immunodeficiency virus (HIV)** is the virus that primarily infects cells of the immune system and that causes AIDS. **Acquired immune deficiency syndrome (AIDS)** is the disease that is caused by HIV infection, which weakens the immune system.

HIV infection is an infection in which HIV has entered the blood and is multiplying in a person's body cells. HIV specifically infects cells of the immune system. HIV eventually destroys the body's ability to fight off infection. After someone is infected with HIV, the virus

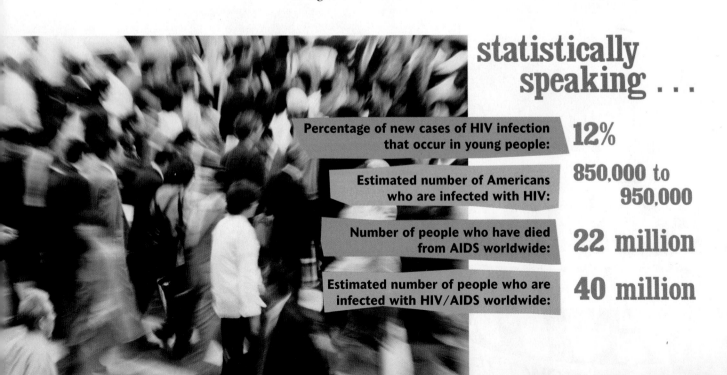

statistically speaking . . .

Percentage of new cases of HIV infection that occur in young people:	**12%**
Estimated number of Americans who are infected with HIV:	**850,000 to 950,000**
Number of people who have died from AIDS worldwide:	**22 million**
Estimated number of people who are infected with HIV/AIDS worldwide:	**40 million**

starts making new copies of itself inside the immune system cells. The new copies of the virus destroy the cells they infect. The copies of the virus are then released into the bloodstream and enter other immune system cells. The destructive cycle then continues.

Getting AIDS Being infected with HIV doesn't mean the person has AIDS. A person is said to have AIDS when the virus has destroyed many immune system cells and has badly damaged the immune system. It usually takes 5 to 10 years for a person who is infected with HIV to develop AIDS if the person has not received treatment. People with AIDS cannot fight off illnesses that a healthy person's immune system could easily defeat. AIDS patients suffer from and often die from these illnesses.

There is still no cure for AIDS. Once the virus infects a person's body, there is no way to remove the virus. Most people with HIV infection eventually develop AIDS. So, learning about HIV and AIDS and protecting yourself from being infected are very important.

www.scilinks.org/health
Topic: AIDS
HealthLinks code: HH4005

HEALTH LINKS. Maintained by the National Science Teachers Association

HIV Around the World

AIDS is a **pandemic,** a disease that spreads quickly through human populations all over the world. More than 20 million people throughout the world have died from AIDS in the last 20 years.

HIV was first discovered in the United States in the early 1980s. Most scientists think that HIV came from central Africa. The virus spread very quickly from Africa to other regions and countries. HIV is still spreading rapidly in many parts of the world, including Asia and Eastern Europe (especially in the Russian Federation). However, the hardest hit area is Africa. AIDS is now the leading cause of death in sub-Saharan Africa. To get an idea of how widespread HIV and AIDS are in the world, look at the statistics in **Figure 1.**

Figure 1

These statistics show that AIDS has spread through populations around the world.

ACTIVITY *If the population size of North America is 316 million, what percentage of the population is infected with HIV/AIDS?* **MATH SKILL**

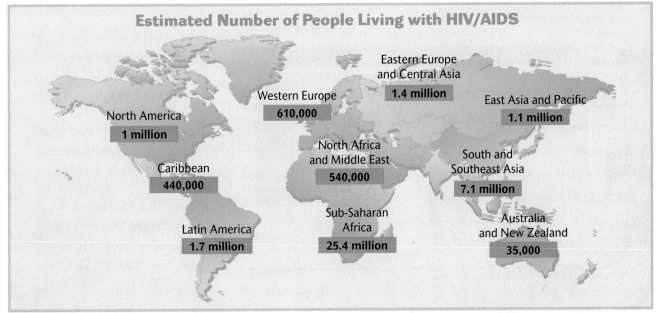

Estimated Number of People Living with HIV/AIDS

- Eastern Europe and Central Asia — 1.4 million
- Western Europe — 610,000
- East Asia and Pacific — 1.1 million
- North America — 1 million
- North Africa and Middle East — 540,000
- South and Southeast Asia — 7.1 million
- Caribbean — 440,000
- Latin America — 1.7 million
- Sub-Saharan Africa — 25.4 million
- Australia and New Zealand — 35,000

Source: Joint United Nations Program on HIV/AIDS.

In some African countries, more than 30 percent of adults are infected with HIV. Nearly all infected people will die because treatment is not readily available or affordable. Many children are left without parents. The loss of human life will also affect the economies of these countries. Many important jobs in fields such as teaching and farming will be left without anyone to fill them.

The AIDS epidemic is also very serious in the United States. An estimated 850,000 to 950,000 people are currently living with HIV infection. Of those infected with HIV in the United States, more than 400,000 people are living with AIDS. Each year, another 40,000 people are infected with HIV.

Teens and HIV

AIDS is most common among young adults, but many of these adults became HIV-infected as teens. Many teens do not know they are infected and may be passing the virus to others. Teenagers are one of the fastest-growing groups to become infected with HIV. More than 10,000 teens between 13 and 19 years of age have been diagnosed with HIV in the United States. More than 4,000 of these kids have developed AIDS. Furthermore, these numbers may underestimate the real numbers, because not all cases are reported.

Analyzing DATA

U.S. Teens with AIDS

1 The horizontal (*x*) axis shows the independent variable, *Year*.

2 The vertical (*y*) axis shows the dependent variable, *Number of teens*.

3 Each bar represents the number of teens with AIDS at each of the four time intervals.

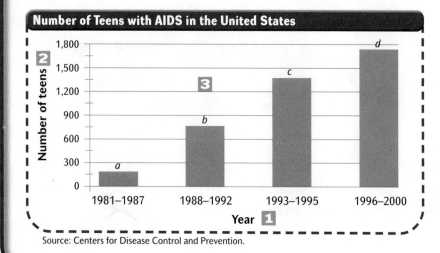

Number of Teens with AIDS in the United States

Source: Centers for Disease Control and Prevention.

Your Turn

1. How many teens were diagnosed with AIDS between bars *b* and *c*? **MATH SKILL**

2. What is the percentage increase in the number of teens with AIDS between bars *a* and *b*? **MATH SKILL**

3. **CRITICAL THINKING** Why do you think that the number of AIDS cases in teens has increased steadily since 1981?

4. **CRITICAL THINKING** Why do you think that the current number of teens with HIV is likely to be greater than the number of teens with AIDS?

HIV Is Rising in Teens HIV cases are rising in teens because many do not take the risks of HIV and AIDS seriously, and thus, engage in high-risk behaviors. Many believe common myths. For example, some teens believe that one can tell by looking at someone if that person is infected. However, many HIV-infected people look "normal" and healthy, especially in the early stages of infection.

Another myth teens have is that HIV/AIDS is a problem only for homosexual males. However, HIV can happen in anyone who engages in high-risk behavior, regardless of sexual orientation, gender, or age. In fact, heterosexual females represent a growing number of new cases. The face of the HIV epidemic is changing, and individuals from all populations are being infected. So, you not only need to know the facts about HIV/AIDS but also need to take the risks seriously.

> **Teens may think that they are not at risk for HIV and AIDS, but teens are one of the fastest-growing groups of people being infected with HIV.**

SECTION 1

REVIEW *Answer the following questions on a separate piece of paper.*

Using Key Terms

1. **Identify** the term for "the virus that causes AIDS."

2. **Define** the term *acquired immune deficiency syndrome.*

Understanding Key Ideas

3. **Describe** the relationship between an HIV infection and AIDS.

4. **Identify** which of the following geographic areas has the highest number of people infected with HIV/AIDS.
   a. Latin America
   b. Western Europe
   c. sub-Saharan Africa
   d. North America

5. **Compare** the number of people in the United States living with HIV infection to the number of people in the United States living with AIDS.

6. **Summarize** why the number of new cases of HIV infection is increasing in teens each year.

Critical Thinking

7. **LIFE SKILL** **Practicing Wellness** State three ways you can help other teens take the risks of HIV and AIDS seriously.

8. Your friend tells you, "My boyfriend is a star athlete. He couldn't be infected with HIV." What could you tell your friend?

9. Your friend tells you that she heard on the radio that HIV infection is not the cause of AIDS. What could you tell your friend?

Understanding HIV and AIDS

OBJECTIVES

Describe how HIV infects the body's immune system.

Summarize the symptoms in each of the phases of HIV infection.

Identify three ways that HIV is spread.

List five ways that HIV is not spread.

State how a teen can know if he or she is at risk for HIV infection.

KEY TERMS

helper T cell (CD4+ cell) the white blood cell that activates the immune response and that is the primary target cell of HIV infection

opportunistic infection (OI) an illness due to an organism that causes disease in people with weakened immune systems; commonly found in AIDS patients

asymptomatic stage a stage of an infection in which the infectious agent, such as HIV, is present but there are few or no symptoms of the infection

Many new viruses (shown as red dots) are being released from an HIV-infected helper T cell.

Have you ever been near someone with a contagious infection, such as a cold, but you didn't get sick? One possible reason you didn't get sick is that your body's immune system was able to fight the infection. Now, imagine what life would be like if your immune system did not work properly. This is what happens after HIV infects the body.

HIV Infects the Body

HIV is found in the body fluids, including blood, of an infected person. After HIV enters the bloodstream, the virus attaches to specific white blood cells. The white blood cells are an important part of the body's immune system, which fights infection and protects us from disease.

HIV Infects Helper T Cells

Helper T cells (CD4+ cells) are the white blood cells that activate the immune response and that are the primary target cells of HIV infection. Healthy people carry about 500 to 1,500 helper T cells in a milliliter of blood (about 20 drops).

After HIV attaches to a helper T cell, the virus's genetic material enters the cell. The virus then forces the T cell to make many copies of HIV in a process called *replication*. After viral replication, the new viruses are released from the T cell and attach to other new helper T cells. The process of viral attachment, entrance, replication, and release is then repeated.

At first, the immune system fights the HIV infection. However, HIV infection isn't like a cold in which the immune system completely kills the virus in time. The immune system of a person infected with HIV cannot defeat all the viruses. Eventually, HIV destroys enough helper T cells to cripple the body's immune system.

Helper T Cell Counts Drop In most HIV-infected people, the virus takes years to destroy the immune system. As more helper T cells are lost, the immune system is less able to fight off other infections and certain cancers. The number of new viruses made and the number of immune cells destroyed determine how quickly a person develops AIDS. **Figure 2** shows how the number of T cells drops as an HIV infection progresses.

AIDS is diagnosed when the number of helper T cells falls below 200 per milliliter of blood or when at least one AIDS-defining condition is present. AIDS-defining conditions include opportunistic infections and other diseases, such as cervical cancer. An **opportunistic infection (OI)** is an illness due to an organism that causes disease in people with weakened immune systems. OIs are commonly found in people with AIDS. One example of an OI is a special kind of pneumonia.

Phases and Symptoms of HIV Infection

HIV infection doesn't progress to AIDS on a specific timetable, but people tend to go through three phases of infection.

Phase I Phase I of HIV infection is called the asymptomatic phase. The **asymptomatic stage** is a stage of an infection in which the infectious agent, such as HIV, is present but there are few or no symptoms of the infection. Phase I can last from the initial infection for as long as 10 years or more. Some infected individuals will briefly develop a short flu-like illness, swollen glands, fatigue, diarrhea, weight loss, or fevers. These mild symptoms may be ignored because they are common to many diseases. However, although infected people may feel well, they can still transmit the virus to others.

HEALTH Handbook For more information about infectious diseases, see the Express Lesson on pp. 542–544 of this text.

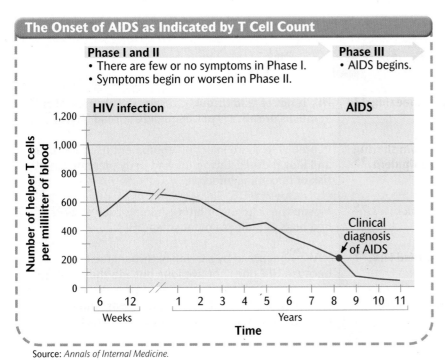

The Onset of AIDS as Indicated by T Cell Count

Phase I and II
• There are few or no symptoms in Phase I.
• Symptoms begin or worsen in Phase II.

Phase III
• AIDS begins.

Source: *Annals of Internal Medicine.*

Figure 2

The graph shows that the number of helper T cells in the bloodstream of a person with AIDS decreases gradually over time.

ACTIVITY *How many years after infection does the onset of AIDS occur in this AIDS patient?*

People with AIDS have a severely weakened immune system and often suffer from AIDS-defining conditions.

Phase II The beginning or worsening of symptoms marks the start of the second phase of HIV infection. As the immune system fails, lymph glands become swollen, and fatigue, weight loss, fever, or diarrhea develop or worsen. Some infected people may notice mental changes, such as forgetfulness and abnormal thinking patterns.

Phase III The third phase of HIV infection marks the beginning of AIDS. This phase is characterized by a helper T cell count of 200 or less and the development of AIDS-defining conditions such as opportunistic infections.

Opportunistic infections are caused by organisms that survive and flourish in an HIV-infected person. These organisms usually do not cause problems in people with a healthy immune system. Opportunistic infections include pneumocystis pneumonia, tuberculosis, and a rare infection of the brain called *toxoplasmosis*. Kaposi's sarcoma is an example of a cancer found in AIDS patients that causes purple-red blotches on the skin.

Gradually, an AIDS patient may appear chronically ill and show weight loss, malnutrition, and little movement. Drug therapy can slow the progress from HIV infection to AIDS. However, AIDS is fatal. Many people with AIDS die from opportunistic infections.

Ways That HIV Is Spread

The body fluids that carry enough of the HIV virus to infect other people are blood, vaginal fluid, semen, and breast milk. HIV infection can occur when the virus from these infected body fluids enters the bloodstream of another person. On the contrary, saliva, sweat, tears, vomit, feces, and urine do not contain enough of the virus to spread HIV to another person.

Beliefs Vs. Reality

"HIV is spread by coughing or sneezing."	HIV is not spread through the air. The amount of HIV in mucus or saliva is not enough to spread HIV.
"A person can't get an HIV infection from sharing needles or other injection equipment."	People who share injection equipment used for legal and illegal drugs, tattooing, and body piercing are at risk of becoming infected.
"HIV is spread by mosquito and tick bites."	Mosquitoes and other biting animals such as ticks, bed bugs, and fleas do not spread HIV.
"Sharing toilet seats can spread HIV."	HIV is not spread by sharing bathroom facilities because HIV does not live long outside the body.
"Teenagers seldom get HIV infection."	HIV does not discriminate by age. Teens who practice risky behaviors are at risk of becoming infected.

Transmission of HIV There are three main ways to spread HIV. Each is a high-risk behavior for getting HIV infection. Remember, HIV must enter a person's bloodstream for an infection to occur. The way that the virus enters the bloodstream depends on the way it is transmitted.

1. **HIV is spread during sexual activity, which includes vaginal, oral, and anal sex, with an infected person.** Infected fluids may enter the bloodstream of an uninfected person through tiny cuts, open sores, or tears in the lining of the mouth, vagina, rectum, or opening of the penis. If either the HIV-infected person or the uninfected person has another sexually transmitted disease (STD), the risk of contracting or spreading HIV increases. This is because helper T cells are more abundant in cervical mucus of women and semen of men who have an STD.

2. **HIV is spread through sharing needles or other intravenous injection equipment with an infected person.** This includes needles used to inject drugs as well as needles for body piercing and tattoos. When an HIV-infected person uses injection equipment, small amounts of infected blood may remain on the equipment. If an uninfected person uses the same equipment, the infected blood may be injected directly into his or her bloodstream.

3. **HIV is spread from an infected mother to her infant before or during the birth process or by breast-feeding.** During the birth process, an HIV-infected mother can spread HIV to her baby through one of the baby's body openings or through a small break in the skin. Infected mothers who breast-feed can also pass the virus to their infant through breast milk. However, mother-to-infant transmission has been reduced to just a few cases each year in the United States because pregnant women are tested for HIV.

Risks to Healthcare Workers Healthcare workers are also at risk for HIV infection if they come in contact with body fluids from an infected person. This may occur if they are accidentally stuck with an infected needle. This may also happen if infected body fluids enter their bloodstream through open cuts or sores. Although such events are rare, the risk for people with these jobs is real.

Behaviors That Are Safe Getting a blood transfusion from an infected person used to be a common way to get an HIV infection. Early in the HIV/AIDS epidemic, many patients received blood or blood products that contained HIV. However, screening the blood supply for HIV in the United States has practically eliminated the risk of infection through blood transfusion. Also, potential high-risk blood donors are discouraged from donating blood. Furthermore, you will not get an HIV infection if you donate blood at a blood bank or any established blood collection center. This is because sterile, single-use needles are used by medical professionals in the United States.

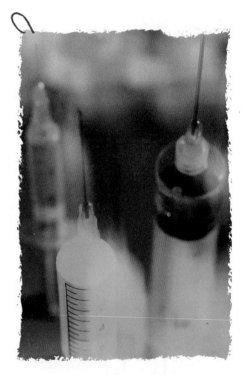

Ways HIV Is Spread

1 Sexual activity with an infected person

2 Sharing needles, syringes, or any other injection equipment with an infected person

3 Contact with body fluids from an HIV-infected mother to her infant before or during birth or by breast-feeding

There are many ways that HIV cannot be spread. For example, you cannot get HIV by playing contact sports with your friends.

Casual contact does not result in significant HIV exposure or HIV infection. Casual contact includes shaking hands, holding hands, kissing, hugging, or playing sports with friends.

HIV is not spread by sharing bathroom facilities or utensils. You will not get an HIV infection by using the same toilet seat as an infected person. You will also not contract an HIV infection by sharing a water glass or spoon, using the same water fountain, or drinking from the same can of soda. Furthermore, you will not get an HIV infection by eating in the same restaurant or by working alongside an infected person.

Teens at Risk for HIV

Teens are at risk of getting an HIV infection. Almost a third of the 40 million people living with HIV/AIDS are teens and young adults. HIV remains the tenth leading cause of death in the United States for teens between the ages of 15 and 24. The situation is worse for teens in Africa.

How do you know if *you* are at risk for HIV? Most teens that are infected acquire the virus through high-risk behavior. If you engage in behaviors known to spread HIV, you are putting yourself at high risk of being infected. You are not at risk if you do not engage in any behaviors known to transmit HIV.

How does a person know if someone he or she knows is at risk for HIV? If a person has engaged in behaviors known to spread HIV, he or she is at risk of being infected with the virus. If someone you know has participated in risky behaviors before, the only way to know if he or she is infected is an HIV test. Encourage this person to be tested for HIV and other STDs. You will read more about HIV testing later in the chapter.

SECTION 2

REVIEW   *Answer the following questions on a separate piece of paper.*

Using Key Terms

1. **Identify** the term for "the white blood cell that activates the immune response and is the primary target cell of HIV infection."

2. **Define** the term *opportunistic infection*.

Understanding Key Ideas

3. **List** the events that occur when HIV infects a helper T cell.

4. **Classify** each of the following symptoms or illnesses as part of Phase I, Phase II, or Phase III of HIV infection:
   a. AIDS
   b. mental changes
   c. opportunistic infections
   d. flu-like symptoms

5. **Name** the body fluids of an HIV-infected person that can spread HIV to another person.

6. **Compare** the ways that HIV can and cannot be transmitted.

7. **Identify** which behavior does *not* put a teen at risk for HIV.
   a. sexual activity   **c.** holding hands
   b. oral sex   **d.** sharing needles

Critical Thinking

8. Your friend tells you that she could not possibly have been infected by HIV because she feels healthy. What do you tell her?

Protecting Yourself from HIV and AIDS

OBJECTIVES

List four ways to protect yourself from HIV and AIDS.

Describe the process of getting tested for HIV.

Summarize the treatment for HIV infection and AIDS.

State three ways a person living with HIV infection can delay the progression from HIV infection to AIDS.

Identify four ways you can help an HIV/AIDS program in your community. **LIFE SKILL**

KEY TERMS

universal precautions the set of procedures used to avoid contact with body fluids and to reduce the risk of spreading HIV and other diseases

HIV-antibody test a test that detects HIV antibodies to determine if a person has been infected with HIV

HIV positive describes a person who tests positive in two different HIV tests

drug combination therapy an AIDS treatment program in which patients regularly take more than one drug

Since AIDS first appeared in the 1980s, doctors have learned a lot about treating HIV infection. New drugs can keep HIV under control for years. However, even with treatment, AIDS is still fatal because there is no vaccine or a cure. The only defense against HIV and AIDS is to prevent infection.

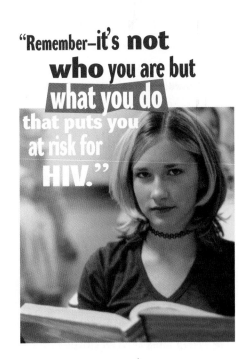

"Remember–it's **not who** you are but **what you do** that puts you at risk for **HIV.**"

Preventing HIV and AIDS

The most important thing to know about HIV infection is that it is preventable. You can avoid HIV infection by learning about how HIV is spread and by avoiding those behaviors and situations that put you at risk for HIV infection. You have the responsibility to take care of yourself. If you don't take care of yourself, who else will?

Get Educated The first thing to do to prevent HIV infection is to educate yourself. There are many good sources of information about HIV infection. For example, many health professionals have information about HIV and AIDS. The Centers for Disease Control and Prevention (CDC) also provides reliable information about HIV and AIDS. In addition, many communities have education and service organizations devoted to HIV and AIDS education and care.

Eliminate the Risks The only way to eliminate the risks of HIV infection is to avoid risky behaviors. Don't take a chance with your life!

1. **Practice abstinence.** Make the decision now to practice abstinence until marriage. Abstinence is the only method that is 100 percent effective in preventing the sexual transmission of HIV. Try to avoid all situations in which you may be pressured to engage in sexual activity. For example, avoid being alone with someone you do not know very well. Instead, go out in groups of friends.

A new student transfers to your school. You become friends with her. She tells you and others that she is HIV positive. Another group of your friends is planning a big party, but these friends say they don't want your new friend to come. They say they are worried about getting AIDS by being around her. You know they are wrong. However, you are worried that they'll get mad at you if you speak up for her. What would you do?

Write on a separate piece of paper the advice you would give your friends. Remember to use the decision-making steps.

Give thought to the problem.

Review your choices.

Evaluate the consequences of each choice.

Assess and choose the best choice.

Think it over afterward.

2. **Be Monogamous in Marriage.** To prevent the risk of spreading diseases such as HIV to each other, neither partner should be sexually intimate with anyone else. When a couple is ready for marriage, both partners should maintain a monogamous relationship.

3. **Don't share needles, syringes, drug injection equipment, or any items that may put a person in contact with blood.** If an HIV-infected person uses these devices, infected blood may remain on or in the equipment and can infect another person. If a person gets a tattoo or body piercing, he or she should choose a professional who uses single-use needles. Single-use needles are sterile and are disposed of properly after one use.

4. **Test to be sure.** When a couple is ready for marriage, an HIV test is the best way to determine that both partners are free of HIV. Because HIV can be transmitted by means other than sexual activity, even those who have been abstinent may have other risk factors.

Practice Universal Precautions
Universal precautions are the set of procedures used to avoid contact with body fluids and to reduce the risk of spreading HIV and other diseases. Health professionals regularly practice this prevention method to protect both the health professional and the patient. Each person examined or cared for in any way by a healthcare professional is assumed to be possibly infected with a pathogen that can be spread through body fluids. This assumption allows the provider to take the necessary actions to prevent the spread of disease. **Table 1** shows examples of universal precautions.

Table 1 | **Universal Precautions for Health Professionals**

Procedures of universal precautions

▶ Wear latex or vinyl gloves when touching the patient or handling potentially infected fluids.

▶ Wear protective clothing such as laboratory coats, goggles, face masks, and hats during activities that may cause exposure to the patient's body fluids.

▶ Handle and dispose of all bodily fluids or tissues in a safe manner.

▶ Handle safely and dispose of properly all supplies and equipment that have been contaminated with body fluids.

▶ Use single-use supplies or equipment when practical.

▶ Clean and sterilize equipment that will be used on more than one patient.

Testing for HIV

People infected with HIV may have few or no symptoms for many years after infection. Without symptoms to indicate infection, the only way to know if one is infected is to get tested. If you have engaged in any high-risk behaviors, get tested. When you are ready for marriage and a sexual relationship, make sure you and your partner get tested.

HIV-Antibody Tests HIV tests are readily available at doctors' offices, clinics, hospitals, and specific AIDS-testing places. All HIV tests are confidential. First, call for an appointment. Once you arrive, you will meet with a counselor. The counselor will ask you to fill out a questionnaire and ask you questions about risk behaviors. It is important to answer those questions honestly.

Next, the counselor will prepare you for the HIV test. A test that detects antibodies to determine if a person has been infected with HIV is known as an **HIV-antibody test.** Antibodies are proteins that are made when the immune system prepares to attack an infectious agent in the body. If the initial test is positive for HIV antibodies, a different test is done to confirm the result. A person who tests positive in two different HIV tests is **HIV positive,** and thus, HIV-infected.

HIV-antibody tests require a blood sample. Newer HIV tests use urine, saliva, and other body fluids instead of blood, but the blood test is the most accurate and reliable test. While the current HIV-antibody tests require a laboratory, some of the newer tests can be performed at home. The FDA has recently approved these newer tests. Furthermore, counseling by a healthcare professional that precedes and follows a lab test is important for answering a person's questions.

A Retest for HIV Is Best HIV antibodies may be found within 6 to 12 weeks after infection with HIV. However, antibodies may not be present until 6 to 12 months after infection. An initial negative test can be misleading if the test is done too soon after infection. If a person thinks he or she has had a recent exposure to HIV, then this person should avoid all high-risk behaviors and be tested. After 6 months, this person should be retested. If the test is negative again and the person has not been exposed to additional risks, he or she is probably not infected.

Lab Tests for HIV-Infected People Two lab tests can help doctors monitor the health of their patients who are HIV positive. One test measures the number of helper T cells in the blood, a value called a *T cell count* or CD4+ count. The result of this test can show the strength of the patient's immune system. This test can also tell whether a person has developed AIDS.

Another lab test measures viral load. *Viral load* is a measure of the number of viruses in the blood. The higher the viral load, the more infectious the person's body fluids are likely to be and the closer that person is to having AIDS.

Myth

A negative HIV test is a guarantee that you are not infected.

Fact

Antibodies to HIV may not show up until 6 to 12 months after infection.

Treating HIV and AIDS

When a person first discovers that he or she is HIV positive, that person should see a doctor as soon as possible. Like almost all other chronic viral infections, no cure exists for HIV infection and AIDS. However, drugs have been developed that can keep the virus under control for years.

Importance of Treatment
All HIV-infected people whose immune system shows signs of impairment or who have developed AIDS should consider a drug treatment plan. Today, many drugs are used to treat HIV infection and AIDS. The key decision is when to start the drugs. Once the decision has been made to start the medications, the doctor will help select a drug regimen and a treatment plan.

The availability of these new HIV and AIDS drugs has caused the average survival time of AIDS patients to increase and the AIDS death rate to drop. New drugs can decrease the viral load, maintain the person's helper T cell counts, and even treat some opportunistic infections. In some rare cases, treatment can reverse the disease and allow the body's immune system to repair itself. However, HIV and AIDS drugs can cause serious side effects, the drugs do not work for every patient, and no drug can cure AIDS.

Drug Combination Treatment
Drug combination therapy is an AIDS treatment program in which patients regularly take more than one drug. Researchers have learned that three or more drugs given at the same time are more effective than one drug by itself. These different drugs stop HIV from multiplying at different steps in the virus's replication process.

A common drug used in drug combination therapy is called *azidothymidine* (AZT). Another group of powerful drugs are called protease inhibitors. AZT and protease inhibitors prevent HIV from making copies of itself inside a T cell. However, even combination drugs cannot completely eliminate the virus from the body.

HIV and AIDS drug treatment plans may require taking many pills each day. This is the medicine cabinet of a person who has been living with HIV since 1980.

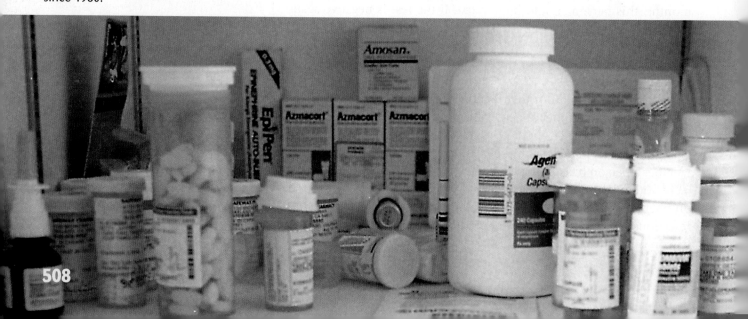

Limits of HIV/AIDS Drugs   After drugs for HIV infection have been started, the patient is checked for side effects. Drugs are continued until side effects become serious or the HIV infection worsens. Side effects can include kidney and liver damage. About 30 percent of the people who start taking some of these drugs become so sick that they have to stop taking them. Because of these side effects, doctors wait to prescribe drugs until the virus has caused noticeable damage to the patient's immune system.

In addition to side effects of the drugs, taking HIV/AIDS drugs can be difficult for the following reasons:

▶ These drugs can lose their effectiveness over time because the virus can develop resistance to the drugs.

▶ The cost of these drugs and of treatment is very high.

▶ The drug treatment plans are very complicated and require taking many pills per day on a strict schedule.

▶ The lab tests that monitor treatment progress require that patients be motivated, committed, and involved in their progress.

Drugs may slow the development of the disease and extend the quality of life for AIDS patients. However, drugs do not cure the disease.

> **Drugs to treat one person with AIDS cost between $10,000 and $15,000 per year.**

LIFE SKILL Activity

Using Community Resources

HIV and the Community

You may be saying to yourself, "I want to do my part to help stop the HIV/AIDS epidemic. But what can I do?" Here are some ways to get started:

1. Make a commitment to yourself to tell one person that you won't put yourself at risk of becoming infected. Write down a plan about how you will avoid risky behaviors.

2. Educate your friends about preventing HIV infection. Encourage them to avoid risky behavior.

3. Make a commitment to participate in preventing HIV/AIDS in your community. Write down three community organizations that support HIV/AIDS education and prevention. Find out if there is an AIDS hot line. If so, find out how you can help.

4. Find out if an organization in your community sponsors an AIDS walk and when the walk is scheduled. Find out if the AIDS walk provides opportunities for walkers to raise funds for local AIDS organizations or patients. Sign up for the walk, and encourage your friends to participate.

5. One way people honor those who have died of AIDS is by making an AIDS quilt. Find out other ways to honor people who have died of AIDS in your community.

LIFE SKILL Using Community Resources

1. What can you do to support HIV/AIDS education and prevention programs in your community?

2. How might you help raise funds for an AIDS education program?

Living with HIV Infection

Maintaining good health through treatment, diet, exercise, and rest is important for delaying the progression from HIV infection to AIDS. Counselors at clinics and in health facilities can provide information about keeping healthy. Counselors can also help people deal with the emotional aspects of finding out that they are infected. Support groups and outreach programs for HIV and AIDS patients and their families are available in most large communities.

Most HIV-infected people continue doing almost everything they did before they got infected. Infected people continue to work, go to school, participate in sports and other activities, and be around others. However, all HIV-infected people should remember that they can transmit this deadly virus to others. To avoid infecting others, HIV-infected people must avoid participating in activities that may expose others to infected body fluids.

Some HIV-infected people become activists and spokespeople for HIV/AIDS prevention. Ervin "Magic" Johnson is a former basketball star who is HIV positive. He speaks to many people every year about preventing HIV infection. Johnson often talks about how he denied being at risk for HIV. He encourages others to realize the risk of HIV infection. He stresses that HIV infection can happen to anyone, even a famous athlete. We can all make a difference in small ways and in big ways in the fight to stop the spread of HIV and AIDS.

Many people infected with HIV, such as "Magic" Johnson, become AIDS activists and speak to groups about HIV and AIDS prevention.

SECTION 3

REVIEW   *Answer the following questions on a separate piece of paper.*

Using Key Terms

1. **Define** the term *universal precautions.*

2. **Identify** the term for "describes a person who tests positive for two different HIV tests."

Understanding Key Ideas

3. **List** four things a person can do to prevent HIV infection and AIDS.

4. **Identify** which of the following is *not* a universal precaution procedure.
   a. wearing gloves when handling blood
   b. disposing of blood-contaminated supplies
   c. avoiding single-use equipment
   d. sterilizing supplies

5. **Describe** the relationship between the HIV-antibody test and being HIV positive.

6. **Propose** which of the following responses a person should have if he or she may have been exposed to HIV but tested negative for HIV. He or she should
   a. take the test again 6 to 12 months later.
   b. repeat the test next week.
   c. take an at-home HIV test.
   d. none of the above

7. **Name** one advantage and one disadvantage of drug combination therapy.

8. **Propose** four things an HIV-infected person can do to delay the development of AIDS.

9. **LIFE SKILL** **Using Community Resources** State four things you can do to contribute to a community HIV and AIDS program.

Critical Thinking

10. You and your friend find a syringe in the school parking lot. Your friend thinks it's OK to pick it up. What would you do?

CHAPTER 21

Highlights

Key Terms

The Big Picture

✔ Human immunodeficiency virus (HIV) is a virus that primarily infects cells of the immune system and that causes AIDS.

✔ Acquired immune deficiency syndrome (AIDS) is a fatal disease that results from HIV infection.

✔ AIDS is a worldwide epidemic that continues to spread.

✔ An estimated 850,000 to 900,000 Americans are living with HIV infection.

✔ Teenagers are one of the fastest-growing groups with HIV and AIDS because they engage in high-risk behaviors.

✔ HIV primarily infects important immune cells called helper T cells. The number of helper T cells decreases as HIV increases in the body.

✔ There are three phases of HIV infection. In the early stages of HIV-infection, people often do not know they are infected because they have few or no symptoms.

✔ The most common ways HIV is spread is through sexual contact, through shared drug injection equipment, and through contact with body fluids from a mother to her baby before or during birth or by breast-feeding.

✔ HIV is not spread by casual contact.

✔ Teens are at risk for HIV infection if they engage in high-risk behavior.

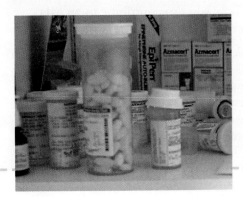

✔ HIV can be prevented by abstinence and avoiding the high-risk behaviors known to transmit HIV.

✔ If a person has engaged in any behaviors that put him or her at risk for an HIV infection, he or she should get an HIV-antibody test.

✔ Although drug combination treatment can slow down the replication of HIV in the body, drugs cannot cure AIDS.

✔ People living with HIV can delay the progression from HIV infection to AIDS by getting treated, eating well, and getting support from the community.

✔ You can contribute to a community AIDS program by volunteering for an AIDS hot line, joining an AIDS walk, or just talking to your friends about what you know about preventing HIV infection.

Review

Using Key Terms

acquired immune deficiency syndrome (AIDS) (496)
asymptomatic stage (501)
drug combination therapy (508)
helper T cell (CD4+ cell) (500)
HIV-antibody test (507)
HIV positive (507)
human immunodeficiency virus (HIV) (496)
opportunistic infection (OI) (501)
pandemic (497)
universal precautions (506)

1. For each definition below, choose the key term that best matches the definition.
   a. an AIDS treatment program in which patients regularly take more than one drug
   b. a stage of an infection in which the infectious agent is present but there are few or no symptoms
   c. the white blood cell that is the primary target of HIV infection
   d. the virus that causes AIDS
   e. a disease that spreads quickly through human populations all over the world

2. Explain the relationship between the key terms in each of the following pairs.
   a. *HIV-antibody test* and *HIV positive*
   b. *HIV* and *universal precautions*

Understanding Key Ideas

Section 1

3. How does HIV cause AIDS?

4. Which geographic area has the greatest number of people with HIV/AIDS?

5. About how many people in the United States are infected with HIV?
   a. 100–200
   c. 850,000–900,000
   b. 10,000–12,000
   d. 3,000,000

6. Why is HIV infection on the rise in teens?

7. **CRITICAL THINKING** Propose possible ways that teens can help reduce the rate of HIV infection among teenage populations.

Section 2

8. What happens when HIV infects helper T cells?

9. What can happen during Phase III of HIV infection?
   a. opportunistic infection   c. low T cell count
   b. few symptoms   d. both (a) and (c)

10. Name three ways that HIV is spread.

11. Which of the following behaviors has the highest risk for spreading HIV?
    a. shaking hands with an infected person
    b. sexual intercourse with an infected person
    c. using a glass used by an infected person
    d. kissing an infected person

12. State five behaviors that do not put someone at risk for an HIV infection.

13. How would a teen know if he or she is at risk for HIV infection?

Section 3

14. Which of the following is one way you can eliminate the risks of HIV and AIDS?
    a. drug use   c. sexual activity
    b. abstinence   d. sharing needles

15. What is the relationship between alcohol and other drugs and the risk of HIV infection?

16. How does the HIV-antibody test work?

17. Which of the following statements is true about drug combination therapy?
    a. It is not costly.   c. It can prolong life.
    b. It is a cure for AIDS. d. It has few side effects.

18. How can people living with HIV infection delay the progression of HIV to AIDS?

19. Propose how you can contribute to an AIDS program in your community. **LIFE SKILL**

20. **CRITICAL THINKING** Which of the following do you think shows that drug combination therapy is working?
    a. increased T cell count
    b. increased viral load
    c. reduced T cell count
    d. pneumonia

Interpreting Graphics

Study the figure below to answer the questions that follow.

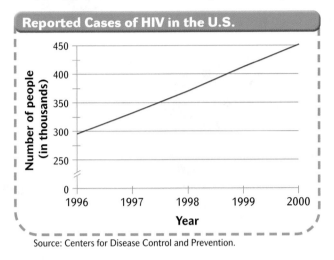

Reported Cases of HIV in the U.S.

Source: Centers for Disease Control and Prevention.

21. How many reported cases of HIV infection occurred in the United States in 1999?

22. What is the percentage increase in the reported number of people with HIV infection from 1999 to 2000? **MATH SKILL**

Activities

23. **Health and You** Write a short report about the benefits of abstaining from sexual activity and other high-risk behaviors for contracting HIV. **WRITING SKILL**

24. **Health and You** Research one of the following AIDS-related illnesses: Kaposi's sarcoma, "thrush," or pneumocystis pneumonia. Write a short report describing the infection. Include information on the causes, symptoms, and treatment of the infection. **WRITING SKILL**

25. **Health and Your Community** Research one local HIV/AIDS community program, and write down some ways the program can help reduce the number of new cases of HIV infection. **WRITING SKILL**

26. **Health and Your Community** Research HIV infection rates in your state, and compare that number to the national figure.

Action Plan

27. **LIFE SKILL** **Practicing Wellness** Discuss at least four things you can do to contribute to HIV and AIDS education and prevention.

Standardized Test Prep

Read the passage below, and then answer the questions that follow. **READING SKILL** **WRITING SKILL**

My name is Lena. At the age of 18, I was on my way to college. The year was 2002. I needed to find housing, learn my way around the campus, and sign up for the right classes. I was not thinking about HIV. I never thought anyone around my age would get HIV. I thought we were invincible and that nothing would happen to us. I now know about HIV, and I am <u>livid</u> that it took my brother Mario away from me. Why didn't someone tell Mario about HIV?

28. In this passage, the word *livid* means
 A feeling very cold.
 B feeling very angry.
 C feeling very sick.
 D feeling very happy.

29. What can you infer from reading this passage?
 E Mario had cancer.
 F Mario had AIDS.
 G Mario had an alcohol problem.
 H Mario survived to tell us his story.

30. Write a paragraph describing some of the things Lena can do to protect herself from HIV and AIDS.

31. Write a paragraph describing some of the things Lena can do to help stop the spread of HIV and AIDS in her community.

Visit go.hrw.com for a list of health agencies and organizations. Enter the keyword *HH4 Agencies*.

Nervous System

The nervous system is your body's control center and communications network.

What does the nervous system do?

The nervous system works with the endocrine system to control how your body works and to help your body respond to changes in its surroundings. Messages picked up from inside and outside of the body cause the nervous system to create signals (nerve impulses). These signals coordinate the body's thoughts, senses, movements, balance, and many automatic responses. Specialized cells, called **neurons,** receive and send the signals. Neurons form most of the tissues of the nervous system.

What are the parts of the nervous system?

The brain, the spinal cord, and many nerves make up the nervous system. **Nerves** are bundles of tissue that carry signals from one place to another. The **spinal cord** is the column of nerve tissue that runs through the backbone. The nervous system is divided into two main parts.

The brain and spinal cord make up the **central nervous system (CNS).** The nerves that connect the brain and spinal cord to other parts of the body make up the **peripheral nervous system (PNS).**

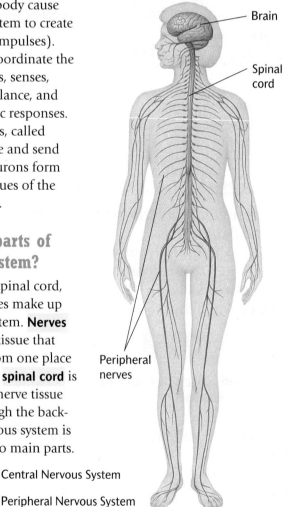

Brain

Spinal cord

Peripheral nerves

Central Nervous System

Peripheral Nervous System

How do the parts of the nervous system work together?

Some nerves of the PNS gather messages from inside and outside the body and carry signals to the CNS. The CNS interprets the incoming signals. If a response is needed, the CNS sends signals back to the muscles and the organs of the body through other nerves of the PNS. The signals from the CNS cause a response.

The nervous system enables these volleyball players to coordinate their movements.

What do neurons look like?

Most neurons (nerve cells) have three parts. The central part of a neuron is the *cell body*. Branches from the cell body, called *dendrites*, receive signals. A long extension of the cell body, called an *axon*, carries signals to the next cell. One neuron meets another neuron or other cell at a synapse. A **synapse** is a point between a neuron that is sending a signal and the neuron or other cell that is receiving the signal. The ends of axons release chemicals called **neurotransmitters** which move across the *synaptic cleft* and bind to receptors on the surface of the next cell. When the chemicals bind, they pass a signal to the next cell.

How does the nervous system work?

Sensory receptors detect messages for the nervous system and create signals. Examples of these receptors are the taste buds and the receptors for touch, smell, temperature, and light. **Sensory nerves** are nerves that carry the signals from the sense organs toward the CNS, where they are processed or relayed. **Motor nerves** are nerves that carry signals from the brain or the spinal cord to the muscles and glands. These nerves cause the body to respond. The nervous system responds in two basic ways. Some of the responses by the nervous system are voluntary, which means that you can make them happen. These responses include moving your arms and legs to walk or run and turning your head to look in a particular direction. Other responses are involuntary, or automatic. They happen whether you think about them or not. For example, shivering when you're cold and pulling your hand away from a very hot object are involuntary responses. Reflexes and the control of internal body organs are involuntary.

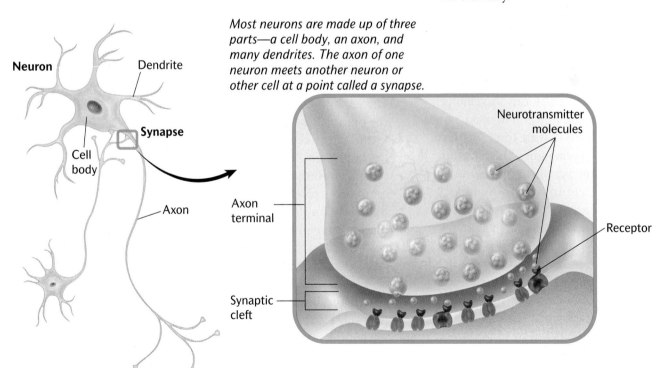

Most neurons are made up of three parts—a cell body, an axon, and many dendrites. The axon of one neuron meets another neuron or other cell at a point called a synapse.

Neuron

Dendrite

Synapse

Cell body

Axon

Axon terminal

Synaptic cleft

Neurotransmitter molecules

Receptor

Nervous System *continued*

Do nerves grow back after an injury?

Doctors once thought that injured nerves could not heal or be repaired. But recent studies now show that some nerve tissue can be repaired or can heal to some degree. Sensory and motor nerves can heal completely, but the process is very slow. Spinal nerves have also shown the ability to grow, but they generally do not grow well enough to repair significant damage. This is why spinal cord injuries and the resulting paralysis are often permanent.

Researchers are studying the nature of the spinal cord and spinal nerves to determine why they do not heal. Nerves of the brain can heal somewhat. Some types of brain cells can also change their function to make up for cells that are lost because of severe injury. The olfactory nerve, which creates the sense of smell, is unique among all nerves. It is able to heal rapidly, even after being completely severed. The mechanism for this healing is not yet known. Intense study is underway to unlock the secret and pass this ability on to other nerve cells.

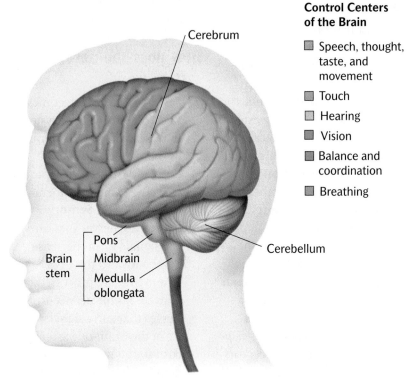

Cerebrum

Control Centers of the Brain

- ■ Speech, thought, taste, and movement
- ■ Touch
- ■ Hearing
- ■ Vision
- ■ Balance and coordination
- ■ Breathing

Pons
Brain stem Midbrain
Medulla oblongata

Cerebellum

What do the parts of the brain do?

The **brain** is the main control center for the body. Three major areas make up the brain. These are the cerebrum, the cerebellum, and the brain stem. The largest, most complex part of the brain is the **cerebrum.** It is the center for thought, imagination, and emotions. The cerebrum has two halves, or *hemispheres.* Each half has four lobes that act as control centers for different activities. These activities include the control of movement and the processing of signals that create vision, hearing, taste, and touch.

The **cerebellum** is the part of the brain that controls balance and posture. It also smooths out movement that requires fine coordination.

The **brain stem** is the part of the brian that guides signals coming from the spinal cord to other parts of the brain. There are three parts to the brain stem. The *pons* is the wider area just below the cerebrum. The *midbrain* is above the pons. Below the pons, the brain stem becomes the *medulla oblongata.* The medulla oblongata helps control many automatic actions such as heartbeat, breathing, digestion, swallowing, vomiting, sneezing, and coughing.

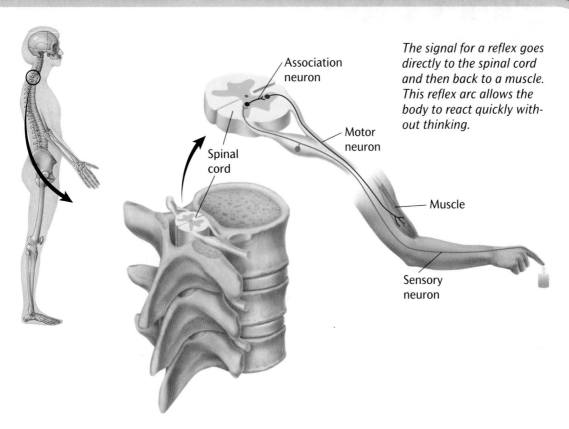

Association neuron

The signal for a reflex goes directly to the spinal cord and then back to a muscle. This reflex arc allows the body to react quickly without thinking.

Motor neuron

Spinal cord

Muscle

Sensory neuron

How does the brain send messages to the body?

The spinal cord is the major line of communication between the brain and the rest of the body. It is a cylinder of nerve tissue about 18 in. long and about as thick as your index finger. The bones of the spine, the spinal fluid, and three layers of tissue surround and protect the spinal cord. **Spinal nerves** are nerves that branch from the spinal cord and that go to the brain and to the tissues of the body. Unfortunately, despite all its protection, the spinal cord is still delicate and subject to injury.

How do reflexes work?

A **reflex** is an involuntary response that enables the body to react immediately to a stimulus, such as a possible injury. Some reflexes involve the brain, but many do not. Many reflexes, such as the reaction to intense pain, result from signals that travel to the spinal cord through one or more sensory nerves. The signals move to the spinal cord and then to a motor neuron. The motor neuron returns a signal that causes you to pull away from the source of the pain.

EXPRESS Lesson REVIEW

1. Summarize the functions of the central nervous system and the peripheral nervous system.
2. Explain how the signals carried by nerves pass from one neuron to the next.
3. Describe the functions of the cerebrum, the cerebellum, and the brain stem.
4. CRITICAL THINKING If all nerves could be made to heal rapidly, what groups of people might benefit?

Vision and Hearing

Your vision and hearing enable you to sense the world around you.

How do we see?

Your eyes and brain enable you to see. The **eye** is the sense organ that gathers and focuses light and that generates signals that are sent to the brain. Light that enters the eye falls on the retina. The **retina** is the light-sensitive inner layer of the eye. Two basic types of cells that respond to light—rods and cones—are found in the retina. *Rods*, which produce black-and-white vision, receive dim light and detect shape and motion. *Cones*, which produce color vision, receive bright light and sharpen your vision.

Rods and cones respond to light by creating nerve signals. These signals leave the eye by the *optic nerve*, which extends from the back of the eye to the area of the brain that processes sight. Your brain interprets the nerve signals created in response to light, which enables you to see the object the light came from.

What is the blind spot?

The *blind spot* is the place where the optic nerve meets the retina. There are no photoreceptors in this area of the retina. So, any image that forms on the blind spot cannot be seen.

Do you see only in black and white if you are colorblind?

No, people who are color-blind see some colors. Three different types of cones collect three basic colors of light—red, green, and blue. A person who is colorblind has a deficiency, but not a total lack, of cones that detect one or more of these basic colors of light.

How does the eye focus?

Light rays enter the eye through the *lens*, which changes shape to focus the light on the retina. It is interesting to note that images form upside down on the retina. The brain corrects the images, and thus we see things right side up.

What happens when you're nearsighted?

If you are nearsighted, your eyes focus distant objects in front of the retina rather than on it. As a result, distant objects look fuzzy. Images of nearby objects are still in focus on the retina. This condition is called *myopia*.

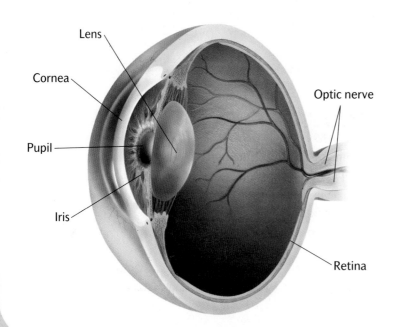

Lens

Cornea

Pupil

Iris

Optic nerve

Retina

How do we hear?

Your ears and your brain enable you to hear. The **ear** is the sense organ that functions in hearing and balance. The *outer ear* gathers in vibrations that cause sound and directs them to the eardrum. The **eardrum** is a membrane that transmits sound waves from the outer ear to the middle ear. Sound vibrations cause the eardrum to vibrate. The *middle ear* has three tiny bones—the hammer, the anvil, and the stirrup—that transmit vibrations from the eardrum to the inner ear. The bones also increase the force of vibrations.

The *inner ear* contains the fluid-filled semicircular canals and the cochlea. The **cochlea** is a coiled, fluid-filled tube. Tiny hairs in the cochlea are the receptors for sound. Signals created by the receptors go through the *auditory nerve* from the cochlea to the temporal lobe of the brain. There, the brain interprets the signals as different sounds.

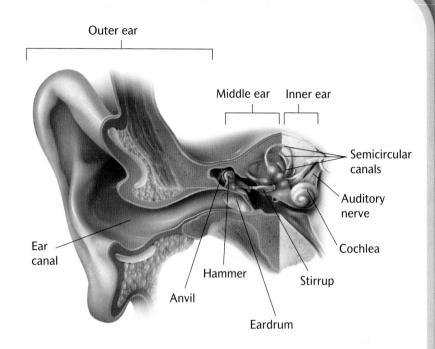

Outer ear

Middle ear   Inner ear

Semicircular canals

Auditory nerve

Cochlea

Ear canal

Hammer

Anvil

Stirrup

Eardrum

What part of the ear controls balance?

Movement of the sensory receptors in the inner ear controls balance. Some of the receptors detect gravity and changes in speed. Receptors in the semicircular canals detect rotational motions, such as spinning.

Why do ears pop in an airplane?

A tube called the **eustachian tube** connects the middle ear to the throat. The eustachian tubes maintain equal air pressure on both sides of your eardrums. Air pressure is much lower at high altitudes, where airplanes fly. You do not usually notice any changes in air pressure as you slowly gain altitude. But when you experience a rapid change from high altitude to low altitude, the air pressure on your eardrums increases suddenly. This causes the eardrums to be pushed inward, impairing your hearing temporarily. When the pressure on both sides of an eardrum is equalized, the eardrum moves back to its normal position. As a result, you hear a popping sound, and normal hearing is restored.

EXPRESS Lesson REVIEW

1. List and describe the two basic types of light receptors in the retina of the eye.

2. Explain what causes a person to be nearsighted.

3. List in order the series of structures through which sound vibrations pass in the ear.

4. **LIFE SKILL** **Practicing Wellness** Research several causes of deafness. What can a hearing person do to protect himself or herself from hearing loss?

Male Reproductive System

The male reproductive system makes male reproductive cells and hormones that cause male characteristics to appear.

What does the male reproductive system do?

The male reproductive system makes sperm and delivers them to the female reproductive system. **Sperm** are the sex cells that are made by males and that are needed to fertilize an egg.

Where are sperm made?

Sperm are made in **testes (testicles),** the male reproductive organs that also make testosterone. Inside the testes, there are tightly coiled tubes called *seminiferous tubules*, which make

sperm. About 100 million sperm are made each day! The testes must be kept cooler than normal body temperature. Sperm made at high temperatures are defective and cannot fertilize eggs. The testes, therefore, are not inside the body cavity but outside of it. Testes are found in a skin-covered sac called the **scrotum.** The scrotum contracts and relaxes to make the testes move closer to or farther from the body. When the testes are away from the body, sperm stay cooler.

What do sperm look like?

Sperm are the smallest cells in the human body. Each mature sperm is made up of three basic parts: a head, a midpiece, and a tail. The head contains substances that help the sperm enter an egg. The head also holds half the genetic information required to start a new life. The midpiece of the sperm contains structures that release the energy needed for the long trip through the female reproductive system. The tail is made of proteins that help the sperm move.

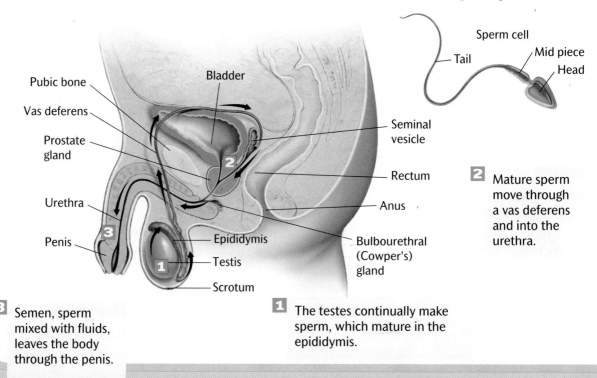

Pubic bone
Vas deferens
Prostate gland
Urethra
Penis
Bladder
Epididymis
Testis
Scrotum
Seminal vesicle
Rectum
Anus
Bulbourethral (Cowper's) gland

Sperm cell
Tail
Mid piece
Head

3 Semen, sperm mixed with fluids, leaves the body through the penis.

1 The testes continually make sperm, which mature in the epididymis.

2 Mature sperm move through a vas deferens and into the urethra.

What happens to sperm once they are made?

Once sperm are made, they move into a coiled tube called the *epididymis*. Here, immature sperm take 2 to 10 days to fully mature. The mature sperm then travel into another tube, called the *vas deferens*. The sperm are stored here until they leave the body or are reabsorbed.

How do sperm survive the long travel?

As sperm move through the body, several organs add fluids to the sperm. These organs are the *seminal vesicles*, the *bulbourethral glands* (Cowper's glands), and the prostate gland. The **prostate gland** is a gland in males that adds fluids that nourish and protect sperm when the sperm are in the female body. Sperm and the added fluids make up *semen*.

How do sperm leave the body?

Sperm leave the body during ejaculation via the *urethra*, a tube that passes through the penis. The **penis** is the organ that removes urine from the male body and that can deliver sperm to the female reproductive system. A flap in the urethra prevents urine and semen from going through the penis at the same time.

What does testosterone do?

Testosterone is the male hormone made by the testes. It causes many of the changes that happen when males reach *puberty*, or sexual maturity. For example, the shoulders get wider, the muscles get larger, hair grows on the face and other parts of the body, and the voice deepens. At this time, testosterone also causes the body to start making sperm.

The male hormone testosterone causes masculine characteristics (such as a mustache) to appear.

EXPRESS Lesson REVIEW

1. Identify the locations where sperm are made and where they mature.
2. List the three main parts of a sperm.
3. List the components of semen.
4. **LIFE SKILL** **Practicing Wellness** Prostate cancer is one of the leading causes of cancer in men. Read more about the prostate gland. What are other problems that can affect the prostate?

Female Reproductive System

The female reproductive system makes female reproductive cells and hormones that cause female characteristics to appear.

What does the female reproductive system do?

The female reproductive system makes eggs and gives them a place to develop. **Eggs,** or *ova*, are the sex cells of females and can be fertilized by sperm. When an egg and a sperm join, a new life begins. Organs of the female reproductive system nurture and protect developing humans. Parts of the system also make female hormones, which cause young girls to develop breasts and other features of women. The female hormones also help eggs to mature and prepare the body for pregnancy.

Where are eggs made?

Eggs are made in ovaries. The **ovaries** are the female reproductive organs that produce eggs and the hormones estrogen and progesterone. Girls already have all their eggs at birth. On average, there are about two million! But the eggs are immature. The eggs begin to mature when a girl reaches *puberty*. One egg matures about every 28 days. The process by which the ovaries release mature eggs is called **ovulation.**

Where are eggs fertilized?

Eggs are fertilized in the fallopian tubes. A **fallopian tube** is a female reproductive organ that connects an ovary to the uterus. After a mature egg is released, it moves into one of the fallopian tubes. The ends of these tubes do not really touch the ovaries. Tiny hairs around the opening of a fallopian tube draw an egg into the tube. If there are sperm in the tubes, a sperm may fuse with the egg and fertilize it.

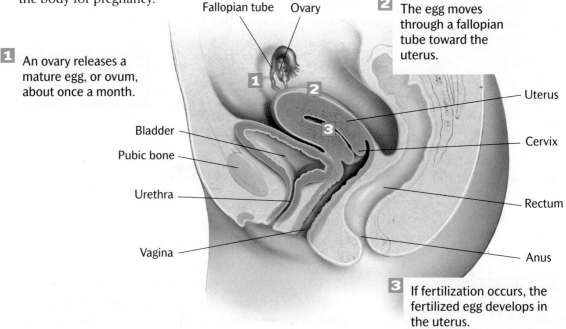

1 An ovary releases a mature egg, or ovum, about once a month.

2 The egg moves through a fallopian tube toward the uterus.

3 If fertilization occurs, the fertilized egg develops in the uterus.

Fallopian tube   Ovary

Bladder
Pubic bone
Urethra
Vagina

Uterus
Cervix
Rectum
Anus

Where do fertilized eggs develop?

Fertilized eggs develop in the **uterus,** which is a muscular organ about the size of a fist. The **cervix** is the narrow base of the uterus. As an egg matures, the lining of the uterus, or the **endometrium,** thickens. Many tiny blood vessels feed this lining. These blood vessels will bring food and oxygen to a growing baby and will carry away its wastes. This exchange happens via the **placenta,** a blood vessel–rich tissue that forms in a mother's uterus.

When a baby is ready to be born, the cervix expands to allow the baby to pass into the vagina. The **vagina** is the reproductive organ that connects the uterus to the outside of the body.

What happens if an egg isn't fertilized?

If an egg is not fertilized, the blood vessels in the endometrium break down. Blood and tissue that built up in the uterus flow out of the body through the vagina in a process called **menstruation.**

What happens during the menstrual cycle?

The **menstrual cycle** is a monthly series of hormone-controlled changes that mature an egg and prepare the uterus for pregnancy.

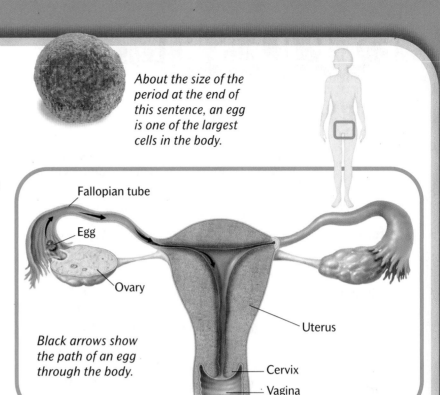

About the size of the period at the end of this sentence, an egg is one of the largest cells in the body.

Fallopian tube

Egg

Ovary

Uterus

Black arrows show the path of an egg through the body.

Cervix

Vagina

Days 1–5 Menstruation begins. Blood and the lining of the uterus (the menstrual fluid) flow out of the body.

Days 6–14 The hormone estrogen helps prepare the body for pregnancy. The hormones FSH and LH cause an egg to mature in an ovary. As the egg matures, the endometrium thickens. Ovulation occurs on about day 14.

Days 15–28 The hormone progesterone helps maintain the lining of the uterus as the uterus waits for a fertilized egg. Hormone levels remain fairly steady for several days. If a fertilized egg has not attached to the wall of the uterus by about day 28, hormone changes cause the blood vessels in the uterine lining to break down.

EXPRESS Lesson REVIEW

1. List the functions of the female reproductive system.

2. Describe the pathway an egg takes after it is released from an ovary.

3. Summarize the steps of the menstrual cycle.

4. **LIFE SKILL** **Evaluating Media Messages** Some products claim to be able to treat premenstrual syndrome (PMS). After reading more about PMS, discuss whether you think these drugs are likely to be effective.

Skeletal System

Your skeletal system gives your body shape and support, provides protection for vital organs, and produces blood cells.

What does the skeletal system do?

The skeletal system gives your body the shape it has. Without bones, you would be a shapeless blob pooled on the floor. The **skeleton** is a framework of bones that support the muscles and organs and protect the inner organs. Bones also serve as points to which the muscles attach and create body movement. Inside some bones, there is a soft tissue that makes new blood cells.

How do bones grow?

At birth, the skeletal system is soft and made mostly of *cartilage*. As a child grows, bone tissue begins to replace the cartilage. At the end of long bones is a band of cartilage called the *epiphysis*, or growth plate. Cartilage that will be replaced by bone tissue grows here. When a person reaches full height, the cartilage stops growing. At this point, bone tissue has completely replaced the cartilage, except at the very tips of the bones in the joints.

What is the "soft spot" on a baby's head?

The bones of an infant's skull are not fully developed. Areas of soft cartilage called *fontanels* separate the bones. These "soft spots" allow the skull bones to move as a baby passes through the birth canal. After birth, the skull bones grow until the soft cartilage is completely replaced. The joints where the skull bones meet are called *sutures*. Some fontanels close up within two months after birth. But the one at the top of the head takes about a year to close completely.

Understanding how the bones act as levers can help a baseball pitcher learn how to throw the ball faster and harder.

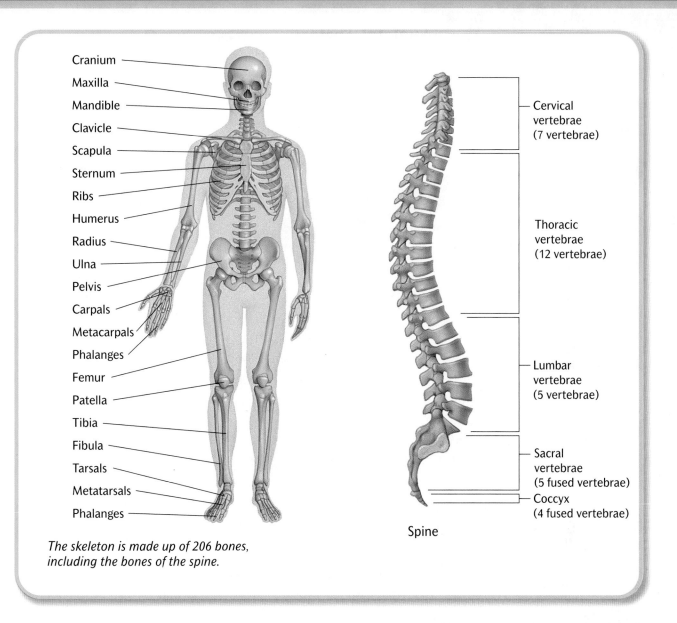

Cranium

Maxilla

Mandible

Clavicle

Scapula

Sternum

Ribs

Humerus

Radius

Ulna

Pelvis

Carpals

Metacarpals

Phalanges

Femur

Patella

Tibia

Fibula

Tarsals

Metatarsals

Phalanges

Cervical
vertebrae
(7 vertebrae)

Thoracic
vertebrae
(12 vertebrae)

Lumbar
vertebrae
(5 vertebrae)

Sacral
vertebrae
(5 fused vertebrae)

Coccyx
(4 fused vertebrae)

Spine

*The skeleton is made up of 206 bones,
including the bones of the spine.*

How many bones do we have?

Your skeleton has 206 bones and has two main parts. The *axial skeleton* is made up of the skull, the spinal column, the rib cage, and the sternum. These central bones work together to provide support and protect vital organs. The bones of the skull, for example, surround and protect the brain. The *appendicular skeleton* is made up of 126 bones. These bones form the frame to which the muscles are attached and enable the body to move about.

Are mature bones alive?

Bone is very much alive. Cells called *osteoblasts* form new bone continuously. This allows bones to heal when they are broken. Lumps of new bone may also form on parts of bones that are repeatedly stressed.

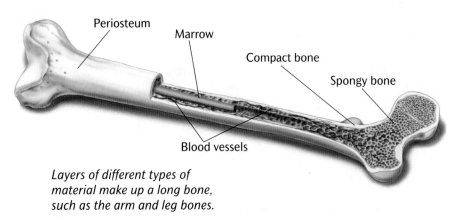

Periosteum

Marrow

Compact bone

Spongy bone

Blood vessels

Layers of different types of material make up a long bone, such as the arm and leg bones.

How do broken bones heal?

The human femur (upper leg bone) is stronger than a bar of iron of the same weight. Even so, bones sometimes break. When a bone breaks, the outer layer tears, causing severe pain and some bleeding. Blood clots form inside the break and seal both sides. Next, white blood cells come and clean out fragments of broken bone and dead cells. Fibrous strands of cartilage begin to fill in the fracture and bridge the gap between the two sides. The final step in the healing process occurs when compact bone replaces the cartilage.

What are bones made of?

The outside layer of a bone is made up of a membrane called the *periosteum*. The periosteum contains blood vessels that supply nutrients to the bone and nerves, which signal pain. Under the periosteum is a hard material called *compact bone*. Compact bone provides support and is made up of living bone cells, minerals, protein fibers, blood vessels, and nerves. Inside compact bone is a network of *spongy bone*, a connective tissue that makes bones both light and strong. Many bones also contain a soft tissue called **bone marrow,** which can be either yellow or red. The inside of long bones is filled with *yellow bone marrow*, which is made mostly of fat that stores energy. Other bones contain *red bone marrow*, in which the production of blood cells begins.

How are bones held together?

Muscles, tendons, and ligaments hold bones together. Two or more bones meet at places in the body called **joints. Ligaments,** which are tough bands of tissue, hold the ends of bones together at joints. **Tendons** are cords of connective tissue that attach muscles to bones. Muscles and tendons attach to the bones on either side of a joint, holding the joint together tightly.

Is it bad to crack my knuckles?

No, the popping or cracking sound made by some joints is very normal. Pulling on a joint creates a vacuum inside the joint. This vacuum causes tiny air bubbles in the joint fluid to burst. The result is a "pop" or a "crack" that you can hear. Popping joints is not clearly linked to getting **arthritis,** a painful inflammation of the joints.

What keeps joints from scraping?

Joints that move contain a very slippery liquid called *synovial fluid*. The pads of cartilage that serve as shock absorbers at the ends of bones also help bones glide smoothly across each other.

Do all joints move?

No, some joints are fixed, such as the ones between the bones in the skull. A *fixed joint* does not allow any movement.

Other joints, such as the *semimovable joints* between most of the *vertebrae* in the spine, allow only a small amount of movement. Several different kinds of joints allow the body to move in different ways. The simplest is the *hinge joint*. This is the type found in your elbows and knees. There, bones attach to each other in such a way that the joint can bend only back and forth.

One more flexible type of joint is the *ball-and-socket joint*. This is the type of joint found in your hips and shoulders. On one bone, a knoblike piece, or ball, sticks out. On the other bone or set of bones, there is a cup that the ball fits into. The ball is free to rotate inside the cup in almost any direction. The first two vertebrae allow your head to rotate right and left. This is called a *pivot joint*. Pivot joints in the elbow enable the forearms to rotate back and forth, as well. The last type of joint allows movement in all ways except rotation. The wrists and ankles are of this type, called an *ellipsoidal joint*.

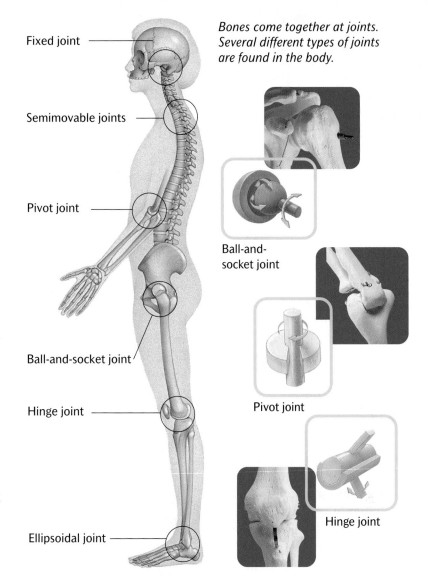

Fixed joint

Semimovable joints

Pivot joint

Ball-and-socket joint

Hinge joint

Ellipsoidal joint

Bones come together at joints. Several different types of joints are found in the body.

Ball-and-socket joint

Pivot joint

Hinge joint

EXPRESS Lesson REVIEW

1. Name the four basic parts of a bone, and identify the function of each.

2. Describe how most long bones grow.

3. List three types of joints.

4. **LIFE SKILL** **Practicing Wellness** Your bones store calcium for your body. If you do not get enough calcium from your diet, calcium will be taken from your bones for use where it is needed. Research the roles of calcium in the body, the sources of calcium in your diet, and the consequences that may result for your skeletal system if you eat a diet that is deficient in calcium.

Muscular System

Your muscular system moves all your moving parts.

What does the muscular system do?

The muscular system accounts for all of the ways that the parts of the body move. This includes actions such as running, eating, breathing, digesting food, and pumping blood. The muscular system also helps protect your joints and helps create the heat that keeps your body warm.

What are muscles made of?

Bundles of special cells called *muscle fibers* make up the muscles. Muscle fibers are made up of long, paired strands of proteins. Muscle fibers are able to contract because of the way their paired strands of proteins are linked. Two paired protein strands latch together like the two sections of an extension ladder. One section of each protein ladder moves along the other section, causing the muscle fiber to contract. When the muscle fibers contract, the whole muscle shortens.

Are all muscles the same?

There are three types of muscle tissue in the body. *Skeletal muscle*, or striated (striped) muscle, is the type that you can move voluntarily. *Smooth muscle* causes the involuntary movements of the eyelids, internal organs, and blood vessels. *Cardiac muscle* is a special kind of involuntary, striated muscle found only in the walls of the heart.

How do skeletal muscles move the body?

Skeletal muscles move the body by pulling on bones that meet at joints. Skeletal muscles are connected to the bones by tendons. Muscles at a movable joint either pull the joint into a bent position or pull it straight. Muscles usually work in pairs, one on either side of the joint. When one contracts, the other relaxes.

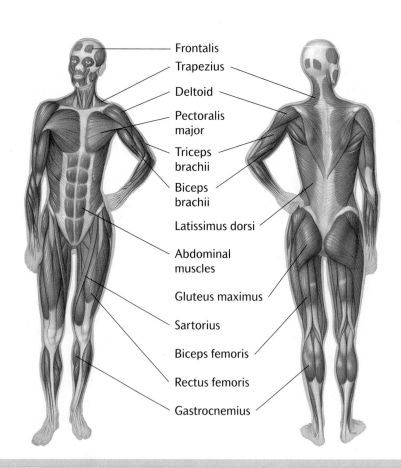

Frontalis
Trapezius
Deltoid
Pectoralis major
Triceps brachii
Biceps brachii
Latissimus dorsi
Abdominal muscles
Gluteus maximus
Sartorius
Biceps femoris
Rectus femoris
Gastrocnemius

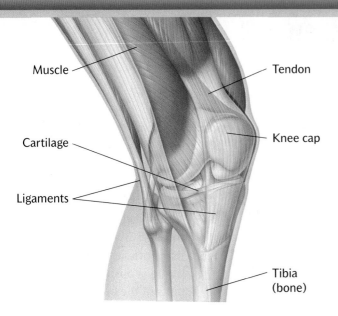

Muscle

Tendon

Cartilage

Knee cap

Ligaments

Tibia
(bone)

Muscles help hold bones together in joints such as the knee. Strong muscles help prevent knee injuries in soccer players and other athletes.

What causes muscles to get bigger when you exercise?

When you exercise a muscle by lifting something heavy, the muscle fibers in the muscle contract. Repeated strong contractions cause the muscle fibers and the muscle itself to grow in diameter and strength. In contrast, moderate contractions, such as those that result from walking, do not increase the diameter of a muscle as much. However, repeated moderate exercise greatly increases a muscle's endurance by enabling it to obtain more oxygen.

Why do muscles get tired?

Your muscles need oxygen in order to produce the energy needed for contracting. Muscles that are working very hard use up all the oxygen at hand. When this happens, less energy is available for creating contractions, which makes you feel weak or tired. But if you're running from a tiger, you can't quit just because your muscles run out of oxygen.

In order for muscles to keep working without oxygen, a process that makes the chemical *lactic acid* provides a small amount of energy. Unfortunately, lactic acid is poisonous to cells. Muscle cells need extra oxygen to get rid of lactic acid before they can make more energy. The extra oxygen needed to rid the body of the lactic acid is called an *oxygen debt*. Only time and rest can erase an oxygen debt.

EXPRESS Lesson REVIEW

1. Identify the components of muscle tissue.
2. Name the tissue that connects muscle to bone.
3. Explain how the process that causes muscle tiredness can be reversed.
4. **LIFE SKILL** **Practicing Wellness** In the past, people thought that they couldn't build muscle without going into an oxygen debt. Think about how muscles increase in size, and explain why this belief is not true.

Circulatory System

Your circulatory system is your body's internal transport system.

What does the circulatory system do?

The circulatory system moves blood all through the body. **Blood** is a tissue that is made up of cells, fluid, and other substances. Blood carries oxygen, carbon dioxide, and nutrients in the body through tubes called **blood vessels.** The **heart** is the organ that pumps the blood through the body.

Is blood really red and blue?

Hemoglobin is the oxygen-carrying pigment in the red blood cells of the blood. Hemoglobin is bright red when oxygen is attached to it. Blood is very dark red when the hemoglobin in it does not carry oxygen. Some veins are close enough to the surface of your skin to be seen. These veins appear to be blue because different colors of light reach different depths in the skin. Red light penetrates farther into the body than other colors of light. Blue light does not go very far before being reflected back by the veins. Arteries are usually so deep that they cannot be seen.

How does the heart work?

The heart beats constantly without rest. With every beat, the heart pushes blood through the vessels of the body. Blood that carries carbon dioxide returns from the body and enters the right atrium of the heart.

An **atrium** is a chamber of the heart that receives blood from the body. The blood in the right atrium is pushed through an *A-V valve* (atrioventricular valve) into the right ventricle. A **ventricle** is one of the two large, muscular chambers that pump blood out of the heart. The right ventricle squeezes blood out of the heart and pushes it toward the lungs. There, carbon dioxide leaves the blood and oxygen enters the blood.

Oxygen-rich blood comes back to the heart at the left atrium. The blood in the left atrium is pushed through an A-V valve into the left ventricle. From there, blood is pushed out to all parts of the body.

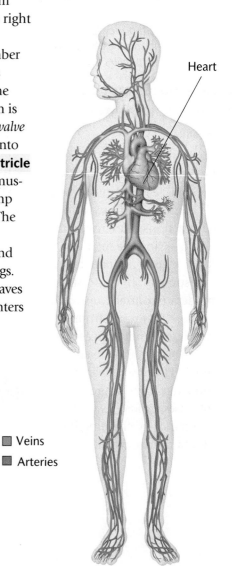

Heart

■ Veins
■ Arteries

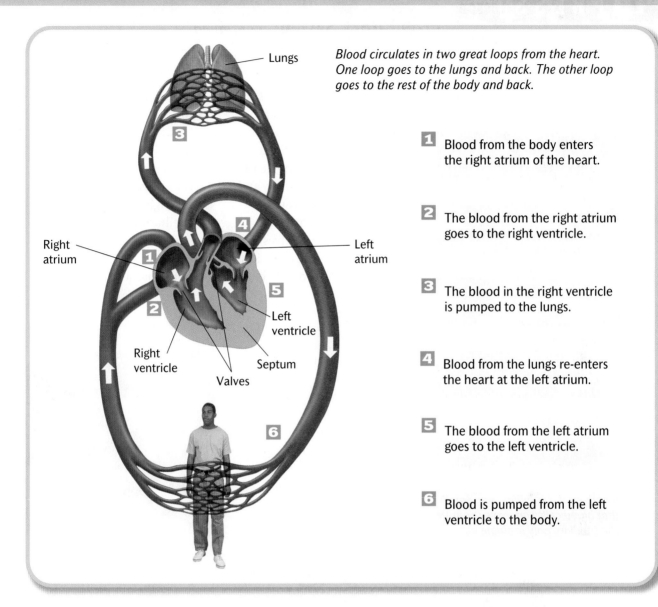

Lungs

Blood circulates in two great loops from the heart. One loop goes to the lungs and back. The other loop goes to the rest of the body and back.

1 Blood from the body enters the right atrium of the heart.

2 The blood from the right atrium goes to the right ventricle.

3 The blood in the right ventricle is pumped to the lungs.

4 Blood from the lungs re-enters the heart at the left atrium.

5 The blood from the left atrium goes to the left ventricle.

6 Blood is pumped from the left ventricle to the body.

Right atrium

Left atrium

Right ventricle

Left ventricle

Septum

Valves

What makes the heart beat?

The heartbeat is a rhythmic contraction of the heart. Signals that begin at the top of the heart cause the heartbeat. A group of cells at the top of the right atrium, called the **cardiac pacemaker,** starts a signal. This group of cells is also called the *S-A node* (sinoatrial node). First, the signal causes the atria to contract. Then, the signal goes down through the heart to another group of cells near the bottom of the septum between the two atria. This group of cells, the *A-V node* (atrioventricular node), passes the signal along to the ventricles. As a result, the ventricles contract a split second after the atria.

What causes the sound of a heartbeat?

As it beats, the heart makes two distinct sounds that are caused by the closing of the valves in the heart. The closing of the A-V valves makes the first sound, or S1. The closing of the valves that allow blood from the ventricles to enter the arteries that leave the heart makes the second sound, or S2.

What is the difference between arteries, veins, and capillaries?

Three types of vessels carry blood through the body. **Arteries** are blood vessels that carry blood away from the heart to all parts of the body. Thick walls help these vessels withstand the pres- sure of the blood that is pushed out of the heart. **Veins** are blood vessels that carry blood from all parts of the body back to the heart. Their walls are thinner, and the blood inside is not under as much pressure. Some veins have valves that open in only one direction to help bring blood back up to the heart. The valves keep the blood from flowing backward. **Capillaries** are tiny blood vessels that con- nect arteries to veins. Blood cells pass through capillaries in single file. The walls of capillaries are very thin, which allows nutrients and wastes to pass into and out of the blood.

The inset shows red blood cells moving through a capillary. The diameter of a capillary is so small that blood cells can move through the capillary only in single file.

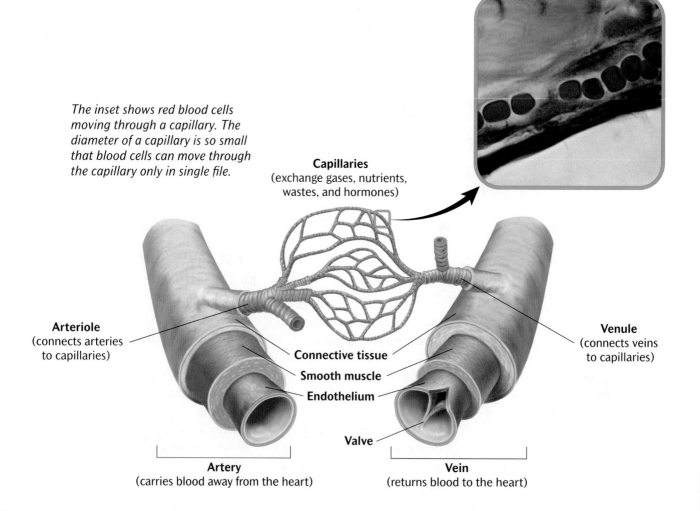

Capillaries
(exchange gases, nutrients, wastes, and hormones)

Arteriole
(connects arteries to capillaries)

Connective tissue

Smooth muscle

Endothelium

Venule
(connects veins to capillaries)

Valve

Artery
(carries blood away from the heart)

Vein
(returns blood to the heart)

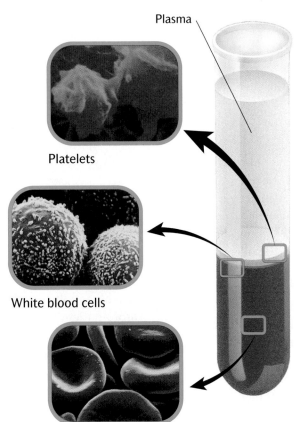

Plasma

Platelets

White blood cells

Red blood cells

Aerobic exercise, such as running, increases blood flow, which supplies more oxygen to body cells.

Blood separates into a liquid part, called plasma, and a solid part that is made up of three types of cells.

What is blood made of?

About 55 percent of blood is plasma. *Plasma* is a clear liquid that is about 92 percent water. Plasma also has nutrients, salts, proteins, and other chemicals. Three kinds of blood cells make up the rest of the blood. **Red blood cells** are full of hemoglobin and carry oxygen to the body. Red blood cells also return carbon dioxide to the lungs. **White blood cells** are blood cells that protect the body from disease. **Platelets** are cell fragments that cause blood to clot, which stops blood loss.

How do white blood cells fight disease?

White blood cells, or *leukocytes*, protect the body from disease by recognizing and destroying matter that does not belong to the body.

Some types of white blood cells kill bacteria and other invaders by surrounding and digesting them. Other types of white blood cells kill invaders by producing antibodies.

E X P R E S S Lesson REVIEW

1. Diagram the path that blood takes through the heart.
2. Describe how the heartbeat is produced.
3. List the differences between arteries, veins, and capillaries.
4. **LIFE SKILL Practicing Wellness** Research sickle cell anemia. What advantage does a person have if he or she carries the genetic trait for this disease?

Respiratory System

Your respiratory system brings oxygen in and lets carbon dioxide out of the body.

What does the respiratory system do?

The respiratory system brings life-giving oxygen into the body. It also helps the body get rid of carbon dioxide, a waste product made by cells. The process of bringing in oxygen and getting rid of carbon dioxide is called *respiration*. The **lungs** are the main organs of gas exchange in the respiratory system.

What path does air take as it enters my body?

Air enters the body through the mouth and *nasal cavities*. The air is warmed and moistened so it does not dry out the delicate lung tissue. Air then flows into the *pharynx*, or *throat*. At the base of the pharynx is the *larynx*, or voice box, where the vocal cords are located. Attached to the voice box is the **trachea,** or windpipe, which carries air to the lungs. Rings of cartilage strengthen the trachea and protect it from injury and collapse.

The trachea branches into two tubes. Each tube, called a **bronchus,** sends air to a lung. In the lungs, the bronchi branch many times into smaller and smaller tubes. The smallest of these tubes is called a **bronchiole.** At the end of each bronchiole is a cluster of thin-walled air sacs. Each air sac, called an **alveolus,** is a site for gas exchange. Capillaries around each alveolus pick up oxygen and get rid of carbon dioxide.

How does oxygen get into my blood?

Oxygen molecules naturally move from the alveoli, where oxygen is more plentiful, into the capillaries, where there is less oxygen. Alveoli and the capillaries around them have very thin walls that gases easily move through. Red blood cells pick up the oxygen molecules and release carbon dioxide.

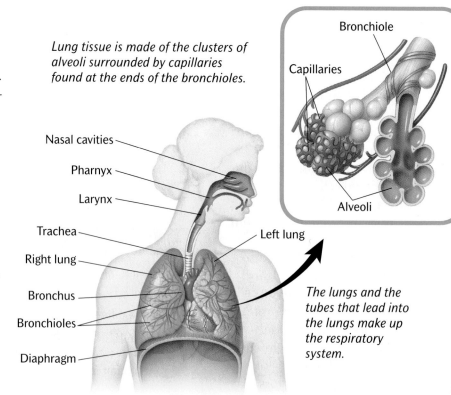

Lung tissue is made of the clusters of alveoli surrounded by capillaries found at the ends of the bronchioles.

Nasal cavities

Pharnyx

Larynx

Trachea

Right lung

Bronchus

Bronchioles

Diaphragm

Bronchiole

Capillaries

Alveoli

Left lung

The lungs and the tubes that lead into the lungs make up the respiratory system.

What makes air flow into and out of my lungs?

Movement of the rib muscles and the diaphragm pull air into the lungs and push air out. The **diaphragm** is a sheet of muscle that separates the chest cavity, which holds the lungs and heart, from the abdominal cavity, which holds the digestive system. When you breathe in, the diaphragm contracts and moves downward. The rib muscles contract and pull the chest wall up and outward. This causes air to rush in and fill the lungs. When the diaphragm and rib muscles relax, the diaphragm bows upward and the chest cavity becomes smaller, forcing air back out of the lungs.

What controls how fast I breathe?

Breathing rate is controlled by centers in the brain stem that detect carbon dioxide in the blood. Because carbon dioxide is toxic to tissues, it must not build up in the blood. When the amount of carbon dioxide in the blood rises, the breathing center in the brain stem signals the diaphragm to contract more often. So, you breathe faster. The reverse happens when the amount of carbon dioxide in the blood drops.

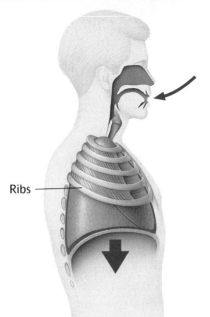

Ribs

When you breathe in, your diaphragm moves down, and your chest cavity gets larger.

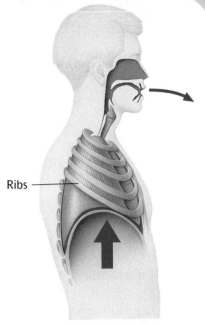

Ribs

When you breathe out, your diaphragm moves up, and your chest cavity gets smaller.

Why does the respiratory system make mucus?

Mucus is a thick, slimy fluid that coats the lining of organs and glands. Mucus lines the bronchi, trachea, and nasal passages. It serves two purposes. First, it adds moisture to the air entering the lungs. Second, it traps particles and bacteria that might otherwise clog the tiny bronchioles or cause infection in the lungs.

What causes hiccups?

Hiccups are tiny spasms of the diaphragm. We do not know for certain what causes the diaphragm to spasm. Irritation of the diaphragm is one possibility. Many studies have been done to try to find guaranteed cures for the hiccups.

EXPRESS Lesson REVIEW

1. Trace the path of air through the lungs.
2. Name the region of the airway that contains the voice box.
3. Identify the small tubes that lead to the alveoli.
4. **LIFE SKILL** **Practicing Wellness** When you run, your body automatically starts breathing faster. What causes this increase in breathing rate?

Digestive System

Your digestive system breaks down food into the nutrients your body needs.

What does the digestive system do?

The digestive system breaks down food into the things it is made of. This process is called *digestion*. As a result, the body is able to absorb and use the nutrients in food for energy, growth, and repair. The digestive system also eliminates undigested food from the body.

How are teeth involved in digestion?

Teeth begin the process of digestion. They break food down into smaller pieces that can be swallowed. Teeth also help mix food with saliva, which has an enzyme that begins to break down starch. **Enzymes** are proteins or other types of molecules that help chemical processes happen in living things.

What path does food take in the body?

Food taken in by the mouth is chewed and swallowed. The food then moves down through the long, straight tube called the **esophagus** and into the stomach. From there, it passes through the small intestine.

Finally, food moves through the large intestine. From there, the food moves into the **rectum,** the last part of the large intestine where undigested waste is stored until it leaves the body. This series of organs through which food passes is called the **digestive tract.**

How does food move through the digestive tract?

Waves of rhythmic motion, called *peristalsis,* run through the walls of organs in the digestive tract. These waves gently push food through the digestive tract.

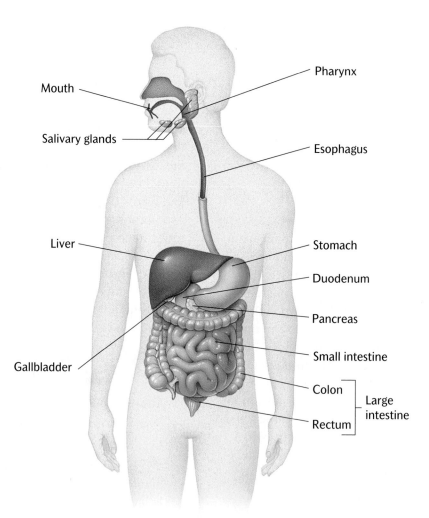

Pharynx

Mouth

Salivary glands

Esophagus

Liver

Stomach

Duodenum

Pancreas

Small intestine

Gallbladder

Colon

Large intestine

Rectum

What happens as food moves from the stomach to the colon?

In the *stomach,* a strong acid and powerful enzymes mix with the food. These chemicals kill bacteria that can be harmful and begin to break down proteins. A mixture of partly digested food and stomach enzymes, called *chyme,* results.

Digestion continues in the *small intestine,* where secretions from the small intestine itself, the liver, and the pancreas finish breaking down carbohydrates, fats, and proteins. The lining of the small intestine has millions of tiny, fingerlike projections, called villi. Capillaries in the villi take up nutrients as the digested food works its way to the *large intestine.*

The major part of the large intestine is called the **colon.** There, bacteria that live on the undigested food make important vitamins, such as vitamins A, B_6, and K, for the body. The vitamins, along with water and minerals, are taken from undigested food before the waste is removed from the body.

What do the liver and pancreas do?

The liver and pancreas are important to digestion but are not part of the digestive tract. Chemicals secreted by the *liver* help with the digestion of fats in the small intestine. Your body also depends on the liver in other ways. The liver stores energy reserves, iron, and vitamins A, D, and B_{12}. The liver also takes chemical wastes and poisons from the blood and breaks them down. Enzymes secreted by the *pancreas* break down carbohydrates and proteins in the small intestine. The pancreas also produces *insulin* and *glucagon,* which together regulate blood-sugar levels.

Why doesn't stomach acid burn the stomach?

The acid in your stomach is strong enough to "dissolve" metal. Luckily, the lining of the stomach secretes a coat of mucus that protects the wall of the stomach.

The uncomfortable feeling of heartburn results when stomach acid leaks into the esophagus.

Mucus is a thick, slimy fluid that coats the lining of organs and glands. Without a coat of mucus, the stomach would digest itself. Sometimes, stomach acid leaks into the esophagus, which does not have a protective lining of mucus. The result is *GERD* (gastroesophageal reflux disorder), or *acid reflux.* **Heartburn** is the pain that is caused by GERD and has nothing to do with the heart.

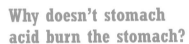

EXPRESS Lesson REVIEW

1. Name the process that moves food through the digestive tract.
2. List the major organs of the digestive tract, and describe what each organ does.
3. Describe the functions of the liver and the pancreas.
4. **LIFE SKILL** **Practicing Wellness** When a person has cirrhosis of the liver, the healthy liver tissue turns to scar tissue and stops working. Look up some of the problems that can arise if a person's liver is not working properly.

Excretory System

Your excretory system removes harmful wastes from your body and maintains the body's water and salt balance.

What does the excretory system do?

The excretory system takes the wastes made by cells out of the blood and moves the wastes out of the body. It also keeps up the body's proper salt content, water content, blood pressure, and acid-base balance. The **kidneys** are the main organs of the excretory system. They filter about 1,200 mL of blood per minute. The lungs and the skin are also part of the excretory system. Carbon dioxide is excreted by the lungs. Many substances are excreted by the skin through the *sweat glands.*

How do the kidneys work?

The kidneys filter all of your blood about 10 times every day. A kidney has millions of tiny blood filtering units called **nephrons.** Blood with wastes is brought to the kidneys by *renal arteries.* Each nephron takes water, salts, minerals, and cell wastes out of the blood. If wastes were released from your body at this stage, you would lose too much water.

Before wastes leave a kidney, capillaries in the kidney reclaim about 99 percent of the water removed by the nephrons. The concentrated liquid waste that leaves the kidney is called **urine.** *Renal veins* carry filtered blood back to the heart.

What is the urinary tract?

The *urinary tract* is the path taken by urine as it exits the body. A tube called a *ureter* takes urine from each kidney to the urinary bladder. The **urinary bladder** is the hollow, muscular sac that stores urine until there is enough to release. Another tube, called the *urethra,* leads from the urinary bladder to the outside of the body.

Lungs
The lungs excrete carbon dioxide and water vapor in exhaled air.

Kidneys
The kidneys excrete nitrogen wastes, salts, water, and other substances in urine.

Skin
The skin excretes water, salts, small amounts of nitrogen wastes, and other substances in sweat.

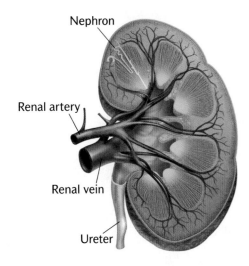

Nephron

Renal artery

Renal vein

Ureter

Inside the kidney, filtering units called nephrons filter wastes from the blood.

Drinking several glasses of water daily replaces the water lost as the kidneys, skin, and lungs do their work. Not drinking enough water can lead to dehydration and the buildup of toxins in the body.

What is urine made of?

Urine is mostly water mixed with things your body needs to get rid of. These things include minerals such as sodium, calcium, and potassium and cellular wastes such as urea, and uric acid. Urine may also contain bacteria that have been killed by the immune system and dead blood cells that must be removed.

How much urine can the bladder hold?

On average, the bladder can hold about 600 mL of urine. You feel the need to urinate at about 200–300 mL. At 600 mL, holding the urine becomes painful. With more than 1,000 mL, the bladder may become dangerously swollen.

How does the body control urination?

Two circular muscles control the flow of urine out of the bladder. Adults have voluntary control of these muscles and can hold or release urine at will. Stretching of the bladder triggers a reflex that gives you the urge to urinate. Stress and illness can interfere with the voluntary control of urination. Loss of voluntary control of urination is called **incontinence.**

What can happen if you are unable to urinate?

If a person is unable to urinate, for example because of spinal cord injury, his or her bladder can become too stretched to hold its shape. If the bladder is emptied too suddenly, there is a risk that it will collapse. If the bladder is not emptied, stress on the body can raise the person's blood pressure. If the problem is not resolved, this condition can lead to a *stroke.*

EXPRESS Lesson REVIEW

1. Name the structures that filter blood in the kidneys.
2. List the parts of the urinary tract.
3. Describe how urine is made in the kidneys.
4. **LIFE SKILL** **Setting Goals** Drinking plenty of water can help you keep your urinary tract healthy. Make a chart to monitor your water-drinking habits. Set a goal to drink six to eight glasses of water a day, and evaluate your progress.

Immune System

Your immune system protects you from disease.

What does the immune system do?

The immune system defends the body against disease. It works by recognizing, attacking, and destroying foreign invaders such as viruses and bacteria. It also destroys dead and damaged body cells and stops some cancer cells before they can spread. The cells of the immune system move about the body in the fluids of the circulatory and lymphatic systems.

What does the lymphatic system do?

The lymphatic system is a network of fine vessels that pick up the fluid, called lymph, that leaks through blood vessels and fills the spaces around the body's cells. **Lymph** is a clear, yellowish fluid that is made up of water, nutrients, and white blood cells. A net of *lymphatic vessels,* which are similar to veins and capillaries, collect lymph from the body and return it to the circulatory system.

What is a lymph node?

Lymph nodes are small, bean-shaped masses that can be found at certain places along the lymphatic vessels. Lymph nodes hold many lymphocytes. **Lymphocytes** are white blood cells that destroy bacteria, viruses, and dead or damaged cells. This process removes these particles from lymph before it re-enters the circulatory system. Groups of lymph nodes can also be found in the armpits and groin and at the base of the neck. The "swollen glands" that go with some infections are lymph glands that have grown larger from filtering out many germ particles and damaged cells. The **tonsils** are the masses of lymph tissue found in the throat.

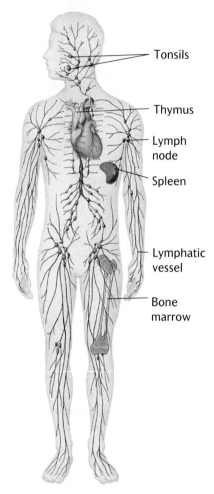

- Tonsils
- Thymus
- Lymph node
- Spleen
- Lymphatic vessel
- Bone marrow

How is the spleen part of the immune system?

The spleen does the same thing for the blood that the lymph nodes do for lymph. It serves as a filtering station where white blood cells rid the blood of particles that should not be there. The filtered blood then returns to the circulatory system.

This image shows a macrophage engulfing the bacterium Neisseria gonorrhoeae.

Types of White Blood Cells

Type of white blood cell	What it does
Neutrophils	engulf and destroy bacteria and release enzymes that kill bacteria
Monocytes (mature into larger macrophages)	engulf and digest damaged body cells and disease-causing agents
Eosinophils	attach to parasites and release substances to kill them
Basophils	function in allergic reactions; release histamine
Lymphocytes (develop into B and T cells)	direct the immune system to react to foreign antigens by attacking and destroying particles that carry the antigens; B cells develop into antibody-forming plasma cells

How is bone marrow part of the immune system?

Bone marrow is the main place where blood cells form. Red blood cells, white blood cells, and platelets are all made in the marrow of your bones. **Leukemia** is a cancer of the tissues that make white blood cells. The cancer causes the tissues to make white blood cells that never mature. Immature white blood cells take over the bone marrow and keep it from making the other blood cells that the body needs. Bone marrow or stem cell transplants can help the body replenish blood cell supplies. But there is still no cure for most leukemias.

What are white blood cells?

White blood cells (WBCs) are the blood cells whose main job is to defend the body against disease. The five types of WBCs (*neutrophils, monocytes, eosinophils, basophils,* and *lymphocytes*) are summarized in the table above. Each type of WBC defends the body in different ways. There are two different types of lymphocytes. **B cells,** which are made in bone marrow, make antibodies that attack viruses in the blood. **T cells,** which are made in the bone marrow and mature in the thymus, attack cells that have been infected by viruses.

How does the body recognize bacteria and virus invaders?

Bacteria, viruses, and cells that have been infected by viruses all have something in common that lets the body know they do not belong. The coating of every cell and virus has identifying proteins called **antigens.** The antigens on viruses and bacteria are not found on any of the body's own normal cells. White blood cells can recognize antigens that do not belong to the body and attach to them. Anything that carries an antigen that is foreign to the body is then destroyed.

Immune System *continued*

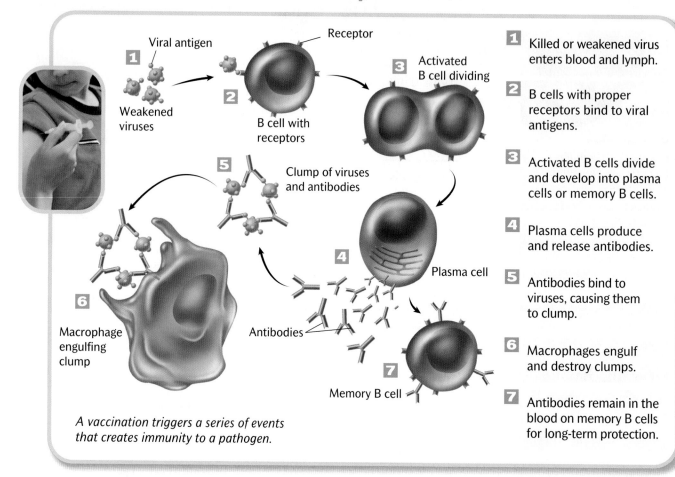

1 Viral antigen

Receptor

3 Activated B cell dividing

Weakened viruses

2 B cell with receptors

Clump of viruses and antibodies

5

4

Plasma cell

Antibodies

6 Macrophage engulfing clump

7 Memory B cell

A vaccination triggers a series of events that creates immunity to a pathogen.

1 Killed or weakened virus enters blood and lymph.

2 B cells with proper receptors bind to viral antigens.

3 Activated B cells divide and develop into plasma cells or memory B cells.

4 Plasma cells produce and release antibodies.

5 Antibodies bind to viruses, causing them to clump.

6 Macrophages engulf and destroy clumps.

7 Antibodies remain in the blood on memory B cells for long-term protection.

How do antibodies fight disease?

Antibodies are proteins the immune system makes in response to specific antigens. White blood cells that are exposed to a bacterium or to a virus make antibodies that can attach only to that bacterium or virus. In this way, antibodies stop bacteria and viruses from invading body cells and keep them in the bloodstream. This process gives white blood cells time to locate and destroy these disease-causing agents.

Can the immune system work against you?

Yes, your immune system will attack a transplanted organ if it carries antigens that differ from your own.

An **autoimmune disease** is one in which the immune system attacks the cells of the body that the immune system normally protects.

E X P R E S S Lesson REVIEW

1. Describe three body parts that help the immune system.
2. List the types of white blood cells.
3. Explain how the immune system identifies invaders.
4. **LIFE SKILL** **Practicing Wellness** Does your immune system respond to stress? Keep a calendar and a journal. Write in advance all the tests, reports, projects, and extracurricular activities that you have coming up for a month. In your journal, keep track of how you feel each day. Are there any patterns?

Endocrine System

Your endocrine system regulates your growth, development, and body chemistry.

What does the endocrine system do?

The endocrine system works with the nervous system to coordinate and regulate the body. Hormones do the work of the endocrine system. **Hormones** are substances that are secreted by cells and that act to regulate the activity of other cells. Organs that release hormones are called **endocrine glands.**

How is the endocrine system different from the nervous system?

The nervous system reacts instantly to a stimulus but has a short-lived effect. The endocrine system responds more slowly and has a longer-lasting effect. Both nerves and chemical messengers carry signals in the nervous system. These signals affect only certain parts of the body. But only hormones carry signals for the endocrine system. The chemical messengers in the nervous system work only at the gaps between nerve cells. Carried by blood, hormones can spread all over the body and can affect many organs.

How do hormones work?

Hormones work by binding to receptors either outside or inside a cell. Each kind of hormone molecule has a shape that fits only certain receptors. Each organ has cells with receptors for certain kinds of hormones. When a hormone binds to a receptor on a cell, the cell reacts. The result depends on the kind of hormone and the organ the cell is in.

What are the endocrine glands?

Several different endocrine glands are scattered about your body. They include the pituitary gland, the thyroid gland, parathyroid glands, adrenal glands, gonads, the pancreas, the thymus gland, and the pineal gland. The table on the next page shows the hormones and functions of some endocrine glands.

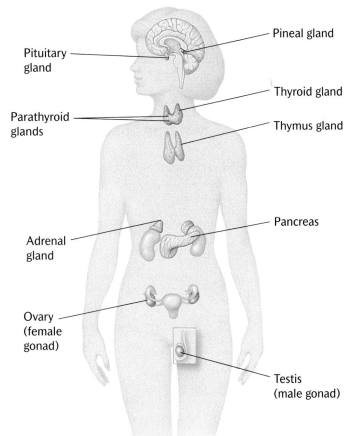

Pituitary gland

Pineal gland

Thyroid gland

Parathyroid glands

Thymus gland

Adrenal gland

Pancreas

Ovary (female gonad)

Testis (male gonad)

Endocrine System *continued*

Glands of the Endocrine System

Gland	Hormone	Function
Pituitary (anterior)	human growth hormone (HGH) thyroid stimulating hormone (TSH) adrenocorticotropic hormone (ACTH) follicle stimulating hormone (FSH) luteinizing hormone (LH) prolactin	regulates growth directs thyroid gland directs adrenal glands directs reproductive organs directs reproductive organs stimulates production of breast milk
Pituitary (posterior)	antidiuretic hormone (ADH) oxytocin	regulates amount of water released by the kidneys stimulates uterine contractions and breast-milk flow
Thyroid	thyroxine calcitonin	regulates metabolism, body-heat production, and bone growth lowers blood calcium levels
Adrenal (medulla)	epinephrine, norepinephrine	stimulate "fight-or-flight" response
Adrenal (cortex)	cortisol aldosterone	regulates carbohydrate and protein metabolism maintains salt and water balance
Pancreas	glucagon, insulin	regulate blood-sugar level
Parathyroid	parathyroid hormone (PTH)	regulates blood-calcium level
Thymus	thymosin	influences maturation of some immune system cells
Pineal	melatonin	controls internal clock and sleep rhythm
Gonads	estrogen, progesterone, testosterone	stimulate development of sex characteristics, affect egg and sperm formation, and control reproductive cycles

Do all diabetics have to take insulin?

No, usually only type 1 diabetics have to take insulin injections. Type 2 diabetics control their blood-sugar level with oral medications, diet, and exercise. Most diabetics have type 2 diabetes, which normally develops after the age of 40. Low blood sugar, or *hypoglycemia*, is also related to insulin and is more common in teens. A high-carbohydrate diet can stimulate the release of too much insulin, which causes the body to use blood sugar too quickly. Low blood sugar makes you feel weak and interferes with your ability to think.

Is it true that everyone has both male and female hormones?

We used to think that only men had male hormones and that only women had female hormones. Now we know that both men and women have both kinds of sex hormones but in different amounts. The male hormone *testosterone* governs the changes in boys as they mature. In women, the "male" hormone causes the normal growth of body hair. The female hormones *estrogen* and *progesterone* govern the changes in girls. In men, the "female" hormones help keep body fat at a safe level.

What determines how tall I am?

Nutrition and other environmental factors affect growth, but genes ultimately determine how tall you are. Genes act by causing the body to make hormones. *Human growth hormone* (*HGH*) is the main hormone that promotes growth in children. HGH is made by the pituitary gland. *Dwarfism* is an inherited trait that results from the underproduction of HGH. *Gigantism* is an inherited trait that results from the overproduction of HGH.

An event such as taking a test causes stress. Your body responds to this stress in the same way that it responds to fear.

What is the "fight-or-flight" response?

Your body responds to stressful situations by getting ready to either fight or run away to protect itself. This "fight-or-flight" response is directed in part by two hormones made by the adrenal glands. **Epinephrine** (EP uh NEF rin) is one of the hormones released by the body in times of stress. Epinephrine is also known as adrenaline. Norepinephrine is another hormone released in times of stress. These stress hormones raise your heart rate, blood pressure, and breathing rate and slow your digestion. As a result, more blood flows to your muscles, bringing them plenty of oxygen—just in case you have to run for your life!

EXPRESS Lesson REVIEW

1. Compare the endocrine system and the nervous system.
2. List three glands of the endocrine system.
3. Describe the way that hormones work.
4. **LIFE SKILL** **Evaluating Media Messages** A new trend in athletic training involves using human growth hormone (HGH) to increase muscle growth. After researching the topic, explain whether you think this is a safe practice.

Environment and Your Health

There was a big meeting tonight at Daniel's school. The community wanted to discuss what to do about the recent news that the water supply might be contaminated. What's the big deal, thought Daniel.

Why should I care about the environment?

The **environment** is the living and nonliving things that surround an organism. The environment includes plants, animals, air, water, and land. Your health and the health of your community is affected by your environment. If the environment in which you live is unhealthy, the chances increase that your health and the health of your community will suffer.

What makes an environment healthy?

A healthy environment is one in which the air is clean, the water is safe, and the land is fertile. It is one in which there is plenty of food for all the inhabitants. A healthy environment is free of pollutants and wastes that can make water, air, and land unsafe for living things. A healthy environment is a balanced environment.

Why are ecosystems important to our health?

An **ecosystem** is a community of living things and the nonliving parts of the community's environment. The living and nonliving parts of an ecosystem interact and depend on each other. If one part of an ecosystem is damaged, the whole ecosystem could become unhealthy. We depend on the ecosystem we live in to produce the resources we need to survive. We can be healthy only if our ecosystem is healthy.

How can pollution be harmful?

Pollution can harm your ecosystem and thus, your health in several ways, as shown in the table. For example, many air pollutants such as smog can cause respiratory problems and eye irritation.

Gases produced by the burning of fossil fuels can react with water vapor in the air and produce acid rain. **Acid rain** is any precipitation that has a below-normal pH (acidic).

Chlorofluorocarbons (CFCs) are pollutants released by certain coolants and aerosol sprays. Chlorofluorocarbons are another type of pollution that can harm your health. CFCs can increase your risk of skin cancer because they move into the Earth's upper atmosphere and destroy ozone. *Ozone* is a gas in the upper atmosphere that reduces the amount of ultraviolet radiation from the sun. **Ultraviolet (UV) radiation** is radiation in sunlight that is responsible for tanning and burning skin. Excessive exposure to UV radiation increases your risk of skin cancer and premature aging of the skin. The ozone layer which is high in the atmosphere is beneficial because it absorbs harmful UV radiation.

Pollution and Your Health

Pollutants	Effects on your health
Water pollutants	
Sewage	breeds pathogens that cause hepatitis, cholera, typhoid fever, and amebic dysentery
Pesticides	cause brain and nerve disorders, birth defects, and cancer
Fertilizers	cause damage to ecosystems and death of fish, birth defects
Mercury and other metals	cause brain damage, mental retardation, nerve disorders, kidney disorders, paralysis, and loss of vision
Indoor and outdoor air pollutants	
Smog and other gases	cause or worsen respiratory illnesses such as asthma
Carbon monoxide	prevents red blood cells from carrying oxygen; loss of consciousness, brain damage, or death
Tobacco smoke	causes lung cancer, asthma, emphysema, and sudden infant death syndrome (SIDS)
Radiation	causes sunburn, cataracts, and cancer
Noise	causes hearing damage
Radon	causes lung cancer
Soil pollutants	
Acid rain	causes lower soil fertility, damages vegetation and buildings, and causes famine
Pesticides and herbicides	cause brain disorders and nerve disorders, birth defects, and cancer

What is conservation?

A *resource* is a material that can be used to meet a need. **Conservation** is the wise use and protection of natural resources. To protect our health and improve our environment, we need to conserve several specific resources in the environment.

▶ **Water** Fresh, clean water is needed for us to live; to keep clean; to grow, prepare, and process our food; and to make items we use.

▶ **Air** To live, we need certain gases that are in the air. For example, we need oxygen in order to get energy from our food. Carbon dioxide is used by plants to make food. Ozone, in the upper atmosphere, reduces the amount of UV radiation from the sun.

▶ **Minerals** We need minerals such as iron, phosphorus, calcium, and sodium to carry out our bodies' activities. We get minerals from the plants and animals we eat and from our drinking water.

▶ **Food** Our bodies need energy in order to live. We get nutrients for energy from plants and animals.

▶ **Land** All living things need a certain amount of land in order to live. Land also provides a growing space for plants. Plants provide food for animals, shelter from the weather, and oxygen.

Why should we conserve natural resources?

Conserving our natural resources helps ensure that resources will be available in the future. A natural resource that can be replaced over a short period of time is called a **renewable resource.** Trees and crops are renewable resources.

Nonrenewable resources are natural resources that can be used up faster than they can be replenished naturally. Oil and natural gas are examples of nonrenewable resources.

Some renewable resources can also be used up too quickly to be replaced. Resources such as fresh water, topsoil, timber, and ocean fish must be conserved.

How does overpopulation affect our health and environment?

The point at which a population is too large to be supported by the available resources is called **overpopulation.** Earth's human population has been increasing rapidly. Overpopulation can lead to many problems.

Low food supplies Overpopulation makes it difficult to find and produce enough food to support the community. Famine is common in overpopulated areas.

Polluted water Polluted water from bathing, washing, and dumping wastes is a frequent result of overpopulation. Drinking, swimming, and bathing in polluted water spread disease.

Poverty, poor sanitation, and disease These problems are common in overpopulated parts of the world.

Overuse of the land and resources In order to feed, clothe, and shelter a growing population, we must use more natural resources. Nonrenewable resources can become depleted because of overuse, which results from supplying a large population.

Deforestation Many countries do not have enough farmland to feed their populations. Populations in tropical areas have little clear land for farming. **Deforestation** is the clearing of trees from natural forests to make space for crops, grazing, or development. When crops are grown on soil from tropical forests, the nutrients in the soil are depleted quickly. More forest must be cleared for people to continue farming.

Overfishing Overpopulation can also lead to overfishing. Because oceans do not belong to any one country, regulating the amount of fishing in oceans is difficult. Our government places limits on the fishing industry in the United States to preserve species. However, not all countries do the same.

How does our government protect our environment?

One approach to protecting our environment has been to make pollution more expensive by placing a tax on it. The gasoline tax is a good example of such a tax. A second approach has been to pass laws. The United States has many laws aimed at protecting the environment.

▶ The Clean Air Act of 1970 limits the release of pollutants into the environment and sets safe levels of several air pollutants.

▶ The Clean Water Act of 1972 limits the release of sewage and chemicals into water in the United States.

The U.S. Environmental Protection Agency (EPA) is the agency that sets and enforces the standards established by these laws.

Who else protects the environment?

A number of local, national, and international organizations also work to protect the environment. Members of these organizations talk to lawmakers, raise money to help preserve land, and publish educational material to teach people about the importance of protecting the environment.

How can you help improve the environment?

▶ **Recycle or reuse products.** Recycling is reusing materials from used products to make new products.

▶ **Conserve electricity and water.** Take showers instead of baths, water lawns in the evenings to prevent evaporation, and fix leaky faucets.

▶ **Become involved in a local environmental issue.** Support recycling and conservation projects in your school. Join or start a group that keeps litter off school and neighborhood lawns.

internet connect

www.scilinks.org/health
Topic: Solving Environmental Problems
HealthLinks code: HH4128

HEALTH LINKS Maintained by the National Science Teachers Association

---

E X P R E S S Lesson REVIEW

1. What do living things need from their environment to live a healthy life?

2. How do pollution and overpopulation affect an ecosystem?

3. **CRITICAL THINKING** What are three ways you can help reduce each of the following: water pollution, air pollution, and soil pollution?

4. **LIFE SKILL** **Using Community Resources** Describe how you can plan a school or community effort to improve the environment around your school.

Public Health

Nurse García was concerned. Another patient came into the Emergency Room with nausea, vomiting, and diarrhea. It could be food poisoning, she thought. This patient was the seventh one in 2 days with these symptoms. She worried that this could be the beginning of an epidemic.

Why is public health important?

Public health is the practice of protecting and improving the health of people in a community. Because the people living in a community interact with one another, they affect each other's health and well-being.

The public health system is important in fighting infectious diseases and preventing other health problems, many of which are related to people's behaviors. The public health system includes people who work in local, state and national health departments, hospitals, clinics, or other health agencies.

Infectious diseases can spread rapidly through a community and cause many people to become ill. This unexpected increase in illness is called an **outbreak.** The cause of an outbreak must be identified and treated quickly to keep the disease from becoming an epidemic. An **epidemic** is the occurrence of many more cases of a disease than expected.

Noninfectious diseases are caused by genetic, environmental, or behavioral factors. Noninfectious diseases often affect a community because the people in the community have many behavioral and environmental factors in common. Noninfectious diseases are harder to eliminate because their treatment requires an improvement in the environment or a change in people's lifestyle.

Restaurant inspections by public health workers help to ensure our food is safe.

Why do epidemics spread?

A **high-risk population** is any group of people who have an increased chance of getting a disease. Populations that have a high risk of developing an epidemic may have the following:

▶ **Poor sanitation Sanitation** is the practice of providing sewage disposal and treatment, solid waste disposal, clean drinking water, and clean living and working conditions. Disease causing bacteria are carried in wastes and unsanitary water.

▶ **Poor nutrition** Poor nutrition makes it difficult for the body to fight disease.

▶ **Low rates of immunization** Many diseases can be controlled through immunization.

▶ **Overcrowding Overcrowding** is the condition in which there are too many inhabitants in an area to live healthily. When many people live and work in a crowded environment, diseases spread easily.

Public Health Agencies

Agency	Function
Centers for Disease Control and Prevention (CDC)	works with state health departments to monitor health trends, detect health problems, and control epidemics
Food and Drug Administration (FDA)	works to ensure that food and medicines are safe, healthy, and effective
National Institutes of Health (NIH)	directs and promotes research on prevention, diagnosis, and treatment of disease
Substance Abuse and Mental Health Services Administration (SAMHSA)	researches problems related to alcohol, drug abuse, and mental health issues
World Health Organization (WHO)	works to control AIDS worldwide, monitors emerging infections, such as Ebola and Hanta virus, and administers childhood immunizations in many countries
United Nations Children's Fund (UNICEF)	assists children with healthcare, nutrition, education, and sanitation

What public health concerns do we have in the United States?

Cardiovascular disease, cancer, stroke, and respiratory diseases are leading causes of death in the United States. These diseases threaten public health because the behaviors that can lead to them are common among many members of the community. These are **lifestyle diseases**—diseases that are caused partly by unhealthy behaviors and partly by other factors. Preventing infectious diseases is also a major concern.

What do public health agencies do?

Public health agencies at several levels of government help protect public health.

Local and state health departments These agencies protect the health of the community in many ways. They regulate community food and water supplies, help prevent infectious and lifestyle diseases, work to control epidemics, educate the public to improve personal and community health, and keep health statistics to watch for trends in illness or injury.

The Food and Drug Administration (FDA) works to ensure the food we eat is safe.

The International Red Cross works to help those in need around the world.

Government laws and regulations help prevent our water from being contaminated.

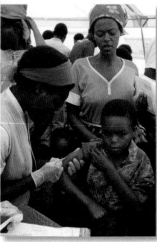

Health clinics offer immunizations to help keep children healthy and diseases under control.

National health agencies These agencies set broad public health objectives; regulate food and drug production; fight epidemics; organize, fund, and conduct research to find cures for diseases; regulate healthy work practices; and sponsor programs that help people stay healthy.

International health agencies International health agencies such as the World Health Organization (WHO) work to fight global health problems. Some of the issues they address include poor nutrition, lack of basic medical care, poor sanitation, lack of clean water supplies, natural disasters, and disease.

How do private health organizations affect public health?

Private organizations also provide important public health support around the world. The International Red Cross, for example, provides food, clothing, temporary shelter, and medical care to people affected by wars, other acts of aggression, and natural disasters.

Many other private organizations work to solve public health problems. Usually, they focus on a specific group in the population or a specific disease. Private organizations depend on donations and volunteers to fund their work.

How do public health policies affect public health?

Public health policies are based on laws designed to protect citizens and promote the health of a community. Examples of these policies are as follows:

▶ **Laws and programs that promote mass immunization** All states have laws that require children to be immunized before they can attend public schools. These laws and programs have been very effective in eliminating diseases such as smallpox and polio and controlling other diseases such as measles and whooping cough.

Goals of Healthy People 2010

- ▶ Reduce the number of deaths from heart disease.
- ▶ Reduce the number of deaths from cancer.
- ▶ Reduce the number of deaths from AIDS.
- ▶ Reduce the percentage of overweight people.
- ▶ Increase the percentage of people who exercise regularly.

- ▶ Reduce the percentage of adolescents who smoke cigarettes.
- ▶ Reduce the number of children exposed to cigarette smoke.
- ▶ Reduce the number of women who smoke while pregnant.
- ▶ Reduce the number of deaths from car accidents.
- ▶ Reduce the number of deaths from drunk driving.

▶ **Waste disposal laws** Laws regulating waste disposal and dumping prevent an increase in rat, mice, and insect populations, which spread disease.

▶ **Standards for health and safety practices** Safe standards for food preparation, seat belt use, and blood-alcohol concentrations are public health policies. The Occupational Safety and Health Administration (OSHA) is a federal agency that sets safety standards in the workplace.

▶ **Requirements for medical licensing** Doctors must have a license to practice medicine in the United States. Licensing ensures that doctors have the knowledge and training to provide medical treatment for a community.

What is Healthy People 2010?

Healthy People 2010 is a set of health objectives established by the U.S. Department of Health and Human Servies for improving the nation's health by 2010. These objectives are goals based on risk factors for diseases that are at least partly preventable.

Eliminating risk factors usually requires significant changes in personal habits, such as eating, smoking, and exercising. The benefits from making these changes are improvements in both personal and public health.

☑ internet connect

www.scilinks.org/health
Topic: Modern Epidemics
HealthLinks code: HH4099

HEALTH Maintained by the
LINKS National Science
Teachers Association

E X P R E S S / Lesson REVIEW

1. What kinds of factors increase the risk of an epidemic spreading throughout a population?
2. Summarize the functions of local, state, and national public health agencies.
3. **LIFE SKILL Using Community Resources** You recently noticed that the water in your school has an unpleasant taste and smell. What could you do to start an investigation of the cause?
4. **LIFE SKILL Practicing Wellness** Name two behaviors you can change today to reach one or more of the Healthy People 2010 goals.

Selecting Healthcare Services

After spending the weekend hiking with his friends, Isaac woke up Monday morning to find his legs covered with red, itchy bumps. His mom opened the phone book to look for a doctor and discovered three pages of listings for doctors. How could they choose which doctor to see?

How do I select a healthcare provider?

Selecting a healthcare provider usually begins with choosing a primary care physician. A **primary care physician (PCP)** is a family doctor who handles general medical care. This doctor is the first one you see when you have a health concern. If your parents plan to use insurance to pay for your visit, your doctor must be able to accept payment from your insurance company.

What kind of healthcare provider can I choose?

There are several different types of healthcare providers from which to choose:

▶ **Doctor of medicine (M.D.)** An M.D. is a physician who is trained in the diagnosis and treatment of disease.

▶ **Doctor of osteopathy (D.O.)** A D.O. is a doctor who has the same training as an M.D. but also specializes in the care of the muscular and skeletal system.

▶ **Physician's assistant (PA)** A PA carries out medical procedures under the supervision of a physician. In rural areas, physician's assistants have become very popular providers of healthcare.

▶ **Nurse practitioner (NP)** An NP is a registered nurse who has additional training and expertise in certain medical practices.

Depending on your needs, you and your parents may choose any of these kinds of medical professionals.

What is a specialist?

If your primary care physician encounters a complex or serious condition or a condition that he or she cannot identify or treat, he or she will send you to a specialist for an accurate diagnosis. A *specialist* is a doctor who studies and becomes an expert in one specific area of medicine. A specialist will have extensive knowledge of a certain body part or illness. The process of sending a patient from one healthcare provider to another is called a *referral*.

How do I know my doctor is qualified?

You and your parents or legal guardians should check your healthcare provider's qualifications. According to the law, your doctor must be licensed. It is illegal for a doctor to practice medicine without a license in the United States. It is a good idea to choose a doctor who is board certified. This means that the doctor has passed special tests given by a physicians' association to verify his or her skill and knowledge.

You may also want to talk with other medical professionals to find out who they would recommend. Family and friends can also help by telling you what they like or don't like about their doctors.

How do I prepare for my visit to the doctor?

Patients meet doctors through get-acquainted visits or during the first checkup. At that time you'll meet the doctor's office staff. The staff will schedule appointments and answer questions about insurance and referrals.

Find out from the office staff how the doctor's practice operates. Will a nurse obtain routine medical information from you? Are sick patients separated from well patients while waiting to see the doctor? Do several doctors share patient care responsibilities? Are there specific hours to speak to the doctor by phone? How are emergencies handled during evening and weekend hours?

Making out a fact sheet like the one on the next page will help you prepare for your visit. Your list should include the following:

▶ your basic medical history

▶ any medications you are taking

▶ any allergies you have, especially if you have an allergy to a medicine

▶ a list of questions you want to ask your doctor

▶ the reason for your visit

Questions to ask:

Choosing a Doctor

▶ Is this doctor a member of your insurance plan?

▶ Where did this doctor attend medical school?

▶ How long has this doctor been practicing medicine?

▶ Is the doctor board certified?

▶ Is this doctor recommended by people you respect?

▶ Does this doctor communicate in a way that you understand?

▶ Do you feel comfortable with this doctor?

▶ Are this doctor's office hours and location convenient?

▶ Are the prices fair and reasonable?

▶ How long do you have to wait for an appointment?

▶ How long do you usually wait in the doctor's office?

Selecting Healthcare Services (continued)

How do I make sure I understand my doctor?

When speaking with your doctor, make sure your doctor explains your illness so that you understand the problem and the recommended treatment plan. If your doctor's advice is unclear, you may not be able to follow the treatment plan.

Ask your doctor to clarify anything you do not understand about your visit. If your doctor is in a hurry to see another patient, something important may be overlooked.

Make sure your doctor takes the time to answer your questions. You must feel comfortable and confident with your doctor.

How do I evaluate my doctor?

Choose a few of these questions to ask your family physician. Discuss his or her answers with your parents, and decide as a family whether you are happy with your doctor or would like to choose another.

▶ How long do you have to wait for an appointment?

▶ How long do you have to wait in the waiting room?

▶ Does your doctor seem to be rushed when seeing you?

▶ Do you feel comfortable asking your doctor questions?

▶ Does your doctor explain the diagnosis and treatment clearly?

HEALTHCARE PROVIDER VISIT FACT SHEET

Date: _____ Healthcare Provider: _____

1. Reason(s) for seeing doctor: _____

2. Symptoms and when they started: _____

3. Current medicines and dosage: _____

4. Family health history: _____

5. Allergies: _____

6. Recommended treatment: _____

7. Cost of treatment: _____

8. Other treatment options: _____

9. Questions and concerns: _____

What are a patient's rights?

Every patient has the right and responsibility to

▶ receive accurate, easily understood information

▶ receive assistance in making informed healthcare decisions

▶ have a choice of healthcare providers

▶ have access to emergency health services when and where the need arises

▶ participate in all health-related decisions

▶ make wishes about healthcare known, such as being an organ donor

▶ receive considerate, respectful care

▶ not be discriminated against in the delivery of healthcare services

▶ have confidential communication with healthcare providers

▶ have a fair and efficient process for resolving complaints or disagreements

What should I do if my doctor is too busy to see me?

Many times the healthcare providers are very busy. If your doctor has to rush through your evaluation to hurry on to the next patient, you may not feel that you're getting the best care. Feeling rushed may also keep you from asking questions and making sure you understand your doctor's advice and treatment. When you choose your primary care physician, make sure your doctor has enough time to spend with you. You and your parents may need to visit with several doctors before choosing one who will be your primary care physician.

What types of patient care are available?

Inpatient care is medical care that requires a person to stay in a hospital for more than a day. **Outpatient care** is medical care that requires a person to stay in the hospital only during his or her treatment. **Home healthcare services** are medical services, treatment, or equipment provided for the patient in his or her home.

EXPRESS Lesson REVIEW

1. **LIFE SKILL** **Being a Wise Consumer** If you were dissatisfied with your healthcare provider, what steps could you take to find a new provider you would be happy with?

2. Explain why a patient might need a referral.

3. **LIFE SKILL** **Communicating Effectively** What information should you take to the doctor with you if you have a health problem? What are three questions you could prepare to ask your doctor?

Financing Your Healthcare

A visit to the emergency room can cost from 150 dollars to several thousand dollars. Very few people can afford to pay medical bills without any help. Having health insurance can help you afford medical costs.

What does health insurance actually do?

Many healthcare services are too expensive for people to afford on their own. Health insurance allows people to pay a set amount of money each month in exchange for protection against large medical bills. If you were ever to have an accident or become seriously ill, health insurance would help you pay your medical bills.

How do I get health insurance?

There are many ways people can get health insurance in the United States. One way is through work. Many companies offer insurance as a benefit to their employees by paying all or part of the cost. Other people purchase their own health insurance.

What kind of health insurance is available?

The three major types of health insurance plans are
▶ fee-for-service plans
▶ managed-care plans
▶ government-assisted health plans

What is a fee-for-service plan?

Fee-for-service insurance plans are traditional insurance plans, in which the patient must pay a premium and a deductible. A **premium** is a monthly fee for insurance. A **deductible** is the amount that the subscriber must pay before an insurance company begins paying for medical services. Fee-for-service plans can be expensive, but patients are free to choose any healthcare provider they wish to see.

Questions to ask:

Choosing Health Insurance

▶ Can I afford this insurance?
▶ Do I have to pay a deductible? How much is the deductible?
▶ Do I have to pay a copayment? How much is the copayment?
▶ Do I get hospital, surgical, medical, and prescription benefits?
▶ Can I visit any doctor, or do I have to choose from a list of doctors?
▶ If I have a preexisting condition, is the condition covered?

▶ How much does going to the emergency room cost?
▶ What conditions or services are excluded?
▶ Is part of the cost of insurance covered by my job or parent's job?
▶ Can I get a cheaper rate by belonging to a group of subscribers?
▶ Can I continue my insurance if I lose my job?
▶ Can I cancel my insurance if I need to?

What are managed-care plans?

Managed-care plans are plans in which an insurance company makes a contract with a group of doctors to provide care and services at a lower fee to patients who have this insurance. Usually, the patient pays a yearly (or monthly) premium and a copayment for each doctor visit. A copayment is the amount that the patient pays each time medical care is received. Managed-care plans include HMOs and PPOs. They can be less expensive than other types of insurance, but offer a limited choice of providers.

What is an HMO?

A **health maintenance organization (HMO)** is a managed-care plan in which patients must use a doctor who contracts with the insurance company. If the patient uses a doctor who is not part of this contract, the insurance company will not pay for the services. The only exception is in the case of an emergency.

What is a PPO?

A **preferred provider organization (PPO)** allows the patient to see a doctor who does not contract with the insurance company. The patient pays a higher fee to do this.

What happens if you can't afford health insurance?

Local health departments provide many health services, including information, immunizations, and HIV/AIDS testing and counseling, either free or for a very small fee. The Children's Health Insurance Program (CHIP) provides health insurance for children who are not covered by insurance. This program helps ensure that all children receive quality healthcare.

What is government-assisted healthcare?

Medicare and Medicaid are healthcare programs provided by the government. **Medicare** is a healthcare program for people who are 65 years old or older and for younger individuals who are disabled. **Medicaid** is a healthcare program for people who are on welfare or have low incomes, have dependent children, or are 65 years or older, blind, or disabled.

internet connect

www.scilinks.org/health
Topic: Healthcare Systems
HealthLinks code: HH4075

HEALTH LINKS. Maintained by the National Science Teachers Association

EXPRESS Lesson REVIEW

1. Describe three types of health insurance.

2. List three groups of people who can receive healthcare through Medicaid.

3. **LIFE SKILL** **Being a Wise Consumer** Your family has been offered a fantastic deal on a traditional health insurance policy. What questions should you ask the insurance agent before purchasing the policy?

Evaluating Healthcare Products

Lose 20 pounds in 5 days! Get rid of acne while you sleep! **If you have been tempted by claims like these, don't be embarrassed. Each year, consumers are cheated out of billions of dollars for healthcare information, services, and products that don't work.**

How can companies sell fraudulent products?

Fraud is the marketing and selling of products or services by making false claims. **Quackery,** a type of fraud, is the promotion of healthcare services or products that are worthless or not proven effective. Several government agencies watch for fraudulent products. However, these agencies do not have enough money or staff to check every reported case of fraud.

Why do people buy fraudulent products?

People believe false advertisements and buy fraudulent products for several reasons. Companies use scientific-sounding phrases to make their ads seem legitimate. Some ads use exaggerations, vague statements, opinions, and pressure to convince people to buy the product. People with severe illness may be desperate for a cure. Companies take advantage of people's emotions, illnesses, weaknesses, and fears to sell fraudulent products.

Is quackery really dangerous?

Most quackery only wastes people's money and gives them false hopes. However, quackery can injure or kill people who are seriously ill by convincing them to buy useless products instead of effective, proven medical treatment. In addition, the product itself may be harmful.

How does the government protect us from fraud?

Several government agencies protect us from fraud.

▶ **U.S. Food and Drug Administration (FDA)** The FDA regulates the content and labeling of foods, drugs, cosmetics, and medical devices. The FDA can use law enforcement action to seize and prevent the sale of products that are falsely labeled.

Questions to ask:

Identifying Fraudulent Products

▶ Does the ad claim the product will treat a variety of health problems?

▶ Does the ad promise the product will provide a quick cure or miracle?

▶ Is the product unavailable anywhere else or at any other time?

▶ Is the product marketed as a secret remedy or miracle drug?

▶ Is the only proof that the product works the story of someone who used it?

▶ Do the methods seem strange or unconventional but promise to produce results?

▶ Is the product sold door-to-door by a so-called health advisor?

▶ Is the product marketed through the use of scare tactics?

▶ Is the product available through the mail only?

▶ Does the company have a post office box number but no street address?

▶ Does the ad claim that the product is a scientific breakthrough that the medical community has held back or overlooked?

This **all-new, revolutionary** formula brings you the secret that South American natives have used for centuries! It is 100% natural and has no harsh chemicals!

Zit-Away
Acne Cream
NET WT 4 OZ.
113 g

Zit-Away

takes care of all of your skin needs! Liz Wilson, a 16-year-old from Alvin, Texas, writes, *"I tried every product on the market, and nothing would get rid of my acne. Zit-Away worked in 48 hours!"*

BUY ONE FOR $9.99 AND GET A 2ND FOR FREE

This price is available only for a limited time.

This cream not only clears acne in two days, but also heals dry skin, reduces wrinkles, and, when used properly, removes unwanted facial hair! Don't put up with zits for another day. Get *Zit-Away* !!!

There is no evidence and no information to verify these statements.

This tactic is often used to make you think you're getting a great value when you're not.

At a grocery store, look at the price of two similar products. Find the price per unit on the label.

ACTIVITY *How can you use this information to decide which product is a better value?*

Testimonials are often used in place of scientific evidence that the product works.

This statement gives people the impression that there is no time to investigate the product.

Be wary of ads that promise a quick cure-all for a wide variety of problems.

▶ **U.S. Federal Trade Commission (FTC)** The FTC works to prevent unfair, false, or untrue advertising and marketing of foods, over-the-counter drugs, medical devices, and healthcare services.

▶ **Consumer Product Safety Commission (CPSC)** The CPSC protects consumers from harmful products. The CPSC can require companies to remove dangerous products from stores. This removal is called *recalling* a product. They can also require companies to place health warnings on labels.

How can I protect myself from quackery?

Talk with your parents or a physician before buying any medical product. If you suspect a product or service is fraudulent, you should investigate the product, service, or information more carefully. You can also call the Better Business Bureau or Consumer Affairs Office.

internet connect

www.scilinks.org/health
Topic: Fraud, Quackery, and Health
HealthLinks code: HH4067

HEALTH LINKS. Maintained by the National Science Teachers Association

EXPRESS Lesson REVIEW

1. Why are people willing to believe false advertising claims?
2. Name four questions you should ask as a healthcare consumer if you suspect a product is fraudulent.
3. **LIFE SKILL** **Being a Wise Consumer** Look through a magazine or newspaper for three ads that you suspect are fraudulent. What tactics or phrases does the ad use that would make you doubt the validity of the product?
4. **LIFE SKILL** **CRITICAL THINKING** How do you think marketing and advertising influence a person's choice of products?

Evaluating Health Web Sites

If a health Web site claimed that fluorescent lightbulbs are scientifically proven to cause pink eye, would you believe that claim? Probably not. Sorting out accurate health information on the Internet can be confusing if you don't know what to look for.

How can you tell if a health Web site is reliable?

Anyone can give health information or sell health-care products through the Internet. Some Web sites may seem very reliable and may be full of health advice that sounds very convincing. Some Web sites may sell healthcare products by giving information that sounds scientific.

To determine if a health Web site is reliable, assess the following features.

Author Who sponsored or created the Web site? Be careful if you cannot tell who the author is. Is the author qualified to publish health information? Health information is generally more reliable if it comes from a medical professional. Does the author objectively present health information? Be wary if the author is trying to sell a product.

Information Is the information outdated? When was the Web site last updated? Information more than a year old may not be accurate. Is the health Web site trying to inform or advertise? Web sites that are providing reliable information usually have links to other reliable Web sites.

Web sites that sell products based on only the testimony of people who used the product are often fraudulent. This fact may seem strange. However, there is no way to prove that any of the people listed ever actually used the product.

References The Web site should provide the reader with complete references. Make sure the references are from science journals or U.S. government publications.

Questions to ask:

Identifying Fraudulent Health Web Sites

- Is the Web site designed primarily to promote or sell a product?
- Is the purpose of the Web site unclear?
- Does the Web site give health advice without identifying a source of information?
- Does the Web site use evidence based mostly on the testimony of users?
- Does the Web site have a lot of "pop-up" advertising?

- Are you required to open a membership and give your credit card number?
- Were you linked to the Web site by unsolicited e-mail?
- Does the Web site promise free trial offers?
- Does the Web site send e-mail that says you were referred to them by an unidentified friend?
- Is the content of the Web site outdated?

Which health Web sites can I trust?

Health information that you can trust is provided by government agencies such as

▶ the National Institutes of Health (NIH)

▶ the Centers for Disease Control and Prevention (CDC)

▶ the Food and Drug Administration (FDA)

Health information found on educational Web sites sponsored by universities is also probably trustworthy.

Is there any group that monitors health Web sites?

The **Health on the Net (HON) Foundation** is an organization of Web sites that agree to follow a code of ethics regarding health information. The *HONcode* lists rules that its member Web sites must follow regarding the health information they provide, which include the following:

▶ The Web sites must offer health advice from trained health professionals unless a clear statement is made that the advice is from a nonmedical individual or organization.

▶ The Web sites are required to honor doctor-patient confidentiality.

▶ The Web sites are required to provide information about who wrote the text and paid for the Web site.

▶ Any claims relating to a specific treament or commercial product or service must be supported with scientific evidence.

A complete list of *HON-code* rules can be found at the HON Foundation Web site. Web sites that are members of the Health On the Net Foundation are allowed to add a symbol to their Web site so that readers know they follow *HONcode* rules.

What else can I do to make sure health Web sites are providing reliable information?

Other ways that you can evaluate health Web sites include the following:

▶ Always cross-check information between several reliable Web sites.

▶ Do plenty of research before you believe anything as fact.

▶ Check with your parents, your doctor, or your pharmacist before you try any health recommendations from a Web site.

EXPRESS Lesson REVIEW

1. List three health Web sites that would be likely to have accurate information.

2. List five signs that a health Web site is not a reliable source of information.

3. **LIFE SKILL** **Being a Wise Consumer** Explain why a health Web site that is selling a product might not offer accurate information.

Caring for Your Skin

Ouch! Jim's skin felt like it was on fire. The day at the beach was fun, but Jim was sorry he forgot to use sunscreen.

What does skin do?

The skin has more functions than any other organ of the body does. The skin

▶ helps control your body temperature

▶ keeps germs from getting into your bloodstream

▶ senses temperature, texture, pressure, and pain

▶ releases oils, wastes in sweat, and excess salts

▶ protects you and keeps you warm

▶ shields you from ultraviolet (UV) rays and uses these rays to make vitamin D

▶ provides a waterproof covering that prevents dehydration

What is your skin made of?

Your skin has two main layers. The outermost layer of the skin is made of one to several layers of dead cells and is called the **epidermis.** Beneath the epidermis is the functional layer of skin, called the **dermis.**

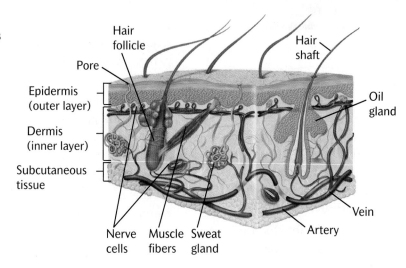

The epidermis is the layer you see when you look in a mirror. The dead cells of the epidermis contain keratin. **Keratin** is a strong, flexible protein found in skin, hair, and nails. Keratin makes skin tough and waterproof. The epidermis has small openings called *pores*. Pores deliver oil and sweat to the skin's surface.

The epidermis also contains **melanin,** a pigment that gives skin its color and shields skin from ultraviolet radiation. *Ultraviolet (UV) radiation* is radiation in sunlight that is responsible for tanning and burning skin.

The dermis is the thick inner layer of the skin, which has nerves, blood vessels, sweat glands, oil glands, and hair follicles. Protein fibers that make skin flexible, called **collagen,** are also found in the dermis.

Under the two layers of the skin is the *subcutaneous layer.* This fatty tissue insulates the body, acts as a shock absorber, stores energy, and connects the skin to the body.

What causes body odor?

Sweat makes a perfect home for bacteria, which are always present on your skin. The waste products of these bacteria are what cause body odor. The best way to prevent body odor is to bathe regularly and use antiperspirant or deodorant.

Foot odor is also caused by bacteria growing in the sweat on your feet. Washing your feet daily, wearing cotton socks, and wearing shoes that allow sweat to evaporate can help prevent foot odor. Deodorant powders and shoe inserts with charcoal can also help eliminate this problem.

What causes acne?

Acne is an inflammation of the skin that occurs when the openings in the skin become clogged with dirt and oil. Acne is the most common skin problem during adolescence. Acne can take the form of whiteheads, blackheads, or pimples.

Whiteheads and *blackheads* are pores that are plugged with oil. Blackheads get their color from melanin in dead skin cells that are plugging the pore. A *pimple* forms when oil builds up inside the clogged pore. Bacteria living in the oil release wastes that add to the buildup. This waste irritates the skin and causes redness around the pimple.

Acne is a normal part of being a teen. Hormones released during adolescence cause the oil glands to produce excess oil. Usually, acne goes away on its own when the body stops producing such large amounts of hormones.

People used to think that chocolate, French fries, and other foods could cause acne. Research now shows that they do not cause acne. However, avoiding greasy foods, eating more fruits and vegetables, and drinking plenty of water help skin look and feel better.

How do I get rid of acne?

Acne can be managed with proper skin care. The best way to reduce acne is to wash your face twice a day with a gentle soap and warm water. Using astringents and medicated products may also help.

Do not scrub, pick, or squeeze your pimples. Popping pimples can lead to permanent scars. Severely infected acne may need to be treated with antibiotics. Consult a *dermatologist* (a doctor who specializes in skin care) if you have severe or persistent acne.

Caring for Your Skin (continued)

If I tan easily, do I still need sunscreen?

Melanin is the body's natural protection against UV radiation. The skin produces more melanin when it is exposed to the sun. However, melanin can't completely block the sun's UV rays. Prolonged exposure to the sun will lead to sunburn in even the darkest-skinned people. Sunburns can lead to skin cancer and premature aging of the skin. So, even if you tan easily, you should still use sunscreen.

What causes sunburns?

Ultraviolet radiation is divided into two types, UVA and UVB rays. Both types of radiation are found in sunlight. UVB rays cause sunburn when you spend too much time outside. If a burn is not too severe, the skin will be red but will not have blisters. Aloe vera gel or cool, wet cloths can soothe the burn until the skin has healed. If your sunburn causes blistering or affects your vision, you should see a doctor right away.

Are all sunscreens the same?

Everyone should use some form of sunscreen when spending prolonged time outside. For most people, a sun protection factor (SPF) of 30 or more will prevent burning for about 1.5 hours. Babies and people who have pale skin should use an SPF of 45 or more.

Are tanning beds safe?

Even though UVA rays do not cause sunburn, they are not safe. The UVA radiation, which is used in commercial tanning beds, penetrates deeper into the skin than UVB rays do. This kind of radiation damages DNA and has been linked to some types of skin cancer.

What causes skin cancer?

Skin cancer can be caused by several factors, including genetics and UV radiation. The most common types of skin cancer are carcinomas (KAHR suh NOH muhz). *Carcinomas* are masses of cells that begin in the skin or layers that line organs. Carcinomas originate in skin cells that do not produce pigments. If they are detected early, carcinomas can be treated. In its early stages, a carcinoma may look like a wart.

A small percentage of skin cancers are caused by mutations that occur in pigment-producing skin cells. These cancers are called melanomas (MEL uh NOH muhz). *Melanomas* are cancerous tumors that begin in the cells that produce melanin. Melanomas may spread quickly to other parts of the body. A melanoma often looks like a mole with an unusual color and shape.

You can reduce the risk of skin cancer by avoiding overexposure to both natural and artificial UV radiation. Use sunscreens and wear long sleeves and a hat when exposed to the sun for an extended period of time.

Are tattoos and body piercings safe?

Tattoos and body piercings have become very popular forms of decoration. However, because tattooing and body piercing involve puncturing the skin, they can pose health risks. Diseases such as hepatitis and AIDS are spread easily through needles. Using sterile practices can help reduce the risk of contracting such a disease. A tattoo or piercing artist should

▶ wash his or her hands for 15 to 20 seconds with an antibacterial solution before and after each session

▶ wear protective latex or vinyl gloves at all times during the procedure

▶ use individual sterile needle packets and materials (which should be opened in front of the client)

▶ have a machine for sterilizing equipment on site

▶ properly dispose of contaminated materials after each session (needles should be discarded in biohazard containers)

▶ provide adequate information for proper care of tattoo or piercing

What other problems can piercing and tattooing cause?

Some body parts are more prone to infection than others. The upper ear is mostly cartilage and has little blood flow. If bacteria enter here, it is difficult for the body to fight the infection.

The navel is also very prone to infection. This area heals slowly and is constantly rubbed by clothing. Piercing in areas that have naturally high bacteria counts, such as the tongue and nose, can cause severe infections.

Tattoos can also become infected if not cared for properly. Infected tattoos are very painful.

Some people develop large scars as a result of piercings and tattoos. These large, raised scars are called *keloids*.

What if I change my mind about a piercing or tattoo?

Most holes from body piercing will eventually close if left alone. However, it is easier to get a tattoo than to remove one. Laser removal is expensive, very painful, and causes scarring. Be sure to carefully consider the dangers and consequences before doing anything permanent to your body.

☑ internet connect

www.scilinks.org/health
Topic: Skin Cancer
HealthLinks code: HH4126

HEA*L*TH*LINKS*® Maintained by the National Science Teachers Association

EXPRESS Lesson REVIEW

1. What should you do to get rid of acne?

2. How can you protect yourself from overexposure to the sun?

3. **LIFE SKILL** **Being a Wise Consumer** Check the phone book for tattoo artists. How many advertise that they comply with the U.S. Environmental Protection Agency (EPA) standards?

Caring for Your Hair and Nails

Chrishelle wanted a completely different look for summer. She wondered if extensions would damage her hair. How do you know what's healthy for your hair?

Why should I care about my hair?

Everyone has heard the saying "When you look good, you feel good." But, besides affecting your appearance, taking good care of your hair is an important part of your total health. In addition, your hair is one of the features by which people identify you. Your hair reflects your individual style and shows your unique personality.

What is hair made of?

Hair is made of dead cells that grow from the hair root. The roots of hairs are made up of living cells. The root of a hair is found in a tiny pit in the skin called a **follicle.** A folicle is embedded in the layer of skin called the *dermis.*

Hair cells are made of a protein called *keratin.* Keratin is a strong, flexible protein found in skin, hair, and nails. The visible part of the hair is called the shaft.

The shape of the hair shaft determines whether hair will be straight, curly, or waxy. **Sebaceous glands** are glands in the skin that add oil to the skin and hair shaft to keep skin and hair looking smooth and healthy.

What is a split end?

A single strand of hair has three layers. The inner layer, called the *medulla,* is made of large cells that are partially separated by air spaces. The middle layer is called the *cortex.* The outer layer is the *cuticle.* The cortex and cuticle are made of overlapping rings of dead cells.

When hair strands are damaged, the cells in the cuticle separate from each other and the hair splits open, which forms a "split end." Hot blow-dryers, curling irons, and harsh chemicals can dry out hair and cause split ends.

Hair Care Tips

▶ Most people should shampoo every 2 days. Shampoo oily hair more frequently and delicate or dry hair less frequently.

▶ When shampooing, massage your scalp gently with your fingertips.

▶ Use a comb instead of a brush on wet hair.

▶ Brush your hair by starting at the ends and working your way up to the scalp.

▶ Avoid frequent use of blow-dryers and curling irons if possible.

▶ Avoid harsh bleaches and dyes.

▶ Use conditioner to improve the appearance of dry or damaged hair.

▶ Get your hair trimmed regularly.

Harsh bleaches and hair dyes can also damage your hair. Trimming your hair regularly will get rid of most split ends and will keep your hair from looking frayed and dull.

How do I get rid of dandruff?

Dandruff is made of flaky clumps of dead skin cells from the scalp. Cold or very dry weather can cause skin to flake. The little white specks of skin fall out of your hair and onto your shoulders. Dandruff can be treated with a medicated shampoo. If you have severe dandruff, you may need to consult a dermatologist.

What are head lice?

Head lice are tiny parasites that feed on blood vessels in the scalp. They crawl onto the hair shaft to lay their eggs. The egg sacs are visible as white spots in the hair.

Lice can be spread by sharing brushes or hair accessories, pillows, or clothing. You should never share combs, brushes, hats, or hair accessories. Getting rid of lice requires treatment with a medicated shampoo. You should also wash and dry anything that may have come in contact with the lice.

Nail Care Tips

▶ **Keep your fingernails and toenails clean and dry.**

▶ **Use a soft brush to clean under nails.**

▶ **Use lotion regularly.**

▶ **Cut your nails straight across top, and file the tip and corners smooth to avoid ingrown nails.**

▶ **Use a nail clipper to clip hangnails.**

▶ **Do not bite your fingernails.**

▶ **Notify your parents at the first sign of an infection, and visit your doctor or dermatologist.**

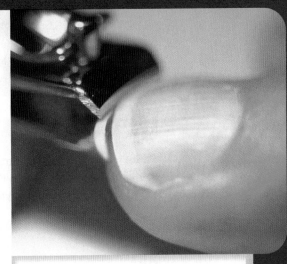

How fast do fingernails grow?

Fingernails grow from the base of the fingernail, which is called the *matrix*. Fingernails grow about an eighth of an inch per month, depending on the person's age, gender, genetics, activity level and the season.

Why do fingernails break and split?

Proper nutrition plays the biggest role in keeping fingernails strong and healthy. Moisturizer can also help keep nails from becoming dry and splitting.

Are artificial nails safe?

Artificial nails can pose some health risks.

▶ Some nail glues and nail glue removers contain poisonous substances.

▶ Artificial nails can damage the natural nails if they are left in place too long.

▶ The chemicals used to apply artificial nails are highly flammable.

▶ The tools used in a salon can spread bacterial and fungal infections.

internet connect

www.scilinks.org/health
Topic: Head Lice
HealthLinks code: HH4072

HEALTH
LINKS. Maintained by the National Science Teachers Association

EXPRESS Lesson REVIEW

1. Name four ways to keep your hair healthy.

2. Name four ways to keep your nails healthy.

3. **LIFE SKILL** **Practicing Wellness** Why should you take good care of your hair and nails?

Dental Care

Have you ever noticed that a model's teeth are always perfect? Models spend lots of money on dental work to improve their teeth. But if you take care of your teeth now, you can have beautiful teeth without spending a lot of money.

What are the parts of a tooth?

A tooth can be divided into three parts—the visible part, called the *crown,* the *neck* of the tooth just below the gum line, and the *root* below the gum line. The root holds the tooth in the jaw.

A tooth also has three layers. Enamel, the outermost layer, protects the crown and is the hardest substance in the body. The middle layer is cementum—a thin, bone-like layer that covers and protects the root. The innermost layer is dentin—a hard tissue that makes up most of the tooth and surrounds the pulp. The pulp is the living center of the tooth and contains nerves and blood vessels.

How do I whiten my teeth?

Certain substances, such as coffee, tea, and tobacco stain the enamel of teeth. Dentists use special bleaches to remove stains from teeth. Some over-the-counter products claim to remove these stains. Consult a dentist to make sure any product you use is safe for your teeth.

What causes cavities?

If you don't brush your teeth after you eat, bacteria that live in your mouth will digest food stuck to your teeth. The mixture of food particles, saliva, and bacteria on the tooth is called **plaque.** If plaque is not removed by brushing and flossing, it will harden into tartar. Tartar must be removed at a dentist's office.

Both plaque and tartar are slightly acidic. The acid irritates the gums and slowly dissolves the hard surfaces of the teeth. This process is called **tooth decay.** Eventually, the acid from tartar will eat through the dentin and into the pulp of the tooth.

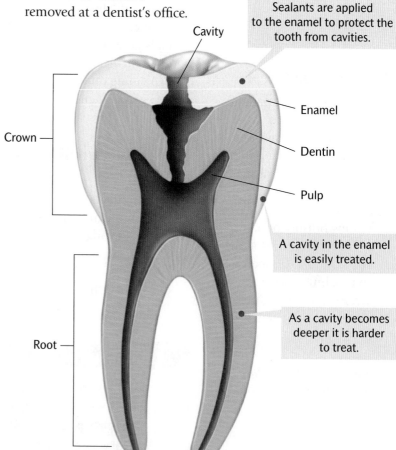

Cavity

Crown

Root

Sealants are applied to the enamel to protect the tooth from cavities.

Enamel

Dentin

Pulp

A cavity in the enamel is easily treated.

As a cavity becomes deeper it is harder to treat.

The hole in the tooth produced by tooth decay is called a **cavity.** When decay reaches the pulp, the pulp becomes infected with bacteria. Because the pulp contains nerves, cavities can be painful.

How are cavities treated?

Dentists can put a plastic sealant on teeth to keep acids from damaging the enamel. If a cavity is treated early, a dentist can clean the hole and fill it with metal or other hard substances to prevent further decay.

When a cavity reaches the pulp, the dentist must drill into the pulp of the tooth to remove the infection caused by a cavity. This procedure is called a **root canal.** If the infection is too deep for a root canal to be effective, the tooth must be removed.

What is gum disease?

Bacteria on the teeth can irritate and infect the gums, which can lead to gingivitis. **Gingivitis** is a condition in which the gums become red and infected and begin to pull away from the teeth. Once you have gingivitis, more bacteria can fill the pockets between the teeth and gums. If gingivitis is not treated, the tooth will become loose and will eventually fall out.

Proper Brushing Technique

▶ **Place a soft-bristled toothbrush at a 45-degree angle to your gums.**

▶ **Gently, brush teeth in short strokes away from the gum.**

▶ **Brush the outer, inner, and top surfaces of your teeth.**

▶ **Brush your tongue.**

▶ **Rinse your mouth with water.**

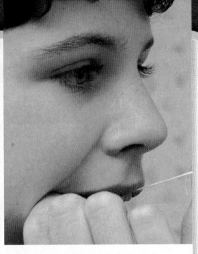

Proper Flossing Technique

▶ **Use about 18 inches of dental floss.**

▶ **Wind the ends of the floss around your middle fingers.**

▶ **Gently, insert the floss between two teeth.**

▶ **Rub the side of the tooth with the floss.**

▶ **Repeat steps 1 through 4 on the rest of your teeth.**

▶ **Rinse your mouth with water.**

What other problems can teeth have?

Tobacco use, chronic infections, and poor oral hygiene increase a person's chances of developing oral cancer. Oral cancer must be surgically removed. If it is not removed, it could spread to other parts of the body.

How can I protect my teeth?

You can easily prevent bad breath, cavities, and gum disease. Follow the guidelines listed to brush and floss your teeth after every meal. Eat a balanced diet. Avoid food high in sugar or acid and foods that stick to your teeth. Get dental checkups twice a year.

EXPRESS Lesson REVIEW

1. Describe the process that leads to a cavity.

2. Explain why gingivitis can cause you to lose a tooth.

3. **LIFE SKILL** **Practicing Wellness** List three things you can do that will help prevent tooth decay.

Protecting Your Hearing and Vision

After the rock concert, Julie's ears were ringing. "That's how you know you were at a good concert!" Julie shouted. "I'm not so sure about that," said her best friend, "I heard loud music can make you deaf."

Can loud music make me lose my hearing?

The ears are delicate and sensitive organs. Unfortunately, they have no way to shut out loud noises. Sounds above a certain level can permanently damage the ear. That's why you must protect your hearing.

How can I tell if I've damaged my hearing?

By the time teens become young adults, many have already suffered some degree of hearing loss. After the ears have been exposed to loud noise, the ears may ring and words may seem muffled. The effect usually disappears in a day or two, but damage from noise adds up over time. A buzzing, ringing, or whistling sound in one or both ears that occurs even when no sound is present is called **tinnitus** (ti NIET es). Some people are born with tinnitus; others may develop it as a result of damage to hearing.

How loud is too loud?

Sound is measured in units called **decibels** (DES uh BUHLZ). The abbreviation for decibels is dB.

A person can hear sounds above 0 decibels. Prolonged exposure to noise above 70 decibels may begin to damage hearing. Serious damage occurs if a person is exposed to sounds above 120 decibels. Sounds of 140 decibels or more can cause pain. Sounds of 180 decibels or more cause immediate and irreversible hearing loss.

The length of time you are exposed to sounds is also important. For example, listening to loud music for a couple of hours is just as damaging as hearing a much louder sound for a short time.

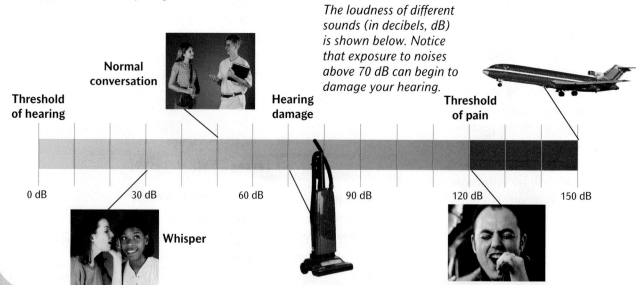

The loudness of different sounds (in decibels, dB) is shown below. Notice that exposure to noises above 70 dB can begin to damage your hearing.

Normal conversation

Threshold of hearing

Hearing damage

Threshold of pain

0 dB   30 dB   60 dB   90 dB   120 dB   150 dB

Whisper

How can I protect my hearing?

Following these tips can help you make sure you can enjoy a good concert for many years to come.

▶ Keep your ears clean. Use a soft cotton swab to remove dirt and wax.

▶ Do not push a cotton swab into your ear canal.

▶ Never use a pencil or sharp object to clean your ear.

▶ Protect your ears from the cold to prevent frostbite and inner ear infections.

▶ Avoid loud noises and keep volume low when using headphones.

▶ Have your hearing checked once a year.

Can using a computer damage my eyes?

Reading in dim light or from a computer screen cannot damage your eyes. However, these activities do cause temporary eye strain. Part of the reason for the strain is that people engaging in these activities do not blink as often as they usually would. Not blinking enough can cause the eyes to feel dry and irritated. Refresh your eyes by taking frequent breaks to blink. Look up from your work, and focus on distant objects to relieve eye strain.

How can I protect my vision?

Follow these tips to keep your eyes as healthy as possible.

▶ Be sure to eat a healthful diet rich in dark green and orange vegetables.

▶ Take regular breaks when you are reading or using the computer. Focus your eyes on distant objects.

▶ If you have glasses or contacts, wear them. Trying to focus without your corrective lenses will strain your eyes.

▶ Choose sunglasses that block 90 to 100 percent of UVA and UVB radiation (the two types of ultraviolet radiation from the sun).

▶ Any time you're working with chemicals or power tools, be sure to wear safety goggles.

▶ Sit at least 5 feet from the television.

▶ Use a room light and a reading lamp to reduce glare.

▶ Because infections can be spread by your hands, avoid touching or rubbing your eyes unless your hands have been washed with soap and water.

▶ To avoid infection, do not share contacts or contact solutions.

▶ Visit your eye doctor once a year.

What should I do if I hurt my eyes?

Even the best protection can't ensure you'll never injure your eyes. Any injury to the eye should be treated seriously. Often, the eye may seem fine at first, but symptoms of vision loss may begin to appear later. If you experience any eye injury, you must see a doctor immediately. Eye injuries can be treated, but only if you get professional medical help.

EXPRESS Lesson REVIEW

1. Name five things you can do to protect your vision.

2. According to the figure on the pervious page, what noises fall within the range of 120 to 150 dB?

3. **LIFE SKILL** **Practicing Wellness** What activities do you do that may put your eyes at risk for injury? What can you do to decrease this risk?

4. **LIFE SKILL** **Assessing Your Health** What noises are you exposed to in your daily life that could possibly damage your hearing?

Responding to a Medical Emergency

Sam was riding his bike along a trail near a campground. He suddenly came upon someone who was unconscious and bleeding. What should he do?

What should I do if I encounter a medical emergency?

Quickly survey the scene for hazards that might harm you or the victim. Call out to bystanders for help. Determine how many people (if there is more than one victim) are injured or ill. Ask each person, "Are you OK?" If a person does not respond, you or a bystander should immediately call for medical help.

Check for life-threatening injuries. Then ask, "May I touch you?" Do not touch the person without consent.

If there is no response, you have implied consent to help. Try to determine the cause of the injuries or illness to tell medical personnel when they arrive. Check to see if the victim has a medical-alert necklace or bracelet.

What medical conditions should I look for?

If needed and if you can do so safely, give life-saving first aid and then obtain medical help if you have not already done so. If the person might have a head or spinal injury, do not allow the head or neck to move. Remain with the person until help arrives.

How do I know whether to go for help if I am alone with a victim?

A person needs medical attention if he or she is not alert, is not aware of the surroundings, and does not respond to questions.

If you can easily get to a phone or to others and safely return, then go for help. If not, stay with the victim, check for life-threatening injuries, and give life-saving first aid.

After these measures, if the victim remains unresponsive or needs medical attention, you must decide whether it is better to go for help or to stay. Consider factors such as the following:

▶ how long it might be before someone finds you

▶ whether the person will survive if you leave

▶ whether the person will survive if you do not obtain medical help

Do not risk your own safety.

Steps to Take

When You Encounter a Medical Emergency

1 Look for hazards and remove them.

2 Determine the cause of injury or nature of illness.

3 Determine the number of victims.

4 If the victim is unresponsive, seek medical help.

5 If the victim is responsive, obtain consent to touch him or her.

6 Check the ABCs (Airway, Breathing, Circulation).

7 Give first aid for life-threatening conditions.

8 Seek medical help if not done previously.

9 Stay with the victim until help arrives.

*Do not risk your own safety in order to rescue or provide first aid to another person. For more information on these and other topics, see the Express Lessons on pp. 576–613.

How to Check the ABCs of Life-Threatening Conditions in an Unresponsive Person

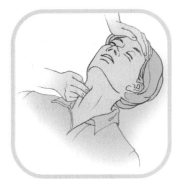

A *Airway—Open the airway by tilting the head back and lifting the chin. Make sure the tongue is not blocking the airway.*

B *Breathing—Look for movement of the chest. Listen and feel for air movement by placing your ear and then your cheek at the mouth and nose of the victim.*

C *Circulation—Place your index and middle fingers into the groove of the neck next to the voice box to feel the carotid artery pulse.*

What can I do to aid the victim until help arrives?

To aid the victim, you must know what is wrong. First, check the **ABCs.** ABC is an acronym to remind you to check three important vital signs during an emergency. The **A** reminds you to check whether or not a person's **a**irway is obstructed (blocked). The **B** reminds you to check if the person is **b**reathing. The **C** reminds you to check the person's **c**irculation by assessing the carotid pulse.

How do I check if a person's airway is obstructed?

If a person is talking or crying, his or her airway is open. If the person cannot talk but is alert and aware, he or she might have an obstructed airway. In this case, administering abdominal thrusts (the Heimlich maneuver) may clear the airway. **(See the Express Lesson "Choking" on p. 586.)**

If the person is unresponsive and does not appear to have a spinal injury, place the victim face up. Open the airway by tilting the head back and lifting the chin. If the victim appears to have a spinal injury, ask others to help you roll the victim so that no twisting of the body occurs. Place the tips of your fingers behind the angle of the jaw and move the jaw upward and forward. Remove any visible object or vomit from the mouth. Wear disposable gloves if available.

How do I determine if the victim is breathing?

Always ask the victim, "Are you all right?" If there is no response or if he or she is breathing fewer than 8 times per minute or more than 24 times per minute or is having trouble breathing, seek medical assistance.

To detect breathing in an unresponsive person, look for movement of the chest. Then, listen and feel for air movement by placing first your ear and then your cheek at the mouth and nose of the victim. If the victim is not breathing, keep the airway open and provide rescue breathing. **(See the Express Lesson "Rescue Breathing" on p. 580.)**

How do I check for circulation?

To check circulation, check the victim's carotid pulse. The **carotid pulse** is the pulse felt at the carotid arteries, the major arteries of the neck. A carotid artery runs along each side of the voice box (Adam's apple). Take the carotid pulse by placing your index and middle fingers into the groove of the neck next to the voice box. Do not use your thumb; it has a pulse of its own. Do not take the pulse on both sides at the same time, as it can cut off blood flow to the brain.

What if there is no pulse?

If the victim has no pulse, has no other signs of circulation, and is not breathing, perform CPR **(see the Express Lesson "CPR" on p. 582)** if you are certified in this technique and call for medical assistance. If you are not certified to perform CPR, call for medical assistance immediately, and then remain with the victim until help arrives.

Can I be held responsible for the death or injuries of the person I am trying to help?

Good Samaritan laws have been designed and enacted to encourage people to help others in an emergency. These laws vary from state to state. Generally, if you provide help during an emergency, you are protected from lawsuits if you obtain consent, act in good faith, are not paid, use reasonable skill and care, are not negligent (careless), and do not abandon the person.

Shock can be a life-threatening event if not treated properly.

Symptoms of Shock

A person experiencing shock may

▶ appear anxious, restless, or combative

▶ be lethargic, difficult to arouse, or unconscious

▶ have pale, cold, and "clammy" skin

▶ become nauseated and vomit

▶ experience increased pulse and respiration rates

▶ have a bluish tinge to his or her skin

▶ be thirsty

▶ have dilated (enlarged) pupils

What is shock, and when do people usually experience it?

Many types of trauma can cause a person to go into shock, which can be life threatening. **Shock** is a condition in which some body organs are not getting enough oxygenated blood. Shock may occur when the heart is not pumping properly, when a considerable amount of blood is lost from the body because of hemorrhaging, dehydration, or a systemic infection, or when the nervous system is damaged because of injury or drugs. Significant injuries usually cause shock, so automatically treat injured victims for shock.

What should you do if someone is in shock?

▶ First, check the ABCs and treat a victim for any injuries you know how to.

▶ Lay the victim on his or her back.

▶ Raise the legs 8 to 12 inches.

▶ Cover the victim with blankets, coats, or other coverings.

▶ Call for medical assistance.

▶ Do not give the victim anything to eat or drink.

How should you treat someone for shock if he or she has head or spinal injuries or is having trouble breathing?

If the victim has head injuries, assume the neck and spine are also affected. If the victim has spinal injuries, do not raise the head or feet. Place victims with breathing difficulties, chest injuries, eye injuries, or a heart attack in a half-sitting position. This position will help breathing.

How should you treat an unconscious person for shock?

If a shock victim becomes unconscious, put the person in the *recovery position*. To do this, lay the person on his or her back. Kneel next to the person. Place the arm closest to you straight out from the body. Place the far arm with the back of the hand against the near cheek. Grab and then bend the person's far knee. Roll the person toward you by protecting the head with one hand (make sure the hand is under the cheek) and pulling the far knee over and to the ground. Tilt the head up so that the airway is open. In the case of a head or ear injury, keep the injured side down.

internet connect

www.scilinks.org/health
Topic: First Aid
HealthLinks code: HH4063

HEALTH LINKS. Maintained by the National Science Teachers Association

EXPRESS Lesson REVIEW

1. List the steps you should take when encountering an emergency medical situation.

2. If you were alone with an accident victim, how would you determine whether to stay and help the victim or go for help?

3. Describe the steps you should follow to help someone in shock.

4. **LIFE SKILL** **Communicating Effectively** Imagine that you found someone who was injured in an accident. A bystander has gone to seek help. What questions would you ask the victim if he or she is responsive? What would you tell emergency medical help if he or she is unresponsive?

Rescue Breathing

Naveen saw flames coming from David's house. Then he saw David stumble from the house and collapse on the lawn. David wasn't breathing. David needed Naveen's help quickly!

What is rescue breathing?

Rescue breathing is an emergency technique in which a rescuer gives air to someone who is not breathing. To perform rescue breathing, a person blows air into a victim's lungs to give him or her oxygen. You may hear rescue breathing referred to as *artificial respiration* or *"mouth to mouth."*

How do I know if a person has stopped breathing?

In responding to a medical emergency, you will need to determine if a person has stopped breathing by checking the person's ABCs (airway, breathing, and carotid pulse). To determine if a person has stopped breathing, **see the Express Lesson "Responding to a Medical Emergency" on p. 576.** If the victim is not breathing, keep the airway open and provide rescue breathing.

How do I help an adult who has stopped breathing?

Follow these steps to help an adult:

Tilt Head Be certain that the head is properly tilted by gently pressing the victim's forehead back with one hand while raising the chin with the other.

If the person appears to have a spinal injury, do not tilt the head. Instead, lift the jaw by placing your palms on the victim's cheekbones and lifting the jaw with your fingers.

Administer Breath Now that the airway is open, pinch the victim's nostrils closed, and seal your mouth around the mouth of the victim. Blow gently into the victim's mouth for 2 seconds and watch for the chest to rise. Unpinch the nostrils, and remove your mouth so that the victim can "exhale." Watch for the chest to fall, listen for air sounds, and feel for a flow of air from the victim's mouth and nose.

Performing Rescue Breathing on an Adult

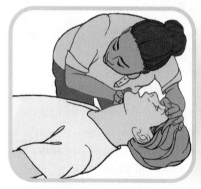

If the person does not have a spinal injury, tilt the head back and raise the chin.

Administer breath as described above.

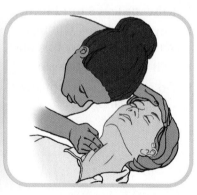

Check for pulse and signs of breathing.

If the chest rose and fell, give another rescue breath. If not, retilt the head and check the mouth and nose seals; try another rescue breath.

If air is still not entering the victim's lungs, check the head tilt, check for an airway obstruction, and administer abdominal thrusts. **(See the Express Lesson "Choking" on p. 586.)** Then try rescue breathing again.

Check for Signs of Breathing
After two successful rescue breaths (chest rises and falls), look, listen, and feel for signs of breathing. Also, check the victim's pulse. If the victim is still not breathing, give rescue breaths once every 5 seconds.

How do I help a young child or infant who has stopped breathing?

Rescue breathing for a young child ages 1 to 8 years or for an infant is performed as for an adult, with these exceptions:

▶ First, tilt the head of a child less than the head of an adult, and the head of an infant less than the head of a child.

▶ Second, in the case of an infant, seal your mouth around its mouth and nose.

▶ Third, each rescue breath should last only 1 second rather than the 2 seconds for an adult. CAUTION: blow slowly and gently, using only enough air to make the chest rise.

Performing Rescue Breathing on a Young Child

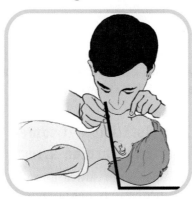

To position a child for opening of the airway, tilt the child's head less than you would tilt an adult's. Blow gently once every three seconds. Each rescue breath should last only one second.

To position an infant for opening of airway, tilt the infant's head less than you would a child's. Blow gently once every three seconds for only one second. You should seal your mouth around the infant's mouth and nose.

▶ Fourth, breathe into the victim once every 3 seconds, rather than the once every 5 seconds for adults.

How do I know when to stop rescue breathing?

After performing rescue breathing for 1 minute, look, listen, and feel for signs of breathing. If the victim is breathing on his or her own, stop rescue breath-

ing. If not, continue rescue breathing until the victim is breathing on his or her own or until medical help arrives.

internet connect

www.scilinks.org/health
Topic: Rescue Breathing
HealthLinks code: HH4118

HEALTH LINKS Maintained by the National Science Teachers Association

EXPRESS Lesson REVIEW

1. What is rescue breathing?

2. When is rescue breathing used?

3. Compare rescue breathing in adults with rescue breathing in young children and infants.

4. **LIFE SKILL** **Practicing Wellness** In a short paragraph, describe two situations that may cause a person to stop breathing.

CPR

Nigel's grandfather grabbed his chest and fell to the floor. Nigel thought that his grandfather was having a heart attack and that his heart may have stopped. Panicked, he didn't know what to do.

What is CPR?

CPR stands for **cardiopulmonary** (heart-lung) **resuscitation. CPR** is a life-saving technique that combines rescue breathing and chest compressions. During CPR, the rescuer performs the job of the heart, artificially pumping blood to the body. The pumping helps move oxygenated blood around the body.

What is the difference between a heart attack and cardiac arrest?

A heart attack is the damage and loss of function of an area of the heart muscle. A heart attack occurs when part of the heart muscle does not receive enough oxygen as a result of insufficient blood flow. As the heart muscle dies, it may cause a cardiac arrest. A cardiac arrest is a sudden stoppage of effective heart action. During cardiac arrest, heart muscle contractions may be rapid and irregular or stop altogether. Other causes of cardiac arrest include electrical shock, drug overdose, chest trauma, drowning, and suffocation.

How do I know if someone is in cardiac arrest?

A person in cardiac arrest is unconscious, has no pulse (a throbbing that can be felt in certain arteries as the blood rushes through), and has no signs of circulation. Therefore, victims who are alert and responsive are not in cardiac arrest.

If a victim is unresponsive, quickly look for signs of circulation, which include pinkness of the nail beds and warm skin. If the nail beds or skin are blue-gray, or if the skin is cool, circulation may be poor or may have stopped. Next, turn the victim face up and check the carotid pulse. The **carotid pulse** is felt at the carotid arteries, the major arteries of the neck. One carotid runs along each side of the voice box (Adam's apple). Take the carotid pulse by placing your index and middle fingers into the groove of the neck next to the voice box. Do not use your thumb; it has a pulse of its own. Do not take the pulse on both sides at the same time.

What should I do if a person is in cardiac arrest?

A victim can die from cardiac arrest in minutes. Therefore, get medical help immediately for an adult, or after 1 minute of CPR for a child or infant.

Perform CPR only if you are certified in this technique. CPR is a technique that cannot successfully be learned from a book. Any training that you might receive in CPR or any other emergency procedure will help you perform competently and effectively in case of an emergency situation.

Warning: Do not perform CPR unless you have been trained to do so.

How do I give CPR to an adult?

Only give CPR to a victim in cardiac arrest and only if you are certified to perform this technique. To perform CPR on an adult, do the following steps:

1. **Open and clear the airway.** Do this by tilting the head back and lifting the chin. Remove any objects or vomit blocking the throat.
2. **Give two slow rescue breaths.** Be sure to pinch the nostrils and seal your mouth around the victim's mouth.

Watch for the chest to rise, and then unpinch the nostrils and remove your mouth to allow the victim to "exhale." **(See the Express Lesson "Rescue Breathing" on p. 580.)**
3. **Perform chest compressions.** Place the heel of one hand in the center of the victim's chest between the nipples, and place the heel of the other hand on the back of the first. Depress the chest 1 1/2 to 2 inches. Give 15 chest compressions at a rate of about 5 every 3 seconds. After 15 chest compressions, repeat cycle steps 2 and 3.

4. **Check for signs of circulation and breathing.** After 4 cycles of compressions and breaths (about 1 minute), check the carotid pulse and other signs of circulation and breathing.

If the victim still has no pulse, continue with cycles of compression and breathing, rechecking the signs of circulation every few minutes. Continue until medical help arrives or until you are unable to continue.

Giving CPR to an Adult

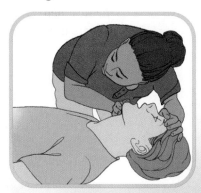

1 Open and clear the airway.

2 Give two slow rescue breaths.

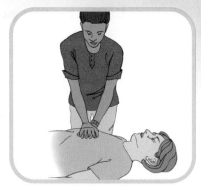

3 Perform chest compressions.

4 Check for signs of circulation and breathing.

How do I give CPR to a child or infant?

To perform CPR on a child between the ages of 1 and 8 years or on an infant younger than 1 year, do the following:

1. **Tilt head to open and clear the airway.** Do this by tilting the head back and lifting the chin. Clear the throat.

2. **Give two slow rescue breaths.** For a child, pinch the nostrils and seal your mouth around the child's mouth. For an infant, seal your mouth around the infant's mouth and nose. Blow slowly and gently. When the chest rises, unpinch the nostrils and remove your mouth.

3. **Perform chest compressions.** Place the heel of one hand in the center of the child's chest between the nipples, and place the other hand on the child's forehead.

For an infant, place the middle and ring finger of your hand nearest the infant's feet in the center of the infant's chest, one finger width below the nipple line. Rest the other hand on the infant's forehead.

Depress the chest 1 inch for a child and 1/2 to 1 inch for an infant. Give 5 chest compressions at a rate of about 5 every 3 seconds for the child and at a slightly faster rate for the infant.

4. **Check for signs of circulation and breathing.** After 5 chest compressions, give one slow rescue breath. Repeat the cycle of 5 compressions and one rescue breath for 1 minute. Check the carotid pulse in the child and the brachial (arm) pulse in the infant. The brachial pulse can be felt on the inside of the arm between the elbow and the armpit. Check for signs of breathing. If the victim still has no pulse, continue with cycles of compressions and breathing, rechecking the pulse every few minutes. Continue until medical help arrives or until you are unable to continue.

Giving CPR to a Child or Infant

1 Tilt head to open airway. Check for breathing.

2 Give two slow rescue breaths.

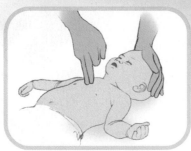

3 Perform chest compressions.

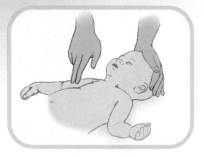

4 Locate infant's brachial artery to check pulse.

Chest Compressions During CPR

	Adult (>8 years)	Child (1–8 years)	Infant (<1 year)
Hand position	Place heel of hand in center of chest between nipples. Place heel of other hand on back of first hand.	Place heel of hand nearest the victim's feet in center of chest between nipples. Rest other hand on child's forehead.	Place middle and ring finger of hand nearest feet in center of chest one finger width below nipple line. Rest other hand on infant's forehead.
Compression depth	1 1/2 to 2 inches	1 to 1 1/2 inches	1/2 to 1 inch
Cycle	2 breaths after every 15 chest compressions	1 breath after every 5 chest compressions	1 breath after every 5 chest compressions
Rate	About 5 compressions every 3 seconds	About 5 compressions every 3 seconds	About 5-6 compressions every 3 seconds
When to call for medical help when alone	Immediately with an unresponsive victim	After 1 minute of CPR or immediately if you are not certified for CPR	After 1 minute of CPR or immediately if you are not certified for CPR

I've heard about shocking the heart into beating again. How is that done?

Shocking the heart into beating again is called *defibrillation.* Defibrillators are instruments that deliver an electrical current to the heart, which can help restore a regular rhythm to the heart. Today, portable defibrillators, which are designed to be used by minimally trained people, are available in many public areas. These defibrillators are known as *automated external defibrillators* (AEDs). The AED first determines whether shocking the heart is necessary. If so, it guides the rescuer through the defibrillation procedure. The American Heart Association estimates that defibrillating a victim within minutes after cardiac arrest could raise his or her chances of survival to 30 percent or higher. Currently, the national survival rate of victims of cardiac arrest is 5 percent.

internet connect

www.scilinks.org/health
Topic: CPR
HealthLinks code: HH4038

HEALTH LINKS. Maintained by the National Science Teachers Association

EXPRESS Lesson REVIEW

1. What is CPR, and when is it used?

2. Compare CPR for adults with CPR for young children and infants.

3. **LIFE SKILL** **Using Community Resources** Find out where CPR training is offered in your community.

EXPRESS Lesson

Choking

Elisa and Carlos were having lunch when Elisa suddenly stopped talking, looked scared, and put her hands up to her throat. Carlos wasn't sure what to do.

How do I know if someone is choking?

Choking occurs when the windpipe is partly or completely blocked. A choking person usually grabs his or her throat, the universal sign of choking. As the victim coughs, wheezes, and gags, his or her face turns red. A choking person cannot breathe or talk. The face of this person will turn bluish.

The universal sign for choking will let people know you are choking when you are unable to speak.

How do I help a person who is choking?

If a person eight years of age or older is choking, conscious, and can speak, ask him or her to try to cough up the object. After a few minutes, seek medical help if the person is unsuccessful.

If the victim cannot cough, speak, or breathe, or if a victim's ability to breathe decreases, use abdominal thrusts immediately. **Abdominal thrusts** (also known as the **Heimlich maneuver**) are the act of applying pressure to a choking person's stomach to force an object out of the throat.

To give abdominal thrusts, stand behind the victim, facing his or her back. Position a fist just above the navel (bellybutton). Grab your fist with your other hand. Quickly and forcefully press inward and upward with your fist (not your arms).

With a pregnant or obese person, give chest thrusts like abdominal thrusts but position your fist in the center of the chest. Continue thrusts until the object is dislodged or until the victim becomes unconscious because of a lack of oxygen.

For a child between the ages of 1 and 8 years, kneel behind the child to administer abdominal thrusts.

What should I do if the choking person becomes unconscious?

If the victim becomes unconscious, lower him or her to the floor. Send someone for medical help immediately. Open the victim's mouth and look for the object blocking the airway. If you see it, try to remove it with your finger. Try to administer rescue breathing. **(See the Express Lesson "Rescue Breathing" on p. 580.)** Or if you are certified in CPR, give CPR if needed. **(See the Express Lesson "CPR" on p. 582.)** Each time you give a breath, first look for an object in the throat and try to remove it with your finger.

Knowing how to administer abdominal thrusts (Heimlich Maneuver) could help save a life.

How do I help an infant who is choking?

If an infant (child under 1 year) suddenly has trouble breathing, suspect choking. If the infant is coughing, allow the coughing for a few min-utes. If the object is not coughed up, seek medical help right away.

If the infant cannot breathe, is wheezing, or starts to turn blue, you must administer chest thrusts and back blows immediately. Turn the infant face down. With the infant's head lower than the rest of the body, use the heel of your hand to give five forceful back blows. Turn the infant face up, reversing the procedure for turning the infant face down. Place your middle and ring finger in the center of the infant's chest, one finger width below the nipple line. While holding the infant's head lower than his or her chest, give five chest thrusts. Continue giving back blows then chest thrusts until the object becomes dislodged or until the infant becomes unconscious.

If the infant loses consciousness, send someone for medical help immediately. Attempt rescue breaths or CPR if there is no pulse (if you are certified). **(See the Express Lesson "CPR" on p. 582.)**

Try to clear the infant's airway.

Turn the infant face down.

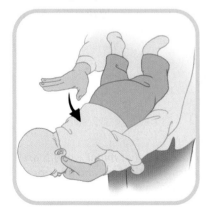

Administer back blows.

If you are choking and are alone, lean over a chair and press your abdomen upward and inward.

What should I do if I am choking and alone?

If you are alone, are choking, and cannot cough up the object blocking your airway, self-administer abdominal thrusts. Place your fist just above your navel. Cover your fist with your other hand and thrust upward and inward. If a chair, table, or other firm object is available, lean over the back of the chair or edge of the object and swiftly press your abdomen upward and inward.

internet connect

www.scilinks.org/health
Topic: Choking
HealthLinks code: HH4032

HEALTH LINKS Maintained by the National Science Teachers Association

EXPRESS Lesson REVIEW

1. Describe the steps you should follow to help a choking adult who becomes unconscious while you are giving him or her abdominal thrusts.

2. What should you do if you are alone and choking?

3. **LIFE SKILL** **Communicating Effectively** Compare the steps you should follow when helping a choking adult with those you should follow when helping a choking infant.

EXPRESS Lesson

Wounds and Bleeding

Stopping severe bleeding can save a person's life. Rapid blood loss can lead to shock and even death.

What are the different types of wounds?

A **wound** is a break or tear in the soft tissues of the body. An open wound breaks the surface of the skin. Open wounds, such as cuts, result in **external bleeding,** or bleeding at the body surface. A *closed wound* does not break the surface of the skin. Closed wounds, such as bruises, result in **internal bleeding,** or bleeding within the body.

How should I care for a minor wound?

Minor wounds usually stop bleeding by themselves after a few minutes. If not, follow these steps:

1. Wash your hands, and put on disposable gloves if you have them.
2. Wash the wound with soap and water. If you are unable to wash all the dirt and grit from the wound, seek medical help.
3. Place a sterile or clean cloth on the wound and apply direct pressure.
4. After the bleeding has stopped, remove dressing and apply antibiotic ointment to the wound.

5. Cover the wound with a sterile or clean *dressing* (a protective covering), and secure it with a *bandage* (something used to hold the dressing in place). Change the dressing at least once a day, keeping the wound clean and dry. If the wound becomes tender, swollen, and red, it may be infected. Seek medical help.

Make sure that minor wounds are washed until clean and free from debris.

How should I care for a person who has a serious wound with severe bleeding?

1. Seek medical help immediately, if possible. Protect yourself from the blood by wearing disposable gloves or other protection.
2. Lay the victim down, and elevate the feet and legs. If the bleeding is from a head wound, place the victim in a reclining (half-seated) position.
3. Follow the blood to find the wound. Expose the wound if it is covered with clothing.
4. Place a dressing, such as a clean cloth, handkerchief, or towel, over the wound, and apply direct pressure with your hand.
5. If an arm or leg is wounded, raise the wound above the level of the heart, and continue to apply direct pressure.

6. If bleeding continues, apply pressure at a pressure point. A *pressure point* is a place where an artery near the skin's surface lies over a bone. Using your hand to press the artery against the bone reduces blood flow. Use the pressure point that lies between the heart and the wound while maintaining pressure on the wound itself.

7. When the bleeding stops, release the pressure point and secure the dressing with a bandage. Do not remove any dressings. Place new dressings on top of the blood-soaked ones. Victims with puncture wounds (those made with blunt or pointed instruments) may need a tetanus booster (an injection that prevents tetanus, otherwise known as "lockjaw").

How do I recognize internal bleeding?

You may not be able to see internal bleeding unless it is near the surface of the skin, as in a bruise. If a person has blood coming from the ears, nose, mouth, or eyes or if the victim is coughing up or vomiting blood, he or she is likely to be bleeding internally. Also, look for signs of shock as a sign of possible internal bleeding. Lay the person down and raise the legs 8 to 12 inches unless he or she has a head injury. If the person has a head injury, put him or her in a reclining position. Lay a vomiting person in the recovery position. Cover the victim for warmth, and seek medical help immediately, as this may be a life-threatening condition.

◯ pressure points

Pressure Points

To stop severe bleeding, apply pressure to a pressure point between the heart and wound. If there is more than one pressure point between the heart and wound, apply pressure to the pressure point nearest the wound, if this will not traumatize the wound or the victim.

EXPRESS Lesson REVIEW

1. Describe how to clean a minor wound.
2. Where do you apply pressure to stop bleeding?
3. **LIFE SKILL** **Practicing Wellness** List the steps you would take to stop bleeding in a severe wound.

Heat- and Cold-Related Emergencies

People who spend time outside in either extreme heat or extreme cold have special concerns regarding their health.

What is hyperthermia?

Hyperthermia is a condition in which the body's internal temperature is higher than normal. It occurs in two stages—heat exhaustion and heatstroke.

What is heat exhaustion?

Heat exhaustion is a condition in which the body becomes heated to a higher temperature than normal. Heat exhaustion can occur when people exercise or work in a hot, humid place where body fluids are lost through heavy sweating. Heat exhaustion may result in a mild form of shock.

Symptoms The physical symptoms of heat exhaustion include cold, moist skin, normal or below-normal body temperature, headache, nausea, and extreme fatigue.

Treatment People experiencing heat exhaustion need to have their bodies cooled. The victim should be moved to a shady place or an air-conditioned room. Cool the victim by removing his or her clothes and applying cool, wet towels. A fan will help speed up the cooling process. Give the victim something cool (not cold) to drink, about half of a glass of cool water every 15 minutes. Observe the victim closely for changes in his or her condition. Seek medical attention if the person's condition does not change. A person suffering from heat exhaustion left untreated may suffer heatstroke.

What is heatstroke?

Heatstroke is a condition in which the body loses its ability to cool itself by sweating because the victim has become dehydrated.

Symptoms The symptoms of heatstroke include hot, dry skin; higher than normal body temperature; rapid pulse; rapid, shallow breathing; disorientation; and possible loss of consciousness.

Treatment Because heatstroke is life-threatening, seek emergency medical help immediately. If there are no emergency facilities nearby, move the person to a cool place, and try to cool the body gradually. The victim can be cooled by immersing him or her in a cool (not cold) bath or by the methods for cooling a heat exhaustion victim. If the person is vomiting or unconscious, do not give him or her water or food. Seek medical attention as soon as possible.

Keeping oneself hydrated is the best way to prevent heat exhaustion and heatstroke.

How can I prevent heat exhaustion and heatstroke?

Heat exhaustion and heatstroke can best be prevented by drinking 6 to 8 ounces of water at least 10 times a day when you are active in warm, humid weather.

What is frostbite?

Frostbite is a condition in which body tissues become frozen. Ice forms within the tissues and cuts off circulation to the area. Frostbite can involve the skin and much deeper tissues.

Symptoms Symptoms of frostbite include a change in the skin color to white, gray, or blue. The part of the body that has been frostbitten may feel numb. When warmth is restored to the body part affected, the pain can be severe.

Treatment Warm the affected part of the body. Do not rub the area; rubbing can cause damage to the tissue. Handle the areas gently. Remove wet or tight clothing. Cover the affected area with a dry, sterile dressing. If you are unable to get medical attention immediately, warm the affected area slowly in warm (not hot) water. Bandage the body part loosely with gauze and seek medical attention as soon as possible.

What is hypothermia?

Hypothermia is a condition in which the internal body temperature becomes dangerously low because the body loses heat faster than it can generate heat. When hypothermia occurs, the brain loses its ability to function at cold body temperatures, and body systems shut down. Hypothermia is usually associated with cold weather, but can also occur in windy or rainy weather when the body becomes cold and can't warm itself.

Symptoms Symptoms of hypothermia include stiff muscles, shivering, weakness, dizziness, cold skin, and slow breathing and heart rate.

Treatment To treat a person experiencing hypothermia, first, seek shelter—do not treat hypothermia outside. Remove any wet clothing and then wrap the person in blankets, towels, or newspapers. Offer warm food or drink. Do not try to heat the

body with hot drinks, hot water, or electric blankets. Seek medical attention as soon as possible.

How can I prevent frostbite and hypothermia?

Frostbite and hypothermia can best be prevented by wearing several layers of warm clothing and a warm hat. Also, going inside frequently to warm oneself will help prevent frostbite and hypothermia.

E X P R E S S Lesson REVIEW

1. How can you tell if someone is suffering from heat exhaustion or heatstroke?

2. What should you do to treat someone with heatstroke?

3. **LIFE SKILL** **Practicing Wellness** Describe what you would do to prevent frostbite and hypothermia if you were going to be out in cold weather for a long period of time.

Bone, Joint, and Muscle Injuries

Bill injured his arm while he and Tim were mountain biking. Tim wasn't sure whether or not he should splint Bill's arm.

What are fractures?

A **fracture** is a crack or break in a bone. In a *closed fracture,* the skin is unbroken. In an *open fracture,* the skin is broken and bone ends may stick out from the skin. An open fracture has the obvious signs of the wound and visible bones. Signs and symptoms of a closed fracture include one or more of the following: pain and tenderness, loss of function, deformity, unnatural movement, swelling, bruising, and a grating sensation or sound. An X ray usually determines with certainty whether a bone is fractured.

How do you treat a fracture?

Check for bleeding and call for medical help. Splint the area of the fracture. A **splint** is a device used to stabilize (hold secure) a body part. Stabilizing a fracture will help reduce pain, prevent further damage to tissues surrounding the fracture, and reduce bleeding and swelling.

Splint the area in the position it was found. Cover any open wounds with a clean, dry dressing, and apply the splint, placing padding between the splint and the body. Be certain that the splint is long enough to extend beyond the joint above and the joint below the fracture. (joints are places where two bones meet.)

Things you can use to make a splint include heavy cardboard, rolled newspapers, or even an adjacent body part (for example, you can tape two fingers or two legs together).

Tie the splint or self-splint to the body tightly enough to prevent movement but not so tightly as to cut off circulation. When possible, place splints on both sides of the injured part.

What is a dislocation?

A **dislocation** is an injury in which a bone has been forced out of its normal position in a joint. Usually the joint is swollen and looks deformed. A dislocation is usually painful, and the dislocated joint may be "locked" in position. Splint a dislocation as you would a bone fracture, and seek medical help.

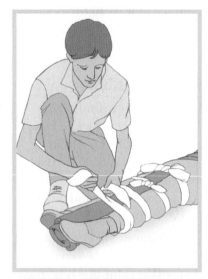

How to Apply a Splint

▶ Find materials to make a splint.

▶ Hold the splint close to the injured area.

▶ Place padding between the splint and the body.

▶ Use extra padding in body hollows and around deformities.

▶ Be sure that the splint extends beyond the joint above and the joint below the fracture.

▶ Tie the splint comfortably to the body.

What are the differences between sprains and strains?

A **sprain** is an injury in which the ligaments in a joint are stretched too far or torn. Ligaments are bands of connective tissue that hold bones to bones. A **strain** is an injury in which a muscle or tendon has been stretched too far or torn. Tendons are bands of connective tissue that hold muscles to bones.

What should you do to treat injuries to bones, joints, and muscles?

Use the RICE technique:
Rest—don't use the injured area
Ice—use an ice pack or cold pack on the injured area to reduce swelling
Compression—wrap the injured area with an elastic bandage to prevent movement and swelling
Elevation—raise the injured area above heart level when lying or sitting down

How do you know if someone has a neck or spinal injury?

A person with spinal injuries may have no obvious signs and symptoms. However, some signs and symptoms of spinal injuries are swelling and bruising at the site of the injury; numbness, tingling, or a loss of feeling in the arms and legs; inability to move the arms or legs; pain; difficulty breathing; shock; and unconsciousness. If the victim was injured in a way that is likely to have caused a neck or spinal injury, assume that such an injury exists.

How do you treat an injury to the neck or spine?

An injury to the bones of the neck or spine can damage the spinal cord and the nerves that branch out from the spine. Therefore, do not move a person that may have a neck or spinal injury. Get medical help immediately. If the person must be moved, steady and support the head and neck by holding it in the position in which you find it. To keep the head from moving, place objects on either side of the head. Steady and support the victim's legs and feet as well.

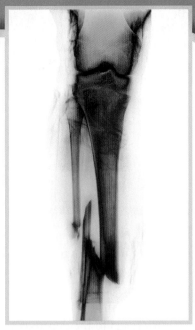

How To Care For Fractures and Dislocations

▶ Check for bleeding. Cover open wounds with a clean, dry dressing.

▶ Seek medical help.

▶ Stabilize the fracture or dislocation with a splint.

internet connect

www.scilinks.org/health
Topic: Joints and Muscles in the Body
HealthLinks code: HH4090

HEALTH LINKS. Maintained by the National Science Teachers Association

EXPRESS Lesson REVIEW

1. Explain the difference between a fracture, a dislocation, a strain, and a sprain.

2. What danger exists in moving a person with a neck or spinal injury?

3. **LIFE SKILL** **Practicing Wellness** Make a list of things in your home that could be used for splints. Identify objects of various sizes.

Burns

Recognizing burns and giving proper, immediate burn treatment will reduce tissue damage and relieve pain.

What are the different types of burns?

Burns are injuries to the skin and other tissues caused by heat, chemicals, electricity, or radiation. The degree of a burn refers to the depth of tissue damage.

▶ **First-degree burns** are burns that affect only the outer layer of the skin and look pink. First-degree burns include minor sunburns and burns caused by a very short exposure to intense heat, such as an explosion. First-degree burns take about 3 to 6 days to heal, and they heal without scarring.

▶ **Second-degree burns** are burns that extend into the inner skin layer and are red, swollen, and blistered. Second-degree burns are caused by brief exposures to flashes of intense heat, such as spilling hot liquid on yourself or grabbing a curling iron by the heated end. Second-degree burns usually take less than 3 weeks to heal. Deeper second-degree burns may take longer to heal. Scarring is possible if the wounds are not treated properly.

Recognizing and Treating Burns

1st degree burn

Treatment
▶ Apply cool water until the pain stops.
▶ Apply moisturizing lotion.

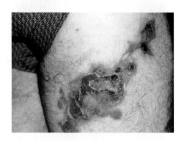

2nd degree burn

Treatment
▶ Apply sterile dressing.
▶ Seek medical attention.
▶ Applying water or ointment to a serious 2nd degree burn can increase the risk of wound infection.

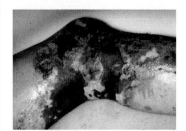

3rd degree burn

Treatment
▶ Seek medical attention immediately.
▶ Cover with a clean, dry cloth.
▶ Treat victim for shock (raise feet if safe; cover with blanket)

▶ **Third-degree burns** are full-thickness burns. They penetrate all skin layers as well as tissue beneath the skin. These burns appear pearly white, tan colored, or charred. Third-degree burns, which can be fatal, are often caused by extended exposure to steam or fire or to immersion in scalding water.

There is usually no immediate pain because of damage done to underlying nerves, but there is severe pain later. A skin graft must be performed if healing is to occur. Some scarring is inevitable, and these burns can take years to heal.

What should I do if I or someone else receives a burn?

For first- and minor second-degree burns only, cool the burn immediately. Do this by immersing the burn in cool water, pouring cool water over the burn, or covering the burn with a clean, cool, wet cloth. Cool the burn until it is pain free both in and out of water.

You may apply a moisturizing ointment to a first-degree burn.

For third-degree burns, cover the burn with a clean cloth. (Do not cool the burn.) Seek medical assistance immediately. Treat the victim for possible shock.

What are the major sources of burns?

There are three major sources of burns. The source of the burn will influence how it should be treated.

1. **Thermal burns** Thermal burns are caused by contact with open flames, hot liquids or surfaces, or other sources of high heat.
2. **Chemical burns** Contact with certain chemicals can burn the skin.
3. **Electrical burns** Direct exposure to electricity can also cause burns.

Do I treat thermal, chemical, and electrical burns in the same way?

No. For thermal burns, remove the victim from the heat source and for first or minor second-degree burns, cool the burn with water. Check for bleeding and for shock, and seek medical attention immediately.

For all chemical burns, contact a Poison Control Center. Chemical burns caused by liquid chemicals should be flushed with large amounts of cool water to remove the chemical from the body. For chemical burns caused by dry or powdered chemicals, brush the chemical off of the skin with a clean cloth. Water may activate a dry chemical and cause more damage than has already occurred.

For electrical burns involving an appliance, shut off the current to the house. Be sure the area is safe before approaching. Cool the burn with cool water. Check the victim's breathing, and stop any bleeding. Treat for shock if necessary, and seek medical attention immediately.

Special Considerations for Burns

▶ Obtain medical attention immediately, for facial burns, severe second-degree burns, third-degree burns, chemical burns, or electrical burns.

▶ Seek medical attention for severe sunburns.

▶ Never apply ointment or cream to a severe burn.

▶ Never try to remove clothing that is stuck to a burn wound.

▶ Always treat burns on the face, hands, and feet as severe, and seek prompt medical attention.

internet connect

www.scilinks.org/health
Topic: Burns
HealthLinks code: HH4026

HEALTH LINKS. Maintained by the National Science Teachers Association

EXPRESS Lesson REVIEW

1. Differentiate between first, second, and third degree burns.
2. What is the first thing you should do to treat first- and second-degree burns?
3. **LIFE SKILL** **Practicing Wellness** List three ways that you can prevent thermal, chemical, and electrical burns in your home.

Poisons

In 2000, over 2 million poisonings were reported by poison control centers in the United States. Nearly all poisonings happen in the home, and over half occur among young children.

What are the different types of poisoning?

A **poison** is a substance that can cause illness or death when taken into the body. Poisons can be swallowed (ingested), inhaled, absorbed through the skin by contact, or can occur as a result of being bitten or stung by an insect or animal. The table shows these types of poisonings.

What are the signs of poisoning?

Suspect poisoning whenever someone becomes ill suddenly and for no apparent reason. Search for clues, such as chemical odors, leftover food, or suspicious containers. Any poisoning victim may lose consciousness and have trouble breathing, but other signs and symptoms depend on the poison and how it entered the body.

Signs and symptoms of ingested poisons include nausea, vomiting, abdominal cramps, diarrhea, discoloration of the lips, burns in and around the mouth, and an odor on the breath.

Signs and symptoms of inhaled poisons include breathing difficulty, coughing, chest pain, headache, and dizziness.

Signs and symptoms of contact poisons include reddening of the skin, blisters, swelling, and burns. Poisons injected through the skin usually irritate the spot where they were injected.

Types of Poisoning and Their Possible Sources

Inhalation

Possible Sources
- paints
- solvents
- toxic gases
- gasoline
- glue

Bites and stings

Possible Sources
- bites from spiders, snakes, etc.
- stings from wasps, bees, hornets, and scorpions

Contact

Possible Sources
- chemicals
- plants

POISON HELP!
©CHospPoh®
1-800-222-1222

Ingestion

Possible Sources
- medications
- household products
- chemicals
- certain plants

What should I do if someone has been poisoned?

You should seek medical assistance immediately, then call a **Poison Control Center**. Staff there can judge the seriousness of the poisoning and provide advice.

If you suspect inhaled poisoning, first make sure it is safe to enter the area. Then, move the victim away from the poison and into fresh air. Seek medical help promptly if the victim is unconscious. Take the container of the suspected poison along with you to the emergency room to aid the staff in treating the poisoning. Check the victim's ABCs. **(See the Express Lesson "Responding to a Medical Emergency" on p. 576).**

If you need to give rescue breaths or administer CPR (if you are certified in this technique), be certain that no poison is on the victim's mouth; otherwise, you could become contaminated too. (If there is poison in the victim's mouth or nose, wait for professional medical help.) **(See the Express Lesson "CPR" on p. 582.)** Hold the victim's mouth closed, seal your mouth around the victim's nose, and provide rescue breaths through the nose. Open the victim's mouth to allow him or her to "exhale."

How can I prevent poisonings from occurring in my home?

There are many areas of the home where poisonings can occur. Taking precautions can help stop poisonings from occurring. In households with small children, install child-safety latches on all cabinets and drawers containing harmful products.

Kitchen Keep products in original containers and out of reach of children. This includes detergents and other cleaning products.

Bathroom Keep all medications in their original, child-proof containers. Discard all old medications. Keep all medications, cosmetics, petrochemical-based lotions, and grooming products out of reach of children.

Garage Keep all products in their original containers with their original labels. Lock up all harmful products, or at least place them out of reach of children. This includes gasoline and other products for your car, solvents, and pesticides.

The best way to avoid an accidental poisoning is to avoid exposure to sources of poison.

☑ **internet** connect

www.scilinks.org/health
Topic: Poisons
HealthLinks code: HH4114

HEALTH LINKS
THE WORLD'S A CLICK AWAY
Maintained by the
National Science
Teachers Association

EXPRESS Lesson REVIEW

1. Find the number of the poison control center in your area. Post this number by the phone at home. Remember to ask for permission first!

2. List the steps you should follow to help an individual who appears to have been poisoned.

3. **LIFE SKILL** **Practicing Wellness** Make a list of things in your home that may be considered poisons and where they are located. What can be done to keep these items from small children? Check your responses with information you obtain from the poison control center.

Motor Vehicle Safety

Brittany read the headlines: "Automobile accidents are the leading cause of death for 15- to 20-year-olds." She wondered what she could do to drive more safely.

What factor contributes most often to automobile accidents?

The factor that contributes most often to automobile accidents is driver behavior. Unsafe driving behavior may be due to a lack of driving skills or due to inexperience behind the wheel. Therefore, it is important for young drivers to take a driver education course and to gain driving experience with a skilled driver in the car. Additionally, driving behaviors that should be avoided include speeding, aggressiveness, impaired driving, and distractions such as cell phones and adjusting stereos.

Speeding The greater the speed of a car, the longer it takes to stop. Therefore, driving more slowly helps a driver avoid crashes because he or she can stop more quickly. Although many automobile accidents occur at low speeds, these accidents are more likely to result only in injuries or property damage. Accidents occurring at 45 miles per hour (mph) or faster are more likely to result in death than those occurring under 45 mph.

Aggressiveness Aggressive drivers not only speed but also tend to tailgate, make frequent or unsafe lane changes, disregard traffic signals, fail to signal when changing lanes or making turns, and fail to yield the right of way. These behaviors are all unsafe driving practices. They increase the chances of having an automobile accident.

Impaired Driving Alcohol, other drugs, and sleepiness can impair driving abilities. The chances of being involved in a car crash and the seriousness of a crash increase with alcohol involvement. Additionally, drivers who have been drinking are less likely to use seat belts. Wearing seat belts cuts the risk of dying in car crashes in half. Young people are also at risk for drowsy-driving crashes. Drivers aged 29 years and younger are involved in nearly two-thirds of all drowsy-driving crashes.

Even single car accidents can be very devastating.

What does it mean to be a "defensive driver"?

A *defensive driver* practices behaviors that help avoid car crashes. Follow these steps to be a defensive driver:

▶ Do not drive while under the influence of alcohol or other drugs that may impair your reflexes, judgment, and ability to stay awake.

▶ Avoid fatigue by getting plenty of rest. On long drives, stop at least once every three hours and rotate drivers.

▶ Stay far behind the car in front of you. Leave at least 1 car length for every 10 mph you are traveling. When roads are wet, snowy, or icy, leave more room.

▶ Drive within posted speed limits, and slow down during poor weather. Use your directional signals when making turns and changing lanes. Obey all traffic laws.

▶ Continually monitor the road for pedestrians, cyclists, stopped vehicles, or other persons or obstacles. Be aware of the space around you to determine where you could move if a person or obstacle suddenly appeared.

▶ Be a courteous driver. If someone else makes unwanted gestures or unsafe driving maneuvers near you, avoid that driver. Do not engage in unsafe driving practices for revenge.

What else can I do to keep myself and others safe when I am driving?

1. **Maintain your vehicle properly.** Complete maintenance and safety checks as suggested by the manufacturer. Be certain that your tires are appropriate for the weather conditions in your area.

All persons traveling in a vehicle should use proper safety restraints.

2. **Insist that all passengers in your vehicle wear seat belts.** Put children under 12 years in the back seat, away from air bags. Use child safety seats according to manufacturer's instructions. Persons in the front seat should sit back 10 inches from air bags.

3. **Plan your route.** Be sure that you are familiar with maps and directions in order to avoid confusion. For long trips, tell others what your route is and when you plan to depart and arrive.

4. **Have necessary emergency and first-aid equipment in the car.** See the list "Things You Should Carry in Your Car."

Things You Should Carry in Your Car

In all types of weather:

▶ Flashlight
▶ Jumper cables
▶ Warning devices
▶ First-aid Kit
▶ Cell phone

In addition, in cold and snowy conditions:

▶ Shovel
▶ Ice scraper/snow brush
▶ Sand, kitty litter, or traction mats
▶ Blanket(s)

In addition, for long trips:

▶ Water
▶ Food
▶ Medications, if needed

Motor Vehicle Safety *continued*

Are there any unique safety concerns for driving a motorcycle?

Yes, a motorcycle provides no protection for its driver or passenger, unlike a car. A motorcyclist has no vehicle surrounding him or her, no air bag, and no seat belts.

If a motorcycle crashes, the persons on the motorcycle are ejected. Therefore, motorcyclists should wear

▶ protective clothing, including a properly designed helmet and eye protection

▶ a leather or heavy denim jacket

▶ long pants and gloves

▶ sturdy low-heeled boots that extend above the ankles.

Motorcycles are also less visible than cars. Motorcyclists can increase their visibility by wearing brightly colored clothing and applying reflective material to their motorcycles and helmets. Also, motorcyclists should have their vehicle lights on when operating the motorcycle, even in the daylight.

Along with following the defensive driving tips mentioned previously, motorcyclists should be particularly watchful at intersections, where most motorcycle-automobile collisions occur.

Motor Vehicle Safety

▶ Operate the vehicle only if you are skilled and experienced and have a required license.

▶ Operate the vehicle at reasonable speeds.

▶ Operate the vehicle in a courteous and defensive manner, not in an aggressive manner.

▶ Do not operate the vehicle while drowsy or under the influence of alcohol or other drugs.

▶ Wear protective clothing, headgear, and footgear when operating open vehicles.

▶ Be certain that your vehicle is in proper working condition.

What can I do to be safer on a motorcycle?

Additionally, many of the causes of motorcycle crashes are linked to the driver's inexperience or inability to handle the vehicle properly. Therefore, motorcyclists should attend motorcycle training courses prior to obtaining their motorcycle licenses.

What safety precautions should I take when operating recreational vehicles?

Before using any recreational vehicle, such as a snowmobile, mini-bike, personal watercraft, or all-terrain vehicle, be sure that it is in top-notch mechanical condition. If your vehicle is small, use a safety flag to help others see you.

Wear protective clothing appropriate for the weather and the vehicle, and check weather reports before you leave. When riding any of these vehicles, wear a helmet with goggles or a face shield to protect yourself from flying debris, such as twigs, stones, and ice chips. Avoid trailing clothing, such as a long scarf, which can get caught in vehicle parts.

What do I need to know about the terrain I will drive over?

If you are unfamiliar with the terrain over which you'll be riding, discuss its characteristics with someone who has traveled it. If you are riding over frozen lakes, ponds, or streams, be sure that the ice is thick enough to support your weight and that of your vehicle. On a personal watercraft, it is important to know where tree stumps or other obstacles may lie hidden in the water. Always ride with another person; never ride alone.

As with the operation of other types of vehicles, do not operate recreational vehicles while under the influence of alcohol or drugs or while drowsy. And before you drive a recreational vehicle, receive instruction from an experienced driver.

Are there any general rules for driving that apply to all motor vehicles?

Yes, some rules that apply when driving any type of motor vehicle are as follows:

▶ **Don't eat while you are driving.** You can't pay full attention to the road when you are trying to handle food. If you have something to drink, make sure you have a proper cup holder and a cup that has a lid.

▶ **Don't wear headphones.** It is difficult to hear what is going on around you in traffic even if you have the volume turned down low.

▶ **Don't talk on the phone while you are driving.** If you need to talk on the phone, pull over to a safe area on the side of the road or into a rest stop.

▶ **Don't look down, even for a second.** If you drop something on the floor, pull over to a safe area on the side of the road to pick it up, or do without it until you stop.

▶ **Don't try to tend to children in the back seat while you are driving.** Again, pull over to a safe area and tend to the children.

▶ **Don't drive if your vision is obstructed.** If it is raining too hard to be able to see, pull over to a safe area and wait for the rain to subside. Turn your hazard lights on if you pull over to the side of the road so that you will be visible to other drivers.

Your windshield may become covered with bugs, pollen, dirt, or other things that can obstruct your vision.

Clean your windshield each time you put gas in your car, and carry some window cleaner and paper towels along in your car for emergencies.

internet connect

www.scilinks.org/health
Topic: Motor Vehicle Safety
HealthLinks code: HH4101

HEALTH LINKS. Maintained by the National Science Teachers Association

EXPRESS Lesson REVIEW

1. List and describe three unsafe driver behaviors.

2. List three things you should do to protect yourself while operating a small, open vehicle that you would not have to do while driving a car. Explain.

3. **LIFE SKILL** **Making GREAT Decisions** While driving on the highway, a passing motorist makes an angry gesture toward you because you are driving 5 mph below the speed limit. How should you respond?

Bicycle Safety

Four out of five collisions involving bicycles and cars are caused by bicyclists who do not follow traffic and safety rules. Read the information below to learn how to protect yourself while riding your bike.

What can I do to be safer on a bicycle?

Most bicycle accidents are caused by rider error. The following guidelines will help reduce your risk of unintentional injury while bicycling.

1. Ride solo on a bicycle designed for one person.
2. Ride responsibly. This includes obeying traffic signs and signals. Ride in the same direction as the traffic, do not weave in and out of parked cars, and signal before you make a turn or stop. Keep both hands on the handlebars except when signaling. If cycling in a group, always remain in single file while on roadways.
3. Remain visible. Install reflectors on the back of your bike and a light on the front for nighttime riding. Wear bright colors in the daytime, and don't ride in between lines of cars where you may not be seen.
4. Remain watchful. Look out for pedestrians and turning cars at intersections. Mid-block, watch for cars pulling out of driveways and parking spaces. Stay away from the curb to avoid debris in the gutter. Leave 3 feet between you and parked cars to avoid being hit by an opening car door. And don't wear audio headphones; they impair your ability to hear cars driving near you.
5. Do not ride while under the influence of alcohol or other drugs. Drugs and alcohol impair your judgment and reflexes.
6. Keep your bike in proper working condition. Make sure that it is the right size for you, and adjust your seat so that your toes touch the ground when you are stopped.
7. Finally, ALWAYS wear a bicycle helmet when you ride.

Bicycle-related head injuries account for about

▶ 500 deaths per year
▶ 17,000 hospitalizations
▶ 153,000 emergency room visits
▶ two-thirds of bicycle-related deaths
▶ one-third of nonfatal bicycle injuries

Source: Centers for Disease Control.

Left turn hand signal

Right turn hand signal

Stop or slow hand signal

What should I consider when buying a bicycle safety helmet?

Buy a helmet that is comfortable and that fits your head properly. Follow the guidelines for selecting a helmet as suggested by the Snell Memorial Foundation, The American Society for Testing and Materials, or the American National Standards Institute.

What are bicycle hand signals?

Bicycle **hand signals** show pedestrians, automobile drivers, and others on the road when you intend to make a turn or stop. Look at the three photos above showing bicycle hand signals. The photo on the left shows the hand signal for a left turn. The arm is extended from the body at a 90° angle, with the palm facing down toward the road.

The center photo shows a right turn hand signal. The left arm is extended out away from the body at a 90° angle, and the forearm is bent upward at a 90° angle at the elbow, with the palm facing forward.

In many states, you may also signal a right hand turn by using your outstretched right arm and hand to point right, similar to using the left hand to signal a left turn. The right photo shows the signal for a slow down or stop. Extend the left arm out at a 90° angle to the body, and bend the arm down at a 90° angle from the elbow with the palm facing backward.

Are bicyclists supposed to follow the same traffic rules as cars?

Yes. Obey all traffic laws, signs, and signals as if you were driving a car. Drive on the road instead of the sidewalk, and always yield to pedestrians. Such behavior assures continuity and predictability for bicyclists and other drivers alike.

internet connect

www.scilinks.org/health
Topic: Bicycle Safety
HealthLinks code: HH4017

HEALTH LINKS. Maintained by the National Science Teachers Association

EXPRESS Lesson REVIEW

1. List seven behaviors that will reduce your risk of unintentional injury while bicycling.

2. Describe the proper hand signals to use when riding a bike.

3. **LIFE SKILL** **Making GREAT Decisions** After school, your friend asks you to give him a lift home on your bike. What would you tell your friend? Why?

Home and Workplace Safety

Test your fire detectors regularly.

Because most people spend their days at home or work, it is no surprise that many unintentional injuries occur in these places.

What are the most common types of unintentional injuries in the home?

The most common types of unintentional injuries in the home are electrocution, suffocation, and injuries from fires and falls. **Electrocution** is a fatal injury caused by electricity entering the body and destroying vital tissues. **Suffocation** is a fatal injury caused by an inability to breathe when the nose and mouth are blocked or when the body becomes oxygen-deficient.

What can I do to help prevent unintentional injuries in my home?

Preventing Injuries from Fires First, prevent fires from occurring. Never leave the stove unattended when cooking. Be sure that portable heaters are 3 feet from anything that can burn, and never leave them on when you go out or go to bed. Keep matches and lighters away from children. Unplug and repair any electrical appliance that has an unusual smell, and do not overload electrical outlets.

Second, plan your escape route from every room in the house and where everyone will meet outside. If your clothes catch fire when you are escaping, stop, drop, and roll. Crawl out of the house to avoid breathing smoke and poisonous gases. Install smoke detectors on every floor of your home, test them periodically, and change the batteries once a year.

Preventing Injuries from Falls About 40 percent of fall-related deaths occur in the home. Some of the things you can do to help prevent falls include installing handrails on stairways; getting rid of clutter on stairs and floors; keeping lamp, extension, telephone, and other cords out of walkways; and refinishing slippery surfaces.

Preventing Suffocation This type of unintentional injury occurs most frequently with infants and small children. To lower the risk, be sure that infant bedding is safe. Use a firm, flat mattress that fits the crib snugly. Do not use pillows and comforters. Additionally, make sure that no places exist that a small child

Unplug all appliances that are near water.

Clean up clutter on stairs and floors.

could enter, become trapped, and suffocate, such as a plastic bag, a lidded toy chest, an old refrigerator, or an unlocked car trunk. And finally, keep all drape cords short and fasten down electrical extension cords.

Preventing Electrocution

One aid to preventing electrocution is the ground fault circuit interrupter (GFCI). A GFCI turns off electricity before electrocution can occur. Install and test GFCI outlets or plug-ins in places where both water and electricity are used, such as kitchens and bathrooms. When small electrical appliances are not in use, unplug them. And never reach into water to get an appliance unless it is unplugged. If small children are in the house, cover unused electrical outlets with child-safety plugs. Finally, do not remove the grounding pin (third prong) from power tools or other electrical items. Instead, use a three-prong adapter to connect a three-prong plug to a two-hole outlet.

What are the most common types of unintentional injuries in the workplace?

The most common types of unintentional injuries in the workplace are the result of a travel-related accident. Workers are also injured from falls, from fires and explosions, by exposure to harmful substances, and by contact with equipment or electricity.

Every workplace has its own safety concerns.

What responsibilities do employers have regarding safety in the workplace?

The **Occupational Safety and Health Administration (OSHA)** is a government agency created to prevent work-related injuries, illness, and death. Since the creation of OSHA in 1970, work-related injuries have dropped by 40 percent and work-related deaths have been cut in half. Employers must obey OSHA regulations, properly train workers, and provide appropriate safety gear.

What responsibilities do employees have regarding safety in the workplace?

Employees are expected to follow OSHA and employer health and safety guidelines. They are expected to wear or use the protective equipment given them, report hazardous conditions, and report and seek treatment for job-related injuries or illnesses.

internet connect

www.scilinks.org/health
Topic: Fires
HealthLinks code: HH4062

HEALTH LINKS. Maintained by the National Science Teachers Association

EXPRESS Lesson REVIEW

1. What safety concerns are particularly relevant in homes with small children?

2. **LIFE SKILL** **Communicating Effectively** Describe what you would do if you saw a co-worker committing serious safety violations at work.

Gun Safety Awareness

While Ashley was jogging along a path in the woods, she spotted a gun among the leaves under a tree. The gun scared her, and she wasn't sure what she should do.

What should I do if I find a gun?

If you find a gun, do NOT touch it. Also, do not disturb anything in the area surrounding it. Along with being unsafe to handle, the gun may be evidence in a crime. Other things in the area may provide evidence as well. Note landmarks so that you can lead the police to the location. Leave the area and call the police, or have a responsible adult call the police.

Where can I enroll in a gun safety class?

There are many groups throughout the country that offer courses in firearm safety as well as many other courses. These firearm safety courses explain how different types of firearms operate and how to handle and store them safely. To find firearm safety classes in your area, contact your local wildlife conservation office or local law enforcement agency.

What are safe ways to store guns?

Firearms should be stored so that unauthorized persons, such as children, cannot use them. First, firearms should be stored separately from their ammunition. Second, firearms should be stored in a locked gun case, gun cabinet, or safe. Unloaded guns may be stored with a locking safety cable or a **trigger lock,** a device that helps prevent a gun from being fired. However, even with these safety devices, a firearm can sometimes still be fired, so always be cautious.

How do I increase my safety while walking in the woods during hunting season?

Try to avoid walking in hunting areas during hunting season. If you must, carry a whistle. If you hear shots, blow the whistle until the hunter acknowledges your presence and leaves the area. Avoid being mistaken for game by wearing bright colors, such as blaze orange or fluorescent yellow.

Always respect firearms, and take a firearm safety course.

In the movies and on TV, I see people fire guns into the air. Is that safe?

No. A bullet fired upward will come down. It could severely wound someone on its descent. This is especially dangerous in urban areas and in crowds.

I inherited a gun from my grandfather. Is it safe to shoot?

You cannot know whether a used gun from any source is safe to shoot. The gun could misfire, causing severe injury. Always take a used gun to a reputable gunsmith who can determine its safety and make any repairs that may be necessary.

Why do I need to wear ear and eye protection when firing a gun?

Exposure to gunfire can cause hearing damage or loss if proper ear protection is not worn. Different types of hearing protection devices can be purchased at sporting goods and drug stores. Additionally, guns can emit debris and hot gas when fired. These substances can cause eye injury without the protection of proper shooting glasses.

Firearm Safety Awareness

Mishaps with guns can be avoided by following some basic safety rules, which include the following:

▶ Always assume the gun is loaded.

▶ Never point a loaded or unloaded gun at anything you do not want to shoot.

▶ When handling a gun, always point the barrel in a safe direction.

▶ Keep the safety on until you are ready to shoot.

▶ Keep firearms and ammunition stored separately under lock and key and away from children.

▶ Know how to use a firearm

safely; enroll in a firearm safety course.

▶ Wear eye and ear protection when shooting.

▶ Keep a record of firearm serial and model numbers stored in a secure place.

▶ Know and obey all gun laws for your state.

▶ Make sure you are aware of what lies in front of and beyond your target.

▶ Never use alcohol or other drugs prior to or when shooting.

☑ internet connect

www.scilinks.org/health
Topic: Gun Safety
HealthLinks code: HH4607

HEA*l*TH
LINKS. Maintained by the National Science Teachers Association

EXPRESS Lesson REVIEW

1. Describe a safe way to store a gun.

2. List four rules for the safe use of firearms.

3. **LIFE SKILL** **Using Community Resources** Speak with a policeman, a judge, or another official in your community to find out about local gun laws.

Safety in Weather Disasters

Every year about 800 tornadoes occur in the United States. Knowing what to do in tornadoes or other hazardous weather conditions could mean the difference between life and death.

What is meant by the terms hazardous weather and natural disaster?

Weather is the state of the atmosphere at a particular place and time. It includes factors such as temperature, cloudiness, sunshine, wind, and precipitation. **Hazardous weather** is dangerous weather that causes concerns for safety. It puts property and human life in peril. Hazardous weather may result in a natural disaster. A **natural disaster** is a natural event that causes widespread injury, death, and property damage. An example of a natural disaster produced by weather is the severe flooding of a city. An example of a nonweather-related natural disaster is widespread destruction resulting from an earthquake.

What should I do to remain safe from lightning?

Lightning is caused when there is a separation of different charges. For cloud-to-ground lightning, the ground has an excess of positive charges, and clouds usually have negative charges. Just as a spark can jump from your finger to a doorknob to reunite separate charges, a lightning bolt can result.

A lightning bolt can strike when a storm is approaching, during a storm, and after a storm has passed. If you can hear thunder, you are close enough to be struck by lightning.

To reduce your risk of being struck by lightning, avoid being

▶ the tallest thing in the area (as in standing in an open field) or near the tallest thing, such as a lone tree

▶ near metal things, such as metal fences or buildings

▶ in a small, open structure, such as a baseball dugout or a gazebo

▶ near water

Seek shelter inside a large, enclosed structure or inside a car or school bus. When inside, avoid water and conductive substances. Therefore, do not use the phone, put any part of your body in water, or touch metal doors or window frames during a storm.

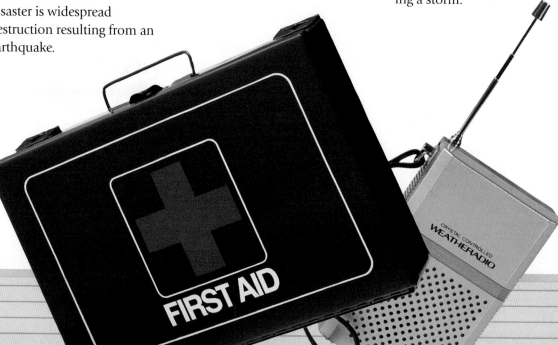

How do I know if a tornado is likely to strike?

A tornado is a violently rotating funnel-shaped column of air associated with a thunderstorm. The National Weather Service (NWS) issues a *tornado watch* when tornadoes are possible in an area. The NWS issues a *tornado warning* when a tornado has been sighted or indicated by weather radar. However, a tornado may develop quickly, without warning. Or you may not hear the warning. Therefore, look for these tornado signs: dark, greenish sky; large hail; and a loud roar. You may or may not be able to see the tornado.

What safety measures should I take if a tornado is likely to strike?

If a tornado warning has been issued or you see signs of a coming tornado, go immediately to an underground shelter, a basement, or a small interior room without windows on the lowest floor. Stay away from windows and corners. If you are in a mobile home, leave it and seek shelter in a nonmobile building. If you are in a car, seek shelter in a building if possible. Otherwise, get out of the car and lie in a ditch or other low area, covering your neck and head with your arms.

What do I need to know about safety and hurricanes?

A hurricane is a type of storm that forms over tropical areas of oceans. However, it can move inland along the coastline.

In the United States, hurricane season runs from June through November. In a hurricane, rain is heavy and winds blow greater than 75 miles per hour.

A *hurricane watch* means hurricane conditions are possible within 36 hours.

A *hurricane warning* means hurricane conditions are expected within 24 hours.

If you live in or visit hurricane-prone areas, be sure to prepare an evacuation plan prior to hurricane watches or warnings.

If a hurricane watch or warning has been issued, bring in all outdoor items that could be blown by the wind. If a hurricane warning has been issued, listen to

Items Needed During Any Weather Emergency

- ▶ weather radio or other battery-powered radio or television
- ▶ battery-powered lights and flashlights
- ▶ candles and dry matches
- ▶ extra batteries
- ▶ gallon of water per person per day for at least 3 days
- ▶ first-aid kit
- ▶ medicines family members might need
- ▶ blankets and/or sleeping bags
- ▶ canned food and a manual can opener

the radio or television for evacuation instructions.

Close hurricane shutters or board windows from the outside with plywood. If you do not have to evacuate, stay indoors and away from windows.

Safety in Weather Disasters *continued*

What should you do in case of a blizzard?

A blizzard is a heavy snowstorm with high winds and dangerous wind chill. If you live in or visit an area prone to severe winter weather, be sure that each family member has a warm coat and hat, insulated gloves or mittens, and water-resistant boots. Add extra blankets to your weather emergency items (see list).

A *winter storm watch* means a winter storm is possible in your area. A *winter storm warning* (or *blizzard warning*) means that a winter storm (or blizzard) is headed for your area.

If a winter storm watch is issued, listen to the radio or television for updates, and note any change in weather conditions. If a winter storm warning is issued, stay indoors if possible, wear layers warm of clothing and cover your nose and mouth if you go outside, and avoid travel by car. If you do travel by car, keep emergency items in the trunk, tell someone when you are leaving and where you are going, and carry a cell phone to call for help should you get stuck.

What do you need to know about safety and floods?

Floods occur when water accumulates faster than the soil can absorb it or rivers can carry it away. If you live in a flood-prone area, add raingear to your weather emergency items (see list). During periods of heavy or prolonged rain, listen to the radio or television for flood information. A *flood watch* means a flood is possible.

A *flood warning* means flooding is already occurring or will occur soon.

If you live in or visit flood-prone areas, be sure to prepare an evacuation plan prior to flood watches or warnings. Check for flash flooding (sudden flooding) in your area. When a flood warning is issued, evacuate immediately. Move to higher ground. If your car stalls in rising water, abandon it and walk or climb to higher ground.

E X P R E S S /Lesson REVIEW

1. Make a list of at least seven things that you and your family should have ready in case of a weather-related emergency.

2. What should you do if you think that a tornado might be approaching?

3. **LIFE SKILL** **Using Community Resources** Find out how to get emergency weather information in your community.

4. For which types of weather-related emergencies should you have a pre-planned evacuation route and destination?

5. In general, what is the difference between a weather-related watch and a warning?

6. What is the best course of action to avoid being struck by lightning?

Recreational Safety

Recreational activities are meant to be fun, relaxing, and good exercise. However, many people are injured each year during these activities because they fail to follow a few safety precautions.

What should I know about safety and water sports?

Water sports include swimming, diving, and watercraft sports. To be safe while swimming, do the following:

▶ Always swim with a buddy.

▶ Do not swim in unknown waters or where "no swimming" or other swimming warning signs are posted.

▶ Do not swim outdoors when an electrical storm is approaching.

▶ Avoid swimming in frigid water; it could cause your body temperature to drop.

▶ Avoid running and horseplay near water. Slips and falls can cause serious injury.

▶ Never throw anyone into a pool or other body of water.

▶ Wear a life jacket and swim in shallow water if you are just learning to swim.

▶ Learn drownproofing, a survival floating technique.

▶ Do not swim while under the influence of alcohol or other drugs.

▶ Never dive into water that may be shallow or have concealed hazards, such as tree stumps or rocks.

Four Stages of Drownproofing

1 Don't panic. Relax while you float with your face in the water, and dangle your arms and legs freely.

2 After a few seconds, slowly raise your arms, separate your legs, raise your head so your mouth is out of the water, and exhale.

3 Slowly press your arms down, bring your legs together, and raise your head well out of the water. Take a big slow breath.

4 Slowly relax your body to the natural floating position.

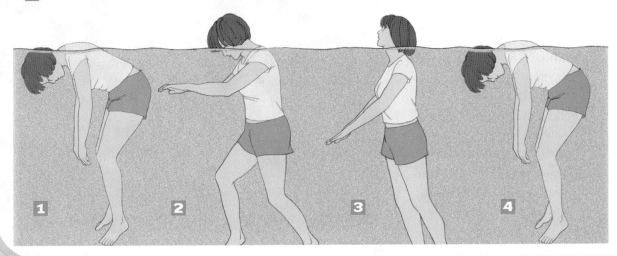

What should I know about diving into water?

There are certain things you need to consider before diving into water. To be safe while diving, dive only into water you are certain is deep enough and free of obstructions. In pools, the water must be a minimum of nine feet deep for a dive.

If you swim and dive in natural bodies of water, remember that water levels may change. Therefore, walk into the water first, and check water depth. Also check for hidden objects in the diving area. Do not dive in unfamiliar waters.

What should I know about operating personal watercraft?

Here are some general safety tips for persons operating watercraft, such as motorboats, personal watercraft, canoes, and kayaks.

▸ Make sure that the watercraft is working properly.

▸ Know how to navigate and operate your watercraft properly.

▸ Take an approved water safety or boating class before operating any watercraft.

▸ Have all safety equipment required by law on board and in working condition.

▸ Always wear a life jacket, and be sure that it fits properly.

▸ Tell a friend or relative where you will be.

▸ If you are in a motorized boat, maintain a safe speed at all times.

▸ Be alert for changing weather conditions, and head to shore if conditions look threatening.

▸ Always scan the waterway in the front and on the sides of you, giving a wide berth to other watercraft.

▸ Obey federal and state boating laws and laws applying to other types of watercraft.

▸ Never operate a watercraft while under the influence of alcohol or other drugs.

How can I keep myself safe when playing sports?

There are a few general safety tips to keep in mind to play any sport safely. Always make sure to warm up before and cool down after your activities. Warming up helps your muscles to extend easily, your joints to be more flexible, and your heart and breathing rates to increase gradually. Cooling down slows your heart rate, relaxes your muscles, and helps your body recover from the stress of the physical activity. Warming up and cooling down may reduce the likelihood of injuries.

Wearing the proper safety gear when doing any sport is essential.

Another general safety rule for sports activities is to wear the proper safety equipment. Many sports, such as biking, football, ice hockey, and skateboarding, require helmets. A helmet that fits well touches your head all around, is comfortably snug but not tight, and should not move more than an inch in any direction. Other types of safety equipment are specific to the sport, such as knee pads and elbow pads for skateboarding, riding scooters, and inline skating.

Containing a campfire is important to your safety as well as preserving the surroundings

What should I know about safety in the wilderness?

If you will be hiking or camping in the wilderness, it is essential to have proper training. Take an approved wilderness-survival and first-aid course to learn how to handle serious emergencies. Plan your trip carefully. Know the trail conditions and weather forecasts before you set out. Bring water with you but also know the water availability and quality where you will be.

Leave detailed plans of your trip with a responsible adult, including when you will return. Bring a cell phone, emergency numbers, and a weather radio with you, and carry a whistle and a small mirror for emergency use. Always have a map of

the area and a compass. Bring the proper camping equipment for the terrain and weather conditions. Wear sturdy hiking boots and appropriate hiking clothes along with sunscreen, insect repellent, sunglasses, and a hat. Additionally, carry extra food and water, a flashlight with extra batteries, a first-aid kit, a fire starter, and matches.

Learn to build, maintain, and extinguish campfires so that they do not pose a forest fire danger. Some tips include the following:

▶ Check that fires are permitted where you will be camping.

▶ Clear an area 3 feet wide of dead leaves and debris around the site of the fire.

▶ Do not build fires under overhanging tree branches.

▶ Find an area shielded from strong winds.

▶ Never leave the fire unattended.

▶ Never burn anything inside a tent.

▶ Extinguish a campfire with water or dirt.

▶ Before you leave the area, feel for heat from the fire. Be certain that it is out and completely cool.

internet connect

www.scilinks.org/health
Topic: Water Safety
HealthLinks code: HH4143

HEALTH LINKS® Maintained by the National Science Teachers Association

EXPRESS Lesson REVIEW

1. List the basic safety guidelines you should observe while playing sports.

2. What are some things that should cause you to cancel an activity involving a watercraft?

3. **LIFE SKILL** **Practicing Wellness** Choose your favorite recreational activity. Discuss things that can affect your safety doing this activity, such as the weather.

4. John and his family own a cottage at a lake. John likes to run the length of the pier and dive into the water as soon as they arrive. Why is this unsafe to do?

The 10 Skills for a Healthy Life

Some people have the skills needed for working with computers. Others have the skills for playing music or sports. There are also skills that are needed for leading a healthy life.

What is a healthy life?

A healthy life is a life where the components of health—physical, emotional, social, mental, spiritual and environmental—are in balance. Leading a healthy life requires some skills that are easily learned. The 10 skills for a healthy life are called life skills. **Life skills** are tools for building a healthy life. You will find these life skills throughout this textbook and be able to use them throughout your life. The life skills are identified by this icon:

LIFE SKILL

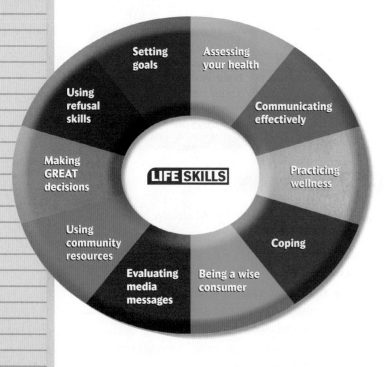

How does each of the 10 life skills help me to lead a healthy life?

LIFE SKILL **Assessing Your Health** This life skill requires that you evaluate the actions and behaviors that affect your health. Learning the things that have negative effects on your health and avoiding them is very important.

LIFE SKILL **Communicating Effectively** This life skill is important in dealing with family, friends, teachers, and anyone else you encounter throughout the day. Communicating effectively will help you to get your point across and avoid misunderstandings with others. You will also learn listening skills. Being able to listen to someone is as important as being able to express yourself.

LIFE SKILL **Practicing Wellness** This life skill will help you practice healthy behaviors, maintain good health, and avoid sickness. You can do this by doing such things as getting enough sleep, choosing nutritious foods, and avoiding risky behaviors.

LIFE SKILL **Coping** Coping means dealing with troubles or problems in an effective way. Things don't always go the way that we would like them to. Accepting this fact is important to your overall health. This life skill will help you deal with emotions such as anger and depression.

LIFE SKILL **Being a Wise Consumer** A consumer is a person who buys products or services, such as food, clothing, or CDs. A consumer also does things like get his or her car repaired. Being a wise consumer will allow you to buy health care products and services without paying too much money. It will help you decide what products are appropriate for you. It will also help you to determine if the claims an advertiser makes are true or false.

LIFE SKILL **Evaluating Media Messages** The media is all public forms of communication, such as TV, radio, movies, newspaper, and advertising.

Many times you are influenced by messages the media sends. This life skill will give you the tools to analyze media messages so you can make better judgments about the accuracy and validity of the message.

LIFE SKILL **Using Community Resources** A resource is something that can be used to take care of a need. Most communities offer a number of services that can help you maintain good health. This life skill will show you where to find these services and describe how they can keep you healthy.

LIFE SKILL **Making GREAT Decisions** Making decisions is something that you do every day. Making the right decisions can affect every aspect of your life. If you make the wrong decisions, the consequences can be tough. Use the Making GREAT Decisions model to help you make decisions and the STOP process to correct your mistakes.

LIFE SKILL **Using Refusal Skills** A refusal skill is a way you can decline to do something you don't want to do. Learning how to say no to others will help you make better decisions. Base your decisions on your values and on what is best for you— not necessarily what is more fun for you or for others.

LIFE SKILL **Setting Goals** A goal is something that you want to do or hope to achieve in the future. Setting goals helps you stay focused on the future. This life skill will show you how to set your long- and short-term goals.

 For more information about the ten skills for a healthy life, see Chapter 2.

Making GREAT Decisions

Should I study for my exam or hang out with friends? Should I get a tattoo? Am I willing to smoke if it makes me look cool?

MAKING GREAT DECISIONS

Give thought to the problem.

Review your choices.

Evaluate the consequences of each choice.

Assess and choose the best choice.

Think it over afterward.

What's so GREAT about decision making?

Every day teens are faced with some very difficult choices. Some of the decisions you make can affect you for the rest of your life. The Making GREAT Decisions model is a tool that you can use to help make these difficult decisions a little easier. Taking the time to consider your goals and values can assist you in making the decisions that are right for you.

So how does using this model work in the real world?

Imagine you were trying to decide whether you should study for your exam or go to the movies. Look at the table below to see how the Making GREAT Decisions model can guide you through this decision-making process.

GIVE thought to the problem. Stop to think about the situation before making any hasty decisions.

REVIEW your choices. In this case, your choices are to stay home and study or go to the movies.

EVALUATE the consequences of each choice. Staying at home and studying will help you to get a good grade. If you go to the movies and then do poorly on the exam, you may not be allowed to participate in sports and other extracurricular activities.

ASSESS and choose the best choice. Staying home to study will help your grade and keep you out of trouble. If you do poorly on the exam, you'll probably lose privileges

THINK it over afterward. If you decided to study, think about how not only did you improve your chances for a good grade, you can go see the movie later. If you decided to go to the movie, think about how important your grades are and how your decision will affect you down the road.

If I use the Making GREAT Decisions model, will I always make the right decision?

Even if you use the model when you are trying to make a decision, it is still possible (and completely normal!) that you will make a wrong decision.

Sometimes the results of making the wrong decision can be embarrassment or humiliation. Don't worry! The feeling of embarrassment will pass, and friends won't hold your mistake against you or think less of you.

Sometimes, however, making the wrong decision can have serious consequences. When this happens, you can use the **STOP, THINK, GO** process. This process has three simple steps and can be very helpful in turning around the damage caused by a wrong decision. The steps of the process are as follows:

1. **STOP** and admit that you made a wrong decision. Take responsibility for what you've done. Stop whatever it was you were doing that was undesirable. This will help minimize the damage from the wrong decision and will allow you to start taking control of the situation again.

2. **THINK** about with whom you can talk about the problem. Usually a parent, guardian, or other responsible adult can help you. Tell this trusted adult about your decision and what its consequences are. Discuss with them ways to correct the situation, and what the possible outcomes are.

3. **GO** and do your best to correct the situation. Sometimes just walking away is the best way to deal with a situation. It may prevent the problem from getting worse.

Sometimes the only way to correct a situation is to "tell on" someone. Many times the decisions that we make are influenced by the actions of other people. Other times, it may be that you need to apologize to someone that you have hurt. This can be difficult, but both you and the other person will feel better afterward.

 TOPIC link For more information about making GREAT decisions, see Chapter 2.

Using Refusal Skills

Have you ever heard any of the pressure lines below? Every now and then, you may feel pressured to do something that you don't want to do or that goes against your beliefs and values. When you need to stand up to someone, it helps if you already know what you're going to say.

"Don't be such a baby."

"Where's your sense of adventure?"

"It'll be our secret"

"I've done it a million times."

"Nothing bad ever happens the first time."

"Everyone is doing it."

How do I stand up to someone who is pressuring me?

Refusal skills are strategies a person can use to avoid doing something they do not want to do. Sometimes, certain strategies are more appropriate for certain situations. Sometimes, you might have to refuse in a couple of different ways for people to accept your answer.

Why do I need to practice using refusal skills?

Most people are a little uncomfortable saying no to their friends. Practicing refusal skills can help you know what to do if you are ever in a "real life" refusal situation. Practicing these skills in low-pressure situations increases the odds that you'll have the confidence to hold your ground when it really matters to you.

How can I resist pressure?

▶ Say no, and mean it. Keep saying no.

▶ Make up an excuse to leave the situation.

▶ Arrange a code beforehand with a parent or someone you trust that indicates that you need to be picked up to get out of a bad situation.

▶ Make a joke out of the situation, and change the subject.

▶ Practice responses like those in the table.

Some things crack under pressure. Will you?

If you hear this . . .	You can say this . . .
Do you always do what your parents tell you to?	Do you HAVE to do everything that everyone else does?
Come on, please? For me?	No! I'm thinking about ME because obviously YOU'RE not!
No one has to know.	I'll know, and that's one too many people for me.
You're just chicken.	It takes a lot more guts to hold out than to give in.
Don't you want to know what it's like?	Sorry guys, but I need to get going.
If you loved me, you'd let me.	If you loved me, you wouldn't ask.

What do I do if someone is pressuring me and won't stop?

The first thing you should do is seek help and advice from a trusted adult. See if the two of you can figure out why someone is so concerned with pressuring you. If the person pressuring you has been a friend in the past, you may need to stop hanging out with him or her. If the person is not a friend, you may need to take steps to try and avoid seeing this person.

How do I say no and still sound cool?

Here are 10 ways to insist that you do things your way:

1. **Blame someone else.** My parents would ground me for life. Besides, it's just not worth it.

2. **Give a reason.** No, my dad said he'll pay me if I stay home and help him.

3. **Ignore the request or the pressure.** Pretend you don't hear them and avoid talking about the issue.

4. **Leave the situation.** Sorry, guys, but I need to get going.

5. **Say no thanks.** No, thanks. I'm just not interested.

6. **Say no, and mean it.** No, I mean it! How many times do I have to say no?

7. **Keep saying no.** How many times do I have to tell you no? Forget it!

8. **Make a joke out of it.** Do you guys HAVE to do everything everyone else does?

9. **Make an excuse.** I can't tonight. I have football practice.

10. **Suggest something else to do.** Why don't we go get some pizza or something else instead?

11. **Change the subject.** So, anyway, what was Angela talking about today at lunch?

12. **Team up with someone.** Sarah and Marcia don't want to go either, so we're going to do something else. Do you want to come with us?

 TOPIC link For more information about practicing refusal skills, see Chapter 2.

10 Tips for Building Self-Esteem

How many times has there been something that you really wanted to do? Maybe you've wanted to try out for the track team or the band, but you just didn't feel like you had what it takes to make it. Feeling confident about yourself and your abilities is one important part of self-esteem.

What is self-esteem?

A very important part of your personality is your self-esteem. Self-esteem is a measure of how much you value, respect, and feel confident about yourself. The better you feel about yourself, the more self-confident you will feel and appear to others.

Where does self-esteem come from?

Self-esteem, as the name implies, comes from within a person. Others may help lift your self-esteem by giving compliments or by cheering you on, but you are the only one that will feel self-esteem's influence. You gain self-esteem by trying new things or by trying to improve the things that you already do.

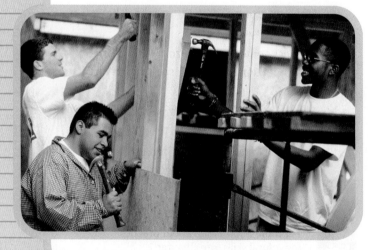

What are the benefits of high self-esteem?

People who have high self-esteem respect themselves and take better care of themselves. They are more likely to stick with their goals and try new things. People who have high self-esteem are also more likely to be valuable members of their family, school, and community.

How can I improve my self-esteem?

There are many ways that you can build your self-esteem.

1. **Make a list of your strengths and weaknesses.** Identify the things you are successful at and try to find time to do those things.

2. **Develop a support system of friends.** Choose friends who will support you and encourage you to do your best. Avoid people who put you down, even if they are joking.

3. **Practice positive self-talk.** Substitute positive thoughts like "I'll figure this out" for negative thoughts like "I'll never figure out how to do this."

4. **Practice good health habits.** A healthy diet, regular exercise, and good grooming habits will help you feel good about yourself. If you look bad, you'll probably feel bad.

5. **Avoid doing things just to "go along with the crowd."** Sometimes people with low self-esteem do things they normally wouldn't do, just to fit in. In the short run, this may work, but in the long run, you'll feel better about yourself when you do the things that support your values.

6. **Give credit where credit is due.** Reward yourself for doing something well. Treat yourself to a movie, a meal at a restaurant, or a new CD. You worked hard and deserve a treat.

7. **Set short-term goals that will strengthen your weaknesses.** Map out a plan to help you reach your goals. Even small improvements are better than not trying at all.

8. **Don't be afraid to try something new.** Sign up for the class you have always wanted to take. Take a swimming or dance lesson. You'll never know if you're good at something until you try it.

9. **Nothing puts things in perspective better than volunteering for those in need does.** Spend time working at a soup kitchen, deliver meals to those who can't leave their homes, or spend time visiting people at a nursing home. Your problems will probably seem less significant than those of the people you help. Helping others can also give you a sense of purpose.

10. **If you experience defeat, don't dwell on it.** Try to learn something positive from the experience and move on. Don't make the mistake of running it over and over again in your mind. Remember, "If at first you don't succeed, try, try again!"

 For more information about self-esteem, see Chapter 3.

Calorie and Nutrient Content in Selected Foods

This table is organized into 14 categories: beverages; breads and grains; cereals; condiments; crackers; dairy and eggs; desserts; fast foods; fruits; meat, fish, poultry, and eggs; mixed dishes; nuts and seeds; snack foods; and vegetables.

Food and serving size	Calories (kcal)	Calories from fat (kcal)	% Calories from fat (%)	Total fat (g)	Saturated fat (g)	Cholesterol (mg)	Total carbohydrate (g)	Dietary fiber (g)	Protein (g)	Calcium (mg)	Iron (mg)	Vitamin C (mg)	Vitamin A (µg RE)
BEVERAGES													
Carbonated beverage (soda)													
12 fl oz	184	0	0	0.0	0.0	0	38	0.0	0.0	13	0.0	0	0
24 fl oz with ice (approximate values)	221	0	0	0.0	0.0	0	57	0.0	0.0	16	0.5	0	0
32 fl oz with ice (approximate values)	295	0	0	0.0	0.0	0	76	0.0	0.0	25	0.6	0	0
diet, 12 fl oz	0	0	0	0.0	0.0	0	0	0.0	0.0	0	0.0	0	0
Fruit punch, 1 cup	117	0	0	0.0	0.0	0	30	0.3	0.0	20	0.5	4	0
Milk													
chocolate, 2%, 1 cup	179	45	25	5.0	3.1	17	26	1.2	8.0	285	0.6	2	143
lowfat, 1%, 1 cup	102	27	26	3.0	1.6	10	12	0.0	8.0	300	0.1	2	144
reduced fat, 2%, 1 cup	122	45	37	5.0	2.9	18	12	0.0	8.1	298	0.1	2	139
skim (fat free), 1 cup	91	0	0	0.0	0.0	4	12	0.0	8.0	301	0.1	2	149
whole, 1 cup	149	72	48	8.0	5.1	33	11	0.0	8.0	290	0.1	2	76
Milkshake, 12 fl oz	414	90	22	10.0	6.0	25	60	1.5	10.6	459	0.4	0	72
Orange Juice, 1 cup	105	0	0	0.0	0.0	0	25	0.5	2.0	20	1.1	147	43
Sports drink, 24 fl oz	150	0	0	0.0	0.0	0	42	0.0	0.0	0	0.0	0	0
Tea, unsweetened, 1 cup	2	0	0	0.0	0.0	0	1	0.0	0.0	8	0.0	0	0
Water, bottled, 12 fl oz	0	0	0	0.0	0.0	0	0	0.0	0.0	5	0.0	0	0
BREADS AND GRAINS													
Bagel, plain, 4 in. diameter	314	16	5	1.8	0.3	0	51	0.1	10.0	50	2.4	0	0
Biscuit, 1 medium	101	45	45	5.0	1.2	1	13	0.4	2.0	67	0.8	7	0
Bread													
white, 1 slice	76	9	12	1.0	0.4	1	14	0.6	2.0	24	0.8	0	0
whole wheat, 1 slice	86	9	10	1.0	0.3	0	16	2.4	3.0	25	1.2	0	0
Donut													
cake type, with chocolate frosting	211	117	55	13.0	3.5	26	21	0.9	2.0	22	0.7	0	10
cake type, plain	204	99	49	11.0	1.8	18	25	0.8	2.0	15	0.6	0	16
yeast, with glaze	242	126	52	14.0	3.5	12	27	0.7	4.0	20	1.6	0	16
French toast, plain, 1 slice	149	63	42	7.0	1.8	75	16	0.1	5.0	65	1.1	0	86
Fried rice, no meat, ½ cup	132	54	41	6.0	0.9	21	17	0.7	3.0	15	0.9	2	10
Muffin, blueberry	155	36	23	4.0	0.8	17	27	1.5	3.1	32	0.9	1	5
Pancake, 4 in. diameter	86	0	0	0.0	0.0	4	19	0.7	2.4	26	0.7	0	4
Pasta, noodles, ½ cup	99	0	0	0.0	0.1	0	20	1.2	3.0	5	1.0	0	0
Pita bread, wheat, 1 medium	165	9	5	1.0	0.1	0	33	1.3	5.0	52	1.6	0	0
Rice													
brown, ½ cup	110	9	8	1.0	0.2	0	23	1.8	2.0	11	0.7	0	0
white, enriched, ½ cup	133	0	0	0.0	0.1	0	29	0.3	2.0	3	1.5	0	0

Food and serving size	Calories (kcal)	Calories from fat (kcal)	% Calories from fat (%)	Total fat (g)	Saturated fat (g)	Cholesterol (mg)	Total carbohydrate (g)	Dietary fiber (g)	Protein (g)	Calcium (mg)	Iron (mg)	Vitamin C (mg)	Vitamin A (µg RE)
Roll													
dinner	141	31	22	3.4	0.8	0	24	1.0	3.0	1	1.0	0	0
hamburger/hot dog	123	20	16	2.2	0.5	0	22	1.3	3.0	56	1.3	0	0
Tortilla													
corn, plain, *6 in. diameter*	58	6	10	0.7	0.1	0	12	0.0	2.0	52	0.4	0	0
flour, *8 in. diameter*	104	20	20	2.3	0.6	0	18	1.7	3.0	71	1.9	0	0
Waffle, from frozen, plain	88	25	28	2.7	0.5	11	14	1.2	2.0	38	0.0	0	150

CEREALS

Food and serving size	Calories	Calories from fat	% Calories from fat	Total fat	Saturated fat	Cholesterol	Total carbohydrate	Dietary fiber	Protein	Calcium	Iron	Vitamin C	Vitamin A
Cereal													
cornflakes, not sweetened, *1 cup*	91	0	0	0.0	0.0	0	22	0.7	2.0	1	7.8	12	188
cornflakes, presweetened, *1 cup*	146	0	0	0.0	0.1	0	34	0.8	1.0	1	5.5	18	274
Oatmeal													
flavored instant, *½ cup*	125	9	7	1.0	0.3	0	26	2.5	3.0	104	3.9	0	305
plain, *½ cup*	72	9	13	1.0	0.2	0	13	2.0	3.0	0	0.8	0	2

CONDIMENTS

Food and serving size	Calories	Calories from fat	% Calories from fat	Total fat	Saturated fat	Cholesterol	Total carbohydrate	Dietary fiber	Protein	Calcium	Iron	Vitamin C	Vitamin A
Butter, *1 tsp*	36	33	93	3.7	2.4	10	0	0.0	0.0	1	0.0	0	33
Honey, *1 Tbsp*	64	0	0	0.0	0.0	0	18	0.0	0.0	1	0.1	0	0
Ketchup, *1 Tbsp*	16	0	3	0.1	0.0	0	4	0.2	0.2	3	0.1	2	15
Margarine, stick or tub, *1 tsp*	34	34	101	3.8	0.7	0	0	0.0	0.0	1	0.0	0	50
Mayonnaise, regular, *1 Tbsp*	57	44	77	4.9	0.7	4	4	0.0	0.1	2	0.0	0	32
Salad dressing, Italian, *1 Tbsp*	69	64	93	7.1	1.0	10	1	0.0	0.1	1	0.0	0	11
Salsa, *1 Tbsp*	4	0	8	0.0	0.0	0	1	0.3	0.2	5	0.2	2	22
Spaghetti sauce, *½ cup*	136	36	26	4.0	1.5	0	21	4.0	2.2	35	1.4	13	96
Sugar, white, *1 tsp*	16	0	0	0.0	0.0	0	4	0.0	0.0	0	0.0	0	0
Syrup													
chocolate, *2 Tbsp*	50	1	3	0.1	0.1	0	12	0.7	0.6	4	0.0	0	0
pancake, *1 Tbsp*	25	0	0	0.0	0.0	0	7	0.0	0.0	0	0.0	0	0

CRACKERS

Food and serving size	Calories	Calories from fat	% Calories from fat	Total fat	Saturated fat	Cholesterol	Total carbohydrate	Dietary fiber	Protein	Calcium	Iron	Vitamin C	Vitamin A
Crackers													
cheese with peanut butter, *6*	210	90	43	10.0	2.5	0	23	1.0	5.0	80	0.9	0	0
graham, *4 crackers*	59	2	3	0.2	0.0	1	11	0.5	1.0	11	0.6	0	0
soda crackers, *5 squares*	70	18	26	2.0	0.0	0	12	0.6	1.0	18	0.7	0	4
Matzo, *1 matzo cracker*	111	1	1	0.2	0.0	0	22	0.8	3.5	11	0.8	0	0

DAIRY AND EGGS

Food and serving size	Calories	Calories from fat	% Calories from fat	Total fat	Saturated fat	Cholesterol	Total carbohydrate	Dietary fiber	Protein	Calcium	Iron	Vitamin C	Vitamin A
Cheese													
American, prepackaged, *1 slice*	70	45	64	5.0	2.0	15	2	0.0	4.0	100	0.0	0	46
cheddar, *1 oz*	114	81	71	9.0	6.0	30	0	0.0	7.1	204	0.2	0	78
cottage, lowfat, *½ cup*	102	12	12	1.4	0.9	2	4	0.0	7.0	78	0.2	0	82
cream, *1 Tbsp*	51	45	89	5.0	3.2	32	0	0.0	1.1	12	0.2	0	55
cream, fat free, *1 Tbsp*	13	1	8	0.1	0.0	0	1	0.0	2.0	26	0.0	0	130
string, *1 stick*	72	45	63	5.0	2.9	16	1	0.0	7.0	183	0.1	0	50
Egg, boiled, *1 large*	78	48	61	5.3	1.0	212	0	0.0	6.0	25	0.6	0	84
Egg, scrambled, plain, *¼ cup*	74	45	61	5.0	1.0	212	0	0.0	6.0	25	0.6	0	84
Frozen yogurt													
cone, chocolate, *1 single*	157	63	40	7.0	3.9	1	22	1.1	4.0	115	0.6	1	42
nonfat, chocolate, *½ cup*	104	9	9	1.0	0.5	1	21	1.5	5.0	163	0.9	1	2
Whipped cream, *2 Tbsp*	15	14	90	1.5	1.0	4	1	0.0	0.0	0	0.0	0	0
Yogurt, lowfat, fruit flavored, *1 cup*	231	27	12	3.0	2.0	12	47	0.0	12.0	372	0.2	1	27

Food and serving size	Calories (kcal)	Calories from fat (kcal)	% Calories from fat (%)	Total fat (g)	Saturated fat (g)	Cholesterol (mg)	Total carbohydrate (g)	Dietary fiber (g)	Protein (g)	Calcium (mg)	Iron (mg)	Vitamin C (mg)	Vitamin A (µg RE)
DESSERTS													
Brownie, *1 square*	227	90	40	10.0	2.0	14	30	1.4	1.5	11	0.9	0	6
Cake, chocolate with chocolate frosting, *1 piece*	411	153	37	17.0	5.0	45	61	3.1	4.6	48	2.5	0	25
Candy, candy-coated chocolate, *10 pieces*	34	9	26	1.0	0.9	0	5	0.2	0.0	1	0.1	0	4
with peanuts, *10 pieces*	103	45	44	5.0	2.1	1	12	0.7	2.0	20	0.2	0	5
Candy, chocolate bar, *1.3 oz*	226	126	56	14.0	8.1	10	26	1.5	3.0	84	0.6	0	24
Cheesecake, *1 piece*	660	414	63	46.0	28.0	220	52	0.2	11.0	106	2.0	1	520
Cinnamon roll with nuts and raisins, *2 oz*	217	63	29	7.0	1.4	8	34	1.1	3.2	36	1.6	0	60
Cookies													
chocolate chip, *1 cookie*	59	23	38	2.5	0.8	3	8	0.2	0.6	3	0.3	0	7
oatmeal, *1 cookie*	113	27	24	3.0	0.8	9	20	0.3	1.0	10	1.3	0	1
sugar, *1 cookie*	72	27	38	3.0	0.8	7	10	0.1	0.8	3	0.3	0	4
Fruit juice bar, *1 bar*	63	0	0	0.0	0.0	0	16	0.0	0.9	4	0.1	7	22
Gelatin dessert, flavored, *½ cup*	80	0	0	0.0	0.0	0	19	0.0	2.0	0	0.0	0	0
Ice cream bar, vanilla with chocolate coating, *1 bar*	171	99	58	11.0	6.4	1	17	0.3	2.0	136	0.4	25	0
Ice cream cone, one scoop regular ice cream, *1 single*	178	72	40	8.0	4.9	32	22	0.1	3.0	102	0.2	0	84
Ice cream, chocolate, *½ cup*	143	40	28	4.5	22.4	7	19	0.8	2.5	72	0.6	0	275
Ice slushy, *1 cup*	151	0	0	0.0	0.0	0	63	0.0	1.0	4	0.3	2	0
Pie, apple, double crust, *1 piece*	411	162	39	18.0	4.0	19	58	0.0	3.7	11	1.7	3	9
Pudding, chocolate, *½ cup*	160	27	17	3.0	1.8	5	27	1.2	3.2	153	0.6	2	43
FAST FOODS													
Burrito, beef and bean	520	207	40	23.0	10.0	150	55	11.0	24.0	150	2.7	5	600
Cheeseburger ¼ *lb*, on bun, with lettuce, tomato, mustard, ketchup, and pickles	520	261	50	29.0	12.6	97	37	1.7	28.0	127	4.3	2	33
regular size mustard, ketchup, onions, pickles	319	117	37	13.0	5.6	42	36	1.9	15.0	144	2.7	2	64
Chicken nuggets, *4*	198	108	55	12.0	2.5	42	10	0.0	12.0	9	0.6	1	0
Chicken sandwich													
breaded chicken breast on bun, with lettuce, tomato, and mayonnaise	492	261	53	29.0	5.5	52	42	1.7	17.0	129	2.5	1	29
grilled chicken breast, on bun, with lettuce, tomato, and mayonnaise	361	63	17	7.0	2.0	54	44	2.6	27.0	132	2.5	4	19
French fries													
1 small order	199	90	45	10.0	2.0	0	26	2.0	2.0	10	0.4	10	1
1 large order	430	198	46	22.0	5.0	0	56	5.0	5.0	23	0.9	20	2
1 extra-large order	545	234	43	26.0	6.0	0	67	6.0	6.0	27	1.0	25	2
Hamburger, regular size, on bun, with mustard, ketchup, and pickles	266	81	30	9.0	3.2	28	36	1.9	12.0	126	2.7	2	23
double meat, double bun, cheese, sauce, lettuce, and tomatoes	510	234	46	26.0	9.3	76	46	3.3	25.0	202	4.3	3	66

Food and serving size	Calories (kcal)	Calories from fat (kcal)	% Calories from fat (%)	Total fat (g)	Saturated fat (g)	Cholesterol (mg)	Total carbohydrate (g)	Dietary fiber (g)	Protein (g)	Calcium (mg)	Iron (mg)	Vitamin C (mg)	Vitamin A (µg RE)
Sub sandwich													
Italian, *6 in. long*	467	216	46	24.0	9.0	57	38	3.0	20.0	40	4.0	15	169
vegetarian, *6 in. long*	222	27	12	3.0	0.0	0	38	3.0	9.0	25	3.0	15	120
Taco													
crispy, with ground beef, cheese, lettuce, and tomato	180	90	50	10.0	4.0	25	12	3.0	9.0	80	1.1	0	100
soft, with beans and rice and no cheese	218	27	12	3.0	0.0	0	19	3.0	7.0	60	0.8	1	60
soft, with chicken, cheese, lettuce, and tomato	212	63	30	7.0	2.6	37	22	2.1	15.0	85	0.8	1	64

FRUITS

Food and serving size	Calories (kcal)	Calories from fat (kcal)	% Calories from fat (%)	Total fat (g)	Saturated fat (g)	Cholesterol (mg)	Total carbohydrate (g)	Dietary fiber (g)	Protein (g)	Calcium (mg)	Iron (mg)	Vitamin C (mg)	Vitamin A (µg RE)
Apple, raw, with skin, *1 medium*	81	1	1	0.1	0.1	0	21	3.5	0.2	9	0.2	8	7
Applesauce, unsweetened, *½ cup*	52	0	1	0.0	0.0	0	14	1.5	0.2	5	0.4	2	14
Banana, fresh, *1 medium*	114	9	8	1.0	0.2	0	27	2.7	1.0	7	0.4	10	9
Blueberries, *½ cup*	41	0	1	0.0	0.0	0	10	2.0	0.5	4	0.1	10	7
Cantaloupe, *¼ medium*	44	1	2	0.1	0.0	0	10	1.0	1.1	14	0.3	53	403
Cherries, sweet, fresh, *1 cup*	84	2	3	0.3	0.0	1	19	2.7	1.4	18	0.5	8	25
Grapes, *½ cup*	62	1	2	0.1	0.0	0	16	0.9	0.6	13	0.3	4	9
Mango, *½ medium*	68	1	1	0.1	0.0	0	18	1.9	0.5	1	0.0	23	321
Olive, ripe, *1 large*	5	9	178	1.0	0.1	0	1	0.2	0.0	4	0.1	0	1
Orange, fresh, *1 large*	85	0	0	0.0	0.0	0	21	4.3	1.7	52	0.1	70	28
Peach, fresh, *1 medium*	37	0	0	0.0	0.0	0	9	1.7	1.0	4	0.1	6	42
Pineapple chunks, canned in juice, *½ cup*	84	0	0	0.0	0.0	0	22	1.1	0.6	20	0.4	13	18
Plum, fresh, *1*	36	0	1	0.0	0.0	0	9	1.0	0.5	3	0.1	6	21
Raisins, seedless, dry, *1 cup*	495	2	0	0.2	0.0	1	131	6.6	5.3	81	3.4	6	1
Strawberries, fresh, *1 cup*	46	0	1	0.0	0.0	1	11	3.5	0.9	21	0.6	86	41
Watermelon, *½ cup*	26	0	0	0.0	0.0	0	6	0.4	0.0	6	0.1	8	30

MEAT, FISH, POULTRY, AND EGGS

Food and serving size	Calories (kcal)	Calories from fat (kcal)	% Calories from fat (%)	Total fat (g)	Saturated fat (g)	Cholesterol (mg)	Total carbohydrate (g)	Dietary fiber (g)	Protein (g)	Calcium (mg)	Iron (mg)	Vitamin C (mg)	Vitamin A (µg RE)
Bacon, *3 slices*	109	81	74	9.0	3.3	16	0	0.0	6.0	2	0.3	0	0
Beef jerky, *1 piece*	81	46	56	5.1	2.1	10	2	0.4	6.6	4	1.1	0	0
Bologna, beef and pork, *1 slice*	73	58	80	6.5	2.5	13	1	0.0	2.7	3	0.3	0	0
Chicken breast													
fried with skin, *1 split breast*	364	166	46	18.5	4.9	119	13	0.4	34.8	28	1.8	0	17
grilled and skinless, *1 split breast*	142	27	19	3.0	0.9	44	73	0.0	27.0	13	0.9	0	5
Chicken drumstick, fried, *meat and skin of 1 drumstick*	193	102	53	11.3	3.0	62	6	0.2	15.8	12	1.0	0	19
Chicken strips, breaded white meat, no skin, *2 strips, 3 in. × 1 in.*	218	54	25	6.0	1.7	102	0	0.0	37.0	18	1.3	0	33
Chicken wing, fried, *meat and skin of 1 wing*	159	96	61	10.7	2.9	39	5	0.1	9.7	10	0.6	0	12
Chorizo, *1 link*	273	207	76	23.0	8.6	53	1	0.0	14.5	5	1.0	0	0
Corndog, chicken	272	117	43	13.0	3.0	65	26	0.0	13.0	90	2.0	0	30
Ham, lunchmeat, *2 ounces*	70	27	39	3.0	1.0	30	1	0.0	10.0	0	0.7	0	0
Hot dog													
regular, *no bun*	220	153	70	17.0	6.0	50	5	0.0	6.0	0	0.7	0	0
low fat, *no bun*	70	23	32	2.5	1.0	2	7	0.0	6.0	0	0.7	2	0

REFERENCE Guide

Calorie and Nutrient Content in Selected Foods (continued)

Food and serving size	Calories (kcal)	Calories from fat (kcal)	% Calories from fat (%)	Total fat (g)	Saturated fat (g)	Cholesterol (mg)	Total carbohydrate (g)	Dietary fiber (g)	Protein (g)	Calcium (mg)	Iron (mg)	Vitamin C (mg)	Vitamin A (µg RE)
MEAT, FISH, POULTRY, AND EGGS (continued)													
Pork chop, 3 oz	300	216	72	24.0	9.7	72	0	0.0	19.7	9	2.0	0	0
Ribs, pork, 3 oz	315	306	97	34.0	12.6	100	0	0.0	20.6	38	1.2	1	2
Roast beef, 3 oz	179	58	33	6.5	2.3	86	0	0.0	28.1	8	3.2	0	0
Sausage, breakfast, pork, 1 link or patty	70	57	81	6.3	2.3	15	1	0.0	2.3	40	0.4	0	0
Shrimp, breaded and fried, 4 large	73	32	43	3.5	0.6	4	3	0.1	6.4	20	0.4	0	57
Steak, beef, broiled, 6 oz	344	126	37	14.0	5.2	152	0	0.0	52.0	18	5.8	0	0
Tuna													
canned in oil, 3 oz	158	62	39	6.9	1.4	26	0	0.0	22.6	3	0.6	0	18
canned in water, 3 oz	109	23	21	2.5	0.7	36	0	0.0	20.1	12	0.8	0	16
Turkey													
lunch meat, 2 oz	83	36	43	4.0	1.2	24	0	0.0	11.0	23	0.7	0	0
roasted, 3 oz	145	38	26	4.2	1.4	65	0	0.0	24.9	21	1.5	0	0
Vegetable burger	70	9	13	1.0	0.5	0	7	3.0	10.0	80	1.8	1	16
MIXED DISHES													
Chicken chow mein, crispy noodles, 1 cup	155	36	23	4.0	0.5	8	24	2.4	7.0	47	1.7	12	29
Chicken noodle soup, canned, 1 cup	60	18	30	2.0	0.5	10	8	0.0	3.0	0	0.4	0	32
Chili with meat and beans, 1 cup	286	126	44	14.0	6.0	43	30	11.2	15.0	120	8.8	4	87
Couscous, ½ cup	100	11	11	1.2	0.0	0	21	1.2	3.0	0	0.2	0	0
Egg roll, shrimp, 3 in. long	190	54	28	6.0	1.0	10	29	3.0	5.0	20	0.4	4	20
Fajita, flour tortilla, chicken and vegetables, 1 cup	418	126	30	14.0	3.0	66	42	3.0	30.0	104	3.0	30	50
Falafel, 1 patty	67	27	40	3.0	0.5	10	7	1.0	2.3	9	0.6	0	5
Lasagna, with meat, 1 cup	382	135	35	15.0	7.8	56	39	3.3	22.0	258	3.2	16	158
Macaroni and cheese, packaged, 1 cup	410	164	40	18.2	4.6	9	47	1.0	11.0	100	2.7	0	120
Pizza													
frozen, with pepperoni, regular crust, ⅓ of 12 in. pizza	440	252	57	28.0	8.0	15	33	1.0	15.0	250	2.7	12	120
restaurant, thick crust, with vegetables, 2 slices	360	90	25	10.0	4.6	19	52	3.0	15.0	286	4.4	13	99
restaurant, hand tossed, pepperoni, 2 slices	452	135	30	15.0	7.6	46	55	3.8	23.0	192	3.0	12	177
Quesadilla	199	90	45	10.0	3.6	14	21	1.2	6.0	123	0.7	3	55
Spaghetti and meatballs, 1 cup	258	90	35	10.0	2.2	22	28	5.8	12.0	52	3.2	5	100
Tuna salad, ½ cup	192	81	42	9.0	1.6	13	10	0.0	16.0	17	1.0	2	28
NUTS AND SEEDS													
Mixed nuts, roasted and salted, ¼ cup	219	180	82	20.0	3.1	0	8	3.2	6.0	38	1.1	0	1
Peanut butter, 2 Tbsp	190	144	76	16.0	3.0	0	7	2.0	8.0	12	0.7	0	0

Food and serving size	Calories (kcal)	Calories from fat (kcal)	% Calories from fat (%)	Total fat (g)	Saturated fat (g)	Cholesterol (mg)	Total carbohydrate (g)	Dietary fiber (g)	Protein (g)	Calcium (mg)	Iron (mg)	Vitamin C (mg)	Vitamin A (µg RE)
Peanuts, dry roasted, salted, ¼ cup	207	153	74	17.0	2.3	0	7	3.2	9.0	31	0.6	0	0
Sunflower seeds, ¼ cup	208	171	82	19.0	2.0	13	5	2.3	7.0	19	2.3	0	2
SNACK FOODS													
Cheese puffs, 1 oz (½ cup)	160	90	56	10.0	2.5	0	15	1.0	2.0	0	0.4	0	3
Granola bar, plain	134	51	38	5.6	0.7	0	18	1.5	2.9	17	0.8	0	43
chocolate coated	132	64	48	7.1	4.0	1	18	1.0	1.6	29	0.7	0	11
Nachos, 1 cup	330	162	49	18.0	5.9	22	33	6.6	10.0	110	2.0	3	73
Popcorn, microwave, butter, ⅓ bag	170	108	64	12.0	2.5	0	26	3.0	2.0	20	0.7	0	10
Potato chips, 1 oz (15 chips)	150	90	60	10.0	3.0	0	10	1.0	1.0	0	0.0	6	0
Pretzels, 10 twist	229	19	8	2.1	0.5	0	48	1.9	5.5	22	2.6	0	0
Tortilla chips, plain, 1 oz	140	66	47	7.3	1.4	0	18	1.8	2.0	43	0.4	0	55
Trail mix with chocolate chips and nuts, ¼ cup	169	100	59	11.2	2.1	1	16	0.0	5.0	38	1.2	0	15
VEGETABLES													
Asparagus, cooked, 4 spears	14	0	0	0.0	0.0	0	3	1.0	1.6	12	0.4	15	49
Beans													
baked, with pork, ½ cup	134	18	13	2.0	0.8	9	25	7.0	7.0	67	2.1	3	23
green, cooked, 1 cup	44	3	7	0.4	0.0	0	10	4.0	2.4	58	1.6	12	84
refried, canned, ½ cup	127	9	7	1.0	0.1	0	23	9.3	8.0	65	2.5	0	0
Broccoli, cooked, 1 cup	27	0	0	0.0	0.0	0	5	2.8	3.0	47	0.5	37	174
Carrot, raw	28	1	4	0.1	0.0	0	7	1.9	0.7	17	0.6	6	1800
Celery, raw, 4 small stalks	10	1	8	0.1	0.0	0	2	1.0	0.5	24	0.2	4	8
Cole-slaw, ½ cup	41	14	34	1.6	0.0	5	7	0.9	0.8	27	0.4	20	38
Collards, cooked, 1 cup	49	6	12	0.7	0.0	0	9	5.3	4.0	226	0.9	35	595
Corn, cooked, 1 ear	83	9	11	1.0	0.0	0	19	2.1	2.6	2	0.5	5	16
Cucumber, raw with peel, ⅛ cup	25	1	5	0.1	0.0	0	6	0.4	0.6	1	0.1	2	3
French fried potatoes, homemade, 20 each	257	117	46	13.0	2.0	0	28	3.0	3.0	11	0.5	0	1
Hummus, ¼ cup	106	47	44	5.2	0.0	0	13	3.2	3.0	31	1.0	5	16
Mixed vegetables, cooked, ½ cup	53	1	2	0.1	0.0	0	12	4.0	2.6	23	0.7	3	389
Mushrooms, raw, slices, ¼ cup	5	1	12	0.1	0.0	0	1	0.2	0.5	1	0.2	1	0
Onions, raw, sliced, ¼ cup	11	0	4	0.0	0.0	0	3	0.5	0.3	17	0.3	3	3
Pepper, chili, raw	18	1	5	0.1	0.0	0	4	0.7	0.9	8	0.5	109	43
Pepper, green, raw, 1 medium	12	1	6	0.1	0.0	0	3	0.8	1.0	4	0.2	40	40
Potato salad with mayo, 1 cup	358	185	52	20.5	1.0	170	28	3.3	6.7	48	1.6	24	82
Potatoes													
baked with skin, ½ cup	66	1	1	0.1	0.0	0	15	1.5	1.4	6	0.8	8	0
hash browns, 1 cup	326	162	50	18.0	7.0	0	33	3.1	3.8	24	2.6	9	0
mashed with whole milk and butter, 1 cup	223	80	36	8.9	6.0	4	35	4.2	3.9	55	0.5	20	44
Salad, mixed green, no dressing, 1 cup	10	9	90	1.0	0.0	0	2	1.0	0.0	15	0.4	4	75
Spinach, fresh, 1 cup	7	1	14	0.1	0.0	0	1	0.8	0.9	30	0.8	8	360
Tofu, ½ cup	97	51	52	5.6	0.8	0	4	0.5	10.1	204	1.8	1	0
Tomatoes, raw, 1 cup	31	4	14	0.5	0.0	0	7	1.6	1.3	7	0.7	28	93

Medical and Dental Careers

Medical workers provide different types of care to improve a person's health. Many medical workers diagnose illnesses and injuries and provide specialized treatment. Others operate highly specialized medical equipment or work in laboratories.

Physician

What Physicians Do

Physicians perform medical examinations, diagnose, and treat patients who have illnesses and injuries. They help people understand how to prevent disease. Physicians are also known as medical doctors (MDs) and they are licensed to perform surgery and prescribe medications. General practitioners or family doctors treat patients for a variety of illnesses. Other doctors choose an area of specialization, such as obstetrics and gynecology, dermatology, and neurological surgery.

Where Physicians Work

Some physicians have their own private practice. Others are employed at hospitals, research facilities, and different specialty clinics.

What Is Required to Become a Physician

▶ a bachelor's degree
▶ 4 years of medical school
▶ 3- to 5-year residency to specialize and be certified

Registered Nurse

What Registered Nurses Do

Registered nurses (RNs) interpret and respond to a patient's symptoms, reactions, and progress. They teach patients and families about proper healthcare, assist in patient rehabilitation, and provide emotional support to promote recovery. RNs use a broad knowledge base to administer treatments and make decisions about patient care. RNs may be responsible for supervising aides, assistants, and LPNs. Often nurses choose to work in specialized areas such as obstetrics (childbirth) or public health.

Where Registered Nurses Work

Registered nurses are employed in places such as hospitals, public health departments, nursing homes, and public schools.

What Is Required to Become a Registered Nurse

▶ associate's degree or bachelor's degree
▶ individual state licensing

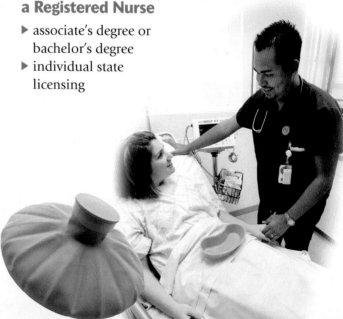

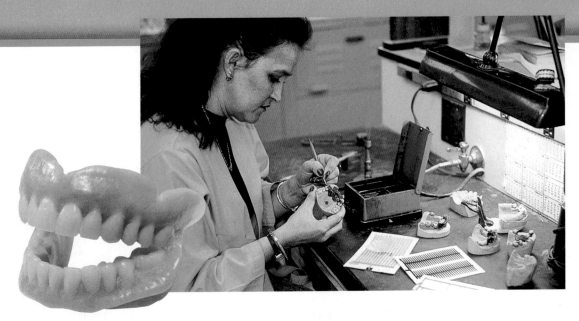

Emergency Medical Technician (EMT)

What Emergency Medical Technicians Do

Emergency medical technician (EMT) is a broad term used to address emergency medical staff. These technicians respond to healthcare crises. They drive ambulances, give emergency medical care, and, if necessary, transport patients to hospitals. EMTs respond to emergencies such as heart attacks, unexpected childbirth, car accidents, and fires. They explain the situation to local hospital staff. Under the direction of a physician, EMTs are told how to proceed with medical care. They perform CPR (cardiopulmonary resuscitation), control bleeding, place splints on broken bones, and check pulse and respiration. Paramedics receive additional training and therefore may be given more responsibilities.

Where Emergency Medical Technicians Work

Emergency medical technicians work in hospitals, for fire departments, or in an ambulance if they have more advanced training.

What Is Required to Become an Emergency Medical Technician

▶ training appropriate to duties
▶ basic classes for certification
▶ numerous college courses, depending upon career goal

Dental Laboratory Technician

What Dental Laboratory Technicians Do

Dental laboratory technicians construct and repair dentures, crowns, and other dental appliances for missing, damaged, or poorly positioned teeth. They follow a dentist's prescription to make plaster models of the patients' jaws and teeth. The technicians then use acrylic, molding equipment, and porcelain to create an exact copy of the teeth.

Where Dental Laboratory Technicians Work

Some dental laboratory technicians work in dentists' offices. Other technicians work for hospitals, including U.S. Department of Veterans Affairs' hospitals. Still other technicians work in laboratories or within their own homes.

What Is Required to Become a Dental Laboratory Technician

▶ a high school diploma
▶ 3 to 4 years as an apprentice or 2 years of college in an associate's degree or certification program

Healthcare Administration

Hospitals and other healthcare facilities must employ administrators to coordinate the activities of all employees—both medical and nonmedical—so that patients receive the best possible care. Healthcare administrators range from housekeepers and computer specialists to hospital directors.

Medical Transcriptionist

What Medical Transcriptionists Do

A medical transcriptionist listens to an audio-recorded summary of a patient's condition and treatment. The transcriptionist types the information and then places the information in the patient's permanent record. This typed information provides a clear, concise, written record, which must contain correct spelling, grammar, and punctuation. Transcriptionists use computers and word processors to complete many medical documents, which include medical histories, physicals, consultations, and operative reports. They record procedures and treatments for the medical record and for the medical staff's reference.

Where Medical Transcriptionists Work

Medical transcriptionists are employed by clinics, hospitals, insurance companies, physicians' offices, and private transcription companies, or they may be self-employed.

What Is Required to Become a Medical Transcriptionist

- high school diploma or equivalent
- classroom and clinical experience (from 9 months for a certificate to 2 years for an associate's degree)
- pass certification exam of the American Association of Medical Transcriptionists to become a certified medical transcriptionist (CMT)

Medical Coder

What Medical Coders Do

A medical coding professional uses a classification system to assign code numbers and letters to each symptom, diagnosis, disease, procedure, and operation that appears in a patient's chart. These codes are used for insurance reimbursement, for research, for health planning analysis, and to make clinical decisions. A high degree of accuracy and a working knowledge of medical terminology, anatomy, and physiology are important skills for these professionals to have.

Where Medical Coders Work

Medical coders are employed by hospitals, insurance companies, doctors' offices, and health maintenance organizations (HMOs).

What Is Required to Become a Medical Coder

- high school diploma or equivalent
- associate's degree or a 24- to 36-month home study course through the American Health Information Management Association
- certification by the American Health Information Management Association to work in certain states

Medical Claims Examiner

What Medical Claims Examiners Do

Medical claims examiners review charges on health-related claims to see if the costs are reasonable based on the diagnosis. If a medical claims examiner feels that an error has been made on an insurance claim, he or she will try to work out the problem before the insurance company will pay the claim. Examiners will then either authorize the appropriate payment or refer the claim to an investigator for a more thorough review.

Where Medical Claims Examiners Work

Medical claims examiners work for insurance companies.

What Is Required to Become a Medical Claims Examiner

▶ a bachelor's degree (no specific course of study is required, but business or accounting courses may be useful)
▶ a general understanding of medical terminology and procedures

Systems Analyst

What Systems Analysts Do

Systems analysts solve computer problems and enable computer technology to meet the individual needs of an organization, including health care agencies. They help an organization realize the maximum benefit from its investment in equipment and personnel. Systems analysts also work on making the computer systems within an organization compatible so that information can be shared. This process may include planning and developing new computer systems or devising ways to apply existing systems' resources to additional operations. Systems analysts may design new systems, including both hardware and software, or add a new software application to harness more of the computer's power.

Where Systems Analysts Work

Most systems analysts work with a specific type of system such as business, accounting, financial, scientific, or engineering systems that varies with the type of organization they work for. Systems analysts who have a general knowledge of healthcare facilities and the functions the facilities perform usually find jobs in hospitals, insurance agencies, and health maintenance organizations.

What Is Required to Become a Systems Analyst

▶ a bachelor's degree in computer science, information science, or management information systems (MIS)
▶ other qualifications that vary with area of service

Health Education

There are many types of healthcare professionals who specialize in educating people about how to improve their overall physical and mental health. Education is part of almost any healthcare worker's job.

Community Health Educator

What Community Health Educators Do

Community health educators try to improve the general health of the community by informing people about important topics such as pollution, disease, drug abuse, nutrition, safety, and stress management. Community health educators try to teach people how to avoid contracting diseases and how to manage the disease when it is contracted. These educators lead presentations and write educational brochures and reports to teach people about health and disease and ways to meet specific health needs.

Where Community Health Educators Work

Community health educators usually work for local or state governments or for private organizations.

What Is Required to Become a Community Health Educator

▶ training appropriate to duties
▶ usually a bachelor's degree or a master's degree focusing on public health or education

Mental Health Counselor

What Mental Health Counselors Do

Mental health counselors help people and their families cope with emotional and mental trauma. In individual or group counseling sessions, these counselors help patients learn how to manage problems with family, depression, stress, addiction, substance abuse and more. The counselors work closely with other health professionals to recommend treatments and assistance programs to patients. Mental health counselors are often referred to as therapists, psychologists, and analysts. Many mental health counselors specialize in areas of counseling such as family and parent-child relationships, domestic violence, or chemical dependency.

Where Mental Health Counselors Work

Some places where mental health counselors may work are private practices, clinics, and mental hospitals.

What Is Required to Become a Mental Health Counselor

▶ a bachelor's degree
▶ at least 2 years postgraduate study to achieve a master's degree or 3 to 5 years to achieve a doctoral degree (Ph.D)

Dietitian

What Dietitians Do

Dietitians help people learn about and follow healthy eating habits. These professionals often create personalized diets for patients according to the person's health status and nutritional needs. Dietitians may also oversee a hospital or health clinic's food preparation service. Dietitians help to prepare and inspect food and help clients improve or create a personalized healthy eating plan. For example, a dietitian may work in a clinic or hospital teaching patients who have diabetes or high blood pressure about which types of food they should eat or try to avoid.

Where Dietitians Work

Dietitians work at places such as hospitals, health clinics, schools, public health agencies, or businesses, such as a food service management company.

What Is Required to Become a Dietitian

▶ a bachelor's degree in dietetics or nutrition (the program must be approved by the American Dietetic Association)
▶ a master's degree or doctoral degree, depending on career goals

Health Writer and Editor

What Health Writers and Editors Do

Health writers and editors research, write, and communicate health information. They contribute articles and other forms of writing to health-related publications such as hospital newsletters and medical journals. Health editors and writers also work writing and editing for health sites on the Internet. They may write about a specific health topic such as cancer or health insurance issues, or they may write about many different topics. They will often write for a specific audience (such as medical doctors). Therefore, they know how to use the same medical terminology and language used by doctors.

Where Health Writers and Editors Work

Health writers or editors work for publishing companies, radio or television stations, professional medical journals, Internet companies, universities, health foundations, or government agencies.

What Is Required to Become a Health Writer and Editor

▶ a bachelor's degree and coursework in science and health-related classes

Community Service

Many people working in community service provide services and products to medical personnel, patients, and the general public. Some of these professions require extensive training, while others only require a few courses after high school.

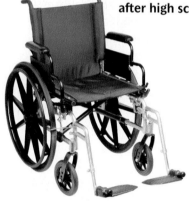

Home Health Aide

What Home Health Aides Do

Home health aides provide personal care in the home to people who are elderly, handicapped, or recovering from an illness or injury. The responsibilities of home health aides include getting the patient out of bed, as well as helping the patient bathe and groom, dress, and exercise. The aide also helps the patient remember to take his or her medication, helps with housecleaning and meal preparation, and provides emotional support.

Where Home Health Aides Work

Home health aides are usually employed by an agency but work in their patient's homes.

What Is Required to Become a Home Health Aide

▶ certification and training, which vary by state (federal law requires a person to have at least 81 hours of classroom and practical training under the supervision of a registered nurse for the person to be eligible to take the national certification exam)

Medical Social Worker

What Medical Social Workers Do

Medical social workers assist patients and their families with health-related problems and concerns. These social workers lead support group discussions, help patients locate appropriate healthcare and other health services, and provide support to patients who have serious or chronic illnesses. These professionals help patients and the patient's families find resources to overcome unhealthy conditions, such as child abuse, homelessness, and drug abuse. Social workers also help patients find legal resources and financial aid to pay for health services.

Where Medical Social Workers Work

Medical social workers usually work for hospitals, nursing homes, health clinics, or community health agencies.

What Is Required to Become a Medical Social Worker

▶ a bachelor's degree or a master's degree

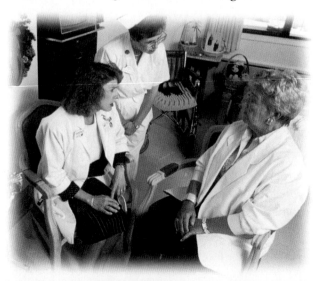

Biomedical Equipment Technician

What Biomedical Equipment Technicians Do

Biomedical equipment technicians specialize in electronic and mechanical equipment used to diagnose and treat diseases. These technicians work with equipment ranging from electronic switches to sophisticated diagnostic equipment. Biomedical equipment technicians adjust and test equipment for proper operation. They periodically inspect and repair machines. They also install new equipment, such as electrocardiographs (EKGs) and artificial kidney machines. These technicians also perform safety inspections on electrical and radiation equipment, demonstrate the use of equipment for other medical personnel, and propose new equipment purchases or modifications.

Where Biomedical Equipment Technicians Work

Biomedical equipment technicians work in places such as hospitals, clinics, and medical equipment manufacturing plants.

What Is Required to Become a Biomedical Equipment Technician

▶ 1 to 3 years in a technical program or a bachelor's degree

Health Insurance Agent

What Health Insurance Agents Do

Health insurance agents sell health insurance to the public. Health insurance is used to help pay for medical expenses if a person needs to go to the doctor or hospital or to receive some other type of medical treatment. A health insurance agent helps people determine what the proper insurance policy for them would be. They consider factors such as how many people are to be covered, what the ages of the people to be covered are, and what level of coverage is needed. Health insurance agents also help their customers by answering questions and acting as a liaison between the insurance company and a customer who needs to file a claim.

Where do Health Insurance Agents Work?

Health insurance agents are located throughout the country and usually work in a private office or in the office of an insurance agency.

What Is Required to Become a Health Insurance Agent

▶ a bachelor's degree or education needed per company of employment
▶ specified amount of continuing education (required per state)

Sports and Recreation

Helping people maintain life-long health through sports and recreation is a rapidly growing area in health careers. The ability of exercise to reduce stress has also created an important new field of jobs. Occupations in this area range from trainers to therapists.

Occupational Therapist

What Occupational Therapists Do

Occupational therapists help patients adjust to and recover from physical illnesses and injuries, such as spinal cord injuries or partial paralysis. Occupational therapists lead patients through rehabilitative exercises and show the patients new ways to perform simple tasks such as getting dressed, cooking, and eating. These professionals also help people who have been injured at work find care and resources and to learn new work duties if necessary. Depending upon the patient's needs, the therapists provide each patient with a personalized rehabilitation plan and may teach him or her how to use equipment such as wheelchairs, walkers, and other aids.

Where Occupational Therapists Work

Occupational therapists work in hospitals, in clinics, or in private business.

What Is Required to Become an Occupational Therapist

▶ a bachelor's degree or a certification program in occupational therapy followed by passing a national certification exam

Certified Athletic Trainer

What Certified Athletic Trainers Do

Athletic trainers are health professionals who work with athletes from sports teams and organizations to prevent, recognize, treat, and rehabilitate sports-related injuries. They provide first aid and nonemergency medical services at sporting events and practices, and they help team members get long-term medical help, if needed.

Where Certified Athletic Trainers Work

Certified athletic trainers usually work for college or professional sport teams, or train amateur athletes.

What Is Required to Become a Certified Athletic Trainer

▶ a bachelor's degree from a National Athletic Trainer's Association (NATA) program or attendance at an NATA internship (Either path requires training in CPR and NATA certification.)

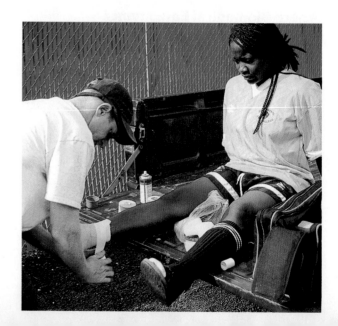

High School Coach

What High School Coaches Do

High school coaches are responsible for training young athletes to play sports well and safely. Coaches usually coach one or more sports, and they may have other duties, such as teaching or working in school administration. Coaches also teach sportsmanship, leadership, and how to work together as a team. High school coaches are responsible for the safety and well-being of their players both on the field and in transit to and from games or competitions.

Where High School Coaches Work

High school coaches work at public and private high schools.

What Is Required to Become a High School Coach

▶ a bachelor's degree
▶ sometimes a master's degree or a Ph.D.

Recreational Therapist

What Recreational Therapists Do

Recreational therapists plan and carry out treatment programs for people who have physical, mental, or social disabilities or for individuals recovering from substance, sexual, and physical abuse. Therapists use art, music, recreation, and dance to help patients relieve stress, express themselves, and build self-confidence. Motivational and creative programs are used to encourage behavior change, improve coordination, and increase social skills.

Where Recreational Therapists Work

Some places where recreational therapists work include hospitals, adult and child day care centers, and nursing homes.

What Is Required to Become a Recreational Therapist

▶ a bachelor's degree
▶ at least 6 months of clinical training

CHAPTER 1
Leading a Healthy Life

1. true
2. false, there are many behavioral risk factors for heart disease. You can follow healthy behaviors to help reduce your chances of developing heart disease
3. true
4. true
5. true
6. false, physical health is just one aspect of overall health

Knowledge—What's Your Health IQ? Scoring

Calculate the percentage of questions you answered correctly by dividing the number of questions you answered correctly by the total number of questions. Then, multiply that number by 100. Check your percentage correct below:

80–100 percent correct Excellent! Your high score shows you have a strong knowledge with the health topics in the chapter. Use this knowledge to make good health choices and you'll be on your way to leading a healthy life!

60–79 percent correct Good You are aware of some of the health topics in the chapter. Learning more about these issues can help you to make better decisions about your health.

0–59 percent correct Needs Improvement It is important to understand the health issues that affect you. Having a high health knowledge can influence you to choose healthy behaviors so you can enjoy a healthy life. Read the chapter carefully, and then retake the What's Your Health IQ? to see if your score improves.

CHAPTER 2
Skills for a Healthy Life

If you scored:

20–28 points You are doing an excellent job of evaluating and learning from the decisions you make that relate to your overall health.

11–19 points You are doing well overall. However, you have a number of areas in which you can improve decisions about your health.

0–10 points You may need to make some major changes in the way you make decisions. You can learn to make changes in your decision-making by reading Chapter 2.

CHAPTER 3
Building Self-Esteem and Mental Health

If you scored:

19–24 points You show respect for yourself and others and probably have high self-esteem.

10–18 points You probably have a healthy self-esteem but could improve the way you treat yourself and others.

0–9 points You should make some major changes in the way you treat yourself and others. You can learn about factors that affect your self-esteem and how to improve it by reading Chapter 3.

CHAPTER 4
Managing Stress and Coping with Loss

If you scored:

19–24 points You are doing an excellent job of managing stress.

10–18 points You are doing very well overall but have areas in which you can improve how you manage stress.

0–9 points You should be making some major changes in the way you deal with stress or you may develop a stress-related illness. You can learn more about how to manage stress by reading Chapter 4.

CHAPTER 5
Preventing Violence and Abuse

If you scored:

19–24 points You are doing an excellent job of avoiding conflict and violence.

10–18 points You are doing very well overall but have areas in which you could improve your interactions with other people.

0–9 points You should be making some major changes in the way in which you interact with other people. You can learn more about how to better avoid conflict and violence by reading Chapter 5.

CHAPTER 6
Physical Fitness for Life

1. false, benefits can be obtained from exercising less often (5 days a week)
2. true
3. false, girls will increase their muscle mass but will not develop bulky muscles typical of males
4. false, lifting weights is anaerobic exercise
5. false, the body needs rest from exercise or injury will occur
6. false, anabolic steroids are used to treat medical problems, but their use to improve athletic performance is illegal
7. true

To check your score, refer to Knowledge—What's Your Health IQ? Scoring on p. 638 under Chapter 1.

CHAPTER 7
Nutrition for Life

1. true
2. false, plant foods do not contain cholesterol
3. false, fiber enables food to move through the intestines smoothly and efficiently
4. false, your body can't produce all vitamins and minerals, so you need to consume them in the diet
5. true
6. true
7. false, choosing the right kinds of snacks can provide energy and nutrients

To check your score, refer to Knowledge—What's Your Health IQ? Scoring on p. 638 under Chapter 1.

CHAPTER 8
Weight Management and Eating Behavior

1. true
2. true
3. true
4. false, a weight management program includes healthy eating and exercise habits that maintain a healthy weight

5. true
6. true
7. false, most food-borne illnesses are caused by foods that are prepared or eaten at home

To check your score, refer to Knowledge—What's Your Health IQ? Scoring on p. 638 under Chapter 1.

CHAPTER 9
Understanding Drugs and Medicines

1. false, minor side effects of OTC medicines are common
2. true
3. true
4. true
5. true
6. false, all drugs, despite their source, are made from chemicals
7. false, people can become addicted to prescription drugs such as painkillers

To check your score, refer to Knowledge—What's Your Health IQ? Scoring on p. 638 under Chapter 1.

CHAPTER 10
Alcohol

1. true
2. true
3. true
4. true
5. true
6. false, alcoholism affects all people who know the alcoholic
7. false, motor vehicle accidents are the No. 1 cause of death among teens; the majority of these accidents are alcohol related.

To check your score, refer to Knowledge—What's Your Health IQ? Scoring on p. 638 under Chapter 1.

CHAPTER 11
Tobacco

1. true
2. false, chewing tobacco causes serious problems to mouth, throat, and stomach
3. false, herbal cigarettes do contain nicotine

4. false, smoking can harm your lungs the first time you smoke
5. true
6. false, chemicals from cigarette smoke readily pass through the placenta
7. true

To check your score, refer to Knowledge—What's Your Health IQ? Scoring on p. 638 under Chapter 1.

CHAPTER 12
Illegal Drugs

1. false, most people try drugs for various reasons such as peer pressure despite the fact that they are dangerous
2. false, marijuana leads to physical dependence and possibly addiction
3. false, while stimulants increase energy, stimulants can also cause restlessness, hyperactivity, anxiety, and even sometimes loss of awareness of reality
4. false, anabolic steroids can cause baldness, shrinking of testes, growth of breasts, and even infertility
5. false, medicinal barbituates are given under physician supervision; however, they are still dangerous and addictive
6. true
7. false, damage to the brain due to drug use is usually permanent

To check your score, refer to Knowledge—What's Your Health IQ? Scoring on p. 638 under Chapter 1.

CHAPTER 13
Preventing Infectious Diseases

If you scored:

22–32 points You are doing an excellent job of preventing the spread of infectious diseases and of protecting yourself from infectious diseases.

11–21 points You are doing well overall. However, there are a number of areas in which you could improve your behavior to prevent the spread of infectious diseases.

0–10 points You should make some major changes in your behavior to protect yourself from infectious diseases and prevent the spread of infectious diseases.

You can learn to protect yourself from infectious diseases by reading Chapter 13.

CHAPTER 14
Lifestyle Diseases

If you scored:

20–28 points You are doing an excellent job of protecting yourself from lifestyle diseases.

11–19 points You are doing well overall but have areas in which you could improve your health-related behaviors and protect yourself from lifestyle diseases.

0–10 points You have a number of areas in which you could make improvements in your health-related behaviors. You can learn how to protect yourself from lifestyle diseases by reading Chapter 14.

CHAPTER 15
Other Diseases and Disabilities

1. false, the development of some hereditary diseases is influenced by behavioral factors
2. true
3. false, autoimmune diseases are caused primarily by defective genes
4. false, allergies and asthma are types of immune disorders while rheumatoid arthritis is an auto-immune disease
5. true

To check your score, refer to Knowledge—What's Your Health IQ? Scoring on p. 638 under Chapter 1.

CHAPTER 16
Adolescence and Adulthood

1. true
2. false, girls naturally have more body fat than boys
3. true
4. false, the leading cause of death in young adults is unintentional injuries; in middle adulthood, the leading cause is cancer
5. false, most older adults do not experience Alzheimer's disease
6. true

To check your score, refer to Knowledge—What's Your Health IQ? Scoring on p. 638 under Chapter 1.

CHAPTER 17
Marriage, Parenthood, and Families

1. false, it's not realistic to expect one's spouse to meet all of his or her partner's needs
2. false, the consequences can also be felt by the couple's children, family, and friends
3. false, a mature person initiates resolution to marital conflicts
4. true
5. true

To check your score, refer to Knowledge—What's Your Health IQ? Scoring on p. 638 under Chapter 1.

CHAPTER 18
Reproduction, Pregnancy, and Development

1. false, sperm are made in the testes
2. true
3. false, most cases of testicular cancer occur among men aged 15 to 35
4. false, testosterone is the primary hormone in males
5. true
6. true
7. false, women typically produce and release only one mature egg each month
8. true
9. true

To check your score, refer to Knowledge—What's Your Health IQ? Scoring on p. 638 under Chapter 1.

CHAPTER 19
Building Responsible Relationships

1. false, differences in values and personality are significant issues to consider when dating someone
2. false, as in any situation in life, each individual has choices, and there are a host of ways to avoid the pressures of becoming sexually active

3. true
4. true
5. true

To check your score, refer to Knowledge—What's Your Health IQ? Scoring on p. 638s under Chapter 1.

CHAPTER 20
Risks of Adolescent Sexual Activity

1. true
2. false, only about 20 percent of teen mothers eventually marry the father of the child
3. true
4. true
5. false, abstinence eliminates all of the risks of teen sexual activity

To check your score, refer to Knowledge—What's Your Health IQ? Scoring on p. 638 under Chapter 1.

CHAPTER 21
HIV and AIDS

1. true
2. true
3. false, HIV is not transmitted through casual contact, such as shaking hands
4. false, HIV is not transmitted through casual contact, such as drinking from a water fountain after a person infected with HIV has
5. true
6. true
7. false, sterile, single-use needles are used during blood donations in the U.S., so blood donors are not at risk of HIV infection
8. false, many HIV-infected people are unaware of their infection and therefore cannot warn anyone else of their infection

To check your score, refer to Knowledge—What's Your Health IQ? Scoring on p. 638 under Chapter 1.

GLOSSARY

A

abdominal thrusts (Heimlich maneuver) the act of applying pressure to a choking person's stomach to force an object out of the throat

abstinence the conscious decision not to participate in sexual activity and the skills to support that decision

abuse physical or emotional harm to someone

acid rain any precipitation that has a below-normal pH (acidic)

acne an inflammation of the skin that occurs when the openings in the skin become clogged with dirt and oil

acquired immune deficiency syndrome (AIDS) the disease that is caused by HIV infection, which weakens the immune system

action plan a set of directions that will help you reach your goal

active ingredient the chemical component that gives a medicine its action

addiction a condition in which a person can no longer control his or her drug use

adolescence the period of time between the start of puberty and full maturation

advocate to speak or argue in favor of something

aggressive hostile and unfriendly in the way one expresses oneself

alcohol the drug in wine, beer, and liquor that causes intoxication

alcohol abuse drinking too much alcohol, drinking it too often, or drinking it at inappropriate times

alcoholism a disease that causes a person to lose control of his or her drinking behavior; a physical and emotional addiction to alcohol

allergy a reaction by the body's immune system to a harmless substance

alveolus a thin-walled air sac that is found in clusters in the lungs and that is the site of gas exchange

Alzheimer's disease a disease in which a person gradually loses mental capacities and the ability to carry out daily activities

amebic dysentery (uh MEE bik DIS uhn TER ee) an inflammation of the intestine that is caused by an ameba

Americans with Disabilities Act (ADA) wide-ranging legislation intended to make American society more accessible to people who have disabilities

anabolic steroid a synthetic version of the male hormone testosterone that is used to promote muscle development

anorexia nervosa an eating disorder that involves self-starvation, a distorted body image, and low body weight

antibiotic resistance a condition in which bacteria can no longer be killed by a particular antibiotic

antibody a protein that is made by the immune system in response to a specific antigen

antigen an identifying protein on the coating of every cell and virus

appetite the desire, rather than the need, to eat certain foods

artery a blood vessel that carries blood away from the heart to other parts of the body

arthritis inflammation of the joints

assertive direct and respectful in the way one expresses oneself

asset a skill or resource that can help a person reach a goal

asthma a disorder that causes the airways that carry air into the lungs to become narrow and to become clogged with mucus

asymptomatic showing no signs of a disease or disorder even though an infection or disease is present

asymptomatic stage a stage of an infection in which the infectious agent, such as HIV, is present but there are few or no symptoms of the infection

atherosclerosis (ATH uhr OH skluh ROH sis) a disease characterized by the buildup of fatty materials on the inside walls of the arteries

atrium a chamber of the heart that receives blood that is returning to the heart

autoimmune disease a disease in which the immune system attacks the cells of the body that the immune system normally protects

bacteria tiny, single-celled organisms, some of which can cause disease

basal metabolic rate (BMR) the rate at which energy is used to keep the body alive when in a rested and fasting state

B cell a type of lymphocyte that is made in bone marrow and that makes antibodies

benign tumor (bi NIEN TOO muhr) an abnormal, but usually harmless cell mass

binge drinking the act of drinking five or more drinks in one sitting

binge eating/bingeing eating a large amount of food in one sitting; usually accompanied by a feeling of being out of control

blood a tissue that is made up of cells, fluid, and other substances that carries oxygen, carbon dioxide, and nutrients in the body

blood alcohol concentration (BAC) the amount of alcohol in a person's blood, expressed as a percentage

blood pressure the force that blood exerts against the inside walls of a blood vessel

blood vessels the tubes, including arteries, veins, and capillaries, through which the blood moves through the body

body composition the proportion of body weight that is made up of fat tissue compared to lean tissue

body image a measure of how you see and feel about your appearance and how comfortable you are with your body

body mass index (BMI) an index of weight in relation to height that is used to assess healthy body weight

bone marrow a layer of soft tissue at the center of many bones

brain the main control center of the nervous system that is located inside the skull

brain stem the part of the brain that filters and guides signals coming from the spinal cord to other parts of the brain

bronchiole the smallest of the tubes that branch from the bronchus in a lung

bronchus one of the two tubes that branch from the trachea and send air into each lung

bulimia nervosa an eating disorder in which the individual repeatedly eats large amounts of food and then uses behaviors such as vomiting or using laxatives to rid the body of the food

bullying scaring or controlling another person by using threats or physical force

burn an injury to the skin and other tissues that is caused by heat, chemicals, electricity, or radiation

cancer a disease caused by uncontrolled cell growth

capillary a tiny blood vessel that carries blood between arteries and veins and through which nutrients and waste pass into and out of the blood

carbohydrate a class of energy-giving nutrients that includes sugars, starches, and fiber

carbon monoxide a gas that blocks oxygen from getting into the bloodstream

carcinogen (kahr SIN uh juhn) any chemical or agent that causes cancer

cardiac pacemaker a group of cells that are at the top of the right atrium and that control the heartbeat

cardiopulmonary resuscitation (CPR) a life-saving technique that combines rescue breathing and chest compressions

cardiovascular disease (CVD) a disease or disorder that results from progressive damage to the heart and blood vessels

carotid pulse the pulse that is felt at the carotid arteries, the major arteries of the neck

cavity a hole in the tooth produced by tooth decay

central nervous system (CNS) the part of the nervous system made up of the brain and spinal cord

cerebellum the part of the brain that controls balance and posture

cerebrum the largest, most complex part of the brain that receives sensations and controls movement

cervix the narrow base of the uterus that leads to the vagina

chemotherapy (KEE moh THER uh pee) the use of drugs to destroy cancer cells

chlamydia (kluh MID ee uh) a bacterial STD that infects the reproductive organs and that causes a mucous discharge

chlorofluorocarbons (CFCs) pollutants released by certain coolants and aerosol sprays

choking the condition in which the trachea (windpipe) is partly or completely blocked

chronic disease a disease that develops gradually and continues over a long period of time

circadian rhythm the body's internal system for regulating sleeping and waking patterns

cirrhosis (suh ROH sis) a deadly disease that replaces healthy liver tissue with scar tissue; most often caused by long-term alcohol abuse

club (designer) drug a drug made to closely resemble a common illegal drug in chemical structure and effect

cochlea a coiled, fluid-filled tube that is found in the inner ear and that is involved in hearing

codependency a condition in which a family member or friend sacrifices his or her own needs to meet the needs of an addict

collaborate to work together with one or more people

collagen protein fibers that make skin flexible

colon the major part of the large intestine

consequence a result of one's actions and decisions

conservation the wise use and protection of natural resources

consumer a person who buys products or services

coping dealing with problems and troubles in an effective way

cross-contamination the transfer of contaminants from one food to another

Daily Value (DV) the recommended daily amount of a nutrient; used on food labels to help people see how a food fits into their diet

dandruff flaky clumps of dead skin cells from the scalp

date rape sexual intercourse that is forced on a victim by someone the victim knows

decibels (DES uh BUHLZ) the units used to measure sound

deductible the amount that the subscriber must pay before an insurance company begins paying for medical services

defense mechanism an unconscious behavior that is used to avoid experiencing unpleasant emotions

deforestation the clearing of trees from natural forests to make space for crops, grazing, or development

dehydration a state in which the body has lost more water than has been taken in

depressant a drug that causes relaxation and sleepiness

depression sadness and hopelessness that keeps a person from carrying out everyday activities

dermis the functional layer of skin beneath the epidermis

designated driver a person who chooses not to drink alcohol in a social setting so that he or she can safely drive himself or herself and others

diabetes a disorder in which cells are unable to obtain glucose from the blood such that high blood-glucose levels result

diabetic coma a loss of consciousness that happens when there is too much blood sugar and a buildup of toxic substances in the blood

diaphragm the sheet of muscle that separates the chest cavity from the abdominal cavity and that functions in respiration

Dietary Guidelines for Americans a set of diet and lifestyle recommendations developed to improve health and reduce nutrition-related disease risk in the U.S. population

dietary supplement any product that is taken by mouth, that can contain a dietary ingredient, and that is labeled as a dietary supplement

digestive tract the series of organs through which food passes

direct pressure the pressure that results from someone who tries to convince you to do something you normally wouldn't do

disability a physical or mental impairment or deficiency that interferes with a person's normal activity

discipline the act of teaching a child through correction, direction, rules, and reinforcement

dislocation an injury in which a bone has been forced out of its normal position in a joint

distress a negative stress that can make a person sick or can keep a person from reaching a goal

divorce the legal end to a marriage

domestic violence the use of force to control and maintain power over a spouse in the home

drug any substance that causes a change in a person's physical or psychological state

drug abuse the intentional improper or unsafe use of a drug

drug combination therapy an AIDS treatment program in which patients regularly take more than one drug

drug interaction a condition in which a drug reacts with another drug, food, or dietary supplement such that the effect of one of the substances is greater or smaller

drug tolerance a condition in which a user needs more of a drug to get the same effect

ear the sense organ that functions in hearing and balance

eardrum a membrane that transmits sound waves from the outer ear to the middle ear

ecosystem a community of living things and the nonliving parts of the community's environment

egg (ovum) the sex cell that is made by the ovaries and that can be fertilized by sperm

electrocution a fatal injury caused by electricity entering the body and destroying vital tissues

embryo a developing human, from fertilization through the first 8 weeks of development

emotion the feeling that is produced in response to life experiences

emotional intimacy the state of being emotionally connected to another person

emotional maturity the ability to assess a relationship or situation and to act according to what is best for oneself and for the other person in the relationship

empathy the ability to understand another person's feelings, behaviors, and attitudes

emphysema a respiratory disease in which air cannot move in and out of alveoli because they break down and lose their elasticity

enabling helping an addict avoid the negative consequences of his or her behavior

endocrine gland an organ that releases hormones into the bloodstream or into the fluid around cells

endometrium the lining of the uterus

environment the living and nonliving things that surround an organism

environmental tobacco smoke (secondhand smoke) a combination of exhaled mainstream smoke and sidestream smoke

enzyme a protein or other type of molecule that helps chemical processes happen in living things

epidemic the occurrence of more cases of a disease than expected

epidermis the outermost layer of the skin, made of one to several layers of dead cells

epinephrine (EP uh NEF rin) one of the hormones released by the body in times of stress; also called adrenaline

esophagus a long, straight tube that connects the pharynx (throat) to the stomach and through which food moves to get into the stomach

estrogen a hormone that regulates the sexual development and reproductive function of females

eustachian tube the tube that connects the middle ear to the throat

eustress a positive stress that energizes a person and helps a person reach a goal

extended family the people who are outside the nuclear family but are related to the nuclear family, such as aunts, uncles, grandparents, and cousins

external bleeding bleeding at the surface of the body

external pressure pressure that a person feels from another person or group to engage in a behavior

eye the sense organ that gathers and focuses light, generates signals that are sent to the brain, and allows one to see

GLOSSARY

F

fad diet a diet that requires a major change in eating habits and promises quick weight loss

fallopian tube the female reproductive organ that connects an ovary to the uterus and that transports an egg from the ovary to the uterus

family counseling counseling discussions that are led by a third party to resolve conflict among family members

fat a class of energy-giving nutrients; *also* the main form of energy storage in the body

fee-for-service insurance plan a traditional insurance plan in which the patient must pay a premium and a deductible

fertilization the process by which a sperm and an egg and their genetic material join to create a new human life

fetal alcohol syndrome (FAS) a set of physical and mental defects that affect a fetus that has been exposed to alcohol because of the mother's consumption of alcohol during pregnancy

fetus a developing human, from the start of the ninth week of pregnancy until delivery

first degree burn a burn that affects only the outer layer of the skin and looks pink

FITT a formula made up of the four parts of fitness training: frequency, intensity, time, and type

follicle a tiny pit in the skin that holds the root of a hair

food allergy an abnormal response to a food that is triggered by the immune system

food-borne illness an illness caused by eating or drinking a food that contains a toxin or disease-causing microorganism

fracture a crack or break in a bone

fraud the marketing and selling of products or services by making false claims

frostbite a condition in which body tissues become frozen

funeral a ceremony in which a deceased person is buried or cremated

fungus an organism that absorbs and uses nutrients of living or dead organisms

G

gene a segment of DNA located on a chromosome that codes for a specific hereditary trait and that is passed from parent to offspring

generic medicine a medicine made by a company other than the company that developed the original medicine

gene therapy a technique that places a healthy copy of a gene into the cells of a person whose copy of the gene is defective

genetic counseling the process of informing a person or couple about their genetic makeup

gingivitis a condition in which the gums become red and infected and begin to pull away from the teeth

goal something that you work toward and hope to achieve

gonorrhea (GAHN uh REE uh) an STD that is caused by a bacterium that infects mucous membranes, including the genital mucous membranes

grieve to express deep sadness because of a loss

H

hallucinogen a drug that distorts perceptions, causing the user to see or hear things that are not real

hand signals signals used by cyclists that show pedestrians, automobile drivers, and others on the road when they intend to make a turn or stop

hazardous weather dangerous weather that causes concern for safety

hazing harassing newcomers to a group in an abusive and humiliating way

head lice tiny parasites that feed on blood vessels in the scalp

health the state of well-being in which all of the components of health—physical, emotional, social, mental, spiritual, and environmental—are in balance

health literacy knowledge of health information needed to make good choices about your health

health maintenance organization (HMO) a managed-care plan in which patients must use a doctor who contracts with the insurance company

Health on the Net (HON) Foundation an organization of Web sites that agree to follow a code of ethics regarding health information

health-related fitness fitness qualities that are necessary to maintain and promote a healthy body

Healthy People 2010 a set of health objectives established by the U.S. Department of Health and Human Services for improving the nation's health by 2010

heart the organ that acts as a pump that pushes the blood through the body

heart attack a sudden loss of blood flow to the heart muscle

heartburn the pain that is felt behind the breastbone and that is caused by GERD (gastric esophageal reflux disorder)

heat exhaustion a condition in which the body becomes heated to a higher temperature than normal

heatstroke a condition in which body loses its ability to cool itself by sweating

helper T cell (CD4+ cell) white blood cell that activates the immune response and that is the primary target cell of HIV infection

hemoglobin the oxygen-carrying pigment in red blood cells

hepatitis an inflammation of the liver

hereditary disease a disease caused by abnormal chromosomes or by defective genes inherited by a child from one or both parents

heredity (huh RED i tee) the passing down of traits from parents to their biological child

high-risk population any group of people who have an increased chance of getting a disease

HIV-antibody test a test that detects HIV antibodies to determine if a person has been infected with HIV

HIV positive describes a person who tests positive in two different HIV tests

home healthcare services medical services, treatment, or equipment provided for the patient in his or her home

hormone a substance that is secreted by a cell that acts to regulate the activity of other cells

Human Genome Project a research effort to determine the locations of all human genes on the chromosomes and to read the coded instructions in the genes

human immunodeficiency virus (HIV) the virus that primarily infects cells of the immune system and that causes AIDS

human papilloma virus (HPV) a group of viruses that can cause genital warts in males and females and can cause cervical cancer in females

hunger the body's physical response to the need for food

hypothermia a condition in which the internal body temperature becomes dangerously low

incest sexual activity between family members who are not husband and wife

incontinence loss of voluntary control of urination

indirect pressure the pressure that results from being swayed to do something because people you look up to are doing it

infectious disease (in FEK shuhs di ZEEZ) any disease that is caused by an agent that has invaded the body

inflammation a reaction to injury or infection that is characterized by pain, redness, and swelling

inhalant a drug that is inhaled as a vapor

inpatient care medical care that requires a person to stay in a hospital for more than a day

insomnia an inability to sleep even if one is physically exhausted

insulin a hormone that causes cells to remove glucose from the bloodstream

integrity the characteristic of doing what one knows is right

internal bleeding bleeding within the body

internal pressure an impulse a person feels to engage in a behavior

intervention confronting a drug user about his or her drug abuse problem to stop him or her from using drugs

intoxication the physical and mental changes produced by drinking alcohol

joint a place where two or more bones meet in the body

keratin a strong, flexible protein found in skin, hair, and nails

kidney organ that filters water and wastes from the blood, excretes products as urine, and regulates the concentration of certain substances in the blood

lactose intolerance the inability to completely digest the milk sugar lactose

leukemia cancer of the tissues that make white blood cells

life expectancy the average length of time an individual is expected to live

life skill a tool for building a healthy life

lifestyle disease a disease that is caused partly by unhealthy behaviors and partly by other factors

ligament a type of tissue that holds the ends of bones together at joints

lung the main organ of the respiratory system in which oxygen from the air is exchanged with carbon dioxide from the blood

lymph the clear, yellowish fluid that leaks from capillaries, fills the spaces around the body's cells, and is collected by the lymphatic vessels and nodes

lymphatic system a network of vessels that carry a clear fluid called *lymph* throughout the body

lymph node a small, bean-shaped organ that contains small fibers that remove particles from the lymph

lymphocytes white blood cells that destroy bacteria, viruses, and dead or damaged cells

mainstream smoke smoke that is inhaled through a cigarette and then exhaled by a cigarette smoker

malignant tumor (muh LIG nuhnt TOO muhr) a mass of cells that invades and destroys healthy tissue

managed-care plan a plan in which an insurance company makes a contract with a group of doctors

marijuana the dried flowers and leaves of the plant *Cannabis sativa* that are smoked or mixed in food and eaten for intoxicating effects

marriage a lifelong union between a husband and a wife, who develop an intimate relationship

media all public forms of communication, such as TV, radio, newspaper, the Internet, and advertisements

Medicaid a healthcare program available to people who are on welfare, have dependent children, or are elderly, blind, or disabled

Medicare a healthcare program available to people who are 65 years old or older and for younger individuals who are disabled

medicine any drug used to cure, prevent, or treat illness or discomfort

melanin a pigment that gives skin its color and shields skin from ultraviolet radiation

memorial service a ceremony to remember the deceased person

meningitis an inflammation of the membranes covering the brain and spinal cord

menopause the time of life when a woman stops ovulating and menstruating

menstrual cycle a monthly series of hormone-controlled changes that prepare the uterine lining for a pregnancy

menstruation the monthly breakdown and shedding of the lining of the uterus, during which blood and tissue leave the woman's body through the vagina

mental disorder an illness that affects a person's thoughts, emotions, and behaviors

mental health the state of mental well-being in which one can cope with the demands of daily life

midlife crisis the sense of uncertainty about one's identity and values that some people experience in the middle of their lives

mineral a class of nutrients that are chemical elements that are needed for certain body processes, such as enzyme activity and bone formation

motor nerve a nerve that carries signals from the brain or spinal cord to the muscles and glands

mucus a thick, slimy fluid that is secreted by the lining of organs and glands

multiple sclerosis an autoimmune disease in which the body mistakenly attacks myelin, the fatty insulation on nerves in the brain and spinal cord

MyPyramid a food guidance system that encourages healthy food choices and daily activity

natural disaster a natural event that causes widespread injury, death, and property damage

neglect the failure of a caretaker to provide for basic needs, such as food, clothing, or love

negotiation a bargain or compromise for a peaceful solution to a conflict

neonatal abstinence syndrome drug withdrawal that occurs in newborn infants whose mothers were frequent drug users while pregnant

nephron a tiny, blood-filtering unit in the kidney

nerve a bundle of nerve cells (neurons) that carry electrical signals from one part of the body to another

neuron a specialized cell that receives and sends electrical signals

neurotransmitter a chemical released at the end of a neuron's axon

nicotine the highly addictive drug that is found in all tobacco products

nicotine replacement therapy (NRT) forms of medicine that delivers small amounts of nicotine to the body to help a person quit using tobacco

nonrenewable resource a natural resource that can be used up faster than it can be replenished naturally

nuclear family a family in which a mother, a father, and one or more biological or adopted children live together

nutrient a substance in food that provides energy or helps form body tissues and that is necessary for life and growth

nutrient deficiency the state of not having enough of a nutrient to maintain good health

nutrient density a measure of the nutrients in a food compared with the energy that the food provides

nutrition the science or study of food and the ways in which the body uses food

obesity (oh BEE suh tee) the state of having a significant amount of excess body fat; the state of weighing more than 20 percent above one's recommended body weight

Occupational Safety and Health Administration (OSHA) a government agency created to prevent work-related injuries, illnesses, and death

opiates a group of highly addictive drugs derived from the poppy plant that are used as pain relievers, anesthetics, and sedatives

opportunistic infection (OI) an illness that is due to an organism that causes disease in people with weakened immune systems; commonly found in AIDS patients

outbreak an unexpected increase in illness

outpatient care medical care that requires that a person stay in the hospital only during his or her treatment

ovary the female reproductive organ that produces eggs and the hormones estrogen and progesterone

overcrowding condition in which there are too many inhabitants in an area to live healthily

overdose the taking of too much of a drug, which causes sickness, loss of consciousness, permanent damage, or even death

over-the-counter (OTC) medicine any medicine that can be bought without a prescription

overpopulation the point at which a population is too large to be supported by the available resources

overtraining a condition that occurs as a result of exceeding the recommendations of the FITT formula

overweight heavy for one's height

ovulation (AHV yoo LAY shuhn) the process in which the ovaries release a mature egg every month

GLOSSARY

pandemic a disease that spreads quickly through human populations all over the world

parental responsibility the duty of a parent to provide for the physical, financial, mental, and emotional needs of a child

passive not offering opposition when challenged or pressured

pathogen any agent that causes disease

peer mediation a technique in which a trained outsider who is your age helps people in a conflict come to a peaceful resolution

peer pressure a feeling that you should do something because that is what your friends want

pelvic inflammatory disease (PID) an inflammation of the upper female reproductive tract that is caused by the migration of a bacterial infection from the vagina

penis the male reproductive organ that removes urine from the body and that can deliver sperm to the female reproductive system

peripheral nervous system (PNS) the part of the nervous system made up of the nerves that connect the brain and spinal cord to other parts of the body

physical dependence a condition in which the body relies on a given drug in order to function

physical fitness the ability of the body to perform daily physical activities without becoming short of breath, sore, or overly tired

placenta a blood vessel–rich organ that forms in a mother's uterus and that provides nutrients and oxygen to and removes waste from a developing baby

plaque a mixture of food particles, saliva, and bacteria on the tooth

platelet a cell fragment that is needed to form blood clots

poison a substance that can cause illness or death when taken into the body

preferred provider organization (PPO) a managed-care plan that offers the patient an option to see a doctor who does not contract with the insurance company; the patient pays a higher fee to use this option

premium the monthly fee for insurance

prenatal care the healthcare provided for a woman during her pregnancy

prescription (pree SKRIP shuhn) a written order from a doctor for a specific medicine

primary care physician (PCP) family doctor who handles general medical care

prioritize to arrange items in order of importance

prostate gland a gland in males that adds fluids that nourish and protect sperm as the sperm move through the female body

protective factor anything that keeps a person from engaging in a harmful behavior

protein a class of energy-giving nutrients that are made up of amino acids, which are needed to build and repair body structures and to regulate processes in the body

psychoactive describes a drug or medicine that affects the brain and changes how a person perceives, thinks, or feels

psychological dependence a state of emotionally or physically needing a drug in order to function

puberty the period of human development during which people become able to produce children

public health the study and practice of protecting and improving the health of people in a community

public service announcement (PSA) a message created to educate people about an issue

purging engaging in behaviors such as vomiting or misusing laxatives to rid the body of food

quackery a type of fraud; the promotion of healthcare services or products that are worthless or not proven effective

Recommended Dietary Allowances (RDAs) recommended nutrient intakes that will meet the needs of almost all healthy people

recovering the process of learning to live without drugs

rectum the last part of the large intestine in which undigested wastes are stored

recycling reusing materials from used products to make new products

red blood cell blood cell that carries oxygen to the body cells and that returns carbon dioxide to the lungs

reflex an involuntary and almost immediate movement in response to a stimulus

refusal skill a strategy to avoid doing something you don't want to do

relapse a return to using drugs while trying to recover from drug addiction

renewable resource a natural resource that can be replaced over a short period of time

repetitions the number of times that an exercise is performed

rescue breathing an emergency technique in which a rescuer gives air to someone who is not breathing

resiliency the ability to recover from illness, hardship, and other stressors

resource something that you can use to help achieve a goal

resting heart rate (RHR) the number of times that the heart beats per minute while the body is at rest

retina the light-sensitive inner layer of the eye, which receives images formed by the lens and transmits nerve signals through the optic nerve to the brain

risk factor anything that increases the likelihood of injury, disease, or other health problems

root canal a procedure in which a dentist drills into the pulp of a tooth to remove the infection from a cavity

salmonellosis a bacterial infection of the digestive system that is usually spread by eating contaminated food

sanitation the practice of providing sewage disposal and treatment, solid waste disposal, clean drinking water, and clean living and working conditions

scrotum a skin-covered sac that holds the testes and that hangs from the male body

sebaceous gland gland in the skin that adds oil to the skin and hair shaft to keep skin and hair looking smooth and healthy

second-degree burn a burn that extends into the inner skin layer and is red, swollen, and blistered

sedentary not taking part in physical activity on a regular basis

self-actualization the achievement of the best that a person can be

self-concept a measure of how one views oneself

self-esteem a measure of how much one values, respects, and feels confident about oneself

semen a fluid made up of sperm and other secretions from the male reproductive organs

sensory nerve a nerve that carries signals from a sense organ to the central nervous system, where the signals are processed or relayed

set a fixed number of repetitions followed by a rest period

sexual abuse any sexual act that happens without consent

sexual assault any sexual activity in which force or the threat of force is used

sexual harassment any unwanted remark, behavior, or touch that has sexual content

sexual intercourse the reproductive process in which the penis is inserted into the vagina and through which a new human life may begin

sexually transmitted disease (STD) an infectious disease that is spread by sexual contact; also referred to as a *sexually transmitted infection* (STI)

shock a condition in which some body organs do not get enough oxygenated blood

sibling a brother or sister related to another brother or sister by blood, the marriage of the individuals' parents, or adoption

side effect any effect that is caused by a drug and that is different from the drug's intended effect

sidestream smoke smoke that escapes from the tip of a cigarette, cigar, or pipe

skeleton a framework of bones that support the muscles and organs and protect the inner organs

sleep apnea a sleeping disorder characterized by interruptions of normal breathing patterns during sleep

sleep deprivation a lack of sleep

sperm the sex cell that is made by the testes and that is needed to fertilize an egg from a female

spinal cord the column of nerve tissue that runs through the backbone from the base of the brain

spinal nerves nerves that branch from the spinal cord and that go to the brain and to the tissues of the body

splint a device used to stabilize (hold secure) a body part

sprain an injury in which the ligaments in a joint are stretched too far or are torn

stimulant a drug that temporarily increases a person's energy and alertness

strain an injury in which a muscle or tendon has been stretched too far or has torn

stress the body's and mind's response to a demand

stressor any situation that is a demand on the body or mind

stroke a sudden attack of weakness or paralysis that occurs when a blood vessel in the brain bursts or becomes blocked

suffocation a fatal injury caused by an inability to breathe when the nose and mouth are blocked or when the body becomes oxygen-deficient

suicide the act of intentionally taking one's own life

symptom a change that a person notices in his or her body or mind and that is caused by a disease or disorder

synapse a tiny space across which nerve impulses pass from one neuron to the next

syphilis (SIF uh lis) a bacterial STD that causes ulcers or chancres; if untreated, it can lead to mental and physical disabilities and premature death

tar a sticky, black substance in tobacco smoke that coats the inside of the airways and that contains many carcinogens

target heart rate zone a heart rate range within which the most gains in cardiorespiratory health will occur

T cell a white blood cell that is made in red bone marrow, matures in the thymus, and that attacks cells that have been infected by viruses

tendon a strong connective tissue that attaches muscles to bones

testis (testicle) the male reproductive organ that makes sperm and testosterone

testosterone the male hormone that is made by the testes and that regulates male secondary sex characteristics and the production of sperm

third-degree burn a burn that penetrates all layers of skin as well as the tissue beneath the skin and appears pearly white, tan colored, or charred

tinnitus (ti NIET es) a buzzing, ringing, or whistling sound in one or both ears that occurs even when no sound is present

tolerance the ability to overlook differences and to accept people for who they are; *also* a condition in which a user needs more of a drug to get the same effect

tonsils small, rounded masses of lymph tissues found in the throat

tooth decay the process in which acid from plaque and tartar slowly dissolve the hard surfaces of the teeth

trachea the long tube that carries air from the larynx to the lungs; also called the windpipe

trigger lock a device that helps prevent a gun from being fired

ultraviolet (UV) radiation radiation in sunlight that is responsible for tanning and burning skin

universal precautions the set of procedures used to avoid contact with body fluids and to reduce the risk of spreading HIV and other diseases

urinary bladder the hollow, muscular sac that stores urine

urine waste liquid excreted by the kidneys, stored in the bladder, and passed through the urethra to the outside of the body

uterus the female reproductive organ that provides a place to support a developing human

vaccine a substance that is usually prepared from killed or weakened pathogens or from genetic material and that is introduced into a body to produce immunity

vagina the female reproductive organ that connects the outside of the body to the uterus and that receives sperm during sexual intercourse

value a strong belief or ideal

vegetarian dietary pattern that includes few or no animal products

vein a blood vessel that carries blood toward the heart

ventricle one of the two large, muscular chambers that pump blood out of the heart

violence physical force that is used to harm people or damage property

virus a tiny disease-causing particle that consists of genetic material and a protein coat

vitamin a class of nutrients that contain carbon and that are needed in small amounts to maintain health and allow growth

wake a ceremony to view or watch over the deceased person before the funeral

weight management a program of sensible eating and exercise habits that keep weight at a healthy level

wellness the achievement of a person's best in all six components of health

white blood cell a blood cell whose primary job is to defend the body against disease

withdrawal uncomfortable physical and psychological symptoms produced when a physically dependent drug user stops using drugs

wound a break or tear in the soft tissues of the body

A

abdominal thrusts (Heimlich maneuver)/empuje abdominal acción de aplicar presión al estómago de una persona atragantada para lograr que un objeto salga por la garganta

abstinence/abstinencia decisión consciente de no participar en actividades sexuales y las capacidades necesarias para respaldar esa decisión

abuse/abuso daño físico o emocional a una persona

acid rain/lluvia ácida toda precipitación que tenga un pH inferior a lo normal (acídico)

acne/acné inflamación de la piel que se produce cuando los poros de la piel se tapan con suciedad y grasa

acquired immune deficiency syndrome (AIDS)/ síndrome de inmunodeficiencia adquirida (SIDA) enfermedad producida por la infección del VIH, que debilita el sistema inmunológico

action plan/plan de acción conjunto de instrucciones que te ayudarán a alcanzar una meta

active ingredient/ingrediente activo componente químico que hace que un medicamento tenga efecto

addiction/adicción estado de dependencia a una droga

adolescence/adolescencia período de tiempo entre el comienzo de la pubertad y la maduración completa

advocate/defender hablar o discutir a favor de algo

aggressive/agresivo modo hostil y poco amable de expresarse

alcohol/alcohol droga presente en el vino, la cerveza y el licor, que produce intoxicación

alcohol abuse/abuso de alcohol beber demasiado alcohol, con demasiada frecuencia o en horarios no adecuados

alcoholism/alcoholismo enfermedad que hace que una persona pierda el control de su conducta como bebedor; adicción física y emocional al alcohol

allergy/alergia reacción exagerada del sistema inmunológico a una sustancia del medio ambiente que es inofensiva para la mayoría de las personas

alveolus/alvéolo bolsa de aire de paredes delgadas que se encuentra en grupos en los pulmones y es el lugar donde se produce el intercambio de gases

Alzheimer's disease/enfermedad de Alzheimer enfermedad que hace que una persona pierda poco a poco las capacidades mentales y la habilidad de realizar las actividades cotidianas

amebic dysentery /disentería amibiana inflamación del intestino producida por una amiba

Americans with Disabilities Act (ADA)/Ley de Estadounidenses Discapacitados (ADA, por su nombre en inglés) ley de amplio alcance que se creó para que sea más accesible la sociedad estadounidense a las personas con discapacidades

anabolic steroid/esteroide anabólico versión sintética de la hormona masculina testosterona que se utiliza para aumentar el desarrollo muscular

anorexia nervosa/anorexia nerviosa trastorno alimenticio en el que la persona deja de comer, tiene una imagen distorsionada de su cuerpo y sufre una pérdida de peso extrema

antibiotic resistance /resistencia al antibiótico condición en la que un antibiótico en particular ya no puede matar a una bacteria

antibody/anticuerpo proteína que produce el sistema inmunológico en respuesta a una antígeno específico

antigen/antígeno proteína que se encuentra en la superficie de todas las células y virus y sirve para identificarlos

appetite/apetito deseo, más que necesidad, de comer algunos alimentos

artery/arteria vaso sanguíneo que transporta la sangre desde el corazón hacia otras partes del cuerpo

arthritis/artritis inflamación de las articulaciones

assertive/acertado directo y respetuoso en la manera de expresarse

asset/don habilidad o recurso que ayuda a una persona a lograr sus metas

asthma/asma trastorno que hace que las vías respiratorias que transportan aire hacia los pulmones se estrechen y se obstruyan con mucosidades

asymptomatic/asintomático que no presenta síntomas de enfermedad o trastorno pero padece una infección o enfermedad

asymptomatic stage/estado asintomático estado de una infección en el que el hay un agente infeccioso, tal como el VIH, pero se presentan pocos o ningún síntoma de la infección

atherosclerosis/aterosclerosis enfermedad caracterizada por la formación de materia grasa en el interior de las paredes de las arterias

atrium/aurícula cámara del corazón que recibe la sangre que regresa al corazón

autoimmune disease/enfermedad autoinmune enfermedad en la que el sistema inmunológico de una persona ataca a ciertas células, tejidos u órganos del cuerpo

bacteria/bacteria organismos unicelulares muy pequeños, algunos de los cuales pueden causar enfermedades

basal metabolic rate (BMR)/índice metabólico basal (IMB) tasa a la que se consume energía para mantener el cuerpo con vida en estado de reposo y ayuno

B cell/célula B tipo de linfocito que se produce en la médula ósea y fabrica anticuerpos

benign tumor/tumor benigno masa celular anormal, pero generalmente inofensiva

binge drinking/beber compulsivamente acción de beber cinco o más bebidas en un corto tiempo

binge eating/bingeing/comer compulsivamente acción de comer una gran cantidad de alimentos en una comida; generalmente acompañada por una sensación de descontrol

blood/sangre tejido formado por células y líquidos que transportan oxígeno, dióxido de carbono y nutrientes en el cuerpo

blood alcohol concentration (BAC)/concentración de alcohol en la sangre (CAS) cantidad de alcohol en la sangre de una persona, expresada en porcentaje

blood pressure/presión arterial fuerza que la sangre ejerce en el interior de las paredes de un vaso sanguíneo

blood vessels/vasos sanguíneos tubos, incluyendo las arterias, las venas y los capilares, a través de los cuales la sangre circula por el cuerpo

body composition/composición corporal proporción del peso corporal formada por tejido de grasa en comparación con los huesos, músculos y órganos

body image/imagen corporal medición de cómo te ves y te sientes con respecto a tu aspecto y qué tan a gusto te sientes con tu cuerpo

body mass index (BMI)/índice de masa corporal (IMC) índice de peso con relación a la altura que se utiliza para evaluar el peso de un cuerpo sano

bone marrow/médula ósea tejido blando que está dentro de los huesos

brain/encéfalo centro de control principal del sistema nervioso que está ubicado dentro del cráneo

brain stem/tronco encefálico parte del cerebro que filtra y dirige señales desde la médula espinal hacia otras partes del cerebro

bronchiole/bronquiolo tubo respiratorio que envía aire desde la tráquea a cada pulmón

bronchus/bronquio tubo respiratorio delgado que se ramifica a partir de un bronquio dentro del pulmón

bulimia nervosa/bulimia nerviosa trastorno alimenticio en el que una persona come constantemente una gran cantidad de alimentos y luego vomita o toma laxantes para eliminar la comida del cuerpo

bullying/intimidación acción de asustar o manipular a otra persona mediante amenazas o la fuerza física

burn/quemadura lesion de la piel y otros tejidos producida por calor, sustancias químicas, electricidad o radiación

cancer/cáncer enfermedad en la que las células crecen de manera incontrolable

capillary/capilar pequeño vaso sanguíneo que transporta sangre entre las arterias y las venas, y por donde los nutrientes y los desechos entran y salen del torrente sanguíneo

carbohydrate/carbohidrato tipo de nutriente que aporta energía e incluye azúcares, féculas y fibras

carbon monoxide/monóxido de carbono gas que impide que el oxígeno ingrese al torrente sanguíneo

carcinogen/carcinógeno toda sustancia química o agente que causa cáncer

cardiac pacemaker/marcapasos cardíaco grupo de células que se encuentran en la parte superior de la aurícula derecha y controlan los latidos del corazón

cardiopulmonary resuscitation (CPR)/resucitación cardiopulmonar (CPR, por su nombre en inglés) técnica para salvar la vida que combina la recuperación de la respiración y compresiones en el pecho

cardiovascular disease (CVD)/enfermedad cardiovascular trastorno del sistema circulatorio causado por daño al corazón y vaso sanguíneo

carotid pulse/pulso carotideo pulso que se siente en las arterias de las carótidas, arterias principales del cuello

cavity/caries cavidad en la dentadura de una persona producida por la degeneración dental

central nervous system (CNS)/sistema nervioso central (SNC) el cerebro y la médula espinal

cerebellum/cerebelo parte del cerebro que controla el equilibrio y la postura

cerebrum/cerebro parte más grande y compleja del encéfalo que recibe sensaciones y controla el movimiento

cervix/cuello de la matriz base angosta de la matriz que conduce a la vagina

chemotherapy/quimioterapia uso de drogas con la finalidad de destruir células cancerosas

chlamydia /clamidia ETS causada por una bacteria que infecta los órganos reproductores y provoca la secreción de una sustancia mucosa

chlorofluorocarbons (CFCs)/clorofluorocarbonos (CFC) contaminantes que despiden ciertos pulverizadores en aerosol y líquidos refrigerantes

choking/atragantamiento trastorno en el que el tubo digestivo se obstruye de manera parcial o total

chronic disease/enfermedad crónica enfermedad que se desarrolla poco a poco y continúa durante un período prolongado de tiempo

circadian rhythm/ritmo circadiano sistema interno del cuerpo encargado de regular los patrones de sueño y actividad

cirrhosis/cirrosis enfermedad mortal que reemplaza los tejidos sanos del hígado por tejidos cicatrizados inservibles; en la mayoría de los casos es causada por el abuso de alcohol durante un largo período de tiempo

club (designer) drug/droga de club (de diseño) droga elaborada de modo que su estructura química y efectos son similares a los de una droga ilegal común

cochlea/cóclea tubo en forma de espiral, lleno de líquido, que se encuentra en el oído interno y participa en la audición

codependency/codependencia condición en la que un integrante de la familia o un amigo sacrifica sus necesidades para satisfacer las necesidades de un adicto

collaborate/colaborar trabajar juntos con una o más personas

collagen/colágeno fibras de proteínas que hacen que la piel sea flexible

colon/colon porción principal del intestino grueso

consequence/consecuencia resultado de las acciones y las decisiones de una persona

conservation/conservación uso correcto y la protección de los recursos naturales

consumer/consumidor persona que compra productos o servicios

coping/sobrellevar manejar los problemas y los inconvenientes de manera eficaz

cross contamination/contaminación cruzada traspaso de contaminantes de un alimento a otro

Daily Value (DV)/Valor Diario (VD) cantidad diaria recomendada de un nutriente; se utiliza en las etiquetas de los alimentos y permite a las personas saber qué aporta un alimento a su dieta

dandruff/caspa trocitos escamosos de células de piel muertas en el cuero cabelludo

date rape/violación en una cita relación sexual forzada por alguien que la víctima conoce

decibels (dB)/decibeles (dB) unidades utilizadas para medir el sonido

deductible/deducible monto que el abonado debe pagar antes de que una compañía de seguro comience a pagar los servicios médicos

defense mechanism/mecanismo de defensa pensamiento o conducta inconsciente que se utiliza para no experimentar emociones desagradables

deforestation/deforestación eliminación de árboles de los bosques naturales con la finalidad de hacer lugar para cosechas o construcciones

dehydration/deshidratación condición en la que el cuerpo no contiene suficiente agua

depressant/depresivo droga que produce relajación y somnolencia

depression/depresión trastorno del ánimo en el que una persona se siente muy triste y desesperanzada durante un período largo de tiempo

dermis/dermis capa funcional de la piel debajo de la epidermis

designated driver/conductor asignado persona que decide no beber alcohol en un evento social para poder manejar de manera segura, ya sea que viaje solo o acompañado

diabetes/diabetes trastorno en el que las células no pueden obtener glucosa de la sangre y que resulta en niveles altos de glucosa en la sangre

diabetic coma/coma diabético pérdida del conocimiento que ocurre cuando el nivel de azúcar en la sangre es muy alto y se forma una acumulación de sustancias tóxicas en la sangre

diaphragm/diafragma lámina de músculo que separa la cavidad torácica de la cavidad abdominal y que participa de la respiración

Dietary Guidelines for Americans/Guía Alimenticia para los Estadounidenses conjunto de recomendaciones alimenticias y sobre el estilo de vida desarrollado para mejorar la salud y reducir el riesgo de enfermedades relacionadas con la nutrición en la población estadounidense

dietary supplement/suplemento alimenticio todo producto que se tome vía oral y contenga un ingrediente dietario y lleve una etiqueta que lo identifique como un suplemento dietario

digestive tract/tracto digestivo serie de órganos por los que pasan los alimentos

direct pressure/presión directa presión ejercida por una persona para de convencer a otra de que haga algo que normalmente no haría

disability/discapacidad incapacidad o deficiencia mental o física que afecta la actividad normal

discipline/disciplina acción de enseñar a un niño a través de la corrección, indicaciones, reglas y refuerzo

dislocation/dislocación lesión en la que un hueso sale de su posición normal en una articulación

distress/alteración estrés negativo que puede hacer que una persona se enferme o no logre alcanzar una meta

divorce/divorcio terminación legal de un matrimonio

domestic violence/violencia doméstica uso de la fuerza para controlar y mantener poder sobre el conyuge en el hogar

drug/droga toda sustancia química que provoca un cambio en el estado físico o emociónal de una persona

drug abuse/abuso de drogas uso indebido e intencional de una droga legal o uso de una droga ilegal

drug combination therapy/terapia de combinación de drogas programa de tratamiento para el SIDA en el que los pacientes toman más de una droga regularmente

drug interaction/interacción de drogas condición en la que una droga reacciona al ser combinada con otra droga, un alimento o un suplemento alimenticio; por ejemplo, el efecto de una de las drogas puede ser mayor o menor

drug tolereance/tolerancia a la droga condición en la que una persona necesita aumentar la dosis de droga para obtener el mismo efecto

E

ear/oído órgano sensorial que participa en la audición y el equilibrio

eardrum/tímpano membrana que transmite ondas de sonido del oído externo al oído medio

ecosystem/ecosistema comunidad de seres vivos y los elementos no vivientes de su entorno

egg (ovum)/óvulo célula sexual producida por los ovarios que puede ser fecundada por un espermatozoide

electrocution/electrocución lesión fatal que ocurre cuando ingresa electricidad al cuerpo y se destruyen tejidos vitales

embryo/embrión ser humano en desarrollo, desde el momento de la fecundación hasta la semana 8 de gestación

emotion/emoción sentimiento producido como respuesta a un hecho de la vida

emotional intimacy/madurez emocional conjunto de emociones ordenadas según el grado de placer que proporcionan

emotional maturity/espectro emocional capacidad de evaluar una relación o una situación y actuar según lo que resulta más favorable para uno mismo y para la otra persona involucrada en la relación

empathy/empatía capacidad de comprender los sentimientos, conducta y actitudes de otra persona

emphysema/enfisema enfermedad respiratoria en la que el aire no puede entrar ni salir de los alvéolos porque estos se rompen y pierden elasticidad

enabling/habilitar ayudar a un adicto a evitar las consecuencias negativas de su conducta

endocrine gland/glándula endocrina órgano que libera hormonas en el torrente sanguíneo o en el líquido que rodea las células

endometrium/endometrio pared interior de la matriz

environment/entorno seres vivos y elementos no vivientes que rodean a un organismo

environmental tobacco smoke/humo de tabaco ambiental (HTA) combinación del humo exhalado por el fumador y el emanado por el cigarrillo

enzyme/enzima proteína u otro tipo de molécula que permite el desarrollo de procesos químicos en los seres vivos

epidemic/epidemia desarrollo de más casos de los esperados de una enfermedad

epidermis/epidermis capa más externa de la piel formada por una o varias capas de células muertas

epinephrine/epinefrina una de las hormonas de estrés que el cuerpo libera en situaciones de estrés

esophagus/esófago tubo recto y largo que conecta la faringe con el estómago y a través del cual pasan los alimentos para llegar al estómago

estrogen/estrógeno hormona que regula el desarrollo sexual y la función reproductiva de las mujeres

eustachian tube/conducto de Eustaquio tubo que conecta el oído medio con la garganta

eustress/estrés positivo estrés positivo que energiza a la persona y le ayuda a alcanzar una meta

extended family/familia extendida personas que no están incluidas dentro del núcleo familiar pero están relacionadas con el éste, tales como, tías, tíos, abuelos y primos

external bleeding/sangrado externo sangrado en la superficie del cuerpo

external pressure/presión externa presión que una persona siente de parte de otra persona o grupo de personas para actuar de una manera determinada

eye/ojo órgano sensorial que recoge y enfoca la luz y genera señales que se envían al cerebro

fad diet/dieta de moda dieta que requiere un cambio importante en los hábitos alimenticios y prometa bajar de peso rápidamente

fallopian tube/trompas de Falopio órgano de reproducción femenino que transporta al óvulo desde el ovario hasta la matriz

family counseling/consejería familiar charlas de asesoramiento a cargo de un tercero para resolver conflictos entre los integrantes de una familia

fat/grasa tipo de nutrientes que aportan energía; *también* es la principal forma de almacenamiento de energía en el cuerpo

fee-for-service insurance plan/plan de seguro de pago por servicio plan de seguro tradicional en el que el paciente debe pagar una prima y un deducible

fertilization/fecundación proceso mediante el cual un espermatozoide y un óvulo y el material genético del que están compuestos se unen para crear una vida humana

fetal alcohol syndrome (FAS)/síndrome de alcohol fetal (SAF) conjunto de defectos físicos y mentales que afectan a un feto que estuvo expuesto al alcohol debido al consumo de alcohol de la madre durante el embarazo

fetus/feto ser humano en desarrollo, desde el inicio de la novena semana de embarazo hasta el parto

first-degree burn/quemadura de primer grado quemadura que afecta sólo la capa externa de la piel y deja una marca de color rosa

FITT/FITT formula para los cuatro componentes del entrenamiento físico: frecuencia, intensidad, tiempo y tipo

follicle/folículo orificio muy pequeño en la piel que sostiene la raíz del cabello

food allergy/alergia a alimentos respuesta anormal a un alimento que manifiesta el sistema inmunológico

food-borne illness/enfermedad por alimentos enfermedad causada por comer o beber un alimento que contiene una toxina o un microorganismo capaz de provocar una enfermedad

fracture/fractura fisura o rotura de un hueso

fraud/fraude comercialización y venta de productos o servicios sobre los que se da información falsa

frostbite/congelación daño a la piel y a los tejidos debajo de la piel provocado por un frío intenso

funeral/funeral ceremonia de entierro o cremación de una persona fallecida

fungus/hongo organismo que absorbe y utiliza nutrientes de organismos vivos o muertos

gene/gen segmento de ADN ubicado en un cromosoma que lleva el código de un rasgo hereditario específico y que se transmite de padres a hijos

generic medicine/medicamento genérico medicamento elaborado por una empresa diferente a la empresa que creó el medicamento original

gene therapy/terapia de genes técnica que coloca una copia sana de un gen en las células de una persona cuya copia del gen tiene algún defecto

genetic counseling/asesoría genética proceso de informar a las personas o parejas sobre su composición genética

gingivitis/gingivitis trastorno en el que las encías se infectan y se enrojecen y empiezan a separarse de los dientes

goal/meta algo por lo que te esfuerzas y que esperas alcanzar

gonorrhea/gonorrea ETS causada por una bacteria que infecta las membranas mucosas, incluyendo las membranas de la mucosa genital

grieve/estar de duelo expresar una profunda tristeza por una pérdida

hallucinogen/alucinógeno una droga que desfigura percepción, capaz de hacer que la persona que las toma vea o escuche cosas que no son reales

hand signals/señales manuales señales que utilizan los ciclistas para indicar a los peatones, automovilistas y demás personas que transitan las calles cuando van a cruzar o detenerse

hazardous weather/clima peligroso clima peligroso que despierta preocupaciones sobre la seguridad

hazing/novatadas acoso a los nuevos integrantes de un grupo de manera abusiva y humillante

head lice/piojos parásitos muy pequeños que se alimentan de los vasos sanguíneos del cuero cabelludo

health/salud estado de bienestar en el que todos los componentes de la salud (físicos, emocionales, sociales, mentales, espirituales y ambientales) están en equilibrio

health literacy/educación para la salud conocimiento de la información sobre la salud necesario para tomar decisiones acertadas sobre ésta

health maintenance organization (HMO)/organización de mantenimiento de la salud (HMO, por su nombre en inglés) plan de salud administrado en el que los pacientes deben utilizar los servicios de un médico que trabaje bajo contrato con la compañía de seguro

Health on the Net (HON) Foundation/Fundación Salud en la Red (HON, por su nombre en inglés) organización de sitios Web que aceptan seguir un código de ética con respecto a la información de la salud

health-related fitness/estado físico relacionado a la salud cualidades de estado físico necesarias para mantener y promover un cuerpo sano

Healthy People 2010/Gente sana 2010 conjunto de objetivos para la salud establecidos por el Departamento de Salud y Servicios Humanos de Estados Unidos con el propósito de mejorar la salud de la nación para el año 2010

heart/corazón órgano que funciona como una bomba que hace fluir la sangre a través del cuerpo

heart attack/ataque al corazón súbita interrupción del flujo de sangre que llega al músculo cardíaco

heartburn/acidez estomacal dolor que se siente detrás del esternón provocado por el TREG (trastorno de reflujo esofagogástrico)

heat exhaustion/agotamiento por calor trastorno de salud en el que el cuerpo adquiere una temperatura superior a la temperatura normal

heat stroke/insolación trastorno de salud en el que el sistema que controla la capacidad del cuerpo para enfriarse mediante la transpiración deja de funcionar

helper T cell (CD4+ cell)/célula T colaboradora (célula CD4+) glóbulo blanco que activa la respuesta inmunológica y que es la célula objetivo principal de la infección por VIH

hemoglobin/hemoglobina pigmento presente en los glóbulos rojos encargado de transportar oxígeno

hepatitis/hepatitis inflamación del hígado

hereditary disease/enfermedad hereditaria enfermedad causada por cromosomas anormales o por genes defectuosos que un niño hereda de uno o ambos padres

heredity/herencia transmisión de rasgos de los padres a sus hijos biológicos

high-risk population/población de alto riesgo todo grupo de personas que tienen mayores probabilidades de contraer una enfermedad

HIV-antibody test/prueba de anticuerpo del VIH prueba que detecra los anticuerpos del VIH, lo que permite determinar si una persona está infectada por el VIH

HIV positive/VIH positivo describe a una persona que tiene dos pruebas diferentes de VIH con resultado positivo

home healthcare services/servicios de salud en el hogar servicios médicos, tratamientos o equipo que se le proporcionan al paciente en su casa

hormone/hormona sustancia química que se elabora y se libera en una célula y que regulariza los actividades de otras células

Human Genome Project/Proyecto del genoma humano trabajo de investigación con el objetivo de determinar las ubicaciones de todos los genes humanos en los cromosomas e interpretar las instrucciones codificadas en los genes

human immunodeficiency virus (HIV)/virus de inmunodeficiencia humana virus que infecta principalmente las celulas del sistema inmunológico y causa el SIDA

human papilloma virus (HPV)/virus de papiloma humano (VPH) grupo de virus que puede causar verrugas genitales en hombres y mujeres y cáncer de cuello de la matriz en las mujeres

hunger/hambre respuesta física del cuerpo a la necesidad de alimentos

hypothermia/hipotermia temperatura corporal inferior al valor normal

incest/incesto relación sexual entre los integrantes de una familia que no son marido y mujer

incontinence/incontinencia pérdida del control voluntario de la orina

indirect pressure/presión indirecta presión para hacer algo porque las personas que admiras lo hacen

infectious disease/enfermedad infecciosa toda enfermedad causada por un agente o un patógeno que invade el cuerpo

inflammation/inflamación reacción a una lesión o infección caracterizada por dolor, enrojecimiento e hinchazón

inhalant/inhalante una droga que se inhala en forma de vapor

inpatient care/hospitalización atención médica que requiere que una persona permanezca en el hospital durante más de un día

insomnia/insomnio incapacidad para dormir aun si la persona está físicamente agotada

insulin/insulina hormona que permite que la glucosa pase del torrente sanguíneo a las células

integrity/integridad característica de hacer lo que uno sabe que es correcto

internal bleeding/sangrado interno sangrado dentro del cuerpo

internal pressure /presión interna impulso que siente una persona de actuar de una manera determinada

intervention/intervención acción de enfrentar a un consumidor de drogas con su problema para que deje de consumirlas

intoxication/intoxicación cambios físicos y mentales producidos por beber alcohol

joint/articulación parte del cuerpo en la que dos o más huesos se encuentran

keratin/queratina proteína fuerte y flexible que se encuentra en la piel, el pelo y las uñas

kidney/riñón uno de los órganos que filtra el agua y los desechos de la sangre, elimina productos en forma de orina y regula la concentración de ciertas sustancias en la sangre

lactose intolerance/intolerancia a la lactosa incapacidad de digerir completamente la lactosa, el azúcar de la leche

leukemia/leucemia cáncer de los tejidos del cuerpo que producen glóbulos blancos

life expectancy/esperanza de vida tiempo de vida promedio que se espera viva una persona

life skill/destreza para la vida herramienta para construir una vida sana

lifestyle disease/enfermedad causada por el estilo de vida enfermedad causada en parte por conductas no saludables y en parte por otros factores

ligament/ligamento tipo de tejido que mantiene unidos los extremos de los huesos en las articulaciones

lung/pulmón órgano principal del aparato respiratorio en el que el oxígeno del aire se intercambia con el dióxido de carbono de la sangre

lymph/linfa líquido transparente y amarillento que sale de los capilares, llena los espacios alrededor de las células del cuerpo y es absorbido por los vasos y ganglios linfáticos

lymphatic system/sistema linfático red de vasos que transportan la linfa por todo el cuerpo

lymph node/ganglio linfático órgano pequeño en forma de frijol que contiene fibras pequeñas que eliminan partículas de la linfa

lymphocytes/linfocitos glóbulos blancos que destruyen bacterias, virus y células muertas o dañadas

mainstream smoke/humo emanado por fumador humo que un fumador inhala a través de un cigarrillo y luego exhala

malignant tumor/tumor maligno masa de células que invade y destruye el tejido sano

managed-care plan/plan de atención de salud administrada plan en el que una compañía de seguros firma un contrato con un grupo de médicos

marijuana/marihuana flores y hojas secas de la planta *Cannabis sativa*

marriage/matrimonio unión para toda la vida entre marido y mujer, quienes mantienen una relación íntima

media/medios de comunicación todas las formas públicas de comunicación; por ejemplo, televisión, radio, periódicos, Internet y avisos publicitarios

Medicaid/Medicaid programa del cuidado de la salud disponible para personas que tienen un plan de asistencia, tienen hijos dependientes, o son ancianos, ciegos o discapacitados

Medicare/Medicare programa de salud para personas de 65 años de edad o mayores y para personas más jóvenes con discapacidades

medicine/medicamento droga que se utiliza para curar, prevenir o tratar un dolor, una afección o una enfermedad

melanin/melanina pigmento que da color a la piel y la protege de los rayos ultravioleta

memorial service/funeral ceremonia para recordar a una persona fallecida

meningitis/meningitis inflamación de las membranas que recubren el cerebro y la médula espinal

menopause/menopausia etapa de la vida de una mujer en la que deja de ovular y menstruar

menstrual cycle/ciclo menstrual serie mensual de cambios controlados por hormonas que preparan el interior de la matriz para el embarazo

menstruation/menstruación proceso mensual de desprendimiento del recubrimiento interior de la matriz durante el que la sangre y los tejidos salen del cuerpo de la mujer a través de la vagina

mental disorder/trastorno mental enfermedad que afecta los pensamientos, las emociones y la conducta de una persona

mental health/salud mental forma en la que una persona piensa y responde a hechos de su vida

midlife crisis/crisis de la segunda edad sensación de incertidumbre sobre los valores y la identidad propios que algunas personas experimentan entre los 40 y 60 años de edad

mineral/mineral clase de nutrientes que son elementos químicos necesarios para ciertos procesos del cuerpo, tales como la actividad de las enzimas y la formación de los huesos

motor nerve/nervio motor nervio que transmite señales desde el cerebro o la médula espinal a los músculos y glándulas

mucus/mucosa líquido espeso y viscoso segregado por el interior de los órganos y las glándulas

multiple sclerosis/esclerosis múltiple enfermedad autoinmune en la que el cuerpo ataca por error la capa de aislación grasosa de los nervios del cerebro y la médula espinal

MyPyramid/Mi pirámide sistema de orientación alimenticia que alienta a los consumidores a elegir alimentos más saludables y a realizar ejercicio físico a diario

natural disaster/desastre natural acontecimiento natural que causa muchas lesiones, muertes y daños a propiedades

neglect/negligencia incumplimiento de una persona encargada del cuidado de un niño en su deber de satisfacer las necesidades básicas del niño, tales como comida, ropa o protección

negotiation/negociación trato o concesión para solucionar un conflicto de manera pacífica

neonatal abstinence syndrome/síndrome de abstinencia neonatal supresión de drogas que experimenta el bebé recién nacido de una madre que consumía drogas frecuentemente durante el embarazo

nephron/nefrón unidad muy pequeña que funciona como filtro de sangre en el riñón

nerve/nervio conjunto de células que transmiten señales eléctricas desde una parte del cuerpo a otra

neuron/neurona célula especializada que recibe y envía señales eléctricas

neurotransmitter/neurotransmisor sustancia química liberada en el extremo del axón de una neurona

nicotine/nicotina droga altamente adictiva que se encuentra en todos los productos con tabaco

nicotine replacement therapy/terapia para reemplazo de nicotina medicamentos que dan cantidades seguras de nicotina para ayudar a una persona parar el uso del tabaco

nonrenewable resource/recurso no renovable recurso natural que se puede utilizar más rápido que lo que se puede reponer naturalmente

nuclear family/familia nuclear familia en la que la madre, el padre y uno o más hijos biológicos o adoptados viven juntos

nutrient/nutriente sustancia en los alimentos que aporta energía o contribuye en la formación de los tejidos del cuerpo y que es necesaria para vivir y crecer

nutrient deficiency/insuficiencia nutricional estado de no tener la cantidad necesaria de un nutriente para mantener una buena salud

nutrient density/densidad nutricional medida de los nutrientes en un alimento en función de la energía que ese alimento aporta

nutrition/nutrición ciencia o estudio de los alimentos y la forma en que el cuerpo los utiliza

obesity/obesidad estado en el que una persona tiene una cantidad significativa de grasa corporal en exceso; estado en el que el peso corporal de una persona supera en más de un 20 por ciento su peso corporal recomendado

Occupational Safety and Health Administration (OSHA)/Administración de la Salud y la Seguridad Ocupacional (OSHA, por su nombre en inglés) organismo gubernamental que ayuda a prevenir lesiones, enfermedades y muertes relacionadas con el trabajo

opiates/opiáceos drogas muy adictivas producidas a partir de la adormidera de amapola que se usan como analgésicos, anestésicos, y sedativos

opportunistic infection (OI)/infección oportunista (IO) enfermedad causada por un organismo que provoca enfermedades en personas con sistemas inmunológicos débiles; se encuentra frecuentemente en pacientes con SIDA

outbreak/brote aumento inesperado de una enfermedad

outpatient care/atención a pacientes externos atención médica que requiere que la persona permanezca en el hospital sólo mientras se le realiza el tratamiento

ovary/ovario órgano reproductor femenino que produce los óvulos y las hormonas estrógeno y progesterona

overdose/sobredosis consumo excesivo de una droga que produce enfermedad, pérdida del conocimiento, daño permanente o hasta la muerte

over-the-counter (OTC) medicine/medicamentos de venta sin receta (VSR) todo medicamento que se puede comprar sin receta médica

overpopulation/sobrepoblación cuando una población es demasiado grande para ser cubierta por los recursos de asistencia disponibles

overtraining/sobreentrenamiento condición causada por el exceso de ejercicio

overweight/sobrepeso excedido de peso en relación a su estatura

ovulation/ovulación proceso mensual mediante el cual los ovarios liberan un óvulo maduro

pandemic/pandémica enfermedad que se transmite rápidamente a través de las poblaciones humanas en todo el mundo

parental responsibility/responsabilidad de los padres el deber de los padres de satisfacer las necesidades físicas, financieras, mentales y emocionales de un niño

passive/pasivo que no presenta oposición ante desafíos o presiones

pathogen/patógeno todo agente, especialmente un virus u otro microorganismo, que provoca una enfermedad

peer mediation/mediación de pares técnica en la que un tercero de tu misma edad, capacitado en el tema, ayuda a las personas involucradas en un conflicto a solucionarlo de manera pacífica

peer pressure/presión de pares sensación de que debes hacer algo porque así lo quieren tus amigos

pelvic inflammatory disease (PID)/enfermedad inflamatoria de la pelvis (EIP) inflamación del tracto reproductivo superior femenino causada por la migración de una infección bacteriana en la vagina

penis/pene órgano reproductor masculino que elimina la orina del cuerpo y que puede colocar espermatozoides en el aparato reproductor femenino

peripheral nervous system (PNS)/sistema nervioso periférico (SNP) nervios que conectan al cerebro y la médula espinal con otras partes del cuerpo

physical dependence/dependencia física estado en el que el cuerpo químicamente necesita de una droga para funcionar normalmente

physical fitness/buen estado físico capacidad de realizar actividades físicas todos los días sin sentir falta de aire, dolor o cansancio extremos

placenta/placenta organo rico en vasos sanguíneos que se forma en la matriz de la madre, proporciona nutrientes y oxígeno al bebé en desarrollo y elimina sus desechos

plaque/placa mezcla de bacterias, saliva y partículas de alimentos que se deposita en los dientes

platelet/plaqueta fragmento de célula necesario para formar coágulos de sangre

poison/veneno sustancia que puede ocasionar enfermedad o muerte si ingresa al cuerpo

preferred provider organization (PPO)/organización de proveedor seleccionado (PPO, por su nombre en inglés) plan de salud administrado en el que el paciente tiene la opción de consultar a un médico que no tiene contrato con la compañía de seguro; el paciente paga una tarifa más elevada por uilizar esta opción

premium/prima tarifa mensual de un seguro

prenatal care /atención prenatal cuidado de la salud que se proporciona a una mujer durante el embarazo

prescription/receta orden escrita de un médico para un medicamento específico

primary care physician (PCP)/médico de cabecera (PCP, por su nombre en inglés) médico personal o de la familia que se encarga de los cuidados médicos generales

prioritize/dar prioridad disponer elementos por orden de importancia

prostate gland/próstata glándula masculina que aporta líquidos que nutren y protegen a los espermatozoides a medida que se desplazan por el cuerpo de la mujer

protective factor/factor protector cualquier cosa que impide a una persona adoptar una conducta ofensiva

protein/proteína clase de nutrientes que brindan energía y están formados por aminoácidos, sustancias necesarias para construir y reparar estructuras del cuerpo y regular procesos del cuerpo

psychoactive/psicoactivo describe a una droga o un medicamento que afecta al cerebro, que cambia cómo percibimos, pensamos o sentimos

puberty/pubertad período del desarrollo humano durante el que las personas adquieren la capacidad de tener hijos

public health/salud pública práctica de proteger y mejorar la salud de personas en una comunidad

public service announcement (PSA)/anuncio de servicio público (PSA, por su nombre en inglés) mensaje creado para educar a las personas sobre un tema

purging/purgar llevar a cabo acciones tales como vomitar o consumir laxantes de forma indebida para eliminar la comida del cuerpo

quackery/charlatanería un tipo de fraude; promoción de servicios o productos de salud sin valor o comprobación

Recommended Dietary Allowances (RDAs)/cuotas dietarias recomendadas (CDR) consumo de nutrientes recomendados que satisfacen las necesidades de casi todas las personas sanas

recovering/recuperando proceso de aprender a vivir sin drogas

rectum/recto porción final del intestino grueso donde se almacenan los desechos no digeridos

recycling/reciclaje reutilización de materiales a partir de productos usados para elaborar productos nuevos

red blood cell/glóbulo rojo célula de la sangre que transporta oxígeno a las células del cuerpo y que transporta dióxido de carbono de regreso a los pulmones

reflex/reflejo movimiento involuntario y casi inmediato en respuesta a un estímulo

refusal skill/habilidad de negación estrategia para evitar hacer algo que no quieres hacer

relapse/recaída regresar a utilizar drogas mientras se recupera de una adicción

renewable resource/recurso renovable recurso natural que se puede reemplazar en un período corto de tiempo

repetitions/repeticiones número de veces que se realiza un ejercicio

rescue breathing/respiración de rescate técnica de emergencia mediante la cual una persona le proporciona aire a la que no respira

resiliency/resilencia capacidad para recuperarse de una enfermedad, una dificultad u otro factor estresante

resource/recurso algo que puedes utilizar para alcanzar una meta

resting heart rate (RHR)/índice de pulsaciones en reposo (IPR) número de veces que el corazón late por minuto mientras el cuerpo está en reposo

retina/retina capa interna del ojo que es sensible a la luz, recibe imágenes formadas por el cristalino y transmite señales nerviosas a través del nervio óptico al cerebro

risk factor /factor de riesgo todo aquello capaz de aumentar la probabilidad de lesión, enfermedad u otros problemas de salud

root canal/endodoncia procedimiento mediante el cual un dentista perfora la pulpa dental para eliminar la infeccíon producida por una caries

salmonellosis/salmonelosis infección del aparato digestivo causada por una bacteria que suele contraerse al comer alimentos contaminados

sanitation/saneamiento práctica de proporcionar drenaje y tratamiento de aguas residuales, el desecho de residuos sólidos, agua potable limpia y condiciones de trabajo y vivienda limpias

scrotum/escroto bolsa de piel que contiene los testículos

sebaceous gland/glándula sebáceas glándula que aporta grasa a la piel y al cuero cabelludo para mantenerlos suaves y saludables

second-degree burn/quemadura de segundo grado quemadura que atraviesa la primera capa de la piel y produce enrojecimiento, inflamación y ampollas

sedentary/sedentario persona que no practica ninguna actividad física regularmente

self-actualization/autorealización máximo potencial de una persona

self-concept/autoconcepto medición de cómo una persona se ve a sí misma

self-esteem/autoestima medición de cuánto se valora, respeta y cuánta confianza en sí misma se tiene una persona

semen/semen líquido formado por espermatozoides y otras secreciones de los órganos reproductores masculinos

sensory nerve/nervio sensorial nervio que transmite señales desde un órgano sensorial al sistema nervioso central, donde se procesan y se organizan

set/serie número fijo de repeticiones seguidas por un período de descanso

sexual abuse/abuso sexual acto sexual que se produce sin el consentimiento de una persona

sexual assault/agresión sexual toda actividad sexual en la que se utiliza la fuerza o se amenaza con hacerlo

sexual harassment/acoso sexual todo comentario, comportamiento o contacto no deseado que tenga contenido sexual

sexual intercourse/relación sexual proceso de reproducción en el que el pene se introduce en la vagina, y mediante el cual se puede dar comienzo a una vida humana

sexually transmitted disease (STD)/enfermedad de transmisión sexual (ETS) enfermedad infecciosa que se transmite por contacto sexual; se conoce también como *infección de transmisión sexual* (ITS)

shock/choque respuesta del cuerpo a un flujo de sangre reducido

sibling/hermano hermano o hermana relacionado con otro hermano u otra hermana de sangre, el casamiento de sus padres o la adopción

side effect/efecto secundario todo efecto producido por una droga que es diferente al efecto intencional de la droga

sidestream smoke/humo del cigarrillo humo que emana la punta de un cigarrillo

skeleton/esqueleto estructura de huesos que sostiene los músculos y órganos y protegen los órganos internos

sleep apnea/apnea del sueño trastorno del sueño caracterizado por interrupciones de los patrones de respiración normales durante el sueño

sleep deprivation/ausencia de sueño falta de sueño

sperm/espermatozoide célula sexual producida por los testículos necesaria para fecundar el óvulo de una mujer

spinal cord/médula espinal columna de tejido nervioso que recorre la espalda desde la base del cerebro

spinal nerves/nervios espinales nervios que se ramifican de la médula espinal y llegan al cerebro y a los tejidos del cuerpo

splint/férula elemento utilizado para estabilizar (mantener firme) una parte del cuerpo

sprain/esguince lesión en la que los ligamentos de una articulación se estiran demasiado o se desgarran

stimulant/estimulante droga que aumenta temporalmente la energía y capacidad de atención de una persona

strain/distensión lesión en la que un músculo o un tendón se estiró demasiado o se desgarró

stress/estrés respuesta del cuerpo y la mente a una amenaza real o percibida

stressor/factor estresante toda situación que es una amenaza o que se percibe como una amenaza

stroke/apoplejía ataque repentino de debilidad o parálisis que se produce cuando se rompe o se obstruye un vaso sanguíneo del cerebro

suffocation/sofocación lesión fatal causada por la incapacidad de respirar cuando la nariz y la boca están obstruidas o cuando el cuerpo tiene una deficiencia de oxígeno

suicide/suicidio acción intencional de quitarse la vida

symptom/síntoma cambio que una persona nota en su cuerpo o mente, causado por una enfermedad o un trastorno

synapse/sinapsis espacio muy pequeño que atraviesan los impulsos nerviosos al pasar de una neurona a otra

syphilis/sífilis ETS bacteriana que ocasiona úlceras o chancros; si no se trata, puede ocasionar discapacidades físicas y mentales y muerte prematura

tar/alquitrán sustancia negra y pegajosa del humo del tabaco que cubre el interior de las vías respiratorias y que contiene muchos carcinógenos

target heart rate zone/zona de frecuencia cardíaca deseable rango de frecuencia cardíaca en el que se obtiene los mayores beneficios para la salud cardiorespiratoria

T cell/célula T glóbulo blanco que se forma en el timo y ataca a las células que han sido infectadas por virus

tendon/tendón tejido conectivo fuerte que une los músculos a los huesos

testis (testicle)/testículo órgano reproductor masculino que produce espermatozoides y testosterona

testosterone/testosterona hormona masculina que elaboran los testículos y que regula características sexuales masculinas secundarias y la producción de espermatozoides

third-degree burn/quemadura de tercer grado quemadura que penetra en todas las capas de la piel y los tejidos subyacentes y tiene una apariencia de color blanco perlado, color tostado o carbonizada

tinnitus/zumbido de oídos sonido semejante a un zumbido, timbre o silbido en uno o ambos oídos que ocurre aun cuando no se oye ningún ruido

tolerance/tolerancia capacidad de aceptar a las personas por lo que son a pesar de las diferencias; *tambien* una condición en la que una persona necesita más cantidad de una droga para sentir sus efectos originales, condición en la que una persona necesita más cantidad de una droga para sentir sus efectos originales

tonsils/amígdalas masas pequeñas y redondas de tejido linfático que se encuentran en la garganta

tooth decay/degeneración dental proceso en el que el ácido de la placa bacteriana y el sarro destruyen lentamente las superficies duras de los dientes

trachea/tráquea tubo largo que transporta aire de la laringe a los pulmones

trigger lock/traba de seguridad del gatillo dispositivo que ayuda a impedir que un arma se dispare

ultraviolet (UV) radiation/radiación ultravioleta (UV) radiación de la luz solar capaz de broncear o quemar la piel

universal precautions/precauciones universales conjunto de precauciones que se utilizan para evitar el contacto con líquidos del cuerpo y reducir el riesgo de transmisión del VIH y otras enfermedades

urinary bladder/vejiga urinaria bolsa hueca y muscular que almacena orina

urine/orina líquido segregado por los riñones, que se almacena en la vejiga y atraviesa la uretra al salir del cuerpo

uterus/matriz órgano de reproducción femenino que proporciona el lugar donde se contendrá al ser humano en desarrollo

vaccine/vacuna sustancia utilizada para hacer que una persona sea inmune a ciertas enfermedades

vagina/vagina órgano de reproducción femenino que conecta el exterior del cuerpo con el útero y que recibe espermatozoides durante la relación sexual

value/valor una creencia fuerte o ideal

vegetarian/vegetariano una dieta alimenticia que incluye poco o nada de productos derivados de animales

vein/vena vaso sanguíneo que transporta la sangre hacia el corazón

ventricle/ventrículo una de las dos cámaras musculares grandes que bombean sangre hacia afuera del corazón

violence/violencia fuerza física que se utiliza para dañar a una persona o una propiedad

virus/virus partícula pequeña capaz de causar enfermedades, formada por material genético y un revestimiento de proteína

vitamin/vitamina una clase de nutrientes que contiene carbono y que es necesaria en pequeñas cantidades para mantener la salud y permitir el crecimiento

wake/velatorio ceremonia para ver a una persona fallecida antes del funeral

weight management/manejo del peso programa de hábitos alimenticios y de ejercicios razonables que permite mantener el peso a un nivel sano

wellness/bienestar estado en el que una persona logra los mejores niveles en los seis componentes de la salud

white blood cell/glóbulo blanco célula de la sangre que tiene como función principal defender el cuerpo contra enfermedades

withdrawal/supresión síntomas psicológicos y físicos molestos que se producen cuando una persona que tiene dependencia a una droga deja de consumirla

wound/herida rotura o desgarro de los tejidos blandos del cuerpo

Boldface page numbers indicate primary discussions. Numbers followed by a *t* indicate tables, and numbers followed by an *f* indicate figures.

Acknowledgments

ACADEMIC REVIEWERS

(continued from p. iv)

Richard Storey, Ph.D.
Professor of Biology
Colorado College
Colorado Springs, Colorado

Marianne Suarez, Ph.D.
Postdoctoral Psychology Fellow
Center on Child Abuse and
 Neglect
University of Oklahoma Health
 Sciences Center
Oklahoma City, Oklahoma

Nathan R. Sullivan, M.S.W.
Associate Professor
College of Social Work
The University of Kentucky
Lexington, Kentucky

Josey Templeton, Ed.D.
Associate Professor
Department of Health, Exercise,
 and Sports Medicine
The Citadel, Military College
 of South Carolina
Charleston, South Carolina

Marianne Turow, R.D., L.D.
Associate Professor
The Culinary Institute of America
Hyde Park, New York

Martin Van Dyke, Ph.D.
Professor of Chemistry Emeritus
Front Range Community College
Westminster, Colorado

Graham Watts, Ph.D.
*Assistant Professor of Health
 and Safety*
Indiana University
Bloomington, Indiana

MEDICAL REVIEWERS

David Ho, M.D.
Professor and Scientific Director
Aaron Diamond AIDS Research
 Center
The Rockefeller University
New York, New York

Ichiro Kawachi, Ph.D., M.D.
*Associate Professor of Health
 and Social Behavior*
School of Public Health
Harvard University
Boston, Massachusetts

Leland E. Lim, M.D., Ph.D.
Clinical Instructor
Department of Neurology and
 Neurological Sciences
Stanford University School
 of Medicine
Stanford University
Palo Alto, California

Iris F. Litt, M.D.
Professor
Department of Pediatrics and
 Adolescent Medicine
School of Biomedical and
 Biological Sciences
Stanford University
Palo Alto, California

**Ronald G. Munson, M.D.,
F.A.A.F.P.**
*Assistant Clinical Professor,
 Family Practice*
Health Sciences Center
The University of Texas
San Antonio, Texas

**Alexander V. Prokhorov, M.D.,
Ph.D.**
Professor of Behavioral Science
M.D. Anderson Cancer Center
The University of Texas
Houston, Texas

Gregory A. Schmale, M.D.
Assistant Professor
Department of Orthopaedics and
 Sports Medicine
University of Washington School
 of Medicine
Seattle, Washington

Hans Steiner, M.D.
*Professor of Psychiatry and
 Behavioral Sciences*
Division of Child Psychiatry
 and Child Development
Department of Psychiatry and
 Behavioral Sciences
Stanford University School
 of Medicine
Palo Alto, California

PROFESSIONAL REVIEWERS

Toni Alvarez, L.P.C.
Counselor
Children's Solutions
Round Rock, Texas

Nancy Daley, Ph.D., L.P.C., C.P.M.
Psychologist
Austin, Texas

Sharon Deutschlander
Executive Director
Alcohol and Drug Abuse Services
Port Allegany, Pennsylvania

Terry Erwin
*Hunter Educational Coordinator
 for the State of Texas*
Texas Hunter Education Program
Texas Parks and Wildlife
 Department
Austin, Texas

Linda K. Gaul, Ph.D.
Epidemiologist
Texas Department of State Health
 Services
Austin, Texas

Georgia Girvan
Research Specialist
Idaho Radar Network Center
Boise State University
Boise, Idaho

Linda Jones, M.S.P.H.
*Manager of Systems Development
 Unit*
Children with Special Healthcare
 Needs Division
Texas Department of State Health
 Services
Austin, Texas

William Joy
President
The Joy Group
Wheaton, Illinois

Edie Leonard, R.D., L.D.
Nutrition Educator
Portland, Oregon

Jo Ann Cope Powell, Ph.D.
*Learning Specialist and Licensed
  Psychologist*
Learning Skills Center
The University of Texas at Austin
Austin, Texas

Hal Resides
Safety Manager
Corpus Christi, Texas

Eric Tiemann, E.M.T.
Emergency Medical Services
Hazardous Waste Division
Travis County Emergency
  Medical Services
Austin, Texas

Lynne E. Whitt
Executive Vice President
National Center for Health
  Education
New York, New York

TEACHER REVIEWERS

Dan Aude
Magnet Programs Coordinator
Montgomery Public Schools
Montgomery, Alabama

Andrew Banks
Sexuality Educator
LifeGuard Character and Sexuality
  Education
Austin, Texas

Robert Baronak
Biological Sciences Teacher
Donegal High School
Mount Joy, Pennsylvania

Judy Blanchard
District Health Coordinator
Newtown Public Schools
Newtown, Connecticut

David Blinn
Secondary Sciences Teacher
Wrenshall High School
Wrenshall, Minnesota

Johanna Chase, C.H.E.S.
Health Educator
California State University
Carson, California

Michelle Deery
*Health and Physical Education
  Teacher*
Donegal High School
Mount Joy, Pennsylvania

Donna DeFriese
Communications Teacher
Soddy Daisy High School
Soddy Daisy, Tennessee

Stacy Feinberg, L.M.H.C.
Family Counselor for Autism
Broward County School System
Coral Gables, Florida

Arthur Goldsmith
Secondary Sciences Teacher
Hallandale High School
Hallandale Beach, Florida

Calvin Gross
Sports Coach and Health Teacher
Rochester High School
Rochester Hills, Michigan

Jacqueline Horowitz-Ostfeld
Exceptional Student Educator
Broward County School District
Fort Lauderdale, Florida

Jay C. Jones
Sports Coach and Health Teacher
Olathe North High School
Olathe, Kansas

Lincoln LaRoe
*Coach, United States Olympic
  Rowing Team*
Milwaukee, Oregon

Steward Lipsky
Secondary Sciences Teacher
Seward High School
New York, New York

Alyson M. Mike
Department Chair
East Valley Middle School
East Helena, Montana

Donna Norwood
Secondary Sciences Teacher
Monroe High School
Monroe, North Carolina

Jenna Robles
Health Teacher
Escondido High School
Escondido, California

Denice Lee Sandefur
*Secondary Sciences and Health
  Teacher*
Nucla High School
Nucla, Colorado

Bert J. Sherwood
Science and Health Specialist
Socorro Independent School
  District
El Paso, Texas

Carla J. Thompson
Health Teacher
Lakes Community High School
Lake Villa, Illinois

Dan Utley
Sports Coach and Health Teacher
Hilton Head High School
Hilton Head Island, South
  Carolina

Alexis Wright
Principal
Rye Country Day School
Rye, New York

Joe Zelmanski
Curriculum Consultant
Rochester Community Schools
Rochester Hills, Michigan

CREDITS

Photography Credits

Abbreviations used: (t) top, (b) bottom, (c) center, (l) left, (r) right, (bkgd) background

Border design on Contents in Brief page, Table of Contents pages, Analyzing Data features, Real Life Activity features, and Life Skills features, Digital Image ©2004 EyeWire

i (c), Scott Van Osdol/HRW; ii (tr), ©Chad Slattery/Getty Images/Stone; v (all), Peter Van Steen/HRW; v (bl), Peter Van Steen/HRW

TABLE OF CONTENTS: vi (tl), Corbis Images; vi (bl), David Young-Wolff/PhotoEdit; vii (br), John Langford/ HRW; viii (tl), ©Clay Patrick McBride/Photonica; viii (cl), Digital Image ©2004 Artville; ix (cr), Digital Image ©2004 EyeWire; ix (bl), ©Ariel Skelley/CORBIS; x (tl), John Langford/HRW; xi (tl), ©Don Smetzer/Getty Images/ Stone; xi (cr), Catrina Genovese/Index Stock Imagery/ PictureQuest; xi (br), Digital Image ©2004 PhotoDisc; xii (bl), K. Beebe/Custom Medical Stock Photo; xiii (tr), ©Ariel Skelley/CORBIS; xiv (tl), Mary Kate Denny/ PhotoEdit; xiv (bl,bc), ©2004 Luciano A. Leon c/o MIRA; xiv (br), Michael Newman/PhotoEdit; xv (cr), ©Bob Daemmrich/The Image Works; xvi (c), Digital Image ©2004 PhotoDisc

UNIT 1: 2-3 (all), ©Werran/Ochsner/Photonica **Chapter 1:** 4-5 (all), ©David Stoecklein/CORBIS; 6 (bl), Grantpix/Index Stock Imagery, Inc.; 8 (t), John Langford/ HRW; 11 (cr), Digital Image ©2004 Artville; 12 (tc), ©David Young-Wolff/Getty Images/Stone; 14 (bc), Corbis Images; 16 (tl), Victoria Smith/HRW; 17 (cr), ©Richard Radstone/Getty Images/Taxi; 18 (tcr), ©Martin H. Simon/ Corbis SABA; 18 (tr), ©Rob Gage/Getty Images/Taxi; 18 (tcl), ©Saturn Stills/ SPL/Photo Researchers, Inc.; 18 (tl), ©V.C.L./Getty Images/ Taxi; 19 (br), David Young-Wolff/ PhotoEdit; 20 (tl), ©Jeff Greenberg/PhotoEdit **Chapter 2:** 24-25 (all), ©Nancy Richmond/The Image Works; 29 (br), Robert Wood/HRW; 31 (br), Jonathan Nourok/PhotoEdit; 32 (cl), Corbis Images/HRW; 33 (cr), Spencer Grant/PhotoEdit; 34 (tr, cr), Digital Image ©2004 PhotoDisc; 34 (cl), John Langford/ HRW; 35 (tr), Myrleen Ferguson Cate/Photo Edit; 36 (bl), Mary Kate Denny/PhotoEdit; 39 (tr), Peter Van Steen/HRW; 40 (b), ©Bob Daemmrich/The Image Works; 41 (br), ©Bob Daemmrich/The Image Works; 42 (tl), Peter Van Steen/ HRW; 43 (tr), Robert Wood/HRW; 43 (cl), Corbis Images/ HRW; 47 (tr), Sam Dudgeon/HRW **Chapter 3:** 48-49 (all), David Young-Wolff/PhotoEdit; 50 (cl), ©Paul Conklin/PhotoEdit; 51 (all), ©Stockbyte; 52 (tr), Michael Newman/PhotoEdit; 53 (br), Victoria Smith/HRW; 55 (cr), Spencer Grant/PhotoEdit; 56 (cl), John Langford/HRW; 58 (bl), John Langford/HRW; 59 (tr), ©Reed Kaestner/CORBIS; 60 (tl), ©Bruce Ayres/Getty Images/Stone; 61 (cr), Digital Image ©2004 EyeWire; 64 (bl), Digital Image ©2004 PhotoDisc; 65 (tr), ©Jeff Greenberg/PhotoEdit; 67 (tr), Ralf-Finn Hestoft/Index Stock Imagery, Inc.; 68 (cl), ©Lisette Le Bon/SuperStock; 69 (tl), ©Arthur Tilley/Getty Images/ Taxi; 70 (bl), ©Charles Nes/Getty Images/Stone; 72 (tl), Victoria Smith/HRW; 73 (tr), ©Lisette Le Bon/SuperStock; 73 (cl), ©Paul Conklin/PhotoEdit; 73 (bl), ©Arthur Tilley/Getty Images/Taxi **Chapter 4:** 76-77 (all), Digital Image ©2004 PhotoDisc; 78 (cl), ©Benelux Press/Getty Images/Taxi; 80 (tl), ©Chris Shinn/ Getty Images/Stone; 81 (all), John Langford/HRW; 83 (br), ©Lori Adamski Peek/Getty Images/Stone; 84 (cl), ©Jack Hollingsworth/CORBIS; 86 (bl), ©David Rosenberg/Getty Images/Stone; 88 (tl), ©Color Day Production/Getty Images/ The Image Bank; 89 (cr), age fotostock/Jonnie Miles; 90 (b), ©Ewa Grochowiak/Corbis Sygma; 91 (br), Mike Derer/AP/Wide World Photos; 93 (cr), ©Richard Lord/The Image Works; 94 (b), ©Laurence Monneret/Getty Images/Stone; 96 (tl), ©Christian Lantry/Getty Images/Stone; 97 (tr), ©Benelux Press/Getty Images/Taxi; 97 (cl), ©Ewa Grochowiak/Corbis Sygma; 97 (bl), ©Richard Lord/The Image Works **Chapter 5:** 100-101 (all), ©Lucidio Studio Inc./CORBIS; 102 (tl), ©Chris Ladd/Getty Images; 103 (bl), Will Counts/AP/Wide World Photos; 104 (tl), ©Spencer Rowell/ Getty Images/Taxi; 105 (tr), Robert F. Bukaty/AP/Wide World Photos; 106 (b), John Langford/HRW; 108 (cl), ©Robert Essel/Corbis Stock Market; 109 (bc), ©Lawrence Manning/ CORBIS; 110 (tl), ©Karine Dilthey/Getty Images/Taxi; 111 (bl), Digital Image ©2004 PhotoDisc; 112 (br), John Langford/HRW; 113 (tr), ©Bruce Ayres/ Getty Images/Stone; 114 (cl), ©Denis Felix/Getty Images/ Taxi; 117 (br), ©Image 100/CORBIS; 118 (tl), SW Production/Index Stock Imagery, Inc.; 119 (tr), ©Lawrence Manning/CORBIS; 119 (cl), Digital Image ©2004 PhotoDisc; 119 (bl), ©Denis Felix/Getty Images/ Taxi

UNIT 2: 122-123 (all), ©Dick Clintsman/Getty Images/ Stone **Chapter 6:** 124-125 (all), ©Lori Adamski Peek/ Getty Images/Stone; 126 (cl), Scott Vallance/HRW; 127 (bc), John Langford/HRW; 127 (cl), ©V.C.L./Getty Images/Taxi; 127 (cr), ©SPL/Photo Researchers, Inc.; 127 (br), ©Photo Researchers, Inc.; 128 (bl), ©Lawrence Migdale/Getty Images/Stone; 129 (tr), ©Michael Darter/ Photonica; 130 (bl), AP Photo/Dawn Dietrich; 131 (tl), David Young-Wolff/ PhotoEdit; 132 (tl), Mary Steinbacher/ PhotoEdit; 132 (cl), Bob Daemmrich/ Stock Boston, Inc./PictureQuest; 133 (cr), ©James Muldowney/Getty Images/Stone; 134 (bl), Michael Newman/PictureQuest; 136 (cr), Mark Gibson Photography; 136 (cl), ©Joaquin Palting/Photodisc/gettyimages; 136 (br), Steve Fitzpatrick/Masterfile; 136 (bl), Andrew Olney/ Masterfile; 140 (b), ©Altrendo Images/Getty Images; 141 (tr), ©Terje Rakke/Getty Images/The Image Bank; 142 (bl), ©Bob Daemmrich/The Image Works; 144 (cl), Custom Medical Stock Photo; 146 (cl), ©David Lassman/ Syracuse Newspapers/The Image Works; 147 (tr), Digital Image ©2004 PhotoDisc; 147 (br), ©Malcolm Piers/Getty Images/The Image Bank; 149 (tr), Bob Daemmrich/Stock Boston, Inc./PictureQuest; 149 (cl), ©James Muldowney/ Getty Images/Stone; 149 (bl), ©Bob Daemmrich/The Image Works **Chapter 7:** 152-153 (all), Carl A. Stimac/ The Image Finders; 154 (cl), Scott Lanza/FoodPix; 155 (tl, br, bl), Sam Dudgeon/HRW; 155 (tr, bc), Digital Image ©2004 PhotoDisc; 156 (cl), Peter Van Steen/HRW; 157 (tr), Digital Image ©2004 PhotoDisc; 157 (tc), Sam Dudgeon/HRW; 158 (tc), Digital Image ©2004 PhotoDisc; 159 (cr), Digital Image ©2004 PhotoDisc; 160 (all), Sam Dudgeon/HRW; 161 (cr), Sam Dudgeon/ HRW; 162 (tr), Sam Dudgeon/HRW; 162 (c), Corbis Images; 162 (br, bc), Digital Image ©2004 PhotoDisc; 163 (tr), ©Stockbyte; 163 (cr, bc), Digital Image ©2004 PhotoDisc; 164 (cl), Peter Griffith/Masterfile; 164 (tr, br), ©Dr. M. Klein/Peter Arnold, Inc.; 165 (tr, br), Sam Dudgeon/ HRW; 165 (tl), John Langford/HRW; 166 (tl), ©Robert Daly/Getty Images/Stone; 168 (tl), Victoria Smith/HRW; 171 (b), U.S. Department of Agriculture/MyPyramid.gov; 172 (tl, tr, c), U.S. Department of Agriculture/MyPyramid.gov; 172 (tc), Sam Dudgeon/HRW; 172 (tcr, bcr, br), Peter Van Steen/HRW; 173 (tl, tc, c), Peter Van Steen/HRW; 173 (tr, cr, bc), U.S. Department of Agriculture/MyPyramid.gov; 173 (br), ©Photodisc/gettyimages; 175 (br), John Langford/HRW; 177 (b), ©Jon Riley/Getty Images/ Stone; 178 (b), U.S. Department of Agriculture/MyPyramid.gov; 179 (cr), ©Tom Hauck/Allsport/ Getty Images; 180 (tr), ©Peter Cade/Getty Images/Stone; 181 (tr), Sam Dudgeon/HRW; 182 (tl), Peter Van Steen/HRW; 183 (tr), Digital Image ©2004 PhotoDisc; 183 (tl), Peter Van Steen/HRW; 183 (bl), ©Tom Hauck/Allsport/Getty Images; 186 (bl), Victoria Smith/HRW; 187 (tr), Digital Image ©2004 PhotoDisc **Chapter 8:** 188-189 (all), Rubberball Productions®; 191 (t), Ed Lallo/HRW; 193 (tl, cl), Digital Image ©2004 PhotoDisc; 193 (c, cr), ©Scott Markewitz/Getty Images/Taxi; 193 (br), Jonathan Nourok/ PhotoEdit/PictureQuest; 194 (tl), Victoria Smith/HRW; 195 (tr), Merritt Vincent/PhotoEdit/PictureQuest; 196 (cl), ©Layne Kennedy/ CORBIS; 197 (br), ©V.C.L./Getty Images/Taxi; 200 (br), Peter Van Steen/HRW; 202 (cl), Digital Image ©2004 PhotoDisc; 203 (br), Ed Lallo/ HRW; 204 (b), ©Royalty Free/Corbis; 205 (tr), Nina Berman/SIPA Press; 207 (cr), Victoria Smith/HRW; 208 (cl), ©Zigy Kaluzny/Getty Images/ Stone; 209 (bc, br), John Langford/HRW; 210 (tl) Copyright 2004 Partnership for Food Safety Education; 211 (tr), ©Scott Markewitz/Getty Images/Taxi; 211 (cl), Digital Image ©2004 PhotoDisc

UNIT 3: 214-215 (all), ©David Job/Getty Images/Stone **Chapter 9:** 216-217 (all), ©Romilly Lockyer/Getty Images/ The Image Bank; 218 (cl), Bob Daemmrich/Stock Boston; 219 (tc), Digital Image ©2004 Artville; 219 (tl), ©Richard Hamilton Smith/CORBIS; 219 (tr), ©R. Laurence/Photo Researchers, Inc.; 222 (cl), Sam Dudgeon/HRW; 223 (tr), ©LWA-Stephen Welstead/CORBIS; 225 (t), Victoria Smith/HRW; 226 (bl), ©Dr. P. Marazzi/Photo Researchers, Inc.; 227 (tr), ©Color Day Production/Getty Images/The Image Bank; 229 (cr), Digital Image ©2004 Artville; 230 (cl), Courtesy Dr. Adriana Alcantara; 232 (br), ©Clay Patrick McBride/ Photonica; 235 (tr), Bob Daemmrich/Stock Boston; 235 (cl), Digital Image ©2004 Artville; 235 (bl), ©Clay Patrick McBride/Photonica; 238 (bl), Victoria Smith/ HRW; 239 (tl), Victoria Smith/HRW **Chapter 10:** 240-241 (all), © Gordon M. Grant/Alamy Photos; 242 (cl), Sam Dudgeon/ HRW; 243 (tr), ©Chad Slattery/Getty Images/ Stone; 244 (bl), ©Simon Battensby/Getty Images/Stone; 247 (bl), Digital Image ©2004 PhotoDisc; 249 (tr), ©Nick White/Getty Images/Taxi; 250 (cl), Peter Byron/ PhotoEdit; 252 (tl), Mary Kate Denny/PhotoEdit; 253 (br), Paul Conklin/PhotoEdit; 255 (b), Digital Image ©2004 PhotoDisc; 256 (cl), Steven Skjold/Painet; 257 (br), ©Syracuse Newspapers/Kevin Jacobus/The Image Works; 258 (tr, tc), ©2004 Luciano A. Leon c/o MIRA; 258 (tl), Michael Newman/PhotoEdit; 259 (tr), ©Syracuse Newspapers/Kevin Jacobus/The Image Works; 259 (cl), Peter Byron/PhotoEdit; 259 (bl), Digital Image ©2004 PhotoDisc **Chapter 11:** 262-263 (all), ©SuperStock; 264 (cl), ©Terry Williams/Getty Images/The Image Bank; 265 (tr), Photo courtesy of Oral Health America/Romano & Associates; 266 (tr), Louie Balukoff/AP/Wide World Photos; 268 (tl), ©Bob Daemmrich/The Image Works; 269 (tr), Gladden Willis/Visuals Unlimited; 269 (bc), ©Martin M. Rotker/Photo Researchers, Inc.; 269 (tc), Carolina Biological/Visuals Unlimited; 269 (bl), Visuals Unlimited; 269 (tl), Custom Medical Stock Photo; 269 (c), Victoria Smith/HRW; 270 (br), Custom Medical Stock Photo; 271 (tr), ©Collection CNRI/ Phototake; 272 (cl), ©Peter Poulides/Getty Images/Stone; 273 (bl), Bruce Coleman, Inc.; 275 (tr), Courtesy Texas Department of Health, Chronic Disease and Tobacco Prevention; 276 (bl), ©Image 100/ CORBIS; 277 (br), Don Couch/HRW; 278 (tl), Bill Haber/AP/Wide World Photos **Chapter 12:** 282-283 (all), ©Spencer Rowell/Getty Images/Taxi; 284 (tr), ©Ted Horowitz/Corbis Stock Market; 284 (cl, cr), ©2002 PhotoAlto; 284 (bl), ©Ariel Skelley/ Corbis Stock Market; 284 (br), Corbis Images; 285 (tl), Digital Image ©2004 PhotoDisc; 286 (tl), ©COMSTOCK, Inc.; 287 (br), Darrin Jenkins/Pictor/Image State; 289 (b), ©Phil Schermeister/CORBIS; 292 (tl), Eric Mason/AP/Wide World Photos; 293 (cr), © Bob Rowan/ Progressive Image/Corbis; 294 (tl), Corbis Images/ HRW; 295 (br), William F. Campbell/TimePix; 297 (tr), Chuck Nacke/Woodfin Camp/Picture Quest; 298 (b), Victoria Smith/ HRW; 299 (tr), Gari Wyn Williams/Pictor/Image State; 300 (tl), ©Clay Patrick McBride/Photonica; 301 (cr), Robert F. Bukaty/AP/Wide World Photos; 302 (bl), Don Couch/HRW; 303 (tr), ©Annie Griffiths Belt/ CORBIS; 304 (br), Akos Szilvasi/Stock, Boston Inc./ PictureQuest; 305 (tr), Paul Conklin/ PhotoEdit/PictureQuest; 305 (tl), ©Moritz Steiger/Getty Images/The Image Bank; 306 (b), Mary Kate Denny/PhotoEdit; 307 (br), Digital Image ©2004 PhotoDisc; 308 (tl), ©Lori Adamski Peek/Getty Images/Stone; 309 (tr), ©2002 PhotoAlto; 309 (cl), Eric Mason/AP/Wide World Photos

UNIT 4: 312-313 (all), ©R.W. Jones/CORBIS **Chapter 13:** 314-315 (all), ©Jim Sulley/The Image Works; 316 (bl), ©Dr. P. Marazzi/SPL/Photo Researchers, Inc.; 316 (br), ©Lowell Georgia/Photo Researchers, Inc.; 316 (bc), ©Oliver Meckes/ Photo Researchers, Inc.; 316 (c), ©Oliver Meckes/ Gelderblom/Photo Researchers, Inc.; 317 (cl), ©John Watney/Photo Researchers, Inc.; 317 (cr), NMSB/Custom Medical Stock Photo; 317 (br), ©Oliver Meckes/Photo Researchers, Inc.; 317 (bl), ©David Scharf/Peter Arnold, Inc.; 317 (c), ©Meckes/Ottawa/ Photo Researchers, Inc.; 317 (bc), ©Mark Clarke/SPL/ Photo Researchers, Inc.; 319 (cl), ©Matt Meadows/Peter Arnold, Inc.; 319 (bc), Michael Newman/ PhotoEdit; 319 (cr), John Langford/HRW; 319 (br), ©Jack K. Clark/The Image Works; 323 (tc), ©Don Smetzer/Getty Images/ Stone; 323 (tl), Custom Medical Stock Photo; 323 (tc, tr), Sam Dudgeon/HRW; 324 (cl), ©Bill O'Conner/Peter Arnold, Inc.; 325 (tr), Michelle Bridwell/PhotoEdit; 326 (b), Kenneth Jarecke/Contact Press Images; 327 (br), Peter Van Steen/HRW; 328 (tl), Digital Image ©2004 PhotoDisc; 329 (bl), Davis Barber/PhotoEdit; 330 (bkgd), Sam Dudgeon/ HRW; 330 (bl), Bob Daemmrich/ Stock Boston; 332 (tl), Mary Kate Denny/PhotoEdit; 333 (br), ©Andrew Syred/ SPL/Photo Researchers, Inc.; 334 (tl), ©S. Nagendra/Photo Researchers, Inc.; 335 (tr), NMSB/Custom Medical Stock Photo; 335 (cl), Sam Dudgeon/HRW; 335 (bl), ©S. Nagendra/ Photo Researchers, Inc. **Chapter 14:** 338-339 (all), ©Peter Cade/Getty Images/The Image Bank; 341 (bl), Digital Image ©2004 EyeWire; 342 (tl), Digital Image ©2004 PhotoDisc; 343 (cr), Peter Van Steen/HRW; 344 (c), Victoria Smith/HRW; 344 (cl), Art & Science/Custom Medical Stock Photo; 344 (bc), ©Adamsmith/SuperStock; 345 (tr), Digital Image ©2004 PhotoDisc; 347 (tr), Brand X Pictures/Picture Quest; 348 (tl), Mark Gallup/Pictor/Image State; 349 (br), AP Photo/Midland Daily News/Jan-Michael Stump; 351 (bc), ©Triller-Berretti/Barts Medical Library/ Phototake; 351 (tr), ©Photo Researchers, Inc.; 352 (bl), Courtesy M.D. Anderson Cancer Center; 353 (br), Sam Dudgeon/HRW; 355 (br), ©Yoav Levy/Phototake; 356 (cl), Michael Newman/PhotoEdit; 357 (tl), Jan Sonnenmair/ Aurora; 358 (tl), ©Tim Bieber/Getty Images/ The Image Bank; 359 (tr), ©Photo Researchers, Inc.; 359 (cl), Peter Van Steen/HRW; 359 (bl), Michael Newman/ PhotoEdit; 362 (bl), Laurie

Models are for illustrative purposes only. Models do not directly promote, represent, or condone what is written within the text of the book, and are not ill.

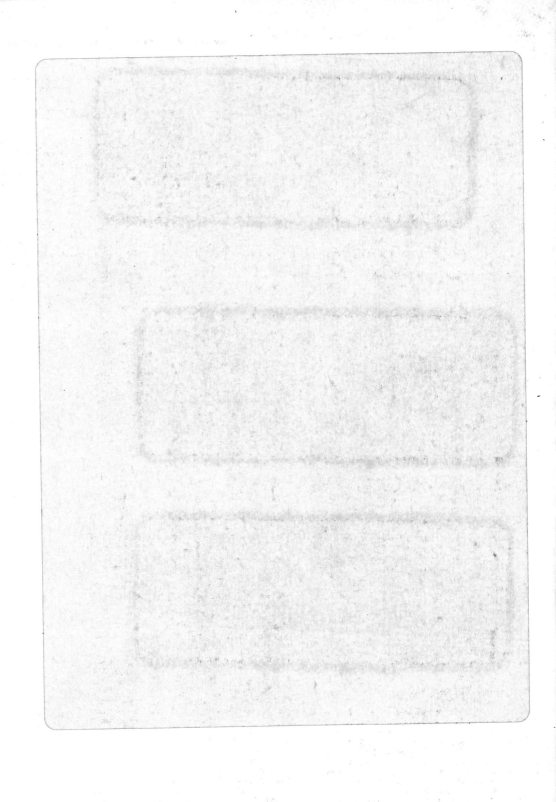

THE DOMESTIC WORLD

TimeFrame

TIME®
LIFE
BOOKS

This volume is one in a series that tells the story
of humankind. Other books in the series include:

THE DOMESTIC WORLD

TimeFrame

BY THE EDITORS OF TIME-LIFE BOOKS

TIME-LIFE BOOKS, ALEXANDRIA, VIRGINIA

TIME-LIFE BOOKS

EDITOR-IN-CHIEF: Thomas H. Flaherty
Director of Editorial Resources:
Elise D. Ritter-Clough
Executive Art Director: Ellen Robling
Director of Photography and Research:
John Conrad Weiser
Editorial Board: Dale M. Brown, Janet
Cave, Roberta Conlan, Robert Doyle,
Laura Foreman, Jim Hicks, Rita
Thievon Mullin, Henry Woodhead
Assistant Director of Editorial Resources:
Norma E. Shaw

PRESIDENT: John D. Hall

Vice President and Director of Marketing:
Nancy K. Jones
Editorial Director: Russell B. Adams, Jr.
Director of Production Services:
Robert N. Carr
Production Manager: Prudence G. Harris
Director of Technology: Eileen Bradley
Supervisor of Quality Control: James King

EUROPEAN EDITOR: Ellen Phillips
Design Director: Ed Skyner
Director of Editorial Resources:
Samantha Hill
Chief Sub-Editor: Ilse Gray

Correspondents: Elisabeth Kraemer-Singh
(Bonn); Maria Vincenza Aloisi (Paris);
Ann Natanson (Rome). Valuable assis-
tance was also provided by: Louise D.
Forstall (Alexandria, Virginia); Josephine
de Brusle (Paris); Michal Donath (Prague);
Elizabeth Brown (New York); Mary
Johnson (Stockholm).

TIME FRAME
(published in Britain as
TIME-LIFE HISTORY OF THE WORLD)

SERIES EDITOR: Charles Boyle

Editorial Staff for *The Domestic World*
Editor: Charles Boyle
Designer: Lynne Brown
Assistant Designer: Rachel Gibson
Researchers: Caroline Lucas (principal),
Sheila Corr, Louise Tucker
Sub-Editors: Luci Collings, Tim Cooke
Editorial Assistant: Molly Sutherland

Picture Department
Administrator: Amanda Hindley
Picture Coordinator: Liz Turner

Editorial Production
Production Assistant: Emma Veys
Editorial Department: Theresa John,
Juliet Lloyd-Price

U.S. EDITION

Assistant Editor: Barbara Fairchild
Quarmby
Senior Copy Coordinators: Jill Lai Miller,
Anthony K. Pordes
Picture Coordinator: David Beard

Editorial Operations
Production: Celia Beattie
Library: Louise D. Forstall
Computer Composition: Deborah G. Tait
(Manager), Monika D. Thayer, Janet
Barnes Syring, Lillian Daniels
Interactive Media Specialist: Patti H. Cass

Special Contributors: Stephen Ball, James
Chambers, Ellen Galford, Michael Kerrigan
(text); Caroline Alcock, Lesley Coleman
(research); David E. Manley (index).

CONSULTANT

N.J.G. POUNDS, Professor Emeritus of History and Geography, Indiana University
(1950-1976), and President of the Royal
Archaeological Institute, London
(1987-1990).

**Library of Congress Cataloging in
Publication Data**

The Domestic world / by the editors of Time-
Life Books.
    p.   cm.—(Time frame)
    Includes bibliographical references and
index.
    ISBN 0-8094-6684-8
    ISBN 0-8094-6685-6 (lib. bdg.)
    1. Home—History. 2. Family—History.
    3. Dwellings—Social aspects—History.
    4. Community—History.
I. Time-Life Books. II. Series: Time frame.
HQ503.D66 1991
307.3'36—dc20   91-23672
                                          CIP

CONTENTS

SHELTERS FROM THE ELEMENTS

"The huts here were circular with a pointed thatched roof overhanging the particolored mud walls, whitewashed halfway up. There was one door and sometimes a window; in the middle of the floor were the ashes of a fire which would be lit again at sunset from a communal ember and fill the room with smoke; the smoke kept out mosquitoes, kept out the fleas and bugs and cockroaches, but not the rats."

Thus the novelist Graham Greene described the houses of the first village that he encountered while he was on an expedition into the interior of the West African nation of Liberia in the 1930s. Meager dwellings, these were typical of the villages that Greene stayed in throughout his journey. But "however tired I became of the seven-hour trek through the untidy and unbeautiful forest, I never wearied of the villages in which I spent the night: the sense of a small courageous community barely existing above the desert of trees, hemmed in by a sun too fierce to work under and a darkness filled by evil spirits—love was an arm round the neck, a cramped embrace in the smoke, wealth a little pile of palm-nuts, old age sores and leprosy, religion a few stones in the centre of the village where the dead chiefs lay."

What Greene was observing was life lived at the level of bare subsistence—the domestic experience, that is, of the vast majority of humans who have inhabited the Earth, for whom the comforts and accouterments of modern civilization were impossible dreams. And the bedrock of this life consisted of the minimum facilities and arrangements necessary for its continuance: shelter, food, and the procreation and raising of children.

While the rise of cities from the third millennium BC and the technological advances they prompted have transformed the living conditions of most of humanity, there still exist some peoples who—usually because of their remoteness from urban centers—have been bypassed by material progress. The photographs on the following pages show some of these peoples—the !Kung of southern Africa, the Bhutia of Nepal, and the Yanomami of South America—in their distinctive domestic environments, following the same round of daily activities as their ancestors had followed for generations before them.

In the same way that the first human populations of Europe and North America constructed their shelters from the most accessible materials and learned to hunt and gather the particular foods with which their locality was blessed, so the homes and diets of the !Kung, the Bhutia, and the Yanomami are largely determined by the natural resources of their habitat. But, in adapting to these physical constraints, each people has evolved patterns of daily life whose sophistication belies the apparent simplicity of their conditions.

At the same time that Graham Greene was trekking through the Liberian forests, the French anthropologist Claude Lévi-Strauss was traveling in the interior of Brazil. Living in a village of the Borero Indians, he found that the twenty-six individual family huts—which were inherited by the women—were arranged in a wide circle around a communal hut reserved for the men. An imaginary line ran across the circle: Those living in one half were obliged to perform duties for those in the other, and a man had to marry a girl from the opposite sector. The placement of the huts also reinforced divisions into castes and into hereditary groups descended through the female line. When some Borero Indians were forced by missionaries to build their shelters in parallel lines or other arrangements, their entire world-view and sense of communal identity were shattered.

Similar patterns of social organization are woven into the everyday lives of all peoples maintaining a centuries-old lifestyle. They allocate precise roles to each member of the community regarding the gathering and sharing of food, the maintenance of shelters, and the upbringing of the following generation.

Where resources are scarce, the needs of the community as a whole necessarily take precedence over individual desire for privacy or the accumulation of wealth. But for the inhabitants of remote settlements such as the Bhutia village shown at right, perched on a Himalayan escarpment, play is no less important than work, and their daily routine is frequently punctuated by the enjoyment of music, dancing, and communal feasts. When Graham Greene returned to England from his African expedition, his memories amounted almost to a nostalgia for a lifestyle that once was known but now is lost: "the complete simplicity on the edge of subsistence: the little groves of rice birds, the graves of chiefs, the tiny fires at sundown, the torchlight, the devils and the dancing."

A Bhutia brother and sister prepare their breakfast of buckwheat bread on a heated skillet. The Bhutia live in scattered settlements almost 10,000 feet above sea level in the Himalayan mountain valleys along the borders of Nepal and Tibet, and their diet is restricted to products derived from the few hardy crops and animals that can survive in this bleak environment. A staple is coarsely ground, lightly roasted barley flour, which is sometimes added to tea and kneaded to form a dough. Yaks and goats are occasionally killed for their meat—which is preserved by smoking—but are valued chiefly for their milk, which is turned into curds, whey, cheese, yogurt, and butter. As well as providing nourishment, the butter is worked into hides to make them waterproof, rubbed on the face as a screen against the sun and wind, clarified to provide oil for lighting, and molded with dough into votive cakes for the gods.

Deep in the Amazonian rain forest near the border between Brazil and Venezuela, a Yanomami man relaxes in his hammock with some of his children and grandchildren. Communities of up to 400 Yanomami live in circular compounds—sometimes 130 feet in diameter—in clearings in the forest. The center of each compound is open to the sky, but a wide canopy of thatched palm affords shelter to the individual family hearths arranged around the circumference. The leader of each community is often the man with the most relatives—especially marriageable sisters and daughters—and its social organization is based entirely on cooperative relationships within and among families. During their first years, children remain close to their parents, being carried everywhere on their mothers' backs in slings, but from the age of three they roam freely with other children around the compound and among the hearths of other families. By observation and imitative play they learn the skills necessary to take on adult work and privileges, and to start families of their own.

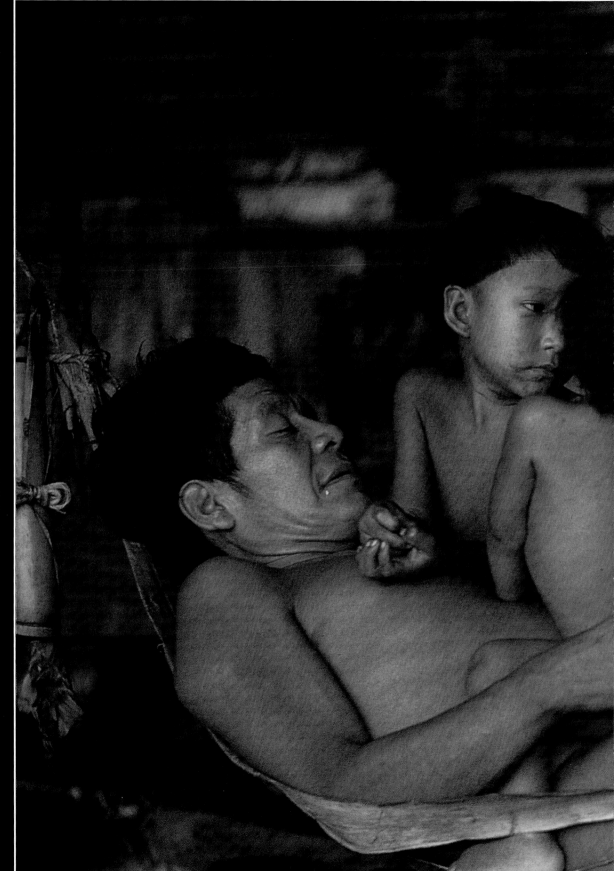

THE INVENTION OF HOME LIFE

Nineteen years after leaving his home to fight in a foreign war, a man returns to his native island. After a decade of testing adventures that have deflected him from his homeward course, he is weary and yearning for peace, but the countryside is shrouded in mist and at first he does not recognize it. "What part of the world is this?" he asks a young shepherd, and it is only when the shepherd reveals himself to be a goddess in disguise that the returning warrior is persuaded of the truth: The island is indeed the realm over which he once ruled as king. "And now joy came at last to the gallant, long-suffering Odysseus. So happy did the sight of his own land make him that he kissed the generous soil."

The long and interrupted journey home of Odysseus, king of Ithaca, after the Trojan War is the subject of the *Odyssey,* one of the earliest masterworks of world literature, composed by the ninth-century-BC Ionian poet known to succeeding ages as Homer. But the landing of Odysseus on Ithaca occurs just over halfway through the tale, and is by no means the end of the hero's adventures. His kingdom is in danger, his faithful wife, Penelope, is beset by jealous suitors, and the story has several twists and turns to come before Odysseus's authority is finally reestablished.

Entering his palace in the guise of an anonymous beggar, Odysseus is recognized only by his former nurse—who catches sight of a familiar scar on his thigh—and by his now-ancient and flea-ridden hunting dog, which pricks up its ears as its master approaches. Odysseus strings a mighty bow that each of the greedy suitors in turn has failed to bend, and he and his son Telemachus wreak vengeance on the suitors until "they lay in heaps in the blood and dust, like fish that the fishermen have dragged out of the gray surf in the meshes of their net onto a bend of the beach, to lie in masses on the sand gasping for the salt seawater till the bright sun ends their lives." Then comes the reunion with Penelope, who still cannot reconcile the appearance of the returned Odysseus with the image she retains of her husband as he set sail from Ithaca almost twenty years before. Odysseus convinces her, however, by describing in detail their marriage bed, constructed around the trunk of an olive tree in an inner court, knowledge that only he could have possessed. Odysseus and Penelope tearfully embrace, and "glad indeed they were to lie once more together in the bed that had known them long ago."

The consummation of Odysseus's homecoming has an inevitability that gives shape and meaning to all of the events that have gone before. In retrospect, the apparently random adventures of the cunning and footloose hero are seen to be stages along the way to the only possible destination. The story as a whole reveals itself as a celebration of the universal experience of home—a place, that is, to which a person's social and moral identity is intimately linked, a place where a person knows that he or she most truly belongs.

Depicted on a fifth-century-BC stone relief erected over a grave, a Greek woman named Hegiso selects an item of jewelry from a box held by her maid. In Greek and Roman households, servants—who included foster mothers, nurses, and tutors—were usually slaves but were often given considerable responsibility: In Homer's *Odyssey,* for example, the servant Eurycleia, purchased by Odysseus's father for twenty oxen, became in her old age the trusted palace housekeeper. And as in all societies in which women were confined to the home and excluded from public affairs, more of their lives might be known to their maids than to their husbands.

17

That place, of course, need not be a royal palace built of stone of the kind to which Odysseus returned. At least since the time of Homer, the physical structure of home has varied widely among different societies, and among different groups in any one society. Most inhabitants of ancient Egypt lived in impermanent houses built of sun-dried mud bricks; in China, Japan, and the well-forested countries of northern Europe, simple wooden dwellings have been home to the majority of the population through much of recorded history. By the late twentieth century a city could present a miscellany of homes within a few square miles, ranging from luxury apartments in high-rise concrete buildings to shantytown huts built of corrugated iron sheets. And for many people the idea of home is not necessarily restricted to the particular building or location they happen to occupy: Nomadic tribes may regard as home the vast tract of territory over which they range, while exiles and other displaced people may dream of a homeland they will never again see.

It is precisely because of this variety of physical structures, however, that the details of any one type of dwelling are so significant. Although the meanings of home are complex and wide-ranging, most people's mental image of home is highly specific: It is an open blue door in a weathered brick house with a garden to the side, the smell of chicken roasting in the oven, the voices of neighbors through a common wall. Such details testify to the degrees of prosperity, comfort, and privacy taken for granted by a building's occupants. And the alterations that are made from one generation to the next—a garage added on, the kitchen extended to accommodate a washing machine and other appliances—are a concrete record of the development of people's aspirations and conceptions of their own identity.

Over a much longer timespan, changes in the physical setting in which men and women carry out their domestic activities demonstrate the human progression from the status of—in Shakespeare's phrase—"poor bare forked animal" to modern-day affluence. The rate of such changes has varied at different times and in different parts of the world. For Homer's audience in the ninth century BC, Odysseus's stone palace represented a degree of luxury they could only dream of: Most people in the Mediterranean lands lived in simple wooden huts that were scarcely more than shelters from the elements. Yet while similar material levels remained the norm in most of the rest of the world, the Greeks and the Romans developed domestic lifestyles to a peak of sophistication that, following the demise of the Roman Empire, would not be equaled in the Western world for another 1,500 years.

In the Europe of the Middle Ages, the majority of people counted themselves lucky if they could feed, house, and clothe themselves and rear enough children to look after them in their old age. As the climate improved and trade expanded, the fortunate few built homes that befitted their new prosperity, and after the European discovery of the New World this wealth fed through to other social strata. The emergent middle classes could afford to indulge their appetites for new pleasures and fashions, setting a pattern that nineteenth-century technology made available to increasing numbers. So pervasive was the appeal of such Western models in the late twentieth century that domestic arrangements had become ever more standardized across the world: American business executives who visited their counterparts in Japan, for example, may have felt comfortably at home, the physical evidence of their cultural differences having been largely smoothed away.

Largely, but not completely. And the longer the Americans stayed in Japan, the more they may have become aware of particular features of the Japanese households,

THE GREEK HOUSE

Because the ancient Greeks—the men if not the women—lived mostly outdoors, and because private life was secondary to the public world of temple, theater, and stadium, their houses were rarely elaborate. Instead they were simple units providing shelter for work and leisure but little else—for water, inhabitants had to walk to a public fountain house; for latrines, they used a back alley or a communal cesspool.

Most urban houses were packed tightly together in blocks, as shown in the reconstruction below of dwellings in the town of Priene on the coast of Asia Minor. But the straight external lines of each block hid a wealth of internal variety: The buildings here, for example, include stores and artisans' workshops as well as private homes. The rich could afford more space, as evident in the reconstruction overleaf of a house in the mainland town of Olynthus, but they enjoyed no additional comforts.

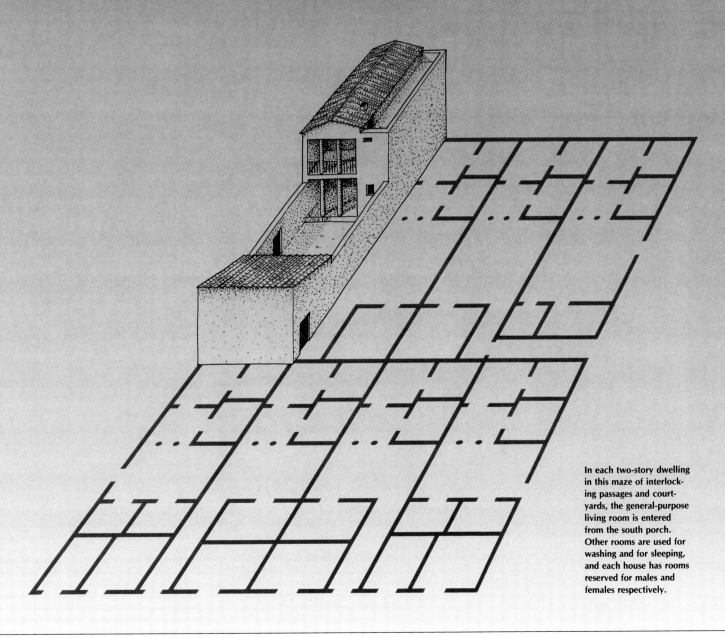

In each two-story dwelling in this maze of interlocking passages and courtyards, the general-purpose living room is entered from the south porch. Other rooms are used for washing and for sleeping, and each house has rooms reserved for males and females respectively.

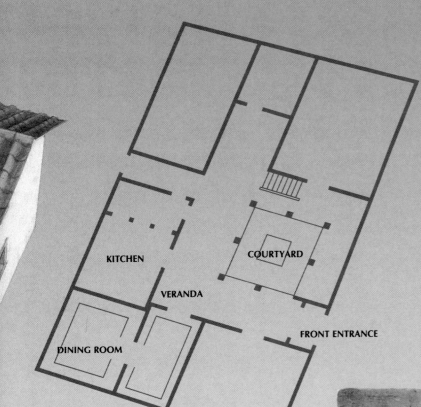

As shown in the accompanying ground plan, this spacious family house built in the late fifth century BC comprises a series of rooms clustered around a small cobblestone courtyard that probably contained a water cistern and an altar. The cutaway section reveals a mosaic of black-and-white pebbles on the floor of the dining room. The walls are built of sun-dried bricks covered with rough plaster; the external windows and doors have timber frames, and the structure is roofed with terra-cotta tiles.

KITCHEN

COURTYARD

VERANDA

FRONT ENTRANCE

DINING ROOM

A fifth-century-BC terra-cotta relief shows a woman placing a neatly folded garment in a chest; hanging on the wall behind her are a basket, a mirror, and two vases. Chests, beds, tables, and chairs or stools constituted the basic furniture of Greek houses, although only the rich could afford the elaborately decorated examples shown here. These items were often covered with textiles woven on the household loom, which was also used to make the family's clothes—simple, rectangular pieces of cloth that could be draped on the body without the need for cutting to shape.

and of unfamiliar social customs, that expressed different relationships to the outside world and among the family members from those they were used to. Most likely, however courteous the hosts, the Americans looked forward to eventually returning to their native land.

The stone palace to which Homer had Odysseus return at the end of his travels was an early literary version of a modern Hollywood film set: a fictional edifice larger than life in every respect, yet still recognizable and appealing to its audience. In real life, conditions for many contemporary Greeks were hard: Their lives were a constant struggle to produce enough food to support themselves against the handicaps of almost-unarable land, barren hillsides, and hot, rainless summers. The way most Greeks lived was reflected more realistically by another poet who wrote more than a century later than Homer. Hesiod, in his poem entitled *Works and Days,* described a harsh world in which famine was a constant threat for the poor farmer; Hesiod talked in longing terms of a golden age when life was comfortable for all. Part of the appeal of Homer's poem lay in a similar nostalgia. Odysseus's residence embodied folk memories of the palaces of the Mycenaean kings who had ruled in southern Greece in the last centuries of the second millennium BC. Homer was also concerned mainly with the exploits of the aristocratic warrior class—Achilles, the hero of his poem the *Iliad,* imagined the life of a landless laborer as the most miserable existence possible. Yet that existence, rather than the lives of the noble warriors, would have been closer to that of Homer's audience. The allure of Homer's description of such grand settings as Odysseus's palace depended on the stark contrast between the glamour of myth and legend and the meager dwellings to which his listeners returned after the tale was told.

Most people in Europe at the beginning of the first millennium BC lived in simple square, rectangular, or round huts built of wood; stone was employed only in parts of southern Europe and Scandinavia where timber was scarce. Many among them were skilled in working these materials, and also in making pottery and in smelting iron to fashion tools or weapons. The majority lived off the land, growing just enough crops to feed themselves and their dependents. But the impact of cities—pioneered in Mesopotamia and Egypt around 3000 BC—was beginning to be felt, and it was the development of urban ways of life in the Mediterranean region that was to promote advances in domestic conditions far exceeding anything even Homer had imagined. Only cities offered an alternative to backbreaking labor on the land; only cities enabled ordinary men and women to invent for themselves more varied, comfortable, and rewarding lives.

In Greece, as Iron Age villages coalesced into larger centers, these urban concentrations further developed into the key institution of the classical world—the polis, or city-state. In its heyday, between about 600 and 400 BC, the city-state spawned most of the extraordinary intellectual, cultural, social, and political achievements of Greek civilization. In turn, these achievements directly shaped all of Western civilization until the influence of Rome gave way to Christianity in the middle of the first millennium AD. For more than ten centuries, a great many features of everyday life remained largely unchanged.

The polis rolled into one all the attributes of village, city, community, country, and nation-state. At its heart was a town or small city, probably surrounded by a defensive wall, but the polis also comprised the surrounding hinterland and outlying villages. Thus the polis of Athens, for example, encompassed the whole district of Attica, an area of some 965 square miles, and its population by around 400 BC may have numbered as many as 350,000.

By the fifth century BC, Athens was effectively the cultural capital of Greece. Yet there were many other important and distinctive poleis. Some—such as Corinth, strategically placed on the neck of Peloponnesus—were commercial and trading centers. Others grew up around the manufacture of special products. Sparta, a law unto itself, was distinguished by its exclusively military character: Every citizen was a soldier and all other callings were forbidden. In fact, Greece was not a single nation at all: Hellas, the word that referred to the Greek mainland territories as a whole, had emotional but no political meaning, for each polis functioned as an independent state, as often as not at loggerheads with its neighbors.

For all their differences, most poleis shared a similar plan. Outside the walls were cemeteries, sacred groves and shrines, and small farms and gardens. Those closest to the walls were owned and worked by citizens living within; farther away would be the plots of hard-working peasant farmers. Inside the walls, the traditional heart of the polis was the acropolis, a defensive retreat on a convenient hill that frequently also boasted a temple or two, especially to a deity of local importance. The hill was also a favorite place for the open-air Greek theater, the slope forming a convenient base for the banked seating. But the social focus of the entire community of the classical polis was the agora, a large open space in which were concentrated all of the many facets of Greek public life. It was often approached down a flight of steps that doubled as seats for an assembled crowd.

The limitations of Greek technology meant that large buildings like assembly halls were rare. But the lack of indoor gathering places had little effect on everyday life, because from first light until dusk the Greek citizen lived largely out-of-doors. All of his daily activities—meeting friends, shopping, exercising in the gymnasium, attending religious festivals, running the affairs of the polis—took place in the open air. The warm climate of Greece made possible something that was wholly impractical in other parts of the world: Public affairs were conducted in public space, not in the seclusion of a council chamber or chieftain's hut.

Greek cities were always compact, usually for defensive reasons, and housing districts were squeezed into the space left around the all-important public areas, graphically reflecting the priorities of Greek thinking: the political and social first, the domestic last. The restricted city sites produced the incidental effect that different classes lived closely together; there was insufficient space to allow the rich to escape to exclusive districts.

Houses were built in blocks, typically approximately 100 feet deep and 150 feet or more long, and were undistinguished from the outside. Most ordinary houses were constructed of dried mud bricks reinforced with timbers, and they were joined to their neighbors in continuous rows. This configuration could have unexpected benefits: In 431 BC, according to the historian Thucydides, a contingent of enemy soldiers infiltrated the central Greek city of Plataea by night; relaxing in an open square, the invaders were overcome by Plataean defenders who had secretly advanced "by knocking holes through the party walls of the houses, that they might not be seen walking through the streets."

Each home usually had only one entrance, commonly facing south, which in all except the smallest houses led into a small cobbled courtyard. Here there would be a domestic altar, and usually a large earthenware pot or stone cistern for water

storage. External windows were small and high up in the walls of the rooms. These were often fitted with wooden shutters, which, in the deforested lowlands of Greece, were considered precious possessions. When an Athenian citizen moved from a house, he took his doors and shutters with him.

Upper stories were reached by an external staircase and probably housed bedrooms under their pitched roofs of terra-cotta tiles. The removal of these tiles was a favorite method of housebreaking; another was to tunnel under the very shallow wall foundations, a practice celebrated in the Greek word for *burglar,* which literally translates as "wall excavator."

The often dull and uniform external appearance of Greek houses was deceptive. No two had the same internal organization. As in all times, the rich were able to command more space, and hence might have a dozen rooms instead of the more usual five or six. They also had more scope in the choice of materials and decoration: stone instead of burned brick, cemented or even mosaic floors instead of tamped earth, and painted walls. But even the homes of the affluent were sparsely furnished: One room suitable for entertaining guests might be lined with simple benches, another would contain a bed, yet another a brazier or stone hearth.

All Greek homes had a separate gynaeceum, or women's quarters. Depending on the size of the house, this consisted of one or more rooms set apart from the guest rooms and the more public area at the front of the house. The separation was nominal rather than the result of special walls or locked doors, but its effect was the same. One reason for the gynaeceum might have been to monitor the behavior of the female slaves who lived there—and to control male access to them. But its principal inhabitant was the woman of the house. Here was where the cloistered wives of Greek citizens were expected to spend a large part of their time.

Almost without exception, citizenship—which in a democratic polis such as Athens included the right to elect and serve as leaders, and to sit in the public assembly—was open only to freeborn men. Women had to content themselves with being the relatives of citizens, enjoying a social status similar to that of their fathers or husbands—but with no political rights. The lot of slaves was even more circumscribed: They, along with beggars, were at the very bottom of both the Greek and the Roman

A Roman bone hairpin *(right)* bears the image of a woman with a layered hair style of a kind worn by many highborn ladies for formal occasions. Such creations often required the addition of false hair—black from India and blond from Germany were especially favored. A third-century Roman marble relief *(left)* shows a woman an attended by her hairdresser while servants hold a mirror and jars of perfume and water.

THE ARTS OF ADORNMENT

The dressing tables of fashionable ladies, noted the Greek poet Lucian, contained enough "jars full of mischief" to stock an apothecary shop. But the women of Greece and Rome, who spent hours each day on personal adornment, were following a tradition that dated back to ancient Egypt and beyond, and they were not easily put off.

Shown here and overleaf are some of the accessories in common use. A woman's complexion was improved with face packs and conditioning creams, then beautified with a wide repertoire of makeup—Pliny the Elder recommended a mascara of bear's fat and lampblack, and also mentioned ants' eggs and squashed flies. Teeth were cleaned with powdered horn; hair was dyed, tied with ribbons, and even shaped with curling irons; body hair was removed with pumice stone and razors. Nor were the men immune from vanity: Beards, for example, became fashionable in Rome after the emperor Hadrian grew one to hide blemishes on his face.

social structure, below the highborn aristocracy, the largely educated middle classes who composed the bulk of the citizenry, and the laboring classes of artisans, tradespeople, and manual workers.

Although slaves made up much of the work force, there were large numbers of free men and women who worked just as hard, and slaves were probably of secondary importance economically. Nevertheless, they were considered a social necessity, as much a part of the natural order of life on earth as animals and birds. To the Greek way of thinking, the idea of a state without slaves was incomprehensible: The leisure that was deemed appropriate to the life of the upper classes would not have been possible, nor would so many citizens have been able to participate in government by attending the public assembly. The slave trade flourished for more than 1,000 years, many of the victims being prisoners of war and other captured foreigners, although large numbers were natives of Greece, born into slave families and destined to follow the occupations of their forebears.

One estimate suggests there was one slave for every two free adults in Athens by about 400 BC. Many poorer people had no slaves at all. The small farmers, for example, found it cheaper to hire freeborn day laborers for seasonal work than to feed a slave all year round. Some slaves developed skills and worked as artisans, and a minority worked in the employ of the state—for example, as street watchmen or as oarsmen in naval galleys. But most acted as domestic and personal servants, and in Greece, female slaves—usually destined to be maidservants, housemaids, and concubines—were more plentiful than males.

Whatever their work, slaves were subject to the absolute authority of their masters. Two particularly unfortunate groups were the helots—Sparta's enslaved subject population acquired by military conquest—and the mineworkers of Athens. The former were treated with great brutality; the latter were permanently shackled with leg irons, and frequently died in rockfalls or from suffocation in poorly ventilated tunnels. Those who attempted to escape risked flogging—a favorite all-purpose punishment for the errors of slaves—and branding on the face.

In the more intimate surroundings of the home, slaves were treated less like animals

A Minoan bath of the second millennium BC *(right)* and a first-century-AD Roman athlete's flask *(below)* both contained liquid for cleansing the body. Olive oil from the flask was rubbed on the skin together with pumice, then scraped off with the two attached strigils.

or inanimate possessions and more as children. The Roman master actually gave them children's names; Greeks preferred simply to call them "boy" or "girl." If they were lucky and served well they might be freed; occasionally, loyal favorites were given grants to start them on a new life.

The wealthy owned enormous numbers of slaves as a sign of social status. Maintenance costs were minimal: A slave's diet was composed of the poorest food—barley bread, cornmeal, salted fish, and occasional leftovers from the master's table. This frugal diet tempted some slaves to seek out other sources of food: Those working in bakeries are known to have worn special collars designed to keep them from sampling the bread.

Within prosperous households, slaves performed most of the menial domestic tasks, but the opportunities for women to indulge their leisure were nevertheless extremely limited. The prime duties of a respectable Greek woman were to manage the house and to raise children. Wives were therefore required to stay at home, where their pale complexions—often prized as a sign of gentility—were in stark contrast to the tanned features of their outdoor-living husbands. They did not eat at the same table as the men and generally kept to the women's quarters.

Women managed nearly all aspects of the Greek household economy. They produced both food and clothing at home: Grain was pounded and milled; yarn was spun, dyed, and woven into cloth; milk from sheep and goats was made into cheese. The Greek wife was also expected to cook and clean for her family, although if her husband was reasonably well off, she could delegate the work to one or more of the household's female servants.

There were few opportunities to leave the house, even to meet other women, and certainly none to meet other men. Greek husbands did the shopping, bringing the produce home in the folds of their tunic or sending it back with one of their slaves. This was motivated not by helpfulness or kindness but by the desire of the men to protect their wives from the disreputable surroundings of the market. Public activities and achievement were therefore completely denied to women, although there is evidence that respectable women did occasion-

Attached to this chatelaine, once worn by a lady in Roman Britain, are manicure tools, cosmetic scoops, and tweezers for plucking hairs.

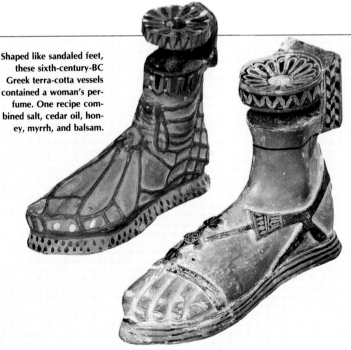

Shaped like sandaled feet, these sixth-century-BC Greek terra-cotta vessels contained a woman's perfume. One recipe combined salt, cedar oil, honey, myrrh, and balsam.

ally get out. Some writers worried that certain plays might not be fit for them, for instance, and the fourth-century-BC philosopher Theophrastus felt it necessary to warn women of street characters like the "coarse buffoon," because "when he sees a lady coming he will raise his dress and show his private parts." In general, however, a Greek wife had very little to console herself with beyond her jewelry, clothing, and daily beautification rituals.

What the Greek woman wore would depend upon her husband's ability to buy her fine things. Care of her hair and body often occupied a lengthy period in the morning. Maidservants were very useful at bath times, and for coaxing a woman's long hair into the elaborate styles favored in classical Greece. Women also shaved their bodies regularly; razors were regarded as part of the female rather than the male toilet. Perfumed oils and cosmetics provided the final touch, and then a lady was ready to face the day—a day in which, ironically enough, she would see almost no one beyond the members of her household.

But not all women were wives or domestic servants. A significant number in Greek society—mostly slaves, but also some freeborn women—were known as hetaerae, or "companions." They made up a disparate group of escorts and courtesans who could at one extreme be the fashionable companions of leading statesmen and at the other ordinary prostitutes. The more fortunate moved freely in the privileged public society of the men and, having no reputation to lose, could follow immodest careers as dancers or musicians. They alone were able to dine with the men, and were often taken home for that purpose, even by married men. The hetaerae were another fact of life that the Greek wife had to cope with.

Because their prospects declined rapidly as they grew older, some hetaerae married as soon as they could. Others retired on the money they had managed to wring from their male customers—an understandable objective but one that caused some men to view them as excessively mercenary. Always in demand, hetaerae achieved a worldliness and cultivation denied to the housebound wives.

The fifth-century-BC Athenian statesman Pericles declared that "the best reputation a woman can have is not to be spoken of among men either for good or evil." Aristotle was even more blunt: "By nature the male is superior, the woman inferior"—although what this donnish philos-

In a detail from a fifth-century-BC Greek vase decoration, uninhibited guests quaff wine, declaim, and play a lyre at a symposium—a male dining-and-drinking party for which female entertainers were hired. Many Roman banquets offered more exaggerated delights: The fare at Trimalchio's house in Petronius's novel *Satyricon,* for example, included a hare embellished with wings and a wild sow stuffed with live thrushes. But by encouraging animated and stimulating discussion, the ideal host of such gregarious occasions intended to nourish the mind no less than the body.

opher knew of women is open to question: He once claimed they had fewer teeth than men. In the fourth century BC, the orator Demosthenes summed up the conventional attitude of his time: "Hetaerae we keep for the sake of pleasure, female slaves for the daily care of our persons, wives to bear our legitimate children and to be the trusted guardians of our households."

While their women were virtually domestic prisoners, men enjoyed considerable sexual freedom. Intercourse with both slave girls and hetaerae was considered unremarkable and normal; one of the few ways of creating sexual scandal was to attempt a liaison with a married woman. And pederasty—homosexual relations between adult men and adolescent boys, ideally wellborn youths from the ages of twelve to about sixteen—was commonly regarded as part of the education of the aristocratic citizen.

To many people, pederasty was just another aspect of everyday behavior. Others did not approve: Aristotle, for example, regarded it as an aberration, albeit one that sprang from habit rather than any innate defect of character. And for the Athenian comic dramatist Aristophanes, pederasty was not just the mark of the dissipated and idle aristocrat, but the identifying characteristic of the whole class. In the face of such disapproval the Athenians blamed the Spartans, among whose all-male military enclaves the practice was endemic. Later, the Romans, whose taste for the so-called Greek vice was no less marked than that of their Greek forebears, blamed the practice on the Athenians.

In general it was not so much pederasty itself that attracted moral disapproval as the scale on which it was practiced. To indulge in any sexual behavior to excess—with either sex—was regarded as weakening. Incontinence, or lack of self-control, did not befit the pursuit of virtue, for to control others, whether as aristocrat or cultivated democrat, first required control of the self. The conventional Roman view was that sexual activity was enervating and that in excess it would lead to effeminacy. Worst of all was any sexual activity—again, with men or women—that put the citizen in a passive role.

Because sexual relations between the men of the house—especially the husband—and the female slaves were routine, homes quite frequently contained both the legitimate offspring of the wife and the children of her

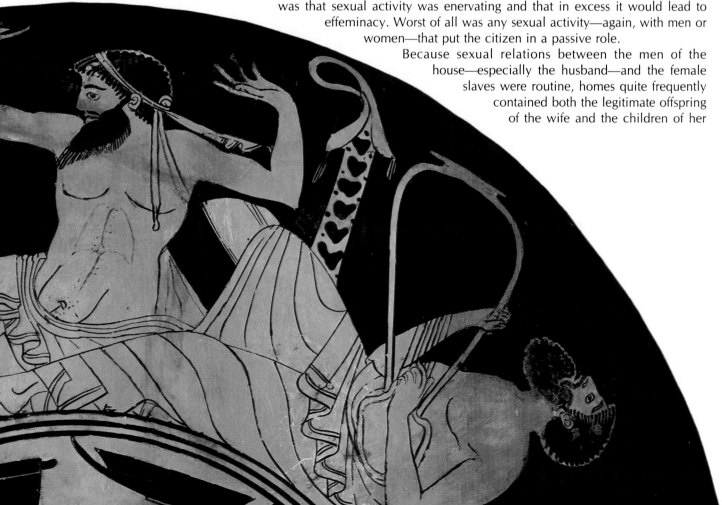

servants. The latter were not always destined to be slaves themselves: A man was relatively free to decide whom to bring up and whom to adopt as an heir, and the child of a servant, especially if it was a boy, could supplant the legitimate children of the household. A rejected child might continue to live with the family but could be sent away for adoption elsewhere.

So important were children to both the Greeks and the Romans that the alleged barrenness of a wife was a ground for divorce. A wife could be renounced fairly informally, because divorce, like marriage, was a private arrangement rather than a public one. There were virtually no grounds available to wives seeking divorces from husbands until the later days of the Roman Empire.

Family size was regulated by natural factors as well as by the whim of the master of the house. The short childbearing life of many women, perinatal and childhood mortality, and the sexual habits of the day all contrived to keep numbers down. Birth control was also practiced. Aristotle recommended one contraceptive method that has reputedly proved effective under modern conditions: A concoction based on olive oil should be applied to "that part of the womb where the seed falls." Other methods were more bizarre: The Roman historian Pliny the Elder recommended an ointment based on mouse droppings and potions containing the excrement of snails. A remedy from the second century AD advises the woman to squat immediately after intercourse and then to sneeze violently in an effort to expel the semen.

Whatever the method of birth control, it is clear that there was a high rate of failure. The exposure of unwanted babies in baskets and earthenware crocks was widely practiced in Greece. The ancient laws of Rome required all boys and firstborn girls to be brought up, but exposure also continued there until it was outlawed in the fourth century AD. It was not considered particularly immoral or inhumane. In Sparta the

PLEASURE GARDENS

In the hot, dry, and often rocky lands of the Mediterranean, gardens were both interludes of beauty and the status symbols of the wealthy few who could ignore agriculture's first claim on fertile soil.

Shown on a papyrus *(left)* dating from 1300 BC, an Egyptian scribe and his wife salute the god Osiris in a garden whose essential features—water and trees arranged in a regular fashion—provided a pattern for later developments such as those overleaf. Greek residential plots were rarely large enough to accommodate private gardens, but their public meeting places were adorned with fountains and shady trees. Interior gardens were a common feature of the town houses of wealthy Romans, who also practiced topiary and built conservatories in which to nurture foreign plants and grow roses out of season.

state decided who would survive, and unwanted female babies, as well as the weak and deformed, were exposed at birth or thrown over a cliff. Elsewhere, exposure might not mean death if the child was found and taken away, although it would probably end up as a slave. Children could also be intentionally given away or sold; a childless noble who craved an heir might supplement the income of a poor family by buying its unwanted children.

A Roman father signaled his acceptance of a newborn child simply by lifting it from the floor where the midwife had placed it after the birth. There would then follow a period of about ten days before the child was named, in case some new reason emerged for not accepting it. Then, provided its health was good, the Greek or Roman child could often look forward to a happy five or six years before its education began. In the case of Greece, large numbers of vase paintings and literary references testify to the undoubted affection in which children were held.

The education of Greek and Roman children was organized along similar lines, differing only in detail. In most of Greece, children were reared by the mother: The father's outdoor life kept him away from the house. The care of grandparents was considered to be valuable and was easy to manage since they frequently lived in the same house. At about the age of seven, boys were put into the charge of a tutor who either was hired for the purpose or was a responsible slave who was already a member of the household. He would supervise a boy's education until adolescence. How much teaching a boy received would depend on the wealth of the household. By the fifth century BC in Greece, especially in Athens, teachers who were specialists offered their services in such subjects as grammar and music; outside the home, in the agora, itinerant professional teachers made a living by teaching rhetoric and argument to those who could afford to pay. Youths also practiced military and athletic skills, such as wrestling.

This first-century-BC painting of a garden wall, from an underground room in the villa of Livia, wife of the Roman emperor Augustus, was designed to give an impression of cool luxuriance during the heat of summer. At right, women on a painted Greek vase play ball, and birds sip from an ornate garden bowl on a Roman mosaic from Pompeii—scenes suggestive of the freedom from daily chores and the natural tranquillity that only gardens provided.

As in so many other areas of life in classical Greece, Sparta was an exception. The most important values of Spartan culture were discipline, courage, obedience, modesty; the intellectual aspects of life were not considered important. Boys lived at home with their families until they were seven years old and then left to enter a strict, communal military life until the age of thirty. Toward the end of his training, a Spartan youth spent a period of time living alone in the countryside, where he preyed on the unfortunate slaves who worked the land; he was required to kill at least one of them before being admitted to manhood. Then he resumed his barracks existence as part of Sparta's standing army.

Spartan girls and women were allowed to indulge in naked exercise in the gymnasium, an exclusively male pastime in most poleis. Elsewhere, however, Greek girls received no education other than in housekeeping skills, probably at the hands of a trusted slave. Secluded in the women's quarters, girl children were brought up to be good wives and mothers, and competent housekeepers—the only fit roles for females in the eyes of Greek society.

In Rome, where many teachers were Greek immigrants, part of the purpose of an expensive education was to set the elite apart from the common people. Teachers sought to inculcate a knowledge of both Greek-inspired culture and an appropriate superior manner—right down to the smallest physical gesture—to fit the wellborn for future power. The emphasis on this rigid notion of cultural attainment did not completely overshadow the still-valued athletic and martial skills, but these were no longer designed to prepare every citizen for military service.

Wellborn Roman girls, like their mothers, enjoyed a little more freedom than was thought proper in Greece, but they too were reared with only one eventual aim in mind: a good marriage. These were usually arranged without consulting the parties: The closeted Athenian bride, for example, probably saw her future husband for the

first time only on her wedding day. Throughout, the woman was treated virtually as property; she would pass from the "ownership" of her father's family into that of her husband's kin and would become the responsibility of her husband. With her came a dowry of cash or possessions, an important and expensive consideration for a man with a daughter.

As a girl passed from one family to another, so she also passed from virginity to wifehood, a transition marked by various rituals in the wedding ceremony. After a day of feasting in the separate houses, the bride was symbolically seized from her old home and taken at night in a cart—its quality appropriate to her station—to the groom's house. Once across the threshold, the bride and groom moved to the hearth, the symbolic center of the home. There, in the Greek version of the ceremony, they were showered with nuts and small cakes for good luck. At last, the marriage could be consummated. The terrors that this might hold for a girl—often no more than twelve or thirteen years old, and away from her childhood home for the very first time—can only be imagined.

Rich or poor, a wife had little opportunity to vary her family's diet or experiment with new foods. Barley was the mainstay of ancient Greece, and because the grains had a coarse outer husk they had to be roasted and then pounded in a wooden mortar before being ground between the two stones of a quern, a simple hand mill. Barley meal found its way into cakes and a porridgelike gruel, but did not make good bread—"fodder fit only for slaves," as one Greek commentator put it. The Romans preferred wheat, much of it imported from North Africa and other parts of the empire to satisfy the enormous demands of Rome and other major cities. So great was the importance of wheat in keeping the populace of Rome well-fed and contented that emperors organized free distribution of grain to Roman citizens. The emperor Tiberius warned the Roman Senate in the early decades of the first century AD that if the wheat dole were discontinued, "the utter ruin of the state will follow." At that time around 330,000 tons of grain were being shipped yearly to the port of Ostia at the mouth of the Tiber River, from where it was ferried about twenty miles upstream to Rome by a shuttle service of specially built flat-bottomed boats. Even so, there were constant grain shortages in Rome and other major cities.

Two kinds of wheat were in general use. The superior husk-free varieties that could be ground without prior processing, and that made good bread, were reserved for the rich. Poorer people still lived on a kind of porridge, usually eaten with vegetables, that was made from a primitive and inferior husked wheat that had all the drawbacks of barley. After the first century AD, flour and bread were increasingly produced by donkey-powered stone grinding mills and public bakeries, and the strenuous pounding of husked grains fell to gangs of prisoners shackled together.

The Greek and Roman diet was supplemented by vegetables and fruit, meat and fish. For the Greeks, the olive was as important as it had been as early as the third millennium BC for the Minoan civilization on the island of Crete. Valued because of its resistance to the droughts that killed off cereal crops and its ability to thrive in barren soil on hillsides where little else could grow, the olive tree's berries yielded oil that—as well as fuel for lamps and a basis for perfumes and cosmetics—provided a nutritious food that was far more dependable than grain. The Romans, in their turn, began to develop better varieties of fruits and nuts, including walnuts, sweet chestnuts, cherries, and apples. The elaborate network of paved Roman roads that crisscrossed most of the empire also made it possible for a much wider range of produce, including exotic spices from distant provinces, to find its way to Roman tables. Under favorable conditions, reasonably fresh fish could be enjoyed by Romans living fifty miles from the sea; most Greeks living away from the coast, however, had had to be content with dried or salted fish.

Throughout the classical period, meat was eaten in large amounts only on special occasions such as religious festivals, which usually involved the sacrifice of animals. The celebration of the founding day of a city, for example, held in honor of the town's patron god, would warrant at least one ox. All the gods needed was the smoke from the roasting fire; the officiating priests sometimes reserved a share of a sacrificed animal for their own private use, but most of the carcass was divided up among the crowd. Women and slaves attended public festivals even in Greece; for the latter, and for the poorest among the free citizens, these celebrations provided what was probably the only meat they tasted. When the festival was over, the priests would leave a small selection of poorer cuts of meat on the altar, ostensibly for the gods. Under cover of darkness these would be spirited away by beggars.

If grain was the staple food, the most important drink, after water, was wine. The milk of sheep and goats was quickly made into cheese, which gave it a longer life; beer was known to the Romans after their conquest of the beer-drinking Germanic tribes to the north, but wine remained the principal drink of all classes in both Greece and Rome. Beer had been a common drink in early civilizations such as Sumer in Mesopotamia, where it had been used to form part of the army's pay, and where a significant proportion of the grain production had been reserved for brewing into alcohol rather than making food. Vines had grown wild on the island of Crete, where the stimulating effects of the fermented juice of their grapes were discovered by the Minoans, for whom wine became one of their chief exports. The grapes were usually

On a fifth-century-BC gravestone from the island of Póros, a girl cradles two tame pigeons. Although offerings of food were left on family graves at certain times of the year, the official religions of Greece and Rome prescribed no set beliefs concerning an afterlife. Many citizens commissioned private memorials such as the one shown here, portraying with affection the deceased enjoying the pleasures of everyday life.

EMBELLISHING A SETTING

The wealthiest Roman homeowners, disdaining the spare and functional interiors that had characterized the homes of their Greek forebears, projected on the walls and floors of their town houses and villas—centers of their work as well as of their family lives—pageants of luxury: paintings of ideal landscapes and scenes from mythology, molded reliefs of gods and heroes, mosaics of abundant food at the moment of ripeness. Such was the skill and inventiveness of Roman artisans that for the audience of protégés and business associates, willing conspirators in this theater of indulgence, the two-dimensional appearance often equaled the real thing. The profession of interior decoration had been born.

Painted on an interior wall of a Roman villa in Pompeii in the first century AD, a wide-angle view of the building's colonnaded courtyard *(above)* awes the viewer with the scale of the host's domicile. A trompe l'oeil painting *(left)* in another villa uses more artful means to produce the impression of receding space and of an upper floor that was divided into intimate chambers.

The studied, casual elegance of this athlete *(above)* with a bowling hoop, a detail from a composition in stucco, imparts an air of refinement to the room it adorns.

The decorative motifs of this intricately worked mosaic on a dining-room floor constitute a realistic scatter of fish bones, shells, leaves, kernels, and other refuse—the discarded remnants of a feast.

trodden by foot, but by Roman times, a mechanical press was used to squeeze the juice from the resultant mash.

In both Greece and Rome the wine was usually combined with water, in proportions that probably varied from class to class—slaves could expect a very high water content. There were various types: One was a resinous wine not unlike the retsina of modern Greece, while the Romans preferred madeira-like sweet wines. Haphazard and often unsanitary wine-making techniques produced a harsh end product, so Roman vintners added grape syrup. This sweetener was made by the dangerous expedient of boiling the grape liquid in lead pots. Modern estimates put the alcohol content of Roman wines as much as 50 percent higher than their modern equivalents, so drinking this strong, lead-rich brew was doubly risky.

Perhaps not surprisingly, drunkenness was common. Poets celebrated the virtues

Clay statuettes of minor deities such as the three Mycenaean examples on the right—two nursing mothers and one with arms outspread in a gesture of protection, all dating from around 1300 BC—once presided over private households and were buried with their owners. Household gods remained the most immediate focus of private worship in classical Greece and Rome, members of a hierarchy of tutelary deities who protected the family, the neighborhood, and the state. Before domestic altars such as that on the opposite page, from a house in Pompeii, the family prayed each morning and laid offerings on festival days. After the eruption of Vesuvius in AD 79, the citizens of Pompeii who had escaped burial built a temple to appease their household gods and give thanks for their own survival.

of wine, and it was universally associated with conviviality and well-being. Wealthy people could afford to drink it in vast quantities: The Roman poet Martial talked casually of drinking three quarts at one sitting.

In Greece, wine was frequently enjoyed at a form of evening supper party known as a symposium, characterized by good conversation and music. Such occasions were strictly for men—usually, the only women there would be hetaerae, as companions or entertainers. The Romans took over this custom and provided lavish banquets at which male guests reclined on couches; any wives attending usually sat upright as a mark of their inferiority. This status distinction was preserved right down the social scale: The poorer Roman sat upright at mealtimes, while his wife served him and remained standing.

Several courses, interspersed with entertainment provided by hired musicians, were served during the eating phase of a banquet. Joints of meat were usually boiled and served with elaborate sauces that were often spicy and—in line with Roman tastes—sweet. Then the drinking began, sometimes continuing until dawn. Because wheeled transportation was hardly ever used in Greek and Roman cities, slaves were left with the problem of escorting their hopelessly drunk masters through the dark and dangerous streets on foot.

In spite of the obvious appeal of banquets, there was an unwritten convention that the good Roman citizen should eat at home. For the poor people, living in overcrowded tenements in the large urban areas, this was unfortunate: Their homes usually had no ovens, and public taverns were the only source of warm food. During the period of the Roman Empire, however, the men of the poorer classes did manage to enjoy an occasional night out: In every town and city, groups of artisans, tradesmen, and even slaves banded together in *collegia*—dining clubs that also functioned as mutual-aid associations. Members of the club paid a subscription fee, which allowed them to attend the tavern drinking sessions and feasts—and also entitled them to a decent funeral.

The frequency of disease, the uncertainty of cure, the ever-present possibility of wars and skirmishes—all made death a commonplace event for Greek and Roman families. And a funeral was an important opportunity to display a family's status: People probably worried more about the quality of their own funeral than about any supposed afterlife. The procedure began with the washing and anointing of the body, a task for the women of the household. The body was then wrapped in a shroud, and a coin was placed in the mouth—this was for the ferryman, who would take the deceased across the river separating the world of the living from the underworld of the dead. While the body lay on its bier, bereaved relatives clad in black indulged in bouts of wailing and lamentation to mark the passage of the deceased; women often cut their hair short, and cut and scratched their own flesh as further dramatic marks of the occasion. Finally, the body was carried in procession to its tomb. For the housebound Greek wife, a funeral was one of the few occasions on which she could wear her finest clothes in public.

A major cause of disease and death was poor personal hygiene and lack of sanitation facilities. For bathing, washing clothes, and good sanitation, a constant supply of clean running water is essential—and in the dry Mediterranean world, water was a precious commodity.

Small settlements had originally grown up around natural sources of water—streams, springs, or wells—but the developed polis, and especially the large Roman city, needed something more. The Greeks were knowledgeable water engineers but built nothing to rival the great Roman aqueducts whose remains still stand in France, Spain, and Italy. The Romans enjoyed political as well as technological advantages.

A highly visible external water supply is vulnerable to sabotage in times of war; a Roman city was part of the republic, later the empire, and was not likely to be attacked by its neighboring cities. The same was not true for the Greek polis, even in its heyday, and what water systems there were in ancient Greece were short and usually buried underground.

In the Greek polis, water supplies were taken to public fountain houses, where individuals could fill containers for their own use. Public buildings and larger houses usually had their own cisterns, or at least large jars, for short-term storage. Bathhouses were available but were usually small establishments in side streets, their baths merely shallow tubs containing water heated by a variation on the potter's kiln. They were not considered proper places for the polite citizen; bathhouse attendants, who probably also made and sold soap, were socially on a par with brothelkeepers. Moreover, bathing was not associated with health, and the dramatist Aristophanes ridiculed the Athenian aristocratic youth for their love of warm water. To them the bath was a symbol of leisure, and hence of the aristocratic life; to Aristophanes it meant the idleness and effeminacy of men who bathed daily, kept their hair long, and used scented cosmetics.

In the public gymnasium, men washed in cold water after exercising their military and athletic skills, but bathing was generally a private affair, to be indulged in as often as individual conscience dictated. For Greek wives in better-off homes, bathing would have been part of the morning beautification ritual. A small, shallow tub was used. Without abundant water a deep bath was not possible; maidservants poured water over their mistresses instead.

Few Greek houses had any sanitary provision other than a narrow passageway between the backs of adjoining rows that probably served as an open sewer. Most people used latrines dug somewhere in the yard or on a communal site nearby. All domestic wastewater was simply thrown out of the window into the streets, which were always in poor condition, dusty when dry and muddy when wet. In rural surroundings this primitive arrangement may have been tolerable; in the crowded residential areas of the polis it must have created foul smells and squalid

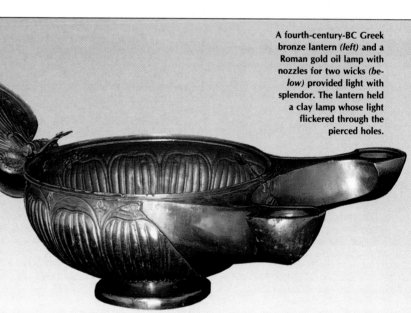

A fourth-century-BC Greek bronze lantern *(left)* and a Roman gold oil lamp with nozzles for two wicks *(below)* provided light with splendor. The lantern held a clay lamp whose light flickered through the pierced holes.

conditions. Nor were the interiors of Greek houses notably clean: Dogs and chickens wandered freely through the house, and even pigs were kept indoors. Flies, rats, and mice would have found conditions congenial. And because neither Greek nor Roman homes had chimneys—at best there was a hole in the roof—cooking always filled the house with wood smoke.

In Roman times matters improved: Every city and town of any size throughout the sphere of Roman influence had at least one public bath, and the old associations of idleness and weakness largely disappeared. Roman baths contained a variety of rooms at different temperatures and humidities, from steam rooms to cold pools. Romans of both sexes cleansed themselves with the strigil, a blunt metal scraper, and olive oil, using a method that had not changed since the early days of Greece. The scraper removed the dirt and the dead outer skin, while the olive oil cleansed, lubricated, and soothed. Men and women paid regular, sometimes daily, visits to the baths, which became important social centers and meeting places.

Cleanliness was clearly an important matter to most Roman citizens. Servants and slaves were sent to the baths, and also accompanied their masters and mistresses there—the sweet-smelling citizen was unlikely to tolerate an unwashed household. The Roman poet Catullus showed no mercy to some of his personal enemies who neglected to wash: He wrote of one man, "plagued by a goat under his armpits," whose unfortunate lover "passes out under the malodor," and mocks one of Julius Caesar's entourage for his "half-washed legs." Other victims, with bad teeth or halitosis, fared no better.

As for teeth, the large proportion of grain in the Greek and Roman diet, much of it coarsely ground flour, doubtless caused rapid wear, and many people must have suffered from dental problems. Greek dentists tied loose teeth with gold wire and used ligatures to bind artificial ones to adjacent teeth. The Roman poet Martial alluded to artificial teeth of ivory, bone, and wood, and also testified to the use of dentures: Addressing a lady named Galla, he wrote, "And you lay aside your teeth

BANISHING THE COLD AND DARK

After sunset, light and heat cost money, and most Greeks and Romans went to bed early. Both the olive oil burned in clay lamps and the tallow employed to make candles—a Roman invention—could be used in cooking, and to consume them for light was considered wasteful by many thrifty citizens. But if keeping late hours was a sign of wealth, then those who could afford it made a virtue of the expense, adorning their apparatus—as shown here

and overleaf—with elaborate decoration.

The rich had bronze, silver, or even gold lamps with as many as fourteen wicks: One such, according to the Roman poet Martial, could "light up an entire feast with its flames." Their rooms were heated by braziers or stoves such as that on the left, made of bronze and dating from around the first century AD. The most luxurious villas were equipped with underfloor heating *(pages 46-47)*.

at night as you do your silken dress." Other dental techniques were less advanced: Pliny the Elder recorded the beliefs that a frog tied to the jaws would make loose teeth firm and that toothaches could be relieved with drops of an oil in which earthworms had been boiled.

All water supply systems in classical times were of the constant-flow type—water flowed into the city without interruption, not only when it was needed, as is the case in a modern demand-based system. It was up to the ingenuity of the water engineers to make the best use of the water as it flowed through. Unused water at one Greek fountain would be piped to another a little way down the hill; and in Rome, waste-water from the bathhouses and fountains was often channeled into tanneries, dye-works, or underground sewers. The sewers flowed into the Tiber River, where the effluent must have created a noticeable stench when times of low river flow coincided with hot weather.

Sewers permitted the development of rudimentary water-flushed toilets. These were little more than open channels kept clean by the constant water flow, but they were more advanced than anything achieved by other societies until the mass production of the flush toilet began at the end of the nineteenth century. Large, communal versions could be found in public places; on a smaller scale they were also a feature of well-appointed homes. The Romans used a shared brush, which was rinsed in the running water after use, rather than any kind of toilet paper. However, few of the multistory apartments of the Roman poor had running water, and those that did had it only at ground level. Upstairs residents had to carry their water up flights of steps and resorted to the traditional expedient of throwing the contents of chamber pots out of the window.

In spite of the Roman interest in cleanliness, little was known about the principles of hygiene. Disease was often rampant, and returning cargo vessels and soldiers coming home from foreign campaigns introduced new diseases to populations that had no natural immunity. In the second century AD, some Italian cities lost one-third of their population to smallpox; in Rome itself, at the height of a measles epidemic in the third century AD, 5,000 people a day died from the disease.

Methods of medical treatment were haphazard. The Romans inherited their medical theories from the Greeks, and these theories were an often-dangerous mixture of scientific understanding and ancient doctrine. If a man's wife was sick, he would mix her a remedy himself or buy one from a local herbalist. Physicians applied poultices and fomentations, and tool kits unearthed by archaeologists suggest that surgeons could perform some drastic operations. Beyond these remedies, there was little that could be done for those who were very ill—except perhaps the hopeful sacrifice of a rooster to Asclepius, the god of healing.

In the early years of the first century BC, Rome—originally a small, polislike city in central Italy—extended its citizenship throughout Italy, all of which it then controlled, and thereby shed the last vestiges of the old

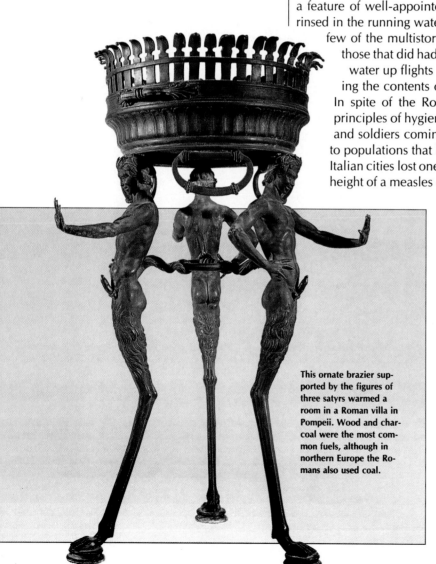

This ornate brazier supported by the figures of three satyrs warmed a room in a Roman villa in Pompeii. Wood and charcoal were the most common fuels, although in northern Europe the Romans also used coal.

city-state. It was then the hub of a nation and an expanding empire. It was to become, in the heyday of the empire, the world's first megalopolis, a city whose population exceeded one million. (The next city to reach this figure was London in the nineteenth century.) Nor was Rome the only major city: The urban centers of the Greek world were Romanized and expanded, and new towns and cities were established, often to serve as regional and commercial centers in the new empire. More than ever before, the city was the place where life was lived and experienced to the full, the site of modernity and progress.

The small houses of the working population were not much of an improvement on their Greek counterparts; many of the multistory apartment houses, cramming as many people as possible into small areas of land, were probably worse. But the rich lived elsewhere, some of their marbled mansions occupying whole blocks. They created their own exclusive residential areas, wishing to emphasize their separateness from the urban poor. And Roman technology, less restricted by terrain and technique than its Greek counterpart, could not only oblige their wishes, it could also be exported to alien climates and lands where it functioned just as successfully as on the Italian mainland.

The Greek tradition of architecture was turned inside out. It is as though Greek buildings were intended to be experienced from the outside, Roman ones from the inside. Two deceptively simple developments made the change possible: the arch and reliable forms of concrete. Neither of these was a Roman invention—like much of Roman civilization, they were forceful developments of the existing knowledge of the ancient Egyptians, Babylonians, Etruscans, and other peoples. The semicircular arch and its three-dimensional derivatives, the tunnel vault and the dome, allowed the Romans to capture internal space on a scale much greater than that permitted by Greek post-and-lintel construction. And new and durable cements, especially a strong waterproof variety that used volcanic dust from the Naples area, allowed the new forms great scope.

As far as official culture was concerned, the Romans simply poured old wine into new bottles. Roman gods were Greek gods under new names; Roman philosophy was Greek philosophy with a few minor additions; statuary was often slavishly copied from Greek originals. The Romans saw nothing strange in this: Much of the world they inherited was already run along Greek lines, and for the newcomers, Greek civilization was simply civilization itself, which the Romans embellished and promoted in their own distinctive manner. But beneath this guise of similarity, social changes were evident.

One change, facilitated by the new mastery of interior space, was a shift from public to private. This affected all walks of life, from the governmental down to the domestic. In terms of public life, state matters were now remote from the ordinary citizen: They were decided by senators or the emperor, administered by regional governors and a civil service, and enforced by a huge professional army. In professional life, commerce—deemed vulgar by the Greeks—was now respectable, and a multiplicity of urban trades thrived among the free and slaves alike, providing new opportunities for enterprising individuals. The countryside faded into the background, a mere service region whose sole function was to provide for the needs of the city and its expanding population. And in private life, the citizen now regarded his home as a fit place to inhabit during the day.

The well-off Roman citizen needed more than a residence, and certainly more than just a place to lay his head. He had private business to transact, private affairs to manage, his wealth and influence to oversee. His home therefore had to serve many purposes. It was a showplace of conspicuous consumption, proclaiming his wealth to the world. It also had to provide an appropriate setting for the family of which he was the autocratic head. And it needed to combine the functions of a business office with those of the state residence of a minor potentate.

Such a home was the domus, the urban residence of the successful Roman. Like the Greek house it looked inward, but onto courtyards and colonnades, and perhaps pools and fountains. The main room was called the triclinium—a combined dining room, banqueting hall, and reception chamber, designed to impress the visitors entertained there. Other, smaller rooms served as offices or private reception chambers. As in Greece, there was no clutter of furniture, but there were plenty of painted statues and other works of art. Plain, bare surfaces were buried under a profusion of decoration and color—wall paintings, mosaics, shell-encrusted plasterwork, elaborate draperies. Some of the draperies served to divide rooms and other spaces; the imaginative use of curtains and doors created an adaptable and versatile interior. Curtains were no less potent symbols of privacy than doors; a Roman would not dream of passing through a closed curtain uninvited.

The water that supplied the pools and fountains also served private baths and flush latrines—essential facilities in the eyes of wealthy Romans, and one more means of keeping apart from the public crowd. Sometimes the pools were used to breed exotic fish, a fashionable pastime for the man of affairs. Farther inside the house, the bedroom was a private inner sanctum at some distance from the more public rooms—a far cry from the Greek bedchamber, where a man was likely to be surprised by early-morning visitors.

Only the wealthy and the aristocratic could afford to build, furnish, and maintain an up-to-date domus—but the ideals of Roman domestic life were embodied in these mansions, and the less fortunate aped the homes of the rich as far as they could.

Outside the city limits, the domus was paralleled by the villa, a comfortable rural residence often surrounded by an agricultural estate. In the Italian homelands the villa served primarily as a retreat or holiday home; homebred Romans were city dwellers at heart. Pausanias, a geographer and historian of the second century AD, expressed a typical scorn for the countryside, being unable to understand the appeal of "a place that has neither public buildings, nor gymnasium, nor theater, nor square, nor water to supply a single fountain, and where people live in huts perched on the edge of a ravine." But farther away from the center of the empire things were different: The upper classes born and raised in provinces such as Gaul and Africa were unaccustomed to city life, and in those places small communities sprang up around the principal villa, probably the home of a local noble, which became a center for local industry, commerce, and security.

Overseas villas made free use of local materials and fostered a quality of life that was uniformly high. In colder climates, for example, where houses needed a form of heating more efficient than the portable braziers used by the Greeks, the Romans developed the hypocaust, a form of underground furnace whose heat and exhaust gases were passed through ducts under the floors of rooms at ground level. Many villas had sophisticated bathing facilities: That belonging to Apollinaris Sidonius in Gaul, for instance, possessed, in the words of its owner, "a hot bathing room the same size as the adjoining anointing room, apart from the space taken up by the roomy semicircular bathing tub, where hot water in plenty gurgles through a maze of lead pipes coming through holes in the wall. In the hot room it is full daylight: Modest people feel more than naked!"

As wealthy Romans discovered the material pleasures of living apart from the masses, and of spending a greater portion of their lives within their private domains, time-honored social conventions gradually eroded. Although marriage was the fundamental institution of the domestic world, the only legitimate framework for raising the next generation of citizens, it was not universal: Many Roman men preferred to live alone or to enjoy the company of other men. Women, although in all spheres of life still less free than men, were eventually granted a comparable power to end an unsatisfactory marriage. By the first century AD, people were divorcing almost non-chalantly. And the cost of a divorce, whether initiated by the husband or the wife, was borne by the man, for the dowry brought by the wife when she married had to be repaid to her family. For the Roman consul and orator Marcus Tullius Cicero, this was a hard lesson to learn. He was delighted, after divorcing his wife, to be able to say that he would never marry again, because he could not manage "philosophy and a wife at the same time." Nevertheless, he soon remarried—the only way he could repay his ex-wife's family was by getting his hands on another dowry.

The dowry system had other consequences. Fathers faced the prospect of large expense on the marriage of a daughter. This increased the likelihood that any infants exposed or killed would be girls, and the result was a serious shortage of marriageable women. Her scarcity value, the dowry, and the ability to divorce her husband gave a woman some power. Her husband was unlikely to view the loss of a wife and her dowry with equanimity, so prudence dictated that he treat her with some indulgence—indeed, if not with kindness.

Some women, pressing their new advantage, managed to lead scandalous lives in the heyday of the empire, and a minority acquired great power behind the scenes. Livia, the second wife of the emperor Augustus, not only managed to survive her husband and several of his successors, but was reputed to have had a hand in the deaths of some of them. Poison was suspected, and indeed was often associated with women: Among uneasy and suspicious men who were used to an unquestioned authority over women, and in an age of poor hygiene when food poisoning was doubtless a frequent occurrence, rumors of poison were all too eagerly believed.

Despite the successes of women who could turn the system to their advantage, however, the system itself remained largely unchanged. The master of any house, the paterfamilias, was an absolute authority in his own home and could deal with its members as he saw fit. He might have a mistress or two outside the house and would probably take his pleasure with the female servants as a matter of course. He might also dabble in pederasty, perhaps because of its old aristocratic associations. And if a man caught his adulterous wife in the act and murdered her on the spot he would almost certainly get away with it, although his fellow citizens might disapprove of his lack of self-control. The same general approach to morality applied as in Greek times, although by now the citizen would probably no longer link his pursuit of virtue to the needs of the state—it had become a purely private affair.

The simplest explanation for this survival of Greek patterns of social behavior was that it suited those in power, and therefore there was no reason to change. And the

ISLANDS OF AMAZING LUXURY

In provincial towns within the Roman Empire, colonists and wealthy natives alike were able to draw upon local resources for the furtherance of their domestic ambitions rather than for defensive needs. They lived in villas that ranged in scale from the simplest of stone farmhouses to virtual palaces; the artist's reconstruction *(above)* of a villa at Müngersdorf in the German Rhineland shows a dwelling of moderate size with ancillary farm buildings set within a ten-acre walled estate.

Plowed fields, orchards, and barns for livestock indicate that the villa was first of all a commercial enterprise. But for its owner, having a comfortable environment in which to live was as important as profit: Within his residence, murals and mosaics adorned the walls and floors; a suite of rooms in one wing, fitted with Belgian marble veneer, contained hot and cold baths, a steam room, and flush toilets; some of the ground-floor rooms were heated by ducts that contained hot air coming from an underground furnace, and some of the windows were glazed. The earliest buildings on this estate date from the first century, and their benefits were enjoyed by successive generations over a period that lasted for more than 300 years.

Of the rooms shown in this ground-floor plan, only the main hall rose the full height of the building. Including the second floor, the villa contained twenty-nine rooms.

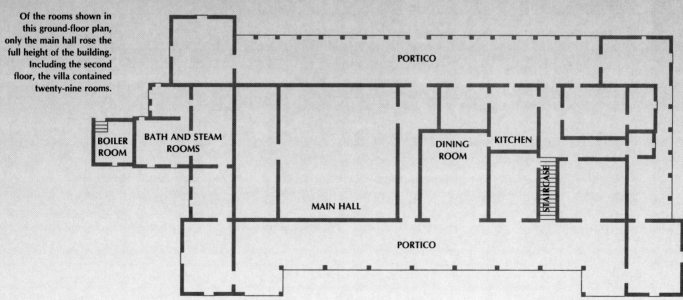

PORTICO

BOILER ROOM

BATH AND STEAM ROOMS

DINING ROOM

KITCHEN

STAIRCASE

MAIN HALL

PORTICO

On a Roman funerary relief dating from around the third century, a landowner records the produce rendered to him by the tenant farmers on his estate. In both Greece and Rome, leisure was a mark of high social status and work of low, and much of the manual labor in the countryside and towns was performed by slaves. These were regarded as property, in the same way as land or animals: The lettering on the fourth-century bronze slave tag on the opposite page records the name of the wearer's master and that of his estate. Slavery in the classical world withered away with the fall of the Roman Empire, but in many other societies it survived until modern times—it was not formally abolished in Saudi Arabia, for example, until 1962.

extent of this power now far exceeded the limits of Greek civilization. The territories ruled by Rome at its height covered the entire Mediterranean region and southern Europe, and its influence reached from Syria in the east to Spain and Britain in the west and north. From the death of Augustus in AD 14 to the death of the philosopher-emperor Marcus Aurelius Antoninus in AD 180, this empire enjoyed an unprecedented period of stability, during which the ideals and mores of the Greco-Roman world were spread to the farthest provinces. This dissemination was not without its critics. Some more perceptive observers noted that along with the advantages of "civilization" the Romans were also exporting its disadvantages. The historian Tacitus, writing about the influence of the emperor Agricola on newly conquered Britain, recorded that "little by little, the Britons went astray into alluring vices: to the promenade, the bath, the well-appointed dinner table." As he summed up the situation: "The simple natives gave the name of 'culture' to this factor of their slavery." Generally, however, it was the Romans' positive contributions to the empire that were most visible.

In terms of domestic life also, more people than ever before shared in the material wealth created by thriving urban industries. As the rich accumulated elegant items of furniture, some inlaid with ivory or metal, simpler furniture spread down the social scale to houses that had previously been bare. The mass production of pottery channeled simple consumer goods into the homes of increasing numbers. Glass, which in Greece had been a luxury item reserved for the wealthy, was now used to make large quantities of bottles and vases for sale at affordable prices.

The comforts enjoyed in the domus or villa, however, depended on the maintenance of economic prosperity, which in turn was dependent on the continued production of agricultural surpluses to feed the growing population and on military security. When the chain was broken, it was hard to repair without advances in technology—and in this field, neither the Romans nor the Greeks before them were conspicuously inventive.

From the beginning of the third century AD, the superstructure that supported the luxurious lives of the Roman rich began to fall apart. The empire broke into two halves, the Latin-speaking west and the Greek-speaking east. There were stirrings around the edge of the empire—in northern Europe, in Parthia, and in troublesome provinces such as Judaea and Egypt. The increasing gap between rich and poor, and the slow decline of rural life, created tensions that the overstretched administration could not resolve. It is even possible that lead—widely used to make water pipes, cooking utensils, and cosmetics—was slowly poisoning the citizens of the empire. As the old world sank into sterility, Christianity rushed in to fill the spiritual and cultural void. The borders of the empire shrank back in the face of barbarian invasions. And in AD 410 the unthinkable happened: Rome was sacked by the Visigoths.

The ruling elite and its culture had almost vanished. So too had one of its most characteristic social institutions: Slavery was never abolished, but as the empire broke up and Roman influence declined, it simply withered away. There was nothing to distinguish the freeborn poor from the slaves once the masters had gone.

The high material standards of the Romans hung on in some provinces. Villas continued to be built in the third and fourth centuries. But by the following century Roman-style life had retreated into the towns—now fortified against raiders—in remote areas such as Britain. The embattled populations of the old Roman world were now living on borrowed time. Cut off from any central government, they had to fend for themselves. And whereas towns could be surrounded by walls, farms in the countryside were easy prey to raiders. Farmers fled to the safety of the towns, and the economic basis of the precarious society broke up altogether.

When the towns finally fell, the high standards of Roman domestic life went with them. The conquerors who stepped or rode into the hastily abandoned houses and villas were mostly nomadic warriors, wholly unaccustomed to urban life, lacking the knowledge and experience necessary to keep the buildings and towns they had seized in working order. A modified version of the culture of Rome was preserved in local regions—in Byzantium, in parts of Italy, and within the monasteries of the Church—but elsewhere the turmoil of the Dark Ages had begun. The essential conditions for high standards of domestic life—for comfort and leisure, for decorative arts and fine food and conversation—had to be developed anew.

AT THE MEDIEVAL HEARTH

2

"The poorest folk are our neighbors, if we look about us—the prisoners in dungeons and the poor in their hovels, overburdened with children, and rack-rented by land-lords." The English poet William Langland, writing toward the end of the fourteenth century, was reminding his audience of how the world stood, and he was not sparing in his details. "For whatever they save by spinning they spend on rent, or on milk and oatmeal to make gruel and fill the bellies of their children who clamor for food. And they themselves are often famished with hunger, and wretched with the miseries of winter—cold, sleepless nights, when they get up to rock the cradle cramped in a corner, and rise before dawn to card and comb the wool, to wash and scrub and mend, and wind yarn and peel rushes for their rush lights. The miseries of these women who dwell in hovels are too pitiful to read, or describe in verse."

The dungeons that Langland had in mind were those of great feudal landlords, against whose arbitrary justice the poor had little recourse. And the hovels he de-scribed scarcely differed from those that had sheltered the majority of the population of Europe a thousand years before, during the period when the Roman Empire began to disintegrate and the inhabitants of its former provinces were left without the security and comforts of the material civilization they had come to know. As Roman towns and cities shrank and decayed, as trade diminished and paved roads disap-peared beneath shrubs and weeds, the peasantry—who constituted around 85 per-cent of the population—were left with only the natural resources of their local environment from which to make a living. From dawn to dusk they worked in the fields, many of them with wooden implements that were too weak for anything but the lightest and least fertile soil, and by night they sheltered in villages that were seldom more than clusters of shabby huts.

Around the beginning of the second millennium, those who had survived succes-sive waves of invasion by the Vikings of Scandinavia and other marauders still lived precariously in isolated rural settlements. Across the center of the continent, where villages and fields were interspersed with forests, most men built wooden frames for their homes; the roofs were covered with thick thatch that sloped almost to the ground, and in the walls below, the gaps between the timbers were filled with wattle and daub, made by interlacing twigs and branches and plastering them with a mixture of mud and straw. Most houses contained only one room, and the walls on either side were so low that it was seldom possible to stand upright anywhere other than in the middle. If there was a window, it was only a hole in the wall. The entrance was more often closed with a curtain made out of leather or linen than with a wooden door. The floor was simply the bare earth strewn with rushes, and the hearth was a circle of stones in the center, with a small opening in the roof above it to let out the smoke.

The only pieces of furniture were a few stools and a board laid across two trestles

A sixteenth-century German stained-glass window de-picts Tobias and Sarah—protagonists of the Book of Tobit, included in the Old Testament Apocrypha—slumbering peacefully with their dog on a well-appointed bed. By the end of the Middle Ages such beds, covered with thick draperies and often overhung by canopies, had become hallmarks of the privacy and comfort enjoyed by well-to-do married couples. During the preceding centuries, beds had been no more than functional platforms for sleeping: Whole families often shared a single straw mattress supported by cords stretched across a wooden frame up to nine feet wide, while their servants slept on the floor nearby.

or tree trunks, which served as a table. At night the entire family slept together, fully clothed, on thin mattresses filled with straw or heather, and they shared their dismal shelter with their hens and pigs. In winter, if they were rich enough to own cows or sheep, they brought these in as well. In cold weather, despite the hole in the roof, the room filled up with smoke from the damp log fire in the hearth. When it rained, the rushes—which were seldom changed—rotted on the muddy floor, and throughout the year they were almost always thick with the stinking excrement of animals.

In the rest of Europe the houses and the conditions were similar. In the warm climate around the Mediterranean there was no need to bring in livestock during the winter, and the rush-strewn floors were a little less unsanitary. But the only major difference was in the building materials. In rocky country, stones were used to build sturdier walls. In the coldest parts of the north, houses were insulated by piling dirt and turf against the sides and roof. And in the south many houses were made out of brick and tiles, some of which came from the nearby ruins of Roman towns and villas.

In such primitive and unsanitary conditions, death, while not exactly a member of the family, was a constant visitor. Cold weather, an inadequate and poorly balanced diet, and the rats, lice, and fleas that bred in the woodwork and unwashed clothing all took their toll. The true cause of infection was unknown (and would remain so until the nineteenth century); preventive medicine even in the late Middle Ages was limited to quarantine, and although a host of herbal and plant infusions were taken to alleviate sickness, most were at best neutral in their effect.

Those most at risk were infants. Women often gave birth on soiled bedclothes—to protect the good ones from damage—and were commonly expected to return to their household or field duties within hours. Those who did without the aid of a midwife were often the lucky ones: Midwives might wash their hands before a delivery but had no idea of the need for sterilization, and their folk remedies could do as much harm as good. Throughout the medieval period and in many areas up until the advent of improved medicine in the nineteenth century, between a quarter and a third of all children died within a year of birth. Many more died before they reached their tenth year. From every two live births a single healthy adult might result.

William Langland was himself no stranger to poverty and death. He lived in a simple cottage with his wife and daughter, "dressed like a beggar," and made a meager living by reciting the Office of the Dead for wealthy patrons. But for Langland as for many others, the more meager and demeaning the physical conditions of his daily life, the more mysterious and challenging was the relationship between his existence on earth and what he considered to be his ultimate destiny. Langland was a minor cleric and was probably educated in a monastery, one of the chief institutions through which the Christian church in Europe had kept alive a tradition of learning and a hope of spiritual salvation through the centuries of privation that followed the collapse of the Roman Empire. And during his own lifetime, material changes were occurring in parts of Europe and in certain strata of society that would eventually improve the lot of most of the population.

Between the eleventh and the early fourteenth century, favorable climatic conditions permitted the expansion of agriculture and the growth of Europe's population. And as trade grew and new urban communities began to flourish, the wealth they accrued allowed increasing numbers to better their conditions—to build warmer and more comfortable houses, to enjoy a more varied and plentiful diet, to provide a secure inheritance for their children. By the sixteenth century, the success of many people's lives was measured not just by their ability to provide for their family's survival, but by their provison of luxuries far in excess of basic needs. A new elite had filled the vacuum left by the vanished patricians of Rome, and while the course of public affairs was still stained by violence and bloodshed, in the courts and mansions of the rich, conduct was marked by growing civility and decorum. Most members of this elite were no less devout than their ancestors and accepted the hardships of life on earth as preparation for a glorious afterlife. But they held a far more optimistic view than their forebears of the capacity of humans to better their worldly existence. The life of men and women was no longer as cheap as that of beasts. "O highest and marvelous felicity of man," apostrophized the Italian count Pico della Mirandola, "to him it is granted to have whatever he chooses, to be whatever he wills."

At the beginning of the eleventh century, the edge of the familiar world for the peasant inhabitants of Europe's scattered villages was defined by two boundaries: that of the manor and that of the parish. The two sometimes overlapped, but by no means always. At the hub of the manor was the manor house, occupied by the local lord; this was the center of secular authority for the surrounding villagers. The church, at the center of the parish, was the focus of spiritual authority—although because the concerns of parish and manor overlapped and intertwined, many villagers probably made no absolute distinction between the two.

The manor was the local manifestation of the social system of dependence and obligation known as feudalism, which had spread through western Europe during the two previous centuries and which was steadily moving into eastern Europe also. The system was based on ownership of land and the need to defend it. The most powerful feudal landlords—the kings and their barons—granted estates to individual knights or landholders, in return for which each knight swore allegiance to his lord and undertook certain solemn duties, the most important usually being the obligation to serve as a member of his lord's military entourage for up to forty days each year. At the lowest level this feudal contract was echoed in the relationship between the local lords and the peasants on their estates. In return for the lord's nominal protection and the right to be heard in his manorial court, the peasants paid him a substantial share of their harvest and their profits, or else worked for him on his land.

Only a few of the peasants were freemen, and these were usually tenant farmers or essential craftsmen such as blacksmiths or millers. The majority—the ones who provided the bulk of the labor force—were serfs, owning almost nothing and entirely dependent on the lord of the manor. He allowed them to graze their livestock on some of his pastures and allotted them strips of arable land on which to grow the crops that fed their families, but in return he required them to work his own fields for up to three days every week. Serfs were effectively the chattels of the manorial lord: They could not move away from the estate or even marry without their master's permission, and it was often they who bore the brunt of any conflict between their overlords. Early in the twelfth century, for example, when a renegade French baron raided some of his king's domains, the king retaliated by invading the baron's estates, burning all his crops, and slaughtering his animals and serfs. So widespread was the indifference to the suffering of serfs that even the abbot of the great monastery of Saint Denis near Paris described the loss of their lives as no more than just and salutary retribution. "It was," he wrote, "an excellent deed."

To the serfs, the manor was their entire existence. They knew nothing of the world

A LORDLY CHAMBER

The long, all-purpose hall that often provided the complete basic structure of the home of a manorial lord, and that comprised the main communal living area of a baron's castle, was at first the locus of all domestic activity: cooking and eating, entertaining and sleeping. As complex social hierarchies developed, interiors became increasingly elaborate: Wooden screens, first erected to bar drafts from open doorways, became permanent features, often surmounted by galleries from which musicians played to an assembled company; the master's table was elevated on a low platform, sometimes framed by tapestries or dramatically illuminated by an arched window, and his gold and silver dishes were displayed in a specially constructed cabinet. But although every feature of the hall—including wall paintings, decorative tracery in the windows, and soaring timber roofs—enhanced its owner's prestige, eventually his desire for comfort and privacy outgrew the confines of a single chamber. Separate kitchens and bedrooms were built, leaving the hall for pomp and ceremony.

While minstrels play trumpets and a sackbut, a cupbearer serves his lord at table in this fifteenth-century Flemish painting. Elaborate ritual governed the setting of the table and the serving of food: Salt, an expensive commodity, was the first item to be placed upon the tablecloth, and fanfares announced the appearance of each course, which was placed before diners in strict order of rank.

A chestnut-timbered roof soars sixty feet high above the great hall of Penshurst Place in southeast England, home in the fourteenth century to Sir John de Pulteney. The life-size carved wooden figures at the foot of each main roof brace represent the peasants who worked the surrounding estate. At the rear of the hall, a minstrels' gallery is built over screens around the servants' entrances. In the foreground, logs are arranged over a central octagonal hearth—the most effective means of heating this 2,000-square-foot room.

beyond and were fiercely suspicious of anyone who came from it. The only way of life they understood was the communal life of the village. Not one of them was rich enough to own a plow as well as an ox or a horse, but among them they could find both a plow and a team of animals to pull it. The one way in which they were able to grow enough grain to feed the whole village was by working the land together, with each providing whatever he could, even if it was only labor. Apart from labor, bread and produce were almost their only currency. They had little money and little need for it. The herdsman who watched over their livestock on the common pastures might be paid in loaves of bread; the miller took a share of the grain as payment; and on the occasions when they needed a craftsman to mend their tools or wagons, they paid him with a chicken and a few eggs.

Besides these routine expenses, the peasants were required to contribute a tenth of their produce or income to the local church. This tax, known as the tithe, was used to provide a living for the priest—who was himself generally a peasant appointed by the lord of the manor—to maintain the church building, and for the relief of the poor. In many parishes additional fees were charged for baptisms, weddings, and funeral services. Of necessity priests were often ruthless in their enforcement of the tithe, although the fourteenth-century English poet Geoffrey Chaucer wrote of a priest who "much disliked extorting tithe or fee." Such reluctance was understandable, for in the small, intimate community of the village it was in no one's interest that relations between individuals turn sour.

The village church was far more than a place of assembly for weekly worship or the rites of marriage or death. Many churches were constructed at least in part as places of refuge, where the whole village could shelter; their towers provided useful vantage points from which to warn of approaching danger. The cemetery outside each church building linked the villagers to their past, giving them a sure sense of local roots. And the annual cycle of religious festivals celebrated in the church—Christmas, Candlemas, Easter, Pentecost, and numerous saints' days—marked the rhythm of the villagers' lives, echoing the parallel cycle of the seasons and their associated agricultural activities.

It was by these religious festivals that villagers told the passing of time: Events in the recent past or near future would be dated by their coincidence with or proximity to a particular saint's day or festival. Few knew the exact year according to the Christian chronology, and even literate men and women living in the manor houses tended to reckon the years in terms of the monarch's reign. The hours of the day were calculated by the position of the sun or by a sundial on the church tower.

Because the seasonal tasks were the same every year, and because only a major public or private event—a plague epidemic, perhaps, or a drought or the death of a family member—distinguished any one year from all the others, time was perceived as cyclical rather than linear or progressive. Few people were aware of any differences or improvements in the physical conditions of their lives compared with those of their grandparents—and indeed, over a span of just two or three generations, any such differences were minimal. But from the eleventh century, changes were in fact occurring at a rate far faster than in the previous 500 years.

First of all these developments involved agriculture: Large areas of forest and wasteland were cleared and sown with crops or turned into pastures; heavy iron plows that could dig deep through the richest soil were introduced, and productivity increased still further as farmers discovered that their new soil need lie fallow for only

The head of John the Baptist, made from painted and gilded alabaster, forms the central motif of a private fifteenth-century English altarpiece standing just sixteen inches high. A ubiquitous presence in medieval life, Christianity provided a focus for all artistic and intellectual endeavor: Figures and episodes from the Scriptures were the almost exclusive subject matter of artists and sculptors, and from craftsmen and manuscript illuminators wealthy patrons commissioned reliquaries, Psalters, and books of hours—anthologies of devotional literature—as aids to meditation. From the thirteenth century, the clicking of rosary beads increasingly accompanied the private recitation of prayers.

one year in every three instead of every other year. In some regions farmers also learned to rotate their crops, planting a winter crop such as wheat or rye in one field and a spring crop such as beans or barley in another. The peasants' diet still comprised chiefly bread and vegetables occasionally enlivened by cheese, eggs, or meat, but food supplies gradually became more reliable. Commercial expansion increased the amount of money in circulation, and some landlords began to collect their rent in cash rather than produce and to pay wages for labor on their land. A determined serf might even be able to earn enough money to buy his freedom and a small plot of land, and to build a sturdy two-room dwelling. Eventually, as market towns became ever more prosperous, and as a class of merchants trading in surplus produce slowly emerged, the ties of manor and parish would be loosened still further.

At the top of the feudal structure were the barons, whose power was based on the land worked by the peasants. At the beginning of the twelfth century, the homes of even the greatest landlords were hardly impressive: Most of the castles built by the barons throughout Europe to house their men-at-arms and guard their estates were simply earth mounds surmounted by wooden towers and surrounded by ditches and stockades. But during the course of the next two centuries the barons became rich enough to replace the perishable and inflammable wood with impenetrable stone. In many castles the central building was transformed into a massive tall tower known as a keep, with walls that were often several yards thick. In the walls of the ground-floor storehouse and the guardroom above it the windows were narrow slits through which an archer could shoot his arrows. On the second floor, where it was more difficult for an assailant to break in, larger windows admitted light to the great hall that rose through the rest of the building. In small towers at the corners of the keep,

The common feature uniting these disparate furnishings—a French tapestry dated 1506 depicting ladies embroidering in a flowery meadow, a fifteenth-century table with liftoff top and collapsible legs, and a sturdy sixteenth-century oak coffer—is their portability. When a medieval nobleman moved from one castle or manor to another, he took his household with him: furniture, linens, pots and pans, and musical instruments as well as squires, grooms, cooks, and other servants. The contingent could comprise more than a hundred people, together with strings of packhorses. Reaching its destination, the household brought the hubbub of human occupation into buildings that for much of the year might be bare-walled shells cared for by a skeleton staff.

circular staircases wound up to galleries and bedchambers. Outside the keep the stockade became a high stone wall joining the towers that watched every approach, and within this wall were stables, an armory, and a blacksmith's forge.

The households living within a castle became larger as landowners themselves became richer. By the fifteenth century many of the most powerful noblemen in Europe were attended by more than a hundred followers, and only the humblest of the followers were peasants. The steward, the chamberlain, the treasurer, the keeper of the wardrobe, and even the yeomen of the wine cellar and the pantry all came from landowning families and regarded themselves as the social equals of knights. It was considered an honor to wear clothes embroidered with the coat of arms of a great lord, and serving in his household was one of the ways in which the younger sons of knights could earn enough to buy land of their own.

The most nobly born of all the servants were often the youngest—the pages, some of whom were no more than eight years old. The pages were the sons and in many cases the heirs of other barons, and within the walls of a castle they had tutors experienced in every skill that a nobleman needed. They learned riding and hunting from the knights lodged at the castle, reading and writing from a grammar master, and dancing and manners from the ladies. And in carving meat, serving wine, and generally waiting on the baron's every whim, they learned a measure of humility. In the same way, barons and the richer knights sent their daughters to other men's castles to learn the domestic and social accomplishments required of a wellborn wife. In most great castles there was a group of young ladies who sat demurely in the hall at dinner, danced before guests, and slept in the one well-guarded dormitory.

The castle's day began at dawn with mass in the chapel for all the household. After a breakfast of bread, fruit, and wine, the knights spent the morning hunting or practicing military skills. Two or three mornings a week the pages might watch or ride with them; on the other mornings they sat with the grammar master. Meanwhile the cooks and their staff prepared the dinner, which was usually served well before noon. With so many mouths to feed and so little ventilation, a castle's kitchen could be as hot as a blacksmith's forge. In the summer the boys who turned the roasting joints on spits often stood naked before the fire.

For dinner—the most important event of the day—the entire household dressed in finery. Clothes were a sign of rank: They were dyed in bright colors that were forbidden to the peasantry and were made of the costliest cloth the wearer could afford. A gentleman's costume always fitted tightly, to show that he was a man who might at any moment have to don a coat of mail or armor.

In the eleventh century, clothes were much the same as they had been during the previous 600 years: Women wore long, shapeless dresses, and men wore woolen tunics and trousers covered with cross-gartering. But the Crusades, beginning at the end of the eleventh century, introduced to the European aristocracy luxurious Oriental silks, damasks, and other fabrics. Soon the men's tunics and trousers were replaced by the doublet, which had buttons down the front and which itself was to change in style and shape over the course of time. Many doublets were embroidered with heraldic designs, and when hose were worn with different colors on each leg, the doublet was often made with the same two colors on opposite sides. The overgarment worn on top of the doublet also became subject to frequent changes of fashion: In the fifteenth century, for example, tailors slashed its sleeves to reveal underneath the contrasting colors of the doublet. For women, changes in the shape and cut of their long gowns were usually more subtle, and the most conspicuous variations were in their often exuberant headgear. Sometimes gold and jeweled tiaras were in fashion, and there were times when the most extravagant ladies sprinkled their hair with gold dust. In Italy, where blond hair was the most admired, ladies sat out in the sun for days on end to bleach it and then wore hats with no crowns to them.

The midday dinner for which the household assembled was served on long, cloth-covered tables running the entire length of the hall. At one end, at a right angle to the other tables, the baron's table stood on a raised platform. His gold-and-silver goblets and plates were displayed on a separate table at the side; the goblets from which he and his guests actually drank were usually made out of pewter, while the plates were often flat pieces of wood, known as trenchers, or else large slices of bread that soaked up the sauces and were then thrown to the hounds. Spoons were the only cutlery to be found on the table; forks were not used until the sixteenth century, and the baron's guests were expected to bring their own knives.

The dishes were many and rich. Beef, mutton, pork, swan, and peacock were served together. Duck, pheasant, and chicken were combined with stuffings of egg yolks, currants, mace, cinnamon, and cloves. Small birds such as sparrows and starlings were served in heavily spiced stews. And there were often one or two novelties, such as a pie with live birds in it or a huge sugary confection fashioned to represent a heraldic or legendary scene. The dishes were served by a procession of servants, first to the baron's high table and then to the other diners in order of rank.

The formality and ceremony of the daily regimen in a castle could be daunting for a young knight who had known nothing but the simpler life of the manor house or an army camp. In many kingdoms, books were written to advise both knights and pages on every detail of dignified behavior at a court or among ladies, and the authors knew from experience that they often had to begin from scratch: Don't eat with your knife, don't fondle the dogs under the table, don't lick your plate, don't butter your bread with your thumb, and don't clean your teeth with the tablecloth.

Sheep are led out to graze and a woman milks a cow while another churns butter in this sixteenth-century Flemish manuscript illustration. The accommodation of animals and people alike consisted of thatched, timber-framed buildings with walls of dried mud and rough plaster; in northern Europe only the rich could afford dwellings of more durable stone. When villages were abandoned—sometimes because of a change from crop growing to sheep farming, and subsequent eviction by landlords—all visible trace of their presence often quickly disappeared from the landscape.

In southern Europe a siesta followed dinner, and then—as everywhere—hunting and training in martial sports continued until supper, which was usually served around sunset. Supper was a lighter meal than dinner, but there were still several kinds of meat, and when it was over, the evening's entertainment began. The household sat until bedtime listening to a traveling storyteller or reciter of verses, or watching acrobats, jugglers, or trained animals. If there were no professionals available, the household amused itself, the ladies playing chess or checkers while the men played dice. Light flickered from the fire in the open hearth, from torches made of resinous twigs, and from guttering candles of animal fat. In the countryside beyond the castle walls, the surrounding villages were already wrapped in darkness.

A nineteenth-century English hymnist encapsulated the apparently unchanging verities of the feudal system:

> The rich man in his castle,
> The poor man at his gate,
> God made them, high and lowly,
> And order'd their estate.

The privileged life of the nobleman's castle was vulnerable to the depredations of war, but for generations the wealth of the nobles cocooned them from the effects of new social and economic forces in society. For the peasants and serfs likewise, wholly at the beck and call of their masters, the conditions of their lives must have

This reconstruction of the facade and interior of a peasant's cottage illustrates one distinctive method of building with timber: arching beams, or crucks, serve as structural supports for both roof and walls. Crucks could support a dwelling up to thirty feet wide, but few cruck-framed buildings were erected after the sixteenth century. The upper stories that were increasingly demanded could more easily be built using the box-frame type of construction shown on the opposite page.

seemed God-given and unalterable. In the houses of the manorial lords, too, change was slow to take effect; but it was in these homes, midway along the social spectrum of the feudal system and supplied with gradually increasing comforts, that forms of domestic life developed that would be familiar to later ages.

Many manors were supervised by stewards on behalf of barons or bishops; and there were some, often the best managed, that belonged to monasteries. But often the manor was held by a knight, who lived on the edge of the village in the only house that was larger than those of the peasants and the priest. At the start of the eleventh century, in the parts of northern Europe that had been settled by Saxons and Vikings, the lord of the manor's home was commonly a long, wooden-framed hall divided into separate sections for his animals, his servants, and his family. Such halls lacked light and were often filled with smoke, but were the scenes of frequent feasting. The Saxons in particular were famous for their hospitality. After the Normans had conquered the Saxon kingdom of England in 1066, the Norman chronicler William of Malmesbury recorded their habits disdainfully. "The custom of drinking together was universal," he wrote, "the night as well as the day being passed in this pursuit. They spent great sums on it while living in small and contemptible homes, unlike the French and Normans, who live at a moderate rate in large and splendid buildings."

In fact the type of house that knights inhabited in France and southern Europe, and that the Normans were about to introduce into England, was neither large nor splendid, being little more than a bigger and better-built version of a peasant's house. Surrounded by a stockade and sometimes by a moat, it often comprised just one large room. Even in the few stone houses that were built on two floors, the ground floor was used only for storage and stabling, and the hall above was reached by an external wooden staircase that could be knocked down if the house was attacked.

Like everyone else in the village, the lord of the manor, his family, and his servants all ate and slept together in the same room. Their furniture was better than that of the peasants: The trestle table was sturdier, there might be a chair at one end for the master, and there were benches on either side instead of stools. There was also one large bed in which, unlike the peasants, the lord and his lady slept naked, and there was a pole wedged into the wall on which they hung their clothes. The major difference between a lord's and a peasant's house was that hounds were the only animals with which the lord shared his living quarters. Livestock was sheltered in a room below or elsewhere in the stockade.

One of the first improvements to appear in manorial houses all over Europe was the wood- or stone-seated latrine, which was built into a wall at one end of the hall. Most had a shaft that carried their contents down through the wall to a cesspool, but a few simply protruded far enough to allow waste to fall outside the house. Toward the end of the twelfth century, in a first attempt to create a degree of privacy for their sleeping area, many lords installed leather curtains or wooden screens, which could be pulled out in the evening to cut off one end of the hall. And then, at the beginning of the thirteenth century, a few took the next step and built houses with separate rooms, a hall and a chamber.

During the thirteenth and fourteenth centuries some lords of the manor built towers with rooms on several floors, while others built wings on either end of their halls, adding chapels, parlors, guest chambers, storage rooms for their wine, and pantries for their bread. To minimize the danger of fire, the kitchen often comprised a separate building; over its open hearths broths and stews simmered in cauldrons, joints and poultry roasted on turning spits, and bread was baked in a wood-heated oven. When the lord and household dined, the food was carried into the hall along a covered walkway and through a passage between storerooms. Since this meant that the door was constantly opening and shutting, screens were used again to stop the draft from blowing smoke from the central hearth onto the high table, where the master and his family sat. At first the screens were movable, but by the fourteenth century they had become permanent architectural features of the halls, many decorated with elaborate carvings in their heavy wood, and some with galleries above them for minstrels who sang to the household in the evenings.

By the end of the fifteenth century many screens were purely ornamental, for the problem of billowing smoke had been eliminated by installing carved stone fireplaces, not only in the hall but also in all the important chambers. Tall brick or stone chimneys boastfully proclaimed their presence above the rooftops. The manor house had grown up. Lodgings for guests and senior servants, kitchens, stables, and a gatehouse reached out to enclose a courtyard in front of the hall. Windows became larger and moats were generally dispensed with, as most parts of Europe had become more peaceful and the need for fortifications had diminished.

The floors of bedchambers were still strewn with rushes, but their walls were now brightly painted with heraldic designs or scenes from legends or the Scriptures. In rich houses the lower parts of the walls were paneled in wood and the upper parts were hung with tapestries. And as always in the bedchamber, the most imposing and elaborate item of furniture was the bed itself. Since the twelfth century beds had been surrounded by curtains, which were suspended either from the ceiling or from long poles protruding from the wall. In the thirteenth century, beds acquired canopies, followed soon afterward by feather mattresses, linen sheets, and silk counterpanes. By the fifteenth century, there were many different designs, particularly in France, where the most popular type was shaped like a sofa with high wooden panels around three sides. At the end of the century, the most fashionable bed was the new Venetian fourposter, with slender columns rising at each corner to support the canopy.

A few of the finest bedchambers had their own latrines, but most were equipped only with portable commodes. When a member of the family or a guest took a bath, servants had to fill clay jars with water, heat them over the fire in the kitchen, and carry them up to the bedchamber; there the jars were emptied into round wooden tubs, sometimes lined with cloth padding or containing a stool for the occupant to sit on. Only the wealthiest palaces could boast separate bathrooms, and few of these had hot and cold running water, even though the simple technology was available. As early as 1351, King Edward III of England built a bathroom in his palace at Westminster with two large bronze taps above the bath, one fed by a tank of cold water and the other by a hot tank with a fire burning beneath it.

An inventory of the bedchamber of Sir John Fastolf, a landowner in eastern England, listed some of the items with which the rich could afford to surround their slumbers in the fifteenth century:

A fifteenth-century English stained-glass roundel from a series illustrating the months of the year depicts a February scene: a man warming his bare hands and feet at an open fire.

THE TAMING OF FIRE

A fire in winter was almost life itself: Most windows had no glass, only rags or wooden shutters to keep out the wind and rain, and thick, ankle-length clothes only partially insulated the wearer from drafts. But a fire burning on a central hearth, diffusing choking clouds of smoke about the room, gave warmth and discomfort in equal measure. Not until the hearth was moved to the side of the room and set in a niche of nonflammable stone with a conduit to guide the smoke directly upward was fire fully domesticated. Such fireplaces changed both the insides and the outsides of buildings.

In primis, a feather bed. Item, a mattress of fine blue.
Item, a bolster. Item, two blankets of fustian.
Item, a pair of sheets. Item, one stitched coverlet.
Item, one set of Arras hangings for the bed.
Item, one canopy. Item, one supporting framework.
Item, one covering.
Item, three curtains of green worsted.
Item, one piece of tapestry to throw over a seat.

The list continued: a pair of bellows for the fire, a pair of andirons, six cushions, a trestle table, two chairs, a candlestick, two bells. The word *Arras* in the inventory referred to the town in northeastern France that gave its name to the tapestries exported from the region, which covered the rough walls of other rooms in Sir John's house besides the bedroom. They depicted a range of subjects including a military siege, a hunting scene, and classical legends.

The furniture in the hall or main living room of a house such as Sir John's was generally limited to tables, benches, stools, and accessories for the fireplace. Chairs were a luxury and were usually reserved for the master and mistress and honored guests. But windows made up of small panes of glass—a product so precious that it had previously been used only in palaces, cathedrals, and some churches—were becoming increasingly common. The windows were often fitted to detachable frames and were regarded as the personal property of a tenant, who took them with him when he moved.

The management of the domestic regime fell to the lord's wife, who had to have both stamina and good business sense. Almost every job required planning, and none more so than the feeding of the household. The meat for the entire winter had to be killed and cured before the cold set in, and everything that could not be supplied by the manor farm or its herb garden had to be ordered and transported from a nearby town or port. The children of the household and the servants had to be clothed, often with garments made of cloth woven and spun on the manor. When the clothes were

In a detail from a 1494 painting by Vittore Carpaccio, a chorus of flared chimneys rises from the rooftops of Venice. The number of stacks seen here indicates that the Venetians, determined to banish the chill of the lagoon, had installed fireplaces not just in their main halls but in most rooms in their homes.

washed in tubs or in nearby streams, they were rubbed with a soft soap made of mutton fat from the manor-house kitchen and wood ash from its hearth; a more effective hard soap was available—made of olive oil, soda, lime, and aromatic herbs, and manufactured chiefly in the Spanish kingdom of Castile—but was much too expensive to be used on anything but the bodies of the master and mistress. And always the kitchen stores had to be replenished. The surviving letters of the Paston family, who lived in a manor house in East Anglia in England in the fifteenth century, show that Margaret Paston was constantly watching the markets for the best time to buy. When one of her sons went to London on business, she made use of his trip by asking him to purchase dates and figs and to check the price of certain costly spices. And when her husband was absent, Margaret had to take on the additional responsibility of looking after the family affairs: Several letters record her successful conduct of a lawsuit, and on one occasion she had to resist the armed retainers of a neighboring lord who laid spurious claim to the family house.

As the Paston correspondence indicates, the writing of letters was becoming an increasingly common activity. Not just the lord and lady of the manor but often some of their servants too were able to read and write, although most people found letter writing an awkward business and preferred to employ a professional scribe. To send their letters, correspondents made use of their servants or of a carrier or traveler who happened to be journeying in the right direction. The letters were folded and sealed to prevent their being read by strangers en route. Even so, there was no guarantee that a letter would reach its desired destination: Roads in the countryside were often overgrown, impassable, and infested with bandits. An Italian envoy in London in the fifteenth century wrote, "There is no country in the world where there are so many thieves and robbers as England; insomuch that few venture to go alone into the country, excepting in the middle of the day." Many of the Paston letters took a little more than three days to travel between

The mantel of this massive fifteenth-century French fireplace is decorated with lords and ladies representative of the homeowners who first built these imposing hearths.

This fancifully decorated sixteenth-century hand warmer, probably German, could be opened so that hot embers could be placed inside.

London and Norwich or vice versa, an average of around thirty miles per day. The family house was thus still comparatively remote from the center of the nation's affairs—but the increasing quantity of letters indicated that the isolation of village communities was being eroded, rendering them open to new influences from outside.

Obsessed with the hierarchical nature of the feudal system, many medieval writers in Europe described their society as made up of three categories of citizens: worshipers, warriors, and workers. A fourth, often unacknowledged category existed as a marginal component of all the others—women. Where women were included in the hierarchy, it was often at the bottom: One twelfth-century French abbot, for example, ranked women in his celestial order beneath the apostles, hermits, perfect monks, good bishops, and good laymen. Women were considered almost as a separate species, and the perspectives that determined how they were perceived and treated were largely those of the Church.

Informing all of the Church's pronouncements were the opposing archetypes of womanhood enshrined in the Christian scriptures: the Virgin Mary, representing absolute chastity, and the temptress Eve. In almost no sphere of life were either churchmen or laymen able to reconcile these images, and it was the latter archetype that was constantly more emphasized and developed. The official Church view was that it was Eve who seduced Adam and thus brought about the Fall; woman was therefore the mother of all sin, and desire for a woman not only made a man dependent on her but was a sin in itself. Medieval art often expressed an association between woman and the devil, the female body being a symbol of lust: A carving in the abbey church of Vézelay in Burgundy, for example, depicted Satan playing upon a woman as upon a musical instrument, and one in the twelfth-century cathedral of Autun showed a woman being seized by a demon while a snake twists about her body and sucks at her breast.

The belief that woman was created inferior to man—and, consequently, was prone to a host of weaknesses and vices ranging from limited intelligence and frivolity to avarice and cunning—was used to justify the exclusion of females from positions of authority in both ecclesiastical and secular institutions. "Let your women keep silence in the churches," Saint Paul had written in his Epistle to the Corinthians, "for it is not permitted unto them to speak; but they are commanded to be under obedience, as also saith the law." Women could not officiate or preach in churches and could not advance in the Church hierarchy beyond the level of deaconess—a position that had been created largely to ensure modesty in the early days of Christianity, when adult baptism was common. In secular life, women were prohibited in most countries from holding political office, from serving as judges and lawyers, and from participating in royal councils or representative assemblies. They had property rights, but their rights to bring suits in courts of law were restricted.

Given that the Church considered sexual activity itself a sin, the institution of marriage posed a taxing theological problem. But of necessity, a compromise was reached. Officially, marriage was regarded as second best to chastity, following the words of Saint Paul: "I say therefore to the

In this fifteenth-century French manuscript illustration, Isabelle of Bavaria, wife of Charles VI of France, receives a volume of poems from their author, Christine de Pisan, whose works also included a treatise on the education of women. Bedchambers were used by the wealthy in the late Middle Ages for the entertainment of guests as well as for sleeping. The room shown here boasts furnishings appropriate to its owner's status: carpets, soft chairs and cushions, a glazed and shuttered window, and wall hangings that bear the fleur-de-lis of France and the diamond of Bavaria.

unmarried and widows, it is good for them if they abide even as I. But if they cannot contain, let them marry: For it is better to marry than to burn." The prime purpose of marriage was deemed to be the prevention of sin—that is, it was a safeguard against the danger of promiscuous, unfettered sexual relationships. The ideal marriage was that of Joseph and Mary—married but celibate. Mutual companionship and the procreation of children were conveniently added to the list of marriage's worldly functions but were not by themselves sufficient justification for marriage. The fourth-century patriarch of Constantinople, Saint John Chrysostom, had written that "marriage was founded after the Fall as consolation for death. Man, who was destined to die, could perpetuate his being through his offspring. The Resurrection vanquished death. The world is full. We are on our way to a better life. There is no need for offspring." A twelfth-century theologian declared that a husband who loved his wife too enthusiastically was in fact an adulterer, and one of his followers added that to take pleasure in sex even for procreation was a sin. Nevertheless, as a concession to human weakness, marriage was transformed by the Church in the eighth century into a sacrament, thereby raising sexual activity within marriage from the realm of sin to that of sanctity.

But even within marriage, woman was not to lose sight of her inferior status. As Saint Paul admonished, "Wives, submit yourselves unto your own husbands, as unto the Lord. For the husband is the head of the wife, even as Christ is the head of the Church." Such

Beside a meandering river on the outskirts of a town, English women soak, pound, lay out, fold, and hang up their linen to dry. The preparation for such communal laundry days, which might take place no more than two or three times a year, involved as much work as the washing, as indicated by the number of tubs and the size of the fire needed to heat the cauldron of water. The making of soap from mutton fat and wood ash was itself a day's work; not until long after the Middle Ages was this expensive commodity widely available from commercial soap boilers in towns.

Eyes modestly downcast, French housewives in two manuscript illustrations sweep a tiled passageway and smooth down bed linen with a rod. In addition to cleaning and cooking, other household chores that fell to women included tending the kitchen garden, drawing and carrying home water, making cheese, brewing ale, and spinning yarn to make garments and furnishings.

opinions translated easily into secular customs and beliefs: "Let not the hen crow before the rooster," ran a popular proverb. These attitudes could sometimes work to the wife's benefit: An English jurist, for example, recorded a case involving a married couple accused of forgery in which the man was sentenced to be hanged but his wife was acquitted, on the ground that she had had no choice but to do as her husband bid her. For the most part, however, the woman suffered the consequences of her subordinate role, and a husband who beat his wife was generally allowed to have acted within his rights as long as he did not severely injure her. In the fourteenth century the legal code of one Flemish town stipulated that a man could beat his wife, slash her body from head to foot, and "warm his feet in her blood"; if she could then be nursed back to health, the man had not done anything wrong.

Male enmity toward or fear of women was manifest in many popular superstitions. Menstruation was a particular bugbear. It was widely held that menstrual blood was harmful to the penis and that a menstruating woman would blight any plant she might touch, while Saint Thomas Aquinas wrote that a mirror could dim and crack under the gaze of a menstruating woman. In popular literature—especially in the rhymed humorous tales known as fabliaux—the pleasures of sex both within and outside marriage were celebrated with gusto, but married women were commonly portrayed as stereotypical shrews: domineering, demanding, jealous, and quarrelsome.

In the more elevated literature of the troubadours—a school of sophisticated lyric poets that flourished in Provence and northern Italy from the eleventh century to the thirteenth—a very different type of woman was celebrated, and a contrasting type of male-female relationship was portrayed. But here too the appeal of the literature was founded upon a female stereotype: In this case, that of the virtuous wellborn lady, more Virgin Mary than Eve. The poems of the troubadours traded on the concept of courtly love, which involved the romantic idealization of woman and the development of a complicated code of secret courtship considered spiritually ennobling for the knights who submitted to it. Ideally, the object of a knight's desire had to be pure, powerful, and unattainable, which usually meant she had to be married. Everything that the knight did was done for her: For her sake, he was brave in battle and elegant and witty at court, and for her he sang songs and composed poems, or at least paid someone else to do so. If the lady acknowledged his devotion, which did not necessarily mean that she was ready to surrender to it, the couple went through a ceremony imitative of that in which a knight swore allegiance to his feudal lord. Kneeling before the lady with his hands clasped between hers, the knight swore to serve and defend her until death; and in return the lady promised her affection, put a ring on his finger, and raised her devotee to his feet.

The great leader of courtly love was the formidable Eleanor of Aquitaine. Divorced from the king of France, in 1152 she married Henry Plantagenet, England's king from 1154 to 1189. As a proud and unattainable queen, she was the object of many unrequited passions and the subject of an anonymous German poem that epitomized the spirit of the cult:

> *If the whole world were mine*
> *From the Elbe to the Rhine,*
> *I would count it little worth*
> *If England's queen would lie in my arms.*

THE PURSUIT OF CLEANLINESS

The smell of unwashed bodies permeated every dwelling: Even the monks of Cluny, the most lavishly endowed monastery in Europe, bathed only twice a year, before Easter and Christmas. But although the connection between poor hygiene and the spread of disease was not properly understood, certain measures were taken to alleviate people's physical discomfort and freshen their appearance. Delousing, as depicted in a carving *(left)* from an English monastery, was a regular family activity. In the countryside, a rain shower often sufficed to wash away domestic ordure, but as towns expanded and growing numbers of people lived in close proximity, the benefits of cleanliness and of household latrines—used in addition to chamber pots, which were emptied directly out of open windows—became more widely appreciated.

At her castle in Poitiers, Eleanor presided over a court of love, where the proceedings of the ladies and their chivalrous admirers were recorded by her daughter's chaplain, André le Chapelain. In his book *The Art of Courtly Love*, le Chapelain emphasized the necessity for secrecy: "He who wishes to keep his love intact for long must see to it above all that it is not divulged to anyone and kept hidden from all eyes. For as soon as several people have knowledge of it, it ceases at once to develop naturally and will go into decline." And he stressed also the need for restraint and self-control. "Pure love goes so far as the kiss and the embrace and the modest contact with the naked lover, omitting the final solace, for that is not permitted for those who wish to love purely."

Even le Chapelain must have realized that this was a rule begging to be broken, and in the most celebrated tales of courtly love it was. The knight Lancelot, for example, the hero of Arthurian legends, among them Chrétien de Troyes's *Conte de la Charette*, not only proved his nobility by his unlimited devotion to the lady of his lord but eventually consummated his love. By doing so Lancelot became an adulterer and thereby posed a conundrum, although admittedly one that has taxed critics and scholars more than Chrétien de Troyes's contemporary audience: How could a man who had violated the religious and secular moral norms of his society remain a hero? The answer lay, most probably, in the tale's truth to life—for courtly love was a decadent game, and while the ideals of chastity and unrequited devotion that it proposed undoubtedly had a strong influence on the courtship behavior of upper-class men and women, their transgression was by no means uncommon.

Although popular fabliaux and the lyric poems of the troubadours por-

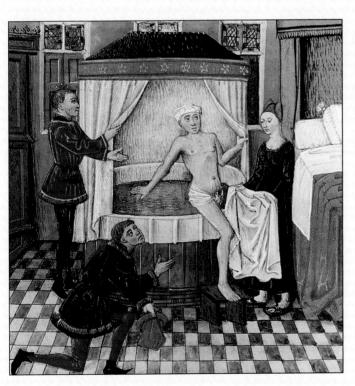

In a fifteenth-century French illustration, a wealthy homeowner steps from his steam bath to be enfolded in a towel held out by a maid. Gradually, bathing became associated less with effeminacy and more with respectability, although a reputation for loose morals still clung to many bathhouses.

A half-dressed man picks himself out of a cesspool, having fallen through a rotten floorboard while using the latrine. This fifteenth-century French miniature illustrated an episode from one of the earthy tales in Giovanni Boccaccio's *Decameron*.

trayed women at opposite poles of the conventional spectrum, they shared a common assumption that true love was not to be found within marriage. Nor indeed was love—at least in the idealized form depicted by the troubadours—commonly expected by either of the two partners who took wedding vows. Marriage among the nobility was primarily a political alliance between two families, and the most important ingredient was not love but land. Even a humble knight could acquire a second manor by marrying the brotherless daughter of another knight, and the fact that an additional estate might require him to furnish more fighting men was not a problem. At first he could send his sons or hire other knights, and most kings became willing to accept a cash payment—known as scutage, or shield money—which they used to hire professional soldiers. The powerful barons always had a surplus of land, and by the beginning of the fifteenth century many lesser lords also had sufficient property to use it as a bargaining counter.

The bargaining was an essential prelude to every marriage. A man who could offer titles and prestige was unlikely to accept a wife for his son unless she came with a large dowry. Even though a wife's land often reverted to her family after her death, her husband had the use of the income during her lifetime. Neighbors negotiated for months, and in order to cement these important alliances as soon as possible they pledged their sons and daughters to each other as children—sometimes while they were still in their cradles—and married them off in their early teens. According to canon law, a girl could be married at the age of twelve and a boy at fourteen years.

On occasion, passion might override more worldly factors. In 1476, for example, when Margery Brews, the daughter of an English knight, realized that her father was determined not to increase her dowry, she wrote in desperation to her betrothed, a member of the Paston family. "Right reverent and worshipful and my right well beloved Valentine . . . my mother has labored the matter to my father full diligently, but she can get no more than you know of, for which, God knows, I am full sorry. But, if you love me, as I trust verily you do, you will not leave me theretofore. For, if you had not half the livelihood that you have, and I had to work as hard as any woman alive might do, I would not forsake you." Despite continuing negotiations, her dowry never did get any larger, but finally the thirty-two-year-old John Paston defied his parents and married the sixteen-year-old Margery against their will.

Economic considerations were paramount in marriage arrangements not just in the upper reaches of society but among the more prosperous peasantry also. In addition, the lord of the manor could himself determine the marriage partner of a widow or the daughter of a serf, and had the right to a fee on the occasion of most marriages of peasants within his domain. In many regions, if the daughter of a serf married a man from outside her lord's manor and moved to his village, some of her children were considered serfs of her original lord and had to return to his manor. Nevertheless, among the peasantry the choice of marriage partner was often more free than it was among the landed classes, and many took advantage of the Church's recognition of private marriage—that is, a wedding celebrated privately by a consenting couple, sometimes in front of witnesses but sometimes not, and not solemnized in church. For example, of 101 marriages registered at the ecclesiastical court of Ely in eastern England between 1374 and 1382, 89 were private. If no one contested the legitimacy of these marriages, the couples were neither punished nor compelled to solemnize their wedding in church, although they were encouraged to do so. The majority of these private arrangements were probably love matches, but marriages so lightly

DIVERSIONS FROM THE EAST

According to the household regulations of Cowdray Manor in Sussex in 1596, the chief steward of the great hall was responsible for supplying "cards and tables for such strangers as shall be willing to play and pass the time thereat." Many of the games that diverted guests at Cowdray Manor were introduced to Europe during the Middle Ages by merchants and knights returning from abroad but had their origins in the more ancient civilizations of Asia and the Middle East.

Backgammon developed from a board game played in Mesopotamia as early as 3000 BC and later modified by the Egyptians and the Romans. Chess is thought to have been first played in India; introduced to Persia around the sixth century, it retained its popularity through successive dynasties—as shown in the miniature at right, dated 1468, in which one player strokes his beard pensively while pondering his next move. A version of the game of go, illustrated overleaf, was played in China in the third millennium BC.

Board games became fashionable among upper-class men and women looking for amusement to speed their idle hours. But many of the games enjoyed by the lower orders had no less lengthy pedigrees: Dice, for example, probably evolved from the prehistoric religious practice of throwing animal bones and predicting future events from the pattern in which they fell. Not every game was won by luck or skill: In Egyptian tombs, dice have been found with edges shaved down to ensure that one side ended faceup more often than the others.

A detail from an illustration to the Japanese novel *The Tale of Genji,* painted around 1610, shows two noble ladies swathed in a sea of silks concentrating on a game of go. On a checkered board each player in turn places a counter on a point where any two lines intersect; the aim is to conquer territory by enclosing squares, while at the same time preventing the opposing player from enclosing one's own counters.

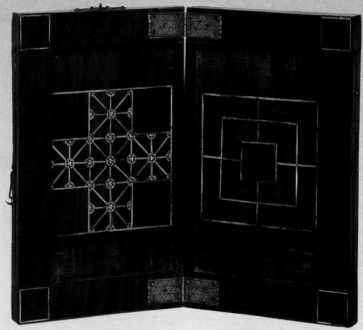

A French portable game kit dating from the fifteenth century includes boards for four different games: On the inside of the folding case are games known as nine men's morris and fox and geese; below, removed from the wings of the case into which they fit, are a board for a version of roulette and a standard chessboard. The outside of the case was stamped with a board for backgammon.

In this 1594 painting, the elder sons of an English nobleman play chess while their younger brothers play cards. Playing cards possibly originated in China; they were in use in Spain and Italy in the fourteenth century, and in England they became so well established that in 1465 card manufacturers sought to impose a protective tariff on imports.

A single candle on what is probably a tavern table illuminates a game of dice in this painting by the seventeenth-century French artist Georges de La Tour.

entered into could as easily be left, and many men who tired of their partners simply walked out and commenced a new life with a woman in another parish.

If love was not to be expected in marriage—and even in private marriages was often a shifting and transient state of affairs—then those who craved it sought it elsewhere. This was a dangerous game. Those caught in adultery faced punishments from the ecclesiastical courts, which imposed fines and sentences of fasting, prayer, and temporary celibacy, and from the secular courts, which varied widely in the severity of their punishments; adulterers also faced the consequences of private vengeance. Among the nobility, revenge was an accepted privilege, although laws were passed to mitigate its brutality. Henry III of England, for example, stipulated that only the husband himself should be allowed to castrate a man who had slept with his wife, and fathers and brothers of adulterous women were forbidden to take revenge. In some parts of Spain the husband was permitted to murder his wife and her lover, but only if he caught them in the act.

Given the superior status of men in society in general, it is not surprising that many courts of law were more lenient to adulterous men than to women. It was commonly determined, for example, that a husband was guilty of adultery only if he had slept with a married woman, while a wife was considered guilty if she had slept with any man, whether he was married or not.

The opportunities for women to conduct extramarital affairs were in any case far more restricted than they were for men. Chastity was thought to be the most important virtue of all women, regardless of class, and married men took great care to protect their women. Wives were not allowed to travel without an escort; daughters were never left alone. The most extreme method of protecting a lady's honor was the use of a chastity belt, a padded metal frame that denied access and was locked on the woman's hips with a key. Introduced in Italy during the fourteenth century, the chastity belt came too late to be used by the Crusaders—who had to abandon their wives for years on end—and it was seldom proof against ingenious lovers or unscrupulous locksmiths, but it was at least a protection against rape. That rape was an ever-present hazard—and that the chastity belt was designed as much to inhibit women from following their own desires as it was to protect them from the desires of others—was illustrated by the experience of the lady of the French manor of Montaillou at the beginning of the fourteenth century. During her first marriage she was raped in her bedchamber by a villager, who subsequently became her lover. After she was widowed, her chamberlain hid one night under her bed and attempted to climb in beside her, but the lady roused her servants, who were also sleeping in the room. During her second marriage she made love to a young priest while her maid stood watch, and on a later occasion she seduced another young priest.

Nevertheless, despite all the restrictions imposed on women by the attitudes of a society that saw no reason to grant them equality in either public or private life, harmony and tenderness between men and women was by no means unknown. The French poet Christine de Pisan, for example, who was born around 1365, was married at the age of fifteen to a man of twenty-four: On her wedding night, she later wrote, her husband did not approach her, allowing her time to become accustomed to his presence, and on the following day he kissed her tenderly and assured her that God had created him to be kind to her. He never lied to her, Christine affirmed, and encouraged her in everything she did.

The possibilities of love and compassion were also evident in a manual written in the late fourteenth century by an elderly Frenchman known as the Goodman of Paris for his fifteen-year-old wife. The Goodman followed convention in his view of the proper subservience of a wife to her husband: "Copy the behavior of a dog who always has his heart and his eyes upon his master; even if his master whip him and throw stones at him, the dog follows, wagging its tail." But he also took a realistic view of marriage as a partnership in which affection and trust between man and wife should be nourished for their mutual benefit: "The source of their pleasure and joy will be to bring each other pleasure, in love and in mutual obedience." Describing how a wife should greet her husband when he returned home, the Goodman recommended that she offer a smiling face, a lit fire in the hearth, clean clothes, food and drink, warm sheets, and, not least, love play in bed. And he told many stories in which good sense and affection triumphed over the often brutal code to which couples were supposed to conform. One story concerned a wife who confessed to her husband that one of their children was not his; the husband forgave her to preserve her honor and refused to inquire which child it was that she referred to. Another tale concerned a woman who left her husband to follow her lover. The husband told his friends that she had gone on a pilgrimage, and when her brothers discovered her destitute and abandoned, he forgave her willingly and welcomed her home with joy.

Such stories almost certainly represent a host of other marriages in which, under cover of the official precepts that gave all power to the man, an enduring harmony was achieved. That these marriages did not feature prominently in the most famous poems of the age was an indication that, in literature as in law and society in general, adequate conventions for the expression of companionship and equality between the sexes had not yet been devised.

For much of the medieval period the feudal system, based on the ownership and working of rural estates, had neither need nor place for towns. The few towns that existed in the eleventh century were mostly small trading settlements sited along the coasts of northern Europe and clustered around the mouth of the river Rhine, or longer-established settlements in Italy and around the Mediterranean that had survived after the collapse of the Roman Empire. Surrounded by walls, they were as much refuges for the people of the surrounding region in times of danger as they were commercial centers. But as the volume of both local and international trade increased in the wake of agricultural expansion, so did the economic importance of towns.

A fourteenth-century Flemish chronicler described the sequence of events that had led to the founding of the city of Bruges some three centuries earlier: "In order to

With jingling bells around his knees and cap, a costumed wooden figure, made in Germany around 1480, executes a crouching step in a morris dance, which developed from both ancient fertility rites and a dance popular among the Moors of North Africa. Itinerant bands of dancers, acrobats, jugglers, and minstrels traveled throughout the villages of medieval Europe, giving public shows at fairs and seasonal festivals and private performances in the great halls of the wealthy.

The female figure in this detail from a fifteenth-century Flemish altarpiece, although representing the Virgin Mary, takes her ease in a room furnished in a style to which increasing numbers of prosperous citizens were becoming accustomed. Engrossed in her studies, she enjoys a degree of privacy that was both new and valued—and that was guarded by locks, bolts, and keys such as the fifteenth-century example shown below. In a story by Boccaccio, a jealous husband taking leave of his wife warns her to "bolt the door to the street, the door to the stairway, and the door to the bedroom"—a sequence of domestic spaces of increasing intimacy.

satisfy the needs of the castle folk," he wrote, there began to gather near the castle and the bridge "traders and merchants selling costly goods, then innkeepers to house and feed those doing business with the prince." Newcomers who needed more permanent accommodation constructed houses, which "increased to such an extent that there soon grew up a large town which in the common speech of the lower classes is still called Bridge, for Bruges means bridge in their patois." From both Flanders and northern Italy merchant adventurers sent out ships to bring back cargoes of luxury goods such as spices as well as wool and other raw materials. Elsewhere the traveling merchants who had previously bought in small quantities from village craftsmen expanded their operations and set up warehouses and workshops within the security of city walls. Serfs and free peasants flocked from the countryside in search of new employment. In Flanders itself, a great cloth industry was born when weavers, dyers, and fullers migrated from their villages to the towns where the merchants were importing wool, dyes, and soap.

In the old Roman towns of southern Europe, many early medieval inhabitants lived in the remnants of Roman buildings, but most town houses were built in the same fashion as their contemporaries in the countryside. In the commercial centers of the towns, where space was at a premium, they were built in rows, often with their longest walls as common walls and only their gable ends facing the street. Many houses had two floors, but if the house was a shop, the owner and his family lived only on the upper floor. Sparks rising from the kitchens to the rear of the houses frequently set light to the wooden frames and roofs of thatch, and such fires could spread with devastating speed. After one particularly terrible fire in London toward the end of the twelfth century, the city council issued building regulations that required all adjoining houses to have tiled roofs and common walls made of stone.

Despite such regulations it was not until the middle of the fourteenth century that London and other cities in northern Europe replaced most of their thatched roofs with tiled ones. By that time, town houses had become more substantial. In much of southern Europe all but the poorest homes were being built of stone or brick, and in the north the timber frames had become strong enough to support several stories. Much of their stability came from the use of overhanging jetties, which also increased the floor space. In order to prevent the second floor from sagging in the middle, its huge timber joists projected by three feet or so over the top of the supporting walls at the front and back of the house; with the weight of the walls that supported the upper part of the house resting on their outer ends, the centers of the joists became rigid. Jetties made the second floor larger than the ground floor; and when similar jetties were built above, the third floor became even larger. From some upper floors, the apprentices who lived in the attics of merchants' houses could reach out over the narrow street and shake hands with their fellows on the opposite side; and sometimes the second floors hung out so low and so close that it was impossible to drive a cart full of hay between them.

Most town houses had courtyards or gardens, where the owners built their kitchens, grew vegetables, and sometimes kept pigs or chickens. Since they also dug cesspools in their gardens, the city councils often had to enact ordinances forbidding them to dig too close to their neighbors' property. Some homeowners avoided the need for a cesspool altogether by having a latrine at the front of the house, projecting over the street. But by no means every house had its own latrine. A contract dating from the early fifteenth century records that a certain citizen of Rouen built "a seat for the relief of the body" on the second floor of his house, put a door in the common wall, and charged his neighbor and his wife a high fee for the right to use the toilet.

For the less fortunate there were public facilities built over rivers or cesspools, the latter sometimes lined with wickerwork or stone. One of the largest, having parallel rows for men and women with sixty-four seats in each, was built in London at the beginning of the fifteenth century at the lord mayor's expense. London was eventually provided with sixteen such communal latrines, but even this number was scarcely sufficient for a population of around 25,000. The public cesspools were cleaned out

In a detail from a painting by Giovanni Mansueti, dated around 1506, Italian women peer eagerly down from windows and balconies toward the center of a square, where a procession is taking place. As in the classical world of Greece and Rome, respectability was for many women a dubious honor: Regarded by their fathers and husbands as precious possessions, and by society generally as the weaker, more sin-prone sex, they were confined to their homes and chaperoned on their rare excursions. Seclusion for these women was not a refuge from worldly distraction but a cell that denied them access to the world's full range of experience.

at intervals, and their contents were carted to the surrounding fields to be used as fertilizer. Those who did not live close to a public convenience simply chucked the contents of their chamber pots into the street. And there the waste lay for a week or longer with rotten fish, blood from the butcher's shop, and the rest of the domestic refuse, until a local farmer came to collect it in his cart.

Linked to the problem of sanitation was that of the supply of clean water for drinking, washing, and cooking. The contents of cesspools frequently seeped through the soil to contaminate wells, and often water from rivers was polluted by waste from tanneries and slaughterhouses and general household refuse. Conduits of stone, wood, or lead were sometimes constructed to channel water from rural springs, but most towns had to wait until the technological advances of the late nineteenth century for adequate supplies of water.

Life in town was scarcely hygienic. Epidemics were recurrent hazards. But there were also ways in which life in towns was more comfortable and convenient than life

in the country. Since the typical house was close to a public bakery, there was no need for an oven. Since it was close to a bathhouse, there ought to have been no need to carry water up to the bedchamber. In fact, however, many bathhouses in European towns were not all that they seemed. In some institutions, such as the public baths at Baden in Switzerland, scores of people of both sexes and all ages bathed together in wooden tubs as a matter of course. But in less respectable bathhouses there were also private rooms and tables for dining, and the women who brought the soap and massaged weary limbs also charged for other services. When a reputable merchant took a bath, he generally did so at home.

The way of life in a merchant's house was similar to that in a manor house. Family, servants, craftsmen, and apprentices all ate together in the hall. The merchant, his wife, and his younger children slept in the chamber on the first floor. Their other children slept in the attic; and if the house was large enough, the apprentices slept there also, instead of in the hall with the servants. The major distinguishing feature of an urban dwelling was the use of the front room on the ground floor: This was where the merchant carried on his business, and for most tradesmen it was both a factory and a shop. Craftsmen and apprentices worked at the back; at the front, a large wooden shutter folded out into the street on hinges fixed at the bottom to form the counter where goods were sold.

For the poorest inhabitants of the towns, living conditions did not compare favorably with those they had sought to leave behind in the countryside. Many casual laborers shared kitchens and kept their families in single attic rooms or in huts in the courtyards. Even for the rich, the scarcity of accommodation meant that urban couples married later than their rural contemporaries—for example, in the French city of Dijon in the middle of the fifteenth century, men did not marry until they were around twenty-five, and the average bride was eighteen. Moreover, the stresses and temptations of city life took a toll on many relationships—marriages were said to last for a shorter time in the towns than in the country.

In the independent cities of Italy, many knights and members of the aristocracy were also merchants, but in the rest of Europe the great landowning families who had rested comfortably at the top of the feudal system were contemptuous of trade. Most merchants were the sons of peasants or serfs, and the gentry despised them for it. But by the middle of the fifteenth century, the leading merchants in Europe's largest cities were powerful enough to return the contempt. The balance of economic power was shifting away from the land and into the towns. The men who manufactured and those who bought and sold were beginning to make more money than the men who produced the raw materials. Cloth merchants, for example, were becoming richer than the farmers from whom they bought wool. The best houses in the cities were as fine as most manor houses, and many merchants were making use of facilities unknown to their country cousins—sending their sons to school, for example, to learn the literacy and numeracy essential for success in commercial life.

In cities and towns across Europe, patterns of life were developing that resembled those of the better-off urban citizens in the Roman Empire. And it was in Italy, the original heartland of that empire, that the new developments were brought to their most exuberant and spectacular fruition. Throughout the Middle Ages, Italy, although no less troubled by warfare and plague than its northern neighbors, had profited from its position at the fulcrum of maritime trade routes between western Europe and the Byzantine and Arab countries to the east and south. Also, as warfare and the administration of prospering cities became more costly, and as the wealth and expenses of the Church also increased, many Italian merchants transformed themselves into bankers and financiers—dealing with taxes and with loans for war throughout Europe, and amassing vast personal fortunes at the same time. Cities flourishing on commerce—Venice, Florence, Milan, Rome, and others—came to replace kings and princes as the political centers of the country. And as intellectual cargoes as well as trade goods entered this increasingly wealthy society—including new ideas in science, philosophy from Byzantium and the Arab world, and old ideas newly recovered in the form of translations of classical Greek and Latin—conditions became right for the explosion of social change that came to be known as the Renaissance.

Much of the wealth of the Italian merchant princes was put to work to transform the urban landscape. In Rome, broad streets were driven through the chaotic maze of slums that huddled among the debris of antiquity. Thick-walled towers, which had sheltered citizens during centuries of local strife, were razed and replaced by the opulent palaces of the patrician families who ruled the cities. Many of the palaces imitated the austere classical style developed by the leading architect of the age, Filippo Brunelleschi. Some had as many as thirty rooms, including apartments for married sons and their families and separate chambers for the elder unmarried children. And villas sprang up in the countryside of Tuscany that were no less luxurious than those of the aristocrats of ancient Rome.

Not content with the grandeur of their palaces alone, the Italian merchant princes—and the cardinals and the popes also—were determined to outbid one another in colorful exhibitions of their wealth and power. Display, indeed, had become part of the art of government. The subjects of the powerful were treated to elaborate and colorful pageants, processions, and tournaments. Their guests were honored with masquerades and revels, and with banquets that must have impressed the most gluttonous. A chronicler described the fare provided by Pope Sixtus IV—who had been born in poverty—for the entourage of the daughter of the king of Naples: "Before them were carried wild boars, roasted whole in their entire hides, bucks, goats, hares, rabbits, fish silvered over, peacocks with their feathers, pheasants, storks, cranes, and stags; a bear in its skin, holding in its mouth a stick; countless were the tarts, jellies, candied fruits, and sweetmeats. An artificial mountain was carried into the room, out of which stepped a liveryman with gestures of surprise at finding himself in the midst of such a gorgeous banquet; he repeated some verses and then vanished. . . . Castles made of sweetmeats and filled with eatables were sacked and then thrown from the loggia of the hall to the applauding crowd. Sailing vessels discharged their cargoes of sugared almonds."

Excess was one of the hallmarks of this new society—in violence no less than in conspicuous consumption. When enmity between families erupted into conflict, no limits were adhered to. In 1445, the people of Bologna, seeking vengeance for the slaughter of the Bentivoglio family, hunted down their enemies and nailed their steaming hearts to the doors of the Bentivoglio palace. In Foligno a cuckolded prince hurled his wife from a turret of his castle and killed her lover's brothers; in return, every member of his own family was murdered and their severed limbs were paraded through the streets. In Milan, the wife of a nobleman assassinated in church was concerned that her husband had died without confession, so she drew up a list of his sins: Her spouse had been, she noted, "versed in warfare, both lawful and unlawful; in pillage, robbery, and devastation of the country; in extortion of subjects; in neg-

82

ligence of justice; in injustice knowingly committed; in the imposition of new taxes which even included the clergy; in notorious and scandalous simony and numerous other crimes." She sought the help of the pope, who granted absolution in return for a subsidy from the widow's family for the papal army.

Yet against this backdrop of gaudy magnificence and bloody retribution, the more durable passions unleashed by the Renaissance were directed toward beauty and justice, learning and discovery. The finest palaces were adorned with bronze and marble statues and with paintings of a quality never before seen in Europe; and from the mid-fifteenth century, when the first printing presses came into operation in Germany, the libraries of these palaces were stocked with the works of both classical and contemporary Italian authors. By 1500, the press of Aldus Manutius, which produced the first elegantly designed, comprehensive, and standardized sets of books at a moderate price, was just one of more than 200 printing presses in Venice alone. One prince, Federigo da Montefeltro, who ruled the small state of Urbino from 1444 to 1482, "had a mind to do what no one had done for a thousand years or more; that is, to create the finest library since ancient times. He spared neither cost nor labor," wrote the Florentine bookseller Vespasiano da Bisticci, "and when he knew of a fine book, whether in Italy or not, he would send for it. It is now fourteen or more years since he began the library, and he always employed, in Urbino, in Florence, and in other places, thirty or forty scribes in his service." Federigo's library included a choice collection of erotica, which he later bequeathed to the Vatican. Nor were books Federigo's only intellectual interest: He employed sculptors and architects from other Italian states, painters from Spain, and tapestry workers from Flanders. He maintained a choir and an orchestra, and oversaw their repertoire himself—"He preferred delicate to loud instruments," noted Vespasiano, "caring little for trombones and the like."

One of many men of learning drawn to the court of Federigo at Urbino was Baldassare Castiglione, who came from an ancient but impoverished noble family and who was acutely aware of the social skills needed for advancement in the new high society of princes who knew as much about books as about battles. In his *Book of the Courtier,* a record of conversations that supposedly took place in Urbino at the beginning of the sixteenth century, Castiglione laid down the principles of correct conduct for modern courtiers. The traditional knightly virtues of courage and strength were still applicable, and a gentleman should ensure his physical fitness by constant exercise in riding, fencing, wrestling, and swimming. But the mind was now no less important than the body: A courtier must be knowledgeable about music, painting, and the works of the classical authors. He must be eloquent in his speech and supple in his dancing. Above all, while the model courtier must excel in all things, he must avoid the appearance of effort: All his activities must be performed with a studied but easy nonchalance, or *sprezzatura*—"so as to conceal all art and make whatever is done and said appear to be without effort and without almost any thought about it."

In practice few courtiers could achieve all that Castiglione demanded of them, but they had been set a new ideal to aspire to: that of the all-around gentleman, the cultivated amateur, as versed in the arts of peace as in those of war. In comparison with this ideal, the warrior knight celebrated by the traditional code of medieval chivalry was a crude, unsophisticated character. Indeed, in the satirical novel *Don Quixote,* written at the beginning of the seventeenth century by the Spanish author Miguel de Cervantes, he was to become a comic rather than a noble figure.

THE PALACES OF ITALY

The merchant princes of Renaissance Italy, enjoying riches unknown to their forebears, did more than ape the grandeur of the landed nobility: By spending lavishly, they created new spaces in which to satisfy their desire for luxury and new codes of behavior to match. In the two decades between 1450 and 1470, they commissioned some thirty palaces in Florence alone, setting standards of elegance and extravagance that soon spread to neighboring cities and states. As the architect Leon Battista Alberti apostrophized, "How many towns that were built of wooden planks when we were children are now all marble?" The rooms in the palaces, often forty feet high and decorated with frescoes, paintings, and sculptures, celebrated the material and intellectual ascendancy of a new elite.

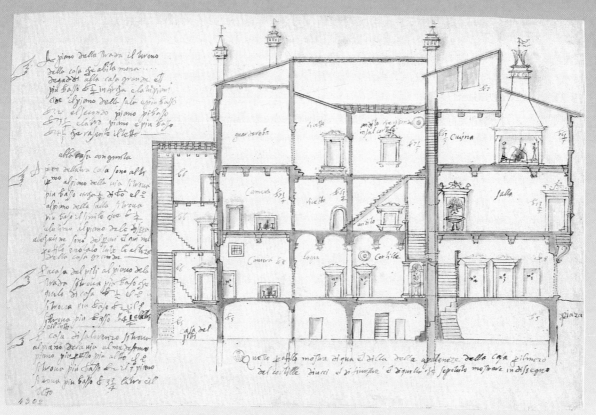

A detail from a sixteenth-century painting *(above)* shows the sumptuous Pitti Palace in Florence, at the time of its construction in the previous century the largest private residence in the world—the facade measured 180 feet wide by 118 feet high. Luca Pitti, who commissioned the palace, used his political influence to have the houses that originally occupied the site demolished. The Gaddi family, also of Florence, was less extreme: the sketch *(left)* shows the architect's proposal for expanding and adapting an existing block of houses to create a palace in the new fashion. The kitchen has been positioned in the top right corner to minimize the risk of fire to the rest of the building.

Castiglione would not have claimed that his principles of conduct expressed a revolution in manners, an overthrow of aristocratic customs by those of the rising merchant classes. The Italian nobles, their wealth enhanced by commercial activities, remained secure enough to maintain their privileged status, and the new ideals were essentially the old ones redefined for a more literate society. But as increasing numbers of ordinary city dwellers enjoyed new degrees of prosperity and material comfort, the ideals were further adapted to their own level and in modified form came to represent standards of correct behavior for bourgeois homes as well for the courts of princes. Educators such as Vittorino da Feltre taught the principles of gentlemanly conduct to children—both girls and boys—from humble homes as well as to those from the families of the nobility. And manuals of etiquette proliferated. Some of the rules included in a book published by Giovanni della Casa in 1558 show that in many cases education had to proceed from a very elementary level: The well-mannered man, decreed della Casa, must not pick his nose, spit, break wind, examine the contents of his handkerchief, or thrust stinking fish under the noses of his friends. Also: "Refrain as far as possible from making noises which grate upon the ear, such as grinding or sucking your teeth." But even della Casa's pupils were encouraged to be "very desirous of beautiful things, well-proportioned and comely." And the principle of sprezzatura still held: "A man must not be content to do things well but must also aim to do them gracefully."

In essence, the educators and treatise writers of Renaissance Italy were teaching people how to live together in towns without unnecessary friction. In the isolated rural settlements of early medieval Europe, traditions of hospitality to guests were sufficient, and good table manners were superfluous: Most people knew everyone they met and were taken as they were found. In towns, however, people constantly had to work and negotiate with complete strangers, and it made good business sense to create a favorable impression—that is, to appear trustworthy, and to show courtesy and respect to others. Urban life had rendered the principal medieval ideals of conduct—that of the chivalric knight and that of the reclusive monk—largely irrelevant. And while schools were available for only a minority of the population, the place in which the new manners were taught could only be the family home.

Urban populations were not large by later standards. At the beginning of the sixteenth century only Paris and the great independent city-states of Italy such as Venice, Florence, and Milan contained more than 50,000 inhabitants. London, Brussels, and the other major trading capitals of northern Europe each contained only around 40,000 citizens; few other towns had populations of more than 5,000, and most of them numbered between 1,000 and 1,500 inhabitants. But it was towns—and the capital engendered in them—that now forced the pace. At the beginning of the millennium, land had been the only meaningful form of wealth; since then, the expanding production of mainly agricultural goods had led to the emergence of a new class of merchant entrepreneurs and the collapse of the rigid hierarchies of a feudal society. The discovery and exploitation of distant lands, especially the gold-rich countries of Central and South America, had injected yet more wealth into the European economy and yet more things to spend it on—including new foods and spices, and new fabrics and dyes for clothing. Efforts were made to maintain social differences by updating the regulations—known as sumptuary laws—that forbade inferior ranks to wear furs, silks, and other materials previously reserved for the aristocracy, but these laws proved increasingly difficult to enforce.

Most of the new wealth stayed in the hands of either the accumulating merchants or the landed gentry, whose traditional status still gave them leverage in the new, more open society. They used it to build large mansions whose ceilings were encrusted with rich plasterwork and whose walls were lined with delicately carved paneling. Tapestries were replaced by ancestral portraits, trestles by tables with heavy carved legs, and benches by rows of chairs. Grand staircases led up to a great chamber where the family now dined separately from their servants. Outside the towns the new homes of the wealthy were often still built in the shape of castles, but their walls were thin and filled with windows, and their moats and battlements were only decorative symbols of their owners' feudal heritage. The eagerness of these classes to learn appropriate standards of conduct and consolidate their position made Castiglione's *Book of the Courtier* a bestseller throughout Europe.

But some wealth filtered down, changing the lives of people who for generations had neither expected nor received more comfort than mere subsistence. "Our fathers and we ourselves," wrote the English author William Harrison in 1577, in the wake of a boom in the construction of new houses, "have lain full oft upon straw pallets, covered only with a sheet." But now, he declared, "the furniture of our houses . . . is grown in manner even to passing delicacy: and herein I do not speak of the nobility and gentry only, but likewise of the lowest sort in most places of our south country." The "costly furniture" of former times had been restricted to the houses of the most wealthy—"whereas now it is descended yet lower, even unto the inferior artificiers and many farmers, who . . . have for the most part learnt also to garnish their cupboards with plate, their joined beds with tapestries and silk hangings, and their tables with carpets and fine napery."

Harrison, infected by the optimism of his time, was exaggerating: There were still many who lived in hovels, and whose successors would do likewise until at least the mid-nineteenth century. But his enthusiasm was understandable, for many sectors of society were now enjoying new opportunities. Not least among them were women: The increased and more varied employment offered by urban industries, especially the silk trade, provided certain women with chances to improve their economic position. More people than ever before had the power to determine the conditions in which they lived their lives, and the Renaissance pride in the human potential was well grounded. Even space and time, it could be claimed, had been domesticated: The richest houses could now be furnished with maps of the world—maps showing continents whose existence had not even been suspected just a century before—and with mechanical clocks that counted every minute ticking by.

THE MARRIAGE BOND

In 1434, the Italian merchant Giovanni Arnolfini posed with his bride, Giovanna Cenami, for the Flemish painter Jan van Eyck. In the painting that van Eyck created *(above)*, every detail—the placement of the newlyweds' hands, their unshod feet, the witnesses, who are visible only in the mirror—documents some aspect of the ceremony by which the couple were united and acquired a new status in their society.

Primarily, marriage is an institution for the creation of an identifiable family unit for procreation and inheritance, for the forging of alliances between clans, and for the pooling or exchange of land and other forms of wealth. Communities have felt that romance and passion were of little significance, and throughout history, most societies have considered marriage far too important an agreement to be left to the individuals. In Chaldea during the third millennium BC, brides and grooms came before the magistrates to record their mutual contract on clay tablets; a variety of other traditions concerning betrothal and the wedding ceremony itself are illustrated on the following pages.

The ceremony of betrothal—the ritual confirmation of a couple's decision to marry—has often been performed with as great a degree of solemnity as the nuptials themselves. In some parts of ancient China, for instance, even the death of one of the partners before the wedding took place did not release the unfortunate survivor from his or her vows. In many cultures the engagement was—and still is—made not by the couple themselves but by the parents, acting on behalf of their juvenile offspring or even for those yet unborn. And the prospective husbands—or, in some societies, hopeful brides—frequently have had to prove the seriousness of their intentions in a number of ways that have satisfied their communities: by exchanging gifts as tokens of their commitment, by performing a series of specific tasks in their future in-laws' fields or households, by accumulating supplies of bedding or kitchen utensils with which to furnish their future homes, or by purchasing their new mates with precisely calculated payments in cash or kind.

Flowers, symbols of the zodiac, and Biblical figures adorn a Jewish marriage contract drawn up in Modena, Italy, on Friday, October 1, 1557. Signed by the prospective groom in front of witnesses, this document—still an essential part of Jewish wedding ritual—sets out the responsibilities and obligations of the new husband.

To symbolize the betrothal of two Hindu children—which, according to tradition, may take place years before they are old enough to consummate the match—a consecrated cord links their flower-bedecked heads. Prayers and days of lavish feasting mark this early step on the road to matrimony.

RITES OF BETROTHAL

Attesting to the wealth of her ancestral home, the lacquered and gilded trousseau of a nineteenth-century Japanese bride includes requisites for upper-class married life. Plum blossom and water plantain—her husband's family crest—decorate the cosmetic boxes, writing case, bookshelves, mirror, washbasin, and clothes racks for the new house.

On a painted chest dating from the Renaissance, a procession approaches the baptistery of San Giovanni in Florence. The massive coffer contained the new clothes and household linen assembled by a well-born maiden in anticipation of her marriage.

From the time that the first temple priest in ancient Sumer pulled a thread each from the garments of a bride and groom and tied these filaments together in a knot, wedding ceremonies have consisted of a series of symbolic acts. To mark the moment when two single people become a married couple, hands may be joined to affirm physical union, a ring offered to the bride as a relic of some ancient custom of purchase, a drink taken from the same consecrated cup, ritual foods consumed, specific promises exchanged aloud, or veils lifted as a statement of intimacy and exclusivity.

The attendance of a priest or other holy official has not always been considered a requisite. Equally important, and far more universal, has been the participation of family and friends. These companions have filled traditional roles as bridesmaids or attendants for the groom, as living links with ancestors, and as witnesses to the fact that the marriage has been solemnized in accordance with the customs of a particular time and place.

Sculpted in marble on the side of a sarcophagus dating from the second century, a Roman groom clasps his bride's right hand in his own to signify that the maiden has now passed into his possession. Behind, a maid of honor oversees the handing over of the bride in a ceremony that was a civil rather than religious occasion.

An eighteenth-century Indian painting illustrates a scene from Hindu lore: the nuptial rites of the future parents of Krishna, the human incarnation of the god Vishnu. In accordance with ancient Hindu practice, the bride and groom sit side by side in the open air while priests chant holy Vedic texts and add ghee—clarified butter—to the sacred fire to make its flames flare.

THE CEREMONY OF UNION

In a detail from a fifteenth-century Flemish altarpiece, a bridal couple under the supervision of a priest perpetuates the old Roman custom of joining hands. During the Middle Ages, the Church in Europe gained increasing control over the nuptials of its communicants.

Flanked by black-clad attendants, the Chinese newlyweds in this 1850 watercolor kneel before the shrine of the groom's departed ancestors. According to Confucian custom, this act of homage was the traditional start to a couple's married life.

The Jewish bridegroom in this eighteenth-century Portuguese engraving *(right)* prepares to crush the glass from which the couple has ceremonially drunk wine. Jews believe the act to be either a token of the bride's imminent loss of virginity or a commemoration of the destruction of the temple in Jerusalem. The edifice on the fourteenth-century Jewish wedding ring below may also be a memento of that sacred place. Such rings were often owned by the community and lent to brides.

Figures in a wedding party adorn this fifth-century-BC Greek vase, intended to carry water for a bridal couple's ritual baths. Similar purifications have been practiced by Arabs, Jews, Thais, and others into modern times.

To shield her from evil spirits, the Chinese bride in a nineteenth-century painting is conveyed to her new home in a closed sedan chair. The chair, like the unseen bridal veil, is red—the Chinese color of joy and good luck.

Leaving the church after the ceremony, a Bolivian bride and groom are showered with rice by family and friends *(right)*. Foodstuffs have been showered on newly married couples in many societies to encourage fertility: The Greeks threw pomegranate seeds, while the ancient Romans used nuts. In Scotland, an oatcake broken over the bride's head expresses the same wish for her fecundity.

Jeweled ornaments dangle from a wedding crown worn by a Norwegian bride in a 1905 drawing *(above)*. To assuage male fears, a Japanese bride's headdress *(above, right)* is designed to hide the horns of willfulness and spite, which—it is believed— sprout from female heads.

Good luck charms—such as a horseshoe and an old boot—adorn this three-tier Western wedding cake. Custom decrees that the newlyweds make the first cut in the cake together to guarantee marital harmony in the years ahead.

TOKENS OF GOOD FORTUNE

Because it is one of the major crossroads on life's journey, marriage has long been perceived as a time when unseen forces, working for good or ill, were particularly potent. To protect the couple from harm, to ensure their well-being and guarantee their fertility, certain rules and restrictions had to be scrupulously observed. The particular color of a bride's costume, the position of the stars and planets on the wedding day, the people seen or touched by the principal participants before and after the ceremony—any or all of these might well turn out to be the decisive factors in deterring any evil spirits and encouraging Lady Luck to smile upon the match.

An English bride is kissed by a chimney sweep to bring her good luck and to encourage her—by negative example—to keep her home spotlessly clean.

Laden with domestic utensils, this German dowry cart ferried a bride's new goods to her marital home in a public show of her family's wealth.

A COMMUNAL CELEBRATION

For many newly married couples, the ceremony itself is merely the beginning of the wedding, as strict formality gives way to exuberant festivities that in some societies can last for days or even weeks. Male guests in Western cultures often insist upon their prerogative to kiss the bride; their counterparts among the Bugti people of Pakistan exhibit their prowess in camel races and in displays of marksmanship. The festivities culminate in the departure of the bride and groom—either in stealth or with much ribald fanfare—for the marriage bed. Privacy for this purpose has not always been allowed. Among the Teutonic peoples of northern Europe it was long thought necessary to send the pair to bed in the presence of witnesses, while Chinese mothers-in-law took pride in displaying the bloody marks of defloration on the nuptial sheets.

Two Italian aristocratic families celebrate the wedding of their offspring at a banquet painted by Sandro Botticelli in 1483. Apart from the groom, who faces his spouse, the members of each sex sit separately, with a display of elaborately carved plates and ewers—possibly wedding gifts—between them.

At an open-air gypsy wedding in Spain in the 1950s, the bride dances with a guest. In many European societies it is customary for the bride to dance with every man at the marriage feast, and the groom with every woman.

To protect a Tartar bride from the evil eye, her male kinsmen have helped her onto a camel's back and concealed her from view beneath a richly decorated canopy *(left)*. Thus secured, she can travel without danger to her marital home.

In a bedroom typical of the Middle Ages in Europe, the Greek hero Jason and the enchantress Medea prepare to consummate their union in this fifteenth-century miniature. In Greek legend, Medea bore Jason two children, but the match was star-crossed: He was later to abandon her.

THE FAMILY DOMAIN

3 An apparently true tale that caused much amusement among foreign travelers in Amsterdam in the mid-seventeenth century concerned a magistrate who neglected to wipe his shoes before knocking on the door of the household where he had an appointment. The maid—a "strapping North Holland lass," according to the English diplomat Sir William Temple—"took him by both arms, threw him upon her back, set him down at the bottom of the stairs, pulled off his shoes, put on him a pair of slippers that stood there, all this without saying a word." Only then was the distinguished visitor permitted to enter the chamber of the maid's mistress.

Temple's Dutch informant told this story as a joke against his own countrymen, but both were well aware that the episode also embodied a wholesome moral. Foreigners were served notice that whatever might be the state of affairs in their own country, in Holland the age-old conventions of high society were likely to be overruled by certain domestic imperatives. In this particular story, a clean floor was obviously more important than the rank of the visitor. More generally, in the republic of the United Provinces of the Netherlands an individual's worth was judged as much by his conformity to the domestic virtues of cleanliness, moderation, and thrift as by his achievements in public life.

To visitors from older and more socially stratified nations, even the most illustrious Dutch citizens seemed remarkably free of pomp or pretension. Temple noted that Grand Pensionary De Witt, chief legislator of the province of Holland, "was seen usually on the streets on foot and alone, like the commonest burgher of the town." And he marveled at the modest demeanor of Admiral De Ruyter, commander of the redoubtable Dutch fleet: "I never saw him in clothes better than the commonest sea captain. . . . And in his own house neither was the size, building, furniture, or entertainment at all exceeding the use of every common merchant or tradesman."

The conception of the plain, well-ordered household as a paradigm of good society was one of the most significant consequences of Dutch political and economic successes in the early seventeenth century. In the late 1500s, the inhabitants of this damp, low-lying corner of western Europe had risen in revolt against the heavy-handed rule of imperial Spain and in 1609 had constituted themselves a loosely federated republic. With few natural resources beyond its human ones, the Netherlands soon came to dominate the commerce of the continent. Perspicacity, hard work, good seamanship, and a genius for building superior ships paid handsome dividends: The Dutch grew rich. And with no monarch or royal court to skim the cream, the wealth spread wide. By the middle of the seventeenth century, the mass of Netherlanders enjoyed a standard of living that excited the envy—and sometimes the wrath—of their neighbors.

In the populous maritime regions of Holland and Zeeland, the majority of men and

Equal partners in learning and affection, a French intellectual couple relax together in the privacy of their library in this painting of the late 1760s. Sequestered from the public gaze, husbands and wives enjoyed a new intimacy and developed self-awareness both as individuals and as married couples. Displaying the influence of feminine taste, the flowing lines of the rococo table and chairs indicate a concern with style as much as with function, with luxury as much as need.

Architecture in seventeenth-century Holland reflected the simple, unpretentious tastes of the new bourgeoisie. Constructed of brick and wood rather than the heavier stone employed in England and France, and pierced by large windows that allowed light to penetrate deep into the interior, Dutch town houses were often built on narrow plots, their steep, red-tiled roofs and stepped gable ends forming distinctive silhouettes—as in the engraving above of Amsterdam's Keizersgracht. The fact that most households had few servants, and the increasing separation of work premises from the home, contributed to the emergence of small, private family houses, although those belonging to the wealthy might extend upward to as many as seven stories, their height corresponding to the prosperity of their owners. Furniture comprised chiefly tables, chairs, and cabinets, neatly arranged on tiled floors beneath walls hung with tapestries. The interior scene on the left, painted in 1662, shows a sequence of chambers receding to a fireplace at the rear, but any impression of extravagance is countered by the inclusion of cat, dog, and broom, and a fallen scrap of paper on the staircase leading off to the right.

women were neither peasants nor landed aristocrats, but town dwellers, carving out their own economic niche. They were the inhabitants of a broad and comfortable middle ground: artisans and shopkeepers; notaries, lawyers, physicians, and architects; scholars, clerics, and schoolmasters; merchants and seafarers; speculators waxing fat on foreign trade. Worldly ambition was tempered by a strong Protestant faith, but this piety was accompanied by a degree of religious and cultural tolerance that was rarely seen in this age.

Foreign observers attributed Dutch success to good financial management and plain common sense. "Their common riches," announced one, "lie in every man's having more than he spends; or, to say it more properly, in every man's spending less than he has coming in, be that what it will." And the money that was spent was not lavished on public display but put to productive use—as seed corn for building even greater fortunes; as the source of charity; as the means for ensuring cleanliness, comfort, and good domestic order.

Untrammeled by old power structures or the weight of encrusted tradition, the burghers of the Netherlands created a new society that reflected their own passions, preoccupations, and deepest needs. In doing so they defined anew and took pride in the pleasures of home and family and pioneered new patterns of domestic life that, with local variations and emphases, were taken up by the prosperous classes of other European nations also. For the seventeenth and eighteenth centuries saw profound and widespread upheavals in material and intellectual life throughout the continent. In the physical world, the Renaissance explorers had done their work, and now the colonizers took over, reaching out to grasp the wealth of the newly discovered continents. Increased affluence and mounting confidence allowed a similar redrawing of mental maps: Old beliefs were challenged, making way for new inventions and fresh ideas. Nor were these developments the sole preserve of any political or intellectual elite. The seventeenth and eighteenth centuries saw profound and lasting changes in the lives of ordinary people—in the arrangement and contents of their homes, the pattern of their work and leisure time, the composition of their households, and in the very nature of the human bonds between them.

Amsterdam, the largest and most prosperous city of the United Provinces, was in the first half of the seventeenth century Europe's fastest-growing town: Between 1612 and 1650, the population swelled from 50,000 to 200,000. Its harbor bristled with masts, and the air was pungent with the spices, timber, wheat, and salt herring carried in the vessels' holds. In the counting houses clerks sat calculating loss and profit, or dispatched their juniors to compile inventories within the warehouses lining the canals. Rivers of gold flowed through the banking halls, and within the arcades of the city's bourse clusters of whispering investors traded in lucrative rumors. Along the Warmoesstraat—where the shops of dealers in luxury goods adjoined the offices of the wealthiest merchants—Chinese porcelain, Italian majolica, silks from Lyons, and taffeta from Spain vied for attention with masterpieces of local provenance: tables inlaid with mother-of-pearl in floral patterns or Leiden linens so white they made the eyes dance.

Such delights did not go begging for buyers: The well-to-do citizens of the young republic may have been thrifty, but they were not parsimonious, and the judicious purchase of an Oriental carpet, a tapestry, or a set of silver spoons was an acceptable way to spend the wealth that remained after the community's conscientious tax

collectors had claimed their hefty dues on grain, wine, beer, butter, flour, fruit, fish, soap, tobacco, firewood, lead, bricks, roof tiles, and all the rest of life's necessities. Temple noted that "what they can spare, besides the necessary expense of their Domestic, the public payments, and the common course of still increasing their stock, is laid out in the fabric, adornment, or furniture of their houses."

Space was at a premium, but the urban Dutch avoided the overcrowding suffered by their counterparts elsewhere in Europe. Throughout the seventeenth and eighteenth centuries a typical household in Paris comprised as many as twenty-five persons, with parents, children, dependent relatives, domestic servants, and the apprentices and journeymen attached to the family business all crammed together under the same roof. During the same period some 90 percent of Netherlanders lived in small nuclear units of husband, wife, and those children not yet old enough to leave the nest, and most households consisted of no more than four or five members. As the economy of the Netherlands boomed, even a relatively modest Dutch artisan could raise the funds to buy his own house instead of renting a part of someone else's, and to set up separate commercial premises instead of living over the shop in the manner of his counterparts elsewhere.

As in most of northwestern Europe, the typical residential plot was deep but narrow. Behind the brick facade, across a threshold scoured clean of any invading speck of outdoor grime, lay halls and rooms floored with black-and-white tiles scrubbed to a mirrorlike polish. The tall house of an affluent burgher might boast four spacious chambers on each story, two at the front and two at the back, illuminated by many-paned windows set high in the exterior walls. As general prosperity increased, the occupants of smaller houses contrived by whatever means they could to augment their limited space with such improvised additions as attics, alcoves, tacked-on annexes, and "hanging rooms" projecting from an upper floor. The usual access to the rear of these tightly packed buildings was a long corridor leading to a small yard, sometimes containing a lean-to or washhouse where the heavier domestic work was done and, beyond it, a compact garden. Here, those who could afford it built little summerhouses or outdoor pavilions; a humbler family might opt for a hencoop as a more practical use of space.

Many families established small flower gardens in their yards, planting separate beds of roses and irises, hyacinths and lilies. Their scents mingled with the odors rising from the canals. Certain moralists inveighed against the Dutch passion for flowers, but many gardens were not the frivolous indulgence they might have seemed. Because of the excellence of the alluvial soil, some gardeners were able to grow species still unknown in the rest of Europe, and sell cuttings and seedlings to other enthusiasts. On a larger scale, horticulture became a major Dutch industry. Tulips in particular, imported from Turkey in the sixteenth century and associated throughout northern Europe with aristocratic delicacy, became the subject of frenzied speculation. This particular variety of flower fetched ever-higher prices until the market finally collapsed in the 1630s.

Inside houses, rooms were not crammed with furniture; the uncluttered simplicity of the typical mid-seventeenth-century Dutch interior reflected the unpretentious tastes of its inhabitants. But the individual pieces were as well made as their owners could afford: A Turkish rug, glowing with subtle colors, might cover a sturdy table; a set of richly embroidered draperies shields a built-in box bed from the chill of damp, ill-heated houses. An average home was likely to contain a dozen or twenty straight-backed wooden chairs, perhaps some cushions, and a couple of mirrors—which sold rapidly when local craftsmen learned how to copy the elegant frames of Venetian masters. But the most important items of furniture in any burgher's household were the imposing carved chests and cabinets for the family's worldly goods—colored glassware, silver-handled tankards, brass candlesticks, sacred and secular books, and an enormous supply of domestic linen. Even an artisan's family of relatively modest means found it necessary to own a dozen tablecloths, eighteen or twenty sets of bedsheets, and scores of starched white napkins and handkerchiefs, all crisply folded and kept sweet with bouquets of dried herbs.

Even more remarkable than the Netherlanders' linen cupboards were their domestic art collections. The penchant for owning pictures spanned all classes. One rich patron, whose fortune came from merchant ventures in the West Indies and the Levant, not only hung dozens of paintings in all the hallways and reception rooms within his mansion, but even installed them in the servants' quarters: A maid's room boasted seven works of art. Less wealthy families snapped up the works of a flourishing army of native artists: seascapes and townscapes, dramatic moments in Dutch history, detailed maps of the republic, rural panoramas of grazing livestock and farmers laboring in the fields, bird's-eye views of bustling city squares. At the lower end of the market, satirical and scatological scenes were popular, with a whole genre of works depicting tavern and brothel life or the misdeeds of servant girls.

Most popular of all were the lovingly detailed scenes of ordinary life within the houses and gardens of the burghers themselves. In these works, painters meticulously re-created the familiar minutiae of everyday existence to celebrate the cult of domesticity. This art was essentially secular, reflecting the Dutch Calvinist aversion to images that smacked of idolatry. Instead of the lives of saints, it recorded the lives of the Netherlanders themselves, in their yards or at their breakfast tables; instead of papist madonnas, it glorified earthly wives and mothers, quietly reading in the light from a high window or smiling as they searched their children's heads for nits.

These idealized, though far from unrealistic, images of home and family became a symbol, for the newly independent Dutch, of their national and private aspirations. They spoke of tranquillity, good order, the virtues of simplicity. Even more, they affirmed the worth of individual human beings going about the humdrum business of their everyday lives. There was no detail too unimportant to catch the painter's eye: the glimpse of a street through an open door, the crumbs on a breadboard, the folds of a woman's apron, the bloom on a bowl of fruit. The spectator could almost hear the laughter and smell the simmering soup.

Daily life in most prosperous Dutch families followed a broadly similar pattern, whether the head of the house was a wealthy man whose most arduous task was to follow the progress of

Two paintings by Pieter de Hooch, both from the 1660s, pay homage to the Dutch housewife's attention to cleanliness. Above, a mistress and her maid transfer a pile of freshly laundered sheets to a linen closet, an item of furniture accorded almost the status of household altar. The external altar was the water pump, shown on the right in a scrupulously scrubbed backyard. Some wealthy homes boasted interior pumps, and a few had tanks that supplied a constant supply of piped water. Failure to maintain an immaculate house, both inside and out, was regarded as a form of social treason.

his investments, an ambitious young trader anxious to make his mark in Baltic grain, or a lawyer hoping to gain from any disputes between the other two. The burghers of Amsterdam went early to bed—most householders snuffed out their candles by 9:00 p.m. and rose at a correspondingly early hour. They slept, when space allowed, in upstairs bedchambers, which by the middle of the seventeenth century served no other purpose. On weekday mornings, they descended their steep staircases to begin the day with a family Bible reading and a meal of bread, cheese, fish, and savory pies, washed down with buttermilk or beer, at a table set with pewter utensils.

After their breakfast, family members separated to pursue the tasks deemed appropriate to their genders and generations: father to his shop or other place of business, children to school to acquire the literacy needed to read the Bible and the numeracy needed to calculate profit and loss. Meanwhile the woman of the house, if she was to fulfill what the republic's moralists deemed her natural destiny, waved off her loved ones and turned her prodigious energies to the maintenance of a perfect home.

To the contemporary writer Jakob Cats—who combined a distinguished political career as grand pensionary of Holland with authorship of several vastly popular works of moralizing verse—the Dutch wife was the angel of the hearth:

The husband must be on the street to practice his trade.
The wife must stay at home to be in the kitchen.
The diligent practice of street wisdom may in the man be praised
But with the delicate wife, there should be quiet and steady ways.
So you, industrious husband, go to earn your living
While you, O young wife, attend to your household.

Attending to this household in a manner that Jakob Cats—and her own watchful neighbors—would approve required the "delicate wife" to possess the wisdom of Solomon and the strength of an ox. Delegation of her responsibilities to a troop of domestic servants was unthinkable: The proper bourgeois housewife, no matter how prosperous, rolled up her sleeves and did the work herself, with the aid of a single maidservant. Nor—unless her strength had been sapped by a difficult childbirth—did she hand her offspring over to a nurse, to be reared out of sight and earshot. She fed her infants with her own milk, guided their tottering steps, and—as numerous painters of the time cheerfully recorded—wiped their dirty bottoms without any assistance.

In a seventeenth-century Flemish painting, sunlight warms a mother feeding her baby while her husband works at a loom in the background. Only in poorer homes such as this did the front room double as a work and living area; the bed might also be in the same room, in an alcove screened off by a curtain. The door was usually left open and merchandise was displayed beneath a canopy outside.

The wife had sole command of the domestic treasury and controlled her budget with as much attention to economy as her husband exercised within his counting house. But her most important task was the physical maintenance of the house, and she organized its cleaning with religious zeal.

Cleanliness was a Dutch obsession. "Every door," marveled an English traveler, "seems studded with diamonds. The nails and hinges keep a constant brightness." To maintain this legendary standard of hygiene, the dedicated homemaker consulted such manuals as the widely circulated *Experienced and Knowledgeable Housewife*, which reinforced the lessons that every good Dutch girl should have learned at her mother's knee. These texts prescribed a strict routine. The first priority, without question, was to empty the family's chamber pots into the canal. This should be followed by vigorous daily scrubbing of entrance hall, threshold, steps, and the very pavement of the street outside. Indoors, floors were swept before a speck or crumb could sully them. Dishes were to be washed as soon as breakfast was over, followed by the laundering of the household's prodigious linen collection. But these daily tasks were only the first item on the agenda. Mondays and Tuesdays called for a campaign of dusting and polishing every surface; Wednesdays demanded a thorough going-over for the entire house; Thursday brought the concentrated cleansing and scouring of candlesticks, cutlery, and cooking pots; Fridays signaled an attack on any grease or grime that dared to trespass in the storage cellars and kitchen.

The kitchen itself was a showplace of gleaming ceramic tiles and immaculate implements: huge cast-iron stew pans, kettles, pewter plates, pottery, baking pans, and griddles. Some women ensured that the room retained its pristine shine by relegating the actual untidy business of food preparation to some dark corner of the house's nether regions or to a makeshift hearth in the backyard.

Meals were simple but substantial: The Netherlanders prided themselves on their liking for plain, old-fashioned fare. At midday, all but the poorest citizens indulged their hearty appetite for meat, often in the form of a *hutsepot,* a long-simmered stew that had acquired the status of a national dish. Variety was provided by the hardy vegetables that thrived in the cool, wet climate—beets, carrots, parsnips, and greens—and by several species of fish: herring, haddock, and cod from the sea; perch, carp, and smelt from the rivers. The evening meal was lighter, often not much more than a soup of bread cooked down to a porridge and sweetened with a little sugar. The usual beverage, as for breakfast, was beer.

To provide these comforts, a burgher's wife worked at least as hard as her husband. But if her routine was well ordered and her servant reliable, she might still find time to read, play music, visit friends, or engage in charitable work. The hospitals, orphanages, homes for the aged, and other benevolent institutions that were the pride of the republic could not have survived without her.

In return for these contributions to public and private well-being, Dutch women enjoyed legal rights and freedoms far in advance of their European sisters. A wife was entitled to inherit property in her own name and to dispose of it in her will, to hold any wealth acquired during her marriage jointly with her husband, and to sue for separation or divorce on grounds of physical abuse or infidelity. Any adult woman, married or not, was entitled to negotiate contracts, sign legal documents, and take an active part in commercial life. Many women either worked alongside their husbands or ran enterprises of their own. In an eighteenth-century tax survey, assessors found that nearly a quarter of the taxable businesses in the city of Leiden, and 15 percent of those in Amsterdam, were operated by women.

"In our Netherlands, God be praised," rejoiced Jakob Cats, "there are no yokes for the wife, nor slaves' shackles or fetters on her legs." Foreign observers formed the theory that the Dutchwoman's remarkable degree of autonomy derived from the fact that she could be trusted, whereas their own women could not, to conduct herself with full propriety. Married women, observed Sir William Temple, "live with very general good fame: a certain sort of Chastity being hereditary and habitual among them, as Probity among the men."

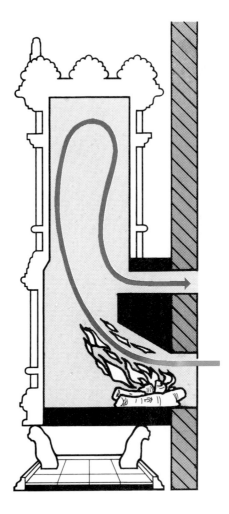

This seventeenth-century Swiss stove, covered with tin-glazed tiles and standing eight feet tall, is of a design common throughout central and northwestern Europe from the fifteenth century. In wealthy households the rear of the stove projected through a wall into an adjoining room; from there, as shown in the diagram, servants could add wood to the fire, whose smoke circulated through the stove before exiting by a separate conduit. Tiles adorning the outside of the stove retained and radiated heat. An English traveler in Poland in 1641 was impressed by one such stove "built in the form of a turret, a pretty little structure, adorning the room," which "casteth a heat to the farthest part of the room."

An emergent egalitarianism, mirroring the political climate of the republic itself, was a conspicuous feature in Dutch family life. The home was no longer a little kingdom, governed by a despotic patriarch. The bonds between husband and wife, parents and children, were those of affection instead of authoritarian control. Contemporary portraits of married couples show husbands and wives in attitudes of relaxed informality—exchanging intimate glances, caressing each other or their children, smiling quietly together at some private joke. Travelers' observations bore out the truth of these painted images. Marriage among the Netherlanders, reflected one admiring French visitor, "is as charming as it is holy."

The customary division of labor—man the breadwinner, woman the domestic manager—was leavened by an atmosphere of mutual support. Parenthood in particular was a shared concern: An engraving from the 1620s shows a nightgowned father pacing the bedroom with an infant in his arms, soothing the crying child while its exhausted mother sleeps. Other nations, in earlier ages, may have loved their children as intensely—and worried over them as tenderly—as did the Dutch, but none had given such powerful expression to these emotions. The younger generation springs to life in hundreds of meticulously detailed paintings and drawings: An ailing child, hollow-eyed, sprawls on a woman's lap; a pair of urchins play cards, in gleeful imitation of the grownups; a little girl intently watches a maidservant peeling parsnips; another dances with excitement when street musicians appear at the door.

At a time when their contemporaries relied heavily on corporal punishment to hammer knowledge into children and beat the devil out of them, most Netherlanders shunned such violent methods. The strictest Calvinists warned against sparing the rod and criticized the dangerously sentimental practice of sending the young to bed with goodnight kisses, but the consensus across the religious spectrum was that gentleness and patience were the most effective tools for turning young savages into worthy citizens of the republic.

In neighboring countries high infant mortality may have led to a deliberate hardening of the heart: There was little point in wasting tears over those who were unlikely to survive to adulthood. The Dutch, even those within the poorest and most marginalized sectors of the community, seemed to feel differently: In a period when the Parisian authorities gave shelter to some 300 abandoned children in a year, the city of Amsterdam—half the size of Paris—found only 20 waifs in need of shelter.

Concern for the welfare of the new generation began before the moment of birth. Popular medical manuals, published in cheap editions, used simple language to advise pregnant women on the best ways to foster the development of the child in the womb. Other guides taught new parents everything they needed to know to keep a baby healthy, clean, and safe. Infants were to be washed regularly all over their bodies, with careful cleansing of every orifice, then rubbed with almond oil or butter to lubricate their tender skins. Ivory teething rings or small, hard biscuits would soothe the agonies of teething, help the little milk teeth come through quickly, and ensure that they were strong and healthy. Toilet training was best accomplished by gentle coercion rather than threats, and parents were well advised to place the child on its potty and allow it to amuse itself with a few toys, unhurried, while nature took its course. Nor should children be scolded or punished when they wet their beds: They all grew out of it sooner or later, and fear of recriminations would only make the situation worse.

Parents could purchase a wide range of items to protect, entertain, and educate their offspring. Wheeled highchairs, with wide trays full of toys, kept infants portable, amused, and out of danger. Sturdy wooden walking frames helped them stand upright and allowed them to take their first tentative steps in safety. And once a toddler could stagger about unaided, a wide, well-padded bumper bonnet protected the little head from cuts and bruises. Older children soon learned the whereabouts of the nearest toy stall, with its tantalizing array of lavishly costumed dolls, drums, trumpets, windmills, and hobbyhorses, and even the most frugal mother readily dipped into her purse. Toys, after all, were tools of learning. Moralists such as the writer Johan van Beverwijck emphasized the value of creative play and warned against force-feeding the young with too much knowledge too soon. "In all this upbringing and education," he counseled, "children should not be kept on too tight a rein, but allowed to exercise their childishness, so that we do not burden their fragile nature with heavy things and sow untimely seed in the unprepared field of understanding. Let them freely play and let school use play for their maturing . . . otherwise they will be against learning before they know what learning is."

Foreigners brought up by sterner methods clucked in disapproval over such proofs of the burghers' overindulgent attitudes. The Englishman William Aglionby despaired over his Dutch hosts' inability to see the error of their ways: "When anybody tells them of their fondness to children, they presently say, 'Does anyone spoil their own face or cut off their nose?' " He consoled himself by reporting that such excessive liberalism caused many children to "rebel against their parents and at last go away to the Indies"—although in fact most of those who did depart for the Indies went with their parents' blessing, to further the family business.

Other foreigners noted with smug satisfaction that for all the orderly habits and high-minded ideals of their hosts, Dutch society was not without its sordid underside. City taverns did a roaring trade in Holland's gin, first distilled by a seventeenth-

From the sixteenth century on, the widespread circulation of printed material freed individuals from dependence on the community for the interpretation of the written word. Literacy rates rose fast both in the Western world and farther afield, as shown on the following pages. Reading democratized learning and opened up new intellectual vistas; at the same time it promoted the pursuit of solitude and the development of rooms for private study, sealed off from domestic hubbub. In libraries and studies, literate men and women could pen letters to distant friends and articulate their intimate thoughts on the pages of diaries.

In this 1660 painting by Dutch artist Jan Vermeer, a young woman reads a letter by the light of an open window.

GATEWAY TO AN INNER LIFE

century professor of medicine at Leiden University. Many men and women of all classes were addicted to tobacco: They cherished their clay pipes, argued over the relative merits of tobacco blends perfumed with scores of different fruits or spices, and kept their supply of the precious weed in boxes carved of the costliest ivory. And those inclined to vice were dogged in pursuit of dissipation.

Amsterdam, city of preachers and politicians, was also a boisterous seaport; and of all the industries that flourished near its harbor, one of the most prosperous was prostitution. The city's ladies of easy virtue entertained a cosmopolitan trade, and their collective reputation traveled far and wide along the sea routes. So extensive were the city's red-light districts that an enterprising publisher issued a detailed guidebook, entitled *Amsterdam's Whoredom,* which was printed in many editions and translated into several languages. And this underworld too had its visual chroniclers who, with unsparing realism and encyclopedic detail, recorded scenes of brothel and tavern life: wrinkled procuresses haggling with clients, a leering soldier pressing a coin into a young girl's hand, drunkards asleep in pools of spilled wine.

The Calvinist preachers wasted little effort on reforming these lost souls. Their prime concern, as the nation waxed fat and the seventeenth century waned, was to preserve the simplicity, frugality, and asceticism that had, in their eyes, been the making of the Dutch. They saw dangerous signs all around them: bare scrubbed wood disappearing under layers of sensuous, soft furnishings; exotic spices creeping into the diet; modest clothing of plain cut and somber colors giving way to frivolous

Printed in 1665, this Bible belonged to the daughter-in-law of William Penn, the founder of Pennsylvania. Facing the title page are handwritten references to passages that inspired private meditation.

In this eighteenth-century French painting a valet reads aloud to his mistress as she eats her otherwise solitary meal. The preference in France for educated domestics resulted in a high rate of literacy among male servants.

ornament. By the late seventeenth century, even the most respectable pillars of the community were adopting the sophisticated tastes of their more decadent foreign contemporaries, filling their houses and adorning their persons with whatever luxuries they could afford. In the 1630s, the charitable ladies who managed the city orphanage of Amsterdam had sat for their group portrait uniformly dressed in neat caps, dark gowns, and stiffly frilled lace collars; in a similar portrait of their successors painted in 1683, the canvas shimmered with curled ringlets, bare arms, low-cut necklines, and plenty of jewels. The good ladies of the Dutch Republic had discovered fashion. And, together with so many of their counterparts elsewhere in western and central Europe, wealthy Netherlanders now looked to France, the new fountainhead of style, for inspiration.

Fashions—in dress, in furniture, in architecture, and in etiquette—spread slowly but inexorably across Europe's ever-improving network of trade and communications. For centuries Italy had held sway as the prime source of new ideas and artistic innovation; its painters and craftsmen produced works that dazzled the eyes and loosened the purse strings of the affluent, while its social mentors taught the rules of good manners and aristocratic behavior to an audience eager to affirm its own gentility. But by the end of the seventeenth century, Italian cultural hegemony was on the wane, and France had assumed its position as the arbiter of elegance. "In the art of living," asserted one eighteenth-century English traveler, "the French have

An eighteenth-century Japanese book illustration *(right)* depicts two girls studying texts created for educational purposes. Shown above is the cover of a Japanese novel from the same period. Prose fiction in Japan, often dealing with the lives of the newly literate merchant classes, became popular at the same time that the novel was developing into a distinctive genre in Europe.

generally been esteemed by the rest of Europe to have made the greatest proficiency, and their manners have been accordingly more imitated, and their customs more adopted, than those of any other nation.''

This new supremacy was no accident, but the result of a conscious policy on the part of the French crown. Jean-Baptiste Colbert, chief minister to Louis XIV, energetically fostered vast industries devoted to the decorative arts. He felt certain that once the international marketplace took note of the magnificent creations of his nation's craftsmen, the desire for beautiful things would take its natural course. As the reputations—and then the carefully wrapped bundles—of France's excellent tapestries, handsome furniture, and extravagant ornaments traveled outward, so the gold of those who purchased these objects would flow in, to the benefit not only of the makers but also of the state.

At home, the market for these luxuries was a small but fabulously wealthy elite. Unlike the Dutch Republic, with its prosperity spanning a wide band of the social spectrum, the kingdom of France housed sharp extremes of poverty and riches. During the eighteenth century, 10 percent of the population of Paris was reckoned to be destitute. Throughout the manufacturing towns of the northern provinces, male artisans—even if fully employed—teetered on the brink of poverty, and the dominant industries relied heavily on armies of barely subsisting female labor. In the town of Bayeux, for instance, workers who married and began to raise children knew themselves to be courting financial disaster: The joint earnings of such couples could never sustain even the most modest of households or cope with feeding a single extra mouth. The situation was even bleaker in rural regions, where some parishes reported that two-thirds of their inhabitants depended totally on charity to survive.

Meanwhile, the aristocrats who clustered around the royal court clothed, fed, and housed themselves in an atmosphere of almost suffocating opulence, and the mem-

Under the watchful gaze of a marble bust, children in this eighteenth-century French painting read and converse in a book-lined library. The acquisition of books brought delight as well as instruction, and many libraries were places of entertainment as well as of serious scholarship.

bers of the innermost royal circles served as role models for ambitious souls of lesser rank. The cut and colors of aristocrats' garments; the arrangement and adornment of their houses; and their manners, fads, and fancies were assiduously copied by a rising class of increasingly powerful bourgeois families, whose wealth had brought them into the orbit of the court.

There was nothing particularly new about this phenomenon. In the 1560s, Jean Bodin had noted that the sumptuary laws—a legislative attempt to end mounting extravagance in dress—were blithely ignored by both courtiers and their faithful imitators. "Edicts have been passed, but to no purpose. For since people at court wear what is forbidden, everyone wears it," wrote Bodin. "Besides, in matters of dress he is always considered a fool and a bore who does not dress according to the common fashion." The excruciating torment of social ostracism and general contempt lay in wait for those who did not take careful note of current modes. Style became as significant a social indicator as the antiquity of a title or the size of a fortune.

In the provinces before the sixteenth century, rich and poor alike had traditionally purchased their goods from the same local artisans, and although the items commissioned by a wealthy household were likely to be more intricate in execution and consequently higher in price than their humbler equivalents, there was otherwise little difference between them. With the rise of the luxury market, however, the upper classes found a new way to set themselves apart. They acquired their furniture, clothing, and ornaments from a completely different set of craftsmen, purveyors of the choicest, costliest objects, whose urban workshops lay within easy reach of the capital and court. The very shape, design, and decoration of these articles differed radically from those turned out in the humbler suburbs or the countryside. And only the rich could afford to keep up with changing fashion; every item within their

111

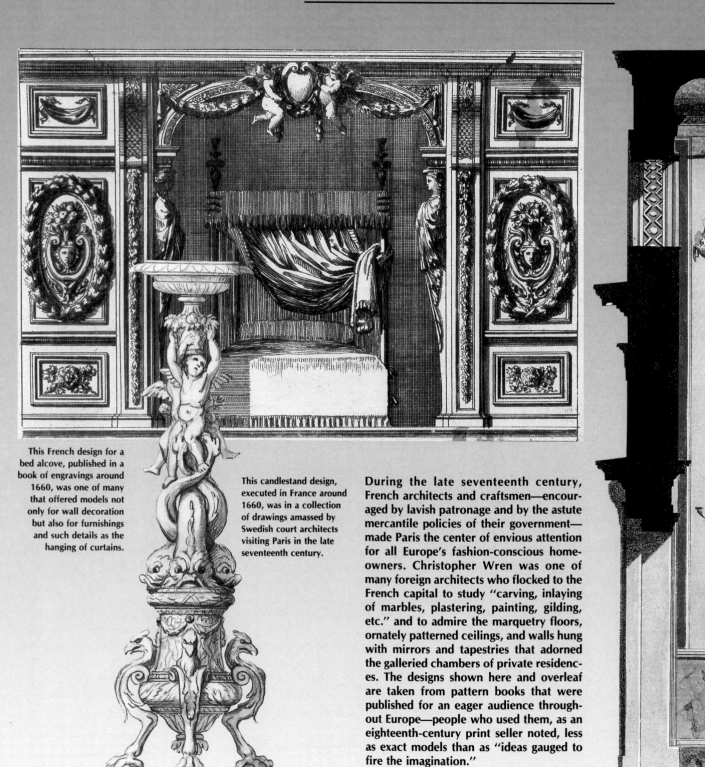

This French design for a bed alcove, published in a book of engravings around 1660, was one of many that offered models not only for wall decoration but also for furnishings and such details as the hanging of curtains.

This candlestand design, executed in France around 1660, was in a collection of drawings amassed by Swedish court architects visiting Paris in the late seventeenth century.

During the late seventeenth century, French architects and craftsmen—encouraged by lavish patronage and by the astute mercantile policies of their government—made Paris the center of envious attention for all Europe's fashion-conscious home-owners. Christopher Wren was one of many foreign architects who flocked to the French capital to study "carving, inlaying of marbles, plastering, painting, gilding, etc." and to admire the marquetry floors, ornately patterned ceilings, and walls hung with mirrors and tapestries that adorned the galleried chambers of private residences. The designs shown here and overleaf are taken from pattern books that were published for an eager audience throughout Europe—people who used them, as an eighteenth-century print seller noted, less as exact models than as "ideas gauged to fire the imagination."

Classic Roman motifs appear in this hand-colored engraving from a 1790s German fashion journal that shows a wall design for a garden pavilion.

One of around 300 plates in George Hepplewhite's pattern book, published in 1788, this chair design exhibits the simple elegance of English Georgian furniture. In 1786, a German magazine, noting the emergence of distinctive national styles, observed that "English furniture is almost without exception solid and practical; French furniture is less solid, more contrived, and more ostentatious."

Nature and artifice are elegantly combined in this design for printed textiles by William Kilburn, published in London in the late eighteenth century. Some of Kilburn's designs—which were printed on high-quality cotton by a London wholesaler—were copied, printed on coarser cloth, and sold by rival firms within ten days of their appearance.

houses, or upon their backs, expressed its owner's social and economic superiority.

Manners, too, gave clues to rank. A new fastidiousness percolated downward, from court to bourgeoisie. Gone were the days when nobles and their humble followers jostled together at a hospitable board, dipping their grubby hands into communal platters. Diners now shrank from such promiscuous intimacy; they required plenty of room on either side, individual place settings, finger bowls, clean plates, and cutlery for their exclusive use. A knowledge of the proper conduct at meals, and the proper use of a whole armory of new eating utensils, was a badge of membership within the elite. In this increasingly snobbish and stratified milieu, the peasant was used to personify all crude, coarse, and unclean habits. For one thing, the lower orders could never afford the battery of utensils now thought essential for decorous dining.

This mounting desire for increased personal space, coupled with a display of social superiority, was not limited to mealtimes. The upper classes desired homes that would reflect the changes in their tastes. The architects of the age responded, evolving designs and theories equally appropriate to a royal palace or to the Parisian mansion of a merchant prince. By the late seventeenth century, residences were constructed as showplaces of pomp and drama, sporting imposing curved staircases, long internal vistas created by sequences of interconnecting galleries, antechambers, and salons; rooms were built with curved walls and in varying shapes. The interior of a house, said its designers, should be agreeable and lively, with masses of intricate detail to divert the eye. Ornamentation, accordingly, became an extravaganza of gilded paneling, much white paint, and the liberal use of large mirrors; interiors, pierced by elongated windows, glittered with borrowed or reflected light.

Now that fashion reigned above mere necessity, however, no single style could endure for long. Within a few decades, architects such as Jacques-Francois Blondel created houses that placed more emphasis on simplicity of design. Grandeur and elegance were as important as ever, but rooms with unusual shapes now fell from favor; the new preference was for symmetry and order, with the interior and exterior of a house planned as a harmonious whole. Practicality rather than theatricality became the governing principle in arranging the layout of a house: People wanted sensible use of space and floor plans and room sizes that were well suited to their personal requirements and preferences.

Foremost among these was the thirst for greater privacy. Residences were divided into public rooms—for the formal reception of guests on ceremonial occasions—and more private spaces. Instead of vast baronial halls for the mass feeding of all comers, dining rooms were scaled down to accommodate the family and its selected guests. Studies and libraries provided silence and solitude for contemplation, intellectual exercise, and the conduct of confidential business, free from the risk of eavesdroppers. Bedchambers and boudoirs in turn provided intimate retreats—although aristocratic custom still transformed morning ablutions into a social occasion. New items of furniture filled these spaces: little daybeds and couches, dressing mirrors, toilet tables of extravagant design.

Writing to her daughter in 1677, the marquise de Sévigné described the house into which they were about to move together. If her daughter took the ground floor, she would be more independent of her mother, who was to take the second floor; on the other hand, the upstairs rooms were much lighter, and the marquise proposed that both she and her daughter should live on the second floor. "There is a big room in common, which I shall furnish, then a passage, then another big room—that is yours.

From this room you pass into . . . mine. And from this big room you go into a small one that you don't know, which I shall furnish for you and where you can sleep if you like. The big room will also have your bed in it; I shall have enough tapestry. . . . People who want to see us both won't upset you much by going through your large room. Those whom I shall want to take off your hands so as to skim your pot will come by a quite separate staircase straight into my little room."

The back staircase described by the marquise was also intended "for my servants, workmen, creditors," and near it were two small rooms "for my maids." When they were not required to powder a nobleman's wig or adjust his lady's corsets, servants were now kept at arm's length. The old, easy relationship between a feudal lord and his personal attendants—who were often the sons of his peers, receiving their knightly education within his house—had long since vanished. The new servants of the aristocracy were regarded as social inferiors; they might live under the same roof as their employers, but they were no longer regarded as members of the family. New devices such as bell ropes, for signaling servants from distant parts of the house, and wine coolers, which made it unnecessary for table attendants to hover, meant that servants could wait, out of sight and earshot, until their presence was required.

Sanitation posed a particular problem. The old fortified castles had had privies built into their walls; in the new mansions, the purpose was served only by freestanding close-stools and chamber pots. These were not always hidden away from view: One of Louis XIV's courtiers had the dubious privilege of attending upon his master at all times of the day with the royal *chaise percée*. The French aristocracy's new love for privacy did not necessarily extend to the performance of bodily functions, and many upper-class households boasted beautifully crafted double commodes, which allowed two people to enjoy an intimate conversation while relieving themselves. All of these vessels had to be removed by servants and carried out of the house to be emptied on some distant dunghill. It would hardly further the cause of elegance, however, if house guests encountered such receptacles on their outward journey. Special service corridors provided a solution, allowing the domestic staff to go about these and other tasks virtually unseen.

Safe from prying eyes, in apartments marked out as private territory, the French upper classes began to learn how to relax. In some Paris mansions physical comfort was enhanced by an ingenious heating system that drew air into ducts behind the hearth, warmed the currents and sent them back into the room through metal grilles set into the mantelpiece. Metal hoods or canopies built over fireplaces minimized heat loss, and many more houses made use of freestanding porcelain stoves of a type first used in the Netherlands and northern Germany.

Without the need to spend half the year huddled next to inefficient fires, the French upper classes spread themselves across their spacious rooms, discovering new and pleasant modes of seating. They sank into easy chairs with cushions and back rests, and sprawled on well-padded settees. When one of the unmarried daughters of Louis XV was asked why she did not follow an older sister's example and enter a convent, she unblushingly confessed that "an armchair was my undoing."

Another cause of the new variety of reclining chairs was the increased prominence of women in both aristocratic and middle-class social circles, a position they had obtained chiefly through their skillful management of the social institution known as the salon. This institution was virtually invented in the early seventeenth century by the marquise de Rambouillet, who designed for herself a house with a number of

The eighteenth-century *tabouret d'aisance*—"stool of ease"—shown on the opposite page, fancifully decorated with humanized monkeys and shaped at the rear to fit neatly into the corner of a room, was a sufficient toilet for even a wealthy homeowner. Louis XIV's palace at Versailles was furnished with around 300 close-stools for the convenience of guests and residents, and the duchess of Orléans complained in her diary of men who "piss into all the corners." Toilet bowls that emptied into cesspools and that contained water seals to eliminate smells became available in the eighteenth century but were not widely adopted because of the conservatism of the rich and because few homes were equipped with running water.

ornately furnished rooms leading to a grand chamber hung with paintings, Venetian mirrors, and blue patterned tapestries. By encouraging learned conversation and insisting on the highest standards of courtesy, the marquise created an environment in which women could meet with men as intellectual equals, and her home soon outshone even the royal court as a center of fashion and the arts. The marquise herself, who had suffered a mysterious illness following the birth of her seventh child, presided over her animated gatherings from a blue, damask-hung bed in an alcove of the room, where she lay swathed in furs to offset the chill. By refusing all sexual liaisons, the marquise and certain other women attending her salon acquired a status above that of wife or courtesan and a moral authority that enabled them to dominate their social circle.

Other women, aware that they could obtain more material rewards by forming sexual alliances with rich and titled men than by refusing them, did not hold to such standards of chastity. Courtesans and aspiring hostesses competed to attract the most talented and powerful men to their salons, creating a new niche in the hierarchy of French society in which women could both increase their personal status and influence political affairs. The life of fashionable women became a continuous social whirl: "Dinner, grand supper with M. and Mme. de Chaulnes, a thousand duty calls and convent ones, coming, going, paying compliments, wearing oneself out, and going quite out of one's mind," complained the marquise de Sévigné to her daughter in 1680. "I long most passionately to be out of here, where they are doing me too much honor; I am totally famished for fasting and silence." Just as women in the Netherlands had been instrumental in pioneering a new domesticity, so Frenchwomen established themselves as the arbiters of etiquette and introduced a relaxed intimacy into social behavior.

The very design of furniture was softening. By 1700, rigid rectangles, straight lines, and sharp right angles had given way to graceful, sensuous curves: Tables and cabinets rested on gently bowed cabriole legs; chairs had rounded arms and backs. Functionalism gave way to frivolity, in the new fluid, highly ornamented style known as rococo. The luxury-loving aristocrats of France and their bourgeois imitators were not at all interested in spare utilitarianism: Their preference was for riotous decoration, the glitter of gold and ormolu, the sheen of rich veneers and colored inlays. New branches of the furniture trade sprang up to cater to the desires of this free-spending market: experts in marquetry and gilding, cabinetmakers, dealers in exotic decorative materials such as lacquer from China, Japan, or the Coromandel Coast. Specialized craftsmen imported shiploads of Oriental screens and cabinets, then took them apart, to cut and reshape their lacquered panels into pieces that were deemed more suited to European tastes.

Across the gray strip of sea that divides the British Isles from continental Europe, the English were not immune to the changing attitudes and fashions of the age. England, too, possessed its minor gentry and rising middle classes, who shared the new enthusiasm for privacy and comfort within their residences, but they had, as always, their own distinctive methods of expressing such preferences. They did not have the Gallic passion for flamboyant decoration and display. While he was visiting the opulent house of a French nobleman in the southern city of Toulouse, the English traveler Arthur Young blinked at interiors encrusted with ornament and noted, "To those who are fond of gilding here is enough to satiate; so much that to an English eye it has too gaudy an appearance."

For his hosts' cuisine, Young had only admiration: "Of their cooking there is but one opinion: For every man in Europe that can afford a great table either keeps a French cook or one instructed in the same manner. That it is far beyond our own I have no doubt in asserting." Nevertheless, even in matters of food, English preferences tended to be more conservative than those indulged on the continent. For many, an enthusiasm for rich sauces and exotic delicacies boded ill for the moral health, as well as the digestion, of the nation. Commentators such as Robert Campbell, writing in 1747, lamented the dear dead days of Good Queen Bess, "when mighty Roast Beef was the Englishman's food, and our cookery was plain and simple as our manners." The English inclination in cookery as well as in architecture, furniture design, dress, and etiquette was toward a studied simplicity. Elegance, in the cut of a gown or the curve of a staircase, could be achieved by restraint and the rational use of line.

One likely explanation for the difference between French and English style lay in the contrast between the two nations' upper classes. French nobles and rich bourgeois families took their cues about fashion from the royal court. This was the center of power and the source of wealth, with all its inward-looking frivolity, extravagance, and lust for novelty. The gentlefolk of England were considerably more austere in

A 1774 design for a London town house, colored with the architect's recommendations for wallpaper and other furnishings, displays the characteristic interior plan of the English Georgian style: The primary rooms open off a central staircase, affording more privacy than the French arrangement of a sequence of rooms leading from one to another. But elegant appearance was not matched by efficient technology: The Anglo-Irish writer Jonathan Swift, visiting a similar house in London earlier in the century, detected "a thousand stinks in it."

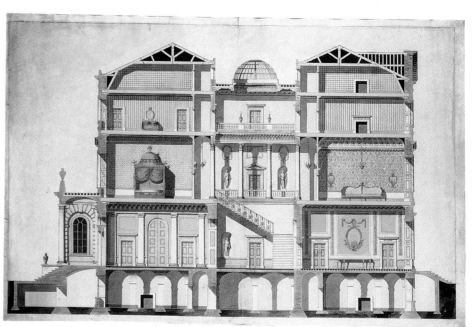

their tastes. The roots of their wealth lay for the most part in the countryside: As agricultural improvements and new intensive farming methods extracted more profits from the land, prosperous yeoman farmers and rural squires turned into gentlemen. Their counterparts in the cities were members of the rising professional and mercantile class: lawyers, physicians, and merchants who had grown wealthy through overseas trade. And as the newly rich climbed the social ladder, they did not necessarily look toward the English court—which was ruled during most of the eighteenth century by a dynasty of imported German princes—but instead formed their own distinctive style.

The landed gentry of Georgian England were becoming a migratory breed. A growing number of them lived for only part of each year on their rural estates in the shires, then routinely transferred themselves to the capital for the months when Parliament sat, the courts of law were in session, and upper-class social life focused on the extremely active round of balls, receptions, and intimate dinner parties known as the London season. Their enthusiasm for building comfortable new country mansions, and their need for suitable residences in town, fostered the rise of a generation of gifted architects and craftsmen.

An oil-painted screen of 1746 displays some of the favorite leisure activities of an English country gentleman: fox hunting, cockfighting, game shooting, and fishing along the top, and, on the bottom panels, card playing, horse racing, dice throwing, and swimming. His wife relied more on the indoor hearth than on physical excercise for warmth. Chairs were pulled away from the walls and arranged informally around the fireplace, but folding screens such as that shown here were still required to shield a seated group from drafts.

In London, entire new residential quarters rose from the clay and gravel—sweeping crescents, circles, garden squares, and long terraces designed as a single, harmonious whole. Both urban residences and large country houses were constructed according to classical principles of symmetry and perfect proportion. Buildings were rectilinear, with flat frontages; exterior ornamentation displayed an elegant restraint. A stone pediment—ancient Greek in inspiration—might crown a facade, or an elaborate fanlight lend drama to a doorway.

These features demonstrated the influence both of the classical theories of the Italian architect Andrea Palladio and of English building legislation. Laws such as the London Building Acts of 1774 were enacted to serve two purposes. The first impetus was fire prevention: Repetition of such catastrophes as the Great Fire of London in 1666, when much of the capital had gone up in smoke, was to be averted at all costs. The logical solution was to ban wood as a building material; after the fire all London houses were constructed only of brick or stone. The 1774 laws added new precautions, banning the use of decorative wood on house fronts and stipulating the distance that the wooden casings of windows had to be set back from the facades.

The legislators' second motive was their wish to ensure the soundness of the expanding city's housing stock. Residential buildings were divided into six categories known as rates, with precise rules governing their size and construction. The first four rates covered terraced houses with floor areas ranging upward from 315 to 810 square feet. The fifth and sixth rates applied to freestanding properties, which—given the rising cost of building land in London—were likely to be erected only for the very grandest of rich families, or in outlying districts where hens still could be seen scrabbling in the unpaved roads.

The typical town house was a three-story edifice, with a semibasement or a basement and an attic. Within these buildings, rooms were well proportioned but designed to a relatively small scale, typically around 144 square feet. The grandest houses belonging to the very rich might occupy a double frontage, with four rooms on each story symmetrically arranged on either side of a central staircase. A certain flexibility was possible: Some houses had a single large reception room running across the width of the property on the first floor, illuminated by tall windows overlooking the street; others linked adjoining front and back rooms by double doors that could be thrown open to create a more spacious effect. More modest terraced houses had two rooms on each floor, with entrance hall, stairs, and passageway running along the common wall.

Whatever the scale of a town house, the top and bottom levels were devoted to servants' quarters and domestic purposes. As in France, the low-paid workers available to serve a well-to-do establishment were segregated within the house. Kitchens, larders, and scullery were relegated to the basement, with exterior access provided by a flight of stone steps or via an alley at the rear: The butcher's boy or the coal man would not have been enthusiastically received at the fanlit front door.

According to its personal preferences and its budget, a family might use its space in several different ways. Some people retained a formal sitting room in which to receive their guests, but passed their time and took their meals in a more intimate back parlor. The practice of setting aside one room exclusively for eating was still, in some quarters, looked upon as a novelty. In 1750, a lady named Mrs. Delany referred, somewhat equivocally, to "my dining-room, vulgarly so-called." Yet the term was by then sufficiently familiar for Samuel Johnson to create an entry for it in his *Dictionary of the English Language,* which was to be published five years later.

Certain privileged women used their homes to entertain regular gatherings of guests distinguished in the arts or politics, on the model of the French salon. Elizabeth Montagu initiated the practice in London in the mid-eighteenth century, forbidding her guests to play cards and seating them in a large semicircle to facilitate conversation. Other hostesses were less formal: Mary Monckton took care "to prevent a circle," noted the English novelist Fanny Burney in 1782, and "pulled about the chairs and planted the people in groups with as dextrous a disorder as you would desire to see." English salons, which drew their members primarily from the upper reaches of the middle classes, generally tended to be more casual than their aristocratic French counterparts.

As in France, salons enabled women to further their social or artistic ambitions, often through patronage. In 1758, for instance, when an English poet named Elizabeth Carter discovered herself to be out of money while translating the work of a Greek philosopher and had to support herself by taking in sewing, members of the salon of Elizabeth Montagu raised money to enable Carter to complete and publish her book. But all efforts to better the position of women in society more generally came up against strong resistance. The reason for this was not least because of the influence that powerful women could now wield, particularly in France, where, reported the Scottish philosopher David Hume, "the females enter into all transactions and all management of church and state: and no man can expect success, who takes not care to obtain their good graces." In the year 1795, Napoleon Bonaparte noted that "a woman, in order to know what is due her and what power she has, must live in Paris for six months."

LIFE IN AN ENGLISH COUNTRY HOUSE

"John Sperling is going to be married to that horrid Miss Hanson—I am sure she has got him and I fear he will repent at his leisure." The voice speaking in this early-nineteenth-century letter was that of Diana Sperling, who was born in 1791. Her childhood and youth were enlivened not by the alarums of the Napoleonic Wars but by the gossip and domestic activities and accidents that punctuated everyday life in an English country house. Among her own pastimes was sketching her family and friends in a series of notebooks, from which the illustrations here and on the following two pages are taken. She married late, at the age of forty-three, and moved to London, leaving behind forever the life she had recorded with such innocent affection.

The artist's mother busies herself with needlework by an open doorway in the company of the family dog, Brisk. Most items of female clothing were homemade, and women spent many hours perfecting their needlework; sewing machines did not become common in private households until the second half of the nineteenth century. Other accomplishments expected of an English gentlewoman included playing a musical instrument and painting in watercolors.

To most men such strength appeared to upset the natural order of society, and even the philosophers of the Enlightenment agreed with John Locke in upholding "the subjection that is due from a wife to her husband." The increasing influence of women was perceived as dangerous to public morality—it could lead to, in the words of a French moralist in 1750, "luxury, revelry, gambling, love, and all the consequences of these passions"—and articles appearing in learned periodicals advocated the maintenance of traditional distinctions between the roles of men and women. Although it was often by their wit and learning that the women of the salons had won the respect of men, too forward a display of intellect was considered unseemly. Lady Mary Wortley Montagu advised her granddaughter to "conceal what learning she attains, with as much solicitude as she would hide crookedness or lameness. The parade of it can only serve to draw on her the envy, and consequently, the most inveterate hatred, of all he and she fools, which will certainly be at least three parts in four of all her acquaintance."

If knowledge and intelligence were not considered appropriate virtues for a woman, however, elegance and fine manners were, and it was through their practice that privileged women were able most acceptably to make their mark on society. "The women seem to take the lead in polishing the manners everywhere," ruefully reflected the English writer Mary Wollstonecraft after traveling in Scandinavia in 1795, "that being the only way to better their condition." Wollstonecraft herself argued vigorously for the improvement of education for girls, insisting that current attitudes were based on "mistaken notions of female excellence" and made women "more artificial and weak in character than they would otherwise have been." But after her death, at the age of thirty-eight, she was remembered by her contemporaries more for the impropriety of her life—she had an illegitimate child by an American adventurer who later abandoned her—than for her subversive ideas.

Younger members of the Sperling family and friends engage in a game of charades. At times charades resembled amateur theatricals, involving props, rehearsals, costumes, and even printed programs. Three of the participants here are clearly dressed for their roles.

At the home of a friend of the Sperling family on the evening of September 17, 1816, the guests have cleared a space in the drawing room for dancing to the music of a harpsichord. While two ladies fan themselves after their exertions, the hostess dances merrily alone in the center of the room. Far removed from the elegant formal balls of high society, such dances took place often when friends were gathered together and put to good use the musical skills of the ladies.

With new money percolating through the economy, considerable elegance was now attainable, even in unfashionable houses. John Wood, writing in 1749, enumerated the handsome fixtures and fittings within the new terraces going up in the spa town of Bath, where country gentry and well-to-do citizens from the capital resorted annually to take the waters. "Floors laid with finest class deals, or Dutch oak boards; the rooms were all wainscotted and painted in a costly and handsome manner; marble slabs and even chimney pieces became common; the doors in general were not only made thick and substantial, but they had the best sort of brass lock put on them . . . nor did the proper chimneys or piers of any of the rooms long remain without framed mirrors of no inconsiderable size." The furniture devised for such houses was as handsome as the architecture itself. Master craftsmen such as Thomas Chippendale, George Hepplewhite, and Thomas Sheraton created pieces that were decorative in line but never overburdened with ornament or grandiose in scale, lest they overwhelm the modest proportions of so many contemporary rooms. They also published pattern books, enabling provincial furniture makers far from the metropolis to copy their designs.

Unlike the French, the English had never made a rigid division between popular and classical traditions of furniture design. In France, where there were sharp extremes of poverty and wealth, furniture making was a luxury trade, with its products intended only for the native rich, or for export to those continental neighbors whose upper classes looked avidly to France to determine their tastes and furnish their salons. In England, with prosperity spread more widely through the population, more modest craftsmen also found a market for their creations. The well-made piece, turned out by a local carpenter, that graced the parlor of a rural parson's home might be seen to bear more than a passing resemblance to a similar article found in a great duke's London residence. The ducal version might be wrought of wood that was

much more expensive, but both items expressed the identical aesthetic principles.

In towns and shires alike the age saw a proliferation of specialized furniture. Tables of all descriptions reflected new modes of social behavior and new ways of spending time. Dining tables of various sizes could accommodate any domestic situation from an intimate family breakfast to a glittering formal dinner for a large party of guests; card tables allowed the racier members of a company to pass an evening pleasantly or gamble away their fortunes; writing tables gave the would-be hostess a convenient place to compose invitations and provided her more literary sister with a discreet corner in which to write novels satirizing the contemporary social scene. An ingenious piece known as a lady's cabinet combined a small surface for needlework or writing with a built-in fire screen, which allowed its owner to warm her feet without drying her complexion in the heat given off by the fire.

Because people now had more possessions, furniture makers turned out a variety of pieces for storage and for display. The spread of literacy, and the swelling numbers of printed books, required shelves to accommodate the household's growing library; ingenious revolving bookcases made it possible for a bibliophile to store a considerable number of volumes neatly but accessibly within a limited space. Chests of stacked-up drawers provided an efficient way to store textiles in rooms that proved to be too small for huge linen cupboards. Cabinets with glazed doors and locks kept prized porcelain and other collected treasures visible but secure, while small occasional tables increased the comfort and the convenience of a sitting room.

Children take advantage of their governess's absence to play in this 1820 painting of a private schoolroom, equipped with books and a globe, in a London house. The importance in education of play and discovery through sensory perception was increasingly recognized. "Children are not to be taught by rules which are always slipping out of their minds," wrote the English philosopher John Locke as early as 1693. "The chief art is to make all that they have to do sport and play too."

Visiting London in 1786, a German noblewoman named Sophie von la Roche wrote a letter to her daughter. In her missive, she praised the convenient little novelties now gracing her hostess's parlor: "I will just mention the neat stands for work baskets which have just arrived at Lady Fielding's, consisting of three smooth round legs made of mahogany, or of any other wood attractively painted, placed next to one another and fastened. The pretty embroidered work baskets or neat flower vases placed on them in the corner of the room form a charming decoration; they are very convenient to carry to and fro for working purposes, and take up very little space."

The well-bred ladies that Sophie von la Roche met during her extended stay in England typified the changes that had taken place since the 1600s in the home life of the middle and upper classes. They were reasonably literate, of comfortable means, and—most important—had plenty of time on their hands. Unlike the wives of Dutch burghers, they left the cleaning of their households and the care of their young children in the hands of their servants. Yet neither they, nor their husbands,

Shielded by low curtains from the gaze of pedestrians in the leafy square outside, a couple dines in a breakfast room in this English watercolor of around 1800. The atmosphere of domestic tranquillity is disturbed only by the presence of two tame monkeys dressed in livery. Breakfast rooms were used for light meals and for informal entertaining. Similarly, other specialized rooms in a well-proportioned Georgian town house—library, study, gallery, conservatory—were often put to wider use than their names implied.

were remote and uncaring parents. While rarely demonstrating the intense sentiment expressed so readily by the Dutch, their own attitudes were clearly softening. The traveler Arthur Young, returning from his long French journey, could not have been entirely atypical when he confessed that "I have more pleasure in giving my little girl a French doll than in viewing Versailles."

The leisure enjoyed by the wives of prosperous Georgian gentlemen was a badge of their husbands' material success and social position. To fill their time, they kept their hands busy with fine needlework (the maids saw to the mending) and entertained themselves with a highly ritualized round of social calls. Sophie von la Roche enthusiastically painted for her daughter a picture of a typical English gathering, in the company of the esteemed novelist Fanny Burney. It was "a first-class English tea party. The tone was intimate and refined. The hostess busied herself delightfully, and just enough to allow of grace and deftness."

The ceremonious brewing of the tea was one task that was considered far too delicate and too important to delegate to the servants. While the lady of the house devoted her complete attention to the infusion of the precious leaves, the guests "continued their fancywork, sewing bands of fine muslin. While we sipped at our tea, pretty and practical discussions took place, in the course of which I was asked a number of questions. . . . Imagine me now between Mrs. Fielding and Miss Burney on the sofa; the oldest Miss Fielding pouring out tea; a younger one handing round bread and butter. . . . Education is being discussed; the value of knowing geography, chronology, and history."

La Roche, sitting at a writing desk in her lodgings, recording her memories of these conversations, was herself a symbol of far-reaching social change. She and her thoughtful English friends were entirely literate. Their reading skills were not simply a means of gaining access to Scripture, but an avenue into a vast universe of opinions and ideas. Literacy was becoming available to all levels of society throughout the continent of Europe. It was no longer the sole preserve of a religious elite, of wealthy merchants, or of the male sex. The number of men and women of all classes who could sign their names to marriage documents, commercial contracts, and wills was rising rapidly, and in some European countries virtually doubled between the early 1600s and the end of the eighteenth century.

The practice of reading aloud as a public and communal act still flourished: Pious households gathered daily to hear a Biblical text; families of a less spiritual bent entertained themselves with readings of poetry, essays, or the latest romantic novel. In humble villages the schoolteacher might read from a chapbook—a collection of popular stories and ballads—to his illiterate fellows. But the relationship between the individual and the written word was becoming a thoroughly private matter, and an ever-increasing supply of new publications issued from the printing presses to satisfy the voracious demands of the new readers.

From the beginning of the eighteenth century, a range of journals and periodicals spread learning out of the colleges and into clubs, coffee houses, and private homes. Among them was the *Spectator,* founded in London in 1711, whose purpose, the editor advised his several thousand readers, was "to make their instruction agreeable, and their diversion useful. For which reason I shall endeavor to enliven morality with wit, and to temper wit with morality." National and international current affairs were reported in newspapers—among them the *Times* of London, first published as the *Daily Universal Register* in 1785 and assuming its present title three years later. In the 1750s, the number of newspapers sold annually in England was around 7.5 million; by 1767 this figure had risen to more than 11 million. In France—where the literacy rate was seven out of ten adults—the *Mercure de France* achieved a circulation of 13,000 copies in 1790, and the *Journal de Paris,* first published in 1777, claimed a circulation of more than 20,000 copies.

The novel, a genre of literature dealing not with knowledge and hard facts but with a range of previously unexamined personal feelings and motives, came of age. Significantly, the first outstanding example in Europe was written by a woman— Marie-Madeleine de La Fayette, the hostess of a celebrated literary salon in Paris, who in 1678 published *The Princess of Clèves,* with a historical setting but portraying manners and behavior that were wholly contemporary. English novels in the first half of the eighteenth century held to a more robust and racy pattern, recounting the often-bawdy adventures of ebullient heroes and heroines on the make, but later in the century it was feelings rather than action that held the attention. In France, Jean-

A prosperous Boston family takes tea in a drawing room in this painting dated around 1788 by a German emigrant artist. Although Boston had been a focus of opposition to British rule up to American independence, its wealthy citizens emulated English customs and manners in their homes. The custom of drinking tea with a light meal in midafternoon had become fashionable in England in the early eighteenth century, and tea was one of many goods exported to America from England. The carpet shown here probably originated in England, as did the china figures on the mantelpiece. The mahogany furniture would have been made locally, following closely the style of an English original.

Jacques Rousseau's *La Nouvelle Héloïse,* dealing with the conflict between passion and duty experienced by a woman whose former lover reappears in her life to tutor the sons of her decent but unexciting marriage, rapidly went through seventy-two editions following its publication in 1761. In Johann Wolfgang von Goethe's *The Sorrows of Young Werther,* published in 1774, the hero's feelings of despair and alienation caused by his love for a woman who marries another man drive him eventually to suicide. This novel was said to have been read by Napoleon Bonaparte seven times, and young men of fashion throughout Europe took to wearing Werther's costume of a blue frock coat and yellow breeches.

Both *La Nouvelle Héloïse* and *The Sorrows of Young Werther* were epistolary novels, written in the form of an exchange of letters between fictitious correspondents. They transformed private sentiments and reflections into public property, and enabled their readers to recognize and articulate their own private feelings as never before. Other forms also contributed to this revelation of the life of the emotions, notably autobiography and memoirs. By focusing almost exclusively on sexual activity, the memoirs of the Italian adventurer Giovanni Giacomo Casanova and the pornographic novels of the French writer and soldier the marquis de Sade took this exposure of the private to even further extremes.

In 1781, Samuel Johnson noted that England had become ''a nation of readers.'' Books were still expensive, but those who could not afford their own collections could now borrow their reading matter from lending libraries—Tunbridge Wells, for example, then a minor spa town in the south of England with a population of around 4,000, had two libraries and daily deliveries of the London newspapers. And because the enjoyment of novels was essentially a private and silent activity, people wanted places to go where they might read and write in solitude. In the houses of the rich and the prosperous middle classes, rooms were set aside specifically for such purposes—studies and libraries, with doors that not only closed but locked. Inside these havens of quiet, men and women kept detailed and intimate diaries, in which they recorded not only the great events of the day but the minutiae of their daily lives: what they read, whom they met, what they ate, and even the state of their digestion. And as communications improved and people traveled in increasing numbers across a widening world, the art of letter writing flourished. Individuals discovered new ways of making their voices heard.

In their thoughts, as in the very structure and contents of their houses, people started to develop a highly particularized sense of self. The hunger for privacy was at once a cause and an effect: Those who had the wealth to make choices opted to maintain a distance between themselves and the crowd, and only the poorest now lived the greater part of their lives in public view. The family was no longer merely a unit within a larger entity—a nation, tribe, or band of coreligionists—but a tiny community of individuals.

The home had developed into an environment in which people possessed both the time and the space to reflect upon their actions and to become more aware of themselves. For example, in Jane Austen's novel *Mansfield Park*, published in 1814, the heroine, Fanny Price, had an upstairs room to which she could retreat "after anything unpleasant below, and find immediate consolation in some pursuit, or some train of thought at hand." The room was furnished with Fanny's own books, plants, and writing desk, and "if indisposed for employment, if nothing but musing would do, she could scarcely see an object in that room which had not an interesting remembrance connected with it."

Outside the home lay the battleground of economic competition and political maneuver, where people fought for their share of wealth and power; inside they could let down their guard and live as they wished, pursuing their private goals and pleasures. When they walked across their thresholds at the end of the working day, they became whoever they imagined themselves to be: saint or scholar, poet or loving parent, hero of their own secret romances. The front door of a house, with its locks and—now more often than not—its peephole, was no longer merely the access to a place of warmth, food, and shelter, but was also the barrier that stood between two increasingly separate worlds.

PLEASURES OF THE TABLE

Fish, game, and fowl pass through the hands of a merchant, a Dutch housewife, and her assistants in this kitchen scene painted by Cornelius Delff in 1597.

Mealtimes are the hub of domestic life: The preparation of food accounts for much of the work undertaken in the home, and its consumption brings together all members of the household to satisfy their common hunger. Yet a traveler abroad who is invited to dine with a local family does well to watch and wait, for it is often in the matter of food that cultures most sharply reveal their differences.

Diet is ruled first of all by geographical factors, but by the time the food arrives on the table these have been overlaid by a host of other influences—by religious taboos, for instance, or by customs that determine what types of food are eaten at what time of day and in what order. Such factors conspire to give food a social meaning: They confirm a people's sense of their own identity and distinguish them from outsiders. So important is the reassurance provided by

food customs that they are often part of the baggage of migrating peoples: It was the Mogul conquerors of India in the sixteenth century, for instance, who introduced to the subcontinent kebabs, pilaf, and other traditional Persian dishes. In the same way, immigrant communities in modern times often hold fast to the dietary customs of homelands they have left.

Cultural traditions are most apparent in the case of religious festivals: the ritual meal eaten by Jews on the eve of Passover, for example, or the great feast eaten by Muslims at the end of the thirty-day period of fasting known as Ramadan. But a similar sense of community often becomes attached to even weekday meals—for example, in the practice of saying a family grace before eating, or in the fact that favorite recipes are handed down from one generation to the next.

A nineteenth-century Kashmiri drawing *(left)* shows cooks frying chapati—disks of unleavened bread—in a well-equipped kitchen. Other methods of food preparation also are shown: On a French misericord from around 1500 *(above, left)*, meat is turned on a spit before an open fire; a sixteenth-century German woodcut and a fourteenth-century English manuscript illumination *(above)* show a cook tasting broth from a cauldron and a batch of loaves being placed in a village oven.

The Chinese, according to one account, first tasted roast pork when a pig trapped in a burning house could not be recovered until the flames had died down. True or not, it was by such felicitous accidents that the several uses of fire—tamed by humans around 500,000 BC—to make raw food more palatable were first discovered.

Baking was first carried out in shallow pits lined with hot embers or pebbles—a method still used in the American clambake. Boiling was facilitated by the development of pottery around 10,000 BC. Fire also enabled the preservation of meat by smoking; other preserving methods, including drying and salting, were familiar to the ancient Egyptians.

Often some techniques proved more applicable than others: The practice of fast cooking at high temperatures, for example, was probably first used in regions where fuel was in short supply. It was the constraints of climate and habitat that led to the development of specific local cuisines.

The fish being grilled in the seventeenth-century German painting above were probably bought from vendors such as those shown in a detail from a Prague manuscript illustration *(right)*. The merchants are checking and repacking herring, which were preserved in barrels of salt and brine during their transportation from the coast.

A detail from a fifteenth-century Flemish illustration shows servants passing a bread trencher—a thick slice of four-day-old bread shaped to contain food. Diners often equipped themselves with a stack of trenchers for each meal; when the bread became sodden, it either was discarded or given to the poor.

In this seventeenth-century painting, the family of a Swiss provincial governor gives thanks to God as food is carried to the table. Each diner has a wooden trencher and a knife, but only the parents and some of their sons have forks, which were still uncommon throughout Europe. A low table at the back bears a wine flagon and cooler; in a niche on the left is a cistern and a basin for washing hands.

A dinner table set for eight in this illustration from an 1873 British textbook entitled *Domestic Economy* boasts an elaborate array made up of silverware, cutlery, and napkins.

Wooden chopsticks resting on a stand and a Japanese lacquered wooden bowl for soup or rice conform to a style unchanged through the centuries.

The eighteenth-century English writer Dr. Samuel Johnson did not enjoy eating fish when he was in company: He was near-sighted, and had difficulty extracting the bones without using his fingers.

If Johnson had lived a few centuries earlier, he need not have worried. In medieval Europe each diner served himself from large uncovered dishes; he used a knife to cut meat when necessary, but his fingers and thumb to carry the food to his mouth. By 1700, however, meals had become much more ordered occasions, involving a sequence of separate courses and a complete set of cutlery.

In Europe, the elaboration of both table settings and manners accompanied the rise of a professional middle class anxious to assert its status. In many other cultures, such standards of sophistication were attained far earlier: Chopsticks were used in China, for example, in the fourth century BC, and their handling was governed by precise rules of etiquette.

FESTIVAL FARE

In medieval Europe, the Christian church enjoined an alternating cycle of feasting and fasting: A midwinter Christmas banquet, for example, might include boar's head, swan, pheasant, spiced pies, and other luxuries, celebrating God's plenty, while during the forty days of Lent preceding Easter the eating of all flesh was forbidden on pain of death. Other religions have also sought to regulate the consumption of food—by banning certain meats deemed unclean, for example, or by endorsing celebratory feasts on holy days. And secular and religious customs often merge, as in the American Thanksgiving Day meal, at which the serving of a roast turkey commemorates the wild turkeys eaten by the Pilgrim Fathers at their harvest feast in 1621. Such observances are a means of socializing appetite, and even after their original cause may have been forgotten they carry the sanction of tradition.

A detail from a fourteenth-century French illustration shows the preparation of crepes for the feast of Candlemas in February. Pancakes were also eaten on Shrove Tuesday, the day preceding Lent, to use up stocks of eggs before fasting began.

At the start of the Jewish celebration of Passover, shown in this fourteenth-century Spanish illustration, a celebrant prepares to uncover a dish of unleavened bread—commemorating that eaten by the Israelites during their exodus from Egypt.

Early-twentieth-century greeting cards from England and Germany display a plum pudding bedecked with Christmas holly and, at right—for Easter—an egg, the symbol of fertility and new life.

Ein Osterei sollst Du nicht missen,
Ich sende Dir mit besten Grüssen
Hier Ostereier frisch vom Nest,
Glückauf zum frohen Osterfest!

A CASTLE FOR EVERYONE

"Every family is a little state, an empire within itself, bound together by the most endearing emotions, and governed by its patriarchal head, with whose prerogative no power on earth has a right to interfere." To these words written by the American clergyman Herman Humphrey in 1840, the vast majority of his prosperous middle-class readers in both the United States and Europe no doubt nodded in silent assent, for no other group in history, before or since, has so clearly defined and so strenuously dedicated itself to the ideals of family life. The cult of home—the family's private universe, and a place, as Humphrey implied, wholly separate from the outside world of work—had become almost a religious institution. "A private shelter to cover two hearts dearer to each other than all in the world; high walls to exclude the profane eyes of every human being; seclusion enough for the children to feel that mother is a holy and peculiar name—this is home," wrote a contributor to a ladies' magazine in 1856. "This is the true nature of home," echoed the English writer and art critic John Ruskin in 1865: "It is the place of Peace; the shelter, not only from all injury, but from all terror, doubt, and division."

The physical features of this temple of family life varied according to the income of the patriarchal head, but it is not difficult to reconstruct a representative setting that Humphrey and Ruskin would have recognized and approved of. All families with any claim to respectability maintained a ground-floor front room for the reception of visitors and for important family occasions to which a degree of formality was appropriate. The furnishing of this drawing room, or parlor, reflected its status as a household shrine.

In mid-nineteenth-century London, a visitor would be ushered into the drawing room by a maid dressed in black with white apron and cap. Left alone while waiting to be received, the visitor might note rich crimson wallpaper, a luxurious vermilion carpet and velvet curtains, and sumptuously upholstered, plush-covered armchairs arranged about the room. The large, leatherbound book that lay upon a massive table of carved mahogany was more likely to be the family photograph album than the more traditional Bible. Great glass-fronted bookcases and a little rosewood writing desk punctuated the walls. The household's impressive collection of silver plates, salvers, and tureens would be displayed on a massive sideboard. Like the great gilt mirror set above the fireplace, the lacquered Japanese fans arranged on either side of it, the brass-headed fire irons in the hearth, the framed family photographs that crowded the walls, and the host of decorative snuffboxes, china statuettes, and other ornaments that thronged every available surface, the family silver would be polished to perfection. Every object in the room would shine in the shimmering light that cascaded from a candlelit crystal chandelier hanging from the ornate plasterwork ceiling and caught the vibrant red glow of a coal fire that crackled companionably

In this illustration from *The Art and Craft of Homemaking*, a manual of advice for housewives without servants published in England in 1913, a wife stands framed in a welcoming glow of light to greet the returning breadwinner. The trim garden and generous size of the dwelling are typical of the new housing being built at the time on the outskirts of industrial cities, to which men traveled to work by public transport. For the families that lived in such houses, enjoying the benefits of urban facilities but removed from the noise and dirt of city centers, suburbia was already becoming as much a way of life and state of mind as a physical location.

137

THE DOMESTIC HIERARCHY

By the late nineteenth century, the houses of the prosperous middle classes reflected a range of interwoven domestic hierarchies. Even in the limited sample of rooms exhibited in the English dollhouse of the 1890s shown above, contrasts in furnishings indicate that some rooms—such as the laundry room *(top right)* and the kitchen and pantry *(bottom right)*—were the servants' domain, while others were the preserve of their employers. Bedrooms, nurseries, and every-day living rooms were for private use, leaving more formally decorated drawing rooms for the reception of visitors. Drawing rooms and boudoirs were female territory; billiard rooms (such as that shown here on the middle floor), libraries, and smoking rooms were male. In the larger houses of the wealthy, this segregation was developed even further, with separate staircases and corridors for bachelors and for unmarried women.

in the grate. For all its grandness, this was a room calculated to set the visitor at ease.

Comparable rooms were common in North America. The class system was somewhat different, as Edgar Allan Poe noted in an essay entitled *The Philosophy of Furniture*, written in 1840: "We have no aristocracy of the blood, and having therefore as a natural, and indeed as an inevitable thing, fashioned for ourselves an aristocracy of dollars, the display of wealth has here to take the place and perform the function of the heraldic display in monarchical countries." Poe, however, went on to describe a room that resembled its English counterpart in many ways. Measuring thirty by twenty-five feet, this room boasted "curtains of an exceedingly rich crimson silk, fringed with a deep network of gold, and lined with silver tissue," and a deep carpet "of the same crimson ground." The walls were covered "with a glossy paper of a silver gray tint, spotted with small Arabesque devices of a fainter hue of the prevalent crimson." The room's furniture included "two large low sofas of rosewood and crimson silk, gold-flowered," two light conversation chairs, an open piano, and an octagonal table "of the richest gold-threaded marble." Four Sèvres vases, "in which bloom a profusion of sweet and vivid flowers," occupied "the slightly rounded angles of the room."

Although they were less lavishly furnished, similar rooms were often maintained even in working-class homes. Here, among the family's most-prized possessions and furniture, guests were welcomed and the household assembled on formal occasions. A contemporary architect decried the practice among the poorer classes of taking space from the living room, "where it will be used every day and every hour, to form a parlor, where it will be used only once or twice a week." But for such households the display—and thus, assurance—of respectability was clearly more important than simple convenience.

The wealth that supported such standards of domestic life, and that enabled privileged families to contrive an entirely new habitat at some distance from the world of public affairs, derived chiefly from the Industrial Revolution. The gradual rise of industrialism in Britain through the latter part of the eighteenth century had brought a veritable explosion of social change in the first half of the nineteenth, as the ways of an agricultural nation were swept away before a rising tide of economic progress. An ever-growing middle class grew up in the favorable climate that capitalism provided, from wealthy bankers and lawyers who serviced the industrialists down to humble bookkeepers and clerks who worked in their offices, teachers and doctors who looked after their families, and shopkeepers and tradesmen who supplied their material wants. Such people did not delay in improving the quality of their lives with the benefits of the factory age: mass-produced furnishings that provided fair imitations of the old, craftsman-made articles at an affordable fraction of their cost; coal fires and cooking ranges to keep them warm and cook their food; improved sanitary arrangements to protect their health; and, as the century wore on, gas and electricity to flood their homes with light.

By the century's end other countries were following in Britain's economic footsteps, in some cases catching up. Trade among the nations of the industrialized world—in continental Europe, North America, and Japan—and between the developed countries and their colonies in Africa, Asia, and Latin America brought further prosperity to the industrial societies. While conditions for the majority still lagged behind those of the middle-class minority, many of the advances the latter enjoyed were gradually filtering down into the homes of skilled workers.

A New York City family of grandparents, parents, and eleven children relax in an elegant mansion in this 1871 painting. The rising incomes and improved diet and medical care that accompanied industrial prosperity in America and Europe at first caused an increase in the size of families; toward the end of the nineteenth century, as the bills began coming in, small families became the norm among the middle class. By this time, children were becoming less an appendage to adult society and more a separate category of the population, with their own educational and imaginative needs.

Altered conditions changed attitudes toward home and family life. Factory and office jobs for women lured domestic workers out of service, accelerating a trend toward smaller homes, simpler in design and less cluttered in their furnishing, which could conveniently be looked after by the servantless housewife with the assistance of a wide range of new "laborsaving" appliances. After staffing the workshops and offices of the industrial world through two world wars while men fought in the armed services, housewives—and their roles and expectations—could never be quite the same. An increasingly vocal feminist movement had already won women in the United States the right to vote in 1920, and middle-class housewives were soon insisting upon their right to take full-time jobs away from home. Their poorest counterparts, through sheer necessity, had always done this, but soon even relatively prosperous families were discovering that as radios and televisions—and all the cars, vacuum cleaners, washing machines, refrigerators, and other appliances that the new broadcasting media advertised so incessantly—became accepted as essentials rather than as luxury items, the standard of living they had come to expect made the woman's extra income vital.

The gradual introduction and acceptance of improved contraceptive measures permitted families to maintain their standard of living by limiting their size—and gave women new independence. As divorce—once an expensive and humiliating process available only to the very rich—became a routine procedure, many commentators argued that the institution of the family itself was threatened, undermined by an ethic that placed individual liberty, self-gratification, and materialist acquisitiveness before the well-being of dependents and society as a whole.

Yet for better or worse, by the middle of the twentieth century Western consumerism and individualism were being promoted through television, radio, film, and other media to the poorest nations of the Third World. Traditional cultures and economic systems came under mounting pressure as the impoverished population of the world at large began to crave the comfort, affluence, and apparent sexual freedom of the privileged few.

For many these goals proved more difficult to achieve than the advertisements and television programs suggested, and even for those who did succeed, they often turned out to be mixed blessings. It was too late now, however, to turn back to the certainties—real or imagined—of the past. Whatever ideas of home and family people entertained, they had to be adapted to the demands and possibilities of ever-faster material and social change.

Even in the nineteenth century, the life of comfort and order expressed by the accumulations of possessions displayed in middle-class households was not as tranquil as it seemed on the surface. In Britain, the middle classes were not a homogeneous and static sector of society: Their members ranged from wealthy industrialists with stately houses and staffs of perhaps half a dozen indoor servants plus others for the garden and private carriage to, at the lower end of the scale, clerks and shopkeepers and teachers living in small houses and employing at best a single domestic servant. Each layer in this complex middle-class society was keenly aware of its precise social standing, of subtle grades of distinction in matters of domestic routine, and of the need to keep up appearances.

For the middle-class married woman, life was apparently easy: Women might work, it was felt, but ladies visited friends, entertained guests, brought up their children, and soothed their husbands' cares. Prized as it was, however, the lady's idleness was more illusion than it was reality. The young bride could look forward to two grueling decades of exhausting (and frequently dangerous) childbirth and the care of infants. With child mortality rates high even among the comfortable classes, families had a tendency to be large, and even with domestic help, the middle-class wife often had to struggle hard to look after her family while at the same time maintaining a busy social life founded on the fallacious assumption of the lady's endless leisure time, and the equally questionable assumption that the bearing and rearing of children was so much woman's natural role that it could not be counted as work at all, but was rather a source of continual joy.

Moreover, the new large houses built for the growing middle classes, while moving with the times in the increased use of brick and slate, tended to imitate in the essentials of design the houses built for the aristocrats of earlier times, whose social eminence the new rich were anxious to attain for themselves. Their technology—systems of heating, lighting, and ventilation, and sanitation facilities—lagged far behind the modernity of their decoration and furnishings.

Throughout the nineteenth century most of the work of running a middle-class household devolved on domestic servants. A rising young professional couple could usually afford only a single young "maid-of-all-work," who had to be on call at all hours and who lacked both the leisure and the money for an outside social life. In England, the most prosperous households were managed by a hierarchy of specialized employees. The king and queen of the realm "below stairs," the basement quarters where much of the work of the servants was performed, were the male butler, who looked after the master's stock of wine and received callers, and the female cook. Beneath them in rank came the coachman, an assortment of kitchenmaids to assist the cook in her duties and to cook for the servants, and parlormaids to clean the house. A young boy might drop in daily after school to polish the family's shoes and clean its cutlery. The ladies' maids who looked after their mistresses' appearance occupied a high but precarious position in the hierarchy: Chosen for their decorative appearance and manner, they enjoyed considerable privileges, often including their employers' castoff finery, but this exalted status was often temporary, being lost with advancing age and fading looks.

The governesses who educated the family's children were in an even more ambiguous position. Normally the daughters of genteel families whose fortunes had declined, they were emphatically "ladies," and dined with the family rather than in the servants' hall. Their subservient status was never forgotten, however: Their pay was low, they were frequently victims of their masters' sexual harassment and their mistresses' jealousy, and their prospects of escaping into marriage within their own social class were severely limited.

Long hours—approximately eighty hours a week for the average housemaid—meager accommodations in unheated attics, and the difficulty of conducting any sort of outside social life made domestic service a grim option. Throughout the nineteenth century, however, it represented the only realistic choice for thousands of young country girls. In Britain in midcentury, live-in servants made up 14 percent of the entire working population; more than twice as many women worked as domestic servants than in the other main female occupations (cotton manufacture, dressmaking and millinery, agricultural labor, laundry work, and teaching) put together. The lot of the houseworker, moreover, was in many ways worse than that of the servants of the

In an American drawing room of the 1880s *(above)*, no surface is left bare of ornament—even the chairs are artfully bedecked with ribbons. Most of the furnishings shown here could by this time be purchased from department stores and mail-order catalogs. Another new development, the invention of photography, is evident in the framed portrait photograph on top of the desk. An increase in housework proved no deterrent to the accumulation of consumer goods, for there was a plentiful supply of cheap female labor to clean, manage the still-backward heating and plumbing systems, and as shown at left, look after kitchen chores.

past. In the United States, it was not forgotten that the domestic tasks that fell to paid servants had, in the past, often been the work of slaves, and indeed servant girls were frequently addressed as "slavey." The contempt that employers displayed toward their domestic staff was often echoed by the disdain with which other working-class men and women regarded them. Hard as their lives were, factory workers enjoyed shorter hours and greater leisure time, higher rates of pay, and above all, independence: They too tended to view the life of the domestic servant as one of virtual slavery.

Because the presence of servants allowed a comfortable existence amid the most antiquated facilities, the wealthy saw little point in improving the technology of their homes. Those inventions that seemed to offer direct improvements in the middle-class standard of living met with some interest, but on the whole, domestic work throughout the nineteenth century remained largely unaffected by the innovations that year by year were transforming industry and commerce. Hence, while the invention of gas-lighting in the early years of the century, and its subsequent refinement, offered far brighter, steadier light than the candles or oil lamps used previously, it was adopted only very gradually in the private home (though it was eagerly seized upon by industrialists who realized that it could make their factories productive day and night). Middle-class homeowners did not mind the inconvenience of the old ways, since the constant tending that candles required, or the endless trimming, cleaning, and replenishing necessary to keep oil lamps burning properly, had never fallen upon them. European aristocrats were accustomed to living in gloomy conditions, as their ancestors had done for centuries, and were far more concerned about the disadvantages of the new system: the faint smell of gas, or the damage to wallpaper and decorations that an imperfectly fitted jet might cause.

It was not until the 1890s, when gas companies began offering prospective consumers free installation of pipes, meters, and fittings, that domestic gas-lighting became at all widespread in London, and even then provincial cities lagged far behind the capital. As homes were connected for gas-lighting, gas ranges followed, though regarded with a good deal of suspicion at first: Again, convenience was not a priority for the classes that employed servants. In the United States, the wealthy in the major cities on the eastern seaboard proved to be more receptive; by the 1820s windows in the most prosperous neighborhoods blazed with light. Here too, however, gas-lighting spread down the social scale very slowly—the cost of installing and running the new system was by itself greater than the yearly rent paid by most poor families. And even among the rich gaslight was widely considered in bad taste: "Its harsh and unsteady light offends," declared Edgar Allan Poe in 1840. "No one having both brains and eyes will use it."

Electric lighting, first successfully demonstrated in 1878 by Thomas Edison, was cleaner and even more convenient than gas-lighting, illuminating the home at the flick of a switch, but it too penetrated the domestic sphere only very gradually. By 1910 a mere two percent of Britain's homes had been connected to the mains, and it was not until after the First World War that the use of electricity began to spread more quickly, encouraged by the development of gas-filled light bulbs with tungsten filaments that burned more brightly and steadily—and for much longer—than the carbon-filament bulb originally developed by Edison himself. Countless electrical appliances for cooking, cleaning, and heating were developed during the last decade of the nineteenth century, but the public at large remained unmoved by their inventors' enthusiastic claims: Such items were out of the reach of poor families, and of little interest to those who had servants to look after their kitchens and carry coal for their fires. There was fear, too, of this mysterious but powerful new form of energy that few could understand.

If improved lighting was by the turn of the century beginning to dispel the prevailing gloom of the middle-class home, there was relief for other senses too. Since the end of the eighteenth century, when the British inventor Count Rumford had improved the standard square fireplace along scientific lines, sloping off the sides so that they tapered up into the chimney, further refinements had been made. Taller chimneys, often with adjustable air regulators, hoods, and canopies above the fire and tightly fitting ash pans for insertion beneath the grate, not only made consumption of coal more economic and room temperature more controllable, but also helped prevent the billowings of acrid choking smoke that had all too often filled family rooms during the winter months.

At a church-run cooking class in New York in 1905, girls in numbered pinafores learn the homemaking skills essential for the maintenance of middle-class status. As opportunities for working women expanded, large staffs became less common, but hostesses were still expected to provide lavish fare. A page from an 1881 edition of Isabella Beeton's *Book of Household Management (below)*, first published in England in 1861, shows arrangements of exotic fruits. A typical dinner menu for twelve prescribed by Beeton called for two soups, two fish dishes, seven meats, two kinds of fowl, seven desserts, and fruit, ice cream, nuts, and cake.

Some of the more offensive smells that had always pervaded the home were also beginning to be banished as sanitation improved. During the early part of the nineteenth century, most middle-class English families had relied upon privies in their backyards and, for overnight use, ceramic chamber pots kept in bedrooms. The toilet in its modern form, with S-bend waste pipe and overhead cistern and valves, had been developed in the late eighteenth century but was not much used until the 1850s. Even then, middle-class habits died hard, and chamber pots remained common (servants, not those who used them, had to empty the chamber pots each morning). In new houses built for middle-class occupiers from the 1860s onward, however, indoor toilets, usually placed on the main bedroom floor, were becoming standard features. But they would remain rare in British working-class dwellings well into the twentieth century: Of 10,000 houses in the Lancashire mill town of Rochdale in 1910, for example, only 750 had toilets.

Despite a tenfold increase in soap production in Britain between 1830 and 1875, and similar increases in other parts of western Europe—made possible by the import of cheap vegetable oils from colonies in the tropics—standards of personal hygiene rose only very slowly. With indoor plumbing a rarity everywhere but in the homes of the very rich, the middle classes shared their humbler contemporaries' robust indifference to bodily odors and cheerfully settled through much of the nineteenth century for washstands. A marble-topped stand with a basin of hot water brought by servants, a pitcher of cold water, and a towel rack alongside, the washstand had underneath an enclosed cupboard in which a slop jar and foot bath were discreetly concealed. In poorer homes tin baths were set up before the kitchen fire and filled with cold water warmed up with a dash of boiling water; wealthier people had fixed baths in special bedroom recesses, for which water had to be carried laboriously upstairs by servants, then taken away by hand afterward.

Bathing was therefore a time-consuming and complicated operation, so people tended not to bother very often. In any case, the virtues of bathing were by no means universally accepted, even by the medical profession. While many enthusiasts swore by the feeling of freshness and glowing health they derived from their baths, critics warned of dire consequences. Baths were "zinc coffins," according to one leading physician. Another commentator counseled strict moderation in cleanliness: "A wet towel applied each morning to the skin, followed by friction in pure air, is all that is absolutely needed." In such a climate it was not surprising that bathrooms with plumbing began to be installed in middle-class homes only in the 1880s; piped water warmed on kitchen ranges or in separate water heaters was not introduced until the end of the century.

While an abundance of personal service ensured that the middle classes remained largely unconcerned about the more functional areas of their houses and acted as a brake on innovation, the compelling desire for status among a still socially insecure group prompted an almost obsessive preoccupation with the appearance of the more public areas of the home. Visiting Britain in the 1850s, the American essayist and poet Ralph Waldo Emerson was struck by the Englishman's zeal in this respect: "If he is in the middle condition he spares no expense on his home. . . . Within it is wainscoted, carved, curtained, hung with pictures and filled with good furniture." Yet in the United States too, as in the cities of Europe, decoration and redecoration had become a mania.

The furnishing and decoration of drawing rooms where formal visits were received and soirees and afternoon "at homes" given, and of dining rooms for formal dinner parties and special family meals, were matters of absorbing interest and often of constant revision. Newspaper advertisements, features in so-called ladies' magazines, and a burgeoning literature on interior design ensured that demand for new furnishings was maintained by constant changes in fashion. An extravagant clutter was not merely tolerated but highly sought after, as homeowners packed all the items they possibly could into the space available: "Providing there is space to move about, without knocking over the furniture, there is hardly likely to be too much in the room," complained one commentator.

Elaboration flourished as chairs, tables, and other furniture sprouted baroque scrolls and arabesques, and functional items from paperweights to coal scuttles broke out in a rash of often grotesque ornamentation. But however determinedly applied, such superficial decorativeness could not satisfactorily conceal the main disadvantage of mass-produced factory objects that mimicked handcrafted originals: their anonymity. If factories could provide an approximation of the appearance of handcrafted goods, they could never hope to reproduce the individuality and personal style of the craftsmen they were steadily putting out of business or the limitless diversity of their products.

Concern over this decline into banal uniformity was voiced by the English artist, poet, and political radical William Morris. Despairing of any attempt by industry to bring real beauty into the home, Morris went into business himself in 1861, hiring a group of craftsmen in cooperation with whom he designed and manufactured furniture, carpets, wallpaper, and tapestries in a "medievalist" style that contrasted with the pseudoclassical symmetry and rococo elaboration of the mass-produced furniture of the day. Soon his goods were all

The flush toilet in this advertisement from an 1894 British catalog features ornamental decor appropriate to its thronelike status. Enclosed behind the bowl is a water-filled trap to eliminate odors rising from the waste pipe.

AUTOMATING THE HOME

By 1900, much of the work that would have taken hours for servants to do could, in the best-equipped houses, be performed automatically at the flick of a switch or by pulling a lever. Improved plumbing made efficient use of piped water, which had become a standard feature of new housing in the 1860s. The still-mysterious forces of gas and electricity, as shown overleaf, provided energy on demand to heat water, cook food, or light rooms. And as well as easing domestic chores, these facilities made possible an improvement in hygiene: Laundering clothes and bathing became more frequent activities; dirt and ordure were quickly disposed of. Houses both looked and smelled clean.

the rage, and while the richest could have the interiors of their houses entirely redesigned and decorated by Morris & Co., even those of more moderate means saved so as to be able to feature at least one Morris item in their drawing rooms. Morris himself was aware of the ironies of his position as left-wing revolutionary (within a few years he was to embrace Marxism) and, at the same time, well-paid darling of the capitalist oppressors; yet he perhaps failed to foresee another irony. It did not take industry long to sense the opportunities that lay in medievalism: Very soon factories were churning out their own imitations, as crude and uniform as any of the monstrosities that had first spurred Morris into action.

Although an artist like Morris may have considered its products vulgar and tasteless, industrialism was nevertheless bringing into the homes of the working classes a range of furnishings they had never known before and in middle-class houses was providing a degree of splendor that had once been the privilege of only the very richest. The spheres of home and work were—as many commentators of the time were well aware—interdependent: While respectable home life would have been impossible without the earnings brought in from work, the money spent on improving and maintaining the material fabric of the home was essential to industry and to the economy as a whole. In addition, the responsibility men felt toward their families, as well as the sympathy and understanding that they received from them, helped them to endure the stresses of working life at all levels of society and thus ensured the continued smooth running of the economic system.

"Good society," noted the English author

..und inzwischen wäscht der PROTOS

A German advertisement from around 1920 shows a housewife about to plug her new washing machine into an electric outlet. Released from the labor of laundering clothes by hand, the elegantly attired woman is on her way out of the house to enjoy an evening of pleasure.

In this illustration from a late-nineteenth-century French manual on household uses of gas, a woman relaxes in a portable tub filled with water heated by a stationary gas appliance.

George Eliot in her novel *The Mill on the Floss*, published in 1860, "has its claret and its velvet carpets, its dinner-engagements six weeks deep, its opera and its fairy ballrooms; rides off its ennui on thoroughbred horses, lounges at the club, has to keep clear of crinoline vortices, gets its science done by Faraday, and its religion by the superior clergy who are to be met with in the best houses." But, she further observed, "good society, floated on gossamer wings of light irony, is of very expensive production; requiring nothing less than a wide and arduous national life condensed in unfragrant, deafening factories, cramping itself in mines, sweating at furnaces, grinding, hammering, weaving under more or less oppression of carbonic acid—or else, spread over sheepwalks, and scattered in lonely houses and huts on the clayey or chalky corn-lands, where the rainy days look dreary."

Precisely because they had been able to cocoon themselves in mass-produced luxury, the comfortable classes were shocked and often deeply disturbed by an explosion of information in the mid-nineteenth century concerning the dire conditions under which many members of the laboring classes lived. Government commissions of inquiry, medical reports, and statistical societies brought to the notice of the middle classes matters to which they had preferred to remain oblivious—despite the fact that outside the confines of home rich and poor continuously rubbed shoulders. "In the midst of the most extraordinary abundance," wrote an American visitor to London in 1849, "here are men, women, and children dying of starvation; and running alongside of the splendid chariot, with its gilded equipages, its silken linings, and the liveried footmen, are poor, forlorn, friendless, almost naked wretches, looking like the mere fragments of humanity."

The rural homes left behind by the work-hungry millions who flocked to Europe's industrial cities during the early decades of the nineteenth century had been far from idyllic. Except on a very few of the largest estates, where wealthy philanthropic landlords constructed experimental "model villages" for their tenants, the country cottages of agricultural laborers were often no better than rural slums: dark, often windowless one-room huts with earthen floors, without piped water, and with no sanitary facilities—except where a village shared a communal cesspool, which overflowed in wet weather and reeked disease all year round. Typhus and malaria were common visitors, especially where landlords had thrown up cottages heedlessly on marshy ground to save their more valuable farming land. But for many of the poor, conditions in the cities were even worse.

In London, private landlords subdivided the old city town houses deserted by aristocrats moving to the leafier environment of the suburbs and rented the resulting apartments to the new arrivals. Crowded one on top of the other in the tiny rooms of such "rookeries," poor families, the sharper landlords quickly discovered, were far more profitable as tenants than their wealthy predecessors. Large numbers could be housed in these buildings, and maintenance was minimal; anybody who objected to the inhuman conditions could leave, and the landlord would have no difficulty in finding replacements among the armies of homeless arriving in the city day by day. Exploring the rookeries of London in 1850, the philanthropist Thomas Beames found one house in St. Giles that had an average of seventeen occupants for each room. The furniture in such rooms amounted at best to a single bedstead upon which the whole family would sleep; more often, the occupants had to content themselves with straw or wood shavings strewn upon the wooden floorboards.

In the Italian bedroom depicted in this painting of around 1905, the clutter of the previous century has been largely suppressed in favor of bare, white-painted surfaces. Simplicity and functionalism became the creed of most modernist architects and designers. "Demand built-in fittings to take the place of much of the furniture, which is expensive to buy, takes up too much room, and needs looking after," advised the French architect Le Corbusier in 1923. "Teach your children that a house is habitable only when it is full of light and air, and when the floors and walls are clear."

In the industrial towns of the Midlands and northern England, old aristocratic houses suitable for subdivision were uncommon, and new housing had to be provided for the workers by the industrialists who employed them or by private landlords. Railways and improved roads made the large-scale transportation of bricks, mortar, and roofing slate economical as it had never been before; local traditions of centuries were discarded, and ranks of uniform terraced houses were constructed in the shadows of the mills in which their inhabitants toiled. Back-to-back housing—in which terraces of small houses shared side and back walls as well as roofs—precluded ventilation by the breeze, although these houses did offer working-class families a degree of privacy undreamed of in London's rookeries. Many of the new houses, built of cheap materials by poorly qualified workers, were structurally unsound: A storm in 1822, for example, blew down rows of houses in the expanding seaport of Liverpool, where the term *jerry-building*—implying shoddy construction and derived from sailors' slang for an inferior, temporary piece of equipment used only in an emergency—originated.

In the industrialized regions of North America and continental Europe, similar conditions prevailed. Whether squeezed several families at a time into the lightweight, timber-framed houses that spread out from the heart of America's great cities along streets piled high with garbage, or eking out an existence in the inner-city tenements and peripheral shantytowns of Europe, the fast-growing working classes were as one in having exchanged rural squalor for urban.

The implications for family life were profound: Indeed, for many industrial workers domesticity was a luxury they could not afford. Husbands, wives, and children often worked full time, out of the house all day, leaving infants—sometimes drugged into groggy docility with the patent opiates sold by pharmacists—in the care of older siblings or their grandparents. Orderly and harmonious family life was well-nigh unthinkable in these conditions. Privacy was virtually nonexistent; the sounds of dogs barking, rats scurrying, children yelling, and their parents fighting in poverty and desperation traveled freely up and down staircases or through thin walls. Even worse than the noise were the smells: In the absence of water supplies, sanitary arrangements, or refuse collection, the atmosphere festered with the sickly odor of human excrement and decaying rubbish. When cholera struck one overcrowded English tenement in 1842, workmen sent to clean out the courtyard had to remove seventy-five cartloads of human and animal manure.

The nuclear family unit of husband, wife, and children, moreover, formed only a small part of a much wider network of social bonds. Relatives tended to live close together, and children to see almost as much of grandparents, aunts, and uncles as they did of their parents. Bonds outside the family were also close: Working together in the factories and sharing facilities at home, the poor of the industrial cities identified strongly with their coworkers and neighbors, supporting one another through times of illness or particular financial hardship and relaxing together during the evenings. Even where their accommodations did not, like the back-to-back courts of Britain or the tenements of Europe, encourage in their very design a physical sense of inward-looking isolation from the world outside, the poor of the industrialized world were thrown upon their own communal resources. Friedrich Engels, the future collaborator of Karl Marx, who was sent to the English industrial city of Manchester by his German father to learn the textile business, wrote in 1844 of the "separate territories assigned to poverty. Removed from the sight of happier classes, poverty may struggle along as it can."

The districts that encompassed the poorest housing, especially those that became notorious as havens of vice, crime, and disease, were shunned by the general public—that is, by all better-off and respectable members of the working classes as well as by those above them. But as knowledge of such abject conditions became widely available—through the polemical writings of Engels and Marx, the more clinical reports of investigators such as Edwin Chadwick, and the novels of Charles Dickens and Émile Zola—ignorance ceased to be an excuse for inaction. Measures of social reform were enacted, by both private philanthropists and government agencies, that would change the lives not only of those whom they were designed to succor, but also of those who sponsored their progress.

Evangelical Christianity, which many of the new middle class had embraced—in place of the laxer Catholic or Protestant creeds that were associated with the preindustrial days of elitist rule—moved many to compassion. There were also more self-interested reasons for the affluent to look to the position of the great mass of the working class. Repeated outbreaks of cholera during the 1840s and 1850s, tearing through the poorer districts of cities in Europe, Britain, and America, did not leave the middle class unscathed and played havoc with local economies. Stranded in New York during the great epidemic of 1832, which brought industry, commerce, and social life to a virtual halt for two months, publisher Henry Dana Ward wrote to his parents safe in the New England countryside: "Deaths exceed a hundred a day.

People are sad, some out of employ that know not how to live without day labor, others have sick friends to nurse while trembling for their own lives, and others are taken like lightning from the midst of their families and daily work.'' Shocked into belated action, and assisted by the development of cheap, nonporous ceramic piping that made the construction of sewage systems relatively inexpensive, governments throughout the industrialized world embarked on large-scale programs that would by the end of the century leave cholera—along with a host of other waterborne diseases—a thing of the past.

Other diseases bred in the squalor of the slums were also felt as a threat. Vice, drunkenness, criminality, and political unrest—even revolution—were clearly liable to flourish in degrading, overcrowded surroundings. "So long as twenty, thirty, or even forty individuals are permitted—it might almost be said compelled—to reside in homes originally built for the accommodation of a single family or at most two families," noted John Simon, a London medical officer, "so long will the evils of ignorance, of indecency, immorality, intemperance, prostitution, and crime continue to exist almost unchecked." As the middle class found itself living in fear of street crime and burglary, as industrialists struggled to keep their factories running in the face of absenteeism and accidents caused by drunken workers, and as the purity of the family shrine itself was blasted by sexually transmitted diseases contracted from prostitutes by erring husbands, it was clear that the lives of the poor had to be reformed, if only for the sake of the rich.

The languorous reader in the French painting of the 1880s shown above has imbued her room with Eastern exoticism: Japanese prints and masks on one wall complement the parasol and dagger on the other, above a lacquered cabinet. The Japanese, after trade between their country and the rest of the world opened up in the 1860s, were no less enamored of Western goods, often adapting their furniture, dress, and hair styles to foreign models. In this 1887 Japanese painting *(opposite)*, an accompanist plays a Western-style organ. During the 1880s, collections of songs combining edifying Japanese lyrics with Western melodies were published for use in both schools and private homes.

Hence the ruthless laws of laissez-faire capitalism came to be tempered by a spontaneous outpouring of charitable work and funds. Prominent citizens founded schools, hospitals, public libraries, orphanages, and shelters for the homeless. Distinguished ladies visited prisons and campaigned for reform in all areas of social life. In America, voluntary work as nurses tending the wounded of both armies in the Civil War left many middle-class American women with a new sense of their duty to those who suffered, and when an unusually harsh winter aggravated the effects of economic slump in 1873 and 1874, soup kitchens established by charitable foundations fed 7,000 indigent New Yorkers a day. Evangelical missionaries labored heroically to spread the word of Christ—and with it the cardinal middle-class virtues of prudence, thrift, and temperance—in godless slums.

Ideas of home life and the family were central to these reforms: Behind the genuine desire to save the souls and improve the quality of life of the poor lay an assumption that society could be saved from anarchy only if the mass of the people could be induced to accept the spiritual and material aspirations of their middle-class employers. The good man feared God and strove to live as a good Christian: He owed his loyalty not to his coworkers but to his wife and children; he worked hard and obediently to support them; he did not drink, but instead saved his money to see them through hard times in the future; he did not jeopardize their welfare by going out on strike, but rather strove to educate and better himself so as to be a more effective breadwinner. While such strictures were calculated to benefit the middle class, they also caught the imagination of thousands among the poor, and the lot of countless families was eased by a father's embracing of temperance, and his substitution of the

Bible or books for beer. And while it was often humiliating for the poor to take parcels of food and clothing from middle-class benefactors, such donations could make all the difference for families on the bread line.

During the final decades of the century, many members of the working classes also enjoyed some relief from unremitting toil in the form of vacations. Although an annual week's vacation was not to be institutionalized until the next century, many employers allowed their workers time off while factories or mills closed for repairs and maintenance, or for the duration of local celebrations. While the rich in Europe traveled to the French Riviera or the coastal towns of Italy as well as to inland spa resorts, the working classes also began to flock to the seaside—to visit the amusement parks, to consume cotton candy in large quantities, to paddle in the sea with hitched-up skirts and trousers.

The great programs of charitable reform that marked the late nineteenth century represented only a part of a wider mood of sympathy—not only for the poor at home but for the supposedly primitive peoples of the European colonies in Africa and Asia, starved of the spiritual nourishment that Christianity could bring. Although compassion was often vulgarized into extremes of mawkish sentimentality—especially over the period of Christmas, which became at this time as much a family as a religious festival—it was no less genuine for that. And within the middle-class home itself, high-minded masters and mistresses discovered another community ripe for the message of moral virtue: their own offspring.

Over the preceding century, writers of the

Romantic movement such as William Wordsworth and Jean-Jacques Rousseau had promoted new views of childhood as a time of natural, unaffected innocence. Such views now found expression in a careful attention to the upbringing and education of children in the home. While earlier ages had seen children past their earliest infancy as miniature adults and treated them accordingly, to a large extent allowing them to bring themselves up with minimal parental interference, childhood was now regarded as a distinct and important phase in which diligent tending and nurturing were necessary for the safeguarding of childish innocence and the preparation of the happy, successful, virtuous adult. Parents spent money on a wide range of toys: dollhouses, puppets and miniature theaters, model trains and ships, and optical toys such as the zoetrope, in which a spinning series of pictures mimicked the natural movements of the figures depicted. Board games proliferated, many of them designed to inculcate the moral virtues of honesty and piety. Spelling books and stories and tracts of moral import lined the shelves of the nursery, which soon became as cluttered as the parents' drawing room. The scope of children's imagination was more generously recognized by a large number of writers who provided this new readership with a literature of its own: Charles Kingsley, Robert Louis Stevenson, Lewis Carroll, Mark Twain, Jules Verne, Louisa May Alcott, and Anna Sewell.

Meanwhile, as previously deprived sectors of society benefited from new attitudes and provisions, material advances continued to accumulate. Diet, once a monotonous regimen enslaved to the circling seasons, was transformed by the advent in the late nineteenth century of canning and refrigeration, which allowed year-round variety. Improved transport by rail and steamship meant that previously unobtainable foodstuffs could be delivered easily to the family dinner table and permitted the leisured classes to travel farther and more frequently beyond their known, familiar territory. Improved hygiene, along with medical improvements such as vaccination and antiseptics, which followed upon the discovery that infection could be transmitted by germs, reduced rates of childhood mortality. In most classes in most countries of the industrialized world—which now included Japan and parts of Russia as well as Europe and North America—the generation that came of age in 1900 could begin life expecting to live longer, more comfortable, and more rewarding lives than their counterparts a century before.

But if the young of 1900 expected their benefits to comprise simply more of the same, they were mistaken. A decade and a half into the new century, a major part of a European generation would be slaughtered on the battlefields of the First World War, in which the family squabbles of the European dynasties escalated into an unprecedented maelstrom of violence. And in domestic life—which is the sector from which most people take their bearings, and in which they find meaning and direction—less spectacular but equally unforeseen developments were in the offing. These would affect the role of women in particular.

In the last decades of the nineteenth century, a tendency toward smaller families among the upper and middle classes especially became apparent. Among the reasons were the decline in child mortality and better child care: The chances that any child would survive into maturity were better than ever before, so a couple needed to produce fewer children to achieve a desired family size. But equally important were economic reasons. The cost of raising and educating children was making increased inroads into middle-class budgets. So too was the cost of servants. Never an attractive prospect for a young girl, work as a servant seemed even less so in a world in which alternatives were opening up all the time: New factories offered shorter hours and better conditions than domestic service; by the 1890s the typewriter was transforming office life, and male clerks were finding themselves replaced by female typists, while an expanding education system afforded young women opportunities for work in teaching. As the pool of domestic labor dwindled, those who did work as servants could demand higher wages.

The presence of servants in the home was also increasingly seen as conflicting with the ideals of home life, their presumed coarse language and low sexual morals posing a constant threat to the sanctity of the family shrine. The middle classes had never been able to manage the aristocrats' breezy indifference to servants as nonpersons, in whose presence no discretion need be maintained and no embarrassment felt; and as a sense of the individual's personal identity grew stronger through the closing decades of the nineteenth century, it became even harder to discount servants in this way. The conduct of the impeccably respectable eighteenth-century French noblewoman who had a footman standing by with a towel while she took her bath would have astonished and appalled the new middle classes. So strong a sense of sexual modesty had religious puritanism instilled in them, indeed, that they believed privacy had to be maintained even from themselves: For example, middle-class parents sprinkled special powders into their daughters' baths to cloud the water so that the girls would not catch a glimpse of their own private parts. Servants, untrammeled by such modesty, were liable to corrupt the jealously guarded innocence of their employers' children.

A world without servants was still a daunting prospect. Manuals were written to advise and reassure the hesitant housewife. The author of *First Aid to the Servantless*, published in London in 1913, addressed her task with cheerful enthusiasm: While admitting that servants were still essential for "the very rich householder, the striving working mistress, the solitary woman, the helpless, the thriftless, the shiftless, and the cross-grained," she claimed that "all other people might possibly be happier, healthier, and wealthier if servantless." Her advice covered newfangled household equipment such as mechanical vacuum cleaners, shoe polishers, and "The Dreadnought Dishwasher," advertised as "saving labor, breakages, time, space, and temper"; the benefits of gas and electric ovens and water heaters; and quick recipes for providing a meal when the man of the house arrives home with unexpected guests. Husbands should be trained to empty their pockets and fold their own clothes before going to bed, and in emergencies to do some shopping. Even the clothes worn by the housewife could contribute to efficiency: "The present fashion of extremely short skirts is most favorable to our purpose. Not only does it allow freedom to flit quickly, and to run upstairs—for example with both hands occupied by the tray—but also it prevents dust or fluff from being carried through the house."

In the United States, where reliance upon servants had never been as great as it had been in Europe, a new movement began that placed housework at the center of the middle-class woman's life and conferred respectability in the form of university courses in "domestic science" or "home economics." No longer to be regarded as unskilled drudgery, housework was redefined as an exact science that could not be entrusted to uneducated, lazy servants; housewives were to become skilled professionals. American domestic pioneers such as Christine Frederick and Lillian Gilbreth applied the techniques of time and motion study—recently developed for rational-

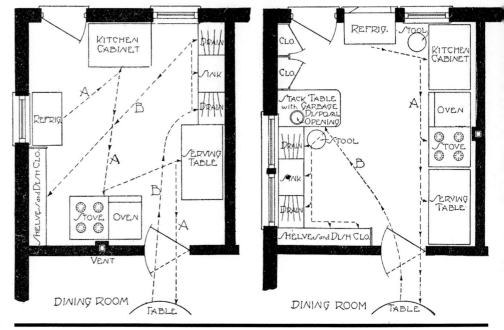

A pair of diagrams from *Scientific Management in the Home,* published in America in 1920, illustrate a poorly planned kitchen *(right)* in which the housewife wastes energy by continually having to walk from one appliance or fixture to another, and an efficient layout *(far right)* that minimizes her movements. The author of the book, Christine Frederick, was inspired by the time and motion studies being carried out at her husband's place of work to undertake similar studies of the domestic habits of herself and her friends. Aiming to combine efficiency with comfort, she established a correspondence course for housewives, dealing with the organization of storage, the placement of appliances to reduce fatigue, and the correct height for work surfaces.

izing work in industry—to analyze household chores such as washing up, sweeping, and scrubbing, breaking them down into their constituent movements and eliminating unnecessary expenditure of energy. Thus Christine Frederick, for instance, found that she made "eighty wrong motions in dishwashing alone, not counting others in the sorting, wiping, and laying away."

As a profession governed by its own fast-growing literature, housework needed equipment that would confirm its new status. The electrical appliances first developed decades earlier—but ignored at the time by their intended purchasers, who saw no need for expensive machines when servants were cheap—now came into their own. In the 1920s and 1930s especially, electric irons, vacuum cleaners, refrigerators, and washing machines began to fill the middle-class kitchens of the industrialized world, their widespread adoption ensured by a bombardment of advertising in newspapers, women's magazines, and on the new wireless sets that seemed to be appearing in every home.

Armies of salesmen, drilled in their routines with military precision, reinforced the work of advertising, pressing home to the housewife her duty to give the members of her family the ideal home they deserved, to preserve them from the menaces of dust and germs. Convenient installment terms were offered to convince the waverer. Expensive as they were, the new appliances were designed to look like necessities rather than extravagant luxuries: Refrigerators and washing machines had hospital white enameled surfaces trimmed with gleaming chrome to proclaim their role in preserving hygiene, and curved corners for easier cleaning (also to permit manufacturers the most economic use of pressed steel).

The homes in which these appliances were installed were themselves transformed. From the beginning of the century there was a trend toward smaller, more easily cleanable houses. Extensive new suburbs of diminutive bungalows sprang up around the peripheries of the great cities of the industrial world, from which male breadwinners commuted to work by public transport or, more and more, by automobile.

Inside the new houses the most crucial change was the increased importance of the kitchen. Up until the nineteenth century there had often been no physical division between the activities of cooking and heating, both of which were associated with the main hearth in the all-purpose living room. The advent of cast-iron stoves, gas and electric ranges, and an expanded array of pots and pans during the late nineteenth century forced a separation, with the kitchen being expanded to accommodate the new facilities. Gradually the kitchen came to rival the drawing room as the focal point of family life: It was now placed not in the basement as previously but on the ground floor, where it was also within easy reach of the dining room. More thought was given to its design, and it was furnished with easily cleaned wallpaper and counters, their height carefully planned to ensure the easiest possible working conditions. This trend was now accelerated, and the space—and financial investment—allotted to the

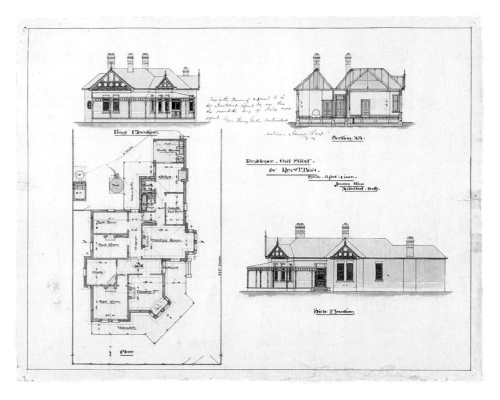

An architect's drawing for a three-bedroom bungalow with extensive verandas, dating from around 1900, provides a blueprint for European-style domesticity in Perth in Western Australia. In the wake of mass immigration to Australia in the 1850s and a boom in house construction, a version of the European way of life quickly took root in a continent that offered more space and a warmer climate than most of the new inhabitants had ever known. Except in the poorest districts, at the turn of the century, single-family houses accounted for two-thirds of all urban buildings.

kitchen reflected the enhanced importance of the woman's role in the home.

Nor was the kitchen the only site in which women became more dominant: New rights were also claimed in the bedroom. Since the 1880s an increasingly vociferous feminist movement had been campaigning to improve the lot of women: Its goals included entry to the professions, political representation on equal terms with men, and, not least, the right of women to control their reproductivity, to choose whether they should bear children or not. In the twentieth century the means to achieve this final goal at last became available.

During the nineteenth century the most widely practiced methods of birth control were abstinence and withdrawal. A variety of sponges, douches, pessaries, and syringes were available, as were condoms—which were commonly made of animal intestines until the 1870s, when rubber was substituted—but reliable information

about contraception was not generally available, and many couples found the recommended methods too complicated or expensive. It was not until the massive distribution of condoms to servicemen during the First World War in an attempt to check venereal disease that the use of prophylactics became at all widespread. Abortifacients were also available in the nineteenth century: "Perfectly harmless, never fails to bring about the desired result, as testified by thousands of married and single females," ran the newspaper advertisement for one patent mixture in the 1890s. But again, authoritative information was hard to come by, and many desperate women were forced to resort to dangerously unsafe methods. Because both the medical profession and the clergy continued to denounce all forms of birth control, and because open discussion of sexual matters was largely taboo, many women remained ignorant of the means by which they could control their own bodies until well into the twentieth century.

Campaigns for contraceptive advice to be made widely and freely available continued to be fought, however, and the advent in the 1950s of hormonal contraceptives designed to be taken in pill form signaled a watershed in relationships between the sexes. The "Pill" was hailed as a great sexual liberator: No longer were women dependent on men to initiate the practice of contraception. Not all were pleased. Conservative critics argued that effective, easily used contraceptives and accessible, affordable abortions were encouraging promiscuity, dulling the individual's sense of responsibility, and destroying the moral fabric of the developed world, while some feminists believed that women's vaunted sexual "freedom" merely left them more vulnerable to exploitation by men. But within fifteen years of coming onto the market, the pill was being used by more than twenty million women; the intrauterine device commonly known as the coil was being used by another ten million.

In Britain, by the late 1950s, women were also beginning to enjoy more legal rights, not least in matters of divorce, where many legislative inequalities that discriminated against them were removed. Until at least the middle of the nineteenth century, obtaining a legal divorce was both difficult and extremely expensive—so much so that between 1715 and 1852 the average number of divorces in England was just two per year. The end of a marriage was usually signified simply by the man's walking out, leaving the woman—and any children—to support themselves as they might. Again, the liberalization of divorce laws was not welcomed by everyone: While for some commentators it was a mark of freedom and common sense, others were highly critical and lamented the easing of obstacles to divorce, believing that it would lead to the undermining of the family as an institution, and therefore of society as a whole. In all countries that have made divorce inexpensive and readily available while protecting the rights and interests of all parties involved, the legal facilities have been used by increasing numbers of people.

One of three such communities built by the company founded by Abraham Levitt, the son of Russian Jewish immigrants, this suburban development outside New York City comprised by 1951 more than 17,000 houses as architecturally simple as a child's drawing. Stores, playgrounds, pools, schools, and churches were integrated into each development, and after living in one Levittown, sociologist Herbert Gans concluded that the inhabitants "take pleasure from the large supply of compatible people, without experiencing the boredom or malaise ascribed to suburban homogeneity."

Clearly, during the first half of the twentieth century the autocratic rule of the nineteenth-century patriarch had been considerably undermined. Not only was his wife demanding an equal say in the planning of the family size and the spending of the family income, but his children too—especially those born during or just after the Second World War, who enjoyed greater spending power at an earlier age than any previous generation—were forming loyalties outside the home and rebelling against their parents' authority. But traditional ideas of the home as a comfortable shelter for harmonious family life remained as strong as ever, and from the 1950s the version of home that had the widest appeal was that to be seen in a million consumer magazines, on movie screens and on the larger-than-life billboards that lined the highways of the Western and increasingly the non-Western world, and on the television sets that were becoming a standard feature of middle-class living rooms the world over—the American Dream.

Sustained by a booming economy—evident in the surging production of domestic appliances, furniture, and automobiles as well as military hardware—postwar Americans appeared to be on a limitless spending spree. They were also producing babies at an unprecedented rate. New housing developments in semirural areas allowed increasing numbers of people to purchase single-family homes on their own plots of land; inside, these houses were furnished with all the latest luxuries and appliances, many of them now made of plastic—a badge of modernity. Improved healthcare and educational opportunities fed a national mood of optimism: "You were given a sense that every American had a personal mission, the idea of personal destiny," recalled one inhabitant of Texas—which, "in the fifties, was a special state: It was the growingest, the biggest."

This new, affluent, open-ended American way of life appeared to many to be the most desirable on earth and attracted millions of immigrants from poorer countries to the United States—or to the almost equally prosperous nations of western Europe. Its characteristic status symbols were coveted equally by Americans themselves and have had an enduring appeal. In the 1980s, one twenty-seven-year-old American attorney stated his ambitions simply: "I want to get married, have two kids, two cars, two color TV sets, and live in the suburbs outside Los Angeles."

"But I want to maintain my individuality," continued the attorney—and there lay the catch. In many ways the wider the fruits of affluence were spread, the more restricted became the scope for personal choice, for the development of ways of life distinct from the norm. In the expanding suburbs especially, homes and patterns of domestic life were becoming increasingly standardized; so too, as market research guided the production of goods that would appeal to the widest possible audience, were fashions in interior decoration and clothes. A contemporary of the attorney, living in a wealthy suburb of a large American city, described the bland routine of husbands returning home on the evening commuter train:

> All these men with their briefcases come zooming out of the cars of the train, scurrying in all directions. All their wives have a certain place that they wait. . . . The little wives in the waiting cars, if you lined them up, they'd look like little penguins in a row. The same topcoat, ubiquitous beige. The same style shoes, the same style skirt, almost the same color hair, a little light brown with a little bit of gold in it.

For the suburban wife during the daytime, while her husband was away at work and her children were at school, her well-furnished home could seem chill and empty. In many cases her husband's work had taken her far from her parents, relations, and school friends, and she became prone to depression and inertia. While linked with friends and relations by telephone, and given a window into a broader world by television, her social life remained impoverished. The introduction of the welfare state and the wide adoption of private medical insurance plans further increased her isolation: Doctors and impersonal hospitals now took the place of parents and neighbors in seeing the woman through the traumas of pregnancy, childbirth, and illness. Psychiatrists, to whom American women—and often men too—turned by the thousand, attempted to provide the sort of emotional support previously offered by families, though the number of patients who became addicted to tranquilizers or remained in treatment for years without appreciable benefit suggested that psychiatry was unable to cope with so widespread a problem.

For women who did not have jobs outside the home—and despite women's success in traditional male occupations during the war years, returning men soon displaced the majority of women from the work force—domestic appliances turned household tasks into a form of endless, often pointless make-work. Work it never-theless was, for "laborsaving" devices had never ultimately lightened the housewife's work. Instead, while easing individual tasks, they had from the first set ever-higher standards of perfection—standards that were now reinforced by sophisticated advertising campaigns calculated to appeal to the housewife's sense of inadequacy. Carpets formerly taken outside and beaten once a year now had to be vacuumed daily; automatic washing machines replaced the weekly labors of washday with constant washing of small loads. In any case, researchers for the manufacturers found that appliances that promised really effective labor savings tended not to sell: Labor, even unnecessary labor, had come to be necessary to the housewife's sense of purpose and self-image. By the 1960s, concern about housewives' obsessive over-conscientiousness was being expressed not only by feminists but by more conservative critics in government and the establishment. America's mothers, it was argued, were pampering their children: supervising and organizing their activities from morning to night, indulging their moods, anticipating their wishes, arranging treats, and, in short, robbing them of all initiative and self-reliance.

Moreover, while divorce rates soared during the 1960s, women were discovering that for all the advantages new domestic technology and reliable birth control methods had given them, power in the home no less than in the outside world was based on money. And the traditional roles of male breadwinner and female homemaker were resistant to change. Even when women went out to work—and in the United States the number of married women who worked more than doubled between 1950 and the mid-1980s—they were expected, and generally took it upon themselves, to do the housework also. When husbands took on household tasks these were usually gender-defined: Men repaired cars and roofs while women washed and vacuumed. For both sexes the stereotypes were hard to break out of. "I understand," wrote the heroine of Sue Kaufman's 1967 novel *Diary of a Mad Housewife*, "that unless I wanted to divorce Jonathan, or have Jonathan divorce me, I had to jump when he said Jump. Since the very word divorce brought on an avalanche of bewilderment . . . I knew I would jump. And jump and jump." For men to take on household chores was to invite ridicule or contempt from their peers.

Divorce, the only possible escape from a marriage in which the strains and difficulties outweighed the rewards, was no simple solution. Children might suffer severe emotional disturbance. The wife was likely to fare worse than the husband: A study made in California during the 1980s showed that after a year of divorce the average

I am thankful for my good health and faith in God, and such material possessions as two cars, two TVs, and two fireplaces," declared the heroine of a story published in an American women's magazine in the 1950s. In the postwar years, abundance and mobility became the defining characteristics of an increasing number of households. Affluence created new strains, however: A newly married woman moving into a single-family house, for example, could feel isolated from the larger family network. By the 1960s, many of the young, who enjoyed improved educational opportunities, had begun to seek alternatives to what they considered a shallow, materialistic lifestyle.

THE AMERICAN DREAM

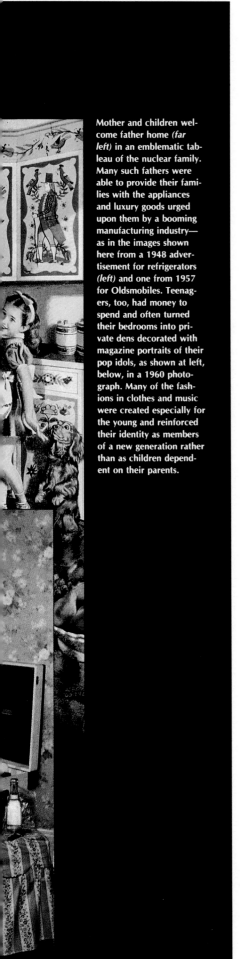

Mother and children welcome father home *(far left)* in an emblematic tableau of the nuclear family. Many such fathers were able to provide their families with the appliances and luxury goods urged upon them by a booming manufacturing industry—as in the images shown here from a 1948 advertisement for refrigerators *(left)* and one from 1957 for Oldsmobiles. Teenagers, too, had money to spend and often turned their bedrooms into private dens decorated with magazine portraits of their pop idols, as shown at left, below, in a 1960 photograph. Many of the fashions in clothes and music were created especially for the young and reinforced their identity as members of a new generation rather than as children dependent on their parents.

man's standard of living had risen by 49 percent, while the average woman's had fallen by 74 percent. High rates of remarriage suggest that even those who have been unhappy once still regard marriage and the family as the preferred way of life.

The strains imposed by Western models of family life have led many to seek alternatives. The Oneida Community, for example, founded in New York in 1848 by fifty-eight adults with their children, banned private property among its members, and attempted to weaken the exclusive bonds of emotion that held individual families together and to replace them with a broader loyalty to the community. Members of the community practiced group marriage—all males being considered married to all females—and produced all their own food and clothing until, shortly after the death of its founder, the community was disbanded in 1879. Also in America, the religiously motivated Shakers—numbering 6,000 by 1850—lived together communally in small groups, practicing celibacy and sexual equality. But while such groups might prove liberating and fulfilling for their members, and were sometimes durable, they remained an irrelevance to society as a whole, by whom they were treated with scorn or simply ignored.

In the twentieth century, more large-scale alternatives have been attempted. The father of the Russian Revolution of 1917, Vladimir Ilich Lenin, inveighed against the "bourgeois" family on account of what he saw as its exploitation and enslavement of woman: "Petty housework crushes her, strangles, stultifies, and degrades her, chains her to the kitchen and nursery, and she wastes her labor on barbarous, unproductive, petty, nerve-racking, stultifying, and crushing drudgery." Lenin's communist government sought to break this bondage by encouraging women to take jobs outside the home, and by instituting new patterns of communal living in which the exclusivity of the nuclear family would be weakened, and the labors of childcare, cleaning, and cooking would be shared more widely.

Yet as Lenin's successor, Joseph Stalin, embarked on a crash program of industrialization in the hope of transforming the underdeveloped Soviet Union into the economic giant of the world, he found that his interests tallied with those of the Western capitalists of the nineteenth century: Strong bonds of loyalty and responsibility between the male breadwinner and his dependent family would be necessary if the worker was to remain docile and diligent. Wider networks of communal support tended to encourage feelings of independence and waywardness, and lax performance and absenteeism.

In China, too, attempts to replace loyalty to the family with loyalty to the state have foundered on the rock of tradition, according to which the family unit of parents and children—linked to extended networks of lineage and clan—is the basic building block of society. The communist family has therefore remained in all essentials a thoroughly bourgeois institution.

At the end of the twentieth century, leftist governments have by and large been content to leave the fundamentals of family life alone. While healthcare programs and free birth control have made life easier for most of these countries' inhabitants, the basic structures of home life have remained the same. Though the revolutionary government of Fidel Castro's Cuba, for example, assured its male citizens that their manhood, far from being compromised by participation in housework and childcare, was rather "reaffirmed" by such labor, and it has emphasized that "femininity" is "not counterposed to any activity of work, of educational improvement, or of the

In a 1969 American credit-card advertisement, a city street becomes an ingenious collage of office buildings, traffic, and giant consumer goods—toys, sports equipment, toiletries, tools, and domestic appliances. Using a credit card and a telephone, homeowners could purchase goods and services without even having to step out of their front doors. This marketplace innovation tempted many to live more luxurious lifestyles than their incomes could support. By 1989, there were more than one billion credit cards in circulation in the United States, an average of nine per citizen; the debt owed on these cards amounted to more than $225 billion.

responsibilities of daily life," there has been little sign of any significant change in attitudes: Housework is still, it seems, for housewives.

Israel's kibbutzim represent a more radical experiment. In these communities children are brought up as a separate group from within a few days of birth. While parents have frequent access to their young sons and daughters, it is only for brief periods. The routine work of childcare is seen to by qualified helpers, leaving the mother free for productive labor in workshop, office, or field, while her time with her child can be devoted to breast-feeding and play. Helpers are changed regularly to prevent the formation of exclusive bonds. Kibbutz children grow up with playmates around them all day, while knowing that their parents are near at hand. Far from being damaged or made vulnerable by the experience, they seem to grow up no less cheerful, self-confident, and mature than children brought up in the confines of the nuclear family. But those who live on kibbutzim constitute only about three percent of the Israeli population.

Elsewhere, in the rapidly industrializing countries of the Third World, systems of family life have been thrown into often-painful confusion by the new conditions. People in such countries have witnessed in the space of just a few years the sort of transformations that took place over many generations in Europe and North America. The astonishing affluence and personal freedom of the lifestyles promoted by Western television, films, and magazines have inevitably proved irresistible to many young people, and traditions of family life that evolved over many centuries have suddenly begun to seem cramping and out-of-date. The result has often been tension or rupture among formerly tight-knit families and communities. Teenagers demand the right to meet friends of the opposite sex without being supervised by chaperones; young men and women reject the marriage partners selected for them by their parents, craving instead the romantic love matches they have seen in the Western media; daughters insist on their right to go out to work, while the growing number of divorces in many countries has appalled the older generation.

Contraception has proved to be another problem area. In regions where high infant mortality has traditionally led to large families, the use of contraception has been widely rejected, and among the few women who have sought to limit their fertility in this way contraception has caused feelings of guilt. Meanwhile, as most women in such regions continue to bear large families, and as improved medical techniques progressively reduce levels of child mortality, the populations of many Third World countries are rising far faster than those of the Western world.

How fully to embrace the moral codes of Western societies and how far traditional social values should be sacrificed to the demands of industrial development have been matters of fierce debate throughout the Third World. Some governments have rejected the ways of the West completely. The Islamic fundamentalist government that came to power in Iran in 1979, for instance, has swept away programs of Westernization in culture and family life, and blames the United States not merely for economic exploitation and political repression under the previous regime, but for the dissolution of traditional Muslim morality and law and their replacement with laxity and decadence. Third World immigrants in developed Western societies—Asians in

An American mother teaches her children how to use a home computer. In many Western nations in 1990, around one-fifth of all households owned a computer. A link between home and the outside world, they enabled their owners to tap into a wide range of educational and research resources. Also, direct communication between personal computers and office terminals allowed increasing numbers of employees to work at home, reversing the trend of the previous two centuries.

Britain, North Africans in France, Turks in Germany, and Latin Americans in the United States, for example—have had to face similar dilemmas of how far to adapt their traditional lifestyles to a new context. While their material lot has on the whole been better than it was in the nations they left behind, the psychological pressures have been far greater. Anxious to succeed in their new homes and to do the best they can for their children, they have nonetheless been disturbed by the very new moral environment in which they have found themselves. Steering a middle course—gaining the advantages of participation in the host society while holding on to the important principles of their own traditional moralities, with all the security they have provided—has proved far from easy.

Not that domestic life, the day-to-day scenario of both rich and poor that is compounded of work and routine and tiredness and frustration as well as of love and affection and hospitality and enjoyment, has anywhere ever been easy. Technological advances—in house construction and furniture, heating, and lighting—and extensive welfare programs have provided for new degrees of comfort, but at the same time have always created new challenges to inherited patterns of home life. Hence, in a modern industrial nation, improved healthcare and welfare provision mean that people are living longer than ever before—yet they often live in poverty and solitude, neglected by children who would once have looked to them for support through the difficult stages of their own lives, such as childbirth and illness, and then in turn looked after them through their old age. The same system of care that has permitted the elderly their longer lives has also usurped their privileged position as respected providers of advice and nurture—a position that the aged still retain in many less materially advanced societies.

But if domestic life has always been difficult terrain—an area in which the dividing lines between the private life of the individual, the life of the family, and that of the wider community have never been fixed, and in which the demands of each sector have often conflicted—one peculiarly modern cause of strain and often of disillusion has been the high expectations with which young couples embark when setting up their own households and starting their families. During the periods of scarcity and want that have been the lot of most ordinary people in the past, to be able to house, feed, and clothe itself was often the best a family could hope for. In the Western world in the nineteenth and twentieth centuries, as automation and affluence have caused the family to become less a unit of production and more a unit of consumption, the manufacturing, service, and media industries dependent on families as consumers have conspired to establish models of family life specifically designed to raise the expectations of as many people as possible.

Most such models have been unrealistically standardized, creating and reinforcing stereotypes of family life that fail to correspond with the range of actual experience. The nuclear family, for example—at its most basic, a married couple and its children living together—although the dominant image of the family among politicians, clergy, and advertisers alike, is just one of many current household arrangements. In the United States in 1989, for example, 17 percent of all family households were maintained by women with no husband present; the number of nonfamily households, consisting mostly of single persons living alone, more than doubled between 1970 and 1989. In Britain in 1988, more than 25 percent of all households comprised single persons living alone; 14 percent of all families with dependent children were single-parent households. These statistics themselves conceal wide variations: Differences of race, class, and religious background make for markedly contrasting patterns of family life even within statistically comparable groups. In the meantime, changing conditions in society as a whole exercise their own influence on events within the home, as political upheavals, economic recessions or booms, advances in medical care, or modifications in education or divorce law affect the individual family. Perhaps the most basic and enduring of all human institutions, the family is also among the most complex and fluid.

An Indian couple wearing the traditional dress of their country relax in a room furnished in a style developed in Western nations but now common throughout the world. The dominating presence is that of the television set: By 1987, there were 9.3 million TVs in India, more than twice the number of telephones. Most are owned by urban families, although community sets in the countryside allow the poorest villagers to observe the lifestyles of the rich as portrayed in Indian-made comedies and soap operas. As in most Third World countries with low literacy rates—that of India is less than 40 percent—television and radio reach a far larger audience than books and newspapers.

ACKNOWLEDGMENTS

The following materials have been reprinted with the kind permission of the publishers: Page 8 and *passim*: "The huts here were circular . . .," quoted from *Journey without Maps* by Graham Greene, © 1936, renewed © 1964 by Graham Greene, by permission of Viking Penguin, a division of Penguin Books U.S.A. Inc. Page 17 and *passim*: "What part of the world . . .," quoted from *The Odyssey* by Homer, transl. by E. V. Rieu, London: Penguin Books, 1946, © the estate of E. V. Rieu. Page 51: "For whatever they save . . .," quoted from *Piers the Ploughman* by William Langland, transl. by J. F. Goodridge, London: Penguin Books, 1966,

© J. F. Goodridge. Page 64: "In primis . . .," quoted in *The Pastons and Their England* by H. S. Bennett, Cambridge: Cambridge University Press, 1968. Page 103: "The husband must be on the street . . ." and page 107: "In all this upbringing . . .," quoted in *The Embarrassment of Riches: An Interpretation of Dutch Culture in the Golden Age* by Simon Schama, New York: Random House, Inc., 1988. Page 115 and *passim*: "There is a big room . . .," quoted from *Selected Letters* by Madame de Sévigné, transl. by Leonard

Tancock, London: Penguin Books, 1982, © Leonard Tancock. Page 123: "Floors laid with finest class deals . . .," quoted from *The Georgian House*, by Richard Reid, London: Bishopsgate Press, 1989.

The editors wish to thank the following individuals and institutions for their valuable assistance in the preparation of this volume:
England: London—David M. Gaimster, Department of Medieval and Later Antiquities, British Museum; Christopher Middleton; Christine Noble; Eugénie Romer; Peter Thornton, Sir John Soane's House and Museum.
Nepal: Katmandu—Thomas Kelly.

PICTURE CREDITS

BIBLIOGRAPHY

Anderson, Bonnie S., and Judith P. Zinsser, *A History of Their Own: Women in Europe from Prehistory to the Present,* 2 vols. London: Penguin Books, 1989, 1990.

Anderson, Michael, *Approaches to the History of the Western Family 1500-1914.* Basingstoke, Hants, England: Macmillan, 1980.

Ariès, Philippe, and A. Béjin, eds., *Western Sexuality: Practice and Precept in Past and Present Times.* Transl. by A. Forster. Oxford: Basil Blackwell, 1985.

Ariès, Philippe, and Georges Duby, general eds., *A History of Private Life.* Transl. by Arthur Goldhammer. 4 vols.:
Vol. 1, *From Pagan Rome to Byzantium.* Ed. by Philippe Ariès. Cambridge, Massachusetts: The Belknap Press of Harvard University Press, 1987.
Vol. 2, *Revelations of the Medieval World.* Ed. by Georges Duby. Cambridge, Massachusetts: The Belknap Press of Harvard University Press, 1988.
Vol. 3, *Passions of the Renaissance.* Ed. by Roger Chartier. Cambridge, Massachusetts: The Belknap Press of Harvard University Press, 1988.
Vol. 4, *From the Fires of Revolution to the Great War.* Ed. by Michelle Perrot. Cambridge, Massachusetts: The Belknap Press of Harvard University Press, 1990.

Barley, Maurice, *Houses and History.* London: Faber and Faber, 1986.

Barrett, Helena, and John Phillips, *Suburban Style: The British Home, 1840-1960.* London: Macdonald, 1987.

Bell, R. C., *Board and Table Games from Many Civilizations.* London: Oxford University Press, 1960.

Bennett, H. S., *The Pastons and Their England: Studies in an Age of Transition.* Cambridge: Cambridge University Press, 1968.

Berrall, Julia S., *The Garden: An Illustrated History.* London: Penguin Books, 1978.

Bloch, Marc, *Feudal Society.* Transl. by L. A. Manyon. London: Routledge & Kegan Paul, 1962.

Boorstin, Daniel J., *The Americans: The Democratic Experience.* London: Cardinal, 1988.

Braudel, F.:
Capitalism and Material Life. London: Weidenfeld & Nicolson, 1973.
The Structures of Everyday Life. London: Collins, 1981.

Briggs, Asa:
The Age of Improvement. Harlow, Essex, England: Longman, 1979.
Victorian Cities. London: Penguin Books, 1990.
Victorian Things. London: Penguin Books, 1990.

Brucker, Gene Adam, *Florence 1138-1737.* London: Sidgwick & Jackson, 1984.

Burnett, John, *A Social History of Housing 1815-1985.* London: Methuen, 1986.

Burnett, John, ed., *Useful Toil: Autobiographies of Working People from the 1820s to the 1920s.* London: Allen Lane, 1974.

Chapelot, J., and R. Fossier, *The Village and House in the Middle Ages.* London: Batsford, 1985.

Coontz, Stephanie, *The Social Origins of Private Life: A History of American Families 1600-1900.* London: Verso, 1988.

Cowell, F. R., *Everyday Life in Ancient Rome.* London: Batsford, 1961.

Drummond, J. C., and A. Wilbrahim, *The Englishman's Food.* London: Jonathan Cape, 1957.

Ehrenberg, V., *The People of Aristophanes: A Sociology of Old Attic Comedy.* Oxford: Basil Blackwell, 1943.

Farb, Peter, *Humankind.* London: Triad Paladin, 1978.

Filbee, Marjorie, *A Woman's Place: An Illustrated History of Women at Home from the Roman Villa to the Victorian Town House.* London: Ebury Press, 1980.

Finley, M. I., *The World of Odysseus.* London: Chatto & Windus, 1964.

Forty, Adrian, *Objects of Desire: Design and Society 1750-1980.* London: Thames and Hudson, 1986.

Frazer, J. G., *First Aid to the Servantless.* Cambridge: W. Heffer & Sons Ltd., 1913.

Friedan, Betty, *The Feminine Mystique.* London: Penguin Books, 1982.

Gathorne-Hardy, Jonathan, *Love, Sex, Marriage and Divorce.* London: Jonathan Cape, 1981.

Girouard, Mark, *Life in the English Country House: A Social and Architectural History.* London: Penguin Books, 1980.

Gloag, J. A., *A History of Furniture Design.* London: Cassell, 1966.

Greene, Graham, *Journey without Maps.* London: Penguin Books, 1971.

Hale, J. R., *Renaissance Europe.* London: Collins, 1971.

Haley, K. H. D., *The Dutch in the Seventeenth Century.* London: Thames and Hudson, 1972.

Hanawalt, B. A., *The Ties That Bound: Peasant Families in Medieval England.* New York: Oxford University Press, 1986.

Heer, Friedrich, *The Medieval World.* Transl. by Janet Sondheimer. London: Weidenfeld & Nicolson, 1961.

Holme, Bryan, *Advertising: Reflections of a Century.* London: Heinemann, 1982.

Holmes, U. T., *Daily Living in the Twelfth Century.* Madison, Wisconsin: University of Wisconsin Press, 1952.

Homer, *The Odyssey.* Transl. by E. V. Rieu. London: Penguin Books, 1946.

Hufton, O. H., *Bayeux in the Late Eighteenth Century.* Oxford: Oxford University Press, 1967.

Jalland, Pat, *Women, Marriage and Politics 1860-1914.* Oxford: Oxford University Press, 1988.

Jenkins, Ian, *Greek and Roman Life.* London: British Museum Publications, 1986.

Jones, A. H. M., *The Later Roman Empire 284-602: A Social, Economic and Administrative Survey.* Oxford: Basil Blackwell, 1964.

Kamen, H., *The Iron Century.* London: Weidenfeld & Nicolson, 1971.

Kitto, H. D. F., *The Greeks.* London: Penguin Books, 1951.

Koenigsberger, H. G.:
Early Modern Europe 1500-1789. Harlow, Essex, England: Longman, 1987.
Medieval Europe 400-1500. Harlow, Essex, England: Longman, 1987.

Lacey, W. K., *The Family in Classical Greece.* London: Thames and Hudson, 1968.

Ladurie, Emmanuel Le Roy, *Montaillou: Cathars and Catholics in a French Village 1294-1324.* Transl. by Barbara Bray. London: Penguin Books, 1980.

Langland, William, *Piers the Ploughman.* Transl. by J. F. Goodridge. London: Penguin Books, 1966.

Larkin, Jack, *The Reshaping of Everyday Life 1790-1840.* New York: Harper & Row, 1988.

La Roche, Sophie von, *Sophie in London.* London: Jonathan Cape, 1933.

Laslett, Peter, *The World We Have Lost.* London: Routledge, 1988.

Le Goff, J., *Medieval Civilisation.* Transl. by Julia Barrow. Oxford: Basil Blackwell, 1988.

Le Goff, J., ed., *The Medieval World.* Transl. by Lydia G. Cochrane. London: Collins & Brown, 1990.

Lévi-Strauss, Claude, *Tristes Tropiques.* Transl. by John Weightman and Doreen Weightman. London: Penguin Books, 1976.

Lockwood, Charles, *Bricks & Brownstone: The New York Row House, 1783-1929, An Architectural & Social History.* New York: McGraw-Hill Book Co., 1972.

Lucie-Smith, Edward, *Furniture: A Concise History.* London: Thames and Hudson, 1979.

McGee, Harold, *On Food and Cooking: The Science and Lore of the Kitchen.* London: Unwin Hyman, 1986.

McKay, A. G., *Houses, Villas and Palaces in the Roman World.* London: Thames and Hudson, 1975.

McNeill, William H., *Plagues and Peoples.* London: Penguin Books, 1979.

Marshall, Dorothy, *Industrial England 1776-1851.* London: Routledge & Kegan Paul, 1973.

Marshall, Peter, *Cuba Libre: Breaking the Chains?* London: Victor Gollancz Ltd., 1987.

Marwick, Arthur, *British Society since 1945.* London: Penguin Books, 1990.

Matthew, D. J. A., *The Medieval European Community.* London: Batsford, 1977.

Miles, Rosalind, *The Women's History of the World.* London: Paladin, 1989.

Mingay, G. E., *The Transformation of Britain 1830-1939.* London: Paladin, 1987.

Mingay, Gordon, and Diana Sperling, *Mrs. Hurst Dancing and Other Scenes from Regency Life 1812-1823.* London: Victor Gollancz Ltd., 1981.

Murray, I. J., *Amsterdam in the Age of Rembrandt.* Norman, Oklahoma: University of Oklahoma Press, 1967.

Murray, Peter, *The Architecture of the Italian Renaissance.* London: Thames and Hudson, 1969.

Oakley, Ann, *Housewife.* London: Penguin Books, 1976.

Ogden, Annegret S., *The Great American Housewife: From Helpmate to Wage Earner, 1776-1986.* Westport, Connecticut: Greenwood Press, 1986.

Poe, Edgar Allan, "The Philosophy of Furniture." In *Collected Works of Edgar Allan Poe*, ed. by Thomas Ollive Mabbott, vol. 2. Cambridge, Massachusetts: The Belknap Press of Harvard University Press, 1978.

Pounds, Norman J. G.:
Hearth & Home: A History of Material Culture. Bloomington, Indiana: Indiana University Press, 1989.
An Historical Geography of Europe 450 B.C.- A.D.1330. Cambridge: Cambridge University Press, 1973.

Power, E., ed., *The Goodman of Paris.* London: Blackwell, 1938.

Praz, Mario, *An Illustrated History of Interior Decoration: From Pompeii to Art Nouveau.* London: Thames and Hudson, 1964.

Quiney, Anthony, *House and Home: A History of the Small English House.* London: BBC Publications, 1986.

Rawling, Marjorie, *Everyday Life in Medieval Times.* London: Batsford, 1968.

Reid, Richard, *The Georgian House.* London: Bishopsgate Press, 1989.

Rörig, Fritz, *The Medieval Town.* Transl. by Don Bryant. London: Batsford, 1967.

Rybczynski, Witold, *Home: A Short History of an Idea.* New York: Viking, 1986.

Schama, Simon, *The Embarrassment of Riches: An Interpretation of Dutch Culture in the Golden Age.* London: Fontana Press, 1988.

Sévigné, Madame de, *Selected Letters.* Transl. by Leonard Tancock. London: Penguin Books, 1982.

Shahar, Shulamith, *The Fourth Estate: A History of Women in the Middle Ages.* Transl. by Chaya Galai. London: Methuen, 1983.

Shapiro, Rose, *Contraception: A Practical and Political Guide.* London: Virago, 1987.

Stambaugh, John E., *The Ancient Roman City.* Baltimore: The Johns Hopkins University Press, 1988.

Starr, C. G., *A History of the Ancient World.* New York: Oxford University Press, 1974.

Sutherland, Daniel E., *The Expansion of Everyday Life 1860-1876.* New York: Harper & Row, 1989.

Tannahill, R.:
Food in History. London: Eyre Methuen, 1973.
Sex in History. London: Hamish Hamilton, 1980.

Temple, William, *Observations upon the United Provinces of the Netherlands.* Cambridge: Cambridge University Press, 1932.

Terkel, Studs, *American Dreams: Lost and Found.* London: Paladin, 1982.

Thompson, F. M. L., *The Rise of Respectable Society: A Social History of Victorian Britain 1830-1900.* London: Fontana Press, 1988.

Thornton, Peter, *Authentic Decor: The Domestic Interior 1620-1920.* London: Weidenfeld & Nicolson, 1984.

Wacher, J., *The Towns of Roman Britain.* London: Batsford, 1974.

Webster, T. B. L., *Everyday Life in Classical Athens.* London: Batsford, 1969.

White, K. D., *Greek and Roman Technology.* London: Thames and Hudson, 1984.

Williams, Dyfri, *Greek Vases.* London: British Museum Publications, 1985.

Wood, Charles T., *The Age of Chivalry.* London: Weidenfeld & Nicolson, 1970.

Wycherley, R. E., *How the Greeks Built Cities: The Relationship of Architecture and Town Planning to Everyday Life in Ancient Greece.* New York: Norton, 1962.

Yarwood, Doreen, *The British Kitchen: Housewifery since Roman Times.* London: Batsford, 1981.

Young, G. M., *Victorian England: Portrait of an Age.* London: Oxford University Press, 1936.

Zumthor, Peter, *Daily Life in Rembrandt's Holland.* Transl. by Simon Watson Taylor. London: Weidenfeld & Nicolson, 1962.

INDEX